Are you **AWARE** of how healthy your attitudes are about intimate relationships?

Discover your attitudes and knowledge about close relationships. By taking AWARE, you will also learn about how your ideas about relationships compare with marriage experts.

www.awareonline.net

What is **AWARE** Online?

AWARE contains 15 categories that match the chapters in the Marriage & Family book. Your Personal Report provides a chapter by chapter summary of your knowledge and insight into relationships.

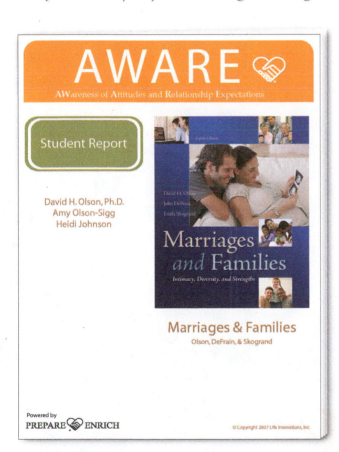

AWARE
AWareness of Attitudes and Relationship Expectations

Student Report

David H. Olson, Ph.D.
Amy Olson-Sigg
Heidi Johnson

Eighth Edition

David H. Olson
John DeFrain
Linda Skogrand

Marriages *and* Families
Intimacy, Diversity, and Strengths

Marriages & Families
Olson, DeFrain, & Skogrand

Powered by
PREPARE ENRICH

© Copyright 2007 Life Innovations, Inc.

You receive an **AWARE Personal Report**
(20 pages)

After answering 150 questions about relationships, you will be able to view and print (in color or black/white) your AWARE Personal Report.

Advantages of **AWARE** to you:

- Helps to personalize the course by highlighting your attitudes and knowledge.
- Identifies your strengths and growth areas regarding relationships.
- Generates insight into your personal style and your past and current relationships.
- Stimulates your interest and curiosity about relationship issues.
- Helps you discover more about your family of origin and better understand your family dynamics.

www.awareonline.net

Marriages & Families

Intimacy, Diversity, and Strengths

Eighth Edition

David H. Olson
University of Minnesota

John DeFrain
University of Nebraska

Linda Skogrand
Utah State University

McGraw Hill Education

MARRIAGES AND FAMILIES: INTIMACY, DIVERSITY, AND STRENGTHS, EIGHTH EDITION

Published by McGraw-Hill Education, 2 Penn Plaza, New York, NY 10121. Copyright © 2014 by McGraw-Hill Education. All rights reserved. Printed in the United States of America. Previous editions © 2011, 2008, and 2006. No part of this publication may be reproduced or distributed in any form or by any means, or stored in a database or retrieval system, without the prior written consent of McGraw-Hill Education, including, but not limited to, in any network or other electronic storage or transmission, or broadcast for distance learning.

Some ancillaries, including electronic and print components, may not be available to customers outside the United States.

This book is printed on acid-free paper.

4 5 6 7 8 9 QVS/QVS 20 19 18 17 16

ISBN 978-0-07-802692-8
MHID 0-07-802692-X

Managing Director: *Gina Boedeker*
Brand Manager: *Courtney Austermehle*
Executive Director of Development: *Lisa Pinto*
Managing Editor: *Sara Jaeger*
Editorial Coordinator: *Adina Lonn*
Marketing Manager: *Alexandra Schultz*
Freelance Development Editor: *Erin Guendelsberger, ANSR*
Direct, Content Production: *Terri Schiesl*

Content Project Manager: *Mary Jane Lampe*
Buyer: *Jennifer Pickel*
Designer: *Studio Montage, St. Louis, MO*
Media Project Manager: *Sridevi Palani*
Compositor: *Aptara®, Inc.*
Typeface: *9.5/12 Palatino*
Printer: *Quad/Graphics*

Text Credits: Multi-generational Asian family blowing bubbles outdoors; credit text: Hill Street Studios/Blend Images LLC. Pregnant Hispanic couple looking at ultrasound printout; credit text: Tetra Images/Getty Images. Parents with their son and daughter on the beach; credit text: Purestock/SuperStock. Hispanic family having video chat with military father; credit text: Ariel Skelley/Getty Images. Two men with girl sitting on sofa in living room; credit text: © Image Source/PunchStock.

Library of Congress Cataloging-in-Publication Data

Olson, David H. L.
   Marriages and families: intimacy, diversity, and strengths / David H.
Olson, University of Minnesota, John DeFrain, University of Nebraska,
Linda Skogrand, Utah State University.—Eighth edition.
      pages cm
   ISBN 978-0-07-802692-8 (alk. paper)—ISBN 0-07-802692-X (alk. paper)
 1. Families—United States—Psychological aspects. 2. Marriage—United States—Psychological aspects. 3. Intimacy (Psychology).
4. Communication in families—United States. I. DeFrain, John D. II. Skogrand, Linda. III. Title.
   HQ536.O46 2014
   306.850973—dc23

                              2013025998

The Internet addresses listed in the text were accurate at the time of publication. The inclusion of a Web site does not indicate an endorsement by the authors or McGraw-Hill Education, and McGraw-Hill Education does not guarantee the accuracy of the information presented at these sites.

www.mhhe.com

Dedication

This book about marriages and families is dedicated to our marriages and families.

Brief Contents

Preface xxi

PART I   The Social Context of Intimate Relationships 1

Chapter 1   Perspectives on Intimate Relationships 1
Chapter 2   Cultural Diversity and Diversity in Family Structure: Family Strengths and Challenges 34
Chapter 3   Understanding Marriage and Family Dynamics 70

PART II   Dynamics of Intimate Relationships 107

Chapter 4   Communication and Intimacy 107
Chapter 5   Conflict and Conflict Resolution 134
Chapter 6   Sexual Intimacy 159
Chapter 7   Gender Roles and Power in the Family 193
Chapter 8   Managing Economic Resources 220

PART III   Stages of Intimate Relationships 246

Chapter 9   Friendship, Intimacy, and Singlehood 246
Chapter 10   Dating, Mate Selection, and Living Together 276
Chapter 11   Marriage: Building a Strong Foundation 303
Chapter 12   Parenthood: Joys and Challenges 329
Chapter 13   Midlife and Older Couples 373

PART IV   Challenges and Opportunities 404

Chapter 14   Stress, Abuse, and Family Problems 404
Chapter 15   Divorce, Single-Parent Families, and Stepfamilies 458
Chapter 16   Strengthening Marriages and Families Worldwide 490

APPENDICES

Appendix A   Couple and Family Scales A-1
Appendix B   Family Science and Family Research Methods A-7

Glossary G-1
References R-1
Credits C-1
Name Index I-1
Subject Index I-9

Contents

Preface xxi

PART I · The Social Context of Intimate Relationships 1

1 Perspectives on Intimate Relationships 1

Three Themes of Intimacy, Strengths, and Diversity 2

Defining Marriage and Family 3
  What Is Marriage? 3
  What Is a Family? 4

Trends in Marriage and the Family: Change and Continuity 6
  Trends in Marriage and Cohabitation 8
  Trends in Divorce and Remarriage 9
  Trends in Family Structure 11
  Continuity in Marriage and the Family 14

Focus on Marital and Family Strengths 14

  BOX 1.1 Putting It Together: *Learning to Focus on Strengths* 15

Advantages of Marriage 15

Impact of the Social Environment on Relationships 18
  Stress, Change, and Materialism 19
  Lack of Time for Oneself and Significant Others 20
  Increasing Use of Child Care Outside the Family 21
  Instability of Couple and Family Relationships 22
  Violence, Criminal Victimization, and Fear 22
  Use of Alcohol, Tobacco, and Other Drugs 24
  The Internet and Human Relationships 26
  Changing Gender Roles and the Balance of Power 27
  Urban Migration and Overcrowding 28
  Financial Problems and the Global Economy 29

Changing the Social Environment 30

Positive Responses to the Social Environment 30

Summary 31

Key Terms 32

Activities 32

Suggested Readings 32

---

2 Cultural Diversity and Diversity in Family Structure: Family Strengths and Challenges 34

Diversity and Strengths in Family Structure and Cultural Context 35

Why Culture Matters 35

Intimacy and Diversity 36

Gay and Lesbian Couples and Families 36
  Same-Sex Couple Relationships and Marriage 37
  Gay and Lesbian Families 38
  The Challenges of Gay and Lesbian Couples and Families 39

The Concepts of Race, Culture, and Ethnicity 41

  BOX 2.1 Diversity in Families: *Race Has No Place* 42

U.S. Demographics and Future Trends 43
The Hispanic Population 43
The African American Population 44
The Asian American Population 45
The American Indian and Alaska Native Populations 45
Immigration and Family Life 45
What the Future Will Bring 46

Challenge to Researchers and Practitioners 47
Research 47
Practice 47

Cultural Competence 48
Awareness 48
Knowledge 48
Skills 49

Kin Relationships Across Cultures 49

Family System and Sociocultural Characteristics 51
Three Family System Characteristics 51
Three Sociocultural Characteristics 52

Family Strengths and Challenges Across Ethnic Groups 53
Strengths of White Families 53

BOX 2.2 Self-Assessment: *Rate the Strengths in Your Family 54*
Strengths of African American Families 55
Strengths of Latino Families 56
Strengths of Asian American Families 57
Strengths of American Indian Families 59

BOX 2.3 At Issue: *Historical Trauma and American Indians 61*

BOX 2.4 Diversity in Families: *The Tables Are Turned: Going from the Majority to the Minority 62*

Cross-Cultural Family Studies 62

Challenges for Ethnic Families 63
Assimilation, Acculturation, and Segregation 63
The Advantages of Being in the Majority 64
Marriage Outside the Group 65
Relationships Between Men and Women 66
Relationships Between Parents and Children 67

Summary 67
Key Terms 68
Activities 68
Suggested Readings 68

3
Understanding Marriage and Family Dynamics 70

The History of Family Science 71
Family Science in the Early Years 72
Family Science Today 73

Models of Couples and Families 74
Family Systems Theory 74

BOX 3.1 Putting It Together: *Reorganization of the Family System After a Car Accident 78*

BOX 3.2 Diversity in Families: *Cultural Conflicts for a Female Chicana College Student 79*
International Family Strengths Framework 81
Family Development Framework 86
Symbolic Interaction Framework 88
Social Construction Framework 89
Feminist Framework 90

Three Key Relationship Concepts 91
Cohesion in Couples and Families 91

BOX 3.3 Putting It Together: *Theories and Research 92*
Flexibility in Couples and Families 96
Communication in Couples and Families 98

Couple and Family Map 98
Balanced Versus Unbalanced Families 99
Balanced Relationships Are More Healthy 99
Value of Couple and Family Map 101

Dynamics Change in Relationships over Time 102

Summary 103
Key Terms 104
Activities 104
Suggested Readings 104

PART II   Dynamics of Intimate Relationships 107

4
Communication and Intimacy 107

Couple Strengths and Issues in Communication 108

Perspectives on Communication 109
Gender Differences in Communication 109
BOX 4.1 Self-Assessment: *Your Gender Communication Quotient* 113
Cultural Differences in Communication 114

BOX 4.2 Putting It Together: *All Together at Family Mealtimes* 115

Using Communication to Develop Intimacy 116
Communication as a Cooperative Endeavor 117
Content and Relationship Messages 118
Nonverbal Communication 118
Mixed Messages and Double Binds 119
Metacommunication: Clarifying Your Communication 120
Continuous Partial Attention 121

Using Communication to Maintain Intimacy 121
Speaking: The Art of Self-Disclosure 122
Listening: A Difficult Skill 125
Assertive, Passive, and Aggressive Communication 127

BOX 4.3 Putting It Together: *Using Communication to Increase Intimacy* 128

Positive and Negative Communication Cycles 129
The Positive Influence of Assertiveness 129
The Negative Influence of Avoidance 130

Summary 131

Key Terms 132

Activities 132

Suggested Readings 132

5
Conflict and Conflict Resolution 134

Couple Strengths and Issues in Conflict Resolution 135

Conflict and Anger: An Overview 136
The Hierarchy of Conflict 136

Anger and Conflict Taboos 138
Myths, Theories, and Facts About Anger 140

BOX 5.1 Putting It Together: *Anger: Myths and Facts* 141

Intimacy and Conflict 141
Intimacy Breeds Conflict 141
Love and Anger in Balance 142
The Dance of Anger 143

BOX 5.2 At Issue: *Determining Styles of Conflict Resolution in Happy Versus Unhappy Couples* 146
Conflict and Supportiveness in Heterosexual, Gay, and Lesbian Couples 146

Approaches to Conflict Resolution 146
Fighting Fairly 147
Constructive and Destructive Approaches 151
Styles of Conflict Resolution 151
Resolving Conflict: Six Basic Steps 153

Summary 157

Key Terms 157

Activities 157

Suggested Readings 157

6
Sexual Intimacy 159

Intimacy, Strengths, and Diversity 160

Couple Strengths and Sexual Issues 160

Sex and Society: An Overview 161
Sexuality, Sex, and Gender 162
Historical Perspectives on Sex and Society 162
Gay and Lesbian Couples 163
Sexuality Across Cultures 165
HIV/AIDS—Three Decades Later 168

American Sexual Health and Behavior 169
National Survey of Sexual Health and Behavior 169
ABC News Survey 170
Sexuality in the Later Years 171
Gay-Male and Lesbian Sexual Behavior 172

Sexual Behavior Among Adolescents and Young Adults 173
Unintended Consequences: Teen Pregnancies and Sexually Transmitted Infections (STIs) 174
Education for Sexuality 175
Sexuality Education and Parents 176

BOX 6.1 Putting It Together: *Father–Child Communication About Sex* 178
Is Sex Education Effective? 179
Sexual Behavior, Alcohol, and College 179

Marital and Extramarital Sexual Behavior 181
Sex Within Marriage 181
Marital Styles and Sexual Behavior 183
Infidelity 183

Toward Sexual Health 185

BOX 6.2 Diversity in Families: *Extramarital Sex Around the World* 186
Sexual Dysfunction 187
Sex Therapy 189

Summary 190

Key Terms 191

Activities 191

Suggested Readings 191

7

Gender Roles and Power in the Family 193

Intimacy, Strengths, and Diversity 194

Gender Roles 194

Gender Norms and Family Life 196
Distribution of Family Work by Gender 198
Emotion Work in Marriage and Family 199
Maternal Gatekeeping 199
Gallup Survey of Male and Female Traits 200
Traditional Versus Contemporary Views of Gender Roles 201

BOX 7.1 At Issue: *The Work–Family Interface* 202
The Move Toward More Egalitarian Roles 203
An International Perspective 205

BOX 7.2 Diversity in Families: *Gender Roles in Japan* 207

Gender Roles Across Ethnic Groups 207
Latino/a Culture 207
African American Culture 208
American Indian Culture 208
Asian American Culture 209
Gender Issues for Immigrant Couples 210

Theories About Gender Roles 210
Social Learning Theory 210
Cognitive Development Theory 211
Family Systems Theory 212
Feminist Framework 212

BOX 7.3 At Issue: *Gender Inequality as a Global Problem* 213

Power in Families 214
Types of Power Patterns 215
Egalitarian Roles and Marital Satisfaction 216
Suggestions for Minimizing Power Issues 217

Summary 218

Key Terms 219

Activities 219

Suggested Readings 219

8

Managing Economic Resources 220

Money and Happiness 221

Marriage and Money 224

BOX 8.1 At Issue: *The Effects of Debt on Newlyweds* 226

Diversity and Financial Style 226

The Cost of Divorce 228

Why Do Finances Cause Problems? 229

BOX 8.2 Putting It Together: *Steps to Financial Freedom* 230

Family Income and Expenses 231
Family Income 231
Annual Household Expenses 235
Family Net Worth 235

BOX 8.3 At Issue: *The Cost of Having and Raising a Baby* 236
Does It Pay to Work Outside the Home? 236

Smart Money Management 237
Creating a Budget 237
Pooling Money: Pros and Cons 238

Credit: Uses and Abuses 239
Credit Cards—Dangerous Plastic 239

BOX 8.4 At Issue: *The Credit Card Trap and How to Avoid It* 240
Advantages and Disadvantages of Credit 240
Purchasing a Home 240
Avoiding Debt and Bankruptcy 243
Financial Counseling 244

Summary 244

Key Terms 245

Activities 245

Suggested Readings 245

PART III — Stages of Intimate Relationships 246

9
Friendship, Intimacy, and Singlehood 246

Friends Versus Lovers 247
  The Fabric of Friendship 247
  The Tapestry of Love 249
  The Love Triangle 249

  BOX 9.1 Putting It Together: *Ten Traits of Love 250*
  Jealousy: A Green-Eyed Monster or Real Love? 252

  BOX 9.2 At Issue: *Love and Science 253*
  Looking for Love on the Internet 254

Exploring Intimacy: From Experience to Relationship 255
  Paths to Intimacy Differ in Males and Females 255
  Intimacy and Communication 256
  Intimate Experiences Versus an Intimate Relationship 257
  The Paradox of Marriage and Intimacy 257

Developing Intimacy in Couple Relationships 258
  Communication Skills 258
  Couple Closeness 259
  Couple Flexibility 259
  Personality Compatibility 259
  Conflict Resolution 260

Intimacy Games 260
  Constructive Intimacy Games 262
  Destructive Intimacy Games 262
  Limiting Destructive Games 264

Attachment Theory and Intimacy 265

Being Single 267

  BOX 9.3 Diversity in Families: *Definitions of Singlehood 268*
  A Historical Perspective on Being Single 269
  Being Single Today 270

Summary 273

Key Terms 274

Activities 274

Suggested Readings 274

10
Dating, Mate Selection, and Living Together 276

Courtship Patterns 277
  Parent-Arranged Marriages 277
  Dating: An American Creation 280
  Hooking Up: The Contemporary Trend 281
  Internet Dating and Matchmaking Services 285

  BOX 10.1 Putting It Together: *Dating Do's and Don'ts 286*
  Dating Among Older People 286

Choosing a Mate 288
  Physical Attractiveness 288
  Age and Finding a Mate 289
  Birth Order 290
  Similar Personalities or Different Personalities 290
  Interracial and Interfaith Marriages 290
  Finding a Good Mate 293

Patterns of Mate Selection 294

Conflict and Violence in Dating 295

Living Together 296

  BOX 10.2 At Issue: *Dating Violence Warning Sign 297*
  Cohabitation's Dramatic Increase 297
  Reasons for Cohabiting 299

  BOX 10.3 Putting It Together: *Ten Ideas to Consider Before Cohabiting 300*
  Difficult Choices 300

Summary 301

Key Terms 301

Activities 301

Suggested Readings 301

11
Marriage: Building a Strong Foundation 303

Intimacy, Strengths, and Diversity 304

Perspectives on Marriage Today 304
  The Benefits of Marriage 305
  Marriage and Black Americans 306
  When Marriages Do Not Work 306
  The Decline in Marriage 307

Components of a Successful Marriage 308

Marriage Education 310
  Premarital Education 311
  What Constitutes an Effective Premarital Program? 312

  BOX 11.1 Putting It Together: *The PREPARE Program for Premarital Counseling* 313

  BOX 11.2 At Issue: *Predicting Marital Success* 314
  Predicting a Successful Marriage 314

The Importance of Families of Origin in Marriage 315
  Kathy's Family of Origin 315
  Jim's Family of Origin 316
  Goals for the Marriage 316

Newlywed Years 317

Keeping Marriages Strong 320
  Five Types of Marriage 320
  Changes in Marital Satisfaction over Time 322
  Why Marriages Fall Apart 323
  Keeping Your Marriage a Top Priority 323
  The Role of Forgiveness in Marriage 324
  The Role of Sacrifice in Marriage 325

Federal Healthy Marriage Initiative 325
  Changes in Policy and State Laws to Strengthen Marriage 326

Summary 327

Key Terms 327

Activities 327

Suggested Readings 328

12
Parenthood: Joys and Challenges 329

Roots and Wings 330

Children and Happiness 330
  Children and Individual Happiness 330
  Children and Couple Happiness 331

Couple Strengths and Issues in Parenting 331

The Challenge of Parenthood 333
  Myths and Realities of Parenthood 333
  The Transition to Parenthood 335
  Financial Issues and Children 337

Adoption 338

The Child-Free Alternative 339

Styles of Parenting 343
  Democratic Style 344
  Authoritarian Style 345
  Permissive Style 345
  Rejecting Style 345
  Uninvolved Style 345
  Democratic Parenting Works Best 346

Theories of Childrearing 347

Issues in Parenting 349
  The Need for Positive Discipline Today 349
  Corporal Punishment and Its Consequences 350

  BOX 12.1 Putting it Together: *The Mother's Book by Mrs. Child* 353
  Child Care 354

  BOX 12.2 Diversity in Families: *Child Care for the Growing Hispanic Population* 355
  Coparenting 357

  BOX 12.3 At Issue: *Looking for a Very High Quality Child Care Program and Positive Caregiving* 358
  Single Mothers 360
  Gay and Lesbian Parenting 360
  Fatherhood and Motherhood Today 361
  When a Child Dies 365
  Educational Programs and Resources for Parents 365

The Joy and Enduring Satisfaction of Parenthood 369

  BOX 12.4 Putting It Together: *Owl Moon Walk* 370

Summary 370

Key Terms 371

Activities 371

Suggested Readings 371

13
Midlife and Older Couples 373

Intimacy, Strengths, and Diversity 374

Family Life in the Middle Years 375
  Defining Middle Age 375
  Middle Age: A Crisis or An Opportunity? 376
  The Middle-Aged Person and the Working World 377
  Sexuality in Middle Age 377
  BOX 13.1 Diversity in Families: *Childlessness: The Invisible Group* 378
  The Middle-Aged Marriage 380
  Divorce During the Middle and Later Years 381
  Empty Nest, Spacious Nest, or Cluttered Nest? 382
  Caught in the Middle: The Sandwich Generation 383
  Grandparenthood 383
  Grandparents Raising Grandchildren 385

BOX 13.2 Diversity in Families: *Grandparents and Grandfamilies* 387

Family Life in the Later Years 388
Defining Old Age 389
Conventional Wisdom About Old Age 390
Retirement 393

BOX 13.3 At Issue: *Alzheimer's* 395
Long-Term Marriages 396
Losing a Spouse 397

Couple Relationships in the Later Years 398

BOX 13.4 At Issue: *I Am Aware That I Am No Longer Anyone's "Most Important Person": The Desolation of Grief* 399
Changes in Family Dynamics in the Later Years 400

Summary 401

Key Terms 402

Activities 402

Suggested Readings 402

PART IV — Challenges and Opportunities 404

14 Stress, Abuse, and Family Problems 404

Intimacy, Strengths, and Diversity 405

Cross-Cultural Perspectives on Couple and Family Stress 406

What We Know About Stress 406
Coping with Stress 407
Stress and Life Events 407
Top Five Stressors for Couples 409

BOX 14.1 At Issue: *Ambiguous Loss: When We Are Uncertain If a Person Is In or Out of Our Family* 410
Five Tips for Dealing with Stress in Your Relationship 412
The ABC-X Family Crisis Model 412
Life as a Roller Coaster 413
A Roller Coaster Course of Adjustment 414
Family Systems Changes Before and After the 9/11 Attacks 414

War and Its Effect on Families 416
Couples 417

BOX 14.2 At Issue: *The Impact of War on Families Left Behind* 418
Children 422
The Role of the Community in Supporting Military Families 422
Posttraumatic Stress Disorder and War 423

Family Coping Strategies 424
Theoretical Perspectives 424
Coping with 9/11 425

BOX 14.3 Putting It Together: *Strategies for Managing Stress* 427

Domestic Violence 427

Incidence of Domestic Violence 428
Diversity and Domestic Violence 429
National Survey of Domestic Violence 430
Relationship of Physical Abuse and Psychological Abuse 431
Factors Contributing to Domestic Violence 432
Patterns of Domestic Violence 435
Treatment and Prevention of Domestic Violence 435
Domestic Violence and Children 437

Child Abuse and Neglect 437
Incidence of Child Abuse and Neglect 438
Psychological Aggression and Spanking 438
Alternatives to Spanking 440
The Long-Term Consequences of Child Abuse and Neglect 441

BOX 14.4 Putting It Together: *Surviving and Transcending a Traumatic Childhood: The Dark Thread* 442
Transcending Abuse 442
Families at Risk 443
Treatment and Prevention of Child Abuse 445

Sibling and Child-to-Parent Abuse 445
Sibling Abuse 445

BOX 14.5 Diversity in Families: *Family Violence from a Global Perspective: Strengths-Based Research and Case Studies* 446
Child-to-Parent Abuse 448

Alcohol Problems in Families 449
Alcohol and Family Violence 450
The Family's Reaction to Alcohol Abuse 450
Treatment and Prevention of Alcoholism 452
Acknowledging the Dangers of Legal Drugs 454

Summary 455

Key Terms 456

Activities 456

Suggested Readings 456

15

Divorce, Single-Parent Families, and Stepfamilies 458

16

Strengthening Marriages and Families Worldwide 490

Intimacy, Strengths, and Diversity 459

Divorce in Today's Society 460
Historical Trends 460

BOX 15.1 Diversity in Families: *The Globalization of Divorce 462*
Divorce Laws and Views on Divorce 462

BOX 15.2 At Issue: *Dissolution of Interracial Marriages 465*

Understanding Divorce 466
The Culture of Divorce 466
The Impact of Divorce on Adults 466
The Impact of Divorce on Children 468

Single-Parent Families 471
Fathers 473
Strengths of Single-Parent Families 475
Challenges of Being in Single-Parent Families 476
Benefits of Being in Single-Parent Families 478
What Resources do Single-Parent Families Rely On? 479

Stepfamilies 480
Differences Between Nuclear Families and Stepfamilies 481
Children in Stepfamilies 482
Couples in Stepfamilies 484
Stepfamilies in Diverse Populations 485
Boundary Ambiguity in Stepfamilies 486
Stepfamilies in Later Life 486
Building Stepfamily Strengths 487

Summary 488

Key Terms 489

Activities 489

Suggested Readings 489

Global Perspectives on Family, Community, and Cultural Strengths 491
Family Strengths 492
Community Strengths 492
Cultural Strengths 492
Two Visual Models Integrating Family, Community, and Cultural Strengths 493

BOX 16.1 Diversity in Families: *The Perennial Philosophy 495*

Premarital and Marriage Programs 496
Premarital Programs for Marriage 497
Couple Education Programs 498

Marital and Family Therapy 499
Common Problems in Couple Relationships 499
Problems Related to Closeness and Flexibility 500
Common Questions About Marital and Family Therapy 501
Family Therapy Case Study 503

BOX 16.2 Putting It Together: *Building a Stronger Marriage 507*

Strengthening Your Marriage and Family Relationships 507
Building a Stronger Marriage 507

BOX 16.3 Putting It Together: *Building a Stronger Family 508*
Building a Stronger Family 508

The Future of Your Family 509

Summary 510

Activities 511

Suggested Readings 512

Appendices

Appendix A
Couple and Family Scales A-1

Appendix B
Family Science and Family Research Methods A-7

Glossary G-1

References R-1

Credits C-1

Name Index I-1

Subject Index I-9

Boxed Features

Box 1.1   **Putting It Together:** *Learning to Focus on Strengths 15*

Box 2.1   **Diversity in Families:** *Race Has No Place 42*

Box 2.2   **Self-Assessment:** *Rate the Strengths in Your Family 54*

Box 2.3   **At Issue:** *Historical Trauma and American Indians 61*

Box 2.4   **Diversity in Families:** *The Tables Are Turned: Going from the Majority to the Minority 62*

Box 3.1   **Putting It Together:** *Reorganization of the Family System After a Car Accident 78*

Box 3.2   **Diversity in Families:** *Cultural Conflicts for a Female Chicana College Student 79*

Box 3.3   **Putting It Together:** *Theories and Research 92*

Box 4.1   **Self-Assessment:** *Your Gender Communication Quotient 113*

Box 4.2   **Putting It Together:** *All Together at Family Mealtimes 115*

Box 4.3   **Putting It Together:** *Using Communication to Increase Intimacy 128*

Box 5.1   **Putting It Together:** *Anger: Myths and Facts 141*

Box 5.2   **At Issue:** *Determining Styles of Conflict Resolution in Happy Versus Unhappy Couples 146*

Box 6.1   **Putting It Together:** *Father-Child Communication about Sex 178*

Box 6.2   **Diversity in Families:** *Extramarital Sex Around the World 186*

Box 7.1   **At Issue:** *The Work–Family Interface 202*

Box 7.2   **Diversity in Families:** *Gender Roles in Japan 207*

Box 7.3   **At Issue:** *Gender Inequality as a Global Problem 213*

Box 8.1   **At Issue:** *The Effects of Debt on Newlyweds 226*

Box 8.2   **Putting It Together:** *Steps to Financial Freedom 230*

Box 8.3   **At Issue:** *The Cost of Having and Raising a Baby 236*

Box 8.4   **At Issue:** *The Credit Card Trap and How to Avoid It 240*

Box 9.1 **Putting It Together:** *Ten Traits of Love 250*

Box 9.2 **At Issue:** *Love and Science 253*

Box 9.3 **Diversity in Families:** *Definitions of Singlehood 268*

Box 10.1 **Putting It Together:** *Dating Do's and Don'ts 286*

Box 10.2 **At Issue:** *Dating Violence Warning Signs 297*

Box 10.3 **Putting It Together:** *Ten Ideas to Consider Before Cohabiting 300*

Box 11.1 **Putting It Together:** *The PREPARE Program for Premarital Counseling 313*

Box 11.2 **At Issue:** *Predicting Marital Success 314*

Box 12.1 **Putting It Together:** *The Mother's Book by Mrs. Child 353*

Box 12.2 **Diversity in Families:** *Child Care for the Growing Hispanic Population 355*

Box 12.3 **At Issue:** *Looking for a Very High Quality Child Care Program and Positive Caregiving 358*

Box 12.4 **Putting It Together:** *Owl Moon Walk 370*

Box 13.1 **Diversity in Families:** *Childlessness: The Invisible Group 378*

Box 13.2 **Diversity in Families:** *Grandparents and Grandfamilies 387*

Box 13.3 **At Issue:** *Alzheimer's 395*

Box 13.4 **At Issue:** *I Am Aware That I Am No Longer Anyone's "Most Important Person": The Desolation of Grief 399*

Box 14.1 **At Issue:** *Ambiguous Loss: When We Are Uncertain If a Person Is In or Out of Our Family 410*

Box 14.2 **At Issue:** *The Impact of War on Families Left Behind 418*

Box 14.3 **Putting It Together:** *Strategies for Managing Stress 427*

Box 14.4 **Putting It Together:** *Surviving and Transcending a Traumatic Childhood: The Dark Thread 442*

Box 14.5 **Diversity in Families:** *Family Violence from a Global Perspective: Strengths-Based Research and Case Studies 446*

Box 15.1 **Diversity in Families:** *The Globalization of Divorce 462*

Box 15.2 **At Issue:** *Dissolution of Interracial Marriages 465*

Box 16.1 **Diversity in Families:** *The Perennial Philosophy 495*

Box 16.2 **Putting It Together:** *Building a Stronger Marriage 507*

Box 16.3 **Putting It Together:** *Building a Stronger Family 508*

About the Authors

David H. Olson, Ph.D.

David Olson is professor emeritus of family social science at the University of Minnesota. He is founder and president of Life Innovations. He is a past president of the National Council on Family Relations (NCFR) and a past president of the Upper Midwest Association for Marriage and Family Therapists (UMAMFT) and a fellow of the American Psychological Association (APA). Olson is also a member of the editorial boards of multiple family journals. He has received numerous awards, including the Distinguished Contribution to Family Therapy Research Award from both AAMFT and the American Family Therapy Association (AFTA).

Olson has written or edited more than 20 books, including *Couple Checkup; Remarriage Checkup; Empowering Couples; Building Relationships; Families: What Makes Them Work; Circumplex Model; Power in Families; Treating Relationships;* and 10 volumes of the *Inventory of Marriage and Family Literature*. He has published more than 100 articles with the theme of bridging family research, theory, and practice.

Olson and his colleagues at the University of Minnesota are well known for having developed the Circumplex Model of Marital and Family Systems and a variety of couple and family assessment tools, including PREPARE, ENRICH, FACES, PAIR, and AWARE.

John DeFrain, Ph.D.

John DeFrain is a professor emeritus of family studies at the University of Nebraska-Lincoln. His professional focus through a long career has been the development of couple and family strengths nationally and internationally.

DeFrain's research on family strengths and challenges from a global perspective has been recognized around the world. He holds an Honorary Appointment as Conjoint Professor of Family Studies at the University of Newcastle, Callaghan, New South Wales, Australia; serves as a research scientist in the Center for Family Studies, Shanghai Academy of Social Sciences, People's Republic of China; received an Onassis Foundation Fellowship to work at Aristotle University of Thessaloniki, Greece; was a Fulbright Scholar at the University of the South Pacific in Suva, Fiji; regularly attends the World Public Forum *Dialogue of Civilizations* conferences in Rhodes, Greece; consults with the Department of Family Development of the federal government of Mexico; and works with the MISS Foundation based in Phoenix, Arizona, part of an international network helping to develop programs for families whose child has died.

DeFrain is a co-founder of the Global Consortium for Education in Family Studies, developing an international family studies graduate program for students around the world. The Global Consortium links universities in America, Australia,

China, Greece, India, and Korea, making it possible for students to learn about how to strengthen families from teachers in many countries.

DeFrain's research has been published in 160 professional articles in books, journals, and Extension publications; and he has co-authored and co-edited 35 books, including: *Coping with Sudden Infant Death; Secrets of Strong Families; Stillborn: The Invisible Death; On Our Own: A Single Parent's Survival Guide; Parents in Contemporary America; Sudden Infant Death: Enduring the Loss; Building Relationships; and We Cry Out: Living with Developmental Disabilities*. His most recent books are: *Surviving and Transcending a Traumatic Childhood: The Dark Thread; Family Treasures: Creating Strong Families; Strong Families Around the World: Strengths-Based Research and Perspectives; The Strengths and Challenges of New Immigrant Families: Implications for Research, Education, Policy, and Service; Getting Connected, Staying Connected: Loving Each Other Day by* Day; and *Family Violence from a Global Perspective: Strengths-Based Perspectives*.

Linda Skogrand, Ph.D.

Linda Skogrand is a professor and family life extension specialist at Utah State University in Logan, Utah. She began her professional career as a social worker in the inner city of St. Louis, Missouri, and throughout her career has enjoyed a balance between academic institutions and social service organizations. Her current position as an Extension specialist allows her to take knowledge and research findings and make them available to people in communities in Utah and throughout the nation. She is a member of the working group for the National Extension Relationship and Marriage Education Network (NERMEN), which provides relationship education materials nationally for Extension educators and others who provide relationship and marriage education.

Skogrand's social service experiences include providing HIV/AIDS education programs for street kids, people in prison, and gang members, and overseeing the design of an AIDS house for the Latino population. She also taught family courses at St. Olaf College in Northfield, Minnesota, for 17 years and was adjunct faculty at the University of Minnesota.

She has authored numerous journal articles focusing on topics such as transcending a traumatic childhood, diversity, strong Latino marriages, strong Navajo marriages, strong African American marriages, relationship and marriage education for low-income and diverse populations, and benefits of stepfamily education for Latino and low-income audiences.

Skogrand is nationally known for her work with diversity—hearing the voices that are not typically heard in family research. With that focus in mind, she has conducted research with Latino couples and Navajo couples and created curricula for these populations based upon this research. These curricula include *Strong Latino Couple Relationships* for the Latino population and *Strong Marriages for Navajo Couples* for the Navajo people so members of these populations can strengthen their couple relationships in ways that are consistent with their cultural values. Currently, she is collaborating with the 4-H director in Alaska in conducting research in order to ultimately bring 4-H to youth in remote Native villages in culturally appropriate ways.

Preface

Our colleague and friend, the late Dr. David R. Mace, once said, "Nothing in the world could make human life happier than to greatly increase the number of happy couples and strong families." Throughout eight editions, our goal in writing *Marriages and Families: Intimacy, Diversity, and Strengths* has been to provide students with information about marriage and family relationships that will help them move toward Mace's goal.

We have tried to make the concepts and ideas presented in this book useful and meaningful so students will be able to apply them to their own lives. We hope to help students integrate intellectual ideas and personal experiences, thereby enriching both. Although the text deals with some complex ideas and materials, it is written in a style that is accessible to students new to the field of family studies and to those wishing to learn more about intimate relationships.

Intimacy, Strengths, and Diversity

Three distinctive themes have guided our efforts in writing this book, and they are woven throughout the text. The first is *intimacy,* and our focus is on how to develop and maintain close relationships. Most people seek connectedness and want to be involved in intimate relationships, the most intimate being marriage and family. This book is full of ideas, principles, and suggestions for building and keeping intimate relationships in your life. As a result, this is a book that you will want to keep and refer to throughout your life.

The second key theme is *marital and family strengths.* The family strengths perspective is based on the premise that if you approach relationships from a "problem-oriented" perspective, you will find problems. If you look for strengths, you will find strengths. Growing numbers of family educators and family therapists are using this approach today, helping families recognize their own strengths and use them as a foundation for positive growth. In Chapter 1, we identify a number of strengths that have been found to be present in healthy marriages and families all over the world. Throughout the book, we show how these strengths help families provide healthy and nurturing settings that promote the growth and well-being of individual family members, better enabling them to face the challenges and solve the problems they encounter.

Although the theme of marital and family strengths is integrated throughout the book, three chapters focus especially on this theme: Chapter 2 highlights the couple and family strengths of diverse ethnic and cultural groups, as well as gay and lesbian couples and families; Chapter 14 examines how families can use their strengths to manage stress, abuse, and other family issues; and Chapter 16 looks at how families, communities, and cultures can work together to build a healthier world in the future.

The third key theme is *diversity,* and, wherever possible, we consider how concepts, research, and theories about the family apply to couples and families of diverse ethnic and cultural backgrounds. We also focus on the diversity in structure that characterizes families today, looking at the many different forms that *family* can take. Diversity in sexual orientation—gay and lesbian relationships and families in our society—is another type of diversity we explore. The theme of diversity is introduced in Chapter 1, discussed in detail in Chapter 2, and integrated into discussions throughout the book. One of the four categories of the boxes throughout the text is dedicated to exploring diversity in families.

Family Systems and Family Strengths

We present innumerable theories of family in this book, but we focus especially on family systems theory. Recognizing that the family unit is a system of interdependent parts, we look at how families maintain themselves, yet change; how family members can be separate, yet connected; and how communication facilitates the processes of change and growth. We focus on communication and conflict resolution skills as essential tools for creating healthy intimate relationships. We also look at how families can learn to function well within the larger systems of community and society.

The family strengths perspective was developed by Nick Stinnett, John DeFrain, and many of their colleagues across the country and around the world. We use this perspective throughout the text as a model for understanding and evaluating families. With it, we identify and focus on six key qualities of healthy families: commitment, appreciation and affection, positive communication, enjoyable time together, spiritual well-being, and the ability to cope with stress and crisis. The research driving this model has involved thousands of family members in the United States and other countries around the world.

In Chapter 3, we introduce the Couple and Family Map, an assessment tool that was developed by David Olson and his colleagues. The Couple and Family Map is based on concepts from family systems theory, and it focuses on the three dimensions of cohesion, flexibility, and communication. It has been used in hundreds of studies to help researchers understand and evaluate families. Throughout the text, we cite studies that have used the map as a theoretical base. An ongoing family case study, described in the Instructor's Manual, can be used to show students how the Couple and Family Map is applied. Appendix A contains the instructions and materials to apply the map to couple and family relationships.

Updates in the Eighth Edition

Like a healthy couple and family, a good textbook needs to identify major issues and change over time. We have tried to describe the current issues in marriage and families today and identify changes in these relationships.

The field of relationships, especially marriages and families, is increasingly changing and becoming more diverse and complex. Marriage is being preceded and/or replaced by cohabitation, and two-parent families are becoming less common. Same-sex couples are increasing, as are single parents and people who are choosing not to marry. We will now highlight some of the changes we have made in each of the 16 chapters.

Overall, it is important for the reader to know that as we work on a new edition of the textbook, we check every citation to be sure that it is the most up-to-date source available. In addition, worldwide databases are tapped, organizations that collect the most recent data about marriages and family are searched, and the most reliable research and commentary are chosen to help keep the book current. This process takes 18 months.

Part I: The Social Context of Intimate Relationships

In **Chapter 1, Perspectives on Intimate Relationships,** we have completely updated national statistics on marriage and divorce in America. We have added some new definitions of *family* for the reader, and discussed the controversy between the so-called *exclusionists* and *inclusionists*. The latest developments in the struggle over same-sex marriage in the United States are discussed, followed by new statistics on cohabitation and remarriage. We present several propositions on how to look at couples and families from a strengths-based perspective, and go on to discuss why, from a statistical perspective, marital relationships look stronger than cohabiting relationships. New statistics are featured that show Americans are generally pessimistic about the prospects for the country's economy and for international peace in the near future, but the vast majority are optimistic about how they and their family will do in the coming year.

A number of major challenges Americans face in the broader social environment are described. This section includes the latest statistics on who's minding the kids, looking at the percentages of young children in the care of their parents, other relatives, child care centers, or nonrelatives in home-based arrangements. Violence and domestic abuse in this country are reviewed using very recent research. The latest data on the problems caused in families by tobacco use and excessive alcohol use are reviewed. New research is presented on how family socialization has dropped dramatically in recent years, attributed to increased Internet use. And finally, we look at the increase in single-parent families, the decrease in the number of children, and the decrease in the percentage of women who are stay-at-home moms. For the new Eighth Edition, Chapter 1 has been extensively revised and strengthened.

In **Chapter 2, Cultural Diversity and Diversity in Family Structure: Family Strengths and Challenges,** we have added a discussion about *why culture matters* and we conclude that everything that happens in couple and family relationships happens within a cultural context. This chapter, therefore, is very important in understanding how couples and families function based upon their own cultural values and experiences. Updated information about the ethnic population distribution in the United States is included. Additionally, new information about the increase of gay and lesbian couples and families is provided, and the newest research in this area included.

Chapter 3, Understanding Marriage and Family Dynamics, features a section on the *Family Strengths Perspective,* and we clarify the subsection on *Spiritual Well-Being and Shared Values* by explaining the distinction between spiritual beliefs and religious beliefs. In the subsection on the *Family Development Framework* we discuss the controversy surrounding the exact number of stages involved in the family life cycle, numbering 4 stages to 24 stages, depending on the theoretical model.

Part II: Dynamics of Intimate Relationships

In **Chapter 4, Communication and Intimacy,** the Gender Communication Quotient has been revised and updated, and seven new *Suggested Readings* have been added at the end of the chapter.

In **Chapter 5, Conflict and Conflict Resolution,** new research is featured on the relationship between how well an individual controls anger and the person's health. Also, the terms *fight, fighting,* and *fair fighting* are discussed, drawing attention to the notion that verbal disagreements are serious business and should be treated with caution and good sense.

Chapter 6, Sexual Intimacy, includes a new study about differences and similarities between men's and women's sexual behaviors. In addition, new research about same-sex and opposite sexual behaviors has been included. Findings about the long-term impact of teen pregnancy have also been added to this chapter.

Chapter 7, Gender Roles and Power in the Family, provides the most up-to-date information about gender roles, including information about why women still do most of the work in the home. The latest findings indicate that *attitudes* about such work seem to be different for men and women. This may explain why women do more housework—they enjoy it and have a positive attitude about it. New research about gender roles internationally is also provided.

Chapter 8, Managing Economic Resources, includes new research about the impact of the recession on poverty rates, credit card use, and bankruptcy. How the low interest rates affect the cost of buying a home is also discussed, as well as how financial issues affect couple and family relationships.

Part III: Stages of Intimate Relationships

Chapter 9, Friendship, Intimacy, and Singlehood, provides a new discussion with new citations about the unique friendship patterns of new immigrants and other cultural groups. A new phenomenon in our country is that there are an increasing number of women of child-bearing age who are choosing to have children and who are not getting married. These women are either choosing not to marry or are not finding the right person to marry. The implications for children and families are provided in this chapter. The chapter also discusses new research about the feelings and perceptions of single women in today's society.

Online dating has become increasingly pervasive in today's society. In **Chapter 10, Dating, Mate Selection, and Living Together,** we talk about what we are learning through research about this experience. Also, as our population is aging, dating in the older years is becoming increasingly prevalent. This results in new challenges for this segment of the population and we provide new information about how individuals and couples are addressing these challenges. A new section about theories of mate selection has been added. Research about those from diverse populations is added in multiple places throughout the chapter.

In **Chapter 11, Marriage: Building a Strong Foundation,** the latest marriage statistics from the U.S. Census Bureau are reported; new facts about marriage are presented from the Pew Research Center analyses of government data; and five new *Suggested Readings* are added.

Although children can often bring challenges to married life, **Chapter 12, Parenthood: Joys and Challenges,** draws on a recent study that shows couples with certain characteristics actually have improved couple relationships after they have children. This is groundbreaking research. This chapter also contains new information about the benefits of family education classes addressing the transition to parenthood. There is also new research about the use of punishment and its impact on children from differing cultures in this chapter.

In **Chapter 13, Midlife and Older Couples**, a new section on *Divorce During the Middle and Later Years* has been added, along with a new box on *Grandparents and Grandfamilies*. Also, new research is included on life satisfaction across the lifespan; the economic well-being of older families; the health of older Americans; loneliness and the elderly; and the myth that most older adults end up in nursing homes. There is also a new section on *Losing a Spouse*; and nine new *Suggested Readings*.

Part IV: Challenges and Opportunities

In **Chapter 14, Stress, Abuse, and Family Problems,** new thinking has been added on cross-cultural perspectives of couple and family stress. The *Stress Across the Family Life Cycle* section has been revised and updated with new research. A section on the classic ABC-X Family Crisis Model has been included. The latest research has been added about family members left behind when a person is deployed to a war zone. Up-to-date statistics on domestic violence are now included. The relationship between physical abuse and psychological abuse has been clarified. New sections have been added on alternatives to spanking and the long-term consequences of child abuse and neglect. New material on sibling abuse and child-to-parent abuse has been added. A section is now included on family violence from a global perspective, based upon a new study. The latest statistics on alcohol abuse and families are provided, plus up-to-date information on treatment and prevention of alcohol problems. The discussion on the importance of acknowledging the dangers inherent in the misuse of legal drugs has been strengthened. The list of *Suggested Readings* is filled with current resources, showing how much new research and thinking has appeared in the past few years.

Chapter 15, Divorce, Single-Parent Families, and Stepfamilies, includes 25 new citations, since this is an area of increasing change in our society. There is new information on the effects of divorce, how people manage stepfamily relationships, and how individuals and couples function in same-sex relationships. Much of this new information focuses on the impact on children as family structure changes. Because single-parent families have become so prevalent, a significant section has been added about what we know about this family structure, including a component about the strengths of single-parent families.

Chapter 16, Strengthening Marriages and Families Worldwide, has many new resources related to couple education programs. A new section entitled *Common Questions on Marital and Family Therapy* has been included. The section on *Strengthening Your Marriage and Family Relationships* has been revised. The *Suggested Readings* section has been revised and updated.

Appendices

Appendix A, Couple and Family Scales, based on research over the past 30 years that continues today, remains helpful to students who want to learn how to describe and assess couples and families from a family systems perspective. Having students use these scales to evaluate their own family or another family is a very useful and insight-producing assignment. See the *Activities* section at the end of Chapter 3 for more details on the assignment.

Appendix B, Family Science and Family Research Methods, has been reviewed and all the references have been updated to include the most recent citations.

How We Do Our Job

The field of family studies or family science continues to grow dramatically. Thanks to advances in computer technology and search engines scouring massive databases, we have been able to update this text to include the most current statistics and cutting-edge research studies. More than 350 new sources are cited in this volume, carefully gleaned from computer-driven searches, searching the top journals in the field of marriage and family, and keeping our eyes open literally every day of our lives for interesting new material for this textbook.

The tools listed below have proven to be especially useful as we do our job:

- *Google Scholar* is a Web search engine owned by Google Inc., and is a widely used search engine on scholarly work on the Internet. Google receives several hundred million queries each day through its various services. We have found Google Scholar especially useful when trying to track down the source of different ideas, quotations, or data that we have run across.
- *U.S. government Web sites* of the federal government provide a wealth of information about families that proves useful for textbook writers. Some of our favorite Web sites include Administration on Aging; Centers for Disease Control and Prevention; CIA *World Factbook;* Library of Congress; National Center for Health Statistics; National Council on Alcoholism and Drug Dependence; National Institutes of Health; U.S. Bureau of the Census; U.S. Department of Health and Human Services; National Youth Violence Prevention Resource Center; U.S. Office of Justice; Statistical Abstracts of the United States.
- *Professional organizations and other useful Web sites* include the Alan Guttmacher Institute; Alliance for Children and Families; American Academy of Pediatricians; American Association for Marital and Family Therapy; American Psychological Association; Child Trends; Compassionate Friends; Mayo Clinic; M.I.S.S. Foundation; National Healthy Marriage Resource Center; National Council on Family Relations; National Marriage Project; Pew Research Center; Planned Parenthood.
- *The media* provide some of our favorite sources, including *The New York Times, The Economist, The Nation, AARP Magazine, Time, Newsweek, The New Republic, The Atlantic Monthly, Business Week, Money Magazine, NPR,* and *PBS.*

Finally, but probably most importantly, to update this and every edition of *Marriages and Families: Intimacy, Diversity, and Strengths,* we literally go through every issue of the following 12 professional journals, searching for solid and interesting new research and thinking: *Journal of Marriage and Family, Family Relations, Marriage and Family Review, Journal of Family Issues, Journal of Marital and Family Therapy, National Council on Family Relations Report, Journal of Family Communication, Child Development, Journal of Family Psychology, Family Process, Families in Society,* and the *Journal of Family and Economic Issues.*

Online Resources

The Eighth Edition of *Marriages and Families: Intimacy, Diversity, and Strengths* is accompanied by a number of supplementary learning and teaching available on the Online Learning Center Web site at www.mhhe.com/olson8e.

For the Student

AWARE Online. AWARE is a computerized assessment that contains 15 categories that match the chapters in the book. After completing the AWARE Online assessment, the student receives a 19-page *AWARE Personal Report* that identifies relationship areas and issues that are strengths for the student and problematic issues that need to be considered. AWARE helps personalize the course by showing students how their current relationship attitudes compare with professionals in the field. It also stimulates students' interest and involvement in the class by highlighting current relationship issues. To learn more about AWARE, go to the Online Learning Center Web site at www.mhhe.com/olson8e.

Additional Student Resources. The Online Learning Center Web site that accompanies this text offers a variety of resources for the student. Students will find interactive multiple choice and true/false chapter quizzes, and an annotated list of other online resources. Please visit the text OLC site at www.mhhe .com/olson8e.

For the Instructor

The password-protected instructor side of the Online Learning Center Web site includes AWARE Online, the Instructor's Manual, Test Bank, internet exercises and PowerPoint® lecture slides. Go to www.mhhe.com/olson8e.

Instructor's Manual. For each chapter of the text, the Instructor's Manual provides a chapter outline, learning objectives, a chapter summary, a list of key terms, lecture notes, suggested activities, and suggested readings. The Instructor's Manual also can be downloaded from the Instructor's Online Learning Center.

AWARE Online. AWARE is an acronym for **AW**areness of **A**ttitudes and **R**elationship **E**xpectations. AWARE contains 15 categories that match the chapters in the textbook. After the students have completed the AWARE Online assessment, the instructor can view online and print a 20-page *AWARE Instructor Summary.* The summary provides an overview of the background areas, along with the strengths and issues for the class on 15 categories and the Couple and Family Map. There are several advantages for using AWARE with a class.

- First, the instructor can quickly and efficiently learn about the relevant relationship attitudes of the students in the class.
- Second, by knowing the strengths and growth areas for the class, the instructor can tailor the class to better serve the needs of that class.
- Third, AWARE provides background information about the students that an instructor could not easily ask in a class.
- Fourth, the instructor can provide the class with summary feedback about their relationship attitudes for each chapter in the book.
- Fifth, AWARE personalizes the class for the students and stimulates their interest and involvement in the class.
- Last, AWARE helps engage the students in the class and facilitates greater class interaction. For more information about AWARE, go to www.mhhe .com/olson8e.

Test Bank. The Test Bank offers multiple-choice, true/false, short-answer, and essay questions for each chapter in the text. The Test Bank can be downloaded as a Word file from the Online Learning Center Web site at www.mhhe.com/olson8e. A Computerized Test Bank is also available on the Web site.

PowerPoint® Slides. A collection of tables and figures from the text, augmented by additional graphics, allows instructors to add visual content to their lectures. The PowerPoint® slides are also available on the Web site.

Additional Online Resources. The Instructor's side of the OLC offers access to the student chapter quizzes, an annotated list of other online resources and Internet exercises. The Instructor's Manual, PowerPoint® slides, and more can be accessed on this Web site at www.mhhe.com/olson8e.

Acknowledgments

We are grateful to the following reviewers for providing us with their helpful comments and suggestions during the development of the eighth edition:

Glee Bertram, University of Central Oklahoma
Crystal Bossard, Cincinnati State Technical & Community College
Kelly Champion, Northern Illinois University
Jeffrey Dew, Utah State University
Anne B. Edwards, Purdue University Calumet
James P. Guinee, University of Central Arkansas
David Law, Utah State University
Dandy Levy-Cullins, Texas Southern University
CoSandra McNeal, Jackson State University
Jackie Wiersma, University of Arkansas
Xiaolin Xie, FCNS, Northern Illinois University

David Olson
John DeFrain
Linda Skogrand

1 *Perspectives on Intimate Relationships*

Three Themes of Intimacy, Strengths, and Diversity

Defining Marriage and Family

Trends in Marriage and the Family: Change and Continuity

Focus on Marital and Family Strengths

Advantages of Marriage

Impact of the Social Environment on Relationships

Changing the Social Environment

Positive Responses to the Social Environment

Summary

Key Terms

Activities

Suggested Readings

Three Themes of Intimacy, Strengths, and Diversity

Most people need *intimate relationships* with other people. Intimacy is sharing intellectually, physically, and/or emotionally with another person. In this text we will focus on intimacy in marriage and family relationships and on how they are maintained and how they become broken.

Intimacy usually occurs when individuals disclose information about themselves, allowing themselves to become vulnerable, and involves trusting that the other person will not use that information to cause harm. Sharing information that involves intimacy usually results in receiving support from that person or persons.

Intimacy will be discussed throughout this book in terms of dating and courtship, sexual relationships, communication, dealing with conflict, and other aspects of marriage and couple relationships. Intimacy may look different at different times in the life cycle. In addition to having intimacy in couple relationships, intimacy occurs in parent–child relationships, relationships with extended family, and relationships with others who take the place of family. Most intimate relationships go through periods when that closeness is threatened or destroyed. Our goal is to provide you with ideas and exercises to help you improve your ability to develop and maintain intimate relationships throughout life.

Identifying and focusing on *strengths* and building on those strengths are essential for developing and maintaining successful marriage relationships. The focus of this textbook on couple and family strengths provides evidence from the United States and many other countries around the world on how families succeed in the face of life's inherent difficulties (DeFrain & Asay, 2007). By concentrating only on a family's problems and a family's failings, we ignore the fact that it takes a positive approach in life to succeed. The family strengths perspective is a worldview or orientation toward life and families that is positive and optimistic, grounded in research conducted among thousands of couples and families globally. It does not ignore family problems but restores them to their proper place in life: as vehicles for testing our capacities as families and reaffirming our vital human connections with each other. Not all families are strong, of course, but all families have strengths, and these strengths can be a foundation for continued growth. When one only looks for problems in marriages and families, that is all that one will find. By looking for a relationship's strengths, we create a more balanced and realistic picture of the couple and family situation. Finally, looking for what makes families strong helps us discover knowledge that is useful in helping other families. The strong families identified by researchers around the world become the experts for teaching other families how to create a happy and resilient family environment.

Focusing and building on strengths in relationships will be evident throughout this book in relation to couples, marriage relationships, single-parent families, gay and lesbian relationships and families, parenting practices, relationships in diverse cultures, and life in the middle and later years.

There is more *diversity* in family and couple relationships than ever before. There are a variety of family structures that are described in this book, including married couples, cohabiting couples, gay and lesbian couples, single-parent families, stepfamilies, and grandparents raising grandchildren. There is also greater cultural and ethnic diversity in the United States than ever before, with minority cultural groups becoming a greater proportion of the total population. These cultural groups bring a wide array of values, beliefs, and practices to our understanding of how marriages and families work. It is increasingly challenging to understand the diversity of couple and family relationships that exist today and will continue to increase in the future.

The three themes of intimacy, strengths, and diversity are critical in understanding couple and family relationships today. These themes and the research and literature surrounding these themes are essential for developing healthy and happy relationships. Knowledge about the latest research in each of these areas will help you develop healthy relationships and better understand and appreciate those around you.

Defining Marriage and Family

Not as many people today live in the so-called traditional family, with a dad at work and a mom at home with the kids—only about 20% of all families in the United States match this model (Tavernise, 2011, May 26). In addition to the diverse types of family structure, families may vary in cultural or ethnic background, income, size, and longevity. There are many possible family structures rather than one "right" way for a family to be organized.

What Is Marriage?

Marriage is by nature a multifaceted institution. We define **marriage** as *the emotional and legal commitment of two people to share emotional and physical intimacy, various tasks, and economic resources.*

The following nine characteristics of marriage were identified by the late Carlfred Broderick (1992, 1993). A former president of the National Council on Family Relations, Broderick found these characteristics to be common across income levels, educational levels, and ethnic and cultural groups in the United States:

- *Marriage is a demographic event.* Each marriage creates a social unit in society.
- *Marriage is the joining of two families and social networks.* When individuals marry, they marry not only each other but their partner's family and friends. Their social network may comprise friends of both partners, but only those friends liked by both partners tend to remain friends of the couple.
- *Marriage is a legal contract between the couple and the state.* Each state specifies the rights and responsibilities of the partners.
- *Marriage is an economic union.* A married couple usually becomes a single financial unit for most purposes. As a group, married couples are probably society's most important financial decision makers—buying, selling, borrowing, and sharing resources as one.
- *Marriage is the most common living arrangement for adults.* Few people choose to live alone. Marriage is also the most popular living arrangement for adults.
- *Marriage is the context of most human sexual activity.* Most married couples rate sexual activity positively, especially in the early years.
- *Marriage is a reproductive unit.* Most married couples become parents and see parenting as an important goal and a valued purpose in their lives.
- *Marriage is a unit that socializes children* (although children can also be raised by single parents, extended families, grandparents, and other caregivers).
- *Marriage is an opportunity to develop an intimate, sharing relationship.* Although many marriages fail, many others provide a supportive context in which people develop and maintain intimacy.

Same-sex marriage. Historically speaking, the first laws in modern times recognizing same-sex marriage took effect during the first decade of the 21st century. As this textbook goes to press in the summer of 2013, 13 countries on five continents allow same-sex couples to marry (Argentina, Belgium, Brazil, Canada, Denmark, France, Iceland, Netherlands, Norway, Portugal, Spain, South Africa, Sweden). Several subnational jurisdictions (parts of Mexico and the United States) also allow same-sex marriage. Freedom to marry legislation has also passed in Uruguay, France, and New Zealand, and when these laws take effect in these three countries, same-sex couples will have the freedom to marry, regionally or nationwide, in 17 countries around the world. Bills to legally recognize same-sex marriage have also been proposed, are pending, or have been passed in at least one legislative body in Andorra, England and Wales, Finland, Germany, Ireland, Luxembourg, Nepal, Scotland, and Taiwan, as well as parts of Australia, Mexico, and the U.S. (Freedom to Marry, 2013a).

On June 26th, 2013 the U.S. Supreme Court in Windsor v. United States struck down Section 3 of the so-called Defense of Marriage Act, a 1996 law passed by Congress and signed by President Bill Clinton that denied legally married same-sex couples over 1,100 protections and responsibilities of marriage. By striking down Section 3 of DOMA, the court affirmed equal legal respect and treatment for all married couples, straight or gay (Freedom to Marry, 2013b).

Gay rights advocates hailed the decision as a major step in the struggle for equal protection under the law, while opponents decried the decision. Both sides saw that the struggle would now continue in the U.S., state by state. As this textbook goes to press, 13 states representing about 30% of the U.S. population grant the freedom to marry for same-sex couples (California, Connecticut, Delaware, Iowa, Maine, Maryland, Massachusetts, Minnesota, New Hampshire, New York, Rhode Island, Vermont, and Washington, plus Washington, D.C.) In 2012 New Jersey passed a freedom to marry bill, and there is work underway to override the governor's veto. New Mexico explicitly recognizes out-of-state marriages of same-sex couples, though the state does not grant gays the freedom to marry. Six other states offer broad protections for gays, short of marriage: Colorado, Hawaii, Illinois, and New Jersey allow civil union, while Oregon and Nevada offer domestic partnership (Freedom to Marry, 2013b).

What Is a Family?

Family can be defined in many ways. One dictionary offers the following definitions (*American Heritage Dictionary of the English Language*, 2012):

1. A fundamental social group in society typically consisting of one or two parents and their children.
2. The children of one of these groups.
3. A group of persons related by descent or marriage.
4. People in the same line of descent; lineage.

There are innumerable other definitions of family, and following is a collection that represents a diversity of perspectives:

- A family consists of two or more people (one of whom is the householder) related by birth, marriage, or adoption residing in the same housing unit (U.S. Census Bureau, 2011, Sept. 13).
- The term *family* is an inclusive term for people who "care, support and protect each other" (Australian Government, 2008).
- A family is defined as two or more persons who share resources, share responsibility for decisions, share values and goals, and have a commitment

Strong families are good for raising healthy and happy children. Extended families are a great source of support in raising children.

to one another over time (American Association of Family and Consumer Sciences, 2004).

- The family is the most important unit of society and functions to fulfill its members' needs for both survival and well-being. "Families" come in many forms. A well-functioning family enhances its individual members' ability to function both within the family and in the larger community; such a family provides emotional, physical, and economic mutual aid to its members. Ideally, family is characterized by intimacy, intensity, continuity, and commitment among its members throughout the life cycle (Family Service Association, 2012).

- The definition of a family "should not rest on fictitious legal distinctions or genetic history" but instead should be based on the functional and psychological qualities of the relationship: the "exclusivity and longevity" of the relationship; the "level of emotional and financial commitment"; the "reliance placed upon one another for daily family services"; and how the couple (members) "conducted their everyday lives and held themselves out to society" (New York State Administrative Regulations, 1995).

- Definitions of the family vary along a continuum with biological conceptions on one end of the continuum and social conceptions on the other (Holtzman, 2005). Having a child through birth would be on the biological end, and adopting a child would be on the social end of the continuum. Both are legitimate definitions of family.
- Voluntary family or voluntary kin. People who care for us, support us, and feel like family to us, but are not related by blood or law (Braithwaite, 2008).
- Call it a clan, call it a network, call it a tribe, call it a family. Whatever you call it, whoever you are, you need one (Howard, 2002).

How Americans define *family* is clearly evolving. A research team at Indiana University led by sociologist Brian Powell surveyed more than 2,300 people between 2003 and 2010 (Berman, 2010, Sept. 15). The researchers found that "people are moving away from a traditional definition of family towards a modern definition of family," Powell said. "That includes a greater array of living arrangements. They're including a much broader group of people, broader combination of people as families."

The Indiana research team identified three clusters of Americans, when it comes to defining family: *exclusionists* who hold onto a more narrow definition of family; *moderates* who are willing to count same-sex couples as family if children are involved; and *inclusionists* who have a very broad definition of family. In 2010, the researchers found that almost everyone—99.8%—agreed that a husband, wife, and kids count as a family. Ninety-two percent said that a husband and wife without the kids made a family. "Children provide this, quote, 'guarantee' that move you to family status," Powell said. "Having children signals something. It signals that there really is a commitment and sense of responsibility in a family."

The researchers also found that 83% of Americans say unmarried couples with children are a family. Only 39.6% said that an unmarried man and woman living together were a family, but adding kids jumped the number up to 83%. Thirty-three percent said a gay male couple was a family. Sixty-four percent said they became a family when they added children. This number rose from 54% to 64% between 2003 and 2010. "People right now are really reevaluating their views about same-sex couples," Powell said.

Sixty percent of Americans in 2010 said that if you considered yourself to be a family, then you were one.

We personally believe that any definition of family should be broad enough to encompass a range of family structures, dynamics, and functions. Our definition of family is *two or more people who are committed to each other and who share intimacy, resources, decision-making responsibilities, and values*. This definition is inclusive and allows for diversity in family structure, family values, and ethnic and cultural groups. At a Wimbledon tennis match, sisters Venus and Serena Williams were going to play each other and a sports writer asked, "Will this match hurt your relationship with your family?" The immediate answer was: "Tennis is just a game. Families are forever."

Trends in Marriage and the Family: Change and Continuity

What are marriage and the family like today? Current trends include fewer marriages, later age of marriage, fewer children, continued flattening of divorce rates, more single-parent families and stepfamilies, a greater need for day care, more child abuse, more spouse abuse, and less connection to kin networks (National Marriage Project, 2012).

Strong families enjoy leisure activities together.

Statistics on divorce, domestic violence, and alcohol and other drug abuse, as well as stories of families in crisis, paint a rather negative picture of marriage and family life today. These snapshots of troubled families may be newsworthy, but the situations they describe are not new. For decades, many respected social scientists have predicted that the institutions of marriage and the family would not survive. For example, in 1927, psychologist John B. Watson predicted, "In 50 years, unless there is some change, the tribal custom of marriage will no longer exist." He believed marriage would disappear because family standards had broken down. In 1937, Pitirim Sorokin, a respected Harvard sociologist, wrote, "The family as a sacred union of husband and wife, of parents and children, will continue to disintegrate." Ten years later, Carl Zimmerman, also a Harvard sociologist, noted, "There is little left now, within the family itself or the moral code, to hold the family together" (Bernard, 1970, p. 42).

Although some professionals emphasize the decline of marriage and the family, others see them as being in a state of transition. As Ernest Burgess and his colleagues stated in 1954, "Certainly marriage and the family in the U.S. are in the process of rapid change. But is it change for the worse? Perhaps it may be for the better" (Bernard, 1970, p. 43). In a similar vein, David and Vera Mace, pioneers in the marriage and family enrichment movement in Great Britain and the United States, argued that "marriage has not failed—it is simply in transition" (Mace & Mace, 1980, p. 260). Skolnick and Skolnick (1977), in their classic study *Family in Transition*, clearly illustrated the dramatic changes in family life over the centuries. In fact, one of the salient characteristics of the family is its ability to adapt to changing times and new challenges.

Today, pessimists and optimists disagree about how to interpret these trends and what to do about them. The pessimists see recent changes as an indication that marriage and family are in serious trouble and are declining in their significance to society. They believe that we need to return to a more traditional value system to curtail these negative trends. The optimists, on the other hand, see recent changes as a reflection of the flexibility of marriage and family and the ability of these institutions to adapt to the increasing stresses of modern life. They believe marriage and the family will survive and thrive.

In fact, marriage and the family have survived over time despite all the predictions of their imminent collapse. Moreover, marriage remains the most popular voluntary institution in our society, with about 85% of the population marrying at least once (Popenoe & Whitehead, 2004).

Trends in Marriage and Cohabitation

There are several important trends in the United States that will be briefly described in this section: a decline in the percentage of those who are married, an increase in the number of those delaying marriage until they are older, an increase in the number of the never married, and an increase in the number of couples who choose to cohabit before—or instead of—marrying.

Marriage. Although marriage remains popular in the United States, it is not as popular as it once was. The percentage of people over the age of 18 who are married has steadily declined. In 1970, 68% of adults were married; in 1980, 66%; in 1990, 62%; and about 60% in 2000 (see Figure 1.1). In 2006, homes headed by married couples dipped to 49.7% (Roberts, 2006). This is the first time that married-couple households dipped below 50%, thus making married couples a minority in the United States. There are two reasons for this change: Many couples are choosing to stay single longer or are choosing to cohabit. There are also increased numbers of elderly people who have lost their spouse, which is adding to the number of single-family households. In addition, there are increasing numbers of same-sex couples who are not typically counted as being married.

More individuals are delaying marriage until their late 20s. Today, the median age for first marriage is 28.7 years for men and 26.5 years for women, the oldest in U.S. history. Age at marriage has been on the increase for more than 4 decades. In 1960, the median age for a first marriage was 22.8 years for men and 20.3 years for women (National Marriage Project, 2012; U.S. Census Bureau, 2010).

Cohabitation. The number of unmarried couples who are living together in the United States has increased dramatically over the past five decades. Most

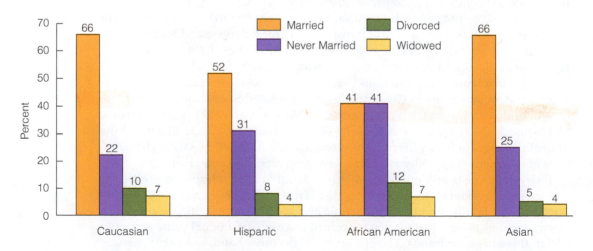

FIGURE 1.1

Marital Status of U.S. Population

Source: U.S. Census Bureau, 2005e, table 54.

younger Americans are spending some time living together outside of marriage, and cohabitation commonly precedes marriage. Between 1960 and 2011 the total number of cohabiting couples increased 17-fold. Unmarried cohabitation, defined as the status of couples who are sexual partners, not married to each other, and sharing a household, is particularly common among young people (National Marriage Project, 2012). An estimated 60% to 75% of first marriages are preceded by cohabitation, and up to 80% to 85% of remarriages (U.S. Census Bureau, 2003b).

Trends in Divorce and Remarriage

Although marriage is still popular, it is not necessarily lasting, with new estimates indicating that the lifetime probability of divorce or separation now falls between 40 and 50 percent (National Marriage Project, 2012, p. 67). However, the majority of those getting divorced will remarry.

Divorce. The majority of people who divorce eventually remarry. However, the increases in divorce rates in the United States and decline in remarriage rates have led to a steep increase in the percentage of adults in this country who are currently divorced. This percentage was only 1.8% for males and

Cohabitation was once rare, but today a majority of young men and women of marriageable age live together without being married for some time, and about 40% of all children before reaching age 16 will spend some time in a cohabiting family.

2.6% for females in 1960, but quadrupled by the year 2000 and remains high today. The percentage of divorced persons is higher for females than for males, because divorced men are more likely to remarry than divorced women. Also, among those who remarry, men tend to remarry sooner than women (National Marriage Project, 2012, p. 69).

As we have seen, the chances of divorce for a first marriage entered into in recent years remains high—between 40 and 50%. But the likelihood of divorce varies considerably among different segments of the American population: the figures are higher for Blacks than for Whites, and higher in the South and West than in other parts of the country. These differences, however, are diminishing. The trend toward a greater similarity of divorce rates between Blacks and Whites has been largely attributed to the fact that fewer Blacks are marrying (National Marriage Project, 2012, p. 72).

There has been little change in such traditionally large divorce rate differences as between those who marry as teenagers and those who marry after the age of 21. Teenagers still have higher divorce rates than the rest of the population. And the divorce rate for the religiously committed remains lower than the divorce rate for the nonreligious (National Marriage Project, 2012, p. 72).

Why are there so many divorces and unhappy marriages in our society? Here are a few things to think about:

1. Many people enter marriage with unrealistic expectations.
2. Many marry the wrong person for the wrong reasons.
3. Marriage is a challenging type of relationship, even if one chooses a partner wisely.
4. Little time or effort is put into developing the relationship skills needed to create and maintain a strong marriage.

Remarriage. A remarriage occurs when a previously married person marries again. The National Healthy Marriage Resource Center (2013) has shared a wide variety of remarriage statistics and trends in the United States that are worth reviewing. Much of these data are dated to the early 2000s, because national surveys and databases that allowed for analyses of marriage patterns no longer exist:

- In 2001, 10,232,000 American wives were in their second marriage (17.7% of all marriages) and 2,106,000 wives were in their third or later marriages (3.6% of all marriages).
- Many Americans have remarried at least once: 12% of men have married twice; 13% of women have married twice; 3% of Americans have married three or more times.
- The median time between a divorce and a remarriage (second marriage) is 3.5 years.
- The median age at second marriage is 35.1 for men and 32.7 for women.
- About half of women in remarriages give birth to at least one child.
- Of all divorced people 25 years old and older, 55% of the men and 44% of the women have remarried.
- The rate of remarriage for women 45 to 64 is half the rate for men the same age.
- Remarriage rates for women with children and women without children are not significantly different.
- Five years after a divorce, 58% of White women have remarried; 44% of Hispanic women have remarried; and 32% of Black women have remarried.

- Ten years after a divorce, 81% of women who were under age 25 at the time of their divorce remarried; 68% of women at age 25 or older at the time of their divorce remarried.

The National Healthy Marriage Resource Center (2013) reports that though remarriages have always existed in the United States, until recently the majority of remarriages followed the death of a spouse rather than a divorce. From early colonial times until as late as the 1920s, remarriage was more likely to follow widowhood than divorce. But the trend changed and by 1987, only 9% of men and women remarried due to the death of a spouse. Remarriages also show higher divorce rates than first marriage. Researchers have found that 20% of first marriages end in divorce within 5 years, while 25% of second marriages end within this same time frame.

The presence of children is one factor associated with the failure of a second marriage. About 40% of remarriages involve children from a previous relationship, and women who had children before their second marriages were more likely to see that marriage fail within 10 years than women without children before the second marriage. Women who reported their children were *not wanted* were more likely to see the second marriage fail within 10 years than those who said their children *were wanted*. Also, failure of a remarriage is associated with remarriages in communities with higher poverty rates, low median family income, and a low proportion of college-educated residents (National Healthy Marriage Resource Center, 2013).

Table 1.1 provides some statistics on marriage and divorce trends. Divorce and remarriage will be discussed in greater detail in Chapter 15.

Trends in Family Structure

Family structure is becoming more complex through divorce and remarriage, which creates new kinship relationships. Contemporary families are more varied today than ever before. There are stepfamilies, same-sex parents and couples,

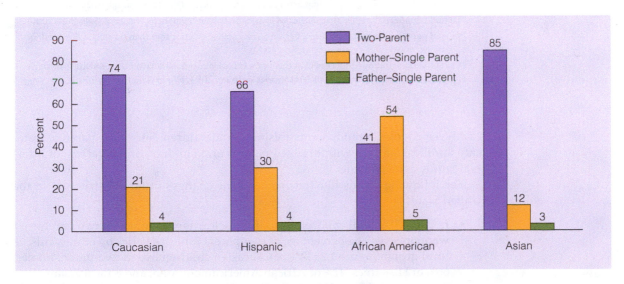

FIGURE 1.2

Family Structures with Children Under 18

Source: U.S. Census Bureau 2012, Table 67.

TABLE 1.1	Statistics on Marriage and Divorce

- 85% of the U.S. population will marry at least once (U.S. Census Bureau, 2008).
- Age at marriage has been on the increase for more than four decades. In 1960, the median age for a first marriage was 22.8 years for men and 20.3 for women. In 2009 the median age for first marriage was 28.4 years for men and 26.5 years for women (U.S. Census Bureau, 2011a).
- Over 75% of Americans report a belief that *being married* is an important value (Popenoe & Whitehead, 2010).
- Marriage among those with college degrees appears to be getting stronger, while marriage among those with a high school degree or less is becoming increasingly unstable and unhappy (Popenoe & Whitehead, 2010).
- In 2010 there were 2,096,000 marriages and 872,000 divorces (Centers for Disease Control and Prevention, 2013a).
- 23.2 million Americans—about 9.1% of the U.S. population—are currently divorced (U.S. Census Bureau, 2009).
- People marrying today have a 40–50% chance of divorcing. Statistically, 40% of first marriages, 60% of second marriages, and 73% of third marriages end in divorce (Popenoe & Whitehead, 2010; U.S. Census Bureau, 2006).
- About 75% of those who divorce will eventually remarry (U.S. Census Bureau, 2008).
- Of the marriages that do not end in divorce, the quality of some of those may be poor (Popenoe & Whitehead, 2010).
- After 10 years of marriage, it has been predicted that only 25% of couples will still be happily married (Popenoe & Whitehead, 2010).
- Most divorces involve children, and more than 1 million children are affected by divorce each year (U.S. Census Bureau, 2008).
- Approximately 40% of children will experience divorce before adulthood (Amato, 2007).
- Women are more likely than men to file for divorce (Popenoe & Whitehead, 2010).
- Most adults adjust well to divorce over time. 30% feel their lives were negatively impacted (Hetherington & Kelly, 2002).
- Divorce and unmarried child bearing are highly related to child poverty (Rank & Hirschl, 1999).
- A small number of studies have found positive individual benefits of divorce such as greater autonomy, personal growth, and happiness (Amato, 2000).
- Married people live longer than unmarried or divorced people (Waite & Gallagher, 2000).
- Married people are happier than single, widowed, or cohabiting people (Waite & Gallagher, 2000).
- Married people have more sex and a better quality sexual relationship than do single, divorced, or cohabiting individuals (Waite & Gallagher, 2000).
- Married people are more successful in their careers, earn more, and have more wealth than single, divorced, or cohabiting individuals (Antonovics & Town, 2004; Waite & Gallagher, 2000).

child-free couples, grandparents raising grandchildren, surrogate parents, foster care families, families with disabled parents and children, and a variety of informal family arrangements.

The following trends illustrate some of the changes in family structure in the United States:

- In 2010, 70% of all children lived in a nuclear family in which two parents were present. The percentage of two-parent families varies by ethnic/cultural group (Figure 1.2): 74% of Caucasian children live in two-parent homes; 66% of Hispanics; 41% of African American children; and 85% of Asian American children (U.S. Census Bureau, 2012).
- Single-parent families with children under the age of 18 have dramatically increased in number. In 1970, only 12% of children lived in a single-parent

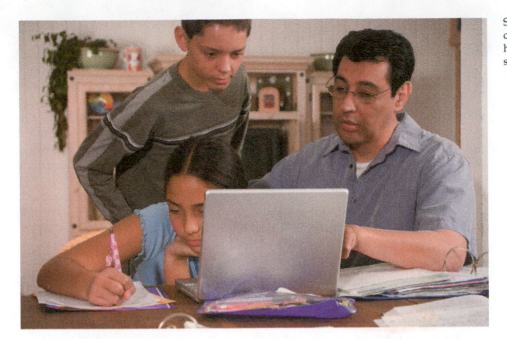

Single-parent families with children under the age of 18 have dramatically increased since 1970.

home. The latest available figures indicate that 35% of children are living in a single-parent home (Child Trends Databank, 2013).

- About half (52%) of all African American families are headed by a single mother, while 25% of Hispanic families, 18% of Caucasian families, and 10% of Asian American families are headed by a single mother (Fields, 2003, p. 5). A small but growing number of families in the United States (3% to 6% of families across ethnic/cultural groups) are headed by a single father (Fields, 2003, p. 5; U.S. Census Bureau, 2005b). Some social scientists have predicted that 60% of children in the United States will have lived in a single-parent household by the time they are 18 years old, if current divorce and remarriage rates hold.

- Families are typically having fewer children today, compared to earlier generations. A woman in the early 1900s in the United States could expect to give birth to about four children during her childbearing years, considered to be ages 15 to 44. A woman living during the Great Depression of the 1930s could expect to have only two children. After World War II, the number of births per woman climbed to 3.7 in 1957, but fell to 1.8 by the mid-1970s. Since then, the birth rate in the United States has hovered around two births per woman, with the most recent number at about 2.1 births per woman. This is a rate that is slightly below the long-term replacement level (Day, 2011; U.S. Census Bureau, 2004b, p. 4-1).

- The number of stay-at-home moms has declined since the 1950s, with more and more women choosing to enter the workforce (Family Focus, 2005). Most recent figures from 2011 indicate that there were 5 million stay-at-home moms in the United States, which is 23% of all the mothers in married-couple family groups with children under age 15 (U.S. Census Bureau, 2012, May 19).

Continuity in Marriage and the Family

Although we tend to focus on how marriage and the family have changed, in many ways these institutions have remained the same over several decades and continue to provide stability in our lives. For example, most people in the United States want to marry, and most couples who do so see marriage as a lifelong commitment and do not plan to divorce. Many couples want to have an egalitarian marital relationship, but equality does not mean that they will share exactly the same roles around the house. Rather, equality means that they work together to accomplish the many tasks and responsibilities required by family life on a regular basis and divide these responsibilities fairly.

Most couples who marry want to have children. Parenthood is an important goal for many couples, a fact that becomes more evident when a couple is not able to have a child. Most parents want their children to have a good education and to be at least as successful as they, the parents, are in society. In fact, most parents would like their children to do better than they have in all aspects of life.

Most family members also have a commitment to each other, although they might not always get along. They have an emotional connection to their immediate and extended family network and feel it is appropriate to call on them in times of need. This family network is an important support system, although it is often taken for granted until a crisis arises. The family is an interdependent system of people who are emotionally connected to each other.

Most families also have a value system that encompasses spiritual and/or moral beliefs that provide the foundation for their attitudes and behaviors. These values become even more important to couples after they have children or in times of crisis. Also, there is an ongoing commitment and connection between parents and their children, even after divorce. This is particularly true if the parents are given joint custody of their children. Most people also feel that the family is the most effective and efficient way of socializing children.

In summary, marriage and family provide significant continuity in our society. Unfortunately, overemphasis on marriage and family problems can overshadow the stability and continuity that these intimate relationships offer us in our daily lives.

Focus on Marital and Family Strengths

A major theme of this book is strengths and the importance of focusing on strengths in a marriage and a family. This means paying attention to the good things your partner or children do and giving praise for the things you appreciate. Too often, married couples and family members tend to shift their focus from the positive to the things they do not like about each other.

Box 1.1 summarizes a number of important observations about relationship strengths. This includes the idea that all families have strengths, and you will observe them if you look for them rather than look only for problems. A strong marriage is the foundation for a strong family. This does not mean that single-parent families cannot be strong, but it is often harder for one parent to manage all the stressors and maintain the strengths. Strengths develop over time and are tested by struggles and ongoing issues that inevitably arise in marriage and parenting. Strengths also provide a framework for dealing with crises and for growing and changing over time.

BOX 1.1   Putting It Together

Learning to Focus on Strengths

Over the past 40 years, researchers looking at couples and families from a strengths perspective have developed the following propositions (Asay, DeFrain, Metzger, & Moyer, 2013; DeFrain & Asay, 2007):

- *Families, in all their remarkable diversity, are the basic foundation of human cultures.* Strong families are critical to the development of strong communities, and strong communities promote and nurture strong families.
- *Not all families are strong, but all families have strengths. If one looks only for problems in a family, one will see only problems.* If one also looks for strengths, one will find strengths.
- *Function, not structure, is most important.* When talking about families, it is common to make the mistake of focusing on external family structure or the type of family rather than internal family functioning.
- *Strong marriages and intimate partners are the center of many strong families.* The couple relationship is an important source of strength in many families with children who are doing well. Parents need to find ways to nurture a positive couple relationship for the good of everyone in the family.
- *Strong families tend to produce great kids.*
- *If you grew up in a strong family as a child, it will probably be easier for you to create a strong family of your own as an adult.* But it's also quite possible to do so if you weren't so lucky and grew up in a seriously troubled family.
- *The relationship between money and family strengths is weak.* Once a family has adequate financial resources the relentless quest for more is not likely to increase the family's quality of life, happiness together, or the strength of their relationships with each other.
- *Strengths develop over time.* When couples start out in life together, they sometimes have considerable difficulty adjusting to each other, and these difficulties are quite predictable. Adjusting to each other is not an easy task. Many couples who are unstable at first end up creating a healthy, happy family.
- *Strengths are often developed in response to challenges.* A couple and family's strengths are tested by life's everyday stressors and also by the significant crises that all of us face sooner or later.
- *Strong families don't think much about their strengths, they just live them.* It is, however, useful to carefully examine a family's strengths from time to time and discuss precisely how family members use these strengths to great advantage.
- *Strong families, like people, are not perfect.* Even the strongest of families have difficulties and disagreements. A strong family is a work of art continually in progress, always in the process of growing and changing.
- *When seeking to unite groups of people, communities, and even nations, uniting around the cause of strengthening families can be a powerful strategy.*
- *Human beings have the right and responsibility to feel safe, comfortable, happy, and loved.*

Sources: Asay, DeFrain, Metzger, & Moyer, 2013; DeFrain & Asay, 2007.

Advantages of Marriage

Although people are delaying marriage and some are choosing not to marry, most people still value marriage. In one survey of adults, 93% rate having a happy marriage as one of the most important or very important objectives (Waite, 2001, 2003; Waite & Gallagher, 2000; Waite & Lehrer, 2003; Waite, Luo, & Lewin, 2009). For college freshmen, 94% said they personally hoped to get married, and they had a negative view of divorce. Over 70% agreed that children do better with both parents, and over 60% felt that children develop more emotional problems if their parents divorce.

But until recently, the positive impacts of marriage on the persons in the marriage have not been emphasized. Linda Waite and Maggie Gallagher (2000) made a major contribution in that regard in their book, *The Case for Marriage,* where they summarized over 200 studies that clearly demonstrated the major positive impacts of marriage.

First, Waite and Gallagher (2000) found that married people live longer than unmarried or divorced people. In fact, Waite and Gallagher stated, "Not being married can be hazardous to your health" (2000, p. 47). Nonmarried women have a 50%

higher mortality rate than married women, and nonmarried men have a 250% higher rate than married men.

Married people live longer partially because they lead a healthier lifestyle. Single men typically engage in more risky behavior, including drinking, smoking, and drug use. Although single women typically have lower levels of risky behavior compared to men, being married also lowers the rate at which women participate in unhealthy behaviors. In addition, marriage improves a man's health as well as a woman's health. Married partners also tend to monitor each other's health more closely than cohabiting couples.

Married people are happier than single, widowed, or cohabiting people. About 40% of married people said they were very happy with their lives, whereas only 18% of divorced people, 15% of separated people, 22% of widowed, and 22% of cohabiting people were very happy.

On the basis of two national surveys, married couples have sex more frequently and find their sexual relationship more satisfying physically and emotionally than singles (Waite, 2001, 2003; Waite & Gallagher, 2000; Waite & Lehrer, 2003; Waite, Luo, & Lewin, 2009). In one study, 43% of the married men reported having sex at least twice a week, whereas only 26% of the single men who were not cohabiting had sex this often. The findings were similar for women; very few married women reported never having sex. Almost half (48%) of married men said sex is extremely satisfying emotionally compared to 37% of cohabiting men who found sex satisfying. There was less of a difference for married women compared to cohabiting women (42% for married versus 39% for cohabiting) who reported that sex was extremely satisfying.

Married sex is better sex because of four factors: *proximity, a long-term contract, exclusivity,* and *emotional bonding* (Waite & Gallagher, 2000). In terms of proximity, being married means your partner is more available, and partners are more comfortable with each other. Because they plan to remain married, married couples are often more willing to invest time, money, and energy in the relationship. By being more sexually exclusive, married couples are more willing to develop a mutually agreeable relationship. Emotionally, married couples feel more connected to each other than cohabiting couples.

Being married is also good for men in regard to their career and financial earnings (Waite, 2001, 2003; Waite & Gallagher, 2000; Waite & Lehrer, 2003; Waite, Luo, & Lewin, 2009). They argue that marriage is almost as important as education in predicting a man's success in a career. Their explanation of why this is so may raise the hackles of some readers, so let's discuss what they are saying in some depth. Why would marriage statistically predict a man's success in a career as much as his level of education? Waite and Gallagher propose that many married men are more successful because they can focus more on earning money and know that other tasks such as meals, laundry, and child care will be handled by their wives. Also, a wife often contributes ideas about her husband's job and generally supports the career of the husband.

The controversy ignites when wives don't feel equally supported in their careers, of course. And if an egalitarian relationship is not created—a genuinely 50/50 marriage—a couple runs the risk of ending up with two marriages, rather than one. Jessie Bernard, an eminent family sociologist, explained her two-marriages concept quite compellingly four decades ago in her classic book *The Future of Marriage* (1972). Bernard argued that marriage was simply better for men than for women because women take care of men, but men in a male-dominant society aren't as willing or capable or inclined to take care of women. She argued that in many cases there are two marriages: *his* marriage and *her* marriage, and his marriage is a much better deal because the wife attends to the husband's needs with more energy and interest than the husband attends to hers.

The argument looks like this behind closed doors, and it is still being fought today in some households:

She: "Well, I took your suits to the Laundromat and got them cleaned and pressed. And I got a great present for your secretary's birthday. Oh, your mom called, and I told her you were too busy to go out to dinner this week, but I would take her to lunch Friday."

He [distracted as he looks through the mail]: "Oh, yeah, thanks. . . ."

She [miffed as blood pressure rises]: "I could use a good wife!"

He [startled and angered by her sarcasm, responds in kind]: "You couldn't afford one!"

[And on and on.]

The concept of two marriages helps explain why women today are more likely to file for divorce than men: In essence, more women feel let down by marriage than men. The solution, of course, is not to bog down in *his* marriage and *her* marriage, but to work together to create *our* marriage. This, however, is no simple task.

Married couples accumulate more financial wealth, which is a total of their assets (home, car, investments, savings) after deducting their debts (mortgages, other loans, credit card debt). Married couples are able to combine their incomes, which is helpful inasmuch as more women work outside the home and increasingly are earning as much as or more than the husband. This pooling effect is worth 12% to 14% for couples at the age of 30 and it increases to 30% for retired couples compared to single individuals. Married couples are also more responsible in their spending because they have another person involved in the decision about spending. Conversely, if a person gets divorced the wealth is divided and each person starts over again (Waite, 2001, 2003; Waite & Gallagher, 2000; Waite & Lehrer, 2003; Waite, Luo, & Lewin, 2009).

Married people, especially women, are less likely to experience domestic abuse than cohabiting and separated women. The abuse rate for separated women is about 3 times higher than that for divorced women and 25 times higher than that for married women. Also, arguments between couples tend to lead to physical abuse in 4% of married couples compared to 13% for cohabiting couples.

Children generally fare better in families where their parents are married (Manning & Brown, 2006). Children from homes where the parents are married tend to be more academically successful, more emotionally stable, and more likely to assume leadership roles. This is, in part, because of the stability and guidance of two parents. Also, a married couple can model communication and collaborative behaviors, which helps childhood learning.

Marriage is much different from cohabitation (Waite & Gallagher, 2000). Cohabitation is seen by society and sometimes by the partners themselves as a temporary arrangement, whereas marriage is still seen as a lifelong commitment. Marriage is seen as a sexually exclusive relationship, and cohabitation is sometimes perceived as more sexually open to others. People who are cohabiting are typically less willing than married couples to be financially responsible for their partners. For married couples there are higher expectations to be seen and to operate as a couple socially than is true for cohabiting couples. Cohabiting couples have less-positive attitudes toward marriage and more-positive attitudes toward divorce than married couples.

In summary, marriage seems to have multiple benefits for both the husband and the wife. Married people live longer, are healthier and happier, and feel better emotionally. They also have more sex and a better sexual relationship. Married people are also more successful in their careers, earn more, and have more wealth. Married women experience less domestic abuse. Children raised by married parents tend to be more emotionally stable and academically successful. So, in many ways, married persons do experience numerous positive outcomes from being married that single and cohabiting couples do not receive.

This is not to say, of course, that if you are unhappy with the person you are living with and rush out and get married everything will work out fine. And this is not to say that if you are unhappy as a single person and rush out and get married you will suddenly be happy as a married person. All this is saying is that for many reasons marital relationships from a statistical perspective look stronger than cohabiting relationships, and married people tend to do better in life in many ways, compared to single people. This is not always the case when looking at individual situations, but on average it is true.

Impact of the Social Environment on Relationships

Human beings do not live and love in a vacuum. Just as we are connected to the special people in our lives—our friends and loved ones—so we are inextricably embedded in our social environment. The **social environment** comprises all the factors in society, both positive and negative, that impact on individuals and their relationships, such as the mass media, the Internet, changing gender roles, and growing urban crowding. As individuals, we each have a modest influence on society, yet society clearly shapes our personal attitudes and behaviors and ultimately our couple and family relationships.

There is emerging interest about the interface between individual and family lives and community life. Basically, it has been found that the strengths of the community enhance life in the family (DeFrain & Asay, 2007). A good example of this is a study showing that when neighborhood factors were controlled, African American students were less likely to drop out of school than White students (Van Dorn, Bowen, & Blau, 2006). Bámaca, Umaña-Taylor, Shin, and Alfaro (2005) found that psychological outcomes for Latino adolescents were related to community assets, with more positive outcomes occurring in neighborhoods that had more assets. This occurred even when parenting influences stayed the same. Other researchers found that problem behaviors for African American children decreased when social assets in the neighborhood increased (Caughy, O'Campo, Nettles, & Lohrfink, 2006). It has also been found that the incidence of teen cohabitation and nonmarital births increased as ties with the community decreased (Houseknecht & Lewis, 2005). These studies make it apparent that there is an interface between families and the communities in which they live and that community strengths enhance family strengths.

We may be drawn to the Western ideal of rugged individualism—going boldly where no man or woman has gone before—but the reality of our lives is probably closer to the East Asian notion that each of us is but a drop of water in the ocean of life. Cultural norms and expectations have a powerful impact on us, especially if we try to behave against these norms. Visiting another culture is one way to experience the pervasive influence the social environment has on our lives, as the following personal account illustrates.

Stress, change, and materialism

Instability of couple and
family relationships

Urban migration and overcrowding

Use of alcohol,
tobacco, and
other drugs

Financial problems
and the global
economy

Violence in our
society

The Internet and
human relationships

Lack of time for self and significant others

Increasing use of child
care outside the family

Changing gender roles
and the balance of power in
relationships

Although families work
and play together to create
a haven in a sometimes
bewildering and hazardous
world, countless elements in
the social environment can
challenge a family's drive
for balance and stability.

"When my husband and I were living in China, everything was so different from what we were used to: the language, the food, the music, the dress, everything. Now this is a hard thing to explain to someone who has not already experienced it, but being out of my own culture, my own environment, I started to feel after a few months in China like my identity as a person was disappearing.

"It was like I was shrinking. Without my family and my friends at home, without our dog Jessie, without my music, without my food, without our crummy old car, I felt so disconnected, so insignificant. One day I would have given $50 for a genuine American cheeseburger. It sounds crazy talking about it now.

"We both finally did adjust pretty well to China. After about a year or so I kind of turned an emotional corner. And after 2 years I felt like an old hand at surviving culture shock. Today, I love China. But we also love home. And I learned something very important from all this: The social environment I'm used to is very, very important to me. I felt like a fish out of water for a while when taken away from what's familiar to me. I'm not the great individualist I thought I was."

In general, the social environment shapes us much more than we can shape the social environment. However, we are not puppets of the social environment. Growing up in an alcoholic family is not an excuse for being an alcoholic. Similarly, being abused as a child does not justify abusing one's own children. Countless people grow up in violent families but are able to rise above those life experiences. Individuals can make positive choices in their lives, regardless of their past lives.

Stress, Change, and Materialism

"Whatever you're doing," one anonymous observer noted, "it's not enough." The velocity of life in this country appears to many people to be increasing exponentially, and our inner demons press us to perform, to produce, to consume, to move. These voices accelerate as social change presses upon us. **Stress** is the body and mind's reaction to life. Stress is directly related to change, and the greater the change, the higher the level of stress. The continuous cascade of new developments in society today can be defined broadly as *progress* perhaps, but many of these developments add stress to our lives.

We now want and expect things to happen fast. We now have voice mail, e-mail, and texting, and we even call regular mail snail mail. We used to have telephones in our homes and offices. Now we carry them in our pockets, purses, and packs and attach them to our belts. We also do multiple tasks at one time. We drive cars while we talk on the phone (though this act is now illegal in many states), put on our makeup, sing along with the CD player, eat a cheeseburger, plan our day, and of course text. Not only have these technological changes increased the volume of information we receive and must respond to, but the time in which we are expected to respond has been shortened—from a few days to return a letter to a few hours to return an e-mail to seconds as we answer our ubiquitous cell phones and read our text messages.

As a society, we also have a great appetite for material possessions—for *stuff*. In fact, everything has to be new, if we were to believe media sales pitches: We need new cars, new houses, new clothes, perhaps a new nose. The business world is brimming with stories of corporate takeovers and downsizing. Companies come and go every day, and workers are cast off like old furniture. In this kind of consumer culture, it's not such a stretch to imagine that finding a new partner is the easiest option when there are problems with the old relationship. As the old male chauvinist joke goes, "I'm tired of my 40-year-old wife. I'm going to trade her in for two 20-year-olds."

Combined, technology and materialism increase our level of stress in all areas of life. We feel pressured to do more and to have more—and to run faster while grasping for all of it. The first casualty in such an environment is our individual sense of well-being. The second casualty is our bond of affection and closeness with each other.

You can counter these trends by being more proactive in your personal life. You can look for ways to be less materialistic and less caught up in the hectic pace of life. This is a personal choice that you can make, which will influence how much you let these factors affect you.

Lack of Time for Oneself and Significant Others

According to family researchers, one of the most difficult qualities to develop in many American families is the ability to spend enjoyable time together. Not only do we find ourselves challenged by a busy and competitive social environment outside the home, but once we return home, we often feel we need time to unwind from a hectic day before reconnecting with others.

For many in today's society, the boundaries between the home and work are being blurred. As sociologist Arlie Hochschild (Hochshild, 1997, 2009, 2010). observed, work becomes more like home and home becomes more like work. Caught in the time bind, the more time we work, the more stressful home life becomes. The more stressful home life becomes, the more we want to escape back to work. Hochschild argues that we must challenge the economic and social system that invites or demands long hours at work, and focus our efforts on investing less time in the job and more time in couple and family relationships.

Families that have discretionary income can purchase labor such as child care and people who care for the household in order to free up time for families to eat out or engage in recreational or leisure activities. Low-income families may not have the option to purchase services and may experience greater challenges in finding time for themselves and other family members. Researchers have found that low-income families are less likely to spend time in activities outside the home but instead intentionally build relationship time into mealtime and other household activities (Tubbs, Roy, & Burton, 2005).

You can counter these trends by purposefully setting time aside for yourself and also time to be with your significant others. Some people have found their alone time is to have 15 minutes with coffee in the morning; others look for time alone at the end of the day, going for an hour-long walk or exercising at the recreation center. For couples, it is important that they purposefully find time to reconnect after a hectic day, even though on some days it might be for only 10 to 15 minutes together. Families also need time to be with each other, and although it is often hard to find time, more families are taking time to set up regular rituals, eating together as often as possible, and not allowing the world to steal their time together.

Increasing Use of Child Care Outside the Family

What do we do about our kids when both parents work outside the home? This is one of the most challenging questions our society faces today. In the United States today more than half of mothers with young children work outside the home, compared to about one in three in the 1970s. Working mothers are now the rule rather than the exception. Women have been moving into the workforce not only for career satisfaction but also because they and their families need the income. Many women who are married have husbands who make less than $30,000 a year (American Academy of Pediatrics, 2013).

While parents are working, who's minding the kids? The U.S. Census Bureau reports that there are approximately 20 million children in the United States under 5 years of age. In a typical week, 12.7 million children (63% of the total) are in some type of regular child care arrangement, defined as at least once a week; 37% of the families had no regular child care arrangement (Laughlin, 2010). These preschoolers were more likely to be cared for by a relative (41%) than by a nonrelative (35%), while 11% were regularly cared for by both. Twenty-three percent of preschoolers were regularly cared for by their grandparent, and 16% were cared for by their father. The survey only asked about child care provided by the father for the time the designated parent was working. Care by other relatives (7%) or by the mother while she worked (4%), or by siblings (3%) was less frequent.

Nearly one-fourth of all young children were cared for in organized facilities, with day care centers (14%) being more commonly used than nursery or preschools (6%). Overall, other nonrelatives provided home-based care to 13% of preschoolers, with 6% cared for by family day care providers. More than one-third of the young children (7.3 million) were not in a regular child care arrangement when the research was conducted.

Mothers and fathers struggle with questions about day care:

- Do I need to work outside the home? Is employment essential for our family's well-being? For my well-being? And how will it affect our child's well-being?
- Will I be able to develop a bond with my child if she spends so much time away from me?
- Will I spend more money on child care, extra clothes, lunches, and transportation than I make on the job?
- How will the stresses of the job affect me personally? Our family? Can all this be balanced effectively?
- How will our child adapt to outside care? Will he receive good care? Will it be as good as the care we can give him?
- Will our child enjoy being with other children? Will the child's social development be enhanced by these opportunities?

For parents, finding satisfactory answers to these and countless other child care–related questions is a considerable challenge.

Parents now are becoming more active in finding ways to balance time away from their children and quality child care. Parents are checking out day care centers more carefully and are looking more critically at teachers and their relationship with their child.

Instability of Couple and Family Relationships

Many observers have argued that our fast-moving and competitive social environment is directly responsible for the high rate of marital dissolution and the increase in single-parent families and stepfamilies. Although personality conflicts and troubles within a marriage clearly contribute to marital breakdown, societal factors and values also influence our intimate behavior.

Rather than come home from work and sit on the front porch to talk with family and neighbors, we often hide behind closed doors in a cocoonlike atmosphere, plopped down in front of the television or a computer. As a result, many of our personal impressions come from the media. We may know more about our favorite actor's marriage than we know about how the couple is doing next door. Perhaps we are choosing to live like this, of course, in the name of personal privacy. But married life on television and in the tabloids is far different from the average couple's life. It can be argued that the steady diet of extramarital affairs and marital conflict we receive from the media helps create a *culture of divorce* in this country.

However, we believe that more people are feeling the need to maintain their close personal relationships. People are seeking more stability in their relationships and are trying to stay more connected. Married couples are more interested in building a stronger marriage, and families are trying to find ways to spend more quality time together.

Violence, Criminal Victimization, and Fear

Violent and abusive behavior continues to be a major cause of death, injury, stress, and fear in our country. More than 1.2 million violent incidents were reported in 2011, according to the FBI, while property crimes hit a 9-year low (Frieden, 2012). The Gallup Poll has found that despite a sharp decline in the United States' violent crime rates since the mid-1990s, the majority of Americans continue to believe that the crime problem in this country is getting worse rather than better, as they have believed for most of the past decade. The latest statistics indicate that 68% of Americans say there is more crime in the United States than the year before, 17% say less, and 8% volunteer that crime is unchanged. In contrast to the 68% who say it is getting worse on the national level, 48% say crime in their local area is getting worse, and 38% say there is an area within a mile of where they live where they would feel unsafe walking alone at night. Why do people tend to feel that crime is increasing rather than decreasing? Gallup argued that this unwarranted pessimism may stem from the imperfect views of crime that Americans receive from the news and other sources, as well as Americans' overall mood (Saad, 2011).

Sexual violence, stalking, and intimate partner violence are major public health problems in the United States, according to the National Intimate Partner and Sexual Violence Survey conducted by the Centers for Disease Control and

Prevention (2011, November). Consequences for survivors of these forms of violence can include mental health problems such as depression, anxiety, low self-esteem, and suicide attempts, and other health consequences including gastrointestinal disorders, substance abuse, sexually transmitted diseases, and gynecological or pregnancy complications. These can lead to hospitalization, disability, or death. Women are more likely to be affected by sexual violence, intimate partner violence, and stalking:

- 1.3 million women were raped during the year preceding the survey.
- Nearly one in five women have been raped in their lifetime, and one in 71 men have been raped during their lifetime.
- One in six women have been stalked, and one in 19 men.
- One in four women have been the victim of severe physical violence by an intimate partner, and one in seven men have experienced severe physical violence by an intimate partner.

Nationwide in 2011, there were an estimated 681,000 victims of child abuse and neglect, according to the U.S. Department of Health and Human Services (2011). The unique victim rate was 9.1 victims per 1,000 children in the population. Victims in the age group of birth to 1 year had the highest rate of victimization at 21.2 per 1,000 children in the national population. Victimization was split between the sexes with boys accounting for 48.6% and girls accounting for 51.1%. Fewer than 1% of victims were of unknown sex. Eighty-seven percent of the victims were comprised of three races or ethnicities: African American (21.5%); Hispanic (22.1%), and White (43.9%). More than 75% of the victims suffered neglect (78.5%). More than 15% suffered physical abuse (17.6%). Less than 10% suffered sexual abuse (9.1%). Child fatalities are the most tragic consequences of maltreatment. An estimated 1,570 children died from abuse and neglect in the United States. This is 2.10 deaths per 100,000 children in this country.

Most recent statistics on suicide indicate that 34,598 people took their own life in the United States (National Institute of Mental Health, 2013). The overall rate was 11.3 suicide deaths per 100,000 people. An estimated 11 suicide attempts occur for every person who actually ends his or her life. Risk factors for suicide include: depression and other mental disorders, or substance-abuse disorder; a prior suicide attempt; family history of mental disorder or substance abuse; family history of suicide; family violence, including physical or sexual abuse; firearms in the home, the method used in more than half of all suicides; incarceration; and exposure to the suicidal behavior of others, such as family members, peers, or media figures.

Gun violence in the United States is far greater than gun violence in any other of the G-8 countries that collect data. The Group of Eight includes the eight largest economies in the world (ABC News, 2012). There are an estimated 88.8 civilian guns per 100 people in the United States, according to the Small Arms Survey, a number unparalleled in the rest of the world and higher than the other G-8 countries for which there are data. The United States also has a much higher rate of homicides by gun—3.2 homicides by firearm per 100,000 people, according to the United Nations Office on Drugs and Crime Homicide Statistics. Italy, the G-8 country with the second highest rate of homicides by firearm, comes in far behind the United States. According to United Nations data, a person is 4.5 times more likely to die from gun violence in the United States than in Italy. In France, the homicide by firearm rate is 0.1 per 100,000. That is one in a million.

Use of Alcohol, Tobacco, and Other Drugs

Drinking and smoking are woven into the very fabric of American culture, and yet the use of legal substances—alcohol and tobacco—kills hundreds of thousands of Americans every year, far more deaths than can be attributed to illegal drugs.

Some statistics compiled by the Centers for Disease Control and Prevention (2013b), give a good picture of the situation concerning alcohol:

- There are approximately 80,000 deaths attributable to excessive alcohol use each year in the United States, making alcohol use the third leading life-style-related cause of death in our country.
- Excessive alcohol use is responsible for 2.3 million years of potential life lost each year, or an average of about 30 years of potential life lost for each death.
- In 2006 there were more than 1.2 million emergency room visits and 2.7 million physician office visits due to excessive drinking.
- In 2006 the economic costs of excessive alcohol consumption were estimated at $223.5 billion.
- Excessive alcohol use increases the risk of unintentional injuries, including traffic injuries, falls, drownings, burns, and unintentional firearm injuries.
- Excessive alcohol use increases the risk of violence, including intimate partner violence and child maltreatment. About 35% of victims report that offenders are under the influence of alcohol. Alcohol use is associated with two out of three incidents of intimate partner violence. And alcohol is a leading factor in child maltreatment and neglect cases, and the most frequent substance abused among these parents.
- Excessive alcohol use increases the risk of miscarriage and stillbirth among pregnant women, and a combination of physical and mental birth defects among children that last throughout life.
- Excessive alcohol use increases the risk of alcohol poisoning, a medical emergency resulting from high blood alcohol levels that suppress the central nervous system and can cause loss of consciousness, low blood pressure and body temperature, coma, respiratory depression, or death.

CATHY

BY CATHY GUISEWITE

Cathy © Cathy Guisewite. Reprinted with permission of Universal Uclick All rights reserved.

- Long-term health risks associated with excessive alcohol use include neurological problems (dementia, stroke and neuropathy); cardiovascular problems (myocardial infarction, cardiomyopathy, atrial fibrillation, and hypertension); psychiatric problems (depression, anxiety, and suicide); social problems (unemployment, lost productivity, and family problems); cancer of the mouth, throat, esophagus, liver, colon, and breast; liver diseases (alcoholic hepatitis, cirrhosis, Hepatitis C virus); and other gastrointestinal problems (pancreatitis and gastritis).

The research-based evidence on the negative effects of tobacco use is also overwhelming, regardless of what the advertisers say. Statistics from the Centers for Disease Control and Prevention (2013c):

- Tobacco use is the single most preventable cause of disease, disability, and death in the United States. Each year, an estimated 443,000 people die prematurely from smoking or exposure to secondhand smoke, and another 8.6 million live with a serious illness caused by smoking.
- Despite these risks, about 46.6 million U.S. adults smoke cigarettes. Smokeless tobacco, cigars, and pipes also have deadly consequences, including lung, larynx, esophageal, and oral cancers.
- Smoking harms nonsmokers as well. An estimated 88 million nonsmoking Americans, including 54% of children aged 3–11 years, are exposed to secondhand smoke. Even brief exposure can be dangerous, because nonsmokers inhale many of the same poisons in cigarette smoke as smokers.
- Secondhand smoke exposure causes serious disease and death, including heart disease and lung cancer in nonsmoking adults and sudden infant death syndrome, acute respiratory infections, ear problems, and more frequent and severe asthma attacks in children. Every year, primarily because of exposure to secondhand smoke, it is estimated that 3,000 nonsmoking Americans die of lung cancer, more than 46,000 die of heart disease, and about 150,000–300,000 children younger than 18 months have lower–respiratory tract infections.
- Add to this enormous health toll the significant economic burden of tobacco use: more than $96 billion each year in medical costs and another $97 billion a year from lost productivity.
- Cigarette companies spend about $13 billion per year on advertising their products. This comes to $36 million per day (Centers for Disease Control and Prevention, 2009c, d).

The number of deaths caused by alcohol is dwarfed by the number of deaths caused by tobacco, as we have seen: approximately 80,000 alcohol-related deaths in a recent year, compared to 443,000 tobacco-related deaths. These are legal drugs, killing 523,000 Americans each year. Illegal drugs claim the lives of an estimated 10,000 to 20,000 Americans each year (Centers for Disease Control, 2007). Thus, an estimated 22 to 44 times as many people are killed by legal drugs in this country each year, compared to the number killed by illegal drugs.

You can counter these trends by limiting or eliminating altogether your use of tobacco and alcohol, which is easier if you choose friends who also have a similar lifestyle. By limiting your use, you can minimize the addicting quality of these drugs, which are very difficult to stop using once one is addicted. Because drugs negatively affect your body in the short and long run, adopting a lifestyle without them will bring you a healthier life.

The Internet and Human Relationships

In our continuous quest to market technological solutions to human problems, much has been made of the computer's potential for connecting human beings. In the movie *You've Got Mail*, Meg Ryan and Tom Hanks fall in love via e-mail. It is a charming notion, but research tells a more complicated story.

The Internet is used extensively by people of all ages. Some of the trends we see for adults using the Internet include the following (U.S. Census Bureau, 2005d):

- People 35 to 54 years of age use the Internet more than other adult age groups.
- Men and women use the Internet about equally.
- Married people use the Internet more than single people.
- College graduates are more likely to use the Internet than people who do not have college degrees.

Research indicates that more than 68% of households used broadband Internet access service, and approximately 80% of households had at least one Internet

Too much time on the Internet can create problems in relationships for many people.

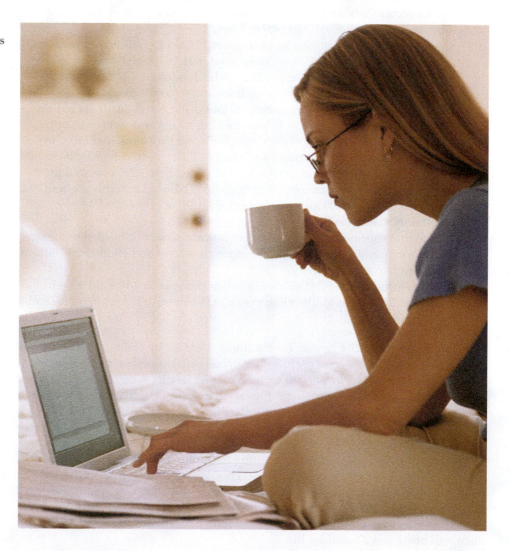

user, either at home or elsewhere (Economics and Statistics Administration, 2011). Parents and children use the Internet for e-mailing, text messaging, listening to music, reading the newspaper, shopping online, and many other activities. Monitoring children's use of the Internet is increasingly difficult as young people rely on it to do homework, which means they also have access to unsuitable Web information.

Research at the University of Southern California indicates that more and more of America's Internet-connected households report erosion of face-to-face family time, increased feelings of being ignored by family members using the Web, and growing concerns that children are spending too much time online (Annenberg Center for the Digital Future, 2009). The USC research team reported that the percentage of people who say they spend less time with household members since being connected to the Internet nearly tripled, from 11% in 2006 to 28% in 2008. Total hours devoted to family socializing dropped by more than 30% over the 3-year period, from about 26 hours per month to 17.9 hours per month.

According to a study by Wolak, Mitchell, and Finkelhor (2006), one in seven youths have received unwanted sexual solicitations on the Internet, one in three have experienced unwanted exposure to sexual material, and one in 11 have been subjected to threatening or other offensive behavior. The good news is that these numbers were lower than they were 5 years before, as a result of national Internet safety programs.

Pedophiles often use the Internet to lure children into participation in sexual behavior. Sexual exploitation of children on the Internet is an increasing concern for parents, law enforcement agencies, and legislators (Wolak et al., 2006). Research indicates that parents have made efforts to monitor young people's use of Internet sites, with one study indicating that 61% of parents regulated their teen's Internet use (Wang, Bianchi, & Raley, 2005).

What about adult access to pornography on the Internet? What affect does it have on marriage and family lives? It is estimated that 15% of individuals visiting Internet porn sites develop sexual behaviors that interfere with their lives (Gustafson, 2005). On a very basic level, pornography is viewed in secret, which creates deception in marriage and contributes to divorce (National Coalition for the Protection of Children and Families, 2007). In addition, Dr. Mary Anne Layden, a psychotherapist and expert on sexual addiction, concludes that involvement in pornography is the common theme in sexual violence. Layden says that pornography increases the likelihood of sexual addiction, and 40% of sex addicts will lose their spouse, 58% will have financial difficulties, and 27% will lose their jobs or be demoted (Gustafson, 2005).

Sex is big business, and some say it has become a national obsession. This trend has been fueled by an increase in Internet sex reaching deep into our homes, causing problems for children and for marriage and family relationships.

Changing Gender Roles and the Balance of Power

There has been a dramatic increase in the number of mothers working outside the home. This development has helped fuel an ongoing discussion of the roles of women and men in America and how power should be allocated in society as a whole and between household partners in particular.

Though 22 governments around the world currently have female heads of state, the United States has yet to elect a woman president (Institute for Women's Leadership, Rutgers University, 2011). Nevertheless, women are serving as associate justices in the Supreme Court, as senators and representatives of Congress, and in countless other positions of power and influence in both government and the business world. With the emergence of women in traditionally male roles, particularly in positions of power, **gender roles** (the traits and behaviors assigned to males and females in a culture) are being redefined.

Just as *supermoms* struggle to find a meaningful balance between work and family, so too men are challenged by their own changing world. Years ago, a man's home may have been *his* castle; today it's an *egalitarian haven.* Just how fairly power and work should be shared in American households is a topic of considerable discussion today. Some observers suggest that men still have a long way to go before true equality is reached in the home.

Many maintain that women have been the true pioneers of the gender revolution, arguing that wives have more quickly changed their roles *outside* the home than men have changed their roles *inside* the home. Still others question how equal we really want males and females to be in our society. They assert that females and males are biologically different and that wives should stay at home to better socialize our children. Regardless of one's position, it's impossible to deny that gender roles and relationship power balances are evolving in today's society.

Urban Migration and Overcrowding

"The history of American agriculture," according to Rex Campbell, a rural sociologist at the University of Missouri at Columbia, "is the history of technology in rural areas" (Campbell, cited in Graham, 1998, p. 9; also, Campbell, 2010). When farmers depended on animals for work and transportation, small towns dotted the rural landscape in the heartland about 6 miles apart. Eventually, trucks and tractors replaced horses and mules, farms got bigger, and the number of farmers and farm families declined steadily over the years. Small towns also shrank in size.

What do we lose when a small town vanishes? What do we lose when the kids grow up and leave the farm or ranch for the city? A realist, focusing solely on harsh economic forces, might say that the young person is leaving the farm to find work and a more stable life in an urban environment. An idealist might argue that we lose a little bit of the fabric of America, a small piece of the American dream. American rural societies tend to be caring environments in which many honest and hard-working individuals live and join together to help each other and their communities to succeed (Struthers & Bokemeier, 2000).

Another trend is that more people are moving away from the large cities to smaller communities within commuting distance. Although it may take a village to raise a child, a villagelike atmosphere can also be created in an urban neighborhood, in an apartment building, or among relatives and friends scattered about a city. The impersonal forces of urban living can be countered by the creation of villagelike social structures in the neighborhood, in the workplace, in religious institutions, and in community settings. Villages today are also being created in cyberspace. Many people enrich their already vibrant social lives by connecting to loved ones, friends, and colleagues globally via the Internet. One's neighborhood may reach out through several continents.

Financial Problems and the Global Economy

Financial issues are the most common stressors couples and families face, regardless of how much money they make. Researchers have consistently found that economic distress and unemployment are detrimental to family relationships. More than one in five children in this country live in poverty (22%), and more than one in three poor people are children (36%) (National Poverty Center, 2010).

Food security in American households and communities is defined as access by all people at all times to enough food for an active, healthy life. The latest data indicate that 85.1% of U.S. households were food secure throughout 2011, while 14.9% were food insecure at least some time during that year (United States Department of Agriculture, Economic Research Service, 2013).

The National Coalition for the Homeless argues that it is very difficult to estimate how many people are without a home in the United States, but the best approximation comes from a study conducted by the Urban Institute, which found that 3.5 million people are likely to experience homelessness in a given year, and 1.35 million of these people are children. The most recent statistics available indicate that children under age 18 account for 39% of the homeless population; and that 42% of homeless children were under the age of 5. It is argued that two trends are largely responsible for the rise in homelessness in the past 20 to 25 years: a growing shortage in affordable rental housing and, at the same time, an increase in poverty (National Coalition for the Homeless, 2009, July).

Many Americans today are doing well financially, and yet many other Americans live close to the edge, lacking savings and chronically spending more than they earn. Easy credit lines have contributed to mounting debt and difficulty. Credit card debt, which carries extraordinarily high interest rates, plagues many Americans, and many are in over their heads from housing payments spurred, again, by easy credit. As we have seen, debt threatens not only individuals and families but also the well-being of the lenders and, eventually, the economy as a whole.

Although economic survival is challenging for many people in the United States, residents of many countries around the world are in far worse straits. Nonetheless, their economic problems do not exist in isolation; as business commentators and politicians frequently point out, we are living in a global economy. The strength of the American economy is inextricably linked in complex ways to the economies of many other nations.

Thus the employment situation in Asia, Europe, or Latin America influences marriage and family relationships not only in those corners of the world but in this country as well. For example, if American farmers can't find markets for their produce in the United States or elsewhere, they aren't going to be able to buy American cars, Japanese televisions, or shirts crafted in Malaysia. Likewise, if the Japanese or Malaysians can't find markets for their products at home or abroad, income and employment will drop in those countries, and Malaysians won't be going to college in California and Japanese won't be vacationing in Hawaii.

Although individuals cannot directly influence the economic changes in the United States or internationally, they can control their own spending. The most positive approach is that people should have a saving and investment plan, which is only possible if a person stays out of debt by limiting credit card spending and other overspending.

Changing the Social Environment

Recently, there have been a number of initiatives with the goal of improving the social environment in order to improve the lives of individuals and families in communities. An example of one of these initiatives is the Search Institute in Minneapolis, Minnesota, a nationally known organization that conducts research and creates programming around assets that promote healthy growth and development of young people (Search Institute, 2013). Twenty of the 40 assets that have been known to help youth have to do with positive experiences that young people receive from interactions in their communities. Several communities have enhanced community assets, such as schools, neighborhoods, and youth organizations, with the goal of ultimately improving the lives of young people.

William Doherty, a family scholar at the University of Minnesota, has developed the Families and Democracy Model, which provides strategies to engage citizens to make changes in their communities (Doherty, 2013). The model provides direction to family professionals and community citizens to come together to solve problems that affect individuals and families. After hearing from a family professional about the loss of family time in today's busy society, community members in one neighborhood decided to do something to change this societal trend. Using the Families and Democracy Model, the community developed and implemented the Putting Family First initiative, which encourages families and community institutions to make family time a high priority. One of the outcomes of this initiative was the cancelation one night a week of all community activities so that families could spend time together.

Many communities have schools, organizations, and religious institutions that provide positive experiences for the individuals and families who live in those communities. Even when those institutions are not present, community initiatives can create a social environment that will benefit the community's residents.

Positive Responses to the Social Environment

Because the social environment in which we live poses many problems for couples and families, it is important that couples and families be more proactive, beginning with their own relationships. There is growing evidence that people are happier, healthier, and wealthier if they are in a marriage (Waite & Gallagher, 2000). And a strong marriage brings even more positive benefits for the individuals, the couple, and their family.

Fortunately, there are countless ways to provide for oneself and one's close relationships and at the same time help make the world a better place. There are types of work and lifestyle that provide not only financial security but also emotional satisfaction and the comfort of knowing that one's life actually makes a difference. The following account illustrates the reciprocal value of giving to others. This is what Raedene, 20, an undergraduate student and volunteer in a Big Brothers Big Sisters program, had to report:

I felt it was my job as a college student as well as a citizen to give something that I had always received, a little love and attention. I signed up for training in the program and was contacted by one of the organizers. After attending many long hours of training, I wondered if I had gotten myself into something more than I had bargained for. They required me to spend at least 5 hours a week with my match. I didn't think that I possibly had time but decided to give it a shot.

About 5 days after training, I received a phone call that I was going to be matched with a little 5-year-old girl. I met my supervisor at the home of Elizbeth, my new little friend. A little nervous, I walked into their home. It was really strange. The minute I sat down, Elizbeth jumped up on my lap like she had known me for years. "Could you read this book to me? … Watch this! … Come into my room!" She just couldn't stop talking.

I did know from that minute on that this young child needed my love and attention more than 5 hours a week. I felt a sense of warmth come over me. To think that I was second-guessing 5 hours a week to give to a child who needed me. We played for a couple of hours until her mom felt comfortable with the match. I told Elizbeth that I would phone her Monday. Her response was, "Don't forget." When I left all I could do was smile. I knew I was in for some fun.

Over the semester I have seen much growth in her, socially and intellectually. She's in kindergarten and is always telling me how much she likes it, and I always try to reinforce how much fun school is. I understand what she talks about, and I listen to what she has to say. I feel she has gained so much trust in me over the past 4 months.

I am able to communicate openly with her mother. I offer suggestions to her on many topics. I am very honest with her mother, and her mother trusts me a lot, too. I have learned how difficult a time their family has dealing with finances, stepparents, and stepsiblings. I have seen much growth in their family over the past 4 months. I am very happy that I chose to volunteer my time. I wish everyone would volunteer because not only does the child benefit from the experience, but you do, too.

The late Betty Friedan (1921–2006), a pioneer in the latest wave of the feminist movement, said, "People's priorities—men's and women's alike—should be affirming life, enhancing life, not greed." She argued for a basic restructuring of our economy and society, putting the lives and interests of people first. The restructuring cannot be accomplished in terms of women versus men, Blacks versus Whites, old versus young, conservative versus liberal. "It can't be done by separate, single-issue movements now, and it has to be political to protect and translate our new empowerment with a new vision of community, with new structures of community that open the doors again to real equality and opportunity" (Friedan, 1997; National Women's Hall of Fame, 2013).

Summary

- The family today is not in danger of extinction, but it is changing. The American family is more diverse today, in terms of family structure and ethnicity, than ever before.

- Somewhat under half the people marrying today will probably divorce at some time in their lives, often because they enter marriage with unrealistic expectations, marry the wrong person, marry for the wrong reasons, or have few skills to deal with the many challenges of marriage.

- Marriage is the emotional and legal commitment of two people to share emotional and physical intimacy, various tasks, and economic resources. A family is two or more people who are committed to each other and who share intimacy, resources, decision-making responsibilities, and values.

- Some of the major trends in family structure, marriage, divorce, and remarriage are the following: There are both more families headed by single women and more stepfamilies today than there were in the 1950s and 1960s; families are smaller today; women are more likely to work outside the home after marriage; both men and women are marrying at a later age; cohabitation before marriage has increased dramatically; the divorce rate increased but has now stabilized at somewhat under 50%; and about 75% of those who divorce later remarry.

- Though not all families are strong, all families have strengths, and strengths develop over time. Strengths help families cope with stress and problems and help families better manage change.
- Marriage has many advantages for individuals, including a longer life, better health and healthier lifestyle, more money and wealth, a better sexual relationship, less domestic abuse for women, and more successful children.
- Human beings do not live and love in a vacuum. Besides being connected to special people in our lives, we are inextricably embedded in our social environment. As individuals, couples, and families, we have little influence on society, but society has a great deal of influence on our personal attitudes and behaviors.
- There are many elements in our social environment that pose difficult challenges for couples and families. These include stress, change, and materialism; lack of time for oneself and significant others; the increasing use of child care outside the family; instability of couple and family relationships; violence; the use of alcohol, tobacco, and other drugs; the Internet's effects on human relationships; changing gender roles and the balance of power in intergender relationships; urban migration and overcrowding; and financial problems and the effects of the global economy on families.
- Community initiatives led by community members and family professionals have made some communities more supportive of youth development and building strong family relationships. These initiatives can be models for other communities.
- Surveys over the years indicate that the majority of Americans think their marriages and families are doing pretty well and that their lives are generally satisfying.

Key Terms

marriage	stress
family	gender role
social environment	

Activities

1. In small groups, write down your own definition of the family. Share your responses within the group and compare how your ideas are similar and/or different.
2. What is your definition of marriage? After writing your definition, compare it with the definition used in this book.
3. Interview a grandparent or a great-grandparent (or another older person you would like to get to know better) about family life in *the old days*—both positive and negative aspects. Some interesting areas to explore might be (1) growing up in a family, (2) a *woman's place*

in the world 50 or more years ago, (3) gender roles, (4) the Great Depression of the 1930s, (5) World War II, (6) major family crises, (7) religion, and (8) philosophies of child rearing.
4. What are the major stressors in your social environment? Make a list and discuss it with others. How did you deal effectively with these stressors?

Suggested Readings

Al-Anon/Alateen. (2013). "For over 55 years, Al-Anon (which includes Alateen for younger members) has been offering strength and hope for friends and families of problem drinkers. It is estimated that each alcoholic affects the lives of at least four other people . . . alcoholism is truly a family disease. No matter what relationship you have with an alcoholic, whether they are still drinking or not, all who have been affected by someone else's drinking can find solutions that lead to serenity in the Al-Anon/Alateen fellowship." Web site: http://www.al-anon.alateen.-org/english.html.

Alcoholics Anonymous. (2013). In their own words, AA is "a fellowship of men and women who share their experience, strength and hope with each other that they may solve their common problem and help others to recover from alcoholism. The only requirement for membership is a desire to stop drinking." AA charges no dues or fees for membership and is self-supporting through member contributions. It is not allied with any sect, denomination, politics, organization, or institution. AA does not wish to engage in any controversy, and neither endorses nor opposes any causes. "Our primary purpose is to stay sober and help other alcoholics to achieve sobriety." Web site: http://www.aa.org/lang/en/subpage.cfm/page=1.

Asay, S. M., DeFrain, J., Metzger, M., & Moyer, B. (2013). *Family violence from a global perspective: A strengths-based approach*. Thousand Oaks, CA: Sage.

Bryant, J., & Bryant, J. A. (2001). *Television and the American family*. (2nd ed.). Mahwah, NJ: Erlbaum.

Cherlin, A. (2009). *The marriage-go-round: The state of marriage and family in America today*. Clashing values have caused more partnering and repartnering in the United States than elsewhere in the world, Cherlin argues. The reason, in part, is that Americans value both marriage and individualism.

Dalla, R., DeFrain, J., Johnson, J., & Abbott, D. A. (2009). *Strengths and challenges of new immigrant families: Implications for research, education, policy, and service*. Lanham, MD: Lexington Books/Rowman & Littlefield. Explores the lives of East Indian, Sudanese, Somali, African, Asian Indian, Korean, Irish, Egyptian, Israeli, Chinese, Mexican, and other immigrants. "A wonderful introduction for those wanting to study or work with immigrant families."

Deal, R. L., & Olson, D. H. (2010). *The remarriage checkup: Tools to help your marriage last a lifetime.* Minneapolis: Bethany House. Ways in which remarried couples can build on their strengths and overcome relationship problems.

DeFrain, J., & Asay, S. M. (Eds.). (2007). *Strong families around the world: Strengths-based research and perspectives.* London and New York: Haworth Press/Taylor & Francis.

Esteinou, R. (2009). *Construyendo relaciones y fortalezas familiares: Un panorama internacional.* Mexico, D.F.: Centro de Investigaciones y Estudios Superiores en Anthropologia Social. This book, published in Spanish in Mexico City, is the first book in Latin America to focus on family strengths. The book is the result of the Mexican Family Strengths Conference held in Cuernavaca, and includes articles from Mexico, Australia, Botswana, China, Italy, Korea, and the United States.

Freedom to Marry. (2013a). What's happening now with marriage. Web site: http://www.freedomtomarry.org.

Freedom to Marry. (2013b). Marriage at the Supreme Court in 2013. Web site: http://www.freetomtomarry.org/landscape/entry/c/supreme-court.

Kartemquin Films. (2008). *The new Americans.* Web site: kartemquin.com. Follows 4 years in the lives of a diverse group of contemporary immigrants and refugees as they start new lives in America. An Indian couple is viewed through the dot-com boom and bust in Silicon Valley. A Mexican meatpacker struggles to reunite his family in rural Kansas. Two families of Nigerian refugees escape government persecution. Two Los Angeles Dodgers prospects follow their big dreams of escaping the barrios of the Dominican Republic. And a Palestinian woman marries into a new life in Chicago, only to discover that in the wake of September 11, she cannot leave behind the pain of the conflict in her homeland.

National Marriage Project. (2012). *The state of our unions: Marriage in America 2012.* Web site: http://www.nationalmarriageproject.org.

National Stepfamilies Resource Center. (2013). Web site: http://stepfamilies.info.

Northern Territory Government. (2008). *Strong families: Sharing cultural parenting knowledge.* Darwin, N.T., Australia: Department of Health and Community Services. Focuses on four strong families in Australia: the Ahmed family from Somalia; the Albert family from Thailand and Australia; the Gray family from Papua New Guinea; and the Casimiro-Branco family from East Timor. The families share their personal stories, their family traditions, and how they have dealt successfully with the challenges of life they face in Australia today.

Olson, D. H., Olson-Sigg, A., & Larson, P. J. (2008). *The couple checkup.* Nashville: Thomas Nelson. Based on a survey of 50,000 couples, the book is an effort to help couples find the strengths in their relationship and build on these strengths.

Straus, M., Gelles, R., & Steinmetz, S. (2006). *Behind closed doors: Violence in the American family.* New Brunswick, NJ: Translation Publishers.

Visit the text-specific Online Learning Center at **www.mhhe.com/olson8e** for practice tests, chapter summaries, and PowerPoint slides.

2 Cultural Diversity and Diversity in Family Structure: Family Strengths and Challenges

Diversity and Strengths in Family Structure and Cultural Context

Why Culture Matters

Intimacy and Diversity

Gay and Lesbian Couples and Families

The Concepts of Race, Culture, and Ethnicity

U.S. Demographics and Future Trends

Challenge to Researchers and Practitioners

Cultural Competence

Kin Relationships Across Cultures

Family System and Sociocultural Characteristics

Family Strengths and Challenges Across Ethnic Groups

Cross-Cultural Family Studies

Challenges for Ethnic Families

Summary

Key Terms

Activities

Suggested Readings

Diversity and Strengths in Family Structure and Cultural Context

Our goal in this chapter is to point out some of the major strengths of various **ethnic groups** in the United States. Although most of the information in this chapter is about ethnic diversity, we are also including information about an increasingly common diverse family structure, gay and lesbian couples and families. One of the reasons our country has prospered is that the various ethnic groups have different strengths. The strengths of each of these groups can be seen at the individual level, family level, and cultural level. Some ethnic groups place a high value on the importance of kin networks and are very group oriented; other cultures emphasize more individual achievement. Some ethnic groups value both individual achievement and group connection relatively equally.

Diversity and strengths are also interconnected. There are strengths in diversity, and diversity helps build further strengths. The different abilities, interests, attitudes, and values of each diverse group provide a broad range of options and ideas that can improve the ability to solve problems and create new ideas. These diverse strengths can help people at all levels of society from the personal level, to school, and at work.

When we see people from different ethnic groups, we typically do not focus on their strengths. When we see gay and lesbian couples and families, we typically do not focus on their strengths. The more common reaction is to notice how they are different from us. The next reaction can be that the difference is seen as interesting or it could be perceived as a potential problem. But after getting to know someone who is different from yourself, you will be able to see that some of the differences can be both personal strengths and things you value about your relationship with them.

So one way to increase our appreciation of diversity is to seek out opportunities to talk with people who have ethnic backgrounds different from our own. Sharing feelings about oneself with someone who is different can be a mutually rewarding experience, an opportunity to learn more about others and their uniqueness.

Why Culture Matters

Families are families, right? Does it really matter that families have cultural histories? Yes, it does. For example, strong marriages look different in Navajo (Skogrand et al., 2008), Latino (Skogrand, Hatch, & Singh, 2008), and African American (Skogrand & Chaney, 2010) cultures. The findings of a study of Latino couples who had strong marriages indicated that in order to have strong marriages, couples needed to have children (Skogrand et al., 2008). The African American couples indicated that prayer, God, and church were highly important to have a strong marriage (Skogrand & Chaney, 2010). Everything that happens in families happens within a cultural context. Family members learn, and pass on to their children, the definition of family, how intimacy is expressed, what it means to be male and female, and role expectations (Waldegrave, 2009).

Most often programs and policies focus on the values evident in mainstream society (Waldegrave, 2009). In the United States that is primarily white, middle-class individuals. White, middle-class individuals and families typically focus on individualism and self-determination, whereas, many members of diverse cultures think more collectively in that they value the group over oneself, and the group may be family or the community (Waldegrave, 2009). The result is that programs do not fit the values and needs of diverse populations. An example is that in the field of family finance, it is expected that you save money, plan for retirement, and take care of yourself. However, based upon one study of strong African American couples, it was sometimes more important to help others, such as family and friends, than have financial security for oneself (Anderson, 2010). Most financial education programs would not provide information that would be consistent with these collectivist values. The result is the African Americans know they are not going to get their needs met in programming, so they do not attend. Or if they do attend, they do not see the relevancy of the information to their lives. This lack of fit is also evident in family policy, therapy, and counseling.

To be effective and relevant in the lives of individuals and families from diverse cultures, we need to understand their values and experiences. This chapter provides information to begin the process of understanding members of diverse populations. It will become clear, however, that understanding cultural differences is a long process.

Intimacy and Diversity

While some people have relatively stable family lives evidenced by two-parent families, some do not. Poverty, prejudice, education level, and life experiences affect the ability to maintain intimate family relationships such as extended-family relationships, parent–child relationships, and couple relationships (Bent-Goodley, 2005; Perreira, Chapman, & Stein, 2006; Sarkisian, Gerena, & Gerstel, 2006).

Some people had historical experiences that have long-term effects on their ability to maintain intimate family lives today. For example, American Indians in the United States historically had land, language, and culture taken from them (Caldwell et al., 2005). In the mid-1900s, children were taken from their homes and put in boarding schools where they were to become "civilized" and adopt the ways of White Americans. These experiences created a legacy of trauma, which contributed to multiple psychiatric disorders such as alcoholism and violence (Caldwell et al., 2005). These issues affect intimacy in American Indian families.

How members of **cultural groups** entered the United States, when they entered the country, and how they were received may also impact their ability to develop intimacy among family members. Did they come as refugees with nothing but the clothes on their backs? If so, these refugees will need to focus on survival with little time or energy to develop intimate relationships. The following example is a real event that could impact close and intimate family relationships:

> Recently, there was a raid by immigration officials at a food processing plant in a small community that employed a large number of Latino immigrants. A significant number of Latino breadwinners were arrested for prosecution and deportation. Members of the Latino community were afraid to leave their homes, go to work, and send their children to school, and many had limited or no financial resources. In some cases both parents were arrested, and children were being cared for by friends or relatives.
>
> Financial, social, and emotional stress prevailed for these families. Survival and safety were foremost in the minds of these family members, which negatively impacted their intimate family relationships.

Gay and Lesbian Couples and Families

Although most of this chapter is about ethnic diversity and families, we also want to include information about a family form that is increasing in this country—gay and lesbian couples and families. There has been increased contention about whether or not gay and lesbian people have a right to legally marry and raise children. People's views about these issues often have roots in religious beliefs. Religious groups are not all opposed to gay and lesbian marriages and families. Some religious groups have struggled internally with these issues, and splits within denominations have resulted.

In 1996 the federal government passed the Defense of Marriage Act, which defines marriage as a legal union exclusively between one man and one woman, and says that a gay or lesbian marriage that takes place in one state will not be recognized across state lines and those married in states were same-sex marriages are legal would not benefit from federal laws which benefit married couples. However, in a June, 2013 ruling by the Supreme Court of the United States, The Defense of Marriage Act was struck down and now any couples legally married in states where it is allowed are recognized as married by the federal government. Currently, 13 states and the District of Columbia recognize same-sex marriages. By the time this textbook is published, this number may have changed. Clearly, this is a controversial and fluid issue.

Although there are studies about same-sex couple relationships and families, most of this research is focused on samples that are European American and middle class (Goldberg, 2007). We know very little about ethnic minority same-sex couples and families. Gay and lesbian same-sex couples and families who are from ethnic minorities not only are dealing with discrimination related to their family structure, but also are dealing with issues around racism. Low-income couples and families have the added stress of financial insecurity to contend with.

Same-Sex Couple Relationships and Marriages

There is no way of knowing how many gay and lesbian people are in relationships. It is estimated, however, that 40% to 60% of gay men and 45% to 80% of lesbians are involved in romantic relationships (Kurdek, 2004). Because being public about being in a same-sex relationship can result in discrimination, it is likely these estimates are low.

Studies generally conclude that healthy gay and lesbian couple relationships are similar to healthy heterosexual couple relationships (Kurdek, 2004; Porche & Purvin, 2008). According to findings provided by Kurdek, same-sex couples functioned as well, relationshipwise, as heterosexual couples. On some relationship variables, same-sex couples functioned better than heterosexual couples. Kurdek did find, however, that gay and lesbian couples experienced less social support than heterosexual couples.

It is reasonable to assume that gay and lesbian couples could benefit from couple education in the same way heterosexual couples benefit. In fact, because of the lack of social support same-sex couples experience, these couples may need it even more. However, couple education for this population is typically not available. In a very small, nonrepresentative sample of therapists and researchers, researchers asked about existing relationship education and needed modifications (Whitton & Buzzela, 2011). Their research revealed three things. First, relationship skills used in couple education of heterosexual couples, such as communication skills, conflict resolution skills, developing and maintaining positive couple connections, and individual self-regulation, were found useful for same-sex couples. Second, the clinicians who have provided couple education for same-sex couples found they needed to modify the information presented. One example of such changes was the use of gender terms and another was the issue of commitment as symbolized through marriage. Third, clinicians found that there were unique issues experienced by same-sex couples that were not addressed in curricula developed for heterosexual couples. An example of one of these issues was how to deal with discrimination and stigma for themselves and their children. In addition, in one study of the benefits of stepfamily education developed with heterosexual couples in mind, two lesbian couples found the course very useful (Skogrand, Mendez, & Higginbotham, 2012). In fact, these two same-sex couples felt they shared many of the same issues as heterosexual couples and experienced a feeling of normalcy by attending the class. In this case no modifications were made to the course.

Because same-sex marriage is so new and available in only a few states, we know very little about the effects of couples entering into a legal relationship versus living in a cohabiting relationship. Historically, gay and lesbian couples have been more likely to dissolve their relationships than married heterosexual couples (Kurdek, 2004). This may be because there have been no legal barriers to dissolving the relationship. What will the effect of legalization of same-sex marriages be over time (Oswald & Kuvalanka, 2008)? Will these couples be happier? Will they receive more social support from friends and family? Will they be less likely to break up?

Gay and Lesbian Families

The number of same-sex couples raising children has risen in the past 20 years with individuals feeling more comfortable coming out and being open about being in **gay and lesbian families**. Approximately one-fourth of gay and lesbian couples have children, and approximately 45% want to have children (Gates, 2008). The majority of the children of same-sex couples are a result of previous heterosexual relationships. Although we may think of gay and lesbian families as being primarily European American, African American and Latino men are three times more likely to be raising children in same-sex relationships than are European American men. More than half of the children being raised by same-sex couples are non-White.

Children being raised by same-sex couples have not been studied until recently. In the 1990s, researchers wanted to know if children raised by gay and lesbian couples would, in some way, be damaged by the experience of growing up in a gay family (Berkowitz, 2009). The answer was that there was no difference in developmental outcomes—there were no adverse effects. In the 2000s, other researchers (Stacey & Biblarz, 2001) criticized the earlier work, suggesting that these researchers have been so concerned that "there was no difference" between children raised by same-sex parents and those raised by heterosexual parents that they missed differences that might be viewed as positive.

Although there is no typical gay and lesbian family, Brenda and Lori provide one example of what family life might be like:

> *Lori and Brenda have lived together for 5 years. They met at work, dated for about a year, and then moved in together. Each had two children from prior heterosexual relationships, ranging in age from 7 to 15. Lori and Brenda also have a 2-year-old child together through assisted reproduction with an unknown donor.*
>
> *At one point Brenda was not allowed to have any contact with her children because her former husband obtained sole custody of the children, as a result of the claim that she was an unfit mother because she was lesbian. Later, however, she got visitation rights and now has the children for 1 month in the summer and two weekends out of each month. Lori has shared custody of her children, and they spend the majority of their time with Brenda and Lori.*

Generally speaking, their family has been well received in their suburban neighborhood, schools, and the church they attend. Both Brenda and Lori teach Sunday School and attend other church events. They both attend their children's school conferences. There is one other lesbian couple in the neighborhood with whom they spend lots of time.

There have been challenges. Although Lori's extended family is supportive of their relationship, Brenda's extended family members blame Lori for Brenda's being gay. Their relationships with Brenda's extended family members are strained, and they spend little time with them. This has resulted in Brenda's children having limited time with their grandparents.

Because they are a stepfamily, their biggest challenge is parent/child relationships. It has been difficult having all the children together and disciplining effectively and treating them all fairly. Brenda and Lori feel their relationship is strong, but if things do not go well for the children, it could put stress on their couple relationship. There has been a problem with Brenda's ex-spouse who says derogatory things about her to the children. Brenda and Lori have decided to "take the high road" and not say negative things to Brenda's children about their father. They have both worked hard to put the children's needs first, and the children are generally doing well. One of the children has learning disabilities and struggles with school. This means both Brenda and Lori spend considerable time each evening helping him with schoolwork.

Someday they want to become married legally, but currently it is not possible in the state where they live. Although they have considered having a religious ceremony, they have decided to wait, with the hope that they can be legally married at some point in the future.

They try to do things together like any other family. They go on camping trips, generally around some theme. For example, one year they visited several historic homes of Laura Ingalls Wilder. Before the trip the family members read several of her books to learn about her life and her books.

One of the questions often asked is, "Don't children need both a mother and a father?" In other words, does the gender of parents matter? Biblarz and Stacey (2010) reviewed studies comparing same-sex families, opposite-sex families, and single-mother and single-father families. They found that the long-held conviction that children need both a mother and a father did not hold true. After looking at the studies that have been conducted, these researchers suggested that children who had two mothers did as well as children who had a mother and a father. There is not enough research to conclude the same is true for children who had two fathers. Single-parent families did less well. These authors concluded that two parents provide advantages over a single-parent trying to raise children. These findings, however, are looking at averages, and single-parent families also have strengths and children can do just fine in these families. These authors concluded that two parents can do well raising children and it is not dependent on gender or marital status. It appears that committed and compatible parents are most important in providing strong families. In some aspects of raising children, Biblarz and Stacey (2010) found that lesbian parents actually outperformed heterosexual couples. According to these authors, this may be due to women typically having better parenting skills than men.

The Challenges of Gay and Lesbian Couples and Families

Many of the challenges of gay and lesbian couples and families center on the fact that couples cannot be legally married (Allen, 2007). That means that unless a state has some other domestic partnership rights for unmarried couples, they have no right of inheritance (unless specified by a will), have no right to visit their partner in hospitals or prisons, and do not have spousal health insurance coverage. Because couples are typically not legally married, they cannot become legally divorced. Therefore, there is no prescribed or legal process for families that dissolve.

It is obvious that same-sex relationships can be more difficult because of societal pressures. Researchers have addressed how the stigma of being in a same-sex relationship affects intimacy in the couple relationship because these relationships are not seen as equal to heterosexual relationships (Frost, 2011). When Frost interviewed 99 individuals about their gay and lesbian relationships, he found that individuals in couple relationships developed six different ways to allow intimacy and stigma to coexist in their lives:

- Many individuals in this study said stigma weighed heavily on their relationships. These individuals described stigma from society and family members as an ever-present negative force on their relationships. This weight was not only difficult to endure but contributed to couples' thoughts about ending the relationships because it was just too difficult to stay together.
- Other individuals did not describe negative stigma as ever-present but, rather, were generally able to maintain normal family relationships. They were able to have children, buy houses, and attend family events. There were times, however, when these experiences were "contaminated" by family members or individuals in society. Even though they could do typical couple things, people could dampen their happiness. For example, even though a couple had a commitment ceremony that was generally very positive, it could be dampened by parents' not attending because they did not approve.
- Another group of individuals said that stigma had, at one time, been a significant factor in their lives, but currently they did not allow it to affect their couple relationships. These individuals were most likely to live in accepting and liberal communities and neighborhoods.
- Some individuals said they almost never experienced discrimination, and then went on to describe a very difficult situation. It appears these individuals were reluctant to acknowledge that negative things happened. Therefore, it appears these couples distanced themselves from it and did not let stigma affect their couple relationships.
- Other individuals described experiencing discrimination and stigmatization in their relationships, but they did not view these experiences as negatively affecting their couple relationships. Rather, these individuals used these experiences to strengthen their couple relationships and solidify their commitment to each other. They also saw this societal discrimination as coming from the outside and did not let it affect their intimacy.
- Some individuals recognized the stereotypical heterosexual relationship models that existed. For themselves, however, they developed their own process for becoming a couple and a family even though it mirrored the heterosexual norm. These individuals redefined what was important in their relationships and created opportunities for commitment and public recognition of their relationships.
- Finally, some individuals described discrimination and intimacy but indicated no connection, either positive or negative, between the two in their couple relationships. Frost (2011) speculates that these individuals deliberately distanced themselves from the stigma and did not allow it to affect their couple relationships.

This study (Frost, 2011) makes it clear that society's stigma can positively or negatively affect intimate, same-sex couple relationships. It is important to note from this study that most couples are able to maintain a positive couple experience, even in the context of discrimination.

Gay and lesbian couples having children adds another layer of complexity to family life (Hare & Skinner, 2008). To give birth to a child in a lesbian relationship, there must be a sperm donor. This donor can be anonymous, which gives no rights to the father. However, many states do not give any rights to the lesbian partner and do not allow same-sex adoption. If the sperm donor is a person selected by the couple, the father's involvement in the child's life must be negotiated and in some cases legally defined. Because neither partner in a gay male relationship can give birth, gay men having children is even more complicated (Berkowitz & Marsiglio, 2007). One option is to employ a surrogate mother to carry and deliver the child. Again, multiple legal issues must be resolved, and same-sex adoptions may not be legal in the state in which they reside. It is clear that family policy and family law have not caught up with the increased number of gay and lesbian couples who want to have children.

Once a couple brings children into the relationship, solidifying their family identity in society becomes an issue (Suter, Daas, & Bergen, 2008). Sometimes the couple creates a common family last name, typically the hyphenated last names of both partners. They often create regular family activities (Suter et al., 2008). These regular events are recognized by others as ordinary family interactions. The events can include such things as taking regular walks as a family, attending school or church events as a family, or putting up family pictures in the workplace. Families often create their own family rituals around holidays or other celebrated events. These events help family members and members of society see their family as a cohesive group.

The Concepts of Race, Culture, and Ethnicity

Race refers to the common physical characteristics of a group and generally describes skin color and the texture of hair (Murry, Smith, & Hill, 2001). The concept of race originally arose as a way to explain the diversity of the human population worldwide but can be problematic, since it does not describe what happens to people regarding socialization and environment (Murry et al., 2001). These authors indicate that ethnicity, on the other hand, refers to nationality or ancestry. Further, culture is usually used to describe how people make sense of their environment and their experiences. It describes their values, beliefs, and practices. Toni Morrison, the Nobel Prize–winning author of such novels as *Song of Solomon, Beloved*, and *Tar Baby*, puts it this way: "Race is the least reliable information you can have about someone. It's real information but it tells you next to nothing" (cited in Gray, 1998, p. 67). With the recent influx of Latinos into the United States, many people talk about cultural groups or use the term *ethnicity* because Latinos are not a race (Murry et al., 2001). Selections from a creative play about the problems with the concept of race are provided in Box 2.1.

Therefore, we will try to avoid using the term *race* in this book; rather, we will use the terms *culture* (or *cultural group*) or *ethnicity* (or *ethnic group*) when referring to different groups of people. Because of the great diversity within groups, however,

BOX 2.1   Diversity in Families

Race Has No Place

The following are segments selected from a play called VOICES, created by Twin Cities Youth (in collaboration with Stacey Parshall) from Minneapolis and St. Paul for an exhibition on the concept of "race" at the Minnesota Science Museum in 2007.

"The words you hear, the stories, the definitions, the statements and wishes, are those of some of your teenage youth across the Twin Cities. A sacred space was created for them to write these words. They were told their voices are absolutely necessary for all of us to move forward, beyond the pain and confusion that the subject of race conjures up. . . .

Will you tell me about race. R. A. C. E. What does that mean to you? What does that stand for?

Respect All Colors Everywhere
Respect All Cultures Equally
Radical Awesome Cultures Everywhere
Rare Assortment of Color and Ethnicity
Rights And Confusion Expressed
Race Always Changes Everything
Rage Amongst Conflicting Ethnic groups

Revolutionize All Concepts that Enslave
Real Answers Can (help shape) Equality
Race Absolutely Costs Everybody

Race is just another word.
Race is just a title.
Race is not necessary.

Black, White, yellow, tan and they're just colors.
Color is what you get when White light is broken up.

Color defines merely what is on the outside.
Skin color? In my mind means nothing.
There is a saying, "it's only skin deep."
I always try to look deeper.

People are different races and come from different places, but we all have faces. Treat all with respect, no matter their races, even in tough cases. We are one human race."

Source: Adapted from *VOICES* (Science Museum of Minnesota, St. Paul, Minnesota, 2007). Adapted with permission.

even calling them *ethnic* or *cultural* groups can be misleading. Jews, for example, are often classified as an ethnic group, but doing so stretches the imagination considerably, for a number of reasons: (1) Jews hold a wide variety of religious views, from very conservative to very liberal—some are Orthodox believers, and others are atheists; (2) Jews speak a variety of languages, and many Jews today cannot

Ethnic or cultural differences are not always evident. A mother may look like her child but may have adopted this child from a country where everything is different from the U.S., including language, religious beliefs and traditions, and cultural values.

speak Hebrew, the language of tradition; (3) Jews are of many nationalities as a result of Judaism's expanding influence worldwide over the centuries; and (4) Jews exhibit a variety of physical characteristics, ranging from dark-skinned, black-haired African Jews to light-skinned, blue-eyed, blond European Jews. From a cultural viewpoint, a nomadic Jewish shepherd in Ethiopia has much more in common with other Africans than he does with a Jewish dentist in suburban Chicago.

Perhaps the key issue in determining membership in an ethnic or cultural group is whether the individual *believes* he or she is a member of that group. Clearly, human beings are diverse. Classifications cannot be based solely on religious views, language, ancestry, or physical characteristics.

U.S. Demographics and Future Trends

The United States is more ethnically diverse than ever before, with the Hispanic population making up the largest ethnic group, followed by African American, Asian American, and American Indian. The 2010 Census provided new information on the population distribution in the United States. The most recent census indicated the population distribution is as follows: White 72%, Hispanic or Latino 16%, African American or Black 13%, Asian 6%, and American Indian or Alaska Native 1% (Humes, Jones, & Ramirez, 2011). More than half of the U.S. population growth between 2000 and 2010 was due to the increase in the Hispanic or Latino population. In addition, Humes and colleagues found that minority populations are growing at a faster rate than the non-Hispanic White populations. The non-Hispanic White population grew at a rate of 1% from 2000 to 2010, and the minority populations grew at a rate of 29% during the same period of time.

There are differences in minority population changes by regions in the United States (Humes et al., 2011). The fastest rate of increase of minority populations was in the West, with the next largest increase in the South. As of 2010, California has the largest *total minority* population of any state, followed by Texas and New York. States with the *largest percentage* of minority populations, which are all over 50% minority, are Hawaii (77%), California and New Mexico (60%), and Texas (55%). These states have what is called a "majority-minority" population (Humes et al., 2011). Our nation's capital, Washington, D.C., also has this majority-minority status with a 65% minority population.

See Figure 2.1 for some demographic characteristics of families from various ethnic groups.

The Hispanic Population

The Hispanic population, also referred to as "Latino," includes people from Spanish-speaking cultures. In 2005, the Hispanic population became the largest ethnic group, surpassing the African American population for the first time in U.S. history (U.S. Census Bureau, 2006a). The Hispanic population is the fastest-growing minority population, and growth is primarily due to new births and secondarily immigration.

The largest number of Hispanics in the United States immigrated from Mexico (63%), with the remainder coming from other Central American, South American, or other Hispanic countries (Ennis, Rios-Vargas, & Albert, 2011). The Hispanic population in this country is very young, with a median age of 27 years in 2012 as compared with 37 years for the population as a whole (Infoplease, 2012).

Income*
(Median household)

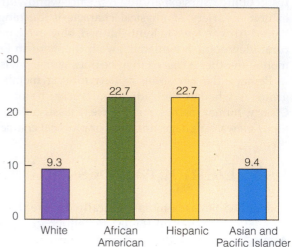

Poverty*
(Percentage of families living below poverty line)

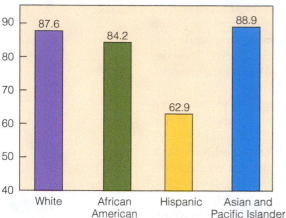

Education
(Percentage of people age 15 and older who
completed high school)

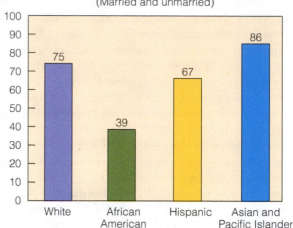

Two-Parent Families*
(Married and unmarried)

FIGURE 2.1

Characteristics of Families from Various Ethnic Groups

*U.S. Census Bureau, *The 2012 Statistical Abstract*, tables 696, 715, 229, 69.

The African American Population

The African American population is the second-largest minority population in the United States. African Americans, or Blacks, refer to people having origins in any of the Black race groups of Africa. Although many African Americans came to the United States as slaves years ago, 8% of African Americans were foreign born in 2007 (Grieco, 2010). These new immigrants are very diverse and very different culturally from African Americans who have lived in the United States for several generations. These refugees and immigrants have come from the Caribbean and African countries such as Nigeria, Ghana, and Ethiopia and have very little in common with their native-born counterparts. Because of this increasing diversity in the Black population, we need to be more aware of the diversity of cultural values and beliefs in what we once thought of as a relatively homogeneous cultural group.

In 2000, the median age for African Americans was 30 years, which was 6 years younger than the population as a whole (McKinnon & Bennett, 2005). Blacks have the lowest median income of any cultural group (DeNavas-Walt, Proctor, & Lee, 2006).

The Asian American Population

Asian Americans refer to people having origins in the Far East, Southeast Asia, or the Indian subcontinent. The Asian American populations differ greatly in their culture, language, and length of residency in the United States. More recent immigrants and refugees include Hmong, Vietnamese, Laotians, and Cambodians, while people coming from China and Japan typically have been in the United States for several generations.

The median age of Asian Americans is 36 years. Asian Americans have the highest income level of all the minority groups and higher than that of Whites. It is important to note, however, that there is a wide disparity in education and affluence among different groups who identify themselves as Asian American. For example, the Hmong are, on average, very poor with limited education, whereas Asian Indians are, on average, highly educated and affluent (DeNavas-Walt et al., 2006).

The American Indian and Alaska Native Populations

There are over 560 tribes that make up the American Indian and Alaska Native (AI/AN) population in the United States (Caldwell et al., 2005), with a wide range of tribal cultures. The largest tribe by population is the Navajo tribe in Arizona, New Mexico, and Utah (Norris, Vines, & Hoeffel, 2012, January).

One of the unique characteristics of the AI/AN population is that their communities are sovereign political entities with tribes having their own form of governance, culture, and history (Caldwell et al., 2005). Many AI/AN people live on tribal land or reservations (36%), with the remaining population living in rural and urban communities throughout the country (Ogunwole, 2006). The median age for American Indians and Alaska Natives is 29 years, which is lower than other U.S. minority groups.

Immigration and Family Life

According to Cherlin (2010), immigration has continued to be at record highs in recent years. In 2006 those who were foreign born made up 12% of the U.S. population. The ethnic composition of the immigrant population is primarily Latino and Asian, with Mexicans making up the majority of Latinos coming into the United States. Historically, men made up the majority of immigrants, but more recent data indicate that immigrants are about equally male and female. The increasing numbers of women who have come to the United States have left their own children behind in their country of origin to care for children and clean houses of the more wealthy in this country. These women are leaving their children behind in the care of extended family members and send money to their families back home (Cherlin, 2010).

Many immigrants come to the United States without documentation or have allowed their documentation to expire (Glick, 2010). There are indications that one-third of children who have immigrant parents have at least one parent that is undocumented. These parents may not have access to services for themselves or their children and are very vulnerable because they risk deportation if they ask for help.

FIGURE 2.2
Increasing Diversity in
America from 2000 to
2050
Source: U.S. Census Bureau,
2004a.

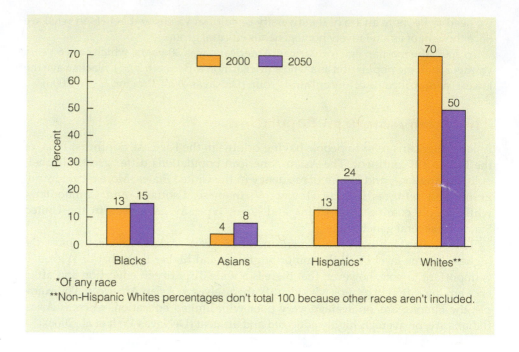

*Of any race
**Non-Hispanic Whites percentages don't total 100 because other races aren't included.

Refugees make up another group of folks who come to the United States. Refugees come to the United States because conditions in their country of origin are unsafe (Glick, 2010). They often come to this country as families and are able to access social and financial services, but often face other challenges. Refugees have often experienced trauma due to war or other kinds of oppression prior to their arrival in the United States. Many come having spent years in refugee camps that provided for their physical safety, but that in no way provided for optimal family life.

These families come to the United States with enormous issues and challenges as they begin their lives anew. They need to learn about the American culture, find ways to make a living, and help their children enter a world that is foreign to them. In addition to challenges for their families, there are also challenges for the communities where they reside. Social services are not always prepared to meet the extreme variety of needs presented by these new neighbors (Martinez-Brawley & Zorita, 2011).

What the Future Will Bring

Estimates have been made about what the White and ethnic populations might look like in the year 2050 (Figure 2.2). The minority populations will grow faster than the White population. The nation's Hispanic and Asian populations are predicted to triple over the next half century, and non-Hispanic Whites will represent about one-half of the total population (U.S. Census Bureau, 2004a).

If the trend of multiracial marriages and relationships continues to increase as they have in recent history (Qian, 2005), there will be increasing numbers of multiracial children in the country. This combined with the increase in minority groups means it is possible that by the year 2050 cultural groups may cease to be an issue that will be written about in marriage and family textbooks.

Challenge to Researchers and Practitioners

Most research that informs programs and services is based on White, middle-class families, and, yet, this research is typically used to provide programs and services for all ethnic groups (Skogrand, Hatch, & Singh, 2008). Most of these programs and services are not a good fit for families from other cultures, because the information is not culturally relevant. There is, therefore, a need for research to be conducted within a cultural context to inform programming for the members of diverse ethnic groups.

Research

Mohatt and Thomas (2006) indicate that we need to include members of diverse cultures in decision making about how we conduct research, analysis of findings, and interpretation of results. There are a variety of things we should be doing differently when conducting research with minority populations, which will take a shift in our thinking (Trimble & Fisher, 2006):

- We need to be respectful of the wishes of cultural groups regarding the research we do, how it should be used, and how those communities might benefit from the research findings.
- We need to collaborate with and develop partnerships with members and organizations in diverse cultures and accept the conditions imposed by the community when conducting research.
- We need to know about belief systems and show respect for these values in conducting research.
- Participants in research studies need to provide informed consent in a language and reading level that they understand.
- Interpretation of findings requires involving members of the population studied, because cultural meanings may not be understood by the researchers.

Practice

We might ask, Why is it important to address the issue of marriage and family from the perspective of one's culture? There are two responses to this question. First, if there is a cultural clash between the information and services provided and the values of a cultural group, people will usually not participate. If they do participate, they will not benefit from the information provided. Harm to members of the cultural group may result if individuals embrace programming ideas that destroy aspects of their cultural heritage (Fowers & Davidov, 2006; Skogrand et al., 2008).

Second, there is evidence that relying on one's cultural heritage, the way one's people deal with struggles, is the most effective way for people to be resilient and capable of handling difficulties (Skogrand et al., 2008). Several studies have shown that a positive **ethnic identity** has a positive influence on the lives of youth (Kiang, Gonzales-Backen, Yip, Witkow, & Fuligni, 2006; Perreira et al., 2006; Spencer, 2006). Consequently, it is important to draw on and reinforce the existing family values that are evident in minority cultural groups. In addition, there is evidence that maintaining one's cultural heritage and also learning about the dominant culture contribute to positive mental health (Chapman & Perreira, 2005; Kiang et al., 2006; Perreira et al., 2006).

Cultural Competence

With the increasing numbers of people of diverse cultures becoming part of society, it is critical that professionals develop culturally appropriate ways to provide effective family education and services. This ability has been described as **cultural competence**. Cultural competence has been defined in a variety of ways. A general definition is that one is effective in working with a variety of cultural groups. Cultural competence is often viewed as having three parts: awareness, knowledge, and skills. Fowers and Davidov (2006) discuss these three components and also emphasize the importance of having an *openness* to learning about oneself and others throughout the process.

Awareness

According to Fowers and Davidov (2006), a person must begin with self-exploration, which leads to self-awareness. This is a process that starts with an understanding of one's own cultural heritage and belief system, which leads to the ability to recognize how one's own culture affects how one views those from other cultures. People who are African American have values and beliefs that come from a long history of racial and ethnic experiences, and a person who is African American sees others based on those cultural experiences.

People who are German or Norwegian also have cultural perspectives that affect how they view people from other cultures. Many who have a European ancestry see themselves as blending into the dominant culture in the United States and may not think of themselves as having a culture, but everyone has values and beliefs with which they grew up that affect how they view the world.

To better understand our own belief system, we might ask ourselves the following questions:

- What are my basic beliefs about family, children, and extended family?
- Do I think the individual or the collective group has the higher priority?
- How do religion and spirituality play into my belief system?
- What rituals do I carry out, and how and why have I developed these rituals?
- What foods do I eat and what kinds of clothes do I wear that make me feel like I am part of my family or community?

How we think about these questions may be influenced by a variety of things, but many of the answers might have resulted from our cultural experiences. Once we understand who we are and how our concept of self has been developed, we can think about how those views affect how we interact with those who are different from us.

Knowledge

The second component described by Fowers and Davidov (2006) is gaining the knowledge or factual information necessary to understand another person's culture. Knowledge may be general in nature and may include understanding discrimination, prejudice, and oppression and how these experiences affect a person or group of people. Specific knowledge about a cultural group might include the group's history, cultural beliefs and values, and family dynamics. The knowledge that one gains contributes to being more open to work with members of a culture because there is cross-cultural understanding. Not everyone within a cultural group is the same, but having knowledge about some cultural characteristics and features is necessary for one to become culturally competent. Once a person has knowledge about a culture as a whole, there can be additional learning about the subcultures within the larger group.

How does a person gain knowledge about a cultural group? Several strategies have been identified by Skogrand (2004) that are useful in learning about a cultural group. First, reading scholarly information that describes the history of the culture, beliefs and values, and family organization will provide much needed knowledge about a cultural group. A second strategy is to attend activities, markets, art galleries, or places of business that are frequented by members of the culture. For example, attending events such as pow-wows and Juneteenth Day celebrations would help one learn about history and spiritual practices. Visiting markets, art galleries, or places of business would provide information about food preferences, clothing worn, and other cultural beliefs. Learning about family life will also occur as we pay attention to who goes to the market, how mothers and fathers interact with their children, and the presence or absence of extended-family members. Respectfully attending these events can contribute to learning about family life, customs, and heritage.

Skills

Developing and practicing appropriate skills in effectively working with people who are culturally different from us is the third component of cultural competency (Fowers & Davidov, 2006). Being aware and having knowledge are of little use unless they are put into action.

Cultural competence skills can be demonstrated by the language used and by showing knowledge of history, beliefs and values, and cultural practices in implementing programs and providing services. Fowers and Davidov (2006) make it clear that it is not easy to teach skills in being culturally competent, but, rather, these skills are an outcome and are expressed naturally and in individual ways once one is self-aware and has knowledge about a cultural group.

Kin Relationships Across Cultures

Most of us learn about kinship early in our lives, with little or no theoretical explanations. We learn, for example, about brothers and sisters and about aunts, uncles, and cousins; but we identify with them as people rather than focus on specific kinship principles. We know who Uncle Jack and Aunt Libby are long before we understand the concepts of "mother's brother" or "father's sister."

All cultures recognize **kinship**, the relatedness of certain individuals within a group, and have norms and expectations that structure and govern kin behavior. The diversity of these norms is wide ranging. These kinship concepts describe kinds of kinship groups and the norms that govern marital forms, family structure and organization, inheritance, authority, and residence.

Kinship groups range from nuclear families to various forms of extended families and may even include symbolic relationships. The **nuclear family**—the smallest, most elementary kinship unit—usually consists of two parents and their dependent children. Even in societies in which the nuclear family is embedded within a larger group, it is recognized as a distinct entity. The nuclear family is a **conjugal family system**, one that emphasizes the relationships formed through marriage. Typically, a conjugal system comprises only two generations and is relatively transitory, dissolving when the parents die or the children grow up and

As people get divorced and remarried, forming new stepfamilies, family and kin relationships become more complex.

leave. Because nuclear families are comparatively small and short lived, they are less likely to develop traditions that are handed down through the generations.

Many family functions are better performed by composite family groups, or **consanguineal family systems**, which emphasize blood ties more than marital ties. In consanguineal systems, married couples and their children are embedded in a larger kinship group of three or more generations related by blood. Consanguineal systems can include extended families or families resulting from plural marriages. An **extended family** consists of a nuclear family and those people related to its members by blood ties, such as aunts, uncles, cousins, and grandparents.

A **plural marriage**, or **polygamy**, is a marriage in which a man has more than one wife (**polygyny**) or, more rarely, a marriage in which a woman has more than one husband (**polyandry**). In **monogamy**, a man or woman has only one mate. Although people from monogamous societies often perceive potential hazards in plural marriages, family patterns appear to operate in a relatively smooth fashion in groups in which plural marriages are the norm.

A third kind of kinship group is a **pseudo–kin group**, in which relationships resembling kinship ties develop among unrelated individuals. Relationships within these groups range in intensity, from close friendships to godparent–godchild connections to individuals living together and caring for each other without any legal or blood relationship.

Cultural norms influence family structure, but they also influence concepts of **lineage** or lines of descent; of who holds authority in a family; and of where newly married couples should reside. Lineage is important in determining membership in a particular kinship group, patterns of inheritance, and kinship obligations or responsibilities. In some societies, descent is traced by gender: **matrilineal societies** trace descent through females, and **patrilineal societies** trace descent through males. In a matrilineal society, for example, a man inherits group membership through his mother; lines of descent through his sister(s) are also important. Although a man may live with his wife or wives, he perceives the households of his mother and sisters as his true home. In a patrilineal society, a man's sister will be in his descent group but her children will not; they belong to their father's descent group.

Bilateral descent is common in many Western societies, with children tied equally to relatives of both the mother and the father. In this "family tree" approach to descent, in which ancestors and descendants multiply geometrically, true descent kinship groups are not formed unless limited by generation or to particular ancestors and descendants.

Norms for lines of descent may or may not be linked to lines of authority within a kinship group. If females exercise the authority, a kinship group is considered a **matriarchal group**. If males are dominant and exercise the authority, the kinship group is considered a **patriarchal group**. Note that these terms emphasize femaleness and maleness rather than motherhood and fatherhood. In a patriarchal group, for example, the grandfather is likely to wield more authority than the father of a nuclear family. But the criterion of gender always supersedes that of age in matriarchal and patriarchal kinship groups.

In **egalitarian groups**, such as those found in the United States, the ideals of democracy suggest that the rights and perspectives of both genders and all generations be respected. A given family's structure and interactions may lean toward the patriarchal or matriarchal, but the norms of the group would most likely be considered egalitarian.

Norms of residence for newly married couples can also be categorized by a society's emphasis on biological sex. In a **matrilocal society**, newly married couples normally live with or near the wife's kin, especially her mother's kinship group. Newly married couples in **patrilocal societies** are expected to live with or near the husband's kin, usually his father's kinship group. In a **neolocal society**, norms encourage newly married couples to establish a separate, autonomous residence, independent of either partner's kinship group.

Although a society may have norms regarding marital and family organization and interaction, diversity is generally also evident within that society's families and kinship groups. Understanding the concept of kin relationships, however, enables observers to compare and analyze the structure and dynamics of a broad range of kinship groups.

Family System and Sociocultural Characteristics

Family system framework is very useful for understanding and improving the quality of life for couples and families. These family system characteristics are cohesion, flexibility, and communication. Three sociocultural characteristics that also give us insight into families are the extended family, the social system, and the belief system. Figure 2.3 graphically illustrates how the family system characteristics and the sociocultural characteristics can be synthesized.

Three Family System Characteristics

There has been a great deal of research looking at the characteristics of strong families, focusing on their family system. The three dimensions (clusters of concepts) of family systems that have been found are cohesion, flexibility, and communication (Olson, 2011; Walsh, 2006). These three dimensions also relate directly to the six characteristics of strong families described by DeFrain in the international family strengths model (DeFrain, 2006).

FIGURE 2.3
Family System
and Sociocultural
Characteristics

Family cohesion is *the emotional closeness a person feels to other family members*. Cohesion includes both commitment and spending enjoyable time together from the family strengths model. Commitment to the family includes trust, honesty, dependability, and faithfulness. Spending time together means committing a considerable amount of quality time to sharing activities, feelings, and ideas, and enjoying each other's company.

Family flexibility is *the ability to change and adapt when necessary*. Flexibility also relates to dealing effectively with stress and having helpful spiritual beliefs from the family strengths model. Coping abilities include using personal and family resources to help each other, accepting crises as challenges rather than denying them, and growing together by working through crises. Spiritual well-being includes happiness, optimism, hope, faith, and a set of shared ethical values that guide family members through life's challenges.

Family communication is *the sharing of information, ideas, and feelings with each other*. Communication is generally positive in strong families because angry outbursts and other negative interchanges simply don't work well. Appreciation and affection are regularly shared. Positive communication includes having open, straightforward discussions, being cooperative rather than competitive, and sharing feelings with one another. Appreciation and affection include kindness, mutual caring, respect for individuality, and a feeling of security.

Three Sociocultural Characteristics

In describing successful families, we have emphasized three important family system characteristics, but it is also important to consider the sociocultural context in which families live. The three sociocultural characteristics that are particularly useful in describing and understanding families from diverse ethnic groups are the *extended-family system*, the *social system*, and the *belief system* (Walsh, 2006).

The **extended-family system** encompasses *relatives, kin, and other family members connected to the family system*. These are very important resources for most families and are a particularly important resource for families of color (McAdoo, 2007).

The **social system** includes *the economic, educational, and other related resources available*. Families of color are often at a disadvantage in the social system because they are more likely to be of middle or lower socioeconomic status. Because of their relative lack of both education and economic resources, the social system is often more a liability than an asset to families of color.

The **belief system** refers to *a family's spiritual beliefs and values*. All families have a value system, and families of color often have a spiritual belief system that helps them maintain a strong and successful family.

Family Strengths and Challenges Across Ethnic Groups

This section describes some of the most salient family strengths and family challenges of the major ethnic groups in the United States. The summary lists that follow were created from reviewing several hundred publications related to the various ethnic groups. We tried to rely on studies done by *insiders* rather than *outsiders*—studies done by researchers who were members of the particular ethnic group under study, rather than studies done by researchers on the outside looking in. Although the characteristics in each list are commonly found in a particular ethnic group, it does not mean that every family has these particular characteristics. Each family in the world is a culture all to itself. It is unique and different from all the other families in the world, even though it is quite likely to share many similarities with other families in its own ethnic group and similarities with families outside its ethnic group.

So that you may identify the strengths in your own family, we have put together a short quiz you can take. Box 2.2 lists 10 characteristics that you can use to rate your own family. We hope you find it a useful way to think about the good things in your family.

Strengths of White Families

Strengths of White families in the United States have been highly influenced by the work of John DeFrain and Nick Stinnett at the University of Nebraska and David Olson at the University of Minnesota. Citations of their collective work are provided throughout this text. Their work began in the mid-1970s and resulted in six major themes about what makes families strong.

- *Commitment to family.* Strong White families are very committed to one another and are able to give all family members the freedom and support they need to achieve their individual goals.
- *Enjoyable time together.* White families that remain strong throughout the family life cycle find ways to spend time together and enjoy each other.
- *Ability to manage stress and crisis effectively.* Although all families encounter marital and family stress, strong families see stress as a challenge and deal directly with issues as they occur.
- *Spiritual well-being.* Strong White families have spiritual beliefs and values, often including religious beliefs, that help them deal with ongoing life issues.

BOX 2.2   Self-Assessment

Rate the Strengths in Your Family

This Family Strengths Inventory was developed by researchers who have studied strengths as perceived by more than 21,000 family members in 27 countries. Put an "S" for *strength* beside the qualities you feel your family has achieved, and a "G" beside those qualities that are an area of potential *growth*. If the particular characteristic does not apply to your family or is not a characteristic that is important to you, put an "NA" for *not applicable*.

——— 1. We enjoy expressing appreciation and affection for each other.

——— 2. We are committed to our well-being as a family and the well-being of each individual.

——— 3. Communication is usually positive, straightforward, and honest.

——— 4. We share an adequate amount of enjoyable time together.

——— 5. We share beliefs and values that give us meaning and a sense of belonging in the world.

——— 6. We see challenges in life as opportunities for growing closer together.

——— 7. We love one another.

——— 8. Life in our family is satisfying to us.

——— 9. We are happy as a family.

——— 10. All things considered, we are a strong family.

How Can a Family Use This Inventory?

Partners or family members can fill out a copy of this Family Strengths Inventory separately and then share their answers with each other. If discussed in a positive manner, they will be able to identify those areas they would like to work on together to improve, and those areas of strength that will serve as the foundation for their growth and positive change together.

Source: From John DeFrain, *Family Treasures: Creating Strong Families* (iUniverse, 2007). Reprinted by permission.

- *Positive communication.* One of the most important characteristics of healthy Caucasian families is that they feel good about their communication with one another.
- *Appreciation and affection.* Sharing the positive feelings they have about one another helps keep relationships positive in strong White families.

Enjoyable time together is critically important for families in American society. In a fast-paced environment, loved ones need to s-l-o-w d-o-w-n and relearn why they care for each other so much.

Strengths of African American Families

Throughout the past 4 decades researchers have been interested in strengths of African American families (Billingsley, 1992; Hill, 1971; McAdoo, 2007). In recent years there has also been increased interest in strengths of African American marriages (Chaney and Skogrand, 2009; Marks et al., 2008). Both areas of research help us identify and better understand the strengths of this population:

- *Strong kinship bonds.* The extended family is very important to many African American families, and African Americans tend to take relatives into their households (Hine, 2007; Marks, Nesteruk, Hopkins-Williams, Swanson, & Davis, 2006; Sarkisian, 2007).
- *Flexibility in family roles.* Role flexibility serves as an effective coping mechanism in healthy African American families. Because it has been necessary for many mothers to work outside the home, Black mothers tend to have considerable power in the family. The typical strong African American family is not matriarchal or patriarchal but is egalitarian in style. African American families have a longer tradition of egalitarian marriages than White families. Compared with African American couples, White couples as a group are relative newcomers to the dual-job arena (Sarkisian, 2007).
- *Strong motivation to achieve.* African American parents believe education is important, and many would like to see their children go to college.
- *Strong religious orientation.* African American churches provide emotional, spiritual, and intellectual satisfaction to African American families. Church work provides meaning and purpose for many African Americans. One study showed that Black adults who had church-based networks shared an emotional closeness to individuals in the church community, had frequent interaction with church members, and received substantial amounts of help from members of the church. These authors concluded that churches may function as families and supplement the efforts of the family network (Taylor, Lincoln, & Chatters, 2005).

In 2011 the Martin Luther King, Jr., Memorial was dedicated. Dr. King's leadership in the civil rights movement of the 1960s brought hope to many Black Americans that freedom and liberty could be a reality for all people. Martin Luther King has become a symbol of civil rights for people around the world.

- *Egalitarian marriages.* A sixth family strength is the observation that many successful African American marriages are defined as loving partnerships between equals. An egalitarian marriage does not necessarily mean that both partners contribute to the family in the same ways and that they both do the same things in life. In many couples, role responsibilities are somewhat different. For example, one partner might be especially good at cooking and the other might be especially good at balancing the checkbook. An egalitarian marriage, therefore, is marked by the fact that power and influence are shared between the partners, and each is held in high regard and respected by the other (McAdoo, 2007).

Recent research about African American marriages has found other strengths in addition to those already identified. For example, Marks et al. (2008), in a qualitative study of 30 couples who had strong marriages, found that these couples relied upon their faith when facing challenges in their marriages. In preliminary findings of a study of 38 African American couples who had strong marriages, communication, God/church/prayer, commitment, and respect were key components of their marriages (Chaney & Skogrand, 2009).

Strengths of Latino Families

Because Latinos have recently become the largest U.S. minority group (U.S. Census Bureau, 2006a), there has been increased literature about the cultural characteristics of this population. Although family strengths can vary depending upon country of origin and migration experience, there are several strengths that most Latinos have in common, and several of these characteristics are also common in families from other cultures:

- *Familism.* The family is highly valued in Latino culture and is viewed as sacred. There is cohesion among family members, and family members usually include the extended family or friends that might be viewed as family (Skogrand, Barrios-Bell, & Higginbotham, 2009).

Latinos in the United States have managed to preserve a strong family system in spite of the difficult challenges they face. As in other ethnic and cultural groups, Latino families are changing as mothers become more involved in the workforce and fathers become more involved in family responsibilities at home.

- *Children are highly valued.* Children are sometimes viewed as more important than the marriage relationship (Skogrand, Hatch, & Singh, 2008). Children are typically not left with child care providers, and if children need to be cared for by someone other than parents, it is often an extended family member (Olsen & Skogrand, 2009).
- *Religion.* Members of the Latino culture are highly likely to self-identify as having a religious affiliation, with the majority identifying as Catholic (Skogrand et al., 2009). Religion influences decisions about marriage, having children, and divorce.

Family members provide support to each other. The Latino culture is collectivistic, which means that the group, or the family, is more important than the individual. Therefore, family members provide social and financial support for those in need, sometimes at the expense of their own well-being (Halgunseth, Ispa, & Rudy, 2006).

Linda Skogrand and colleagues interviewed 25 Latino couples who had strong marriages to find out what made their marriages strong (Skogrand et al., 2009). The study was conducted using open-ended interview questions with the questions being developed within a cultural context. These couples indicated three things that were essential in making their marriages strong: children, communication, and religion.

Children were important to these Latino couples because they were the reason for getting married and they were the "glue" that kept the marriages together. These couples saw there marriages subsumed within and a part of their family lives—marriage relationships were not separate, but a part of their family. Participants in the study also said communication was essential for a strong marriage. Finally, religion was important in making a marriage strong. Religion provided a strong base for the relationship with support from other congregational members. Religious beliefs were also the context for their strong sense of commitment in the marriage. Making a commitment before God and the church helped the couples stay in the marriage even through difficult times (Skogrand et al., 2008).

The Latino marriage study supported extensive literature identifying family and religion as important values in the Latino culture. These values provide resources and strength to Latino families.

Researchers have found that Mexican American families and Anglo families share two strengths. Using an assessment scale called FACES (Family Adaptability and Cohesion Evaluation Scales), William Vega and colleagues (1986) studied cohesion (togetherness) and adaptability (flexibility) in a group of low-income Mexican American parents and a group of middle-income Anglo parents. The researchers expected to find differences between the two groups, based not so much on culture but on social class. In short, they hypothesized that money helped family life run a bit more smoothly. They were surprised to find that even though the Mexican American families had the additional challenges that come with low income, their group scored no differently on cohesion and adaptability than the middle-income Anglo families.

Strengths of Asian American Families

Families of Asian descent are another very resilient group in this country. Although Asian Americans have faced prejudice and discrimination throughout their history in the United States, they have fared better than other ethnic minorities economically and have managed to preserve their family ties, traditions, and

A tradition of hard work, discipline, high regard for education, and commitment to the family has translated into a valuable and important strength for many Asian American families. This graduate honors his family with his achievement, but he has probably also enjoyed their wholehearted support and encouragement as he worked toward it.

values. Asian Americans come from many diverse national origins and also represent diverse economic backgrounds (Zhou & Lee, 2008). Asian Americans who come here to get additional education and seek high-paying jobs do very well economically in this country. Others, however, have come as refugees with minimal skills and have settled in poor inner cities.

A period of disruption occurred in the 1940s, which affected many early Asian American immigrants. Following the bombing of Pearl Harbor, fear of further attacks by Japan led the U.S. government to resettle Japanese Americans—even those born in this country—in what were essentially prison camps until the war ended. Four decades later, the federal government agreed to modestly recompense surviving family members for the ill treatment they had suffered.

Many Asian Americans share a cultural heritage that values discipline, family commitment, hard work, and education (Qian, Blair, & Ruf, 2001). Young people reared in such an environment become challenging competitors in a society such as ours, which values competition and individual initiative. Asian American families are very diverse, but they commonly share many of the strengths of other cultural groups. Following are six major strengths of Asian American families:

- *Strong family orientation.* Both the nuclear and the extended family are very important historically and today.
- *Filial piety.* The great respect Asian American families have for their elders is noteworthy. It helps explain the high level of mutual support each generation receives from the other generations.
- *High value on education.* Asian American families emphasize the importance of education, from nursery school through college.
- *Well-disciplined children.* Traditionally, children are expected to be quiet, well behaved, and somewhat passive.

- *Extended-family support*. Financial and emotional support is provided by the extended family when the nuclear family needs it.
- *Family loyalty*. Family members support each other and protect each other's privacy.

Strengths of American Indian Families

American Indians and Alaska Natives (AI/ANs) are people having origins in any of the original peoples of North and South America (including Central America) and who maintain tribal affiliation or community attachment (U.S. Census Bureau, 2000c). The greatest concentrations of American Indians and Alaska Natives are in the West, Southwest, and Midwest, especially in Alaska, Arizona, Montana, New Mexico, Oklahoma, and South Dakota. American Indian families in the United States are members of 569 federally recognized tribes, plus an unknown number of tribes that are not federally recognized (U.S. Census Bureau, 2000a).

The 2000 Census classifies American Indians and Alaska Natives together. Native Hawaiians and other Pacific Islanders are included in a separate group. In this section on the strengths of American Indian families, we are looking only at the groups living in North America.

There is great diversity within the American Indian population based upon tribal affiliation and whether they live on reservations or in metropolitan communities. Several strengths of American Indians have been identified by researchers and others who write about the cultural characteristic of this population (Cross, 1997; Red Horse, 1997; Trimble & Gonzalez, 2008).

- *Extended-family system*. The extended family is very strong in American Indian families.
- *Spiritual beliefs*. The belief system of American Indian tribes focuses on harmony with nature and the value of contentment.
- *High family cohesion*. The connectedness of the family is important. The family is broadly defined to include the nuclear family, the extended family, and the tribal community.
- *Respect for elders*. Elders are the most respected individuals in traditional American Indian tribes, and the family reinforces this attitude.
- *Bilingual language skills*. Most American Indians work hard to maintain their native languages, but this objective is becoming more difficult because the children attend school off the reservations and are increasingly exposed to television and other mass media.
- *Tribal support system*. Many American Indians rely on their tribal support system for all types of problems. Only when that is inadequate do they turn to outside support.

Spirituality is probably one of the most pervasive themes in the American Indian culture (Limb & Hodge, 2008). Health and wellness are based upon the ability to create balance and harmony among the mental, physical, and spiritual aspects of one's life, and thus spirituality is an integral component of most aspects of one's life. One of the authors was conducting research with one of the tribes and after several attempts could get no answer about how to ask about spirituality. This author concluded that spirituality is so much a part of individual and collective lives in this tribe that it is not talked about as a separate concept—it is part of all that is. Historically, efforts have been made to destroy the spiritual expressions and practices of American Indians, but these beliefs remain for many. Spiritual practices have been a source

American Indian families have many strengths on which they rely, including a strong extended-family system, traditional beliefs that focus on harmony with nature and the value of contentment, high family cohesion, respect for elders, bilingual language skills, and the tribal support system.

of strength by reminding American Indians where they came from, giving them strength from their ancestors, and also contributing to the maintenance of a cohesive bond between the individual, the community, and the Creator. There is an increase in research about historical trauma (See Box 2.3), and the impact of this trauma as well as the importance of reconnecting with cultural to address this trauma.

Although American Indian families are characterized by diversity (Stauss, 1993), some investigators have asserted that the family remains the basic unit of the American Indian community and that the American Indian family can be characterized as having traditional beliefs, practices, and languages and a unique history and lifestyle. American Indian families derive support from both individual family members and the clan or tribal group to which they belong.

The extended family is still a source of strength for many American Indians, but this is changing as more family members leave the reservation to seek opportunities elsewhere. American Indian youths may have a wider array of people to whom they are attached than do non-Indians. In times of crisis, support from both the extended family and the tribal community helps people survive. Nuclear families are important, but the tribal community also acts as a safety net, assuming a great deal of responsibility for the welfare of its individual members. Many fathers actively care for their own children along with the mothers and serve as father substitutes for children whose fathers have died or deserted the family.

How an individual behaves, in both positive and negative ways, reflects upon the individual's family and tribe. The group is in part collectively liable for the transgressions of its individual members, so the group provides a collective conscience and consciousness that emphasize individual responsibility. Respect for elders is common among American Indian tribes, and grandparents often hold a unique position, passing on cultural values and beliefs to their grandchildren and educating the young about the physical, social, and spiritual world. Social shame (that is, embarrassment) is a common tool for disciplining children. In general, physical punishment is not encouraged or condoned. Parents usually praise their children only for special accomplishments. The young are not socialized to expect praise, and it is not given lightly.

A number of tribes stress marriages based not only on an attraction between two people but on the consensus of their relatives and the tribal community. This

BOX 2.3   At Issue

Historical Trauma and American Indians

In recent years several researchers have written about the trauma American Indians have experienced through history with the loss of land, language, and culture (Jervis et al., 2006; Trimble & Gonzalez, 2008). This trauma has at times been referred to as **historical trauma**, historical consciousness, intergenerational trauma, or unresolved grief. These terms generally refer to the result of what has been taken from them by European Americans over several generations. Land—often sacred land—was taken when American Indians were placed on reservations. Language was taken from them when children were put in boarding schools and were not allowed to speak their native language or practice their traditional ways. They experienced genocide when large numbers of people died due to exposure to illnesses for which they had no immunity. Promises were made and were broken. These multiple losses have gone on for several generations, and the trauma that resulted has affected individual and family lives.

These losses, sometimes referred to as "soul wounds" (Trimble & Gonzalez, 2008), have resulted in social and individual problems such as alcoholism, suicide, homicide, abuse, and domestic violence. In essence, part of their selves has been taken, resulting in tremendous loss. Many believe that to recover, and to address the social problems such as alcoholism, they must reclaim their culture—reestablish rituals and traditional practices, sometimes called "cultural recovery" (Trimble & Gonzalez, 2008).

Many tribes are making efforts to heal themselves. Some are teaching children their almost lost tribal language, because culture is embedded in language. Many are becoming gatekeepers of research, which can be done on the reservation, such as the Navajo Nation, in order to control what is said about them in research findings. Some tribes have their own schools and colleges so that what young people learn is taught within a cultural context. In essence, many American Indians are "taking back

their culture" as a way to address social issues and become healthy. Here is the true story of one man:

A 50-year-old Lakota man was adopted as a child into a European American family. He took on the ways of White society from living in a White home, attending White schools, learning White history, and attending White churches. Even though he had dark skin, he did everything he could to fit in as a White person.

As an adult he drank heavily and became an alcoholic. He went through alcohol treatment several times with little success. Finally a case worker said that he needed to find out who he was as an American Indian man before he could become healthy. The process was long because he had to create an entire new identity. He had to get over his internal shame about being Indian and learn Lakota ways. For a period of time he cut off contact with his White family and friends and became immersed in his Lakota culture. It was very difficult to be proud of being Indian. Through a long, painful process he developed his American Indian identity—he knew who he was. Only then could he remain sober.

Although most researchers focus on historical trauma as it relates to the lives of American Indians, one might wonder if historical trauma might also be evident in the lives of members of other minority groups. For example, African Americans experienced multiple and painful losses when children, spouses, parents, and other family members were separated during slavery. It took years before Blacks were allowed to own land or participate in the social life of White communities. The civil rights movement brought hangings and other trauma to many who fought for their rights. Did the Hmong and other refugees who came to this country after the Vietnam War experience similar losses as they left family members behind and sailed on boats that had little hope of bringing them to safety? Future research may address such questions, and others may better understand how historical trauma may have impacted their lives.

---

approach to marriage recognizes the fact that an individual marries not only another individual but also that person's family and cultural community. Research suggests that these officially sanctioned marriages are more stable than those not recognized by the couple's family members or the tribe.

The bilingual childrearing seen in some tribes and families is also identified as a strength of American Indian families. Although most American Indians learn English for survival in a White-dominant culture, they often find strength in sharing their own common languages. The family strengths and culturally adaptive patterns of American Indians deserve more extensive study in the years ahead.

BOX 2.4 **Diversity in Families**

The Tables Are Turned: Going from the Majority to the Minority

In the following story, a father tells what it felt like when his family moved from being members of the dominant White majority in the United States to being members of the tiny White minority in the small country of Fiji in the South Pacific.

Living as a minority in another country was one of the most vivid experiences our family has ever had. It gave us all a great deal of insight into what it feels like to be an "outsider." We went from a city in which we were part of the 89% White majority and we were "insiders," to a village in which we were part of the 2% Caucasian minority.

We were used to being accepted, to being "normal," to "fitting in." When we arrived, everything was different to us, and it was clear that we just did not fit in. Instead of seeing the middle-class midwestern suburban neighborhood with well-kept homes, manicured yards, and new cars, we moved into an indigenous settlement. The settlement was set in a river valley ringed by low mountains that were covered with tropical rain forest. It rained 200 inches a year. The settlement was a 10-minute walk from a tropical lagoon where tiger sharks swam and women hunted for eels and shellfish to feed their large families.

The first evening we moved into our house we heard drums begin to beat a few hours after we had fallen into bed, exhausted; faint chanting was coming from the settlement. Lying underneath the mosquito netting in bed, we laughed about how the drums sounded like some kind of celebration. The islanders had given up cannibalism more than a century before: "Perhaps they're reviving the old ways to introduce us to the culture," we joked to each other, falling into cultural stereotypes that made us feel guilty for dredging them up. The next day we found out the drums were traditional instruments carved from large logs. They were being used to call members of the local church choir to Wednesday evening practice. We felt even stupider then.

The people of color who dominated the country had a different language than we did. They ate different foods, sang different songs, danced different dances, wore different clothes, held different religious beliefs, made different rules for their families and their communities and their government. And the color of their skin was different from ours. Frankly, everything was different to us.

At first these differences seemed exotic and interesting. After a while, we were worn down by being different, and a kind of chronic fatigue set in upon us, sprinkled with occasional outbursts of anger that we felt we should not express. You could see the stress on the faces of other Whites who were either visiting the small island or had decided to live there. Being different meant that they didn't quite understand all the cultural rules—all the patterns of behavior and thought and speech, all the do's and don'ts.

Being a member of the 2% White minority in our little South Pacific country turned the tables on us. When we visited with other Whites on the island, the conversation often focused on how difficult it was to live in a culture dominated by people of color. "You can't trust them. They're always trying to take advantage of you. They run the government. They make the rules. There's no way we can get ahead in this country," and so forth. The minority Whites often seemed sick and tired and miserable, though they put on brave, smiling faces when around the majority.

Fortunately, my family and I met people of color there who took us into their homes and their hearts, and served as our cultural guides, helping us understand their world and the wonderful things about life the islanders knew that we didn't know. Without these cultural guides, our life on the island would have been much more difficult. Instead, it turned into an unforgettable experience in seeing the world from the perspective of an ethnic minority.

Reprinted with the permission of John DeFrain.

Cross-Cultural Family Studies

Cross-cultural family studies tend to focus on two interrelated questions. First, how are families in the United States different from those in other parts of the world? Second, how are they similar? At first glance, people are often struck by the obvious differences between family cultures. Clothing styles, food preferences, religious beliefs, housing, music, education—all these aspects of culture vary from one society to another. When visiting a new culture, people often look for the differences between it and their own culture. Eventually, they also begin to see the similarities. When learning about another culture, then, the key is to look for both similarities and differences.

Cross-cultural family studies focus on how particular cultural contexts influence a wide variety of issues: family values and behaviors, courtship patterns and weddings, marital and parent–child communication, power and gender roles, work and the family, ethical and religious values, childrearing patterns, sexuality, the role of grandparents and the extended family, and the role people outside the immediate family play in helping families in crisis.

We are all ethnocentric to some extent; we see others through unique lenses that are shaped by our own culture. **Ethnocentrism** is the assumption that one's own culture is the standard by which other cultures should be judged. Our ethnocentricity influences the extent to which we judge other people, families, and cultures as similar to or different from us. Tolerance of the traditions and values of other cultural and ethnic groups is the first step in transcending our overconcern with human differences. Understanding other ways of looking at life and the world around us can lead to genuine, mutual appreciation among people of different backgrounds (see Box 2.4).

Related to the issue of ethnocentrism is what anthropologists have called *perspective*. When one looks at a society from the outside, or from an **etic perspective**, one sees its characteristics in isolation rather than as they relate to the structure of the society as a whole. On the other hand, when one looks at a society from the inside, or from an **emic perspective**, one analyzes behaviors in terms of the internal structural elements of the society. The etic perspective tends to focus on and exaggerate differences, whereas the emic perspective makes it easier to see similarities between cultures.

Family researchers attempt to combine these two perspectives, recognizing the differences between cultures but also trying to identify similarities. Researchers from one culture can never completely discard their personal lenses. They can, however, try to become more open to new ideas and behaviors by submerging themselves in another culture, even learning that culture's language and living within that culture.

Challenges for Ethnic Families

Ethnic families in the United States face many challenges. Among them are intercultural marriage, the issue of assimilation, and relationships between men and women and between parents and children. Ethnic families do not experience the "advantages of being in the majority" that White Americans in the predominant culture do.

Assimilation, Acculturation, and Segregation

Newcomers to any society face a difficult set of choices: Should they swiftly reject their former life and the culture from which they came? Should they downplay their ethnic origins in an effort to fit the mainstream view? Or should they build their own ethnic enclave and try to create a safe microworld that reflects their cultural heritage? These questions are extremely difficult to answer, and minority-group members often disagree on how to proceed. Some families are torn apart by controversies of this nature.

There are three important processes that help explain what happens when a cultural group from another country encounters the dominant culture of the new country. **Assimilation** is *the process in which old cultural traits and values are relinquished and replaced by those of the dominant culture.* **Acculturation** is *the process whereby cultural traits and values from one ethnic group become blended with those of the dominant culture.* **Segregation** is *the process in which an ethnic group isolates itself or is forced into isolation within the dominant culture.* All three of these processes can occur in an interactive way as a family adapts to living in another culture.

Members of the majority culture whose families have been in the United States for two, three, or more generations sometimes do not understand why immigrants are hesitant about assimilation—adopting the values of the dominant culture. But it is clear that immigrants are in a difficult psychological position. They see and are attracted by the strengths of American culture, especially its abundance of economic resources. But they also see the weaknesses of American culture—materialism, competitiveness, wasteful exploitation of the natural world, a fast-paced and often impersonal existence. Immigrants are in some ways in a better position to see America's strengths and weaknesses than are Americans, for they have another culture with which they can compare this one.

Unfortunately, most of what people know about ethnic and cultural groups other than their own is based on **stereotypes**—standardized, oversimplified, and mean-spirited views. When a person from one group describes people from another, the description is often a stereotype. **Prejudice**, which literally means prejudging, is also closely linked with stereotyping; both attitudes reinforce each other. As a society, we need to move beyond stereotypes and focus on each group's strengths and challenges. Recognizing others' strengths helps reduce prejudice.

Racism is closely related to ethnocentrism and may even be a by-product of it. All the various "isms" tend to distance human beings from each other by accentuating differences and ignoring fundamental similarities, which, in turn, leads to tension and conflict. **Racism** develops when the most powerful group in a society creates an elaborate mythology (a set of beliefs that grossly distort reality) about a minority group. These prejudices often endure because of the need of the dominant group to feel superior to others. These prejudices can be significant stressors for members of the minority group, having serious psychological, social, and physiological effects (Clark, Anderson, Clark, & Williams, 1999).

The Advantages of Being in the Majority

If you're a member of the predominant culture in any society, there are innumerable benefits that accrue to you. You receive these benefits every day of your life, regardless of whether you worked for them—and, thus, "deserve" them—or didn't do anything at all to gain them. They are a birthright, like being born into a wealthy family. If you're a member of the majority culture, you take these benefits for granted. In fact, you hardly ever think about them.

We're not just targeting American culture here; we believe this is a cross-cultural phenomenon. Many countries throughout the world have a dominant culture. The dominant culture does not necessarily have to comprise the largest population, but it does hold most of the power.

What, in essence, are we talking about here? If you're a member of the majority culture:

- People speak the same language you speak.
- The educational system is patterned after your ways of thinking and honors your history, your beliefs, and your values.

- The job market is more open to you because you are the "right" color, gender, religion, sexual orientation, political affiliation, or social class, and you don't have a disability that makes the majority culture uncomfortable.
- People will not discriminate in renting an apartment to you or selling you a house in their neighborhood.
- The laws, the police, and the courts are sensitive to your cultural values and tend to deal with you in a relatively open-minded fashion.
- Religious and spiritual values of the culture are ideals that you can agree on and live with.
- Music, literature, movies, and art reflect your tastes and values.

The list of advantages accruing to those in the majority culture is almost endless. What advantages can you add to this list?

Marriage Outside the Group

In many countries throughout the world, marriage is seen primarily as an agreement between two families. An alliance through marriage between two successful families can enhance the power, prestige, and well-being of all the members of both families. In this sense, one marries not just an individual but also that person's family.

Because American culture stresses individuality, the importance of a good "fit" between families is often overlooked, and individuals who wish to marry often purposely ignore advice from family members. Sometimes that advice is based on ignorance of the proposed partner's personal strengths and/or on prejudice toward the cultural group from which the proposed partner comes. The greater the differences between the two families, the more likely the chance for conflict.

As our society becomes more ethnically diverse, marriage across ethnic groups has increased and, in turn, expanded ethnic diversity. According to Qian (2005), who relied on the 2000 Census, 9% of African American marriages are multiracial, 39% of Hispanics, 56% of American Indians, and 59% of Asian Americans. Only 4% of Whites are in **multiracial marriages** (marriages between two people from two different cultural or ethnic groups). Recent studies indicate that there are increasing numbers of interracial marriages between Whites and Blacks, and slower increases in interracial marriages between Whites and Latinos (Qian & Lichter, 2011). There has also been a decline in the number of White and Asian interracial marriages. These authors speculate that the rate of interracial marriages is impacted by the numbers of people in an ethnic group in this country. Because of the increase in Latino and Asian populations, these individuals are more likely to find a larger pool of potential marriage partners within their own cultural group. The number of marriages between foreign-born and U.S.-born has also increased because Latinos born in the United States are now likely to marry new immigrants. This is also the reason why there is such a low percentage of Whites in interracial marriages. They have a large pool of potential marriage partners from which to choose from within their own culture.

The number of multicultural couples cohabiting has increased and is approximately twice as high as the number of multiracial marriages (Batson et al., 2006; Qian, 2005). Some couples choose to live together to avoid disapproval from extended family. The number of multiracial marriages is increasing, and the trend is expected to continue as public attitudes become more accepting of such unions.

A survey conducted by the *Washington Post*, the Henry J. Kaiser Family Foundation, and Harvard University indicates that biracial couples report widespread tolerance and even acceptance of their relationships. The survey also found

es interviewed said they had intro-
ther family members, and felt com-
survey also found that the majority
disadvantaged by having parents

rveys with 1,709 randomly selected
adults. They found that 53% of Whites, 77% of Blacks, 68% of Latinos, and 67% of
Asians said it makes no difference whether a person marries someone of their own
ethnic group or a different group. About 40% of those interviewed in the random
sample said they had dated someone of another ethnic group. The researchers also
found that 46% of Black–White couples said being married to someone of a different group makes married life harder, compared to 30% of Latino–White couples and
32% of Asian–White couples. And 65% of Black–White couples said a parent at first
had a problem with the relationship, compared to 24% of Latino–White couples and
24% of Asian–White couples ("Biracial Couples Find More Tolerance," 2001).

Relationships Between Men and Women

Regardless of nationality or cultural background, friction occurs between men and
women in intimate relationships. Although couples strive for mutual love and caring,
different socialization processes and biological inheritances produce misunderstanding and conflict. Women in developed countries, because of greater education
and more employment opportunities outside the home, tend to have more options.
If they are dissatisfied with their marriages and can support themselves, they are
not as likely to stay in these marriages. Women in rural areas and in developing
countries have fewer options, even though they may be just as unhappy as their
divorcing counterparts in developed countries. As a result, divorce rates tend to
be higher in industrialized, urban-oriented societies around the world and lower
in less-developed, agrarian societies. But the lower divorce rates in the more rural
societies do not necessarily indicate happier marriages.

Ethnic identity is a social
construction rather than a
biological fact. The children
in this family are of mixed
European American and
Asian heritage; their ethnic
identity depends not on
their physical characteristics
but on the tradition within
which they are being raised.
Many young parents such
as these work to rear their
children in a bicultural
environment, respectful of
both family traditions.

Relationships Between Parents and Children

Children often develop into adults much like their own parents. In the process of growing up, however, children and parents often experience much conflict. The younger generation strives to create a relatively independent life, and the older generation tries to maintain control of the children. These struggles are played out in countless cultures around the world. Family power structures in various cultures seem to change gradually over time, as societies move from agriculturally oriented economies to industrialized economies. In an agriculturally oriented family, the father, who is responsible for making sure the farm runs smoothly, has more control over his children. In the city, the father's influence lessens, and the influence of others (peers, school, the workplace) increases. Rural societies generally emphasize respect for the authority of the dominant males. In more modern societies, the rights of the individual, whether female or male, receive more weight because the family is more likely to succeed if all its members become well educated and find good jobs.

When a family moves from one culture to another, parent–child relationships can be especially strained, because the youngsters struggle to fit into the new culture and inevitably lose touch with past traditions. Kim, a 35-year-old woman who married an American and emigrated to the United States from Korea, explains why it is important for their children, born in Korea but being raised in the United States, to be able to speak not only English but her native language as well. It will be a delicate balancing act for the family to maintain connections to both Korean and American cultures, but the benefits of such an accomplishment can far outweigh the difficulties.

"Of course, they need to know English. They're going to end up being Americans. That's obvious. We aren't going back to Korea to live, only to visit.

"It's hard for them. They speak English in school and in the neighborhood, but in the home we speak Korean. They get confused sometimes and mix languages. Sometimes the neighbor kids tease them about it. It's especially difficult for Jared, our son, but Emily is doing great. I think they'll both catch on and see why it's important in the long run.

"I want them to appreciate their roots, to remember the wonderful civilization they come from. And, most important, I want them to know me, their mother. I live in the United States but probably always will be Korean deep down, because that's where I grew up. I can't help it. That's home. The language of emotion, the language of love is your native language. How can I show my true emotions, my true love for my children if they cannot understand my Korean? How can they really know me?"

Summary

- When viewing people from different ethnic groups, it is important to look beyond their physical qualities and get to know their personal and family strengths.
- In families we learn what it means to be a family, how intimacy is expressed, what it means to be male and female, and gender roles. Families, however, exist within a cultural context—therefore culture matters.
- Most of what we know about gay and lesbian couples and families has come from samples that are primarily European American and middle-class.
- Approximately one-fourth of gay and lesbian couples have children, and approximately 45% want to have children.
- Gay and lesbian couples experience society stigma as they develop and maintain intimate relationships. Individuals and couples develop a variety of ways to allow stigma and intimacy to coexist.
- Cultural identity evolves from shared beliefs, values, and attitudes.
- Ethnic identity refers to the geographic origin of a particular group.
- Race is based on the physical characteristics of a group of people and is a concept that is losing value.

- The Hispanic, or Latino, population recently became the largest minority population in the United States, followed by African American, Asian American, and American Indian and Alaska Native populations.
- Historically, research has been primarily conducted with White, middle-class populations. Not only is there a need to include minority population in research studies, but there is also a need to include members of these populations in all aspects of research, including planning, analyzing data, and interpreting results.
- Professionals need to become culturally competent in order to more effectively provide family education and services.
- Strong families share the three family system traits of cohesion, flexibility, and communication. Three sociocultural characteristics are also useful for understanding families: the extended-family system, the social system, and the belief system.
- The strengths of White families in the United States include commitment to the family, enjoyable time spent together, the ability to manage stress and crisis effectively, spiritual well-being, positive communication, and appreciation and affection for each other.
- The strengths of African American families include strong kinship bonds, flexibility in family roles, strong motivation to achieve, strong religious orientation, and egalitarian marriages.
- The strengths of Latino families include familism, a supportive kin network system.
- The strengths of Asian American families include strong family orientation, filial piety, a high value on education, well-disciplined children, extended-family support, and family loyalty.
- The strengths of American Indian families include an extended-family system, spiritual beliefs, high family cohesion, respect for elders, bilingual language skills, and a tribal support system.
- Multiracial marriage can be challenging for families, but it can also be the source of considerable learning and personal growth.
- Male–female relationships and parent–child struggles are common issues in families from a variety of ethnic groups.
- The issues of assimilation, acculturation, and segregation must be faced by any new ethnic or cultural group.

Key Terms

cultural identity	gay and lesbian families
ethnic identity	race
cultural group	cultural competence
ethnic group	kinship

nuclear family
conjugal family system
consanguineal family system
extended family
plural marriage
polygamy
polygyny
polyandry
monogamy
pseudo–kin group
lineage
matrilineal society
patrilineal society
bilateral descent
matriarchal group
patriarchal group
egalitarian group
matrilocal society
patrilocal society

neolocal society
family cohesion
family flexibility
family communication
extended-family system
social system
belief system
historical trauma
cross-cultural family study
ethnocentrism
etic perspective
emic perspective
assimilation
acculturation
segregation
stereotype
prejudice
racism
multiracial marriage

Activities

1. Make a list of your family's strengths. How do they compare with the strengths identified by family researchers?
2. This chapter compares collectivistic values versus individualistic values. Reflect upon your own family's values. Are they more collectivistic or individualistic?
3. Find people in your class or on campus who have different ethnic backgrounds than yours. Talk with them about what positive and negative things they have experienced because of their membership in this ethnic group.
4. Try to learn more about the challenges and strengths of living in a gay or lesbian family. You might find a family through a gay and lesbian group on your campus who might be willing to talk with you about their family life. Pay particular attention to examples of family members being stigmatized and how they deal with it.

Suggested Readings

Bergstron, A., Clery, L. M., & Peacock, T. D. (2003). *The seventh generation: Native students speak about finding the Good Path.* Charleston, WV: Educational Resources Information Center (ERIC), Clearinghouse on Rural Education and Small Schools.

Chang, I. (2003). *The Chinese in America: A narrative history.* New York: Viking. The 150-year history of a people's search for a better life.

Coles, R. L., & Green, C. (2010). *The myth of the missing Black father.* New York, NY: Columbia University Press.

Coontz, S. (Ed.). (2008). *American families: A multicultural reader.* New York: Routledge.

Dalla, R., DeFrain, J., Johnson, J., & Abbott, D. A. (Eds.). (2009). *Strengths and challenges of new immigrant families: Implications for research, education, policy, and service.* Lanham, MD: Lexington Press.

Dreby, J. (2010). *Divided by borders: Mexican migrants and their children.* Berkeley, CA: University of California Press.

Garcia, A. M. (2003). *Narratives of Mexican American women.* Walnut Creek, CA: AltaMira Press. This is an insightful narrative of Chicana college students' struggle with their personal and family lives.

Graves, J. L., Jr. (2004). *The race myth: Why we pretend race exists in America.* New York: Dutton. Dr. Graves, an evolutionary biologist at Fairleigh Dickinson University in New Jersey, argues,

> We have paid dearly for the policies of racism, and are continuing to pay in a currency of despair, unfulfilled dreams, and blood. . . . Every time we pay, we slide closer toward hell on a road paved with our racial misconceptions. We will continue to pay until we reject the notion that there are biological races in the human species, and that race determines an individual's worth.

Hammack, P., & Cohler, B. (2009). *The story of sexual identity: Narrative perspectives on the gay and lesbian life course.* New York, NY: Oxford University Press.

Hao, L. (2007). *Color lines, country lines: Race, immigration and wealth stratification in America.* New York, NY: Russell Sage Foundation.

McAdoo, H. P. (Ed.). (2007). *Black families* (4th ed.). Thousand Oaks, CA: Sage.

Mohatt, G., & Thomas, L. (2006). "I wonder, why would you do it that way?" In J. E. Trimble & C. B. Fisher (Eds.), *The handbook of ethical research with ethnocultural populations and communities.* Thousand Oaks, CA: Sage.

Qian, Z. (2005). Breaking the last taboo: Interracial marriages in America. *Contexts, 4,* 33–37.

Skogrand, L. (2004). A process for learning about and creating programming for culturally diverse audiences. *Forum of Family and Consumer Issues, 9.* Online Journal: http://www.ces.ncsu.edu/depts/fcs/pub/forum.html.

Skogrand, L., Hatch, D., & Singh, A. (2008). Strong marriages in Latino culture. In R. Dalla, J. DeFrain, J. Johnson, & D. Abbott (Eds.), *Strengths and challenges of new immigrant families: Implications for research, policy, education, and service.* Lexington, MA: Lexington Books.

Skogrand, L., Mueller, M. L., Arrington, R., LeBlanc, H., Spotted Elk, D., Dayzie, I., & Rosenband, R. (2008). Strong Navajo marriages. *American Indian and Alaska Native Mental Health Research: The Journal of the National Center, 15,* 25–41. Retrieve from http://www.ucdenver.edu/academics/colleges/PublicHealth/research/centers/CAIANH/journal/Documents/Volume%2015/15(2)_Skogrand_Strong_Navajo_Marriages_25–41.pdf.

Suárez-Oronzco, C., Suárez-Oronzco, M., & Todorova, I. (2008). *Learning a new land: Immigrant students in American society.* Cambridge, MA: Belknap Press of Harvard University Press.

Tudge, J. (2008). *The everyday lives of young children: Culture, class, and child rearing in diverse societies.* New York, NY: Cambridge University Press.

Visit the text-specific Online Learning Center at **www.mhhe.com/olson8e** for practice tests, chapter summaries, and PowerPoint slides.

3 Understanding Marriage and Family Dynamics

The History of Family Science

Models of Couples and Families

Three Key Relationship Concepts

Couple and Family Map

Dynamics Change in Relationships over Time

Summary

Key Terms

Activities

Suggested Readings

There are a variety of perspectives or ways of describing marriage and family dynamics. These perspectives are like different lenses through which we can observe the various aspects of close relationships. Each perspective, or framework, is built on different assumptions and has specific concepts that help define the relevant elements of each framework.

In this chapter we will present six major conceptual frameworks for describing marriage and family dynamics: *the family systems theory, the international family strengths framework, the family development framework, the symbolic interaction framework, the social construction framework,* and *the feminist framework.* We will also take a look at three major dimensions of couple and family dynamics that integrate many of the concepts from the six frameworks; these three central dimensions are cohesion, flexibility, and communication. To conclude, we will discuss the Couple and Family Map, which helps integrate and apply these more abstract frameworks and concepts to specific couple and family relationships.

Before we begin exploring the conceptual frameworks, we will define some of the relevant concepts related to conceptual and theory development. A **conceptual framework** is a set of interconnected ideas, concepts, and assumptions that helps organize thinking from a particular perspective. A **theory** consists of general principles that are composed of interrelated concepts, and **hypotheses** are presumed relationships between variables. A **research study** can be designed to test one or more specific hypotheses.

Most family professionals maintain that there are many ways of looking at families. They use ideas and principles from several conceptual frameworks to help them understand marriage and family life. This open-minded approach to learning and to life is often termed an *eclectic* approach, and most family researchers, family life educators, and family therapists subscribe to it. However, professionals with an eclectic approach can sometimes be too open and accepting of contradictory ideas.

There are two contrasting approaches to understanding how individuals and families operate: the idiographic approach and the nomothetic approach. Some family scientists maintain that human beings are unique and that it is difficult to construct a broad conceptual framework or theory that applies to all couples and to all families. This view has been labeled the **idiographic approach**, which focuses on the unique aspects of individuals or families. Professionals who use this approach are more interested in individual case studies and tend to have a clinical focus.

On the other end of the theory spectrum is the **nomothetic approach**, which focuses on ideas that apply to the majority of individuals or families. Researchers using this approach try to develop a broader understanding of couples and families and to work toward a general theory. Both of these approaches have value and usefulness, because every marriage and every family *is* unique and yet has much in common with others.

The History of Family Science

Family science began many years ago, focusing on family relationships. Currently it is a multidisciplinary field integrating research from multiple areas. There have been changes in focus and content over the years, but many of the issues remain the same.

Family Science in the Early Years

Family science is a relatively new multidisciplinary field that originated more than 70 years ago. Many of the leaders in the field came from sociology, which had been established earlier. The National Council on Family Relations (NCFR), one of the major professional organizations in the field, was founded in 1938 and focuses on family research, practice, and education (ncfr.org). The first journal published by NCFR was called *Living*, and has evolved to a journal called *Journal of Marriage and Family*. In 1952, NCFR added a second journal that focused less on research and more on the application of research to family life. The earliest version of the journal was called *The Coordinator*; this evolved into a journal that is currently known as *Family Relations*. In 2009, NCFR added a third journal entitled *Journal of Family Theory & Review*, which focuses on all aspects of family theory.

The American Association for Marital and Family Therapy (AAMFT), which was founded in 1942, is made up of marriage and family therapists who focus on increasing understanding, research, and education and on helping individuals, couples, and families who have problems (aamft.org). Although most of their work involves therapy with individuals and families, marriage and family therapists also provided education for couples and families. They began publishing a journal entitled *Journal of Marital and Family Therapy* in 1975.

There are several journals in addition to those published by NCFR and AAMFT that are well known in the family science field and are widely read by family social scientists. Some of those journals include *Marriage and Family Review, Journal of Family Issues,* and *Family Process*. Others come from psychology and include the *Journal of Family Psychology*. Because family science is an interdisciplinary field, there are also journals in social work, education, communication studies, anthropology, and many other fields that have relevance for family science.

Family life education has also evolved as a part of family science. Early work included sex education for youth, with later education focusing on parent education. In recent years there has been an increased focus on couple and relationship education (Administration for Children and Families, n.d.), with federal funding supporting marriage education.

A study of the first three volumes of *Living* (Volume 1, 1939; Volume 2, 1940; Volume 3, 1941), which evolved into what is currently the *Journal of Marriage and Family*, places family science in the historical context. Many of the issues in these first three volumes are similar to the issues that we still highlight in current family science literature. For example, there were concerns about the impacts of poverty and inadequate housing on family life. There were concerns about family instability, focusing on the high divorce rate of that time (18%, compared to about 50% today). There were discussions about the need for casework and family counseling to help all families, but particularly poor families. There were also articles about what it takes to have a good marriage and the importance of healthy relationships to avoid divorce. Having healthy parent–child relationships also received attention in family science in the early years.

There were also topics that are no longer focused on in current family science literature. For example, there were several articles about **eugenics**, which refers to breeding to improve inherited characteristics. There was concern that contraception be available to limit births in cases where genetic defects would likely be inherited (Osborn, 1939). These articles used terms such as "superior heredity capacity," "physical, mental and social inadequacy," and "hereditary defectives, borderline cases, and persons with marked ability" (p. 34). There were also several articles describing marriage courses that had been successfully implemented at colleges and universities and explaining why these courses were successful. Authors indicated concerns about youth and the problems they were encountering. Mention is made of the Civilian Conservation Corps (CCC), which provided work and structure for young men and at the same time provided service to the country.

Although the concerns about the demise of the family were similar to what we experience today, the cause of those concerns might have been different. An article by Goldstein (1940, p. 9) describes the reasons for the "disorganization of the family":

> That the family is in danger today there can be no doubt in the minds of those who know the facts. Growing tensions and discords and disruptions in family relationships; the deepening rebellion of children; the widening revolt of women; the increasing restlessness of men; the almost incredible multiplication of estrangements, separations and divorces—and these are the symptoms of a serious disorganization in family life.

One author, in an article entitled *Seven Pillars of Family Strength*, identified the seven things that made families strong in the early years of family science (Faris, 1940). The seven pillars were (1) laws of the land about marriage and family life, (2) church, (3) schools, (4) neighborhoods, (5) communities, (6) welfare organizations, and (7) what they were learning through research about the problems of human nature, personality, and family life. It is interesting to note that six out of seven of these pillars are social structures and institutions outside of the family itself. Because research about marriage and family was just beginning and was very limited, it was viewed as only a small part of what helps families.

Although some of the articles provided very limited research evidence, and this research was both qualitative and quantitative, many articles reported the thoughts of the authors, making arguments for a stand they were taking. Where we came from as a science provides a foundation for where we are today.

Family Science Today

The growing impact of the family profession is indicated by how many other professional groups now focus on family-oriented topics. Table 3.1 illustrates the topics

TABLE 3.1	Disciplines Contributing to Family Science
Discipline	**Topics in Family Science**
Anthropology	Cross-cultural studies; kinship; diversity in families
Biology	Conception and reproduction; growth, development, and aging
Child development	Development of infant and child; parenting
Communication studies	Family communication
Economics	Family finances; consumer behavior
Education	Family life education; marriage education
English	Marriages and families in literature (present and past)
History	Historical perspectives on the family throughout time
Human ecology	Ecosystem perspectives on family, nutrition, housing, and clothing
Law	Marriage and divorce laws; child custody laws
Medicine	Families and health; family practice
Psychiatry	Family therapy
Psychology	Family psychology; assessment of couples and families
Social work	Treating problem families; family policy
Sociology	Marriage and divorce statistics; sociological theories about families

and issues that the traditional disciplines are now studying and are providing significant contributions. Increasingly, professionals from these other disciplines are now specializing in marriage and family. For example, there are lawyers who now specialize in family law. Even in the medical profession, there is a specialty that focuses on the family called *family practice*.

There is a growing awareness of the importance of close relationships in a person's life. Studies of personal happiness have consistently revealed that close relationships are the most important aspects of life and are essential to emotional well-being and good physical health (Berscheid, 2006). Conversely, many studies have documented that a troubled relationship, especially a distressed marriage and family, is the most common presenting problem of those seeking therapy.

While psychologists have traditionally focused on understanding individuals, family science is focused on *relationships*. The growing interest in relationship science was identified by Ellen Berscheid, a well-known social psychologist, who emphasizes the importance of studying interactions and interconnections between people (Berscheid, 2006). Relationship science assumes that a relationship is dynamic and resides between people and not within a person.

Relationships are the essence of life. "We are born into relationships, we live our lives in relationships with others, and when we die, the effects of our relationships survive in the lives of the living" (Berscheid, 2006). It is for this reason that there is increasing interest in family science, which focuses on studying, understanding, and helping all types of close relationships.

Models of Couples and Families

This chapter will describe a variety of models or ways of understanding couples and families, which are called *conceptual frameworks*. The most popular of the conceptual frameworks is the *family systems theory*, which focuses on the family as an ongoing system of interconnected members. (Because it is a broad and comprehensive set of principles, this perspective is referred to more often as a theory than as a conceptual framework.) The *international family strengths framework* is becoming more accepted because it highlights the positive aspects of couples and families rather than only looking at their problems. The *family development framework* looks at how couples and families change over time. The *symbolic interaction framework* has historically been valuable to family professionals because it examines how family members learn roles and rules in our society. The *social construction framework*, which is growing in popularity, maintains that our views as partners and family members are shaped by our social world and that each of us has a different life experience and therefore a unique view of our own close relationships. The *feminist framework* is increasingly important to the family field because it emphasizes the value of women's perspectives on marriage and family life and on society.

Family Systems Theory

Everything that happens to you, happens to me.

—Nikki DeFrain

According to **family systems theory**, everything that happens to any family member has an impact on everyone else in the family (Goldenberg & Goldenberg, 2011). Because family members are interconnected and operate as a group, the group is called a **family system**. This approach to describing the family as a system has become very popular in both theory and practice, particularly with family therapists who work with couples and families having relationship problems.

A pioneer family therapist Carl Whitaker (1992) was fond of saying that in a metaphorical sense "there are no individuals in the world—only fragments of families." In other words, individual human beings are inextricably tied to their family. How people think and behave is deeply influenced by their family background, and people are best understood by understanding their family. From a family therapist's standpoint, an individual can most effectively change if his or her family also changes. If a family is in trouble, both parents and children need to become involved in family therapy.

When an individual has a problem, not only the family but also the whole community is often involved in finding a solution, an idea echoed in the popular statement "It takes a whole village to raise a child." A family simply cannot do it all alone. Troubled families often live in troubled communities, and if individuals are to be well, the community must find a way to create health for all its members.

Family systems theory grew out of the general systems theory, a conceptual framework developed in the 1960s by Ludwig von Bertalanffy (1968), and family therapists applied these ideas to marriage and family as a system. The **general systems theory**, a broad-based model used in a variety of fields, is a set of principles and concepts that can be applied to all types of systems, living and nonliving. The dictionary defines a **system** as (1) a set or arrangement of things so related or connected as to form a unity or organic whole and (2) a whole made of interacting parts.

Family systems theory was created by family therapists because family therapists working with troubled individuals over the years discovered that working with an individual alone did not produce long-term change in a child's behavior. A problem child might make some improvements in her or his functioning by working alone with the therapist, but the child often reverted back to problem behaviors unless the family changed. This is because the family system has such a powerful impact on a child's behavior.

Another important finding by family therapists was that when a child has problems, often there are problems in the family system. For example, family therapists have found that if there is a disturbed child in a two-parent family, there is often a troubled marriage which contributes to the child's difficulties.

A Hierarchy of Connected Systems. Proponents of the family systems theory have expanded on ideas and terminology developed by general systems theorists, and family therapists use these ideas in their practice. Several concepts of the general systems theory are particularly relevant to family systems. The idea of **multiple system levels** is that systems are embedded within other systems. Whenever attention is focused on a given system, a **suprasystem** (a larger system) and a **subsystem** (a smaller system) are usually also involved. If you are focusing on the couple as the system, the suprasystem is the family and the subsystem consists of the two individuals. If you are focusing on the nuclear family as the system, the suprasystem is the extended family and the subsystem is the couple or any other dyadic (two-person) unit, such as parent and child.

Systems are both connected to and separated from other systems by **boundaries**. The notion of a boundary also implies a hierarchy of interconnected systems, each system being separated by invisible boundaries from other smaller or larger systems (Goldenberg & Goldenberg, 2011). Considering the family, there is a boundary between the family and the larger kin system and a boundary between parents and the children.

Human systems have many different system levels that can be characterized as a set of concentric circles (Figure 3.1). For example, the smallest circle at the center would be the individual; encircling this in graduated rings would be the couple (a dyad, or two-person human system), the family, the local neighborhood (including businesses, schools, etc.), the town, the nation, the continent, the world, and so on. Families do not function in a vacuum because they are a part of larger systems.

Thinking about human systems is considered an ecological approach; **ecology** is the study of how all the organisms in a system are related to each other. As Figure 3.1 illustrates, all the concentric circles are connected to one another and the people in each of the circles influence the people in the other circles—creating a **human ecosystem**. To really understand a specific family system, you also need to consider the various system levels it influences and that influence it. For these reasons, helping a middle-class, suburban family through a crisis would be very different from helping a family living in poverty in the inner city.

Another concept from general systems theory is **wholeness**, the concept that the whole is more than the sum of its parts. From a family systems perspective, the whole family is more than the total of all its individual members. This means that you cannot know the family simply by knowing each person as an individual because each individual will behave differently outside the family (Goldenberg & Goldenberg, 2011).

FIGURE 3.1

An Ecological Approach to Human Systems

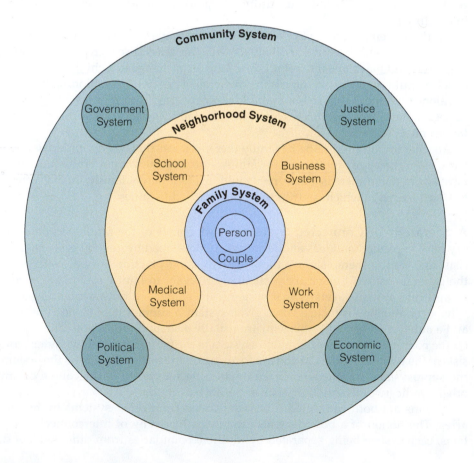

For example, Carla, a student living in an apartment, has a certain identity related to her life at college and another identity back home with her family. If you observe Carla very carefully in her college environment, you get a good understanding of what she is like at college. But when Carla goes home to visit her family for a holiday break, she becomes a different person in many ways. She is transformed into a daughter, a granddaughter, a big sister, a little sister. At home she may return to some of the ways she previously behaved at home, even though she does not continue that pattern at school. This is partly because, although she might have changed in college, the family did not change, and when the family is all together again she fills the role she played in the family to create the wholeness of the family.

A good cook takes individual herbs, spices, and vegetables and combines them to create a wonderful and zesty sauce that has flavors of the individual ingredients but is more than and different from the separate ingredients. The whole family system is also more than the sum of its parts, and the family's behavior cannot be predicted from knowing only the individual persons. Conversely, it is difficult to predict the behavior of the individuals by knowing about the family as a whole.

Another concept of the general systems theory is the **interdependence of parts**: The parts or elements of a system are interconnected in such a way that if one part is changed, other parts are also affected (Goldenberg & Goldenberg, 2011). Visualize for a moment a mobile, an artistic creation suspended in midair, made up of many carefully balanced elements. Each element in the mobile is weighted and placed in such a way as to create not only an aesthetic effect but also a delicate system that can be easily set in motion by a slight ripple of wind or a soft touch. Anything stronger might knock it out of balance.

Healthy families, in a sense, are like a mobile: Each member fits into the whole in a unique way and adds to the beauty of the whole. If one individual changes— for better or worse—the total creation is affected. Consider how one event changed the family in the story presented in Box 3.1.

Flexibility: Balancing Stability and Change. Flexibility is the ability of a system to balance both stability and change. A flexible couple or family is like a flower in the wind because it is able to bend with the wind. General systems theorists use the term **open system**, or **morphogenic system**, when referring to a system that is open to growth and change. A **closed system**, or **morphostatic system**, is one that has the capacity to maintain the status quo, thus avoiding change (Goldenberg & Goldenberg, 2011).

Family therapists have discovered that many couples and families are highly resistant to change, even though they need to adapt to solve the problems they face. They are likely to want to maintain the status quo out of habit, lack of insight, or fear of something new. A common observation is when one family member changes, there is also change in the other family members.

As an example of a morphostatic system, consider the following story. By failing to deal openly and effectively with their relationship problems, Katherine and Ken are beginning a free fall into despair. They are an example of a morphostatic family system, unable or unwilling to change. A morphogenic system, one open to growth and change, might have been able to prevent such a scenario.

Ken and Katherine have been married for 15 years. Ken is an alcoholic, though he manages to hold on to his job as a floor supervisor at a printing plant. Ken has been having an extramarital affair with Winona, a co-worker at the plant, for 6 months. When Katherine discovers the affair, she tells Ken she is leaving him. He responds by begging for forgiveness and promising to give up the relationship with Winona.

BOX 3.1   Putting It Together

Reorganization of the Family System After a Car Accident

Like other families affected by sudden changes, Julia's family will probably never return to the way things were before an accident occurred. But as Julia's case shows, the nuclear family, with the help of extended-family members, is capable of establishing a more connected family system.

Julia was a single parent living with her two young children, Camille and Katy. Their life together was a hectic but satisfying round of school, work, family visits, and activities with friends. A year ago, Julia was involved in an auto accident and was seriously injured. She could neither work nor care for her children. Her family's delicate balance was upset until her mother, Eloise, her brother Tim, her sister Allison, and her best friend at work, Sheryl, all stepped in to help create a new sense of family balance.

These four adults spent countless hours at the hospital, reassuring Julia and listening to her express her uncertainty and pain. They also worked out some new arrangements to make up for her absence. Camille and Katy temporarily moved in with Eloise. She took care of them, prepared their meals, made sure they had clean clothes

for school, and took over many details of their lives. Tim, who lived nearby, drove Camille and Katy to and from school and took care of them afterward. Allison, who still lived at home, got them to bed at night and took them on outings on the weekends. Camille and Katy took on some new responsibilities themselves, like walking the dog and doing their homework without prompting. Sheryl kept things going at the office by taking on several of Julia's responsibilities herself.

After an initial period of confusion and difficulty, all these individuals became familiar with their new roles and proud of their new skills. Julia was hospitalized for several weeks and had physical therapy for several months, but eventually she regained her strength and her courage. When she returned home, the whole family celebrated. In the months that followed, she established a new balance with her children, assimilating the experiences they had all had since the accident. She also had a stronger network of friends and family than she had had before the accident.

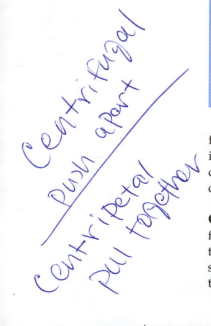

He wants to avoid divorce for a number of reasons: embarrassment at work, shame in his extended family, and financial consequences. Besides, although the thrill is gone from the marriage, he and Katherine have a long history together, and she is a good mother to their three children. Katherine is skeptical of Ken's promises. She tells him that she wants him to give up drinking as well. He says he can control his drinking and just drink "socially." He doesn't really need to go "cold turkey," he argues.

Katherine remains skeptical; she has heard such arguments many times before. In spite of her skepticism, however, Katherine decides to forgive Ken, as she has before, and to stay. She genuinely loves him, even though she hates his drinking and, now, his seeing another woman. And he provides a good income for her and the children. Katherine also fears being on her own, both socially and financially. She dreads the thought of going back into the workplace after so many years at home. Whatever she has now, she feels, is better than what she would have as a divorced mother of three.

The family systems framework assumes that systems operate on a continuum from extreme morphostasis to extreme morphogenesis. In a healthy system, there is a balance between these extremes. The couple or family needs to be open to change, but not to the point of being rootless or chaotic. Conversely, it needs to be centered and stable, but not to the point of being rigid.

Cohesion: Balance of Separateness and Connectedness. Couples and families need to find a balance between their separateness as individuals and their connectedness as a system. The dynamics that help systems maintain this separateness–connectedness balance are the opposing forces of centrifugal and centripetal interactions. **Centrifugal interactions** tend to push family members apart,

BOX 3.2 Diversity in Families

Cultural Conflicts for a Female Chicana College Student

I am a Chicana graduate student who wants to complete a Ph.D. in family studies so I can teach at the college level and help the family field be more inclusive and up-to-date regarding Chicano families. Fortunately, the choices I've made are not in conflict with my family of procreation.

It was very difficult for my family of origin initially to understand why I wanted or needed to go to school for so long. Since my grandparents and parents struggled just to provide for adequate housing, food, and clothing, they find it difficult to see why education is so important. They were also somewhat threatened by the fact that I wanted to study families because I might learn too much.

Another conflict was regarding my interest in my own development versus their emphasis on the whole family. They felt I was focusing too much on myself and not giving back enough to the family. Also, they felt this was making me more competitive and less cooperative, which is a quality valued highly. Another issue is the use of the Spanish language and whether I would use both Spanish and English in my home. Since we decided to raise our children using English only, some family members viewed that choice as rejecting our heritage. Also, as my years of college education increased, my relatives tended to distance themselves more from me.

Fortunately, my husband, who is also Chicano, is totally supportive and is a house husband for our two small children. He takes care of the children, and I am the primary wage earner. This is not the traditional family model for most Chicanos, and so it does challenge some of our other family members and kin.

While I was not initially aware of the importance of my mother's support, I have lately become even more appreciative of her encouraging words. I have finally been giving her more credit for her support. She also served as a positive role model since she began working full-time when I was young. She also has strongly encouraged me to work outside the home and even to try to seek a career.

In general, I have made it because I am determined to have a professional career and have the strong support of my husband and my mother. My other relatives are less understanding and supportive since they question my goals and values. In spite of it all, education is necessary for me to help advance myself and my family.

Source: Unpublished manuscript by Julie Palacio, 1992, former graduate student in Family Social Science, University of Minnesota, St. Paul, MN. Reprinted by permission.

---

thereby increasing separateness. **Centripetal interactions** pull family members together and increase family closeness (Goldenberg & Goldenberg, 2011).

Family therapists have found that a family crisis can push families to an extreme of either centripetal or centrifugal interactions. Faced with a death of a family member, one family may pull together and come out stronger as a result of the loss, whereas another family may find itself torn apart by the events. The first family resolves to hold onto each other, communicate about feelings, and help each other. These centripetal interactions strengthen the bonds of love and concern. The members of the second family are afraid, cannot talk with one another, and attempt to deal with the death as individuals. They separate from the family and look for comfort outside it, or they bury themselves in personal despair.

An important aspect of understanding cohesion is whether a family system permits family members to develop their own independence from the family. In the personal account of a young Chicana woman recounted in Box 3.2, you will see that in her close Chicano family, most of the family system is opposed to a female (Julie) getting too much education. However, her mother and her husband are very supportive and enabled Julie to continue graduate school and develop her own independence within a very close family system.

Family therapists agree that a healthy balance of separateness and connectedness works best for families in crisis. In the face of death, family members can draw on each other's strengths and skills for comfort and at the same time seek out

Families that spend time together and enjoy fun activities build stronger relationships.

positive people in the community who can be growth enhancing for the family as a whole. If family members choose to go their separate ways as a result of the crisis, the likelihood of a positive outcome for the family as a whole lessens considerably.

Feedback Within the System (Communication). Another basic principle of the general systems theory is that communication in the system is essential. No matter how hard one might try, one simply cannot *not* communicate (Becvar & Becvar, 2009). Even if we completely withdraw from our family, we are communicating an important message: the family is not a safe, healthy, or happy place to live.

Family systems function better when important information is regularly exchanged among the members, which is the essence of communication. General systems theorists talk about information feedback loops, which can be either positive or negative (Goldenberg & Goldenberg, 2011). **Positive feedback** in families is intended to create change, whereas **negative feedback** is designed to minimize change and keep things the same. Feedback can come either from family members or from people outside the family.

Positive and negative do not connote value judgments or indicate whether a change is good or bad but rather whether change occurs in the system or not. For example, Sandy suggests that the members of her family exchange jobs around the house to add variety and give everyone a better understanding of what the various jobs entail. If Sandy's family members accept this idea and change their routine, then Sandy's feedback to the system is considered positive. However, if they resist her idea of change, the system feedback is negative.

In sum, openness to change is a key concept in the family systems framework. A common reaction of some couples and families under stress is to look inward and try to prevent new information or people from coming into the system. This would be an example of negative feedback because they are resisting change. When under stress, families would be helped if they were more open to change, which is an example of positive feedback.

International Family Strengths Framework

The **international family strengths framework** focuses on how couples and families succeed rather than on why they fail, from a global perspective (DeFrain & Asay, 2007; DeFrain et al., 2012). This perspective arose from the notion that strong families can serve as models for other families wanting to succeed. One advantage of the international family strengths framework is that it tends to change the nature of what one finds in families. Simply stated, if one studies only problems, one finds only couple and family problems. Similarly, if researchers and therapists are interested in couple and family strengths, they have to look for them. When these strengths are identified, they can be the foundation for continued growth and change.

Family therapists and other counselors are finding the international family strengths framework helpful in treating family problems (DeFrain, Cook, & Gonzalez-Kruger, 2005; Marsh, 2003). Many professionals have found that just solving problems is not enough. They need a model of healthy family development as a goal for troubled families to work toward. Identifying a family's strengths also boosts morale among family members.

The most extensive series of studies of family strengths has been conducted by Nick Stinnett, John DeFrain, and colleagues (DeFrain et al., 2006, DeFrain & Asay, 2007). In more than 35 years of study, the researchers have collected data from more than 28,000 family members in every state of the United States and 38 countries around the world. Stinnett and DeFrain propose that six major qualities are commonly present in strong families (Table 3.2). These qualities are appreciation and affection,

TABLE 3.2	Qualities of Strong Families
Appreciation and Affection	**Commitment**
Caring for each other	Trust
Friendship	Honesty
Respect for individuality	Dependability
Playfulness	Faithfulness
Humor	Sharing
Positive Communication	**Enjoyable Time Together**
Giving compliments	Quality time in great quantity
Sharing feelings	Good things take time
Avoiding blame	Enjoying each other's company
Being able to compromise	Simple good times
Agreeing to disagree	Sharing fun times
Spiritual Well-Being and Shared Values	**Ability to Manage Stress and Crisis**
Hope	Adaptability
Faith	Seeing crises as challenges and opportunities
Compassion	Growing through crises together
Shared ethical values	Openness to change
Oneness with humankind	Resilience

Source: From John DeFrain and S. Asay (eds.), *Strong Families Around the World: The Family Strengths Perspective.* Copyright © 2007 by The Haworth Press, Inc. Reprinted by permission of Taylor & Francis Group, LLC, a division of Informa plc.

commitment, positive communication, enjoyable time together, spiritual well-being and shared values, and the ability to manage stress and crisis effectively.

All these family strengths are interrelated, overlap to some degree, and interact. Appreciation and affection for one another make family members more likely to spend time together, and time together is enhanced by positive communication. Communication enhances commitment, and commitment leads to spending more time together. A feeling of spiritual well-being gives people the confidence to weather a crisis, and the ability to manage crises makes family members appreciate each other more. Family strengths are thus interconnected like a large, complex puzzle. Let's look at each strength in more detail.

Appreciation and Affection. People in strong families care deeply for one another, and they let each other know this regularly. Many people, however, don't express **appreciation and affection** in their families. Consider the response of one spouse: "She cooked dinner every evening, but it never occurred to me to thank her for it. She doesn't thank me for going to work every day." Such an attitude is unfortunate, because expressing affection and giving and receiving sincere thanks foster a positive atmosphere and help people get along better. A pat on the back, a smile, or a hug builds a bond of caring. One member of a strong family explained it this way: "He makes me feel good about me and about us as a couple. Very few days go by without him saying something positive."

People in dysfunctional families more often focus on the negative. These people gain energy by feeding off the self-esteem and good feelings of others. They believe that by putting other people down they can build themselves up. The approach usually backfires, however, often producing only countercriticism.

Researchers have found that sexual behavior in strong marriages is often a form of expressing appreciation for each other. "Foreplay does not begin at 10:30 P.M. on Saturday night," one husband explained. "It begins when I take out the garbage on Wednesday morning, when I cook dinner on Friday night, and when I help Jeannie solve a problem at her work on Saturday afternoon." Sex is a natural way to express warm feelings for the partner. Another person reported, "The times when sex was

The international family strengths framework focuses on the positive qualities of families. Apparent in this family are such strengths as warmth, caring, appreciation, affection, trust, commitment, and enjoyment of each other's company.

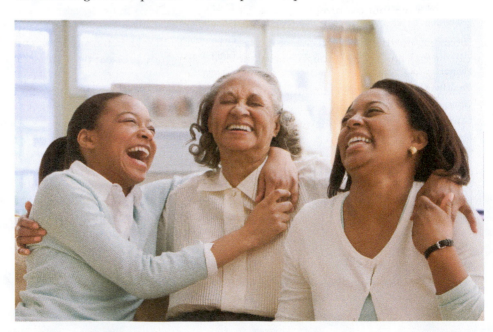

best have been times when we've felt especially close and in tune with each other, when we'd solved a problem or when we were working on a project together."

Commitment. Members of strong families generally show a strong **commitment** to one another, investing time and energy in family activities and not letting their work or other priorities take too much time away from family interaction. "My wife and kids are the most important part of my life," one father said in describing commitment. Another noted that "what we have as a family is a treasure." Commitment does not mean, however, that family members stifle each other. "We give each other the freedom and encouragement to pursue individual goals," one wife noted. "Yet either of us would cut out activities or goals that threatened our time together."

Commitment includes sexual fidelity. Some of the people interviewed by the researchers admitted to having engaged in an extramarital affair earlier in the marriage. Some believed the affair precipitated a crisis that in the final analysis led to a stronger marriage. But marriages can change for the better without a crisis of such major proportions. "Being faithful to each other sexually is just a part of being honest with each other," one young woman noted. Honesty, indeed, is the best policy.

Positive Communication. When people are asked to list the qualities they consider essential to a strong family, most list **positive communication**. Yet many families don't spend much time talking to one another. Although successful families are often task oriented, identifying problems and discussing how to solve them, family members also spend time talking with and listening to one another just to stay connected. Some of the most important talk occurs when no one is working at communication. Open-ended, rambling conversations can reveal important information. How does your teenager feel about sex? Her grades? Her future? When parents and children get comfortable with each other, important issues arise.

Communication does not always produce agreement in strong families. Family members have differences and conflicts, but they speak directly and honestly about them without blaming each other. They try to resolve their differences but may agree to disagree. Dysfunctional families, on the other hand, are either overly critical and hostile in their communication with each other or deny problems and avoid verbal conflict. Although verbal hostilities are not productive, neither is avoidance of problems.

Studies reveal that communication in healthy families has several important aspects. Members of strong families are good at listening. "I'd much rather listen to other people talk," one father explained. "I learn a lot more when I'm listening to my loved ones than I do when I'm talking *at* them." Family members are also adept at asking questions, and they do not try to read one another's minds. Members of strong families also understand that people's views of the world change, and this can be a good thing.

Humor is another important aspect of healthy family communication. Strong families like to laugh. A study of 304 mothers, fathers, and teenagers revealed that humor is a valuable source of family strength. Wuerffel, DeFrain, and Stinnett (1990) reviewed the scientific literature on humor and found that humor can be used in many different positive and negative ways. Humor can reduce daily tension, facilitate conversations, express feelings of warmth and affection, lessen anxiety, point out mistakes made by others, and entertain. It can also help put others at ease and help maintain a positive outlook on life.

The study found positive correlations between the use of humor and how strong the families were based on their responses to a family strengths inventory. The stronger the family, the more likely the family members were to use humor to maintain a positive outlook on life, to entertain each other, to reduce tension, to express warmth, to put others at ease, to facilitate conversations, to lessen anxiety, and to help cope with difficult situations. The stronger families in the study reported negative effects, however, when humor was used to put down other family members. Put-downs and sarcasm were used less often by the stronger families.

The study concluded that families benefit from humor that points out the incongruous aspects of life—the inconsistent, bizarre, silly, illogical things that happen to people every day. Families, however, do not benefit from humor that places someone in a superior position or from sarcasm aimed at demeaning a family member. Sarcasm is often an attempt to mask anger; it is rarely used out of love.

Enjoyable Time Together. "What do you think makes a happy family?" a researcher asked 1,500 schoolchildren. Few replied that money or cars or fancy homes or television sets made a happy family. The most frequent response? A happy family is one that does things together and spends **enjoyable time together**. Although the response seems simple enough, family therapists see many couples and families who haven't figured this out. "I don't have a lot of time with my family," many people like to say, "but I try to make it quality time."

Happy memories result from quality time spent together in considerable quantity: "I remember stories Mom and Dad told me when they tucked me into bed." "Going with Dad to work on the farm. I felt so important." "Singing together—we

Spending fun time together and expressing love and affection are key components of strong families.

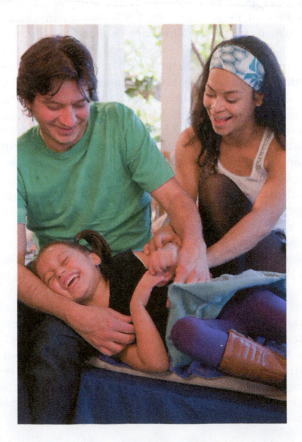

had an old piano, and I learned to play, and we would all sing corny old songs." "Vacation. We would go 50 miles to the lake and rent a cabin, and Dad would swim with us."

These happy memories share common threads. First, happiness often centers on activities that are shared as a family. Second, pleasurable time together often centers on simple activities that don't cost a lot of money. Strong families identified these popular family activities: meals together, house and yard chores, and outdoor recreation, including camping, playing catch and other yard games, canoeing, hiking, and picnicking.

Meaningful family rituals are one of the ways family members are brought together. Family rituals have been linked with positive outcomes for families, including greater marital and family satisfaction and better adjustment in children (Leon & Jacobvitz, 2003). Family rituals range from daily and weekly events like family dinners and weekend routines to family traditions like celebrating birthdays and holidays. These rituals contribute to a greater feeling of connection and stability in the family.

Spiritual Well-Being and Shared Values. Perhaps the most controversial finding of the family strengths researchers is the importance of religion or spirituality in strong families. Some families call this **spiritual well-being**. Others talk about faith in God, hope, or optimism about life. Some say they feel a oneness with the world. Others talk about their families in almost religious terms, describing the love they feel for one another as sacred. Others express these kinds of feelings in terms of ethical values and commitment to important causes.

Spiritual well-being can be the caring center within each individual that promotes sharing, love, and compassion. Spiritual well-being is the feeling or force that helps people transcend themselves. "I feel my family is a part of all the families of the world," said one respondent. An important aspect of membership in a religious or spiritual group is the caring, supportive community it provides. When illness strikes, a baby is born, or an accident occurs, friends in the group are often quick to help each other.

It is important to distinguish between *spiritual* and *religious* when talking about spiritual well-being. Spiritual beliefs can be seen as very personal, private beliefs individuals hold. Religious beliefs, in contrast, can be seen as being linked to a particular religious denomination or faith. Thus, some people would think of themselves as being spiritual but not religious, indicating that they have a strong personal belief system but are not connected to a religious institution. And other people would think of themselves as being *both* spiritual and religious, having a very personal belief system while being active in a religious institution. While spiritual beliefs focus on private and more universal beliefs, religious beliefs emphasize the public and external system linked more with denominations than with family dynamics. Families that are grounded spiritually have often integrated these beliefs into their family behavior and traditions.

Agreement by a married couple on spiritual beliefs has been found to be strongly linked to a more successful marriage (Larson & Olson, 2004). In a national study with 24,671 married couples who took the ENRICH couple inventory, couples with high agreement on spiritual beliefs not only were more happily married, but also had many other strengths in their marriages, including better communication, greater ability to resolve conflict, and feeling more couple closeness; they also had higher levels of couple flexibility.

Ability to Manage Stress and Crisis Effectively. Strong families are not immune to trouble, but they are not as crisis prone as dysfunctional families tend to be. Rather, they possess the **ability to manage stress and crisis effectively**. Strong families are often successful at preventing troubles before they occur, but some stressors in life are inevitable. The best a family can do is meet the challenge as efficiently as possible, minimizing its damage and looking for opportunities for growth together in the process.

Among the strategies strong families use to weather crises is pulling together rather than pulling apart. Each person, even a very young child, has a part to play in easing the burdens of the others. Additionally, strong families seek help if they cannot solve the problem themselves. Although this may surprise some people, members of strong families do get counseling in an attempt to learn better ways of coping with a crisis. In contrast, truly troubled families often do not have the strength to admit that they have troubles and need to seek advice.

Family Development Framework

Family development as a conceptual framework was originally designed to describe and explain the process of change in couples and families. Researchers and clinicians working from a **family development framework** are primarily

Many cultures embrace a form of family and community life that reflects what theorists think of as extended family systems. Among many American Indian tribes, for example, significant life events are marked with community-wide ceremonies. Individual problems are considered problems that can be solved only within the context of the group.

interested in how partners and family members deal with various roles and developmental tasks within the marriage and family as they move through various stages of the life cycle. The family development framework assumes that the more efficient a family is at completing these tasks, the more successful the development of the various family members will be.

Evelyn Duvall, a major creator (with Reuben Hill) of the family development approach, has described some of the advantages of this framework (Duvall, 2001). For one thing, it focuses on development and change in individuals and the family over time. It also encourages attention to process. It approaches the family not as a static and unchanging group but as a dynamic system.

Some controversy surrounds the exact number of stages involved in the family life cycle. Duvall originally identified eight stages: Stage 1, The Married Couple; Stage 2, Childbearing; Stage 3, Preschool-aged Children; Stage 4, School-Aged Children; Stage 5, Teenage Children; Stage 6, Launching the Children; Stage 7, Middle-Aged Parents; and Stage 8, Aging Family Members. Her traditional family development framework in the early years assumed that a couple would marry and have children, raise the children until they are launched, retire, and become grandparents. The complexities of life as we witness them today were not really addressed in Duvall's early work: divorce, single parenthood, remarriage, voluntary childlessness, and so forth. Other family science professionals following in Duvall's footsteps have identified four to 24 stages in the family life cycle. The sequence of stages is clearest and easiest to apply when there is only one child in the family. The number of stages and the complexity of overlapping stages increase when there is more than one child or when the couple gets divorced and one or both partners remarry.

Recent research identifies a new stage of development, **emerging adulthood**, between childhood and adulthood, which is the age from 18 to 25 (Arnett, 2000; Nelson & Barry, 2005). This is a prolonged period of role exploration focusing on identity, and time is spent trying out career and relationship possibilities (Arnett, 2004). This is also a period of risk taking with substance abuse and alcohol. Sexual activity is also common during these years, with the majority of young adults engaging in and approving of sex before marriage. In a study by Willoughby and Dworkin (2009) it was found that most emerging adults engaged in sexual activity, although they typically used condoms or birth control, and marriage was not a high priority. It will be interesting to see if emerging adulthood will develop as a well-recognized stage of development in future family science literature.

The family development framework is a useful framework for thinking about stages of the family life. However, it does not address the complexity of families today, which do not follow a traditional pattern of marrying, having a child or children, raising the children until they are launched, and retiring and becoming grandparents. Today's families often begin without marriage, and even those that begin with marriage often end in divorce. There is often remarriage that may include stepchildren from one or both parents, who might then have their own children.

Today there is a renewed interest in the family development framework (Hunt, 2005), likely because our longer life span affects many areas of social life. People born in the 1900s would have expected to live to about 65 years of age, while those born in the mid-1900s are living into their late 70s. In the near future, life expectancy might be 110 years—medical advances and the ability to eliminate infectious diseases increase life expectancy.

Life cycle and *life stages* are terms we are familiar with in social science literature. These terms usually refer to specific age categories such as childhood or adolescence. However, according to Hunt (2005), **life course** is a more accurate term to describe the transitions one makes through life. *Life course* is more fluid, reflecting the unpredictable changes such as divorce, remarriage, or early retirement that are not tied to traditional age stages. That the family development framework has evolved and adapted to the changing roles, family structures, and life expectancy is evident in today's society.

Using Duvall's traditional family life cycle stages as a starting point, how would you adapt her model to fit the family life cycle stages that your parents and you are moving through? How traditional is your family, in this regard? And how nontraditional or more contemporary is your family?

Symbolic Interaction Framework

As the name indicates, the **symbolic interaction framework** focuses on symbols, which are based on shared meanings, and interactions, which are based on verbal and nonverbal communication (White & Klein, 2002). This framework helps explain how we learn through communicating with each other about various roles in our society. The family is seen as a unit of interacting personalities, which according to Ernest Burgess (Burgess & Wallin, 1943) explains the importance of family interaction in creating an ongoing group.

A **role** is the expected behavior of a person or group in a given social category, such as husband, wife, supervisor, or teacher. Every family member plays a variety of roles at different times. For example, a man can be a parent, spouse, manager at work, and coach of a baseball team. A woman can be a parent, spouse, manager at work, and chairperson of a fund-raising committee. A young girl can be a daughter, student, and musician.

Roles are learned in society by **role taking**, the process whereby people learn how to play roles correctly by practicing and getting feedback from others. **Role making** involves creating new roles or revising existing roles. For example, as a couple's relationship changes from husband led to a more egalitarian relationship, the partners need to change the way they interact with each other.

One assumption is that meaning arises in the process of interaction between people. Shared meaning helps people understand each other and learn how to play various roles. Another important concept is **definition of the situation**, developed by William Thomas: Each person subjectively interprets a given situation, and different people will interpret an interaction or situation in different ways. This helps explain why there are often different perceptions of a marriage; there can be "his" marriage and "her" marriage, as initially described by Jessie Bernard (1970).

Another assumption is that people learn about themselves and develop a self-concept based on their interaction with others. An early theorist, Charles Cooley (1864–1929), developed the concept of the **looking-glass self**, the idea that you learn about yourself based on the feedback you receive from others who are reacting to your behavior. In other words, your feelings about yourself are derived from how others react to you. Another important theorist was George Mead (1863–1931), who described how the self-concept emerges in childhood. The child plays out a certain role, which helps him or her learn to take the role of the generalized other—to understand and even predict the feelings of another person. This ability can be valuable in any situation because it enables a person to understand another's feelings.

Social Construction Framework

According to the **social construction framework**, human beings are profoundly immersed in the social world; our understanding of this world and beliefs about this world are social products. Similar to the earlier thinking of the symbolic interactionists, social construction theorists argue that because the self is a product of social processes, individuality is most difficult to develop because we live in a social environment: We are born into and live within social settings, as members of particular social groups. Our identities are shaped over time through our life experiences.

Social construction theories, which are compatible with the postmodernist and multicultural intellectual movements, are gaining attention today. **Postmodernism** thinking emphasizes the notion that we live in a complex world and that multiple perspectives or "truths" are in constant interaction and conflict with each other (Weinberg, 2008). In a postmodern era, then, there is no objective, universal truth that can be seen, once and for all, and readily agreed upon; rather, there is a collection of subjective truths shaped by the particular subcultures in which we live. These multiple subjective truths are constantly competing for our attention and allegiance.

When we look at the world, we are looking through a lens colored by our own beliefs and values, which we have developed in our own particular social worlds. In other words, we do not see the world the way *it is,* we see the world the way *we are.* Any "truth statement" is a statement about the observer as well as about what is being observed. The various perspectives on life that we encounter are called *knowledge-positions.* When one knowledge-position gains more power than the others in a particular culture, it becomes dominant and its adherents sometimes refer to it as the truth with a capital *T.* Traveling around the world, however, we find that there are innumerable truths from country to country; even within a particular country or particular family there are many different brands of truth.

From a postmodernist perspective, a dominant truth in a particular cultural group is simply the most popular and widely accepted story or narrative explanation about the way life is or should be. This story serves two purposes: to reinforce and maintain the power and cohesiveness of the particular group and to eliminate or minimize the stories and explanations of competing groups. But because this story or truth or knowledge-position is socially constructed, as society changes over time and countless new influences emerge, the story continuously evolves.

From an individual family's perspective, the truth about who the family is and what the family does can change as time passes. A troubled family can learn how to create a new, more positive story about who they are and where their family is going. Narrative therapy, which developed out of social constructionist and postmodern thinking, seeks to develop a new story for the individual and the family that works better than the old approach (Cook & DeFrain, 2005; White & Morgan, 2006). The family, as storyteller, relates the current perspective on reality that the family holds. In addition, the family therapist, in concert with the family members, helps develop a new narrative, or story, that helps the family meet its goals in a more effective manner.

Finally, from a social constructionist and postmodernist point of view, this textbook represents not necessarily the truth about marriage and family today but rather the perspective of three family scholars who see the world through particular conceptual lenses and whose worldviews are shaped by the unique sociocultural context in which they live. The articles and books we choose to quote in this textbook and the personal comments we make all reflect the social environment that has heavily influenced us.

Feminist Framework

I myself have never been able to find out precisely what feminism is: I only know that people call me a feminist whenever I express sentiments that differentiate me from a doormat, or a prostitute.

—Rebecca West, 1913

The feminist framework has grown in importance and has had a significant impact on theorizing about marriage and the family in recent decades (Switala, 2012). Central to the **feminist framework** is the notion that women are exploited, devalued, and oppressed and that society should commit to empowering women and changing their oppressed condition (Tong, 2009).

The feminist framework grew out of the feminist movement, which began with the struggle for the right to vote, considered to be the first wave of the movement in the United States. The second wave was stimulated by women like Betty Friedan who wrote the important book *The Feminine Mystique* (1963). She argued that women needed a more active voice in decisions that affect them. She also pointed out that women are burdened by the guilt that they often feel because they are unable to balance motherhood and working outside the home.

The second wave occurred in the 1960s and 1970s, and the movement is now in the third wave, which is now led by women in their 20s and 30s. A clear difference between the second and third waves is that the former was more a collectivist movement, whereas the current wave is more an individualistic approach. There is currently some conflict between the second and third wave in terms of how the movement should proceed as well as how much effort should be put into individual versus collective efforts (Friedlin, 2002).

Feminist theories have a common interest in understanding the subordination of women with the goal of changing it (Fox & Murry, 2000). Feminists assume that women's experiences are central, not less important than those of men, and that gender must be explicitly used as a central focus. **Gender** is defined as the learned behaviors and characteristics associated with being male or female in a particular culture. Feminist theories examine gender differences and how gender-based distinctions legitimize power differences between men and women.

Feminists have also challenged the definition of family that is based on traditional roles. They see the family as a dynamic, changing, and open system that does not restrict roles and opportunities. They have criticized the structural/functional framework, which prescribed the roles of males and females. Parsons and Bales (1955) assumed that the family was most functional if the male played the **instrumental role**, being in charge of tasks, and the wife played the **expressive role**, being nurturing. Feminists maintain that both men and women can play both roles. This perspective provides couples with more flexibility because both members can play roles based on their unique skills and interests.

Even though some men today are offended and threatened by feminist thinking, feminism may have certain benefits for both men and women in family relationships. Some suggest that to be healthy, all human beings need to exhibit a full range of masculine and feminine qualities (Tong, 2009). It encourages men to express their feelings, to share wage-earning responsibilities, and to focus less on their careers and more on their children. For men, the pressure of being the only wage earner is reduced when both partners are working outside the home. At the same time, working outside the home helps women enjoy an identity separate from their role within the family. It also provides them with independent economic security. Sharing the responsibility for child rearing allows men to participate in their children's development and women to pursue professional and personal interests. When work and power are shared, both partners have more opportunity to develop their full potential.

Feminism has affected thinking and research about family science in many ways (Tong, 2009). For some, feminist theory is about oppression and domination in many aspects of society, such as classism, racism, or ageism—not just sexism. Also, multicultural feminism focuses on how prosperity for women in developed nations might be achieved at the expense of women in developing nations. **Ecofeminism** is about the domination of nature or the nonhuman world. This has taken the form of environmentalism with concerns about global warming, waste disposal, and animal farming. Therefore, feminism can be about the voices not heard in a world of domination and oppression.

Three Key Relationship Concepts

[Authors' Note: In order for you to more easily understand the three dimensions of family cohesion, family flexibility, and family communication, it would be useful to assess your own family of origin before reading the following section. Complete Activity 1 at the end of the chapter and then read the following section.

Also read about the Couple and Family Scales in Appendix A at the back of the book.]

There is considerable agreement among theorists who have studied couples and families that the dimensions of cohesion, flexibility, and communication are central to understanding relationship dynamics. Although the descriptive terms vary from theorist to theorist, the majority of concepts relate to the three dimensions of relationships that we will now describe in more detail.

Cohesion in Couples and Families

Cohesion is a feeling of emotional closeness with another person (Olson, 2003). Four levels of cohesion can be described in couple and family relationships: disengaged, connected, cohesive, and enmeshed (Figure 3.2). The extreme low level of

FIGURE 3.2
Four Levels of Family Cohesion: Balancing Separateness and Togetherness

DISENGAGED System	*Separateness* vs. *Togetherness* — **Too much separateness**	**Unbalanced**
CONNECTED System	Separateness vs. Togetherness — **More separateness than togetherness**	Balanced
COHESIVE System	Separateness vs. **Togetherness** — **More togetherness than separateness**	Balanced
ENMESHED System	Separateness vs. **Togetherness** — **Too much togetherness**	**Unbalanced**

BOX 3.3 Putting It Together

Theories and Research

We have described the differing models or theories that are used to provide a context for conducting research and explaining findings. When students read journal articles, they will see evidence of these models or theories because authors will usually indicate that a study was conducted within the context of a specific model or theory. For example, research may have been conducted from the perspective of a family development framework, which means that the researchers are focusing on change in individuals or families over time. The study might be about couples who make the transition to becoming parents or may focus on later stages of life such as older adulthood or aging. In the discussion section of an article, the findings are likely to be interpreted from the perspective of the same theory. Following are examples of studies being conducted within the context of each model or theory.

Family Systems Theory

A study conducted by Dolbin-MacNab and Keiley (2009) focused on relationships of adolescents who were raised solely by their grandparents. The specific relationships that were analyzed were those between the child and the parents who did not raise the child and the child and the grandparents who did raise the child. The study used the ecological approach of systems theory to create the context of multiple environmental systems that influenced the child. Adolescents who were raised by grandparents became the most important people within the inner circle of the family system. The parents may be in one of the outer circles, depending upon their involvement with the adolescent. In the discussion, these authors

described the importance of community services and organizations in the outer circles that could be of help to these adolescents as they experience several sources of stress.

International Family Strengths Framework

A study conducted by Skogrand, Mueller, Arrington, et al. (2008) focused on the components of strong marriages in the Navajo (Dineh) culture. This study used research about positive cultural characteristics of American Indians to develop the interview questions for the study, and the questions focused on what was going well in these marriages within their cultural context, rather than what was not going well. Navajo couples were interviewed so they could tell their stories about their marriages, and five components of strong marriages were identified: maintaining communication, nurturing the relationship, learning about marriage, being prepared for marriage, and having a strong foundation. The findings of this study were used to create a couple activity book (Skogrand, Mueller, Crook, et al., 2007) that other Navajo couples could use to strengthen their marriages.

Family Development Framework

The transition to parenthood has been identified as a key transition in the life cycle of families. This transition has been found to be stressful because of the reorganization that must occur in the family. The need to care for the child can also decrease marital happiness. Claxton and Perry-Jenkins (2008) examined the effects of becoming parents on leisure patterns for dual-earner, working-class

cohesion is called *disengaged*, and the extreme high level, *enmeshed*. Although being disengaged or enmeshed is appropriate at times, relationships become problematic when they are stuck at one of these extremes. The two middle levels of cohesion—*connected* and *cohesive*—seem to be the most functional across the life cycle, in part because they balance separateness and togetherness. Both connected and cohesive relationships are classified as balanced family systems.

Balancing Between Separateness and Togetherness. Balance between separateness and togetherness is the essence of family cohesion. Family members need to balance between being intimate with and feeling close to other family members and being independent from the family so that they can develop as individuals. The concept of balance entails both autonomy and intimacy—and the ability to move back and forth between the two. Establishing a dynamic balance between the two requires shifting back and forth on a weekly, daily, or even hourly basis.

couples. They found that both husbands and wives experienced a decline in independent and shared leisure immediately after the birth of the child. Couples began to increase their leisure activities when the wife returned to work, but couples never fully returned to their previous level of leisure before the baby was born. These authors also found that a decrease in shared leisure during the transition to parenthood was associated with more positive marital outcomes.

Symbolic Interaction Framework

The role of trust in intimate unions of low-income mothers was the focus of a study conducted by Burton, Cherlin, Winn, Estacion, and Holder-Taylor (2009). This study was guided by the symbolic interaction framework and examined trust in developing intimate relationships. They found that although these women generally did not trust men, they developed differing types of intimate relationships depending upon the role and function men played in their lives. These researchers found that four forms of interpersonal trust emerged in the women: suspended, compartmentalized, misplaced, and integrated. This study was conducted within the context of shared meanings and definitions of the situations and the roles men played in their lives.

Social Construction Framework

One study examined how lesbian mothers perceived their young children's parental preferences when one mother was the biological parent and the other mother was not (Goldberg, Downing, & Sauck, 2008). The findings of the study indicated that as infants these children preferred the birth mother, due to factors such as breast-feeding which resulted in differing amounts of time spent with the birth versus the nonbiological mother. As children grew older, however, they typically did not have a preference. In this case the social processes of the children changed when time spent with their mothers was not based upon biology. The children's social world changed, and so did the relationships with their mothers.

Feminist Framework

Hill, Freedman, and Enright (2007) have written a journal article about feminist theory and forgiveness. They describe a forgiveness therapy model that includes the uncovering phase, the decision phase, the work phase, and the deepening phase. It has been suggested that the use of this model with clients in therapy has yielded positive results. Feminist critics have said this model should not be used with some women clients who have been exploited by men, because it perpetuates traditional gender roles—that is it advocates change for women victims by having them forgive rather than having male offenders make changes. The authors provide an in-depth description of how the forgiveness therapy model could be modified to include and address the issues identified by feminist critics. For example, the therapist should make sure that there is no pressure, but rather free choice, for a woman to forgive a male offender, since women have historically been expected to forgive men.

Table 3.3 illustrates the four levels of family cohesion, from low to high. There is a balance between separateness and togetherness at both the connected and the cohesive levels of cohesion. *Connected relationships* place more emphasis on the individual than on the relationship. Levels of closeness are often low to moderate in a connected family system, with lower levels of loyalty; there is often more independence than dependence and more separateness than togetherness. *Cohesive relationships* place more emphasis on togetherness and less on separateness. There is some loyalty to the relationship, and there is often more dependence than independence.

Disengaged relationships (those with a low level of cohesion) emphasize the individual. There is often very little closeness, a lack of loyalty, high independence, and high separateness. *Enmeshed relationships* emphasize togetherness: very high levels of closeness, loyalty, and dependence on one another. Enmeshed relationships are often typical of couples in love. When this level of intimacy occurs between a parent and a child (for example, an enmeshed father–daughter

TABLE 3.3	Levels of Couple and Family Cohesion			
Characteristic	**Disengaged (Unbalanced)**	**Connected (Balanced)**	**Cohesive (Balanced)**	**Enmeshed (Unbalanced)**
Separateness–togetherness	High separateness	More separateness than togetherness	More togetherness than separateness	Very high togetherness
I–we balance	Primarily I	More I than we	More we than I	Primarily we
Closeness	Little closeness	Low-to-moderate closeness	Moderate-to-high closeness	Very high closeness
Loyalty	Lack of loyalty	Some loyalty	Considerable loyalty	High loyalty
Activities	Mainly separate	More separate than shared	More shared than separate	Mainly shared
Dependence–independence	High independence	More independence than dependence	More dependence than independence	High dependence

relationship or an enmeshed mother–son relationship), the relationship often becomes problematic.

Kahlil Gibran describes a balance between separateness and togetherness in his poem "On Marriage":

Love one another, but make not a bond of love:
Let it rather be a moving sea between the shores of your souls.
Fill each other's cup, but drink not from the same cup.
Give one another of your bread, but eat not from the same loaf.
Sing and dance together and be joyous, but let each one of you be alone,
Even as the strings of a lute are alone though they quiver with the same music.
Give your hearts, but not into each other's keeping.
For only the hand of Life can contain your hearts.

And stand together yet not too near together:
For the pillars of the temple stand apart,
And the oak tree and the cypress grow not in each other's shadow.
But let there be spaces in your togetherness,
And let the winds of the heavens dance between you. (1923/1976, pp. 16–17)

(Kahlil Gibran, "On Marriage" from *The Prophet*. Copyright 1923 by Kahlil Gibran and renewed 1951 by Administrators C.T.A. of Kahlil Gibran Estate and Mary G. Gibran. Used by permission of Alfred A. Knopf, a division of Random House, Inc.)

The relationship Gibran describes is an ideal. In the real world of loving relationships, few find this perfect balance with their partners. It is a useful goal but one that is difficult to maintain for long. It is also important to note that in intimate relationships, people can experience and even enjoy, at least for a short time, both extremes on the togetherness–separateness continuum. Couples can remain in love with each other while also enjoying being apart for periods of time.

Extreme Togetherness and Extreme Separateness. Too much togetherness can lead to relationship fusion, or enmeshment. People "in love" often feel they need each other. Although this feels good for a while, soon the enmeshment begins to prickle. After too much togetherness, lovers can get on each other's nerves.

Especially in the early stages of a relationship, couples enjoy being totally together. When two people are "falling in love," being away from each other for very long literally hurts. Each one aches and pines and feels pent-up emotion in the expectation of seeing the other again. Couples in this type of situation are enmeshed; being together so totally can be very exciting for a time. To expect to be totally sheltered from the storms of life by a loved one is a nice fantasy—but it *is* a fantasy. Judy Altura has expressed it poetically:

EXTREME TOGETHERNESS POEM

We do everything together.
I am here to meet all your needs and expectations.
And you are here to meet mine.
We had to meet, and it was beautiful.
I can't imagine it turning out any other way. (1974, p. 20)

(Judy Altura, "Extreme Togetherness Poem" from Jerry Gillies, *My Needs, Your Needs, Our Needs.*
Copyright © 1974 by Judy Altura. Used by permission of Doubleday, a division of Random House, Inc.)

Two of the most common reasons an enmeshed relationship becomes trouble-some are jealousy and personification. People feel jealous when they fear they might lose their partner to another person. Tied closely to jealousy is **personification**, the notion that everything one's partner does is a personal reflection on oneself. A person who personifies his or her partner's actions will try to control the other's behavior. This may work in the short run, but it can destroy intimacy in the long run.

Enmeshment is problematic both for the people in the relationship and for the relationship itself because it romanticizes the relationship and puts impossible

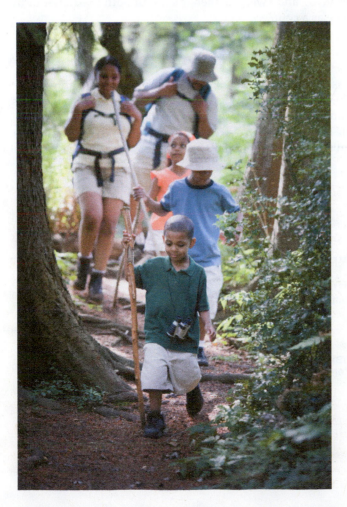

Within every family, each member must find a balance between autonomy and intimacy. If their family is like other families, these five people will experience periods of greater and lesser separateness and togetherness over the course of their lives.

expectations upon the partners. It also tends to stifle individual development. One way to improve an enmeshed relationship is for each person to develop individual interests and abilities.

In the 1970s, one cultural theme in American society was "doing your own thing." Young people were dubbed "the me generation." This overfocus on self was problematic for relationships. "Doing your own thing" can lead to a disengaged relationship, in which there is very little emotional closeness.

A disengaged couple or family typically has very little emotional closeness. There is so much separateness that each person is mainly focused on himself or herself and not on each other. As a result, they have difficulty developing and maintaining intimacy with others. Most couples with marital problems have low levels of emotional connection as do families with problem children. Emotional closeness is the glue that helps couples and families stay connected even during difficult times. When emotional closeness is missing, individuals care more about themselves and there is little commitment and few resource to help the couple or family thrive.

A young former prostitute described the family she grew up in as very chaotic, saying, "It was like a sieve. Anybody could come into it, and anybody could leave, and anybody could fall through the gaps. The family wasn't safe or reliable for anybody at all."

Successful couples tend to be those who have figured out how to balance effectively between "I" and "we." Partners maintain both their own individuality and their intimacy as a couple.

Flexibility in Couples and Families

Flexibility is the amount of change that occurs in leadership, role relationships, and relationship rules (Olson, 2003). Like cohesion, flexibility has four levels, ranging from low to high. Those levels are rigid, structured, flexible, and chaotic (Figure 3.3). The extreme types of family systems—the *rigid* and the *chaotic*—can work well in the short run, but they have difficulty adapting over time. Conversely,

FIGURE 3.3
Four Levels of Family Flexibility: Balancing Stability and Change

RIGID System	*Stability vs. Change* **Too much stability**	**Unbalanced**
STRUCTURED System	*Stability vs. Change* **More stability than change**	Balanced
FLEXIBLE System	*Stability vs. Change* **More change than stability**	Balanced
CHAOTIC System	*Stability vs. Change* **Too much change**	**Unbalanced**

Characteristic	Rigid (Unbalanced)	Structured (Balanced)	Flexible (Balanced)	Chaotic (Unbalanced)
TABLE 3.4	**Levels of Couple and Family Flexibility**			
Leadership	Authoritarian	Sometimes shared	Often shared	Lack of leadership
Discipline	Strict discipline	Somewhat democratic	Democratic	Lenient discipline
Negotiation	Limited discussion	Organized discussion	Open discussion	Endless discussion
Roles	Roles very stable	Roles stable	Role sharing	Dramatic role shifts
Rules	Unchanging rules	Few rule changes	Some rule changes	Frequent rule changes
Change	Very little change	Some change	Moderate change	Considerable change

the balanced types—the *structured* and the *flexible*—are more able to adapt to change over the family life cycle.

Balance Between Stability and Change. The essence of family flexibility is balancing stability and change. Families need a basic foundation that gives them stability, but they also need to be open to change when necessary. Change is particularly important when families are under stress and need to adapt in a crisis.

The two balanced levels of change are called *structured* and *flexible*. Of the two, structured relationships have more moderate levels of change, with leadership that is sometimes shared. Discipline is often democratic, and the roles are stable. In flexible relationships, there is more change. Often both the relationship between the couple and the relationships among family members are more democratic, and there is also more role sharing between the partners, as shown in Table 3.4.

The two extremes of change are described as *rigid*, indicating a very low degree of change, and *chaotic*, indicating an extremely high degree of change. Both extremes are unbalanced and problematic because families are often stuck at these extreme positions. In rigid relationships, the leadership is often authoritarian. As a result, the discipline is strict, and the roles are very stable. In chaotic relationships, there is too much change, often because there is a lack of leadership. Discipline is erratic and inconsistent, partly due to dramatic shifts in family roles.

Extreme Stability and Extreme Change. Families by nature tend to resist change; they are basically rigid. Most families function primarily to maintain the status quo: "When an organism indicates a change in relation to another, the other will act upon the first so as to diminish and modify the change" (Haley, 1958, p. 361; see also Haley, 2012; and Zeig, 2001).

In short, when one partner tries to make changes in a relationship, the other partner's first reaction is often to defend against the change or at least to slow it down until he or she can better understand what is happening. People often fear that the change will bring more harm than good. The family, which is maintenance oriented and conservative in its approach to change, often creates even more problems for itself. As Lyman Wynne sees it, "Families that rigidly try to maintain homeostasis [the status quo] through successive developmental phases are highly disturbed and atypical. Enduring success in maintaining family homeostasis perhaps should be regarded as a distinctive feature of disorder in families" (1958, p. 89).

Characteristic	Poor	Good	Very Good
TABLE 3.5	Levels of Couple and Family Communication		
Listening skills	Poor listening skills	Appear to listen, but feedback is limited	Give feedback, indicating good listening skills
Speaking skills	Often speak for others	Speak for self more than for others	Speak mainly for self rather than for others
Self-disclosure	Low sharing of feelings	Moderate sharing of feelings	High sharing of feelings
Clarity	Inconsistent messages	Clear messages	Very clear messages
Staying on topic	Seldom stay on topic	Often stay on topic	Mainly stay on topic
Respect and regard	Low to moderate	Moderate to high	High

Extreme stability is seen in rigid families, those in which there is little room for change. The family rules are always the same, even though the game of life outside the family continuously changes. This rigidity manifests itself in such relatively trivial matters as scheduling family meals. Family members do not permit one another to make even the slightest changes, even if the changes helped one or more members. The rigidity may also be evidenced by resistance to changes in family roles. For example, a mother wants to find work outside the home but the father opposes it, or a son wants to become a musician but his parents are not supportive.

On the other extreme of change are chaotic families. These families are almost completely without structure, rules, and roles. No one knows what to expect. For example, a chaotic family operates on the premise that nothing is constant in life but change. It is difficult to go through life without some change—and individuals and relationships often do better if they are open to some change over time. However, constant change is problematic for most people.

Communication in Couples and Families

Communication is the grease that smoothes frictions between partners and family members. Family communication is linear: The better the communication skills, the stronger the couple and family relationship (Olson, Olson-Sigg, & Larson, 2009).

The following six dimensions are considered in the assessment of family communication: listening skills, speaking skills, self-disclosure, clarity, staying on topic, and respect and regard (Table 3.5). Positive *listening skills* involve empathy and giving feedback. *Speaking skills* include speaking for oneself and using "I" statements rather than speaking for others. *Self-disclosure* entails sharing personal feelings and ideas openly. *Clarity* involves the exchange of clear messages. *Staying on topic* is another important aspect of interpersonal exchanges. Last, *respect and regard* reflect the good intentions of family members and keep communication positive.

Couple and Family Map

The **Couple and Family Map** is built on the three major dimensions of cohesion, flexibility, and communication. Four levels of cohesion and four levels of flexibility are integrated to create a model that is useful for describing and understanding couple and family dynamics. The Couple and Family Map (otherwise known in the field of family research as the *Circumplex Model of Marital and Family Systems*) was developed by David Olson and his colleagues at the University of Minnesota, especially Douglas Sprenkle and Candyce Russell, who worked on the original model. The model offers a way of mapping and understanding couple and family relationships. It can also be applied by therapists, counselors, and family members interested in understanding and changing the dynamics within a couple or family experiencing difficulties.

The Couple and Family Map is built primarily on principles and concepts from family systems theory, but it also has features in common with other frameworks. As a graphic model, it clearly represents the dimensions of cohesion and flexibility; the third dimension, communication, serves as a facilitating function.

It is through communication that family members identify and work out their concerns about cohesion—issues of spending time together versus having enough separateness to retain a sense of oneself—and flexibility—issues of adapting to the demands of change versus minimizing such demands if they threaten the stability of the relationship. Communication thus helps families move between the extremes of cohesion and flexibility to find a balance that works for them. If couples or families have good communication skills, they are more likely to be able to maintain their cohesive structure, adapt to change, and work out whatever problems confront them (Olson, Olson-Sigg, & Larson, 2009).

Balanced Versus Unbalanced Families

The Couple and Family Map identifies 16 types of couple and family relationships (Figure 3.4). The logic is quite simple: The dimensions of cohesion and flexibility are broken down into four levels each, and 4 × 4 = 16. A marriage or family relationship can be classified according to one of these 16 types depending on how a given family or couple relationship operates.

The 16 types of family relationships can be clustered into three general types of family systems: balanced families, midrange families, and unbalanced families. **Balanced families** are those that fit into the four central categories (yellow section) on the relationship map in Figure 3.4. Balanced families are labeled flexibly connected, flexibly cohesive, structurally connected, and structurally cohesive. **Midrange families** (orange section) are extreme on one dimension (e.g., cohesion) but balanced on the other (e.g., flexibility). **Unbalanced families** (red section) are those that score at extreme levels on both dimensions. In the Activities section at the end of this chapter, you will have the opportunity to classify your own family using the Couple and Family Scales.

Balanced Relationships Are More Healthy

The Couple and Family Map is a valuable model because it is scientifically verifiable; in other words, researchers can validate (or invalidate) the Couple and Family Map by testing hypotheses derived from it. A few of the most important hypotheses that have been developed and tested in numerous studies are discussed next.

One hypothesis is: *Balanced couple and family systems* (those that fall under two central levels of cohesion and flexibility) *generally function more adequately across the family life cycle than unbalanced types* (two extremes on cohesion and flexibility).

FIGURE 3.4
Couple and Family Map

Families balanced on cohesion allow their members to be both independent from and connected to the family. Families balanced on flexibility maintain some stability but are also open to change. Although balanced family types are located in the central area of the model, they can experience the extremes of the dimensions when necessary to deal with a situation, but they do not typically function at those extremes for long.

Conversely, couples and families with problems are more typically found at the extremes of the dimensions; they are unbalanced types. Problem families often experience too much separateness (disengaged type) or too much togetherness (enmeshed type) or cohesion. On flexibility, problem families tend to have too much stability (rigid type) or too much change (chaotic type).

There is considerable support for the main hypothesis derived from the Couple and Family Map: *Balanced family types are healthier and more functional than unbalanced family types.* One systematic study that found strong support for this hypothesis was by Volker Thomas and David Olson (1993). They tested four groups of families with an adolescent, videotaping each family while they discussed some family topics. The four samples included 35 families with an emotionally disturbed child, 25 families in family therapy for a variety of problems, 62 healthy families with a Down syndrome child, and 60 healthy families.

The findings strongly supported the hypothesis (Figure 3.5). As hypothesized, only 16% of the families with an emotionally disturbed child and 12% of the

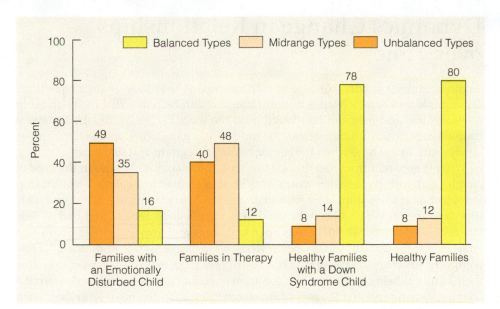

FIGURE 3.5

Degree of Balance in Problem and Healthy Families

families in therapy were balanced types, whereas about 78% to 80% of the healthy families were balanced types. Conversely, almost half (49%) of the families with an emotionally disturbed child and 40% of the families in therapy were unbalanced. Only 8% of the healthy families were unbalanced.

Value of Couple and Family Map

There are several advantages to using the Couple and Family Map to understand marital and family life. First, *the model provides a common descriptive language for talking about real couples and real families—a language the expert and the layperson can use to talk with each other.*

Second, the Couple and Family Map *draws on concepts and ideas from three of the major frameworks we have discussed—family systems, family strengths, and family development.* It offers a means of bringing together and applying all three frameworks to the examination of real families and their interactions. It grounds theory in examples of relationships based on intimacy and commitment.

Third, the Couple and Family Map *can help describe how a couple relationship or a family changes as time passes or as stresses and challenges appear.* The relationship map provides information about the present dynamics of a couple or family's relationship and what actions are necessary to bring about change. It provides a means to visualize where one is and where one might wish to be.

Finally, the Couple and Family Map *turns concepts into working themes so one can observe and measure couple and family dynamics.* Just where is a given family on the relationship map? Is this relationship a rigid, inflexible, suffocating environment? Is it an unpredictable, unsafe, chaotic place to be? Or is it flexible and nurturing? Can family members communicate what their problems are and express what kind of family they would like to become? What changes must they make to move toward that ideal or maintain the aspects they wish not to lose as they change others?

Dynamics Change in Relationships over Time

Another important characteristic of relationships is that they change over time. The Couple and Family Map is a useful tool that can help describe the changes in relationships, and they can be plotted onto the map. Figure 3.6 illustrates how a couple's relationship changed from the time they began dating, to marriage and as newlyweds, to the time when the couple became pregnant and had a baby.

What is apparent from viewing Figure 3.6 is the dramatic changes in the type of couple relationship over a few years. This level of change in a couple's relationship is typical as relationships deal with changes, particularly related to major events like parenthood. Jeff and Mary began dating in college as seniors and had a "flexibly cohesive" relationship that was open to change and growing closer. Two years later they got married and as newlyweds were "structurally enmeshed." They were very structured because they both were very organized and wanted to be like their families. Being enmeshed is a common characteristic of many newly married couples. During the first 2 years of marriage, they each got busy with their own careers and had less time with each other. Emotionally, they moved apart more and changed from being enmeshed to being cohesive and then to connected levels of cohesion.

Mary became pregnant and the couple then had a "structurally connected" relationship. Once the baby was born, the couple moved to become a "chaotically cohe-

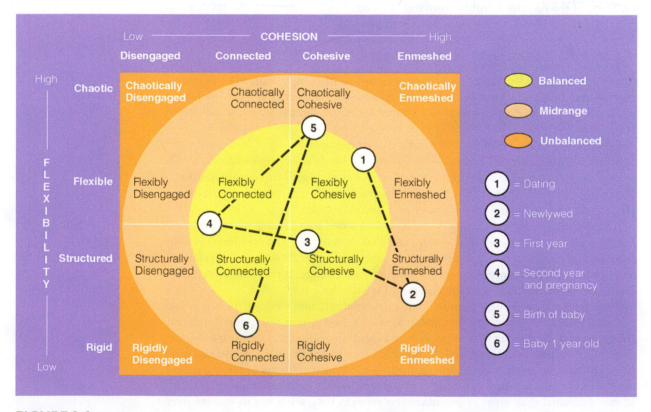

FIGURE 3.6

Couple and Family Map: Change Over Time

sive" family. The birth of their first child brought them closer emotionally as a couple and new family. But the infant also added chaos to their typically stable life because life needed to revolve around the infant, which meant less sleep for both of them. As the child reached 1 year old, the couple was now "rigidly connected." The rigidity came from the need to establish a clear schedule for the child, and the child responded in a positive way to this structure by sleeping and eating at predictable times. But the couple became less close and moved from being cohesive to connected because Mary felt stuck with mainly child care, while Jeff continued to work and get more involved in his professional development.

In summary, this example illustrates how the Couple and Family Map can help a couple understand how their relationship changes over time. In terms of changes in the type of relationship over time, most couples and families simply experience the changes without knowing or thinking about them. But the model can also be used by couples and families in a more proactive way. Couples can jointly decide what type of relationship they want and they can work together to move the relationship toward that goal.

Summary

- Conceptual frameworks help describe different perspectives on couple and family dynamics.
- Family science began more than 70 years ago and focuses on family relationships.
- Early work in the family science field focuses on many of the same issues that receive attention today, such as poverty, housing, divorce, and marital happiness.
- The family systems theory focuses on the family as a system of interdependent parts.
- The international family strengths framework focuses on the positive characteristics of healthy families and couples.
- The family development framework examines how couples and families change across the life cycle.
- Emerging adulthood (18–25 years) has been identified by researchers as a new stage of exploration and identity development.
- The symbolic interaction framework examines the internal perceptions of family members and how they learn social rules and roles.
- The social construction framework emphasizes the importance of multiple perspectives on reality and their use in helping families meet their goals more effectively.
- The feminist framework, which focuses on the world as women perceive it, aims to empower women in all aspects of their lives.
- Family theorists have identified three basic qualities that make couples and families stronger: cohesion,

flexibility, and communication. These three concepts are central to the family systems theory, the international family strengths framework, the family development framework, as well as other theories and frameworks.
- Cohesion focuses on the dynamic balance between the extremes of separateness and togetherness in both couple and family relationships. Balancing these two extremes entails maintaining both autonomy and intimacy but not remaining stuck at either extreme for long periods.
- Flexibility focuses on the dynamic balance between stability and change. The most functional couples and family systems have both characteristics, and they are able to move back and forth between them. Couples and families with problems over time tend to become stuck at one of the extremes, either too much stability (rigid) or too much change (chaotic).
- Communication is a facilitating dimension that can help create change in the levels of cohesion and flexibility when change is necessary.
- The Couple and Family Map is a tool for understanding couple and family relationships. It is based on the family systems theory and is structured on the three dimensions of cohesion, flexibility, and communication.
- The Couple and Family Map describes three general types of family systems—balanced, midrange, and unbalanced—and can illustrate how systems change over time.

Key Terms

conceptual framework
theory
hypothesis
research study
idiographic approach
nomothetic approach
eugenics
family systems theory
family system
general systems theory
system
multiple system levels
suprasystem
subsystem
boundary
ecology
human ecosystem
wholeness
interdependence of parts
open system
morphogenic system
closed system
morphostatic system
centrifugal interaction
centripetal interaction
positive feedback
negative feedback
international family
    strengths framework
appreciation and affection
commitment

positive communication
enjoyable time together
spiritual well-being
ability to manage stress
    and crisis effectively
family development
    framework
emerging adulthood
life course
symbolic interaction
    framework
role
role taking
role making
definition of the situation
looking-glass self
social construction
    framework
postmodernism
feminist framework
gender
instrumental role
expressive role
ecofeminism
cohesion
personification
flexibility
Couple and Family Map
balanced families
midrange families
unbalanced families

cohesion, enter *disengaged, connected, cohesive,* or *enmeshed*).

Cohesion	Flexibility	Communication
Score: _____	Score: _____	Score: _____
Level: _____	Level: _____	Level: _____

d. Now, plot the scores for cohesion and flexibility onto the Couple and Family Map (page 100) and identify the type of family system in which you grew up.

e. After plotting your scores onto the model, consider the following questions:

• What is/was it like to live in your type of family (e.g., flexibly connected, rigidly enmeshed, etc.)?

• In what ways related to cohesion and flexibility is/was your family satisfying and in what ways is/was it frustrating?

• How did your family change on cohesion and flexibility as you were growing up?

• In what ways did communication affect your family's dynamics?

2. Plot on the Couple and Family Map (page 100) how your family changed over the years. Select at least three to five points in time and then plot them on the map. Then link those times and reflect on the changes. Also, were you and your family more happy at certain locations on the map than at others?

3. If you are dating someone, are engaged, or are married, both you and your partner should answer the questions on the Couple and Family Scales twice: first, in terms of your families of origin (as in Activity 1) and second, in terms of your couple relationship. Compare your partner's description of your couple relationship with yours and discuss the similarities and differences. Then compare the descriptions of each of your families of origin with those of your couple relationship.

(For more details on using the Couple and Family Scales, see Appendix A at the back of the book.)

Activities

1. Use the Couple and Family Scales (Table 3.6 on page 105) to describe your family of origin. Select a time period when you were all together (e.g., when you were in high school). Make a list of the people you are including in your family. Then do the following:

   a. Review the six categories shown in the scales (Table 3.6) for assessing cohesion, flexibility, and communication.

   b. On a separate piece of paper, rate your family on a scale of 1 to 8 for each of the categories in the three dimensions.

   c. To determine a total score for each dimension, review the scores and select a number that represents the best average score. Record the score below, and indicate the level for each dimension (e.g., for

Suggested Readings

Arnett, J. J. (2011). Emerging adulthood(s): The cultural psychology of a new life stage. In L. A. Jensen (Ed.), *Bridging cultural and developmental approaches to psychology: New syntheses in theory, research, and policy* (pp. 255–275). New York: Oxford University Press.

Boss, P., et al. (2009). *Sourcebook of family theories and methods: A contextual approach.* St. Paul, MN: Springer. An outstanding collection of family theories and family research methods.

TABLE 3.6	Couple and Family Scales

COHESION							
Characteristic	**Disengaged (Unbalanced)**		**Connected (Balanced)**		**Cohesive (Balanced)**		**Enmeshed (Unbalanced)**	
Score	1	2	3	4	5	6	7	8
Separateness–togetherness	High separateness		More separateness than togetherness		More togetherness than separateness		Very high togetherness	
I–we balance	Primarily I		More I than we		More we than I		Primarily we	
Closeness	Little closeness		Low-to-moderate closeness		Moderate-to-high closeness		Very high closeness	
Loyalty	Lack of loyalty		Some loyalty		Considerable loyalty		High loyalty	
Activities	Mainly separate		More separate than shared		More shared than separate		Mainly shared	
Dependence–independence	High independence		More independence than dependence		More dependence than independence		High dependence	

FLEXIBILITY							
Characteristic	**Rigid (Unbalanced)**		**Structured (Balanced)**		**Flexible (Balanced)**		**Chaotic (Unbalanced)**	
Score	1	2	3	4	5	6	7	8
Leadership	Authoritarian		Sometimes shared		Often shared		Lack of leadership	
Discipline	Strict discipline		Somewhat democratic		Democratic		Lenient discipline	
Negotiation	Limited discussion		Organized discussion		Open discussion		Endless discussion	
Roles	Roles very stable		Roles stable		Role sharing		Dramatic role shifts	
Rules	Unchanging rules		Few rule changes		Some rule changes		Frequent rule changes	
Change	Very little change		Some change		Moderate change		Considerable change	

COMMUNICATION					
Characteristic	**Poor**		**Good**		**Very Good**	
Score	1	2	3	4	5	6
Listening skills	Poor listening skills		Appear to listen, but feedback is limited		Give feedback, indicating good listening skills	
Speaking skills	Often speak for others		Speak for self more than for others		Speak mainly for self rather than for others	
Self-disclosure	Low sharing of feelings		Moderate sharing of feelings		High sharing of feelings	
Clarity	Inconsistent messages		Clear messages		Very clear messages	
Staying on topic	Seldom stay on topic		Often stay on topic		Mainly stay on topic	
Respect and regard	Low to moderate		Moderate to high		High	

Goldenberg, H., & Goldenberg, I. (2011). *Family therapy: An overview* (8th ed.). Belmont, CA: Brooks/Cole.

Holstein, J. A., & Gubrium, J. F. (Eds.). (2008). *Handbook of constructionist research.* New York: Guilford Press.

Hunt, S. (2005). *The life course: A sociological introduction.* New York: Palgrave MacMillan.

Mahoney, A. (2010). Religion in families, 1999–2009: A relational spirituality framework. *Journal of Marriage and Family, 72* (August), 805–827. The role of religion "for better and worse," in marital and parent-child relationships.

Owens, T. J., & Suitor, J. J. (Eds.). (2007). *Advances in life course research: Vol. 12. Interpersonal relations across the life course.* Amsterdam: Elsevier.

Smith, S. R., & Hamon, R. R. (2012). *Exploring family theories* (3rd ed.). New York: Oxford University Press.

Switala, K. (2012). The feminist theory. Web site: http://www.cddc.vt.edu/feminism/enin.html. Research materials and information for students, activists, and scholars interested in women's conditions and struggles around the world.

Tong, R. (2009). *Feminist thought* (3rd ed.). Boulder, CO: Westview Press.

Walsh, F. (Ed.). *Normal family processes: Growing diversity and complexity* (4th ed.). New York: Guilford.

Visit the text-specific Online Learning Center at **www.mhhe.com/olson8e** for practice tests, chapter summaries, and PowerPoint slides.

4

*C*ommunication *C*and Intimacy

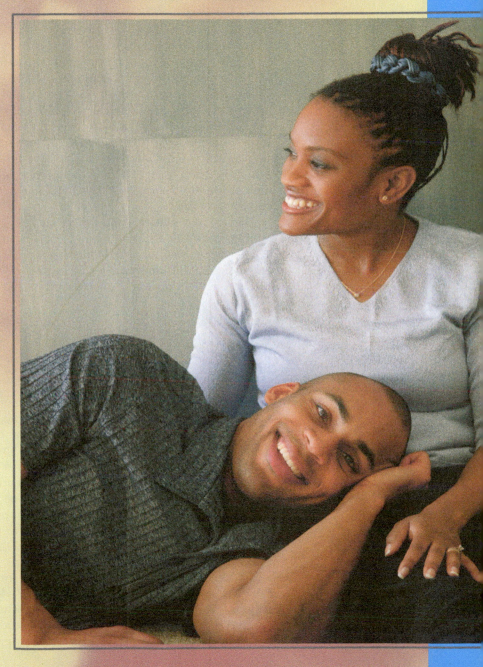

Couple Strengths and Issues in Communication

Perspectives on Communication

Using Communication to Develop Intimacy

Using Communication to Maintain Intimacy

Positive and Negative Communication Cycles

Summary

Key Terms

Activities

Suggested Readings

Communication is at the heart of intimate human relationships—it is literally the foundation on which all else is built. **Communication** is the way humans create and share meaning, both verbally and nonverbally. The ability to communicate is one of a handful of essential skills individuals must master if they are to enjoy close relationships. In fact, the ability and the willingness to communicate have been found to be among the most important factors in maintaining a satisfying relationship.

In this chapter we will look at the art of interpersonal communication, focusing on several important principles of communication, as well as gender and cultural differences in communication styles. We will examine ways for people to become more aware of their communication patterns and styles. Finally, we will explore various approaches and techniques people can use to improve communication in their relationships, thereby increasing the level of intimacy they enjoy with friends, partners, and family members.

Because positive communication is critical to a successful couple relationship, we will open this chapter with some findings from a national survey (Olson, Olson-Sigg, & Larson, 2008). To identify the differences between happy and unhappy couples, the researchers conducted a study involving more than 50,000 married couples. Based on their scores on a marital satisfaction scale, the couples were classified as either *happily married* or *unhappily married*. There were 20,675 classified as happily married and 20,590 couples classified as unhappily married. A middle group of about 10,000 couples were not included in either group because their marital satisfaction scales were moderate or because one partner was high and one was low.

This national survey identified couple strengths in communication by comparing the happy couples and unhappy couples. Responses from the entire sample of 41,265 couples were used to identify specific issues for married couples in terms of their sexual relationship. The quality and quantity of a couple's communication are the key to the quality of other aspects of their relationship.

Couple Strengths and Issues in Communication

In a national study (Olson, Olson-Sigg, & Larson, 2008) comparing the major communication strengths of happy couples with those of unhappy couples, researchers found that happy couples were six times more likely (90%) than unhappy couples (15%) to agree that they are very satisfied with how they talk to each other (Table 4.1). Most happy couples (79%) feel that their partner understands them, but this is true for only 13% of unhappy couples. Almost all happy couples (96%) feel that they can express their true feelings, whereas this is true for only 30% of unhappy couples. Happy couples are good listeners (83%) compared to unhappy couples (18%). Most happy couples (79%) do not make comments that put each other down, but few (20%) unhappy couples could say the same thing.

In terms of problematic issues for all married couples, the survey focused on 41,265 couples regardless of whether they were happy or unhappy. As shown in Table 4.2, the vast majority of couples (76%) wished that their partner was more willing to share feelings. Sixty-nine percent of all couples had difficulty asking the partner "for what I want." Sixty-five percent did not feel understood, and 64% felt that their partner refused to discuss issues or problems. Also, 62% felt the partner

TABLE 4.1	Communication Strengths of Happy Couples vs. Unhappy Couples

Percentage in Agreement	Happy Couples	Unhappy Couples
Communication Issue		
1. I am very satisfied with how we talk to each other.	95%	15%
2. My partner understands how I feel.	79	13
3. I find it easy to express my true feelings to my partner.	96	30
4. My partner is a very good listener.	83	18
5. My partner does not make comments that put me down.	79	20

Source: Adapted from David H. Olson, Amy Olson-Sigg, and Peter J. Larson Ph.D., *The Couple Checkup.* Copyright © 2008 by David H. Olson, Amy Olson-Sigg, and Peter J. Larson. Reprinted by permission of Thomas Nelson, Inc.

TABLE 4.2	Top Five Communication Problems for Couples

Communication Issue	Percentage of Couples Having Problem*
1. I wish my partner were more willing to share his/her feelings.	76%
2. I sometimes have difficulty asking my partner for what I want.	69
3. My partner often does not understand how I feel.	65
4. My partner often refuses to discuss issues or problems.	64
5. My partner makes comments that put me down.	62

*One or both partners indicated this was an issue for them.

Source: Adapted from David H. Olson, Amy Olson-Sigg, and Peter J. Larson Ph.D., *The Couple Checkup.* Copyright © 2008 by David H. Olson, Amy Olson-Sigg, and Peter J. Larson. Reprinted by permission of Thomas Nelson, Inc.

made comments that put them down. Clearly, these are very common issues for the vast majority of married couples; the difference is that happy couples are more able to resolve these problems than unhappy couples.

Perspectives on Communication

Communication difficulties often arise when partners have divergent communication styles. This section sheds light on two significant sources of communication-style differences: gender and culture.

Gender Differences in Communication

> *When you're looking for Mr. Right, make sure his first name isn't* Always.
> —AUTHOR UNKNOWN

Common gender-related differences in communication often cause conflict between men and women. It sometimes seems that there are two separate styles of

TABLE 4.3 — Conversational Style and Gender

LISTENING STYLE		SPEAKING STYLE	
Male	**Female**	**Male**	**Female**
• Irregular eye contact	Uninterrupted eye contact	• Few pauses	Frequent pauses
• Infrequent nodding	Frequent nodding	• May abruptly change topic	Connects information to previous speaker's information
• Infrequent use of "uh-huh"	Frequent use of "uh-huh"	• Speaks until interrupted	Stops speaking when information is delivered
• May continue another activity while speaking	Usually stops other activities while speaking	• Speaks louder than previous speaker	Uses same volume as previous speaker
• Interrupts in order to speak	Waits for pauses in order to speak	• Frequent use of "I" and "me"	Frequent use of "us" and "we"
• Questions are designed to analyze speaker's information	Questions are designed to elicit more information	• Personal self-disclosure rarely included	Personal self-disclosure often included
		• Humor delivered as separate jokes or anecdotes	Humor interwoven into discussion content
		• Humor often based on kidding or making fun of others	Humor rarely based on kidding or making fun of others

Note: This chart was developed by Jane Tear, a New York City–based consultant who specializes in gender dynamics in the workplace. She stresses that although most people have a speaking style fairly typical of their sex, each person's individual style reflects gender-typical tendencies to a greater or lesser extent.

Source: Peg Meier, "War of the Words: Women Talk About How Men and Women Talk" from *Minneapolis Star/Tribune* (January 6, 1991): 8. Copyright © 1991 by Minneapolis Star Tribune.

communication: a masculine style and a feminine style. A better understanding of the differences between these styles can reduce some of the friction between men and women.

Jane Tear (cited in Meier, 1991) summarizes what many authorities believe to be common differences between male and female communication styles (Table 4.3). Men often use conversation in a competitive way, perhaps to establish dominance in the relationship, whereas women tend to use conversation in a more affiliative way, hoping to establish friendship. Females tend to use good listening behaviors (such as making eye contact, nodding frequently, focusing attention on the speaker, and asking relevant questions), whereas men seem less focused on listening and more focused on responding. Men also tend to talk more but to disclose less personal information about themselves. Women tend to speak as a way to connect with people and ideas.

Deborah Tannen's work complements Tear's synthesis of communication styles. In her book *You Just Don't Understand: Women and Men in Conversation*, Tannen (2001) reported a conversation between a couple in their car. The woman asked, "Would you like to stop for a drink?" Her husband answered truthfully, "No," and they didn't stop. He was later frustrated to learn that his wife was annoyed because she had wanted to stop for a drink. He wondered, "Why didn't she just say what she wanted? Why did she play games with me?" The wife was annoyed not so much because she had not gotten her way but because her husband had not considered her preference. From her point of view, she had shown concern for her husband's wishes but he had shown no concern for hers.

Tannen believes that in this instance the spouses had used different but equally valid styles of communication and that both need to learn how to decipher each other's approaches to communication:

> In understanding what went wrong, the man must realize that when [his wife] asks what he would like, she is not asking an information question but rather starting a negotiation about what both would like. For her part, however, the woman must realize that when he answers "yes" or "no" he is not making a non-negotiable demand. (2001, p. 22)

Competition Versus Connection. Men are generally socialized to be competitive; much of their life is spent in a hierarchical world in which each encounter with another person is seen as a challenge to their position. When the match is over, the man often evaluates himself as one-up or one-down. Male conversations are almost symbolic struggles in which the competitor tries to gain the upper hand, protect himself from threatening moves, and not allow himself to be pushed around. Men are therefore more uncomfortable talking about feelings than women are, because feelings can be interpreted as signs of weakness.

Women tend to approach the world not as competing, independent individualists but as individuals intimately interconnected with one another. Women tend to "network"; men tend to "compete." Tannen argues that, for women, conversations are "negotiations for closeness in which people try to seek and give confirmation and support, and to reach consensus" (2001). Women tend to seek out a community and to work to preserve intimacy and avoid isolation. Although they are also concerned with achieving status and avoiding failure, these are not their major focuses in life.

Although we all apparently need to have both a sense of independence from others and a sense of intimacy with others, men lean toward independence and women lean toward intimacy. The greater the difference in communication style between a man and a woman, the greater the potential for misunderstanding. A woman, needing closeness, will naturally want to tell her spouse where she's going, whom she'll be with, and when she'll return. A man, needing independence and control, may find it more difficult to see why it is important to share this information.

Similarly, a woman, being more concerned with building a close relationship, will want to tell her spouse about every purchase she would like to make—even those that are relatively inexpensive. Her husband may resist seeking permission from her for every little purchase, seeing any lessening of control over the family purse strings as a loss of control in life (Tannen, 2001).

Communication in an intimate relationship involves a continuous balancing of competing needs for intimacy and independence. Tannen points out that intimacy implies that "we're close and the same," whereas independence implies that "we're separate and different." Independence can also be the foundation of a hierarchy in a relationship—that is, "If I'm independent of you, and you're dependent on me, I'm higher on the totem pole. I have the power." Perhaps that is why men, socialized to pursue power and control, tend to place more emphasis on independence than women do. Independence fits better into the world in which men have been trained to live (Tannen, 2001).

Tannen explains women's "nagging" by arguing that it comes from a different approach to living. Women are inclined to do what people ask them to do, whereas men tend to resist even the slightest hint that someone else—especially a woman—has the authority to tell them what to do. Women tend to repeat their requests of

Gender differences in conversational style can lead to misunderstandings if people are not aware of them. Women tend to view conversation as an opportunity to connect with another person; men tend to view conversation as an arena for establishing dominance. These young women are probably able to communicate with each other more easily than with a member of the other sex.

men—to "nag"—because they assume men think like *they* think. "He would, of course, want to do what I'm asking if he only understood what I want."

So who's at fault? Neither. Both are simply reflecting masculine and feminine gender roles in their conversational styles. Tannen is careful to point out that women also value freedom and independence but tend to emphasize interdependence and connection more. Similarly, men find comfort in closeness but are socialized to see independence as more important.

Affiliation Versus Action. Women are often seen as the *talkers* in the family, whereas men may play the *strong and silent* role (Tannen, 2001). This phenomenon also springs from differences between masculine and feminine gender roles. Women, seeking to affiliate, do so by talking. Men, being more competitive, tend to be careful about talking. So when men go out with their friends, they are likely to do things together rather than to just talk. Women, on the contrary, tend to seek social situations centered around conversation, such as having lunch together. A good heart-to-heart talk builds intimacy and warm feelings. Many gay men also favor a conversational style that focuses on building intimacy.

In groups of people, men tend to be the talkers, but much of this talk is performance oriented, an attempt to establish dominance. When the topic is politics, sports, or other controversies that can be vigorously disputed, men lead the discussion. This performance-oriented talking is not really about establishing intimacy but about clarifying who has the power.

Men also tend to focus on solutions to problems, whereas women focus on sharing what they are feeling about problems. Because of this difference in focus, men often feel that women *only talk* about problems, rather than being interested in solving them, and women often feel frustrated and misunderstood.

Male and female gender roles begin to influence boys and girls at a young age. Boys generally play outside more, in larger, hierarchically structured groups. Girls tend to play more in small groups or pairs, and their lives often revolve around best-friend relationships. Although males and females are attracted to each other,

BOX 4.1 Self-Assessment

Your Gender Communication Quotient

How much do you know about how men and women communicate with one another? The 20 items in this questionnaire are based on research conducted in classrooms, private homes, businesses, offices, hospitals—places where people commonly work and socialize. The answers appear at the bottom.

	True	False
1. Men talk more than women in the workplace.	___	___
2. Men are more likely to interrupt women than they are to interrupt other men.	___	___
3. There are approximately 10 times as many sexual terms for males as for females in the English language.	___	___
4. During conversations, women spend more time gazing at their partners than men do.	___	___
5. In a heterosexual dating relationship, females are more likely to fall out of love *first* compared to males.	___	___
6. Female managers communicate with more emotional openness and drama than male managers.	___	___
7. Men not only control the content of conversations, they also work harder at keeping conversations going.	___	___
8. When people hear generic words such as "mankind" and "he," they respond inclusively, indicating that the terms apply to both sexes.	___	___
9. Women are more likely to touch others than men are.	___	___
10. In classroom settings, male students receive more reprimands and criticism than female students.	___	___
11. Women are more likely than men to disclose information on intimate personal concerns.	___	___
12. Female speakers are more animated in their conversational style than are male speakers.	___	___
13. Women use less personal space than men.	___	___
14. When a male speaks, he is listened to more carefully than a female speaker, even when she makes the identical presentation.	___	___
15. In general, women speak in a more tentative style than do men.	___	___
16. Women are more likely to answer questions that are not addressed to them.	___	___
17. Women are more likely to cry out of anger and/or frustration than their male counterparts.	___	___
18. Female managers are seen by both male and female subordinates as better communicators than male managers.	___	___
19. In classroom communications, teachers are more likely to give verbal praise to female than to male students.	___	___
20. In general, men smile more often than women.	___	___

Answers: 1. T; 2. T; 3. F; 4. T; 5. T; 6–9. F; 10–15. T; 16. F; 17. T; 18. T; 19. F; 20. F.

Source: "How Wide Is Your Communication Gender Gap?" by Hazel R. Rozema, Ph.D., University of Illinois of Springfield at Springfield, and John W. Gray, Ph.D., University of Arkansas at Little Rock. Reprinted by permission.

they have difficulty understanding each other. These difficulties continue throughout dating and into marriage. It is logical to argue that gender-role differences contribute to the unhappiness many people experience in marriage.

Tannen (2001) concludes that both sexes could learn from each other. Women could learn to accept some conflict and difference without considering it a threat to intimacy; men could learn from women that interdependence is not a threat to personal freedom. Tannen believes that the *best* style of communication is a flexible one: finding that delicate balance between separateness and connectedness. To determine your gender communication quotient, take the quiz in Box 4.1.

Tannen's work has generated a good deal of controversy. According to Elizabeth Aries (Tannen & Aries, 1997), the most common counterargument to Tannen's research is that Tannen unnecessarily polarizes the differences between men and women, deemphasizing the fact that men's and women's styles of communication overlap considerably. This argument is similar to the one that Sandra Bem (1995) makes in regard to gender roles: The differences between individual women and the differences between individual men are greater than the differences between women as a group and men as a group. In effect, even though men and women as groups may differ, there are countless individuals within each group who defy the stereotypes. The key is to recognize that the sexes do seem to differ to a modest degree on average but that averages do not tell the whole story by any means. As a friend of ours likes to say with a wry smile, "The meanest, toughest, most insensitive person in my office is . . . a woman!"

Cultural Differences in Communication

The uses and interpretations of both verbal and nonverbal communication vary widely from culture to culture. In England, for example, nonverbal gestures are considered brash and undesirable. But in Italy, France, and the Polynesian islands of the southwest Pacific, among other places, nonverbal gestures are common.

Culture influences many aspects of communication, including such nonverbal elements as eye contact, facial expression, physical proximity, and touching. These Latino men find it natural to greet each other on the street with a hug, whereas many other men in the United States would be more comfortable with a handshake.

BOX 4.2   Putting It Together

All Together at Family Mealtimes

Researchers studying strong families have known for a long time that mealtimes together are one of the best ways to enhance communication and further develop family strengths (DeFrain et al., 2007). In recent years, family mealtime practices have been examined by researchers in a variety of disciplines, including family studies, psychology, cultural anthropology, history, and nutrition (Larson, Branscomb, & Wiley, 2006).

These researchers have been answering questions such as: What is the history of mealtime practices? Historically, how was mealtime different in differing socioeconomic classes? How does mealtime enhance the language skills of children? What role does mealtime play in the lives of those sitting around the dinner table?

For Linda Skogrand, mealtime on the farm in Minnesota in the 1950s and 1960s meant that work would stop and everyone could eat a large meal of meat, potatoes and gravy, vegetables, dessert, and coffee. The meal would have been prepared by the women in the family, including young girls, while the men and boys did the heavier farm labor outside. The conversation would be about the quality of the crop, whether rain would fall to interrupt the harvest, and how Grandma was doing with her recovery from the flu. There were two major mealtimes, dinner (the noon meal) and supper (the evening meal). Of course, there were lunches between these major meals.

During this same time period of the 1950s and 1960s, immigrant families might be having a different mealtime experience. The newcomers to this country might have been domestic servants providing meals to more affluent families in urban communities (Cinotto, 2006). The family mealtime was a time to serve others, and the domestic help would eat in the kitchen after everyone else had been fed. Those eating at the kitchen table were the hired help, which could include the immigrant workers' own family members.

So, what is family mealtime like today, and what purpose does it serve for family members? We might expect that family mealtime has decreased with all the competition for valuable time. Although the frequency of family mealtimes together has declined somewhat since the 1950s, in more recent years it has remained constant and may have actually increased in the past few years (Larson et al., 2006). Family mealtimes today may be informal and may reflect the diversity of contemporary families today. A family member may have stopped at a restaurant on the way home from work, or families may go out to eat at a restaurant. Family mealtime may involve all members of the family participating in preparation of the meal to accommodate very busy schedules. Or an adult who has the major responsibility for homemaking may prepare the meal.

Mealtime activity can accomplish the goal of enhancing family well-being because family members can connect and share important happenings of the day. It provides opportunities for children to develop as they participate in conversations with other children and adults, solve problems, tell stories, and plan events (DeFrain & Asay, 2007; Larson et al., 2006). It is the place where communication skills are learned and cultural values are transmitted from one generation to the next (Ochs & Shohet, 2006). Although family mealtimes have changed over the years, this important time together is highly valued by most families today.

Cultural differences can affect not only how well a message is understood but also the way in which the messenger is perceived as an individual. A graduate student from India related the following incident, which occurred when he first arrived in the United States. The student was fairly fluent in English, but he was totally unfamiliar with American customs. One day he was walking down the street with a fellow student he had recently befriended. Without giving it much thought, he reached toward his friend and began holding hands with him as they walked down the street. Having assumed his friend was heterosexual, the American student was somewhat startled and asked his friend why he wanted to hold hands. The Indian graduate student became confused and said it was customary in India for two close friends to hold hands to show their friendship.

Clearly, actions may be interpreted quite differently in different cultures. The nature and scope of our nonverbal communication are largely determined by our cultural heritage, as well. For example, studies have documented the different ways in which men react to beautiful women around the world: the American male lifts his eyebrows, the Italian presses his forefinger into his cheek and rotates it, the Greek strokes his cheek, the Brazilian puts an imaginary telescope to his eye, the Frenchman kisses his fingertips, and the Egyptian grasps his beard.

Westerners consider direct eye contact important, but many cultures see it as a personal affront, conveying a lack of respect. In Japan, for example, when shaking hands, bowing, and especially when talking, it is important to glance only occasionally into the other person's face. One's gaze should instead focus on fingertips, desk tops, and carpets. In the words of one American electronics representative, "Always keep your shoes shined in Tokyo. You can bet a lot of Japanese you meet will have their eyes on them" (Axtell, 2007).

In most Latin countries, from Venezuela to Italy, the *abrazo* (hug) is as common as a handshake. Men hug men; women hug women; men hug women. In Slavic countries, this greeting is better described as a bear hug. In France, the double cheek-to-cheek greeting is common among both men and women. A traditional bow from the waist is the standard greeting for the Japanese, who are averse to casual touching. Many Americans, however, feel uncomfortable with bowing, but to the Japanese, it means "I respect your experience and wisdom."

Using Communication to Develop Intimacy

> *People forget what you say,*
> *They forget what you do,*
> *But they don't forget*
> *How you make them feel!*
>
> —AUTHOR UNKNOWN

Good, positive communication is a hallmark of successful close relationships (Markman, Stanley, Jenkins, & Blumberg, 2004). A man might say, "We're best friends. We talk about everything. I don't know what I'd do if she weren't around to listen to my problems. She lets me know, very clearly, when she's upset about something. But I don't feel attacked. We both just sit down and work out a solution." Poor communication, on the other hand, often minimizes the possibility of establishing a close relationship. People may say, "We don't communicate." "He never talks." "She always nags." "He doesn't understand me."

Communication is important in every stage of a close relationship. The seeds of marital failure are often sown early in a relationship—sometimes even before marriage. Poor communication before marriage is likely to continue after marriage. One study of premarital couples assessed individuals' feelings and attitudes toward communication in their relationships. The assessment focused on the level of comfort each partner felt in sharing feelings and in understanding each other. Couples who scored low on communication were more likely to be dissatisfied in their marriage or divorced 3 years later (Olson, Olson-Sigg, & Larson, 2008).

Communication is also important for families across the family life cycle. When children arrive, the complexities of family life increase, and positive communication becomes even more important. One of the significant challenges for families is parent–adolescent communication (Peterson, Steinmetz, & Wilson, 2005).

Communication is a complex process, but understanding certain principles can help individuals improve their interactions with others. For example, it is useful to know that people send subtle verbal and nonverbal messages to each other no matter what they say or do, even when they aren't consciously trying to say or do anything. Therefore, one important principle of communication is that "you cannot *not* communicate." Noncommunication is also a form of communication.

Communication as a Cooperative Endeavor

Communication depends on both the skillful sending and the skillful receiving of messages. Believing that you sent a clear message is no guarantee that it was decoded (understood) in the way you intended. The only way to know whether the message you sent is what was received is to ask the other person what he or she heard. Having the receiver restate what was said tells the sender whether the message was understood (Markman, 2010).

When disagreement and conflicts arise, there is a natural tendency to blame the other person and deny or minimize personal responsibility for creating and maintaining the conflict. For example, a couple has an argument over the husband's refusal to discuss issues in the relationship that are important to the wife. The more she pushes him, the more the husband withdraws. He says to her, in effect, "I wouldn't withdraw so much if you stopped nagging me." To which the wife retorts, "I wouldn't nag you if you would discuss these important things with me." The discussion finally ends with the husband's withdrawing even more, which only reinforces the wife's negative feelings. This potential dialogue ends in two monologues: Each blames the other for what has happened and neither accepts responsibility for the outcome.

One model of interpersonal communication assumes a linear cause and effect. In the battle just described, the husband blames the wife because she nags and the wife blames the husband because he withdraws. This is an example of the **linear causality model**, which states that there is a direct, or linear, relationship between cause and effect. Interpersonal communication that reflects this linear model is usually destructive rather than productive. Both people end up saying, in effect, "If it weren't for you, I wouldn't act this way."

A family systems model better explains both what has happened and how to escape this type of situation. According to the **circular causality model**, both people deny responsibility for what has happened and for changing it and preventing it from happening again. In the circular causality model, one person sends out a message, which causes a change in and a response from the other person. That response causes a new response in the first person, and so on. The communication cycle usually escalates into conflict. The husband's and wife's responses to each other's comments trap them in a vicious circle of causality: He says, "I withdraw because you nag," and she says, "I nag because you withdraw." Each spouse sees her or his behavior only as a reaction to the other's behavior, not as a determining factor in the other's response. In essence, they are both escalating the conflict.

It is best to avoid the *blame game* and to focus on working together to find solutions that are acceptable to everyone involved. Whereas blaming is a competitive endeavor in which one side tries to beat the other, genuine communication is a cooperative endeavor in which the participants focus on agreement. (See Chapter 5 for a detailed discussion of various approaches to conflict resolution.)

Content and Relationship Messages

When people communicate with each other, they send out two kinds of information. The most obvious component of communication is content—that is, the facts, opinions, and experiences people relate to one another. This is also called the *report* component of communication. The report component is usually relatively straightforward and for the most part is given verbally. The other component of communication is the message—that is, what the individual conveys about the relationship at hand—for example, whether it is a friendly relationship. This is called the *relationship*, or *command*, component of communication. More subtle than the report component, the relationship component is often conveyed nonverbally. Although the content of the message being communicated may be straightforward, it is always interpreted in light of the accompanying message about the relationship between the people involved in the communication.

Nonverbal Communication

Verbal communication includes both spoken and written words. Spoken communication has various nonverbal aspects to it: tone of voice, volume, pitch, speed of speech, and rhythm of speech. Written communication also has nonverbal aspects:

People send some their most powerful messages nonverbally. This mother has her hand out with a frown on her face talking to her daughter. The daughter has her back to her mother, paying attention to the pile of clothes, rather than looking at her mother. Anyone looking at this picture can assume that their relationship is strained at this point.

the style of writing (handwritten, printed, typed, sloppy, neat) and the medium (personal stationery, a card, a napkin).

Nonverbal communication takes a wide variety of forms. It includes facial expressions, eye contact, gestures and other body movements, spatial behavior (e.g., how far apart two people stand or sit from each other), body contact, nonverbal vocalizations (e.g., sighs, grunts), and posture. Nonverbal communication is just as difficult to interpret as verbal communication. Is that yawn boredom, or is it a reflexive action?

The relationship component of communication has a central influence on the accurate transmission and interpretation of nonverbal messages (Gottman & Notarius, 2000). For example, if you saw two people hugging at the airport, you would assume that they have a close relationship. In other words, people make guesses about a relationship on the basis of nonverbal behavior and the context in which they observe the behavior.

Mixed Messages and Double Binds

People often send **mixed messages**—messages in which there is a discrepancy between the verbal and the nonverbal components. The receiver hears one thing but simultaneously feels something else. When the verbal and the nonverbal messages conflict, people tend to rely more on the nonverbal information. For example, a person collapses into her or his favorite chair to watch a favorite television show and says to another person, "Is there anything you want me to help you with now?" Although the verbal message conveys a willingness to help, the nonverbal actions express just the opposite. The person sending the message is hoping that the listener notices the discrepancy and responds to the nonverbal cues, enabling the speaker to watch the program while at the same time giving the impression of being willing to help out.

We all send mixed messages for a variety of reasons every day, but they often stem from an unwillingness to be direct and honest in our communication. Mixed messages can become a barrier to real understanding. Directness in communication minimizes misunderstanding and confusion.

Whereas a mixed message is a conflict between the verbal and the nonverbal components of a communication, a **double bind** occurs when the verbal and nonverbal messages (*interaction* component) relay information that causes some question or conflict about the relationship between the speaker and the receiver (the *relationship* component). The receiver is in a double bind when the speaker creates a situation—legitimate or not—that calls into question the type of relationship the receiver has with the speaker.

An example of a double bind is when one person tells a friend a secret and later learns from other people that the friend told them the secret. Because the supposed friend told a secret that was not to be shared, the speaker questions not only the trustworthiness of the friend but also the existence of the friendship. When one questions the relationship, one is caught in a double-bind situation.

Although a double bind can occur in any relationship, the probability of its occurring is greater if the relationship component is unclear. When the relationship between the two parties is established and clearly defined, the relationship component plays a less significant part in the interpretation of the message, and, consequently, the content can be more accurately understood. For example, if you say to someone, "You really are feebleminded," that message could be interpreted in a variety of ways, depending on the relationship you have with that person. If the person is a close friend, she or he would probably realize that you were just joking and might respond in a similar fashion. If, however, the other person was someone you just met, he or she might not only *not* know how to interpret what you said but might also question whether he or she would want a relationship with you at all.

Furthermore, the potential for a double-bind message hinges on the quality and mood of a relationship. If a husband brings his wife flowers, for example, the way she interprets this behavior will depend on the mood of their current relationship. If she is feeling good about the relationship, she will likely interpret the flowers as a sign of affection. Depending on recent events, however, she might also see them as a bribe, an apology, or a preparation for something to come. She might worry about what this act means, an indication that she is unsure or distrustful of her husband's behavior. Again, the interpretation depends on the quality and current mood of their relationship and on past experiences related to this event.

In summary, when the relationship between the two parties is established and clearly defined, the relationship component plays a less significant part in the interpretation of the message, and, consequently, the content is more accurately understood.

Metacommunication: Clarifying Your Communication

The original description of double-bind communications by Gregory Bateson (Bateson, Jackson, Haley, & Weakland, 1956) described a situation in which a mother visited her schizophrenic son in the hospital. When the man tried to embrace his mother, she stiffened, pulled away from him, and asked, "Don't you love me anymore?" On the verbal level, she was implying love, but nonverbally she was rejecting him. Because of his dependent relationship with her, he was unable to respond verbally to the double-bind situation she had created.

The primary way of preventing or unbinding a double bind is known as **metacommunication**—simply, communicating about communicating. It is sometimes easier for children to pick up and respond to conflicting messages than it is for adults, as illustrated in this exchange: A man was talking with an 11-year-old boy he liked very much. The boy was describing how much he disliked girls. The man commented that he really liked girls but disliked boys. After a moment of perplexity, the boy responded, "You're teasing!"—and they both laughed. In spite of the conflicting message about their relationship, the child was able to understand and to point out the incongruence. Because the man acknowledged the discrepancy, they were both able to see the humor in the situation. It did not turn into a double bind.

When a couple wants to really connect with each other, they have to use all their communication skills—speaking honestly, listening attentively, requesting clarification, giving constructive feedback. Such efforts pay off in high-quality moments like the one this couple is enjoying.

It is often more difficult to respond to a double-bind message that occurs within a close and dependent relationship. Because of the significance of the relationship, the possibility exists that metacommunicating might create more problems. Paradoxically, the more dependent the relationship in which the double-bind messages occur, the greater the resistance to clarifying these messages. The dilemma is this: In order to improve a relationship, one must be willing to risk losing it. Consequently, the more one has invested in a relationship, the less willing one is to discuss or change it, even though change is often necessary if the relationship is to remain vital or to grow. Because many individuals are not willing to take this *existential risk,* their relationships become increasingly predictable and routine.

Although double binds are usually seen as detrimental to a relationship, they can also prove beneficial. They can, first of all, create a situation in which one person feels the need for a clearer definition of the relationship. This can be accomplished by discussing the nature of the relationship directly, to clarify and possibly to renegotiate its nature.

Continuous Partial Attention

There can be no doubt that new technologies have improved our lives in countless ways, connecting us with each other in our communities and helping to develop human relationships around the world. These new technologies demand our attention and in many ways have speeded up our lives. Thus, they have become a double-edged sword: in some ways they help to increase human intimacy, and in other ways they diminish human intimacy.

To keep up with the relentless flow of information, ideas, and exchanges, we often find ourselves in a state of **continuous partial attention**. As we attend to our e-mail, smartphone, computer, television, laptop, iPod, iPad, and so forth, we also are often trying to hold a genuine conversation with a friend. This form of multitasking, when it comes to developing and maintaining intimate relationships, simply does not work.

By not really attending to what our partner is saying, we are like someone talking on a cell phone while driving a car: researchers have concluded that continuous partial attention behind the wheel makes us as dangerous as a drunk driver. In the same vein, the guy talking to you at the party while looking over your shoulder to the next person he wants to meet and greet is not making a great impression with you. You feel miffed and slighted.

In terms of loving relationships, continuous partial attention is disrespectful and self-defeating, for it is planting the seeds of the dissolution of our intimate bonds. Continuous partial attention is a strategy we use in a busy world in hopes that we won't miss anything. What happens, however, is that in our efforts to catch hold of the mountains of minutiae that bombard us, we drop the most important thing in life: our friendships.

Using Communication to Maintain Intimacy

Developing and maintaining communication skills are lifelong processes (Gottman, Schwartz Gottman, & DeClaire, 2006). Being good at communicating takes time, practice, and attention to detail. In this section we will focus on specific speaking and listening skills.

Speaking: The Art of Self-Disclosure

It is very important that as a speaker you speak for yourself, not for others. Communication problems often occur when a person tries to speak for another person, especially in a close relationship. A good way to avoid unnecessary friction is to stay away from *you should's* and *we's*. Again, the issue is one of power and control.

Self-disclosure occurs when an individual reveals to one or more people some personal information or feelings that they could not otherwise learn. We acquire information about an individual in many ways—from mutual acquaintances, from the person's behavior, and even from the clothes he or she wears. Self-disclosure differs from these other ways in that the individual willingly and with some forethought discloses the information. (Self-disclosure does sometimes also occur inadvertently.)

Self-disclosure requires both an awareness of information (reactions, goals, feelings, etc.) about oneself and a predisposition to disclose that information. For example, an adolescent may want to discuss her vocational goals with her parents, goals that do not include college. Her parents, however, are set on her going to a particular college. The daughter complies with her parents' wishes to avoid conflict and never discloses her true feelings about going to college. Thus, although she is aware of her feelings, her predisposition to disclose does not overcome her desire to avoid conflict.

Females receive more disclosures from other people than men do. Females also disclose more than men. However, these differences in disclosure can be small and are moderated by the situation and the sex of the other person. Dindia (2000) completed a comprehensive review of studies on gender and disclosure and found the following:

- Females receive more disclosures than do males.
- Females disclose more to females than males do to males.
- Females disclose more to males than males do to females.
- Females disclose more to females than males do to females.
- Females that are attractive receive more disclosure from males.

In general, there is a strong relationship between the amount of disclosure and liking a person. People disclose more to people they like, and the more they disclose, the more the other person discloses in return. More disclosure between people leads to greater feelings of closeness. So self-disclosure helps to build closeness and intimacy between people.

Self-Disclosure and Intimacy. Patterns of self-disclosure vary with each type of relationship, but relationship type is not the sole determinant of self-disclosure. High and low levels of disclosure occur among strangers, friends, and intimates. But factors such as motivation for and frequency of disclosure are likely to be related to relationship type. Let's look at three different relationships—between strangers, between friends, and between intimates—and compare the patterns of self-disclosure among them.

If you were to ask your average city bus rider why he or she never reveals personal information to the bus driver, the answer you'd probably get is "that wouldn't seem right." What this means is that disclosure does not seem appropriate between people who don't really know each other. Personal disclosure to strangers seems inappropriate because there is no relationship history to serve as a foundation for the disclosure. There are, of course, exceptions to the general rule. When one stranger discloses to another, it may be because the discloser knows that he or she will never see the other person again and therefore feels there is little risk.

"I was on a plane trip from Texas to Chicago," related Lydia, a young art student. "I found myself seated next to a young man who, like myself, was a student. We talked casually for a few minutes, mentioning where we had spent our vacations. However, by the time the plane had reached cruising altitude, he began asking me questions about my relationship with my boyfriend, future plans for marriage, motivations for marrying, and a host of other pointed and personal questions.

"I was rather surprised to be asked to reveal such personal information, but I was even more surprised to find myself answering his questions. At first I was wriggling with discomfort at disclosing to a complete stranger. But although the questions were startling, his manner was not at all offensive. In fact, he seemed rather likable. Because he also revealed some information about himself, I revealed more personal information and feelings to him. I guess I felt I had nothing to lose because I would never see him again."

Strangers also engage in self-disclosure in structured support groups such as Weight Watchers, Alcoholics Anonymous, grief groups, or group psychotherapy. Here, self-disclosure is encouraged so that the group may help the person work through feelings related to a specific goal or task. Because the groups's purpose is to help the group member deal with problems that he or she might feel uncomfortable expressing in another situation, there is less concern about the appropriateness of self-disclosure.

Self-Disclosure in Friendships and Intimate Relationships. Although self-disclosure is not expected between strangers, it is expected and desired between good friends. The discloser is usually aware of how the receiver will react to a disclosure on the basis of what has gone on previously in the relationship. Although self-disclosure between friends may be quite selective, it may also become quite intimate and personal as the friends increase their mutual trust and exclusivity.

Some couples, even though they are physically together, are more focused on their cell phones, work, newspaper, etc., and less focused on each other.

In a relationship between friends, self-disclosure increases the listener's obligations because the listener also feels compelled to self-disclose. Mutual disclosure helps the friendship develop more equally on both sides. Their close relationship and previous knowledge about each other allow friends to move quickly from impersonal to personal communication: One moment they may be talking about a mutual friend's wedding and the next about their personal feelings about their own marriages.

In some intimate relationships, including marriages and parent–child relationships, there is unfortunately less self-disclosure than in close friendships. Among married couples, partners often assume they know each other. Some even finish each other's sentences. But this assumption can be problematic, inhibiting communication. Also, couples often allow themselves only *leftover* time to share. At the end of the day, they may exchange pleasantries, review the day's activities, and talk about friends and the children, but they rarely take the time to talk with each other about their relationship, their hopes, and their dreams. Most married couples take their intimacy for granted. Consequently, they stop exploring new aspects of each other's personality and feelings. Some husbands and wives think that love alone will make the spouse understand all their needs and desires: "*If* she (he) loved me, she (he) would know what I want." However, spouses cannot guess their partner's inner feelings. Two people must *tell* each other what they need and want. Revealing new information allows the other partner to share in one's changes and increases the intimacy of the relationship. Failure to reveal changes can result in partners' *growing apart* from each other.

Figure 4.1 summarizes some research on self-disclosure, positive comments, and negative comments in various types of relationships. (The positive and negative comments were about the partner and sometimes about the relationship.) Interactions with strangers tend to involve low-to-moderate self-disclosure and many more positive than negative comments. The greatest degree of self-disclosure and a high level of positive comments are seen in close friendships, which are also characterized by a moderate amount of negative comments. Dating relationships

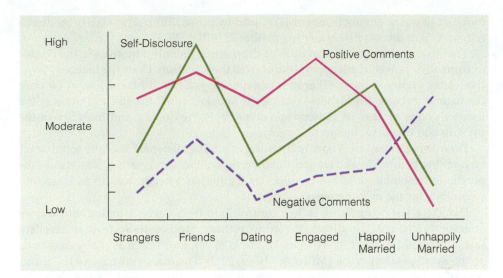

FIGURE 4.1
Self-Disclosure and Positive and Negative Comments by Relationship Type

tend to have a higher level of expression of positive feelings and lower levels of both self-disclosure and negative comments. As couples move toward engagement, positive comments are at their highest, and both self-disclosure and negative comments increase. Happily married couples tend to be moderate to high on both positive and negative comments, as well as on self-disclosure. In contrast, unhappily married couples are very low on positive comments, very low on self-disclosure, and very high on negative comments.

Listening: A Difficult Skill

We hear only half of what is said to us, understand only half of that, believe only half of that, and remember only half of that.

—MIGNON MCLAUGHLIN, Journalist

Comedian Lily Tomlin urges us to "listen with the same intensity reserved only for talking." If one communication skill could be considered a foundation for intimacy, it would be listening. A very perceptive person once said, "Listening is really a lot more fun. When I'm talking, I'm not learning a thing."

People have a tendency to judge one another, listening to what others say and then deciding whether they are "right" or "wrong." "Being right" usually means that we agree with the other person, and "being wrong," that we disagree with the other person. Good listening skills require suspending judgment and spending more energy trying to understand other people. An important listening skill is to restate the speaker's ideas and feelings for verification. Although this approach slows down communication, it minimizes misunderstanding and conflict. When the goal of communication is to control other people, listening skills are of little importance. If the goal is to connect with other people and to develop genuine emotional intimacy, however, listening is essential.

Sherod Miller and his colleagues consider listening to be the process of developing a full understanding of another person's *story* (situation, concern, point of view). Effective listeners are aware of and make choices about how much they will attempt to direct or influence the speaker's telling of the story. Miller and his colleagues note that the listener's motives are paramount and identify three basic motives, or goals, among listeners: (1) to lead by persuading, (2) to clarify by directing, and (3) to discover by attending (Miller & Miller, 2012).

The distinguishing factor of each of these three listening motives is the degree of control, or power, the listener desires over the situation. Does the listener follow the leader, allowing the speaker to relate the story in her or his own way? Or does the listener become the leader—getting the speaker to tell the story in the way the listener wants to hear it? Either approach affects the quality and integrity of the information that is exchanged.

Persuasive listening is hardly listening at all; the "listener" is really looking for an opening to jump in and control the direction of the conversation. Sometimes the persuader resembles a television reporter trying hard to get that 10- to 15-second sound bite for the evening news.

Directive listening involves less control than persuasive listening, but it does attempt to channel, or direct, the conversation. Studies indicate that excellent salespeople (those most likely to make the sale) ask four times as many questions as the average salesperson (Miller & Miller, 2012). The questions control the direction of the conversation, steering it where the directive listener wants it to go. Directive listening has certain advantages. It quickly focuses a conversation, and if the speaker cooperates, it allows the directive questioner to take charge of the dialogue. The major disadvantage of directive listening, however, is that in the interest of efficiency, crucial elements of the story may be lost. Directive listeners who use the approach in a very curt manner often fail to really understand what they are being told. By controlling the direction of the conversation, the directive listener may also lead the speaker down a blind alley into a trap.

Attentive listening is a mode in which the listener simply lets the speaker tell the story spontaneously and without interruption, encouraging rather than directing the teller. Busy people sometimes feel that attentive listening is too time consuming. In fact, it is more efficient than the other approaches because it lets the speaker get to the *real* point, avoiding misunderstanding and confusion. It is clearly the most effective listening mode for building rapport and trust. People

Attentive listening is a rare skill worth cultivating. It not only builds trust and intimacy in a relationship but also most efficiently allows the speaker to get a point across—without interruption or distraction.

who practice this skill, usually described as *good listeners*, find this a positive trait to have in both their professional and personal lives. Here's how one attentive listener, a retired newspaper editor, described the benefits of learning how to listen well:

"I hope I don't sound immodest, but I think the main reason people have always liked me over the years is because I'm a good listener. I really enjoy hearing what other people have to say. I don't have any desire to sit in judgment of them, or to feel superior, or to give out a lot of advice. I simply like to listen and try to understand how their world works. It's always very interesting."

"People take this as a supreme compliment. They smile when they see me coming, and they're always coming up to me to tell me the latest story about their lives because they know I'll appreciate it if it's funny or sympathize with them if it's sad. It's really kind of fun. I always know what's happening, more than anyone else I know. My ability to listen served me well all those years in the newspaper business, too."

Assertive, Passive, and Aggressive Communication

Be careful of your thoughts: They may become words at any moment.

—Proverbs 16:23

Researchers have identified three styles of responses in interpersonal communication: passive, aggressive, and assertive (Olson, Olson-Sigg, & Larson, 2008). Each response style has effects on both the respondent and the partner. Assertive statements were consistently found to be the most accurate, expressive, self-enhancing, and productive in terms of achieving a goal.

Assertive communication involves the expression of thoughts, feelings, and desires as one's right as an individual. Because it is self-expressive, assertive communication frequently uses the personal pronouns *I* and *me*. Assertiveness is associated with feelings of self-esteem, self-confidence, and determination to express opinions or feelings. Assertiveness, in sum, is giving yourself the right to be who

CATHY   BY CATHY GUISEWITE

Cathy © 1992 Cathy Guisewite. Reprinted with permission of Universal Uclick All rights reserved.

BOX 4.3 Putting It Together

Using Communication to Increase Intimacy

Using simple communication techniques like those listed below can help you increase and improve intimacy.

- Look for the good in your partner and give compliments.
- Praise your partner as much as possible.
- Take time to listen, listen, listen.
- Listen to understand, not to judge.
- After listening carefully, summarize your partner's comments before you share your reactions or feelings.
- Be assertive. Share your feelings by using "I" statements (i.e., "I feel," "I think," or "I would like").

- Share personal feelings.
- When issues arise, avoid blaming each other, and talk directly about how to deal with the issue differently.
- If issues persist, focus on creating as many new solutions as you can and then try them one at a time.
- If problems still persist, seek counseling early, when it's easier to find solutions.
- Give your relationship the priority and attention you did when you were dating.

you are without infringing on the rights of your partner to be who he or she is. Assertiveness enables people to feel good about themselves and increases the likelihood of achieving personal goals. Because assertiveness encourages expressiveness rather than defensiveness, it facilitates intimacy between partners.

Passive communication is characterized by an unwillingness to say what one thinks, feels, or wants. Passive behavior is frequently associated with feelings of anxiety about others' opinions, overconcern about the feelings of others ("I just didn't want to hurt her"), and fears about saying or doing anything that can be criticized ("I was afraid of saying the 'wrong' thing"). Passive responses reinforce feelings of low self-esteem, limit expressiveness, leave a well of hurt and anxious feelings, and make achievement of personal goals unlikely. Receivers of passive responses often feel anger at and lack of respect for the sender, realizing that their goals have been achieved at the sender's expense. Passive behavior does little to enhance either person's feelings about oneself or the other and creates distance rather than intimacy.

Aggressive communication aims to hurt or put down another person and to protect the self-esteem of the aggressor. Aggressive statements are characterized by blame and accusation ("You always? . . . ," "You never . . ."). Aggressive behavior is associated with intense, angry feelings and thoughts of getting even. When people act in an aggressive manner with their partners, it reinforces the notion that the partner is to blame for the aggressor's frustration, that it is the partner's responsibility to make things "right." Aggressiveness is expressive behavior, but it is all too often self-enhancing at the other's expense. Goals may be achieved, but only by hurting and humiliating the other. The partner may also retaliate in kind. Because aggressive behavior focuses on the negative aspects of people rather than the negative aspects of the *situation*, it generally escalates in negative spirals, leaving both partners feeling hurt and frustrated and creating distance in the relationship.

Assertiveness, passiveness, and aggressiveness are not personality traits; they are types of responses or behaviors. In most cases, it is inappropriate to label oneself or another an assertive, passive, or aggressive person. Some people use certain types of behaviors in specific situations or with certain people. For example, some women report that they have difficulty expressing their feelings or desires assertively in sexual relationships.

(Box 4.3 offers some excellent suggestions for improving intimacy through communication.)

Positive and Negative Communication Cycles

A study of over 50,000 married couples revealed that a positive communication cycle involves assertiveness and self-confidence and that a negative communication cycle is characterized by avoidance and partner dominance (Olson, Olson-Sigg, & Larson, 2008). The definitions of assertiveness, self-confidence, avoidance, and partner dominance are as follows:

Assertiveness is a person's ability to express her or his feelings and desires to a partner.

Self-confidence is a measure of how a person feels about herself or himself and the ability to control things in her or his life.

Avoidance is a person's tendency to minimize issues and a reluctance to deal with issues directly.

Partner dominance is the degree to which a person feels her or his partner tries to be controlling and dominant in their relationship.

In a positive communication cycle, as people become more assertive with their partner, they also tend to become more self-confident. This occurs, in part, because assertiveness often enables people to get more of what they want from others. Getting more of what they want tends to make them feel more self-confident. And as they gain more self-confidence, they tend to be more willing to be assertive. This positive cycle illustrates how communication skills can help people develop more positive feelings about each other (Figure 4.2).

In a negative communication cycle, as one person avoids making decisions, the other partner will take over and become more dominant, and as one partner becomes more dominant, the other partner may further withdraw (i.e., become avoidant). The combination of avoidance and partner dominance creates the negative communication cycle.

Research has found that couples in which both partners are assertive and self-confident tend to have very happy marriages. Conversely, couples in which one partner is dominant and the other is avoidant tend to have unhappy marriages.

The Positive Influence of Assertiveness

Assertive communication involves the expression of thoughts, feelings, and desires as one's right. It is self-focused and, therefore, favors "I" statements rather than "you" statements. An assertive person is able to ask for what she or he wants

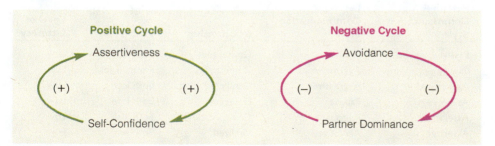

FIGURE 4.2
Positive and Negative Communication Cycles

without demanding it or infringing on the rights of others. Assertive people tend to feel better about themselves because they are able to express themselves.

One goal in helping a couple improve their relationship is to try to help both people become more assertive with each other. Increasing assertiveness tends to increase each person's self-confidence and decrease avoidance and perceived partner dominance. Assertiveness generally has a positive impact on the person and on a couple's relationship (Olson, Olson-Sigg, & Larson, 2008).

In general, assertive individuals feel better about their partners and their relationships than nonassertive individuals. When both persons are assertive with each other, the level of intimacy increases because both partners are able to ask for what they want and, therefore, increase the probability that they will get what they want.

The Negative Influence of Avoidance

Avoidance, or a person's unwillingness or inability to deal with problematic issues, tends to be highest in people who are passive or nonassertive. Conversely, people who are very assertive tend to be low in avoidance.

Increasing evidence suggests that avoidance creates problems in close relationships. John Gottman and his colleagues (Gottman et al., 2006) describe the *avoidant style* quite well. Avoidant couples often minimize conflict by *agreeing to disagree.* Another common technique that avoidant couples use is *stonewalling*—shutting out the other person and not responding to her or him.

In a couple skills program called PREP (Prevention and Relationship Enhancement Program), developed by Howard Markman and Scott Stanley, counselors discovered that avoidance was very problematic for couples. In their book *12 Hours to a Great Marriage* (2004), Markman and colleagues describe the process of avoidance. They define avoidance as the reluctance to have any discussion that would raise problematic issues. When couples regularly avoid talking about risky issues, this is a sign that avoidance is becoming a more common style that will lead to problems in the long run.

The communication style a couple develops influences how intimate and close they will feel toward each other. Table 4.4 lists communication styles and their associated relationship styles, outcomes, and intimacy levels. For example, passive couples typically do not ask for what they want, and so partners usually will not get what they want. The result is a devitalized relationship with a low level of intimacy. When one partner is aggressive and the other passive, the aggressive partner

TABLE 4.4	Communication Patterns and Intimacy			
Person A Communication Style	**Person B Communication Style**	**Relationship**	**Who Wins**	**Level of Intimacy**
Passive	Passive	Devitalized	Both lose	Low
Passive	Aggressive	Dominating	1 wins, 1 loses	Low
Aggressive	Aggressive	Conflicted	Both lose	Low
Assertive	Passive	Frustrated	Both lose	Low
Assertive	Aggressive	Confrontational	Both lose	Low
Assertive	Assertive	Vitalized	Both win	High

tends to dominate the relationship, and this also results in a low level of intimacy. And when both partners use an aggressive style, the relationship is likely to be conflicted and low in intimacy (Olson, Olson-Sigg, & Larson, 2008).

In summary, it is clear that assertiveness (not aggressiveness) has a very positive impact on a couple's relationship, whereas avoidance has a negative influence. Learning assertiveness tends to help people overcome the more negative style of avoidance, so the more both people in a relationship can help each other become assertive with each other, the greater chance they will have in building each other's self-confidence and decreasing their feeling of being dominated by the partner. Couples in which both partners are high in assertiveness and self-confidence will feel better about their communication, how they resolve conflict, and, ultimately, how happy they are with their relationship.

Summary

- Communication, the process of sharing messages, is an integral part of intimacy.
- In a national survey of couple communication strengths, happy couples agreed more often than unhappy couples that they were satisfied with how they talked to each other as partners, had no trouble believing each other, felt their partners did not make comments that put them down, were not afraid to ask their partners for what they wanted, and felt free to express their true feelings to their partners.
- The top five communication issues identified by couples in a national survey were the following: They wished their partners would share their feelings; they had difficulty asking their partners for what they wanted; their partners did not understand how they felt; their partners often refused to discuss issues/ problems; and their partners made comments that put them down.
- Men and women tend to have different communication styles as a result of culturally established gender roles. Although communication styles can vary greatly from one individual to another, in general, men tend to be more competitive in their communication and women tend to be more focused on connecting emotionally with others.
- Basic principles of communication include the following: One cannot *not* communicate; the message sent is often not the message received; when communication fails, both people are responsible for the failure; all messages convey both content information and relationship information; nonverbal communication carries about 65% of the meaning in an interpersonal exchange; incongruent verbal and nonverbal communication can cause misunderstanding; and metacommunication (talking about talking) is useful for unbinding double binds.
- To keep up with the relentless flow of information, ideas, and exchanges, we often find ourselves in a state of continuous partial attention. As we attend to our e-mail, smartphone, computer, television, laptop, iPod, iPad, and so forth, we also are often trying to hold a genuine conversation with a friend. This form of multitasking, when it comes to developing and maintaining intimate relationships, simply does not work. In terms of loving relationships, continuous partial attention is disrespectful and self-defeating, for it is planting the seeds of the dissolution of our intimate bonds.
- Self-disclosure—individual revelations of personal information or feelings—is a key to the development of intimacy.
- Listening is the process of developing a full understanding of another person's *story* (situation, concern, point of view). Persuasive listeners and directive listeners try to control the conversation. Attentive listeners aim at fully understanding the other person's point of view, an approach that encourages the development of genuine intimacy.
- Assertive communication assumes that expressing thoughts, feelings, and desires is the right of the individual. Passive communication is characterized by an unwillingness to say what one thinks, feels, or wants. Aggressive communication aims at hurting or putting down the other person.
- Assertiveness and self-confidence are key elements of a positive communication cycle. A negative communication cycle is characterized by avoidance and partner dominance.
- The more assertive, and less avoidant partners are, the more satisfying their relationship will be.

Key Terms

communication
linear causality model
circular causality model
nonverbal communication
mixed message
double bind
metacommunication
continuous partial attention
self-disclosure
persuasive listening

directive listening
attentive listening
assertive communication
passive communication
aggressive communication
assertiveness
self-confidence
avoidance
partner dominance

Activities

1. Study Jane Tear's chart, Conversational Style and Gender, in Table 4.3. In small groups, discuss the hypothesis that men tend to use conversation in a competitive way in an effort to "win," whereas women tend to use conversation to build relationships. Is this true, or is it a stereotype? What are the values and limitations of each style?

2. Because males and females are socialized differently, adult male culture differs somewhat from adult female culture. What can parents do for their children in the early years to minimize confusion and misunderstanding between the sexes later on?

3. Use the Couple and Family Scales in Appendix A to rate the communication in your family of origin now or at some time in the past. Identify the most positive and most negative aspects of that communication.

4. Use the Couple and Family Scales in Appendix A to rate the communication at various stages of a current relationship (friendship, dating, cohabiting, marriage). How has the communication changed over time on each aspect of the scale?

5. Focus on assertive, passive, and aggressive behavior in this exercise. Form groups of four. Two people will role-play the following styles for 2 to 3 minutes while the other two people observe. After each segment, discuss what it felt like to play the assigned role or to observe the role playing. When your group has role-played all three styles, compare and contrast the various styles.
   a. Passive and aggressive (one person acts passively; one acts aggressively)
   b. Assertive and passive (one acts assertively; one acts passively)
   c. Assertive and assertive (both people are assertive)

Suggested Readings

Axtell, R. E. (2007). *Essential do's and taboos: The complete guide to international business and leisure travel*. Hoboken, NJ: Wiley. A fun and funny book.

Christensen, A., Eldridge, K., Bokel Catta-Preta, A., Lim, V. R., & Santagata, R. (2006). Cross-cultural consistency of the demand/withdraw interaction patterns in couples. *Journal of Marriage and the Family, 68*, 1029–1044. A study of couples in Brazil, Italy, Taiwan, and the United States finds that constructive communication was positively associated with relationship satisfaction, whereas demand/withdraw types of communication were negatively associated with relationship satisfaction.

Gottman, J. M. (2011). *The science of trust: Emotional attunement for couples*. New York: W. W. Norton.

Gottman, J. M., Schwartz Gottman, J., & DeClaire, J. (2006). *Ten lessons to transform your marriage: America's love lab experts share their strategies for strengthening your relationships*. New York: Crown. The latest book from the University of Washington research team.

Journal of Family Communication. Philadelphia: Routledge. JFC publishes original empirical and theoretical papers that advance the understanding of the communication processes within or about families. JFC is also committed to publishing manuscripts that address issues related to the intersection between families, communication, and social systems, such as mass media, education, health care, and law and policy. Web site: http://www.tandf.co.uk/journals/hjfc

Markman, H. (2010). *Fighting for your marriage: A deluxe revised edition of the classic bestseller for enhancing marriage and preventing divorce* (3rd ed.). San Francisco: Jossey-Bass.

Markman, H. J., Stanley, S. M., Jenkins, N. H., & Blumberg, S. L. (2004). *12 hours to a great marriage: A step-by-step guide for making love last*. San Francisco: Jossey-Bass. Most recent popular book from Markman, the marriage communication authority, and his colleagues.

Medved, C. E. (2009). *Journal of Family Communication*. Philadelphia: Routledge / Taylor & Francis Group. This professional journal publishes research on all aspects of communication within and about families, including communication in family systems, communication in family relationships, and families managing communication with social systems such as the mass media, education, health care, and law and policy.

Monaghan, L., Goodman, J. E., & Robinson, J. M. (Eds.). (2012). *A cultural approach to interpersonal communication*. Malden, MA: Wiley-Blackwell.

Olson, D. H., Olson-Sigg, A., & Larson, P. J. (2008). *The couple checkup: Finding your relationship strengths*. Nashville: Thomas Nelson. Based on a national survey of 50,000 marriages.

Seiler, W. J., & Beall, M. L. (2011). *Communication: Making connections* (8th ed.). Boston: Pearson/Allyn and Bacon.

Tannen, D. (2003). *Communication matters. Course one: He said / she said, women, men and language* [sound recording]. Prince Frederick, MD: Recorded Books. Deborah Tannen has focused our attention on the differences between male and female communication styles and how these differences affect our relationships with each other.

Tannen, D. (2005). *Conversational style: Analyzing talk among friends.* New York: Oxford University Press.

Tannen, D. (2007). *You're wearing that? Understanding mothers and daughters in conversation.* New York: Random House.

Tannen, D. (2009). *You were always mom's favorite: Sisters in conversation throughout their lives.* New York: Random House.

Tannen, D. (2012). The official Web site of Deborah Tannen. Web site: http://www9.georgetown.edu/faculty/tannend/

Tannen, D., Kendall, S., & Gordon, C. (Eds.). (2007). *Family talk: Discourse and identity in four American families.* New York: Oxford University Press.

Visit the text-specific Online Learning Center at **www.mhhe.com/olson8e** for practice tests, chapter summaries, and PowerPoint slides.

5 *C*onflict and Conflict Resolution

Couple Strengths and Issues in Conflict Resolution

Conflict and Anger: An Overview

Intimacy and Conflict

Approaches to Conflict Resolution

Summary

Key Terms

Activities

Suggested Readings

Because people view the world from a wide variety of perspectives and have different goals, conflict is an inevitable part of intimate human relationships. In fact, the more intimate our relationships, the more chances there are for interpersonal conflict. Although conflict may be *normal* in a statistical sense, it does not have to escalate into verbal and physical violence. There are many constructive approaches to settling disagreements.

In this chapter we will begin with the results of a national survey (Olson, Olson-Sigg, & Larson, 2008) that identified the strengths of happily married couples versus unhappily married couples in how they resolve conflict. We will also review the five major conflict resolution issues reported by couples in this survey. These data set the stage for the rest of the chapter, in which we will discuss conflict and anger and the relationship between intimacy and conflict. We will also explore 16 rules for fair fighting and some basic approaches for constructive versus destructive conflict resolution.

Couple Strengths and Issues in Conflict Resolution

A national survey of more than 50,000 married couples focused on happy and unhappy couples in the group and revealed the most common strengths for happy couples regarding conflict resolution (Olson, Olson-Sigg, & Larson, 2008). The researchers found that happy couples (78%) are much more likely than unhappy couples (20%) to say that during a discussion of problems their partner understands their opinions and ideas. The survey also found that happy couples (78%) are much more likely than unhappy couples (25%) to say that they can share feelings and ideas with their partner during a disagreement. Happy couples were nearly five times (58%) as likely as unhappy couples (12%) to feel that they are able to resolve their differences. Nearly three-fourths (72%) of happy couples, compared to 28% of unhappy couples, have similar ideas about how to settle a disagreement. Finally, happy couples were nearly four times as likely (54%) as unhappy couples (14%) to feel that their partner takes their disagreements seriously (Table 5.1).

In terms of the most common conflict resolution problems for couples, the national sample of married couples revealed that among the vast majority (80%),

TABLE 5.1	Strengths of Happy Couples Versus Unhappy Couples Regarding Conflict Resolution		
RELATIONSHIP ISSUE	**PERCENTAGE IN AGREEMENT**		
	Happy Couples	**Unhappy Couples**	
1. When we discuss problems, my partner understands my opinions and ideas.	78%	20%	
2. I can share feelings and ideas with my partner during disagreements.	78	25	
3. We are able to resolve our differences.	58	12	
4. We have similar ideas about how to settle disagreements.	72	28	
5. My partner takes our disagreements seriously.	54	14	

Source: Olson, Olson-Sigg & Larson, 2008.

TABLE 5.2	Top Five Conflict Problems for Couples	
Conflict Issue		**Percentage of Couples Having Problem***
1. One person ends up feeling responsible for the problem.		80%
2. I go out of my way to avoid conflict with my partner.		78
3. We have different ideas about the best way to solve disagreements.		77
4. Some of our differences never seem to get resolved.		77
5. We sometimes have serious disputes over unimportant issues.		76

*One or both partners indicated this was an issue for them.

Source: Adapted from David H. Olson, Amy Olson-Sigg, and Peter J. Larson Ph.D., *The Couple Checkup.* Copyright © 2008 by David H. Olson, Amy Olson-Sigg, and Peter J. Larson. Reprinted by permission of Thomas Nelson, Inc.

the partners agreed that during a conflict one person ends up feeling responsible for the problem rather than both. Seventy-eight percent of the couples reported that they go out of their way to avoid conflict with their partner. Most couples (77%) feel that they have different ideas about the best way to solve disagreements, and most couples (77%) report that some of their differences never seem to get resolved. Finally, most couples (76%) said they sometimes have serious disputes over unimportant issues (see Table 5.2).

Conflict and Anger: An Overview

For one human being to love another: that is perhaps the most difficult of all our tasks, the ultimate, the last test and proof, the work for which all other work is but preparation.

—RAINER MARIA RILKE (1904)

If conflict is not resolved, it continues to grow. In this section we will focus on the hierarchical process of conflict and discuss the value of early decision making in preventing problems and crises. We will explore some myths and taboos that limit our ability to express anger in a constructive manner and prevent us from establishing intimate relationships.

The Hierarchy of Conflict

The hierarchy of conflict, illustrated in Figure 5.1, can be thought of as a continuum, ranging from discussions of daily events to crises. The lowest three levels in the conflict hierarchy represent common reasons for individuals to get together to have a discussion: to chat about daily events, to discuss ideas, and to express feelings. These discussions generally operate at a low level of tension and usually entail little or no pressure for making decisions. The next four levels in the hierarchy involve increasing tension and the need for a decision. An awareness of the need for a decision precedes decision making. If a decision that should be made is not made, this could lead to the development of a problem, which would then need to be solved. If the problem is not solved, it could lead to a crisis, which is more difficult to resolve.

FIGURE 5.1
The Hierarchy of
Conflict

As an example of the hierarchical process of conflict, let's consider a couple, Joanne and Gary, who need to make a decision about birth control. The process involves three phases: the decision-making phase, the problem-solving phase, and the crisis-resolution phase.

Decision-Making Phase. If Joanne and Gary are aware that they need birth control, then they need to make a decision about the type of method(s) to use. If they are not aware, then they won't make a decision; this could lead to pregnancy (a potential problem), and an unwanted pregnancy could become a crisis. Even if they are aware of the need for a decision, however, they may not be willing or able to make a decision, which could also lead to crisis. In other words, deciding not to decide *is*, in fact, a decision, but it is one that often produces undesirable consequences. Even if they do make a decision, it may be either effective or ineffective. An effective decision might be to use the birth control pill, which would greatly minimize the chance of an unwanted pregnancy. An ineffective decision would be to choose, say, withdrawal as their sole form of birth control.

Problem-Solving Phase. Problems can arise for Joanne and Gary if they made no decision or if the decision they made was ineffective. If Joanne becomes pregnant and neither Gary nor Joanne wants to have a baby, they have reached the problem level. In the problem-solving phase, Joanne could consider whether to have an abortion. If she does not want an abortion or fails to decide within three months, the problem becomes more serious.

Crisis-Resolution Phase. Not dealing with the unwanted pregnancy could lead Joanne and Gary into a crisis. A crisis has the highest level of tension and creates the most pressure for a decision. Both tension and pressure increase the difficulty of making an adequate decision. The failure to make a decision earlier (to decide, for example, on a type of birth control) or the failure to make an effective decision (deciding, for example, to use a lower-risk, but relatively less reliable, method of birth control) forces Joanne and Gary to make a more difficult decision (whether to have the child or an abortion, whether to get married, whether to relinquish the child for adoption).

One would expect Joanne and Gary to be aware of potential problems and to therefore make an early effective decision to prevent problems and avert crisis.

If this couple is in a situation that requires a decision, they should deal with it as early as possible. When decisions are avoided, problems arise; when problems are ignored, crises develop.

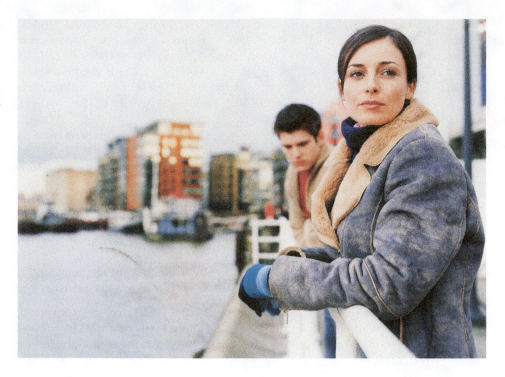

However, many individuals, couples, and families put off making easier, less complex preventive decisions. As a result, they are later faced with problems or crisis situations. This hierarchy of conflict model illustrates the sequential flow toward crisis and points up the importance of awareness and early decision making in preventing problems and crises.

Anger and Conflict Taboos

Most couples are afraid of negative emotions—anger, resentment, jealousy, bitterness, hurt, disgust, and hatred—and have a difficult time learning how to deal with them. A common tactic is to suppress negative emotions, hoping they will disappear with time. There are two predominant reasons for suppressing negative emotions. One is sociological in nature; the other is psychological.

Our culture and many others have a taboo against the expression of anger. This message, transmitted verbally and nonverbally from generation to generation, says that nice and competent people do not show anger, that anger is wrong, and that anger indicates that something is terribly wrong in a relationship. This message requires individuals to deny their genuine feelings and keeps them from being in touch with their true emotions. Repressed anger can lead to high levels of stress for individuals and their relationships, as Doris, a young woman married for five years, describes:

> I don't know what to do or think anymore. I know he loves me . . . I guess. He's just got so many rules he lives by, and so many rules I'm supposed to live by and the kids are supposed to live by. Maybe it's easier for him to live by these rules. Maybe he doesn't really think about them. I don't know. I just can't live by them anymore. The tension in me is volcanic. I find myself crying uncontrollably sometimes. I never have been able to express my feelings. My body expresses them. And now my feelings have built up so I can't seem to keep from exploding.

The psychological reason for suppressing negative emotions has to do with human insecurity. Individuals think, "If I let other people know what I am really thinking and who I really am, they won't love me and I will be abandoned." In intimate relationships, partners struggle to find a delicate balance between dependence on each other and independence from each other. Some observers call that balance *interdependence*. In families, too, children and adolescents struggle to differentiate themselves from their parents and their siblings, to stake out territory and beliefs that are their own. People search for individuality while at the same time trying to maintain close relationships.

Some have been socialized to believe that all disagreements in a relationship are wrong, falsely assuming that the essence of marriage is harmony at any price. Such beliefs can be devastating to a relationship in the long run. Drew, a 30-year-old man, describes his relationship with his wife, Estelle:

> *When I was growing up, my parents gave me the impression that fighting was wrong in a happy family and that kids should be shielded from it. When they wanted to have a good argument, they would wait until we kids were out of the house or asleep. I grew up believing that my mom and dad never fought.*

Fortunately, Drew and Estelle were both intelligent, creative, and committed to the marriage. They stuck with each other long enough to find out how to face and deal with conflict in a positive and productive way.

> *Estelle, my wife, is from an alcoholic family. Her father would get drunk and pull the telephone cord out of the wall, push her mom around, and hit the kids. The meeting of these two approaches to conflict in one marriage was quite perilous for a number of years. My wife sometimes pushed and pushed until I blew up. She expected violence from men and pushed so she could get it over with and ease the tension. I would try to hold in my anger, but eventually I couldn't stand it any longer. One evening I got so mad I picked up a hamper full of clothes and was going to throw it at her.*

People tend to have negative attitudes toward conflict because of the popular assumption that love is the opposite of hate. Both love and hate are intense feelings. Rather than being opposites, however, they are more like two sides of the same coin. The line between the two is a fine one, with feelings of love often preceding those of hate. Nevertheless, when negative feelings are stifled, positive feelings also die. People often say, "I don't feel anything toward my spouse anymore. Not love or hate. I'm just indifferent." Indifference—lack of feeling—is the opposite of anger and love and hate. In the words of one loving father about his children, "If I didn't give a damn, I wouldn't get mad." Anger and love are connected; we often are angriest with the ones we love.

Rollo May (1969) described the dynamic connection between love and hate when he said:

> A curious thing which never fails to surprise persons in therapy is that after admitting their anger, animosity, and even hatred for a spouse and berating him or her during the hour, they end up with feelings of love toward this partner. A patient may have come in smoldering with negative feelings but resolved, partly unconsciously, to keep these as a good gentleman does, to himself; but he finds that he represses the love for the partner at the same time as he suppresses his aggression. . . . The positive cannot come out until the negative does also. . . . Hate and love are not polar opposites; they go together.

Myths, Theories, and Facts About Anger

In all matters of opinion, our adversaries are insane.

—MARK TWAIN (1907)

Bill Borcherdt (1996, 2000) offered an insightful perspective in his discussion of anger: "Of all the human emotions, anger has created the most harm and caused the greatest destruction within individuals, couples, families, and between social groups and nations" (1996, p. 53). Anger is a double-edged sword; just as it is directed at others, so it becomes internalized by the angry individual. As Borcherdt put it: "It is impossible to hate, despise, or resent somebody without suffering oneself." Although anger can sometimes make people feel good, it can also make them feel guilty and less positive about themselves.

Anger can also produce a feeling of strength and power. It deludes people into thinking that they are doing something constructive about the problems they face, when actually they are only making things worse. Anger lets people substitute feelings of superiority for those of hurt and rejection. It also allows them to think anything they want about another person without fear of retaliation.

Four common but false beliefs about anger are that it is externally caused, that it is best to express anger openly and directly, that it can be a helpful and beneficial emotion, and that it will prevent other people from taking advantage of you (Borcherdt, 1996, 2000). Let's take a closer look at these beliefs.

- *Anger is caused by others.* Many people believe that "somebody or something outside of you magically gets into your gut and makes you angry or gets you upset" (Borcherdt, 1996, p. 54). One's happiness or unhappiness, however, is not externally caused, Borcherdt points out. Anger, like any other human emotion, is self-created, usually when someone else does something we don't like.
- *The best way to deal with anger is to let it all out.* Although venting anger may make people feel better for the moment, it won't help them get any better. Letting it all out does not resolve the underlying issues. In fact, it tends to bring out those same feelings in others, increasing both people's anger.
- *Anger is a beneficial emotion.* This is simply not true. Individuals may find in the short run that they get their way by getting angry, but in the long run they will push others away from them or provoke them to get even.
- *You're a wimp if you don't get angry.* Some people believe that if they don't get angry, others will take advantage of them or consider them weak and inferior. Borcherdt urges people to decide how they want to feel, rather than how someone else is going to make them feel. Firm and assertive statements, such as "I disagree" or "I don't like that," let us take more control of situations. We do not *have to* get angry; we *choose* to get angry—and we can therefore choose a different approach.

Common myths and facts about anger are presented in Box 5.1.

Researchers have found that how well an individual controls anger has a powerful impact on a person's health. Investigators at Ohio State University gave 98 study participants blisters on an arm and monitored how quickly the wound healed. The participants, ages 24 to 72, also completed questionnaires that measured how they expressed and managed anger. Those who managed anger well healed faster, within four days. Those who reported that they did not control anger well were four times more likely to take more than four days to heal from the blister. These participants also produced higher levels of cortisol, a stress hormone linked to delayed healing. The consequences of slow healing include an increased risk of infection of the wound, which makes recovery take even longer. The researchers concluded that people who do not deal with anger well end up with a compromised immune system. And, for example, this could affect how quickly an individual heals after surgery (Gouin, Kiecolt-Glaser, Malarkey, & Glaser, 2008).

BOX 5.1   Putting It Together

Anger: Myths and Facts

When it comes to anger, the ability to distinguish fact from myth helps to provide the insight needed to manage anger, promoting both emotional health and a positive and nurturing couple relationship. Below are some common facts and myths about anger to keep in mind:

Facts

- Anger is a feeling, with psychological components.
- Anger is universal among human beings.
- The nonexpression of anger leads to an increased risk of coronary disease.
- The venting of anger—*catharsis*—is of value only when it sets the stage for resolution.
- Aggression leads to further aggression, not resolution.
- Most anger is directed toward those close to us, not toward strangers.

- Depression, shyness, and suicide are expressions of anger at oneself.

Myths

- Venting (by yelling or pounding pillows) *releases* anger and therefore *deals with* it.
- Women get less angry than men.
- Some people never get angry.
- Anger always results from frustration.
- Aggressive behavior is a sure sign of an *angry person*.
- TV violence, active sports, and/or competitive work *release* anger.

Source: Adapted from Robert E. Alberti and Michael Emmons, *Your Perfect Right: Assertiveness and Equality in Your Life and Relationships, Ninth Edition.* Copyright © 2008 by Robert E. Alberti and Michael Emmons. Reproduced with the permission of Impact Publishers, Inc., P.O. Box 1094, Atascadero, CA 93423.

Intimacy and Conflict

Someone once joked, "The major cause of divorce is marriage." Living together as a couple can be one of the most difficult challenges people face in life. In this section we will focus on how intimacy and conflict are bound together, the difficult balance between love and anger, the dance of anger that couples and families perform, and the sources of conflict in intimate relationships. We will also look at the significance of anger in all intimate relationships.

Intimacy Breeds Conflict

The more one knows about another person, the more possibilities there are for disagreement and dislike. If a relationship is to survive and thrive, each of these differences has to be worked through in some way. Folk wisdom tells us that, "You always hurt the one you love." Sociologists who have studied violence in America have argued that, statistically, it is safer to be with strangers than with your spouse or lover. Police officers report that domestic disturbances are among the most dangerous calls to which they respond.

Because intimate relationships are so important in our lives, they can be extremely volatile. It is common to hear a partner or parent say, in exasperation, "I wouldn't get so damned mad if I didn't care so much about her" [or him]. This type of thinking, however, is seriously flawed, because hostile verbal and physical behavior do not solve any problem. They just delay a peaceful solution.

Because many of us fear violent outbursts, we often fall back on the old adage: "If you can't say something nice, don't say anything at all" (Birditt, Rott, & Fingerman, 2009). However, many therapists and researchers going back for decades have reasoned that avoiding issues that cause tension in a family may not

FEIFFER®

be good advice. Instead, family members are encouraged to deal directly with the issues in positive ways—without putdowns or commands. Constructive strategies are indicative of greater relationship quality, while destructive and avoidant strategies predict lower relationship quality.

Love and Anger in Balance

In marriage counseling, couples commonly bring up the issue of balancing separateness and togetherness (the cohesion dimension on the Couple and Family Map). The challenge—or *growing edge,* as family therapists call it—is for couples to learn how to find a way to preserve a workable balance between giving each partner the freedom to grow and change and be a full and capable individual, while at the same time maintaining their deep commitment to each other, and to share life with each other, together. Somehow finding a way to balance *I* and *We*. With too much togetherness, marriage becomes a form of bondage. With too much separateness, the relationship dies from lack of attention. Finding the balancing point is difficult for each and every couple, and the partners are likely to differ in their individual needs and expectations. The balancing point between togetherness and separateness is likely to be quite different from individual to individual, and couple to couple, and that is why togetherness issues are difficult to resolve, but resolution remains crucial.

Similarly, love and anger must be kept in balance. In every marriage it can be argued that these two dynamic forces serve to draw partners together and also drive them apart. Anger, thus, can be a healthy emotion if it helps a couple create a balanced relationship. This is a relationship in which the partners are not too independent of each other, not too dependent upon each other, but a relationship in which they are somewhere in between—*interdependent.*

Anger becomes an ally of the partners when they use it to attend to those areas in the relationship that need work. If the partners do not find a constructive way to use anger, however, they may gradually drift apart. Thus, the most common divorce scenario, many family therapists would argue, is not one of fireworks but one of a gradual loss of closeness. In short, fear of anger and hostilities can lead to disengagement, and disengagement can lead to emotional divorce, which often leads to legal divorce.

People send some of their most powerful messages nonverbally. We don't know the content of this couple's conversation, but we can guess something about their relationship.

In a mature marriage, anger is seen not as an enemy but as a friend. Nevertheless, partners must use it carefully and at appropriate times. Experts suggest that couples make a contract never to attack each other when angry. Feelings of anger signal that something is not right with the relationship. Rather than act on these feelings as they arise, partners should wait until they have calmed down and cooled off, so that they can calmly and rationally work things out. In other words, if they use anger as a barometer that is signaling an impending storm, partners can work together to prevent major damage to the relationship.

The Dance of Anger

It is our job to state our thoughts and feelings clearly and to make responsible decisions that are congruent with our values and beliefs. It is not our job to make another person think and feel the way we do or the way we want them to.

—HARRIET GOLDHOR LERNER (2005)

In her groundbreaking book *The Dance of Anger*, Harriet Goldhor Lerner urges people to closely observe how they manage anger. She graphically describes her own style of managing anger when she is under stress: "When stress mounts, I tend to underfunction with my family of origin (I forget birthdays, become incompetent, and end up with a headache, diarrhea, a cold, or all of the above); I overfunction at work (I have advice for everyone and I am convinced that my way is best); I distance from my husband (both emotionally and physically); and I assume an angry, blaming position with my kids."

Lerner developed a guide to various styles of anger management and labeled these styles pursuer, distancer, overfunctioner, underfunctioner, and blamer. Lerner's styles can be categorized in terms of the Couple and Family Map on the basis of the types of intimate relationships they tend to lead to.

In terms of the Couple and Family Map, **pursuers** tend to want to create connected or enmeshed types of intimate relationships that are very high in cohesion. Lerner describes pursuers as people who react to their anxiety by seeking greater togetherness in a relationship. Pursuers place a high value on talking and expressing feelings, believe other people should do the same, and tend to criticize a partner who can't tolerate feelings of closeness. When the partner wants more emotional space, the pursuer feels rejected and pursues the partner more vigorously before coldly withdrawing.

Although most people have an impulse to blame others when things go wrong, some people habitually avoid responsibility for their part in problems. "Blamers" such as this man tend to expend a great deal of energy trying to get others to change.

Distancers tend to create disengaged or separated types of intimate relationships that are low in cohesion. Distancers want emotional space when stress is high. They are private, self-reliant people rather than help-seekers. They have difficulty showing neediness, vulnerability, and dependency. Partners tend to describe them as being emotionally unavailable, withholding, and unable to deal with feelings. Distancers often manage anxiety by retreating into their work and may terminate a relationship entirely when things become too intense. Distancers tend to open up the most when they are not pushed or pursued.

The **dance of anger** is Lerner's metaphor to describe how human beings relate to each other. Think about the dance of a pursuer and a distancer. As the pursuer moves closer, the distancer retreats. Then, as the pursuer unhappily backs off, the distancer's comfort level increases and the distancer moves toward the pursuer. The pursuer warms up again and moves in on the distancer, who again begins to retreat. Back and forth, ebb and flow. Just as people have different tastes in food, clothing, and cars, so they have different needs and feelings about closeness. In terms of the Couple and Family Map, pursuers and distancers have difficulty finding a comfortable balance between separateness and togetherness. Left to their own devices, family relationships would move back and forth between the extremes of being enmeshed or being disengaged.

Lerner describes **underfunctioners** as people who in many areas of life just can't seem to get organized. These people are too high in flexibility (chaotic). Underfunctioners tend to become less competent under stress, letting others take over or fill in. These people are described at work and in the family as "the fragile one," "the sick one," "the problem," "the irresponsible one." Underfunctioners have difficulty showing their strong and competent side to intimates.

Overfunctioners, on the other hand, know what is best not only for themselves but for everybody else as well. These people are low in flexibility (rigid or structured). In difficult times, overfunctioners move in quickly to advise, rescue, and take charge. They can't seem to stay out of the way and let other people solve their own problems. In this way they avoid thinking about their own problems. Overfunctioners are commonly characterized as "always reliable" and "always together" people. They have difficulty showing their vulnerable, underfunctioning side, especially to people who are having troubles.

In terms of Lerner's dance metaphor, how would a couple composed of an overfunctioner and an underfunctioner dance? The overfunctioner would hide feelings of inferiority and incompetence by swooping in to "save" the underfunctioner, making the underfunctioner's task more difficult in the long run by depriving her or him of the opportunity to develop personal strengths.

Some may think that a couple made up of an overfunctioner and an underfunctioner would be a complementary couple, each helping to meet the needs of the other person. However, this type of relationship is actually quite tenuous. The overfunctioner eventually tires of saving the underfunctioner, or the underfunctioner tires of looking and feeling so incompetent. In both cases, the end result can be the breakdown of the partnership. For the relationship to endure and become strong, the partners need to find relative equality in terms of competence and functionality, both contributing a reasonable share to the common good.

Lerner's fifth style, the **blamer,** is a person who has a short fuse and responds in times of stress with emotionally intense feelings. Blamers often fall in the rigidly enmeshed category, an unbalanced type of family system. Blamers spend a lot of energy trying to change other people. They involve themselves in repetitive cycles of fighting, which may relieve tension but which also perpetuate old patterns. Blamers hold others responsible for their feelings and see others, rather than themselves, as the problem.

Lerner notes that women in our society are encouraged to overfunction in the areas of housework, child care, and *feelings work.* In all other areas of endeavor, however, women are socialized to be pursuers and underfunctioners. Men, on the other hand, are socialized to be distancers and overfunctioners. Both sexes are good at blaming other people, but Lerner believes that women today do it more conspicuously than men because most women still feel they have less power in our society and resent their subordinate status.

All five ways of managing anger can be useful at times, but problems occur when one style dominates. It is important to find a balance between pursuing and distancing, underfunctioning and overfunctioning, blaming and taking the blame. In Lerner's (2005) words, "You will have a problem . . . if you are in an extreme position in any one of these categories or if you are unable to observe and change your pattern when it is keeping you angry and stuck." While many people do get stuck in their habitual styles of dealing with anger, Curt, a perceptive husband and writer, describes his experience with the dance of anger, noting that it *is* possible to change old patterns:

I think dance of anger is a good metaphor for how we operated in the early years of our marriage. It almost seemed choreographed, it was so predictable. Eileen would do her part of the dance, and then I would respond with my part of the dance, back and forth, back and forth, and then all hell would break loose. It could get really ugly. I was so mad at her once, I thought I could kill her.

I think a big part of the problem was we were simply replaying old videotapes of the families we grew up in. Her family in Puyallup was a soap opera par excellence. They loved to fight and did it well all their lives. My dad was an attorney in Bellingham, and he could really pour on the B.S. as well. He'd filibuster over the dinner table in his melodramatic way for ages, and my mother would finally crack and become a bitch on wheels. It was pretty predictable. It made me sick to my stomach. I left home when I was 17.

Fortunately, Eileen and I could see the pattern in our own marriage. We read some books and articles about more positive approaches to settling our differences. We experimented and finally found better ways to get along. Luck probably played a part in it all—as did the fact that we mellowed a bit with age and just simply didn't enjoy a good brawl anymore. For whatever reason, we don't dance and brawl as much. Nobody's thrown anything for a long time. We don't fall into the old habits. We simply sit down and work things out. Thank God.

BOX 5.2   At Issue

Determining Styles of Conflict Resolution in Happy Versus Unhappy Couples

How do the styles of conflict resolution differ in happy versus unhappy couples? For more than 20 years psychology professor John Gottman and his colleagues have been conducting scientific experiments on more than 2,000 couples, using video cameras, EKG monitors, and specially designed instruments for observing what happens when couples interact. These researchers observe how couples talk to each other, examining facial expressions, gestures, fidgeting behaviors, and so on, as well as physiological clues such as changes in heartbeat and respiration during conflict. They also note listening skills and expressions of sarcasm and contempt. The results are like a "CAT scan of a living relationship."

The common denominator of a stable marriage is, according to Gottman, that the couples are "nicer to each other." The ratio of positive to negative moments in their relationship is 5 to 1. "Positive moments nurture the affection and joy that are crucial to weather the rough spots," Gottman says.

And what about divorce-prone couples? If there is a negative interaction for every positive one, the couple is divorce bound. Danger signs include *criticism* (attacking a spouse's personality or character), *contempt* (insulting and psychologically abusing a spouse), *defensiveness* (denying responsibility, making excuses, whining), and *stonewalling* (retreating from the conversation into stony silence). When these behaviors become routine, the marriage has serious problems.

To argue in a healthy manner, Gottman offers these strategies:

- Call a time-out and cool off.
- Edit the argument, responding only to constructive criticisms and ignoring the nastiness.
- Stay focused rather than wandering around verbally.
- Put the fight into perspective and be willing to see that most issues are not all that important.
- Be affectionate, understanding, empathetic, and validating.
- Use humor, and be able to laugh at yourself.

Source: From "Researching and Restoring Relationships" (Gottmann Relationship Institute, 2009), www.gottman.com. Reprinted by permission.

Conflict and Supportiveness in Heterosexual, Gay, and Lesbian Couples

Very few studies have compared couples with different sexual orientations (heterosexual, gay, and lesbian) in terms of their positive and negative communication. A recent study compared these three groups as the couples were videotaped while completing tasks designed to generate couple conflict and encourage supportive behavior (Julien, Chartrand, Simard, Bouthillier, & Begin, 2003). The study found that there was no difference in the level of conflict or supportive behaviors between the heterosexual, gay, or lesbian couples. This was based on their observed communication patterns, and it is consistent with past studies in the field. A surprising finding was that for all the couples, positive communication during conflict was particularly important. Couples who had more positive communication during conflict resolved more issues and had higher couple satisfaction. So, for example, if a partner received positive comments when he or she was talking about a current problem, this helped them resolve the issue and maintain a happy relationship.

Box 5.2 summarizes findings on communication in stable and unstable relationships.

Approaches to Conflict Resolution

So far we have seen that anger is a normal part of intimate relationships, and that disagreements and fights are likely to occur. We believe that differences between partners are better settled calmly and rationally. Long before anger builds up so high in a person that it bursts out in violent verbal and physical attacks, it is important to recognize one's angry feelings, calm yourself down, and then join in with your loved one to find a solution. Together.

Marital and family therapists offer many tips for resolving disagreements couples have. Here are 22 of our favorites (DeFrain & The University of Nebraska Extension Family Action and Research and Writing Team, 2012):

- *Focus on the positive aspects of your partner.* And every day let your partner know how much you appreciate them. Don't get so terribly wound up about a handful of negative things when the vast majority of things your partner does are commendable. Being habitually negative and dwelling on a partner's faults doesn't work. It leads to an endless cycle of hurt and anger. Being habitually positive does work.

- *Call a time-out.* Parents often use time-outs today when children are getting too wound up. Adults sometimes need a time-out, also. To call a time-out with your partner, simply agree that the situation is getting out of hand and that you will get back together in a half hour or a day or two when adrenalin has stopped pumping and you can be reasonable.

- *Listen very carefully to your partner. Check out what he or she is saying:* "Let me see if I understand your point here: are you saying that....?" And then repeat back to your partner what you think she is saying. Many arguments go on needlessly because the partners have no idea what each other are really trying to say.

- *Get to the point. Say what you mean—what you really mean.* Besides listening carefully to your partner, make sure that when you speak you are speaking clearly and to the point. Often times, individuals are afraid to say what they are really feeling, so they mask these feelings by attacking their partner on another front. For example, a husband might disagree with how his wife disciplines the children but he does not know how to talk with her about this, so, instead, he becomes very harsh with the kids when they act up. She then becomes puzzled: "Why is he so angry with little children? What's wrong with him?"

- *Don't expect your partner to be able to read your mind.* You may think that *they should just know,* but this is not realistic.

- *Don't humiliate your partner in front of others.* Shame and embarrassment don't work. The hostilities will simply continue when you're alone together, and the level of anger may be even higher.

- *The dance of nagging-and-avoidance doesn't work.* Couples often get into the trap of nagging and avoiding that can easily escalate. Instead of both partners acting like adults, she acts like his mother, nagging him endlessly to do his jobs around the house, and he acts like her son, ignoring her, avoiding her, running away from her. This type of game usually escalates: she nags even more as he refuses to comply. Finally, he is likely to have a temper tantrum, throw things, hit, and run away. To get out of this trap, sit down together and admit to each other that this is just a childish game each person is playing. Then, find an adult solution to the problem calmly and rationally. She's not his mother and he's not her son, so it's silly to act like it.

- *Avoid giving ultimatums.* Don't get into the game of saying things like, "If you do that again I will *never ever....*" or "You had better do this *or else!*" This is one of the most heavily confrontational ways people have for arguing with each other and such a strategy does not cool things down, it tends to heat things up. When someone gives an ultimatum they are trying to put themselves in an adult position, looking down on the other person, who is supposed to feel like a child. However, the response usually is anger and defiance and the battle escalates.

Couples need to observe certain conventions when arguing with each other; they will feel safer voicing disagreement if they know that it will not get out of hand. The goal is not winning the argument. The goal is to strengthen the relationship.

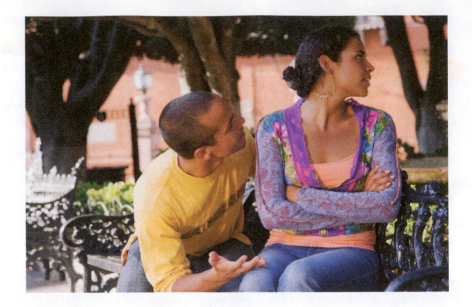

In some cases the situation can get so out of hand that the couple is setting themselves up for one person to walk out or even divorce. Don't give ultimatums because you may find yourself doing something you really don't want to do. Ultimatums are the stuff of silly TV shows but in real-life they don't work.

- *Grow up. Calm down. Act like an adult.* Do we sound like your mother here? We're just trying to get your attention. The trouble is, a sad thing often happens when couples and family members get into a conflict situation. Individuals quickly become reduced to behaving like small children, yelling and throwing tantrums. This is precisely how they look to outsiders. This childish behavior may work when we're little kids but as adults we just look foolish to others.
- *Don't fight dirty. Avoid attacking your partner.* Conflicts in a relationship are not resolved by attacking each other. Things only become worse. Avoid the temptation to fight dirty, to win by damaging your partner. What good can possibly come from making our loved one feel bad?
- *Hate begets hate. Love begets love.* When we are kind to our partner, our partner will be likely to respond with kindness. Similarly, when we are nasty to our partner, we are likely to get nastiness in return.
- *The silent treatment is fighting dirty.* When couples get into the game of "What's-wrong?"—"Nothing..." the likelihood of successfully resolving the conflict goes down dramatically. The silent treatment does not end a conflict. To end a conflict, the partners have to sit down and listen to each other and talk with each other. In a respectful and kind manner.
- *Keep sex out of all this.* Couples often get into the bizarre game of having a big, dramatic and emotional knock-down drag-out fight, followed by tempestuous lovemaking. It is no surprise that this can easily happen, of course, because sex is full of emotion, just as conflicts are full of emotion. However, it is not wise to get into this type of pattern, because it becomes self-reinforcing: if passionate sex follows a big argument, the passionate sex can end up serving as a reinforcer, leading to more big arguments in the future, i.e., "Well, this is an awful argument but I can always hope it will end again in wonderful lovemaking," etc. The problem with this game is that it is way too big a price to pay for sex: if you really want to make love, the road to getting there can be much easier and smoother. Don't pick a fight. Instead, do loving, kind and

thoughtful things all day: listen to your partner and enjoy talking with her or him; help keep the apartment or house clean and orderly; work together preparing a meal; read stories to the kids, do whatever makes the partner's life better. These types of behavior are more happily linked with lovemaking. Don't make the mistake of confusing *anger*-sex and *love*-sex. Love-sex is better.

- *Use "I" statements rather than "you" statements. "I" statements are more gentle and work better.* Blaming each other doesn't work to resolve conflicts effectively and efficiently. It only makes people angry. "You" statements commonly are blame statements: "You shouldn't do that!" or "You always make me so mad!" or "You always sound so stupid when you talk with her!" On the other hand, "I" statements aim toward minimizing blame and working, instead, toward understanding and joint problem-solving. For example, if you are upset about your partner talking with another guy, saying "You do that again and I'll pound both of you" isn't likely to have a positive response. If you say, "I worry that you're losing interest in me" might be able to open the doors of discussion, understanding and positive action.

- *Discuss one thing at a time until it is resolved.* When conflicts get out of hand in relationships, the combatants commonly start throwing everything from the past into the argument. Rather than calmly talking about an issue until it is resolved, they bring up one sore point after another until the chance of anything good happening is almost zero. Instead of falling into this trap, pick the most important issue to talk about and save your discussion of other issues until you have resolved the most important issue.

- *It's hard to talk about all this.* When partners talk about how they communicate with each other and how they resolve conflicts between each other, this is called *metacommunication* by experts in couple and family communication. Metacommunication is very difficult to do, of course, because partners have to be very honest, open, straightforward, objective, and nonjudgmental during metacommunication phases. The partners have to calm down, talk lovingly and reasonably with each other, and develop solutions rather than keep trying to score points in an argument.

- *Win-Win is much better than Win-Lose.* Loving relationships are not athletic contests nor are they wars between ethnic groups or nations. Loving relationships work well when couples in conflict clearly see that they need to join together and work as a team to find a solution to the issue at hand that is good for both partners. Loving relationships fall apart when the couples get into Win-Lose types of conflicts, when each is trying to dominate the other.

  This approach implies that someone in the household is supposed to be the boss and someone is supposed to be the employee. The problem is that people usually don't love their bosses. They might respect or fear their boss, but they are not particularly likely to love their boss. There is usually an emotional distance between the boss and the employee. And who wants to live in a home that feels more like the workplace?

  The reality is, if one partner wins and one partner loses, both are losing. They are losing because a loving relationship between equal partners has broken down. They are acting like they are not playing on the same team but on opposing teams.

- *Solve the conflict, make things better, create a peaceful and harmonious relationship.* Long-term loving relationships are much more important than endless bickering. Find a way to love each other and agree on the vast majority of issues. Life is too short to be spent trying to change each other.

BOX 5.3   At Issue

Ending a Conflict and Learning to Forgive

As we have seen, conflicts within loving relationships are inevitable. Because each of us is a unique and different human being—and often on a different trajectory in life—we view the world differently, and we are puzzled and often frustrated and angered by the differing views our partner has and the strange or thoughtless or hurtful things our partner sometimes does. It needs to be mentioned, of course, that there are different levels of disagreement, different levels of conflict. As partners we forgive and forget mistakes and differences on an almost daily basis. We have to do this to maintain order and civility in the household. Frankly, the vast majority of things that irritate or anger us are simply not that important, not worth mentioning, not worth arguing about. Pick your quarrels carefully, or your life will be one endless battle.

There are, however, genuinely devastating mistakes loved ones make, and hurtful things they do. Forgiveness is much more difficult in these situations. The list includes: infidelities, major lies, drastic unilateral financial decisions, and other similar humiliations and betrayals (Cano, Christian-Herman, O'Leary, & Avery-Leaf, 2002). If partners cannot learn how to forgive each other and effectively resolve the conflict, these betrayals can leave lasting emotional scars on marital functioning, particularly in terms of psychological closeness (Gordon & Baucom, 2003).

What exactly is forgiveness? Professionals who study intimate relationships commonly discuss three elements that comprise forgiveness: 1) regaining a more balanced and compassionate view of the offender and the event; 2) decreasing negative feelings regarding the offender and the event; and 3) giving up the right to seek revenge or lash out toward the offender (Coop Gordon, Hughes, Tomcik, Dixon, & Litzinger, 2009).

Some researchers talk about two dimensions of forgiveness (Fincham & Beach, 2002; Worthington, 2003): 1) a negative dimension which involves the degree to which

a person holds a grudge, withdraws from the relationship, and desires revenge or punishment for the betrayal; and 2) a positive dimension, which involves the degree to which a person experiences a readiness to forgive, an increase in empathy, and a release from anger.

A serious betrayal affects not only the couple relationship but parent-child relationships and the lives of children in the family. For these reasons, the help of professionals in dealing with the wounds should be seriously considered. Some conflicts caused by marital betrayal will not be resolved and the partnership will end in divorce. But even in these cases, parents may need to keep a reasonable working relationship going for the sake of the children. The marriage may not be a good one, but both parents may still be reasonably good parents and children in these cases benefit from positive contact with both parents (American Association for Marital and Family Therapy, 2012a and b; Coop Gordon, Hughes, Tomcik, Dixon, & Litzinger, 2009).

To illustrate the challenges individuals endure when faced with serious betrayal and humiliation in life, we talked at length with two friends who we felt would have some good ideas in regard to forgiveness. Our first friend said that when her husband took off with another woman for several weeks that she was overwhelmed by a feeling of deep hurt: "Why would he do this to me? What have I done?" She hurt and felt somehow she might have contributed to his errant behavior. A few weeks later, however, she concluded that she "was getting high on feeling low." At this point her feelings turned from hurt to anger: "Damn him!" From this point on, she stood up for herself and her sense of honor and what is right, and let her husband know she could live quite happily without him.

When this errant husband did come home a few weeks later, with his tail between his legs, she eventually forgave him, but with qualifications. She would take him back. She would forgive, but she would never forget. And the two

- *Agree to disagree.* People who love each other simply will never agree on everything. Talk about things that are important to you and have the good sense to stop the debate when it is going nowhere. Loving partners don't always vote for the same presidential candidate. So what?
- *If you need help, go get help.* Find a certified marital and family therapist or licensed couples relationship counselor. Researchers have found that the vast majority of couples find counseling sessions helpful. It's not likely to cost much more per session than getting some minor repairs done on your car and, similar to cars, relationships don't fix themselves—the partners have to get involved in the process, sometimes with the help of a skilled professional.

reconciled with the agreement that both of them would carefully guard the sanctity of their partnership by not getting too close to others outside of their marriage. They both agreed to be watchful so that neither would be led into temptation again. The promise held water, and the couple are still together today, many years later.

The second friend we talked with at length had gained several valuable insights from her experience, also. She told her story in the context of her upbringing, which was in a very conservative and religious rural community. Being sheltered and shy, she was knocked a bit off her feet when she left home for the bright lights and big city, and met her husband-to-be, who was significantly older and significantly more experienced in life. She fell for him in a way she would not have fallen if she had been older and wiser.

The marriage was not a good one from early on. Her husband tried to dominate her verbally, physically, and emotionally. She was overwhelmed raising baby after baby pretty much by herself, and he was verbally and physically abusive to her and the children.

Why didn't she leave him? "Where would a mother with many little kids go in those days?" The marriage dragged on year after year, until things finally unraveled when he admitted to a series of affairs over many years. He assumed she would accept the humiliation and his infidelities. But she most certainly did not accept this, and she filed for divorce.

Her main feeling at that point was relief at no longer having to try to make him happy and make the marriage a success.

Now, 14 years later, she has created a happy single life for herself, with support from her children, many friends, and her church family. "Have I forgiven him? In my faith tradition, you have to ask forgiveness from God. My husband never asked to be forgiven by God, or by me. Never.

In his view, I was the one who was wrong. I should simply accept who he is."

She feels today she is reasonably healed from the experience, and said that "You have to forgive yourself, also."

Why would that be? "You keep asking yourself, 'Why was I so stupid putting up with all this?' and I don't know why. I guess I was from another generation of women. When I met him he was exciting, showed me a world I hadn't seen." But all of his running around with multiple sexual partners turned out to be part and parcel of the excitement he embodied. In the beginning she was naïve, she never dreamed this would happen. And when it did happen, she did not have the emotional resources to deal with an errant husband. She raised child after child with little help, only discovering his infidelity after the children were gone.

She agrees with the adage that you need to forgive, but not forget. "If you forget, you're setting yourself up to make the same mistake over and over." But you need to forgive for your own good. Otherwise, your soul is destroyed by anger and hatred: "Anger is poisonous to you, personally."

Looking back over the years, she believes that in the final analysis, "You never get over it. You learn to live with it." She believes a person should let go of the anger and heal. And what does healing mean to her? "You're not angry. You learn to accept what happened. You understand the way the other person looks at the world, but you don't have to agree with that reality. You don't have to join that craziness. You learn to be assertive. You see the truth."

She went on to explain that when she was growing up a long time ago, she was groomed by the community and culture in which she lived to be meek and mild. To be subservient to men. To follow all the rules, even though men don't seem to follow all the rules. But not anymore: "I learned how to be my own person. To stand up on my own two feet. God has really helped me through all this. God doesn't want me to be a doormat."

To learn more about the process of marital and family therapy, and to find a therapist near you, visit the American Association for Marital and Family Therapy website at www.aamft.org.

- *Laugh, have some fun, goof off together.* We get too serious about life, too tightly wound. Make sure you have some fun with each other. Every day.
- *Be kind to each other.* It's really quite simple when you think about it. Treat your partner with the respect, love and kindness they deserve. If we can always strive to be kind to each other, the vast majority of conflicts in our world disappear, as if by magic.

TABLE 5.3	Constructive and Destructive Approaches to Conflict Resolution	
Area of Concern	**Constructive Approach**	**Destructive Approach**
Issues	Raises and clarifies issues	Brings up old issues
Feelings	Expresses both positive and negative feelings	Expresses only negative feelings
Information	Complete and honest information	Selective information
Focus	Conflict focuses on issue rather than on person	Conflict focuses on person rather than on issue
Blame	Accepts mutual blame	Blames other person(s) for the problem
Perception	Focuses on similarities	Focuses on differences
Change	Facilitates change to prevent stagnation	Minimizes change, increasing conflict
Outcome	Both win	One wins and one loses, or both lose
Intimacy	Resolving conflict increases intimacy	Escalating conflict decreases intimacy
Attitude	Trust	Suspicion

Constructive and Destructive Approaches

Peace cannot be kept by force. It can only be achieved by understanding.
—ALBERT EINSTEIN (1931/1988, p. 690)

In destructive approaches to conflict resolution, partners bring up old issues, express only negative feelings, reveal selective information, focus on people rather than on issues, and emphasize differences—all with the goal of minimizing change. There is often a winner and a loser, which decreases intimacy. Conversely, in constructive conflict resolution, partners focus on current rather than past issues, share both positive and negative feelings, provide information in an open manner, accept mutual blame, and search for similarities. Both partners win, and as a result intimacy increases and trust grows in the relationship. Table 5.3 compares constructive and destructive ways of resolving conflict.

Styles of Conflict Resolution

Learning how to deal effectively with conflict is one of the most important steps in creating strong relationships. Because conflict resolution is so critical, many therapists focus their efforts on understanding and describing useful approaches and identifying counterproductive ones.

Figure 5.2 illustrates a useful model for comparing conflict resolution styles. The model is based on the belief that each style of conflict is composed of two partially competing goals: concern for oneself and concern for the other person. Concern for oneself is measured by how aggressive one is, and concern for the other focuses on the level of cooperation. This model of conflict resolution identifies five styles: the competitive style, the collaborative style, the compromise style, the avoidance style, and the accommodating style (Kilmann & Thomas, 1975). There are advantages and disadvantages to all five styles.

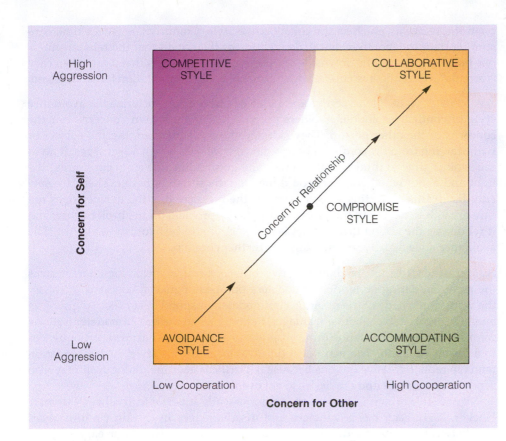

FIGURE 5.2
Styles of Conflict Resolution

Source: From R. Kilmann and K. Thomas, "Interpersonal Conflict: Handling Behavior as Reflections of Jungian Personality Dimensions" from *Psychological Reports* 37 (1975): 971–980. Copyright © 1975 Psychological Reports. Psychological reports by AMMONS SCIENTIFIC LTD. Reprinted with permission of AMMONS SCIENTIFIC LTD. in the format Republish in a book via Copyright Clearance Center.

Competitive Style. People who use a **competitive style** of conflict resolution tend to be aggressive and uncooperative, pursuing personal concerns at the expense of the other. Those with a competitive style gain power by direct confrontation and try to *win* without adjusting their goals and desires in light of the other person's goals and desires. Life is a battleground for people with this type of style. They tend to identify with the following statements: "Once I get wound up in a heated discussion, I find it difficult to stop," and "I like the excitement of engaging in verbal fights" (Wilmot & Hocker, 2011). A competitive style is usually not conducive to developing intimacy.

Collaborative Style. People who use a **collaborative style** of conflict resolution are highly assertive in regard to reaching their goals but have a great deal of concern for the other person. Collaborators would identify with the following statements: "When I get into a conflict with someone, I try to work creatively with them to find new options," or "I like to assert myself, and I also like to cooperate with others" (Wilmot & Hocker, 2011). Collaborators tend to burn out on relationships because they invest so much energy into resolving conflict. Another problem with the collaborative style is that good collaborators are powerful and sometimes use their strength to manipulate others.

Compromise Style. People who use the **compromise style** (which is intermediate on both the aggression and cooperation axes, as shown in Figure 5.2) would identify with these statements: "You have to be satisfied with part of the pie," or "When disagreements occur, you each have to give a little" (Wilmot & Hocker, 2011). The compromise style is more direct than the avoidance style, but it does not push the issues as much as the collaborative style. Compromise is less time consuming than collaboration, but it also reinforces the notion that the relationship is one between equals. The downside of the compromise style is that it favors an easy "formula" for conflict resolution, which may not be the best solution for all involved.

Avoidance Style. Nonassertive and passive behaviors characterize the **avoidance style** of conflict resolution. Avoiders pursue neither their own concerns nor the concerns of the other person. They sidestep the issue by changing the subject or withdrawing from the conflict. The avoidance style has certain advantages: It gives the avoider time to think about whether any good will come from continuing the fight and about whether others could manage the situation better. There are several disadvantages of this style: It conveys the message that the avoider does not care enough to deal with the problem; it puts the problem on the back burner; and it reinforces the notion that conflict is bad and should be avoided at all cost. The avoidance style usually sets the stage for further conflict.

Accommodating Style. Nonassertive but cooperative behavior characterizes the **accommodating style.** Accommodaters put aside personal concerns to satisfy the wants and needs of the other. Accommodaters respond to conflict by giving in and being reasonable—both advantages, but only when the accommodater is in the wrong. Also, accommodation minimizes losses and possible harmful consequences in a losing situation. There are also disadvantages to this style: Accommodation tends to reduce creative options because it sacrifices genuine dialogue; it may also produce resentment and the desire to get even.

No one style of conflict resolution is automatically superior to another (Wilmot & Hocker, 2011). Each has advantages and disadvantages in certain circumstances and between different individuals. Clearly, there are no simple or easy ways to resolve human conflicts. Each situation must be approached with caution and thoughtfulness. People in conflict have to consider many factors, including the personalities of those involved, the merits of the argument, and the level of investment each has in continuing the relationship.

Resolving Conflict: Six Basic Steps

Anything that's human is mentionable, and anything that is mentionable can be more manageable. When we can talk about our feelings, they become less overwhelming, less upsetting, and less scary. The people we trust with that important talk can help us know that we are not alone.

—FRED ROGERS OF MR. ROGERS FAME (1928–2003)

Family therapists assume that most tension and fights between couples signal the need for conflict resolution. In this section we will examine the basic strategies authorities generally agree are useful for successful negotiation within intimate relationships. The steps are: (1) clarifying the issue; (2) finding out what each person wants; (3) identifying various alternatives; (4) deciding how to negotiate; (5) solidifying agreements; and (6) reviewing and renegotiating. We will look at each of these strategies and pay particular attention to the communication skills necessary for effective conflict resolution. It is during periods of conflict that good communication skills take on additional importance.

(1) Clarifying the Issue. Conflicts and fights are probably caused as frequently by misunderstanding as they are by genuine differences. Often people argue over something they don't really disagree on but only thought they did. Clarifying the issue helps;

sometimes true differences get pushed aside or covered over by side issues. These types of misunderstandings can be minimized by using the following techniques:

- Both partners should spend some time alone to think through what is bothering them. During this time, they should ask themselves questions that focus on the issue and on their thoughts, feelings, and desires about the issue: What situation(s) triggered how I'm feeling? What was going on that made me feel uncomfortable? How would I like things to be different? What are some things I want for myself?

- Both partners should try to understand fully what the other partner is saying. Using good listening skills, the listener should repeat back to the speaker what is being *heard*—both its content and its feeling—until the speaker is satisfied that the listener has understood the message. In addition, the listener can ask questions to clarify or to elicit more information from the speaker. By focusing questions directly on what the speaker is sharing, the listener facilitates identification of the conflict.

- Each partner is responsible for keeping the discussion focused. This can be done by agreeing to talk at another time about side issues that may arise or by using reminders such as "Let's refocus" or "Now, where were we?" to keep the discussion from drifting.

- Each partner should sum up what the other has said after each person has had an opportunity to talk. Clearly identifying and echoing the problem ensures that both partners agree on what the issue is.

(2) Finding Out What Each Person Wants. After both people are clear about what the issue is, the discussion should shift to identifying what each person wants. Omitting this part of the process often leads to unsatisfactory negotiations and repetitive fights. This step is important because it helps minimize hurtful exchanges between frustrated couples; each partner has to identify what he or she wants rather than recounting "how bad things have been." Identifying needs can be a difficult process for some couples, but it can be facilitated if both partners genuinely ask each other to express their desires. If one partner says, "I don't know what I want, but I just know I don't want things to be the way they have been," this is a straightforward signal that this part of the process has not been completed.

(3) Identifying Various Alternatives. During this step, partners look at the various options for achieving resolution. This step often leads to new insights. **Brainstorming** ideas can be a fun and creative process because both partners are working together to find ways to deal with an issue. Research indicates that brainstorming increases people's skill at identifying useful alternatives.

(4) Deciding How to Negotiate. After the various alternatives have been identified, it's time to try to work out some agreements, or plans, for change. There are several strategies couples can use to negotiate differences. Each has advantages and disadvantages.

- *Quid pro quo.* A Latin term meaning "this for that," **quid pro quo** is a negotiating strategy by which parties agree that "I'll do this if you'll do that." For example, the Smiths have been bickering over the weekly household chores. Each feels that he or she is doing more than the other. After discussing the alternatives for dividing the tasks more equally, they readily move into a quid pro quo bargain. Jack agrees to do a certain number of the tasks, and Marlene agrees to do the rest. This strategy is effective because it

Brainstorming—thinking of as many solutions to a problem as possible—is a creative way to address conflicts in a relationship. Generating alternatives highlights the fact that many possibilities exist, even when partners think they're at an impasse.

clarifies what each person is going to do. The major disadvantage of this strategy is that it can easily break down if one person fails to keep her or his agreement. Another disadvantage is the difficulty of finding relatively equivalent divisions.

- *Quid pro quid.* A Latin term meaning "this for this," **quid pro quid** is an agreement to do something the other person asks you to do in exchange for being able to do something you want to do. For example, Brent's wife, Nancy, wants him to accept more responsibility for taking care of the children. He agrees to be fully responsible for the children for two nights in exchange for a night out with his friends. This bargaining strategy has advantages over the quid pro quo method in that the consequences for not living up to the bargain are clear and are not based on what the other partner does. This strategy works especially well when one partner is asking the other to change because it enables the partner who agrees to the change to give himself or herself something he or she wants as well. This helps avoid power struggles in which one partner feels she or he has to change simply because the other demands that things be different. The disadvantage of this strategy is that many couples have difficulty reaching any type of mutually acceptable agreement.

- *Agreeing to disagree.* After exploring all the alternatives, a mutually agreeable solution is not always possible; the negotiating strategy then is **agreeing to disagree.** For example, Len wanted to invest the couple's savings in some lakefront property, and Lesley wanted to take a trip to Europe. After long hours of discussion, both felt even more strongly about what they wanted. Because they couldn't agree on either course of action, they agreed to disagree—and left the money in the account. When the issue is not critical to the maintenance of the relationship, agreeing to disagree leaves open the possibility of finding a solution later. When the differences are more basic, however (for example one partner wants children and the other does not), agreeing to disagree will only work in the short run.

(5) Solidifying Agreements. Partners may need to try several negotiation strategies before reaching agreement. But when an agreement is reached, it is important that both people are clear about what has been agreed to and that both do indeed agree. Partners must be careful to avoid bulldozing the other into an agreement. Too often, in their haste to *get things wrapped up* people make agreements they know they can't stick to. Couples should take the time to fully explore what the agreement means for each person before giving it the final stamp of approval. They should be sensitive to each other's reservations. It's a good idea to avoid making agreements while either partner is upset. Pressure tactics, such as implied threats, often win the battle but lose the war. When both partners are in agreement, they should make a contract by writing down everything they've agreed to in simple, clear language. Couples should post the agreement as a reminder of what each is to do. They should also agree to review the situation within a short period of time.

(6) Reviewing and Renegotiating. Once an agreement has been negotiated, it is easy to assume that the issue has been settled once and for all. Unfortunately, this is rarely the case. Carrying out an agreement often brings other issues to light. It is not unusual to discover that the agreement does not really resolve the problem. A timely review ensures that bad feelings about the agreement do not go on too long.

When agreements break down, partners distrust or are disillusioned about each other's genuine interest in working together. Broken agreements should be reviewed as soon as possible. Couples often discover that one or the other simply *forgot* to do what was agreed upon. It is important for people to remind themselves that change is rarely smooth and that it is also rare for any person to live up to any agreement completely. But if both partners are invested in each other's personal well-being and want their relationship to grow, couples can positively resolve just about any conflict.

Summary

- According to a national survey of married couples, happy couples are more able than unhappy couples to understand each other's opinions and ideas when they discuss problems; can share feelings and ideas with their partner during disagreements; are able to resolve differences; have similar ideas about how to settle disagreements; and take disagreements seriously.
- According to the same national survey, the major conflict resolution problems that married couples experience are the following: one person ends up feeling responsible for the problem; they go out of their way to avoid conflict with their partner; they have different ideas about the best way to solve disagreements; some of their differences never seem to get resolved; and they sometimes have serious disputes over unimportant issues.
- Conflict is inevitable in any intimate relationship. It can be thought of as a process that moves from decision making to problem solving to crisis resolution; making decisions when they are called for helps prevent crises.
- Most couples are afraid of negative emotions and have a difficult time learning how to deal with them. A common tendency is to suppress anger for fear of damaging the relationship. Because love and hate are so closely tied, however, the suppression of anger can lead to loss of affection in a relationship.
- Popular myths about anger include the belief that anger is caused by others, that the best way to deal with anger is to let it all out, that anger is a beneficial emotion, and that you're a wimp if you don't get angry.
- Intimacy and conflict are inextricably tied together. Anger keeps people from developing unhealthy dependencies on each other. Interdependence, a balance between dependency and independence, seems to work best.
- People manage stress and anger in a number of ways: Pursuers seek greater togetherness in a relationship; distancers want emotional space when stress is high; underfunctioners become less competent under stress; overfunctioners tend to take charge in tough times; and blamers believe everyone else is responsible for their problems.

- People should observe certain conventions, or *rules for fair fighting* when they are arguing; these rules make the argument safer and more likely to lead to a satisfactory conclusion.
- Some styles of conflict resolution are the competitive style, pursuing personal concerns at the expense of others; the collaborative style, being highly assertive in regard to reaching one's goals while also showing great concern for the other person; the compromise style, an intermediate style between aggressiveness and cooperation; the avoidance style, avoiding conflict by changing the subject or withdrawing; and the accommodating style, which involves nonassertive and cooperative behaviors.
- Family therapists and other authorities generally agree on six steps for resolving conflict: clarify the issue, find out what each person wants, identify various alternatives, decide how to negotiate, solidify agreements, and review and renegotiate.

Key Terms

pursuer
distancer
dance of anger
underfunctioner
overfunctioner
blamer
gunnysacking
passive–aggressive
 behavior
incongruity humor

closure
competitive style
collaborative style
compromise style
avoidance style
accommodating style
brainstorming
quid pro quo
quid pro quid
agreeing to disagree

Activities

1. Using Harriet Lerner's ideas about the various styles of managing anger, focus on someone with whom you have an important relationship. Does one of you tend to be a pursuer or a distancer? An overfunctioner or an underfunctioner? A blamer or a blame taker? Rate each of you on a scale from 1 (low) to 10 (high) on each of the dimensions. Are you performing any dance based on these style differences? If so, how might you create a healthier dance?
2. Use John Crosby's 16 rules for fair fighting as the basis for a small-group discussion. Group members should first rate themselves on each of the rules. Then members should discuss some practical things they can do to become fairer fighters.
3. Think of an ongoing disagreement you have had with someone in an important relationship, one that has been difficult for you both to resolve. Agree to discuss the issue. See if you can work out the disagreement using the six basic conflict resolution steps discussed at the end of this chapter.

Suggested Readings

Alberti, R., & Emmons, M. (2008). *Your perfect right: Assertiveness and equality in your life and relationships* (9th ed.). Atascadero, CA: Impact.

American Association for Marital and Family Therapy (2012a). Infidelity. Web site: http://aamft.org/imis15/content/Consumer_Updates/Infidelity.aspx.

American Association for Marital and Family Therapy. (2012b). Online infidelity. Web site: http://www.aamft.org/imis15/Content/Consumer_Updates/Online_Infidelity.aspx.

Booth, A., Crouter, A. C., & Clements, M. (Eds). (2001). *Couples in conflict.* Mahwah, NJ: Erlbaum. A collection of insightful articles on conflict and conflict resolution in couples.

Borcherdt, B. (2000). *You can control your anger! 21 ways to do it.* Sarasota, FL: Professional Resource Press. A practical guide for people who would like to change.

Coop Gordon, K., Hughes, F. M., Tomcik, N. D., Dixon, L. J., & Litzinger, S. C. (2009). Widening spheres of impact: The role of forgiveness in marital and family functioning. *Journal of Family Psychology*, 23(1), 1–13.

DeFrain, J., & The University of Nebraska Extension Family Action Research and Writing Team. (2012). *Getting connected, staying connected: Loving each other day by day.* Bloomington, IN: iUniverse. A practical guide for couples and families built around the research-based six key couple and family strengths.

Gottman, J. M., Schwartz Gottman, J., & DeClaire, J. (2006). *Ten lessons to transform your marriage: America's love lab experts share their strategies for strengthening your relationships.* New York: Crown.

Lerner, H. G. (2005). *The dance of anger: A woman's guide to changing the patterns of intimate relationships.* New York: Perennial Currents. A new edition of the classic.

Lerner, H. G. (2012). *Marriage rules: A manual for the married and the coupled up.* New York: Gotham Books. Good advice from the much-admired couple and family therapist.

Markman, H. J., Stanley, S. M., Jenkins, N. H., & Blumberg, S. L. (2004). *12 hours to a great marriage: A step-by-step guide for making love last.* San Francisco: Jossey-Bass. Sensual talking, friendship talk, hidden issues, enhancing loving relationship.

Olson, D. H., Olson-Sigg, A., & Larson, P. J. (2008). *The couple checkup: Find your relationship strengths.* Nashville, TN: Thomas Nelson.

Visit the text-specific Online Learning Center at **www.mhhe.com/olson8e** for practice tests, chapter summaries, and PowerPoint slides.

6. *S* Sexual Intimacy

Intimacy, Strengths, and Diversity

Couple Strengths and Sexual Issues

Sex and Society: An Overview

American Sexual Health and Behavior

Sexual Behavior Among Adolescents and Young Adults

Marital and Extramarital Sexual Behavior

Toward Sexual Health

Summary

Key Terms

Activities

Suggested Readings

Intimacy, Strengths, and Diversity

Intimacy in relationships can be expressed in a variety of ways, and the sexual relationship we have with another person can be a key element of intimacy. Men and women differ in the importance they place on the sexual relationship, compared to emotional closeness. They also often view sex and love differently: women are more likely to view sex and love as highly connected, and men are more likely to separate love and sex (Blow & Hartnett, 2005).

Sexual intimacy is an integral part of healthy marriage relationships. Studies show that marital satisfaction and the satisfaction couples have with their sexual relationship are related (Blow & Hartnett, 2005). The quality of the sexual relationship in a marriage relationship can strengthen a marriage, and the quality of the marriage relationship increases the couple's sexual satisfaction (Olson, Olson-Sigg, & Larson, 2008).

Although much of the discussion in this chapter focuses on sexual attitudes and behaviors in the United States, there is evidence that attitudes and behaviors differ in other countries, and these differences will be discussed. There are also differences based on gender and the type of couple relationship (Blow & Hartnett, 2005; Scheinkman, 2005).

New research is described in this chapter about the sexual practices of women and men (Herbenick, 2010). This research indicates that couples experience a variety of sexual practices, but vaginal intercourse is the most common for men and women.

One of the changes that has occurred over the years is that Americans are increasingly more open in their discussions of sex. References to sex are pervasive in the media—we hear about medications that address sexual dysfunction on prime-time television—and discussions of sex and sexuality are common in our daily lives. Many schools are teaching young people about sex, as well as HIV/AIDS and other sexually transmitted diseases. Couples talk about how to improve their sexual satisfaction. We go to doctors to talk about what is not working and get information and treatment about how to make it work. This increasingly open communication about sex means young people and adults know more about sex than ever before in history.

Couple Strengths and Sexual Issues

A major strength for a happily married couple is the quality of their sexual relationship. In a nationwide survey of married couples, researchers revealed distinct differences between happy couples and unhappy couples in terms of their sexual relationships (Olson, Olson-Sigg, & Larson, 2008). Happy couples agreed much more (68%) than unhappy couples (17%) that they were completely satisfied with the affection they received from their partner (Table 6.1). Most of the happy couples (76%) reported that their sexual relationship was satisfying and fulfilling, while only 28% of the unhappy couples reported being satisfied. Happy couples were more likely (82%) than unhappy couples (36%) to agree that their partner does not use or refuse sex unfairly. More than twice as many happy couples (84%) as unhappy couples (40%) did not have concerns that their partner might not be interested in them sexually. Similarly, most happy couples (86%) were not worried that their partner might consider having an affair, as compared to 45% of unhappy couples.

In this same study the researchers looked at the total sample of more than 50,000 couples and identified common sexual problems (see Table 6.2). A majority

TABLE 6.1	Strengths of Happy Couples Versus Unhappy Couples Regarding Sexuality		

SEXUALITY ISSUE	PERCENTAGE IN AGREEMENT	
	Happy Couples	**Unhappy Couples**
1. I am completely satisfied with the affection I receive from my partner.	68%	17%
2. Our sexual relationship is satisfying and fulfilling.	76	28
3. My partner does not use or refuse sex in an unfair way.	82	36
4. I have no concerns that my partner may not be interested in me sexually.	84	40
5. I do not worry that my partner may consider an affair.	86	45

Source: Adapted from David H. Olson, Amy Olson-Sigg, and Peter J. Larson Ph.D., *The Couple Checkup.* Copyright © 2008 by David H. Olson, Amy Olson-Sigg, and Peter J. Larson. Reprinted by permission of Thomas Nelson, Inc.

TABLE 6.2	Top Five Sexual Problems for Couples

Sexual Issue	Percentage of Couples Having Problems*
1. I am dissatisfied with the amount of affection I receive from my partner.	68%
2. Our levels of sexual interest are different.	66
3. Our sexual relationship has become less interesting and enjoyable.	62
4. Our sexual relationship is not satisfying or fulfilling.	58
5. I am dissatisfied with the level of openness in discussing sexual topics.	52

*One or both partners indicated this was an issue for them.

Source: Adapted from David H. Olson, Amy Olson-Sigg, and Peter J. Larson Ph.D., *The Couple Checkup.* Copyright © 2008 by David H. Olson, Amy Olson-Sigg, and Peter J. Larson. Reprinted by permission of Thomas Nelson, Inc.

of couples (68%) were dissatisfied with the amount of affection they received from their partner. About two-thirds of the couples (66%) said the level of sexual interest differed from their partner. More than six in ten couples (62%) said their sexual relationship had become less interesting and enjoyable; 58% said their sexual relationship was not satisfying or fulfilling; and 52% of the couples said they were dissatisfied with the level of openness in discussing sexual topics.

Sex and Society: An Overview

A person's sexual identity is an important part of who she or he is. A number of factors, including biology and culture, influence sexual identity. In this section we will discuss these factors, look at historical and cultural perspectives on sexuality, and explore the ways in which Americans receive information on sexuality.

Sexuality, Sex, and Gender

The formation of a person's sexuality is a complex process, involving continuous interaction among a wide variety of biological influences, family and cultural influences, and each individual's relatively unique set of personality characteristics. **Sexuality** is a broad term that encompasses the set of beliefs, values, and behaviors that defines each of us as a sexual being. One aspect of an individual's sexuality is whether a person identifies himself or herself as **heterosexual, homosexual, bisexual**, or **transgender**. This identity is otherwise known as one's **sexual orientation**.

Heterosexual means that one's sexual orientation is toward members of the other sex. Homosexual means that one's sexual orientation is toward members of the same sex. Bisexual indicates that one is sexually oriented toward both sexes. Transgender refers to people who believe they were assigned a gender at birth based on their genitals, but who feel that is a false or incomplete description of themselves. A majority of transgender persons are biological males who identify themselves as females, usually early in their childhood.

You will notice in these definitions that we did not use the term "opposite sex" because that term is imprecise. This is because males and females are much more similar than different, not only biologically but also in other ways. In fact, in the early phases of an infant's development, there is little visible difference in the genital development of the male and female.

Other aspects of sexuality include a person's interest in having a variety of sexual partners or only one and a person's preference for specific types of sexual acts. There are countless beliefs, values, and behaviors associated with sexuality. Therefore, individuals vary widely in how they define themselves as sexual beings.

In our society, the term **sex** can refer either to being biologically female or male or to sexual activity. The term **gender** refers to the learned characteristics and behaviors associated with being male or female in a particular culture.

Historical Perspectives on Sex and Society

Throughout history, human sexual behavior and thinking about sex have been guided by religious teachings and cultural beliefs. Many religions, including some Christian groups, have attempted to regulate sex outside marriage by condemning it as sinful. Some religions, such as Islam, although also condemning sex outside of marriage, allow men to take more than one wife. Other ideas about sex evolve out of, and are part of, general cultural beliefs. For example, Western male-dominated culture has held the idea that women have little interest in sex. Other cultures—for example, that of the Inuit—consider female sexual activity to be on a par with that of males.

Advances in science as early as the 17th century led to a more technical approach to sex. Little was known about the biological aspects of sexuality until Dutch microscopist Anton van Leeuwenhoek (1632–1723) and his student John Ham discovered sperm swimming in human semen. Oscar Hertwig was the first to observe fertilization of the egg by the sperm in sea urchins in 1875, yet the human ovum was not directly observed until the 20th century.

Today, we have a great deal of scientific knowledge about sex—about conception, contraception, and sexual functioning, as well as about how to treat infertility and sexual dysfunction. We talk openly about sex and are complacent about the ubiquity of sexual images in our society. Yet religion still plays a role in many people's sexual attitudes and behavior, and there is still conflict between those who espouse

In our society, most information about sexual behavior and intimate relationships comes from the media. Not surprisingly, many people have misconceptions and distorted ideas about both the physical and the emotional dimensions of sexuality.

an open, objective, scientific, informational approach to sex and those who wish to regulate people's sexual behavior and their access to information on moral grounds.

Gay and Lesbian Couples

Historically, most of the focus on gays and lesbians has been on their sexual orientation and behavior, with little discussion of other characteristics of gay and lesbian couples. There are an estimated 8.8 million gay, lesbian, and bisexual (GLB) persons living in the United States. The number of same-sex couples in this country grew by more than 30% from 2000 to 2005, from nearly 600,000 couples in 2000 to almost 777,000 in 2005 (Gates, 2006). This change is likely due to the slow, but steadily more accepting, societal view of gay and lesbian individuals. Gays and lesbians have increasingly moved in the direction of developing and maintaining ongoing relationships with one person (Gotta et al., 2011; Kurdek, 2008). Increasingly, both gays and lesbians have had to struggle with coming out and have often experienced considerable rejection by their parents and other relatives. This struggle has helped some of them develop a variety of strengths that are valuable in relationships (Kurdek, 2008). The following are some of the characteristics that have been found to be strengths of gay and lesbian couples:

- *High emotional connection with partner and others*. A common strength for many gays and lesbians is their ability to connect in an emotional way with people of both the same sex and the other sex.
- *High role flexibility*. In their same-sex relationships, they often have a flexible role relationship that gives them the ability to adapt to each other (Green , 2012).
- *Egalitarian decision making*. The ability to negotiate and make decisions in a sharing manner enables them to establish and maintain an egalitarian relationship (Gotta et al., 2011; Green, 2012). Same-sex couples are more egalitarian than heterosexual couples.

- *Positive parent–child relationships.* Gay and lesbian couples are on par with heterosexual couples when it comes to raising healthy, well-adjusted children (Green, 2012).
- *Psychologically perceptive.* Whether it is because they have had to struggle to come out or because of their lifestyle, they often tend to be very perceptive in terms of psychological dynamics.
- *Effective communication skills.* A common characteristic of many of the same-sex relationships is that they have been able to achieve very good communication skills and more equality in communication within their couple relationship (Gotta et al., 2011).

A recent 12-year study of gay and lesbian couples by John Gottman (2010) and his colleagues focused on what makes same-sex relationships succeed or fail. The research demonstrated that all couple types—straight or gay—have many of the same problems and the same approaches to couple satisfaction. The researchers outlined some qualities of strength that are especially critical for same-sex partnerships:

- *Gay and lesbian couples are more upbeat in the face of conflict than heterosexual couples.* Gay and lesbian couples in the Gottman study used more affection and humor when they were engaged in a disagreement.
- *Gay and lesbian couples use fewer controlling, hostile, and emotional tactics than heterosexual couples when communicating with each other.* Fairness and power sharing between partners is more important and more common among gay and lesbian couples, Gottman found.
- *In a fight, gay and lesbian couples take it less personally.* Compared to straight couples, gay and lesbian partners have a tendency to accept some degree of negativity without getting hurt feelings.
- *Unhappy gay and lesbian couples tend to show low levels of physiological arousal.* This is measured by elevated heart rate, sweaty palms, and jitteriness. Straight couples tend to get more aroused during a disagreement than gay and lesbian couples.

It is difficult to study gay and lesbian couples for several reasons. First, many couples are not willing to be open about their sexual orientation and are less willing to be part of a research project. Second, laws and policies are still in place, along with prejudice and oppression, that impact the lives of gay and lesbian couples and families (Chamberlin, 2005; Herek, 2006; Pawelski et al., 2006). For example, most states in the United States still deny gay and lesbian couples the benefits and security of legal marriage. However, some states have the freedom to marry for gay couples, and some states officially pledge non-discrimination toward marriages between same-sex couples (Freedom To Marry, 2010).

Even though there may be an expectation that gay couples function like heterosexual couples, this may be an unrealistic expectation. These differences regarding laws, rights, and the degree of acceptance make it difficult to compare gay and lesbian couples and families with heterosexual couples and families (Meezan & Rauch, 2005; Pawelski et al., 2006). Many gay and lesbian individuals have been in heterosexual relationships and have had children in those relationships. Their extended families may have disowned them, or, at best, they have strained relationships. These past and current life circumstances greatly affect one's family and other network relationships.

Third, we compare gay and lesbian couple relationships to heterosexual relationships with the assumption that heterosexual relationships provide the gold standard for how couple relationships should be—and this may not be a fair way to assess these relationships. Even though these issues are often identified in the literature, the majority of studies continue to compare gay and lesbian relationships to heterosexual relationships.

Kurdek (2006), in a large national study, compared gay couples, lesbian couples, and heterosexual cohabiting couples to heterosexual couples with children regarding their relationship adjustment. The findings of this study showed that these couples did not differ markedly from each other in terms of relationship adjustment. Some relatively insignificant differences were reported. For example, Kurdek found that gay couples were more likely to rely on friends for support, and heterosexual sexual couples were more likely to rely on family for support. Kurdek also found that gay and lesbian couples and unmarried heterosexual couples were more prone to separation than married couples with children. What we know from current research is that children from same-sex couples typically fare about the same as children from other family structures (Chamberlin, 2005; Herek, 2006; Meezen & Rauch, 2005; Pawelski et al., 2006).

While gays and lesbians are increasingly visible in U.S. culture, same-sex relationships are often hidden and forbidden in many other cultures. For example, homosexuality among the men in Afghanistan was recently uncovered and described because of the war in that country (Reynolds, 2002). While the Pashtun literature and the Muslim religion forbid sexual contact between males, it is increasingly happening and the rate could be as high as 50% in some cities such as Kandahar. Because young males are often unable to interact with women or even see their faces, they often turn to other males for sexual fulfillment. Also in the Pashtun culture, a man has to pay for the wedding and gifts for the family, and most men are unable to raise the $5,000 that is expected. So Afghan single men are more sexually involved with other men, and this is predicted to continue until economic conditions improve and women are given more freedom.

Sexuality Across Cultures

Attitudes toward sexuality and sexual behaviors vary markedly from one culture to another, and ethnocentrism encourages people to believe that their culture's thinking and practices are the only "right" or "natural" way to live. An important generalization cross-cultural researchers make about sexuality is that all societies regulate sexual behavior in some way, although the regulations vary greatly from culture to culture (Hyde & DeLamater, 2008). Sex is a powerful force, and societies around the world have found it necessary to develop some rules regarding sexual behavior. For example, **incest taboos,** which prohibit intercourse between parents and children and between siblings, are nearly universal; most societies also condemn forced sexual relations, such as rape (Hyde & DeLamater, 2008).

Standards of Attractiveness. Cultural standards of sexual attractiveness vary widely. In many non-Western cultures, a plump woman is considered more attractive than a thin woman. But in the United States, the ideal woman has a slim body, well-developed breasts, and long, shapely legs; the ideal man is tall and moderately muscular, with broad shoulders and narrow hips. Physical attributes are often more important for women in Western societies because women tend to be judged by their appearance, whereas men are judged by their accomplishments and power.

In some cultures, the shape and color of the eyes are most important; other cultures value good-looking ears. The Nawa of Africa value elongated labia majora (the pads of fatty tissue on either side of the vagina), and Nawa women reportedly tug on them to enhance their length. Although the specifics vary, most cultures identify certain physical traits as attractive and valuable (Hyde & DeLamater, 2008).

Sexual Behavior. Gender roles in sexual behavior differ considerably across cultures. In a few societies, including the Maori and the Kwoma of the South Pacific, females generally initiate love affairs. Although rape in American society is primarily committed by men, the anthropologist Bronislaw Malinowski (1929) reported groups of Trobriand Island women in the South Pacific who regularly raped and sexually humiliated male strangers who were unfortunate enough to wander through the area near their village.

Sexual techniques also vary considerably from culture to culture (Hyde & DeLamater, 2008). Kissing is common in most societies; however, when the Thonga of Africa first saw Europeans kissing, they were amused and could not believe the Europeans were sharing saliva. In some societies, one partner inflicts pain on the other partner during lovemaking. Apinayean women of South America have been known to bite off bits of their partner's eyebrows; Trukese women in the South Pacific poke fingers in the man's ear when sexually excited; and partners in some societies draw blood and leave scars as a result of sexual passion.

In many cultures around the world, the breast is not a sexual object, according to Marilyn Yalom, author of *A History of the Breast* and *A History of the Wife*.

Standards for physical attractiveness, which we take for granted, are actually culturally determined. Although these two women are very different from each other in appearance, each is considered beautiful in her culture.

(a)

(b)

Yalom argues that the breast is over-eroticized in the Western world. In African cultures, breasts are for babies and not for men. In African sexual tradition, the erotic focus is on the buttocks. The Chinese make a sexual fetish of the foot, while the Japanese concentrate on the nape of the neck ("Breasts Shaped by Evolution for Babies, Not Men," 2010).

The frequency of sexual intercourse varies from society to society. American society today is about average when compared with other cultures. The range of frequency of intercourse for married couples runs from a low of about once a month among the Keraki of the South Pacific to a high of a few times a night for young couples among the Aranda of Australia and the Mangaians of the South Pacific.

Sexual Attitudes. Attitudes toward **masturbation,** the self-stimulation of the genitals, vary widely from culture to culture. It is tolerated among children and adolescents in some societies but condemned at any age by other societies (Bhugra, Popelyuk, & McMullen, 2010). Most societies tend to disapprove of adult masturbation; if it is discovered, the consequences range from mild ridicule to punishment.

Similarly, attitudes toward same-sex behavior vary widely from culture to culture. Although some cultures tolerate same-sex sexual activity among children, they disapprove when adults engage in it. Other societies force such behavior on all their male members, most often during puberty rites. (Bhugra, Popelyuk, & McMullen, 2010). Often sexual attitudes are influenced by religious practices and beliefs.

Female Circumcision in Africa. The story of female circumcision is graphically told by the supermodel Waris Dirie in her book *Desert Flower* (1998; see also *Encyclopedia Britannica*, 2010; U.S. Department of Health and Human Services, 2010). She was circumcised at age 5 in Africa as a member of a Somalian tribe and had an arranged marriage to an older tribal member when she was 13. In her teens, she served as a maid in London, England, to an ambassador family and then became a model. After a successful career, she became a special ambassador for the United Nations (UN) to promote cultural change away from female genital mutilation (FGM).

Most African cultures have practiced female circumcision for centuries. The UN estimates that it has been performed on over 130 million women. This still happens to at least 2 million girls a year and over 6,000 women a day. The practice varies by geographic location, cultural group, and tribe. At a minimum, the hood of the clitoris is destroyed. But in over 80% of women in Somalia, the most severe form is infibulation, in which the labia minora and labia majora are also removed, leaving only a small opening to urinate.

The practice of female genital mutilation has been promoted by men and maintained in the culture by women. Men demand a circumcised woman because they feel the woman is otherwise dirty and oversexed. The mothers support it because otherwise their daughters would not be selected by men for marriage.

Female circumcision is dangerous because many women get infected and die from the surgery. They often suffer from immediate health problems from the surgery, including infections and shock. They also suffer long-term problems like chronic urinary infection and depression. In addition, the surgery eliminates the possibility of achieving any sexual satisfaction. Waris Dirie continues to work to eliminate FGM.

Cultural Change. Cultural beliefs and attitudes regarding sexuality change, often dramatically, over time. In China, for example, economic and social reforms have spawned a new sexual permissiveness. The Shanghai Sex Research Center conducted a national survey of 23,000 people and found that the Chinese are having more sex outside marriage and are becoming increasingly adventurous in the ways they make love. The researchers also found an erosion of the strong tie between sex and marriage in the world's most populous nation. Of those surveyed, a vast majority of the people (86%) and about two thirds (69%) of married people approved of extramarital affairs.

HIV/AIDS—Three Decades Later

Three decades after AIDS was first identified among gay men in New York and Los Angeles, the epidemic still continues (Centers for Disease Control and Prevention, 2010). The first case of a mysterious disease was identified in 1981 when researchers were trying to discover what was making gay men sick for no apparent reason. **Human immunodeficiency virus (HIV)** is the virus that causes acquired immunodeficiency syndrome (AIDS). HIV destroys some types of white blood cells and affects a person's immune system. Illnesses that once were fought off with a healthy person's immune system can no longer be fought off. A person with HIV will develop infections, which ultimately results in a diagnosis of AIDS, that make the person unable to work or cause death. People can carry HIV for years before they have any symptoms.

One of the reasons HIV continues to be spreading at alarming rates is that people do not know they are infected and pass it on to others. On average, people carry the virus for 8 to 10 years before they begin to have symptoms. Currently it is estimated that more than 200,000 people are infected with HIV but are unaware they are infected and therefore are unaware that they are passing the virus on to others. The rate of infection increased rapidly in the 1980s, peaked in 1992, and then stabilized in 1998 (Centers for Disease Control and Prevention, 2010a).

The most recent statistics available, from 2006, indicate that an estimated 1.1 million persons in the United States were living with diagnosed or undiagnosed HIV/AIDS. The Centers for Disease Control and Prevention calculated that 56,300 new infections occurred that year.

Most HIV/AIDS cases are among men. In 2006, 74% of HIV/AIDS diagnoses among adolescents and adults were for males, and 24% for females. Figures for 2007 indicated that the largest estimated proportion of HIV/AIDS diagnoses among adults and adolescents was in men who have sex with men. This group accounted for 53% of all HIV/AIDS diagnoses. High-risk sexual contact, defined as sexual contact with persons known to have HIV infection or who have a higher risk of contracting HIV infection, accounted for 11% of all HIV/AIDS diagnoses (Centers for Disease Control and Prevention, 2010a).

HIV is transmitted primarily through sex and injection drug use. The modes of transmission of HIV among men include men having sex with men (71%), injection drug use (10%), heterosexual sex (14%), male-to-male sexual contact and injection drug use (4%), and other (1%). The modes of transmission among women include high-risk heterosexual contact (83%), injection drug use (16%), and other (1%) (Centers for Disease Control and Prevention, 2010a).

The worldwide HIV/AIDS pandemic is staggering in its global scope. The most recent statistics available, from 2008, indicate that an estimated 33.4 million people around the world are living with HIV/AIDS. Approximately 50.1% of these are women and 49.9% are men, and 2.1 million people worldwide living with HIV/AIDS are children under 15 years of age. In 2008, 2.7 million people were newly infected with HIV, including 430,000 children under 15. Approximately 2 million AIDs-related deaths occurred in 2008, and 280,000 of these individuals were children (Joint United Nations Programme on HIV/AIDS and World Health Organization, 2009).

American Sexual Health and Behavior

There have been a handful of large-scale sex surveys in the United States since Alfred Kinsey's landmark study in the early 1950s. These surveys reveal, among other things, information regarding the frequency with which Americans engage in sexual activity and the kinds of sexual activities they engage in.

The first study we will discuss is the National Survey of Sexual Health and Behavior conducted in 2009 and reported on in 2010. We believe this is a landmark study that deserves considerable discussion in this chapter. We will also report the findings of a sex survey conducted by ABC News in 2004. Finally, we will summarize the study commissioned by AARP,* focusing on sexuality in the later years (AARP, 2005). These three studies are the most prominent large-scale studies of sexuality in the United States that we have found in our research literature investigations. Major studies of sexual behavior, as the reader can readily imagine, are not easy to conduct. These investigations are expensive, time consuming, and politically charged because they focus on sensitive and very personal aspects of people's lives. For these reasons, large-scale studies of sexual behavior are not conducted very often.

National Survey of Sexual Health and Behavior

Researchers in this national study surveyed 5,865 randomly selected adults and teens 14 to 94 years of age to understand sexual behavior in the United States. This study included information about masturbation, vaginal intercourse, noncoital sex (i.e. mutual masturbation), anal intercourse, and same-sex behavior.

Men's Sexual Behaviors. Most men (from 28% to 69%) reported masturbating during the past year, with the exception of younger teens and older men (70+ years), and most masturbation was done alone (Herbenick et al., 2010). This research also found that although most men from 18 to 19 years of age had the experience of vaginal intercourse, it was not common. Eighty-five percent of men in their 20s and 30s experienced vaginal intercourse at least once in the previous year, with the percentages dropping to 74% among men in their 40s, and 58% of men in their 50s. Men in the 25 to 49 year age categories experienced vaginal intercourse more often than other sexual behaviors.

Some, but not many, men experienced partnered noncoital behaviors such as partnered masturbation or oral sex, across all age categories (Herbenick et al., 2010). The highest rate of these behaviors happened with men who were between 25 and 49 years of age. Anal intercourse was less common, but not rare, by men across all ages. However, anal sex was most common in men ages 25 to 49 years of age. Almost half of the men between 25 to 59 years reported participating in anal sex during their lifetime.

*The American Association of Retired Persons officially changed its name to AARP in 1999.

Same-sex behavior was not very common, but approximately 6% of men from 18 to 59 years had engaged in same-sex behavior, such as oral or anal sex, with another man in the past year (Herbenick et al., 2010). However, approximately 14% reported such behavior over their lifetime.

Women's Sexual Behaviors. Approximately 40% of women across all age groups reported having masturbated during the past year, except for women over 70 years of age (Herbenick et al., 2010). As was true of men, approximately 43% of women reported vaginal intercourse being the most common sexual behavior with which they engaged. The percentages of women engaging in vaginal intercourse began decreasing in their 30s and continued to decrease through old age. Approximately 80% of women over 70 years had no vaginal intercourse in the previous year.

Masturbating with a partner, or noncoital sex, was reported most often in women between 25 and 49 years of age (Herbenick et al., 2010). Oral sex was more common with women, with more than half of women from 18 to 49 years of age having had oral sex from a male partner in the past year. Anal sex was a behavior approximately 40% of women engaged in during their lifetime, which is similar to the rate of anal sex for men.

Same-sex behavior was reported by less than 5% of women during the past year, again being very similar to men (Herbenick et al., 2010). Oral sex with another woman was the most prevalent same-sex behavior.

Common Findings for both Men and Women. In general, both men and women begin partnered sexual relations at age 14, with sexual activity increasing sharply for 18 to 24 year olds (Herbenick et al., 2010). Findings show these sexual activities continue during the 20s and through the 40s, with a decline beginning in the 50s and continuing into older age. These changes in sexual activity as one ages is considered to be attributed to health issues and the loss of a partner.

ABC News Survey

We would also like to discuss the results of a recent study, the American Sex Survey, conducted by ABC News. The ABC survey confirms much of what the earlier research found, concluding, "the vast majority of Americans are monogamous and happy about it, expressing satisfaction with their sex lives and a broad preference for emotional commitment in sexual relationships. Most by far prefer marriage to the single life" (Langer, Arnedt, & Sussman, 2004, p. 1).

ABC conducted a telephone poll of 1,501 randomly sampled American adults. Differences between men and women were illuminating:

- Forty-three percent of the men in the survey said they thought about sex several times a day; only 13% of the women thought about sex that much.
- Eighty-three percent of the men said they enjoyed sex "a great deal"; 59% of the women said they enjoyed sex "a great deal"; women, however, were equally likely to say they were satisfied with their sex lives.
- Women, on average, reported that they had 6 sex partners in their lifetime; men reported 20. A better measure of sexual activity, however, was the median for both. (The median is the midpoint where half the participants scored higher, and half of the participants scored lower.) Women reported a median of three sex partners, and men a median of eight. ABC explained that the averages are higher than the medians because a small number of individuals, especially men, reported a very high number of sex partners.

Young people become sexually active at an earlier age than in previous generations of Americans, and they also tend to have more sexual partners over a lifetime. But there seems to be a trend toward more conservative sexual behavior, perhaps because of the threat of sexually transmitted diseases.

Five percent of the men in the ABC sample said they had 99 or more sex partners, including four men who reported 200, three who reported 300, and one who reported 400. For the women, 1% reported more than 99 sex partners, and the high was 100 (reported by two women).

- Forty-two percent of the men reported having had sex on a first date, while only 17% of the women reported this.
- Women were more conservative than men on other sexual attitudes and behaviors as well: 84% said there was too much sex on TV, while 62% of the men agreed; 54% of the women condoned sex before marriage, compared to 68% of the men; 31% of the men said they slept in the nude, while only 14% of the women said they did; 51% of the women preferred sex with the lights off, while only 27% of the men liked it this way; 54% of the men thought participating in a sex chat room was cheating on the partner, while 72% of the women thought it was cheating; 15% of all men had paid for sex, and 30% of single men had paid for sex. None of the women reported this.
- About half the women said they had faked an orgasm.

Sexuality in the Later Years

AARP commissioned a research study of individuals age 45 years and older, focusing on attitudes toward and experience with sexual intimacy. The study was conducted in 2004 and included a representative sample of nearly 1,700 men and women. The data were gathered by way of a lengthy questionnaire (AARP, 2005).

The study indicated that, for more than half of those participating in the study, sexual activity contributed to their quality of life. Although we often think of older adults as having no sexual feelings, a vast majority of individuals in this study had a positive attitude about sex. One-half of the respondents said they were extremely or somewhat satisfied with their sex life. As one might expect, those in the younger age groups were more satisfied with their sex life than those who were 70 years and older, and women were more satisfied with their sex life than men.

Approximately one-third of all participants, approximately half of those with regular sexual partners, had sexual intercourse once a week or more. Two-thirds of the participants in this study were married or had a regular sexual partner, and most had been with their partner for more than 10 years (AARP, 2005). Not only do many individuals in the middle and later years of life view a satisfying sexual relationship as being important, approximately two-thirds of participants who had a regular sex partner said they discussed sexual satisfaction with their partner.

The health of the partners in the relationship had an important effect on sexual satisfaction, with health problems identified as the most significant factor affecting sexual satisfaction. Medical conditions and medication were often cited as the reason for sexual dissatisfaction. Some of the health conditions that had a negative affect on sex were high blood pressure, high cholesterol, arthritis or rheumatism, back problems, diabetes, and depression.

Many of the participants in this study wanted to improve their sexual satisfaction. One-fifth of participants, more men than women, have sought treatment for sexual dysfunction. Fourteen percent of the participants, again more men than women, have used medicines, hormones, and other treatments to improve sexual function and activity. Approximately two-thirds of the participants who had used treatments for sexual dysfunction felt it had increased their satisfaction and enjoyment of sex. In addition to health issues, less stress and more initiative from their partner were cited as things that could increase sexual satisfaction.

It is clear from the AARP study that the majority of individuals age 45 and older seek a healthy and satisfying sex life. They talk about improving their sex life with their partner, they seek out medical care for sexual dysfunction, and they take medications to enhance sexual functioning. Sexuality plays an important part in couple relationships.

Gay-Male and Lesbian Sexual Behavior

Homosexuality can be defined as romantic or sexual attraction or behavior among members of the same sex. When speaking of homosexuality as a sexual orientation, this means that an individual has an enduring pattern or disposition to experience sexual, affectional, or romantic attractions primarily with people of the same sex. Sexual orientation also refers to the individual's feelings of personal and social identification as a gay or lesbian, based on these attractions, behaviors expressing them, and membership in a community of other people who share these attractions (American Psychological Association, 2010).

Homosexuality is one of the three main categories of sexual orientation, along with heterosexuality and bisexuality. These three together make up what has been termed the heterosexual–homosexual continuum. Basically, human sexuality is commonly seen by many professionals as not an either/or type of issue, but on a continuum. In essence, researchers have consistently found that some people throughout life have always been heterosexual, some people throughout life have always been homosexual, and other people have had a mix of feelings toward and experiences with both men and women. The most common terms used today are *gay* for a homosexual male and *lesbian* for a homosexual female, though some people prefer other terms or none at all. Sometimes homosexual males and females, when talked about as a group, are called gays.

The number of people who identify as gay or lesbian, and the percentage who have had same-sex sexual experiences, have always been difficult for researchers to reliably determine. This is because individuals are often quite guarded about issues surrounding their sexuality, especially in the case of gays and lesbians. One recent study found that 20% of the participants anonymously reported some homosexual feelings, though relatively few of the participants identified themselves as homosexual (McConaghy, Hadzi-Pavlovic, Stevens, & Manicavasagar, 2006).

According to a study conducted by Gotta et al. (2011), both heterosexual couples and same-sex couples reported having less non-monogamous sex in 2000 compared with 1975. Gay men reported the greatest decrease during that time. Agreements about monogamy are likely to be a result of the HIV/AIDS disease and fears about contacting other sexually transmitted diseases (Gotta et al., 2011).

In many ways, gay male and lesbian relationships are like heterosexual relationships. In the past, gay male couples have been less likely to maintain monogamous relationships (Green, 2012). However, men in general are less likely to have monogamous relationships than women. Over the past 25 years gay men and lesbians have increasingly moved toward developing and maintaining ongoing relationships with one person.

Perhaps the greatest difference between gays and straights in American culture has to do with the stigmatization that same-sex relationships face in this culture. Gay people are frequently the targets of prejudice, have to endure malicious jokes and bullying, and sometimes experience violence against them. They experience discrimination in the employment and housing markets, and in most communities they hold little political power. Gangs of teenagers and young adults have terrorized gays, and stories of brutality against gays by police and military personnel are not uncommon. And as we have seen earlier in this chapter, most states in this country still refuse to recognize the rights of gay and lesbian couples in the same way that the rights of heterosexual couples are honored through marriage.

Sexual Behavior Among Adolescents and Young Adults

Research indicates that by the time adults in this country reach age 44, generally seen as the end of the childbearing years, 99% of Americans have had sex; 95% have had sex before being married; and 74% have had sex before age 20. Even among young people who abstain from sex until age 20 or later, 81% eventually had sex before marriage. (The average age for marriage, as we have seen, is 25 for women and 27 for men.) And, contrary to the widespread public perception that premarital sex is much more common today than in the past, even among women born in the 1940s, nearly 9 in 10 had sex before they were married. In other words, premarital sex is almost universal and has been so for decades (Finer, 2007). (See Figure 6.1.)

Clearly, sex before marriage is statistically normal. Sex among young people is also common. By the time young women in this country reach their 18th birthday, 6 in 10 of them will have had sexual intercourse. By the time young men reach their 18th birthday, more than 5 in 10 of them will have had sexual intercourse (Abma et al., 2004).

FIGURE 6.1
Premarital Sex in
America.
Source: From Boonstra HD,
The case for a new approach
to sex education mounts; will
policymakers heed the message?
Guttmacher Policy Review, 2007,
10(2):2–7. Reproduced with
permission.

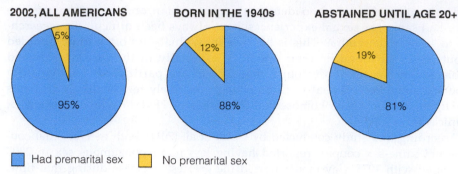

Had premarital sex   No premarital sex

Note: Percentages are of Americans who had premarital sex by age 44.

Unintended Consequences: Teen Pregnancies and Sexually Transmitted Infections (STIs)

Unfortunately, approximately 750,000 teen pregnancies occur each year, and 82% of these are unintended. More than one-fourth of teen pregnancies end in abortion (Guttmacher Institute, 2006; Finer et al., 2006). The pregnancy rate among teenage women in the United States aged 15 to 19 has steadily declined in recent years—from 117 pregnancies per 1,000 young women in 1990 to 75 pregnancies per 1,000 young women in 2002 (Guttmacher Institute, 2006). However, the United States continues to have one of the highest teen pregnancy rates in the developed world—nearly twice as high as teen pregnancy rates in England, Wales, and Canada, and eight times as high as teen pregnancy rates in the Netherlands and Japan (Singh & Darroch, 1998).

So, what is the long-term impact on teen pregnancy? In a recent study, over 500 participants who had a child before the age of 20 were followed until the age of 53 (Taylor, 2009). These participants were compared to delayed child bearers, who had children at an average age for that time. The researcher in this study found that early child bearers were more likely to have less education and less prestigious careers, and were less physically healthy. They also had less stable marriages. These participants who were pregnant as teens were as likely as later child bearers, however, to have satisfying marriages and to feel good about their jobs, and they experienced a high degree of social and psychological support. The author of this research study concludes that there are areas where adolescent pregnancies create vulnerabilities, but there are also areas where individuals adapt and rise to the challenges they experienced with a teenage pregnancy.

Another unintended consequence of sexual activity among adolescents and young adults is a high rate of sexually transmitted infections (STIs) in this country. Every year about 9 million new STIs occur among young people in America. Compared with rates of gonorrhea and chlamydia among teens in Canada and Western Europe, U.S. teens have extremely high rates of infection (Weinstock et al., 2004; Darroch, Frost, & Singh, 2001).

What accounts for these international differences? Researchers have found, for example, that U.S. teens have levels of sexual activity similar to levels among teens in Canada, England, and France. However, American teens are more likely to have shorter and more sporadic sexual relationships and are less likely to use contraceptives than their peers (Weinstock et al., 2004; Darroch, Frost, & Singh, 2001).

Education for Sexuality

Teen pregnancy has declined 40% since its peak in 1990, and is at its lowest level in 30 years (Centers for Disease Control and Prevention, 2009). Two competing approaches to sex education in America have emerged in recent decades: the comprehensive approach to sex education, which stresses abstinence and responsible decision making, but also includes information on contraception and avoiding sexually transmitted infections; and the abstinence-only-until-marriage approach, which argues that nonmarital sex is immoral behavior and people should "just say no."

Both sides are convinced that much of the decline in teen pregnancy can be attributed to their efforts. The abstinence-only proponents have received approximately $1.5 billion since 1996 from the federal government for just-say-no programs in schools (Advocates for Youth, 2010a). The comprehensive sex education proponents report that their research indicates that improved contraceptive use and the use of more effective birth control methods among teenagers explain 86% of the recent declines in teen pregnancy, not teens simply abstaining from sex. They also argue that abstinence-only is unrealistic, because research indicates that 9 out of 10 Americans have sex before marriage and this has been true for decades; and that two decades of research have failed to find evidence that abstinence-only programs delay sexual activity or reduce teen pregnancy (Guttmacher Institute, 2007a, b). A national poll found that Americans overwhelmingly favor broader sexuality education programs over those that discuss only abstinence: 81% said young people should be taught about abstinence, pregnancy, and the prevention of sexually transmitted diseases (STDs); 18% said young people should be taught only abstinence; and 1% had no opinion (Henry J. Kaiser Family Foundation/ABC Television, 1998).

According to interviews the Kaiser Foundation conducted in 2000 with parents, 65% believed that sex education should encourage young people to delay sexual

Because parents tend to be poor at providing their children with clear, useful information about sex, the responsibility for sex education in our society has fallen largely to schools and communities. Sex education is more effective when combined with access to a health clinic where contraceptives are available.

TABLE 6.3	Ten Ridiculous Ideas That Will Make You a Father

- You can count on your partner to use birth control.
- Men have stronger sex drives than women do.
- Men need to have sex with different women to learn to be better lovers.
- If a woman uses birth control, then she has probably been sleeping around.
- A woman would do anything to keep from getting pregnant.
- It is easy for a woman to get on the pill.
- If a man hasn't gone all the way by the time he's 16, then something is wrong with him.

- I don't like condoms.
- When a woman says no, she really just wants to be talked into it.
- I could never talk to my partner about birth control.

Source: Adapted with permission from the brochure "Ten Ridiculous Ideas That Will Make a Father Out of You" (Planned Parenthood of Central Oklahoma, 2000), www.ppcok.org/

activity but also prepare them to use birth control and practice safe sex when they do become sexually active. Among the one-third of parents who said that adolescents should be told "only to have sex when they are married," the overwhelming majority said that schools should teach adolescents how to get tested for HIV/AIDS and other STDs (86%), how to talk with a partner about birth control and STDs (77%), how to use condoms (71%), and where to get and how to use other birth control methods (68%) (Dailard, 2001, p. 5).

Similarly, a subsequent study by NPR, the Kaiser Family Foundation, and the Kennedy School of Government at Harvard University found that only 7% of Americans believed that sex education should not be taught in schools. "The debate over whether to have sex education in American schools is over," NPR declared. "Moreover, in most places there is even little debate about what *kind* of sex education should be taught, although there are still pockets of controversy." (NPR, 2004.)

The most recent study we could find concurred. A random-digit-dial survey of 1,284 California parents found that overall, 89% of the parents reported a preference for comprehensive sex education and 11% favored abstinence-only education (Constantine, Jerman, & Huang, 2007).

Planned Parenthood, a national private nonprofit organization, has developed a wide variety of presentations and materials to benefit young people. A sample of the organization's materials, displayed in Table 6.3, lists some common misconceptions young people have about sex—"ridiculous ideas" that can lead to trouble.

Sexuality Education and Parents

Although people disagree about sexuality, there is agreement on one issue—that education about sexuality should begin in the home. The reason that schools, religious institutions, and agencies such as Planned Parenthood have become involved in sex education is that most parents feel incapable of or uncomfortable about talking seriously with their offspring about sexual matters. A subtle conspiracy of silence exists between parent and child. Parents tell themselves that they are willing to answer any questions their children might have about sex, but children sense that their parents really do not want to talk about these sensitive issues. Because both feel uncomfortable talking about sexuality, they avoid the subject.

Joyce, a 45-year-old single mother of three, describes growing up in a home in which her parents avoided any mention of sex, her early self-consciousness about her own sexuality, and her unease in talking to her own children about sex. Through sexuality education, she overcame her anxieties and can now talk freely about sexual matters.

> "My parents were intelligent, sensitive individuals, and yet they treated the subject of sex like it was the plague. All I knew for sure was this must really be something if it was such a big secret! What happened with my brothers and sister (and me) was there were a lot of misconceptions and a lot of guilt.
>
> "As a parent, what kind of message did I give my children? In my head I knew what I wanted to give them, but in my gut I was still at war with my own sexuality. So I, too, gave mixed messages to my children about sex. It wasn't until I went back to college full-time after my divorce and got into a human sexuality class that the shift really came for me internally. I began to stop feeling self-conscious and began to relax—to enjoy being human. I still have one child living at home, and I'm able to talk openly and honestly with him about any subject regarding sex.
>
> "I feel strongly about good sex education for our children. Two years ago I would have been floored by the idea of showing films on sexual intercourse, masturbation, and gay and lesbian lovemaking to 12-year-olds and their parents in a church setting. Today, I would support it 100%. I wish sex education could be available to all children and their parents at least by the time kids are 12 years old."

Few children receive direct instruction from their parents in the areas of sexuality, sexual intercourse, or birth control (Miller, 2002; Miller, Benson, & Galbraith, 2001; Miller, Sage, & Winward, 2006). See more about father-child communication in Box 6.1. This is sad because good parental communication about sex might forestall or postpone a child's sexual activity. Among those daughters who are sexually active, parental communication appears to help promote more effective contraceptive practices on the part of the adolescent. In one study describing how African American mothers talk to their children about sex, it was found that mothers talk more to their daughters about sex than they talk to their sons (Kapungu, 2010). This finding is consistent with research with other populations. Reasons for this might be that mothers do not know how to talk to sons, talking about menstruation to daughters may be a way to start the discussion, and they experience real concern about their daughters getting pregnant.

There is less pregnancy risk if adolescents have intercourse less often or with fewer partners, as well as by using contraception at first or most recent intercourse and by using contraception consistently over time. Elevated risk of adolescent pregnancy is associated with living with a single parent and living in a lower socioeconomic status family. There is also more risk if a women has older sexually active siblings, has been a victim of sexual abuse, or is residing in a disorganized/dangerous neighborhood (Miller, Sage, & Winward, 2006).

A nationally representative survey of 15- to 17-year-old youth in the United States complements Gordon's findings (Advocates for Youth, 2010b). *Seventeen* magazine and the Henry J. Kaiser Family Foundation in 2002 studied sexual health communication between teens and their parents. The researchers found:

- 51% of teens (61% of females, 42% of males) had discussed with their parents "how to know when you are ready for sex."
- 43% of teens (53% of females, 33% of males) had discussed with their parents how to talk to a boyfriend or girlfriend about sexual health issues, such as pregnancy, birth control, and STIs.

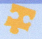

Box 6.1   Putting It Together

Father-Child Communication about Sex

Looking at 49 studies about communication between fathers and children about sex, we know that fathers play an important role in their children's sexual development. Here are some of the findings of studies from 1980 through 2010, with most of the studies conducted in the 2000s:

- In order of the extent to which fathers communicate with their children about sex, Black and Latino fathers communicated the most, then White fathers, and finally Asian fathers. We can conclude that culture impacts father-child communication about sex.
- Generally, fathers who are more educated communicate with their children about sex more often.
- Fathers talk more to their sons than they talk to their daughters about sex.
- Fathers whose parents talked with them about sex are more likely to talk to their children about sex. This positive communication about sex from one generation to the next is worth noting.

- Fathers with permissive attitudes about sex are more likely to talk with their children about safe sex, and more conservative fathers are likely to talk to their children about values.
- The frequency and quality of discussions about sex are related to the extent to which fathers communicate with their children about other issues. If they talk often about nonsexual issues, they are more likely to talk about sexual issues.
- There are no conclusive findings that children's sexual behavior is related to the extent to which they talk with their fathers about sex. Therefore, positive communication about sex does not necessarily affect children's sexual behavior.

Source: Wright, 2009.

- Among male teens, 50% had discussed condoms, but only 35% had discussed other forms of birth control, with parents. Overall, 52% of teens had discussed condoms, and 49% had discussed other forms of contraception.
- 56% of teens (64% of females, 48% of males) had discussed HIV/AIDS with their parents.
- 50% of teens (56% of females, 44% of males) had discussed STIs with their parents.

Why can't parents and teens talk about sex? The study found that:

- 83% of the teens worried about their parents' reaction.
- 88% worried that parents would think they have had sex or are going to have sex.
- 78% cited embarrassment as a big reason.
- 78% of teens (83% of females, 71% of males) said they didn't know how to bring the subject up with parents.

Brent Miller and his colleagues studied how strictness of parenting was related to adolescents' sexual attitudes and behaviors (Miller et al., 2001). These researchers hypothesized and found a curvilinear relationship between flexibility in parenting and sexual behavior. Sexual promiscuity and the experience of intercourse were highest among teenagers who saw their parents as not being strict or as not having any rules (chaotic on the Couple and Family Map; see Chapter 3), lowest among those teens who reported that their parents were moderately strict (flexible on the Couple and Family Map), and intermediate among teenagers who saw their parents as being very strict and having many rules (rigid on the Couple and Family Map). The results of this study suggest that if parents are concerned about adolescent sexual behavior, they can err in two directions: by being either too lenient (chaotic) or too strict (rigid). The more balanced levels (being structured or flexible on the Couple and Family Map) are related to more responsible sexual behavior on the part of adolescents.

Is Sex Education Effective?

In a review of research findings, Advocates for Youth (2010b) concludes that comprehensive sex education helps delay the onset of sexual activity, reduce the frequency of sexual activity, reduce the number of sexual partners, and increase condom and contraceptive use. The organization also says the evidence shows that youth receiving comprehensive sex education are not more likely to become sexually active, increase sexual activity, or experience negative sexual health outcomes. Effective programs have been implemented for young people from a variety of racial, cultural, and socioeconomic backgrounds.

Advocates for Youth began in 1980 as the Center for Population Options and concluded that it could best serve young people by advocating for a more positive and realistic approach to adolescent sexual health. The organization reviewed research on abstinence-only programs and found "little if any evidence" that the programs are effective. Advocates for Youth concluded, "No abstinence-only program has yet been proven through rigorous evaluation to help youth delay sex for a significant period of time, help youth decrease the number of sex partners, or reduce STI or pregnancy rates among teens" (Advocates for Youth, 2010b, p. 2).

The nationwide controversy is not likely to end soon. Because the best sex education of all begins in the home, parents are encouraged to learn quickly how to talk calmly, openly, and honestly with their children from a young age when the questions start coming. Sex education should not be left up to the television set, the movies, the Internet, the pornography industry, or a child's friends on the street. Because schools and religious institutions face so many political obstacles in providing comprehensive sex education, including the discussion of gay and lesbian issues, it is essential that parents begin to prepare themselves to be sex educators for their children.

Sexual Behavior, Alcohol, and College

Most young people (75% of boys and 60% of girls) will have had sex by the time they graduate from high school, and the majority of those who have not will have their first sexual experience while in college. During this developmental period in life, the sexual experience tends to be sporadic, furtive, and poorly managed. Even sexually experienced students entering college therefore have much to learn in the sexual arena (Centers for Disease Control and Prevention, 2010b; Cooper, 2002).

In a culture that glorifies sex and drinking, it is of no surprise that the college campus is probably little different from anywhere else. Alcohol use and risky sexual behavior among college students are strongly linked. Cooper (2002) found that having multiple or casual sex partners, failing to discuss risk issues before having sex, the decision to have sex itself, and inconsistent use of condoms and birth control were all related to alcohol use.

One research team looked at sexual behavior, alcohol, and housing in a northwestern university in the United States (Dinger & Parsons, 1999). The team found that:

It has been estimated that 400,000 college students between age 18 and 24 have had unprotected sex after drinking in a given year, and an estimated 100,000 had sex when they were so intoxicated they were unable to consent.

- 39.4 percent of students living in fraternity/sorority housing reported having six or more sexual partners compared to 22.8% of students in residence halls.
- 15 percent of students living in fraternity/sorority housing reported more than 20 acts of sexual intercourse prior to the study compared to 5% of students living in residence halls.
- 38.2 percent of the students in the study reported drinking alcohol or using other drugs prior to their last sexual intercourse; students living in fraternity/sorority housing were more likely to report this behavior (50%) than students living in residence halls (30.4%).
- 60.3 percent of students reported using a condom at last sexual intercourse; condom use did not differ by residence or fraternity/sorority affiliation.

Estimates indicate that 400,000 college students between the ages of 18 and 24 had unprotected sex after drinking in a given year, and an estimated 100,000 had sex when they were so intoxicated they were unable to consent (Hingson & Howland, 2002). (See Table 6.4.) Another investigator looked at the connection between drinking and teen childbearing and found that teenage girls who binge drink are up to 63% more likely to become teen mothers (Dee, 2001).

TABLE 6.4	Risky Sexual Behavior		

Percentage of sexually active young people who say . . .

	Teens 15 to 17	Young Adults 18 to 24
Alcohol or drugs influenced their decision to do something sexual.	29%	37%
They did more sexually than planned because they had been drinking or using drugs.	24%	31%
They worried about STDs or pregnancy because of something they did sexually while drinking or using drugs.	26%	28%
They used alcohol or drugs to help them feel more comfortable with a sexual partner.	13%	16%
They had unprotected sex because they were drinking or using drugs.	12%	25%

Source: Substance Abuse and Risky Behavior: Attitudes and Practices Among Adolescents and Young Adults: Survey Snapshot by the Henry J. Kaiser Family Foundation and the National Center on Addiction and Substance Abuse at Columbia University, February 6, 2002.

Marital and Extramarital Sexual Behavior

Surveys indicate that most young people have intercourse before marriage; in fact, premarital relationships are often highly sexual. Current research shows that 95% of individuals have had sex before marriage, with 93% indicating they did so by age 30 (Wind, 2006). In fact, this study indicates that this high percentage of people having premarital sex has been evident for a long time, with nearly 9 out of 10 women born in the 1940s indicating they had sex before marriage. The fact that couples are waiting to get married until their late 20s means that individuals have more years available to have sexual relationships before they enter into marriage (Wind, 2006). After marriage, the sexual relationship gradually changes. Some people have jokingly asked, "Is there sex after marriage?" Research indicates there is.

Sex Within Marriage

Years ago when newspaper columnist Ann Landers asked her readers, "Has your sex life gone downhill since you got married?" 82% of the 141,210 people who responded said yes, sex after marriage was less exciting (Landers, 1989). However, intimacy—feelings of warmth and closeness between two people who love each other—does not appear to diminish with time. Within the intimate environment of a happy marriage, sexual experiences can become more satisfying and meaningful—and retain their excitement—over time.

Although most young people have intercourse before marriage, premarital relationships are often highly sexual. But, in many ways it is more meaningful as the strength of the partnership grows. Friendship may deepen, while the sex drive may slowly diminish.

A hectic life often gets in the way of an active sex life. Long hours on the job, caring for children, continual interruptions, and countless other stresses tend to tire people out and decrease their sexual activity. For those couples with two jobs, the phenomenon has been called the **DINS** (double income, no sex) **dilemma**. Therapists have labeled it *inhibited*, or *hypoactive, sexual desire*. In addition to sheer fatigue, boredom is also a factor for some individuals. Most of the time, couples can resuscitate the sexual relationship with some tender care and concern, such as having dinner out together, seeing a movie, or going to bed early. Consulting a marriage and family therapist or a sex therapist may be useful for persistent sexual problems. The preeminent sex researchers and therapists William Masters and Virginia Johnson, along with Robert Kolodny (1998), argued that half of all American couples are troubled at some time by some type of sexual distress, ranging from disinterest to genuine sexual dysfunction.

For many people, sex is not the most important thing in life. A nationwide survey of 815 men found that the most important thing in a man's life is not sex, career, fame, or fortune, but marriage, according to 75% of the married men in the sample. About 90% of these husbands called their wives their best friends. Friendship, based on trust and sharing of responsibilities, becomes more important as life's challenges mount and sexual energy decreases (Hellmich, 1990).

Although sex is clearly not everything, it is important to an intimate relationship. Barry McCarthy (2001, 2003, 2009) explained that when sex goes well, it is 15% to 20% of a relationship; but if there are sexual problems, then it has a much more powerful role of 50% to 75%, and it robs the marriage of intimacy and vitality. Sex is more than a simple physical need; it also impacts the quality of the marriage.

Different people have different needs for sexual intimacy, and those needs affect how they perceive their sexual behavior. For this reason, couples must communicate clearly about sex if they are to maintain a satisfying relationship. The classic movie *Annie Hall* depicts two lovers with different perceptions of their sexual relationship. When friends ask them (separately) how often they have sex, the character played by Woody Allen answers, "Hardly ever, maybe three times a week"; the character played by Diane Keaton replies, "Constantly, three times a week."

Overall, it appears that in many marriages sex is very important for long-term happiness. It has powerful symbolic value in a successful marriage, reaffirming the bond between the individuals. It is an indication that everything is still okay despite wrinkles, sags, and love handles. To keep the spark in their lovemaking, married couples need to keep the relationship alive through communication and sharing. It is very difficult to have a successful sexual relationship if each partner does not feel good about herself or himself or about other aspects of the relationship. Serena, a middle-aged woman in St. Louis, describes the "sexy relationship" she has with her husband, a relationship founded not just on physical attraction but on a number of elements that make her marriage strong and healthy.

> *"Our sexual relationship is great today. It's a lot better than it was early in our marriage. I don't know why exactly, but I think we're more used to each other, more comfortable with each other. Perhaps we really love each other more. As the years pass, you look back and see a long-term tradition of commitment and kindness, and recognize that you have really created a wonderful marriage together.*
>
> *"That's very special, and it makes you feel so very close to each other. It's hard to explain, but we do have a very sexy relationship with each other. Perhaps not as often as before, but it sure can be full of fire and tenderness."*

Marital Styles and Sexual Behavior

Four types of marital dynamics were identified by Barry McCarthy (2001, 2003, 2009), and he found that each style had sexual strengths and problems. The four styles were complementary couples, conflict-minimizing couples, best-friend couples, and emotionally expressive couples. These are not "pure" styles, and couples can sometimes change their styles over time.

Complementary Couples. This was the most common marital style (also called validating or supportive), and each partner has power in certain domains and moderate levels of intimacy. They validate each other's worth and value the marital bond. Sex for them becomes a low priority and often becomes routine, like watching the evening news. Usually the male is in charge of sexuality, and he overemphasizes intercourse at the expense of affection and intimacy. As the couple ages, sexuality drops considerably.

Conflict-Minimizing Couples. These couples are the most stable couple style (also called traditional) and usually have traditional roles. Strong emotional expression is discouraged. The male initiates sex and decides on the sexual style. Sex is very predictable and is rarely discussed.

Best-Friend Couples. This style values intimacy the most and considers friendship to be a strong foundation of their marriage. When the relationship works well, sex is an integral part of the marriage. Sex energizes the relationship and the marital bond is strong. The major pitfall is that it is a difficult style to maintain and it has a high rate of divorce. High expectations and disillusion rob the marriage of its excitement and pleasure.

Emotionally Expressive Couples. This style is full of feelings and can range from intense feelings of love and anger (also called volatile or explosive). Sex is often passionate, exciting, fun, and playful. A healthy pattern can be that sex occurs as a way of making up from conflict or a fight. The problem is that the conflict can often drive the couple apart and it could end in a "divorce from hell."

In summary, each marital style has both positive and negative consequences on the sexual relationship. Most couples develop a style that works for them and find it hard to change it over time, even when they are dissatisfied.

Infidelity

Extramarital friendships are common in American society. As one husband put it, "It doesn't make a whole lot of sense to deny friendships across-the-board to half the human race. If I enjoy talking with a person at work, it doesn't make sense to lose this friendship just because she's a female." Ideally, couples should allow each other the freedom to develop relationships outside the marriage. But if they are not properly handled, friendships with members of the other sex can harm a marriage. These friendships can sometimes develop into extramarital sexual relationships, which are commonly cited as one reason for divorce. Opinion is divided on whether men and women can be friends—loving, affectionate, accepting, and so on—without becoming sexually involved.

Blow and Hartnett (2005) reviewed the research conducted on infidelity from 1980 through 2005. They summarized the research from the perspectives of attitude toward infidelity, prevalence, type of infidelity, infidelity by gender, and several other demographic characteristics. Based on this review, they drew the following conclusions:

- Attitudes about infidelity are related to actions, and those with more positive attitudes about infidelity are more likely to engage in infidelity.
- Attitudes about infidelity differ based on culture, gender, type of couple relationship (e.g., heterosexual, gay/lesbian, dating, marriage), behaviors that make up the infidelity (e.g., kiss, intercourse, emotional connection), and prior experience with infidelity.
- Internationally, differences in attitudes and behaviors vary by country and culture.
- Men are more likely to see a distinction between love and sex than women, with men more likely to view infidelity as only sexual and not emotional.
- Men are more likely to engage in sexual infidelity than women.
- Over the course of married heterosexual relationships in the United States, extramarital sex occurs in less than 25% of committed relationships.
- Dissatisfaction with the marital relationship is related to increased incidence of infidelity.
- There appear to be at least three types of infidelity: emotional-only, sexual-only, and combined sexual and emotional infidelity. Most research is about sexual infidelity.
- Some studies show that gay men are less concerned about infidelity than heterosexual couples. Lesbian couples are less likely to experience infidelity than gay couples.

Emily Brown, a social worker, offers a different perspective on affairs. She identifies six stages in the process of infidelity (Brown, 2000b). The first stage occurs when a climate develops in which infidelity can germinate, such as a couple's allowing hurt, dissatisfaction, and differences to go unresolved. Betrayal occurs in the second stage. The more dissatisfied spouse "slides" into the infidelity. The unfaithful spouse denies it is happening, and the other spouse may collude by ignoring obvious signs. The infidelity is revealed in the third stage. At this stage, both partners realize they will never be able to picture themselves or their marriage again in the same way. According to Brown, this stage requires a lot of time for partners to process; both need to experience the shock and fury of what happened, why it happened, what it means, and what the underlying issues might be. The impact can be as severe as the revelation of sexual abuse. The fourth stage involves admission of a crisis in the marriage. Brown believes that too often the infidelity itself is seen as the crisis rather than the problem she believes underlies the infidelity. In the fifth stage, the partners make a decision either to address all of the issues involved or to bury them and get on with rebuilding the marriage. The sixth and final stage involves forgiveness. Brown believes this can take place only if the preceding five stages have been successfully addressed and resolved.

There is an assumption that couples typically have equal power in a relationship and intervention strategies are carried out with that assumption. However, for some couples and in some cultures, power may not be equal and because of this unequal power, infidelity can be viewed very differently (Williams, 2011). For example, many cultures are male-dominated and there may be an acceptance of infidelity on the part of men, but no acceptance on the part of women. Zhang (2010) found that attitudes and behaviors regarding infidelity were very different between men and women in China. Men had a more permissive attitude and were more likely than women to engage in sex outside of marriage. Therefore, the cultural context of the couple is an important component in understanding how a couple will respond to acts of infidelity and how the issue is resolved, if it is resolved.

The American Association for Marriage and Family Therapy (AAMFT, 2010) argues that the disclosure of infidelity can be devastating to a relationship. Intense emotions and recurrent crises are the norm. But AAMFT also notes that the majority of marriages not only survive an affair but can become stronger and more intimate. Couple therapy can be a useful tool for helping this growth begin. Approximately 50% of couples who seek couple therapy do so because an extramarital involvement has occurred.

Family therapists counsel couples dealing with the crisis of infidelity and try to help them work through the situation in a cautious and rational manner. It is clearly challenging, on the part of family therapists, how to deal with infidelity when the offending partner wants to keep the infidelity a secret (Butler, Harper, & Seedall, 2009). The challenge is whether to honor the confidentiality of the person who wants to keep it a secret, or to honor the rights of the partner for equality and justice in the couple relationship. A professional therapist can be very helpful by encouraging spouses to be calm and honest in disclosing their motives. Infidelity can signal the end of a relationship, or it can be a catalyst for dramatic and positive growth in a marriage. (See Box 6.2.)

A recent study described the benefits of marriage education for couples where there has been history of infidelity in their marriage (Allen, Rhoades, Stanley, Loew, & Markman, 2012). These researchers found that couples who had experienced infidelity and who participated in marriage education showed a significant increase in marital satisfaction and in communication skills, as compared to a control group. However, these couples did not experience an increase in marital satisfaction as high as couples who did not experience infidelity in their marriage. Therefore, these findings suggest that couples who have experienced infidelity can improve their marriage by attending marriage education classes.

Toward Sexual Health

Sex is an important part of human life, health, and happiness. It's a crucial ingredient in individual well-being and in intimate relationships, especially marriage. Problems in sexual functioning therefore need to be addressed if people are to have successful relationships.

A survey of common sexual problems identified the most frequent problems for women and men (Laumann, Gagnon, Michael, & Michaels, 1994). About one-third (33.4%) of women reported a lack of interest in sex, as compared to only 15.8% of men. The second most frequent issue for nearly one-quarter of the women surveyed was an inability to reach orgasm (24.1%) and to find sex pleasurable (21.2%). In contrast, roughly one-quarter of the men reported that they reached climax too early (25.5%) or had anxiety about their sexual performance (17%). These symptoms are very similar to the common complaints heard from married couples in which the male feels the female is not interested in him sexually—often because he climaxes too early and does not satisfy her needs. (See also Gagnon, 2004; Laumann et al., 2004; Laumann & Michael, 2000.)

BOX 6.2   Diversity in Families

Extramarital Sex Around the World

Couple therapists view extramarital affairs as one of the most damaging relationship events a couple can face, and one of the most difficult problems to treat in couple therapy. A review of ethnographic accounts of marital dissolution in 160 societies found that infidelity was the single most common cause of the breakup (Whisman, Coop, Gordman, Chatav, 2007). The global sample of research and commentary below will give the reader a better understanding of how diverse cultures address the issue:

- Worldwide, as many as 60% of all condoms are used outside marriage (*Population Reports*, 1999).

- An extramarital affair is the top cause of divorce in Shanghai, the largest city in the People's Republic of China. A 25-year-old worker in a Shanghai computer company was the first person sentenced to jail for violating the Marriage Law enacted in 2001. Chen Yue, 25, was sentenced to six months in prison after being found guilty of having a live-in girlfriend only months after marrying another woman (China.Org.CN, 2001).

- "When a man is with a woman, it feels like electricity." Men in a rural community in central Mexico believe that male sexuality is a natural force that is difficult to control. For this reason, they are permanently suspicious about the fidelity of their wives and the paternity of their own children. Contraceptive use is experienced with some ambivalence by the men— contraceptives help relieve the economic burdens of a large family but promote the sexual freedom of women (Castro, 2001).

- Indonesia's Justice Ministry drafted laws to ban premarital sex, extramarital sex, living together without being married, reneging on a promise to marry, having sex with a prostitute, performing as a stripper, and witchcraft, among other things (*Gay & Lesbian Times*, 2003).

- Dubai police said they had no evidence supporting a British woman's report that she was raped by a waiter in the Gulf Arab emirate. Instead, the police arrested the woman and her boyfriend for having sex outside marriage. The case was the second time in just over a year that Britons were in the headlines for falling afoul of laws in Dubai, a Muslim emirate country popular with sunseeking Westerners. The couple was arrested for having sex without marriage but subsequently released by authorities. The case was given to the public prosecutor, who would decide whether to bring a court case against the couple (Kasolosky, 2010).

- Two U.S. psychologists studied "human mate poaching," the efforts to romantically attract someone who is already in a relationship. The investigators argued that poaching attempts were relatively common (Schmitt & Buss, 2001).

- The Japanese are more accepting of extramarital sex than are Americans. Or, at least, they are more willing to admit this. While 45% of Japanese adults believed that "extramarital affairs are acceptable under certain circumstances," only 12% of Americans said they felt this way. There were few differences between men and women within each country: Only 14% of American men and 11% of American women agree with the 49% of Japanese men and 42% of Japanese women that extramarital affairs can be acceptable (Taylor, 1998).

- An Islamic court in Lagos, Nigeria, sentenced a 20-year-old woman to 100 lashes with a cane in public for having an extramarital affair (PlanetSave.com, 2001).

- Article 340 of the Jordanian penal code reduces or eliminates punishments for men who claim "honor" as their motivation for murdering a female relative. Women who survive such murder attempts face a life in protective custody, because they have nowhere else to turn. Extramarital sex is one breach of this ancient code (Husseini, 2000).

- Senegal's efforts to prevent AIDS have been successful because husbands have been increasingly likely to use condoms during extramarital sex (amFAR AIDS Research, 2004).

- Twenty-eight percent of husbands surveyed in southeastern Nigeria health care centers said they had engaged in extramarital sexual relationships during their wife's pregnancy. Some of the husbands believed that sex during pregnancy should be less frequent or could cause a miscarriage. Other husbands thought sex during pregnancy enhances fetal well-being (Onah, Iloabachie, Obi, Ezugwu, & Eze, 2002).

- Twelve percent of married or cohabiting men in Brazil reported having had at least one extramarital partner in the previous months, researchers found. Forty percent reported having used condoms during the last time they had extramarital sex. Men who belonged to an evangelical church were significantly less likely to engage in extramarital sex. Brazilian men who lived in the northern part of the country were three times more likely to have extramarital sex than men who lived in southern or central Brazil (Hill, Cleland, & Ali, 2004).

- A German medical researcher studying coronary heart disease and sex sees death in the extramarital bed as a significant problem (Neumaier, 2001).

- An academic studying adultery as it is represented in the literature of the Middle Ages (476 to about 1450) finds evidence for a wide variety of perspectives: from defense of adultery and approval through leniency to condemnation; from joyful sexuality on one side to a crass hostility toward sex on the other (Schnell, 2000).

Sexual Dysfunctions

Sexual dysfunction has been defined as a state in which sexual behavior or the lack of it causes anxiety, anguish, and frustration, which can lead to unhappiness and distress in a couple's relationship (Leiblum, 2002, 2007). A review of research about sexual dysfunction is provided by Simons and Carey (2008), where they summarized the findings of 52 studies. These authors suggest that sexual dysfunction may be among the more prevalent disorders, from a psychological perspective. The use of medications such as Viagra and Cialis for men and estrogen therapy for women indicate this may be true (Mayo Clinic, n.d.).

Researchers believe that it may not be possible to identify the precise cause of a particular form of dysfunction, and that some dysfunctions may have multiple causes. Psychological factors that can result in sexual dysfunction are numerous. Developmental factors include troubled parent–child relationships, negative family attitudes toward sex and sexuality, traumatic childhood or adolescent sexual experiences, and conflict over one's gender identity (one's sense of being male or female). Personal factors include a variety of fears: of poor sexual performance, of pregnancy, of venereal disease, of rejection, of pain, of becoming close to someone, of losing control, or even of success. Interpersonal factors that can be related to sexual problems include poor communication and frequent power struggles between partners; hostility, distrust, and deceit; lack of mutual physical attraction; and gender-role conflicts.

Female Sexual Dysfunction. Many women report that their sex life has lost some of its spark because their body feels unresponsive or they are just not interested. This can happen at any age, but is most common when hormones are in flux—just after having a baby or during the transition into menopause. Sexual concerns also may occur during a major illness, such as cancer.

Symptoms include the following: the woman's desire to have sex is low or absent **(low sexual desire)**; the woman cannot maintain arousal during sexual activity, or cannot become aroused even when she wishes to have sex **(sexual arousal disorder)**; she cannot experience an orgasm **(orgasmic disorder)**; she experiences pain during sexual contact **(sexual pain disorder)**.

Findings vary widely in terms of the prevalence of these disorders for women because so many different criteria are used in the various studies. However, Simons and Carey (2008) found that from 6% to 19% of women experienced sexual arousal disorder, depending upon the study. They also found that from 4% to 9% experienced orgasmic disorder, and approximately 12% experienced sexual pain disorder.

Causes of female sexual dysfunction often are a complex interaction of emotions, past experiences, physiology, beliefs, and lifestyles:

- *Physical conditions* that may contribute to sexual problems include arthritis, urinary or bowel difficulties, pelvic surgery, fatigue, headaches, other pain problems, and neurological disorders such as multiple sclerosis.
- *Hormonal conditions* include lower estrogen levels during menopause, leading to changes in genital tissues and sexual responsiveness. The folds of the skin covering the genital region (labia) become thinner during the menopausal transition and expose more of the clitoris. This sometimes reduces the sensitivity of the clitoris or causes unpleasant tingling or a prickling sensation. The vaginal lining also thins and becomes less elastic, especially if the woman is not sexually active. The vagina requires more stimulation

to relax and lubricate before having intercourse, and this can lead to painful intercourse (dyspareunia). Achieving orgasm may also take longer.

- *Psychological and social causes* include untreated anxiety or depression, and long-term stress. The worries of pregnancy and demands of being a new mother can have similar effects. Long-term conflicts with one's partner—conflicts about sex or any other aspects of the relationship—can lead to lack of interest and diminished sexual response. Cultural and religious issues can also contribute, as well as body image problems the woman might have (Clay, 2009; Mayo Clinic, n.d.).

Male Sexual Dysfunction. This is expressed in a variety of ways. **Erectile dysfunction** (formerly called impotence) is the inability to achieve or maintain an erection that is firm enough for intercourse. (Isolated episodes of the inability to achieve or maintain an erection are nearly universal among men.) **Premature ejaculation**, or rapid ejaculation, is difficult to define precisely, although it is a common sexual dysfunction. It causes problems in a sexual relationship when the woman is dissatisfied because the man reaches orgasm much more quickly than she does. **Orgasmic dysfunction**, the opposite of premature ejaculation, is a dysfunction in which prolonged and strenuous effort is needed to reach orgasm. **Painful intercourse**, often believed to be a problem only for women, can also affect men. Pain can be felt in the penis and/or testicles or internally; the pain is often related to a problem with the seminal vesicles or the prostate gland (Insel & Roth, 2010; Mayo Clinic, n.d.).

According to Simons and Carey (2008), erectile dysfunction is identified as an issue with approximately 25% of men. Erectile dysfunction is more common for people with health issues or who take medicines that can effect the ability to have an erection. These same authors indicated that orgasmic dysfunction ranges from

Sexual interactions can be a source of frustration and disappointment, but they can also be a source of happiness and great joy. A satisfying sexual relationship is an important ingredient in a healthy intimate relationship.

9% to 25%. Premature ejaculation is reported by approximately 25% of individuals and orgasmic dysfunction is evident for approximately 15% of men. Finally, painful intercourse for men is relatively low, reporting pain 8% of the time. Again, these numbers are our conclusions after reading the decade review of 52 studies that used a variety of ways and criteria to gather their data.

Sexual dysfunctions are generally something people are uncomfortable admitting to themselves and discussing with others. We can laugh and leer about sex in our society, but we have a difficult time talking honestly and openly about sex.

Sex Therapy

Many people with sexual difficulties go without help for a long time. This is unfortunate, because most **sex therapy** is simply a process of education. Sex therapists instruct clients (people who seek sex therapy are not called patients) in the gentle art of lovemaking.

Reputable professional sex therapists are trained in the subjects of sex and sexuality and have experience working with many different people regarding sexual needs and dysfunctions. A national organization, the American Association of Sexuality Educators, Counselors, and Therapists (AASECT), has established criteria for certifying sex therapists who have met its training standards. AASECT has also developed ethical principles for the practice of sex therapy. Certified counselors and sex therapists can be found on their Web site (www.aasect.org/).

Sex educators typically work with relatively large groups of people and teach general information and principles that are useful to a variety of individuals. **Sex therapists** typically work with individuals, couples, or small groups of individuals and couples and focus more on individual concerns and problems. On the basis of content alone, a sex therapy session can be difficult to discern from a sex education session. The two approaches overlap considerably, so much so that some professionals do not distinguish between sex education and sex therapy.

Solving Sexual Problems. Sex therapy can involve a number of different components, including the following:

- Learning more about basic anatomy.
- Learning what one's true feelings are about the body.
- Learning what one's basic attitudes toward sex and sexuality are.
- Learning to relax with a partner and to get in a sexually responsive mood.
- Learning to sense one's own body and how the setting affects the body's responses.
- Learning sexual techniques.
- Exploring one's own and one's partner's body.
- Developing new sexual attitudes and techniques and maintaining them over time.

Sex therapists are quick to point out that couples with sexual problems should not rush into intercourse but should take time to enjoy each other's company and to touch each other in a variety of loving ways.

Two of the most common self-help techniques for overcoming sexual problems are body exploration and masturbation. Clinicians have found that masturbation exercises are helpful for treating orgasmic dysfunction in women and lack of ejaculatory control in men. Once a woman learns how to reach orgasm through self-stimulation, she can teach her partner the best ways to bring her to orgasm through intercourse. Self-help techniques that help men slow down during masturbation often help them delay ejaculation while making love with a partner (Kelly, 2008).

Susan Iasenza (2010) has written an interesting article about sex as a queer experience. She suggests that therapists need to expand their way of thinking about sex as they work with clients. She indicates that many sex acts are considered either in the gay or straight category and that individuals often feel guilty if they enjoy or get aroused by what is considered in the domain of same-sex couples, if they are heterosexual. She suggests that sexual behavior does not need to be viewed as gay or straight, but that therapists need to create a safe place for couples to enjoy and express their sexual desires in a variety of ways without guilt.

Behavioral exercises may also be prescribed to help couples enrich and expand their sexual awareness and enjoyment. These exercises include sensate focus, the stop-and-go technique, and the squeeze technique.

- *Sensate focus.* This technique teaches couples how to give each partner pleasure without expecting anything in return. The goal is not sexual arousal or intercourse but education. Each partner directs the other, showing her or him what kinds of touches are the most enjoyable and where the sensitive places are. The exercise helps people learn to communicate better sexually.
- *The stop-and-go technique.* This technique teaches men how to control ejaculation and orgasm. The man's partner manually or orally stimulates his penis until he is just about to ejaculate. Then, the partner stops the stimulation, resuming it only when the man is in control. Stimulation and rest may be alternated several times in a session before orgasm and ejaculation are triggered. Repeated sessions over weeks or months help men control rapid or premature ejaculation.
- *The squeeze technique.* In this variation on the stop-and-go technique, when the partner stops stimulating the man's penis, the partner immediately applies pressure to the penis, squeezing it with the thumb and two fingers until there is a tolerable degree of pain. This pattern is repeated seven or eight times until the man learns to tolerate intense stimulation while delaying ejaculation. The squeeze technique further shortens the time it takes to resolve the problem of premature ejaculation (Hyde & DeLamater, 2008).

Summary

- According to a national survey, happily married couples compared to unhappily married couples reported: they were more satisfied with the affection they receive from their partners; they did not have as many concerns about their partner's level of interest in sex; they were less likely to be concerned that their partner was interested in having an affair; they were less likely to feel the partner used sex unfairly; and they had a more satisfying and fulfilling sexual relationship.

- The most commonly reported problems for married couples in terms of their sexual relationship were differing levels of interest in sex between husband and wife, dissatisfaction with the amount of affection received from one's partner, sexual disinterest between partners, difficulty talking about sexual issues, and an inability to keep the sexual relationship interesting and enjoyable.

- Attitudes toward sexuality, including sexual attractiveness and sexual behaviors, vary markedly from one culture to another.

- Sex surveys—such as the National Survey of Sexual Health and Behavior study, the ABC News Survey, and the AARP study—reveal useful information about the sexual behaviors of Americans.
- Three decades after AIDS was first identified, there is still no cure; however, new drug treatments have helped people live longer. Those infected with HIV can spread the virus to others because they may not know for years that they are infected.
- The most effective sex education programs are those that encourage abstinence but at the same time offer an alternative of effective contraceptives to those who choose to remain sexually active or become sexually active.
- Father-child communication is an important component of sexual development for children.
- Although sexual activity often decreases after marriage, this decline is not inevitable. Key elements in keeping the sexual relationship vital include communication, commitment, and investing time to enjoy each other.
- The majority of individuals, even as they age, seek healthy and satisfying sex lives. Health issues and medication are often reasons for a decrease in sexual behavior as people age.
- Types of male sexual dysfunctions include erectile dysfunction, orgasmic dysfunction, premature ejaculation, and painful intercourse. Female sexual dysfunctions include vaginismus, anorgasmia, rapid orgasm, and painful intercourse.
- Sex therapy involves a number of different components, including learning more about basic anatomy, learning what one's true feelings are about the body, and discovering one's basic attitudes toward sex and sexuality.

Key Terms

sexuality	sexual dysfunction
heterosexual	orgasmic dysfunction
homosexual	psychosocial sexual
bisexual	dysfunction
transgender	erectile dysfunction
sexual orientation	premature ejaculation
sex	painful intercourse
gender	vaginismus
incest taboo	anorgasmia
masturbation	rapid orgasm
human immunodeficiency	sex therapy
virus (HIV)	sex educator
DINS dilemma	sex therapist

Activities

1. Is sex truly everywhere in our society? For a day, keep a log, noting what, when, and where you see or hear something with a sexual theme. Several people in the class can work together and report their findings to the larger group.
2. In small groups, discuss the following situation: You are the parent of a 15-year-old son. He is interested in your views on premarital sex. What would you tell him?
3. What are your personal beliefs about premarital sexual behavior? Write a brief essay articulating and supporting your views.
4. Ask someone whose children are grown how they talked to their children about sex.

Suggested Readings

AARP. (n.d.). Sexuality at midlife and beyond. Web site: http://www.aarp.org.

Advocates for Youth. "Established in 1980 as the Center for Population Options, Advocates for Youth champions efforts that help young people make informed and responsible decisions about their reproductive and sexual health. Advocates believes it can best serve the field by boldly advocating for a more positive and realistic approach to adolescent sexual health." The work focuses on 14- to 25-year-olds in the United States and internationally. Web site: http://www.advocates-foryouth.org.

American Association of Sexuality Educators, Counselors and Therapists (AASECT). A not-for-profit, interdisciplinary professional organization promoting the understanding of human sexuality and healthy sexual behavior. "AASECT members include sexuality educators, sexuality counselors and sex therapists, physicians, nurses, social workers, psychologists, allied health professionals, clergy members, lawyers, sociologists, marriage and family counselors and therapists, family planning specialists and researchers, as well as students in relevant professional disciplines. Web site: http://www.aasect.org/.

American Association for Marriage and Family Therapy. (n.d.). AAMFT is the key national organization for advancing the professional interests of marriage and family therapists, and it has excellent educational resources for professionals and laypersons on its Web site: http://www.aamft.org.

Berzon, B. (2004). *Permanent partners: Building gay and lesbian relationships that last* (Rev. ed.). New York: Penguin. Suggestions by a psychotherapist specializing in same-sex relationships for resolving conflicts over power and control, jealousy, differences in sexual desire, money, and family demands.

Blow, A. J., & Hartnett, K. (2005). Infidelity in committed relationships II: A substantive review. *Journal of Marital and Family Therapy, 31,* 217–233.

Centers for Disease Control and Prevention. (2010). *HIV/AIDS surveillance report, 2010, 17.* Atlanta: Author. Web site: http://www.cdc.gov/hiv/topics/surveillance/resources/reports.

Clay, R. A. (2009). The debate over low libidos: Psychologists differ on how to treat a lack of desire among some women. *APA Online Monitor on Psychology, 40*(4), 32. Website: http://www.apa.org/monitor/2009/04/libidos.html. Is it a medical problem or a relationship problem? An excellent discussion of the issues.

Consumer Reports. (2005). CR's guide to contraception. *Consumer Reports* (February), 34–38. Sections on condoms for extra protection; birth control, more and safer choices; a comparative guide to contraceptives; and abortion options.

Giles, J. (2008). *The nature of sexual desire.* Landham, MD: University Press of America.

Guttmacher Institute. Created four decades ago "to advance sexual and reproductive health in the United States and worldwide through an interrelated program of social science research, policy analysis and public education designed to generate new ideas, encourage enlightened public debate, promote sound policy and program development and, ultimately, inform individual decision making." Web site: http://www.guttmacher.org/.

Harvey, J. H. (Ed.). (2004). *The handbook of sexuality in close relationships.* Mahwah, NJ: Erlbaum. Enhances the dialogue about the centrality of sexual issues in close relationships.

Hyde, J. S., & DeLamater, J. D. (2008). *Understanding human sexuality* (10th ed.). Boston: McGraw-Hill Higher Education. An excellent comprehensive textbook.

Kinsey Institute for Research in Sex, Gender, and Reproduction. The Kinsey Institute at Indiana University promotes interdisciplinary research and scholarship in the fields of human sexuality, gender, and reproduction. Web site: http://www.kinseyinstitute.org/.

Levin, D. E., & Kilbourne, J. (2008). *So sexy so soon: The new sexualized childhood and what parents can do to protect their kids.* New York: Ballantine Books. Sex is everywhere in American commercial culture. How to help children live in such an environment.

Mayo Clinic. (n.d.) Excellent resources on extramarital sex, male and female sexual dysfunction. Web site: http://www.mayoclinic.com.

McCarthy, B. W. (2003). *Rekindling desire: A step-by-step program to help low-sex and no-sex marriages.* London: Routledge Mental Health, Taylor & Francis Group.

McCarthy, B. W. (2007). *Men's sexual health: Fitness for satisfying sex.* London: Routledge Mental Health, Taylor & Francis Group.

National Right to Life Committee. Founded in 1973 in response to a U.S. Supreme Court decision released on January 22 of that year, legalizing abortion in all 50 states. "The ultimate goal of the National Right to Life Committee is to restore legal protection to innocent human life. The primary interest of the National Right to Life Committee and its members has been the abortion controversy; however, it is also concerned with related matters of medical ethics which relate to the right to life issues of euthanasia and infanticide." NRLC does not have positions on other issues, such as contraception, sex education, capital punishment, and national defense. Web site: http://www.nrlc.org/.

Peluso, P. (Ed.) (2007). *Infidelity: A practitioner's guide to working with couples in crisis.* London: Routledge Mental Health, Taylor & Francis Group. When one partner in a relationship is unfaithful to the other, salvaging the relationship takes a lot of work by both parties.

Planned Parenthood Federation of America. Planned Parenthood describes itself as "a trusted health care provider, an informed educator, a passionate advocate, and a global partner helping similar organizations around the world." The organization has delivered reproductive health care, sex education, and information for more than 90 years. Ninety locally governed affiliates nationwide operate 850 health centers. Web site: http://www.plannedparenthood.-org/index.htm.

Sexuality Information and Education Council of the United States (SIECUS). Founded by Dr. Mary S. Calderone in 1964, who was concerned about the lack of information about sexuality for both young people and adults. So, at the age of 60, "with determination to live in a world in which sexuality was viewed as a natural and healthy part of life," she founded SIECUS, which publishes books, journals, and resources for professionals, parents, and the public. Web site: http://www.siecus.org/.

Wincze, J. P. (2009). *Enhancing sexuality: A problem-solving approach to treating dysfunction: Therapist guide* (2nd ed.). New York: Oxford University Press. An excellent overview of sex therapy today.

Visit the text-specific Online Learning Center at **www.mhhe.com/olson8e** for practice tests, chapter summaries, and PowerPoint slides.

7 *G*ender Roles and Power in the Family

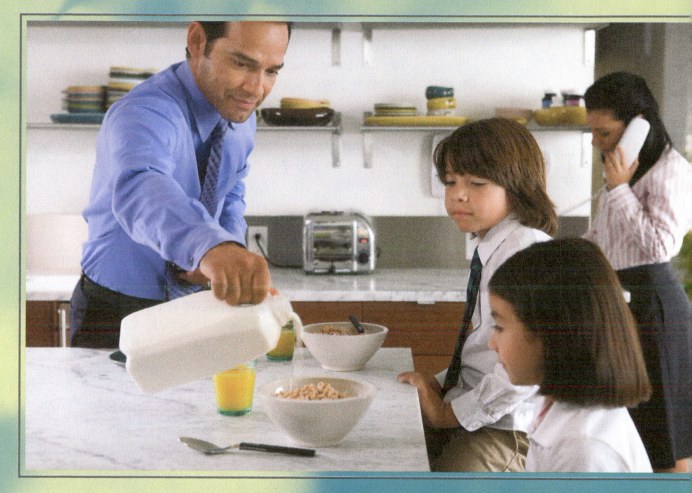

Intimacy, Strengths, and Diversity

Gender Roles

Gender Roles Across Ethnic Groups

Theories About Gender Roles

Power in Families

Summary

Key Terms

Activities

Suggested Readings

Intimacy, Strengths, and Diversity

All animals are equal, but some animals are more equal than others.

—GEORGE ORWELL (1951)

Contemporary models of intimacy stress gender equality in marriage and other types of partnerships. Egalitarianism is the trend among many couples making a serious commitment to each other. But if women continue to make less money for the work they do outside the home and if men continue to avoid child care and household labor, the fabric of intimate relationships is threatened. The fragile bonds of intimacy can easily be damaged when one spouse is subordinate to the other, has more power than the other, or receives less respect and dignity in society.

Individual and couple strengths result when there is equality and a balance of power in family relationships. This chapter provides a description of some of the gender differences between men and women, along with a discussion about the respective influences of nature and nurture to explain these differences. There are clearly cultural differences when it comes to gender roles. Does that mean strengths cannot exist when relationships are not equal? Or does it mean that there can be gender-role differences, but equal power? We will explore the complexity of gender roles and the quality of relationships in the United States and other cultures.

Gender Roles

The different ways in which men and women behave are linked to, but not necessarily determined by, their biological sex. Individuals are identified as male or female on the basis of physical structures, which are determined by chromosomes, gonads, and hormones. This labeling occurs at birth and is the first step in the process of developing **gender identity**—a sense of being male or female and what that means in one's society.

Although nature determines an individual's sex, culture determines the attitudes and behaviors appropriate for an individual on the basis of her or his sex. In each culture, individuals learn to adapt to these expectations as they shape their personal and professional lives. **Gender roles** are expectations about people's attitudes and behaviors in life based on whether they are male or female. When a child is born, **gender-role stereotypes** come into play. People comment, for example, that he is "a strong, healthy boy" or she is "a darling, adorable girl."

Labeling affects a child's psychological development in a variety of ways. The child begins to adopt personality traits, attitudes, preferences, and behaviors considered appropriate to her or his sex, and these affect how he or she walks, talks, eats, exercises, thinks, and later makes love. The gender-role patterns assigned to males and females influence all our roles in life.

Masculinity is the gender-linked constellation of traits that have been traditionally associated with men; **femininity**, the traits associated with women. In our society, the qualities stereotypically associated with masculinity include aggressiveness, independence, dominance, competence, and a predisposition for math and science. Qualities stereotypically associated with femininity include

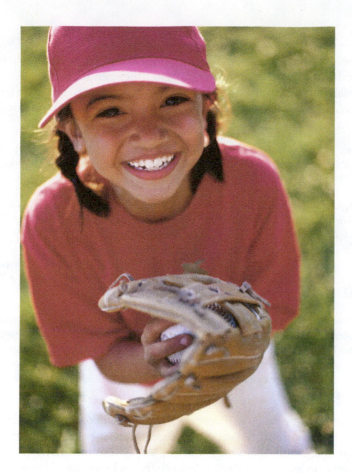

Gender-role behaviors are less distinct today than they were in the past. One example is the degree to which girls play on sport teams that were historically restricted to males.

passivity, dependency, sensitivity, emotionality, and a predisposition for art and literature. These stereotypes are destructive because they imply that all males, and only males, have the so-called masculine qualities and that all females, and only females, possess the so-called feminine qualities. Obviously, any human being can have any of these qualities. Socially imposed gender-role stereotypes create inequality by prescribing—based on whether a person is male or female—certain qualities, behaviors, and opportunities and prohibiting or discouraging others.

Language is one of the most powerful tools people use both deliberately and inadvertently to establish and maintain rigid gender roles. The subtle ways we talk about people of the other sex reinforce stereotypes and segregate people by sex. We talk about men and women as being members of the "opposite" sex, reinforcing the notion that men and women are opposites and accentuating the differences rather than affirming the similarities.

Gender-biased language reinforces the misguided notion that men are more competent and rational than women. Terms used for men are often more positive and affirming, whereas equivalent terms for women are often more negative and degrading. These differences in terminology have an impact on how we perceive and feel about each gender.

Gender Norms and Family Life

Whether we like it or not, families are organized around expectations about gender roles. According to Knudson-Martin (2012), at times gender roles and expectations are so pervasive and ingrained into who we are that they are taken for granted. For example, Colette, age 60, describes how she views gender roles and how they have played out in her life:

"I have been a liberated woman all my life, and have fought for equal rights for women. I have been upset when men opened doors for me because I was perfectly able to do it myself.

"I watched my mother do housework, care for us children, and focus on the family issues, while my father went to work and provided the paycheck. That wasn't all bad, but I wanted things in my life to be different—and they are. I have worked outside the home most all of my life. My husband and I both brought home paychecks. We shared in the raising of children, even though I probably did more than my share of the work in the home. Things weren't always equal, but we both worked hard to make it as equal as possible.

"So, now I am ending my work life, my children are grown, and I like to bake cookies and take care of our house. I like sewing quilts while my husband shovels the drive after a snowstorm. What is the deal? Am I hardwired to enjoy certain things such as quilting, while my husband enjoys shoveling snow? After a lifetime of trying to make gender roles less stereotypical, I can't imagine my husband wanting to quilt, and me wanting to shovel the driveway."

It is a complex question, with complex answers. People who study neuroscience say that boy and girl babies are different, but only slightly different, when it comes to the brain (Knudson-Martin, 2012). Environment most certainly has an impact on gender behavior, especially as behavior relates to language. Environment can be the family environment and the broader social environment. Therefore, parents can insist on a certain behavior in their families, but interaction in one's schools and communities also affects how children respond to gender issues. Therefore, Knudson-Martin (2012) concludes that biology, family, and the environment all interact to determine how one develops views and behaviors regarding gender.

According to a nationwide survey of more than 50,000 married couples, the happy couples agreed more often (82%) than unhappy couples (46%) that both partners are equally willing to make adjustments in their marriage (Olson, Olson-Sigg, & Larson, 2008). As indicated in Table 7.1, happy couples agreed more often (87%) than unhappy couples (54%) that both partners work hard to have an equal relationship. More happy couples (76%) than unhappy couples (42%) believed that both persons are satisfied with the division of housework in their marriage. Happy couples also agreed more often (87%) than unhappy couples (59%) that they make most decisions jointly. Finally, this survey found that household tasks were divided on the basis of preferences rather than tradition more often in happy couples (67%) than among unhappy couples (55%).

Based on the national sample of more than 50,000 married couples, the major role relationship problem that couples faced (49%) was concern about the unfair division of the housework (Table 7.2). Less than half of the couples (44%) disagreed on the issue of whether housework was based on traditional roles versus their interests. Another common problem (44%) was that the husband was not willing to adjust as much as the wife. The couples also disagreed (43%) about whether or not

TABLE 7.1	How Happy Couples Versus Unhappy Couples View Their Roles		

	PERCENTAGE IN AGREEMENT	
Role Issues	**Happy Couples**	**Unhappy Couples**
1. Both are equally willing to make adjustments in their marriage.	82%	46%
2. Both work hard to have an equal relationship.	76	42
3. Both are satisfied with the division of housework.	87	54
4. The partners make most decisions jointly.	87	59
5. Household tasks are divided on the basis of preferences, not tradition.	67	55

Source: Adapted from David H. Olson, Amy Olson-Sigg, and Peter J. Larson Ph.D., *The Couple Checkup.* Copyright © 2008 by David H. Olson, Amy Olson-Sigg, and Peter J. Larson. Reprinted by permission of Thomas Nelson, Inc.

the wife should work outside the home when children are young. And more than a third (36%) disagreed over the issue of whether both work to maintain an egalitarian relationship.

There is an interesting story about the role relationship of Bob and Elizabeth Dole, both former presidential candidates (Fadiman & Bernard, 2000). When Elizabeth Dole was appointed secretary of transportation in 1985, the press was curious about their role relationship because Bob Dole was a senator and she would have a higher political position than he would. A photo was taken of them making the bed together, and a man wrote to Bob complaining, "You've got to stop doing the work around the house. You're causing problems for men across the country." Bob responded, "You don't know the half of it. The only reason she was helping was because they were taking pictures." Perhaps his willingness to do more housework contributed to their still being a married couple in spite of all the stress and public scrutiny they are under as a couple.

TABLE 7.2	Top Five Role Problems for Couples	

Role Issue	**Percentage of Couples Having Problem***
1. Concern about unfair division of housework.	49%
2. Housework is based on traditional roles rather than interests.	44
3. The husband is not willing to adjust as much as the wife.	44
4. Disagree whether or not the wife should work outside the home when children are young.	43
5. Partners disagree that both work to maintain an egalitarian relationship.	36

*One or both partners indicated this was an issue for them.

Source: Adapted from David H. Olson, Amy Olson-Sigg, and Peter J. Larson Ph.D., *The Couple Checkup.* Copyright © 2008 by David H. Olson, Amy Olson-Sigg, and Peter J. Larson. Reprinted by permission of Thomas Nelson, Inc.

Distribution of Family Work by Gender

Extensive research has been carried out in the past several years about gender and the division of labor in the household. A summary of current findings (Meier, McNaughton-Cassill, & Lynch, 2006) include the following:

- Husbands and wives have both decreased the total number of hours spent on housework.
- Wives still do almost two-thirds of the work compared to husbands.
- Having children makes the imbalance even greater.
- Mothers spend twice as much time caring for their children as fathers.
- Even though fathers spend more time with children today than in the past, they still are often seen as "helpers" in providing care for their children.
- Perceptions of fairness regarding the division of household responsibilities are a more likely predictor of marital discord than actual behavior.

Husbands and wives disagree about how much housework each spouse does (Lee & Waite, 2005). These researchers found that wives typically make accurate estimates of husbands' time spent on housework, and husbands overestimate the time they spend. In addition, wives think they spend 13 hours more on housework each week, and husbands see the gap as only half as large. They also found that wives overestimated the numbers of hours worked in the home. These researchers concluded that what happens with housework depends on who you ask, and this gap in perception can lead to marital conflict. They also concluded that wives, in fact, do 9.4 hours more housework per week than their husbands, and the husbands perform about 40% of the work in the home.

So why is it that women still do most of the housework? There are several possible explanations. Poortman and van der Lippe (2009) discuss several factors, based upon past research. According to these authors, research might indicate that the partner that has the least amount of financial resources, such as money from paid employment, will have the least amount of power and, therefore, will be relegated to doing household chores—and in most cases that is the woman in the household. Other observers indicate that as a society we have beliefs about certain behaviors being gender specific, and activities such as cleaning and laundry are women's tasks, whereas household maintenance is relegated to men (Poortman & van der Lippe, 2009). These researchers, therefore, conducted a study to determine whether men and women have differing attitudes regarding household chores. They looked at individuals' enjoyment of household tasks and the standards for how well the chores should be completed.

Poortman and van der Lippe (2009) found that women did, indeed, have more positive attitudes about child care, cleaning, and cooking than men did. Women not only enjoyed these tasks, they felt they had more responsibility for these tasks than men had, and they also had higher standards for how well the tasks should be done. These researchers concluded that, along with power and resources brought into the home, attitudes contributed to the fact that women continue to do more household chores. The findings of the study indicated that attitudes toward the work that needs to be done in the home were more important for men and women, than their attitudes about child care, which tended to be similar. In other words, attitudes about caring for children were less likely to be different for men and women than attitudes about other household chores. The most preferred task for men was caring for children and the least preferred task was cleaning.

It is clear that the issue of who does what in terms of housework and child care is complicated. The studies that are described provide clues about why the inequities continue to occur, but do not provide conclusive answers for the phenomenon.

Emotion Work in Marriage and Family

Although most research on marriages relating to gender has focused on housework and care of children, recent research has conceptualized *emotion work* in families (Erickson, 2005). Emotion work, according to this author, includes such things as listening closely to a spouse's thoughts and feelings, recognizing feelings, offering encouragement, and showing appreciation. Women are deliberate about paying attention to the emotional well-being of other family members. This author concluded that emotion work is a gender issue and looks different to men and women, in that women see emotion work as part of their family work role and they recognize that they are held accountable for performing this work in their families.

Other researchers talk about *mental work* that happens in families, and this work is also divided unequally, with women performing more mental work than men (Meier et al., 2006). Mental work includes worrying about children and household tasks, planning and monitoring children's activities, seeking solutions to child care problems, and managing the division of labor and the delegation of tasks (Meier et al., 2006). This mental work is invisible and is very difficult to measure, but it is estimated that women are doing most of the mental work in families. Meier and colleagues also indicate that the unequal division of mental work affects women's marital satisfaction but not men's marital satisfaction.

Maternal Gatekeeping

Maternal gatekeeping refers to behaviors that affect how women and men collaborate in the work of the family. This was defined by Allen and Hawkins (1999), and has continued to be addressed in literature (Schoppe-Sullivan, 2010). As we have seen, mothers continue to do significantly more child care than fathers, even though both parents realize the importance of father involvement and work at sharing equally in child care. As Schoppe-Sullivan (2010) reviews the recent literature, she speculates that mothers may be ambivalent about giving up their role as the parent with most knowledge about child care. They, in fact, might not want to share the role of being the major caregiver for their children, or they may not feel that the father is doing the caregiving well enough. Mothers may not even realize they send messages to fathers about the fathers' lack of expertise in caring for children.

Examples of maternal gatekeeping can be when a mother rushes in to fix what the father has done such as not putting on a child's hat correctly, or not wiping a child's mouth often enough while feeding. Mothers can roll their eyes in disapproval without even realizing they are doing it. How often does it happen in the media and how often does it happen in the lives of young children? Clearly, this mother-father dynamic is reciprocal. For example, if a father ignores the eye rolling and forges ahead, equality in caregiving can be achieved, and the family system has truly changed.

Schoppe-Sullivan (2010) also proposes that if women can close the gate, they can also open it. Fathers can be complimented as often as they are discouraged by a mother. In her research she found that these positive behaviors can, in fact, make a difference and that fathers are more involved in child care when mothers are encouraging. She indicates that it is only one of many factors that impact father involvement, but maternal gatekeeping should not be underestimated. She concludes that when both parents are invested in providing child care, the child benefits. Equality in child care can happen when:

- Fathers take the initiative some of the time, and do not wait to be invited to provide care.
- Fathers do not give up, even if there are signs of disapproval.
- Mothers think before action is taken or a response is given.
- Mothers give compliments. Society does not always view men as great child care providers, but mothers can change that.

Gallup Survey of Male and Female Traits

In a Gallup poll (2001) of how Americans see males and females, the words that most often were used by both sexes to describe males were aggressive, courageous, and ambitious. Females were most often described by both sexes as emotional, affectionate, talkative, patient, and creative. In 6 out of 10 traits, both genders agreed about the traits for males and females. The one that they both agreed applies more to one gender is men that are more aggressive. The three traits that differed by less than 20% were ambitious, easygoing, and intelligent. Table 7.3 provides a summary of the differences on the major traits survey. It is clear that in most ways both sexes see the major traits of men and women as different.

Although none of the 10 traits surveyed was seen solely as male or female, the trait considered predominantly male was aggressiveness. The country with the highest margin was China, where 81% identified aggression as most characteristic of men and only 3% as most characteristic of women, a difference of 78 points. The differences favoring men were 58 points for the United States and 60 points for Canada and Great Britain. Both men and women across most of the 22 countries surveyed tended to agree with the opinions reported here.

A consistent finding across hundreds of studies is that men of different ages, with different ethnic backgrounds and income levels, are less likely than women to seek professional help for physical and emotional problems. Even though women outlive men by an average of 7 years and have lower rates of most deadly diseases, men still do not typically seek outside help for their problems. Men are also much less likely to seek help for emotional and drugrelated problems, even though they have higher rates than women (Addis, 2008; Whorley & Addis, 2006).

TABLE 7.3	Traits of Males and Females from Gallup Poll		
Trait	**More True of Men**	**More True of Women**	**Advantage for Men**
1. Aggressive	68%	20%	+48%
2. Courageous	50	27	+ 23
3. Ambitious	44	33	+ 11
4. Easygoing	55	48	+ 7
5. Intelligent	21	36	− 15
6. Creative	15	65	− 50
7. Patient	19	72	− 53
8. Talkative	10	78	− 68
9. Affectionate	5	86	− 81
10. Emotional	3	90	− 87

Source: Copyright © 2000 The Gallup Organization. All rights reserved. Reprinted with permission.

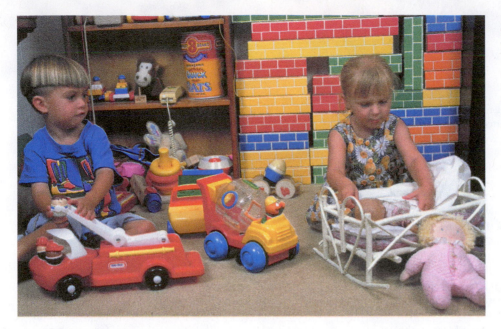

A person's sex is biologically determined, but the abilities, behaviors, activities, social roles, and other characteristics that are considered appropriate for males and females are determined by one's culture.

Traditional Versus Contemporary Views of Gender Roles

In the traditional view of gender roles in our society, males are assumed to be superior to females and to have characteristics that are more desirable. A more contemporary view holds that neither males nor females are superior; both have desirable—and undesirable—traits not based specifically on sex.

To counter the traditional view of men and women in our society, humorist Garrison Keillor ends his radio show, *A Prairie Home Companion,* with the statement that in Lake Wobegon: "All the women are strong, all the men are good looking, and all the children are above average" (Keillor, 2009).

A Traditional View. The traditional view of gender roles in our society grew out of our male-oriented culture, but specific theories have been put forth in its support. One of the best known is that of sociologist Talcott Parsons (1955, 1965), whose theory of the family assumed that highly contrasting gender roles were essential for families and society. Parsons believed that, in this modern family, society required that men be *instrumental* and women be *expressive.* The man's instrumental role was to be the breadwinner, the manager, and the leader of the family. The woman's expressive role was to take care of the emotional well-being of the family through nurturing and comforting. Parsons saw these two roles as separate, one to be performed by the husband and the other by the wife.

The Parsons theory, which has been attacked by innumerable critics, is no longer considered valid. They charged that it was a mistake to assume that the traditional family structure was both a universal and necessary social institution—that only this traditional family structure could fulfill the needs of the individuals within the family and of the greater society. They further argued that the Parsons theory focused on the positive aspects of this traditional family structure but deemphasized potential problems. The traditional model emphasized stability rather than change, focused on harmony rather than conflict, and identified function but

BOX 7.1   At Issue

The Work–Family Interface

Much of the current gender research is centered on dual career couples as they balance their family and work lives. It is appropriate, then, that we explain what the work–family interface looks like.

Managing the responsibilities of work and family life began to be an issue for researchers in the 1970s, as women increasingly entered the workforce. At that time, approximately one-third of women with children under the age of 6 worked outside the home (Halpern, 2005; Raley, Mattingly, & Bianchi, 2006). The issues of work and family in the 1970s focused primarily on how to manage work and child care responsibilities (Halpern, 2005). Researchers found that women became employed but also continued to be the major caretakers of children and other domestic responsibilities.

The number of women with children in the workforce has increased dramatically. Approximately 50% to 66% of heterosexual couples, with and without children, are both employed today (Haddock, Zimmerman, Ziemba, & Lyness, 2006; Meier et al., 2006; Winslow, 2005).

Work-to-Family Influence

When we think about balancing work and family issues, we usually think about the effects of one's work life on one's family life. Work and family researchers often think about the multiple issues work places on family time and include such things as time-based demands and strain-based demands. Time-based demands focus on the idea that time at work means there is less time for family (Voydanoff, 2008). Therefore, when a person works extra hours, does shift work, or travels extensively, there is likely to be less time with the family. In addition, there are often strain-based demands that affect family life. Strain-based demands include such things as job insecurity, workload pressures, time pressures, or dealing with a demanding supervisor. Both time-based demands and strainbased demands have significant effects on family life.

Certainly there are times when both time-based demands and strain-based demands enter into one's work life. For example, when companies go through cycles of downsizing, which has happened in the past several years, employers will decrease the workforce with added responsibilities and longer hours for the workers who remain. In addition, there is the fear of additional downsizing, which also adds stress to the work environment. These stresses together can cause psychological spillover to the family (Voydanoff, 2008).

Family-to-Work Influence

Family-to-work influence refers to how family demands affect work performance (Voydanoff, 2005). The family demands drain one of time and energy to do well at work

ignored dysfunction. The Parsons theory also tended to stereotype masculine and feminine traits, reinforcing differences and denigrating women.

A More Contemporary View. Today, it is more commonly assumed that both sexes are capable and can be successful in a variety of roles at home and at work. Women can be independent, strong, logical, and task oriented; men can be nurturing, sensitive, cooperative, and detail oriented. However, men and women can benefit by learning from each other: Men can learn the value of being more sensitive and caring from women; women can learn the value of independence from men; and both can learn to work together and become interdependent.

Women may be at an advantage in this more cooperative approach to living. Traditional culture has encouraged them to be good listeners and to be empathic, understanding, helpful, and supportive. These caring values fit well with the more cooperative approaches to group decision making that are gaining strength at home and at work.

See Box 7.1 for a closer look at the work–family interface.

and affect one's ability to take advantage of opportunities to advance or take on more responsibilities. The behaviors that might be evident at work because of family demands include such things as absenteeism and lack of ability to concentrate on work tasks.

When family stresses occur at home such as marital issues or divorce, child behavior problems, financial difficulties, or a death, there is less energy for one's work life. For example, a couple may be having marital difficulties. This couple may be fighting more often and constantly feeling stressed over what might happen to the marriage and family life. There is little rest, relaxation, and sleep. Because of the stress the couple is experiencing, there is less quality time for children, and the children feel the stress about what might happen to their family. As a result, the children's behavior deteriorates, and now there is even more stress in the family. As one can imagine, the adults in the family have very little energy for their work. According to Voydanoff (2008), there is a reciprocal and positive relationship between work and family life. It is likely that when things go well at work, it positively affects family life, and when family life is positive, a person is more productive at work.

Current Issues That Affect Work and Family Life

Today, people are living longer, and, in addition to caring for their own children, they are also likely to be caring for aging parents (Halpern, 2005). For example, approximately 50% of working adults plan to assume significant caregiving responsibilities for aging relatives during the next 5 years, and many more are already doing so. Although women are most likely to provide such care, approximately 25% of care is provided by men.

Currently, there are also more family forms than in previous years. For example, there are stepfamilies, single-parent families, same-sex couples, cohabiting couples with children, and grandparents raising grandchildren. These family forms make the work and family relationship even more complex. A single parent balancing work and family will experience different stresses than a two-parent couple. In addition, there are cultural values with new and growing diverse populations that might view the work and family relationship very differently than is described by previous research (Halpern, 2005). For example, members of diverse cultures may be more likely to use extended-family members as a source of childcare, which would affect the stress experienced by a dual-earner couple.

The Move Toward More Egalitarian Roles

American society in many ways is moving away from male dominance and toward **egalitarian roles** (also called *equalitarian roles*)—social equality between the sexes. The process of change has been long and fraught with controversy. The struggle not only occurs in society but is also played out each day in close relationships. Table 7.4 highlights some differences between traditional dating and marriage patterns and more contemporary practices. Looking back through the generations of one's own family illustrates how dramatically times have changed.

One of the most telling indexes of change is the decline of the double standard, the social convention allowing men more sexual and social freedom than women. Women are claiming more freedom for themselves, although some don't realize or acknowledge they are doing so. A number of social scientists have commented that today many women shy away from calling themselves nontraditional or feminist but are clearly living very different lives than their mothers or grandmothers. What is apparently happening is that as women's roles change, the definition of *traditional* also changes.

Working parents are under increasing stress as they try to balance time for their career and family. Too often, the marriage is what suffers.

TABLE 7.4	Contemporary Versus Traditional Dating and Marriage Patterns

Contemporary	Traditional
Both women and men initiate dates.	The man initiates dates.
The woman keeps her maiden name after marriage.	The woman takes the man's last name.
The partners cohabit before marriage or may never marry at all.	The partners live apart before marriage.
Premarital sex is expected.	Premarital sex is not an option.
Both partners continue their education.	The wife supports the husband through school.
The birth of a child might precede marriage.	Children are conceived after marriage.
Both partners work, and both may have careers.	The husband's work is the priority.
Roles are flexible.	Roles are rigid.
Both partners share child care.	The mother is responsible for child care and housework.
Both partners initiate sex.	The husband initiates sex.
Both partners select the couple's friends.	The husband's friends become the couple's friends.

Gender-role stereotypes limit people's choices by dictating what they are believed to be able to do. Today, however, it is more commonly assumed in the United States that both sexes are capable and can be successful in a variety of roles at home and at work.

An International Perspective

Perhaps the classic description of how gender roles are rooted in culture comes from anthropologist Margaret Mead. In *Sex and Temperament in Three Primitive Societies*, Mead (1935) looked at "maleness" and "femaleness" in three New Guinea tribes: the Arapesh, the Mundugumor, and the Tchambuli. In American society, two traditional attributes of females are gentleness and unaggressiveness. Among the Arapesh, Mead found both the women *and the men* to be unaggressive. Not far away, among the Mundugumor tribe, Mead found that both males and females displayed an aggressiveness that Americans would characterize as traditionally masculine. In both the Arapesh and the Mundugumor tribes, Mead found little contrast in temperament between the sexes.

The third New Guinea tribe Mead studied provided further evidence of cross-cultural differences. Among the Tchambuli, both men and women behaved in ways that are opposite to traditional behavior in Western societies. Tchambuli women were independent and aggressive, acting like traditional Western men; Tchambuli men were gentle and sensitive, like traditional Western women. Mead's conclusion was that the varieties in temperament she observed among these three "primitive" societies were not dictated by biology but were largely the creations of the societies.

Mead's work sparked a discussion in America and worldwide that has not ended yet, nor is it likely to ever reach a conclusion, because the discussion and the controversy are too much fun for everyone. One study by psychologist David

Buss is a good example of another important perspective in the discussion of maleness and femaleness. Buss and his colleagues created a questionnaire to be used around the world, asking people to describe their ideal mate. Five categories were included: earning capacity, industriousness, youth, physical attractiveness, and chastity. Buss collected data from 37 groups of men and women in 33 different societies.

The researchers found that even though the participants in the study came from many different geographical and cultural areas, consistent patterns emerged. Females placed more value on wealth and ambition, and males were more interested in signs of youth and fertility. A mate who was a "good financial prospect" was more important to females in 36 of 37 groups, and "good looks" were more important to males than to females in all 37 groups in the study (Buss, Shackelford, Kirkpatrick, & Larsen, 2001).

The Gallup Organization (2001) surveyed men and women in 22 countries around the world regarding gender roles in the family. Residents of nearly two-thirds of the countries believed that their society favors men over women. Countries in greatest agreement with this belief included Germany (76%), Iceland (76%), France (76%), the United States (73%), and Great Britain (72%). In seven countries the consensus leaned toward the belief that men and women are treated equally: El Salvador (63%), China (53%), and Thailand (52%).

The survey showed some potential for change, however, because in five countries, about half those surveyed resented the gender-role expectations their society placed on them. Those countries are Germany (52%), Japan (52%), Thailand (52%), Chile (46%), and Panama (46%). In those five countries, at least half the women and more than 40% of the men expressed resentment. (See Box 7.2, which focuses on Japan's traditional yet evolving gender roles.)

Treas (2011), who has focused her work on how couples internationally distribute the division of housework, concludes that cultural values also contribute to how couples divide up household tasks and that household routines are influenced by the examples that couples see around them. These values may also determine how much time, in total, is spent on housework. For example, she indicates that in countries where hygiene is important, the total time spent on housecleaning may be higher than in other countries where hygiene is less important.

BOX 7.2   Diversity in Families

Gender Roles in Japan

To understand the complex topic of power and gender roles in families in Japan, it is necessary to understand both the social system and the family system. The following overview, which applies to middle- and upper-class urban Japanese families, is provided by Shuji Asai (2004), a Japanese family therapist.

At the societal system level, Japanese culture is patriarchal. The male dominates; he plays the instrumental role in society and tends to be married to his work. Although women make up about 40% of the labor force in Japan, they face discrimination in terms of wages, assignments, and promotions.

Although Japanese society is patriarchal, the Japanese family is more of a matriarchal system, with the mother dominating. This is particularly true of child rearing and finances. Although the husband brings home the money, the wife controls it, often deciding how much spending money the husband receives each month. The woman's financial power also entails making decisions about when and where to invest and how much to pay for a house or remodeling.

In most Japanese families, family cohesion and family communication are also controlled by the mother. Japanese mothers often develop a very strong emotional connection with their children and serve as the communication link between the children and the father; the father may remain disengaged from the family. As a result, the mother dominates the family system, and the father emphasizes his role at work.

Today, more Japanese women are seeking professional careers, and more are delaying marriage and even remaining single. These changes are moving Japan toward a more egalitarian society and are demanding that men and women renegotiate their traditional gender roles at work and at home.

Gender Roles Across Ethnic Groups

It is commonly believed that gender roles do not spring from innate characteristics individuals possess. Rather, they are learned behaviors, rooted in the social context of the particular culture in which people live. The gender roles women and men play vary widely from culture to culture and within each culture. This section examines some examples of cultural gender-role differences in the United States.

Latino/a Culture

Latino males, historically speaking, have often been stereotyped as being *macho*. Male exhibitions of aggressiveness—*machismo*—include bossing women around, being abusive to them, and having numerous extramarital affairs. But this macho attitude is not supported in the research literature (Falicov, 2010). Even though some Latinos act macho, this is not the predominant pattern for this group and it does not display the historical role of Latino men.

After reviewing historical and recent literature, Falicov (2010) concludes that Latino men have multiple ways to be masculine. However, when machismo is thought about within the context of history and the family, the term has positive attributes such as bravery, altruism, and being responsible for and providing for one's family (Falicov, 2010; Skogrand, Barrios-Bell, & Higginbotham, 2009). Being macho often means one does not show emotions. Latino men, however, often show affection, cry, or hug both men and women (Falicov, 2010).

There is also evidence that Latinos are often egalitarian and share equally in decision making, especially around child-rearing or household decisions (Falicov, 2010). This seems to be especially true when Latinos have immigrated to the United States, where the view of women may be different from in their country of origin. Also, many women join the workforce when they enter the United States, and they have more power since they contribute money to the household.

In addition to the unique ways Latino men may show their masculinity, Latinos can come from a variety of countries and these countries can have differing views about gender issues.

African American Culture

The majority of African American families are headed by women and, therefore, extended family members often help out when it comes to caring for children (Sue & Sue, 2008). In addition, the rearing of children can be done by older children, or even close friends. Therefore, the roles of African Americans within the family are flexible and adaptable, and men and women are used to adopting multiple roles.

One of the complexities in gender roles for African American families is that many African American men have been marginalized in their roles as a provider and as a marital partner (Boyd-Franklin, 2003; Franklin, 2006). African American males have often grown up in single-parent homes where they do not have a male model to learn from. African American marriages were most often egalitarian where the couple shared responsibilities and worked together to provide for their family.

Many African American women see feminism from a different perspective than do White women. African American women have rarely served only in the housewife role because economic circumstances have dictated that they work outside the home. African American women are also acutely aware of the disadvantages African American men have faced over the years, making it difficult for them to adopt a wholeheartedly feminist agenda. The dilemma: Am I more oppressed as a woman or as an African American? Because these two factors converge for African American women, life can be especially difficult for them.

American Indian Culture

Native American women confront many of the same problems that African American women face in American society in that there are more female-headed households than in the dominant culture (Sue & Sue, 2008; Sutton & Broken Nose, 2005). Because there are many single-parent families, the extended family members often help in raising children. Native American cultures in the United States vary widely, but some are identified by a matrilineal tradition such as is true in the Navajo, whereas in other tribes men hold the power (Sue & Sue, 2008).

Many Native American families also face racism, unemployment, poverty, and the abuse of alcohol and other drugs (Sutton & Broken Nose, 2005). Native American women play an important role in keeping the family and the tribe together. Some tribal traditions make it difficult for Native American women to attain leadership roles, and some tribes have religious beliefs against both contraception and abortion. But it has also been argued that tribal traditions are a source of strength for American Indian women.

The value orientation of Native Americans has considerable impact on why role relationships in their culture are more complex and less clearly defined (Sutton & Broken Nose, 2005). Native Americans emphasize communal living rather than a nuclear family and communal sharing rather than focusing on individual possessions. As one tribal member commented, "When I was little, I learned very early that what's yours is mine and what's mine is everybody's" (Sutton & Broken Nose, 1996, p. 40). Native Americans also have a tribal identity that puts a high value on the group. Time is also seen differently by Native Americans in that it is cyclical rather than linear, so

Wilma Mankiller, former chief of the Cherokee Nation, was the first woman ever elected to that position. Her election reflected the growing power of women in some Native American tribes.

minutes and hours are less important than seasonal rhythms. In summary, these cultural values greatly influence their lifestyle and how they function as a group.

Asian American Culture

Asian American families as a group have been very successful in the U.S. culture. They value education highly, and they have the highest family income of any ethnic group. They value tradition and respect their elders (called *filial piety*), and their children are well disciplined (Lee & Mock, 2005).

Traditionally, sex roles have been segregated so that the woman is very connected to the children, and the husband is most highly connected to his work. As a result, there is a strong mother–child bond and a weaker husband–wife bond (Asai, 2004). Traditional Asian American families are often hierarchical and patriarchal, with men and older individuals having more power (Sue & Sue, 2008). While marriage is important in Asian families, it is usually not as strong as the family system. Fathers tend be mainly involved with providing the economic base and are typically not very involved with child rearing. One Japanese family therapist described the communication in Japanese families as generally weak with the exception being the mother–child relationship (Vosburg, 2004).

In a study of 849 premarital couples in Japan, it was found that while both the male and the female had a traditional role orientation, the women were more traditional than the males (Asai, 2004). These premarital couples had a clear awareness of the importance of issues related to living arrangements and care of their parents as they age. These premarital couples had more conflict and less awareness of potential issues than premarital couples in the United States.

Gender Issues for Immigrant Couples

New immigrants often face challenges as they come to a new country. They may have had one set of rules regarding gender in their country of origin, and in the United States they not only need to learn the rules, but also must make decisions about adapting gender roles based on new norms. Many women come to the United States with relatively traditional roles, where men make many decisions, and they enter a culture where women often have power equal or nearly equal to men. According to Maciel, Van Putten, and Knudson-Martin (2009), who studied a group of new immigrant couples, such couples usually allow changes to evolve and do this through having lots of couple conversations, interpreting new experiences, and generally interacting with their new world. The end result is that gender roles and power evolve and are often a hybrid of the new and the old.

Often new immigrant women, who have experienced traditional roles in their country of origin, need to work after coming to the United States. This has an impact on power in marriage relationships because they are bringing money into the family. In addition, women see other women in places like the workforce having more power and they challenge past gender roles (Maciel et al., 2009). The researchers found that women gained power in their couple relationships when they had opportunity, access to resources, and legal protection. How much men would let go of traditional gender roles varied greatly, however.

Theories About Gender Roles

Theorists interested in gender roles have focused on how children acquire gender-role identity during the early years of life and how changes in gender-role identity occur. Some observers believe that changes in gender-role identity are possible after early childhood, but it is generally assumed that once gender-role identity is formed, it remains stable and continues throughout adulthood. Four theories about gender-role development and change are described here: social learning theory, cognitive development theory, family systems theory, and the feminist framework.

Social Learning Theory

The **social learning theory** is concerned with how individuals learn the behavior patterns considered appropriate for their sex. Social learning researchers have particularly focused on direct observation of behavior and how people reinforce each other's behavior. Early in life, reinforcement of sex-related behavior by others is of primary importance. As individuals grow and develop, they assess personal situations and develop standards and rules by which to live. In the case of gender roles, individuals begin as very young children to internalize the standards and rules for being a boy or a girl in our society.

Social learning theorist Jerome Kagan (1964) argued that children at a young age dichotomize the world as female versus male and have a strong desire to match their own personal characteristics with the gender-role standards they learn from parents and society in general. Kagan believed that children want to develop a gender-typed identity and that they see variations from the gender-traditional ideal as failures. He noted that certain aspects of gender-role standards cause unnecessary anxiety and restrictions for individuals, and he proposed that perhaps these standards should be changed.

Cognitive Development Theory

The **cognitive development theory** links gender-role development (the progressive acquisition of gender typing) to the more general maturation of the child's thinking processes. Lawrence Kohlberg (1966), the developer of this theory, argued that children themselves actively create gender identity, gender-role stereotypes, and values in their minds in their efforts to understand the world around them (e.g., "I can't do that! Only boys do that!"). He argued that the stereotypes do not necessarily become more rigid over time but follow a curvilinear pattern. In early childhood, the stereotypes develop quickly and are quite rigid. When the child realizes that not all gender-typed characteristics (hair, clothes, sports, etc.) are crucial to maintaining gender identity, the child's thinking becomes less rigid. With increasing maturity, the child learns that variations are possible and becomes more flexible in her or his thinking.

Paul Mussen (1969) synthesized social learning and cognitive processes in looking at gender-role development. Mussen noted that labeling occurs early in the child's life and that the child must see the label as positive, rewarding, lovingly applied, and accepted by the labeler. This linkage between the label and love and acceptance helps motivate the child to perform gender-typed behaviors.

Both the social learning and cognitive development theories have been attacked in recent years. First, critics argue that these early theories erred by assuming that children of the same sex develop very similar gender-role identities (masculine for boys and feminine for girls). In fact, many boys engage in traditionally feminine behaviors, and many girls engage in traditionally masculine behaviors.

Second, the early theories were criticized for characterizing the traditional gender-role identities as desirable and a divergence from the norm as deviant.

Among earlier generations of American women, relatively few had the opportunity to learn skills traditionally assigned to men. Today, people are not limited as much by gender-role stereotypes, though barriers still remain for those who cross traditional gender lines.

Today, many children enjoy the freedom to engage in a broad range of activities, despite the dictates of tradition.

Third, the theories were criticized for assuming that early childhood is a critical period in gender-role development and that an adult's gender-role characteristics spring directly from early-childhood experiences. Dramatic changes in gender-role behavior can take place later in life such as a female homemaker going back to school to become a lawyer and a male engineer retiring early to take care of the home and garden while his spouse begins a new career outside the home. Subsequent theorists have explored human development after childhood and suggest that individuals retain the capacity for growth and change in their gender-role identity.

Family Systems Theory

Family systems theory, as presented in Chapter 1, suggests that the family functions as an interconnected system. A change in one family member necessitates compensatory changes in other family members if the family is to achieve a new balance.

According to family systems theory, change is a difficult process for both individuals and families. If the individual is successful in growing in new directions, sometimes other family members will attempt to bring the individual back "into the fold."

Consider, for example, a young woman who desires more independence in a family wanting to maintain traditional family roles. The daughter feels stifled by the family's long list of rules and beliefs and finds support in feminist writings and rhetoric, but when she expresses her views, her parents react emotionally. "Are you telling me my life has been worthless?" her more traditional mother asks. "Those damned feminists!" her father sputters. Her mother becomes defensive because she has made a career of her children and her marriage. Her father becomes defensive because he feels he has done the right thing by supporting his wife and children.

Family systems that are balanced (on the Couple and Family Map; see Chapter 3) tend to be more open to change and are more supportive of independence in family members. In contrast, some types of unbalanced family systems, particularly rigidly enmeshed types, are resistant to change and restrict independence in family members.

Feminist Framework

Traditional gender-role patterns—stressing the differences between men and women, masculinity and femininity—have been criticized by many feminists, especially since the 1960s. The gender-role constraints under which men and women traditionally have lived have been revised considerably. Many women are doing things their mothers would not have deemed possible. Many men are also gaining the freedom to function outside the traditional boundaries of masculinity. Making these profound changes in life is a struggle, but it would be difficult—if not impossible—for many people to go back to the traditional patterns.

Feminist scholars have focused on the contributions that women have made to society. Feminists point out that, although women have made countless contributions to culture and to human life, the omission of these achievements from the historical record reflects the low status in which women have been held in society. Feminists point out that women have been exploited, devalued, and oppressed. In addition, as a result of their own experiences, feminists tend to be sensitive to other oppressed people.

Another focus of feminists is a commitment to change the conditions of women. Feminists strive to empower women by documenting oppression so that people recognize it when they see and experience it. Feminists take an affirming stance toward women, challenging the status quo of devaluation (see Box 7.3, which

BOX 7.3   At Issue

Gender Inequality as a Global Problem

Thanks in large part to the work of feminists and activists around the world, gender roles have broadened, and many constraints about what is possible and/or appropriate for men and women to do have been lifted in many places. However, even in contemporary American society, the reality is that gender inequality continues.

In 1963, the U.S. Congress passed the Equal Pay Act to "prohibit discrimination on account of sex in the payment of wages by employers engaged in commerce or in the production of goods for commerce."

The act was intended to level the playing field for men and women in the workplace. However, the AFL-CIO and the Institute for Women's Policy Research (1999) found that working families in the United States lose more than $200 billion each year because of the wage gap between men and women, which amounts to an average of $4,000 per year per family.

According to *USA Today* (Dugas, 2012, October 24), women earned 82% of what men earned in this country. The gap was even larger for Latina and African American women.

This kind of gender inequality is by no means exclusive to the United States. In Scotland, for example, the Scottish Trade Union Congress found that as of November 2004, women earned, on average, 19% less than men, and in one city—Aberdeen—the discrepancy was closer to 30% in favor of men in the same job (BBC News, 2004).

The United Nations International Labour Office (2004b), in a report titled "Global Employment Trends for Women 2004," estimated that in 2003 there were 2.8 billion workers around the world, of whom 1.1 billion—or 40%—were women. This represented an increase of nearly 200 million over the past decade. The United Nations International Labour Office (2004a) concluded that women's share of managerial positions in more than 60 countries ranges between 20% and 40%—a figure that has remained the same since 2001.

In almost every country in the world, women are responsible for most of the unpaid, "nonmarket" work. In most societies, women care for the children, the elderly, and the ailing. Women do most of the household chores, which in developing countries can mean walking many miles to fetch water and firewood.

Of course, gender inequality—which exists in every part of the world—isn't limited to gaps in earnings. In an essay published in *Frontline* (India's national magazine), Nobel laureate Amarta Sen (2001) delineated seven kinds of disparity between men and women:

1. *Mortality inequality.* In some areas of the world (e.g., North Africa and Asia), women suffer unusually high mortality rates due to gender bias in health care and nutrition.
2. *Natality inequality.* Where boys are considered more desirable than girls, modern technology can determine the gender of the fetus, and the pregnancy can be terminated if it is a girl. Sex-selective abortion has become a common practice in China, South Korea, Singapore, Taiwan, and several other areas of the world.
3. *Basic institutional inequality.* In many countries women are denied access to education and other social and cultural institutions.
4. *Special opportunity inequality.* In some countries where women do have access to *basic* education, they are denied access to higher education and/or professional training.
5. *Professional inequality.* Even in countries where special opportunities exist, women often encounter great difficulties trying to gain and advance in managerial positions.
6. *Ownership inequality.* In many societies it is very difficult, if not impossible, for women to own land or homes, thus making it much harder for them to become economically independent.
7. *Household inequality.* Family arrangements in most cultures place the burden of unpaid work squarely on women's shoulders and take for granted that, whether they work outside the home or not, they will perform such duties as child care and housework.

One positive note is that many countries exhibiting a high degree of gender inequality are initiating government-led programs to try to reduce the gender gap. However, because gender bias has such a long cultural history and appears on so many fronts, the process ahead to overcome it will no doubt take many more years to accomplish.

describes gender inequality from a global perspective). This affirmation of women does not imply a rejection of men or all things masculine. Instead, both men and women are accorded equal respect and value.

According to feminists, the boxes males and females are put in are too simple and too idealistic. In practice, many individuals—both men and women—feel stifled by the roles they have been assigned and have sought a way to transform the traditional family. The following poem by Nancy R. Smith sums it up nicely:

> For every woman who is tired of acting weak when she knows she is strong,
>
> There is a man who is tired of appearing strong when he feels vulnerable.
>
> For every woman who is tired of acting dumb,
>
> There is a man who is burdened with the constant expectations of "knowing everything."
>
> For every woman who is tired of being called an "emotional female,"
>
> There is a man who is denied the right to weep and be gentle.
>
> For every woman who feels "tied down" by her children,
>
> There is a man who is denied the full pleasures of shared parenthood.
>
> For every woman who takes a step toward her own liberation,
>
> There is a man who finds the way to freedom has been made a little easier.

Nancy R. Smith, excerpt from "For Every Woman." Copyright © 1973 by Nancy R. Smith. Reprinted with the permission of the author.

Power in Families

The fundamental concept in social science is Power, in the same sense in which Energy is the fundamental concept in physics.

—BERTRAND RUSSELL

The words *family* and *power* are inextricably linked. Power, control, and authority are continuously exercised in families, and struggles for personal power in families are exceedingly common. Tradition has dictated that considerable power goes to the males in the family, but women often have more power than they or anyone else admit.

Power can be defined as the ability (potential or actual) of an individual to change the behavior of other members in a social system. By extending this definition to families, we can define **family power** as the ability of one family member to change the behavior of the other family members.

Many of the characteristics of power in close relationships were summarized by Kathleen M. Galvin and Bernard J. Brommel (2000). Power is a system property—a feature of a family system—rather than a personal characteristic of any one family member. Power is an interactive process involving one family member who desires something from one or more other family members; these members may affect all other members in the system. Power is also a dynamic process, not a static one. It creates reciprocal causation (i.e., family members react to power attempts) in which one move leads to another, which leads to another, and so forth. Power also changes over time, particularly when the family is under stress. Power has both perceptual and behavioral aspects: The same power issue may be perceived differently by each family member.

Educational level, occupational prestige, and income are all sources of power in our society—and in relationships as well. This college graduate is very likely to have more power in a marriage relationship than a high school graduate who chooses the role of full-time homemaker and mother.

Types of Power Patterns

According to one classic model (Herbst, 1952), the power balance in a marriage can be characterized in four basic ways: a **husband-dominant power pattern,** in which the man is basically the boss; a **wife-dominant power pattern,** in which the woman is basically the boss; a **syncratic power pattern** (in essence, "to decide together"), in which authority is shared and decisions are made on a joint basis in most areas of endeavor; and an **autonomic power pattern,** in which each spouse has about equal authority but in different areas of life and essentially makes decisions in her or his particular domain independent of the other. These patterns are illustrated in Figure 7.1. Although this work is very old, the concepts still hold true today.

Syncratic: shared authority and joint decision making in most areas

Autonomic: about equal authority, but in different areas of life

FIGURE 7.1

Power Patterns in Marriages

Source: Adapted from P. G. Herbst, "The Measurement of Family Relationships" from *Human Relations* 5 (1952): 3–35. Copyright 1952 The Tavistock Institute, London, UK. Reprinted by permission of SAGE.

In the early stages of a relationship, there can be a great deal of instability as the individuals struggle to work out the balance of power. As time passes, the partners assert themselves to establish some power in the relationship. A male- or female-dominant relationship, with one person leading and the other following, is difficult to maintain. Eventually, the dominant one may tire of leading, and the submissive one may tire of following. The result may be a change to another type of power sharing.

In a syncratic relationship, the sharing of decisions and tasks affords the family system a better power balance. The partners are relatively equal, and couples with children often encourage some sharing of power, especially as the children become older.

In an autonomic relationship, one spouse may have most of the power in one area, such as inside the home, whereas the other spouse may have most of the power in another area, such as outside the home. Both perceive the relationship to be relatively equal in power on the whole, because both domains of endeavor are perceived to be important.

Egalitarian Roles and Marital Satisfaction

When it comes to the importance of an equal relationship versus a traditional relationship to marital satisfaction, the national survey by Olson, Olson-Sigg, & Larson (2008) clearly demonstrated that more equal relationships are highly related to marital satisfaction (see Table 7.5). If both partners perceive their relationship as egalitarian, 81% of the couples describe their marriage as happy and only 19% are unhappy. Conversely, if both partners perceive their marriage as traditional, only 18% feel their marriage is happy and 82% are unhappy. These findings are rather dramatic and demonstrate the importance of an equal relationship for marital happiness.

Two interesting patterns emerged when the partners perceived their relationship differently with one person saying it is equal and the other saying it is traditional. When the husband says the relationship is traditional and the wife says it is equal, half the marriages are happy and half are unhappy. However, when the wife says the relationship is traditional and the husband says it is equal, only about one-third (37%) are happy and two-thirds (63%) are unhappy. It is the wife's perception of equality that is most predictive of couple satisfaction.

TABLE 7.5	Role Relationships in Happy Couples Versus Unhappy Couples	
	PERCENTAGE IN AGREEMENT	
Perception of Relationship	**Happy Couples**	**Unhappy Couples**
Both perceive as egalitarian.	81%	19%
Husband perceives as traditional; wife perceives as egalitarian.	50	50
Wife perceives as traditional; husband perceives as egalitarian.	37	63
Both perceive as traditional.	18	82

Source: Adapted from David H. Olson, Amy Olson-Sigg, and Peter J. Larson Ph.D., *The Couple Checkup.* Copyright © 2008 by David H. Olson, Amy Olson-Sigg, and Peter J. Larson. Reprinted by permission of Thomas Nelson, Inc.

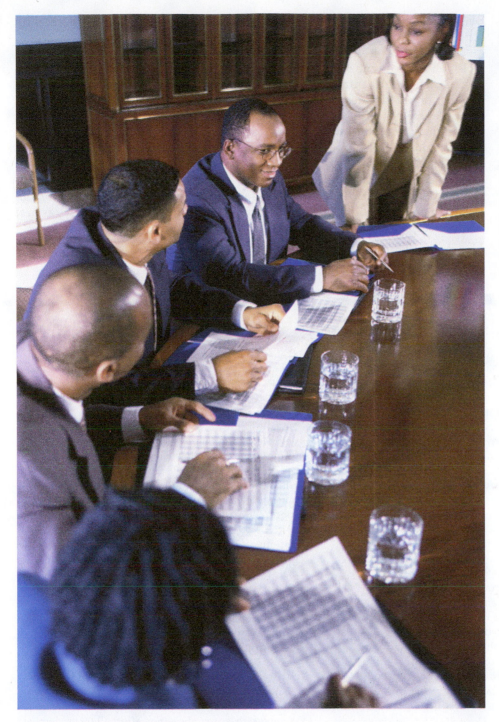

The quest for power, money, and material success in which so many men are immersed is accompanied by higher levels of stress, higher rates of heart disease, and shorter life spans. Some observers believe that over time as women continue to rise in the working world there will also be a concomitant increase in the stress-related health problems that women experience. The current life expectancy at birth in the United States for men is 75.4 years and for women is 80.7 years (Heron et al., 2008).

Suggestions for Minimizing Power Issues

Remember that power is a characteristic of relationships, not of people. Power is always relative, changing, and useful only to the extent that it is legitimate. Many of the conflicts that cause relationship stress are struggles over the power process (the way decisions are made) rather than disagreements about a specific issue. The person holding the authority to make each decision must have the responsibility for following through on the decision.

Decision making should be balanced by the value of the areas each partner controls, not by the number of areas each has. It is more efficient and more realistic to assign each partner primary responsibility for making decisions in certain areas, whether or not the other has veto authority, than to make all decisions a matter of mutual agreement.

Men may think they have a lot to lose by giving up some of their power over women and children, but, in fact, they have a great deal to gain. Men tend to die younger than women, often from a variety of illnesses related to stress and poor lifestyle choices. A macho, "win-at-all-costs" attitude is commonly thought to contribute to men's health problems. Rigid gender roles may have afforded men more power in our culture, but it is lonely at the top. The path toward intimacy is best walked side by side.

Summary

- According to a national survey, happily married couples agree more often than unhappily married couples that both partners are equally willing to make adjustments in roles, that they are satisfied with the division of housework, that it takes hard work to have an equal relationship, and that they make most decisions jointly and household tasks are divided on the basis of preferences rather than tradition.

- The most commonly reported issues for married couples in their role relationship were the following: concern about unfair division of housework, housework based on traditional roles, husband not willing to adjust, wife too involved in housework, and lack of working to maintain an equal relationship.

- Gender roles—the expectations every society has about people's attitudes and behaviors based on whether they are male or female—are rooted in biology but heavily influenced by culture.

- A Gallup poll indicated that males were more often perceived as aggressive, courageous, and ambitious. Females were described as emotional, affectionate, talkative, patient, and creative. There was considerable agreement across genders on these descriptions of men and women.

- Sociologist Talcott Parsons espoused a traditional view of gender roles. His theory of family roles assumed that men should be "instrumental" and women "expressive." Parsons's theory has been vigorously challenged and is no longer well received.

- Persistent gender-role patterns in marriage mean that women do much more of the housework in the family than men do, which often leads to relationship conflict.

- In Latino/a, African American, and American Indian cultures, as in White society, men have often been dominant in their families, but signs of change are also apparent in these cultures.

- New immigrants often have to adapt to new gender role dynamics as they enter the United States. Gender roles often become a hybrid of the new and the old.

- Historically prominent theories of gender-role development include the social learning theory, which is concerned with how individuals learn the behavior patterns considered appropriate for their sex; the cognitive development theory, which links the progressive acquisition of gender typing to the general maturation of the child's thinking processes; the family systems theory, which holds that the entire family must change when an individual member changes; and the feminist framework, which argues that women are exploited, devalued, and oppressed and affirms their equality with men.

- Family power is the ability of one family member to change the behavior of other family members. Power is an interactive process involving one family member who desires something from one or more other family members; these members may affect all other members in the system.

- The power balance in a marriage can be characterized in four basic ways: a husband-dominant pattern; a wife-dominant pattern; a syncratic pattern, in which authority is shared; and an autonomic pattern, in which each spouse has about equal authority but in different areas of life.

Key Terms

gender identity
gender role
gender-role stereotype
masculinity
femininity
egalitarian roles
social learning theory
cognitive development
  theory

power
family power
husband-dominant
  power pattern
wife-dominant power
  pattern
syncratic power pattern
autonomic power pattern

Activities

1. In small groups, discuss whether American society will ever evolve into one in which one's gender is relatively unimportant, except in relation to reproduction. How far can we go in removing the old gender-role stereotypes?
2. Study Table 7.4, Contemporary Versus Traditional Dating and Marriage Patterns. If you are in an intimate relationship, decide which aspects from the "contemporary" list and which from the "traditional" list apply to your relationship. Have your partner do the same exercise and compare your answers.
3. In small groups, discuss family power. How was power distributed in your family of origin? How do you know? (Give examples.) How do you want power to be distributed in the family you hope to create in the future?

Suggested Readings

Bass, B. L., Butler, A. B., Grzywacz, J. G., & Linney, K. D. (2009). Do job demands undermine parenting? A daily analysis of spillover and crossover effects. *Family Relations, 58,* 201–215.

Boyd-Franklin, N., Franklin, A. J., & Toussaint, P. A. (2000). *Boys into men: Raising our African American teenage sons.* New York: Dutton.

Drago, R. W. (2007). *Work, family, life.* Boston, MA: Dollars & Sense Publishers.

Franklin, A. J. (2004). *From brotherhood to manhood: How Black men rescue their relationships and dreams from the invisibility syndrome.* New York: Wiley. Insidious racism still pervades American society.

Gerson, K. (2010). *The unfinished revolution: How a new generation is reshaping family, work, and gender in American.* New York: Oxford University Press.

Gilbert, N. (2008). *A mother's work: How feminism, the market, and policy shape family life.* New Haven, CT: Yale University Press.

Halpern, D. F., & Cheung, F. M. (2008). *Women at the top: Powerful leaders tell us how to combine work and family.* West Sussex, UK: Wiley-Blackwell.

Lippa, R. A. (2001). *Gender, nature, and nurture.* Mahwah, NJ: Erlbaum.

Meier, J. A., McNaughton-Cassill, M., & Lynch, M. (2006). The management of household and childcare tasks and relationship satisfaction in parenting couples. *Marriage and Family Review, 40,* 61–88.

North Carolina Division of Social Services and the Family and Children's Resource Program. (2006). Working with American Indian families. *Children's Services Practice Notes, 11*(2). Web site: http://www.practicenotes.org/vol11_no2.htm.

Pitt-Catsouphes, M., Kossek, E. E., & Sweet, S. (2006). *The work and family handbook.* Mahwah, NJ: Erlbaum.

Saval, M. (2009). *The secret lives of boys: Inside the raw emotional world of male teens.* New York: Basic Books. Listening to boys talking, in a voyeuristic way, parents, teenagers, and especially teenage girls will be fascinated to know that boys care about fashion, cry about girlfriends, and have deep feelings. More important, parents and teenage girls will see aspects of themselves reflected in the stories told by the boys and realize that boys aren't so mystifying after all.

Stone, P. (2007). *Opting out: Why women really quit careers and head home.* Berkeley: University of California Press. This book challenges the media stories about the "new traditionalism" that prompts high-achieving women to make the "choice" to quit work and return to full-time motherhood, "the most rewarding job in the world." Stone argues that women are often forced out of the workplace because it is still designed for "ideal workers" who are available to work 24–7 because they have no caregiving responsibilities.

Treas, J., & Drobnic, S. (Eds.). (2010). *Dividing the domestic: Men, women, and household work in cross-national perspective.* Stanford, CA: Stanford University Press.

Voydanoff, P. (2005). Work demands and work-to-family and family-to-work conflict: Direct and indirect relationships. *Journal of Family Issues, 26,* 707–726.

Visit the text-specific Online Learning Center at **www.mhhe.com/olson8e** for practice tests, chapter summaries, and PowerPoint slides.

8. *M*anaging Economic Resources

Money and Happiness

Marriage and Money

Diversity and Financial Style

The Cost of Divorce

Why Do Finances Cause Problems?

Family Income and Expenses

Smart Money Management

Credit: Uses and Abuses

Summary

Key Terms

Activities

Suggested Readings

In this chapter we will focus on financial issues, particularly as they relate to intimate relationships and to families across the life cycle. The interest and research regarding the interface between couples and families and economic issues has grown substantially in the past 20 years (Dew, 2008b). This interest is expected to continue to grow as baby boomers move into retirement. Some of the topics that have received attention are financial management, women's labor force participation, balancing work and family, and economic issues and their impact on family relationships. The field of study of economic issues and families has, by nature, been interdisciplinary, including such areas as consumer economics, family studies, psychology, political science, nutrition, and sociology. In addition, much research has been done and many resulting journal articles have been written by authors from multiple disciplines. This allows for multiple perspectives to come together to address the issues around families and finances.

The economic recession that began in 2007 is also adding interest to the dynamics between money and families. With the unemployment rate reaching over 10%, many families need to change many aspects of their lives that have implications for family relationships. The recession has affected everyone, and the majority of people expect the effects of the recession to last for several years (*Time*, 2009, April, 27). Money problems are often related to an inability to develop an open and well-organized couple or family system. These financial problems then lead to more stress and conflict in the marriage or family. We will explore the field of financial resource management, whose aim is to achieve economic **goals** and harmony in intimate relationships.

Money and Happiness

Do money and happiness go together? It has been generally felt that when rich and very poor people are compared, the rich are happier. However, it has been thought that once people are out of poverty, the differences in happiness are relatively weak. As we shall see, the findings are mixed.

Some recent reports indicate that there is a strong relationship between money and happiness (*The Economist*, 2007, July 14). In an international study asking people how satisfied they are with their life on a scale of 1 to 10, in general people in wealthier nations (America, Europe, Japan, Saudi Arabia) reported being more happy than those from poor countries (primarily African countries). These findings were also true when it came to looking at those who were wealthy and those who were poor within countries—the wealthy people were happier. Another study, conducted by the Pew Research Center (Stokes, 2007, July 24), indicates that globally, countries that have had rising economic growth have also had rising happiness levels. This report also showed that once people reach a certain level of income, happiness levels off. Some say that after families reach a household income of $50,000, the relationship between money and happiness is no longer strong (*Time*, 2009, April 27).

Another study, which was done in the United States, also showed that money and happiness go together (Pew Research Center, 2006, February 13). In this study, one-third of participants said they were very happy, with another 50% indicating they were pretty happy (see Figure 8.1). According to this study, these numbers have been stable over the past 35 years. Pew also found that annual family income correlated with peoples' happiness responses. For example, only

FIGURE 8.1

About One-Third of
Americans Are Very
Happy

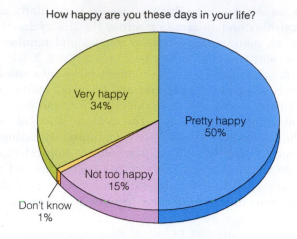

How happy are you these days in your life?

Very happy
34%

Pretty happy
50%

Not too happy
15%

Don't know
1%

24% of those with annual family incomes of less than $30,000 said they were very happy, whereas 49% of families making $100,000 or more said they were very happy (see Figure 8.2). However, just because money and happiness go together does not mean one causes the other. Maybe money leads to happiness, or happiness leads to money. This study also showed that those who were healthiest were more likely to be very happy and those who had poor health were least happy. It may be that those with poor health made less money, and it was health that made the difference, not money. One might ask: Is it the money that makes the difference or is it things that go along with having money that make the difference, such as home ownership, less stress, or having more choices. All we know from these studies is that wealth and happiness seem to go together. With that said, there are many people who would say that when it comes to happiness, there are

FIGURE 8.2

Does Money Buy
Happiness?

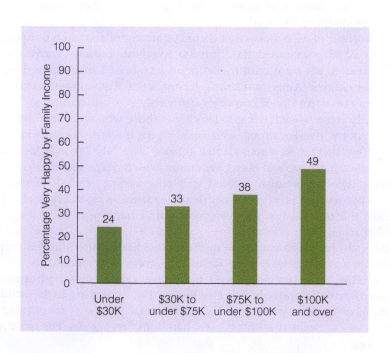

many things more important than money. In fact, two of the wealthiest men in the United States, Warren Buffett and Bill Gates, have weighed in on this issue. Buffet has said, "The true measure of success is the number of people who genuinely care about and respect you when you near the end of your life" (Hoskins, 2005, winter, p. 33). Bill Gates said, "My goal for success outside of work is definitely raising a family. So far I haven't caused any damage; they seem to be doing OK" (Hoskins, 2005, p. 33).

There is also evidence that income is related to social problems. One study indicated that lower income was related to increased environmental and family risk (Jones-Sanpei, Homes, & Day, 2009). In other words, more things can cause problems in the lives of family members who were poor. In another study, poor, rural women who lived in trailer parks told their stories about how they made their way across the life span (Notter, MacTavish, & Shamah, 2008). These women had multiple barriers to overcome, but they managed to be resilient. These women, however, also had persistent economic struggles and experienced social isolation. So poor people can overcome many barriers but still continue to struggle.

What might we conclude from this information? Being poor has multiple stresses, and it is likely that those in this country trying to raise a family on less than $50,000 per year experience many stresses that make them unhappy. They may be living in substandard housing, experiencing crime in their neighborhoods, and sending their children to schools that are unsafe and are not places where children can learn. Once families have earnings beyond a level that provides for basic needs, however, other things factor into happiness. These things may be marital happiness, having a supportive extended family, and doing things that one enjoys.

The economic downturn that began in 2007 had a dramatic impact on most every family in the United States, either directly or indirectly. Many became poor at a time in their lives when they least expected it—and certainly many would consider it a time of unhappiness. This downturn is projected to be like no other, and some of the effects are likely to be long-lasting. Many have lost jobs and homes, and others have been affected by the fear of losing their jobs or their homes and have changed their lifestyle in response to that fear. A *Time* magazine poll found that 57% of people felt that the American dream is harder to achieve (2009, April 27). It was found that 21% of people had become unemployed not by choice. These dramatic economic declines can result in increased substance abuse, increased domestic violence, increased marital tensions, and in some cases divorce (Wilcox, 2009).

There may be, however, a silver lining in this for some families. According to the *Time* poll, one-third of people polled are spending more time with friends and family and are having better relationships with their kids than before the crisis. More people are planting gardens, saving more, going out less, and generally becoming more frugal. These things will all serve families well.

The recession also makes us appreciate things we once took for granted. According to Bradford Wilcox (2009), "The recession reminds us that marriage is more than an emotional relationship; marriage is also an economic partnership and social safety net. There is nothing like the loss of a job, an imminent foreclosure, or a shrinking 401(K) to gain a new appreciation for a wife's job, a husband's commitment to pay down debt, or the in-laws' willingness to help out with childcare or a rent-free place to live" (p. 16).

Many people are assessing what is happening in their marriages and family lives and making decisions about what is really important. This is a good thing.

Marriage and Money

A significant amount of research indicates there is a strong relationship between marital happiness and finances. One large study of over 50,000 couples shows that happy couples have different ways of viewing and managing money than unhappy couples (Olson, Olson-Sigg, & Larson, 2008). This study found that the financial management item that most distinguishes happy couples from unhappy couples is how much they agree on how to spend money (Table 8.1). Other issues that distinguish happy from unhappy couples include concerns about saving, concerns about debt, control of finances, and the use of credit cards. Couples can improve their couple relationship by discussing these issues and come to an agreement about these financial matters.

A national study asked 64 couples who had great marriages to tell, by way of a 31-page questionnaire, what made their marriages great (Skogrand, Johnson, Horrocks, & DeFrain, 2011). They answered questions about many aspects of their couple relationships, including how they managed their finances. Three themes regarding marriage and money emerged from the data. First, for most couples, one of the partners handled the day-to-day finances. The decision was based upon who had the expertise, who had the time, or who enjoyed doing it. When one person managed the money, however, it required trust and communication. Second, these couples with great marriages had little or no debt or had a goal of paying off debt. It was a shared goal to pay with cash or, if credit was used, to pay off the bill as quickly as possible. Third, couples lived within their means, and many considered themselves frugal. There was no trend toward having either joint or separate accounts. Either way seemed to work as long as they were in agreement. Although many of these couples with great marriages had experienced financial challenges during their married life, they had worked them out together. Therefore, one could conclude that managing finances well contributes to a great marriage. The authors of this study provide an alternative explanation, however, and suggest that having a strong marriage, which typically included having good communication and conflict resolution skills, helped couples more effectively manage their money. These strong marriages may have also helped them get through difficult financial times. They also suggest that teaching money management skills alone will not necessarily enable couples to

TABLE 8.1	Strengths of Happy Versus Unhappy Couples Regarding Finances		
		PERCENTAGE IN AGREEMENT	
Financial Issue		**Happy Couples**	**Unhappy Couples**
1. We agree on how to spend money.		85	43
2. I am satisfied with our decision to save.		67	29
3. Major debts are not a problem for us.		69	35
4. My partner does not try to control our finances.		74	43
5. Credit cards are not a problem for us.		69	42

strengthen their marriages. If couples do not know how to solve problems or deal with conflict in the marriages, they are unlikely to be able deal with the conflict that can result with money. It might be that helping couples strengthen their marriage will help them address financial issues. Only further research will address this question. It might be useful, however, for financial counselors and family life educators to work hand-in-hand in helping couples have healthy couple relationships, which would develop skills that will enhance their handling of financial issues—and developing skills in managing finances could enhance their marriage relationships.

A significant amount of data shows a relationship between marital satisfaction and the emotional stress that goes along with finances. In one large sample of nearly 5,000 married couples it was found that couple financial strain contributed to both husbands' and wives' emotional distress (Gudmunson et al., 2007). This stress was related to marital instability. This study also found that there was a direct path from financial strain to disagreements in marriage, and disagreements provide a context for relationship decay. These authors also suggest that couples today have little time to spend together, and if this limited time together is spent arguing about money, it is likely to add to marital instability.

Debt and its relationship to marital happiness has been studied extensively in recent years. Dew's study of newly married couples showed that a change in consumer debt (for goods and services) predicted a change in marital satisfaction (2008a). If couples paid off their debt, their marital satisfaction increased. Dew suggests that having debt affects quality time together, which affects marital satisfaction. Lack of quality time together may be because of need to work more or being unable to spend time together without arguing about finances. Interestingly, changes in mortgage and school debt were not related to changes in marital satisfaction. It may be that mortgage and school debt are viewed as investments.

Along with debt, assets have also been studied in terms of their relationship to marital satisfaction. In another study Dew (2007) compared the impact of debt and assets on marital satisfaction. It was again found that debt was directly related to marital satisfaction—increased debt resulted in decreased marital satisfaction. In addition, however, it was found that assets reduced economic pressure and economic worries, but were not directly related to marital satisfaction. Based upon these findings, Dew suggests that paying down debt has a more direct impact on marital satisfaction than does the accumulation of assets.

Finally, Dew (2009) looked at assets as they related to divorce. The findings of this study showed that for women, assets were related to marital satisfaction, which kept them from wanting a divorce. This relationship was not true for men. It was suggested that assets may enhance wives' marital satisfaction so women do not want to divorce, and these women feel that divorce is not an option. It is possible that wives expect marriage to provide them with economic benefits and these assets, therefore, predict marital satisfaction.

We can conclude from these findings that marital happiness and finances are related. Debt is negatively related to marital satisfaction, and couples who have little or no debt are happier than those with debt. Couples who are happy in their marriages trust each other and communicate about finances. It is expected that future studies will continue to enhance our understanding of this relationship between money and marital happiness.

BOX 8.1   At Issue

The Effects of Debt on Newlyweds

Is it finances in general, or specifically debt, that causes problems for couples? Much has been written about the stress of finances and money in causing problems for couples in their marriages. One study, however, found that it was debt that caused the most problems in newlywed marriages, rather than finances in general.

In a study by Skogrand, Schramm, Marshall, and Lee (2005) of approximately 1,000 randomly selected newlywed couples who had been married from 3 to 9 months, debt brought into marriage was identified as the second-most-cited problem in their marriage by both husbands and wives. In this study, debt brought into marriage was separate from financial decision making, which was much farther down the list of 30 possible problematic areas for couples.

Couples in this study were asked to indicate their level of debt in areas of debt such as medical bills, credit card debt, auto loans, and school loans. Home mortgage debt was not included as a possible problem area in this study, because most newlywed couples do not own a home. Important findings of the study include the following:

- Seventy percent of husbands and wives brought debt into the marriage. Thirty-five percent of husbands and wives had more than $5,000 in debt when they married.

- Fifty-five percent of husbands and wives had automobile debt, 48% had credit card debt, 23% had school debt, and 12% had medical debt when they entered the marriage.
- Of the four kinds of debt, credit card and automobile loan debt had the highest correlation with lower marital satisfaction and adjustment scores for both husbands and wives.
- Higher levels of education were related to lower amounts of debt brought into marriage.
- Medical bills and school loans may have been viewed as necessary debt, because they did not have a high correlation with low levels of marital satisfaction and adjustment.
- The higher the debt brought into the marriage, the lower the marital satisfaction and adjustment scores of participants. Those who brought no debt into the marriage had the highest marital satisfaction and adjustment scores.

According to this study, debt is an important factor in marital satisfaction and adjustment. Why is this true? We suggest that debt and financial difficulties create stress, which takes away from developing and maintaining the marital relationship.

Diversity and Financial Style

Little has been written about how finances are handled by low-income families and families from diverse populations. A major difference between low-income and middle- and higher-income spending practices relates to the difference between a **collective worldview** and an **individualistic worldview** (Skogrand, Hatch, & Singh, 2008). Low-income families and families living in poverty usually view things from a collective worldview. This means a family often gets through life because someone—a family member, friend, or neighbor—helped them when they really needed it. It follows, then, that when this family has a little extra money, it will be shared with the same people who helped them. People with an individualistic worldview typically use resources to better themselves such as buying a bigger house, furthering their education, or investing their money in the stock market.

Diverse cultural groups are also likely to have a collective worldview rather than an individualistic worldview and see helping family and friends as a high priority. This would be true of many Latino families. Family is the highest priority, and family needs would come before personal needs (Skogrand et al., 2008). Family is also viewed as the primary source of financial support. This perspective may be viewed by European American, middle-class folks as being irresponsible when, in fact, it is a cultural strength.

Finances can create difficulties for couples. Discussing financial issues and reaching an agreement about these issues will help the couple's relationship.

Low-income families may have had financial stresses in their lives to the point that they do not have a bank account because of bad credit. Other reasons for not having a checking account include not trusting banks, not trusting technology, or unavailability of banking services in some poorer neighborhoods (Bartholomae & Fox, 2008). Because low-income families often do not have checking accounts, they often pay a fee for using money orders to pay bills or pay a fee for cashing checks. Because they do not have good credit, they may have to borrow money from pay-day loans (loans you pay back when you get a paycheck), which can have interest rates up to 1,000%. These costs add to an already stretched budget.

Because low-income families live from paycheck to paycheck, any unexpected expense has a domino effect. A bounced check of $20 can mean multiple overdraft charges that, according to one researcher, could run as high as 4,000% of the original bounced check (Fusaro, 2008). These overdraft charges can mean a car payment cannot be made, and a loss of a car can mean a loss of a job. There is often no opportunity to recover from an unexpected expense because there is no wiggle room in the budget for emergencies.

Earlier experiences also affect how one manages finances. For example, new Latino immigrants often do not use banks because they were not always trusted in the country from which they emigrated (Holzner et al., 2006). Instead, money may be kept at home—literally under the mattress or in the cupboard, because those are more trusted places than a bank. Having a savings account, investing in a retirement account, or using credit, which involves banks, may not be something Latino families would do. Only a small percentage of Latinos have investment accounts (Holzner et al., 2006). In addition, substantial amounts of money are often sent to family members in their country of origin, rather than being used for improving quality of life for the family that is in the United States.

Somali immigrants have religious views about finances that are in contrast to the majority U.S. population (Solheim, 2008). According to Islamic law, unfair interest cannot be charged on loans, which stems from a belief that there should be economic justice between those who have and those who do not have financial resources. Low-interest loans, however, are acceptable, and paying off credit cards before they accumulate interest is acceptable under Islamic law. Earning interest on savings accounts is also problematic. This issue can be addressed by donating the interest to charity.

The issues that immigrants face in this country are significant, because one in 10 people in America were born in another country, with the number expected to increase (Solheim, 2008). Family finance professionals need to be aware of these cultural differences as they try to help new immigrant families manage money in their new country.

Couples and families use a wide range of strategies that are dependent on social class, family structure, life experiences, and culture. Stepfamilies have to negotiate ways to manage finances that account for each spouse having individual financial responsibilities involving their own children. They may have to manage several pots of money that include yours, mine, and ours to accommodate a complex family system (Stewart, 2007). Child support and other types of financial commitments must be met that were made before the stepfamily relationship developed. Couples who have divorced and remarried later in life may not have young children to financially care for, but may have adult children who do not want their inheritance to go to a new spouse or that spouse's children.

The Cost of Divorce

We have always known that there is a tremendous emotional cost to families who experience a divorce. One researcher recently identified the potential economic cost of divorce. Divorce is necessary and in the best interest of the couple and the family in many cases, and to stay in the relationship would be financially costly as well in terms of physical, emotional, and mental well-being (Schramm, 2006). This study was conducted in 2001 in a western state to determine the cost of divorce to the family and to the state and federal governments, with implications for social policy that would contribute to strengthening marriages.

The personal costs of divorce in the study were calculated based on legal and filing fees for the divorce, divorce education classes that were required in the state where the study was conducted, housing costs with required moves, and lost productivity due to distress (Schramm, 2006). Legal fees for a divorce vary, of course, but a conservative estimate of the costs was $7,000 per divorce for a couple with children, and a filing fee of $95 to start the divorce process. Some states have divorce education classes, especially for couples with children. Although this cost is somewhat minimal, in this western state it was $70 per couple.

Housing may be a substantial cost for divorcing couples. Schramm (2006) indicates that minimally there would be one geographic move in each divorce, and approximately one-third of the couples would have two geographic moves. It is estimated that the average housing cost for a family not going through a divorce would be $15,500, and the equivalent expenses for a divorcing family is estimated to be almost $20,000. Based on estimates of other studies regarding lost productivity related to stress, it is estimated that approximately $3,000 per year per couple is the cost of lost productivity. These costs total approximately $14,000 for the year of the divorce (Schramm, 2006).

Although a personal cost of $14,000 is considerable for any family, this amount would be especially burdensome for low-income families, where the divorce rates are the highest. Many couples may see only the anticipated added benefit of getting out of a marriage without being aware of the added financial costs.

In addition to the personal costs of divorce, Schramm (2006) calculates the cost to communities and local and federal governments and concludes that each divorce has a total average estimated cost of $30,000. Schramm suggests that resources might be invested in education to strengthen marriages, which would result in less money spent than the potential costs of divorce. Couples may also consider the personal investment in marriage therapy and education as being less costly than a divorce.

Why Do Finances Cause Problems?

There are several reasons finances cause problems for families:

- Money is a taboo topic in many families.
- Many couples do not create and stick to a budget.
- Some families overspend and rely too heavily on credit.
- Partners have different styles of spending and saving.
- One partner uses money as a tool to gain power and control over the other partner.
- Partners have different ideas about the meaning of money.

In the dating phase, couples are more likely to talk about any topic other than their financial situations; it's not very romantic to talk about potential income, the use of credit cards, and views on savings. In contrast, among married couples, money matters are the most common sources of arguments. Money can symbolize different things to different people, and if couples don't recognize these differences, they are often unprepared for the resulting friction. That's the situation described by Marcia, a 42-year-old computer technician, in the following account:

"I thought we talked about everything before marriage. But we never seemed to get around to money—what it means to each of us and how it should be spent. Because I saw money as a symbol of security, I wanted to scrimp and save. I wanted to build a house, a nest, and feel safe inside. Because he saw money as a tool to achieve freedom and independence, he wanted to use it for adventure. We were doomed from the beginning to fight over money."

BOX 8.2 Putting It Together

Steps to Financial Freedom

There are some general principles that can help people control their financial resources. These steps can be utilized by individuals, couples, or families. If you are in a couple or family, it would be wise to take time as a couple or have a family meeting and make decisions about implementing these strategies.

Step 1: **Create a budget and stick to it.** Consider the money you have coming in, and identify the expenses that have to be paid. Expenses should include rent or house payments, utilities, loan repayments, groceries, car expenses, and any other regular costs. If you have insurance payments that are only made yearly or quarterly, find a way to put that money away on a monthly basis so that the payments can be made when they come due. It is also wise to put money into savings each month in case of a layoff or other emergency.

Step 2: **Identify your goals.** Think about the goals you have for the next 5 years. These goals will help you identify ways to spend your money in ways that are consistent with your goals. For example, if you want to buy a house, you may need to establish a savings account in order to have a down payment.

Step 3. **Cut up your credit cards.** Credit card debt can get out of hand and result in considerable interest being paid when a balance is maintained. Start paying off the credit cards that have the highest interest rates. When one credit card is paid off, use the money you would normally pay on that credit card to pay on the card with the next highest interest. It is a good idea to have one credit card for emergencies.

Step 4: **Make savings automatic.** If you do not put money aside for savings before other bills are paid, it usually does not happen. Taking a regular percentage out for savings, such as 15%, by way of automatic deposit or some other automatic system, makes it happen.

Step 5: **Protect your credit by making payments on time.** Regular, on-time payments help build good credit. Pay back aggressively if your budget allows for it. Late payments usually result in late fees and may eventually be reported to credit bureaus.

Step 6: **Have a savings account first, then worry about a retirement fund.** The first priority should be making sure you have money set aside for emergencies. Once that is in place, consider putting money away for retirement. It is especially important to contribute to a retirement fund if your employer is matching your contributions. It is free money.

Adapted with permission from: A. Cynkar, "Early-career insights: Seven steps to stomp out debt" from *Monitor on Psychology* 38 (5). Retrieved from http://www.apa.org/monitor/. Copyright © 2007 by the American Psychological Association. No further reproduction or distribution is permitted without written permission from the American Psychological Association.

Money is not just the paper, coin, or plastic used to buy things. It can also be a perceived source of status, security, enjoyment, or control. If partners have incompatible attitudes about money and its uses, extravagant purchases are likely to cause conflicts between them over deeply held beliefs and values.

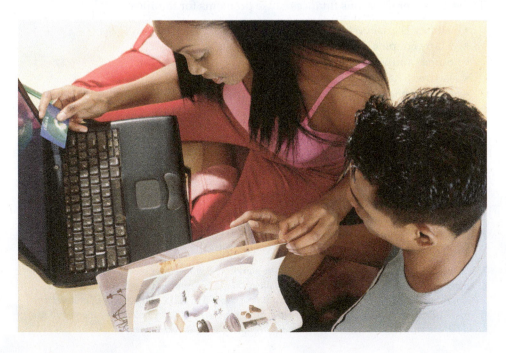

It isn't just married couples, however, who lack communication skills when it comes to finances. The discussion of money between parents and children is often nonexistent. Nonetheless, many financial advisers and counselors argue that it is essential to break the family pattern of financial silence.

Family Income and Expenses

In this section we will focus on the average income of U.S. families and on income variations among different ethnic and cultural groups and between men and women. We will also explore typical family expenses and differences in family net worth. Finally, we will examine the financial feasibility for both spouses to work outside the home, especially if they have children.

What does *living in poverty* mean? It means that people might not have adequate food or a decent place to sleep. (In the case of the homeless, it could mean living in a refrigerator box in an alley or under a bridge.) It means people cannot afford to see a physician when they are ill or to purchase medicine when they need it. Being poor may mean having no telephone, no radio, no television, no means of transportation. It often means that children attend substandard schools or that their parents move so often looking for work that the children do not attend school at all. Poverty is a very stressful state of affairs.

Lower-middle-income families, although not officially "poor" by government standards, also find it quite difficult to make ends meet. In both two-parent and single-parent lower-middle-income families, about three-quarters of all family expenditures can go for housing, food, and transportation. This leaves little money for anything else.

The number of people living in poverty continues to increase. In 2011, there were 46.2 million people, or 15%, in poverty. This was about the same as in 2010. The poverty level is defined by the government and is based on the number of people in the family. For 2011, a family was considered to be living in poverty if a family of five had an annual income of $28,000 or less (U.S. Census Bureau, 2012).

In 2010, the percentage of families living in poverty varied greatly across ethnic groups. While Whites had a poverty rate of 10%, Asians had a 12% rate, Blacks had a poverty rate of 27%, and Hispanics had a rate of 27%. About 22% of children under the age of 18 live in a household that is in poverty (National Poverty Center, n.d.).

Family Income

As one can see from Figure 8.3, there are a significant number of families that earn less than $35,000 per year. Depending upon where in the country one lives, it would be very difficult to support a family on this amount of money.

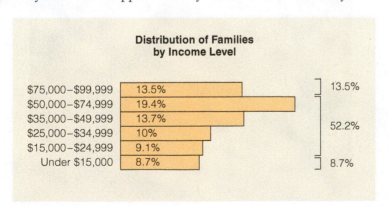

Distribution of Families by Income Level

Income Level	Percentage	
$75,000–$99,999	13.5%	13.5%
$50,000–$74,999	19.4%	
$35,000–$49,999	13.7%	52.2%
$25,000–$34,999	10%	
$15,000–$24,999	9.1%	
Under $15,000	8.7%	8.7%

FIGURE 8.3
Income Levels of U.S. Families, 2009
Source: U.S. Census Bureau, 2009.

TABLE 8.2	Income Levels by Ethnic Group
Ethnic Group	**Median Household Income**
All Groups	$60,088
Asian	$75,027
White	$62,545
Hispanic	$39,730
Black	$38,409

Source: U.S. Census Bureau, 2012.

Ethnic Income Differences. While the average annual income for all groups was $60,088, there are considerable income differences across ethnic groups in the United States (Table 8.2). For example, among all types of family households, the median income for Asian families is $75,027; for White families, $62,545; for Black families, $38,409, and for Hispanic families, $39,730.

Although there is less gender segregation in the workplace than ever before, income differences between men and women still exist.

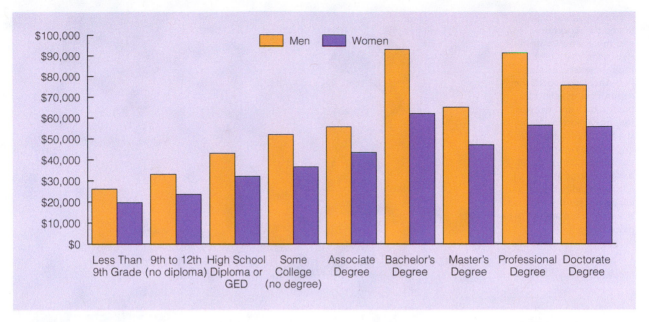

FIGURE 8.4

Median Earnings of Men and Women Age 18 and Older Who Work Full Time, Year Round by Educational Attainment

Source: U.S. Census Bureau, 2012.

Gender Income Differences. There is a large difference in the average income of males and females at all educational levels, with men making more than women at each level. According to a U.S. Census Bureau report (Saving 2 Invest (n.d.), in 2009 the average American male working full time earned $47,100, whereas the average American woman working full time earned only $36,300, a difference of about $11,000.

Education pays off financially as shown in Figure 8.4. As education increases for both males and females, their income progressively increases (U.S. Census Bureau, 2012). Individuals completing 9 years of schooling or less averaged $23,00, those with 9 to 12 years of schooling averaged $28,000, high school graduates averaged $38,000, and college graduates averaged $77,000. Individuals with professional degrees beyond college make even a larger increase in salary, some almost double those of a college graduate.

A continuing issue in our society is the large discrepancy in salary between males and females with the same education level (see Figure 8.4). Males consistently make more money than females across all education levels, and the salary difference increases as the level of education increases. While there are a number of factors that account for this difference, there continues to be a clear case of discrimination in the workplace.

Education is truly a great investment when you look at the total income individuals achieve in a lifetime of working full time. Individuals with a high school education earn about $1.2 million in a lifetime, while those with a college degree earn almost twice that amount, $2.1 million. Those with a master's degree earn about $2.5 million, with a doctorate (Ph.D. or Ed.D.) about $3.4 million, and with a professional degree (such as an M.D.), the total annual income is about $4.4 million over a lifetime.

Economists and other social observers cite a number of reasons for these income differences. Women often drop out of the labor force to have children and then stay at home to care for them for a few years. Meanwhile, men gain seniority in the

As more women have joined the workforce and more families need two incomes to meet their expenses, debates have increased about the differences in salaries paid to men and women for similar kinds of work. If a female office assistant and a male computer technician, for example, have the same amount of education, experience, and job responsibility, why is the office assistant apt to be paid less?

labor force and get more job-related experience. Although it is illegal to pay women less for doing the same job, women have little legal recourse when they are paid lower wages for jobs that may require essentially similar skills. Also, salaries in fields traditionally dominated by women tend to be lower than those in fields traditionally dominated by men. Many people attribute these tendencies to discrimination and sexism.

The "equal pay for comparable work" approach takes a fresh look at "men's" and "women's" work. Proponents argue that pay should be based not on traditional gender-role assumptions but on the comparative difficulty of the job. How much should an office assistant be paid in comparison with a plumber? A child care worker in comparison with a computer service technician? Some states have developed elaborate formulas. A job's worth, in terms of salary, is calculated on the basis of the number of years of education, training, and experience it demands and the difficulty or risk it involves.

Why do Whites tend to make more than African Americans and Hispanics, even when their educational levels are similar? Many observers argue that racism still exists in the United States and that the difference in income can be traced to discrimination. Some believe, however, that a number of other factors also play a part. The first is urban residence. Many jobs sought by minorities have moved from the cities, where most people of color live, to the suburbs, where there are fewer African Americans and Hispanics. The second factor is the type of employment; minorities are more likely than Whites to work in service industries, where salaries are lower. The third factor is tenure; many college-educated minorities are relative newcomers to the labor market and have had less time than Whites to earn promotions and higher pay.

The controversy over the income gap between White males, females, and minorities in our country is not likely to end soon. The disparity in income between the

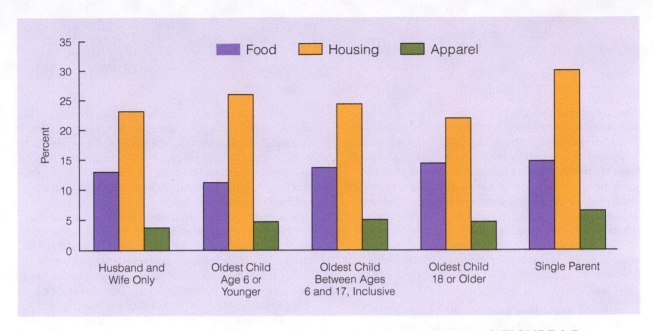

FIGURE 8.5
Annual Expenditures for Necessities
Source: U.S. Census Bureau, 2008.

haves and the have-nots is a problematic issue in a society where millions of people are living at or near the poverty level.

Annual Household Expenses

In terms of annual expenditures, couples and families spend the largest percentage of their income on three items: food, housing, and apparel (Duly, 2003). Figure 8.5 illustrates the income spent on these three items for couples and families across the life cycle. In general, people spend most of their income (about 23% to 30%) on housing, about 15% on food, and about 5% on apparel. However, the amount spent on these items varies by the family structure and stage. One-parent families spend the highest percentage of their income on housing (30%), while the average for other families is about 25%; two-parent households with young children spend the least on food (11%) compared to other families because they eat at home more often.

Family Net Worth

Net worth is defined as the sum of all your financial assets minus all your liabilities. Assets can be liquid (e.g., cash, savings, stock) or nonliquid (e.g., real estate or a trust account). Based on a survey of income by the U.S. Census Bureau (2003b), Whites have by far the greatest family net worth compared to Blacks and Latinos, and this difference has increased over time. In 2001, Whites had a median net worth of $117,722, while Blacks had only $18,510 and Latinos had $11,149 (Robles, 2003).

A revealing fact is the percentage in each ethnic group that had a zero net worth. While 11% of Whites had a net worth of zero, 27% of Latinos and 29% of Blacks had a net worth of zero. This means that when these families encounter any financial problem, they will quickly be in debt. These findings clearly demonstrate why families are so vulnerable to any financial situation.

BOX 8.3 At Issue

The Cost of Having and Raising a Baby

The cost of raising children has been discussed for years, with the cost rising every day. There are several costs to consider associated with the raising of children, and other costs having to do with a stay-at-home parent who might have otherwise earned a substantial amount of money working out of the home. It has also been determined that the cost of a stay-at-home mom or dad could command $138,000 annually for all the work that goes into running a household and caring for a child.

The costs of raising a child, of course, will vary by socioeconomic status and ethnic practices. However, here are some estimated costs for a child raised in a middle-class family:

- It would cost $32,000 to raise a child to age 2.
- It would cost an additional $24,000 for each additional child in a family to raise that child to age 2.
- To raise a child to age 18 costs $191,000.
- Add to the $191,000 the cost of lost wages for a stay-at-home parent and college, and the cost would be $1.6 million.

The medical costs surrounding getting pregnant can also be substantial. With couples waiting longer to have children, fertility costs are a reality for some couples. These costs can be $4,000, or much more.

There is considerable uncertainty when having a child when it comes to costs. For example, a child may have or develop medical problems, which could add substantially to those costs. If there are any special needs, there may be additional educational costs. Once a child is born, parents often begin thinking about life insurance to take care of a child if a parent or parents die.

If both parents choose to work outside the home, they face the substantial cost of day care. The cost can be from $600 to $2,000 per month for preschoolers. The cost of day care varies widely depending upon whether a child is cared for in a day-care home or a day-care center. A live-in nanny would be substantially more. There is also the cost of buying a larger house, for families who need to add space. Private schools can also add $10,000 to $30,000 to the cost of raising a child.

Most parents do not think about all these costs as they consider having children. Instead, they anticipate some of the costs, and beyond that they take what comes. Couples cannot anticipate everything, and couples may need to plan wisely and be open for a few surprises.

Source: Ordoñez, J. (2007, May 14). Baby needs a new pair of shoes, *Newsweek*, 50, 51, 54.

Does It Pay to Work Outside the Home?

One of the sobering facts of life for two-income families is that the second income often seems to disappear when the expenses associated with earning it are paid. A hypothetical example: Assume the second income in the family is a reasonably good one—$28,000 a year, or $2,333 a month. Each month, federal, state, and Social Security taxes could conceivably take about $942. Child care for two children under school age could easily take another $550 a month. Working outside the home also entails increases in clothing expenditures, say, $110 extra a month; personal-care and dry-cleaning bills may also go up an extra $45 a month. Lunch costs may rise about $110 monthly, and transportation to work could add at least $55 a month. After all is said and done, the $2,333 monthly salary is reduced to $521—about $3.25 an hour—in real income.

One woman who quit her $7-an-hour job in a family decision to rely solely on the husband's income said, "I had the feeling that all my money was going for clothes, lunch, and day care for my daughter." It is important to emphasize, however, that there are many reasons beyond financial ones for working outside the home, including personal and professional development, networking with others, and getting a break from child care at home.

The costs of professional child care can be a significant expense for couples in which both partners are working outside the home.

Smart Money Management

Managing money requires knowledge of how to budget, which is really how one manages expenses considering income, and to do this taking into account personal, couple, and family values. It also requires consideration of how two-income couples manage the different pots of money that they bring into the relationship. Smart money management also involves a plan for saving money for future needs, including unexpected crises.

Creating a Budget

Budgeting is the regular, systematic balancing of income and expenses. It is a personal system for making sure there is enough money to cover the essentials and, one hopes, a few extras.

To construct a workable budget, individuals need to examine their personal values about saving and spending; they must also have a good idea of what things really cost. To begin with, couples need to establish how much income they can count on. They should then outline their expenses by category: shelter, transportation, food, clothing, and so forth. After developing categories that reflect their particular circumstances, they must estimate how much money they will need to pay for each category.

Most people don't take the time to create a budget. An accurate budget requires that a couple or family record their expenses on a regular basis (e.g., monthly) so they know how much they are spending in each category. At the end of the month, the couple can look at the recorded expenditures and develop a budget for the next month. Individuals usually find budgeting easier than families do because they don't need to negotiate decisions and work out priorities that are appropriate for the entire family.

Finances are one of the most stressful areas for couples because they reflect couples' power dynamics and values.

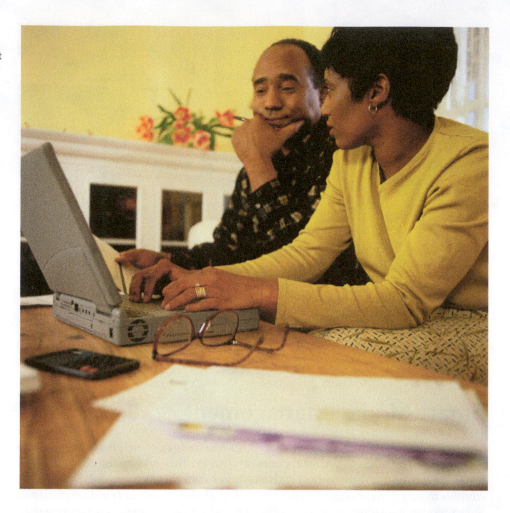

Budgeting is a continuous process of assessment and adjustment. A good budget is simple, realistic, and clear. A good budget builds in some personal control for each family member. It also distinguishes between wants and needs, with needs given priority but a few wants satisfied if possible. A good budget treats credit as debt, not income. Charging something or deciding to pay for it "on time" creates a fixed expense that adds to a family's debt.

Pooling Money: Pros and Cons

Should two-income couples pool their money? This is a difficult question that partners have to answer together, and one they should discuss before marriage. Many newly married couples feel obligated to pool their money, believing that a refusal to do so might be interpreted as a lack of commitment. Married couples tend to favor pooling more than cohabiting couples, but those who remarry after divorce are more likely to maintain separate funds, perhaps because they worry about the permanence of the new relationship.

Pooling is simpler because there are fewer accounts to balance. But because each spouse must keep the other informed about financial transactions, pooling entails some loss of independence. If one partner forgets to record a check written on the joint account and causes an overdraft, a conflict is inevitable.

Another approach is to pool some of the money from each person to cover joint expenses and for each person to also keep a smaller but separate checking account and credit card. The problem with each individual having more freedom is when the total from the joint expenses and the two separate expenses cannot be paid.

In one study of 64 couples who had great marriages it was found that there was not a trend toward either joint or separate accounts (Skogrand et al., 2010). Although some couples had strong feelings about doing things one way or the other, it seemed most couples needed to work it out in a way that worked for them. This choice can depend upon many factors. For example, if couples marry late in life or are in a remarriage, they may want to continue to manage their own money rather than pooling their finances. If there is only one breadwinner in the family, it may make sense to pool their financial resources.

Credit: Uses and Abuses

There are both advantages and disadvantages to using credit. Buying on credit is easy, but it is important not to overdo it. Excessive debt can result in bankruptcy. Financial counseling can help those who have gotten into problems with credit.

Credit Cards—Dangerous Plastic

Having a credit card, actually several cards, has become the norm for most adults and with it has come credit card debt. The average credit card debt for the typical American person was about $3,000 in 2012 (Federal Reserve Bank of New York, 2012). The amount of credit card debt has actually decreased in recent years as people experienced the recession. It may be that people are being careful about incurring debt with the economy being so uncertain. About two-thirds of families carry a monthly balance and the interest rate ranges from 15% to over 20%. These plastic cards are creating a society where having a savings account is rare compared to having credit card debt.

College students are now offered "interest-free" credit cards with unspecified spending limits and these cards are very easy to obtain. College campuses are flooded with a large variety of credit cards that students can sign up to use. Unfortunately, it is too easy to spend money and abuse these cards, and most students find themselves having credit card debt. A common sign of financial problems is when people sign up for additional credit cards, which they use to pay off past credit card debt. (See Box 8.4.) "Twenty-somethings" are the group of individuals who are most likely to get into credit card trouble because they have recently begun living on their own and have new financial obligations (Chu, 2006).

Just paying the minimum amount on a credit card can be very costly. Let us assume that the interest rate is about 17%, which is about the average rate on most credit cards. If you had a monthly balance of only $1,000, it would cost you $2,590 and 17 years to pay off the balance. If you had a monthly balance of $2,500, your total cost would be $7,734, and with a monthly balance of $5,000, the total cost you would pay over 40 years would be $16,305. So the goal should be to pay off your credit card balance every month; otherwise, you will be in a difficult financial position very quickly, which will be hard to resolve. In a recent study by Lucia Dunn (*Chicago Tribune*, 2013), it was found that debt increases at younger ages, peaks when people are in their middle years of life, and tapers off at old age. Younger people not only have more debt, they also pay off their credit cards more slowly than older adults. These differences make sense in that older adults are

BOX 8.4   At Issue

The Credit Card Trap and How to Avoid It

College campuses today are practically overrun with credit card offers. Some banks offer free T-shirts, water bottles, umbrellas, or other incentives to encourage students to sign up for their cards. Actually, many students already have cards before they ever set foot in a college dorm. In his report, "Credit Cards on Campus," Dr. Robert D. Manning (2001) notes that ". . . companies are approving credit lines for students at progressively earlier ages, including high school seniors. Most college freshmen now receive their first credit card before taking their first mid-term exam." And no wonder—marketing these cards to students is now a billion-dollar business, and there is no sign of a slowdown.

Having a credit card in hand makes it so easy, so convenient, to shop for clothes, eat out with friends, and enjoy the good life. But such convenience often comes at quite a price, and every year thousands of college students find themselves caught in the credit trap.

Here are some surprising statistics about college credit card users:

- In 2003, 54% of freshman students carried a credit card. By sophomore year, that number rose to 92% (Lazarony, 2002).
- 47% of college students have four or more credit cards (Lazarony, 2002).
- Between freshman orientation and graduation day, students double their credit card debt and triple the number of credit cards in their wallets (Lazarony, 2002).

- Three out of five students reached or exceeded their credit cards' limits during their freshman year (Singletary, 2003).
- Almost three-quarters of students used their student loans to pay credit card bills (Singletary, 2003).
- Student credit card holders are more likely (12.1%) to be more than 30 days late in paying their bills, as compared to older adult card holders (8.1%) (Singletary, 2004).

There are many reasons students get into trouble with credit cards. One reason is that banks and credit card companies, which used to require parental approval for student cards, no longer do so. Some teens, out from under parental authority for the first time and enjoying the sense of financial freedom that having their own credit card gives them, fail to realize the consequences of letting their spending get out of hand.

Another reason, according to James A. Roberts, associate professor of marketing at Baylor University, is that "research shows that when you use a credit card you overestimate your wealth, you are less sensitive to price and you are more likely to purchase compared to those who write checks or pay cash" (Singletary, 2004).

Students, and some parents as well, argue that it is important to have a credit card in order to build a good credit history so that after graduation they will be able to rent an apartment or finance a car. Thus, building a credit history—a good credit history—can be a good thing.

likely to be living on a fixed income and they cannot assume they can pay off high credit card debt in the future.

Advantages and Disadvantages of Credit

Buying on credit is very popular for a number of reasons. It is convenient, and it also allows people to enjoy something while paying for it, to take advantage of sales, and to have something in case of an emergency. The disadvantages of credit include the generally high interest charges and the potential for overuse. Credit should be used with caution. Unfortunately, it is a very seductive luxury.

Purchasing a Home

The family dwelling has psychological significance in virtually all cultures. It provides the family's space and binds them together as a unit. It can be a haven, a place of rest and enjoyment, somewhere to kick off one's shoes and escape the pretenses of polite society.

A home is usually the most expensive item Americans buy. Careful deliberation should go into its purchase. One rule of thumb is that, whether renting or

However, problems with credit cards—like late or missed payments—stay on your credit reports for 7 years. It isn't necessary to have a credit card to establish credit. Another way for students to establish credit is to sign up for telephone, utility, or retail accounts in their own names (i.e., not their parents') and pay their bills on time (Singletary, 2003).

The best way to *avoid* the credit trap is to be knowledgeable about credit cards before getting one. Think seriously about whether or not you really need one. Many people do just fine in life without them. And, be very cautious if you do choose to have a credit card.

Below are some tips for the wise credit consumer:

- Make sure you're ready to handle your own finances. Open a checking account before you get to school and learn how to track your expenses.
- Get a secured card or a debit card. A secured card requires a security deposit of a certain dollar amount, and that is your credit limit (which can be as low as $200 to $500). A debit card is linked to your checking account balance, so you can't overspend easily.
- Compare rates and fees before you sign up for any card. You can go to Web sites like www.cardtrak.com or www.bankrate.com to make comparisons.
- When comparing rates, look for details like annual fees, late fees, and charges for cash advances.
- Be sure to read the fine print of any credit card offer. Some cards offer a "teaser rate," which is an initial low interest rate that increases sharply after only a few months.
- Take responsibility for paying the card yourself. You're much less likely to rack up the spending if you're footing the bill rather than your parents.
- Negotiate lower rates. Call the credit card company and ask for a lower rate. Companies are competitive, and if you have a good credit history, the company may give it to you (Chu, 2006).
- Pay your bills on time. Finance charges and late fees quickly add up to much more than the cost of the original product or service.
- Visit the Federal Trade Commission Web site at either www.ftc.gov or www.consumer.gov for free information on dozens of topics relating to credit cards.

If you do fall into the credit trap, Poduska (2001) suggests ways to get out of it—for example, by paying cash for as many things as possible, using the credit card only for emergencies, paying off the debt as soon as possible to reduce the compounded interest over the long haul (even if this means asking your parents for help), and reducing your living expenses by buying only what you really need.

When it comes to the credit card trap, the most important thing to remember is that while it is easy to fall into it, getting out of it can prove very difficult.

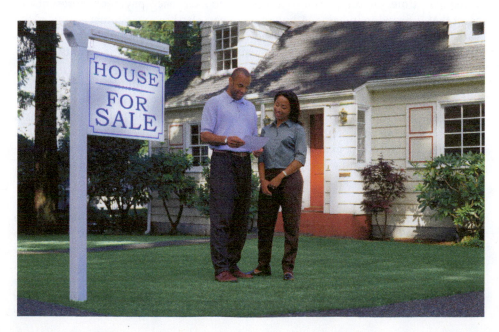

Buying a home is an important aspect of family life. A home can be a great unifying benefit for families and can also be a major cost.

buying, a family should spend no more than 1 week's take-home pay per month for housing expenses. Housing expenses are either rent or the total of all house-payment expenses (mortgage payment, insurance, and real estate taxes). Families who can find adequate shelter for 20% to 25% of their take-home pay are likely to be in relatively good financial health. Unfortunately, many lower-income families find themselves paying 50% of their income or more for housing.

Renting Versus Buying. Generally speaking, it is wiser to buy a home than to rent. Rent money is gone forever, whereas each mortgage payment gradually increases one's equity in the home and inflation increases the net worth of the dwelling. There are, however, many exceptions to this generalization, and families must carefully analyze their unique financial situation to decide if buying a home is the right choice for them. The recent housing crises have taught us that we can sometimes buy a house at a high dollar figure, only to have the home drop in value. The values of homes have stayed low in many areas of the country as a result of the housing crises, which causes problems for people who want to relocate. They find their home is not worth as much as they owe. To sell the house they would need to pay the lender an additional amount when they sell. We call this "being under water." Therefore, owning a home has not been as appealing as it once was, since we are not sure if housing values will continue to decline or if they are on their way up.

There are numerous advantages to both renting and buying. The advantages of renting include mobility, perhaps some amenities (pool, tennis courts, party rooms, laundry facilities), and a lifestyle that involves fewer responsibilities. No large down payment is needed (only a security deposit), and the relatively fixed housing expenditure (rent) makes budgeting easier.

The advantages of buying include pride of ownership, a better credit rating, and a monthly payment that remains constant for many years (that is, with a fixed-rate mortgage). The federal income tax deductions for mortgage interest and real estate property taxes are a major advantage, as is the potential for the home to increase in value over time. Owning a house forces one to save; each payment represents an asset that is growing in value. A homeowner can also borrow against equity as the value of the home increases. Furthermore, owners can make home improvements and alterations, which can increase the value of the home and/or add to the enjoyment of the dwelling.

The disadvantages of renting are that it offers no tax deductions and no potential gain from the rising value of the property. Furthermore, rents rise with inflation, and many rental units have restrictions on noise level, pet ownership, and children. One disadvantage of buying is the substantial down payment that is needed; this can reduce available funds for other things. Also, the cost of maintenance and repairs can be high. A home is a big commitment in time, emotion, and money.

The Cost of Home Loans. The average interest rate in 2012 for a 30-year home mortgage was only about 3.5%, a drop from about 10% to 11% in 2000. This drop has greatly increased the number of people purchasing homes. The savings on a loan with 3.5% interest versus 10% is substantial over the life of the loan, which is typically 15 to 30 years. Even 1% interest difference makes a difference in the interest for the lifetime of the loan. For example, a very modest 25-year mortgage loan of $60,000 will cost the borrower more than $151,000 at 9% interest but more than $157,000 at 10% interest. One percentage point makes a $6,000 difference over the 25-year life of the loan. These figures also show that a $65,000 or $75,000 home (assuming a $5,000 or $15,000 down payment plus a $60,000 loan) really costs more than double its price when the interest on the mortgage is considered. Therefore, it is clear that the low interest rates currently should mean people would be buying homes, and they are. The mortgage crises, however, have made qualifying for home loans more difficult. Buyers need more money down and higher credit scores to qualify for a loan than was true in the past.

Avoiding Debt and Bankruptcy

Bankruptcy is a legal term indicating that a person is financially insolvent and unable to pay her or his debts. In 2011, more than 1.3 million people declared personal bankruptcy in the United States, and about 35,000 businesses filed for bankruptcy (United States Courts, n.d.). Although bankruptcy offers some protection from creditors, it is not a solution to financial problems because bankruptcy blemishes one's financial record for many years, making many financial matters more difficult. In our society bankruptcy signifies an individual's inability to handle money wisely, and society exacts various punishments on those who declare bankruptcy.

To stay out of debt and avoid bankruptcy, it is helpful to know why some people assume too much debt. It is interesting that level of income is not clearly related to debt. Debt-free families and debt-ridden families alike come from all socioeconomic levels.

Excessive debt may be due to any or all of the following reasons: credit spending, crisis spending, careless or impulsive spending, and compulsive spending. Unwise *credit spending* can lead to overextension. *Crisis spending*—resulting from unexpected events in life such as unemployment, uninsured illness, and business income decline or failure—can throw personal finances into turmoil. *Careless or impulsive spending* includes overpaying for items that could be purchased for less, purchasing inferior merchandise that does not last, and buying things one does not really need. *Compulsive spending* occurs because some people simply can't say no to salespeople or because they have an uncontrollable impulse to acquire material things.

Fortunately, there are a number of time-tested strategies for families who have become overextended. Although these solutions are not easy, they are far better than the alternative of bankruptcy:

- Develop and stick to a balanced budget.
- Avoid making any new financial commitments. Do not incur any new debt.
- Destroy all credit cards or lock them up so that they can't be used.
- Develop a plan for repaying all debts. If the budget cannot handle the repayment schedule, try to negotiate lower payments and lower payback periods.
- Pay off debts with the highest interest rates first.
- Work to reduce the total number of debts.
- Make a plan to pay at least a small amount on each debt each month.
- Avoid debt consolidation loans. These can set the stage for new borrowing, especially on credit cards.

Not only does moving toward and experiencing bankruptcy affect one's financial record, it also creates enormous stress for individuals, couples, and families. One study (Thorne, 2010) indicated that as couples moved toward bankruptcy, being in charge of finances meant not only paying the bills, but also increased work on the part of the bill payer. The work involved micro-managing of all debt and spending, dealing with bill collectors, and filing for bankruptcy. In the Thorne study, this work was typically done by wives rather than husbands. Thorne speculates, based upon other research, that marriage relationships are strained and power struggles about spending ensue. Whenever there is financial strain, time spent on finances can take away from other positive interactions in the couple and family relationships.

Financial Counseling

If individuals are overextended and they have made no progress in dealing with their debt in 3 to 6 months, they should seek financial counseling. Many large employers have budget counselors available through the human resources department or an employee assistance program. When financial difficulties are a symptom of a deeper marital or personal problem (alcohol or other drug abuse, depression, violence), a therapist may be the best way to approach the crisis.

For example, a single parent continues to support her 25-year-old son, even though his cocaine addiction is dragging her down financially. The son deals cocaine to come up with some of the $3,000 or $4,000 a month he needs to support his drug habit. He regularly borrows money from his mother and even steals and pawns her possessions. Consumed by guilt, she covers up for him, pays the bills, and lends him money, denying his drug habit. This mother needs not only a competent financial adviser to help her deal with the mountain of debts she has accumulated but also a personal therapist to help her come to grips with her son's drug problem, for which he must take responsibility.

People seeking financial counseling should avoid "credit clinics," which charge fees of $250 to $2,000 or more for their services. Some of these businesses advertise that they will negotiate new repayment schedules with creditors, but people in financial trouble can work directly with their creditors or can find help from nonprofit personal counseling organizations. The human services section of most local telephone books lists resources. Another possible resource is the network of more than 1,000 Consumer Credit Counseling Service (CCCS) agencies across the United States. Each year about a million people seek credit and budget counseling advice from CCCS.

Summary

- Studies about economic issues and family are relatively new. These studies often draw on different disciplines and involve researchers from different disciplines.
- There are studies that show that happiness and money often go together. However, we do not know if one causes the other. It may be that things that go along with having money make the difference, such as health, less stress, or having more choices.
- The economic downturn that began in 2007 has had a dramatic affect on families. Many lost jobs and homes, and lost their hope for achieving the American dream. Some of the results of the downturn, however, resulted in families spending more time together and appreciating each other more.
- According to a national survey of married couples, happy couples—as compared to unhappy couples—agree on how to spend money, have no concerns about how the partner spends money, are satisfied with decisions about savings, major debts are not a problem, and financial decisions are not difficult.
- Numerous recent studies indicate that marital happiness and money are related. One national study showed that couples with great marriages had little or no debt and lived within their means.
- It has been suggested that financial counselors and family life educators work together to help couples address both marriage issues and financial issues.
- It is not only money in general that causes difficulties for couples but debt in particular that causes stress. Research shows that as debt goes down, marital

satisfaction increases. It is suggested that debt affects both the amount of quality time a couple has and also how they spend that time.

- People manage their economic resources in different ways, depending on their worldviews, life experiences, and family structures.
- Although couples often think that things will get better after a divorce, divorce is financially costly, and couples need to be aware of those potential costs as they contemplate this important life decision.
- White families in the United States make more money, on average, than Hispanic and African American families. Asian families have the highest median income. Males make more money than females, and there is a clear relationship between educational level and income.
- Budgeting is the regular, systematic balancing of income and expenses. To budget successfully, individuals need to examine their personal values about saving and spending and to monitor their plan monthly.
- Couples who pool their money are neither more nor less satisfied with money management issues in the relationship than couples who have separate accounts.
- Monthly housing expenses should consume no more than 1 week's take-home pay. Generally, buying a home is a better investment than renting.
- Credit spending, crisis spending, careless or impulsive spending, and compulsive spending are four reasons people go into excessive debt. Families who cannot reduce their debt over a period of 3 to 6 months should seek financial and perhaps personal counseling.

Key Terms

goals
collective worldview
individualistic worldview
budgeting
bankruptcy

Activities

1. Write a few paragraphs describing how money was handled in your family of origin and how you handle money today. Then form groups of five or six for discussion. After having read the essays out loud, identify similarities and differences that emerge.
2. Are you a spender or a saver? How about your partner? Consider the similarities and differences between your style and your partner's style.
3. Think about the relationship between money and happiness in your life. Are there times when you have been very happy and you believe it was because of money? Are there times when you have been very happy and you feel money had nothing to do with it? Based upon what you have learned in this chapter and what you know about life, what advice would you give to your child about money and happiness?
4. Has the economic downturn that began in 2007 affected you either positively or negatively? Has

it affected others in your family, such as your parents?
5. Keep track of your spending for 1 month. Write down everything you spend, including for small items such as snacks, newspapers, or bus fare. At the end of the month, evaluate your spending. Are you spending money in a way that reflects your values and what's important to you? If not, how would you change your spending?
6. Pair off into "couples" and discuss the following questions as if you were planning to marry. Then report your discussions to the class.
   a. Do you expect to share equally in financial decisions? If not, how do you plan to make financial decisions?
   b. Do you plan to use a budget? Why or why not?
   c. How do you feel about each partner's having a personal allowance for which he or she is not accountable to the other?
   d. How do you feel about buying small items on credit? Large items?
   e. Who will be the treasurer? The check writer? The bookkeeper? The investor?

Suggested Readings

Danziger, S., & Rouse, C. E. (Eds.). (2007). *The price of independence: The economics of early adulthood.* Philadelphia: Network on Transitions to Adulthood.

Folbre, N. (2008). *Valuing children: Rethinking the economics of the family.* Cambridge, MA: Harvard University Press.

Holzner, C., Jameson, K., Maloney, T., Abebe, B., Lund, M., & Schaub, K. (2006). *The economic impact of the Mexico–Utah relationship.* University of Utah Study. Web site: http://www.ipia.utah.edu/utah_mexico_final_version.pdf.

Karger, H. (2005). *Shortchanged: Life and debt in the fringe economy.* San Francisco: Berrett-Koehler.

Schramm, D. G. (2006). Individual and social costs of divorce in Utah. *Journal of Family and Economic Issues, 27,* 133–151.

Skogrand, L., Schramm, D. G., Marshall, J. P., & Lee, T. (2005). The effects of debt on newlyweds and implications for education. *Journal of Extension, 43.* Web site: http://www.joe.org/joe/2005june/rb7.shtml.

U.S. Census Bureau (2012). *Money income of families —Percent distribution by income level in constant (2009) dollars: 1980–2009* (Table 696). Statistical Abstract of the United States. Retrieved from http://www.census.gov/compendia/statab/2012/tables/12s0695.pdf.

Xiao, J. J. (Ed.). (2008). *Handbook of consumer finance research.* New York: Springer.

 Visit the text-specific Online Learning Center at **www.mhhe.com/olson8e** for practice tests, chapter summaries, and PowerPoint slides.

9 Friendship, Intimacy, and Singlehood

Friends Versus Lovers

Exploring Intimacy:
From Experience
to Relationship

Developing Intimacy in
Couple Relationships

Intimacy Games

Attachment Theory
and Intimacy

Being Single

Summary

Key Terms

Activities

Suggested Readings

In this chapter we will explore various ways of defining love and the related concept of intimacy. We will also identify a number of constructive and destructive games people play in their intimate relationships. The goal of this chapter is to help you understand love and intimacy and learn how to enhance your own intimate experiences and relationships.

Love and friendship bind society together, providing both emotional support and a buffer against stress and thereby preserving our physical and psychological health. Love is clearly much more than friendship, and thus we treat love relationships more seriously. However, the strongest love relationships have roots in friendship. Satisfying and stable love relationships come from shared interests and values. When friends fall in love, they are adding passion to the emotional intimacy we call friendship.

Love means different things to different people. Definitions of love are almost endless (Table 9.1). No other topic demands so much attention and generates so much confusion in our society. We cannot turn on the radio or TV, pick up a magazine or book, or converse with a friend for long without being confronted with words about love, thoughts of love, acts of love, or images of love. Despite the ubiquitous nature of love, it remains a mystery to many. Many regard it as a strange force that can overpower us and at times take control over our lives: People speak of being "under love's spell" or being "swept away" with passion. New scientific research has identified where love is located in the brain. These findings help us understand new love, sex drive, and couple attachment.

Finding a partner looks different today than in the past. People are using the Internet more than ever before to find partners and develop intimate relationships. This can be an extremely useful and efficient way to identify people who have similar interests and goals in life, though it comes with some risks. Even though most people still want to marry sometime, singlehood is more prevalent today than in the past. Some are very content to be single and take advantage of the multiple opportunities for education and career opportunities.

This chapter reminds us that many aspects of friendship, intimacy, and singlehood have not changed over the years. There are also many ways in which they look very different today, and these are likely to continue to emerge and develop as aspects of society change.

Friends Versus Lovers

Friendship and love are alike in many ways. In fact, if we regularly treated our marriage partners like our best friends, we might have better relationships. There are, however, crucial differences between lovers and friends.

Love, in short, runs deeper and stronger than friendship. And because the stakes are so high with love, the possibility of interpersonal difficulties increases, and we jealously guard this important relationship.

The Fabric of Friendship

When it comes to friendship, we can assume that two individuals participate in a reciprocal relationship as equals (Davis, 2004, 2007). The fabric of friendship includes eight important elements:

- *Enjoyment.* Friends enjoy each other's company most of the time, although disagreements and friction occasionally occur.
- *Acceptance.* Friends accept each other for who they are and don't try to change each other.

TABLE 9.1	On Love

In love the paradox occurs that two beings become one yet remain two.
—ERICH FROMM, *Psychiatrist*

Love doesn't just sit there, like a stone, it has to be made, like bread; remade all the time, made new.
—URSULA K. LE GUIN, *Writer*

Being in love isn't ever really loving, it's just wanting. And it isn't any good. It's all aching and misery.
—JAMES LEO HERLIHY, *Writer*

Love is the history of a woman's life; it is an episode in man's.
—MADAME DE STAËL, *Writer*

He who knows nothing, loves nothing . . . But he who understands also loves, notices, sees . . .

The more knowledge inherent in a thing, the greater the love.
—PARACELSUS, *Philosopher*

The trouble with some women is that they get all excited about nothing—and then marry him.
—CHER, *Actor*

When the satisfaction or the security of another person becomes as significant to one as is one's own security, then the state of love exists.
—HARRY STACK SULLIVAN, *Psychiatrist*

Chains do not hold a marriage together. It is threads, hundreds of tiny threads which sew people together through the years. This is what makes a marriage last—more than passion or even sex!
—SIMONE SIGNORET, *Actor*

Love is a state of perpetual anesthesia.
—H.L. MENCKEN, *Journalist*

There is only one happiness in life, to love and be loved.
—GEORGE SAND, *Writer*

To act intentionally, in sympathetic response to others (including God) to promote overall well-being.
—THOMAS J. OORD, *Scholar*

- *Trust.* Friends assume that they will act in each other's best interest. "Even when he's hassling me, I know it's for my own good." "She would never intentionally hurt me, except in a fit of extreme anger."
- *Respect.* Friends respect each other; they assume the other has good judgment in making choices in life.
- *Mutual assistance.* Friends help and support each other; they can count on each other in times of need.
- *Confiding.* Friends share life experiences and feelings with each other.
- *Understanding.* Friends know each other's values and understand what is important to each other. "I know what makes her tick."
- *Spontaneity.* Friends feel free to be "real" around each other. They don't feel they have to play a role or hold back their true feelings.

According to Goodwin (2009), however, modern-day friendships have changed somewhat. Because of increased geographical and social mobility, friendships may emerge as people move to new situations, rather than being long lasting. There has also been a change from the acceptability of friendships being same sex to friends being from the opposite sex. The Internet, texting, and other modern forms of communication have also affected how we communicate as well as our ability to maintain friendships around the world, if we choose to. Goodwin (2009) indicates that the result is that friendships can be somewhat superficial because we do not always maintain intimate relationships with friends.

According to Goodwin (2009), culture affects how we develop and maintain friendships. For example, in ethnic groups in the United States and around the world, collectivist cultures typically value the group more than the individual. Therefore, friendships may be more important than and look different in individualist cultures. Also, where family is highly valued, friendships may be focused on family members rather than people outside the family. In individualistic cultures, friendships may be less important in general, and individuals may spend more time alone.

Immigrants may also have unique friendship patterns (Goodwin, 2009). For example, friendships for immigrants initially could focus on those who meet certain needs as people transition to a new country. We know that immigrants often relocate in geographical centers with others who came from the same country. Therefore, friendships may develop with people who have the same ethnic values and can provide social support.

The Tapestry of Love

Love is magical, changing, fragile, complex, and paradoxical. Amy and David Olson (2001) describe 10 traits of love that are common in our culture (Box 9.1). There are so many ways to think about love, and this has changed over time and has cultural impacts.

It is assumed that romantic love exists in all cultures (Goodwin, 2009). However, historically, love was not as important in romantic relationships and marriages, and relationships were often arranged or based upon economic considerations. For example, an 86-year-old woman describes her decision to get married some 68 years ago:

> "Paul and I grew up two miles apart in a rural, farming community in central Minnesota. We both grew up on farms, and farming was all we knew as a profession. We had known each other all our lives through church and school. Dating in those days was a challenge because everyone was related to everyone else. We had to find someone to date that was not a relative.
>
> "We were dating, but had not talked about marriage. Then a cash-crop farm became available for rent. Renting a farm in those days meant you gave half the income from the farm to the person who owned the land. It was really a "share cropper" type of arrangement, but we didn't call it that. Since those farms did not become available often, we thought we better get married and rent the farm. It was within a mile of each of our families, so we would have support from them. We eventually bought our own farm.
>
> "It wasn't that we weren't in love, because we probably were when we got married. However, love wasn't the deciding factor in our decision to marry, it was the availability of a farm to rent. In those days, coming out of the recession, we had to make practical decisions. We had to have a means of livelihood. We were married 56 years until Paul died, we raised four children, and had 13 grandchildren. I would definitely say love developed and we had a good life together."

In most countries around the world, arranged marriages are no longer the norm; however, there are many cultures that still seek family consent in marriage decisions (Goodwin, 2009). Therefore, love and romance are becoming more important in couple and marriage relationships.

The Love Triangle

Although the phrase *love triangle* usually brings to mind a relationship in which one person has two lovers, another sort of love triangle was developed by Sternberg and Weis (2008). The three dimensions of the triangle are decision and commitment (the cognitive component), intimacy (the emotional component), and passion (the motivational component).

BOX 9.1   Putting It Together

Ten Traits of Love

These 10 characteristics of love are common in our culture, and knowing about them can help you become more realistic about the complexity of love.

1. **Love is often confused by chemistry**. People often claim to be in "love" when they experience a physical attraction to someone. There are many theories as to why people experience attraction in the first place. Attraction may be biologically/evolutionarily driven where we instinctively choose mates who will ensure survival of the species. Under this theory, men with overt alpha male characteristics and women whose vitality and health indicate she will bear children will be attractive. The social exchange theory says we choose mates whom we see as our equals, not only in terms of physical traits but things such as social status, intelligence, creativity, etc. The persona theory is such that a mate is determined by the degree to which he or she raises our self-esteem, including any pride or embarrassment we may attach to how we believe others perceive us in relation to our partner. To further complicate love, attraction releases chemicals from the human brain and these chemicals create a rush of euphoria lasting from between 6 months to 3 years, which can lead to the next trait.

2. **"Love" is often blind**. Studies show that the early stage of love (the attraction stage) changes the way we think. We can't help this as the brain is triggered to release chemicals and these chemical make us feel energized (physically and emotionally), causing, among other things, an increased experience of joy and sociability and a decrease in appetite. The feeling of "floating on air" and excitement this brings also causes new couples to idealize their partners, seeing only their positive traits and not their flaws. This can make for a fun experience but not a very realistic and lasting one. It turns out that the human brain plays a vital role in the saying, "love is blind." This is one of the reasons why it is important for people to consider the input from family and from close friends about a potential date as they are often better able to "see" the other person with more objectivity.

3. **"Love" changes over time**. The beginning stages of romantic relationships are typically not very realistic due largely perhaps to brain chemistry. Some people find it difficult to sustain a long-term relationship because they become almost addicted to the rush of chemicals associated with the infatuation stage of a relationship. They become serial daters, moving from one partner to another once these chemicals subside (every 6 months to 3 years) in order to maintain this feeling of excitement. But over time if couples remain together upon finding their circumstances, personalities, and many other variables to be compatible, they move to "attachment," which is associated with a different set of brain chemicals. Attachment has been linked to chemicals known as endorphins that produce feelings of comfort and tranquility.

4. **Love-based marriages are more fragile than arranged marriages**. Because "love" is often confused with the chemicals of attraction, and arranged-marriages emphasize family and stability, divorce rates are very low (less than 4%) among arranged marriages. Other possible factors affecting the low divorce rates of arranged marriages may be that they occur in traditional cultures with a more practical view of marriage compared to the romanticized views of marriage in the United States.

5. **Love is not a feeling**. Love is often referred to as a feeling, but feelings are transient and ever changing. Joy and good feelings are one of the byproducts of love, not love itself. Love needs no specific object to receive it, although love is often talked about in the context of an object, such as "I love my dog."

6. **Real love grows over time while superficial love will fade**. With real love, the positive feelings grow with time. With superficial love, the best feelings are usually at the beginning of the relationship. Over time, these feelings fade and the relationship dissolves as well. Real love realizes that love does not just "happen" but takes time, effort and commitment to build.

7. **Our language for love is inadequate**. We are limited by the language we have to describe love. Love is much more complex than what we often express. Can we possibly be expressing the same idea when we say, "I love pizza," "I love football," and "I love you"? Similarly, while Eskimos have many different words to describe what we simply call "snow," we basically have one word to describe love. This vocabulary restraint gives limit to something infinite and beyond definition.

8. **Love is often "misdiagnosed."** Along the same lines as the language barrier in describing love is a common misdiagnosis of love. People often make the mistake of using the word "love" when what they are really describing is passion, excitement, enjoyment, or need. Or people profess to love a person but only when that person is doing what they want. Real love is caring for the happiness of another person without any thought of what we might get in return.

9. **Love is paradoxical**. The "love" we throw around in our language system is paradoxical. We are told that love can conquer anything, yet it often does not. We are told that love is eternal, yet couples who claim to be in love later claim they have "fallen out of love." In a relationship, love may help get it started but it is not enough to make the relationship last.

10. **Giving love is receiving love**. You must give love to receive love. In fact, love is unique in that the more you give, the more you will have to give and the more you will receive.

Source: Adapted from A. Olson and D. H. Olson, *Why Do Fools Fall in Love? Experiencing the Magic, Mystery, and Meaning of Successful Relationships*, edited by J. Levine and H. J. Markman. Copyright © 2001 by Jossey-Bass Publishers, Inc. Reprinted with the permission of John Wiley & Sons, Inc.

A relationship can start off with intimacy (friendship) and develop into love. A relationship can also start off with only passion and later develop the other two components. A relationship (such as an arranged marriage) can also begin simply with a commitment between partners for economic reasons or for reasons dictated by the couple's families; even this type of relationship can later develop intimacy and passion and bloom into love.

Commitment is a cognitive attachment to another person. It develops over time, beginning slowly and increasing at a faster rate if the relationship is positive. If the relationship fails, commitment disappears. People express commitment when they move their relationship to a more advanced stage (from dating to engagement, from engagement to marriage), when they are faithful, or when they stay in the relationship during difficult times.

Intimacy involves sharing feelings and providing emotional support. It usually entails high levels of self-disclosure, the sharing of personal information not ordinarily revealed because of the risk involved. Intimacy gradually increases as closeness grows and deepens as a relationship matures. Few couples are likely to share everything with each other. People need some private space, a bit of their world that is closed to everyone else. But in a mature intimate relationship, most areas are open for discussion and sharing. By opening up, by earning each other's trust and becoming vulnerable to each other, people can build a strong emotional bond of intimacy. The paradox is that by expressing feelings of weakness and vulnerability, individuals can gain support and strength from trusted loved ones.

Passion is usually expressed by touching, kissing, and being affectionate, which are linked to physiological arousal; it is also expressed through sexual interactions. Because of its intensity, passion develops quickly but can also fade quickly. Passion is like an addiction; when it ends, a person can experience withdrawal symptoms such as irritability and depression.

Combining the three dimensions of love in various ways, Sternberg identified eight types of love relationships: non-love, liking, infatuation, empty love, romantic love, fatuous love, companionate love, and consummate love. **Non-love** occurs when there is no commitment, intimacy, or passion. **Liking** begins when there is just intimacy, but no passion or commitment. **Infatuation** involves passion only. In **empty love** there is commitment but no passion or intimacy. **Romantic love** has both intimacy and passion, but it is lacking in commitment. **Fatuous love** occurs when a couple is committed on the basis of passion but has not had the time to develop true intimacy. (For example, two people fall in love and, after seeing each other only on weekends for 2 months, get married.) **Companionate love** is more characteristic of couples who have been married for years. These couples have both commitment and intimacy, but they lack the passion they had when they were first married. Finally, **consummate love** is complete love, containing all three dimensions. It is the goal of most couples.

Most people have experienced several of these types of love and can recognize that each of them feels rather different. Even within one relationship, it is possible to experience two or more types of love over time. A couple, for example, may start out as close friends (liking) and then 2 years later become sexually involved (romantic love); a year later they may decide to live together (consummate love). However, 3 months later he has an affair; she finds out about it and moves out, ending the relationship (non-love).

A further description about what happens to one's brain chemistry is provided in Box 9.2. Science provides another description of how we physically respond in a new relationship.

Jealousy: A Green-Eyed Monster or Real Love?

He that is not jealous is not in love.

—SAINT AUGUSTINE

Love, jealousy, and abuse are all interconnected (McGinley & Sabbadini, 2006; Puente & Cohen, 2003). **Jealousy** is defined as an emotional response to a real or perceived threat to a valued relationship. When a person is in love with another person, there is always the possibility that he or she will feel some jealousy. In fact, some maintain that if there is no jealousy, there is no real love.

Certainly, some level of jealousy is functional in a relationship, but it can become problematic if it intensifies. It can be functional if it encourages a person to think about an intimate relationship and look for positive ways to develop a stronger relationship. But jealousy can be hurtful and can destroy a relationship as it creates more suspicion about the relationship. In the extreme, jealousy can lead to the greater probability of abuse and violence in an intimate relationship.

Both men and women become jealous when their partners become emotionally or sexually involved with other persons; there are no gender differences in the frequency, duration, or intensity of jealous feelings (Levy, Kelly, & Jack, 2006). However, there is often a sex difference as it relates to causes of jealousy. Men are more likely to feel jealous if the partner becomes sexually involved with a new partner, whereas women are more likely to be upset if the partner is emotionally connected with another person (Levy et al., 2006; Pines, 1998).

Jealousy is seen by therapists as a self-defeating emotion, and jealous people are often their own worst enemies. Jealousy leads to feelings of possessiveness, envy, and suspicion. The more jealousy takes over as a factor in an intimate relationship, the more it creates a vicious cycle of greater and greater jealousy. The jealous partner, who is often insecure about the relationship anyway, fears losing the relationship. When the partner tries to control the relationship and seeks greater closeness, the person they most fear losing is often driven away. Thus jealousy often leads to more problematic behavior, including various types of abuse (verbal, physical, sexual), and tends to push many couples apart.

Jealousy can be triggered by both external causes and internal causes. The external causes relate to behavior by a person that demonstrates the partner is (or appears to be) more interested in another person emotionally and/or sexually than in you. While you cannot control your partner's behavior, you can control how you perceive this external behavior. You can perceive it as a threat to your relationship, which will trigger jealousy, or as a sign that your partner is friendly and this person is not a threat to you. The greater your insecurity about the relationship, the greater the chances you will feel jealousy (Marelich, Gaines, & Banzet, 2003).

Jealousy is often related to internal factors that are under your control and relate to such factors as your level of self-esteem, how dependent you are in the relationship, your level of insecurity about the relationship, your past experience about trusting others, and your perceived alternatives for another relationship (Levy et al., 2006). Findings from a variety of research studies have demonstrated that the lower a person's self-esteem, the more easily that person will become jealous. The more dependent you are on your partner or the more involved in the relationship, the more you will tend to become jealous. If you have been emotionally hurt in past relationships, trust in your partner is often not strong, which can lead to feelings of jealousy.

BOX 9.2   At Issue

Love and Science

In February 2006, *National Geographic* ran an article entitled "This Thing Called Love" (Slater, 2006). It provided an overview of chemical changes that occur with people when they fall in love and how those change when couples settle into the more mundane life when passion ends. We all go through it, and when it happens we ask ourselves, "What happened?" The article draws on the most recent scientific data about brain chemistry by way of MRIs and behavior. We are actually beginning to understand where love happens in the brain.

The prominent researchers that have contributed to this knowledge are Helen Fisher, Arthur Aron, and Lucy Brown (2006). These researchers looked at the brains of 17 people who were intensely "in love" as these subjects looked at pictures of their loved one. These researchers found that a part of the brain activates dopamine receptors. Dopamine creates intense energy, focused attention, obsessive following, and exhilaration. It allows one to focus attention and create a motivation to get rewarded. These researchers explain that this process is a brain mechanism for courtship and is true of all humans, and it is comparable to what we see in mate selection for animals.

It is also interesting to note that the serotonin levels in the blood of subjects who are in love are at levels similar to those in people who have an obsessive-compulsive disorder (Slater, 2006). Therefore, one can conclude that love and obsessive-compulsive disorder have similar chemical characteristics and that love and mental illness may be very similar. This author suggests that the use of some mental health medicines, such as those used for obsessive-compulsive behavior, may be useful for treating mental health but may also be jeopardizing a person's ability to fall in love. The medicine does not allow the dopamine receptors to respond and, thus, keeps romantic love from sweeping one away.

Fisher, Aron, and Brown (2006) also indicate that the brain response in new love relationships is different and longer lasting than sex drive. Sex drive is related to increased levels of testosterone, but is not related to romantic love. Sex drive and romantic love are related to two distinctly different aspects of the nervous system but work together to focus on potential mating partners and are also able to focus courtship attention on one individual. A person can sustain attraction and sexual arousal in a way that maintains a romantic relationship for a period of time and can set the stage for a long-term relationship. The sex drive, on the other hand, can be focused on several individuals—even someone on television or in the media—with a specific goal of a sexual union with a partner. It is also possible, then, for people to be sexually aroused and have sexual relationships with partners without having any interest in a romantic relationship. Romantic love, however, is focused on having an emotional union with the other person and does not go away by having sex.

These authors also consider a third neurological component that comes into play in couple relationships (Fisher et al., 2006). As described elsewhere in this chapter, partner attachment has a role in relationship intimacy. Attachment adds sustainability to sex drive and courtship attraction. Although attachment begins in childhood between child and parent, attachment remains active throughout one's lifetime and provides a foundation for the long-term attachment of couples, which ultimately provides a way to provide long-term care for the raising of children. The brain indicates a third neurological response, increased levels of oxytocin, which is related to attachment. Oxytocin is a hormone that promotes the ability to connect and bond with others. Therefore, sex drive, romantic love, and partner attachment occur in different parts of the brain, acting in ways that work together in helping couples form relationships, have children, and raise families.

One of the implications of these scientific findings related to love is that we now have a physiological explanation for why the intense passion evident at the beginning of a relationship moves to a much less intense attachment as time goes on. These findings also make the case for taking one's time when looking for a long-term relationship. Wait until the period of intense emotional feelings transition to partner attachment to see how that feels before getting married or making a commitment.

If you are feeling jealousy in an intimate relationship, it is very important to confront jealousy directly and to talk about it with your partner. Jealousy is a warning sign that things are not going well, and it should not be ignored. The person feeling jealousy should find a time and place to fully discuss the topic, and each person should openly share what he or she is feeling about the relationship. One significant issue to discuss is how much each person is committed to the relationship and wants to maintain it over time. If there is agreement on commitment to the relationship, then the couple should talk about ways that they can both work together to build a closer and more intimate relationship. In other words, jealousy can be a signal that you need to talk about your relationship and explore ways to make it grow.

Looking for Love on the Internet

Because of the increase in dating services and online dating, it has been possible to conduct studies that indicate what people are looking for and what they are attracted to when seeking intimate relationships. Today, professional dating services or Web sites are being used by people of all ages. In a survey by the Pew Research Center (Madden & Lenhart, 2006), 74% of those currently single and looking for romantic partners indicated they had used the Internet to further their romantic interests. In addition, 15% said they know someone who had been in a long-term relationship with, or married, someone he or she met online. Many online daters find happiness with people they met online, with 43% of daters having gone on dates with people they met using the Internet, and 17% entered into long-term relationships with, or married, dating partners they met online. The bottom line is, however, that only 3% of those who are married or in committed relationships met online. So, although online dating is prevalent, people usually marry or develop a committed relationship with people they met in other ways. Because these data are from 2006 and we do not have more current data, we can only speculate that the numbers of people looking for romantic relationships online have risen.

People are looking for dating opportunities, companionship, or potential marriage partners. People might be seeking either long-term or short-term relationships. Here is one scenario about that experience:

> Nancy is a 48-year-old single woman with a 9-year-old daughter. She has been single for 7 years and has decided she wants to have a relationship with a man—mainly for companionship. She is looking for someone who is reasonably attractive and would have a lifestyle that is consistent with hers, which is someone from a small rural community, attends church, does not drink or party excessively, has wholesome values, and is committed to family. Nancy has supported herself most of her adult life and is financially independent, though not wealthy. She wants to be able to go out to dinner, or a movie, and have someone to spend time with. She is open to a relationship becoming permanent, but that is not her goal. She has been married twice before and does not want the legal entanglements of marriage. Currently, her primary goal in life is to raise her daughter in a healthy environment.
>
> She uses a free online dating service. Pictures and personal descriptions of other participants are available. The service allows her to connect with potential dates with a secure e-mail. Multiple men contact her—many with offers for one-night stands, which is not what she is looking for. Others, however, offer what, in her mind, are very respectful invitations to talk or meet over coffee to get to know each other better. After several e-mails, she agrees to have a telephone conversation with one man. After several phone conversations, they agree to meet for coffee. They have agreed to go to a movie together. Where will the relationship go? Time will tell.

What people are looking for in a partner has evolved over time. In the late 1980s and early 1990s, mutual attraction and love were considered important qualities for both men and women (Najman, Dunne, Purdie, Boyle, & Coxeter, 2006). Current literature shows that women are more likely to want a partner with the ability or potential ability to earn money or have a high social status (deVries, Swenson, & Walsh, 2007; Najman et al., 2006). Education has also been viewed as important by women because it indicates potential earning power. Men are more concerned about physical attractiveness. Other studies show that the attractiveness ratings of photographs determined success in attracting dates, with the most attractive people being selected most often. Attractiveness is usually determined by facial features. The self-descriptions, which included such things as resources (financial and nonfinancial), physical health, and social qualities, did not predict dating success (deVries et al., 2007).

It is expected that looking online for potential partners for dating, companionship, or marriage will continue to increase. It is also expected, therefore, that research about this process will increase in the future, and time will tell how this means of developing relationships will evolve. See Chapter 10 for more information about this important topic.

Exploring Intimacy: From Experience to Relationship

Like love, intimacy is also an elusive concept. The word generally brings to mind images of physical closeness and sexuality. But it is really much more than that. Intimacy is the closeness and feelings of warmth we have with certain people. It is an ongoing process of life with other people, and it has many components. Without intimacy with other human beings, life would be boring, cold, and lonely. Many people in our culture place a high value on intimacy. Although intimacy is not restricted to marriage relationships, most of us get married in our search to find and maintain intimacy. It is considered a reward and benefit of marriage.

Paths to Intimacy Differ in Males and Females

Although both males and females agree that the path to greater intimacy is one of greater personal self-disclosure, a variety of studies have found that females are more likely to follow that path (Fehr, 2004). In studying same-sex friendships, women consistently increase their intimacy with higher levels of self-disclosure about themselves. Males feel greater intimacy through doing activities together. So for many men, intimacy with other males is formed through attending sports events or doing activities together.

When seeking intimacy with those of the other sex, both women and men are often disappointed because they falsely assume that they will create intimacy the same way with the other sex that they do with their same-sex friends. So women often assume that they will achieve greater intimacy with a man by mutual self-disclosure, but many men are not very good at self-disclosure. Similarly, men often assume that it is by simply doing activities together that they will increase intimacy with a woman.

A more realistic goal for creating a more intimate relationship with the other gender is that there need to be both higher levels of self-disclosure on the part of the male and greater participation in activities by the female. By participating in activities with the male, females will find that doing things together opens the male up for more self-disclosure. A male will also appreciate the participation of the female in joint activities because this creates a feeling of greater bonding and intimacy to a male. And if men can learn to be more open and share personal beliefs and feelings, say, over lunch with their female partner, they will also benefit from this newfound emotional intimacy.

Intimacy and Communication

Honest communication is essential to true intimacy. We cannot feel close to another person if we are hiding or withholding important thoughts or feelings about that person, or even about ourselves. This doesn't mean, however, that we should lay bare our every thought or emotion. High self-disclosure can be detrimental to the development of intimacy at the beginning of a relationship, and it can damage a more established relationship if the "brutal truth" is too brutal. In the former case, when a relationship is just beginning, opening oneself up may threaten a partner who doesn't have the same commitment to the relationship and who therefore would not share in return. In the latter case, when a relationship is established, "honesty" may be a thin disguise for hostility or anger against the partner or spouse.

Nevertheless, open communication in appropriate doses, at appropriate times, and with good intentions can enhance a relationship and lead to greater

The temptation is to let oneself be swept away by romance, but individuals falling in love should use some uncommon sense: Let things develop slowly, be honest with the other person and oneself, keep an open mind and a sense of humor. It's easier to fall in love than to stay in love.

intimacy. A couple who tries to maintain peace and stability by glossing over disputes or ignoring problems is headed for trouble. Finding a productive way of resolving differences, by meeting them head on and negotiating a workable compromise, is key.

Intimate Experiences Versus an Intimate Relationship

One can feel close to another person in a variety of ways and in different areas of one's life. Some of these ways include emotional intimacy, intellectual intimacy, social intimacy, recreational intimacy, and sexual intimacy.

An **intimate experience** is one in which we feel close or share ourselves with another person. For example, a deep philosophic discussion can be a very intellectually intimate experience. Working together successfully on a project can also lead to an emotionally intimate feeling. The most commonly perceived type of intimacy is sexual intimacy. Nevertheless, people perceive experiences differently, and what one person perceives as an intimate experience may not seem so intimate to another.

An **intimate relationship** is one in which we share intimate experiences in several areas over time, with expectations that this sharing will continue. It is difficult to have and to maintain intimate relationships with more than a few people at once because intimacy is time consuming. For example, how many really good friends, intimate friends, do you have? Probably very few.

Also, it is quite clear from research with couples that no relationship can provide intimate experiences in all areas all the time. With apologies to Abraham Lincoln, "You can please some of the people some of the time, but you can't please all of the people all of the time." This is certainly the case with love relationships. Intimate partners may be able to satisfy each other in a number of ways—emotionally, intellectually, sexually—but both partners will most likely satisfy other intimacy needs outside the relationship. We do not suggest sexual intimacy as one of these areas, because an extramarital affair can destroy intimacy in all other areas of the relationship. But both partners can have friends of either gender at work or in other areas of their lives, friends who are very special and who provide something that the mate does not or cannot provide. These friendships can add to each partner's happiness and thus be a positive force in the couple or marriage relationship as long as the partners can minimize feelings of insecurity and jealousy.

The Paradox of Marriage and Intimacy

Most people in our culture seek marriage in their quest for intimacy. Marriage is an important source of intimacy, but, paradoxically, intimacy too often declines, and sometimes is completely destroyed, after marriage. For many, marriage increases intimacy; for others, however, it becomes an intimacy trap and smothers the very thing the two people desperately seek to enjoy. On the one hand, marriage is extolled as the path to happiness; on the other hand, it can be a source of conflict.

The basic question remains: Does marriage provide intimacy on a permanent basis? The answer is a qualified yes. Marriage can provide intimacy, but the partners must work to make it happen. Marriage in our society has become the classic great escape. People escape into marriage to avoid loneliness and to find intimacy.

Later, when the marriage feels stifling or empty, some people escape from it to maintain their sanity and independence. Single people can feel lonely. So can married people (Rokach, 2005, 2006). In the next section, we'll look more closely at how couples can develop and maintain intimacy.

Developing Intimacy in Couple Relationships

With an extremely large sample, researchers have identified five areas in couple relationships that contribute to couple satisfaction (Olson, Olson-Sigg, & Larson, 2008). Although these findings are based on a study about married couples, they also provide information that is useful for dating couples, cohabiting couples, and premarital couples. These researchers found that there were distinct differences in the scores of five relationship characteristics between happily married couples ($n = 20,675$) and unhappily married couples ($n = 20,590$). These five areas, in order of importance, are communication, couple closeness, couple flexibility, personality compatibility, and conflict resolution. Olson et al. refer to these five areas as the five keys to intimacy, in that it is possible to predict with over 90% accuracy whether a couple will be happy or unhappy based on their scores in these five areas. These data were taken from the **ENRICH** Inventory (PREPARE-ENRICH, n.d.), which has been used by over 50,000 couples who want to improve their couple relationships. These findings are depicted in the graph in Figure 9.1, and a more detailed description of each area is provided below.

FIGURE 9.1

Happily Versus Unhappily Married Couples

Source: From David H. Olson, Amy Olson-Sigg, and Peter J. Larson Ph.D., *The Couple Checkup.* Copyright © 2008 by David H. Olson, Amy Olson-Sigg, and Peter J. Larson. Reprinted by permission of Thomas Nelson, Inc.

Communication Skills

It is not surprising that communication is the area that most strongly distinguishes happy couples from unhappy couples. There is considerable agreement that good

Open communication is an essential component of a successful relationship, but talking about feelings—especially feelings about the relationship—can be a difficult experience for some individuals and couples. Fortunately, communication skills can be learned.

communication is essential for having an intimate relationship. Some people are more comfortable talking about their feelings than others. What appears to be critical for couples is that they are able to share important emotions and beliefs, they are able to both listen and speak, and they are able to communicate openly with their partner.

Couple Closeness

Couple closeness is the degree to which a couple has an emotional connection. It also assumes there is a balance between couple togetherness and couple separateness. People get busy doing their own thing during the day or during the week, and they also need to have the ability to get reconnected when they come back together. Couples who are close often help each other, express feelings of emotional closeness, spend time together, and have their relationship as their top priority.

Couple Flexibility

Couple flexibility is the capacity to change and adapt as situations arise. This includes the ability to deal with stress and to respond when necessary. Couples who do well in this area typically share leadership roles in their relationships and change the rules about who does what as situations change.

Personality Compatibility

Two people are never going to be exactly same, but it is important to respect each other and not try to control or change each other. There are some couple combinations that mesh well. There are others in which individuals need to make slight adjustments in how they interact with others because their personalities are extreme or out of balance. Sometimes there needs to be an understanding and appreciation for personality differences.

Sharing leisure activities is one way couples can build and maintain the intimacy of their relationship. This couple has chosen an activity that allows for companionship and exercise.

Conflict Resolution

Couples who are happy resolve conflict by talking openly with each other and trying to understand each other's opinions and feelings. These couples generally deal with conflict rather than avoiding issues that are difficult to talk about.

Intimacy Games

Two important aspects of any intimate relationship are honesty and straightforwardness. When one partner asks for or tells the other what he or she wants, the other partner is free to comply or not comply. But many people play **destructive intimacy games** with their partner, concealing what they really want and attempting instead to manipulate the partner into doing or giving them what they want. (As we will see later in this section, there are also constructive intimacy games.) Because destructive intimacy games tend to be effective in the short run—people often get what they want using these techniques—they can be rewarding. But in the long run, they undermine relationships. Closeness and sharing suffer, resentment grows, and the relationship may ultimately be destroyed.

Along these lines is what family therapists refer to as the **zero-sum game.** In this type of game, there is a winner and a loser. Unlike more cooperative games in which both people win by working together, the competitive zero-sum game results in one person winning what the other person loses; hence the score of the game comes to zero. For example, if I win by six points and you lose by six points, it all adds up to nothing. In human relationships, zero-sum games usually lead to problems, especially if the rules are constructed so that the same person wins most of the time. One partner might say, for example, that he or she will make the final decisions about how the couple's money is spent because he or she works outside the home and the other spouse doesn't.

Why do people play destructive intimacy games? Sometimes people don't really know what they want from a relationship. Sometimes they're embarrassed or afraid to ask for what they want, or they assume they'll be turned down. Sometimes they perceive a situation to be so difficult that the only way they can see to handle it is by playing a game. Then, because playing games often works in the short run, people tend to play them again and again.

Destructive intimacy games share many elements of such games as chess, bridge, and football: goals, players, rules, and strategies. But in football, for example, everyone knows what the goal is, who the players are, what the rules are, what the rewards and penalties are, when the game is over, and what the outcome is. In a destructive intimacy game, many of these elements are hidden or unclear. Intimacy games can be identified and defined by asking the kinds of questions listed in Table 9.2.

TABLE 9.2	Dimensions of Intimacy Games
Characteristic	**Relevant Questions**
Name of game	What name describes the game?
Players	Who were the players/opponents?
	Who were the spectators?
	Who were the referees?
Playing field	Where was the game played?
	When was the game played?
Objectives	What were the short-term objectives?
	What were the long-term objectives?
Rules	What were the rules?
	Were they implicit or explicit?
Strategies	How was the game played?
	What strategies did the offense use?
	What were the long-term objectives?
	What counterstrategies did the defense use?
Communication style	Did the participants express themselves verbally, nonverbally, or both?
Rewards and penalties	What were the rewards?
	What were the penalties?
Outcomes	How effective was the game in the short term? In the long term?
	How enjoyable was the game?
	Was there a winner and a loser?

Constructive Intimacy Games

Although most intimacy games are destructive, **constructive intimacy games** can enhance a relationship. Too often intimates focus on what they do *not* get from each other rather than on how often they benefit from the other person. This sets up a negative cycle: As one person becomes more negative and less willing to give, the other person reciprocates. Soon neither person in the relationship is giving to the other in a positive way.

One way to reverse this type of negative interaction is to focus on the positive, on what you can do for the other person and what the other person can do for you. Giving to another person in a positive way encourages the other person to do the same. Also, telling the other person what you want increases your chances of receiving it.

Marital therapists often find that when one partner does something positive for the other, the other will respond positively in return relatively soon. Over a period of 2 weeks, if one spouse did ten positive things for the other, the spouse would be likely to receive about the same number of positive gestures in return. In contrast, when individuals are negative, they receive negative responses, and the negative pattern repeats itself. Marital therapists often ask partners to double the number of compliments they give to their spouses each day for a week. Although both spouses commonly feel it would be strange to exchange so many compliments, they find that the recipient not only accepts the compliments but returns about the same number over the next few days. This approach develops a positive complementary cycle. The Beatles put it more poetically when they sang, "In the end, the love you take/Is equal to the love you make."

Unlike destructive intimacy games, constructive games help develop positive cycles. In addition, constructive games have objectives that are specific, rules that are explicit, strategies that are cooperative rather than competitive, and outcomes that are mutually rewarding. A constructive intimacy game called "Giving Compliments" is available on the text's Online Learning Center. Couples who would like instruction in constructive intimacy games can enroll in a couples communication workshop. Constructive games can be especially enjoyable in intimate relationships, which allow for a greater variety of ways in which partners can reward each other and develop more positive feelings toward each other.

Destructive Intimacy Games

As mentioned, many intimacy games are destructive. Identifying and analyzing a few can illuminate their pitfalls and provide the basis for developing more contructive and positive ways of relating. Two destructive intimacy games are "I Don't Care; You Decide" and "The Ties That Bind."

"I Don't Care; You Decide." Many times, when couples are involved in decision making, one partner genuinely wants the other partner to make the decision. However, when one partner knows what he or she wants but is afraid to tell the other person, or when the partner wants to make the decision but have it appear as if the other person has made it, the decision-making process can become a game.

The initiator often begins playing this game when he or she is relatively sure the other person will make the decision the initiator prefers. The initiator often

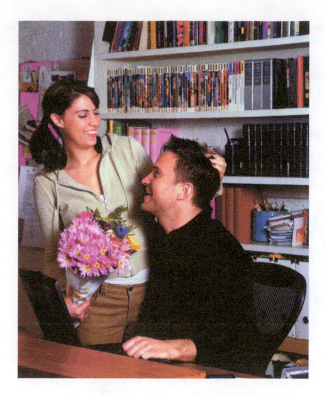

Human relationships are too precious to risk by playing destructive games. Constructive interactions, positive feedback, and honest communication are the keys to successful, long-lasting relationships.

opens the game with a loaded question, such as, "Do you want to stop here for dinner?" This really means, "I want to stop here, and I hope you will know that and make that decision." When the other player says yes, however, she or he can then be held responsible if the food is bad, the service is poor, or the bill is too high.

The following dialogue illustrates another common way this game begins. Jennifer and Tom have received an invitation in the mail from a couple they haven't seen in some time. The party-givers are primarily Tom's friends, whom he has known for years. Jennifer doesn't enjoy them because they argue so much.

Tom: What do you want to do about this party? Should we go?

Jennifer: I don't care . . . [even though she does].

Tom: Wouldn't you like to see them again?

Jennifer: Well . . . don't you have other things you'd rather do this Saturday?

Tom: No, I'd rather go. Okay?

Jennifer: Okay, but . . .

Tom: Are you sure you want to go?

Jennifer: Yes, I guess so.

When Jennifer and Tom go to the party, Jennifer will go reluctantly and will probably be frustrated by the experience. Jennifer had hoped Tom would realize she didn't want to go to the party and would decide they shouldn't go. But by not expressing her true feelings and not actively involving herself in the decision-making process, Jennifer failed to achieve what she intended. This is one of the negative consequences of playing games.

Another negative consequence might be that when she gets home from the party, Jennifer will feel so miserable or annoyed that when Tom wants to make love, she will say quite honestly, "I don't feel like it tonight." Tom, suspecting Jennifer's playing a game, might speculate, "She didn't want to go to their house all along, and now she's punishing me by withholding sex!" The merry-go-round continues, and both people feel frustrated.

"The Ties That Bind." The parent–child relationship is also fertile ground for destructive intimacy games, especially when the children become adults. Although supposedly played in the best interests of all concerned, these games are often disguised, and the players often do not enjoy playing them. Nevertheless, game playing between parents and their adult children is likely to exist. Giving up the role of parent is difficult. Although many parents would agree intellectually with Kahlil Gibran's observations on children, they often have difficulty living this philosophy:

> Your children are not your children.
>
> They are the sons and daughters of Life's longing for itself.
>
> They come through you but not from you,
>
> And though they are with you yet they belong not to you . . . .
>
> You are the bows from which your children as living arrows are sent forth.
>
> The archer sees the mark upon the path of the infinite, and He bends you with His might that His arrows may go swift and far. (1923/1976, p. 24)

Kahlil Gibran, "On Children" from *The Prophet*. Copyright 1923 by Kahlil Gibran and renewed 1951 by Administrators C.T.A. of Kahlil Gibran Estate and Mary G. Gibran. Used by permission of Alfred A. Knopf, a division of Random House, Inc.

The degree and type of involvement parents have with their married children causes difficulty in many families. The prevalence of in-law jokes attests to the significance of this issue in marital and family relationships. Some mutually agreed-upon degree of balance is important. But it can be difficult to successfully balance the dimension of separateness as individuals with that of connectedness to our families of origin. Some parents have difficulty accepting the fact that their children are grown up and desire a more independent lifestyle, one that is free from past traditions. Parents who are frustrated by their dwindling contact with their adult children often play games, such as the destructive intimacy game called "The Ties That Bind," which is also available on the text's Online Learning Center.

Limiting Destructive Games

Over the years, researchers and family therapists have devised a number of useful techniques for limiting gamesmanship in families and maximizing true intimacy. The four central techniques are (1) naming the game, (2) making implicit rules explicit, (3) identifying strategies and counterstrategies, and (4) discussing the disguised objectives and making them clear and specific. Each of these components is described in more detail below.

Naming the Game. Catching yourself and others playing intimacy games can be fun, as well as a way to increase intimacy in your relationships—as long as it is done in a playful and good-natured manner. A destructive intimacy game is a ploy someone uses to get something without directly asking for it. When you catch yourself or a loved one doing this, try very hard to describe what you see honestly. Encourage the loved one to be honest, too. Avoid blame or sarcasm. A matter-of-fact, caring approach is much more effective than a heavy-handed one.

Once the game playing is identified, try to give the game a catchy title. For example, everybody who has been in love is guilty at one time or another of playing the "If You Really Love Me, You'll Know What I Want" game. In this game we assume that the other person can read our mind at all times; if the loved one can't, then he or she must not care about us. Identifying and naming a game and focusing on the problem in a rational and calm manner are major steps in eliminating game playing.

Making Implicit Rules Explicit. Implicit (secret) rules are difficult to reveal, and they add confusion to the destructive intimacy game. Nevertheless, exposing implicit rules is an effective technique for ending the destructive intimacy game. The most common implicit rule is "Don't directly ask for what you want." This rule assumes that if you do ask directly, you will be refused. But playing by this rule puts you in a difficult situation. You don't ask directly because you think you'll be refused, but because you don't ask directly, people have to guess what you want. If they don't guess correctly, you won't get what you want.

By being direct, you give the other person a chance to choose how and when he or she might give you what you want. This places the responsibility for action on the other person and frees that person to give to you. And giving others what they want—making them feel good—makes the giver feel good also.

Identifying Strategies and Counterstrategies. Withdrawing quietly and sullenly from an argument is a common strategy in destructive intimacy games. Its intent is to keep the other player in the argument from continuing on the offensive. The "opponent" may then respond with a counterstrategy by saying, for example, "What's wrong, Dear?" And the obvious counterstrategy to this ploy is for the quiet and sullen "Dear" to respond, "[Sigh] Oh, nothing."

Unveiling game strategies like this isn't easy because, as in cards or tennis, players often try to confuse their opponents. Your intimate opponent may set you up by unveiling one game strategy, only to substitute another. Nevertheless, unveiling strategies can be an important step in building intimacy in a relationship.

Discussing the Disguised Objectives. Rather than directly asking for what they want, some people disguise their objectives. The loaded question is a common technique for disguising what one really wants and for making the partner think that he or she is making the decision. For example, suppose your partner asks, "Wouldn't you like to go to this movie?" To identify the hidden objective, you can ask your partner what movie she or he wants to see.

Attachment Theory and Intimacy

Attachment theory focuses on how children develop attachment to their caregivers, usually their parents, in infancy. The most important tenet of this theory is that a young child needs to develop a relationship with at least one primary caregiver, for social and emotional development to occur normally. Although this theory is a child development theory, since the late 1980s it has been applied to adult attachment, including the development of intimate and love relationships (Cassidy & Shaver, 2008; Mikulincer & Shaver, 2007). There is evidence that attachment follows a developmental trajectory throughout a person's life, beginning with parents, followed by peers, close friends, romantic partners, and a spouse. Romantic love and marriage (including sex), therefore, have recently been viewed as part of the attachment process.

Schachner (2006) also found that long-term singles were most likely to view their siblings or a close friend as attachment figures. Some studies indicate that the extreme negative emotion adults' experience around romantic breakups, divorce, or death parallels what happens with children. When the attachment figure is unavailable, adults express intense anxiety, sorrow, loneliness, and despair (Mikulincer & Shaver, 2007). This intense emotion is comparable to the negative emotion experienced by a child who is separated from a parent.

Substantial research supports the notion that there are several attachment figures during adulthood in addition to romantic partners. For example, it was found that married adults viewed their spouse as their principal attachment figure, and as they got older they also mentioned their children as attachment figures (Schachner, 2006). Parents also continue to be a focus of attachment and serve as a secure base for adults to return to (Mikulincer & Shaver, 2007). For example, when relationships do not work out, some people might go to their parents for comfort and security. During adulthood, siblings and friends are also important attachment figures.

Researchers Cindy Hazan and Phillip Shaver identified three types of attachment responses for adults to characterize their feelings and behaviors in romantic relationships (Mikulincer & Shaver, 2007). These responses parallel attachment theory for children. First, secure romantic attachment involves being comfortable with closeness and interdependence with one's partner and not being fearful of being abandoned by that partner. Second, avoidant attachment is feeling uncomfortable with closeness and interdependence. Finally, anxious attachment involves anxiety over abandonment and frustration over lack of closeness.

Sex is also part of attachment in adulthood, in that romantic love also involves sex (Mikulincer & Shaver, 2007). It is suggested that those who were securely attached as children are more likely to feel comfortable and relaxed and will be more likely to have enjoyable sexual experiences, being able to balance their own and their partner's needs. Insecure adults are likely to have more challenges and more conflict regarding sex in relationships. Avoidant individuals may abstain from sex or may have sexual relationships without intimacy and interdependence.

According to Mikulincer and Shaver (2007), when romantic couple relationships transition from flirtation and dating to a more permanent, long-term relationship, expressions of attachment also change. Mutual support and emotional intimacy become important. There is more disclosure, sharing of personal history, and a focus on long-term goals. The couple is providing a foundation for what they hope will be a committed, lasting, and mutually satisfying couple relationship. They are beginning the process of seeing themselves in a long-term, committed relationship and see their partner as an attachment figure who will be a sensitive and reliable source of comfort and support.

Another study examined the relationship between the family of origin's ritual patterns and the attachment of young adults (Homer, Freeman, Zabriskie, & Eggett, 2007). With a sample of over 200 couples it was found that the more meaningful the family of origin rituals, the more secure and less anxious the adult children were in their romantic relationships. The study also supports the idea that meaningful family rituals are associated with a higher sense of self-worth and greater self-confidence, which contribute to longer-lasting relationships.

Attachment theory provides a context for romantic relationships and marriage, and may provide explanations for happy and unhappy relationships and loss of a partner. Because this area of study is relatively new, it is likely a deeper understanding about the relationship between attachment and intimacy will continue to evolve.

Being Single

Marriage is still very popular in the United States, with the vast majority of people marrying at some time in their lives. The most recent census data, for example, indicate that among Americans 70 years of age and older, 96.7% of the men and 96.7% of the women had been married during their lifetime.

Even though marriage is still in fashion, the census data also show that 51% of American women were living without a spouse in 2005, up from 35% in 1950 and 49% in 2000. Married couples became a minority of American households for the first time. Explanations for these changes include the fact that women are marrying later or living unmarried with partners, and women are living longer as widows or delaying remarriage after divorce because they prefer their new freedom. Census data also indicate that about 30% of Black women are living with spouses, compared to 49% of Hispanics, 55% of White women, and more than 60% of Asian women. Family historian Stephanie Coontz notes that Americans are now spending half of their adult lives outside marriage. Demographer William H. Frey sees

Once considered a sad fate to be avoided at almost any cost, singlehood is today recognized as a legitimate, happy, and healthy alternative to marriage. This single man in his 30s demonstrates some of the benefits of being single, including self-sufficiency and the time and space to cater to one's own tastes.

BOX 9.3 Diversity in Families

Definitions of Singlehood

Being unmarried in the United States, as well as in most other industrialized countries, is not what it used to be—especially for women. Only recently have the words "spinster" and "old maid" gone out of fashion. In the 1950s, for instance, if a young woman wasn't married by the age of 25, she was considered an oddity and was likely to be pitied. Most people were married soon after they graduated from high school or college. It's a different story today. According to the U.S. Census Bureau (2005c), the median age for getting married is now 27 years for men and 25 years for women, compared to 22.8 years for men and 20.3 years for women in 1960 (Glick, 1989).

In an article entitled "Singles Shall Overcome," Bella DePaulo (2004) reports that there are 86 million unmarried people now living in the United States, which represents more than 40% of the adult population.

For U.S. women, singlehood has its upsides and its downsides. On a positive note, increases in education and income have made single women the second largest category of buyers of condos, co-ops, townhouses, and single-family homes. RealEstateJournal.com, an online division of *The Wall Street Journal,* reported in November 2004 that 21% of home buyers were single women (up from 15% in 1993), whereas only 11% were single men (Lisle, 2004).

However, the news for single women is not all good. Single women are often caught in the middle of two worlds. Like the four women on the TV show *Sex and the City,* they enjoy the freedom and sense of adventure that comes with being unattached, yet they spend much of their time searching for the perfect relationship. In an article in the *Journal of Mental Health Counseling,* Phyllis A. Gordon (2003) states that society does not prepare women for singlehood and that "from an early age, most young girls are prompted to think of an adult life that encompasses marriage and motherhood." She also says that although it is fairly acceptable for a man to remain single, women who do so are usually seen as less loving and nurturing, less sexually attractive, and more selfish. They often see themselves as being "less than," as lacking something fundamental, and they frequently experience low self-esteem. Many women feel great societal pressure to be part of a couple.

Traditionally, people married to fulfill parental expectations, for social and economic security, and for religious reasons. Contemporary reasons for getting—or not getting—married are often more personal and include the rise of feminism and the sexual revolution, the fact that many young people are staying in school longer to earn graduate degrees, and the cultural changes that affect the way people search for mates. Many people are no longer so concerned about meeting society's expectations.

That is not to say that intimacy is not still an important issue. Many young adults are postponing marriage until they find that one individual who is just right for them. According to Whitehead and Popenoe (2001) in a report for the National Marriage Project at Rutgers University, young adults are "searching for a deep emotional and spiritual connection with one person for life." The authors went on to say that 94% of never-married men and women ages 20–29 are searching for their soul mates "first and foremost."

In a global context, waiting for Mr. Right is a particularly Western notion. In other places around the world, marriage is often seen as an alliance between families for this as a culmination of post-1960s trends toward greater independence and more flexible lifestyles (Roberts, Sabar, Goodman, & Balleza, 2007).

Following are some other interesting statistics on singles from the U.S. Census Bureau (2004d, 2006b):

- There are 95.7 million unmarried and single Americans.
- Fifty-four percent of the unmarried and single Americans are women.
- 14.5 million unmarried and single Americans are aged 65 and over.
- 28.8 million people in America live alone. These one-person households comprise 26% of all U.S. households.
- Thirty-three percent of births in 2002 were to unmarried women, varying from 89% for unmarried teenagers aged 15 to 19 to 12% for unmarried women aged 30 to 44.
- 683,000 unmarried grandparents are responsible for caring for their grandchildren.

social, political, or economic reasons. The following are views of singlehood in several Asian countries:

- Phyllis A. Gordon (2003) reports in an article in The *Journal of Mental Health Counseling* entitled "The Decision to Remain Single: Implications for Women Across Cultures" that in Korea, choosing not to marry may reflect badly on the family, because it is perceived that the parents have been neglecting their duty to find a suitable mate for their child.
- In China, single women may face numerous problems, according to Philip A. Pan (2000) in a *Washington Post* article entitled "Thoroughly Modern Women Disconcert Many in China." Chinese men who are economically secure may choose to pursue extramarital affairs, but their wives usually choose to stay married to them, because divorced women in China are seen as tarnished. Single women in China are forbidden by law to bear children. And successful single Chinese women often find it difficult to find a mate. According to Pan, successful Chinese women want to marry men at least as successful as they are; however, Chinese men believe wives should be subservient, and ". . . less educated and less successful than their husbands, [and] university professors often advise their female students to get married before they pursue graduate studies, lest they end up 'overqualified' for marriage."
- In Japan, Anthony Faiola (2004) reports in an article in the *Washington Post* entitled "Japanese Women Live, and Like It, on Their Own" that Japanese women are entering the workforce in record numbers (with the percentage of women in the workforce hitting 40.8 in 2003). They are also becoming more financially independent, and many are choosing to remain single. In 2003, according to Faiola, 54% of Japanese women in their late 20s were single—a higher percentage than that found in any other country, including the United States. For many years, their icon was Princess Sayako, daughter of Emperor Akihito, who chose to remain single until she recently announced her engagement at age 35 (although every year on her birthday she was asked by the press about her marriage plans). However, single Japanese women are often criticized strongly for not taking their traditional roles of wife and mother seriously. Faiola quotes former Prime Minister Yoshio Mori as saying, "Welfare is supposed to take care of and reward those women who have lots of children. It is truly strange to say that we have to use tax money to take care of women who don't even give birth once, who grow old living their lives selfishly and singing the praises of freedom."
- In Thailand, a young woman named Saovapa Devahastin, 38, won a beauty contest and became the first woman ever to hold the title of "Miss Spinster." In an article in *The New York Times*, Seth Mydans (2004) reported that Miss Saovapa and ". . . a growing number of successful professional women like her are challenging not only the traditional imperative of marriage and family but also what they see as the delicate egos of Thai men." Not all traditions have changed, however. Before entering the contest, Miss Saovapa asked her father for his approval.

Throughout the world, marriage remains the norm. However, singlehood is increasing, and it is changing the makeup of many of the world's cultures.

- There are 120 single men who are in their 20s for every 100 single women in their 20s (for Hispanics, there are 153 men per 100 women; for Asians, 132 men per 100 women; for non-Hispanic Whites, 120 men per 100 women; and for Blacks, 92 men per 100 women).
- There are 33 single men aged 65 or older for every 100 single women of the same age.

See Box 9.3 for some definitions of singlehood.

A Historical Perspective on Being Single

An increasing number of people in the United States see singlehood as a legitimate alternative to marriage. This outlook represents a major shift in our society's attitude toward marriage. Throughout most of American history, the failure to marry (note how even the terminology is loaded) was considered undesirable. Of course, not everyone married in 18th- and 19th-century America, and many married in their late 20s or their 30s. But social circumstances or pure economics probably contributed to not marrying more than personal desires did, for marriage was highly valued. *Old maid* and *spinster* were certainly not flattering descriptions for unmarried women.

In colonial times in America (the 17th and 18th centuries), virtually all unmarried individuals lived in a family environment of some type—either in their parents' home or as servants in another's home. Unmarried people of all ages usually stayed dependent on the families with whom they lived until they married. Only then did they become fully independent members of society.

In the 19th century, the position of unmarried people began to change. They increasingly became involved in wage labor outside the family and often lived in boardinghouses. During the Industrial Revolution, many young people went to work in factories, often at some distance from the farms they grew up on. The boardinghouses exercised family-type controls but were still quite different from a traditional family environment. Although attitudes toward singlehood may have improved over the 19th and early 20th centuries, social custom held that marriage was by far the preferable state, and those who remained single were stigmatized.

Being Single Today

Being single can mean many things. It includes those who have never married, those who have been married and divorced or widowed, or those who are cohabiting. In 2006, 44% of Americans 18 and over were single—25% had never married, 10% were divorced, 6% were widowed, and 2% were separated (Jayson, 2010). With the age of marriage increasing, currently at 27 years for women and 29 years for men (Marquardt, Blankenhorn, Lerman, Malone-Colon, & Wilcox, 2012), young people who eventually marry spend more years as singles. With the divorce rate at approximately 40 to 50%, many people are single for periods of time after a divorce. The increase in cohabitation also affects the marriage rate, with many people living with a partner but officially single. As marriage rates have dropped, nonmarital cohabitation has increased, with over 50% of women ages 19 to 44 having cohabited for a portion of their lives (Popenoe, 2008).

Although many wish to be married some day, there are also substantial numbers of people who are enjoying being single and taking advantage of the opportunities available when there are no responsibilities to a spouse or family (Jayson, 2010). For example, Nancy, a middle-aged divorced woman in Alabama, is content with being single:

> "I don't know, perhaps I'll never get married again. At first, after the divorce, I was very panicky, like, 'Oh, I've got to be married, I've got to be married!' And then after several months of looking for the ideal mate, I discovered that I like myself quite a bit and actually was quite content having my own private space in the world. I'm a busy professional. Sure it gets lonely sometimes, but I've got lots of friends, male and female. I get on the phone and call someone, and we get together and talk and laugh, and I think, 'Hmmm, it could be a lot worse. I could still be dealing with Jerome's drinking.'"

Historically, people did not buy a house or have a child until they were married. In fact, many did not feel they could get on with their real life until they had someone to share it with. Today, singles buy homes, have babies, and make major career decisions without a spouse. Many singles choose to devote time to careers, with multiple job changes and multiple moves. Some of these lifestyles might be difficult if married.

There is a new phenomenon that has been written about recently, which is the increasing number of women between the ages of 25 and 60 years of age who are not married but are raising children alone (Marquardt, Blankenhorn, Lerman, Malone-Colon, & Wilcox, 2012). These women typically have not been married. This group of individuals is also likely to be less well-educated than those who are married with children. For example, more than half of births among women under age 30 now occur outside of marriage. The average woman who has a child and is not married has a high school diploma and is White. Thus, there is a decline in marriage for approximately 60% of Americans who have high school degrees, but do not have college degrees. These authors have concerns about this trend because we know that children, on average, do less well in single-parent homes than in two-parent homes.

These individuals do not necessarily want to be married or are unable to find the right person, but they do want children. Marquardt et al. (2012) conclude that these homes, with female heads of households with limited education, can quickly fall from being middle-income to low-income. These families, then, are less able to provide for their children and are less able to contribute to their communities. This increase in low-income families results in increased costs to our federal and state governments, which is adding to our financial debt. Therefore, this is not only a family issue, but is also becoming a public policy issue.

It is clear that being single today can mean several things. It can mean, "I am having the time of my life with a great career and few obligations," or it can mean, "I am struggling as I raise a child and am barely getting by."

The movie *Up in the Air*, starring George Clooney, is about a man with a job that has him traveling around the country firing people. A major focus of his life is his loyalty-program memberships and his frequent flyer miles. He loves his job because it leaves him with only a handful of days each year where he is not traveling—it leaves him no time for extended family or friends. When he is not traveling for work, he spends time in a very tiny apartment that is simple and plain, with no evidence of any life beyond his job. Ultimately, he falls in love and begins to have a glimpse of what he might have been missing in terms of relationships. The story ends when he finds out that the person with whom he has fallen in love is married and has no interest in a long-term relationship. One of the messages of this movie might be that this is a wake-up call for singles with a fast-paced career and no time for intimate relationships. Reviews of the movie were mixed, which may reflect the variety of ways singles view this issue. Some say it is, indeed, a wake-up call—if one is not careful, one could miss the most important things in life, having intimate relationships. Others say the man was happy and that he did not need relationships to complicate his life.

A recent study by Sharp and Ganong (2011) provided research findings of interviews conducted with 10 single women in their late 20s and early 30s about their experiences with being single. Even though being single is becoming very common, these women indicated that challenges still exist with family and friends considering them "losers."

These women had feelings of the eligible pool of men decreasing as they got older and were not married. The men who were available might be considered leftovers who could not find a partner earlier, or they had been married and divorced and many had children to bring into the relationship. Family and friends also reminded them regularly that they were on a different trajectory than others when they were not married and did not have children. On the other hand, the things they were accomplishing in their lives such as success in their careers were somewhat invisible to those around them. Although there were times when people acknowledged how lucky they were to be single, these comments were somewhat rare.

The book *Loneliness: Human Nature and the Need for Social Connection* by Cacioppo and Patrick (2008) presents pioneering research by Cacioppo on the physiological and psychological importance of human connections. He indicates that people today are living longer, having fewer children later in life, and are increasingly mobile, which can result in loneliness. Cacioppo's findings show that prolonged loneliness can have damaging effects and can be as harmful to one's health as smoking or obesity. For example, loneliness is related to greater resistance to blood flow through the cardiovascular system, higher levels of stress hormones, higher blood pressure, and increased levels of depression. The authors of this book suggest that mainstream society's focus on competition and individualism, rather than on family and community, is damaging to the health and well-being of individuals.

Many singles are enjoying lives without partners and are living healthy and happy lives. There are others, however, who would like to be in a couple relationship but for one reason or another are not, and these folks may feel lonely. Some advice for those seeking to cope effectively with loneliness:

- *Appraise your strengths.* What are the good things about yourself? If you have difficulty listing your attributes, ask some people who know you.
- *Develop a friendship network.* Spend time developing and connecting with a few close friends who can provide you with a caring network.
- *Take a chance.* Reach out and take risks. You must tell people how you really feel and what you need. Say, "I'm really lonely today. I wish I just had somebody to talk to." Until you do this, people can't help you.
- *Don't expect too much.* When you go out socially, go out just to have fun. Many lonely people go out with a different motive: to find the perfect person, a lifelong friend. Convince yourself, instead, that you can enjoy relationships without long-term commitment.

Women who remain single are likely to be high achievers of above-average intelligence. This can make it difficult for them to find an unattached man of equal status, because men sometimes prefer to marry "down."

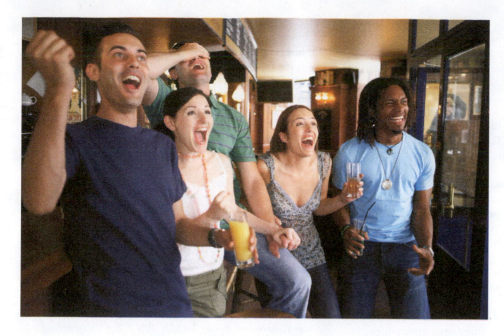

Single people have the same basic desire for sexual intimacy that married people have, but they must take different approaches to fulfilling that need. For some, clubs such as this one offer the right mix of sociability and opportunity. Other singles seek partners in more tranquil settings.

- *Depend on yourself.* Looking for someone else to make you feel all right is seldom effective. You have to depend on yourself and participate in activities you enjoy.
- *Rejoin your family.* Your family can be a great support. Regardless of how you treat your family or how they treat you, you still belong to that family.
- *Find an outside interest.* Try to find something that really interests or excites you and then work at it. If you join an organization, for example, don't just sit in the corner. Take some responsibility. Volunteer for things; really get involved.

In summary, these useful suggestions are not only for singles but also for anyone who wants to maintain healthy relationships with others. These time-tested ideas provide practical ways to live a happy and more connected life.

Summary

- Love and friendship are different. In addition, the dynamics of both have changed recently. Love and friendship can also look different depending on the culture.
- The love triangle, developed by Robert Sternberg, has three dimensions: decision and commitment, intimacy, and passion.
- Science shows that chemical changes occur in the brain when we fall in love and develop long-term relationships. This information may be useful in understanding why we respond as we do in courtship and marriage.
- Men and women are using the Internet to find potential partners more than ever before. In the end, only

3% of people who are married or are in committed relationships found their partner using the Internet.
- Jealousy is very connected with love and intimacy. Although jealousy can be both functional and dysfunctional in a relationship, it is more often seen as problematic. While both men and women get jealous, men are often upset when the partner has a sexual relationship with another person, and women are more often upset when the partner becomes emotionally involved with another person.
- Even though both men and women agree that self-disclosure is related to greater intimacy, it is mainly women who are good at self-disclosure. Men seek intimacy by doing activities with others; women use self-disclosure to create intimacy with others.

- Intimacy involves feeling close to and sharing one-self with another. Although marriage is an important source of intimacy, intimacy often declines after marriage and sometimes disappears completely. Intimacy takes a great deal of time, effort, and hard work to develop and maintain.
- The five keys to intimacy are communication, couple closeness, couple flexibility, personality compatibility, and conflict resolution. These keys are important for dating couples, cohabiting couples, premarital couples, and married couples.
- Attachment theory, based upon infancy development, applies to and can explain attachment in adult love relationships. What happens in childhood attachment affects how we interact in our adult relationships.
- Intimacy games can be either destructive or constructive. To minimize destructive games, it's important to identify them, make their rules explicit, determine the hidden strategies, and make the disguised objectives clear and specific.
- An increasing number of people in today's society see singlehood as a viable alternative to marriage. This represents a major shift in behavior in the last decade.

Key Terms

commitment	consummate love
intimacy	jealousy
passion	intimate experience
non-love	intimate relationship
liking	ENRICH
infatuation	destructive intimacy game
empty love	zero-sum game
romantic love	constructive intimacy game
fatuous love	attachment theory
companionate love	

Activities

1. In a small group, discuss your friendships and how they are similar to and different from love relationships.
2. What does love mean to you? In a small group, share a description of an especially romantic time in your life. What are the similarities and differences among the descriptions group members provide?
3. Consider Box 9.2, "Love and Science." Think about times you have felt you were in love. Did you react in a way that seemed obsessive—like you could not think about anything else but the person you were in love with? Did you experience intense energy around this person? In your experience, is this scientific description about what happens in our brains correct?
4. Take a class survey—using anonymous written responses—to find out how many times each student has been in love. What is the average number? What is the range (lowest to highest)?
5. Interview a divorced or remarried person. Ask how the individual's definition of love changed as she or he went through the following phases: dating, engagement, marriage, marital dissolution and divorce, singlehood, and remarriage. To do this exercise well, spend 45 to 60 minutes with the person to get a good understanding of what happened to the marriage and why.
6. What intimacy games have you personally played? Pick an intimacy game you have played and respond to the questions in Table 9.2. Then discuss your experiences with other members of a small group.

Suggested Readings

Baumbusch, J. L. (2004). Unclaimed treasures: Older women's reflections on lifelong singlehood. *Journal of Women and Aging, 16*(1/2), 105–121. Lifelong single women strongly emphasize their independence and "ability to be alone" as significant benefits, while discussing drawbacks, including loneliness and the absence of a social support network, which became more important as they experienced increasing age and frailty.

Buono, A. J., & Weisenbach, S. (Eds.). (2004). *We met online! Stories of married Catholics who met their spouses on the Internet.* Philadelphia: Xlibris.

Cacioppo, J. T., & Patrick, W. (2008). *Loneliness: Human nature and the need for social connection.* New York: W. W. Norton.

Cassidy, J., & Shaver, P. R. (Eds.). (2008). *Handbook of attachment: Theory, research, and clinical application* (2nd ed.). New York: Guilford Press.

Chiriboga, D., Zettle, L., Connidis, I., Koropeckyj-Cox, T., Bluck, S., Luecking, G., Rook, K., Dykstra, P., DePaulo, B., Morris, W., & Hertel, J. (2004). The never-marrieds in later life: Potentials, problems, and paradoxes. *The Gerontologist, 44*(1), 145. A cross-national perspective on conceptual models and research findings, including discussions of social supports available to never-married men and women, advantages and disadvantages of never being married, how society views individuals representing this role status, and the variety of types of never-marrieds.

DePaulo, B. M. (2006). *Singled out: How singles are stereotyped, stigmatized, and ignored and still live happily ever after.* New York: St. Martin's.

Ferguson, S. J. (2000). Challenging traditional marriage: Never married Chinese American and Japanese American women. *Gender and Society, 14*(1), 136–159. Why do some heterosexual Chinese American and Japanese American women never marry? The four most significant reasons are the effect of their parents' marriages, their status as eldest daughter, their pursuit of education, and the lack of eligible suitors. Parents' traditional marriages and duties as eldest daughter caused many to have negative views of marriage and childbearing. The number of suitors was limited for 46 of 62 respondents because their parents placed strict restrictions on them concerning the types of men they are allowed to marry.

Goodwin, R. (2009). *Changing relations*. New York: Cambridge University Press.

Mashek, D. J., & Aron, A. (Eds.). (2004). *Handbook of closeness and intimacy*. Mahwah, NJ: Erlbaum. Written by scholars in the field, this book provides the most comprehensive summary of a wealth of ideas about closeness and intimacy.

Mikulinger, M., & Shaver, P. R. (2007). *Attachment in adulthood*. New York: Guilford Press.

Oord, T. J. (Ed.). (2008). *The altruism reader: Selections from writings on love, religion, and science.* West Conshohocken, PA: Templeton Foundation Press.

Puente, S., & Cohen, D. (2003). Jealousy and the meaning of violence. *Personality and Social Psychological Bulletin, 29*(4), 449–460.

Sternberg, R. J., & Weis, K. (Eds.). (2006). *The new psychology of love.* New Haven, CT: Yale University Press. The latest hypotheses about love from the researchers studying it.

Sternberg, R., & Weis, K. (2008) (Eds). The new psychology of love. Yale University Press: New Haven, CT.

Straus, J. (2006). *Unhooked generation: The truth about why we're still single.* New York: Hyperion.

Visit the text-specific Online Learning Center at **www.mhhe.com/olson8e** for practice tests, chapter summaries, and PowerPoint slides.

10 *D*ating, Mate Selection, and Living Together

Courtship Patterns

Choosing a Mate

Patterns of Mate Selection

Conflict and Violence in Dating

Living Together

Summary

Key Terms

Activities

Suggested Readings

Regardless of how intense a love relationship is, there are both good and bad reasons for getting married. Similarly, there are both good and bad reasons for remaining single. Today, marriage is a personal choice, not a social dictate. In this chapter we will examine theories that attempt to explain mate selection and the functions and stages of dating. We will focus on mate selection from a cross-cultural point of view, looking at arranged marriages around the world and comparing them with the customary couple-arranged *love matches* of more-developed societies.

In American culture, physical attractiveness is the major factor in choosing a date but not necessarily a mate. We also tend to find mates who are like us in some way, people from our group—ethnic, religious, or socioeconomic. But many of these rules are changing as a result of our increasingly multicultural population. So-called mixed or intercultural marriages are a growing phenomenon, causing many families to examine their attitudes and behaviors toward people outside their particular cultural group.

Later in this chapter we will take a close look at some serious problems in our society today: conflict and violence in dating and the relationship between premarital violence and violence after marriage. Finally, we will conclude with a discussion of the growing trend of couples living together—an arrangement that is becoming a new courtship stage but one with legal and relationship consequences.

Courtship Patterns

One of the chief reasons so many marriages fail is that the functions of a date and a mate differ radically—that of a date is to be charming; that of a mate to be responsible; and, unfortunately, the most charming individuals are not necessarily the most responsible, while the most responsible are just as often deficient in charm.

—SYDNEY HARRIS, Journalist

All societies have created some system for matching individuals for marriage and parenthood. These systems range from the practice of bride purchase, to the selection of a mate by the village shaman according to astrological signs, to contractual systems in which a mate may serve as an indentured servant to the bride's parents, to individual choice based on personal attraction and love. In some cultures, couples are matched while they are still infants; in others, the bride and groom must prove their fertility by producing children before they are eligible for marriage. Although the customs of mate selection vary widely, all perform the necessary function of matching a couple for marriage and eventual parenthood.

Parent-Arranged Marriages

Throughout much of world history, courtships were generally brief. In most cultures, the parents of the bride and groom selected the future spouse and made most of the arrangements for the marriage ceremony. If the prospective couple were granted any freedom of choice, they were expected to complete their arrangements in a few days. The pattern common in modern industrialized nations, in which a couple spends months or even years dating and choosing a mate, developed largely over the past century. Parent-arranged marriages, however, still occur throughout much of the nonindustrialized world (Bhopal, 2008). Although young adults in the United States today might view the practice as archaic and uncivilized, many people worldwide prefer parent-arranged marriages.

Myers, Madathil, and Tingle (2005) compared arranged marriages in India with marriages of choice in the United States. Their study indicated differences in what couples from these two countries thought were important precursors to marriage. For example, couples from the United States felt that love was an important requirement before marriage and couples in India felt love was less important. The important finding from this study, however, was that in the end marital satisfaction between the two groups did not differ significantly. Couples from the United States felt that love was an important component to have before the marriage, whereas, couples from India felt that love could grow. Couples in the arranged marriages also saw the importance of accepting and adjusting to their partner after marriage.

Parent-arranged marriages are based on the principle that the elders in a community have the wisdom to select the appropriate spouse. Parents or elders are more likely to base their decision on economic, political, and social status considerations—to enhance the family's status and position through their choice. Considerations of lineage and family status are generally more important than love or affection in such decisions, although the parents may take the couple's preferences into account to some extent. Arranged marriages thus serve to extend existing family units rather than to create new units. They reinforce ties with other families in the community, strengthening the order and organization of the community (Bhopal, 2008).

Advantages of Arranged Marriages. Parent-arranged marriages are usually very stable, because it is the duty of the whole family to help the new couple get established in life. Divorce is almost unheard of—except for the reason of infertility—because of the potential disapproval a couple would receive from the parents and members of the community who were responsible for the selection. Although love between the couple before marriage is relatively unimportant, affection and respect usually grow through the years; arranged marriages are often quite harmonious. Because there is not really a courtship period, premarital intimacy is minimal or nonexistent.

In parent-arranged marriage systems, couples avoid many of the problems of *American-style* dating. There is virtually no risk of being rejected or of losing one's

Parent-arranged marriages are usually very stable, because it is the duty of the whole family to help the new couple get established in life. Divorce is almost unheard of—except for the reason of infertility—because of the potential disapproval a couple would receive from the parents and members of the community who were responsible for the selection.

true love, and one does not have to determine whether one's partner is committed to the relationship. Although many people might not view these factors as advantages, they effectively ensure a stable marriage. Remnants of arranged courtship and marriage systems are still found in our culture today; for example, a limited number of professional marriage brokers still operate among urban ethnic groups. Further, as most single people know, relatives and friends are often only too eager to help find that "perfect" partner.

Patterns of Change. The world, in general, appears to be moving toward freedom of choice in marriage. This approach is sometimes referred to as the *love match*, though love is not always the goal of marriage in Western industrial societies. Perhaps a better term would be **couple-arranged marriage.** Cross-culturally, the absence of economic means for women to gain financial independence leads to early marriage and little individual freedom. The ability of women to work leads to the decline of arranged marriages, enhances the possibility of love matches, and may slightly diminish the marriage rate. In general, the world is also moving toward monogamous marriage, although the rate of advance varies from country to country.

The movement away from arranged marriage appears to be related to industrialization. As countries shift from more rural to urban industrial societies, love marriages become more common. Data from Africa, India, Israel, and Malaysia indicate that love marriages are more likely among people who marry at a later age, have a higher level of education, have a higher socioeconomic status (or the promise of a higher status), and live in an urban setting. A woman who can support herself financially is more likely to want to decide for herself whom she will marry.

Cultural Variations. The ways people find marriage partners vary from culture to culture. In developing countries that are moving away from arranged marriages, the influence of cultural tradition may be combined with modern sensibilities. In India, for example, it is commonly believed that there is one predestined mate who will share life with the spouse through reincarnation. Therefore parents believe they should supervise their children's marriage choices to avoid mistakes. But many young people are unhappy with this approach, and a compromise is often reached. Semiarranged marriages, in which parental approval is obtained before the marriage, are becoming more common. The case of Dipendra, an Indian sociology lecturer at a university in the South Pacific, provides an example:

> *"I suppose you could call our marriage a 'semiarranged' marriage. My parents had a girl in mind for me, but there was this other beautiful girl in my classes at the uni. I hadn't talked with her much, but she seemed good for me. So, I had my brother talk with her and then he talked with my parents, and the families got together and worked it out. She came from a good family, so my parents were quite pleased. Officially, it was an arranged marriage in the traditional Indian fashion, but I had a lot to say about it!"*

In China, there has been a dramatic change in mate selection from parent-arranged marriage to love-based marriage, as in the United States (Pan, 2002; Xu et al., 2007). Love-based mate selection happens more often in the larger cities than in the small towns and rural areas where parent-arranged marriage continues to occur. A common problem is that many of the young people in China do not know how to date or how to select a mate, and so dating is a challenging adventure for Chinese couples. But China, like many places in the world, is changing rapidly.

Japan, one of the current industrial giants of the Pacific, has generally moved from arranged marriages to love-based marriages. The traditional *nakode*, or matchmaker, is still used in some rural areas of Japan, but the matchmaker's role has become increasingly ceremonial. As more women have entered the labor force and gained financial independence, they have moved away from marriages arranged by their parents. Japanese young people can find dating very awkward and uncomfortable, however, because they often do not have much social contact with members of the other sex.

The Scandinavian countries are perhaps the most liberal in the world in regard to marriage customs. Parent-arranged marriages disappeared decades ago in Scandinavia, and cohabitation has become the most common type of relationship until after the birth of a child. Research in Sweden indicates a steep drop in the marriage rate. Associated with this decline are an increase in cohabitation and an increase in state and parental support for children born outside of matrimony (Cherlin, 2009).

Dating: An American Creation

Dating, historically speaking, is a creation of young people in the United States. It symbolizes couples' efforts to take more control over the process of mate selection. Because the United States was one of the first nations to industrialize, it serves as a good example of the changes in dating behavior that occur when a society evolves from an agrarian culture.

The Emergence of Individual-Choice Courtship. Early in U.S. history, parents typically exercised considerable influence over dating and the choice of a mate. Young people were usually tied to the home and the land, and, except for the occasional community social event, had little opportunity to escape the watchful eyes of their parents. Opportunities for dating were infrequent. Courtship was a rather formal event, often conducted under parental supervision. Males were expected to get the permission of the female's parents and to initiate the acquaintance. Although the couple were generally allowed the privilege of making up their own minds, family members usually announced their approval (or disapproval) before the relationship got too serious. But even then young people were granted much more freedom of individual choice than exists in a parent-arranged courtship system.

As America became more industrialized, families left the farm or ranch to find better opportunities in towns and cities. This has been a long-term trend in America, dating back to colonial times. When parents began to work away from the home, young people gained considerable freedom from parental supervision, as well as the responsibility for organizing their free time. **Dating,** or individual-choice courtship, emerged as an activity in its own right, creating a new institution within the culture. (See Table 10.1 for limitations on the current dating system in the United States.) This pattern, with some variation, appears to be common as societies change from agrarian to industrial.

Along with the emergence of individual-choice courtship and a defined period for dating, permissive behavior also increased. The term **permissiveness** refers to the extent to which couples are physically intimate before marriage. Historically, males were permitted greater freedom and privilege than females and tended to be more experienced in sexual relations than females. However, the same basic forces that revolutionized dating customs in industrial societies also fostered a decline in the **double standard**—different standards of sexual and social behavior for men and women. As customs changed, women engaged in more sexual experimentation. The amount of sexual intimacy women experience before marriage still does not match that of men, but because female sexual involvement has increased rapidly, the difference between male and female sexual behavior is much smaller today

TABLE 10.1 Limitations of Dating

Dating has become the predominant method of finding a potential mate in the United States and other industrialized societies, yet there are numerous limitations to the current dating system. In his book *I Kissed Dating Goodbye*, Joshua Harris (2003) identifies several shortcomings of dating:

- Dating leads to intimacy but not necessarily to commitment.
- Dating tends to skip friendship, which should be the foundation of a stable relationship.
- Dating focuses on romantic attraction, so it lasts only as long as the romantic feelings remain.
- Dating focuses on enjoying love and romance solely for their recreational value.
- Dating often mistakes a physical relationship for love.
- Dating often isolates a couple from other vital relationships, leaving important friendships in disrepair.
- Dating takes a lot of time and energy, which can distract young adults from their primary responsibility of preparing for the future.
- Dating creates an artificial environment for evaluating another person's character.

Source: Excerpt from Joshua Harris, *I Kissed Dating Goodbye*. Copyright © 2003 by Joshua Harris. Used by permission of Multnomah Publishers, a division of Random House, Inc.

than it was in the past. Although many females still expect males to call them, to plan dates, and to propose marriage, females are more assertive and participate to a greater extent in the dating process than they did in earlier generations.

Hooking Up: The Contemporary Trend

A study of more than 1,000 college women (Glenn & Marquardt, 2001) discovered the newer trends of hanging out and **hooking up** as an alternative to dating. These women reported the following trends (see Table 10.2). First, marriage was a major goal of their life and they wanted to marry someone from college. They

TABLE 10.2 Hooking Up, Hanging Out, and Hoping for Mr. Right: College Women on Dating and Mating Today

National Study and In-Depth Interviews of More Than 1,000 College Women

- Marriage is a major life goal for the majority of college women.
- Most women would like to meet a spouse while at college.
- Relationships between college women and college men are often characterized by either too little commitment or too much.
- "Hooking up" is a distinctive sex-without-commitment interaction between college students and has many levels ranging from only kissing to oral sex and intercourse.
- The ambiguity of the phrase "hooking up" is part of the reason for its popular appeal.
- "Hooking up" is widespread on most campuses.
- Dating carries multiple meanings from hanging out (being together) to a high level of commitment.
- It is rare for college men to ask women out on dates or to acknowledge when they have become a couple.
- In areas such as marriage aspirations, getting advice from parents, and "hooking up," college women from divorced families differ significantly from women who grew up in intact families.

Source: From Norval Glenn and Elizabeth Marquardt, *Hooking Up, Hanging Out, and Hoping for Mr. Right: College Women on Dating and Mating Today* (Institute of American Values, 2001), pp. 4–6. Copyright © 2001 by the Institute of American Values, www.americanvalues.org. Reprinted with permission.

Couples may spend time together doing a variety of activities with others, or they may spend time together as couples.

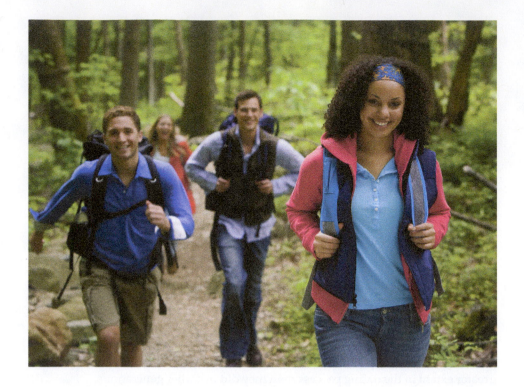

also felt that there was either no commitment in dating or else there was too much. Hooking up was a common term that had a vague definition on purpose so they would not have to reveal the specific details of their relationship. It could range from only kissing to oral sex to intercourse. About 40% of the women said they hooked up, and 10% had done it more than six times. Dating also had multiple meanings, from hanging out, which meant just being together, to a more highly committed relationship. Most college women said it was rare for college men to ask them out on dates. One-third of the women had two dates or less and half had six or more dates since college. So the scene on college campuses is changing from traditional dating to a greater variety of ways of relating, including hanging out and hooking up.

At Stanford University in California, journalist Marisa Milanese (2002) argued that it was a myth that no one dates there. The fact is that "it all depends on what you call a date." The writer noted that 70% of Stanford undergraduates reported having sex, compared to the national average of 72%, but the old adage on campus was that, "No one dates."

The problem may be partially one of semantics. For many students, the phrase "to date" sounds old fashioned, with "let's-split-a-malt-at-the-drive-in overtones." Those students who use the term can be referring to many different types of arrangements: to go out together twice, to be a genuine couple, to be a year away from engagement. The ambiguity of the term, and the ambiguity inherent in human relationships, make students skittish about labeling precisely what is happening.

Commenting on the Glenn and Marquardt study, one Stanford administrator stated that hookups "come with a lack of expectations about emotional depth," but that might not be the students' genuine preference. Stanford Student Health's regular health surveys on campus reveal that relationship concerns regularly top the list of anxieties. And Glenn and Marquardt had found that 63% of women enter college hoping to meet Mr. Right.

Why the confusion in the campus dating situation? Many ideas have been advanced:

- An ever-increasing achievement ethic with rigorous schedules and ambitious goals leaves little time for dating.
- The women's movement eliminated traditional courtship rules but did not present alternative conventions, so that instead of men asking women out now, no one's asking anyone out.
- Coed dorms also figure in the explanation: Men and women brushing their teeth side by side at the sinks may start to see each other more as brothers and sisters rather than as dream dates.
- Finally, there are countless less formal ways to hang out together without generating the anxiety and high expectations of a formal date.

For her book *Hooking Up: Sex, Dating and Relationships on Campus* (2008a), sociologist Kathleen Bogle studied hooking up at two unnamed universities—a large East Coast public university and a smaller Roman Catholic school in the Northeast. She found that hooking up involves a wide range of behavior, from those who do not participate at all to those who participate to a moderate degree to those aspects of hookup culture that might be "cause for alarm (or at least concern)." She argues that it is unfair to characterize college students in general "by what we see on MTV's coverage of spring break."

In her review of research literature, Bogle found that hooking up has been documented by those who study college slang terms and can be traced back to the early to mid-1980s. Researchers perceived a shift from traditional dating in the 1950s and 1960s to group "partying" in the 1970s. Back then it was common for men and women to "pair off" at the end of a party for a sexual encounter, involving anything from kissing to sexual intercourse.

Technology has changed hookup culture to some degree. Instant messaging, Facebook, and text messaging have been added to the tools young people use to connect with each other. Bogle explains that during the traditional dating era, interaction was more formal and required a certain amount of planning. Most likely it was the man who placed the phone call to the woman several days in advance, asking for a date at a specific time and place. Today, things happen on a more spur-of-the-moment, casual basis. Late-night hookups can be arranged if the individuals did not happen to meet at a party or bar.

Comparing a religious institution to a state university, Bogle found that most students she interviewed in the faith-based university did not believe that the religious affiliation affected hooking up in any way. College, by its very nature, is very conducive to hooking up. Bogle describes campuses as homogeneous populations of young men and women living close together with no strictly enforced rules or careful monitoring of their behavior. Students socialize among themselves, and this fosters feelings of safety and comfort. A *let loose and party* attitude pervades campuses, and this makes for an environment in which hookup culture thrives.

In many campus fraternities, freshman males are not allowed to attend a party unless they are a fraternity member, while freshman females are admitted to the party for free. Bogle argues that this practice fosters a *conquest mentality* toward sex among many fraternity members. She also believes that hookup culture more negatively impacts females than males. For one reason, women are far more likely to get a bad reputation for their conduct, including a bad reputation for how often they hook up, whom they hook up with, how far they go sexually during a hookup, and how they dress when they go out at night to a place where hooking up may occur. Men who are active in the hookup game are called *players,* while women are called *sluts.* A second reason hookup culture is harder on women than men is, Bogle believes, that women are not getting what they want out of the hookup system. Women often are seeking a stable, ongoing relationship rather than simply a sexual experience, and are dissatisfied with how often hooking up leads to nothing. Bogle concedes that there are certainly many cases in which a woman is not seeking a serious relationship, "but on average women are far more interested in a hookup turning into 'something more' than men are."

All this puts women in a difficult position. If they don't hook up at all, they are left out of the dominant cultural game on campus and may find it difficult to find opportunities to form sexual and romantic relationships with men. If they do hook up, though, they find themselves walking a fine line as they try to be part of the campus mainstream without being negatively labeled. Bogle observed that campus hookup culture was a 24/7 sexual arena in which students were constantly watching each other, gossiping about each other, and judging each other. When students leave college, Bogle says, there is a discernible shift away from hookup culture to more formal dating and, eventually, marriage, for many. Some college graduates in her study found the more formal dating system a big adjustment.

Several students described to Bogle what they called the *walk of shame.* This refers to a college student, usually female, walking home in the morning after a hookup in the same outfit she was wearing the night before. Because students dress differently when they go out at night, it is obvious to everyone she passes on campus where she has been. Bogle believes that this terminology alone underscores the point that many students on campus are struggling with the hookup system and want more (Bogle, 2008b).

In the past, the pool of eligible partners was often limited by the difficulty of traveling long distances. Today, the Internet allows people from across the country to chat online, making the pool of potential partners less restricted by physical proximity. As in any dating situation, there are both rewards and risks associated with cyberdating.

Internet Dating and Matchmaking Services

Although in an individual-choice courtship system young people make their own selections, many still want help in finding a mate. Today, however, dating services are a more discreet but also more expensive approach. Some services call themselves "relationship services," and their approach is not too much different from that used by employment services. Dating services, popular in many major cities, charge a fee that can reach hundreds of dollars. Applicants fill out forms, describing their traits and the traits they want in a partner; some services videotape applicants' responses. Each customer's file (coded by number, not name, to ensure some privacy) is made available to those who have paid for the privilege. If questionnaire data on "Mr. X" look good to a woman, she might ask to see his videotape. If she is interested in learning more about him, the agency might contact him by phone or postcard, indicating the manner in which he can contact the interested woman. From that point on, what happens in the relationship is up to the individuals involved.

The most popular dating innovation is meeting people online, through subscription services or directly on the Internet. Some services offer chat rooms where strangers can get connected. As with personal ads, there are few safeguards to ensure the accuracy of the information people provide about themselves. Individuals often reveal only positive characteristics that they think will attract others to them. Although the subscription services and/or the Internet might be a simple and inexpensive way to meet someone initially, this approach to dating lacks intimacy and can be risky.

The most extensive study of online dating that we could find was the Pew Internet and American Life Project (Madden & Lenhart, 2006). The researchers found that most online Americans who are single and looking for dates have used the Internet, and millions more Americans know people who have tried and succeeded at Internet dating. That said, most Internet users also believe that online dating is dangerous, because it puts personal information online and open for public view. They also believe that many online daters lie about their marital status. One in 10 Internet users have personally visited dating Web sites. The majority of online daters report good experiences with the sites, and online daters believe dating Web sites help individuals find a better match because they can get to know a lot more people.

In one study about online dating (Wildermuth & Vogl-Bauer, 2007), researchers found that there were five themes that emerged as individuals described their online romantic relationships. These individuals were currently or had been involved in an online romantic relationship. First, these participants indicated that there was intense emotion, both positive and negative, as they talked about these relationships. They talked both about being *swept off their feet* and *becoming very depressed*, depending upon how the online relationship was going. A second theme was that participants warned others to be cautious because you cannot really trust a person to be who they say they are. As a result they gave advice such as not giving out one's phone number online or taking a friend along when meeting in person for the first time. Third, individuals described the power of online connections, in that one gets to know someone to the point that attractiveness does not matter. Fourth, individuals talked about extramarital affairs. Several participants were looking for love on the internet because their real life relationships were unhappy. Others were happy with both their real life relationships and their online relationships. They had differing feelings about the degree to which their online relationships affected their real life relationships. Finally, participants in the study described the negative

BOX 10.1   Putting It Together

Dating Do's and Don'ts

Going out can be fun, but it can also be serious business. Here are some things to think about when dating:

- There are two main reasons for dating, for pleasure and to find a mate.
- Dating should be for fun and for mutual enjoyment. It gives two people a chance to get to know each other and enjoy each other's company.
- Take it slow. Don't jump into things. Gradually reveal more and more about yourself, rather than overwhelming the other person.
- Don't feel the need to become involved physically too soon because it is better for the relationship if you first become friends.
- Friendship is a better foundation to base a relationship on than sex. Sexual attraction and energy often confuse you and prevent you from getting to know each other in other ways.
- It's important to get to know a number of people before getting serious with one.
- In looking for good people to date, be very careful about using a dating service, the newspaper, the Internet, or going to a bar. Dating can be serious business, and you need to exercise caution in how you find prospective dates.
- Friends and relatives sometimes have good suggestions for dating partners.
- Friends and relatives also can give you good feedback about your dates. They often can be more objective about what is happening than someone who thinks he or she is falling in love.
- Get to know the friends and family members of someone you are getting serious about. You often can learn a great deal about a person by visiting with those who have known him or her intimately over a long period of time.
- How do your prospective mate's parents get along? This can give you some clues about how you will get along after marriage.
- Whatever you see that you dislike while dating someone is likely to become magnified after marriage. Small problems before the wedding can become large ones later.
- Be especially cautious about how the prospective mate deals with angry feelings. If the person takes anger out on others, it is only likely to get worse after marriage.
- Notice how your date treats other people. Look for someone who is respectful and kind to everyone.
- Be realistic. Don't look at your prospective mate through rose-colored glasses, seeing only the positives. Sometimes there are serious negatives that have to be considered carefully.
- Be sure to talk with each other about what you like and what bothers you. Being positive is easy, of course, but you need to be honest and express those thoughts that are more difficult to bring up.
- Falling in love is easy. Staying in love takes intelligence, creativity, commitment, and a good heart.
- Trust your feelings and use your brain.

responses from their social networks about their online relationships. Friends and relatives questioned this mode of getting to know someone.

The authors of this study do not indicate whether online romances are good or bad. In fact, if one examines the themes described by Wildermuth and Vogl-Bauer (2007) one could say there are both good and bad aspects of this means of developing connections. Of course, this is also true of other ways in developing romantic relationships.

No matter how one begins the process of dating, some general guidelines about the do's and don'ts of dating are listed in Box 10.1. Basically, dating is a time to learn more about yourself and what you like and don't like in other people. These guidelines are suggestions that can help you make dating a more rewarding and useful experience.

Dating Among Older People

The term *dating* has a decidedly youthful ring, but single people over 65 also date and are sexually active. Interest in dating, especially for older women, is typically the result of divorce; whereas, dating for older men is typically because they have never married (Sassler, 2010). Dating offers the single older person romance, the

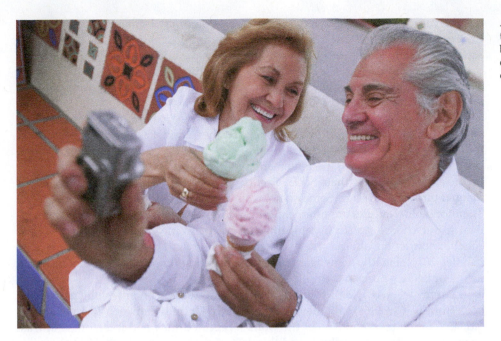

Although we usually think of dating couples as being young, today more older couples are dating, cohabiting, and marrying.

most exciting form of intimacy for human beings, no matter what age. When it goes well, dating can boost an older person's self-confidence and offer the potential for happiness and companionship at an age in life when future prospects are uncertain. When it goes poorly, dating can destroy self-confidence. In sum, dating in the later years can be thrilling, nerve-wracking, and complicated, just as it was in the younger years of life. Older people on a date, just like younger people, can be interesting, smart, attractive, and complex, and they can also be boring, selfish, and superficial (Beers, 2007).

The proportion of older individuals in the American population has increased dramatically since 1900. About 13% of Americans are over 65 (U.S. Census Bureau, 2011). In 2010 there were 50 million women and men over the age of 62 in this country (Howden & Meyer, 2011, May). For every 100 men over age 65 there were 137 women. As life spans lengthen, the percentage of older individuals is expected to increase, to about 20% by the year 2030 (U.S. Administration on Aging, 2009; U.S. Census Bureau, 2009a). We also know that divorced or widowed men are more likely to remarry than women (Sassler, 2010).

Older people date, fall in love, and behave romantically in ways similar to the young. It is very common these days to see proms and dances at retirement facilities. There are also *kings* and *queens* crowned at these events—makeup and formal dress all around. These events are very successful and are well attended. What older people do on dates is similar to what younger individuals do but is often "far more varied and creative." In addition to pizza, movies, and dances, older couples went camping, enjoyed the opera together, and flew off to Hawaii for the weekend. Also, the pace of dating is greatly accelerated. Older people realize they simply do not have much time to play the field. Therefore, they are very direct and forthcoming in their approach in building relationships. Sexual relationships may develop and older people may feel they need sexual intimacy more as they get older than they did earlier in their lives. Sex can reaffirm the fact that one is alive and important to at least one other person in the world.

Like younger individuals, older people face a number of dilemmas and difficulties in dating. Fear of disapproval leads many to be secretive about their dating activities. At this point in their lives, they may have adult children or grandchildren who disapprove of their romantic relationships. Adult children may worry about their aging parents having bad judgment about relationships, or they may feel that their parents are moving into relationships too quickly.

Marriage is another dilemma for older people. They may initially seek a marital partner, but many decide as time goes on that they are not willing to give up their independence. Women, especially, often like the new freedom divorce or widowhood offers (Sassler, 2010). Both men and women sometimes do not want to marry because they will lose their Social Security or do not want to have their assets merged through marriage. Some do not want the hassle of merging two households. Therefore, older adults are often entering into long-term companionship arrangements, but choose not to live together or get married. Older adults often view cohabitation as an alternative to marriage rather than a precursor to marriage (Sassler, 2010). Finally, many fear the burden of caring for someone in deteriorating health or being a burden themselves to someone else.

A survey by AARP, 2005 found that 70% of single baby boomers (the generation born from 1946 to 1964) said they dated regularly. Of those between 40 and 59 years old, 45% of the men and 38% of the women reported they had intercourse at least once a week. The survey also found that 14% of the women said their most important reason for dating was finding someone to live with or marry. Aging baby boomers tend to find dates in the traditional way—through friends, neighbors, and relatives—though a growing number are searching online. All of this dating activity for older individuals is seen as a sea change by sociologist Pepper Schwartz: "You were supposed to stay home and be a grandparent at 50," she argues, but baby boomers today are "very clear about what they want, and they're willing to go looking for it" (Kantrowitz, 2006, p.50).

Choosing a Mate

Americans tend to choose partners who are similar to them in a variety of ways—in ethnic and cultural background, age, educational and religious background, and socioeconomic status. Physical attractiveness also plays a large role in mate selection. This section discusses the criteria that influence mate selection in the United States.

Physical Attractiveness

Physical attractiveness is one of the most important components of mate selection (Herz & Inzlicht, 2002). Researchers have been creative in devising rating scales to measure physical attractiveness. One method is simply to have a panel of judges rate individuals on a scale of attractiveness from low to high. The more physically attractive a person was, the more likely she or he was to have friends of the other sex.

Based on a sequence of studies over 50 years, Buss and colleagues (2001) found that there are several characteristics that both sexes consider very important in a potential marriage partner. Over time, physical attraction became less important for both sexes. Personal characteristics that grew in importance were whether the partner was dependable and had emotional stability and a pleasing disposition. Mutual attraction and love became more important for both sexes over time. The

Appearance makes a difference in a person's life in several ways: Attractive individuals do better in school, believe they have a more promising future, and feel better about themselves than less-attractive individuals. Appearance is one of several features important in mate selection.

characteristics that were significantly different for males and females were that men placed a higher premium on physical attraction. Women placed a higher value than did men on ambition, similar educational background, and being a good financial provider.

In a study of more than 728,000 Match.com members, it was found that being physically attractive was rated as the third most important characteristic; first was being intelligent, and second was being funny (Gardyn, 2002). The percentages that said it was more important to be intelligent were 79% for the total sample and 90% for people with a college degree. Being funny was rated as important by 70%, attractive by 34%, athletic by 12%, and wealthy by only 6%. So being attractive was much less important than being intelligent and funny.

Age and Finding a Mate

It has been estimated that in six out of every seven marriages in the United States, the man is as old as or older than the woman. Why is this the case? Physiologically, males mature more slowly than females and do not live as long. Furthermore, in the United States there are more males than females in their early 20s. Finally, there is the phenomenon social scientists have labeled the **mating gradient**, the tendency of women to marry men who are better educated or more successful than they are. Because men tend to "marry down" in terms of age and status, it can be difficult for successful older women to find an acceptable mate.

Although married men tend to be as old as or older than their spouses, the age difference between partners marrying today isn't very pronounced, especially among younger people. In the United States in the 1960s, the median age for males marrying for the first time was about 23, and the median age for females was about 20, about a 3-year difference in ages. By 2012, the estimated U.S. median ages at first marriage had risen, to 28.3 years for men and 25.8 years for women, about a 2.5 year difference in ages (Copen, Daniels, Vespa, & Mosher, 2012, March).

The term **sex ratio** indicates the relationship between the number of men and the number of women of a given age. Because of differences in birth and infant mortality rates, men have historically outnumbered—and continue to outnumber—women in the U.S. population. Most recent U.S. Census Bureau (Howden & Meyer, 2011, May) figures indicate there are 105 men for every 100 women. If every single man in this country wanted to marry, there wouldn't be enough women to go around. This problem is true for men across all age groups, except those 85 and older when women tend to start exceeding men, since women have a longer life span.

An increasing dilemma for women who want to pursue a career is that it is challenging to develop a career while also trying to find Mr. Right. An insightful discussion of the many issues confronting women today is provided by Barbara Whitehead (2003) in a book entitled *Why There Are No Good Men Left*. As women reach their 30s, there are fewer men available who are personally acceptable and can also match the income and achievements of the women. As a result, many career women are frustrated in their efforts to find and develop a relationship that will lead to marriage and a family.

Birth Order

One might wonder if birth order affects marital satisfaction. Should we be looking for a partner who has similar birth order, or differing birth order from ourselves? Historically, studies have had mixed findings. The assumption is that birth order affects personality and personality affects how we form friendships and select a mate and, thus, there would be a relationship between birth orders of friends and spouses (Hartshorne, Salem-Hartshorne, & Hartshorne, 2009). These authors completed two studies with sample sizes of 1,000 and 2,500 participants and found in both studies that people are more likely to be in long-term relationships, either friendships or romantic, if they share a birth order than if they do not.

In a recent study of a large random sample of 10,000 married couples, a researcher compared couple satisfaction and intimacy for couples who had a spouse with the same birth order with those who had a spouse with a different birth order (Raetz, 2011). This researcher found that there was no significant effect on marriage intimacy and satisfaction.

The answer to the question: Does birth order matter in mate section? We don't know yet.

Similar Personalities or Different Personalities

Are people attracted to personality types that are like themselves or different from themselves? Are relationships likely to work better if a couple is like *two peas in a pod*, or *the odd couple*? Kaufman (2011) conducted a study with 10,000 couples with five different couple types concerning their degree of relationship satisfaction. The first finding was that couples did not, in fact, marry someone like themselves. Two-thirds of the couples had personality scores that did not match up. Second, this researcher found that happily married couples were not significantly different or significantly similar to each other. The findings of this study indicated that whether individuals have similar personalities or different personalities, it does not impact marital satisfaction.

Interracial and Interfaith Marriages

Two other factors that influence mate selection are endogamy and exogamy. **Endogamy** is the culturally prescribed practice or tradition of choosing a mate from within one's own group. These groups might include ethnic, religious, socioeconomic, or general age groups. The principle of endogamy supposes, say, that middle-class Whites will marry middle-class Whites, Catholics will marry Catholics, and young people will marry young people. **Exogamy**—the practice or tradition of choosing a mate from outside one's own group—is typically discouraged in our society. There are no laws against marrying someone of a different socioeconomic status, religion, or ethnic group; however, outside groups tend to be off limits or less desirable as a source of marital partners.

The growing ethnic diversity in the United States and the increasing rate of marriage across ethnic groups are changing the *unwritten rules* regarding exogamy. This change reflects a common belief that in the United States all ethnic and cultural groups can live and work together. This belief is true to a certain degree—we have developed a relatively stable society and share certain democratic values—but the United States is by no means a blended and homogeneous society. Although the ethnic and cultural mix often works rather well, the elements that make it up remain distinct. Ethnic values and identifications endure for generations. When people marry out of their ethnic group, problems can arise; the difficulties inherent in intercultural marriage often intensify if the partners do not anticipate them. We confuse the idea that we are all created equal with the belief that we are all the same.

The marriage rate between members of different ethnic groups is difficult to assess accurately because the concept of race is elusive, and many people cannot be easily classified into ethnic groups. The U.S. Census Bureau does, however, ask people to state their ethnic identity and thus has a means of calculating Black–White marriages, among other things. In 1970 the number of Black–White marriages was 65,000; by 2005, the number had increased to 422,000. Nearly two-thirds of these couples were Black male–White female couples, and over a third were White male–Black female couples (U.S. Census Bureau, 2007).

Parents are often hesitant to bless an intercultural marriage. They may be aware of the problems their children will face, both within the relationship and in our society. They may also think the young partners are naive, idealistic, or blinded by love and need the guidance of their more experienced elders.

Some of these concerns are legitimate. When people marry, they are often idealistic in their beliefs. One common—and unrealistic—belief is that love conquers all. Another is that true love means that the couple either has few differences or that one partner can change the other after marriage. In the words of one family therapist, "Spouses tend to perceive their cultural differences as failings—either badness or madness. With insight, people are able to get some distance from their hurt feelings and stop taking inevitable differences personally." Although differences can be a source of strength in a marriage, they can also cause problems.

One study investigated the experiences of 10 White/Asian Indian mixed race marriages (Inman, Altman, Kaduvettoor-Davidson, Carr, & Walker, 2011). The findings of this study indicated that couples received support from outside the family, but not from families of origin. The most common concern on the part of families of origin was protecting future generations. This concern focused on diluting ethnic pride, not passing on cultural values, and the effect on religious values. For these couples there was often a difference in social class, specifically education and income, which also became a concern for families of origin. These couples also experienced power and cultural differences in their interracial relationships, which required extensive negotiation to resolve and address. The more they learned about each other's culture, however, the more it strengthened their marriages.

Ethnically mixed couples are more likely to divorce and to have a variety of marital and family problems (McGoldrick, Giordano, & Preto, 2005, 2008). Children of intercultural marriages have more personal and relationship problems than children from ethnically homogeneous families. The greater the ethnic differences between individuals, the less likely they are to marry. After marriage, the greater the differences, the greater the difficulty the couple will have adjusting to each other. McGoldrick and colleagues (2005, 2008) identify eight factors that they believe most influence the degree of adjustment:

- *Values*. The greater the discrepancy in values between the cultural groups, the more difficulty the couple will have. For example, a Puerto Rican–Italian couple will probably have less difficulty because of disparity of values than will an Irish–Italian couple.
- *Acculturation*. The greater the difference in the levels of acculturation of each partner, the greater the probability of conflict. For example, a couple is likely to have more difficulty if one is a recent immigrant and the other a fourth-generation American.
- *Religion*. Adding religious differences to cultural differences can compound adjustment difficulties. An Irish–Italian couple will probably have an easier time adjusting to marriage than an Irish–Jewish couple because the Irish and Italian partners are likely to share a common Catholic heritage. This is one less area for misunderstandings.
- *Race*. Interracial couples are the most vulnerable of all couples, sometimes feeling isolated from both groups. The children of an interracial union are also sometimes subject to discrimination from both groups. As interracial children become more commonplace, however, this discrimination may decline. President Obama, the son of a white mother and black father, may be helping our thinking on all this to enolve.

Marriages between individuals of different ethnic backgrounds involve special challenges. Partners must acknowledge and appreciate differences and make them a strength of the relationship rather than a source of conflict.

- *Sex and sex roles.* Because women are generally reared to talk more about their feelings, an Irish wife, for example, will probably have an easier time adjusting to a Jewish husband than a Jewish wife would have adjusting to an Irish husband. Why? Because Jews are traditionally more verbal, and McGoldrick and colleagues presume that matching a verbal Irish wife and a verbal Jewish husband would work out better than matching a verbal Jewish wife and a relatively less verbal Irish husband.
- *Socioeconomic differences.* Partners from different socioeconomic circumstances have added difficulties adjusting to each other. The financial issues with which couples must contend can become even more problematic if the partners have different life experiences and expectations regarding them.
- *Cultural familiarity.* Partners who have some experience with each other's culture before marriage are more likely to understand and adjust to each other. Couples who live in a multiethnic neighborhood after marriage are also less likely to experience pressure and negative reactions from others.
- *Extended-family agreement.* If kin of both partners are supportive, the couple has a greater chance of success. If a couple feels forced to elope or if one partner's family refuses to attend the wedding, this can indicate future difficulties.

Every ethnic group has its own unique heritage, values, and behaviors that make it special. It is important for those who marry someone from a different group to be aware of these differences and to work toward making them an asset rather than a liability.

In the final analysis, it can be argued that couples who engage in a relationship as intimate and enduring as marriage are likely to have transcended the boundary between them to some degree. From this positive perspective, increasing intermarriage can be celebrated as evidence that ethnic and cultural boundaries are weakening. Intermarriage can also be seen as an engine of social change, because children of interracial and interethnic couples are not as likely to identify with a single group, and these children challenge group boundaries by their very existence (Fu, 2008).

Finding a Good Mate

People often meet and date someone, may eventually marry, and ultimately realize the person is not a good partner. In fact, they may realize he or she is really a jerk. A curriculum used around the country helps someone looking for a partner to discern what to look for when seeking a partner. The program is referred to as *How to Avoid Falling for a Jerk (ette)* (Pick Program, n.d.). It was developed by Dr. John Van Epp, a therapist, and the curriculum is research based. This is a 6-hour premarital curriculum for anyone who wants to learn what a couple needs in order to have a healthy relationship. Not only does one learn how to avoid falling for a jerk (ette), but one can also learn to identify how they might, at times, act like a jerk (ette).

Utah State University Extension faculty have used this curriculum in providing classes throughout the State of Utah. The goal of the project was to provide classes for 18- to 30-year-olds, primarily college-age individuals. As the program progressed, however, it became clear the need for such a course went well beyond college-age individuals, and participants have instead ranged from 18 to 80 years of age. Not only do those who want a healthy first marriage take the course, but those who are widowed and divorced one or more times also enroll. High school age youth also benefit from the course as they look forward to having healthy relationships.

Preliminary data with 300 participants indicated that there was a statistically significant positive change after taking the course in knowing how to have a healthy relationship, communicate well with a partner, and have effective conflict management skills (Morrill, Bradford, Higginbotham, & Skogrand, 2013). Also, after taking the course, 68% felt they needed to change how *they* were in relationships. They realized everyone can act like a jerk at times.

Patterns of Mate Selection

Research regarding mate selection is currently more complex than it was years ago. If we are to truly understand mate selection today, we need to be knowledgeable about Internet dating, hooking up, marriage after child birth, cohabitation, and serial partnering, as well as the traditional research that focused primarily on how couples transitioned into marriage. However, the common denominator in selecting a mate is a great desire for sexual and emotional intimacy that is sought after with each of the kinds of romantic relationships listed above. In addition, how this partnering happens also changes throughout the life cycle (Sassler, 2010).

Earlier editions of this textbook have included three theories about mate selection. Today, that does not begin to cover all the theories that are used in explaining how we find intimacy. One of the popular theories used today is attachment theory, which assumes that the same kind of emotional bonds between parents and children are evident in adult intimate relationships (Cassidy & Shaver, 2008). A second theory that is often used is exchange theory, which focuses on how relationships are developed based upon rewards received between partners (Qian & Lichter, 2007; Sprecher, 2001). Equity theory, which focuses on what is fair and unfair in relationships, is also used to explain and describe mate selection behaviors (Sprecher, 2001). Life course theories are also used to describe how individuals and couples transition throughout different stages in life (Waller & Peters, 2008). Feminist theory, which focuses on gender, is also increasingly being used (Smiler, 2008). Additionally, sociobiological theory emphasizes how evolutionary factors affect romantic and sexual preferences (Shoemake, 2007). Certainly this is not an exhaustive list of theories used to understand and explain mate selection; however, it provides an understanding of how varied the use of theory is regarding this topic. In recent years, because there are so many issues around mate selection, many family theories are used. It is beyond the scope of this book to describe them all in detail.

One of the new areas of research is to include the population of emerging adults, that is, those whose ages range from 18 through their mid-20s. This stage of life has received attention because young people are spending more time transiting into adulthood (Willoughby & Dworkin, 2009). Therefore, the adolescent years of mate selection have been expanded to include those into their mid-20s (Sassler, 2010). A summary of the literature in recent years draws the following conclusions about mate selection with teens through young adulthood (Sassler, 2010):

- By mid-teens approximately half of these adolescents have had a romantic relationship.
- By the time they graduate from high school, almost three-quarters of teens have had such a relationship.

- As teens move into emerging adulthood, they move from spending time in friendship groups to dating.
- Spending time together, holding hands, and meeting a partner's parents usually precede sexual activity.
- Those who are in romantic relationships during high school are more likely to marry or enter cohabiting relationships in their 20s.
- Most teens and emerging adults enter into romantic relationships with others who are like them. However, there are a significant number who date across racial lines.
- Teenagers typically date before engaging in sexual intimacy; however, for a minority sexual partnering occurs without a relationship.
- Although hookups are defined as having a sexual encounter, the majority of hookups do not result in intercourse.
- The overwhelming majority of people in this age group plan to marry.

Several other sections in this chapter provide additional research findings about the components of mate selection, such as cohabitation, dating among older people, hooking up, and Internet dating. These topics indicate how complex mate selection is in the 21st century.

Conflict and Violence in Dating

The incidence of reported violence is 25% for women and 10% for men in dating relationships (Luthra & Gidycz, 2006). Jealousy and differences in level of commitment are only two of numerous causes for conflict between dating partners. These conflicts sometimes result in violent behavior, which can then lead to spouse abuse after marriage.

Conflict is an inevitable part of every relationship, but areas of conflict change as partners become more committed to each other. In the early stages of a relationship, jealousy and other personality issues are the greatest sources of conflict; later, conflict arises from such issues as differences in background, the balance of power in the relationship, and parent relationships.

One young woman from Chicago recounts her experience before and after her wedding:

> "I thought it would get better after the wedding. We had planned so long and carefully for it, and I knew the wedding would be wonderful. But even on the day of the wedding, Marty slapped me in the face. I don't know. He was frustrated about something my brother said or something. I don't know.
>
> "After we got married, it really got bad. He would stay out with his friends till all hours and when he came home, if I said even one word about it, he would hit me. Hard. I stayed with him 2 years, but when he pushed me down when I was 7 months pregnant, I couldn't stand it anymore and I left for the domestic violence program shelter. He would have hurt the baby, and I would never have forgiven myself. I ended up leaving town, moving to my sister's in Indianapolis. I didn't have hardly anything . . . Alexis's baby clothes and her toys, my clothes, a small stereo system.
>
> "I didn't have anything, really, but I was free and that was what counted."

A national survey by Jay Silverman (2001) of 4,163 high school students found that 22% of the girls were victims of nonsexual dating violence. Victimized girls were eight to nine times more likely to attempt suicide in the year previous to the survey, four to six times more likely to have been pregnant, three to five times more likely to use cocaine, and three to four times more likely to engage in unhealthy behaviors. It is unclear whether dating violence caused these teens to be involved in these activities or whether troubled girls selected more violent partners. It is clear, however, that many of the males felt that it was their right to control their girlfriends through violence.

In terms of handling conflict, all males and females (100%) used reasoning, and most (87% to 93%) used verbal aggression. In terms of physical violence, more men (32%) than women (29%) were on the receiving end of minor violence. This concurs with the fact that fewer men (3%) than women (19%) reported using severe physical violence. Men are less often hurt than women in violent encounters, however, because women are generally not as physically able to cause serious injury as men.

It is clear that if an individual is violent during dating, it is most likely this behavior will continue after marriage. In general, a violent date is a poor marriage risk. Violence breeds violence and quickly destroys an intimate relationship. It is important, especially for women, to watch for warning signals that a partner might become more abusive as the relationship becomes more serious. See Box 10.2, which lists several very useful warning signals.

It is important for people to trust their own feelings regarding abuse from a partner and not to confuse abuse with love. Following are four relevant questions to seriously consider before committing oneself to a relationship:

Does your love "turn you on" or "turn you off"?
Does your love "tune you in" or "tune you out"?
Does your love "make you sing" or "make you shout"?
Does your love "light your fire" or "put it out"?

Living Together

For many people, marriage is no longer considered a prerequisite for living with a romantic partner. **Cohabitation** is defined by the federal government as two unrelated adults of the opposite sex sharing the same living quarters. A broader definition would include both heterosexual and same-sex unmarried couples who have an emotional and sexual relationship.

BOX 10.2 At Issue

Dating Violence Warning Signs

Young people generally do not tell others when they are involved in a violent relationship, so it is important to be alert for signs that an individual may be involved in a relationship that is, or has the potential to become, abusive. Some of the following signs are just part of being a young person. But when these changes happen suddenly, or without explanation, there may be cause for concern.

- Does the boyfriend or girlfriend lash out, criticize, or insult the individual?
- Do you see signs that the individual is afraid of his/her boyfriend or girlfriend?
- Does the boyfriend or girlfriend seem to try to control the individual's behavior, making all of the decisions, checking up on his/her behavior, demanding to know who the individual has been with, acting jealous and possessive?
- Does the individual have unexplained bruises, scratches, or injuries?
- Does the individual apologize to you and others for the boyfriend or girlfriend's behavior?
- Has the individual casually mentioned the boyfriend or girlfriend's temper or violent behavior, but then laughed it off as a joke?

- Have you seen the boyfriend or girlfriend be abusive toward other people or things?
- Does the individual seem to have lost interest or to be giving up on things that were once important? Has he/she lost interest in school or other activities?
- Has the individual's appearance or behavior suddenly changed?
- Has the individual stopped spending time with friends and family?
- Have you seen sudden changes in the individual's mood or personality? Is the individual becoming anxious or depressed, acting out, or being secretive? Is the individual avoiding eye contact, having "crying jags" or becoming "hysterical"?
- Has the individual recently started using alcohol or drugs?

Source: Adapted from *Dating Violence Warning Signs*, 2009, National Youth Violence Prevention Resource Center.

Cohabitation's Dramatic Increase

Between 1960 and 2009, the number of unmarried couples living together increased by more than fifteen-fold (Wilcox, 2010). Among cohabiting couples, about half of the partners (54%) had never been married, about one-third (37%) had been divorced, and the rest were widowed (U.S. Census Bureau, 2003b).

Cohabitation is more popular than ever as a way for many Americans to move from being single to becoming married. Though it remains a controversial issue for many people, from a statistical standpoint it has become the norm to cohabit before marriage. The majority of all marriages are preceded by cohabitation, with the rate being 68% for first marriages (Copen, Daniels, Vespa, & Mosher, 2012) and up to 80% to 85% for remarriages (U.S. Census Bureau, 2003b).

Even for teenagers, a study of several thousand found that about 66% of the boys and 59% of the girls agreed that it is a good idea for couples to live together before marriage (Popenoe & Whitehead, 2004). Increasingly, young people were agreeing with the concept used in the title of the article about cohabitation—"Sex Without Strings, Relationships Without Rings" (Popenoe & Whitehead, 2000).

A later study concluded that most young adults are not replacing marriage with cohabitation but instead are cohabiting and then marry. The researchers argued that "adolescents are including cohabitation as part of their future life trajectory but rarely envision cohabitation as substituting for marriage" (Manning, Longmore, & Giordano, 2007).

The length of time a couple cohabits varies considerably depending on whether or not they get married. While about half (55%) of cohabiting couples get married within 5 years of living together, 40% breakup and 10% stay together and choose not to marry (Smock, 2000). About 40% of cohabiting women have children with their partner, and many times the pregnancy was not planned (Bumpass & Lu, 2000b). It is predicted that about 40% of all children in our society will at some point in their life live in a cohabiting household.

Cohabitation is likely to spark spirited discussion in your family among the different generations, and it certainly generates controversy and study after study after study among researchers. Some investigators argue that their findings indicate that cohabitation is not a good way to prepare for marriage and that couples who cohabit before marriage have a higher risk of divorce (Popenoe & Whitehead, 2004). Other researchers have found that if the cohabiting occurs after a couple has planned to marry or are engaged, there is no difference in marital success than with couples who did not cohabit (Copen, Daniels, Vespa, & Mosher, 2012; Kline et al., 2004).

The rate of living together is also related to religious orientation with those who are more religious less likely to cohabit (Wilcox, 2010). In addition, those who have been divorced are more likely to enter into a cohabiting relationship, as are those whose parents have been divorced. Finally, those who grew up with marital discord or those who grew up without a father are more likely to cohabit.

Given the predominant rates of cohabitation, it is difficult to believe that in the recent past living together for unmarried heterosexual couples was both illegal and considered immoral by many people. This revolutionary change can be attributed to several factors. First of all, first marriages are occurring at a later age than ever before (median age for females, 25.8; for males, 28.3) (Copen, Daniels, Vespa, & Mosher, 2012). In addition, puberty and sexual activity begin earlier, resulting in an extended singlehood before first marriage. The social stigma that was attached to cohabitation in the past has significantly declined, in part because of the sexual revolution. The saturation of sexuality within the entertainment industry and the media has greatly contributed to this change. Another important reason for cohabitation's growth is the decline in the number of individuals who choose to marry. Though the current divorce rate has declined significantly to 17.5 per 1,000 married women from 22.6 in 1980, the marriage rate has also been on a steady decline: a 50% drop since 1970 from 76.5 per 1,000 unmarried women to 39.2 (National Marriage Project, 2009). Concern over the continuing high rate of divorce may lead couples to choose to live together as either an alternative to marriage or a precursor to marriage.

People cohabit for many reasons and have various types of cohabitation arrangements. Following are some common reasons that couples give for cohabitating:

- Living together enables us to spend more time together.
- Living together allows us to share sexual and emotional intimacy without the commitment of marriage.
- Economic advantage—"We can save money by sharing living expenses."
- We can better learn the habits and character of each other, and if the relationship does not work out, there is no messy divorce.
- We can "test" our compatibility for a potential future marriage—see how we operate on a day-to-day basis.
- Engagement—"We are planning to marry."

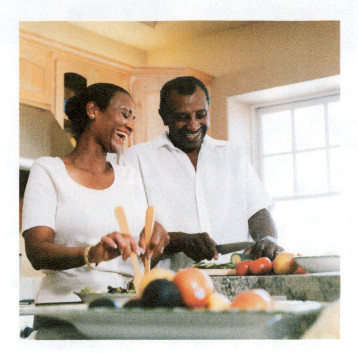

Men have as much to gain from egalitarian relationships as women do. The quest for power, money, and material success in which so many men are immersed is accompanied by higher levels of stress, higher rates of heart disease, and shorter life spans.

Reasons for Cohabiting

In a recent study of working-class and middle-class individuals between 18 and 36, information about the reasons for **cohabiting** became apparent (Sassler & Miller, 2011). In addition, the reasons were different depending upon whether they were working class or middle class. These researchers found that working-class participants moved in with their romantic partners more quickly than did middle-class participants. The reason for this move was primarily financial in that it was cheaper to live together rather than separately. The cohabiting relationships were felt to be *pushed* and were often not a good match. These couples often ended up having an unplanned pregnancy. Middle-class couples often had more resources in order to live independently and often had work requirements that made them slow down their move toward cohabitation. This was less likely to be true for working-class couples.

These researchers also found that middle-class participants were more likely to move in together as a step toward marriage, and that was less likely for working-class couples (Sassler & Miller, 2011). Middle-class couples were also more likely to have plans made for marriage when they moved in together. This was less likely to be true for working-class couples. In fact, some working-class couples eventually concluded that living together could be an acceptable alternative to marriage.

It is clear that cohabiting has differing risks for the two groups of couples. Middle-class couples were often moving toward marriage, whereas, working-class couples were often moving in together as a better financial alternative than living separately. The trajectory toward a healthy marriage is clearly affected depending on the reasons for cohabiting.

Another related study by Dew (2011), with approximately 500 cohabiting individuals, indicated that over time, 40% of participants married their partner, 35% broke up, and 25% remained in a cohabiting relationship. Financial disagreements and

BOX 10.3   Putting It Together

Ten Ideas to Consider Before Cohabiting

1. Make the decision to live with another person with great care—remember it is much easier to move in together than to move out.
2. Before you move in together, clearly define what your expectations are for the relationship. Are you both interested in marriage or is this arrangement just because it feels right?
3. Keep your expectations reasonable. Do not live together to change the other person.
4. Define the amount of time you are planning to cohabit. Is it 1 month, 6 months, 1 year, or whatever?
5. Draw up and sign a "living-together agreement" that clarifies how you plan to handle finances and property.
6. Use birth control and be clear about your interest in having children. Remember that an unplanned pregnancy is a common outcome of living together.
7. Take a couples education class together so that you can get to know each other and see if you can develop and maintain a healthy relationship together.
8. Ask your friends and family to honestly tell you what they think about your relationship and trust their opinion.
9. Remember that love "blinds you" and that love and your relationship will not always be like they are today.
10. Before you decide to marry, seek premarital counseling to build a stronger couple relationship.

Source: Adapted and revised from Solot & Miller, 2009.

perceived unfairness with finances were the only types of disagreements associated with breaking up. Although couples had other disagreements, such as housework, sex, parents, and spending time together, these differences did not predict a breakup.

It seems, therefore, that when finances are the reason for cohabiting, they also might become the reason for breaking up. These issues are complicated, but important to think about as individuals consider cohabiting. Box 10.3 provides additional things to think about when considering cohabiting.

Difficult Choices

The growing rate of cohabitation among couples adds a new step in the mate selection and courtship process. Many counselors have severely criticized traditional courtship because it emphasizes recreation and avoids conflictual issues. Also the strong erotic needs of premarital couples tend to decrease their interest or ability to deal with problematic issues in their relationship. As one husband said in counseling, "When you're in love, you're willing to compromise on anything." Many believe that traditional courtship provides partners with idealized views of each other, making early marriage a period of more severe and difficult adjustments for most couples. In a cohabiting relationship, however, couples are able to experience the realities of life together before they decide to tie the knot.

Just as cohabitation has its supporters, so it has its detractors. Some argue against cohabitation on moral, religious, and philosophical grounds. Others question whether cohabitation is an effective predictor of marital success; because it is not truly a marriage, they contend, it cannot serve as a test of marriage. In the opinion of many observers, it is only "playing house"; to test marriage, they say, you need to actually get married.

Nonetheless, living together won't keep partners from experiencing pain and misery if the relationship breaks up. For many couples who have cohabited, dealing with the hurt of a broken relationship can be as difficult as it would have been if they had been legally married.

This is a difficult decision to make. What do you think?

Summary

- Parent-arranged marriages remain common—and are effective—in many nonindustrialized cultures today, but in the United States, individual-choice courtship is the norm.
- Online dating has been the focus of study recently, indicating that all kinds of new rules apply to this type of partnering. For example, individuals need to make sure they are safe in meeting someone in person after connecting online, and they need to know they cannot always trust what the person says online.
- Research on dating reveals that older individuals experience the same emotions as young people. They may be more direct and move more quickly into a relationship, because they have less time left in their life to develop meaningful relationships.
- Many older adults choose to enter into a cohabiting relationship rather than marriage because of financial and other considerations.
- Premarital programs are effective in helping individuals make wise decisions in choosing a mate.
- Factors that influence mate selection are physical attractiveness, personality, age, life success, and the principles of exogamy and endogamy. The rise in ethnic diversity in the United States is changing the unwritten rules regarding mixed or intercultural marriages.
- Multiple theories are used today to explain and predict the various ways couples enter into relationships. In addition, there has been increased attention to how people choose a mate in different life stages.
- In dating relationships the incidence of reported violence is 25% for women and 10% for men. Violent dates are likely to become violent mates.
- Cohabitation is more popular than ever as a way for many Americans to move from being single to becoming married. Though it remains a controversial issue for many people, from a statistical standpoint it has become the norm to cohabit before marriage. The majority of all marriages are preceded by cohabitation, with the rate being 68% for first marriages and up to 80% to 85% for remarriages.
- Cohabitation is likely to spark spirited discussion in your family among the different generations, and it certainly generates controversy and study after study after study among researchers. Some investigators argue that their findings indicate that cohabitation is not a good way to prepare for marriage and that couples who cohabit before marriage have a higher risk of divorce. Other researchers argue that it depends: they have found that if the cohabiting occurs after a couple has planned to marry or are engaged, there is no difference in marital success than with couples who did not cohabit.

Key Terms

parent-arranged marriage
couple-arranged marriage
dating
permissiveness
double standard
hooking up

mating gradient
sex ratio
endogamy
exogamy
cohabitation
cohabiting

Activities

1. Share your thoughts on these questions in a small group: What forces are pushing you toward marriage? What forces are pulling you toward marriage? What is pushing you toward singlehood? What attracts you to singlehood?
2. What initially attracts you to another person? Rank the following traits from 1 to 5 (1 being the highest and 5 the lowest): physical attractiveness, popularity, social status, personality, and financial security. Discuss your rankings in a small group.
3. Do opposites attract? Or do birds of a feather flock together? Are you attracted to people like you, or people who complement who you are?
4. Discuss violence in dating as a small group. Be sure to address these questions, among others: How frequently have you experienced abuse? What was your reaction to it? What can be done to reduce courtship violence?
5. What are the pros and cons of living together? Make a list of five advantages and five disadvantages.
6. Interview someone who lived with a partner as they moved toward marriage and also interview someone who chose not to live with a partner before marriage. Ask them why they made the decision they did and what were the ultimate pros and cons of their decisions.

Suggested Readings

AARP. (2005). Sexuality at midlife and beyond. Web site: http://www.aarp.org.

Bogle, K. A. (2008a). *Hooking up: Sex, dating and relationships on campus*. New York: New York University Press.

Bogle, K. A. (2008b). The sociology of "hooking up." An interview with Kathleen Bogle. *Inside Higher Education*. Web site: http://www.insidehighered.com /news/2008/01/29/hookups.

Bradford, K., Higginbotham, B., & Skogrand, L. (2013). Evaluation data from pre-marital classes. Unpublished raw data.

Cherlin, A. J. (2009). *The marriage-go-round: The state of marriage and family in America today.* New York: Random House.

Gottlieb, L. (2006, March). How do I love thee? *The Atlantic.* Academic researchers work with Internet dating sites to develop a new science of attraction. The pros, the cons, the questions.

Hamon, R. R., & Ingoldsby, B. B. (Eds.). (2003). *Mate selection across cultures.* Thousand Oaks, CA: Sage. The meaningful processes, traditions, and practices related to couple formation around the world, including chapters from North America, the Caribbean and South America, Africa, the Middle East, Europe, and Asia.

Karis, T. A., & Killian, K. D. (2008). *Intercultural couples.* London: Routledge, Taylor & Francis Group. Cross-cultural relationships were once shunned and assumed to be inherently problematic. But in recent years intercultural couples have grown in numbers and social acceptance.

Marquardt, E., Blankenhorn, D., Lerman, R., Malone-Colon, L., & Wilcox, B. (2012). *The state of our unions 2012: The president's marriage agenda for the forgotten sixty percent.* University of Virginia, The National Marriage Project. Retrieved from http://www.stateofourunions.org/.

Valente, J. (2009, May 9). Hooking up. *PBS: Religion and Ethics Newsweekly.* Interviews and discussion from the Public Broadcasting Service. Web site: http://www.pbs.org/wnet/religion-andethics/episodes/may-8-2009/hooking-up/2896/.

Van Epp, J. (2008). *How to avoid falling in love with a jerk.* New York: McGraw-Hill.

Visit the text-specific Online Learning Center at **www.mhhe.com/olson8e** for practice tests, chapter summaries, and PowerPoint slides.

11 *Marriage: Building a Strong Foundation*

Intimacy, Strengths, and Diversity

Perspectives on Marriage Today

Components of a Successful Marriage

Marriage Education

The Importance of Families of Origin in Marriage

Newlywed Years

Keeping Marriages Strong

Federal Healthy Marriage Initiative

Summary

Key Terms

Activities

Suggested Readings

Intimacy, Strengths, and Diversity

For those who marry, marriage is generally the most intimate relationship people have. It involves emotional and physical intimacy, which has the potential to make us feel happy and fulfilled. Intimacy involves good communication, which requires couples sharing feelings and experiences, and good communication helps couples solve problems and make decisions. Physical intimacy is also an important part of the closeness spouses feel toward one another. The degree of intimacy in a marriage is an important barometer of the health of the couple relationship.

Every marriage relationship has strengths, and it has been determined that focusing on strengths, rather than problems, can be helpful for couples trying to make their marriages better. Marriage education inventories, such as **PREPARE**, help couples identify their strengths and also spend time addressing areas where they want to grow. Recently, there has been an increased interest in promoting healthy marriages through marriage education throughout the country.

Most research and marriage education is focused on White, middle-class couples. We know very little about the effectiveness of existing marriage education programs for low-income couples and couples from diverse populations. Because of the current interest in, and federal funding for, marriage education for such couples, it is likely that we will see an increase in culturally appropriate programming for diverse audiences in the near future.

Perspectives on Marriage Today

Next to parenthood, marriage is the most important, challenging and rewarding relationship we ever undertake. But what happens in this most private of all relationships can have powerful effects on others, and on society as a whole.

—THEODORA OOMS (1998, p. 6)

Based on the latest data from the U.S. Census Bureau, among all people 15 and older in 2009, 55% had been married once, with 30% never having been married at all. At the same time, 15% had married more than once, including 12% who had married twice and 3% who had married three or more times (U.S. Bureau of the Census, 2011).

More than half of currently married couples (55%) had been married for at least 15 years, and 35% had reached their 25th wedding anniversary. Six percent had passed their 50th wedding anniversary, the golden anniversary. These percentages are about one to two percentage points higher than they were in 1996, reflecting the leveling of divorce rates in recent years and increases in life expectancy, the Census Bureau reported.

For most couples (72%) both partners were in their first marriage. Six percent of the people married included a wife in her second marriage and a husband in his first marriage; 8% included a husband in his second marriage and a wife in her first; and 8% of the marriages in which both spouses were in their second marriage. One percent of currently married couples included both a husband and a wife who had both been married three or more times.

Both men and women are delaying when they marry to an older age. Males are now getting married at the average age of 27 years and 25 for women. In 1970, the average age for marriage for men was 23 and 20 for women (U.S. Bureau of the Census, 2004c). In 1970, 77% of women over the age of 15 were married but only 50% of women are currently married. Another indication of the delay in marriage is that for the age group of 25 to 34 years, in 1950 only 19% of men were never married but that increased to 39% in 2000. For women in 1950, only 11% were never married but that increased to 30% in 2000.

The Benefits of Marriage

Society has a large stake in strengthening marriages. Children should be our central concern and, in general, they are better when raised by two parents. Marriage also typically improves the health and economic well-being of adults, stabilizes community life and benefits civic society.

—THEODORA OOMS (1998, p. 4)

Because the media so often focus on the negative aspects of marriage (marital violence, divorce), many people often fail to see the positive effects of marriage, which are numerous. Linda Waite reviewed various studies that examined the positive effects of marriage on individuals (Waite & Gallagher, 2000). By and large, these studies included White middle-class couples. The benefits identified by Waite are as follows:

- *Married people lead a healthier lifestyle.* People who are married tend to avoid more harmful behaviors than do single, divorced, or widowed persons. For example, married people have much lower levels of problem drinking, which is associated with accidents, interpersonal conflict, and depression in women. In general, married people lead a healthier lifestyle in terms of eating, exercise, and avoiding harmful behaviors.

- *Married people live longer.* At every age level, married people live several years longer than do single, divorced, or widowed persons. This is often because they have emotional support in the partner, as well as more economic resources.

- *Married people have a satisfying sexual relationship.* Married couples have sex about six to seven times per month, as compared to an average of seven times for cohabiting couples and only three to four times for singles. In terms of sexual satisfaction, over half (54%) of the married males and 43% of married females are extremely satisfied with their sexual relationships. For cohabiting couples, about 44% of the males and 35% of the females are extremely satisfied.

- *Married people have more wealth and economic assets.* Because a married couple can pool their economic resources, they tend to be more wealthy. In fact, the median household wealth for a married couple is $132,000, as compared to $35,000 for singles, $42,275 for widowed individuals, $33,670 for divorced individuals, and $7,600 for separated individuals. Married couples have greater wealth in part because two can live for the price of 1½ persons by sharing the cost of housing, household appliances, furniture, utilities, and so on.

- *Children generally do better raised in a two-parent home.* Children from two-parent homes tend to do better emotionally and academically. They are half as likely to drop out of school; they have higher grades; and they are less likely to get pregnant. Children from two-parent homes also get more parental attention (such as parental supervision, help with schoolwork, and quality time with each child) than do children from single-parent homes. Also, children from single-parent homes have a much higher probability of growing up in poverty and experiencing a lower quality of life.

In summary, being married has a very positive impact on an individual's emotional and physical health. Some have suggested that the question isn't whether marriage has a positive effect on individuals but whether more healthy and happy people choose to marry rather than remain single. Nonetheless, an extensive analysis from a variety of studies demonstrates that selective factors in who marries do not explain the positive benefits of marriage (Waite & Gallagher, 2000). It is, in fact, the synergy of pooling a variety of resources that makes marriage beneficial to individuals.

It is clear that all African American family members can benefit from stable marriages, however, the couple relationships can be complex.

Marriage and Black Americans

Researchers have reviewed the studies conducted with Black American couples to determine if they benefited from marriage to the same degree as White Americans (Blackman, Clayton, Glenn, Malone-Colon, & Roberts, 2005). The review of the literature found many similarities but some differences with the findings of Waite and Gallagher (2000):

- Marriage for Black Americans was related to more income and less poverty, and couples were more likely to be happy and have better family relationship functioning.
- Physical health did not appear to improve for Black couples who were married.
- Black men benefited more from marriage than Black women in terms of family life and physical health.
- Children in Black families, especially male children, experienced great benefits from parents who were married.
- Black women who were married actually reported *poorer* health than unmarried Black women.
- Black women experienced no benefit in terms of quality of family life when they were married.

Why is it that Black men seem to benefit more in terms of health and quality of family life than Black women? The researchers speculate that Black marriages experience more conflict than White marriages, and women, in general, are more likely to experience stress from this conflict. Therefore, this conflict negatively affects the quality of family life and health for Black women (Blackman et al., 2005).

When Marriages Do Not Work

Even though, on average, individuals do better being married, people should not stay in destructive marriages. Marriages that involve physical abuse or substance abuse often are physically and emotionally damaging to individuals. Even though healthy marriages have positive effects on individuals, marriages with conflict result in negative effects on health and well-being.

Approximately one-third of divorces involve relationships with a high degree of conflict (Schramm, 2006). Couples may try therapy to improve the relationship, and certainly those efforts can have positive effects in developing a healthy relationship. However, if improvements cannot be made to make it a healthy relationship, couples may need to consider divorce.

It is also important to remember that it takes two people to make a marriage work. Even though one person is willing to make changes to improve the marriage, the spouse may not be willing to make changes. Ultimately, individuals must draw their own conclusions about whether the marriage is worth the effort and, sometimes, heartache.

The Decline in Marriage

There is no sign in any nation that cohabitation is in decline; quite the opposite, it is increasing everywhere.

—DAVID POPENOE

Marriage trends in recent decades indicate that Americans are less likely to marry, and the marriage rate in the United States continues to decline. For those who do marry, there has been a moderate drop since the 1970s in the percentage of couples who report their marriages to be "very happy," but in the past two decades this trend flattened out (Wilcox & Marquardt, 2011).

Americans have become less likely to marry, reflected by a decline of more than 50% from 1970 to 2010 in the annual number of marriages per 1,000 unmarried adult women. In real numbers, the total of marriages fell from 2.45 million in 1990 to 2.08 million in 2010. Much of the decline—though researchers cannot say just how much—can be attributed to delaying of first marriages until older ages. The median age of first marriage went from 20 for females and 23 for males in 1960, to about 26 and 28, respectively, in 2010. Researchers argue that the decline in marriage is also affected by the growth of unmarried cohabitation, and a small decrease in the tendency for divorced persons to remarry. The U.S. Census Bureau also reported that the decline in marriage has accelerated in the wake of the Great Recession since 2008 (Wilcox & Marquardt, 2011).

The number of unmarried couples increased dramatically over the past 5 decades. Most younger Americans now spend some time living together outside of marriage, and unmarried cohabitation is common before marriage. Between 1960 and 2010, the number of unmarried couples increased more than 17-fold. About one-fourth of unmarried women age 25 to 39 are currently living with a partner, and another quarter lived with a partner at some time in the past. More than 60% of first marriages are now preceded by living together, though cohabitation was rare 50 years ago (Wilcox & Marquardt, 2011). Reasons people chose cohabitation over marriage are that people now are socially permitted to have sex outside of marriage, and there is greater equality between men and women, so women are choosing careers, education, or other opportunities over marriage.

As these statistics suggest, the popularity of marriage is decreasing. Although most individuals choose to marry at least once, it appears that fewer are choosing to remarry and instead either stay single or choose cohabitation over marriage. Marriage has been on the decline for the last two decades, and it appears that increasingly fewer people will choose to get married or to remarry in future years. See Table 11.1 for more details.

TABLE 11.1 Facts About Marriage

According to a Pew Research Center analysis of U.S. Census Bureau data:

- Barely half of all adults in the United States—a record low—are currently married.

- The median age at first marriage has never been higher for brides (26.5 years) and grooms (28.7).

- In 1960, 72% of all adults ages 18 and older were married; today just 51% are. The share of adults who are currently married will drop to below half within a few years.

- Other adult living arrangements—including cohabitation, single-person households, and single parenthood—have all grown more prevalent in recent decades.

- The United States is not the only nation where marriage has been declining for the past century. The same trend holds true in most other advanced post-industrial societies, and this long-term decline does not appear to be related to the business cycle's ups and downs. The declines have persisted during good and bad economic times.

- The declines in marriage have occurred among all age groups, but are the most dramatic among young adults. Only 20% of adults ages 18 to 29 are married, compared to 59% in 1960. Over the past 50 years, the median age at first marriage has risen by about 6 years for both men and women.

- It is not yet known whether young adults today are abandoning marriage or merely delaying marriage. Even though only 51% of the total adult population is currently married, a much higher percentage, 72% of all adults, has been married at least once.

- However, this "ever married" percentage is down to 72% today from 85% in 1960.

- Public attitudes about the institution of marriage are mixed in the United States. Nearly four out of ten Americans say marriage is becoming obsolete. Yet, the same survey in 2010 found that most people who have never married (61%) would like to marry someday.

- Why has marriage declined? The decline is far less among adults with college educations than among the less educated. And some of the increase in the median age at first marriage over the long term can be explained by the rising percentage of young adults enrolling in college, who tend to marry later in life. Divorce is also a factor in the diminishing percentage of adults who are currently married compared to 50 years ago.

- The decline of marriage is occurring in other developed nations, especially in Europe, and in some cases in less developed nations. The United Nations argues that the decline is due, in part, "to an increasing acceptance of consensual [cohabiting] unions as a replacement for marital unions."

Source: D'Vera Cohn, Jeffrey Passel, Wendy Wang and Gretchen Livingston. (2011, December 14). *Barely half of U.S. adults are married—A record low.* Pew Research Center, Washington, D.C. Web site: http://www.pewsocialtrends. org/2011/12/14/barely-half-of-u-s-adults-are-married-a-record-low/. Copyright © 2011 by Pew Research Center. Used by permission.

Components of a Successful Marriage

Happy wife—happy life.

—A CHINESE PROVERB

A loving relationship can bring two people enormous benefits; it can help them grow as friends and lovers, and it can even heal wounds. Most counselors agree that the chances of marital success are greater if both partners enter marriage as friends; but the chances of achieving a successful intimate relationship are slim for a couple in which one plays the role of therapist and the other the role of patient. A careful review of research and clinical experience reported by many professionals indicates that a marriage has a better chance for success if potential partners meet the following conditions:

- *Both individuals are independent and mature.* The more mature and independent two people are, the easier it is for them to develop an interdependent relationship that can facilitate intimacy. Independence and maturity often increase with age, a good reason for waiting to marry. In fact, the single best predictor of a successful marriage is the age of the couple. This is partly because older people are typically more stable and know what they want in marriage.

- *Both individuals love not only each other but also themselves.* Self-esteem is very important in an intimate relationship. It is difficult to truly love another

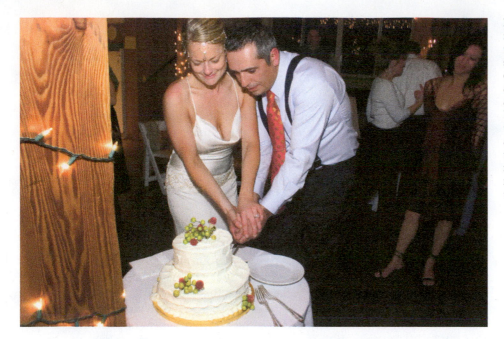

Independent and mature individuals are likely to have acquired the self-knowledge and self-confidence necessary for an intimate relationship and a successful marriage. Because they can express their needs honestly and assertively and respond unselfishly to each other's needs, such couples are more likely to be friends as well as lovers.

person without also loving oneself. People need to feel secure and self-confident before they can be truly giving and loving to another.

- *Both individuals enjoy being alone as well as together.* To balance the separateness and togetherness that an intimate relationship requires, partners need to enjoy separate activities and time apart. Time apart reminds partners of the value of the relationship and increases the importance and value of time together. Too much togetherness can lead to such negative behaviors as attempting to control one's partner and failing to appreciate the partner.

- *Both individuals are established in their work or occupation.* A stable and satisfying occupation or job fosters both financial and emotional security. When people's jobs are going well, they are able to devote more time and energy to their relationships. Conversely, the greater the stress at work, the less positive energy there is for a relationship.

- *Both individuals know themselves.* An intimate relationship requires openness and honesty between partners. They must be able to evaluate their personal strengths and failings objectively and not blame their problems on other people. They must also know what they want from and can give to the partner.

- *Both individuals can express themselves assertively.* One key to developing intimacy is assertiveness—expressing oneself in a direct and generally positive manner. People who are not assertive in their communication often adopt a passive–aggressive approach. The more clearly partners can ask for what they want from each other, the better the chances for compliance. (See Chapter 4 for a detailed discussion on assertive communication.)

- *Both individuals are friends as well as lovers.* When people focus on their lover's needs, they find that the loved one tends to focus on their needs. This has been called the *law of enlightened self-interest.* Developed by social exchange theorists to describe successful relationships, the principle holds that being less selfish is in a person's best interest because it helps build cooperative and intimate relationships that benefit everyone. Nonpossessive caring encourages the partner to grow and to reach her or his potential. Both partners generally benefit.

Marriage Education

The dignity of a vocation is always to be measured by the seriousness of the preparation made for it. How then do we appraise marriage?

—R. Herbert Newton

Marriage education has had an interesting and sporadic history in the United States. In the 1970s, there were a significant number of marriage education programs. Such programs began with the work of David and Vera Mace, who founded the Association for Couples in Marriage Enrichment in 1973 (Doherty & Anderson, 2004). Marriage Encounter emerged during this time, which was used primarily by Catholics but by other denominations as well. Marriage Encounter became the largest national marriage education program during that time (Doherty & Anderson, 2004). Marriage Encounter was led by clergy along with laypeople, and marriage education was taught within the context of spiritual beliefs.

During the 1980s and 1990s, marriage education was less popular (Doherty & Anderson, 2004). Marriage was seen as promoting patriarchal norms and not allowing for the emerging gay and lesbian relationships that were becoming more and more publicly prevalent. In addition, cohabitation was becoming an acceptable partnership model. One program that continued to attract large numbers of premarital couples was PREPARE. During this time, however, new marriage programs began to emerge, such as the Prevention and Relationship Enhancement Program (PREP), Relationship Enhancement, and Couples Communication (Doherty & Anderson, 2004).

In the 1990s, research emerged about the negative effects of divorce and resulted in what we know today as the *marriage movement* (Doherty & Anderson, 2004). Healthy marriages were viewed as a necessary component of society for the benefit of the couples and their children. By 2002 there was the hope of federal funding to support marriage education nationally. This funding materialized in 2006. Today there are several well-known programs throughout the country that are being used to help couples develop marriage skills.

The Healthy Marriage Initiative (Administration for Children and Families, 2010), which was funded at the federal level in 2006, has resulted in marriage and relationship education programs and evaluations of those programs around the country. For example, one study looked at the impact of relationship education for a sample of 340 adolescents from a range of socioeconomic backgrounds who were primarily African American (Adler-Baeder, Kerpelman, Schramm, Higginbotham, & Paulk, 2007). The results of the study indicated that participants had increased knowledge about relationships and decreased destructive verbal and physical conflict strategies, as well as increases in reasoning strategies and positive changes in relationship beliefs that support healthy relationships. These researchers concluded that, in fact, adolescents from a wide range of backgrounds can benefit from relationship education, which can ultimately improve future couple relationships.

Other studies showing benefits of stepfamily education also showed positive results. A stepfamily education program focusing on low-income European American and Latino stepfamilies was implemented throughout the state of Utah using a model that included both children and adults (Higginbotham, Skogrand, & Torres, 2010). Because a major challenge for stepfamilies is to effectively address the needs of stepchildren, this model is recommended so that the entire family can benefit from the educational intervention. In this case children and parents were in separate rooms learning parallel information during most of a class session, and then came together during the last half hour for a family-strengthening activity. A qualitative evaluation study indicated the children in these stepfamilies benefited from their parents' participation in the stepfamily course, because parents became more empathetic about their children's situations, they spent more time with their children, and they were able to communicate more effectively with their children. The children also benefited by learning to express feelings and worries appropriately, being more empathic with their parents' and stepparents' situations, and learning skills that improved their family relationships. By attending the course with other stepfamilies, they also learned they were not alone and that other children shared their experiences.

Although historically much of what we know about marriage education has been based on research with European American, middle-class populations, the two examples above indicate that this is changing. In addition, recent articles have described what marriage education for low-income and diverse populations should look like (Olsen & Skogrand, 2009; Skogrand, Barrios-Bell, & Higginbotham, 2009). For example, Skogrand et al. discuss what stepfamily education should look like for Latino stepfamilies. Religious and family values affect how Latinos view stepfamilies, and stepfamily education needs to be adapted to address those values. For example, divorce and remarriage are often viewed negatively in Latino culture, and advertising for and presenting information to stepfamilies may need to look different than it would for European American families. In fact, many Latinos view the term *stepfamily* negatively, and other terms may need to be introduced.

Because divorce rates are highest in low-income and diverse populations, it is increasingly important that we provide culturally appropriate marriage and couple education for these populations (Skogrand, Hatch, & Singh, 2008). It appears that the federal funding is helping make that happen.

Most of the marriage education programs were based on research with primarily White, middle-class couples. As a result, the usefulness of these programs for low-income and diverse populations is unknown and currently being tested. Developing effective programs for these populations, where the divorce rates are highest, is one of the future challenges for marriage education (Skogrand, Hatch, & Singh, 2008).

Premarital Education

Failing to prepare is like preparing to fail.

—ANONYMOUS

Before the wedding, couples spend hours talking about the wedding flowers, the size of the diamond and the design of its mounting, the color of the groomsmen's ties, and so on, but they rarely discuss such topics as finances, in-laws, and role relationships. Without instruction and preparation, people are no more expert at developing intimate relationships than they are at parenting. Writing about his own family-building experiences, Norbert Wiener, one of the original developers of the modern computer, said, "One has only one life to live and there is not time enough in which to master the art of being a parent" (Wiener, 1956, p. 224).

If it weren't for concerned clergy who insist that couples meet with them at least once before marriage, many couples would have no premarital preparation. About 40% of couples getting married for the first time in a place of worship (church, synagogue, or mosque) receive some type of premarital services or programs. Many of these couples meet only once or twice with their clergy to discuss marriage issues. Some premarital couples attend small-group couples' workshops or retreats where they discuss marriage. Another group of couples complete a premarital inventory and receive some feedback in two or three sessions. However, very few premarital couples receive a comprehensive premarital program that includes all the components mentioned below.

A growing number of couples are now seeking premarital preparation. This is, in part, because they see the large number of divorced people around them, including their parents, relatives, and even friends who had only been married a few years.

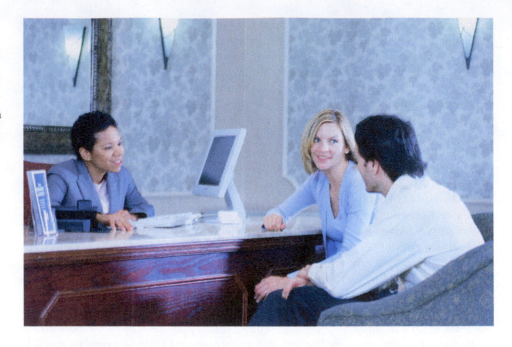

What Constitutes an Effective Premarital Program?

It is evident from the research that there are at least five essential components to an effective premarital program:

- *The couple should take some type of premarital inventory and should receive feedback on the results.* A premarital inventory increases the couple's awareness of the strengths and potential problem areas in their relationship. It also helps them discuss their relationship. In addition, the process establishes a relationship with a clergy member, a counselor, or a married couple with whom the couple can consult should they need intensive counseling for serious problems. Finally, it prepares them for later marriage enrichment.
- *The couple should receive training in communication and problem-solving skills.* These skills help the couple deal with various relationship issues by teaching them empathy as well as techniques for self-disclosure, resolving conflict, and problem solving.
- *The couple should participate in a small discussion group in which couples share their feelings and experiences.* This increases a couple's ability and willingness to share with other couples, lets the couple see how other couples relate and deal with issues, and may foster friendships with other couples.
- *A good premarital program should start 12 months before marriage and last 6 to 8 weeks.* Unfortunately, most premarital couples do not begin marriage preparation until 2 or 3 months before their wedding. When a couple cannot complete a comprehensive program before marriage, they should enroll in some sort of program after marriage.
- *A good premarital program should motivate the couple to want to continue marital enrichment after marriage.* Marriage is a process and one that takes continual effort to make it grow and deal with the stress and changes over time. Couples should ideally seek out couple enrichment programs after marriage to continue to sustain their relationship.

BOX 11.1   Putting It Together

The PREPARE Program for Premarital Counseling

The PREPARE Program is offered by over 100,000 clergy and counselors in the United States and has been taken by over 3,000,000 premarital couples. The PREPARE Program consists of first taking the PREPARE Couple Questionnaire (165 questions) and then receiving feedback using the six couple exercises. During the four to six counseling sessions, the couple also learn how to improve their communication and conflict resolution skills.

The PREPARE Program has been demonstrated to be very effective in improving a couple's communication and ability to resolve conflict and has led to greater couple agreement (Knutson & Olson, 2003). By improving their relationship skills, they get their marriage off to a better start.

Six Couple Exercises

1. To help the couple explore their relationship strengths and growth areas.
2. To help the couple increase their communication skills (assertiveness and active listening).
3. To help the couple learn how to resolve couple conflict using the Ten Step Model.
4. To help the couple discuss their families of origin and what they want to bring, or not bring, from their families into their couple relationship.
5. To help the couple develop a workable budget and financial plan.
6. To help the couple develop their personal, couple, and family goals.

Over 25 Significant Relationship Areas in PREPARE/ENRICH Program

Interpersonal Area	SCOPE Personality Scales	Couple & Family System
Communication	Social	Couple Closeness
Conflict Resolution	Change	Couple Flexibility
Role Relationship	Organization	Family Closeness
Sexual Relationship	Pleasing	Family Flexibility
Financial Management	Emotionally Stable	
Family & Friends		
	Relationship Dynamics	
Intrapersonal Areas	Self-Confidence	
Realistic Expectations	Assertiveness	
Personality Issues	Avoidance	
Spiritual Beliefs	Partner Dominance	
Marital Satisfaction		

To Locate a Professional Offering the PREPARE Program (www.prepare-enrich.com)

To locate a professional trained to offer the PREPARE Program in your area, go to the Web site at www.prepare-enrich.com. You can insert your zip code and find professionals in your area. You can also take a Couple Quiz online, individually or as a couple, and learn more about your couple relationship.

There are a variety of couple programs that contain most of the characteristics that are helpful to couples, both premarital and married couples. Many curriculum resources are available. These can be downloaded from a marriage resource Web site (National Healthy Marriage Resource Center, n.d.). The resources include information for Hispanic couples, empty nesters, singles, and much more. Many of these resources have been developed with funds from the federally funded Healthy Marriage Initiative (Administration for Children and Families, 2010). The most highly recommended programs are Couple Communication, PAIRS Program, PREP Program, PREPARE/ENRICH programs, and the Relationship Enhancement Program. See Box 11.1 for more detailed information about the PREPARE Program.

BOX 11.2 At Issue

Predicting Marital Success

We are taught, through fairy tales, TV movies of the week, romance novels, and our own fantasy lives, that love conquers all. And it does—in fairy tales, TV movies, novels, and fantasies. In real life, relationships (especially marriages) require continual care.

Couples often marry with unrealistic expectations of a life where both partners will always be happy, they will never fight, and conflicts will magically resolve themselves. They don't realize that fighting is an integral part of a relationship. Work conducted at the Gottman Institute (online at Gottman.com) indicates that marriages tend to settle into one of three styles of conflict resolution (Driver, Tabares, Shapiro, Nahm, & Gottman, 2003):

1. *Validating*—couples argue, but they let each other know that they respect the other's points of view and emotions, even if they don't agree with them.
2. *Volatile*—passionate couples have intense fights and then intense make-up sessions; these couples see themselves as equal sparring partners.
3. *Conflict-avoiding*—couples often make light of their differences and learn to live with them.

Driver et al. concluded that no matter what the conflict resolution styles, the predictor of marital success is the ratio of positive-to-negative feelings and actions toward each other. "As long as there is five times as much positive feeling and interaction between husband and wife as there is negative," note the authors, "the marriage [is] likely to be stable over time."

Researchers at the Gottman Institute have been able to predict which couples will get divorced by about 90% after watching and listening to couples' videotaped interaction for just 5 minutes. The following are the specific signs they used to identify couples who would later divorce.

1. *A harsh startup*—the couple begins the discussion by being negative and accusatory of each other.
2. *The four horsemen*—four ways of interacting that can sabotage communication:

   - *Criticism*—negative words that are global about the partner, attacking the partner's personality or character rather than a specific behavior.
   - *Contempt*—being overly critical and using such means of expression as insults, sarcasm, name calling, hostile humor, and mockery.
   - *Defensiveness*—denying one's own role in a problem or issue, thus blaming the partner.
   - *Stonewalling*—failing to respond, or tuning the partner out.

3. *Flooding*—feeling overwhelmed by the partner's negativity leaves the person shell-shocked.
4. *Body language*—men are more physiologically and visibly overwhelmed by conflict than women are.
5. *Failed repair attempts*—failing to break the cycle of negativity or prevent the flood.
6. *Bad memories*—when a marriage isn't going well, the couple rewrites the past in a more negative way.

The goal would be to identify those areas where couples are having difficulties and develop tailored interventions for couples, to help them avoid divorce.

Predicting a Successful Marriage

Love is not enough to make a successful marriage. The truth of this can be seen in divorce statistics. Most people who marry are in love, but roughly half of those who marry eventually divorce. If love at the time of marriage is a poor predictor of marital happiness, what characteristics do predict a happy marriage? Studies demonstrate that the type of relationship a couple has before marriage is very predictive of whether they will have a successful and happy marriage.

Two different approaches to predicting a successful marriage were conducted by two different research teams. Both teams could predict marital outcome (happiness versus divorce) with about 90% accuracy. One team directed by John Gottman (Driver et al., 2003) at the University of Washington focused on videotaping couples talking and resolving conflict based on microanalysis of the videotapes. The findings are summarized in Box 11.2.

The second team was directed by David Olson and colleagues (Olson, Olson-Sigg, & Larson, 2008) at the University of Minnesota, and they used couple questionnaires rather than videotaping couple interaction. The questionnaires are called PREPARE (for premarital couples) and ENRICH (for married couples).

Both studies found that 90% of the time it was possible to predict, on the basis of their PREPARE inventory scores *before* marriage, whether a couple would later be happily married or divorced.

The Importance of Families of Origin in Marriage

When a couple gets married, each partner is also joining the other partner's family. As such, the Couple and Family Map (Olson, D., & Gorall, D. M. (2003). Circumplex model of marital and family patterns. In F. Walsh (Ed.), *Normal family processes* (3rd ed.), pp,. 514-548). New York: Guilford Press.) can be useful for helping partners discuss and compare their **families of origin**—the families in which they were raised during childhood—before they marry. The case study that follows involves Kathy and Jim, a couple whose family backgrounds are quite different. They explored these differences in premarital counseling.

Kathy's Family of Origin

Kathy grew up in a *structurally enmeshed* family (Figure 11.1). She is the third oldest of six children, who at the time of counseling ranged in age from 18 to 27. Kathy's parents have been married for 28 years. All of the children except Kathy live and work in the town in which they grew up. Kathy's family is structured on the

FIGURE 11.1
Family of Origin and Ideal Type of Marriage

flexibility dimension of the Couple and Family Map for the following reasons: While growing up, the children knew what was expected of them. The parents were firm yet fair with discipline and enforcement of family rules. The mother was strong and a thorough organizer, and the father was equally strong and even stubborn at times. The father acted as the head of the household but respected his wife's education, contributions, and ability. The mother was comfortable playing a somewhat traditional role and worked hard at keeping the family organized.

Kathy's family is enmeshed on the cohesion dimension. They are a close-knit Catholic family from a small town. Except for 18-year-old John, all of the children have left home, and all except Kathy have settled in the local community. The children drop by the family home several times a week. On weeknights, they play cards or just sit around and talk. The whole family gets together at least every other Sunday for dinner. The mother is heavily involved in each of her children's lives. She feels excited when they are excited and guilty when they are down, and she is always trying to help them. The father is less involved in the lives of his children but expects them to visit often, especially on weekends.

Jim's Family of Origin

Jim grew up in a *flexibly disengaged* family (see Figure 11.1). He is the older of two children; his brother is 4 years younger. His parents have been married for 27 years but are now separated. After several years of frustration, the mother decided that she had had enough and asked her husband for a separation; he moved out several months ago. He has been asking for a reconciliation, claiming he's changed, but she is suspicious of these "instant" changes and has decided to "wait and see" if they are permanent.

Jim's family is currently flexible in terms of how it functions, but over the past several years, it has undergone certain changes. For many years, it was closer to a structured family: The mother and father had traditional male and female roles; the father handed down the rules, and the mother backed him up. After 15 years as a homemaker, however, Jim's mother went back to school and got a 2-year certificate in bookkeeping. Her self-esteem improved, and she became more confident and assertive in her relationship with her husband. The family system became more flexible. Jim's father began helping out around the house. He became more lenient with the boys when he saw that they were fairly responsible and willing to pitch in around the house.

In terms of cohesion, the family is currently disengaged. When they were young, the boys were very involved in school activities, and the parents each had separate interests. The father hunted and fished, and the mother had her church activities. The father took the boys hunting and fishing when they got old enough, and they went on several canoe trips together. But these outings were the only times they were together. Most of the time, family members went their own ways and did their own thing. Each person in the family had her or his own friends, and these friends were sometimes more important to each person than family members were.

Goals for the Marriage

Kathy and Jim disagree somewhat on how cohesive (close) they want to be in their marriage, in part because of their families of origin. These two diverse family systems present some problems for this couple. Kathy would like a *cohesive* type of marriage but one in which she would have more emotional space and greater autonomy than in her *enmeshed* family of origin. Jim would like an enmeshed marriage, in reaction to his disengaged family of origin (see Figure 11.1). He has experienced a lot of pain and disappointment because of the breakup of his parents' marriage and has vowed not to make the mistakes they did. He doesn't want to be in another disengaged system in which people go their own way and do not connect emotionally.

This couple is struggling to negotiate just how much closeness they want from the relationship. Because it's hard for Jim to say what he is really feeling and to share his need for closeness in a direct way with Kathy, she sometimes interprets his desire for closeness as an attempt to control her. But Kathy wants to avoid the overcontrolling atmosphere of enmeshment that existed in her family. So she sometimes backs away from Jim when he is needy and wants closeness. Jim isn't always aware of how he tries to control Kathy or even why he wants to. He is more aware of the outcome of his efforts—her withdrawal.

What both Jim and Kathy have in common is the desire for a *structured* type of marriage. Although Jim sympathizes with his mother, he emotionally leans toward his father's value of a more structured type of system, with more stable male–female roles and predictable family rules and patterns. This is the level of flexibility with which he is most comfortable. Kathy would also like a structured marriage with fairly stable roles but with a distribution of responsibilities. She likes the predictability of a structured system but does not want it to become rigid like her family of origin. The desire for a structured system is a goal they both share and one they can work together to achieve.

Newlywed Years

The first years of marriage can be stressful, with spouses adjusting to the new relationship and with these marriages being especially vulnerable to dissolution. The newlywed years are also especially important for setting the tone that results

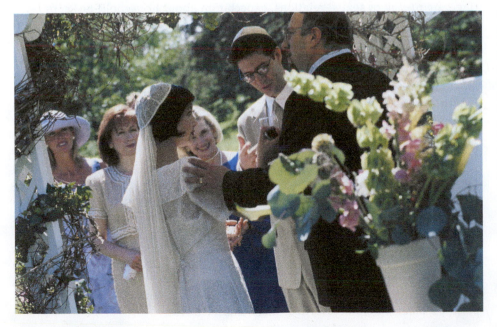

Whether a wedding is simple or extravagant, it is a milestone in the lives of two families and public testimony of a couple's love for each other. Decisions about the date, the place, the kind of ceremony, the size of the wedding party, the guest list, and the reception often require negotiation among the couple and their relatives so that everyone will feel that their preferences have been considered. Preparation for the wedding sometimes becomes the couple's first major challenge together in life.

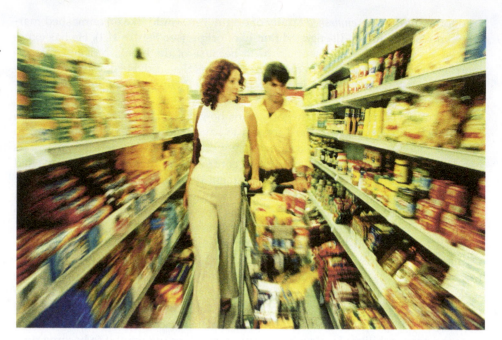

He likes to make a quick circuit of the store, picking up whatever appeals to him. She likes to make a list of what they'll need for the week and shop for bargains. Newlyweds discover differences in their habits and preferences and must find ways to accommodate these differences if their marriage is to succeed.

in high marital satisfaction years down the road (Niehuis, Skogrand, & Houston, 2006; Schramm, Marshall, Harris, & Lee, 2005). Some of the difficulties that are related to later divorce include difficulty with finances, emotional dependence, immaturity, difficulties with families of origin, infidelity, jealousy, and substance abuse—to name a few (Schramm et al., 2005).

In a random sample of over 1,000 couples who had been married for less than a year, Schramm and colleagues (2005) identified the problems most often faced by these newlywed couples. The problems faced by both husbands and wives in order of importance, were debt brought into marriage, balancing job and marriage, frequency of sexual relations, expectation about household tasks, in-laws, financial decision making, and communication (Schramm et al., 2005). It was interesting to note in this study that both husbands and wives generally experienced the same types of problems in the first several months of marriage, with debt brought into marriage and balancing job and marriage being the most commonly reported problems. Other newlywed research supports these findings in that things that affect marital stability and satisfaction are similar for husbands and wives (Kurdek, 2005). Table 11.2 shows how perceptions of the marriage relationship may look very different before the marriage than a year or so after the wedding day.

The study by Schramm and colleagues (2005) showed that between 8% and 14% of these newlywed couples scored in the distressed range of marital satisfaction and adjustment. According to this study, marital adjustment and satisfaction differences were clearly measurable even shortly after that wonderfully romantic wedding day.

Couples in the study by Schramm and colleagues (2005) also indicated that there were positive things going on in the relationship that provided protection from stress even when there were problems. These protective factors were respect, appreciation, commitment, mutual affection, and trust. When these factors were in place, problems did not result in as much marital stress.

TABLE 11.2	Premarital Fantasies and Marital Realities

- She married him because he was such an assertive male;

  She divorced him because he was such a domineering husband.

- He married her because she was so gentle and petite;

  He divorced her because she was so weak and helpless.

- She married him because he could provide a good income;

  She divorced him because all he did was work.

- He married her because she was so attractive all the time;

  He divorced her because she spent too much time in front of the mirror.

- She married him because he was so romantic and sociable;

  She divorced him because he was a fun-loving playboy.

- He married her because she was so quiet and dependent;

  He divorced her because she was so boring and clinging.

- She married him because he was the life of the party;

  She divorced him because he was such a dud at home.

- He married her because she was so sociable and talkative;

  He divorced her because she could only discuss trivia.

- She married him because he was such a good athlete;

  She divorced him because he was always playing or watching sports.

- He married her because she was so neat and organized;

  He divorced her because she was too compulsive and controlling.

Happy couples learn to weather the stresses of life. They are, above all, best friends and enjoy spending time together. In fact, they are likely to find each other more interesting as the years go by.

The study also found that marriage education was an important variable in marital satisfaction and marital adjustment. Having formal marriage education in college resulted in higher marital satisfaction and adjustment. This study indicates how important it is to develop knowledge about issues that cause problems in marriage before the wedding day. Because many couples get married shortly after leaving high school, information about the findings of this study should be introduced in high school.

Keeping Marriages Strong

Five Types of Marriage

Using a national sample of over 50,000 married couples, Olson, Olson-Sigg, and Larson (2008) described five significantly different types of married couples: *vitalized*, *harmonious*, *conventional*, *conflicted*, and *devitalized*. These five types of marriage are described in more detail, and the impact of the type on other aspects of their relationship is described elsewhere. These five types were created with largely White couples (Figure 11.2).

To see if the same types occurred in African American marriages, William Allen completed an analysis of 415 African American married couples from around the United States (Allen & Olson, 2001). He identified the same five types of couples in the African American marriages, and his findings demonstrate the similarity of these couple types across ethnic groups.

Vitalized Couples. These couples composed 18% of the couples in the national survey. They had strengths in communication, conflict resolution, their sexual relationship, and finances. Only a small percentage of these couples had ever considered a divorce.

Harmonious Couples. Twenty-four percent of the couples fit into the harmonious category and had fewer strengths than vitalized couples. They were particularly satisfied with their ability to resolve conflicts and their role relationship.

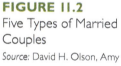

FIGURE 11.2

Five Types of Married Couples

Source: David H. Olson, Amy Olson-Sigg, and Peter J. Larson Ph.D., The Couple Checkup. Copyright 8 2008 by David H. Olson, Amy Olson-Sigg, and Peter J. Larson. Reprinted by permission of Thomas Nelson, Inc.

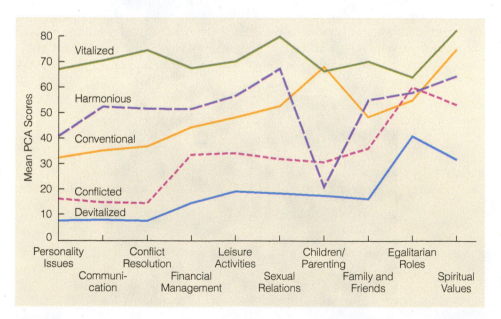

Conventional Couples. Conventional couples made up 17% of the total sample. Although these couples were generally happy, they did not do as well as vitalized and harmonious couples when it came to personality compatibility, communication, and conflict resolution. They had strengths in spiritual beliefs, having traditional roles, and a network of supportive family and friends.

Conflicted Couples. These couples made up 22% of the couples. They were unhappy, with few strengths and multiple areas where they needed growth. Seventy-three percent of these couples had considered divorce. They had low scores in communication and conflict resolution.

Devitalized Couples. These couples were very unhappy and made up 19% of the couples. Almost all had considered divorce. Many of these couples had sought marital therapy or marriage enrichment.

Interestingly, when the same analysis was done with premarital couples, four types of premarital couples were identified (Fowers & Olson, 1992; Olson & Olson, 2000). The devitalized type was missing, which makes sense because premarital couples are typically optimistic and happy with the relationship. The total sample consisted of 5,030 couples; there were roughly 25% to 30% of couples in each of the four types. Researchers subsequently conducted an outcome study to examine the relationship between the four premarital types (vitalized, harmonious, traditional, and conflicted) and the marital relationship 3 years after marriage (Fowers, Montel, & Olson, 1996).

Vitalized couples had the highest level of marital satisfaction, followed by harmonious, conventional, and conflicted couples, in that order (Table 11.3). More specifically, 3 years after marriage, 60% of vitalized couples were very happily married, and only 17% were divorced or separated. Conversely, 16% of conflicted couples were very happily married, and 54% were separated or divorced. Conventional couples were the least likely to divorce or separate, even though half of these couples were less happily married. These results clearly demonstrate that marital stability and satisfaction can be predicted on the basis of premarital relationship quality.

It needs to be noted, however, that couple unhappiness or marital discord can change over time, and unhappy couples can become happy. We all know couples who have gone through rough patches and eventually things improve. Researchers have found that some couples who were unhappy at some point were happy several years later, with no apparent intervention (Fincham, Stanley, & Beach, 2007). These researchers refer to this phenomenon as spontaneous remission of marital discord, or self-repair.

TABLE 11.3	Marital Success of Four Premarital Types			
Four Premarital Types	**Very Happily Married**	**Less Happily Married**	**Separated/ Divorced**	**Total Couples**
Vitalized	60%	23%	17%	100%
Harmonious	46	29	25	100
Conventional	34	50	16	100
Conflicted	16	30	54	100

Source: From B.J. Fowers, K.H. Montel, and D.H. Olson, "Predicting marital success for premarital couple types based on PREPARE" from *Journal of Marital and Family Therapy* 22, no. 1 (1996): 103-119. Copyright © 1996. Reprinted with permission of John Wiley & Sons, Inc.

Changes in Marital Satisfaction over Time

Researchers have consistently found that marriage satisfaction tends to decrease over time. In a longitudinal study of newlywed couples, Lawrence Kurdek (1998) found that over the first 4 years of marriage, the marital satisfaction for both males and females dropped each year and at a similar rate. As marital satisfaction dropped, there was an increase in the severity of depression, especially among women.

Another important study focused on change in marital satisfaction for couples who had firstborn sons; this study followed couples for 5 years. Using the *love scores* from fathers and the *conflict scores* from mothers Jay Belsky and Kuang-Hua Hsieh (1998) found three distinct patterns of change. One group of couples, called the stays good group, maintained a good relationship over 4 years. In this group, the fathers' love level stayed high and the mothers' conflict level stayed low. In another group, the *good gets worse* group, the fathers' love level was initially high and then dropped and the mothers' conflict level was initially low and then became high. In the third group, the *bad to worse* group, the fathers' love level was initially low and went lower and the mothers' conflict level was initially high and stayed high. This typology of couples is very useful because it more clearly demonstrates the dynamics of change than can an instrument that only records average scores across all couples, which is the typical approach to measuring change. What this study reveals is that some couples can maintain a healthy marriage in spite of having a child, whereas other couples' marriages become less loving and more conflicted.

Some couples can maintain a healthy marriage with the advent of children, while others become less loving and more conflicted.

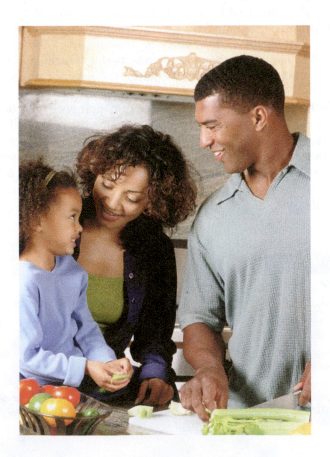

Another type of marriage study examined how marriage changes before and after having a child. Audrey Bryan (1998) assessed married couples as they began a class on childbirth and then reassessed them after their child was born. She administered the ENRICH inventory at the beginning of the class and identified five types of married couples from most happy to least happy: vitalized couples (22%), harmonious couples (27%), conventional (8%), conflicted couples (23%), and devitalized couples (20%).

The percentage of couples who showed no change over time varied greatly by marital type. Over two-thirds (70%) of the vitalized couples stayed the same, and about one-quarter (26%) became traditional couples. For the harmonious couples, about one-quarter (27%) became happier, vitalized couples; another quarter (23%) became traditional couples; and one-third (35%) became less happy, conflicted couples. About half (55%) of the traditional couples stayed traditional, whereas 18% became vitalized and 18% became conflicted. For the conflicted couples, over one-hird (37%) stayed conflicted and another third (37%) became less happy, devitalized couples. About 70% of the devitalized couples stayed devitalized; 20% became conflicted; and 10% became traditional.

So, in general, most of the marriages changed as a result of having children. The least change was seen in the best marriages (vitalized) and the worst marriages (devitalized). The other three types experienced changes for better and worse.

Why Marriages Fall Apart

There are a number of reasons why couples drift apart over the course of the marriage. A major issue is that we begin to take marriage for granted and focus on other priorities in our life. William Doherty in his book *Take Back Your Marriage* (2001) identifies a variety of forces that negatively impact marriage: We are too busy for marriage; we get used to our mate; television and other media come between us; we stop dating, especially after having children; we don't know other couples' strategies for maintaining vibrant marriages; and the difference between spouses in their "work orientation" toward marriage gets resolved in the direction of less work.

This drifting apart is not usually done on purpose but gradually happens as a result of neglecting the marriage. William Doherty uses an interesting analogy in describing this process:

> Ever since I moved to Minnesota, I have thought that getting married is like launching a canoe into the Mississippi at St. Paul. If you don't paddle, you go south. No matter how much you love each other, no matter how full of hope and promise and good intentions, if you stay on the Mississippi with a good deal of paddling—occasional paddling is not enough—you end up in New Orleans. Which is a problem if you wanted to stay north. (Doherty, 2001, p. 11)

Keeping Your Marriage a Top Priority

One of the major things a couple can do to keep their marriage alive and growing is to make it a top priority—preferably number ONE. A good exercise for couples is to sit down and list the various important aspects of life and then rank them in terms of ideal priorities. Then rank them in terms of their actual priority in your life, which will probably be different from your ideal. The more you can keep your marriage the number one priority, the better your chances of marital success will be in the future.

There are a variety of specific things that you can do to keep your marriage a top priority in your life. Doherty (2001) offers these suggestions:

- If you are married, remind yourself repeatedly that your marriage is the foundation of your family and the cornerstore of your children's security.
- Remind yourself repeatedly that your children are apt to be better fighters for their needs . . . than you and your mate are at fighting for the needs of your marriage.
- Limit your family's outside activities so that you have two rare elements for today's families: time to hang out as a family and time to hang out as a couple.
- Have fixed bedtimes for your children, after which you are off duty and can be alone as a couple.
- Don't let children interrupt every conversation you have.
- Carve out private time for yourselves as a couple.
- Get sitters and go out on regular dates.
- Be open with your children about what you are doing for your marriage.

The Role of Forgiveness in Marriage

Everyone says forgiveness is a lovely idea, until they have something to forgive.
—C. S. Lewis

The importance of forgiveness in marriage has become recognized as an important part of couple relationships, and it contributes to marital happiness and stability (Fincham, Hall, & Beach, 2006). In fact, forgiveness is important in our overall well-being and general health in that it helps us deal with everyday hurts (Gordon, Baucom, & Snyder, 2005; Harris & Thoresen, 2005). This has become such an important topic today that a scholarly book entitled *Handbook of Forgiveness* has been published to describe the benefits of forgiveness in all aspects of life (Worthington, 2005).

Forgiveness does not mean you have to be religious or that you forget about or accept the transgressions of your partner (Fincham et al., 2006). A person forgives in spite of the wrongful nature of the transgression and even if the transgressor does not deserve forgiveness (Fincham et al., 2006). An important component of forgiveness can be reconciliation, which may be helpful in allowing a couple to move on to a more positive place in their relationship. Forgiveness is about decreasing the negativity and increasing positive feelings and goodwill toward one's partner.

Forgiveness contributes to marital satisfaction when it becomes a part of conflict resolution (Fincham et al., 2006). Forgiveness helps couples move on from a conflict without having resentments that spill over into future conflicts, resulting in escalation of conflict over time. Forgiveness on the part of the victim involves understanding the impact of the offense, finding meaning for what happened, and moving forward—which may mean a change in the relationship. Here is an example of what the process of forgiving looked like for one couple:

Mary and Louis had been having difficulties in their marriage because each had a stressful work schedule, and they had been unable to spend much time together. Mary was working long hours and spending a considerable amount of time with a co-worker. They ended up having an affair that lasted several months. Louis suspected the affair and confronted Mary. Mary had already ended the extramarital relationship, but admitted that it was true.

Mary said she was sorry and declared her commitment to the marriage. Louis also wanted to stay married, but he was so angry. He both loved and was angry with Mary for betraying his trust. He wanted to forgive Mary, but he wasn't sure he could ever trust her again and have a healthy marriage relationship. He wanted to hurt her as much as she hurt him.

After working with a therapist for almost a year, the relationship began to get back on track. Louis was able to forgive Mary and eventually, with the help of the therapist, was able to have positive feelings toward her. He shared with her how it had deeply wounded him since he had always been vulnerable when it came to being rejected. What happened would always cause him some pain.

Mary and Louis also began cutting back on the hours spent on work and created a relationship that was very different from the one they had had before the affair. They would always set aside time to talk if either of them felt that things were not going well in their relationship. They fixed the problem rather than letting things go. Even though it took a long time, both Mary and Louis ultimately felt their marriage was better than before the affair. Forgiveness was definitely a necessary component of getting their marriage back on track in making their marriage healthy and stable.

The Role of Sacrifice in Marriage

Sacrificing for the other person in a marriage and how it affects relationship functioning has become an area of research in recent years (Stanley, Whitton, Sadberry, Clements, & Markman, 2006). There are two components of sacrifice. First, an individual can make sacrifices for his or her partner, which means that a person puts the partner's needs before his or her own needs. A second component of sacrifice is that the partner puts the relationship above selfish interests, which means a person places the couple or marriage relationship above personal needs (Morrill, 2006).

Stanley and colleagues conducted a longitudinal study of those who were newly married in 1980 and studied the effects of sacrifice on the long-term relationship. They were interested in following newlyweds through the first several years of marriage, because that is the time when many couples experience difficulties in their relationship. These researchers found that sacrifice predicted marital success when those behaviors began early in the marriage. Morrill (2006) also contributed to our understanding of the role of sacrifice in marriage relationships in her qualitative study of couples who had great marriages. She found that couples who thought their marriages were great regularly made sacrifices for their spouse. They gave up personal wants and desires for each other and for the good of the marriage relationship. Here is how one husband from Morrill's study described sacrifice for his wife and his marriage:

> The promise is to always be there, willing to do whatever is needed to help the partnership, and to provide continuous support for, and encouragement to, your mate. . . . You are not the most important, they are. (p. 49)

There is also evidence that sacrificial behaviors appear to be symbols of overall commitment to the marriage and result in mutual trust (Stanley et al., 2006). Sacrificial behavior, then, can be instrumental in affecting several aspects of the marriage relationship in that it can be a tangible way that partners can show commitment on a daily basis.

Federal Healthy Marriage Initiative

In 2006, the federal government passed legislation to fund the Healthy Marriage Initiative, which provided grant money of $100 million per year for 5 years to provide programs to promote healthy marriages around the country. According to the Administration for Children and Families (ACF), which is part of the U.S. Department of Health and Human Services, healthy marriages are the foundation of a successful society and promote the interest of children. Children do better when they are part of a family with two married parents.

Funding was granted to 126 organizations to provide programs for couples, especially those in low-income and minority populations who have high rates of single parents and divorces. The programs were to teach relationship skills and knowledge to couples with the goal of forming and sustaining healthy marriages.

This is what the federal government says about healthy marriages (Administration for Children and Families, 2010):

> "There are at least two characteristics that all healthy marriages have in common. First, they are mutually enriching, and, second, both spouses have a deep respect for each other."

> "It is a mutually satisfying relationship that is beneficial to the husband, wife, and children (if present)."

> "It is a relationship that is committed to ongoing growth, the use of effective communication skills, and the use of successful conflict management skills."

This initiative has been controversial. At a policy level, some question whether the federal government should be involved in something as personal as marriage. Some feel that the initiative is a way to promote marriage rather than promoting *healthy* marriages, and that promoting marriage could result in couples staying married when the marriage is harmful to the partners. Because this initiative is about marriage between a man and a woman, some believe it is a way to promote heterosexual marriage at the expense of same-sex unions and relationships. Because this initiative is supported by conservative religious organizations, some feel this initiative has a religious agenda.

However one feels about this initiative, it is an extensive policy change that can benefit many couples who want to have healthier relationships. Only time will tell if the funding and ultimate marriage education programming will accomplish the goal of couples having healthier marriages that will benefit children in those unions.

Changes in Policy and State Laws to Strengthen Marriage

Because of a growing concern over the rate of divorce (about 50%) in the United States, legislators are pushing for changes in the laws to impose more requirements on couples planning to marry (Ooms, Bouchet, & Parke, 2004). Florida was the first state to pass a comprehensive package of legislation designed to strengthen marriage and reduce divorce. Passed in the Florida State Legislature in 1998, the Marriage Preparation and Preservation Act became effective in January 1999. The bill had four key components:

- High-school students are required to take a course in marriage and relationship skill–based education.
- Engaged couples are encouraged to take a premarital preparation course of at least 4 hours. Those who do so qualify for a reduction in their marriage license fee. Each courthouse is to keep a roster of religious and secular approved courses.

- Each couple applying for a marriage license will be given a handbook prepared by the Florida Bar Association informing them of their legal rights and responsibilities as married partners to each other and to their children, both during marriage and in the event of marital dissolution.
- Couples with children who file for divorce must take a parent education and family stabilization course.

Other states are following this approach in order to develop policies and laws that support premarital education programs. Some of the states that have passed some form of premarital program are Arizona, Florida, Louisiana, Minnesota, Maryland, Oklahoma, Texas, and Utah (Ooms et al., 2004).

Summary

- Marriage offers a number of benefits. As compared to single or divorced individuals, married couples lead a healthier lifestyle, live longer, have a more satisfying sexual relationship, have more wealth and economic assets, and generally do a better job raising children.
- Three trends point to the changing role of marriage in the United States today. First, a decline in the popularity of marriage is indicated by a decrease in the number of marriages to an all-time low. Second, fewer couples who get divorced choose to remarry. And third, the number of couples living together has increased from 500,000 couples in 1970 to more than 5.5 million couples at present.
- Couples have a better chance for a happy marriage when both individuals are mature, love each other and themselves, enjoy being alone and together, are established in their work, are assertive with each other, and are friends as well as lovers.
- A very low percentage of couples in the United States enroll in a comprehensive marriage preparation program. The most useful programs include (1) a premarital inventory to assess strengths and areas of potential growth and a discussion of the assessment results with a trained counselor, (2) a small discussion group in which couples share feelings and concerns with each other, and (3) training in communication and problem-solving skills, which should start 12 months before marriage and last 6 to 8 weeks.
- Emerging research indicates that individuals and couples learn how to make their couple and family relationships better through marriage education. Evaluation studies indicate that these educational interventions can be effective for low-income and diverse populations.
- Researchers have developed an inventory that couples can take before marriage to assess the strengths in their relationship. The inventory can predict a couple's chances of marital success or failure with 90% accuracy.
- A national survey identified five types of marriages: From most to least happy, they are *vitalized, harmonious, conventional, conflicted,* and *devitalized.* Studies suggest that these types exist across ethnic groups.
- Because of a growing concern over the high rate of divorce in our country, legislators are pushing for laws to strengthen marriage, such as offering incentives for engaged couples to attend premarital preparation courses; requiring high-school students to take courses on marriage and relationship skills; giving couples applying for marriage licenses a handbook informing them of their legal rights and responsibilities; and requiring couples with children who file for divorce to take a parent education and family stabilization course. Communities are also getting involved in developing a variety of premarital and marital enrichment programs.

Key Terms

PREPARE	conventional couple
family of origin	conflicted couple
vitalized couple	devitalized couple
harmonious couple	

Activities

1. List what you consider positive and negative reasons for getting married. Share the list with a partner or with others in a small discussion group.
2. How do you know if you are ready for marriage? Discuss this issue with a small group and formulate some guidelines to help people decide whether they are ready to marry.
3. For *dating or engaged couples:* Both partners should write down five things they like about the partner and

five things that sometimes bother them. Then both partners should discuss the items on the lists very carefully and listen to each other so that the exchange is positive and constructive.

4. For those dating or engaged couples interested in taking the PREPARE Program, first contact a counselor or a member of the clergy in your area. If you cannot locate someone trained in PREPARE, go to the Web site to locate one: www.prepare-enrich.com.

Suggested Readings

Administration for Children and Families. (2012). The Healthy Marriage Initiative. Web site: http://www.acf.hhs.gov/healthymarriage/.

Allen, W. D., & Olson, D. H. (2001). Five types of African-American marriages based on ENRICH. *Journal of Marital and Family Therapy, 27*(3), 301–314.

Apter, T. (2009). *What do you want from me? Learning to get along with in-laws.* New York: Norton.

Doherty, W. J., & Anderson, J. R. (2004). Community marriage initiatives. *Family Relations, 53,* 425–432.

Gottman, J. M. (2011). *The science of trust: Emotional attunement for couples.* New York: W. W. Norton.

Gottman, J. M., Gottman, J. S., & DeClaire, J. (2006). *Ten lessons to transform your marriage: America's love lab experts share their strategies for strengthening your relationship.* New York: Crown Publishers.

Knutson, L., & Olson, D. H. (2003). Effectiveness of PREPARE Program with premarital couples in a community setting. *Marriage and Family, 6*(4), 529–546.

Kurdek, L. A. (1998). The nature and predictors of the trajectory of change in marital quality over the first 4 years of marriage for first-married husbands and wives. *Journal of Family Psychology, 12*(4), 594–610.

Lerner, H. G. (2012). *Marriage rules: A manual for the married and the coupled up.* New York: Gotham Books.

National Healthy Marriage Resource Center. (2012). Web site: http://www.healthymarriageinfo.org/index.aspx.

Olson, D., & Gorall, D. M. (2003). Circumplex model of marital and family patterns. In F. Walsh (Ed.), *Normal family processes* (3rd ed.), pp,. 514–548). New York: Guilford Press.

Olson, D. H., Olson-Sigg, A., & Larson, P. (2008). *The couple checkup.* Nashville, TN: Thomas Nelson.

Schramm, D. G., Marshall, J. P., Harris, V. W., & Lee, T. R. (2005). After "I do": The newlywed transition. *Marriage and Family Review, 38,* 45–67.

Stanley, S. M., Whitton, S. W., Sadberry, S. L., Clements, M. L., & Markman, H. J. (2006). Sacrifice as a predictor of marital outcomes. *Family Process, 45,* 289–303.

Waite, L., & Gallagher, M. (2000). *The case for marriage.* New York: Doubleday.

Worthington, E. L. (Ed.). (2005). *Handbook of forgiveness.* New York: Routledge.

Visit the text-specific Online Learning Center at **www.mhhe.com/olson8e** for practice tests, chapter summaries, and PowerPoint slides.

12 *P*arenthood: Joys and Challenges

Roots and Wings

Children and Happiness

Couple Strengths and Issues
in Parenting

The Challenge of Parenthood

Adoption

The Child-Free Alternative

Styles of Parenting

Theories of Childrearing

Issues in Parenting

The Joy and Enduring
Satisfaction of Parenthood

Summary

Key Terms

Activities

Suggested Readings

Roots and Wings

A parent's job is to give a child both *roots* and *wings,* which is no easy task. Rearing children may indeed be life's greatest mixed blessing. It is full of good times and bad times, frustrating challenges and genuine feelings of success. A baby's first stumbling steps and first words, a teenager's first love, a grown child's first baby—all are important transitions that parents remember. At the same time, children bring heavy responsibilities and drain parents of energy, finances, and time.

When we did a search on "parenting" using the Amazon.com Web site, we found over 40,000 books listed in their database. Even so, we are quite confident that there is no book on rearing children that answers all the questions and no clear path to family happiness. The road is difficult, and there are no guarantees.

We begin this chapter with the results of a recent study about how children affect individual and couple happiness (Wilcox, 2011). We will examine the challenge of parenthood and take a look at some of the conventional wisdom that surrounds it. Among the challenges are the effects of parenthood on marriage, the decision whether to have children, and the financial burdens of raising children. We will discuss various parenting styles and how they relate to the family styles of the Couple and Family Map. This will be followed by an exploration of issues in parenting and some practical approaches to raising children, including coparenting. Then, we will touch on the benefits of parent education and family therapy and conclude with a summary of the many satisfactions of parenting.

We will report on the national survey that examined couple strengths and issues for married couples (Olson, Olson-Sigg, & Larson, 2008). We will begin with the results of the survey regarding the parenting strengths of happy couples versus unhappy couples. Next, we will review the five most common parenting issues as reported by more than 50,000 couples.

Children and Happiness

There is conflicting information about the effects of children on individual and couple happiness. A recent study by Bradford Wilcox (2011), using large data sets, looked at these issues, and the findings provide new insights into these issues.

Children and Individual Happiness

Most people want to have children, and yet, children can often create personal stress. Wilcox (2011) found that married men and women were equally happy regardless of their parental status. Parents who are cohabiting are next in terms of happiness, and single parents are least happy. This author concludes that those with a partner, whether that partner is a spouse or a person in a cohabiting relationship, have a higher degree of personal happiness raising children than do single parents.

When it came to being depressed, Wilcox (2011) found that married parents and cohabiting parents had an equal likelihood of being depressed, and single parents had a higher likelihood of being depressed. The similarity in general happiness between married parents and cohabiting parents is an important finding, given that 40% of those who cohabitate will have children (Wilcox, B. 2010). One might speculate that sharing the work, responsibility, financial costs, and stress of raising children is made easier when one has someone with which to share it.

Children and Couple Happiness

According to Wilcox (2011), although marital happiness does decline over time for all couples, it decreases more suddenly for parents versus nonparents. Childless couples have a more gradual decline in marital happiness, whereas for couples with children there is a significant decline that coincides with the birth of their first child. However, it should be noted that children do not create a higher degree of marital conflict or divorce proneness for married couples compared to those without children.

Are there benefits to having children? Both married men and women, according to Wilcox (2011), are more likely to indicate that their life has an important purpose than married couples who do not have children, and this was especially true for women. One might speculate that although marital happiness may decline with the addition of children, a sense of purpose may replace the marital satisfaction.

Wilcox (2011) looked more closely at the minority of couples who had higher levels of marital happiness after children arrived. What makes them have even better marriages than before children? This author identified eight factors that contributed to these couples having high marital quality even with children:

- Higher educational levels
- Higher level of financial resources
- Sharing of work and family responsibilities
- Support from family and friends
- Faith in a higher being
- Shared beliefs about marriage and parenthood
- High levels of sexual satisfaction
- Being generous to each other

Wilcox (2011) also explored differences in the number of children and marital happiness.

He found that couples who had no children and couples who had four or more children were happiest. How could this be, given the added financial and emotional stress of four or more children? This author speculates that several factors were evident with these couples that could have contributed to these findings. Wilcox (2011) found these couples were more likely to attend a place of worship, felt a sense of purpose in their lives, and experienced increased social support, which may have become an integral part of their marriage and family lives.

Couple Strengths and Issues in Parenting

In a national survey of married couples, Olson, Olson-Sigg, and Larson (2008) identified a number of parenting strengths. As Table 12.1 shows, happy couples were more than twice as likely (61%) as unhappy couples (30%) to agree on how

TABLE 12.1	Strengths of Happy Couples Versus Unhappy Couples Regarding Parenting		
		PERCENTAGE IN AGREEMENT	
Parenting Issue		**Happy Couples**	**Unhappy Couples**
1. I am satisfied with how childrearing is shared.		61%	30%
2. My partner focuses as much on the marriage as on the children.		59	31
3. We agree on discipline.		59	33
4. We feel closer since having children.		53	33
5. I am more satisfied in my marriage since having children.		35	19

Source: Adapted from Olson, Olson-Sigg, & Larson, 2008.

to share the responsibilities of raising their children. Happy couples were almost twice as likely (59%) as unhappy couples (31%) to be satisfied with the amount of attention they focus on their marriage versus the amount of attention they focus on their children. Almost twice as many happy couples (59%) reported agreeing on how to discipline their children as did unhappy couples (33%). Happy couples were much more likely (53%) than unhappy couples (33%) to feel that they had grown closer since having children. And 35% of the happy couples reported that they were more satisfied in their marriage since having children, compared to 19% for the unhappy couples.

Table 12.2 identifies the top five parenting issues from this national sample of more than 50,000 couples. The biggest issue for parents (82%) is that children had a negative impact on their marital satisfaction, and they reported feeling more dissatisfied in their marriage since having children. The second most frequently reported parenting issue (65%) was that the father did not spend enough time with the children. Rounding out the top five parenting issues, 64% of the parents were dissatisfied with how childrearing responsibilities were shared; 63% disagreed on how to discipline their children; and 64% felt their partner focused more on their children than on the marriage.

TABLE 12.2	Top Five Parenting Issues for Couples	
Parenting Issue		**Percentage of Couples Having Problems***
1. Having children has reduced marital satisfaction.		82%
2. The father is not involved enough with our children.		65
3. My partner focuses more on the children than on the marriage.		64
4. I am dissatisfied with how childrearing is shared.		64
5. We disagree on discipline.		63

*One or both partners indicated this was an issue for them.

The Challenge of Parenthood

Many authorities have noted that parenthood is the last bastion of amateurism in our society. Plumbers, bookkeepers, computer analysts—all need some kind of formal training, certificate, or license. About the only job that doesn't require some special kind of education is nurturing the young to adulthood.

Our society tends to shy away from "intruding" into family matters, and rearing children is certainly a family matter. But some have gone so far as to argue that education and even something like an internship should be mandatory before people can become parents—that is, that a license should be required for parenthood—although such a proposal has little chance of becoming law. Nevertheless, its proponents underscore the importance of parenting: Society benefits from parents' successes but also suffers from their mistakes.

Adults with problems often had problems as children, and many times they pass their problems on to the next generation. For example, one therapist described a counseling session with an abused woman who had fled from her husband after repeated beatings; the woman's 18-month-old son accompanied her. During the session, the toddler became angered over some minor issue and ran at his mother. In his frustration, he put his hands around her neck and tried to strangle her. He was imitating almost precisely what he had seen his father do a few days earlier. With counseling, this pattern could be changed so that the boy would not repeat his father's behavior.

Myths and Realities of Parenthood

All societies have folk beliefs or myths that are widely accepted and rarely examined. The myths about parenthood in our society often sugarcoat the subject, romanticizing a task that is too important for people to undertake with rose-colored glasses. What follows is a list of commonly held folk beliefs or myths in our society, along with some comments that offer a more balanced and realistic view.

Myth #1: *Children will turn out well if they have "good" parents.*
Reality: Parents are an important factor in a child's development, but they are only one influence among many, including siblings, schools, the mass media, and the child's peer group. The goal of parenting must be to instill values and model positive behaviors that children will internalize and use in their lives. But there are no guarantees. Some good parents work hard at parenting only to see their children get into great difficulty in life.

Myth #2: *Children are sweet and cute.*
Reality: Although children can be adorable, they can also be selfish and destructive, as well as extremely active. In fact, children possess the full range of human qualities—positive and negative—that adults must deal with in each other. Parents who have no break from watching over children can easily become exhausted.

Myth #3: *Good parents can manage any child, no matter what the child's nature.*
Reality: This myth is based on the notion that a human being is born a *tabula rasa*, a blank slate upon which the environment writes its script. But research on infants indicates that to some degree temperament is present at birth. Some babies are calm and content; others are cranky. Although the family environment that parents construct for their young is tremendously

A first haircut is one of the many milestones that mark a child's growing up. Although this toddler may not remember the experience, his mother will likely remember this event in his transition from baby to little boy.

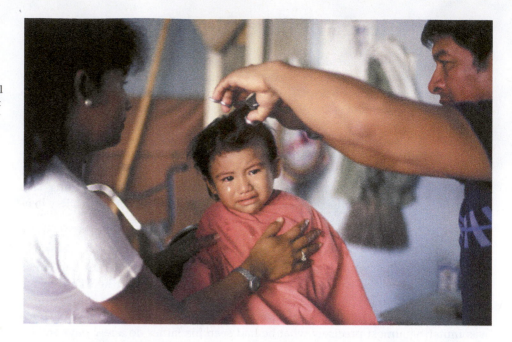

important, it is not the only influence or the sole determinant of a child's developmental outcome. It is important to note that children also strongly shape their parents' behavior. Parents, in sum, raise children. And children in many ways raise parents.

Myth #4: *Today's parents are not as good as yesterday's parents.*
Reality: Standards for raising children have gotten higher, making the challenge for today's parents even greater. Society now expects parents to be more democratic in their approach, to take the child's feelings into account when decisions are made, and to involve older children in the decision-making process.

Myth #5: *One child is too few.*
Reality: Although many believe that an only child is spoiled and selfish, countless studies worldwide have demonstrated that this belief is an unsubstantiated stereotype. The fact is, there are both advantages and disadvantages to having only one child. One child is less expensive to raise, is less demanding on the parents, places fewer limits on the parents' freedom, and receives more parental attention. On the downside, parents of only children sometimes focus too much attention on or overprotect the child, thus limiting the child's exposure to peer companions and possibly even causing the child to feel lonely. Also, having brothers and sisters can be a great source of support and joy throughout life: not only someone to fight with when you are young, but someone to cherish as a dear friend when you are grown up.

Myth #6: *All parents are adults.*
Reality: As reflected in our nation's teenage pregnancy rates, many adolescents unfortunately become parents. Government statistics indicate that 10.5% of all birth mothers are under age 20 (U.S. National Center for Health Statistics, 2009). Childrearing is difficult for adults, but it can be particularly challenging for teenage parents.

Myth #7: *Parenthood receives top priority in our society.*
Reality: Making money—not parenthood—receives top priority in our society. Parents are pressured to put their jobs first if they seek promotions—and sometimes even if they simply want to hold on to their jobs.

Myth #8: *Love is enough to guarantee good parental performance.*
Reality: Love certainly helps parents put up with the many difficulties of childrearing, but success at parenting also requires hard work and good parenting skills.

Myth #9: *Single-parent families are problematic.*
Reality: Single-parent families are often stigmatized in American society today, and the discussion of single-parent families' efforts to create a happy life together too often focuses on the negative. There is little question that many single-parent families face considerable challenges. Money and stress are very prominent on the list. The fact is, however, that there are countless strong single-parent families in which children are growing up happy and healthy. Simply knowing the structure of a family does not tell you how well a family is functioning.

Myth #10: *Parenting gets easier as children get older.*
Reality: Although most parents hope that parenting will get easier as their children mature, they typically find that their parenting issues change and become more difficult. Adolescence is the most challenging stage for many parents, because adolescents are seeking greater autonomy and freedom from parental control.

Myth #11: *Parenting ends when the children leave home.*
Reality: For most parents, parenting does not end when a child leaves home. Adult children often return home to live after a divorce, a job loss, or some other life crisis. Furthermore, parents are often called on to help with the care of their children's children; grandparenting brings joy, but it can also be exhausting.

Myth #12: *The empty-nest syndrome leaves many parents lonely and depressed.*
Reality: One observer noted, "After the kids leave home, some parents suffer from the empty-nest syndrome; others change the locks." Many parents enjoy the freedom that comes with not having adolescents at home. The middle-aged parent may get a job or change jobs, travel, or take up a new avocation. After they leave home, adult children are often surprised to watch their parents blossom and enjoy life in a variety of new ways.

The Transition to Parenthood

Parenthood isn't something that happens gradually; the 9 months of a normal pregnancy should give prospective parents time to think about parenthood and to plan for the arrival of the baby. But many parents are unprepared for the challenges that will confront them when the infant arrives. They may take classes to prepare for childbirth, but few prepare for the responsibilities of parenting itself.

When the baby is born, parenting begins in earnest. For some it is a crisis. E. E. LeMasters gained prominence in the 1950s with his report in the *New York Times* of a study entitled "Parenthood as Crisis." LeMasters argued that because of romantic notions about parenthood, people go through a process of disenchantment when they have children. LeMasters was flooded with letters from parents, most of whom agreed with his findings. In his research, LeMasters interviewed 46 couples and found that 83% defined the coming of a child as a "crisis" for their marriage (LeMasters, 1957). Other researchers have debated these findings ever since, and the definition of the term *crisis* remains controversial (Lawrence et al., 2008; Miller, 2000).

One dictionary defines *crisis* simply as a *turning point*, which parenthood certainly is in the life of mothers and fathers. Ask new parents a few months or years into the process if they can remember what life was like before having a baby, and the responses tend to run like these:

> *"I'm so tired, I can't remember what life was like yesterday, let alone what it was like before Lindy was born. We're just trying to figure out the everyday demands of parenting and do the best we can."*

or

> *"No, I don't remember at all. I know everything changed, but all in all, it's been a good change."*

or

> *"NO, I cannot imagine how life was like before he came. Everybody told me how your perspective and priorities change with a child, and I did not know the extent of it till now. It is the first time I am completely happy and do not feel guilty that I am not working. I used to work, even during vacations. Today, I am more than happy to just enjoy my son."*

Another dictionary defines *crisis* as a time of great danger or trouble. New parents are not likely to use these terms, because they may seem melodramatic or overblown. However, most new parents will agree that life has changed, dramatically. Thus, in this section we will talk about the *transition to parenthood*, even though that may sound a bit dry and academic, not quite capturing the emotion and drama that surround the advent of a child into a new parent's life.

There are several changes that new parents can expect (Cowan & Cowan, 2011). First, as each person takes on the parent role, their identity as a spouse, lover, and successful employee takes second stage. A parent may be too tired to give time to her or his spouse, or may not be able to give 100% at work if the person spent all night taking care of a fussy baby. Second, the relationships with family of origin change. Some new parents want to parent just like their parents did and others want to avoid doing things their parents did in raising them. This may mean these new parents pull away from their parents, whereas others want to draw closer. Third, each new parent develops a new relationship with this child as part of the transition to parenthood. The parent tries to figure out why the child cries and how to satisfy every need. Fourth, there are new stressors as well as new sources of emotional support. Trying to go to work while worrying about a baby in someone else's care can be difficult for both mothers and fathers. Stressors can also come from changes in partners' roles. For example, a couple might have shared most responsibilities equally before the baby was born, and they want to continue this after the birth of the child. However, that typically does not happen and gender roles become quite traditionally stereotypical with a new baby. This change in the family system creates stress for both parents. Finally, the quality of the couple relationship changes, which has been supported by many studies. The couple relationship satisfaction declines after the birth of the first child and continues to decline for several years.

According to Cowan and Cowan (2011), couples who attended family education classes addressing issues around the transition to parenthood were more likely to maintain high couple satisfaction with the birth of the first child, and these results were maintained long term. These authors also have the following suggestions for couples who cannot attend such classes:

- Communicate about issues that are creating stress for each parent.
- Develop a division of labor that is realistic and can work for both parents.
- Take time to keep the couple relationship strong. Take time for each other by building it into each day.

Financial Issues and Children

One of the surprises for most parents is how much children cost, in terms of not just time and energy but also money. Raising children is a very expensive venture, no matter what a family's income. An analysis of the expense of raising a child, based on data from the Family Economics Research Group at the U.S. Department of Agriculture, was summarized by Mark Lino and Andrea Carlson (2009). The data were broken down into six major categories: housing, food, transportation, clothing, health care, and education.

As expected, the amount of money spent on a child varied with the structure and income level of the family: two-parent families tended to spend more on children than one-parent families; and the higher the family income, the more the family spent on the child. The average child in a two-child, husband–wife family cost parents between $11,610 and $13,480 per year to raise. Broken down into three income groups (lower, middle, and higher), yearly expenses for the average child in a two-child, husband–wife family ranged:

- from $8,330 to $9,450, on average (depending on the age of the child), for households with before-tax income less than $56,870;
- from $11,610 to $13,480 for households with before-tax income between $56,870 and $98,470;
- and from $19,250 to $22,960 for households with before-tax income more than $98,470.

As you will recall, the average child in a two-child, husband–wife family costs parents between $11,610 and $13,480 per year. To raise this same average child in a two-child, husband–wife family from birth through age 17 costs these same average parents $221,190. (See Figure 12.1 for details.)

An important aspect of socializing children is helping them learn to understand and manage finances. One careful study of 182 parents by Sharon Danes asked when it was appropriate to introduce children to a variety of financial activities.

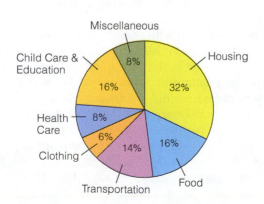

FIGURE 12.1

Cost of Raising a Child from Birth Through Age 17

Source: Lino & Carlson, 2009, U.S. Dept. of Agriculture, Center for Nutrition Policy and Promotion.

About 70% of these parents felt that children 8 years or younger were mature enough to receive an allowance, and 64% felt that they could open their own savings account. Almost half of the parents surveyed felt that 12- to 14-year-olds could be responsible for their own clothing budgets, and 29% believed that they were mature enough to be told about the family's income. About half the parents felt that 15- to 17-year-olds should know about car insurance and have their own checking accounts. More than half the parents believed that by age 18 to 20, adult children should have and be responsible for their own credit cards and be able to apply for and make the payments on a loan (Danes, 1992; Danes & Haberman, 2007; see also CYFERnet, 2010).

Adoption

By most estimates, about 2 million, or 3%, of Americans are adopted. This is not a high percentage, but it has been estimated that 6 in 10 Americans have some kind of experience with adoption: A family member or close friend was adopted, or the individual had adopted a child or placed a child for adoption. Many other Americans consider adopting a child at one point in their life and spend a good deal of time discussing the issue with friends and relatives.

Since the mid-1970s, adoption practices in the United States have changed dramatically (Grotevant, 2003, 2008; Riemer & Siegel, 2007). In the past, confidentiality in adoption was the norm; today, the trend is toward *openness* in adoption, which means that there is increasing contact between adoptive families and birth parents. The contact may be either direct or mediated (e.g., through an adoption agency). Some adoption professionals argue that fully open adoption should be standard practice and that the secrecy of confidential adoptions has been harmful to all those involved. Others argue that openness is experimental and may prove to be harmful: Confidential adoption has worked well, so why change it?

To understand the issue of openness in adoption, Harold Grotevant and Ruth McRoy recruited a nationwide sample of adoptive families and birth mothers with a *target* adopted child between the ages of 4 and 12 when the first interview occurred between 1987 and 1992. The sample included 720 individuals: both adoptive parents in 190 adoptive families, at least one adopted child in 171 of the families, and 169 birth mothers. Families were sampled across the full range of openness in adoption: *confidential* (no information shared between birth parents and adoptive parents); *mediated* (information shared, with the adoption agency as the go-between); and *fully disclosed* (ongoing direct contact between birth parents and adoptive family members). Adoptive families were interviewed in their homes.

As predicted, when compared with parents in confidential adoptions, parents in fully disclosed adoptions reported higher levels of acknowledgment of the adoption, more empathy toward the birth parents and child, a stronger sense of permanence in their projected relationship with their child, and less fear that the birth mother might try to reclaim the child (Grotevant, 2003).

Adoptees face unique challenges, and it is often assumed that these additional challenges increase psychological and interpersonal problems for them. Adoptees are sometimes stereotyped as being unhappy, poorly adjusted, and malfunctioning in life (Sharma, McGue, & Benson, 1998). But research comparing adoptees and a matched group of adult friends who were not adopted indicates more similarities than differences between the two groups. In many ways, adult adoptees "are navigating their adult years no differently than their non-adopted peers," and as a group doing reasonably well (Borders, Penny, & Portnoy, 2000, p. 415).

Another study that compared adopted and nonadopted adolescents found that adopted adolescents are at higher risk in all the areas examined, including school achievement and problems, substance use, psychological well-being, physical health, fighting, and lying to parents. The researchers concluded that their data showed that "more adopted adolescents have problems of various kinds than their nonadopted peers" (Miller, Fan, Christensen Grotevant, & van Dulmen, 2000 p. 1458). Some observers believe there is a so-called adopted child syndrome, which includes problems in bonding, attachment disorders, lying, stealing, defiance of authority, and acts of violence. These observers believe that adopted children are in an at-risk group for developing emotional problems because they are overrepresented in mental health caseloads (Smith, 2003).

Six factors have been identified that contribute to the success of parents adopting a child:

1. Healthy adoptive parents explore their motivations and expectations for adoption in an open and healthy manner and are in agreement.

2. Healthy adoptive parents demonstrate stability and quality in their interpersonal relationships.

3. Healthy adoptive parents demonstrate flexibility and openness in the family system. They can accept and deal with change, they value differences among family members, they readily seek support and resources when help is needed.

4. Healthy adoptive parents know the importance of creating a family environment that openly acknowledges and communicates about adoption.

5. Healthy adoptive parents understand the core issues of adoption that may affect their child and the triggers that may create a crisis. These core issues include the child's grief and mourning over loss of her birth parents; and the child's feelings of loss and control, rejection and fear of abandonment, shame and guilt, loss of personal identity, and feeling different from other children.

6. Healthy adoptive parents understand that adoption is a lifetime commitment and maintain that commitment through difficult times (Schooler & Atwood, 2008).

The Child-Free Alternative

Attitudes in the United States regarding the importance of children to a successful marriage have shifted in recent decades. A Pew Research Survey on marriage and parenting found that children had fallen to eighth place on a list of nine factors that people associate with successful marriages, well behind *sharing household chores, good housing, adequate income, a happy sexual relationship,* and *faithfulness.* In a 1990 World Values Survey, children ranked third in importance among the same eight items, with 65% saying children were very important to a good marriage. Just 41% said so in the most recent study (Pew Research Center, 2007). (See Figure 12.2, which compares the percentages from 1990 and 2007.)

FIGURE 12.2
Factors Americans
Associate with Successful
Marriage

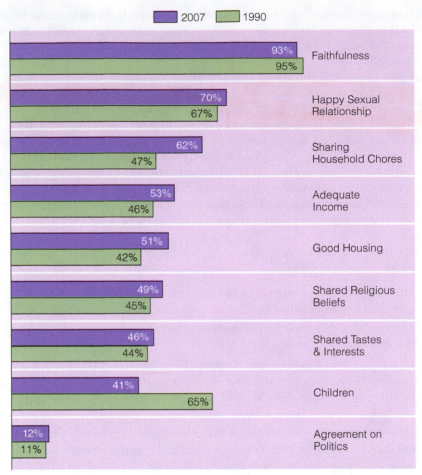

"Modern Marriage." Pew Research Center, Washington, D.C (July 18, 2007). http://www.pewsocialtrends. org/2007/07/18/modern-marriage/. Copyright © 2007 by Pew Research Center. Used by permission.

Various terms are applied to the choice not to have children, including *nonparenthood, voluntary childlessness,* and the **child-free alternative.** Acceptance of childlessness has increased since the 1970s, and researchers have found that women are more accepting of childlessness than men are. More than 86% of adults agreed or were neutral on whether childless adults could have fulfilling lives (Koropeckyj-Cox & Pendell, 2007, 2009).

The percentage of childless, middle-aged women aged 40 to 44—those at the end of their childbearing years—has increased from 10% in 1976 to about 18% (Wilcox, 2011). Rates of childlessness in the United States, including both women who choose not to have children and women who cannot have children, have varied substantially over the years. For example, for White women born in the mid-1880s, slightly over 15% remained childless. For White women born in 1910 and who reached childbearing age during the Great Depression of the 1930s, the childless rate was more than 25%. For White women born in 1935 who reached childbearing age during the baby boom of 1946 to 1964, the childless rate dropped dramatically to 10% (Morgan & Chen, 1992). The current recession has also had its effect on reproductive decisions. It has been found that 64% of women said that with the current economy, they could not afford to have a baby (Sandler, 2010, July 19). It was also found that 44% said they planned to reduce the number of children they plan to have because of the economy.

These fluctuations indicate that even when modern, relatively efficient contraception is not available, parents have responded over the years to changing economic and social conditions. Reviews of research revealed some interesting answers to common questions about childlessness (Dykstra, 2007a, 2007b; Hird & Abshoff, 2000; Koropeckyj-Cox & Pendell, 2007, 2009; LaMastro, 2001).

- *What long-term effects does voluntary childlessness have?* Although adult children are often very important to their parents in old age, older people without children also do quite well. (Aging parents may even find themselves rejected or neglected by their adult children.) Those without children often prepare for their later years by developing a network of friends and relatives to help meet their needs. They also learn how to cope with isolation if necessary (Skutch, 2001).
- *Is there something wrong with people who don't wish to have children?* The majority of studies on this topic concluded that nonparents exhibit no more psychopathology or deviance than a control group of randomly sampled parents. Culture affects one's attitude about whether or not to have children. For example, it has been argued that African Americans, American Indians, and Mexican Americans tend to be more family oriented than Whites and consider children an important part of marital life (Skogrand, Hatch, & Singh, 2009).
- *Do people without children do better in their careers?* Apparently, many people without children do very well. Voluntary childlessness leaves people with time and energy that can be focused on career goals. A disproportionate number of high-ranking businesswomen and professionals are childless.
- *Is the quality of a child-free marriage as good as that of a marriage with children?* Studies have found more vital and happy relationships among child-free couples than among those with children (Olson et al., 1989; Somers, 1993). This is, in part, because child-free couples can devote more time to their marriages and because they are more likely to divorce if they do not have a good relationship than would a couple with children.

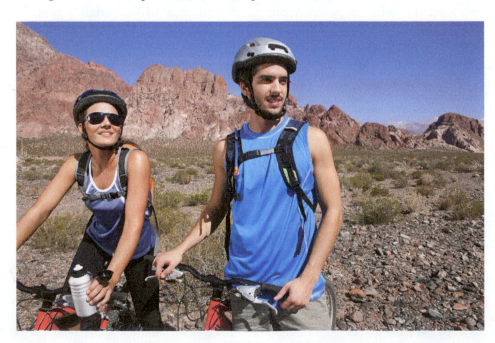

Parenthood is not for everyone. Couples who have decided not to have children can find happiness and fulfillment in life with each other, with their careers and avocational interests, and with friends and family.

- *What are the advantages and disadvantages of voluntary childlessness?* A study of 287 childless individuals aged 55 and over found that 67% reported advantages to childlessness, and 64% reported disadvantages. Perceived advantages included fewer worries or problems, financial benefits, greater freedom, and career flexibility. The major disadvantages included lack of companionship/being alone/loneliness, lack of support and care when older, and missing the experience of parenthood (Connidis & McMullin, 1999).

How do couples decide to remain childless? What is the process they go through to decide not to have children even though there is no known reason why they could not have children? Durham and Braithwaite (2009) conducted a qualitative study, interviewing 32 individuals who were part of couples who were voluntarily childless. They found four trajectories that described the differing ways couples communicated about remaining childless.

The authors identified the first category of individuals who remained childless as being in the accelerated-consensus trajectory (Durham & Braithwaite, 2009). These individuals are deliberate about choosing a partner who wants to remain childless. These individuals often had political or other personal reasons for not wanting children. These couples discussed the issue of not having children early on in their relationship, and the issue typically did not come up with any regularity after that.

The second category of individuals who were childless was identified by the authors as being on the mutual-negotiation trajectory (Durham & Braithwaite, 2009). These individuals came into their relationships without prior discussion about having or not having children. Like those in the accelerated-consensus trajectory, these persons were on the same page as their partner, but in this case they had not made a decision about having children. They described their communication as going on over time about the pros and cons of having or not having children. They experienced times of being undecided or ambivalent about their reproductive preferences. Even though individuals described their relationships as being equal in terms of power, because each individual had uncertainty over the issue, many of the people on this trajectory experienced stress in their communication process. Even after they were beyond childbearing years, they wondered if they had made the right decision.

The third category of individuals in this study was identified as being on a unilateral-persuasion trajectory (Durham & Braithwaite, 2009). These individuals were part of couples where one spouse was committed to being child-free and that person convinced the undecided partner that being child-free was the best option for their marriage. Different from individuals in the mutual-negotiation trajectory who had equal power, one individual in the unilateral-persuasion trajectory had more power and influence in their communications about reproduction. All the individuals in this study in this trajectory resulted in the man being the undecided person and the woman being clear in wanting to remain childless. In many cases the man felt his spouse would eventually change her mind and they would have children. Individuals in this trajectory, as one would imagine, experienced lots of conflict and stress regarding the reproductive issue, and this conflict and stress spilled over into other aspects of their relationships.

Finally, the fourth category of individuals was identified as being on the bilateral-persuasion trajectory (Durham & Braithwaite, 2009). These individuals were in relationships in which they disagreed completely in their family planning perspectives. One spouse wanted to be child-free and the other wanted children. All the individuals who wanted children thought, incorrectly, that they would ultimately persuade their spouse to change their mind and they would have children. Individuals in these relationships described their communication as often being emotionally heated and negatively charged, resulting in lots of emotional turmoil. Often unilateral decisions were made on the part of one partner that resulted in hurt and anger on the part of the spouse. The impact on the marriage relationship was extensive.

Even though voluntary childlessness has increased, the joint decision to remain childless is not always easy. This decision, like all couple decisions, can support the marriage relationship or distract from the relationship. Although the previous study included married couples, the decision to have children or remain childless also impacts the increased number of cohabiting couples who are also making reproductive decisions.

Styles of Parenting

There are two key aspects of parenting: parental support (family closeness on the Couple and Family Map) and parental control (family flexibility on the Couple and Family Map) (Figure 12.3). **Parental support** is defined as the amount of caring, closeness, and affection that a parent exhibits or gives to a child. **Parental control** is defined as the amount of flexibility that a parent uses in enforcing rules and disciplining a child.

There is considerable evidence that higher levels of parental support are related to positive outcomes in children, including better academic performance, higher self-esteem, more social competence, and better psychological adjustment

FIGURE 12.3
Parenting Styles and the Couple and Family Map

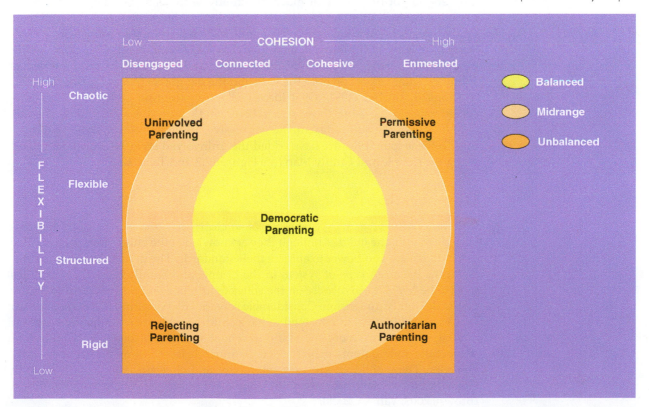

TABLE 12.3	Parenting Style and Children's Behavior
Parenting Style	**Children's Behavior**
Democratic style	Self-reliant, cheerful, achievement oriented
Authoritarian style	Conflicted, irritable, unhappy, unstable
Permissive style	Impulsive, rebellious, underachieving
Rejecting style	Immature, psychologically challenged
Uninvolved style	Solitary, withdrawn, underachieving

(Amato & Booth, 1997; Bean, Barber, & Crane, 2006). However, when you look at the extremes of family closeness using the Couple and Family Map, where there is very low closeness (disengaged) or very high closeness (enmeshed), children from these extremes tend to have more problems emotionally, socially, and academically (Manzi, Vignoles, Regalia, & Scabini, 2006).

Regarding parental control (family flexibility on the Couple and Family Map), there is considerable evidence that parenting that is too lenient (chaotic on the Couple and Family Map) and too strict (rigid on the Couple and Family Map) results in children with more psychological and academic problems (Amato & Booth, 1997). Conversely, parents who have a more balanced style of parenting (central level of the Couple and Family Map where parents are "structured" or "flexible" in parenting) have more positive outcomes with their children (Bean et al., 2006).

Sons and daughters often have different experiences growing up in the same family because they are treated differently by each parent. Although it appears that mothers do not function that much differently with sons and daughters, fathers tend to pay more attention to sons. As a result, daughters often feel closer to their mothers than to their fathers. Both parents have a tendency to punish sons more than daughters, and many still tend to assign tasks on the basis of gender—more boys mow the lawn, and more girls clean the house. In general, parenting style has about the same impact on both the sons and the daughters (Amato & Booth, 1997).

Diana Baumrind (1991, 1995) identified four parenting styles and has done considerable work using those styles. Baumrind's four styles are the democratic (authoritative), the authoritarian, the permissive, and the rejecting styles of parenting. To these four styles we have added the uninvolved style, which we identified using the Couple and Family Map (see Figure 12.3 and Table 12.3).

Democratic Style

In **democratic parenting,** parents establish clear rules and expectations and discuss them with the child. Although they acknowledge the child's perspective, they use both reason and power to enforce their standards. The democratic style is similar to the balanced type of system in the Couple and Family Map; these families tend to be *connected* to *cohesive* on the cohesion dimension and *structured* to *flexible* on the flexibility dimension. Considerable research on parenting has demonstrated that balanced family systems tend to have children who are emotionally healthier and happier and are more successful in school and life (Olson, 1996). Children of democratic-style parents exhibit what Baumrind describes as energetic-friendly behavior. These children are very self-reliant and cheerful. They cope well with stress and are achievement oriented. Many other observers concur with Baumrind (Brown, 2003; Van As, 2003).

Authoritarian Style

In **authoritarian parenting,** parents establish rigid rules and expectations and strictly enforce them. These parents expect and demand obedience from a child. The authoritarian style is located in the lower-right quadrant of the Couple and Family Map; these families tend to be *structured* to *rigid* on the flexibility dimension and *cohesive* to *enmeshed* on the cohesion dimension. As the authoritarian style becomes more intense, the family moves toward the *rigidly enmeshed* style. This type of family system is particularly difficult for adolescents, who tend to rebel against authoritarian parenting. In Baumrind's observations, children of authoritarian-style parents are often conflicted and irritable in behavior: moody, unhappy, vulnerable to stress, and unfriendly. A study of authoritarian parenting (Rudy & Grusec, 2006) in several European countries and the United States found that children from these families have more serious problems in a variety of areas (lower self-esteem, more behavior problems, less academic achievement).

Permissive Style

In **permissive parenting,** parents let the child's preferences take priority over their ideals and rarely force the child to conform to their standards. The permissive style is located in the upper-right quadrant of the Couple and Family Map; these families tend to be *flexible* to *chaotic* on the flexibility dimension and *cohesive* to *enmeshed* on the cohesion dimension. As the permissive style becomes more extreme, the family moves toward the *chaotically enmeshed* style, a style characterized by constant change and forced togetherness, which is not healthy for children. Baumrind observed that children of permissive-style parents generally exhibit impulsive–aggressive behavior. These children are often rebellious, domineering, and underachieving.

Rejecting Style

In **rejecting parenting,** parents do not pay much attention to the child's needs and seldom have expectations regarding how the child should behave. The rejecting style is located in the lower-left quadrant of the Couple and Family Map; these families tend to be *structured* to *rigid* on the flexibility dimension and *connected* to *disengaged* on the cohesion dimension. As the rejecting style becomes more extreme, the family moves toward the *rigidly disengaged* style, which leaves children feeling uncared for even though they are expected to behave and have many rules to follow. As a result, children from these homes are often immature and have psychological problems.

Uninvolved Style

In **uninvolved parenting,** parents often ignore the child, letting the child's preferences prevail as long as those preferences do not interfere with the parents' activities. The uninvolved style of parenting is located in the upper-left quadrant of the Couple and Family Map; these families tend to be *connected* to *disengaged* on the cohesion dimension and *flexible* to *chaotic* on the flexibility dimension. As the uninvolved style becomes more extreme, it moves toward the *chaotically disengaged* pattern, in which children are left on their own without emotional support and a lack of consistent rules and expectations. The uninvolved style of parenting is not often discussed in published research, but it is in many instances combined with the rejecting style. Children of uninvolved parents are often solitary, withdrawn, and underachieving.

Democratic parents are actively involved with their children. They set standards and discuss them with the child. Children of these parents tend to be self-reliant and achievement oriented, and they cope well with stress.

Democratic Parenting Works Best

Diana Baumrind (1991, 1995) completed several studies that linked the four parenting styles and outcomes with children. She has done considerable work using these styles. Baumrind described three styles of behavior in preschool children—energetic–friendly, conflicted–irritable, and impulsive–aggressive—and correlated those behaviors with her parenting styles (Table 12.3). In general, the democratic style resulted in children who were self-reliant, cheerful, and achievement oriented. Children raised with other styles, which are more extreme on cohesion and flexibility, had more problematic behaviors and less academic success.

In a major study of parenting that surveyed 11,669 high school students, the democratic (authoritative) style of parenting had the most positive impact on an adolescent's development (Avenevoli, Sessa, & Steinberg, 1999). Democratic parenting was significantly related to lower psychological distress, higher self-esteem, a higher grade-point average, lower levels of drug use, and less delinquent behavior. The importance of democratic parenting held up across ethnic groups and various levels of income.

In contrast to the positive outcomes of democratic parenting, authoritarian parenting was related to greater psychological distress, lower self-esteem, a lower grade-point average, and—interestingly—lower substance abuse (Avenevoli et al., 1999). Permissive parenting, considered the opposite of authoritarian parenting, was related to higher self-esteem, lower psychological distress, and lower substance abuse but also a lower grade-point average and some delinquency. Neglectful parenting was the most problematic parenting style. It was related to greater adolescent distress, lower self-esteem, a lower grade-point average, and greater drug use and delinquency compared to the other styles.

An important question concerns the importance of parenting style versus family structure (single- versus two-parent) and socioeconomic level (Avenevoli et al., 1999). Although they found that two-parent (intact) families from a variety of ethnic groups and socioeconomic levels were more democratic and less neglectful in their parenting style than were single-parent families, the differences between the two types of families were quite small and practically insignificant. The researchers concluded that the most important finding was "that family structure does not meaningfully moderate the relation between parenting and adjustment across a wide variety of socioeconomic and ethnic groups" (p. 87). The parenting style was the most critical variable in determining adolescent development and adjustment. Thus, regardless of ethnic background, socioeconomic level, or family structure, children of democratic-style parents have the best psychological and educational outcomes.

Theories of Childrearing

Parenting is a complex process that raises many questions: How shall we raise the children? How strict should we be, and how will we discipline our children? How soon should we begin toilet training? Will day care meet all our children's needs if both of us work outside the home? How can we share household and parenting responsibilities so that neither one of us feels overburdened or resentful? Before we tackle the issues surrounding these and other questions, let's take a look at some interrelated and complementary theoretical approaches to parenting.

The family systems perspective is increasingly being used by those studying the parent–child relationship. Earlier work focused on the influence of the parent on the child and some focus of the child on the parent. In the 1980s, a strong consensus developed by child development researchers about the need to study **bidirectional effects**—both the effects of the child on the parent and those of the parent on the child—in order to understand parent–child dynamics. The idea was not new to proponents of family systems theory, but it was a breakthrough for traditional child development researchers. The book by Richard Bell, who described the research in *Child Effects on Adults* (1977), helped stimulate interest in bidirectional research. The family systems perspective takes this one step further, viewing the parent–child relationship as an interactive cycle, a circular process of mutual influence.

Several theories of child development have had an impact on approaches to raising children. Freud and his followers focused on the importance of childhood, when the foundation for later life is laid down. Freudians and other proponents of the **psychodynamic theory** emphasized the importance of providing a positive emotional environment for the child, who needs to believe that the world is a safe and good place and that parents can be trusted to be kind and consistent. Although individuals who have suffered enormously in childhood can make dramatic, positive changes later in life, it is best if we can help children succeed from the very beginning.

Jean Piaget and proponents of **organismic theory** were interested in cognitive development, the development of the mind. Piaget held that the mind develops through various stages over the course of childhood and adolescence. He observed that children think very differently than adults do. Child-thought is primitive and mystical; young children have only the beginnings of logical reasoning. Thought processes develop slowly toward higher forms into adulthood. This theory encourages

Teaching a child appropriate behavior does not necessarily mean punishment for bad behavior. A more effective technique is reinforcing good behavior with praise and a hug.

parents to select toys and activities that are developmentally appropriate for their children and not to expect more than their children are capable of at any given stage.

The **behaviorists,** operating from **learning theories,** have developed some practical, positive approaches for dealing with children's behavior. Rather than focusing on punishment, behaviorists encourage "accentuating the positive," known as **reinforcement.** When a child does something positive, reward the child. Picking the appropriate reinforcer is not easy; "different strokes for different folks" often applies. Most children respond quite well to money, but praise and a hug are usually equally or even more effective. (Adults, too, appreciate praise from a boss for giving that extra effort.) A parent's job is to be creative in developing new reinforcers.

Perhaps the greatest positive reinforcement is simply enjoying each other's company. For example, when invited to speak about our research on strong families at a conference, John DeFrain often goes on a "journey of happy memories" with the audience. He asks people to recall the "best time" they can remember as a child: "Close your eyes. Think back to when you were a kid. Picture the best time you can remember with your family. Go right back to the scene as if you were there once again. What are you doing with your family? What's happening? Who's there? Get into it. Feel it. . . ." Then, we ask them to open their eyes, and we call for volunteers to describe what they just saw in their mind's eye.

Some people recall holidays:

"I'm in the living room. It's Thanksgiving. The whole family is gathered together, standing and sitting around the piano. We're all singing songs. Us kids are giggling and squirreling around, too. It's wonderful."

Some remember family nights together:

"I remember how we'd play games every Friday night. Just lie on the floor in the living room and play simple board games and laugh together."

Some tell about working together:

> *"When I was 12, my job was to scrub the kitchen floor with Mom every Saturday morning. We'd be on our hands and knees—just the two of us—scrubbing and laughing and flicking water at each other. It was great!"*

Some remember times together outdoors in nature:

> *"We're on vacation. We're at the lake 2 hours north of our hometown. We're camping out. We're telling stories around the campfire."*

We have gone on this journey of happy memories with literally thousands of people over the past 25 years, and the most remarkable thing we have found is that adults rarely recall something that cost a lot of money. On only a handful of occasions has anyone recalled an expensive event: a costly vacation to a theme park, a big meal in a fancy hotel. The vast majority of our happiest memories from childhood come from experiences that cost almost nothing. The key element is this: People who love one another are together, enjoying each other's company, being kind to one another.

It's very clear: Simple things can be tremendously reinforcing to a good relationship. These good times not only enhance the bond between parents and children, they also foster cooperation in children.

Issues in Parenting

In this section of this chapter, we will focus on nine important issues that are regularly in the news today: the need for positive discipline; corporal punishment and its consequences; the need for high-quality child care; coparenting; single mothers; gay and lesbian parenting; the relationship between fatherhood and motherhood today; how families endure the death of a child; and educational programs and resources for parents.

The Need for Positive Discipline Today

Are parents today too lenient with their children and letting the children take over more? *Time* magazine featured this question with the theme "Who's In Charge Here?" (Gibbs, 2001). A Time/CNN poll indicated that 80% of parents felt that children are more spoiled today than 10 to 15 years earlier. Seventy-five percent of the parents felt their children did fewer chores. Over two-thirds (68%) of the parents felt that children today are somewhat to very spoiled. Last, 71% of the parents felt that children are exposed to too much advertising, which increases their desires for more things.

In reaction to this trend, a variety of authors have identified the problem and offer some solutions. Bill Doherty (2000) in his book *Take Back Your Kids* describes how parents are almost afraid to discipline their children. He describes how parents are willing to sacrifice time so their children can have endless opportunities for community and school activities. He identifies ways parents can stand up to their children and take more control of their lives. He believes it is important to balance family time together and the needs of the individual children to achieve their personal goals.

Dan Kindlon (2001) sounds a similar theme of parents giving in too much in his book *Too Much of a Good Thing: Raising Children of Character in an Indulgent Age.*

After surveying 1,700 teens and parents, he concluded that parents today want to indulge their children emotionally and with things. He even felt that he was too lax with his children and did not expect enough of them. He compared children where the parents were not indulgent with parents who were indulgent. The study found that the nonindulgent parents used the TLC approach. Time: They spent more time with their children at supper, after school, and at bedtime. Limits: They set firmer limits and expected more of the child in a variety of areas. Caring: They took an interest in all aspects of the child's life. Nonindulgent families also shared four traits:

- Families frequently ate dinner together.
- Parents were not divorced or separated.
- Children were required to keep their rooms clean.
- Children did community service.

In summary, today's parents may be more indulgent and lenient with their children, and this trend can be problematic when carried to extremes. It is interesting that parenting styles may change over time on a scale from parent-dominant to child-centered. Harsh discipline and the old saying that "children should be seen and not heard" are indicators of a parent-dominant approach to childrearing. Letting children do whatever they wish in life would be an indicator of an extreme child-centered approach. We will always be arguing for a more balanced approach, of course. *Positive discipline*, as it is called today, focuses on teaching a child how to behave responsibly in life, while at the same time honoring and loving this child for the unique and beautiful person he or she already is.

Discipline as it is discussed today is often punitive. But why, in our efforts to make children do good in life, do we insist on making them feel bad? Positive discipline, on the other hand, seeks a win-win approach to childrearing: helping a child learn to do good and at the same time feel good about herself or himself for doing good.

Judith Rich Harris (2009) makes an interesting comparison between marriage and parenthood:

> *The relationship between a parent and a child is an important one, but it's important in the same way as the relationship between married partners. A good relationship is one in which each party cares about the other and derives happiness from making the other happy. A good relationship is not one in which one party's central goal is to modify the other's personality.*

Corporal Punishment and Its Consequences

Corporal punishment is the use of physical force as punishment, correction, or behavior control. Corporal punishment usually refers to spanking or slapping but can also include grabbing, shoving, or hitting with an object. Corporal punishment is highest with younger children and decreases as the child reaches adolescence (Straus, 2002). Children aged 2 and 3 are hit about 16 to 18 times a year, and the frequency drops to about 10 times for 10-year-olds, and about 6 times for adolescents 13 to 16. In his research, Straus (2001) found that more men (58%) than women (44%) recall being hit as adolescents. Furthermore, adolescent sons are almost equally as likely to be hit by their fathers as by their mothers,

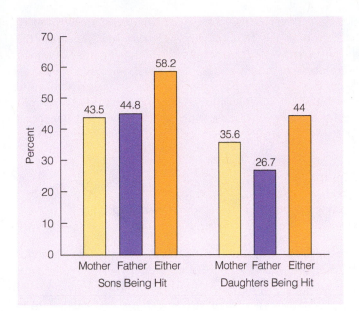

FIGURE 12.4

Frequency of Adolescent Sons and Daughters Being Hit by a Parent

Source: *Beating the Devil Out of Them: Corporal Punishment in American Families* by M. A. Straus, copyright © 2001 Transaction Publishers, New Brunswick, NJ.

whereas adolescent daughters are about a third more likely to be hit by their mothers (Figure 12.4).

There is some evidence that the use of and support for corporal punishment in the United States is decreasing. This is congruent with the trend toward a more child-centered style of discipline that was previously described. Based on data merged from seven national surveys, the percentage of Americans who approve of corporal punishment declined from 94% in 1968 to 68% in 1994 (Straus & Mathus, 1996). Research findings also indicate differences in support of corporal punishment across sociocultural groups. Approval of corporal punishment is more common among African Americans, men, people who are less educated, older age groups, and individuals living in the southern United States.

Straus (2002, 2007) believes that all forms of physical punishment have long-term harmful consequences, not only for children and parents specifically but for society as a whole. By teaching the young that big people have the right to hurt smaller people, spanking contributes in some degree to the relatively high level of violence in American society. Straus (1998) found that the more corporal punishment experienced by the child, the greater the tendency for the child to engage in antisocial and impulsive behavior, and this pattern may contribute to the level of violence and other crime in our society.

In addition, the more corporal punishment experienced as a child, the greater the chance the person will hit his or her spouse (Straus, 2007). If a person experienced little or no corporal punishment as a child, the rate of hitting a spouse ranged from 8% to 14%. But if a child was hit 10 or more times a year, the rate of spouse abuse increased from 20% to 25%.

Several studies have found a direct linear relationship between corporal punishment received as a teenager and levels of adult depression (Christie-Mizell, Pryor, & Grossman, 2008). Even when Straus (2007) controlled for other variables, such as poverty and witnessing violence between parents, Straus still found in his sample of more than 6,000 adults that the more corporal punishment teenagers received, the more depressive symptoms they had as adults. This relationship was stronger

FIGURE 12.5

Relationship Between
Corporal Punishment
Received as a Teenager
and Adult Depression

Source: Straus, 2001.

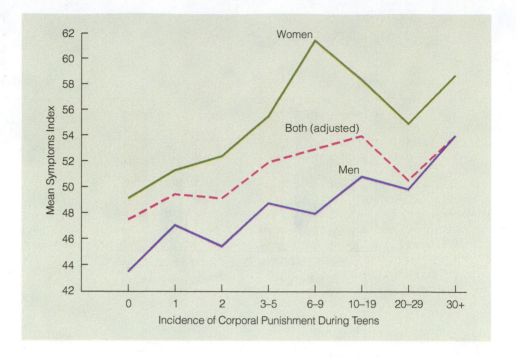

for women than for men (Figure 12.5). Also, adults whose parents hit them a lot as
adolescents were more likely to have suicidal thoughts than adults who were not
hit as adolescents.

Another researcher looked at the relationship between corporal punishment
inflicted by parents and the perpetration of animal abuse by the children (Flynn,
2000a, 2000b). The research found that males who committed animal cruelty in
childhood or adolescence were physically punished more frequently by fathers,
both as preteens and teenagers, than males who did not perpetrate animal abuse.
The relationship did not hold up for males spanked by their mothers or for females
spanked by either their mothers or fathers.

Research on spanking shows that it does work to correct misbehavior. But the
research also indicates that it does not work better than other modes of correction
and control, including *time out, explaining,* and *depriving a child of privileges.* Besides
this, the gains of spanking come at a great cost: these include the weakening of the
ties between children and parents, and increasing the probability that the child
will hit other children, hit their parents, and, as adults, hit a dating or marital partner. Spanking also slows mental development and lowers the likelihood of the
child doing well in school and college. More than one hundred studies of the side
effects of spanking have been conducted, and there is 90% agreement among them
that it is not the best way to discipline children (Straus, 2007).

In 1979 Sweden was the first country to pass a no-spanking law. The Swedes
have no criminal penalty for spanking. Instead, the purpose of the law is to set
a standard for how children should be treated and to make public funds available to educate people about the standards and provide services to help parents
who are having enough difficulty with their children that they feel they need
to spank them. The Swedes believe their law has been very effective. Spanking
has declined tremendously in the country, and fears that children would "run
wild" were not realized. Instead, the rate of youth crime, drug use, and suicide all

BOX 12.1   Putting It Together

The Mother's Book BY MRS. CHILD

The roots of the word *discipline* go back through the millennia to the time of Jesus. The early followers were called disciples—*learners*—and Jesus was their teacher. Thus, the word *discipline* has always had an educational connotation. Similarly, parents, in essence, are teachers of children, and positive discipline techniques as they are defined today focus on ways to help children learn how to live successfully in a complex world. Positive discipline techniques demand that parents search for a reasonable balance between love, kindness, and thoughtful instruction, on the one hand, and firm insistence, on the other. This is not a new dilemma for parents, of course. *The Mother's Book* by Mrs. Child was a popular book on parenting, published in Boston in 1831. Mrs. Child was also the author of *The Frugal Housewife, The Girl's Own Book,* and *Evenings in New England* and the editor of *The Juvenile Miscellany.* As you read what Mrs. Child has to say on discipline, you may readily surmise that many of the challenges parents face today were challenges parents struggled with down through the centuries:

> I have said much in praise of gentleness. I cannot say too much. Its effects are beyond calculation, both on the affections and the understanding. The victims of oppression and abuse are generally stupid, as well as selfish and hard-hearted. How can we wonder at it? They are all the time excited to evil passions, and nobody encourages what is good in them. We might as well expect flowers to grow amid the cold and storms of winter.
>
> But gentleness, important as it is, is not all that is required in education. There should be united with it firmness—great firmness. Commands should be reasonable, and given in perfect kindness; but once given, it should be known that they must be obeyed.

Source: Mrs. Child, *The Mother's Book* (Boston: Carter & Hendee, 1831).

decreased in Sweden. Fifteen nations now prohibit spanking by parents, and an emerging global consensus is building. The United Nations committee charged with implementing the Charter on Children's Rights has asked all nations to prohibit spanking. The UN committee argues that never spanking will reduce the risk of delinquency and mental health problems, and also bring to children the right to be free of physical attacks in the name of discipline. Wives gained the basic human right not to be physically assaulted by a husband more than 125 years ago (Straus, 2007).

It needs to be noted, however, that parental stress can be a factor in physical punishment. Cumulative or **cascading circumstances** can build up to the point that parents use harsh discipline with their children such as hitting, spanking, or yelling (Arditti, Burton, & Neeves-Botelho, 2010). The circumstances that cause the stress can be a parent getting sick, which adds to losing a job, which results in getting evicted from an apartment. This is not uncommon when people are living at or near the poverty line, and one incident can result in a cascade of problems—with no resources with which to stop it. The stress pileup causes frustration and anger, and sometimes children ultimately experience the brunt of it. Stress does not excuse the parental behavior, but it might explain it. As these authors conclude, harsh disciplinary practices should not be condoned; however, suggesting alternative ways of disciplining may not make sense to those living in the context of poverty and extensive stress. Other sources of support in terms of resources might be more useful.

Although research is clear about the harm corporal punishment can cause children, many parents do not think spanking is wrong. According to the findings of a large national study (Ellison & Bradshaw, 2009), 73% of parents agree that a spanking is sometimes necessary. Beliefs about spanking can be associated with income levels, political, and religious beliefs. For example, Ellison and Bradshaw (2009) found that conservative Protestant beliefs are predictive of the use of spanking. These authors also found that parents who are politically conservative are more likely to approve of corporal punishment than those who are liberal or moderate politically.

In addition, internationally the use and results of differing forms of discipline have different results for children. One study drew a sample of almost 300 mothers and children from China, India, Italy, Kenya, Philippines, and Thailand (Gershoff et al., 2010). These parents and children within each country were considered middle class by the standards within those countries, and the sample focused on children from 8 to 12 years of age. The study focused on the relationship between mothers' disciplinary techniques and children's behavior. The study found that using corporal punishment (e.g., spanking, slapping, hitting), expressing disappointment, and yelling or scolding were positively related to children's aggression. The study also found that the use of time-outs, corporal punishment, shaming, and expressing disappointment were positively associated with children's anxiety. It was also interesting to note that expressing disappointment on the part of mothers was more strongly associated with aggression in children in China, Italy, Philippines, and Thailand. So, although the authors do not speculate about the reasons for this, one might conclude that differing cultural views about disciplinary practices might have differing impacts on children. These researchers also found that the effects of certain forms of discipline did not have as strong a relationship with aggression and anxiety if it was considered normative by the child. For example, if children thought other children were experiencing corporal punishment, then they were not likely to be as anxious or aggressive.

So what can we conclude about corporal punishment and other forms of discipline? In the United States, it is clear that for many children corporal punishment has negative effects. However, even in the United States, many of our studies do not include families from diverse cultures and, therefore, we do not even know if these findings are likely to be true beyond White, middle-class families. Research internationally indicates that there may be different standards and expectations about corporal punishment and other forms of discipline, and these differing standards result in different outcomes for children.

Child Care

Relatives regularly provide child care to almost half of the more than 19 million preschool-age children in this country, according to the U.S. Census Bureau (2008, February 28). Among the 11.3 million children younger than 5 whose mothers were employed, 30% were cared for on a regular basis by a grandparent during their mother's working hours. A slightly greater percentage spent time in an organized care facility, such as a day care center, nursery, or preschool. Meanwhile, 25% received care from their fathers, 3% from siblings, and 8% from other relatives when mothers went to work. More specific information about child care for one ethnic group is provided in Box 12.2.

Some parents turn to relatives for child care, not only to save money but also because they prefer care from members of their extended family. Some parents value the developmental education approaches found in selected child care programs. Parents for whom hours, location, and cost of care are important issues often choose care in a home. And parents who think it is important that the child know the caregiver are more likely to choose family care. One research team found that in their sample of parents surveyed on the importance of various characteristics of child care, the top three factors were warmth of the caregivers, educational level of the caregivers, and utilization of a play-based curriculum (Kensinger-Rose & Elicker, 2008).

In addition to the use of relatives and in-home day care, there are multiple centers that provide child care and preschool experiences. Most of these centers are located

BOX 12.2   Diversity in Families

Child Care for the Growing Hispanic Population

With so many mothers in the United States working outside the home, the issue of child care is a pressing concern. It is an issue that cuts across social and ethnic lines, as most families struggle to balance the need for work and the needs of their families.

Current statistics about Hispanic families provide a picture of the rising need for child care among Hispanic families:

- **45.5 million people.** This is the estimated Hispanic population of the United States as of July 1, 2007 (U.S. Census Bureau, 2008, May 1).
- **15.1%.** Hispanics accounted for about 1 in 6 Americans (U.S. Census Bureau, 2008, May 1).
- **16.** The Hispanic population exceeded 500,000 people in 16 states (U.S. Census Bureau, 2008, May 1).
- **One-half.** Hispanics accounted for about 50% of the nation's population growth between 2000 and 2006 (U.S. Census Bureau, 2009, September 21).
- **24.3%.** The Hispanic population growth rate was more than three times the growth rate of the total population (6.1%) (U.S. Census Bureau, 2009, September 21).
- **3.3%.** The Hispanic population increased 3.3% in a recent year. This makes them the fastest-growing minority group in America. Asians were the second fastest growing minority group at 2.9%. The White population group grew 0.3% during the same 1-year period (U.S. Census Bureau, 2008, May 1).
- **24.4%.** The Census Bureau estimates that by 2050, Hispanics will increase from just under 1 in 7 Americans to nearly 1 in 4 Americans (U.S. Census Bureau, 2009, September 21).
- **27.7.** This is the median age for Hispanics in the United States (27.0 for Hispanic males and 27.6 for Hispanic females). The median age for the total U.S. population is 36.8 (35.2 for males and 37.8 for females) (U.S. Census Bureau, 2008, July 1). These numbers indicate that the Hispanic population in America is closer to prime childbearing years than the general population.
- **11%.** Hispanics are the most likely ethnic group in America to be preschoolers (under age 5), with 11% in this age group (U.S. Census Bureau, 2005).

- **High unemployment, lower earnings, more likely to live in poverty, less likely to have health insurance.** The unemployment rate for Hispanics (12.6%) is higher than for any other ethnic group in the United States except African Americans (16.5%). White unemployment (8.7%) and Asian unemployment (8.4%) are lower (U.S. Department of Labor, 2010, February 5). The income level for Hispanic households (a median of $37,913) is lower than for any other ethnic group in the United States except African Americans ($34,218). Median White household income ($55,530) and Asian income ($65,637) are higher. And the poverty rate for Hispanics in America is 23.2%, higher than for any other ethnic group except African Americans (24.7%). The poverty rates for Whites (8.6%) and Asians (11.8%) were lower. Hispanics were the most likely ethnic group to not have health insurance (30.7%). Figures for other ethnic groups: Whites (10.8% do not have health insurance); Blacks (19.1%); and Asians (17.6%) (U.S. Census Bureau, 2009, September 9).
- **25%.** It is projected that by the year 2030 Hispanics will make up 1 in 4 of the total U.S. school-age population (National Child Care Information Center, 2004b).
- **Minorities will be in the majority.** By the year 2050, Hispanics and Blacks under the age of 5 will outnumber non-Hispanic Whites in the United States (National Child Care Information and Technology Assistance Center, 2004a, 2008, June).
- **Lower-quality child care, a lower supply of child care.** Although the Hispanic population is among the fastest growing and youngest segment of American society, families confront lower quality and lower supply of available child care in relation to the general public (National Child Care Information and Technology Assistance Center, 2004b, 2008, June).
- **About 15.5%** of Hispanic children of employed mothers were in organized care (child care centers, nurseries or preschools, Head Start programs, or other schools) (National Child Care Information and Technology Assistance Center, 2004b, 2008, June).

in private or nonprofit entities such as churches or schools and are supported by parents' fees (American Planning Association, 2011). The cost of such child care is often more than parents can handle and high-quality child care is hard to find. The cost of child care in child care centers depends upon the age of the child, with younger children costing more. Another factor is the location, with centers in larger cities being more expensive than in smaller towns. The average cost of center day care in the United States is about $1,000 per month (Babycenter, 2011).

There are also employers, both public and private, who sponsor child care centers for their employees. These centers are either on site or near the place of employment, or companies pay to reserve space for employees' children at public and private care centers. There are a variety of ways employers subsidize the cost, such as providing the building or actually paying part of the cost of the care provided. These types of arrangements can actually benefit the employer by reducing turnover rates and absenteeism (American Planning Association, 2011).

It has been estimated that more than two million American preschoolers attend day care centers. The critical question for the parents of these children—and for our society as a whole—is how day care affects children, both positively and negatively. The National Institute of Child Health and Human Development Study of Early Child Care and Youth Development (NICHD) is by far the most ambitious study of the effects of nonmaternal child care, and about families who use child care as well as those who do not. Researchers tracked more than 1,300 children in various child care arrangements, including staying at home with a parent, being cared for by a nanny or a relative, or attending a large day care center. After the children reached school, the study used teacher ratings of each child, which assessed behaviors such as interrupting class, teasing, and bullying. This government-funded $200 million study began in 1991 (Eunice Kennedy Shriver National Institute of Child Health and Human Development, NIH, DHHS, 2006). Because of the importance of this ongoing research, we will examine it in some depth here.

The major goal of the study is to examine how differences in child care experiences relate to children's social, emotional, intellectual, and language development, and how these differences also relate to children's physical growth and health. Child care, for the purpose of the study, was defined as any care provided on a regular basis by someone other than the child's mother. This did not include occasional babysitting or any type of care for less than 10 hours per week (Eunice Kennedy Shriver National Institute of Child Health and Human Development, 2006).

Researchers, based at universities, collected data at 10 sites around the country. The study population was composed of children who were born healthy from a variety of socioeconomic backgrounds. The features studied were (1) cognitive and language development, (2) social behavior, (3) emotional development and relationships with parents, and (4) health and physical growth.

What were the major findings of the NICHD child care study?

1. *Higher-quality care was associated with better outcomes.* During the first 4½ years of their life, children in higher-*quality* child care had somewhat better language and cognitive development than those in lower-quality care. These children were somewhat more cooperative than those who experienced lower-quality care during the first 3 years of their life.

2. *Amount of time in care mattered to some degree.* Children who spent a higher *quantity* of time in child care (total combined number of hours) showed somewhat more behavior problems while in child care and in kindergarten classrooms than those who spent fewer hours in child care.

3. *The impact of child care type or setting was different for children of different ages.* Center-based child care has both positive and negative effects. This type of care is associated with better cognitive development through age 4½ and with more positive social behaviors through age 3. However, children attending child care centers also showed somewhat more behavior problems just before and just after entry into school than children who experienced other nonmaternal child care arrangements.

4. *Parent and family characteristics were more strongly linked to child development than any aspect of child care.* The researchers looked at the quality of the family environment, parental attitudes, maternal psychological adjustment, and mother's sensitivity. The following characteristics predicted children's cognitive/language and social development: parents' education, family income, and two-parent family compared to one-parent family; mothers' psychological adjustment and sensitivity; and the social and cognitive quality of the home environment.

In the NICHD study, only a small percentage of children received a lot of positive caregiving, and that percentage decreased as children got older, moving from 18% to 13% to 6% during the first 3 years of life. Poor-quality care, in which children received hardly any positive caregiving, also occurred for only a small percentage of children, changing from 6% to 8% to 4% during the first 3 years of life. The data suggest that most child care settings in the United States provide care that is "fair" (between "poor" and "good"). Fewer than 10% of child care arrangements were rated as providing very high-quality child care. At the other extreme, fewer than 10% of child care arrangements were estimated to provide children with very low-quality experiences (Eunice Kennedy Shriver National Institute of Child Health and Human Development, NIH, DHHS, 2006, p. 11). (Box 12.3.)

A follow-up study was conducted including a sample of these same children at age 15 (Vandell et al., 2010). This research was able to determine the longer-term effects of child care on children into their teens. High-quality care predicted increased cognitive and academic achievement for these 15-year-olds, and this was true for all income ranges. The higher quality of care also was predictive of less behavior problems for these adolescents. In addition, consistent with findings with children who were studied when they were 4½ years of age, these 15-year-olds experienced increased behavior problems the longer they were in child care. Those who had been in care longer hours were more likely to take risks and be impulsive. We can conclude, based upon this large national study, that high-quality child care can have positive effects on children more than 10 years later.

Although the interest and need for day care continue to rise, the United States is one of the few countries that does not have national day care policies or standards. Day care workers, who typically earn only minimum wage, often have little direct training. It is a sad commentary on our society that we fail to train and reward the people who are responsible for caring for, teaching, and nurturing so many of our children.

Coparenting

A growing number of parents have adopted a cooperative approach to parenting, known as **coparenting**. Traditional family roles—in which dad was the provider and mom the nurturer; dad was "tough" and mom was "tender"—are changing. More mothers are working outside the home, and more men are sharing in parenting tasks. An increasing number of mothers are providing income for their families and enjoying their connection to the world outside the home. At the same time, an increasing number of fathers are experiencing the joy of watching their children grow and learn.

Coparenting has been defined as the process by which mothers and fathers coordinate and support one another's parenting efforts (Kolak & Volling, 2007). Some couples share the responsibilities equally: Mother and father each do half the child care, half the housework, and half the work outside the home. But most

BOX 12.3   At Issue

Looking for a Very High Quality Child Care Program and Positive Caregiving

Researchers in the pioneering National Institute of Child Health and Human Development Study of Early Child Care found that fewer than 10% of the child care arrangements they studied around the United States provided *very high quality child care*, which promotes the developmental well-being of children. What should parents look for when visiting child care programs? And what constitutes positive caregiving?

Professional Standards for Child Care Recommended by the American Academy of Pediatrics and the American Public Health Association

Adult-to-Child Ratios	Group Sizes	Training and Education of Staff
Children age 6 months to 1½ years—3 children to 1 staff person	Children age 6 months to 1½ years—maximum of 6 children in the group	Formal post–high school training, including certification or college degree in child development, early childhood education, or a related field
Children age 1½ years to 2 years—4 children to 1 staff person	Children age 1½ years to 2 years—maximum of 8 children in the group	
Children age 2 years to 3 years—7 children to 1 staff person	Children age 2 years to 3 years—maximum of 14 children in the group	

Percentage of Child Care Center Classes Observed in the NICHD Study Meeting Recommended Guidelines at Age 6 Months to 3 Years

Standard	6 Months	1½ Years	2 Years	3 Years
Adult-to-Child Ratio	36%	20%	26%	56%
Observed Group Size	35%	25%	28%	63%
Caregiver Training	56%	60%	65%	75%
Caregiving Education	65%	69%	77%	80%

From John DeFrain, Family Treasures: Creating Strong Families (Lincoln, NE: University of Nebraska-Lincoln Extension, 2006). Copyright © 2006 University of Nebraska-Lincoln Extension. Reprinted by permission of the University of Nebraska-Lincoln Extension.

couples do not divide up the tasks exactly equally. One young father explained, "I'm a better cook, so I tend to do more of that. She likes to see a neat, clean house, so she concentrates on that. We both like taking care of the girls, but I do baths and bedtimes because she's so tired at the end of a day of nursing." Flexibility is the key.

Researchers have found a number of advantages to the coparenting model. Parents report greater satisfaction with their marriage and family life than they had before they adopted the coparenting approach. They also report improved relationships with their children. Some partners even considered divorce before they changed their attitudes about childrearing. Coparenting frees men to spend more time relating to, caring for, and relaxing with their children and frees women to pursue outside interests. Both parents have much to gain from active involvement in their children's growth. Parenthood is much too important and much too time consuming to be left to one person (Dienhart, 2001; Risman & Johnson-Sumerford, 1998; Smith, 2009).

What Is Positive Caregiving?

The NICHD researchers found that the more positive the caregiving, the higher the quality of care. When caregivers cared for a smaller number of children, they showed more positive caregiving, which in turn was associated with better outcomes in the children's lives. The same was true for caregiver education level. Caregivers with higher education levels were more positive in their caregiving and the children benefited. Positive caregiving was a primary indicator of child care quality. Positive caregiving behaviors include:

- **Showing a positive attitude**—Is the caregiver generally in good spirits and encouraging when interacting with the child? Is he or she helpful? Does the caregiver smile often at the child?
- **Having positive physical contact**—Does the caregiver hug the child, pat the child on the back, or hold the child's hand? Does the caregiver comfort the child?
- **Responding to vocalizations**—Does the caregiver repeat the child's words, comment on what the child says or tries to say, and answer the child's questions?
- **Asking questions**—Does the caregiver encourage the child to talk/communicate by asking questions that the child can answer easily, such as "yes" or "no" questions, or asking about a family member or toy?
- **Talking in other ways**—such as:
  - **Praising or encouraging**—Does the caregiver respond to the child's positive actions with positive words, such as "You did it!" or "Well done!"?
  - **Teaching**—Does the caregiver encourage the child to learn or have the child repeat learning phrases or

items, such as saying the alphabet out loud, counting to 10, and naming shapes or objects? For older children, does the caregiver explain what words or names mean?

- **Telling and signing**—Does the caregiver tell stories, describe objects or events, or sing songs?
- **Encouraging development**—Does the caregiver help the child stand up and walk? For infants, does the caregiver encourage "tummy time"—activities the child does when placed on his or her stomach while awake—to help neck and shoulder muscles get stronger and to encourage crawling? For older children, does the caregiver help finish puzzles, stock blocks, or zip zippers?
- **Advancing behavior**—Does the caregiver encourage the child to smile, laugh, and play with other children? Does the caregiver support sharing between the child and other children? Does the caregiver give examples of good behaviors?
- **Reading**—Does the caregiver read books and stories to the child? Does the caregiver let the child touch the book and turn the pages? For older children, does the caregiver point to pictures and words on the page?
- **Eliminating negative interactions**—Does the caregiver make sure to be positive, not negative, in the interactions with the child? Does the caregiver take a positive approach to interacting with the child, even in times of trouble? Does the caregiver make it a point to interact with the child and not ignore him or her?

Source: Copyright © 2006 University of Nebraska-Lincoln Extension. Reprinted by permission.

Another important benefit of coparenting is that it brings fathers into the family on an emotional level. Some observers have concluded that fathers often "draw on their life at home to take care of their emotional needs, but . . . distance themselves from the emotional needs of other family members" (Larson, Wilson, Brown, Furstenberg, & Verma, 2002). Some fathers enjoy being nurtured at home but don't want to nurture others in the home or don't have the capacity to do so. The experience of coparenting can help men learn how to attend to the emotional needs of others. This is a skill that has often been neglected because in our culture we tend to socialize men for competition, not cooperation.

A problem with coparenting is that sometimes the marriage gets lost in the shuffle. The mother is working outside the home, caring for the children, doing housework; the father is doing the same. Two outside full-time jobs and the job of maintaining a family and household add up to at least three full-time jobs for only two people. Often the marriage is neglected while the spouses concentrate on their employment responsibilities and their family and household tasks.

The couple might be doing great at the office and great with the kids but still end up getting divorced because they forgot to focus on their relationship with each other. They need to remember that the foundation for the whole operation is a strong marriage.

Single Mothers

There is a growing number of single-parent mothers, primarily because women are having children out of wedlock, and secondly because of divorce from the father (Downs, 2003; Dye, 2008). The number of single-parent births is well over 1 million each year, which is more than one-third of all births. The rate of out-of-wedlock births is highest in the African American population (72%), drops among Hispanic women (36%), is lower in Asians (27%), and is lowest in Whites (25%). Younger women have by far the highest rates of out-of-wedlock births. About 90% of births to teenagers (15 to 19 years old) are out of wedlock, while the rate drops to 50% for women in their twenties and to 12% for women 30 years old and over (Martin, Hamilton, Sutton, Ventura, et al., 2009).

What is common among all single-parent mothers is the high level of stress and the low level of economic and emotional resources that these mothers have in their lives. One qualitative study of single mothers ranging in age from 33 to 44 years old reports the various challenges they face, including time management, coping with sick children as the sole caregiver, and contending with the negative social stigma surrounding their choice. The support of friends and family, in particular, helps them meet the challenges they face and enhances their level of life satisfaction. All 15 participants in this study said they received life's greatest joys from motherhood (Fill, 2002).

In a study of midlife independent single women who intentionally decided to enter solo parenthood, the women said they felt entitled to be single mothers because of four attributes: their age and related maturity, the level of personal responsibility they demonstrated, their emotional security, and their financial capabilities. Presenting a variety of economic, moral, and religious justifications, these women saw themselves as competent mothers (Bock, 2000).

Gay and Lesbian Parenting

Nearly one-quarter of all same-sex couples (lesbian couples and gay couples) are raising children. Nationwide, over one-third (34%) of lesbian couples are raising children compared to 22% of gay male couples (Herek, 2006). In contrast to same-sex couples, almost half (46%) of all married heterosexual couples have children.

After a major review of the studies comparing children of gay and lesbian parents to those raised by heterosexual couples, the American Psychological Association (2004) concluded that there was no difference in the children's adjustment, achievement, and overall well-being between the two groups. In another major review (Meezan & Rauch, 2005) on this topic, four conclusions were made about same-sex parenting. First, when comparing lesbian mothers and gay fathers, few differences were found with children raised by heterosexual parents. In some cases, children with same-sex parents did better in that they were more tolerant of diversity and more nurturing toward younger children. Second, children of lesbian and gay parents are not confused about their gender identity and were not more likely to be homosexual. Third, there were no differences between children in cognitive abilities, behavior, and emotional development in the two types

This is the first generation in the United States where gay and lesbian couples have openly raised children who are now reaching adolescence and young adulthood.

of families. Finally, there appears to be little difference in the parenting style and effectiveness of same-sex parents compared to heterosexual parents.

A relatively new trend is the increasing number of gay and lesbian couples who are having and raising children. Some of the children are the biological offspring of one of the persons, and some are from a previous relationship or marriage. Some lesbian couples have used donor insemination to have their own child, and more gay male couples are choosing to adopt children.

This is the first generation in the United States where gay and lesbian couples have openly raised children who are now reaching adolescence and young adulthood. Studies have found that lesbian parents are very committed to creating a strong family (Herek, 2006). They are also concerned about the social challenges that their children will face when others learn that they are being raised by same-sex parents. The parents have generally found that they have had limited problems raising younger children, but some adolescents have felt embarrassed about their same-sex parents—especially among their peers.

In general, it appears that gay and lesbian couples are increasing their interest in raising children, and these families appear to be doing well. In addition to the normal challenges of raising adolescents, lesbian and gay couples and adolescents have to deal with the issue of social acceptance from others. The question about the eventual lifestyle and overall adjustment of the children will become more clear in the coming years.

Fatherhood and Motherhood Today

Coparenting may be gaining popularity as an ideal, but the reality in many cases is quite different. Although the images of father as breadwinner and mother as nurturer are slowly breaking down, new images—especially for fathers—have not yet taken hold. More than half of American mothers with children under 18 are now in the workforce, but many fathers have not become proportionately involved in nurturing tasks. The value of fatherhood has not increased dramatically.

Margaret Mead once wrote that "motherhood is a biological necessity, but fatherhood is a social invention." James Garbarino explains that parenthood for women is clear, because it is tied to their essential biological role in the process of bringing children into the world. But the role of the father is ambiguous and relies on cultural prescriptions (Garbarino, 2000, p. 11).

Some scholars have gone so far as to ask, Is the father even a part of the family? David Blankenhorn (1999, 2004, 2007) has found that nearly 40% of children live in homes where the biological father is not present. Wade Horn (2010) estimates that 6 out of 10 children born in the 1990s will be "fatherless" before reaching adulthood. What forces are responsible for these trends? And what can be done about them?

The Absent Father. Two major threats to a father's presence in a child's life are divorce and nonmarital childbearing, both of which are increasing. Marriages are continuing to fail at a high rate, and a growing number of families are starting out without a father (Dye, 2008). More than one-third of births are to single women. Virtually all children born outside of marriage live with their mothers, and in two-thirds of these cases, the father never establishes paternity.

In 90% of divorce cases, the children reside with their mothers. Many fathers, no longer living with their children, struggle to stay involved with them. But research has shown a pattern of gradual withdrawal by nonresidential fathers and growing alienation between fathers and children. One large national study found that about two-thirds of children of divorce had poor relationships with their fathers; among children whose parents were not divorced, less than a third (29%) had poor relationships with their fathers (Nord & Zill, 1996). Conflict between the former spouses also affects the quality of the father–child relationship by creating strains on the child that may offset any advantages of having the father actively involved.

When fathers remain in frequent contact and when conflict between the parents is low, fathers are more likely to make regular child support payments. There is a strong association between a divorced father's economic support and the well-being of his children. So frequent contact, low parental conflict, and economic support have a positive effect on the child's well-being. Nevertheless, many fathers would like to have the opportunity to contribute to their children's lives in deeper and more meaningful ways.

When a child is born, a father is born.

—FREDERICK BUECHNER

The Father as Nurturer. Research in child development has shown that fathers are just as capable as mothers in performing nurturing tasks (assuming the fathers are living with their children). Children can establish attachment relationships with fathers as they do with mothers. Fathers respond to the needs of their infants, picking up on their cues, just as mothers do. When mothers are present, however, fathers tend to back off and defer to them.

Fathers are more likely to be involved in the care of children if the parents are dual earners, but especially when the mother works different hours than the father. When parents work the same hours, mothers tend to come home to a "second shift" of family work (DeLuccie, 1995).

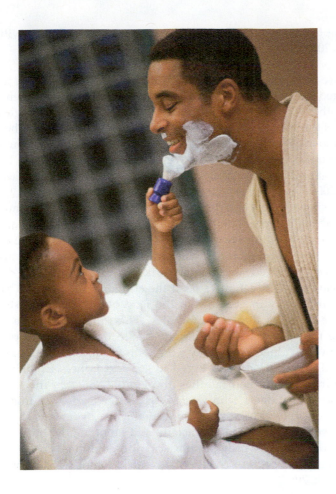

Many fathers are fully capable of nurturing and caring for their children.

Some studies report that women want men to be nurturing in their families, whereas other studies have shown that many mothers do not want increased father involvement (Gaunt, 2008; Goldberg, Downing, & Sauck, 2008; Hogan, 1993). The home is said to be a place of power and control for women, whereas the workplace is where men have traditionally dominated. Some women do not want to share their power or their role as the "more important parent." Men's involvement as fathers can be shaped, positively or negatively, by the mothers' expectations and support.

Schoppe-Sullivan (2010) discussed the gatekeeping of mothers and how mothers can have dramatic effects on how fathers father. This author makes the argument that fathers' behavior affects mothers' behaviors and vice versa. For example, if fathers are hesitant in responding to their children's needs, mothers are likely to step in and address those needs. On the other hand as gatekeepers, mothers can let fathers know that they are not doing things right, or can belittle their efforts. Schoppe-Sullivan suggests that both mothers and fathers should be aware of these possible family dynamics and take initiative to do what they need to do and want to do as parents.

In sum, countless fathers are fully capable of nurturing and caring for their children, but other factors—social, cultural, and interpersonal—tend to discourage them from doing so wholeheartedly. This is particularly unfortunate in light of the belief, put forth by some feminist scholars, that as more men become involved in nurturing tasks, inequalities in the workplace and the family will be reduced (Silverstein, 2010; Silverstein & Auerbach, 2000).

Responsible Fatherhood. What is the appropriate role for a father? It must first be acknowledged that every society constructs and defines roles for men and women; the role of father is no exception. In our society today, there is no single definition or description of this role. If a father is living at home with his children, he may be married and coparenting or single and parenting alone. Living apart from his children, he may be young and unwed, with or without paternity established. If divorced, he may have joint physical or legal custody or just visitation rights (Doherty, Erickson, & LaRossa, 2006; Lee & Doherty, 2007).

Although single fathers and divorced fathers with custody have nurturing roles thrust upon them, it appears that many other fathers in our society are given quite a wide latitude in how involved they want to be in the family. Unlike mothering, fathering appears to be a choice that men make in the face of contextual pressures. They can be very involved—or they can walk away.

To develop new roles, fathers need the support of mothers. They also need the support of society in general—in the workplace, in the courts, and in the social service agencies that serve families. This support may be forthcoming. Recognizing the holistic nature of family health, family service programs now attempt to involve fathers when they work with families. Additionally, new community-based programs have emerged to support fathers in their efforts to be responsibly involved in their families. Jim Levine and Ed Pitt, discussing their experience as practitioners who work with families, advance this definition of paternal responsibility: A responsible father waits to have a child until he is prepared to support the child, financially and emotionally; he establishes legal paternity; and he actively provides physical and emotional care for the child, as well as financial support, in cooperation with the mother (Levine & Pitt, 1995; Levine & Pleck, 2002).

> *The best gift a father can give his children*
> *Is to love their mother.*
>
> —ANONYMOUS

Good Fathering Makes a Real Difference in Children. Kristin A. Moore (Moore, 1998, 2010) of Child Trends, a private organization that monitors research and policies related to children and parenting, conducted a major review of research on fathering. She found that fathers can have a very positive impact on their children's development—whether or not the father lives with the children or is a noncustodial partner. The specific conclusions from this review are as follows:

- The more fathers are involved in the routine activities of their children, the more likely the children will have fewer behavior problems, be more sociable, and do better in school.
- Fathers often promote children's development more through physical play, whereas mothers do it through talking and teaching.
- Across different ethnic groups, fathers tend to assume the important role of economic provider, protector, and caregiver.
- Fathers who provide economically for their children also stay more involved with their children, even if they live apart.
- Fathers who pay child support tend to have children who behave better and do better in school.

When a Child Dies

The loss of a child creates a unique crisis in a family. No individual experiences the crisis in the same way another does, and each family is different. Though common themes of grief and bereavement occur time and time again, each family experiences the crisis in its own desperate way.

We do not use the word *desperate* lightly here, because every parent we have talked with in our work as counselors and researchers over the past 30 years has been plunged into dreadful unhappiness in the aftermath of the child's death. Many parents consider suicide because of the death. Living becomes almost unbearable for most. Mothers and fathers have told us of slitting their wrists, trying to kill themselves in an automobile crash, trying to overdose on drugs, turning on the engine of the car in a closed garage.

The vast majority of parents who have experienced the loss of a child see the death as the most devastating crisis they have experienced in their lives. The child's death is clearly a catastrophe for families—mothers, fathers, brothers, sisters, grandmothers, grandfathers, and other close relatives and friends—and the responsibility falls to each of us in society to help these stricken people in any way we can. They are clearly crushed in a life-threatening and spiritually numbing situation.

And yet, parents do survive the loss of their child. They turn to each other for comfort, to their relatives and friends, and to professionals in their community. Many individuals suffering from the loss of a child say that their belief in God was helpful and that being able to tell themselves that their child was with God was one of the few comforts they received. But others caution that they sometimes couldn't sit back and wait for God to help, "You've got to get out of your rut yourself."

Commitment, togetherness, and the ability of partners and other family members to take turns being strong for each other are also seen as positive ways of enduring the loss of a child. A final common denominator seems to be a person's simple ability to survive—to get up in the morning and get through the day, to force concentration on tasks that may seem irrelevant to the situation. One woman found herself thinking, "How can I scrub this floor? My child is dead." But she knew she had to keep busy and involved, if even on such a basic level.

As the months and years after the death of the child pass, many parents and grandparents express surprise that they have survived the tragedy. Once the realization sinks in that they will live though their child did not, they find strength in themselves they never thought they had. Most of them grimly acknowledge the truth of one mother's words: "Now I can survive anything." (Visit the Web sites of Compassionate Friends and the M.I.S.S. Foundation for excellent resources.)

Educational Programs and Resources for Parents

In meeting the challenges of raising children, parents often turn to professionals for guidance, either for education or for therapy. **Parent education** usually involves a presentation of information in a group setting followed by a group discussion of generic parenting problems, such as communication, discipline, imparting values to children, sibling rivalry, and choosing adequate child care. The focus is on common issues that parents face and general principles that are useful for thinking about and dealing with these challenges.

In **family therapy,** a therapist typically works with a single family with one or more specific problems, including sexual abuse, spouse abuse, child abuse or neglect, a runaway child, a child's attempted suicide, a child's coming out as a gay or lesbian, or the abuse of alcohol or other drugs. Though the dividing line between education and therapy tends to be somewhat blurry, educational programs tend to involve more participants and representatives of many families, while therapy tends to involve a single family and fewer people. Education for parents tends to aim at preventing problems before they begin, while family therapy tends to deal with more severe problems after they have occurred. The American Association for Marital and Family Therapy (AAMFT) is the leading professional organization in the United States specializing in couple and family therapy (2010). The National Council on Family Relations is the leading professional organization focusing on educational programs for parents and families in the United States. Founded in 1938, the NCFR awards Certified Family Life Educator (CFLE) to qualified professionals. This is the only international program that certifies family life educators (National Council on Family Relations, 2010).

Parent education has a long history in America, and has been traced back to 1700 (Bjorklund, 1977). Over the past 300 years, parent educators have developed a remarkable and evolving collection of educational programs for parents, meeting every imaginable need. Following is a sampling of the diverse programs currently available.

Abusive and Neglectful Parents. The explosion of child abuse and neglect reports that began in the 1970s, and the media attention that followed, prompted a nationwide response. Countless programs for parents under stress and in need of parenting advice and support were created and continue to thrive today.

Adoptive Parents. Adoptive parent associations and adoption agencies are teaming up to form support groups for adoptive parents, including support for parents involved in transracial and international adoption.

Alcohol and Other Drugs. AA, Al-Anon, Alateen, and countless other organizations have been created to help individuals and families deal with alcohol and other drug problems. Parent–child issues are common sources of discussion in these groups, of course. Special programs for adolescents who are chemically dependent abound, as do programs for the adult children of alcoholics.

Blue-Collar Parents and Parents with Lower Incomes. These parents have been unfairly criticized for lack of interest in parenting programs, but there is good evidence to indicate that if professionals design programs for the specific needs of these parents, the interest is there.

Bereaved Parents. Many local and national organizations have formed across the country to provide support and education for parents who have lost a child.

Business Community Programs for Parents. Increasing numbers of executives have begun to realize that worker productivity is intimately associated with how well the worker's family is doing. Employee assistance programs have sprung up in businesses and government to deal with the stresses of managing home and work, and wellness programs to focus on social and behavioral health issues, including parenting, are common.

Childbirth Education. Historically speaking, this has been one of the easiest types of parent education programs to get people involved in. Professionals complain all the time that it is difficult to fill a meeting room with parents. But childbirth educators are enjoying tremendous positive response. Perhaps it is the fear of childbirth that motivates many couples to attend prepared childbirth meetings. Whatever their reasons for attending, the classes can be very beneficial.

Couple and Family Enrichment Programs. Professionals are aware that parenting does not occur in a vacuum. The quality of a couple's relationship critically affects how well the partners are doing as parents. Many parent education programs target couple issues, for the couple is the foundation of a two-parent family.

Crisis Nurseries and Respite Care Facilities. Many social agencies around the country run crisis nurseries and other short-term care facilities for children and parents. The goals of the organizations vary, but the general idea is that the parent is helped in tough times, and the professionals get a chance to teach the parent new skills and enhance self-esteem so crises are not as common in the family.

Farm and Ranch Families. Programs for economically vulnerable and distressed farm and ranch families have been created by community-based mental-health teams, church groups, and the USDA's Extension Service. Economic problems of the family often have negative consequences for marriage and family relationships.

Foster Parents. Many communities have developed approaches to helping foster parents, including kin, understand and meet the challenges of this unique type of parenting.

Grandparents. The dramatic increase in past decades in the numbers of grandparents raising grandchildren has motivated the development of educational programs for grandparents.

The Mass Media. We have been rather hard on the media in this textbook, for much of what is seen on television, in the movies, on the Internet, in magazines and newspapers, and on the radio are destructive to positive couple and family relationships. Fortunately, there are some wonderful parent education programs available via the mass media.

Military Families. Millions of families in the United States are relatively rootless, moving from base to base and assignment to assignment for the military. The stresses of picking up stakes regularly, and the enormous stress for families when a father or mother is serving in a war zone, affect parent–child relationships in many ways. Family support programs sponsored by the U.S. Department of Defense and many other governmental and private organizations bring needed resources to these parents under stress.

Minority-Group Parents. Support groups for parents of the various minority groups in our country are relatively common and are affiliated with religious institutions, counseling centers, and associations of various ethnic and cultural groups. These groups unite to reaffirm the beauty and importance of their cultural heritage, to gain strength through numbers in the quest for fair treatment, and to help each other deal with the problems parents of minority children face in America.

Newsletters and Internet Resources for Parents. One fascinating development is a series of newsletters for new parents, delivered in the mail or via the Internet. An agency puts a family's name on its mailing list and sends the newsletter each month as the baby grows. Research has shown that these newsletters can be very popular with the vast majority of parents who receive them.

Useful Web sites with information on parenting programs are innumerable. Here are five of our favorites: Family Action Centre, University of Newcastle, Australia (www.newcastle.-edu.au-/centre/fac); Kansas State University at Manhattan (www.oznet.ksu.edu); the National Council on Family Relations (www.ncfr.org); University of Missouri at Columbia Extension (www.extension.missouri.edu -/main/family/index.shtml); University of Nebraska-Lincoln Extension (www .ianrpubs.unl.edu/-epublic/pages/index.jsp).

Parenthood Decision Making. To be a parent or not to be a parent? That is not an easy decision to make, and there are scattered reports in the professional literature of programs for people on the horns of this dilemma.

Parents of Children with Developmental Disabilities. The unique aspects of raising a child with a physical or mental handicap have created a demand for programs focusing on these issues. Parent support groups satisfy a number of needs: to vent frustrations among people in the same boat; to band together to gain political clout in the struggle to improve programs for special needs children in the schools and society; and to educate members as to the most successful ways of interacting with a special child and enhancing the child's growth and development.

Parents of Sexual Minorities. Over the years countless programs and support groups have been created that help parents of sexual minority children: gays, lesbians, bisexuals, transgender, transsexual, and two-spirited identities. Many parents find it difficult to understand their children, and seek ways to support them in a world that can be hostile to them.

Preparation for Parenting Classes. Colleges and universities offer classes for people who wish to become parents some day and for students who are already parents.

Sexuality Education. Sex education programs for young people are often presented in schools, and the communication about sexuality is between the school teacher and the students. Another model that can be very exciting is an education for sexuality model that links parents and their children. Typically, parents and their teens meet together to discuss the issues in a classroom setting with a professional teacher. Then, on the way home from the session and in the following days, the parents and their teens are more open to communicating about sexual issues. In this particular model of education, the goal is not only information about sex and sexuality, but improved communication between parents and their children. Ideally, parents and their teenage children will feel more comfortable talking about issues that often cause embarrassment and discomfort. This way, education for sexuality is family-centered, rather than driven by the Internet, television, the movies, and other sources that generally have in mind, not the child's best interest, but money.

Single Parents. Parents Without Partners (2010) and many other social support and education groups have been created to help single mothers and fathers through local chapters, programs, and services. Joining the group expands the parent's network of supportive and understanding people to call upon in times of need.

Stepfamilies. Local organizations have developed programs for stepparents and stepchildren, and national stepfamily groups provide educational materials and conferences.

Teen Parent Programs. A good deal of energy has been focused on solving the problems teen parents face, and programs for them abound. The professionals and volunteers working with teen parents focus on enhancing the self-esteem of the young parent, helping to keep the parent in school, providing child care for the parent so she can further her education and have a brief respite from the pressures of parenting, and enhancing her skills in the day-to-day responsibilities of caring for a child.

Welcome Baby Programs and the First Three Years of Life. Motivated by consistent research findings in past decades on the importance of the early years of life, countless programs have been created to take over after the childbirth educators are finished with their work. These so-called Welcome Baby programs help the young family get off to a good start and stay with them until they are well established.

It scarcely needs to be said that some parents will need therapy even though they have attended parent education programs. Such parents should not feel guilty or incompetent—their problems are simply more complex than those that most parents have to face. For the majority of parents, however, it is hoped that educational materials found in the library, on the Internet, and at parent support meetings will suffice to provide the information and emotional encouragement needed to be successful as a parent.

The Joy and Enduring Satisfaction of Parenthood

An enduring challenge for parents is how to translate philosophy into action. One important goal is to provide children with a basic foundation upon which they can build. This is illustrated exquisitely by Kahlil Gibran's poem, *On Children:*

Your children are not your children.

They are the sons and daughters of Life's longing for itself.

They come through you but not from you,

And though they are with you yet they belong not to you.

You may give them your love but not your thoughts,

For they have their own thoughts.

You may house their bodies but not their souls,

For their souls dwell in the house of tomorrow,

which you cannot visit, not even in your dreams.

You may strive to be like them, but seek not to make them like you.

For life goes not backward nor tarries with yesterday.

You are the bows from which your children as living arrows are sent forth.

The archer sees the mark upon the path of the infinite, and He bends you with His might that His arrows may go swift and far.

Let your bending in the archer's hand be for gladness;

For even as He loves the arrow that flies, so He loves also the bow that is stable.

(1923/1976, pp. 18–19)

Each day, parents are confronted with difficult questions that have complex answers. To find these answers, parents must learn to relate their personal philosophy to what is actually occurring with their children:

- "I don't believe in spanking, but this kid is driving me crazy!"
- "I love to watch my children grow, but I also need a life of my own. How do I balance the two?"
- "One child has a soccer game, but we had all planned to go to a children's play."
- "He flunked his math test again. I told him I would help him study for it, but he didn't want to study. Should I let him suffer the consequences of failing?"
- "We have not gone out as a couple to the movies or for dinner for almost a year, but our kids always want more of us."

Objective: To experience the wonders of life as a family

Supplies needed: A moonlit night, the book *Owl Moon* by Jane Yolen and illustrator John Schoenherr, snow (optional)

Step-by-Step instructions:

1. Read *Owl Moon.* (If you cannot get the book, don't worry, you can still do the rest!)
2. On a moonlit, snowy night, take a walk to hear the owls. It does not matter if you don't hear owls.
3. Listen to the snow squeaking as you walk.
4. Whisper.
5. Find joy in each other.

Discussion Questions:

What did you discover on your walk? (Did you see your breath, hear the sound of the snow, see the stars, see the moon, what was it like being together, etc.?)

What did you like most about your walk?
What are some other things in nature you would like to experience?

Remember, don't get so wrapped up in making it meaningful that you forget to just enjoy.

Variation:

What other books could you read?

Source: Family Treasures: Creating Strong Families (p. 138) by John DeFrain and the University of Nebraska For Families Writing Team, 2006. Lincoln, NE: University of Nebraska–Lincoln Extension. Copyright © 2006 University of Nebraska–Lincoln Extension. Reprinted by permission of the publisher.

"What was life like before you had children?" Many parents respond, "I cannot imagine what it was like anymore. It has been such an emotional and overwhelming journey since the kids came along." Children take control of a parent's life and a parent's heart. They bring a considerable amount of stress to the parent's life; there is no question about that. But we cannot afford to discount the engagement and fascination and joy they spark in our lives. Each day is a new day for a child, and watching the story unfold can be a delight to loving parents. What will the next chapter of the story bring? What will the children do next? What will they become in life? As one father put it so well, "I suppose I could have concentrated on my career more if I hadn't had children, but love has always counted far more to me than money. You can't hold a $100 bill in your lap and read a story to it."

There are joys and challenges when raising children. Sometimes we forget to have a good time and actually enter the child's world and see things from the child's perspective. The activity described in Box 12.4 will help a parent do just that.

Summary

- New research indicates that children add to individual happiness when people are in cohabiting or marriage relationships. Most couples experience a decline in marital satisfaction after the birth of their first child, but a minority of couples experienced increased marital satisfaction.
- A national survey of 50,000 married couples identified five key parenting strengths. Happy couples were more than twice as likely as unhappy couples to agree on how to share the responsibilities of raising their children. Happy couples were almost twice as likely as unhappy couples to be satisfied with the amount of attention they focus on their marriage versus the amount of attention they focus on their children. Almost twice as many happy couples reported agreeing on how to discipline their children as did unhappy couples. Happy couples were much more likely than unhappy couples to feel that they had grown closer since having children. And happy couples reported that they were more satisfied in their marriage since having children, compared to unhappy couples.

- Paradoxically, parenthood is both very challenging and very satisfying emotionally.
- Conventional wisdom and folk mythology on the subject of parenthood in our society abounds. Although many people might believe the conventional "truths," research on parenthood indicates that the picture is more complex.
- Researchers have found that voluntarily childless individuals and couples can have just as satisfying a life as those who have children. New research describes the process couples go through as they make decisions about having children.
- Parenting styles differ, and some are more effective than others. The democratic style is favored today because it appears to produce self-reliant children who cope well with stress. Other parenting styles that are authoritarian, permissive, rejecting, and uninvolved tend to produce children with more behavioral and academic problems.
- Parenting styles can be related to the cohesion and flexibility dimensions of the Couple and Family Map.
- How to discipline children is a major issue for many parents, as well as a source of some debate in our society.
- Corporal punishment is widely used in the United States. Stress can sometimes cause parents to use physical punishment as a result of cascading circumstances.
- Quality of day care can be a key component in determining whether child care is beneficial. These findings are also evident in following children long term.
- Numerous studies demonstrate the important role a father plays in a child's development—whether he lives with the child or is a noncustodial parent. Mothers' and fathers' behavior can affect how involved the other parent is in the lives of children.
- In the United States, many parent education programs have been developed as a response to the challenges of raising children and the diversity of American families. Many trained professionals provide both information and one-on-one therapy.

Key Terms

child-free alternative	psychodynamic theory
parental support	organismic theory
parental control	behaviorist
democratic parenting	learning theories
authoritarian parenting	reinforcement
permissive parenting	cascading circumstances
rejecting parenting	coparenting
uninvolved parenting	parent education
bidirectional effects	family therapy

Activities

1. Read Kahlil Gibran's poem *On Children* carefully and write a brief essay analyzing his philosophy of parenthood. On what points do you agree and disagree?

2. Set a time and place to interview a couple you know well about their beliefs on rearing children and the challenges and joys they have experienced over the years as parents. A good interview takes careful planning: Write down 15 to 20 questions you want to be sure to ask. Make sure to ask about how children affected their relationship. Then write up your interview in a short paper and share it with the class or a small group. You might like to audio-record or video-record the interview. (These might even become family treasures and make great gifts.)

3. Parenthood can be a challenging task; children are often too busy and too overwhelmed by their own problems and concerns to think about their parents' feelings. Write a letter to your parents, thanking them for all the things they have done for you and for their unique human qualities.

4. If you do not have children of your own, spend an afternoon with some children you know—your nieces and nephews, a neighbor's children, or a friend's kids. Reflect on your reactions to this brief "parenting" experience.

Suggested Readings

Bellous, J. E. (2010). *Children, spirituality, loss and recovery*. New York: Routledge.

Belsky, J. (2006). Early child care and early child development: Major findings of the NICHD study of early child care. *European Journal of Developmental Psychology, 3*, 95–110.

Bloch, E. (2007). The daddy difference. *Parenting, 21*(5), 81–84. The author argues that fathers let kids take risks while mothers are too protective because of their attachment to the child, which developed during pregnancy. And fathers trust themselves more than experts, while mothers are more sensitive to getting it right; they tend to compare notes with other parents more than dads do.

Boyd-Franklin, N., Franklin, A., & Toussaint, P. (2000). *Boys into men: Raising our African American teenage sons*. New York: Penguin Putnam. "A convincing argument to parents that educating an African-American teenage son and keeping him alive, healthy, and out of jail past the age of 25 years is no small task."

Clark, R. A., Richard-Davis, G., Hayes, J., Murphy, M., & Pucheu Theall, K. (2009). *Planning parenthood: Strategies for success in fertility assistance, adoption, and surrogacy*. Baltimore: Johns Hopkins University Press.

Compassionate Friends. (2010). Through a network of more than 625 chapters, with locations in all 50 states, as well as Washington, D.C., and Puerto Rico, for the past four decades Compassionate Friends has been supporting bereaved families after the death of a child. Web site: http://www.compassionatefriends.org/.

Crittenden, A. (2001). *The price of motherhood: Why the most important job in the world is still the least valued*. New York: Metropolitan Books. "An easy, informative, enjoyable read."

Diamond, M. (2007). *My father before me: How fathers and sons influence each other throughout their lives.* New York: W. W. Norton. Suggested reading from the American Association for Marital and Family Therapy.

Doherty, W. (2000). *Take back your kids.* Notre Dame, IN: Sorin. How parents can rescue their family from being taken over by outside activities.

Douglas, S. J., & Michaels, M. W. (2004). *The mommy myth: The idealization of motherhood and how it has undermined women.* New York: Free Press. Cultural forces are at work to "return women to the Stone Age."

Eunice Kennedy Shriver National Institute of Child Health and Human Development, NIH, DHHS. (2006). *The NICHD study of early child care and youth development (SECCYD): Findings for children up to age 4½ years (05-4318).* Washington, DC: U.S. Government Printing Office. This government-funded $200 million study, which began in 1991, is by far the most ambitious study of the effects of nonmaternal child care, and about families who use child care as well as those who do not. A free 62-page report is available on the Web site at http://www.nichd.nih.gov/publications/.

Family Action Centre, University of Newcastle, Australia. (2010). Useful information and resources on parenthood. Web site: www.newcastle.edu.au-/centre/fac.

Gottman, J. M. (2007). *And baby makes three: The six-step plan for preserving marital intimacy and rekindling romance after baby arrives.* New York: Crown.

Helburn, S. W., & Bergmann, B. R. (2002). *America's childcare problem: The way out.* New York: Palgrave. A holistic overview of all aspects of child care in America.

Jacobs, N. N. (2006). *Coping with infertility: Clinically proven ways of managing the emotional roller coaster.* Routledge Mental Health. Web site: http://www.routledgemental health.com. For couples trying to better understand and cope with issues involving infertility.

Kansas State University at Manhattan. (2010). Useful information on parenting and families on the KSU Extension Web site: www.oznet.ksu.edu/.

Lino, M., & Carlson, A. (2009). *Expenditures on children by families, 2008.* U.S. Department of Agriculture, Center for Nutrition Policy and Promotion. Miscellaneous Publication No. 1528-2008. Web site: http://www.cnpp.usda.gov/ExpendituresonChildrenbyFamilies.htm.

M.I.S.S. Foundation. (2010). The MISS Foundation is a 501 (c) 3, volunteer-based organization committed to providing crisis support and long-term aid to families after the death of a child from any cause. MISS also participates in legislative and advocacy issues, community engagement and volunteerism, and culturally competent, multidisciplinary, education opportunities. Web site: http://www.missfoundation.org/.

National Center for Health Statistics. (2009). National Vital Statistics Reports. *Births: Final data for 2006, 57(7),* January 7, and *Births: Preliminary data for 2007, 57(12),* March 18.

National Council on Family Relations. (2010). The premier U.S. organization focusing on family life education and the preparation and certification of professionals in the field. Web site: www.ncfr.org.

Rowe, D. (2007). *My dearest enemy, my dangerous friend: Making and breaking sibling bonds.* Routledge Mental Health. Web site: http://www.routledgementalhealth .com. A book for those who have struggled with the pain and pleasure of brotherhood and sisterhood.

Schooler, J. E., & Atwood, T. C. (2008). *The whole life adoption book: Realistic advice for building a healthy adoptive family.* Colorado Springs, CO: NavPress. What to consider before adopting; creating a nurturing family environment; communication about adoption from infancy through adolescence; adopting internationally transracially; understanding attachment and the impact of trauma; when a child wants to search for birthparents.

Sheldon, A. (2009). *Big brother now: A story about me and our new baby* and *Big sister now: A story about me and our new baby.* Magination Press. Web site: http://www .magination-press.com.

Skogrand, L., Hatch, D., & Singh, A. (2009). Strong marriages in Latino culture. In R. Dalla, J. DeFrain, J. Johnson, & D. Abbott (Eds.), *Strengths and challenges of new immigrant families: Implications for research, policy, education, and service* (pp. 117–134). Lexington, MA: Lexington Press.

Smith, J. A. (2009). *The daddy shift: How stay-at-home dads, breadwinning moms, and shared parenting are transforming the American family.* Boston: Beacon Press. What happens when dads stay home? What do stay-at-home fathers struggle with and what do they rejoice in?

Tamis-Lemonda, C. S., & Cabrera, N. (2003). *Handbook of father involvement: Multidisciplinary perspectives.* Mahwah, NJ: Erlbaum. Experts from diverse scientific disciplines share their interests in the topic of father involvement in the lives of children.

University of Missouri at Columbia Extension. (2010). Information on parenthood and families. Web site: www.extension.missouri.edu-/main/family/.

University of Nebraska–Lincoln Extension. (2010). Parenting and family issues from a strengths-based perspective. Web site: www.ianrpubs.unl.edu/-epublic/pages/index.jsp.

Wilcox, B. (2010). *The state of our unions: When marriage disappears.* Retrieved from http://www.stateofourunions .org/2010/index.php.

Wilcox, B. (2011). *The state of our unions: When baby makes three.* Retrieved from http://www.stateofourunions .org/2011/SOOU2011.pdf.

Visit the text-specific Online Learning Center at **www.mhhe.com/olson8e** for practice tests, chapter summaries, and PowerPoint slides.

13 *M*Midlife and Older Couples

Intimacy, Strengths, and Diversity

Family Life in the Middle Years

Family Life in the Later Years

Summary

Key Terms

Activities

Suggested Readings

Intimacy, Strengths, and Diversity

Intimacy in the middle and later years of life looks very different from intimacy in the earlier stages of the life cycle. Freedom from raising children for couples in the middle years of life may pave the way for new sexual and emotional intimacy. For those in later years, sexual intimacy in marriage or couple relationships may change with added health problems. Emotional intimacy in couple relationships, however, may be very solid as couples grow old together. There are strengths in couple and family relationships for people in the middle and later years of life. They have learned many of life's lessons and can pass this knowledge on to others.

Intimate emotional relationships with adult children may increase as these children have children of their own and they now have shared the life-changing experience of having children. Relationships with grandchildren may be deeper and take on new meaning as they see these young people providing a continuation of themselves to another generation.

Couples are likely to find themselves in the sandwich generation, which means they are caring for their aging parents and also have responsibilities for adult children who may have moved back into the home. This may create stress, but it also may create new opportunities to tap into family strengths and unexpected intergenerational family relationships (Skogrand, Henderson, & Higginbotham, 2006). Below is a true story about such a family:

> Sandra and Martin were in their mid-50s and for a couple of years they had been in an empty nest. Their children were off to college, and the major responsibilities of raising children were done. It was great. They could go out when they wanted, take trips on the spur of the moment, or sleep late, with no major responsibilities except their jobs to tie them down. The spark was back in their relationship with limited stress in their lives and more opportunity to spend time together
>
> Several months ago, however, their son, Adam, dropped out of school and moved home to make a decision about career goals and decide where he wanted to continue his education. It was to be temporary, but there was much ambiguity about future plans. He quickly got a low-paying job and lived with Sandra and Martin. He was really not much bother. He took care of his own meals, picked up after himself, and got himself to work. Sandra and Martin were looking forward to spending time with their son who was now an adult.
>
> About the same time Adam moved home, the decision was made that Sandra's mother who lived 800 miles away would move to a nursing home in their town. Both Sandra and Martin viewed the move positively. For the first time in her adult life Sandra would be able to have quality time with her aging mother.
>
> Soon after the move, however, Sandra's mother's health began to decline. She needed daily visits and frequent medical appointments and conferences. Work for Sandra involved long days, ending with several hours spent at the nursing home in the evening. There were many 14- and 15-hour days for Sandra, who would drop into bed exhausted, only to do it again the next day. Martin's days also became longer as he picked up most of the household responsibilities in addition to his job.
>
> Although Adam generally took care of himself, he still counted on his parents' help in buying a new car and applying and making arrangements to enroll in school. He had anticipated that he would have his parents available to help him plan his future, but they were rarely available.

This sandwich generation family was experiencing stress and responsibility at a time when the middle-aged couple expected a less stressful time. As you read this true story, you may be feeling yourself tense up as you think about all the responsibilities in their lives. The couple reflected on this time a year after Sandra's mother died and their son had gone back to college. They said it had been stressful and they did not want to do it again. They also said, however, that there were many positive things that happened in their family relationships during this time. Adam got to know his grandmother as he sat by her bed in the last weeks of her life. Adam's grandmother had talked about how she loved getting to know her grandson as an adult—something that she had not anticipated before she died. Sandra developed the intimate relationship with her mother that she had hoped for. In fact, she says this special time was short and at times difficult, but was also one of the best times of her life. Martin and Sandra developed a closer couple relationship because they agreed that both generations needed them during this time.

The middle and later years of life are filled with surprises, some difficult and stressful, and also some positive things that are never anticipated. Individuals and couples in the middle and later years of life usually have developed skills to weather the storm and appreciate wonderful surprises.

In the middle years and later years of life there is diversity. Couples have been married for 50 or more years—accepting and loving their children, grandchildren, and great-grandchildren who have been married and divorced, who are in stepfamilies, and who may be in gay or lesbian relationships. Many folks in these middle and later years have problems with these new family structures, but many embrace this diversity and show unconditional love to family members.

Family Life in the Middle Years

After the kids leave home, some parents suffer from the empty nest syndrome; others change the locks!

—ANONYMOUS

What images does the term *middle age* conjure up? For most young college students, their mom and dad are the first to come to mind. Middle age can be a relaxing time, a time of thankfulness that the challenges and fears of youth have been overcome. But middle age can bring new pressures, new challenges.

"Life begins at 40," an old saying goes. The kids may leave the nest. Family income may reach a peak. But *middlescence* can set in. In the middle years, some people mourn lost opportunities, the road not taken, and wonder what their lives would have been like if only they had been bolder, smarter, or luckier. Middlescents also often yearn for a taut young body and freedom from the grind.

In Erik Erikson's classic schema, middle age can be a time for generativity or stagnation (1950). The question of middle age is, "Can we remain productive despite boredom and malaise? (Can an old dog learn new tricks?)" Millions of people transform their lives in the middle years by starting new careers or falling in love. Those who are flexible, who can adapt to new circumstances and "roll with the punches," will be much more likely to succeed. The inflexible ones may survive but will probably not excel—and they will be less likely to enjoy the process of living than those who are flexible.

Defining Middle Age

A popular societal definition of **middle age** is the period of life between ages 35 and 65, but age alone does not tell the whole story, especially when applied to the middle years. The eminent gerontologist Bernice Neugarten notes philosophically that the middle years are the time when people begin to think about how many years they have left rather than how many they've already lived (1968). One middle-aged man described life as a rainbow: At the beginning are infancy, early childhood, adolescence, and young adulthood; around the very highest point of the rainbow are the middle years; and nearing the end of the rainbow are the later years of life. When one reaches the crest of the rainbow, the middle years, one can clearly see the remainder of life for the first time. "When I reached middle age," the man explained, "I saw the rest of my life clearly. It looked like more of the same old stuff I had grown tired of over the past 10 years. Some people might call it a middle-aged crisis," he continued. "I thought of it as a middle-aged opportunity, and I've been changing steadily ever since."

The post–World War II baby boom period ran from 1946 to 1964. Now this group of Americans is well into middle age, and the oldest **Baby Boomers** are in their 60s and many are collecting Social Security and even receiving Medicare benefits. This group of aging adults will have a decisive impact on society. For example, the percentage of Americans who are 65 years and older is expected to double in the next 25 years, when one in five Americans will be 65 years or older. Currently the age group 85 years and older is the fastest-growing segment of society (U.S. Census Bureau, 2012).

The growing numbers of Baby Boomers will put increasing pressure on society to focus more on retirement, health care, and empty-nest issues. Their buying power will impact consumer goods and health care systems. While our society is often portrayed as a youth-oriented culture, Baby Boomers will have a growing impact on shifting more attention to their group.

Middle Age: A Crisis or An Opportunity?

For some, **midlife crisis** is an apt term. During their 40s and 50s, many people will experience the death of a parent or family member, career changes, physical changes in appearance and health, and noticeable changes in relationships with a

One of the biggest changes of middle age is the children's departure from home for college or a job. Parents who are flexible usually enjoy the freedom from daily responsibility for their children and are likely to develop new interests or even start new careers.

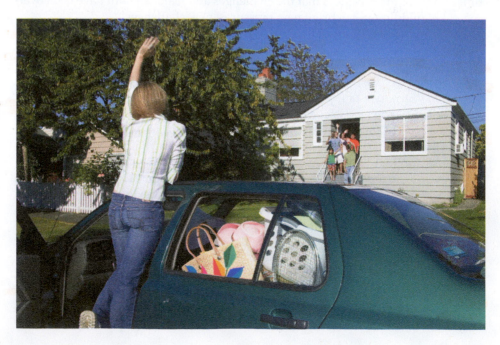

spouse and children. The realization that one's life is half over and that many goals have not been attained or that there is nothing new to look forward to can cause emotional upheaval.

Despite this common perception—and even the popularity of the term *midlife crisis*—evidence does not support the existence of a generalized midlife crisis. Although people do experience crisis and stress at important transition points in life, including midlife, data show that midlife is not any more stressful than other life stages. In fact, midlife is often a time of stability, freedom, and control, as well as a time to redefine life and relationships (Aldwin & Levenson, 2001; Lachman, 2004; Rosato, 2012).

Statistically, midlife does not bring about an increase in divorce, depression, suicide, or alcoholism. In fact, a survey found that people in their 40s find life more exciting than younger or older adults (National Opinion Research Center, 1996). With age comes greater work satisfaction and satisfaction with one's finances, a reduction in depression, and a rise in one's general happiness. Additionally, older people are less likely to divorce than younger people, and suicide rates drop during middle age (National Opinion Research Center, 1996). In fact, *early life* is more a time of crisis than midlife.

The Middle-Aged Person and the Working World

Middle age, especially for those in their 40s and 50s, can be a time when both men and women decide they can make a change in their work lives. Children might be leaving home, and financial obligations may seem less daunting. There are new opportunities for the major breadwinner to make a career change or for the caretaker of the children to go back to work or school. Some have even been able to retire early, in their late 40s and 50s, to explore new hobbies, start a business, or embark on a new career. For example, in 2009, 25% of those in the 45- to 54-year-old age group were already retired (Rainville, 2009, May).

The economic downturn that began in 2008 has made it difficult for some to retire early. Many saw their retirement funds diminish dramatically when the stock market fell. In one study conducted in the middle of the economic crisis, 27% of those approaching retirement (ages 55–64) reported that they were postponing plans to retire (Rainville, 2009). It was also found that 30% of those in the 45–54 age group felt it was somewhat likely that their job would be eliminated within the next year. Many who have lost their jobs are unlikely to find new employment in their current field. Opportunities for trying out new careers in midlife may no longer be an option. We do not know how long the economic downturn will continue, but we do know that it has affected the plans and opportunities for many in their middle years.

Sexuality in Middle Age

As noted in Chapter 6, sexual activity often declines steadily over the years of a marriage. Fortunately, among couples who are creative and committed, sex can remain a source of intense pleasure throughout the middle years. Two issues of concern during this time are menopause and "male menopause."

Menopause. The most dramatic age-related change in female reproductive functioning, after puberty, is **menopause**, the end of monthly menstrual periods. Sheehy

BOX 13.1 Diversity in Families

Childlessness: The Invisible Group

Much of our discussion in this chapter implies that children are part of the lives of those in middle and later years of life. Parenthood is often central to how we think about psychological growth and the life cycle (Dykstra & Hagestad, 2007). What about those who remained childless? What is the pathway to childlessness? What are the lives of those without children like?

The Context

Even though one in five people older than 65 years of age will be without children, this group of people is often invisible and is left out of the family studies literature (Dykstra & Hagestad, 2007). We might feel sympathy for those who involuntarily are childless, and some of us might assume that there is something deviant about those who deliberately made that choice. This stigma was even more evident several decades ago—when those who are now in the later years of life were at childbearing age.

Over the years we have changed how we talk about having children or not having children. In the 1970s, we began using the term *childfree*, implying that for some not having children was a conscious decision (Dykstra & Hagestad, 2007). The women's movement has also contributed to the idea that women have a choice and have control in childbearing. In recent years we have also seen less connection between marriage and having children, with the increase of single parenthood and cohabitation.

Pathways to Childlessness

In addition to consciously choosing to not have children, there are several factors that came into play that affected the ability and decision to have children for men and women who are now in their middle or later years of life. Timing was important, especially for women (Hagestad & Call, 2007). For most who are currently in the middle and later years of life, societal expectations were that marriage came before childbearing. Caring for aging family members, economic conditions, war, and social policy were just a few of the factors that might have affected marriage and, thus, childbearing. For example, one couple who are now in their 80s chose to get married because a farm was available for rent and farms did not often become available in the community. The man had a means of making a living, thus marriage was possible. Another man in this same community enlisted in the military during World War II. After being away for several years, he came back to a community with a limited number of available women to marry. He never married and remained childless.

In addition to infertility or choosing to be childless, some life patterns were more likely to correspond with childlessness than others. For example, those who delayed leaving home were more likely to remain childless (Hagestad & Call, 2007; Koropeckyj-Cox & Call, 2007). Those who were slower to make life transitions, such as

(1998) refers to menopause as the "silent passage" because it is so rarely discussed openly. Menopause occurs, on average, around the age of 50 but can begin as early as a woman's mid-30s or as late as her early 60s. Because of various hormonal changes, menopause signals the cessation of a woman's ability to have children. Reproductive organs shrink, and the amount of fatty tissue in the breasts and other parts of the body decreases. The vulva becomes thinner, losing its capacity to engorge with blood, and the vagina shrinks and loses some elasticity. Vaginal secretions that provide lubrication during intercourse diminish (Boston Women's Health Book Collective, 2006, 2011).

Many women experience distress—including irritability, insomnia, "hot flashes," headaches, and depression—during menopause. Historically, hormones to replace those no longer produced by the body have been prescribed to alleviate some of these effects. In 2002, however, a large clinical trial called the Women's Health Initiative reported that hormone treatment presented more health risks than benefits (Mayo Clinic, 2012). Hormone therapy can increase the risk of heart disease, breast cancer, stroke, and blood clots. The benefits of hormone therapy include decreased risk of osteoporosis or colorectal cancer. Women need to talk to their doctor to determine whether hormone therapy is the best treatment for them. For some, such as women at high risk for osteoporosis, the benefits of hormone therapy outweigh the risks.

leaving home, getting an education, or getting a job, were also more likely to be childless.

The Lives of Those Who Are Childless

What are the lives of childless middle-aged and aging adults like today? Childless couples and individuals have typically been very involved in the lives of children of other family members, including nieces and nephews, siblings, and cousins. In some cultures, such as American Indian and African American cultures, there has been a tendency to share children, especially among the female family members (Dykstra & Hegestad, 2007). With the increasing number of stepfamilies today, some have become stepparents. Others were deeply involved in the lives of children by being foster parents, teachers, or involved with other professions that involve working with children. Therefore, we cannot assume that childless individuals have not had interactions with children.

Research indicates there are some differences between adults who remained childless and those who had children. Women who are childless, and less likely to be married, are more likely to have higher levels of education and occupational status. Childless men, on the other hand, are likely to have lower socioeconomic status (Koropeckyj-Cox & Call, 2007). It has also been found that behaviors that have a negative effect on health, such as smoking and alcohol consumption, are more prevalent for those who did not have children, and this is especially true for men (Kendig, Dykstra, Gaalen, & Melkas, 2007). We might speculate that those with children had developed positive role model behaviors.

We might also expect that childless individuals are less involved in their community than parents, because children might be the impetus for such involvement. However, it has been found that there are no real differences in community participation between those who have children and those who do not (Wenger, Dykstra, Melkas, & Knipscheer, 2007). In terms of relationships with extended family members, these researchers found that childless adults had more contact with siblings, nieces, and nephews than parents, whereas parents had most of their contact with their adult children. It was also found that adults without children were more at risk for loneliness and isolation than parents. In the end stages of life, parents were more likely to depend on a spouse or adult children, and childless adults, who do not have those resources, were more likely to rely on formal institutional services. In general, childless older adults were more likely to live alone or in institutions, and it was more likely that women would fit this pattern than men (Koropeckyj-Cox & Call, 2007)—perhaps because women live longer and are more likely to be widowed, thus not having a spouse to live with.

In general, most women perceive menopause as a transition period rather than a problem. Even though physical responses change, a woman's perception of pleasure and satisfaction during intercourse may remain the same or may decrease or even become painful due to lack of lubrication and thinner vaginal tissues. There may also be a drop in libido with shifting hormones.

"Male Menopause." Sexual changes related to age also occur in men. Production of the male hormone **androgen** declines slowly and steadily in most men until about age 60, when it levels off. For most men, this decline in hormone production does not cause the emotional and physical changes that some women experience during menopause. In other men, the symptoms are so similar to those experienced by menopausal women that physicians label the condition **male menopause**, a term that generates some controversy in the medical community.

As men get older, the amount of fluid ejaculated with orgasm tends to diminish, as does the strength of the ejaculation. The testicles become smaller and less firm; erections become less frequent and also less rigid. By age 50, the average male may

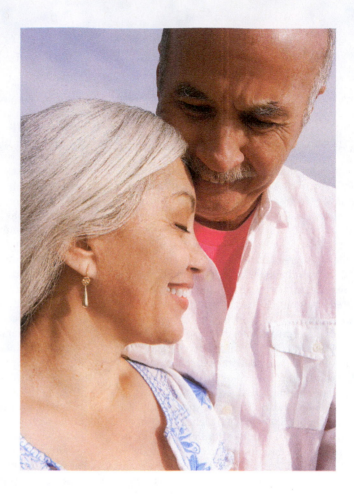

People between the ages of 43 and 50 usually come to terms with life, and are able to more realistically assess their strengths and weaknesses.

require 8 to 24 hours after orgasm before he is capable of having another erection. Most men also require more time to reach orgasm, but this can be viewed as a benefit, as a lengthening of the period of pleasure for both the man and his partner (Hyde & DeLamater, 2011).

The Middle-Aged Marriage

Many marriages are happier before children arrive and after they leave home. For many couples in the middle years, marital satisfaction may reach a low point and then increase as the adolescents leave home.

Strengthening Marriage in the Middle Years. A great deal can be learned about marriage from divorced people. Based on interviews with those who have experienced marital dissolution, here are some suggestions for strengthening marriage in the middle years:

- Establish priorities early in marriage, with the spouse at the top of the list. Do not allow parenthood to overshadow the marriage.
- Be alert for warning signs of marital problems, which include nagging, sarcasm, possessiveness, criticism, and personal discontent.

Successful middle-aged couples tend to be those who have shared feelings and activities throughout their marriage, in spite of the competing demands of jobs and children. They continue to express love and concern both verbally and physically.

- Strive toward equality in all aspects of the marriage. Each partner should feel important and powerful.
- Seek a balance between togetherness and personal growth; either extreme can be harmful to a marriage.
- Good sex in a relationship in the middle years does not come naturally; it is a result of a positive daily life together.
- Develop a network of friendships with other couples who are concerned about maintaining a quality marriage.
- Evaluate the marriage from time to time and attend a marriage enrichment workshop.
- Avoid boring or frustrating work situations; a midlife career change may be beneficial.
- Consider a lifestyle change rather than a partner change in middle age to add pizzazz to the marriage.
- A happy marriage is the key to a content spouse. The best way to deal with infidelity is to prevent it from occurring.

Divorce During the Middle and Later Years

An AARP study of couples who got divorced later in life found the participants emerged from the difficulties of divorce far happier and emotionally healthier than most of them would have dared to hope at the beginning of their journey. The researchers surveyed 1,147 men and women who divorced in their 40s, 50s, and 60s. The researchers found that 66% of the women said they had asked for the divorce, while 41% of the men said they asked for the divorce. More men were caught off guard by the coming divorce than women (26% to 14%). Men were likely to remarry sooner (Montenegro, 2004).

The AARP study found the causes of divorce at midlife and beyond are:

- Verbal, physical, or emotional abuse (34%)
- Different values, lifestyles (29%)
- Cheating (27%)
- Simply fell out of love/no obvious problems (24%)
- Alcohol or drug abuse (21%)
- Being a control freak (16%)
- Money problems (14%)
- Not carrying their weight in the marriage (14%)
- Fell in love with someone else (10%)
- Abandonment (10%)

Less than 5% to 8% of the respondents in the study checked *always being away, sexual problems, stepchildren,* and *in-laws* as reasons for the divorce. Not having children, religious differences, cultural differences, age differences, declining physical health, and homosexuality were named by less than 5% (Montenegro, 2004, p. 20).

The number of people ending long-term marriages after age 50 has increased dramatically. While the overall divorce rate in the United States has declined since 1990 somewhat, the divorce rate for those over age 50 has doubled. The surge spawned the term *gray divorce.* Jay Lebow, a psychologist at the Family Institute at Northwestern University, said, "If late-life divorce were a disease, it would be an epidemic" (Abrahms, 2012, p. 26).

What has caused the increase of divorces in the middle and later years? Sociologist Andrew Cherlin argues that as people's prospects for a long life have increased over the past decades, many are leaving unhappy marriages in quest of many more happy years ahead (Enright, 2004). One woman explained the reason for her divorce in midlife by saying, "If I hadn't been expected to live so long, I would have stayed with him. But I just couldn't see another 30 years in the marriage."

Empty Nest, Spacious Nest, or Cluttered Nest?

The term **empty-nest syndrome** describes the feelings of malaise, emptiness, and lack of purpose that parents sometimes experience when their children leave home. Some parents do suffer from these feelings, and most go through a period of adjustment when their children leave the nest. But the empty nest is a boon for many parents, giving them more time and energy to invest in their marriage. To emphasize the positive aspects of this time, we prefer the term **spacious nest**. There is more room in the home for the parents' things—and more money and time in the marriage for each other. Of course we need to keep in mind that not all couples choose to have children (Box 13.1), and may not experience this aspect of their midlife years.

The opposite of the spacious nest is the parental nest refilled with **boomerang kids**—adult children who return home for economic reasons, because of divorce, the need to find a safety net, extended education, drug/alcohol problems, or during a temporary transition period. The stereotypic image of this situation is of a self-centered young adult returning home to place an unfair economic burden on parents who resent the invasion of their new-found privacy. While this image may represent the experience of some, boomerang children are for the most part well tolerated by parents as long as the return home is temporary and does not happen too many times (Dickler, 2012; Nance-Nash, 2012; New York Life, 2012; Wang & Morin, 2009).

Today, middle-aged parents of young adults are less likely to find themselves with empty nests than were their counterparts 35 years ago. More young adults are postponing marriage or are marrying and divorcing. A phenomenon called the **cluttered nest** occurs when adult children return to the parental nest to live after college graduation while they get established professionally and financially and save enough money to move into their own apartments or homes.

As one middle-aged mother in suburban Washington, D.C., asked rhetorically when recalling the time her daughter had returned home with two preschool-aged children after her divorce:

"What was I supposed to do? Slam the door in her face? She had no money. Her husband's lawyer was threatening to take the kids away, and she was so depressed I thought she might overdose on pills. I had to help. I love my daughter and I love my grandchildren.

"I knew they wouldn't be with us forever. I knew she would be getting back on her feet soon enough. I knew I could help. What are families for?"

Caught in the Middle: The Sandwich Generation

Besides struggling with adolescents, empty or cluttered nests, and boomerang kids, people in their middle years are also apt to have growing responsibilities for their aging parents. For this reason, middle-aged parents have been described as the **sandwich generation**. Researchers agree that daughters are more likely to assume the caregiving role than sons, and somewhere between half and two-thirds of adult women will assume this role at some time in their lives (Cicirelli, 2001, 2003).

Caring for an elderly family member can be a burden for the caregiver, but it can also increase intimacy between a parent and an adult child. One study of 133 pairs of adult caregiving daughters and their elderly mothers reported that about half the mothers and daughters saw their relationship as having been positively affected by the caregiving situation, whereas most of the rest reported no change in the quality of their relationships (Walker & McGraw, 1999).

For some middle-aged parents, though, the stress of caring for their children—whether adolescents or young adults—and for frail aging parents can be too great. Exhaustion and anger can reach a boiling point and can create intergenerational conflicts. These can also produce neglect or abuse of the elderly, which unfortunately is relatively common in the United States (National Center on Elder Abuse, 2012).

Caring for children and aging parents can cause stress for the marriage relationship (Skogrand et al., 2006). A married couple may be looking forward to freedom from caregiving responsibilities and to renewing that spark in their relationship. The opposite happens—instead there is added stress. There is evidence that having a healthy marriage going into the sandwich generation phase of life provides much needed support for the spouse who has the major responsibility for caring for two generations (Skogrand et al., 2006). It is, therefore, important to maintain a strong marriage relationship through the childrearing years, in preparation for what is sometimes a stressful time in life.

Grandparenthood

If I had known grandchildren would be this fun, I would have had them first.
—BUMPER STICKER

There are many ways to describe the experience of being a grandparent. Many grandparents talk about how they can spoil these children in a way they could not spoil their own children. Others describe the unconditional love they can provide to children whom they see only as delightful. In 1972 the anthropologist Margaret Mead shared some thoughts about being a grandparent (Mead, 1995):

> Grandparents and grandchildren get along so well because they have a common enemy. (p. 275)
>
> [Being a grandparent is] the extraordinary sense of having been transformed not by an act of one's own but by the act of one's child. (p. 277)

She went on to explain that grandparents do not have the anxiety and guilt experienced by parents.

The most recent data available from a national survey of people aged 65 or older reveal that 75% have living grandchildren. Many people become grandparents long before age 65; the first grandchild is often born when grandparents are in their early or mid-40s (Aldous, 1998; Troll, 1997), with one-third of one's life being spent as a grandparent (Thiele & Whelan, 2006).

For most people, grandparent–grandchild interaction is very enjoyable. Three-fourths of all grandparents have contact with their grandchildren weekly. Although grandparents are not directly responsible for the well-being of their grandchildren, they do have a vested interest in their development. Research has shown that the resulting emotional closeness continues into adulthood if grandparents have provided support for grandchildren as they go through difficult times, especially when these life events occur before 12 years of age (Wood & Liossis, 2007). Grandparents were typically available to the grandchildren to provide child care, teach life skills, and provide recreational activities for the children, and they were seen as providing a stabilizing source of support and a buffer against stress.

Research has also found that the relationship between grandparents and grandchildren is related to the strength of the relationship between a parent and his or her own parent (Monserud, 2008). In addition, mothers, rather than fathers, are often the gatekeepers when it comes to the strength of the grandchild/grandparent relationship. For example, if a mother is close to her in-laws, it is more likely that the grandchild/grandparent relationship will be strong.

In a summary of the current research about grandparents, several dimensions of the grandparent role have been identified by Thiele and Whelan (2006). These aspects or dimensions include grandparents' attitudes and expectations, grandparent behaviors, the symbolic meaning of grandparenthood, and the affective outcome or feeling of satisfaction of grandparents.

- *Grandparents' attitudes and expectations.* The role is ambiguous, and grandparents have little control over how it plays out. There may be an expectation that there will be frequent contact with their grandchildren and that may or may not happen.
- *Grandparent behavior.* There is no single way for grandparents to behave. In some cultures where the elderly are viewed as authority figures, the relationship with grandchildren may be very formal. In other cultures, the expectation is that grandparents are fun loving and warm.
- *Symbolic meaning of grandparenthood.* Some grandparents view their role as a source of status. Others view their role as emotional self-fulfillment. Still others see the grandparent role as their opportunity to be a teacher to the next generation.
- *Grandparent satisfaction.* How enjoyable or how happy grandparents are in their role varies. The vast majority are very satisfied and happy with their role, but a small minority are not. The greatest satisfaction seems to come when involvement is moderate, not detached, but not providing custodial care.

The role of grandparents may differ greatly in different cultural groups. As Thiele and Whelan (2006) noted, some cultures view the elderly in ways that affect their relationship with grandchildren. For example, in a study conducted with American Indian grandparents, researchers found that these grandparents did many of the typical things all grandparents do such as engaging in a variety of activities with their grandchildren and providing unconditional love (Robbins, Scherman, Holman, & Wilson, 2005). In addition, however, these grandparents also engaged in activities where they had the opportunity to pass on American Indian traditions and knowledge. Almost all of the participants in this study were concerned that tribal culture would be lost if their grandchildren did not learn about it and pass these traditions on to future generations.

Thinking about one's relationship with one's own grandparents might help clarify the dimensions described by Thiele and Whelan (2006). What was your relationship with your grandparents like? What kind of a grandparent do you want to be?

By and large, the grandparent role is mutually enjoyable for grandparents and grandchildren, and it gives the parents a welcome break. Although grandparenting can sometimes overwhelm and tire out grandparents, the role is generally pleasurable: "I can enjoy these kids so much now . . . so much more than I really could my own kids. I don't have to worry about them. Their mom and dad can do the worrying."

Grandparents Raising Grandchildren

One child in 10 in the United States lives with a grandparent, and about 4 in 10 (41%) of those children are also being raised primarily by that grandparent, according to U.S. Census Bureau data. The phenomenon of grandparents serving as primary

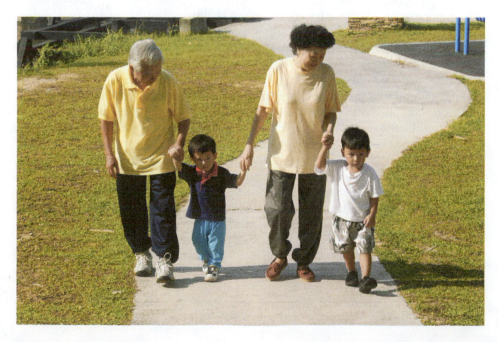

Because they do not have to bother with the daily chores of childrearing, grandparents are free to develop a more creative relationship with their grandchildren, sharing activities and interests with them. For most grandparents, one of the greatest satisfactions of grandparenthood is seeing a continuation of their family through another generation.

caregivers is more common among African Americans and Hispanics than among Whites, but during the Great Recession of 2007–2009, the sharpest rise was among Whites. About 2.9 million children live with a grandparent, and almost half (49%) of children being raised by grandparents also live with a single parent; 8% have both parents in the household, in addition to the caregiver grandparent (Livingston & Parker, 2010). Grandparents are typically raising their grandchildren because of problems that exist with the parents of the grandchildren such as substance abuse, HIV/AIDS, mental illness, neglect or abuse, incarceration, or divorce (Dolbin-MacNab, 2006). For many adults in the grandparenting role, it means that they can care for their grandchildren, spoil them, and then give them back to the parents. For other grandparents, however, grandparenting means caring for their grandchildren in the same way they cared for their own children—taking care of their physical and emotional needs 24/7 (Dolbin-MacNab, 2006). In some cases, grandparents are providing care for several grandchildren, who may come from several different families, and they also may be caring for their own children (Bachman & Chase-Lansdale, 2005).

The amount of stress experienced by grandparents raising grandchildren is extensive with concerns about finances, parenting issues, and their own health (Bachman & Chase-Lansdale, 2005; Goodman & Silverstein, 2006; Ross & Aday, 2006). The majority of grandparents raising grandchildren do so without any formal custody of the grandchild and with resulting anguish about the long-term relationship (Cox, 2007). In addition, many grandparents experience grief if they are dealing with the loss of their own child to antisocial behavior. The emotional stress they are feeling about the family relationships that have gone wrong, or could go wrong, are also adding to the pain experienced by the grandparents raising grandchildren. There is a need for financial and emotional support for grandparents as they are highly committed, but highly stressed as they care for their grandchildren.

African American children are more likely to be raised by their grandparents than children of other cultural groups, including Whites (Gibson, 2005; Goodman & Silverstein, 2006). Statistics show that 5% of White grandchildren are being raised by grandparents, 15% of African American children, and 9% of Latino children (Ross & Aday, 2006). One researcher suggests that custodial grandparenting is more prevalent in the African American community because, historically, members of this cultural group have cared for their own rather than have children placed in the social service system (Gibson, 2005). Black women are most likely to care for their grandchildren because of parental drug use and incarceration (Gibson, 2005).

Goodman and Silverstein (2006) studied the differences among African American, Latina, and White custodial grandmothers. They found that African American and Latina grandmothers raised their grandchildren more often because of financial reasons, and White grandmothers were more likely to raise their grandchildren because of some other dire parental circumstances such as parental substance abuse, child neglect, and parental mental health issues. These researchers also found that Latina and African American custodial grandparents were less likely to experience extreme stress than White grandmothers in raising their grandchildren. These authors suggest that White grandmothers are more likely to expect their adult children to be independent, and, therefore, when they must intervene and become caregivers of their grandchildren, it creates a sense of disappointment in their child, which adds to the stress.

In a qualitative study of 55 American Indian and White grandparents raising grandchildren, it was found the American Indian grandparents had higher

BOX 13.2 Diversity in Families

Grandparents and Grandfamilies

Grandparents have always been central to families. They have provided essential and often simultaneous assistance to two generations, their children and their grandchildren. Grandparents often take the role of the family historian, responsible for passing customs and the family lineage on to the next generations. Increasingly, grandparents are being asked to provide both emotional and instrumental support to their adult children as these children attempt to balance long work hours, distant military service, or other commitments with parenting responsibilities. Some modern grandparents act as co-parents to their grandchildren by assisting their adult children with the daily responsibilities and care for their grandchildren.

Grandparenthood is a mutually reciprocal relationship for all generations interconnected. The grandparents benefit from seeing their family grow and the continuation of their legacy. The younger generations benefit from the past experiences and knowledge shared by the older generation.

Some grandparents have the responsibility of *parenting again* if they parent their grandchildren full-time. Grandparents provide child kinship care for their grandchildren if their adult children are absent, unwilling, or unable to parent (Gibson, 2002). While some grandparents have always cared for their grandchildren, *grandfamilies* are increasing in numbers with an estimated 5 million children residing with custodial grandparents (U.S. Census Bureau, 2010a). Grandfamilies are defined as households where the parents are absent or the grandparent is the head of the household (Saluter, 1996). These custodial grandparents often benefit from an increased sense of purpose in caring for their grandchild.

This is an excerpt from a story written by a custodial grandmother with the pseudonym of Dee:

Becoming a parent and raising your kids is an experience with many rewards, blessings, and disappointments. I had three daughters and desperately wanted a son but did not have one. You know the saying, "Be careful what you wish for because wishes do come true." Little did I know that after my girls were grown that I would literally become a full-time Grandma raising two of my grandsons.

These days there are many grandparents being-full-time caregivers for their children's children. My two grandsons are ages 8 and 6 and believe you me raising boys is a helluva lot harder than raising girls. I thought girls were difficult to bring up dealing with their attitudes and such, but I've discovered that little boys are totally different. They are very loud, extremely active (flying over furniture, very risk-taking requiring many trips to the emergency room) and just plain messy (hiding food, dirty clothes, and the like in places you would not believe).

My grandsons have special needs as they have been diagnosed with Attention Deficit Hyperactivity Disorder (ADHD). Their hyperactivity means their energy level knows no boundaries. They are always on the go like the energizer rabbit! I only wish I could tap into some of their energy, so that I could keep up with them.

I'm often asked, "How do you do it raising two very active grandsons with their special needs?" By the grace of God I've been blessed with a wonderful support system. Even when I have days when I'm not feeling my best, I still find a way to provide the care and guidance for my boys. They sing in the church youth choir, receive honors at school, and yes they can be quite the handful at times, and there are times when I wonder just what have I gotten myself into. But, after the crisis is over, whether it's mine or theirs, we are still a loving family with lots of hugs, kisses, and smiles. I predict the future for them will be very bright, full of rainbows and sunshine after we weather a few storms along the way.

Source: Dr. Toni L. Hill, Department of Family Studies, University of Nebraska at Kearney. Email: hilltl@unk.edu. Reprinted by permission.

---

levels of depression than their White counterparts (Letiecq, Bailey, & Kurtz, 2008). Although American Indians have a rich history of providing care for their grandchildren and teaching them about their culture, these grandparents were providing care for their grandchildren because of a crisis with their own children. The authors of this study speculate that these high levels of depression may have resulted, in part, from the sadness they felt about unemployment, alcohol or drug addiction, or their children's inability to parent. These grandparents were trying to keep their grandchildren out of the foster care system and were overwhelmed with the full-time caregiving responsibility. These researchers also found that White and American Indian grandparents who had more financial resources were less depressed than those who had fewer resources. For more on grandparents and *grandfamilies*, see Box 13.2.

Family Life in the Later Years

The later years of life can be bittersweet. For those who were successful in raising a family and planning for retirement, the later years are easier than for those who have family or financial problems. Some older adults experience loneliness and isolation. Many must make do on limited funds. And elder abuse by younger family members occurs in some families.

Although many studies of older people have focused on the negative aspects of aging, a recent study demonstrated that many people become happier as they age. Mroczek and Spiro (2003) found that older men, especially those who are married, are happier than are younger men. Older men seem to regulate their emotions more effectively and are more able to maximize the positive and minimize the negative. In a sample of 2,727 men from ages 25 to 74, the older men reported having fewer negative emotions and, in general, were happier than the younger men. Younger people reported feeling sad, nervous, hopeless, or worthless more often than did older participants. Thus, aging seems to have some positive aspects when it comes to emotions.

American society is going through a "demographic revolution" as the life span of the population increases. In 1900, the average life expectancy was 47 years; life span has increased to 77.2 now. The gap between males and females was 5.4 in 2001, and the average longevity was 74.4 for men and 79.8 for women (Arias & Smith, 2003).

A subsequent study by the same research team found that life satisfaction generally peaks around age 65 in men (Mroczek & Spiro, 2005). On average life satisfaction dropped in late life after peaking around 65, so that men around age 85 were about as happy as they were in their mid-40s. "But people vary significantly from that overall growth curve," Daniel Mroczek said. "Some people may keep going up, some people may never peak and some just keep going down. Finding a pattern doesn't mean everyone abides by it." The researchers also found that men with high levels of extroversion correlated with high levels of life satisfaction and relative stability in life satisfaction over the years; men with lower levels of extroversion had an overall lower level of life satisfaction and less stability in life satisfaction as the years passed. "So, people with high extroversion are happier throughout life, but importantly, they're also more stable," Mroczek concluded (Kersting, 2005).

More recent research by Gallup (Stone, Schwartz, Broderick, & Deaton, 2010) complements earlier findings. In a telephone survey of 340,000 people nationwide, ages 18 to 85, researchers found among many other things that by almost any measure people get happier as they get older. The researchers developed a global measure of well-being, including enjoyment in life, happiness, stress, worry, anger, and sadness. On this global measure people start out at age 18 feeling pretty good about themselves, on average, and then, apparently, life starts to make life more difficult. People tend to feel worse and worse on average until they reach age 50. At this point, there is a sharp reversal, and they keep getting happier and happier as they age. By the time they are 85, they are even more satisfied with their lives than they were at 18.

American society is going through a demographic revolution as the life span of the population increases. In 1900, the average life expectancy at birth was 47 years. The most recent data available projects a life span of 78.3 years. A baby boy at birth is projected to live to age 75.7 years old, while a baby girl is projected to live to 80.8 years of age, women outliving men by an average of 5.1 years (U.S. Census Bureau, 2012b).

Because of increased life expectancy, American society is growing older. Trends indicate that the population of older persons is increasing rapidly. Most recent data indicate that people over age 65 in the United States make up 12.9% of the total population, about one in every eight Americans. By 2030 there are projected to be about 72.1 million older persons, more than double their number in 2000. In 2030 it is estimated that older people will represent 19% of the total population (Administration on Aging, 2011).

Defining Old Age

Old age is often said to begin at 65, which in our society is the typical age of retirement. But any exact chronological starting point for old age is bound to be arbitrary. In some parts of the world where life expectancy is lower, a person might be old at a much earlier age. Even in our own society, we see enormous variation among older adults. We all know active 75-year-olds and tired 50-year-olds.

Older adults are often divided into distinct groups: (1) the young-old, those between 55 and 65, who are still working and at the peak of their social and vocational status; (2) the middle-old, those between 65 and 75, who tend to be retired and in good health and have abundant time to follow their interests; (3) the old-old, those over age 75, who as a group tend to be the frailest, loneliest, and poorest of the old. Some observers add a fourth group, the frail old. Even though the old-old tend to have the most health problems as a group, there are frail old people represented among the young-old and middle-old groups as well. By adding this fourth category, one is signifying clearly the fact that human beings, for a variety of reasons, grow old at different rates.

Aging is in part a *psychological phenomenon*. How an older person feels depends to some degree on her or his mental attitude toward both the accomplishments of the past and the possibilities for the future. For most purposes, a person who feels "young at heart" is still young. Of course, aging is also a *biological reality*, and some variations among older adults are a result of their different genetic heritages. Aging is also a *social phenomenon*. If society forces people into retirement at 65, it is in effect declaring them to be old. Similarly, there are compelling data to argue that one's social standing or social class directly affects one's health and life expectancy. Similar to chickens, people have a pecking order, and the higher level of status one holds in the human pecking order, the longer, happier, and healthier one's life is likely to be (Marmot, 2004). Finally, aging is part of the family process, one that occurs in the context of ongoing interpersonal relationships with spouses, parents, children, and other family members whose attitudes help us define and redefine ourselves as we grow older.

Despite the challenges of aging—the lower energy levels, the failing eyesight or poor hearing, the serious health problems—many people adapt to these changes and continue to live fruitful lives. How we as individuals, and as members of families and communities, define the later years powerfully influences our well-being during this time.

Conventional Wisdom About Old Age

Grow old along with me! The best is yet to be, The last of life, for which the first was made.
—ROBERT BROWNING (1864/1970, p. 811)

Many people in our society accept the conventional wisdom about old age, most of which is negative. It is important, though, that we set the record straight about these myths or false beliefs, which foster a form of prejudice known as **ageism**, prejudging an older person negatively solely on the basis of age. In the following discussion, we hope to deconstruct some of the most common myths about old age.

> **Myth #1:** *At 65, You're "Over the Hill."*
> **Reality:** Attitude has a good deal to do with how "old" one is. People whose attitudes toward life remain positive generally lead happier and more fulfilling lives in their later years. Many symptoms popularly associated with old age—cognitive impairment, falling, dizziness, loss of bladder control, and loss of appetite—are symptoms of disease, not of normal aging.

> **Myth #2:** *Most Older Adults Are Poor.*
> **Reality:** Actually, the financial situation for most people 50 and above is quite good. The Pew Research Center found that households headed by older adults have made dramatic gains compared to younger adults in terms of economic well-being over the past quarter century. Most recent data show that the typical oldest age household had 47 times as much net wealth as the typical household headed by someone in the youngest age group. Households headed by persons 65 and older had an average net wealth of $170,494, while households headed by persons younger than 35 had an average net worth of $3,662 (Fry, Cohn, Livingston, & Taylor, 2011). Table 13.1 shows clearly how the accumulation of wealth has actually fallen off for young people in recent years, while wealth for 65 and older people has dramatically increased.
>
> It is clear that, on average, older families are doing better than younger families from an economic perspective. However, other researchers have found

Older couples often have more time to enjoy leisure activities together and see renewed happiness in their marriage. They may also return to hobbies or activities they previously did not have time to enjoy while working.

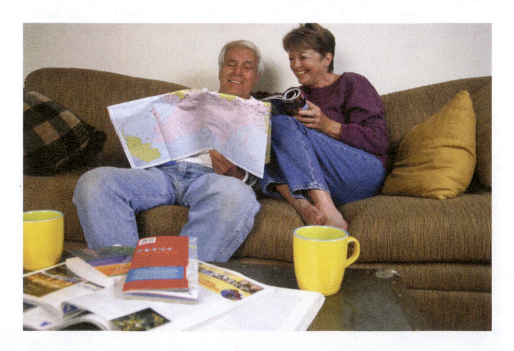

TABLE 13.1	Median Net Worth by Age of Householder, 1984 and 2009 (in 2010 dollars)		
	1984	**2009**	**Change**
All	$ 65,293	$ 71,635	10%
Younger than 35	11,521	3,662	−68%
35–44	71,118	39,601	−44%
45–54	113,511	101,651	−10%
55–64	147,236	162,065	10%
65 and older	120,457	170,494	42%

Source: Pew Research Center tabulations of Survey of Income and Program Participation data and U.S. Census Bureau P–70, No. 7; Household Wealth and Asset Ownership: 1984: Data from the Survey of Income and Program Participation, Table E

that nearly half of all elderly Americans will encounter at least 1 year of poverty or near poverty between the ages of 60 and 90. Also, 58% of those between 60 and 84 will at some time fail to have enough liquid assets to make it possible for them to weather an unanticipated expense or downturn in income (Rank & Williams, 2010).

Myth #3: *Older Adults Are Not Interested in Sex.*
Reality: A major study by Lindau et al. (2007) focused on sexual behaviors of over 3,000 adults from ages 57 to 85 years of age. Men and women were approximately equally represented in the sample. The purpose of the study was to learn about the prevalence of behaviors, sexual activity, and problems in the older population and to learn about the relationship between sexuality and health conditions.

The findings of the Lindau et al. (2007) study indicated that sexual activity, including vaginal intercourse, oral sex, and masturbation, declined with age, and men were more sexually active than women. Women were less likely than men to be in a marriage or other intimate relationship, or more likely to have lost their sexual partner through death, which affected their level of sexual activity. Participants 75 to 85 years of age were involved in sexual activity less than those who were younger, but even at this age 54% were having sex at least two to three times per month, and 23% had sex once per week or more.

Both men and women in this study masturbated, with masturbation declining as age increased, with men masturbating more frequently than women. Approximately half of men and 25% of women in the 75- to 85-year-old age group had masturbated in the previous 12 months. This was true for adults who were in a relationship or marriage and those who were not. Although approximately half of the participants in the study, both men and women, reported sexual problems often related to health, one in seven men reported taking medication to improve sexual functioning.

Based upon the findings from this study, it is clear that older adults are, indeed, sexually active. Medications taken in middle and later years can, however, affect the ability to have and enjoy sex. For example, research shows that medications such as statins, which lower cholesterol, also lower sexual pleasure (Elias, 2009, March 6). Men indicated that their sexual pleasure was reduced by one-half. Women's sexual pleasure was also decreased, but not as dramatically. Many who experienced sexual problems sought solutions through the use of medication.

Myth #4: *Older Adults Are Usually Sick.*

Reality: Actually, older adults are generally in good health. Even in the advanced stages of old age an overwhelming majority have little functional disability, and the proportion of the disabled is going down not up (Alliance for Aging Research, 2012). People over 65 have about half as many acute illnesses as those between 17 and 44. It is true, of course, that chronic conditions tend to accumulate over time, and older adults commonly suffer from sensory losses—hearing, vision, and taste. But as AARP regularly points out, these problems do not keep most older adults from enjoying an active, healthy life. People who have adapted to change throughout life will likely find ways to cope with most of the changes that aging brings (AARP, 2013).

Myth #5: *Older Adults Become Senile.*

Reality: The term *senility* is not often used by gerontologists today, because it has little specific meaning. Although brain damage can be caused by a series of small strokes, most progressive organic brain impairment is caused by disease, such as **Alzheimer's disease** (Box 13.3). Assuming that memory loss or change in behavior in older adults is a function of age can cause one to overlook a disease that might be successfully treated. All too often, people attribute an older person's anger or depression to old age, when, in fact, it may be due to a life occurrence that would cause similar symptoms in a younger individual (U.S. National Library of Medicine, 2010).

Myth #6: *Most Older Adults End up in Nursing Homes.*

Reality: Latest figures indicate there were about 38.9 million people 65 and older in the United States, and the number is steadily growing. This age group accounts for 13% of the total population. The number of people 65 and older who were living in a nursing home or skilled nursing facility at the time of the survey was 1.6 million. These residents comprised 4% of all people in our country over age 65 (U.S. Census Bureau, 2012c).

Research indicates that 43% of Americans over age 65 will enter a nursing home at some time in their lives. Most of these nursing home stays are for relatively short periods of time, as patients recuperate from surgery or illness. The average nursing home stay is between 2 and 3 years (Public Broadcasting Service, 2012). The likelihood of being in a nursing home increases with age: 1.4% of those aged 65 to 74 are in a nursing home; 6% of those aged 75 to 84; and 24% of those 85 and older. Four out of five elderly with long-term care needs live in the community. Only one in five persons with such needs lives in a nursing home. Few families abandon their loved ones in their later years, and few families wantonly "warehouse" older members to a nursing home (American Association of Homes and Services for the Aging, 2012).

Older people are placed in a nursing home for a number of reasons: advancing age; a greater level of chronic disability; deteriorating mental and physical capacities; living alone, or lack of family members to provide help; female gender (women tend to outlive their husbands and end up alone); White race (Whites are twice as likely to enter nursing homes as Blacks); and time spent in a hospital or other health facility. About three out of four nursing home residents are aged 75 or older, and 7 out of 10 are women. The nursing home industry argues that the vast majority of nursing homes have dedicated staffs and try very hard to meet the needs of infirm older people (American Association of Homes and Services for the Aging, 2012).

Myth #7: *Myth: Most Older Adults Are Lonely.*

Reality: The conventional wisdom brings to mind a picture of a frail old man sadly looking off into space, housed in a nursing home with no loved ones or friends visiting him until the day he quietly dies. There are certainly cases like this, but older adults as a group are not necessarily lonely. Some researchers studying loneliness have found that it increases with age, being the strongest among the oldest age groups. Some researchers have found that loneliness decreases with advancing age. And some researchers have found no statistical relationship between age and loneliness (Hall & Havens, 2004).

Loneliness is likely to increase in old age as family and friendship networks become smaller. Social contacts tend to decrease after retirement and may continue to decline with the death of family members, and friends, change in residence after losing one's spouse, mobility difficulties, and poor health. To prevent feelings of isolation and loneliness, it is recommended that individuals keep in regular contact with older family members, friends, and neighbors and help them feel needed and valued. Local communities and groups are advised to increase the availability of programs and services for older people, enhance transportation programs for the elderly, develop low-cost leisure and educational activities, and involve older people in all levels of planning these services (Hall & Havens, 2004).

A study by AARP surveyed 3,012 people ages 45 and above. Using the UCLA Loneliness Scale the researchers found that 35% were chronically lonely, compared to 20% a decade earlier. Loneliness was equally prevalent regardless of race, gender, or level of education. Age, however, did make a difference: those who said they were suffering the most from loneliness were not the oldest but rather adults in their 40s and 50s (Edmondson, 2010).

Myth #8: *Older Adults Are Isolated from Younger Family Members.*
Reality: A national study (Troll, 1997) found that more than half of all people over age 65 who have children live either in the same household with an adult child or in the same neighborhood as a child. Contact with other family members, especially adult children, is rather frequent.

Most older adults enjoy their privacy, preferring not to live in the same house as their adult children and their grandchildren. Of older people who have adult children but live alone, however, half live within 10 minutes from a child. On the day they were interviewed for this study, half of the older people with children reported that they had seen one of their adult children the day they were interviewed, and about three-quarters reported having seen at least one of their adult children during the week preceding the interview. This study also revealed that even in those cases where the geographic distance between them is considerable, older and younger family members tend to stay in contact.

What about the quality of these contacts—a much more difficult characteristic to measure? One way to measure quality is to assess the amount of help family members give each other. In a national study, 7 out of every 10 older adults with children said they helped their children, and 7 out of every 10 older adults said they helped their grandchildren. Five out of every 10 said they even helped their great-grandchildren. Seven out of 10 older people also said they received help from their children. This help included home repairs and housework, care during an illness, and different kinds of gifts. In addition, older people reported that they helped their adult children by caring for grandchildren. In short, it appears that older people are not isolated from younger family members and that these contacts are generally happy ones (Allen, Blieszner, & Roberto, 2000).

Retirement

The stereotypical view of retirement is a dreary, downhill period of life in which people lose their self-esteem and immerse themselves in memories of better days; they stop being productive working citizens and slowly waste away. To the contrary, research shows that retired people are no more likely to be sick or depressed than people of the same age who are still on the job. In fact, most people adapt satisfactorily to retirement, with few long-term changes in their health, psychological well-being, or family relationships.

There are, of course, examples of people who find retirement difficult and depressing. One woman said of her recently retired husband, "He used to be a powerful executive with 200 employees under him. He would work long, hard hours and then come home to relax and enjoy his hobbies. He retired 5 years ago, and ever since he's been terribly depressed."

Fortunately, positive retirement stories are the general rule. Most men and women report they adjust quite well to voluntary retirement, and studies consistently find that satisfaction with life remains fairly high for the majority of retired people. Factors predicting a positive adjustment to retirement include good health (many older people leave the workforce because of poor health), economic security, and a supportive social network (Darkwa, 2004; Elderly Health Services, 2004).

As with any major life transition, retirement takes some adjustment. Retired people report a number of problems associated with this transition, including sleeplessness, aimlessness, and sadness over not seeing work friends and colleagues regularly. But other retirees are quick to point out that they have gotten involved in so many new activities that they have less free time than they did when they were working and would like to slow down a bit.

Retirement affects marriage in different ways. For couples who place a high value on intimacy and family relationships, retirement can bring more freedom to enjoy each other and the family. Some wives—especially those who always assumed traditional roles and traditional divisions of labor—are pessimistic about the husband's impending retirement, perhaps fearing the retiree will intrude on their domestic territory. This perspective is captured on a bumper sticker: *Retirement: Half as much money, twice as much husband.*

Most older people adjust well to voluntary retirement, especially those who get involved in new activities.

BOX 13.3   At Issue

Alzheimer's

What Is Alzheimer's?

Alzheimer's is the most common form of dementia and results when plaques and tangles develop in the brain and interfere with brain functioning (Alzheimer's Foundation of American, n.d.). It is not clear what causes Alzheimer's, and there is no cure. It is progressive, and there is no hope for recovery. The onset of Alzheimer's usually occurs after age 60, with symptoms that include memory loss, decreased thinking and language skills, and behavioral changes. Approximately 10% of all people over the age of 65, and 50% of people over age 85, have Alzheimer's (WebMD, n.d.). It has been estimated that the number of people age 65 and older will double by the year 2030 (Alzheimer's Foundation of America, n.d.). Because people are living longer, we are seeing an increase in the number of people being diagnosed, resulting in an increase in family issues of caregiving and health care costs. For all involved in the lives of those living with Alzheimer's, it is emotionally, socially, and financially difficult.

Those Who Provide Care

Approximately 70% of people with Alzheimer's live at home (Kantrowitz & Springen, 2007, June 18). It is estimated that one to four family members care for each person who has the disease (Alzheimer's Foundation of America, n. d.). Baby Boomers, those born between 1946 and 1964, are typically the caregivers, because it is their parents who are now in the age group most affected. These caregivers are often referred to as "the sandwich generation" because they are caught between caring for their own children, work, and caring for their parents.

People who care for those with Alzheimer's have a heavy burden. One woman talked about how her father could never be left alone, or he would walk out of the house and not know how to get back. Both she and her husband worked, and therefore he had to be in a day care facility during the day. At night they had to lock his bedroom door to prevent him from wandering off. Any change in schedule would mean her children and husband would need to fill in to help with his care. The responsibility was taking a toll on their marriage and family life. An additional component of this story is that he had been an abusive father and husband, which meant caring for him was an unwelcome burden. Her siblings, who lived far away, had no idea how difficult things were, and provided no help, which contributed to resentment toward her brothers and sisters.

Other caregivers include spouses of those with Alzheimer's. These caregivers often still feel love for their spouses, even though the person with Alzheimer's no longer recognizes the person they have been married to for many years. The person with Alzheimer's may become aggressive or even violent, and the weight of what to do next is heavy. One man's wife was relatively easy to care for because, even though she could not carry on a conversation and often did not recognize him, she would accompany him to social events. Even though she did not know what was being said, she would sit quietly and nodded knowingly when engaged in conversation.

Because of the increase in remarriages, there is an increasing number of late-life remarried spouses caring for Alzheimer patients (Sherman & Bauer, 2008). These caregivers sometimes inherit unresolved family issues. The caregiving spouse can end up being on the front lines dealing with family relationships, inheritance issues, and unresolved resentments.

All caregivers can easily become isolated and neglect their own needs. Caregivers often do not feel they have time or resources to have a social life, take time for their own interests, or spend time with family.

Even limited home care is expensive and is usually not covered by Medicare. Ultimately, nursing home care is likely to be necessary, and the cost can run as high as $65,000 to $75,000 per year. Not all nursing homes are equipped to care for elderly Alzheimer's patients, and therefore some patients may need to live in a facility some distance from family, which can add to the cost of care.

How to Prepare

It is important to talk with aging relatives, including parents, before health issues impact their lives. It is a difficult topic to broach. Who wants to talk about health issues, the loss of control, and finances with one's own parents, even though it is likely these issues will need to be faced at some point? It is also likely that aging relatives will not want to talk about these issues. The conversation might begin by asking parents about their wishes if the time should come when they cannot care for themselves. What would they like to have happen, and what resources are available to make that a reality? In the case of a late-life remarriage, it is especially important to have family discussions about these topics.

One of the issues receiving increasing attention is long-term care insurance. It typically covers some or all of the cost of nursing home or in-home care. The insurance is cheaper when it is purchased early in life and before health problems become evident. Most insurance companies can provide information about cost and benefits of such insurance.

Retirement satisfaction in terms of financial resources can be affected by one's marital history. For example, divorce can affect one's wealth accumulation, which has an impact on how much money one has available in retirement. In a national study with a large sample, it was found that divorce affected wealth in retirement (Ulker, 2009). For those who divorced early in life and remarried, there was little effect on their financial resources in later stages of life because they had time to recover. However, for those who remained single, there was less wealth than for those who remained married, and this was especially true for women.

Long-Term Marriages

Stereotypes about older couples abound in our society. One common belief is that if you have survived many years together, you must be getting along extremely well. Counter to this opinion is the anonymous thought that, "Marriage is forever. And forever is a damned long time."

A number of family researchers have studied long-term marriages, trying to get closer to the truth. From their findings, George Rowe and Marcia Lasswell were able to divide **longevous marriages**—marriages that last 50 years or more—into three categories: (1) couples who are very happy and blissfully in love, (2) couples who are very unhappy but who continue the marriage out of habit or fear, and (3) couples in between, who are neither very happy nor very unhappy and accept the situation (cited in Sweeney, 1982). Lasswell estimated the "very happy" number at roughly 20% of the total and the "very unhappy" number at 20%. Both researchers also found a negative relationship between the number of children couples had and marital happiness: Couples with larger families tended to have less happy marriages. "We can't explain that, except the study indicated that a dip in marital happiness is almost always concurrent with the time the children are a heavy responsibility for parents," Rowe said (p. 23). He theorized that the more children a couple has, the longer this period of responsibility lasts and the more the relationship is drained by parenting responsibilities.

In a similar vein, Timothy Brubaker (1985) reviewed 25 studies of older couples' relationships and identified three common patterns in the studies:

1. Some couples experience a decline in marital quality during the middle years of marriage, and then the marriage improves in the later years.

2. For some couples, the marriage declines gradually in quality as the years go by, with the trend line from the newlywed days to later life moving steadily downward.

3. For some couples, the trend line remains stable in the middle years and into the later years. Those who were happy when the children were at home will remain happy when the children leave home and when they retire. Those who were unhappy as a couple when the kids were at home will continue to be unhappy when the nest empties and they retire.

In general, the quality of the marital relationship shows continuity over the years. Couples who did not get along well in their early years together are likely not to get along well in the later years of their marriage. "In the later years, those who have vital, rewarding relationships will most generally experience continued positive interactions within the marriage, while those who have difficult, unsatisfying relationships will most likely experience continued negative marital interactions" (Brubaker, 1991, p. 229).

What can we conclude? Researchers have found that simply because people remain married for a long time is no guarantee that they are happy with the marriage. Some long-term married couples have very happy marriages, while some have very unhappy marriages. Some may have stayed married for so many years simply out of habit. Some may have stayed married for so many years to honor religious and cultural traditions. Some may have stayed married for so many years because they saw no better options in life. And some may have stayed married for so many years because they genuinely loved and cared for each other and enjoyed each other's company.

We could not find more recent research on long-term marriages, which is unfortunate. But we would hazard this guess: Because divorce is common in our society and because divorce is much more acceptable today than it was in the past, we would predict that fewer and fewer couples will stay together for a long time if they are unhappy. And because of this, in the long run, marriages will steadily improve in quality. In a word, because of the option to divorce, there will be fewer and fewer long-term unhappy marriages. And this will mean that a higher percentage of marriages will be happy ones.

Time, of course, will tell.

Losing a Spouse

After the loss of my husband
The years go fast
But the days and nights are long.

—A BEREAVED 90-YEAR-OLD WIDOW

The death of a spouse is a difficult life transition for most, and for some it is a devastating personal crisis. Brubaker (1990) outlined three characteristic stages of the grieving process:

1. **Crisis-loss stage of grief.** In the first few days and weeks after the loss, the survivor is in a chaotic stage of shock. Common reactions are "I can't believe this is happening to me," "I'll do anything to bring her back," "What am I going to do now?"

2. **Transition stage of grief.** In the transition period, the survivor begins trying to create a new life. Grief lessens in its intensity, and the bereaved person sees the possibility of a life ahead.

3. **New-life stage of grief.** The survivor changes her or his lifestyle and proves to the world and to herself or himself that it is possible to live satisfactorily as a single person. The widow or widower develops an identity without the partner.

Grief lasts longer than was long believed to be the case—up to 2 years, according to research on widows. A widow's grief can include a range of feelings, from sadness and anger to fear and anxiety. The prevalence of anxiety in the first 3 years after a husband's death led one researcher to see its role in mourning as crucial. Other researchers see depression as a significant risk among bereaved spouses (Bruce, 2002).

But other studies question whether depression is universal among the bereaved. These studies also indicate that sudden deaths are not necessarily more distressing than expected ones, and have found that bereaved people who had strained marriages actually feel less grief than those who had close and loving ones. Some widows and widowers experience profound depression in the months and even years following their loss. Many are comforted by "confronting and working through their loss." Yet the majority of older bereaved spouses see death as simply a part of life—albeit a sad part—and for them recovery and resilience is the rule and not the exception (Carr, 2006).

In old age, loved ones with whom one had intimate relationships may no longer be alive, but this does not mean that people no longer feel intimate connections (Troll, 2001). Many older people feel connected to their deceased intimate partners through prayer, photos, visits to the cemetery, and other ways they honor the dead. Commitment and caring are maintained after the death. Cognitive intimacy is maintained by thinking of the departed partner. Though physical encounters cannot continue, some individuals substitute heirlooms or pictures to preserve the physical presence of the loved one. And interdependent intimacy is maintained by hearing the voice of the dead speaking through one's own thoughts.

"Do you talk with Joan?" we asked one elderly husband who had lost his wife to cancer 7 years earlier. "Oh, yes," Bill replied. "She's right here in the kitchen with me now, helping get the tea and cookies together." Bill maintained his intimate emotional connections with his wife after death, and found strength in her presence.

In the United States, 11 out of every 12 people who have lost a spouse are women. This is because women live longer than men and because they tend to marry men older than themselves. Three out of four wives can expect to become widows (Daggett, 2002). While past generations of older people often stayed in difficult marriages because of religious or cultural prohibitions against divorce, Baby Boomers today have more freedom to divorce if their marriage proves unsatisfactory. If the baby boom generation dissolves troubled marriages, the remaining Boomers late in life may be more likely to have warm and close relationships, and may be the most grief-stricken upon their loss. It has also been argued that marriage has been idealized in recent decades and we now seek a *soul mate*, who shares our interests and passions, rather than a *helpmate* who just pays the bills or washes the dishes. If our partner is an irreplaceable *soul mate*, the loss can be much more devastating (Carr, 2006).

As one bereaved widow told us, "Society says, 'Get over it. The funeral's over, get off the floor and quit grieving.' But Larry was my best friend for 54 years. You never get over losing your best friend. To hell with society." For one woman's story, see Box 13.4 below.

Couple Relationships in the Later Years

Because people are living longer, there are more opportunities to develop new couple relationships after a late-life divorce or widowhood. Many in their 60s, 70s, 80s, and even 90s begin new relationships that end up in marriage or cohabiting. Others choose an increasingly popular option of maintaining separate homes while in a committed intimate relationship (Levaro, 2011).

Women's life expectancy is greater than men's, so there are more women available than men. In fact, by the time people reach their late 70s, there three times as many women as men, and most of these women are widowed (Levaro, 2009). Some women may believe that their chances of meeting a man are slim and therefore do not see an intimate relationship as feasible, while men report greater loneliness than women and often marry. Marriage is often viewed as the desirable option for couples because it often meets both social and religious expectations.

BOX 13.4   At Issue

I Am Aware That I Am No Longer Anyone's "Most Important Person": The Desolation of Grief

As I write, it is 5 months to the day since my darling died. He died in our home, where I had nursed him for the preceding 7 months, with the loving assistance of family and friends, as well as paid carers. For most of that time, Thomas, as I shall call him, was bedridden and incontinent, and was becoming increasingly demented yet subdued by the morphine which gave him effective relief from pain but did not relieve his anxiety state.

In the months before he came home from hospital to live and then to die, Thomas suffered what in hindsight I believe were multiple TIAs (transitory ischemic attacks—silent, indiscernible little strokes), which gradually took from him his ability to initiate thought, to plan, to process or perform complex thoughts and tasks and which caused confusion, loss of balance and co-ordination and falls. One fall, whilst in the acute specialist hospital in which he was receiving tests, resulted in a fractured femur in an artificial hip joint. Despite the fracture being mended with surgery, he never bore his own weight again. Underlying all these misadventures were his cardiac disease treated by stenting, coronary arterial by-pass surgery and a pacemaker and prostate cancer which had progressed to secondaries in his bones. The compounding effects of all of these factors meant I had to take up the Power of Attorney and Enduring Guardianship which Thomas had earlier entrusted to me, as he was no longer competent to manage his affairs.

It was an honor and a privilege to be able to care for him in our home during his final weeks and months. We both knew death was coming and every moment was therefore intense and precious.

Now, today, there is the void. My emotions are many and varied, but predominately that of desolation, despite being surrounded by dear and caring friends and two willing and helpful brothers, and being kept busy with the many tasks that must occupy one in the immediate days and weeks after the death of a next of kin:

- whom to inform, personal, professional and statutory bodies;
- funeral to arrange;
- clothes and personal items to be distributed amongst his children and other relatives, many of whom are at a distance, with relationships with me and their father strained;
- papers to be prepared for solicitors (probate) and the tax office (inland revenue);
- bank accounts closed;
- and soon, financial assets to be distributed, equitably, if not amicably! ("Where there is a will, there is a relative" has been quoted to me on more than one occasion since his death!)

My emotions: a deep sadness, sense of bewilderment, loss of purpose and focus, and the death of my sense of fun and capacity to enjoy much of anything; anger toward his relatives who stayed away when he so wanted them to visit near to the end. Each morning when I wake, the empty space beside me brings the reality of my loss right back to my consciousness, again and again. I continue to live in the home we have shared for 27 years, and tend the garden in which we were married. Its emptiness makes it a lonely place and yet it is the place richest in our memories. I have surrounded myself with photos of my man, mostly ones of him smiling, at least one in every room, including even at the kitchen sink, so that I can see and talk to him in all those domestic spaces, and as I prepare and eat my meals from which I currently gain little pleasure. I talk to him out loud, voicing my displeasure at his absence, and telling him it is time to come home. I remind him of happy events from our past, and of the debate we used to have about which one of us would die first, so as not to have to empty the attic! (We are both hoarders!) I tell him that it is unfair that he did not let me win that one!

I know that pleasure in eating and in socializing will return in time, but for now, it takes a lot of effort to just do the routine tasks each day. I feel I must keep my "face on," so as to not to pass my sadness on to others and so dampen their spirits. So, sometimes I choose to be alone. Mostly I cry on my own, too. I am aware that I am no longer anyone's "most important person." I am also mindful though, that I have had more happiness from a relationship, for almost half of my life than some people ever have. I am also aware that the effects of chronic stress and fatigue from the caring role I willingly took on will pass and that I will mend.

Source: This story was written by a friend of ours in Australia, a counselor with many years of experience working with grieving families, who wishes to remain anonymous. Printed by permission.

There are many reasons, however, why older individuals might not want to marry (Levaro, 2011). For example, there may be financial considerations, where their respective children's inheritance may be affected. There also may be a loss of pension benefits with remarriage, especially for women. Another concern may be potential medical costs or medical care issues, which are often felt by women more than men because women are likely to live longer.

Cohabitation has become an increasingly acceptable choice for aging adults, just as it has for younger generations. Cohabitation allows couples to have an intimate relationship without the legal ramifications of marriage. This arrangement, however, creates new issues for children and grandchildren, who may not know how to respond to this new arrangement (Levaro, 2011). For example, how are family heirlooms to be handled with a new person living in the home? What are the children's and grandchildren's obligations to this new partner? Many children and grandchildren are delighted that their parent or grandparent has found happiness in later life, and others are concerned about how to respond to the new partner.

Levaro (2011) describes a third option that some elderly couples have chosen—*living apart together.* This term describes the living arrangement for couples who are in a committed intimate relationship but choose to maintain separate homes. Women are typically the driving force behind this arrangement, because they often have the most to lose in marriage or cohabiting. This choice allows couples to have a relationship without the issues around inheritance, and it offers freedom from the potential obligation of medical caregiving. Another benefit is that after so many years, individuals have developed their own habits and preferences about living arrangements. Living apart allows individuals to retain the privacy of their own home and maintain their individual lifestyles.

If we look to aging couples around us, we are likely to see all of these examples of couple relationships. One couple lived together for 15 years, got engaged when both were 61, and at age 62 decided to marry. The bride's maid of honor at the wedding was her granddaughter, age 10, and the best man was the bride's father, who was 90 years old. The priest who married them said he had never conducted a wedding where there was an 80-year age difference between the best man and the maid of honor. Another couple who were both widowed started *dating* when she was 73 and he was 75. They maintained their separate homes but went to dinner and social events together and occasionally took trips together. There are a variety of ways couples develop and maintain relationships in later years of life, and these couples are making choices that fit their life circumstances and preferences.

Changes in Family Dynamics in the Later Years

Sibling relationships in middle and older adulthood have recently become a new area of research. Most sibling relationships remain strong and positive throughout the years and are important for the older adult's well-being. Research indicates in the later years that sisters are the closest, followed by cross-sex siblings, and then brothers (Van Volkom, 2006). Sometimes events in life trigger the opportunity to reconnect in later years, even when siblings had not been particularly close before. A spouse may have died, and relationships with siblings may become closer to fill the void. Here is how two sisters in their 80s developed a closer relationship:

Two sisters, one age 80 and the other age 86, have always kept in touch but have not been especially close. They live 1,000 miles apart and have led very different lives. One was married to a chemist, and the other was married to a farmer. Over the years they would see each other once every year or two and would talk on the phone occasionally. In recent years, as they entered old age, they began calling each other regularly—usually every day—to talk about the mundane, but personal and real, events of daily life.

One was widowed 4 years ago after 56 years of marriage and did quite well in her grief with the help of family and friends in a very close-knit farming community. Recently her sister's husband died suddenly. Because the sister had no family nearby and lived in a large city, she had less family and community support. She began calling her sister in the farming community even more often—sometimes several times a day. They talked about losing husbands, with the one who has been widowed longer providing sage advice for the sister who just recently experienced her husband's death. They developed a very intimate emotional relationship with these frequent telephone conversations, even though they have not seen each other for 2 years.

Summary

- Middle age roughly spans ages 35 to 65, a period during which many couples are (1) still raising teenagers, (2) launching young adults and then coping with their absence from or return to the home, and (3) entering retirement.

- For many, the challenges of middle age include coping with routinization in the job, developing a new or second career outside the home (especially for women), coping with the transition of menopause and "male menopause," maintaining the emotional and sexual health of the marriage, dealing with the empty or the cluttered nest, and managing the demands of aging parents.

- Marriages fail in the middle years for five main reasons: verbal, physical, or emotional abuse; alcohol or drug abuse; cheating; "falling out of love"; or different values or lifestyles.

- Recommendations for strengthening a marriage in the middle years include making one's spouse the number-one priority, being alert to warning signs of marital trouble, establishing an equal partnership, helping the spouse feel important and powerful, balancing togetherness and personal growth, working to keep the sexual relationship exciting, networking with other committed couples, evaluating the marriage and attending marriage enrichment workshops, changing frustrating job situations, and changing one's lifestyle rather than one's partner to revitalize the marriage. Happiness is key to a content spouse and is the best way to prevent infidelity from occurring.

- People in their middle years are often *sandwiched* between two or more competing responsibilities: caring for adolescents, dealing with boomerang kids (adult children returning to the parental nest), and caring for their own aging parents. The results can be both positive (a closer relationship between the caregiver and the aging parent) and negative (too much stress).

- Grandparenting reinforces continuity of the generations and brings pleasure to most grandparents. Of those 65 or older, 75% have living grandchildren.

- Today, one child in 10 in the United States lives with a grandparent, and about four in 10 (41%) of those children are also being raised primarily by that grandparent. These grandparents experience stress related to finances, parenting issues, and their own health.

- U.S. society is undergoing a *demographic revolution* due to the increasing life span of its population. Our average life expectancy is over 78.

- Conventional wisdom about old age includes the following inaccurate beliefs: at 65, *you're over the hill*; most older adults are poor; older adults are not interested in sex; older adults are usually sick; older adults become senile; most older adults end up in nursing homes; most older adults are lonely; and older adults are isolated from younger family members.

- Contrary to stereotypes, retirement is not a negative period of life. Most people who retire voluntarily adapt satisfactorily to retirement, with few long-term effects on their health, psychological well-being, or family relationships.

- Not all marriages of long duration are happy. People stay married out of habit, or fear, or (in about 20% of these marriages) simply because they are very happy or in between or accepting, neither very happy nor unhappy. The fewer the number of children, the happier the marriage seems to be.

- Alzheimer's is a disease that affects many people beginning at age 60, with increasing likelihood as one gets older. Caring for someone with this disease can be overwhelming physically, emotionally, and financially, and often this care is provided by family members.

- The death of a spouse is a difficult life transition for most, and for some it is a devastating personal crisis. If our partner is an irreplaceable *soul mate,* the loss can be especially troubling.
- Because people are living longer, there are many opportunities to develop new couple relationships after a late-life divorce or widowhood. Many in their 60s, 70s, 80s, and even 90s begin new relationships that end up in marriage or cohabitation. Others choose an increasingly popular option of maintaining separate homes while in a committed intimate relationship. This arrangement has been called *living apart together.*
- Most sibling relationships remain strong and positive throughout the years and are important for the older adult's well-being. Research indicates that in the later years sisters are the closest, followed by cross-sex siblings, and then brothers.

Key Terms

middle age	boomerang kids
Baby Boomers	cluttered nest
midlife crisis	sandwich generation
menopause	old age
androgen	ageism
male menopause	Alzheimer's disease
empty-nest syndrome	longevous marriage
spacious nest	living apart together

Activities

1. Discuss career issues with a middle-aged man or woman. Ask the individual to trace her or his career development. What conclusions can you come to?
2. Interview your parents (if they are middle-aged) or other middle-aged individuals about the stresses of midlife and their means of coping with them.
3. Interview a middle-aged person who is "sandwiched" between trying to support adolescent or young-adult children and caring for an elderly family member. Prepare 10 or 15 questions for the interview and record 5 or 6 general conclusions.
4. After reading the section on grandparenthood, prepare some questions and interview a grandparent. This can be an easy and rewarding exercise because grandparents and young adults often have an automatic bond.
5. Interview an older couple. Ask them to tell you the story of their family, including information about their parents and grandparents. Focus part of the interview on intergenerational relationships.
6. Write down your feelings about death and share them in a small-group discussion. Record the similarities and differences in the group's observations.

Suggested Readings

AARP. (2013). Web site: http://www.aarp.org.

AARP. (n.d.). Web site: http://www.aarp.org. AARP is a large, well-known, and politically powerful organization providing information and advocacy for people age 50 and older.

Aiken, L. R. (2004). *Dying, death, and bereavement* (4th ed.). Mahwah, NJ: Erlbaum. A brief but comprehensive survey of research, writings, and professional practices on death and dying.

Aldwin, C. M., Park, C. L., Spiro, A. III, & Abeles, R. P. (2007). *Handbook of health psychology and aging.* New York: The Guilford Press. How biological, psychological, and social factors over the life course affect aging.

Alzheimer's Foundation of America (n.d.). Web site: http://alzidn.org/index.htm.

Booth, S. (2010, February). They're golden. *Real Simple,* pp. 127–135. "There's nothing so nice as a new marriage," the screenwriter Ben Hecht once wrote. But the six couples featured in this magazine story beg to differ. More than 50 years into their marriages, they share their unforgettable moments and secrets of staying together, happily.

Boss, P. (2011). *Loving someone who has dementia: How to find hope while coping with stress and grief.* San Francisco, CA: Jossey-Bass.

Boston Women's Health Book Collective. (2006). *Our bodies, ourselves: Menopause.* New York: Touchstone/ Simon & Schuster.

Brubaker, T. H. (1985). *Later life families.* Beverly Hills, CA: Sage.

Brubaker, T. H. (1991). Families in later life: A burgeoning research area. In A. Booth (Ed.), *Contemporary families: Looking forward, looking back* (pp. 226–248). Minneapolis: National Council on Family Relations.

Bruce, M. L. (2002). Psychosocial risk factors for depressive disorders in late life. *Biological Psychiatry, 52*(3), 175–184.

Daggett, L. M. (2002). Living with loss: Middle-aged men face spousal bereavement. *Qualitative Health Research, 12*(5), 625–639.

Edmondson, B. (2010). All the lonely people. *AARP Magazine.* Researchers find a rise in loneliness in recent years. Web site: http://www.aarp.org /personal-growth/transitions/info-09-2010/all_the_ lonely_people.html.

Fry, R., Cohn, D'V., Livingston, G., & Taylor, P. (2011). The rising age gap in economic well-being: The old prosper relative to the young. *Pew Social & Demographic Trends.* Web site: http://www.pewsocialtrends.org/2011/11/07 /the-rising-age-gap-in-economic-well-being/ Researchers find that households headed by older adults have made dramatic gains over younger adults the past quarter century in terms of economic well-being.

Kornhaber, A. (2004). *The grandparent solution: How parents can build a family team for practical, emotional, and financial success*. San Francisco: Jossey-Bass.

Kuba, C. A. (2006). *Navigating the journey of aging parents: What care receivers want*. New York: Taylor & Francis.

Nadeau, J. W. (1998). *Families making sense of death*. Thousand Oaks, CA: Sage. Well written and provides a rich qualitative analysis of how families make meaning after a significant death.

Niemeyer, R. A. (2011). *Grief and bereavement in contemporary society: Bridging research and practice*. New York: Routledge.

Rank, M. R., & Williams, J. H. (2010). A life course approach to understanding poverty among older American adults. Families in Society. *The Journal of Contemporary Social Services, 91*, 337–341. Nearly half of all elderly Americans will encounter at least 1 year of poverty or near poverty between the ages of 60 and 90.

Rowe, D. (2008). *What should I believe? Why our beliefs about the nature of death and the purpose of life dominate our lives*. London and New York: Routledge. If we use our beliefs as a defense against our feelings of worthlessness, we feel compelled to force our beliefs on other people by coercion or aggression. But if we can create a set of beliefs expressed in religious or philosophical metaphors that are meaningful to us, we can live in peace with ourselves and others.

Silverstein, M., & Giarrusso, R. (2010). Aging and family life: A decade review. *Journal of Marriage and Family, 72* (October), 1039–1058. An excellent overview of recent trends in research.

Skogrand, L., Henderson, K., & Higginbotham, B. (2006). Sandwich generation (fact sheet). Utah State University Cooperative Extension. Web site: http://extension.usu.edu/cooperative.

Troll, L. E. (2001). When the world narrows: Intimacy with the dead? *Generations, 25*(2), 55–58.

Ulker, A. (2008). Wealth holdings and portfolio allocation of the elderly: The role of marital history. *Journal of Family Economic Issues, 30*, 90–108. Death and divorce earlier in life can significantly affect the accumulation of wealth among the elderly.

Van Volkom, M. (2006). Sibling relationships in middle and older adulthood: A review of the literature. *Marriage and Family Review, 40*, 151–170.

Visit the text-specific Online Learning Center at **www.mhhe.com/olson8e** for practice tests, chapter summaries, and PowerPoint slides.

14. *Stress, Abuse, and Family Problems*

Intimacy, Strengths, and
Diversity

Cross-Cultural Perspectives
on Couple and Family Stress

What We Know About Stress

War and Its Effect on Families

Family Coping Strategies

Domestic Violence

Child Abuse and Neglect

Sibling and Child-to-Parent
Abuse

Alcohol Problems in Families

Summary

Key Terms

Activities

Suggested Readings

Intimacy, Strengths, and Diversity

Individuals, couples, and families have extraordinary abilities when it comes to facing the many problems in the world today. Couple and family intimacy is one of the most important components in successfully dealing with life's problems. We know that pulling together as a family—using close couple and family bonds—helps us get through difficult times. Developing and maintaining close and intimate relationships with friends and extended family, and relying on those relationships, is also important in dealing with difficulties. Intimacy involves sharing feelings, sorrows, and joys, which helps people when there is stress in life.

> One individual had grown up learning to be very independent in life. She had learned that she could handle most crises in life, with little help from friends or family. At age 45 she is going through a divorce and a diagnosis of cancer. Even though she had handled most crises successfully, without relying on others for emotional support, she knew this was different—it was going to be more stressful than anything she had experienced thus far in her life.
>
> She approached two close friends and her sister and asked if she could rely on them as she went through the loss of her marriage and her diagnosis with cancer. She already had a close, intimate relationship with each of these people and now she needed to rely on them for support. Each of the people she approached had the same response of surprise. She had never asked for this kind of emotional support before and, of course, they would be there for as long as she needed.
>
> She called or got together with these close friends and family member when she needed to cry, needed to make decisions, or when she just needed the comfortable presence of someone who cared about her. Along the way she wished she had learned to rely on intimate relationships in getting through difficult times earlier in her life. Why did she wait until she was middle aged before she learned this important lesson?

Contrary to the notion that strength means facing a problem without any help, research indicates that the strength to cope with difficulties comes from the close and intimate relationships with loved ones, friends and relatives.

Every couple and family will experience challenges. Strong marriages and strong families will be able to weather difficult times more successfully than people in marriages and families that are not strong. This chapter will describe a study about people who experienced a traumatic childhood and relied on their inner strengths along with using other strategies to become healthy adults. People will also tell you that going through difficult times often makes you a better, more caring person. Facing difficulties and coming through the crisis can also result in stronger marriages and families.

There is variability and diversity in how people define problems and difficulties. One of the models of family stress described in this chapter includes the definition the family or individual gives to the event. For example, some cultures have extended-family networks that provide care for children beyond the nuclear family. In such a culture, an adolescent leaving home to live with a relative may not be defined as a crisis. This may be true, for example, in American Indian families. In a culture where children are expected to live with their parents until they are grown, however, this event might be defined as a real crisis as a child running away from home.

Intimacy, strengths, and diversity all play a part in how people deal with family problems. Close relationships provide resiliency and strength that are not available when one tries to deal with crises alone, and this is likely to be true in all cultures.

Cross-Cultural Perspectives on Couple and Family Stress

The following are some of the aspects of family stress that are common across cultural groups. These are generalized principles that emerged from studying family strengths and stressors in different countries and cultures around the world (DeFrain & Asay, 2007).

1. *All stressors either begin or end up in the family.* No matter what the origin of a stressor, it eventually affects the couple and family system and all its members.

2. *Families from all cultural groups experience couple and family stress.* Although the causes of couple and family stress and the types of issues that are most stressful may vary by cultural group, all couples and families experience and understand the concept of stress.

3. *To manage their stress, couples and families tend to first use internal resources (those inside the family system) before seeking external resources (those outside the family system).* Across many cultural groups, most families rely on their internal resources first, seeking external help only after internal resources have proven to be inadequate.

4. *In many cultures, the extended family system is considered "the family" rather than the nuclear family system. In families with strong extended-family structures, the major resources come from inside the extended family, while fewer resources come from the nuclear family.* For this reason, many researchers and practitioners believe the extended family system, when functioning well, can be much stronger and more resilient than a nuclear family system, which may be weak and isolated from sources of support.

5. *All couples and families have some internal strengths for managing stress in their systems.* However, cross-cultural studies of families have seldom sought to identify family strengths within a cultural group. Instead, they have focused on the problems in families from different cultures. By building on a strengths model, we will be able to more clearly identify useful coping strategies across cultures. And when researchers do this, they are likely to find that approaches to stress and coping from one culture to the next can be remarkably similar.

What We Know About Stress

People lead complicated lives, and the term **stress** is used often in today's society to refer to the daily pressure we all encounter (Monat, Lazarus, & Reevy, 2007). Here we will talk about stress and coping as individuals. Later in the chapter we will describe how families experience and manage stress.

There are three levels of stress. First, there is physiological stress, which is the body's harmful reaction to whatever happens. There is a fast-growing body of evidence that stress causes physical reactions in our bodies, such as increased blood pressure or decreased immune response. Second, there is psychological stress, which involves appraising the threat, resulting in an emotional reaction. Finally, there is sociocultural stress, which is the disturbance of social systems. Examples of sociocultural stress might be war, neighborhood violence, unemployment, or poverty. The effect of the stress of war on individuals and families is discussed elsewhere in this chapter. Stress and emotion are interdependent—where there is stress, there is emotion, and sometimes the reverse is true (Lazarus, 2007).

Coping with Stress

We are coping when we say things like "We're hanging in there" or, as people sometimes say in the Midwest, "It could be worse." Each of us has different ways of coping, and how we cope affects those around us. **Coping** is what we do when we identify something as potentially harmful or stressful (Kleinke, 2007). Coping involves a certain amount of effort or planning, the outcome will not always be positive, and the process takes place over time. Coping can be either problem-focused or emotion-focused. When we do problem-focused coping, we either try to change the situation or behaviors of others or change our attitudes. Emotion-focused coping is managing our own emotional distress and doing such things as exercising or seeking support.

People can respond to stress in a variety of ways, such as confronting the stressful situation, ignoring the stressful situation, or problem solving to change the situation (Kleinke, 2007). Successful coping usually involves being flexible, anticipating long-term effects of a coping response, and making accurate appraisals of the situation. For example, suppose a student faces the possibility of failing a course. Successful coping may include talking to the professor to find out if failing the course is or is not a likely possibility and what the student can do to pass the course. It also means the student may need to look ahead to the next semester and change the current class schedule in order to retake the course. Finally, it means the student needs to look ahead and be realistic about meeting the long-term goal of graduating by a certain date.

Successful coping means you take on life's challenges with personal control and hope (Kleinke, 2007). It means you try to find solutions to problems by developing a plan to address the situation, get advice and support from others, and use the stressful situation as an opportunity to grow. It usually involves a sense of humor and patience. People all have their own personalities that determine how they respond to stress. What we do know is that how we respond can affect our health and can also affect our future opportunities and choices.

Stress and Life Events

The classic work of Thomas H. Holmes, Richard H. Rahe, and their colleagues (Holmes & Ella, 1989; Holmes & Rahe, 1967) has greatly influenced much of the current research on the relationship between life changes and signs of emotional and physiological stress in individuals (Cooper & Dewe, 2007). These pioneering researchers developed a scale of 43 *life events* that require some type of change of behavior, or readjustment. The scale is called the Holmes and Rahe Social Readjustment Rating Scale, but it is often referred to as the Holmes and Rahe Stress Test. These life events include personal, family, financial, and occupational stressors. Table 14.1 lists the top 14 stressors identified by Holmes and Rahe. It is noteworthy that 11 of the top 14 stressors are marriage and family issues. In fact, the scale could legitimately be called a Marriage and Family Stress Test.

Holmes and Rahe found a relationship between life changes and health. Of those people who scored between 0 and 150 points on the scale, more than 30% experienced a serious negative health change in the 2 years that followed. (A serious negative

TABLE 14.1	Stress Test by Holmes and Rahe	
Event		**Points**
* 1. Death of spouse		100
* 2. Divorce		73
* 3. Marital separation		65
4. Jail term		63
* 5. Death of close family member		63
6. Personal injury or loss		53
* 7. Marriage		50
8. Fired at work/lost job		47
* 9. Marital reconciliation		45
*10. Retirement		45
*11. Change in health of family member		44
*12. Pregnancy		40
*13. Sex difficulties		39
*14. Gain of new family member		39

*Stressors related to couples and families.

Note: Impact points indicate the severity of the impact of the stressor on individuals, couples, or families.

Source: "The Social Readjustment Rating Scale" by T. H. Holmes and R. H. Rahe, *Journal of Psychosomatic Research, 11,* p. 213. Copyright 1967 by Elsevier Science Inc. Reprinted by permission of the publisher.

health change might be the development of rheumatoid arthritis, clinical depression, cancer, the onset of alcoholism, or a heart attack.) Of those who scored between 151 and 300 points, about 50% experienced a serious negative health change in the 2 years that followed. And of those who scored more than 300 points, almost 90% experienced a serious negative health change in the 2 years following the rating.

Holmes and Rahe found that physical and emotional problems are likely to occur when individuals experience a cluster of major and minor changes in life. As an example, a middle-aged woman scored above 700 on the Holmes and Rahe Stress Test. She received her divorce in January and remarried in August; her new husband moved out 3 months later; and by late November she had a new live-in companion. Her mother died during the year, and the woman started and lost two jobs. She had a sprinkling of other life changes during the year, including two car accidents and many bills. As might be predicted, she became very depressed and considered suicide. The relationship between stressful events and major health problems in this woman's life is quite clear.

This pioneering work laid the groundwork for what we know today about the link between stress and physical illness (Cooper & Dewe, 2007). There is significant research that connects stress with breast cancer, cardiovascular disease, and the common cold (Jones & Bright, 2007). Some research suggests that all kinds of cancers might be related to stressful life events.

Breast Cancer and Negative Life Events. Research that supports the idea that cancer and stress are related dates back to 1900 (Jones & Bright, 2007). These studies suggested that the loss of a close relative was often the incident that resulted in cancer. More recent work in the 1990s focused on breast cancer and its relation to negative life events. The results of these studies are mixed. Although some studies show a relationship, other studies show no relationship. Many of the studies that show a relationship get national attention, and therefore the public is likely to believe that a relationship exists. Jones and Bright (2007) conclude that, although we simply do not know for sure, it seems likely that the relationship between negative life events and breast cancer is negligibly small compared to the role of biological factors.

Chronic Work Stressors and Cardiovascular Disease. The relationship between work stress and heart disease was a focus of research in the 1980s and 1990s. This relationship was generally supported by research findings and often focused on increased blood pressure, which is a component of heart disease (Jones & Bright, 2007). Findings indicate that the most stress in employment comes from jobs with low control and high demand. For example, people in food service or those in the medical field might fit into this category. Other studies suggest that low control, high demand, and low support are the key factors that affect heart disease. Jones and Bright conclude that, at the very least, a situation of high demand and low control leads to increased risk for heart disease.

Stress and the Common Cold and Influenza. There is evidence that stressful life events contribute to the common cold, even when we do not think we are stressed (Jones & Bright, 2007). Interpersonal conflicts and work-related stress as well as minor hassles are often related to getting a cold. Emotional stress is also related to a greater risk of getting an infection and flu.

Other research has delved into whether stressors are linked to negative health behaviors, which then become the real cause of health problems (Jones & Bright, 2007). For example, stress may cause a person to drink more, smoke more, exercise less, or engage in marital conflict, all of which affect one's health. Stress, therefore, may be indirectly related to health issues. The studies are inconclusive, so it is likely that further research will be needed to sort out this complex issue.

Because stress can affect the immune system, it is important to do things to support your body's natural defenses (Somer, 2007). One important thing you can do is to eat well, which means eating breakfast and including low-fat foods in your diet. It is also important to avoid tobacco and limit your consumption of alcohol and caffeine. It is useful to exercise daily and sleep at least 7 hours per day. Emotionally, it is important to think positively, laugh, and use relaxation techniques that you find useful.

Top Five Stressors for Couples

In a study of 20,000 couples, the purpose was to determine what are the top five most stressful issues that couples experienced (Larson & Olson, 2012). The data were collected from dating, engaged, and married couples using the PREPARE-ENRICH Couple Program (Olson, Larson, Olson-Sigg, 2009) that contains a Personal Stress Profile. The Profile contained 25 of the most frequent stressors that were found in previous research by Olson and colleagues (see Table 14.2).

For dating couples, their jobs were the biggest stressor for both males and females and job security and income were also problematic. While women felt that being emotionally upset was their top issue, it was also in the top five stressors for men. Women also were concerned about feeling overweight. This was not an issue for men.

For engaged couples, much of their stress related to the wedding, including the cost of the wedding and how planning reduced their level of exercise and sleep.

BOX 14.1 At Issue

Ambiguous Loss: When We Are Uncertain If a Person Is In or Out of Our Family

In the 1970s, I was interested in family stress and especially why some families could cope with high stress while others could not. I focused on what I proposed was an immense stressor—**ambiguous loss,** a term I coined, meaning a loss that remained unclear. That is, the loss could not be verified as definite—like a death. Ambiguous loss is a loss without closure, often for years, even for a lifetime. **Boundary ambiguity** is the outcome of ambiguous loss. It means that people are confused about who is in or out of their family system. For example, is a parent who has dementia and no longer knows who you are still perceived as part of your family? Yes, but no longer in the same way. The change is stressful but does not have to mean closing out the ill person. He or she is still present physically and should be visited, talked to, touched, and cared for, even though the relationship is no longer reciprocal. Actually, such a one-sided relationship requires a deeper level of humanity and maturity on our part. We grow deeper and stronger when we are able to stick with such difficult human relationships.

There are two types of ambiguous loss. Type 1 occurs when a loved one is physically absent but kept psychologically present because there is no assurance of death. Examples are loved ones who are missing in action, kidnapped, lost at sea, swept away by floods or a tsunami, vanished without a trace, and so on. More common examples are breakups, divorce, adoption, and uprooting through immigration and migration.

Type 2 ambiguous loss occurs when someone you care about is present but absent psychologically. That is, the person is physically with you but cognitively and emotionally

Pauline Boss

gone. Examples are Alzheimer's disease or other dementias, traumatic brain injury, addiction, depression and other chronic mental illnesses, unresolved grief, autism, and so on. More common examples are homesickness, preoccupation with loss, and obsessions with the Internet, computer games, or work. This type of ambiguous loss is the topic of my latest book, *Loving Someone Who Has Dementia* (Boss, 2011). Indeed, the ambiguous loss of dementia leads to boundary ambiguity in families. It takes a while to know who is in and who is out in such unclear situations of absence and presence. Hopefully, we can tolerate the ambiguity and continue to care for someone even though they are no longer fully present.

I wrote this book especially for families because I believe that theory can be useful for ordinary people, not just academics or professionals. With the theory of ambiguous loss to guide their thinking and actions, family members who love someone who has dementia can find enough resilience for their long journey with ambiguous loss before death brings some measure of finality and clarity.

What I tell family members is this: The lack of clear information about their loved one's absence and presence is immensely stressful and even traumatizing, but the main thing to remember is that the situation is abnormal, not the people experiencing it. The task—when the problem (in this case, dementia) has no solution—is not to seek a solution, but rather, to help people find the strength and resilience to live with the ambiguity. This is not easy in a *can-do* culture that hungers for certainty, but it is possible. I have seen many people find the resiliency to tolerate,

TABLE 14.2	Top Five Stressors for Couples	
Dating Couples	**Engaged Couples**	**Married Couples**
1. My job	My job	My Spouse
2. Feeling emotionally upset	Financial concerns	My Job
3. Inadequate income	Cost of wedding	Feeling emotionally upset
4. Your partner	Lack of exercise	Inadequate income
5. Job security	Lack of sleep	House projects undone

Source: Larson, P. J. & Olson, D. H., Top five stressors for couples, www.prepare-enrich.com. Copyright © 2012 Life Innovations, Inc. Reprinted with permission.

even embrace, their ambiguous loss. They learn to think in both-and terms: With dementia, "My loved one is here but also gone," or in the case of a physically missing relative or friend, "My loved one is probably dead, but maybe not."

Paradoxically, with dialectical (*both-and*) thinking, we find the resilience to live with the imperfections of absence and presence and losses that have no closure. Our loved ones are "gone but still here" or "here but also gone."

As a family therapist, and from the narrative perspective, I see a family's ambiguous loss as a story without an ending. Their family tale has a beginning and middle but no end. So people must socially construct their own ending. With ambiguous loss and the inherent lack of information and facts, that ending most often remains in flux. One day, you see the person as fully gone; the next day, you see them as here again. Back and forth. Ups and downs. To further complicate the situation, family members often see the situation differently, and they fight about what it all means. I tell them it is okay to see the situation differently at this time. They need to tolerate each other's interpretations of ambiguous loss, as there is no certainty here. Hopefully, they find ways to live without a clear answer. This involves *both-and* thinking. When answers are not forthcoming, or when a problem has no solution, the goal is to find the resilience to withstand the ongoing stress.

Ambiguous loss and its subsequent boundary ambiguity create the most stressful kind of loss because there is no possibility of closure or resolution. The stressor (ambiguous loss) goes on and on, often without finality. It immobilizes individuals and couples by confusing the necessary family processes of decision making, boundary maintenance, role assignments, coping, adaptation, and resiliency. Relationships are ruptured by the ambiguity, roles remain unclear, family boundaries remain blurred, and family celebrations and rituals, the guts of family life, are often canceled. Our task is to make sure family processes continue, although with adaptations, despite ambiguous loss.

What we have learned is that the majority of people can and do live with ambiguous loss *if* they are given family and community support. Not everyone needs medical intervention after such a loss, but they do need human connection. Peer groups are useful in providing ongoing human connection and emotional support; professionals are useful in providing ongoing psychoeducation—informational support. Meanwhile, society must be more patient and normalize the sadness and grief that lingers when losses have no clarity or closure. Remember: with ambiguous loss, the situation is pathological, not the person who is experiencing it.

In sum, ambiguous loss is a more common type of loss than we once knew. We need to know what is, how to cope with it, and how to live with it. Unlike with death, there is no closure. For ambiguous losses, the goal is learning to embrace the ambiguity. We can practice this skill by walking an unknown path, by fishing a new river, by improvisation in theater or music, and by going for a drive without an agenda and purposely getting lost just for the adventure of it. Ambiguity does not have to devastate; it can make us stronger even with loss. We can live with the ambiguity of loved ones who are not totally in or out of our family system. We can learn to manage the stress of ambiguity.

Dr. Pauline Boss is a professor emeritus of family social science at the University of Minnesota-St. Paul. She is a former president of the National Council on Family Relations, and her books include: *Ambiguous Loss: Learning to Live with Unresolved Grief* (Harvard University Press), *Family Stress Management* (Sage), *Loss, Trauma, and Resilience: Therapeutic Work with Ambiguous Loss* (Norton), and *Loving Someone Who Has Dementia* (Jossey-Bass).
Source: Pauline Boss, Ph.D., Professor Emeritus, Department of Family Social Science, University of Minnesota; www.ambiguousloss.com; Author of Ambiguous Loss, Harvard University Press, 1999, and Loss, Trauma, and Resilience, W. W. Norton, 2006.

How the couple handles the wedding is often predictive of how they will handle other major stressors in their life. It is important for them to learn from that experience so they don't repeat the problems from the past.

For married couples, both spouses agreed that their most stressful issues were, in fact, their partner. Blaming one's partner is a very common approach when people feel stressed in a relationship. However, this often indicates that they are not able to work together to resolve issues or support each other during difficult times. The next most stressful issues were their jobs, feeling emotionally upset, and inadequate income. Again, only women were stressed out by their weight, while men were more stressed by job security.

Five Tips for Dealing with Stress in Your Relationship

1. *Share what is most stressing each of you.* What is amazing is that most couples do not know how stressed their partner is feeling and what are the top stressful issues for them. In counseling couples using the Personal Stress Profile from PREPARE-ENRICH, David Olson has found that couples are surprised how little they know about their partner's level of stress. So simply talking about stress is a good beginning since it will provide insight and greater mutual understanding.

2. *Prioritize what stressor to tackle first.* It is not realistic to handle more than one or two major stress issues at one time. So talk about what are the specific stressful issues that you want to work on in the next few weeks.

3. *Develop a plan with specific goals to manage the stress together.* First, set one or two specific goals for each of you. Then brainstorm together some ideas about how to achieve these goals. Working together makes it more of a team effort and will increase the chances that you both will succeed.

4. *Use your communication and relationship skills.* This is the time for you to each practice and use the best communication skills that you have to make this process successful.

5. *Support and praise each other for progress.* Set up a time (say Thursday after dinner) to review the progress each of you has made and to praise each other for good efforts. Try not to blame each other, but find ways to support each other in reaching your goals.

In summary, use these five steps for handling one or two stressful issues for you and your partner over a period of 4 to 5 weeks, with weekly reviews. You will be amazed at the progress if you both work together and support each other. After some success with one issue, you can then move on to tackle together another issue. The good news is that being successful in resolving an issue will not only reduce your stress level, it will also bring you closer together.

The ABC-X Family Crisis Model

The late Reuben Hill (1958) was a pioneer in the field of family studies at the University of Minnesota. Hill explained why some families do better than others in hard times with what he called the ABC-X Model. The model argues that:

A = the stressor event
B = the family's crisis-meeting resources
C = the definition the family gives to the event
X = the crisis

Hill defined a *stressor* as "a situation for which the family has had little or no prior preparation," and a *crisis* as "any sharp or decisive change for which old patterns are inadequate." The dictionary defines crisis as simply "a turning point in life," and that works fine, also.

To better understand what Hill is saying here, think about a family in which the mother is driving to her job one morning when a speeding driver runs a red light and broadsides the woman's car, injuring her in the crash. The *stressor event,* A, is the accident that causes multiple injuries to this young mother. But simply knowing that the car crash occurred and resulted in serious injuries does not give you a clue about how the crisis will unfold.

If the family possesses important *crisis-meeting resources*, B, the likelihood that the family will survive the crisis and somehow manage to rise above the tragedy increases dramatically. *If* the family's crisis-meeting resources include invaluable relationship strengths among the family members, *if* the family has adequate financial resources, *if* the family has health insurance and access to high-quality medical care, *if* the family is connected to supportive people at work, in the community, in the neighborhood, and in their own extended family. . . . There are literally countless *ifs* to consider, but the more crisis-meeting resources the family can tap into, the better the outcome of the crisis will be for the family.

C, *the definition the family gives to this event,* also plays an important role in how the crisis unfolds. When family members can find some good to hold on to through the tragedy, when they can find good things mixed in among the wreckage of the crash, they can find a way to look to the future and grow together. If they can reframe the situation in a positive light in some way, the likelihood of a more positive resolution to X, *the crisis,* is likely.

So, back to the basic question: "Why do some families fail in a crisis and some families succeed?" The ABC-X Model helps us understand that it is not just the stressor event but the interaction of the event with the family's strengths, the resources they can tap, and how they think about the situation that all combine to determine how severe the crisis will become in their lives. Hill's model is very useful in helping us see how some families rise above the traumatic events they face in life, while other families sink.

Life as a Roller Coaster

Reuben Hill also observed that the path families follow as they deal with a crisis in life looks in many ways like a roller coaster ride, full of ups and downs. Think back to the young mother severely injured in the car crash. Here's just one example from countless possibilities of how the crisis could unfold: Right before the crash as she is driving to work she is thinking about how wonderful her life is and how much she loves her job, her husband, and her children. Seconds later she is broadsided by the speeding driver running the red light and the young mother's life is torn apart. She almost dies on two occasions, on the way to the hospital and during surgery. Her family is thrown into despair—dad, sister, brother, grandparents—everyone believes the young mother will die, and even as she begins to recover, the family becomes disorganized, not knowing how to function effectively or adjust to all the changes necessitated by the mother's incapacity. She endures two surgeries in the first week, and in the following weeks and months she slowly starts to recover from the devastation caused to her body. Complications arise and 3 months after the accident she is back in surgery for reconstructive work to her face. Finally, she leaves the hospital and intensive rehabilitation services begin. Most important of all, she has returned to the shelter of her loving family, who strive to care for her as best they can.

Now, imagine this possibility: Four years after the crash she has made an amazing recovery. However, the family is *not back to normal,* because no family returns to normal after a profound crisis in life. The family has found *a new normal* in life. Mom, partially disabled, has found a new job, a job that is less physically strenuous than her old job. And everyone in the family loves and values each other more than before the catastrophe. They are all much less likely to take each other for granted, as they often did before the crisis. They have learned that life is, indeed, a slender thread, and we all need to cherish each moment because moments simply do not last forever.

Think back to Reuben Hill's idea about how a family crisis can be likened to a roller coaster ride. In Figure 14.1 we have sketched out a very simplified version of how the

FIGURE 14.1

A Family Endures the Aftermath of a Serious Motor Vehicle Accident

Source: Getting Connected, Staying Connected: Loving Each Other Day by Day (p. 184) by J. DeFrain and the University of Nebraska–Lincoln Extension Family Action Research and Writing Team, 2012. Bloomington, IN: iUniverse. Copyright © 2012 by the University of Nebraska–Lincoln Extension. Reprinted by permission of the University of Nebraska–Lincoln Extension.

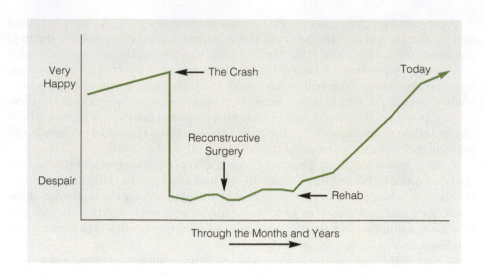

young mother and other family members might draw the roller coaster ride they were on for 4 years after the accident. Before the crash life was looking up for everyone in the family. When the crash occurred it was as if the whole family fell off the edge of a cliff. Their very happy life together was plunged into an abyss of fear and despair, wondering whether the mother would live and how they would go on in life. But as life unfolded they gained strength from the shelter of each other's arms and moved on through the ups and downs of the mother's recovery and countless other challenges the family faced. Four years from the time of the crash the family is almost as happy as it was before the crash, and the trend continues to be in a positive direction.

A Roller Coaster Course of Adjustment

The roller coaster model is very relevant for understanding the attacks on America that happened on September 11, 2001, when the World Trade Center in New York and a section of the Pentagon in Washington, D.C., were destroyed.

In considering the attack this country was caught totally by surprise, which created a period of disorganization, both for the country and for the families who had family members in the area. Soon after the attack, the cities of New York and Washington, D.C., the country, and the families started to begin the process of recovery by mobilizing a large variety of resources. This process of recovery took months and eventually the families, the cities, and the country became reorganized. In the process, the reorganized cities and families were changed and in some cases were better than they had been before the crisis. So a crisis can be problematic in the short run and in the long run can strengthen the various components that were initially attacked.

Family Systems Changes Before and After the 9/11 Attacks

An important aspect of family systems is that the family changes to deal with any crises. Let us consider the Greenberg family before and after the destruction of the Twin Towers (Figure 14.2). The father, Henry, worked on the 72nd floor, and it was initially unclear whether he had been able to escape. He had been married for 26 years and had three children ages 22, 20, and 17.

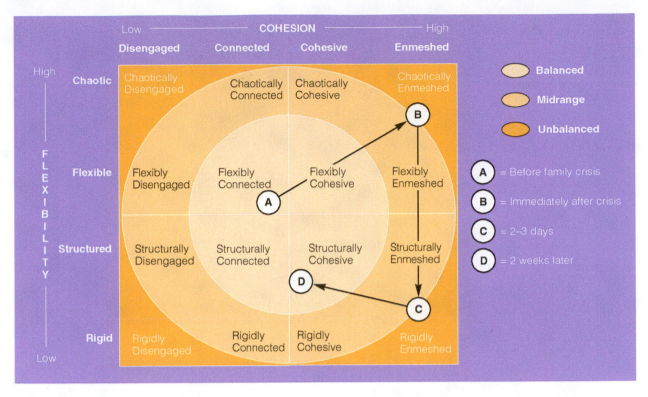

FIGURE 14.2

Family Changes in Response to the 9/11 Attacks Adapted from W.R. Burr and S.R. Klein, Reexamining Family Stress: New Theory and Research. Copyright © 1994 by Sage Publications. Reproduced with permission of Sage Publications Inc. in the format Republish in a book via Copyright Clearance Center.

Before 9/11 (point A), the family was *flexibly connected*, which is appropriate for their stage of the life cycle. Hours after the attack (point B), the family system became *chaotically enmeshed* because the family did not know if the father had escaped from his office. The family, along with close relatives and friends, gathered at their home and huddled together in a mutually supportive way. This high level of closeness and bonding created "enmeshment," and the fact that they did not know if he had survived created a great deal of chaos in their family.

During the next day or two after the attack, the family continued to stay together and were emotionally enmeshed, but they developed a highly organized style of operating, creating a *rigidly enmeshed* system (point C). They got very organized as a group in an attempt to find out what had happened to Henry. This rigidity was an attempt to bring some stability to the chaos by reorganizing some of their family. They decided that their home would be the headquarters and that everyone needed to be in touch by phone. They divided up into teams so they could better search to find out what had happened to Henry. Some family members went to the site of the attack, others went to check out the hospitals, and others stayed at home. They checked in with the home every few hours.

On the third day, a miracle happened from their point of view. They found that Henry was in a downtown hospital but was severely injured in one leg and arm and had some memory loss. He could not remember his phone number but did know his name. That enabled the hospital on the second day to post his name.

Two weeks later, he was home, and the family then changed again, becoming a *structurally cohesive* system (point D). Some of the rigidity was no longer there, but they were still rather organized in order to care for him and to start to get back to their normal routines. Some of the closeness decreased and the family moved from being enmeshed to being cohesive. But the family was closer and more organized

The death of a family member results in a difficult time for that family. The family is likely to experience family disorganization for some period following the death.

than before the attack, which was a useful style during the family's recovery from the stress that they had all experienced.

This example illustrates one family's ability to adapt to a crisis. The family changed system types several times over the 6-week period following the attack, and these changes were beneficial in helping the family more effectively deal with this major stressor.

After studying the impact of stress on several hundred couples and families by plotting the changes on the Couple and Family Map, the following general principles of change related to stress were developed (Olson, 1996). *First,* under stress couples and families often move in the direction of becoming more extreme on both flexibility (a move toward a more chaotic system) and cohesion (a move toward a more enmeshed system). *Second,* communication almost always increases during a stressful event. *Third,* once the stress has abated, couples and families usually return to a similar—but rarely to the same—type of system they had before the stress. *Fourth,* couples and families often require a minimum of 6 months to a year to adjust to a major stress. *Fifth,* balanced couple and family systems tend to become unbalanced during the stress and then return to another balanced system about a year later.

War and Its Effect on Families

The wars that have resulted from the events of 9/11 have affected many aspects of family and community life. One of the issues couples and families face in the military is **deployment**, which is determined by the government and is out of the control of couples. Deployment refers to the time when a military person leaves his or her family and engages in training or combat. Because the couple and family have no control over where or when the family member will be deployed it creates uncertainty. "The only certainty about the deployment of a service member during an era of terrorism, is uncertainty from beginning to end" (Huebner, Mancini, Wilcox, Grass, & Grass, 2007, p. 113).

Those who are deployed may experience the lasting effects of trauma. The family members remaining at home experience effects of separation, reunion, and other difficulties. Finally, communities are faced with the question of how to support these families. There have been many studies about the short-term and long-term effects on military families since the beginning of the wars in Iraq and Afghanistan. It is likely that military deployment and the effects on families will continue for years, and therefore it is likely that research about and services to these families will continue.

Because 55% of military members are married and 43% have children, with nearly half of the children under 5 years of age, family relationships are a major concern for today's military families (Huebner, Mancini, Bowen, & Orthner, 2009). Research regarding the relationship between military deployment and couple and family relationships has been conducted as a result of the current wars in Iraq and Afghanistan.

Couples

Because more than half of military members are married, the marriage relationship for military personnel is a focus of concern. Here is how things worked for one couple anticipating marriage as they dealt with deployment:

> Jenny and Allen were planning to get married in 4 months. Allen was in the National Guard and knew he could be deployed to Iraq. One day he received his deployment orders—he was expected to leave in 1 month for training before going to Iraq. Jenny and Allen were devastated. They'd known that this could happen, but the reality of living apart under these circumstances was overwhelmingly difficult. They were both 24 years old and were totally unprepared to deal with Allen going to war. Their extended families were wonderfully supportive, but even they had little experience with military life and did not know what to expect.
>
> The couple decided to get married before Allen left, and everyone pitched in to put together a lovely wedding in less than a month. This was a bittersweet event, because everyone involved knew that immediately following the wedding Allen would be leaving, and the uncertainty about the couple's future together was difficult for everyone. Jenny was often seen crying as she tried on wedding dresses, selected flowers, and met with the photographer.
>
> The wedding was a very difficult experience and not the happy occasion of most weddings. Even the guests felt the sadness that pervaded the ceremony. "'Til death do us part" took on new meaning and brought tears to everyone's eyes.
>
> Allen left 2 days after the wedding in a very tearful good-bye with Jenny and all extended family members. Jenny moved in with her parents because she did not want to live alone. Allen is currently in Iraq and hopes to be home soon.

Jenny and other spouses deal with many stresses as their spouses are engaged in military operations. Spouses, who may be either men or women, fear for their partner, face challenges of maintaining a household, face coping with being the only parent available for children, and experience the marital strain due to separation with an uncertain return (Mansfield et al., 2010).

The stress that couples feel when one partner is deployed can create mental health issues that interfere with marital well-being. According to Mansfield et al. (2010), wives whose husbands had deployed were more likely to have mental health issues than those whose military husbands had not deployed. The kinds of mental health issues included depression, anxiety, and sleep disorders. These researchers also found that these mental health issues increased with length of deployment—the longer the spouse was deployed, the more symptoms occurred and the more likely it was that the at-home spouse would seek mental health services. See Box 14.2 for more information about the impact of war on the families left behind.

Those who have been deployed and have experienced combat can develop multiple mental and physical health issues that can affect marital or couple relationships.

BOX 14.2   At Issue

The Impact of War on Families Left Behind

When you think about one country going to war against another, your immediate concern is for the soldiers who will be fighting on the front lines and the civilians caught in the crossfire. It's easy to imagine—and often to see—the sacrifices they have made as part of their job and their duty. It is not so easy to see the sacrifices made by the families soldiers leave behind.

The long wars in Afghanistan and Iraq over more than a decade have affected the lives of approximately 2 million U.S. service members and their families in many different ways. A study conducted by the RAND Corporation of reservists who had been deployed found that 63% of the service members said their families coped well or very well with the deployment; 16% coped *moderately well*; 8% *poorly*; and 13% of the service members did not know or gave no answer. In the same study, spouses of the service members said that 62% of the families coped *well or very well*; 20% coped *moderately well*; 7% coped *poorly*; and 10% did not know or gave no answer (Hosek, 2011).

Problems Related to the Deployment

In the RAND study (p. 36) service members and their spouses reported many different problems related to the deployment:

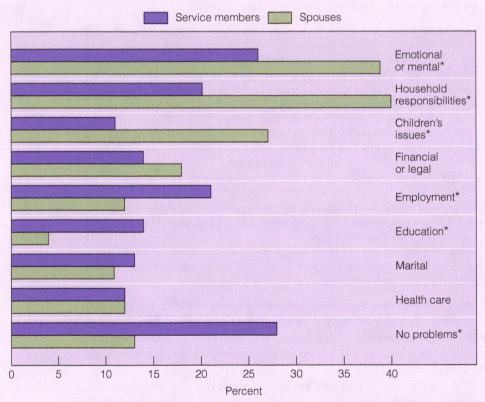

*Statistically significant at p < 0.10.

Positive Aspects of the Deployment

The RAND study (p. 37) also found positive things that were reported by the service members and their spouses in regard to the deployment:

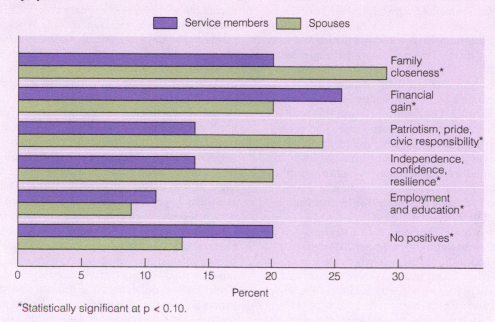

*Statistically significant at p < 0.10.

Do the Service Members Plan to Stay in the Military Until Retirement?

Just over half of the service members and their spouses indicated in the RAND study (p. 38) that the families intended to stay in the reserve component until they were eligible for retirement. As the figure below indicates, more than that plan to leave before they are eligible for retirement.

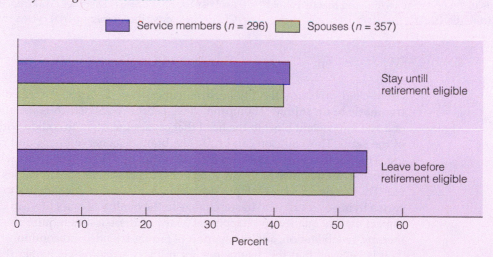

BOX 14.2 *(Contd.)*

The death toll for American military service members continues to mount in Iraq and Afghanistan, and reached more than 6,400 by mid-2012 (*Washington Post*, 2012). Estimates of the number of Iraqi and Afghani people who have died as a consequence of the conflicts run into the hundreds of thousands. No one knows for sure, and there is a great deal of controversy surrounding the numbers (Tirman, 2012).

Early in the Iraq war, one team of journalists tried to put a human face on the conflict by looking closer at the American losses. The reporters found that by the end of 2004, almost 1,400 American troops had been killed and approximately 9,000 wounded, along with thousands upon thousands of Iraqis. Among the Americans killed were 27 women, 6 of whom were mothers. Their 10 children were a fraction of the more than 900 who had lost a parent in Iraq by that time (Hoffman & Rainville, 2004).

The reporters found that more than 40% of the American war dead through November 2004 were married, and 429 had children, many of whom were under the age of 10. There are more "married with children" soldiers in this war than in past wars, partly because of the large numbers of reserve forces in Iraq, who tend to be older and more settled than active-duty soldiers (Hoffman & Rainville, 2004).

The reporters quoted Charles Moskos, a leading military sociologist and Northwestern University professor, who said, "As much as we are concerned about veterans' programs, we now have to be concerned about orphan programs. This is the first time we crossed that threshold" (Hoffman & Rainville, 2004).

Military families have always had to face different challenges than those faced by civilian families. Often, military families move from city to city, or even country to country, as they follow military orders. Children and spouses have to learn to adapt quickly to new environments and to make new friends they may be with for only a few short months. Spouses must learn to be single parents while their husbands or wives are away for long periods. And these are challenges that occur during peacetime.

During wartime, the challenges are even greater as families cope with uncertainty and loss. An article in *Newsday* (Perez, 2004) described three families' struggles to deal with the holiday season. For one family, Christmas would never be the same, as Army Specialist Victor Martinez, 21, was buried on December 24th. He had joined the army to help pay for college and to get a head start on his dream of becoming a police officer. In contrast, the family of Navy Hospital Corpsman Thomas Smith Jr., 23, was celebrating Smith, wounded, who returned home a hero and became a father just five days before Christmas. A third family waited and worried as their only child, Sergeant Francisco Soriano, stationed in Kuwait, waited for his orders to go to Iraq. His mother, who would not put up a tree until her son came home, said, "I don't sleep well. . . . I don't eat well. I can't watch the news. My only desire is to open the door and see his face again."

When soldiers are sent off to war, families undergo emotional cycles. The *Iraq War Clinician Guide,* published by the Department of Veterans Affairs' National Center for Post-Traumatic Stress Disorder (Waldrep, Cozza, & Chen, 2004), describes the emotional cycle's five stages:

Often-cited problems include posttraumatic stress disorder, described below, and **traumatic brain injury** (Thompson, 2008, February 25), which is usually the result of a sudden, violent blow to the head that causes the brain to collide with the inside of the skull. This collision can bruise the brain, tear nerve fibers, and cause bleeding. The resulting symptoms can include severe headaches, problems with memory, confusion, an inability to follow directions, depression, and difficulties concentrating. These issues, along with physical injuries that affect one's ability to continue to earn a living or result in a drastic change in the quality of one's life, can dramatically impact marital quality and happiness. Many of these issues require counseling and therapy, rehabilitation, and the support of family, friends, and community.

It is believed that the divorce rate for military personnel is higher than for civilians. Research on women in the military supports this belief, while studies on men are less clear. The number of women in the military who are divorcing is three times that of men. There is speculation that men who remain at home are at a greater risk

1. *Predeployment.* Between the time the family is notified and the time the soldier leaves, families often go through denial and then intense preparation for and anticipation of the departure.
2. *Deployment.* During the first few a months of the soldier's absence, there can be significant emotional turmoil, including depression and feelings of abandonment. Families must find a new balance as they take on the responsibilities of the absent loved one.
3. *Sustainment.* While the soldier is away, families settle into a new routine. Some families, especially those with little outside support, have a more difficult time with this than others, and children may begin to act out in inappropriate ways.
4. *Redeployment.* Just before the soldier is due to return home, families often experience great excitement and anticipation along with great anxiety.
5. *Postdeployment.* While most homecomings are joyous occasions, they can also be accompanied by unrealistic fantasies about the reunion. Soldiers may find it hard to integrate into the family structure that has formed while they were away, and families may have a difficult time giving up new patterns they have created. It may also take time for couples to reestablish physical and emotional intimacy.

The five stages outline some of the emotional impacts on soldiers' families. But there are economic impacts as well. One team of reporters focused on members of the 1161st Transportation Company, which had been on the longest deployment of any National Guard unit since World War II (Caplin & McGirt, 2004).

In rural areas like Ephrata, Washington, people often join the National Guard for a second income or as a way to pay for college. However, when a unit ships out, that economic advantage often disappears, Despite popular belief, the U.S. Army does not supply all of a soldier's needs, and it's up to the families to make up the difference. One soldier's wife said she had spent about $3,000 on hardware and supplies for her husband, and another $2,200 to ship it all to Iraq. Soldiers and their families also pay for phone calls home. Although they get a discount rate, it often costs more than $1,000 a month to keep in touch (Caplin & McGirt, 2004).

And while federal law requires employers to hold jobs for National Guard troops on active duty, it does not require that their companies pay their salaries or continue to pay heath benefits. The U.S. General Accounting Office issued a report in March 2003 stating that 41% of reservists reported that they earned less on active duty than in their civilian jobs. Spouses left at home often have to seek employment or second jobs in order to support their families (Caplin & McGirt, 2004).

The families in Ephrata, Washington, were planning a huge celebration when their loved ones returned home from the war. As one soldier's wife put it, "We deserve a party, too. I truly believe anyone who was left behind serves their country, too" (Caplin & McGirt, 2004).

for isolation and experience less support than women who stay behind, which may be the reason for this higher percentage of women in the military divorcing (Hull, 2011).

Those who believe divorce is more common among military families cite the increased number of stressors and challenges related to deployment, as well as incentives for early marriage:

1. **Stress:** Repeated and extended family separations; dealing with the soldier's psychological and physical injuries; and difficulty communicating during deployments.
2. **Selection:** The military attracts and selects men and women with pre-existing factors for divorce, including a younger age, lower levels of education, having been victims of abuse, or having divorced parents. Other risk factors include substance abuse, lack of emotional response by the military member, depression, domestic violence, and posttraumatic stress disorder (PTSD) (Hull, 2011).

Children

Researchers have recently focused on the effects of parents' deployment on children. These children experience depression, acting out, poor academic performance, and discipline problems at home (Huebner et al., 2007). Adolescents experience challenges with their parents' deployment because their ability to cope with such stresses is not fully developed and these stressors add to the existing demands of adolescent development. In fact, children younger than age 8 are unlikely even to understand the concept of war and therefore might know that a parent is gone but have no real understanding about where they are (O'Malley, Blankemeyer, Walker, & Dellmann-Jenkins, 2007). For children and adolescents whose parent or parents are deployed, there may be issues of relocation, changes in family roles and routines, and loss of a parental figure for extended and unknown periods of time.

In one study of 107 youths 12 to 18 years of age with a deployed parent, researchers found that the youths experienced several effects directly related to the deployment (Huebner et al., 2007). These youths felt an overall sense of loss and uncertainty. They used words such as *lonely, mad, confused, worried,* and *afraid* to describe these feelings. They also experienced changes in roles and responsibilities because they had to help cover the role filled by their deployed parent. They experienced mental health issues such as depression, changes in sleeping patterns, sadness, crying, and anxiety. Finally, they described conflicts in their relationships at home that often resulted in emotional outbursts. These conflicts were typically focused on the relationships with their mothers, and they talked about how stressed she was. They also talked about how difficult reunions were and how difficult it was to integrate the deployed parent into the family again.

It is generally found that children's ability to cope with the deployment of a parent is dependent upon the adjustment of the at-home parent (Huebner et al., 2009). For example, if the at-home mother is depressed, it is more likely that children will experience problems. It is likely that if the at-home parent is not coping well, the children will experience, to some degree, the loss of both parents.

The Role of the Community in Supporting Military Families

Several recently developed social programs help military families deal with stress (Huebner et al., 2009). Army Child and Youth Services has partnered with National 4-H, which is part of the Extension Service, to provide youth development programs to support military youth and families on U.S. Army installations worldwide. Operation: Military Kids supports military children wherever they live, on or off military bases. The many activities for youth and families focus on recreational, social, and educational programming. The goal is to form friendships and support networks for families. A third program, Essential Life Skills for Military Families, focuses on the relational and practical skills that military reserve families need to help them cope with the uncertainties and challenges of deployment.

Many local communities are creating their own formal and informal support systems for military families. Some help the at-home families of the deployed with house repairs, child care, household bills, or other needs. The overall goal of community programs is to provide military families with support systems to deal with the stress of military life and deployment. These programs help connect potentially isolated family members with services in the community and also provide opportunities for those not in military services to support those who are.

Posttraumatic Stress Disorder and War

With troops deployed in Iraq, Afghanistan, and other places where they are experiencing combat, we have many individuals affected by **posttraumatic stress disorder (PTSD)** and the resulting symptoms. These symptoms are causing stress and disruption in marriage and family relationships (Carey, 2007; Greer, 2005). According to Sammons (2005), "PTSD can be a chronic and debilitating disorder—one closely associated with related problems such as substance abuse, depression, and domestic and occupational dysfunction" (p. 902). It can result from combat or other traumatic events.

Soldiers are exposed to urban fighting, suicide bombers, and guerilla tactics. When these traumatic events are experienced consistently and over long periods of time, it is a predictor of later mental health problems (Carey, 2007; Greer, 2005). It makes sense, then, that mental health problems are the second most common reason for medical military discharge, second only to orthopedic injuries (Sammons, 2005). Some reports indicate that as many as 10% of those serving in combat may have a diagnosis of PTSD, which indicates that problems for family life are also substantial for these troops (Fals-Stewart & Kelley, 2005; Sammons, 2005).

A common symptom of PTSD is domestic violence, with one study indicating that the rate of violence for those diagnosed with PTSD was 5.4 times that of veterans who were not diagnosed with the disorder (Sherman, Sautter, Jackson, Lyons, &

Increased family separation has resulted from recent military deployment. Many families are having a difficult time responding to family members repeatedly being deployed to face difficult war-time combat.

Han, 2006). Those veterans experiencing depression were also more likely to be violent than those veterans who did not experience depression.

Other mental health symptoms related to PTSD, such as substance abuse and occupational dysfunction, are not as well documented. These issues are also likely to be very disruptive to family life and personal well-being. Treatment for PTSD is usually a combination of drugs and therapy (McGirk, 2009, November 30). Studies also show that veterans with PTSD recover faster if they have a supportive social network of family and friends to help them recover.

Family Coping Strategies

The Chinese pictograph or symbol for the word *crisis* is a composite of two other pictographs: the symbols for *danger* and *opportunity* (Figure 14.3). For thousands of years, the Chinese have understood that a crisis can be a dangerous time but also a time to look for new opportunities. Strong families tend to agree with this idea. Professionals working with those under stress have commonly found that in the midst of the hurt and despair of a serious crisis, there are also some positive outcomes as people draw on their strengths.

What good could possibly come out of a disaster? Many families say that after they have weathered a crisis together, their relationships with each other are stronger, more positive, and more loving. People who have gone through a crisis often relate how they became stronger as individuals as well as closer to their partners and families. They grow to appreciate their families more and become more willing to share with them.

Theoretical Perspectives

Pauline Boss (2002) clarified the difference between coping as a family resource and coping as a process. She explains why the concept of **managing stress** is a more accurate description of how families handle stressors than is *coping with stress:* A family's coping resources are considered strengths, but simply having these strengths available is no guarantee the family will use them to *manage* the stress. Boss also noted that resources are derived from all aspects of life: psychological, economic, and physical.

S. E. Hobfoll and C. D. Spielberger (1992) completed an excellent overview of family stress models and research, observing the commonalties and differences among family stress theories and identifying the important family resources across a variety of models. The major resources and strengths were cohesion rather

FIGURE 14.3
The Chinese Pictograph for Crisis

Danger   Opportunity

TABLE 14.3	Major Family Coping Strategies
General	**Specific**
Cognitive	Gain knowledge
	Reframe situation
Emotional	Express feelings
	Resolve negative feelings
	Be sensitive to others' emotional needs
Relationships	Increase cohesion
	Increase adaptability
	Increase trust and cooperation
Community	Seek help and support
Spiritual	Be involved in religious activities
	Maintain faith
Individual development	Develop autonomy, independence

Source: Adapted from W.R. Burr and S.R. Klein, Reexamining Family Stress: New Theory and Research. Copyright © 1994 by Sage Publications. Reproduced with permission of Sage Publications Inc. in the format Republish in a book via Copyright Clearance Center.

than separateness, flexibility/adaptability rather than rigidity, communication rather than privacy, boundary clarity rather than boundary ambiguity, and order and mastery rather than chaos and helplessness.

Burr and Klein (1994) also provided an excellent summary evaluation of past studies of the most useful coping strategies for families. They identified six general coping strategies that encompass numerous specific strategies. The six general **family coping** strategies are cognitive, emotional, relationships, community, spiritual, and individual development (Table 14.3).

Coping with 9/11

In the September 11, 2001, attack by terrorists, many innocent people were killed. People used a variety of coping resources to deal with this major stress, and we will use this example to illustrate how coping resources are used by families.

In terms of cognitive coping resources, Burr and Klein (1994) described gaining knowledge and reframing the situation. Immediately after people learned of the attacks on the World Trade Center and the Pentagon, they wanted more and more information. Fortunately, the media dropped all other coverage and exclusively reported on the events related to this attack. This media coverage continued nonstop for several days.

Reframing is another cognitive resource, and it involves defining the situation as a challenge that can be conquered rather than denying it is a problem. This attack was so dramatic that it immediately put people into a proactive mode that made them want to overcome the challenge.

In terms of emotional coping strategies, expressing feelings and being sensitive to others' emotional needs are important resources that help people cope. In the attack on America, we saw endless examples of New Yorkers and others around the country and world expressing their intense feelings about the events and being

Contrary to the notion that strength means facing a problem without any help, research indicates that the strength to cope with problems comes from close connections with loved ones, friends, neighbors, and relatives. Human beings are, indeed, social beings. Good neighbors provide support in countless ways during both good times and troubled times.

more open than normal to how others were feeling. With the attack came a dramatic shift in the level and intensity of feelings that were expressed and an interest in sharing with others.

Relationship coping resources include increasing cohesiveness or closeness, increasing flexibility or adaptability, and increasing trust and cooperation. Probably no recent event in our history has brought Americans together more dramatically than this attack. People sought out members of their family and often got reconnected with each other. During crises, people are also willing to forget their normal routine and do whatever it takes to deal with the situation. Their trust and cooperation with each other increase as they bond together to deal with the major problem.

The value of the community as a source of support was clearly demonstrated after the attack. New Yorkers pulled together into a caring community, with strangers helping strangers. The city that had a reputation for being arrogant, distant, and noncaring was transformed into a caring network that rushed to help everyone in need.

The importance of spiritual beliefs was clearly evident from the time of the attack. People were comforted by clergy of all denominations, and prayers were offered by people around the country for those lost and their families. Religious services were packed with people who were there both to comfort and be comforted.

In summary, the terrorist attacks were so dramatic and powerful that they required people to use all the resources described above to begin to better manage the major stress created for all Americans. Because America and Americans are resilient and resourceful, they overcome crises and move on to become stronger people and a stronger country. Box 14.3 provides a summary of the most common strategies for managing stress.

BOX 14.3 Putting It Together

Strategies for Managing Stress

The following is a summary of some of the major strategies for managing stress that were found across a variety of studies of couples and families.

- Look for something positive in every situation.
- Pull together rather than apart.
- Try to be open to sharing our feelings.
- Try to be flexible in handling roles and tasks.
- Try to focus on not worrying about what we cannot change.

- Meet the challenges head on.
- Learn how to go with the flow.
- Be able to cry but also look for humor.
- Take on issues one at a time.
- Do not blame each other.
- Think about the meaning and purpose of life.
- Rely on our spiritual beliefs.
- Show our love for each other.

Domestic Violence

Domestic violence has been defined as a pattern of abusive behavior in any relationship that is used by one partner to gain or maintain power and control over another intimate partner (National Center for Victims of Crime, 2012; National Domestic Violence Hotline, 2012; U.S. Department of Justice, 2012; WomensLaw.org). Forms of abuse include physical, sexual, emotional, economic, or psychological actions or threats of actions that influence another person. Abusive behaviors are those that intimidate, manipulate, humiliate, isolate, frighten, terrorize, coerce, threaten, blame, hurt, injure, or wound someone.

> *Physical abuse:* Hitting, slapping, shoving, grabbing, pinching, biting, hair pulling, and so forth are types of physical abuse. This type of abuse also includes denying a partner medical care or forcing alcohol and/or drug use upon her or him.
> *Sexual abuse:* Coercing or attempting to coerce any sexual contact or behavior without consent. Sexual abuse includes, but is certainly not limited to, marital rape, attacks on sexual parts of the body, forcing sex after physical violence has occurred, or treating one in a sexually demeaning manner.
> *Emotional abuse:* Undermining an individual's sense of self-worth and/or self-esteem is abusive. This may include, but is not limited to, constant criticism, diminishing one's abilities, name-calling, or damaging one's relationship with her or his children.
> *Economic abuse:* Is defined as making or attempting to make an individual financially dependent by maintaining total control over financial resources, withholding one's access to money, or forbidding one's attendance at school or employment.
> *Psychological abuse:* Elements of psychological abuse include but are not limited to causing fear by intimidation; threatening physical harm to self, partner, children, or partner's family or friends; destruction of pets and property; and forcing isolation from family, friends, or school and/or work.

Domestic violence is widespread, and can happen to anyone regardless of race, age, sexual orientation, religion, or gender. It affects people in all socioeconomic backgrounds and educational levels. It happens in heterosexual and same-sex relationships, and can happen to intimate partners who are married, living together, or dating (National Center for Victims of Crime, 2012; National Domestic Violence Hotline, 2012; U.S. Department of Justice, 2012; WomensLaw.org, 2012).

The effects of domestic violence are also widespread. Besides affecting those who are abused, domestic violence has a substantial effect on family members, friends, co-workers, other witnesses, and the larger community. Children who grow up witnessing domestic violence are among those who are seriously affected. Frequent exposure to domestic violence predisposes children to numerous social and physical problems and teaches them that violence is normal in life. This increases the child's risk of becoming society's next generation of victims and abusers.

When we hear the term *domestic violence* we often think about a man physically causing harm to his spouse or girlfriend. Many people think of men being the aggressors and women being the victims, with extensive physical harm being done. According to Michael P. Johnson (2008, 2012) domestic violence takes several forms and the aggressor is not always a male.

Johnson (2008) identifies three different types of domestic violence between couples. *Intimate terrorism* is violence enacted when taking control over one's partner. This will likely involve physical harm. This type of domestic violence is most often gender specific, with men being the aggressors. This type of violence is often frequent and brutal. Individuals often end up in shelters or hospitals; occasionally, murder is the result (Fergusson, Horwood, & Ridder, 2005; Holtzworth-Munroe, 2005.

The second type of domestic violence involves *violence resistance* and may be in response to a partner's abuse. An example might be when a person inflicts harm on her or his partner in resisting assaults.

The third type of domestic violence identified by Johnson (2008) is *situational couple violence,* which results when there is a contentious situation or problem in the couple relationship. Situational couple violence is much more common than intimate terrorism. In this type of domestic violence, the aggressor is equally likely to be male or female (Holtzworth-Munroe, 2005). Most studies do not distinguish among the different types of domestic violence, and these distinctions are more likely to be made in future research.

Incidence of Domestic Violence

A wealth of statistics compiled by the National Coalition Against Domestic Violence (NCADV) (2012a) gives a grim picture of domestic violence in the United States. Researchers estimate that one in four women (25%) will experience domestic violence in her lifetime. An estimated 1.3 million women are victims of physical assault by an intimate partner each year. Eighty-five percent of domestic violence victims are women. Though 15% of domestic violence victims are men, because men are generally bigger and stronger than women, the men have higher rates of inflicting the most dangerous and injurious forms of violence on their female partners. Much violence by women appears to be in self-defense. Historically, females have been most often victimized by someone they knew. Women 20–24 years of age are at the greatest risk of nonfatal intimate partner violence. Most cases of domestic violence are never reported to the police.

The NCADV (2012b) also reports that witnessing violence between one's parents is the strongest risk factor for transmitting violent behavior from one generation to the next. Boys who witness domestic violence are twice as likely to abuse their own partners and children when they become adults, compared to boys who do not witness abuse. And 30% to 60% of those who abuse their partners are also likely to abuse children in the household.

One in six women and one in 33 men have experienced an attempted rape or completed rape. Nearly 7.8 million women have been raped by an intimate partner at some point in their lives. Sexual assault or forced sex occurs in 40–45% of violent relationships. One in 12 women and one in 45 men have been stalked in their lifetime. Eighty-one percent of women who have been stalked by a current or former partner were also physically assaulted by that partner, and 31% were also sexually assaulted (NCADV, 2012a).

Nearly one in three female homicide victims reported to police were killed by an intimate partner. In 70–80% of these intimate partner homicides, no matter which partner was killed, the man physically abused the woman before the murder. Fewer than one in five victims reporting an injury from intimate partner violence sought medical treatment following the injury. And intimate partner violence results in 18.5 million mental health care visits a year (NCADV, 2012a).

The economic impact of domestic violence in the United States is considerable, exceeding $5.8 billion each year, with $4.1 billion of this going for direct medical and mental health services. Victims of domestic violence lose nearly 8 million days of paid work because of the violence perpetrated by current or former husbands, boyfriends, and dates. This loss is the equivalent of more than 32,000 full-time jobs. Also, there are 16,800 homicides and $2.2 million in medically treated injuries due to intimate partner violence each year, costing $37 billion (NCADV, 2012a).

Domestic violence is believed to be one of the most chronically underreported crimes. Only about one-fourth of all physical assaults, one-fifth of all rapes, and one-half of all stalkings perpetuated against women by intimate partners are reported to police (NCADV, 2012a).

A dating relationship is apparently more likely to be violent than a marital relationship. According to statistics compiled by the National Dating Abuse Helpline (2012), nearly 1.5 million high school students nationwide experience physical abuse from a dating partner in a single year. One-third of adolescents are victims of physical, sexual, emotional, or verbal abuse from a dating partner. One in 10 high school students has been purposefully hit, slapped, or physically hurt by a boyfriend or girlfriend. One-fourth of high school girls have been victims of physical or sexual abuse.

Girls and young women between 16 and 24 years of age have the highest risk of intimate partner violence—three times the national average. Violent behavior commonly begins between 12 and 18. About 72% of eighth and ninth graders are "dating." Violent relationships in adolescence can have serious ramifications and long-lasting effects. The victims are at higher risk for substance abuse, eating disorders, risky sexual behavior, and further domestic violence. Teen girls who are being physically or sexually abused are six times more likely to become pregnant and twice as likely to get a sexually transmitted disease. Half of young people who have been victimized by both dating violence and rape attempt suicide, compared to 12.5% of nonabused girls and 5.4% of nonabused boys (National Dating Abuse Hotline, 2012).

Only 33% of teens who were in a violent relationship ever told someone about the abuse, and 81% of parents believe teen dating violence is not an issue or admit they don't know if it is an issue (National Dating Abuse Hotline, 2012). Young people who are being abused in a dating relationship are encouraged to talk about their situation with their parents and other loved ones, friends, and other trusted people in their lives, including school counselors and religious professionals.

Diversity and Domestic Violence

We know that cultures where men are considered dominant are likely to have higher rates of domestic violence than cultures where men and women are considered equals. We also know that social class, migration, and female dependence on males affect the rates of domestic violence. These factors are very complex, but there are research findings that are beginning to make these relationships more clear.

Some studies show that domestic violence is more prevalent in Latino and African American cultures (Bornstein, 2006). Frias and Angel (2005) found that among poor women, women of Mexican origin reported similar rates of domestic violence to African American women. They found that Latina women from other countries such as Puerto Rico had significantly lower rates of violence. These authors concluded that there are differing cultural views that affect domestic violence for Latinos depending on the country of origin.

Frias and Angel (2005) also found that Latina women who had immigrated to the United States when they were older than 15 years of age were at lower risk of domestic violence than those who immigrated before age 15. One can only speculate about the reason for this difference, but the timing of migration can also affect the incidence of domestic violence.

We also know that domestic violence is more common among low-income couples (Dingfelder, 2006; Frias & Angel, 2005). Low-income couples are likely to be experiencing considerable stress regarding meeting basic needs, which may affect one's ability to handle issues without violence. It is important to note, however, that domestic violence occurs at all income levels, and the degree to which domestic violence is reported may vary depending on income levels.

There are many factors that affect the willingness to report domestic violence. If a cultural group does not view domestic violence as negative, individuals are less likely to report violence to the police or even self-report violence in research studies. In fact, actions that may be viewed as domestic violence in one culture may not be viewed as domestic violence in another culture. Low-income couples may live in more crowded housing where domestic violence is reported to police by neighbors. Middle- or upper-income couples may live in homes where domestic violence is less likely to be noticed by neighbors and less likely to be reported. Therefore, we must be careful in assuming that reported incidences are an accurate assessment of what is really happening.

National Survey of Domestic Violence

One of the largest national surveys of marriage that also focused on spouse abuse was done by Shuji Asai and David Olson (2004) and is summarized in Table 14.4. This survey of 20,951 married couples from all 50 states had couples

TABLE 14.4	National Survey of Spouse Abuse

- National sample of 20,951 married couples from all 50 states.
- Average age of 35 years for husbands and 32 years for wives who were married 2 to 30 years.
- Classified into nonabusive (61%), only wife abusive (8%), only husband abusive (17%), and volatile—both abusive (13%).
- Greater levels of alcohol use meant a higher level of partner abuse.
- Volatile couples saw more abuse between their parents, more abuse by their parents, and more abuse by others.
- Abused spouses had lower levels of assertiveness and self-confidence and higher levels of avoidance and partner dominance.
- Nonabusive marriages had significantly higher levels of couple closeness, communication, family and friends, personality strengths, couple flexibility, and effective conflict resolution.
- There are five couple types based on the ENRICH inventory: vitalized, harmonious, traditional, conflicted, and devitalized (with ranges from high couple satisfaction to low satisfaction).
- Levels of abuse were highly related to the five couple types: vitalized (5%), harmonious (11%), traditional (20%), conflicted (48%), and devitalized (73%).

Source: Asai, S. G., & Olson, D. H. National couple abuse study. Roseville, MN: Life Innovations. Web site: http://lifeinnovations.com. Copyright © 2004 Life Innovations, Inc. Reprinted with permission.

complete the ENRICH couple inventory. The average age was 35 for males and 32 for females, and they had been married from 2 to 30 years. Couples were classified into one of four groups based on their level of abuse: nonabusive (61%), only wife abusive (8%), only husband abusive (17%), and volatile—both abusive (13%).

Comparing nonabusive marriages with the other three abusive groups, couples in nonabusive marriages had lower levels of alcohol use and abuse, had less abuse from their parents, and saw less abuse between their parents. In terms of personality styles, couples in nonabusive marriages were more assertive, had higher levels of confidence, less often avoided issues, and less often dominated their partners. Nonabusive marriages had higher levels of couple closeness and flexibility, better communication and conflict resolution, and a more supportive family and friendship network.

In summary, in most ways nonabusive married couples had a much stronger marriage relationship in almost all the major dimensions compared to abusive marriages. This seems to demonstrate that having a strong marriage protects the couple from using more abusive approaches with the partner.

Relationship of Physical Abuse and Psychological Abuse

Psychological abuse has been defined as the systematic perpetration of malicious and explicit nonphysical acts against an intimate partner, child, or dependent adult. This can include threatening the physical health of the victim and the victim's loved ones, controlling the victim's freedom, and effectively acting to destabilize or isolate the victim. Psychological abuse frequently occurs before or concurrently with physical or sexual abuse. A number of studies have shown that while psychological abuse increases the trauma of physical and sexual abuse, psychological abuse independently causes long-term damage to its victim's mental health (National Coalition Against Domestic Violence, 2012).

Researchers have found that 95% of men who physically abuse their intimate partners also psychologically abuse them. Psychologically abusive men are also more likely to use a weapon against their partners, have prior criminal arrests, abuse substances, and have employment problems. A woman who is employed and has an unemployed partner is more than twice as likely to be psychologically abused. A woman who has a physical disability is 83% more likely to be psychologically abused. And women who earn 65% or more of their household's income are more likely to be psychologically abused (National Coalition Against Domestic Violence, 2012).

Victims of psychological abuse are more likely to experience poor physical health; difficulty concentrating; emotional and/or mental impairment; poor work or school performance; higher likelihood of illegal drugs and alcohol use; and suicidal thoughts and/or suicide attempts (National Coalition Against Domestic Violence, (2012).

Physical abuse is almost always accompanied by psychological abuse, but psychological abuse is often present in relationships in which there is no physical violence (Arias & Pape, 1999; Street & Arias, 2001). However, abuse has been conceptualized as a developmental process in which psychological abuse occurs first and eventually may progress into physical aggression. Norina, a college co-ed, describes the escalation of abuse in her relationship with her boyfriend Jerry:

"In the beginning I thought Jerry was abusive because he was drunk, but then it happened when he wasn't drunk, too. I ignored it at first. I guess I thought he would quit. I also loved him so much I tried to cover it up.

"He became very demeaning toward me, and there was a lot of mental abuse. I wanted to quit seeing him, but he wouldn't accept it. I needed to get away, but he followed me wherever I went and watched every move I made. I didn't realize how bad the situation had become until one night at a party. He had followed me there but didn't speak to me most of the night. He left—or so I thought. Because I was upset, I started to talk with a male friend of mine. Out of the blue my boyfriend returned, picked me up, and carried me outside behind a building. I was scared and started crying. I was so upset I couldn't listen to him. He kept slapping me and telling me to shut up and listen. A few of my friends were watching. They confronted my boyfriend, and he started fighting with them too."

Although a woman who is psychologically abused will not have bruises or visible signs of injury, she will experience damage to her physical and psychological health. Psychologically abused women have an increased chance of serious or chronic illness, lower levels of relationship satisfaction, and lower levels of perceived power and control. These women experience psychological distress, including fear, low self-esteem, depression, an inability to trust others, nightmares, guilt, feelings of inferiority, pessimism, low ego strength, introversion, and helplessness. They also may experience psychophysiological symptoms such as fatigue, backache, headache, general restlessness, and insomnia. Psychological abuse also compromises mothering skills and thus puts children at risk. Psychological abuse has been found to be a major predictor not only of a mother's depression but also of her children's depression and low self-esteem (Arias & Pape, 1999; Street & Arias, 2001). In fact, data suggest that the psychological and behavioral dysfunction of children exposed to interparental psychological abuse is similar to that found in children exposed to interparental physical abuse.

Many symptoms experienced and reported by battered women mirror symptoms of PTSD (posttraumatic stress disorder). An investigation by Arias and Pape (1999) found psychological abuse to be a significant predictor of women's PTSD symptomatology and intentions to end an abusive relationship. Psychologically abused women with low-PTSD symptomatology were highly associated with intentions to terminate the abusive relationship, but there was no significant association for women in the high-PTSD symptomatology group. Arias and Pape suggest that because psychological abuse targets cognitions and is incorporated into self-concept, higher levels of abuse-related distress may decrease a woman's ability to leave the abusive relationship. Based on these findings, Arias and Pape argue that domestic violence shelters need to increase the duration of stay for women to ensure affective and cognitive improvements and to increase the probability that these women will find the support and strength to leave the perpetrator.

Factors Contributing to Domestic Violence

Researchers and clinicians have hypothesized that a number of factors contribute to the likelihood of spouse abuse in a family. These factors are rather similar to those found in the national survey of spouse abuse previously described in Table 14.4 by Asai and Olson (2004).

Violence in the Family of Origin. The family systems theory attributes a tendency toward domestic violence as an adult to growing up in a violent home, where the child learns to be a victim as well as a potential **victimizer**. Abused male children typically learn to be victimizers. They often develop a sort of "pecking order" attitude toward violence: You get beaten up when you're small; then when you're big, you repeat what you learned. Female children typically learn to be victims in their family of origin and are likely to become victims again in their marriage (Frias & Angel, 2005; Gelles, 2000a). As with child abuse, however, growing up in a home where spouse abuse occurs does not guarantee that one will become a victim or a victimizer as an adult (Gelles, 2000a). People can and do make positive, life-affirming choices.

Theorists with a psychodynamically oriented approach might see some abusers as having a personality disorder that is facilitated by a "willing" victim. The abuser's sadism is reinforced by the victim's masochism. Another way to think of this is that the abuser is a dominating partner whose dominance is maximized because the abused person is passive rather than assertive.

In a similar vein, **learned helplessness theory** postulates that battered women often learned from childhood that they cannot afford to appear competent around competitive men who like to win. These women give power away to men, and this ingrained passivity leads to a lack of options in life. When abused, they feel they have no way out: nowhere to go, no job skills or career opportunities, no choice except to continue to take their punishment.

Low Self-Esteem. Low self-esteem is a factor in domestic violence. The abusive spouse may feel inadequate and may use violence to gain control. The abused spouse may passively accept the violence, feeling that she or he deserves nothing better.

Youth. Age and spouse abuse are statistically related. Marital violence is twice as likely among couples who are under age 30 than among those over age 30 (Center for Problem-Oriented Policing, 2012).

Economic Stress. Although spouse abuse occurs in families at all income levels, economic stress increases the likelihood of wife battering. Spouse abuse is more likely in low-income families, and unemployed men are twice as likely to batter their wives as employed men are (Center for Problem-Oriented Policing, 2012).

Financial Dependency. Financial dependency refers to the degree to which one person relies on another for financial support and in which one member of the couple has considerable control over financial resources (Bornstein, 2006). Financial dependency is positively related to the likelihood of domestic violence. Financial dependency creates an unequal balance of power, which makes it difficult for individuals to move out of the relationship and away from the violence because they have limited or no resources to do so (Bornstein, 2006).

Isolation. Social isolation is also a factor in abuse. Abusers often feel isolated and alone. They have fewer contacts with friends, neighbors, and relatives and engage in fewer social activities than nonabusers do. In stressful times, the abusers have no social support network upon which to call (Gelles, 2000a).

Alcohol. Alcohol is implicated in a high percentage of domestic violence incidents. Many men who assault their wives are found to have been drinking (Asay, DeFrain, Metzger, & Moyer, 2013; Gelles, 2000a; Substance Abuse and Mental Health Services Administration, 2012). Does drinking cause violence? Some observers argue that

Most women who are physically abused by their husbands or partners are reluctant to report the abuse and even more reluctant to end the relationship. One theory for this masochistic behavior is that these women were abused as children and know only the role of victim. Another theory is that throughout their lives they have been conditioned to act passively and as a consequence have few skills and little self-esteem and see no alternative to a brutal relationship.

alcohol facilitates violence by helping break down the abuser's inhibitions. But alcohol is never the sole cause of a violent episode. Drinking is no more an excuse for assaulting another human being than it is for killing someone in a car accident. Our system of social justice would break down if people were not held responsible for their behavior.

Male Dominance. Professionals and clinicians studying abuse from a feminist perspective have identified clues as to why men batter women. They note that many in our culture believe that males have the right to control or try to control their partners. Men have also been socialized to believe that aggression is an acceptable, normal response to stress and anger. A patriarchal family system influences males to assume the head-of-the-household role and women to accept subordinate status. Egalitarian decision making is associated with nonviolence in families. Research shows that levels of wife beating and husband beating are higher among husband-dominant couples than among democratic couples (Asay, DeFrain, Metzger, & Moyer, 2012; Gelles, 2000a).

Other Cultural Factors. In our culture the depersonalization and objectification of women are reinforced by pornography and by advertising that uses sexy women to sell products. Victim blaming is common, as rape trials often reveal. We live in a society with a high tolerance for overt coercion and the use of physical force to gain control over others (Pence & McDonnell, 2000). All of these social factors are viewed as contributing to the epidemic of domestic violence in this country.

Linkage of Animal Abuse and Domestic Violence. There is considerable evidence that mistreatment of animals is a powerful indicator that other forms of violence may be occurring in the home. Seventy-one percent of pet-owning women entering women's shelters reported that their batterer had injured, maimed, killed, or threatened family pets for revenge or to psychologically control victims; 32% reported their children had hurt or killed animals (American Humane Association, 2012). Many abused women have companion animals, and many of these companion animals are abused by the perpetrators as a way to hurt and control the women or their children. Some women may choose not to leave the partner or stay separated for long because of their concern for the safety of their companion animals (Fawcett, Gullone, & Johnson, 2002). Other researchers have found that children who abuse animals are often cruel toward people, and they argue that we can intervene in the cycle of abuse by decreasing a child's potential to be abusive toward animals, and, consequently, promote prosocial behavior toward humans (Mickish & Schoen, 2004; Thompson & Gullone, 2003). One study found that half of all the youths surveyed had abused animals at some time in their lives, with boys being more involved in abuse than girls (Baldry, 2003).

Patterns of Domestic Violence

Clinicians commonly see a three-phase, cyclical pattern to wife battering: (1) a tension-building phase; (2) an explosion phase, in which the actual beating occurs; and (3) a loving or honeymoon phase, in which the battered woman is rewarded for staying in the relationship (Walker, 2009). The third phase can be very pleasant. Many women stay with their spouses or boyfriends because of the promises and gifts that often follow a violent incident.

A common belief in our culture is that venting anger verbally can prevent physical violence. This theory of **catharsis conflict**, as it has been called, is simply not true. Verbal aggression is not a substitute for physical aggression but actually goes hand in hand with physical aggression. The more verbally aggressive a couple is, the more likely they are to be physically aggressive with each other (Gelles, 2000a; Loseke, Gelles, & Cavanaugh, 2005; Straus, Gelles, & Steinmetz, 2006).

Treatment and Prevention of Domestic Violence

Many clinicians and professionals who work in women's shelters are skeptical that batterers can alter their behavior without professional help and without the genuine desire to change. Some argue that battering men "have a good thing going," with a terrified wife and children who jump every time the batterer says jump.

Counselors commonly advise battered women to leave their husbands and go to a relative's or a friend's home or to a shelter for battered women. But this is easier said than done. Some men panic when women leave because they feel they are losing control. Panic can lead to even more violent behavior. "It's extremely rare that you read about a man who has beaten a woman to death while she's living with him," according to Ellen Pence, who works with battered women. "It's when she leaves him that he kills" (Pence & McDonnell, 2000).

Responding to pressure from the women's movement, police departments are now more likely to make arrests in cases of domestic violence. Assault against a spouse is seen as a serious offense. After studying research findings indicating that men who had spent time behind bars were less likely to assault their partners again, the Duluth, Minnesota, police department was the first in the United States to make arrest mandatory for suspected batterers. The Duluth program requires

FIGURE 14.4
Equality Wheel
Source: From Domestic
Abuse Intervention Project,
www.theduluthmodel.org/
wheelgallery.php. Reprinted with
permission.

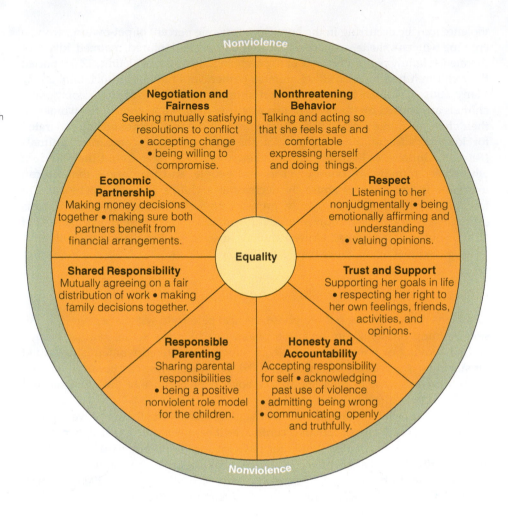

batterers to attend at least 6 months of counseling and classes. If a man misses two meetings, he risks serving up to 10 days in jail. Studies done 2 years after the program was initiated found that 80% of the women whose partners had completed the program were no longer being battered.

Domestic Abuse Intervention Programs (n.d.) in Duluth, Minnesota, has developed models for positive treatment of women who have been involved in domestic violence. The Equality Wheel (Figure 14.4) was created by women who have been abused by their male partners. This model also has implications for treatment of all family members and would be a positive way to view all the people who live together in a home.

To help prevent the next generation from falling into the sexism/violence trap, Myriam Miedzian suggests encouraging schools to teach positive approaches to conflict resolution in the classroom and on the playground, and to show children there are alternatives to violent behavior. Television should be prosocial and nonviolent rather than sexist and violent. We need to restrict violent pornography, which both demeans women and glorifies killing. Also boys should be encouraged from a young age to be empathetic rather than aggressive (Miedzian, 2002).

Domestic Violence and Children

There is a relationship between partner violence, essentially violence between two adult partners, and child abuse (Johnson, 2008). Adults who are involved with partner violence are often abusing their children. Couples who are involved with situational couple violence—couples who become violent as a result of a conflict that turns into an argument, then verbal abuse, then violence—are less likely (31%) to be violent to their children. Those who are involved with intimate terrorism, where a person uses violence to control his or her partner, are much more likely (67%) to abuse their children as well. It is more likely that these adults will abuse their children, because the violence is about control, and children are often a threat to that control. It is also more likely that a perpetrator who is involved with intimate terrorism will create an atmosphere of control in the home by way of emotional abuse of all family members. It is also likely that even though children may not have been physically abused themselves, they are likely to have witnessed the abuse of a parent.

Children who witness violence suffer long-term effects even if they, themselves, have not been physically abused (Johnson, 2008). The fear that a small child experiences when violence is directed at a parent is devastating. Most states, therefore, have domestic violence laws that require reporting domestic violence to human services if a child witnesses domestic violence. The long-term effects for children who witness couple violence include behavioral and social problems, stress, depression, substance abuse, and aggression.

One study by Bradford, Vaughn, and Barber (2008), which focused on youth ages 12 to 18 years, examined the impact of both overt and covert interparental conflict. Behaviors of the parents ranged from passive-aggressive behaviors that put children in the middle to the parents hitting each other. These researchers found that youths were likely to imitate their parents' maladaptive and aggressive behavior and were at risk for antisocial behavior. They were more likely to be aggressive with siblings and peers, and were more likely to show disrespect, yell, and hit. They learned from what they witnessed rather than what they were told. These youths were also more likely to be depressed. The study found that parents and children in these families were also likely to experience conflict.

It is important to realize that, according to the study by Bradford et al. (2008), the effects of conflict, not only violence, can greatly affect children and youth. Parents' treatment of each other can have long-lasting effects on children's social and emotion development.

Child Abuse and Neglect

Child abuse "is any recent act or failure to act on the part of a parent or caretaker, which results in death, serious physical or emotional harm, sexual abuse, or exploitation, or an act or failure to act which presents an imminent risk of serious harm" (Child Welfare Information Gateway, 2012a). Although all states include sexual and physical abuse in their definition of child abuse, not all states include neglect or emotional abuse in their definition.

Child abuse can occur in all kinds of families. We do know, however, that child abuse is reported in low-income families more often than in middle-income families. Reporting could be higher in low-income families because they have fewer resources to cover up the abuse. It is also very likely that the stress related to limited income could contribute to increased abuse in low-income families (Child Welfare Information Gateway, (2012b).

Incidence of Child Abuse and Neglect

The findings of the *Fourth National Incidence Study of Child Abuse and Neglect* (Sedlak et al., 2010) show that reported maltreatment has decreased by 19% since the last comparable study, which was conducted in 1993. All statistics about child abuse from this report were dependent on actual cases being reported, not estimates of the number of children abused and neglected. Based upon this report, one in 58 children experienced abuse or neglect during the year 2005–2006. Forty-four percent of these children were abused, while 61% were neglected. Of those identified as having been abused, 24% were sexually abused.

Some children are more likely to be abused and neglected than others (Sedlak et al., 2010). For example, girls were more likely to be sexually abused than boys. Children under 2 years of age were less likely to be abused than older children. The report suggests that these findings may be a result of underreporting, because younger children are not in school and may not be identified by educational personnel as being abused. Black children were more likely to be abused than White or Hispanic children. Children who were not enrolled in school were sexually abused more often than enrolled children.

There were also differences in the rate of abuse and neglect based upon family characteristics (Sedlak et al., 2010). Not surprisingly, children living with parents who were employed experienced a lower rate of abuse than those whose parents were not employed. Additionally, children living in low-income households, below $15,000 a year, had the highest rate of maltreatment—five times the rate of other children.

Family structure was also related to child maltreatment (Sedlak et al., 2010). Children living with both biological parents had the lowest rate of child maltreatment, and those living with a single parent who was cohabiting had the highest rate, which was eight times higher. Family size was also a factor: families with more than four children and only-child families had the highest rates of abuse. The lowest rates were in families with two children. Finally, rural children were more likely to be abused than urban children.

Some of the factors associated with an increase in child abuse and neglect are related to increased stress and decreased resources, such as not being employed and low income. These findings are not surprising. Other factors, such as living in rural communities versus urban communities, may be less clear. One might speculate that rural communities are more isolating and have limited resources to help parents with parenting issues.

The majority of the abused or neglected children were maltreated by a biological parent (Sedlak et al., 2010). The explanation for this finding might be that children are most often in the care of their biological parents. Consistent with the mother being the primary caregiver is the finding that most children suffer maltreatment by their biological mothers. Sexual abuse, however, was more often committed by males.

Psychological Aggression and Spanking

Psychological aggression by American parents is also quite common. Psychological aggression is yelling, shouting, or threatening a child, but not physically hurting the child. In a nationally representative sample of 991 parents, Straus and Field (2003) found that by the time the child reached age 2, 90% of the parents said they had used one or more forms of psychological aggression during the previous

Everyone Can Help Prevent Child Abuse

Raise the issue.

Call or write your elected officials to educate them about issues in your community and the need for child abuse prevention, intervention, and treatment programs.

Reach out to kids and parents in your community.

Anything you do to support kids and parents in your family and extended community helps to reduce the likelihood of child abuse and neglect.

Remember the risk factors.

Child abuse and neglect occur in all segments of our society, but the risk factors are greater in isolated families and also when parents or caregivers have other social or emotional problems.

Recognize the warning signs.

The behavior of children may signal abuse or neglect long before any change in physical appearance.

Report suspected abuse or neglect.

If you suspect abuse or neglect is occurring, report it—and keep reporting it—until something is done. Contact child protective services (in your local phone book) or your local police department.

For more information go to
http://nccanch.acf.hhs.gov/topics/prevention

gateways to prevention

U.S. Department of Health and Human Services
Administration for Children and Families
Administration on Children, Youth and Families
Children's Bureau
Office on Child Abuse and Neglect

Prevent Child Abuse America
200 South Michigan Avenue, 17th Floor
Chicago, Illinois 60604-2404
312.663.3520 tel
www.preventchildabuse.org

National Clearinghouse on Child Abuse and Neglect Information
800.394.3366 tel
http://nccanch.acf.hhs.gov

Child maltreatment includes child neglect, physical abuse, sexual abuse, and emotional abuse.

12 months, and by age 5, 98% of the parents had done so. From ages 6 to 17 the rates of psychological aggression continued in the 90% range. Rates of what the researchers termed severe psychological aggression were lower: 10% to 20% for toddlers and about 50% for teenagers. Straus and Field found that psychological aggression cut across all social classes and ethnic and cultural groups, indicating that it is a near universal disciplinary tactic of American parents.

Some researchers view spanking as undesirable and see it as the first step in parents' getting out of control and physically abusing their children (Straus,

2008). According to Straus, only a tiny percentage of parents who spank lose control and become physically abusive. However, most of those who become physically abusive began by using spanking as a form of discipline and it got out of control. Therefore, it is argued that preventing spanking will reduce physical abuse.

Currently, 94% of parents with preschoolers spank their children. Some of these parents spank only occasionally; others do it every day. On average, parents spank several times per week (Straus, 2008). Straus found that children experience trauma when spanked often, even if their parents are loving and caring in every other way. Many parents believe that children under 2 years of age sometimes do not respond to anything but spanking. Straus suggests that children this age do not change their behavior easily, no matter what the consequence. Repetition is the only thing that seems to help young children. Parents, however, sometimes think that if spanking did not work, it was because the spanking needed to happen more often or harder—thus, the potential for it to get out of control.

It has been suggested that putting an end to spanking can decrease physical abuse (Straus, 2008). In addition, Straus suggests that spanking has harmful side effects for children. Children who have been spanked may hit other children, and when older may hit other adults, such as a dating or marital partner, or their own children. Straus strongly supports the *never hit a child* approach to enhance the well-being of the child and of all those the child will encounter in life.

Alternatives to Spanking

Perhaps the best argument against spanking is that there are many nonviolent approaches to teaching children how to behave in an acceptable manner. Child development specialists have known these approaches for many years and use them successfully in early childhood programs across the country and around the world.

Four commonly used and effective approaches are:

1. *Accentuate the positive.* Focus on what the child is doing right, instead of focusing always on what the child is doing wrong. Focus on rewarding the positive behavior of children by giving them verbal praise, hugs, and occasional material rewards such as food or small gifts when they do the right thing. This makes it important, then, for parents to be watching their children closely to see when they behave correctly. By spending more time on rewarding good behavior and less time on punishing bad behavior, it sets up a loving and friendly family environment in which children are happier, as well as parents.

2. *Call a time-out.* When the kids get out of hand, have them sit down, calm down, and come back with everyone else when they are under control. Time-outs work best when they are short and don't involve angry lectures. Simply state what the child did wrong and have the child sit down until ready to behave properly. This should last only 2 or 3 minutes, if it is done effectively. Long time-outs generally don't work. While the child is calming down in time-out, the parent is also calming down. If everyone is emotionally upset, everyone ends up suffering, so a time-out is as much for the parent as for the child.

3. *Be consistent in how you discipline children.* Make reasonable rules with reasonable consequences, and stick to them.

4. *Teach your children. Don't hit them.* Parents are much more effective when they act as educators, rather than disciplinarians.

The Long-Term Consequences of Child Abuse and Neglect

The price we pay in our society for child abuse and neglect is staggering. It can be seen as we list some of the most common physical, psychological, behavioral, and societal consequences determined by researchers (Child Welfare Information Gateway, 2012b):

Physical Health Consequences. The immediate physical effects of abuse or neglect can be relatively minor (bruises or cuts) or severe (broken bones, hemorrhage, or even death). Though physical effects in some cases are temporary, the suffering caused to the child cannot be discounted. Long-term physical health consequences include: shaken baby syndrome (bleeding in the eye or brain, damage to the spinal cord and neck, and rib or bone fractures); impaired brain development (important regions of the brain fail to form or grow properly); and poor physical health (allergies, arthritis, asthma, bronchitis, high blood pressure, and ulcers).

Psychological Consequences. The immediate emotional effects of abuse and neglect include feelings of isolation, fear, and an inability to trust. Lifelong consequences include low self-esteem, depression, and relationship difficulties. Depression and withdrawal symptoms are common among children as young as 3 who experience emotional, physical, or environmental neglect. In one study as many as 80% of young adults who had been abused met the diagnostic criteria for at least one psychiatric disorder at age 21: depression, anxiety, eating disorders, and suicide attempts. Other researcher teams found psychological and emotional conditions associated with abuse and neglect include panic disorder, dissociative disorders, attention-deficit/hyperactivity disorder, depression, anger, posttraumatic stress disorder, and reactive attachment disorder. Cognitive difficulties associated with abuse and neglect include lower cognitive capacity, language development, academic achievement, and classroom functioning. Social difficulties include antisocial traits, borderline personality disorders, and violent behavior.

Behavioral Consequences. Not all victims of child abuse and neglect experience behavioral consequences; however, problems are more likely among this group, even at a young age. Clinical or borderline levels of behavioral problems among children ages 3 to 5 are displayed at a rate more than twice that of the general population of children. Later in life, child abuse and neglect appear to make difficulties more likely: juvenile delinquency and adult criminality; alcohol and other drug abuse; and abusive behavior toward their own children.

Societal Consequences. The impact of child abuse and neglect does not end within the family, but spills out into the broader society. Direct costs for society include those associated with maintaining a child welfare system to investigate and respond to allegations of child abuse and neglect. One estimate put this dollar cost at $24 billion per year. Indirect costs of child abuse and neglect include costs associated with juvenile and adult criminal activity, mental illness, substance abuse, and domestic violence. These costs can also include loss of productivity due to unemployment and underemployment, the cost of special education services, and increased use of the health care system. These costs have been estimated at more than $69 billion per year.

BOX 14.4   Putting It Together

Surviving and Transcending a Traumatic Childhood: The Dark Thread

A study was conducted asking 90 volunteers who felt they had survived and transcended a traumatic childhood how they did it (Skogrand et al., 2007). The researchers wanted to know how, as young people, they survived the trauma and how, as adults, they transcended the trauma and became healthy. The participants decided for themselves whether they considered their childhood experience to be traumatic—with the definition of traumatic being that whatever happened to them had long-lasting psychological effects.

Some of the things that happened to the participants included the following:

- A high-school-age youth described how other students tried multiple times to burn her fat off with a Bunsen burner in chemistry class. Taunting and teasing were a routine part of her adolescent life—and no one did anything.
- A 15-year-old boy came home, one more time, to find his mother lying on the floor bleeding as a result of his father beating her up. The young man could not take it any more. He found a gun in the house and shot his father.
- One girl had 17 of her pet dogs killed by her father and stepbrothers—supposedly because she was "bad." She never knew what she had done wrong, but when she was "good" she got a new dog.

Almost all of the 90 who said they experienced trauma as children described abuse—someone abused them and most often they were abused by one or more family members. The trauma/abuse was usually multifaceted. For example, a person may have been sexually and physically abused, lived with a family member who was an alcoholic, and experienced abandonment all over the same time period. These things often went on for years.

As children, they could only survive, getting through life as best they could. They did not have the emotional or cognitive abilities or the physical strength to do anything but live through it. Looking back, the participants in this study said they did several things to survive:

- *They drew on spiritual resources.* They turned to a higher being that loved and cared about them. Usually, this was God, the protector. They believed in angels and did lots of praying. Religious institutions and leaders were typically not helpful.
- *They disassociated.* When they were being beaten or sexually abused, they mentally left their bodies and tuned out the pain. Some said it was like they were watching what was happening to them from a distance.
- *They escaped.* They read books, did well in school, developed their skills in music, or came up with other forms of diversion to get away from what was happening to them.

Transcending Abuse

Many abusive parents were themselves abused as children, but being abused as a child does not necessarily doom a person to pass the misery along to the next generation. Some abused children grow up to be happy and healthy adults, although transcending the pain of a violent childhood is very difficult. Since the early 1980s, researchers and clinicians have begun to focus on these resilient individuals. What they have found is that a nurturing relative, adult friend, or teacher often helped the troubled individual find a more positive approach to living.

Edward Zigler and his colleagues estimated that the rate of "cross-generational transmission" of child abuse is about 25% to 35%. This means that about one-quarter to one-third of those who are physically or sexually abused or neglected as children will subject their own children to similar abuse. However, the majority (65% to 75%) of people abused as children "will care for their offspring as well as the general population." According to the researchers, "many adults abused as children remember the agony they once suffered and have sworn to give their own children a better start." The research team did make it clear, however, that anything else, and they accepted it as part of life.

- *They survived by default.* Later, they realized that, as children, things had happened that kept them afloat. Something happened that kept them from the one beating that could have resulted in death or having their spirit broken to the point that they could not put themselves back together. Someone came to the door when they were being beaten, or someone came into their lives who made things better.

As adults, they could begin the process of healing, transcending, and becoming healthy. They now had the emotional, cognitive, and physical abilities to do things to become healthy, even though it was a long, slow process:

- *They sought out spiritual resources.* They, again, relied on a loving higher being or God to be there for them. Organized religion was helpful for some, but for most it was a personal spiritual connection that helped.
- *They sought out therapy and support groups.* About half of the participants went to counseling and/or attended support groups to help them heal.
- *They got married to a loving spouse.* Many found a loving supportive spouse through a first marriage. Their spouse listened to them, supported them, and some-

this first step of marrying someone who was abusive was a first step in getting away from the abuse.

- *They escaped from the abuse.* As adults, many had to move away from the abuser/abusers to become healthy. Others did not physically move but stopped having contact with those who harmed them.
- *They looked forward, not back.* At some point, many of the participants said they had to let go of what happened to them. This was usually after much healing had already taken place. They had to focus on the future.

We often hear about those who had traumatic childhoods growing up to further the cycle of abuse. But many draw on strengths and are, for a variety of reasons, able to become healthy and have healthy family lives. The "dark thread" of abuse will always be there, but it can become less pervasive in their lives.

A large number of the participants in this study became professionals who helped others in their work. Although no one said they were glad this trauma had happened to them, they said it was all part of what had made them who they are today.

Source: Linda Skogrand, Nikki DeFrain, John DeFrain, and Jean Jones, *Surviving and Transcending a Traumatic Childhood: The Dark Thread.* Copyright © 2007 by The Haworth Press, Inc. Reproduced by permission of Taylor and Francis Group, LLC, a division of Informa plc.

---

individuals with a history of abuse are still about six times more likely to abuse their own children than is the average person, who has about a 5% likelihood of doing so (Zigler, 2004). Clearly, the experience of childhood abuse does not predetermine that an abused child will grow up to abuse others later in life (Skogrand, DeFrain, DeFrain, & Jones, 2007). See Box 14.4 for coping strategies used by survivors of childhood trauma.

Families at Risk

Several of these factors were identified by Sedlak et al., 2010:

- *Economic distress.* Unemployment, low income, illness in the family, and inability to pay for adequate medical care are stressors in the lives of many abusive parents.
- *Inadequate parenting skills.* Abusive parents often have unrealistic expectations of their children, have little knowledge of child development, and demonstrate an inability to bond with infants.

Children are more likely to suffer abuse when their parents are under stress because of unemployment, low income, or illness, especially if the parents are immature and know little about the development of children. During stressful times, parents need friends and other sources of support to help them cope with frustrations, and they need to relate to their children in a positive way.

- *Parental personality problems.* Abusive parents often have low self-esteem and are likely to be more immature, less empathetic, and more self-centered than nonabusive parents. They also tend to be rigid, domineering, self-righteous, moralistic, and prone to anger.
- *Chemical abuse as a means of coping with stress.* Abusive parents often have high stress in their lives but have a difficult time dealing with that stress in a proactive, rational manner. Many turn to alcohol and other drugs to forget their troubles.
- *Social isolation.* Abusive families tend to be isolated from their community, with few friends or sources of outside support.
- *A special child.* Children with a chronic illness, an emotional disturbance, hyperactivity, mental retardation, or a physical handicap are at higher risk for abuse. Children who were unplanned and are unwanted are also more likely to be abused, as are children whose birth was difficult.
- *Domestic violence in the family of origin.* Many abusive parents witnessed domestic violence between their own parents and were likely to have been physically punished themselves as children.
- *A violent subculture.* Some cultures and subcultures appear to be more tolerant of violent behavior toward children. For example, children who live in an unsafe neighborhood characterized by high levels of violence are at greater risk of being abused than are children growing up in a more peaceful neighborhood.
- *A violent marriage.* Parents who abuse their spouse are more likely to abuse their children than are parents whose marriage is peaceful.
- *Single parent.* Children who live with a single parent are more likely to suffer abuse than are those who live with two parents, perhaps because of the stresses often associated with single parenthood.
- *Stepparent.* A child living with a stepparent is more likely to be abused than is a child living with both natural parents, perhaps because the stepparent's lack of a biological tie with the child can foster intolerance. One study (Daly & Wilson, 1996) of preschoolers found the likelihood for abuse to be 40 times greater for stepchildren.

esteem, (2) increasing the parent's knowledge of children and positive child-rearing techniques, and (3) devising community support networks for families under stress.

Parents who mistreat children are commonly viewed as people who need more positive ways of coping with their many problems. Counselors working with abusive parents are often quite successful in facilitating positive behavioral changes. By focusing on these parents' strengths, a therapist can enhance the development of the parents' self-esteem and parenting skills. A counselor can also provide referrals to other community services: financial aid for families in economic distress, food stamps, aid in finding better housing, family planning and adoption services, and day care.

Many programs for troubled parents include a parent discussion and support group among the treatment offerings. A group of parents, often facilitated by a professional, gets together to share stories about life's ups and downs and to offer advice and support to each other. Child abuse hotlines are also available to parents around the clock for help in dealing with difficult childrearing situations.

There are a number of things we as a society can do to prevent the abuse of children (Centers for Disease Control and Prevention, 2012; Prevent Child Abuse, 2012). They include working to reduce sources of social stress, such as poverty, racism, inequality, unemployment, and inadequate health care; eliminating sexism in the workplace and the home; providing adequate child care; promoting educational and employment opportunities for both men and women; supporting sex education and family planning programs in an effort to reduce unplanned and unwanted pregnancies; and working to end the social isolation of families in our culture.

Sibling and Child-to-Parent Abuse

Domestic violence is not initiated only by adults, and it is not directed only at children and partners. Siblings also engage in violence, and children sometimes attack their parents.

Sibling Abuse

The most violent members of American families may be children. Parents often do not recognize sibling abuse for what it is. Parents and society in general tend to expect fights and aggression among brothers and sisters, and because of this parents often don't see sibling abuse as a problem until serious harm has occurred (University of Michigan Health System, 2012).

Sibling abuse has been defined as the physical, emotional, or sexual abuse of one sibling by another. Physical abuse among siblings can range from mild forms of aggression, such as pushing and shoving, to very violent behavior such as using

BOX 14.5 Diversity in Families

Family Violence from a Global Perspective: Strengths-Based Research and Case Studies

Family violence is a core social issue in every country around the world. The historical and political bias that events occurring outside the home are more significant than events occurring within the home and that what happens inside the home is private and not public have helped mask the impact of family violence. Yet, the world is slowly awakening and admitting the fact that family violence is a major problem, and it is hard to conceive how to construct strong nations without creating healthy violence-free families.

Our research team linked more than 50 people in 17 countries, representing every major geocultural area of the world. We worked over a 4-year period, studying the extent of family violence in each country, and how each country responded to family violence. Quite predictably, we found many differences among the countries, and we found many situations quite unique to each country.

But despite these differences, there is a striking commonality, also. All the countries acknowledge that family violence exists in their country; that family violence is wrong; and that there is a need to respond in more effective ways to the problem.

The Nature of the Challenge

Here are some key findings that emerged from this study, and ideas for successfully dealing with the global problem of family violence:

- *Family violence is a serious problem in every country around the world.* The home is often idealized as a haven in a heartless world, a place of security and protection. And yet, the home can be a very dangerous place in every culture and country.
- *Family violence includes physical violence, psychological violence, sexual violence, and economic violence.* Many cultures are working to clearly define each of these forms of violence. Psychological or emotional violence is the most common form of family violence, followed by physical violence, and sexual violence.

- *Family violence occurs in all social classes.*
- *Family violence occurs among all age groups.*
- *Family violence occurs among all ethnic groups.*
- *Women are much more likely to be victims than perpetrators.*
- *Women, however, are by no means perfect.* Mothers are approximately twice as likely to abuse children as fathers. This can be explained by the fact that mothers spend much more time with children, on average, and that in a hierarchical system those above feel entitled to severely punish those below.
- *Abusive men are likely to abuse both their partner and the children.*
- *Women are more likely than men to see that domestic violence is a significant problem in their country.*
- *Causes of family violence commonly cited include:* (1) a history of violence from generation to generation; (2) alcoholism and other forms of substance abuse; and (3) male dominance (a patriarchal belief system). Though alcohol and other drugs are commonly associated with family violence, they should not be used as an excuse to justify family violence. Many men who have not been drinking beat their partners.
- *By objectifying women and children in families and making them inferior to men, a patriarchal belief system gives justification for abusive behavior.* Patriarchy and family violence often go hand in hand.
- *These patriarchal beliefs are deeply embedded in all cultures.* Abusers rarely disclose their abuse, in part because they believe they are justified in using violence.
- *Besides patriarchy, other barriers to change include:* socialization that emphasizes the woman's role as a mother and wife at the expense of her own happiness, independence, and freedom; stigma and social prejudice toward divorce; pressure from family members to return to abusive situations; and a lack of effective community services to support women in their quest for change.

weapons. Similar to child abuse in general, sibling abuse has both immediate effects and long-term consequences that can last into adulthood.

Researchers have found that sibling abuse is quite common, probably even more common than child abuse by parents or spouse abuse. It has been estimated that three children in 100 are dangerously violent toward a brother or sister, and the number of assaults each year to children by a sibling is about 35 per 100 kids. The rates of sibling abuse are similar across income levels and racial and ethnic groups. Sibling incest is believed to be much more common than parent-child incest.

job opportunities will be more likely to try to keep the family together. More contemporary cultures in economically developed nations will be more likely to encourage women and children to seek a shelter and leave their partners, because women will be in a better position to fend for themselves.

- *Empowerment is key.* Implementing strategies and education to help women to develop individual strengths will empower them to rise above their circumstances and move forward in abusive situations.
- *Challenging the power structure is dangerous.* Because families and the broader culture in which they live are deeply embedded in patriarchy, revealing abuse and identifying abusers can be dangerous. While encouraging victims to leave abusive situations is necessary, their safety can be compromised without cultural changes that support the victims' efforts to find a safe environment in which to live.
- *Holding perpetrators accountable is often poorly addressed.* While there have been considerable efforts initiated to help victims of abuse, frequently strategies to hold perpetrators accountable draw less interest, including creating and implementing interventions. The focus, rather, seems to be to stop the perpetrator from brutalizing the rest of the family, and to protect the rest of the family from continuing harm.
- *Stopping family violence also requires changes in policy.* Macro level support from communities and cultures in the form of changes in laws, policies, and procedures must occur to support efforts for change on the micro level of individuals and families. These measures to define family violence, delineate procedures for

the world.

- *Violence against elders in families includes physical abuse, psychological abuse, material or financial abuse, sexual abuse, and neglect.* Data on the occurrence of elder abuse in many countries are still scarce.
- *A great deal of progress has been made worldwide, and there is much more work to be done in all countries.*
- *The process of positive change around the world is accelerating.* These changes are aided by advances in communication technologies, as good ideas transfer rapidly from one culture to another, one community to another, one family to another, one woman to another.
- *The feminist movement around the world has played a significant role in shedding light on the subject of family violence.* In those countries where feminists have been active in this regard, there has been considerable protest and denial from others, including some men, some women, governments, politicians, religious organizations, the media, and other groups.
- *The cycle of family violence can be broken. By bringing together people working on all levels of society—from the local community to the national, international, and global levels—approaches to ending domestic violence can be created that are coordinated, integrated, and holistic.* Government, social and family service organizations, educational and religious institutions, health care facilities, and businesses all have important roles to play in the efforts to end family violence.

Source: Sylvia M. Asay, John DeFrain, Marcee Metzger, and Bob Moyer, *Family Violence from a Global Perspective: Strengths-Based Research and Case Studies.* Copyright © 2013 by Sage Publications, Inc. Reprinted by Permission of Sage Publications, Inc.

All siblings squabble at times and call each other mean names, and some young siblings may "play doctor" with each other. But there is a difference between typical sibling behavior and abuse: If one child is always the victim and the other always the aggressor, it is an abusive situation. Other signs of abuse include: one child always avoids the other sibling; a child exhibits changes in behavior, sleep patterns, eating habits, or has nightmares; a child acts out abuse in play; a child acts out in sexually inappropriate ways; the children's roles are rigid, with one always the aggressor and the other the victim; and roughness or violence between siblings is increasing over time.

Child-to-parent abuse is devastating to a family. Children who abuse their parents are likely to be in their teen years or older.

Sibling abuse can be prevented by reducing the rivalries between the children; setting ground rules to prevent emotional abuse and sticking to these ground rules; not giving older children too much responsibility for younger children; setting aside time to regularly talk with the children, one-on-one; knowing when to intervene in the children's conflicts, to prevent an escalation of abuse; learning how to mediate conflicts; modeling good conflict-solving skills for the children; modeling nonviolence; teaching the children to *own* their own bodies; teaching them to say *no* to unwanted physical contact; creating a family atmosphere where everyone is comfortable talking about sexual issues and problems; keeping an eye on the children's media choices; and, in sum, keeping actively involved in the children's lives and knowing what they are doing.

Child-to-Parent Abuse

Because parents are usually physically and socially more powerful than their children, we assume that parents are immune to abuse by their children. But **child-to-parent abuse** occurs in many families.

In comparison to child abuse and spouse abuse, parent abuse by their adolescent children has received very little attention by mental health professionals, even though its prevalence is comparable. Studies dating back to the 1950s were showing that the physical abuse of parents was a concern. Recent research found that of all the cases of parent abuse reported to the researchers, 57% were categorized as physical abuse; followed by verbal abuse at 22%; the use of a weapon, usually a knife or gun, at 17%; throwing items at 5%. Regardless of gender, 11% of children under age 10 physically abuse their parents, and this percentage stays steady for boys over age 10. For girls it drops to 7%. Mothers are five times more likely than fathers to experience severe physical abuse from their children, and the highest rate of abuse occurs in families with a single mother (Robinson, ing for an aging parent can be great, and abusive adult children sometimes argue that they are paying their parents back for the abuse they suffered as children: "He did it to me. Now I have my chance to get even." Other adult children report they are responding in kind to the abuse their difficult elderly parents have showered on them. Fortunately, many treatment programs are available to help people find positive and satisfying ways to relate to one another across the generations (BBC News, 2012; Buzzetti & Associates, 2010; Purplefairy, 2012).

Alcohol Problems in Families

A family with a drinking problem is always a family in trouble.
— MARCIA LASSWELL AND THOMAS LASSWELL (1991, p. 256)

Alcohol is a drug that acts as a depressant to the central nervous system. It is the mood-altering ingredient in wine, beer, and liquor. Alcohol is absorbed into the bloodstream and travels to virtually every part of the body. When ingested in large amounts or over a long period of time, alcohol can kill. It can damage the liver, heart, and pancreas; other consequences include malnutrition, stomach irritation, lowered resistance to disease, irreversible brain or nervous system damage and can cause cancer (American Cancer Society, 2012; National Institute on Alcohol Abuse and Alcoholism, 2012).

Alcohol abuse is a generic term that encompasses both **alcoholism**, which is the addiction to alcohol characterized by compulsive drinking, and **problem drinking**, which is alcohol consumption that results in a functional disability. More than one-half of American adults have a close family member who has or has had alcoholism or was a problem drinker. That is to say, about half of all adults in this country grew up with an alcoholic or problem drinker or had a blood relative who was an alcoholic or problem drinker (Centers for Disease Control and Prevention, 2012; National Institute on Alcohol Abuse and Alcoholism, 2012).

Alcohol is the most widely used psychoactive drug in the United States. It contributes to the death of 100,000 people every year, making it the third leading cause of preventable death in this country after tobacco and diet/activity patterns. Based on victim reports, 37% of the rapes and sexual assaults in America involved alcohol use by the offender. Fetal alcohol syndrome (FAS), which can occur when women drink during pregnancy, is the leading known environmental cause of mental retardation in Western countries. And it is estimated that more than 7 million children live with a parent with alcohol problems (Centers for Disease Control and Prevention, 2012; National Institute on Alcohol Abuse and Alcoholism, 2012; National Survey on Drug Use and Health, 2012).

Alcohol and Family Violence

Alcohol is commonly associated with marital disruption, domestic violence, and many other family problems (Centers for Disease Control and Prevention, 2012; National Institute on Alcohol Abuse and Alcoholism, 2012). Alcohol abuse is far more common among men than among women, although alcohol abuse by women is growing. Most literature has focused on the husband as the alcohol abuser and the wife and children as victims, but statistics show that alcohol dependence problems among wives are on the rise.

Alcohol abuse and family violence are statistically related. A national sample of more than 2,000 couples found, in general, that the more often a spouse was drunk, the greater likelihood there was of physical violence in the marital relationship. The exception to this finding was when the alcohol abuse was extreme. In this case, when the spouse was "almost always" drunk, the level of physical violence dropped to a lower level.

Even if there is no violence in the family of an alcoholic, there is likely to be a high degree of marital dissatisfaction and a large number of disagreements. Tension and verbal conflict are likely to be frequent. Researchers have estimated that half the divorces and half the juvenile arrests for delinquency in the United States occur in families with at least one alcohol-abusing member.

Spouses and children of alcohol abusers are at risk for developing serious physical and emotional problems. Although the majority of children reared in alcoholic homes are no more prone to suffer some kind of pathology, they are more likely to exhibit a variety of behavioral and emotional problems than are children from families without an alcoholic member. These problems include conduct disorders or delinquency, alcohol abuse, hyperactivity, difficulties with school work, anxiety, depression, or other health problems.

The Family's Reaction to Alcohol Abuse

In a classic article, Joan K. Jackson (1954) was the first to describe the common dynamics of how families attempt to live with an alcohol-abusing father. It is widely recognized today that there are many families with alcohol-abusing mothers, of course, and children in a family frequently have drinking problems because

TABLE 14.5	Warning Signs for Alcohol Abuse

The following are some common warning signs of alcohol abuse. The more warning signs that apply, the greater the severity of the problem with alcohol use.

1. Drinking alone or secretively.

2. Using alcohol deliberately and repeatedly to perform or to get through difficult situations.

3. Feeling uncomfortable on occasions when alcohol is not available.

4. Escalating alcohol consumption beyond an already established drinking pattern.

5. Consuming alcohol heavily in risky situations (e.g., before driving).

6. Getting drunk regularly or more frequently than in the past.

7. Drinking in the morning or at other unusual times.

Sources: From P.M. Insel and W.T. Roth, Core Concepts in Health, Ninth Edition (New York: McGraw-Hill, 2004), p. 268. Copyright © 2004 by McGraw-Hill Education, LLC, reprinted with permission.

the sober adult about the drinking behavior, denies there is a problem. The family accepts this statement and tolerates or rationalizes the abuser's drinking episodes.

- *The family tries to eliminate the problem.* When the drinking can no longer be ignored, the sober spouse tries to control the problem drinker with threats, bribes, and/or by hiding the alcohol. Marital conflict increases, and family members isolate themselves from friends and neighbors in a futile effort to conceal the drinker's problem.

- *The family becomes disorganized.* The sober spouse realizes that the problem cannot be rationalized away or concealed from the children or the drinker's employer and co-workers. The sober spouse also recognizes that it is futile to try to curtail the drinker's alcohol consumption. Conflict increases, with the children often caught between arguing parents.

- *The family tries to reorganize.* The sober spouse recognizes that the drinker cannot function adequately in the family—a recognition often precipitated by the drinker's mismanagement of family funds or by the drinker's violence toward the sober spouse or the children—and takes action. The sober spouse may assume the alcohol abuser's role in the family or may decide to leave the alcohol abuser. The sober spouse may seek assistance from various public agencies, counselors, treatment programs, and self-help groups such as Al-Anon. This network of support helps the sober partner gradually regain self-esteem and find the strength to go on. During this process, the problem drinker is likely to bargain with the family, hoping to regain the lost family role and stature. If the family accepts the drinker's bargain but the drinker continues or resumes drinking, the destructive cycle begins again.

- *The family tries to escape the problem.* The sober spouse seeks a legal separation or divorce. The alcohol abuser often gives up drinking for a while, but the sober spouse may have already shifted from inaction to action.

- *The family tries to reorganize a second time.* After legal separation or divorce, the sober spouse assumes the roles formerly held by the problem drinker, and family life without the problem drinker is generally much better for all family members. The sober spouse may feel guilty for having left the troubled partner. The problem drinker may attempt to reenter the family or may try to get even with the family.

- *The family reorganizes, with the substance abuser seeking help.* If the alcohol-abusing member seeks help and learns to control the drinking, the family may be able to reunite successfully. The process can be difficult, family roles will have to be reassigned once again, and family members will need to reassess their feelings toward the alcohol abuser.

Later therapists built on Jackson's work and outlined a number of coping strategies women commonly use when dealing with alcohol-abusing husbands. These include emotional withdrawal from the marriage; infantilizing the husband; threatening separation or divorce or locking the spouse out of the house; trying to avoid family conflict; assuming control over family finances; and acting out themselves by drinking, threatening suicide, or becoming involved with other men.

Treatment and Prevention of Alcoholism

Some family therapists have been critical of programs that treat the alcoholic outside the context of the family, whereas some alcoholism treatment therapists have criticized family therapists for assuming that alcoholism can be cured simply by eliminating dysfunctional family patterns. It is probably safe to say that problems in families can contribute to alcohol abuse in individual members and that the alcohol abuse then contributes to problems for that family. Those who work with alcohol abusers are becoming increasingly aware that family therapy is an important tool in the treatment of alcoholics and their family system (O'Farrell & Fals-Stewart, 2001, 2007; Rowe, 2003).

Self-help groups such as **Alcoholics Anonymous (AA)** (for alcoholics) and **Al-Anon** (for families of alcoholics) have chapters in most U.S. cities and towns. In some metropolitan areas, many different AA meetings are held at a variety of locations each week. These groups offer advice and support for troubled individuals and families. **Alateen,** founded on the AA model, is a support group for young people with alcoholic parents. In weekly meetings, members discuss their problems and learn from others how to move ahead in life from the experiences of others in similar situations.

Alcoholics need to be confronted about their condition by people they trust and in a form they can receive. Even in the most advanced phases, alcoholics can recognize and accept some reality.

- There are 58,820 AA groups in the United States and 5,025 AA groups in Canada. Total members in North America number 1,384,699 (Alcoholics Anonymous, 2012a).
- Worldwide, there are 114,070 AA groups in 170 countries. Total members in the world number 2,133,842 (Alcoholics Anonymous, 2012a).
- Though we could not find numbers for Al-Anon and Alateen groups in the United States and Canada, worldwide numbers are considerable: there are 24,000 Al-Anon groups and 2,300 Alateen groups in 115 countries around the world (Al-Anon/Alateen, 2012a).

Besides thousands upon thousands of face-to-face support group meetings each week, AA, Al-Anon, and Alateen have well-developed online programs, including e-mail groups, real-time chat meetings, and Internet telephony meetings helping members meet via free conference calls on the Internet (Al-Anon, 2012b; & Alateen, 2012b; Alcoholics Anonymous, 2012b).

Though no one would say the process is easy, many people have been successful in the process of recovery from the disease of alcoholism and other drugs. Perhaps for the first time, there may be an accurate estimate of how many people in the United States are currently in recovery for an alcohol or other drug problem. A national survey conducted by the Partnership at DrugFree.org and the New York State Office of Alcoholism and Substance Abuse Services (OASAS) indicates that 10% of all adults over age 18 in the United States consider themselves to be in recovery. This means that an estimated 23.5 million Americans have found sustained recovery from involvement with drugs and alcohol that they once considered problematic. The researchers also found that 12% of males are in recovery, and 7% of females (About.com, 2012).

The National Council on Alcoholism and Drug Dependence (NCADD) (2012) argues that helping a loved one struggling with alcoholism or drug dependence can be heartbreakingly painful, but with help it also can be remarkably rewarding. At times it can seem so overwhelming that it would be easier to ignore the problem, pretend that nothing is wrong, and just hope it all goes away. But denying or minimizing the problem does not work in the long run and will cause more damage to family and friends and the person who is caught in the trap of addiction.

NCADD (2012) urges family and friends, "Don't wait. Now is the time." To get started, they offer these suggestions:

1. *Learn all you can about alcoholism and drug dependence.* Learn about alcohol, learn about drugs, and learn about family education opportunities.
2. *Speak up and offer your support.* Don't wait for your loved ones to hit bottom. You may be met with excuses, denial, and anger, but be prepared to respond with specific examples of behavior that has you worried.
3. *Don't expect the person to stop without help.* Promises to cut down or stop abusing don't work. Treatment, support, and new coping skills are needed to overcome the addiction to alcohol and drugs, and this journey cannot be made alone.

4. *Support recovery as an ongoing process.* Once your friend or family member is receiving treatment or going to meetings, remain involved. Maintain your commitment to helping them find resources; continue to support their participation in continuing care, meetings, and recovery groups. Continue to show that you are concerned about their successful long-term recovery.

NCADD also lists things you don't want to do:

1. *Don't preach.* Don't lecture, threaten, bribe, or moralize.
2. *Don't be a martyr.* Avoid emotional appeals that may only increase feelings of guilt and the compulsion to drink or use other drugs.
3. *Don't cover up.* Don't lie or make excuses for their behavior.
4. *Don't assume their responsibilities.* Taking over their responsibilities protects them from the consequences of their behavior.
5. *Don't argue when using.* Arguing with the person when they are using alcohol or drugs does not work. They are incapable of having a rational conversation.
6. *Don't feel guilty or responsible for their behavior.* It's not your fault.
7. *Don't join them.* Don't try to keep up with them by drinking or using.

Acknowledging the Dangers of Legal Drugs

Our national fervor to stamp out use of and addiction to illegal drugs has in some ways overshadowed the serious harm legal drugs cause in our society. Alcohol and tobacco cause many times the number of deaths attributable to illegal drugs—and the associated costs, in terms of lost time from work and medical bills, are much greater.

About 570,000 people die every year due to drug use. About 440,000 die from disease related to tobacco use; 80,000 due to alcohol; 20,000 due to prescription drug abuse; and 20,000 due to illegal drugs (National Institute of Drug Abuse, 2012). Looking at those numbers from another angle, they tell us that only 3.5% of drug-related deaths in our country each year are related to the use of illegal drugs, leaving 96.5% of the deaths caused by legal drugs. Why in our society do we focus so much attention on illegal drugs, when legal drugs kill so many more people? What do you think is going on?

Medically speaking, alcohol and cigarette addictions can be very difficult habits to break. Almost all adult smokers began to smoke before age 20. Researchers have found almost half (47.8%) of U.S. adolescents try smoking by the time they are in ninth grade, and most adult smokers (90%) began smoking at or before they were 18 years old (Hood Center for Children and Families, Dartmouth Medical School, 2012). It is also known that family functioning is related to adolescent cigarette smoking. For example, William J. Doherty and William Allen (1994) found that families who were low in cohesion (togetherness) and had a parent who smoked were the most likely to have a young adolescent who smoked. Similarly, Janet N. Melby and her colleagues found that harsh and inconsistent parenting was related to adolescent tobacco use and that nurturant and involved parenting was not (Melby, Conger, Conger, & Lorenz, 1993).

In addition to not smoking themselves, there are a number of other important ways parents can influence their children in the decision to not smoke: by setting rules about movie viewing so that kids don't see a lot of smoking and drinking by the stars (and often subsidized by the tobacco and alcohol companies); communicating positively and regularly with one's children, rather than isolating them effectively. Fortunately, most families find ways to create relatively supportive and satisfying relationships among their members, which helps prevent many problems of all sorts.

Summary

- Some of the aspects of family stress are common across cultural groups. These are generalized principles that emerged from studying family strengths and stressors in different countries and cultures around the world: (1) all stressors either begin or end up in the family; (2) families from all cultural groups experience couple and family stress; (3) to manage their stress, couples and families tend to first use internal resources (those inside the family system) before seeking external resources (those outside the family system); (4) in many cultures, the extended family system is considered "the family" rather than the nuclear family system; the major resources come from inside the extended family, while fewer resources come from the nuclear family; and (5) all couples and families have some internal strengths for managing stress in their systems, and approaches to stress and coping from one culture to the next can be remarkably similar.

- The three levels of stress are physiological, psychological, and sociocultural. Physiological stress is what happens to our bodies; psychological stress is what happens to our emotions; and sociolcultural stress refers to things around us that cause stress, such as war or poverty.

- Coping is how we respond to something that is potentially harmful. Coping with stress can either be problem-focused or emotion-focused. If we focus on the problem, we try to change the situation, the behavior of others, or our attitudes. If we focus on our emotions, we try to reduce or manage our own stress.

- There is a relationship between stress and health. The strongest association is between work stress and cardiovascular disease.

- The roller coaster course of adjustment to stressors, described by Hill, involves a period of disorganization, an angle of recovery, and a new level of organization.

- Families draw on a variety of resources and related coping strategies to deal with stressful issues: cognitive resources (reframing the situation), emotional resources (expressing feelings), relationship resources (increasing cohesion), community resources (seeking help and support from outside the family), spiritual resources (praying; seeking help from a pastor, priest, or rabbi), and individual resources (developing autonomy).

- According to family systems theory, family members' behaviors are all interrelated; each member's actions affect the other members and their actions. As such, the family systems approach focuses on helping families resolve relationship issues rather than on identifying "causes" of family problems.

- War and deployment of soldiers to training facilities or a war zone affect couple and family relationships. Some of the effects for at-home spouses include mental health issues such as depression, anxiety, and sleep disorders. Those deployed often experience multiple mental and physical health issues.

- Divorce rates have increased for military personnel, with military women divorcing more often than military men.

- Children of parents who are deployed experience an overall sense of loss and uncertainty, often resulting in behavior changes and conflict with the at-home parent.

- Community organizations have been formed to help families with a deployed parent. The support of communities is viewed as important in helping families feel less isolated and alone.

- Family violence is a core social issue in every country around the world. The historical and political bias that events occurring outside the home are more significant than events occurring within the home and that what happens inside the home is private and not public, have helped mask the impact of family violence. Yet, the world is slowly awakening and admitting the fact that family violence is a major problem, and it is hard to conceive how to construct strong nations without creating healthy violence-free families.

- Based on a national survey of spouse abuse with 20,951 married couples, nonabusive marriages were compared with abusive marriages. Couples in non-abusive marriages had used less alcohol, had higher levels of couple closeness and flexibility, had better communication and conflict resolution skills, and had a stronger network of family and friends. In terms of personality, nonabusive marriages had partners who were more assertive, had higher levels of self-confidence, and less often tried to dominate their partners.
- Many of the risk factors for spouse abuse in a family are similar to those for child abuse: victimization as a child, low self-esteem, youth, economic stress, social isolation, alcohol abuse, and a male-dominated relationship. Cultural factors that implicitly support the objectification and denigration of women may also play a part.
- Counselors generally advise battered women to leave their husbands. Shelters for abused women and their children offer emotional support and counseling as well as practical help. Police arrest of perpetrators of domestic violence is more common today, and research indicates that men who spend time behind bars are less likely to assault their partners again.
- Child abuse is physical or emotional harm to children or failure to act that results in harm to a child. Abuse includes physical and sexual abuse as well as neglect.
- The number of reports of child maltreatment has decreased since 1993.
- Some researchers have found that spanking is detrimental to the short-term and long-term development of children. It is suggested that hitting children teaches them to hit others—as children and later as adults.
- Parental and family risk factors for child abuse include economic distress, inadequate parenting skills, parental personality problems, chemical abuse, social isolation, a special child, domestic violence in the abuser's family of origin, a violent subculture or marriage, and single parenthood or stepparenthood.
- Sibling abuse and child-to-parent abuse are more common than might be expected. An estimated 75% of siblings are involved in a violent episode each year, and 10% of parents are victims of their children's violent behavior.
- An estimated 80,000 Americans die each year from alcohol abuse, and about 440,000 Americans die from diseases linked to smoking.

Key Terms

stress
coping
family coping
ambiguous loss
boundary ambiguity
deployment
traumatic brain injury
posttraumatic stress
    disorder (PTSD)
managing stress
victimizer
learned helplessness theory

catharsis conflict
child abuse
sibling abuse
child-to-parent abuse
alcohol abuse
alcoholism
problem drinking
Alcoholics
    Anonymous (AA)
Al-Anon
Alateen

Activities

1. Think about how members of your family respond to stress. Ask your parents, siblings, or spouse to describe how your family responds to stress. Are there cultural components to your family's responses? Compare what you have learned from this chapter to what your family does.
2. Identify a family in your community who has a member deployed. Talk to them about what they are experiencing. If it is appropriate and if the parents approve, also talk with the children. Identify ways you can help, and do so.
3. Identify and visit a domestic violence facility in your community. Learn what they do and how they help those who have experienced domestic violence. Or interview a police officer and find out how he or she handles domestic violence calls.
4. In small groups, discuss the extent of alcohol and other drug abuse on campus. Also discuss any violent incidents, such as date rape, related to chemical abuse.

Suggested Readings

Al-Anon/Alateen. (2012a). About us. Web site: http://www.al-anon.org. The volunteers with Al-Anon provide education and support for families of alcoholics. Alateen volunteers work with young people who have drinking-related problems.

Al-Anon/Alateen. (2012b). Online Al-Anon outreach. Web site: http://www.ola-is.org/. Online education and support for families of alcoholics, and for young people.

Alcoholics Anonymous. (2012a). Welcome to AA. Web site: http://www.aa.org/. Education and support for alcoholics from other alcoholics.

look at domestic violence from an international perspective, including 17 countries in all the world's major geocultural areas.

Center for Problem-Oriented Policing. (2012). Factors contributing to domestic violence. Web site: http://www.popcenter.org/problems/domestic_violence/2.

Center for Problem-Oriented Policing. (2013). The problem of domestic violence, Guide No. 45. Web site: http://www.popcenter.org.

Centers for Disease Control. (2012a). Alcohol and public health. Web site: http://www.cdc.gov/alcohol/faqs.htm.

Centers for Disease Control. (2012b). Child maltreatment prevention. Web site: http://www.cdc.gov./ViolencePrevention/childmaltreatment/index.html.

Centers for Disease Control. (2012c). Dating Matters Initiative. Web site: http://www.cdc.gov/ViolencePrevention/DatingMatters/index.html Dating Matters is a new teen dating violence prevention initiative.

Child Welfare Information Gateway. (2012). What is child abuse and neglect? Web site: http://www.childwelfare.gov/can/defining/.

Cullington, D. (2008). *Breaking up blues.* New York: Routledge.

Faces and Voices of Recovery. (2012). Organizing the recovery community. Web site: http://www.facesandvoicesofrecovery.org/about.

Johnson, M. P. (2008). A typology of domestic violence: Intimate terrorism, violent resistance, and situational couple violence. Boston: Northeastern University Press.

Kaminer, Y., & Bukstein, O. G. (2008). *Adolescent substance abuse.* New York: Routledge.

Mickish, J., & Schoen, K. (2004). Colorado Alliance for Cruelty Prevention: Safe pets, safe families, safe communities. *The Colorado Lawyer, 33*(1), 37–40.

National Center for Victims of Crime. (2012). Help for crime victims. Web site: http://www.victimsofcrime.org/.

National Coalition Against Domestic Violence. (2012a). Domestic violence facts. Web site: http://www.ncadv.org/.

National Institute on Alcohol Abuse and Alcoholism. (2012). Alcoholism and health. Web site: http://www.niaaa.nih.org.

National Institute on Alcohol Abuse and Alcoholism. (2012). A guide for marriage and family therapists. Web site: http://www.niaaa.nih.org.

National Institute on Drug Abuse. (2012). General questions about drug abuse. Web site: http://drugfactsweek.drugabuse.gov/chat/chatfaqs_topics/general_questions.php.

Partnership at Drugfree.org. (2012). Support and resources for parents dealing with teen drug and alcohol abuse. Web site: http://www.drugfree.org.

Prevent Child Abuse. (2012). Making the case: Why prevention matters. Web site: http://www.preventchildabuse.org/index.shtml.

Scott, M. J. (2007). *Moving on after trauma.* New York: Routledge.

Skogrand, L., DeFrain, N., DeFrain, J., & Jones, J. E. (2007). *Surviving and transcending a traumatic childhood: The dark thread.* New York: Routledge.

U.S. Department of Justice. (2012). Domestic violence. Web site: http://www.ovw.usdoj.gov/domviolence.htm.

Walker, L. E. (2009). *The battered woman syndrome: With research associates.* New York: Springer.

Willows, J. (2008). *Moving on after childhood sexual abuse.* New York: Routledge.

WomensLaw.org. (2012). Learning about abuse. Web site: http://www.womenslaw.org.

 Visit the text-specific Online Learning Center at **www.mhhe.com/olson8e** for practice tests, chapter summaries, and PowerPoint slides.

15 *Divorce, Single-Parent Families, and Stepfamilies*

Intimacy, Strengths, and Diversity

Divorce in Today's Society

Understanding Divorce

Single-Parent Families

Stepfamilies

Summary

Key Terms

Activities

Suggested Readings

Stepfamily relationships require new and usually more complicated intimate relationships with the addition of stepchildren and new extended-family relationships.

People seek inner strength as they go through a divorce and also as single parents. All types of families can be strong. In fact, single mothers and single fathers can create wonderfully strong family relationships. There is no doubt that life is often more complicated and stressful for single parents and stepfamilies, but many families do well in meeting the challenges.

Stepfamilies are becoming increasingly common as the number of single parents and divorced parents marry.

This chapter is also about the diversity of family forms. This growing family complexity creates challenges for family members, extended-family members, therapists, and policymakers as we try to navigate new territory.

Divorce in Today's Society

Historical Trends

Before the mid-1800s, people married for physical and economic survival. Divorce for most people was not an option (Joanning & Keoughan, 2006). Many marriages were arranged, or women married the farmer down the road with only two or three potential marriage partners available. Very few marriages ended in divorce during this time (Coontz, 2005). By the late 1800s and early 1900s, young people moved from viewing marriage as a way to stay alive to marrying for love (Joanning & Keoughan, 2006). Today, slightly less than 50% of marriages end in divorce. As can be seen by Figure 15.1, the divorce rate has been increasing and then leveling off.

Divorce rates can change as a result of societal events. Some researchers, although not all, believe that part of the increase in divorce in the 1970s was also related to a change in divorce laws, which made it easier to get divorced (Cole & Broussard, 2006). During this time, many states went from fault-based divorce to no-fault divorce, which meant that divorces could be granted without either partner finding fault with their spouse. The highest divorce rates in history occurred in 1979 and 1981, with the rates beginning a decline in 2005 (Cole & Broussard, 2006). But the divorce rate may be increasing as a result of the Iraq War like it did after other wars.

Another factor that also seems to have had a significant effect on divorce rates was women entering the workforce and earning salaries that allowed for economic independence. This earning ability was spurred on by the feminist movement in the 1960s and 1970s, which increased the awareness of equity in economic opportunities (Cole & Broussard, 2006). Some suggest that contraception options, which became more available in the 1970s, also contributed to divorce rates, because women could chose not to have children, and without children they were able to get out of unhappy marriages (Cole & Broussard, 2006).

FIGURE 15.1

Number of Divorces per 1,000 Married Women Age 15 and Older, by Year, United States

Source: Copyright © 2009 by National Marriage Project at the University of Virginia, reprinted with permission.

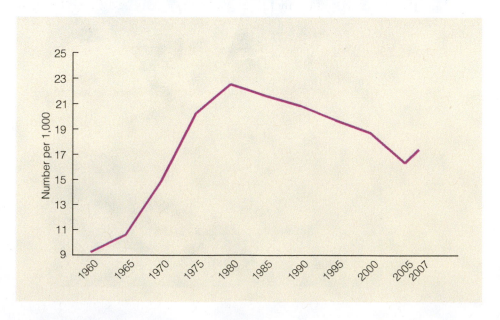

(2009), couples are more likely to weather the economic storm by staying together rather than divorcing. Although there are times when it is most important to have a spouse who meets one's emotional needs, during a downturn individuals may choose to stay with someone who can help contribute to house payments. During financially challenging times, marriage becomes an economic partnership and a safety net.

The number of people who cohabit also affects the divorce rate (Popenoe, 2008). The increase in the number of people who cohabit has caused a decline in the number of people who marry. The divorce rate, therefore, may be declining because the number of people marrying is declining. We do not have any documentation about the number of people who cohabit and then break up, but historically those who break up would have been represented in divorce statistics. This is true to an even greater extent in European countries. For example, the cohabitation rates in Sweden and Denmark have increased to more than 90%, which also results in a decrease in the divorce rates. In some of these countries there is no distinction between marriage and cohabitation, and no one asks if a couple is married or not.

The extent to which people are religious also affects the divorce rate (Popenoe, 2008). Countries where religion is widely practiced are more likely to have higher marriage, lower cohabitation, and lower divorce rates. Spain and Italy are examples where the marriage rate is high, the cohabitation rate is about 3% to 4%, and the divorce rate is also low. These countries are more likely to have more traditional family structures, and religious values affect how couples view marriage. The United States still maintains many religious traditions as compared to some European countries, and thus the U.S. divorce rate is still relatively high.

There are many differences of opinions about whether the decrease in the marriage rate and the high rate of divorce in this country is a bad thing or a good thing. Popenoe (2008) has strong feelings about this trend. He says:

> To improve child wellbeing, modern nations need to foster more long-term, committed relationships among child-rearing couples. This means, essentially, that the institution of marriage, in some form, needs to be strongly encouraged, supported, and protected . . . marriage has had as its primary function the holding together of parents to raise their children, and there is really no other institution in sight than could successfully replace it. (p. 21)

There are, on the other hand, many who choose not to be in marriages. For example, there is an organization called the Alternatives to Marriage Project (www. unmarried .org), which says that they are not opposed to marriage but do not feel marriage is for everyone. The organization supports the notion that people should have choices about marrying and not feel pressured to marry. Individuals must draw their own conclusions about this issue. Those conclusions are likely to be influenced by the individual's religious beliefs, expectations about the role of happiness in marriage, and personal life experiences.

The average age at divorce is 36 for men and 33 for women. The average length of first marriages that end in divorce is about 7 years. So, of the half of all first marriages that end in divorce, half of those end within the first 7 years. In terms of first marriages,

BOX 15.1   Diversity in Families

The Globalization of Divorce

Although America ranks high in the rate of divorce, the rest of the world is catching up. Across Europe, for instance, marriage rates are declining and divorce rates are climbing steadily, with Belgium reporting in 2002 that it had the fewest number of marriages in the European Union (3.9 per 1,000 people) and the highest number of divorces (3.0 per 1,000 people) (UK National Statistics, 2004).

Cultural changes taking place around the world are influencing divorce rates in almost every country. One of the countries changing most rapidly is the Republic of Korea, which in the past 10 to 15 years has become an increasingly open, westernized society.

Prior to 1990, divorce was a cultural and legal taboo in the Republic of Korea (known as South Korea by Westerners), and Korea's divorce rate was one of the lowest in the world (1.1 per 1,000 people). A divorced woman would be ostracized and had a very slim chance of marrying again. She usually lost custody of her children and had a difficult, if not impossible, time finding employment. A divorced man would also have had a hard time finding a job, or if he already had one, would not get promoted. His career path was definitely cut short. His chances at remarriage were not good either, as few women wanted to marry a man who had already shown he could not keep a stable relationship or take care of his family (Lankov, 2004).

The situation began to change in the early 1990s. Within 12 years, Korea's divorce rate rose from 11% in 1990 to 47% in 2002, ranking the country among the top 10 in the world. Some of the reasons for this swift-spreading change include "the collapse of traditional patriarchic values, the rise of a new generation of college-educated women, the growth of employment opportunities for female workers and their ensuing economic independence, and the powerful influence of Western individualism and feminism" (Lankov, 2004).

As a symbol of just how much Korean attitudes toward divorce have changed, in 2004 nearly a quarter of the country's television viewers tuned in once a week to watch a show called *Love and War,* where actors dramatized actual divorce cases and marital conflicts. Viewers could then vote online on whether they thought the couple should stay together or get divorced.

The Republic of Korea isn't the only Asian country to experience a dramatic rise in divorce rates. Below are some divorce statistics and their cultural significance in several other Asian countries:

- *India.* Not so long ago, a woman was so tied to her husband's fate that if he died before she did, she was thrown onto his funeral pyre. Today, that practice is no longer legal, and women in unhappy marriages are now seeking divorce. In 2004, the divorce rate was estimated at 11 per 1,000 people (versus 7.41 in 1991). However, divorce is still not socially accepted by everyone. One divorced woman related to *Time Asia* that divorced women in India always feel a sense of isolation and that "women like her are widely viewed as inferior to those with husbands" (Fitzpatrick, 2004).
- *Japan.* Statistics showed that in 2004 a couple married every 42 seconds in Japan—and that every 2 minutes another couple got divorced. The divorce rate rose from 22% in 1990 to 38% in 2002. The biggest change

divorce most often occurs during the first year or two. By the end of 5 years of marriage, 19% of couples are divorced; by the end of 10 years, 14% more are divorced. Another 7% divorce before 15 years of marriage; 7% more divorce before their 25th anniversary; and 3% more divorce before their 50th anniversary (U.S. Census Bureau, 2004a).

Divorce rates in other countries are different from the United States as described in Box 15.1. We will likely continue to see trends change in these countries because of the cultural changes taking place around the world.

In addition, even within the United States, divorce rates of interracial couples are higher than rates for couples of the same ethnic group. As one can see in Box 15.2, divorce rates are very complex.

Divorce Laws and Views on Divorce

In the early to mid-1900s the granting of a divorce by the legal system was based upon the ability of one of the spouses to successfully place blame on the other

- *China.* In the past 20 years, the divorce rate in mainland China has doubled—and has tripled in Taiwan. As in Japan, many of these divorced couples are in their 40s and 50s and have been married for many years. People over the age of 50 seeking divorce made up 9% of all divorces in 1980, as compared to 14.7% in 2003. The Association for Asian Research suggested four reasons for increased divorce rates among middle-aged Chinese: (1) the concept of marriage is changing and individual pursuit of happiness is seen as more important than stability; (2) the demands of professional success coupled with the demands of raising a family cause strain on relationships; (3) social acceptance of divorce has increased, and more opportunities exist to meet new partners; and (4) familial support systems—where extended families all lived together and shared responsibilities—are weaker than ever before ("Divorce Rate Climbs," 2004).

  In Shanghai, where divorce rates increased by 30% in the 1-year period from 2003 to 2004, the government sent out notices to couples seeking divorce asking them to reconsider the correctness of their decision. One reason for the sharp increase was that procedures for divorce were greatly simplified in 2004, and couples who previously had to wait a month for their divorce agreement now had to wait about 10 minutes ("Divorce Rate on the Increase in Shanghai," 2004).

brings a woman great shame. In contrast, when a woman in the western Sahara gets a divorce, she throws a party, and men who seek the hand of the newly available woman bring presents like camels, perfume, or money (Harter, 2004).

In another part of the continent, Egypt is struggling to find a more equitable system of granting divorce by changing some of its centuries-old laws and traditions. However, as reported by Human Rights Watch (2004), even the new laws are still biased toward the male population. Egyptian men have an unconditional right to divorce without ever having to go to court; they simply have to make an oral renunciation that can later be ratified by a member of the clergy. Women, on the other hand, must go through complicated legal procedures. If they wish to keep full financial rights, they must show evidence that their husbands inflicted physical harm, a claim they are usually required to support with eyewitness testimony. A woman can file for "no-fault" divorce—if she agrees to forfeit all her financial rights and repay the dowry given to her by her husband when they were wed (Human Rights Watch, 2004).

As the westernization of the world continues, as economic growth in poor countries increases, and as women's rights take on greater dimensions, we can expect the rising global divorce rate to continue to be an unintentional by-product.

(Adams & Coltrane, 2007). Divorce was a result of a family breakdown, and there was an effort to control the number of divorces by limiting the available grounds for divorce. Because a divorce could not be granted unless one of the partners had done something to break the union, divorces were by definition adversarial. There were times, however, when everyone involved, including lawyers, fulfilled the legal requirement of placing blame, even when both partners agreed that a divorce was in the best interest of the couple.

No-fault divorce statutes eliminated the need to place blame on one partner or the other (Adams & Coltrane, 2007). Incompatibility and irreconcilable differences were added to the grounds for divorce. The first state to enact the no-fault statutes was California in 1969–1970. By 1985 all states had some provisions for no-fault divorce. No-fault divorce resulted in the following changes in how divorces were obtained:

- *Redefinition of the traditional duties of husbands and wives and establishment of equality between the genders as a norm.* Under no-fault laws, the husband is no

Because divorce can be a traumatic experience for adults and children, lawyers should not act as adversaries doing battle for their clients but should try to facilitate responsible communication. The lawyer's most important task is to help divorcing parents restructure the family and minimize the emotional damage to both themselves and their children.

longer considered by law to be the head of the family. Both spouses are presumed to be equal partners, with equal obligations for financial support and care of their children. Spouses are treated equally with respect to child custody, as well as finances and property. The so-called **tender years doctrine**, which presumed that young children would do better with their mother than with their father, has been replaced by the notion of joint custody as being in the "best interests of the child." Fathers are at least theoretically equal to mothers in questions of custody. In a small number of cases, fathers are winning not only custody but also child support.

- *Elimination of fault-based grounds for divorce.* Under no-fault laws, one spouse does not have to prove the other's adultery, cruelty, or desertion. The concept of *irreconcilable differences* recognizes the irrelevancy of discussing the reasons for the marital dissolution in court.

- *Elimination of the adversarial process.* Proponents of divorce reform argued that the adversarial nature of traditional divorce proceedings was harmful to all parties involved, especially to the children. Under no-fault, by facilitating accurate and responsible communication rather than doing battle, lawyers can help divorcing parents restructure the family and prepare to fulfill their postdivorce parenting responsibilities. Many spouses neither love nor hate each other at the end of a marriage; they are capable of an *amicable divorce* and are good candidates for joint custody of their children.

- *Basing of financial decisions on equity, equality, and economic need rather than on fault or gender-based role assignments.* In a no-fault system, each spouse's economic circumstances are assessed under the principle of equality between the sexes. No-fault laws adhere to the notion that divorced women should be self-supporting and when it is not possible, they should receive fair compensation. Under the newer no-fault divorce laws, older homemakers are more likely to receive alimony than are younger homemakers. In some cases, a woman might receive support while she goes back to school for retraining.

studies of interracial couples have included Black-White marriages and focused on marriage prevalence rather than dissolution rates. This study included interracial couples who were White, Black, Hispanic, and Asian. The study was conducted under the premise that homogeneity is related to marital stability, and that couples who are dissimilar because of racial differences were likely to be at risk for divorce or separation.

The findings of this study showed that mixed marriages involving Blacks were the least stable, followed by Hispanics. Mixed marriages involving Asians were, however, very stable. Black-White marriages were found to be the least stable of all the interracial combinations. Interracial couples involving one Black or Hispanic spouse were more likely to divorce or separate than same-race couples, whereas couples involving an utes to the dissolution of these interracial marriages. The findings also revealed that mixed marriages were likely to have larger differences between spouses when it came to age and education. This could also contribute to the higher risk for marital dissolution. This finding, however, does not explain why White-Asian couples are quite stable.

The study found that interracial marriages did not have marital dissolution rates that were different than the marital dissolution rates of the higher-risk group within the couple. In other words, a Black-White couple did not have a higher risk of marital dissolution than a Black-Black couple would have. As the authors conclude, it takes both partners to make the marriage work, and whatever the factors are that result in higher divorce rates for a particular ethnic group, these factors also affect that interracial marriage.

Attorneys have been forcefully arguing that women who previously put their husbands through professional school are entitled to a share of their earnings for a period of time after the divorce.

Although no-fault divorce was generally viewed as creating more equality between spouses, inequities still remained. Women typically could not earn as much as men, and women typically were awarded custody of the children (Adams & Coltrane, 2007). In the 1970s, fathers began to advocate for more involvement in their children's lives and we began to see research focusing on the benefits of fathers being involved in the lives of their children. Fathers began to gain custody of their children in divorce, or at least began to have shared custody of their children.

In the 1990s we began to see research that supported the view that children need both parents in their lives and that with divorce the children become the victims (Adams & Coltrane, 2007). The result is that states have begun to instigate longer waiting periods and parental counseling to ease the transitions of divorce for children.

Some efforts have been made to put in place safeguards before marriage to reduce the divorce rate (Adams & Coltrane, 2007). Some states charge less for a marriage license for couples who have participated in premarital education. Other states, such as Louisiana, Arizona, and Arkansas, have implemented the option of covenant marriages. They typically focus on the premise that marriage is more than a contract, it is a covenant with God. In a covenant marriage, the couple agrees to premarital counseling and, if a divorce becomes necessary, fault-based divorce provisions and an extended waiting period before finalizing a divorce. Covenant marriages are typically accepted by couples who are conservative Christians, and may be embraced by clergy and promoted in their congregations.

Understanding Divorce

No emptiness on earth can compare with the loss of love.

—PAUL THEROUX (1996, p. 425)

Both partners in a divorce often spend considerable time trying to unravel the reasons why their marriage ended. Although the task is difficult, it is essential to the postdivorce recovery process. The search for the "causes" of a divorce must take into consideration a number of factors and many points of view. In this section we will look at several important issues to understand why people divorce.

The Culture of Divorce

Divorce culture is the notion that divorce has now become so accepted that it is almost the expected outcome of marriage (Adams & Coltrane, 2007). Before the 1950s, divorce was rare, and there was considerable social pressure to stay married, even if it was a bad and abusive marriage. But now divorce is linked with the pursuit of individual satisfaction, and there is less social pressure to stay married. Even the presence of children is not a deterrent to getting divorced as it was in the past. The challenges of divorce are even fodder for comedy, as in the movie *Mrs. Doubtfire,* in which a mother unknowingly hires the separated father (dressed up as a woman) as a nanny to care for their children.

Usdansky (2009) recently concluded that as a society we are less critical of single-parent families when they have resulted from divorce than when they have resulted from nonmarital births. She indicates we currently have an *ambivalent acceptance of divorce.* Other researchers have also contributed to this discussion in that divorce is about individual rights and that in many cases divorce is necessary because of the right to be free of violence or other unfortunate circumstances (Cherlin, 2009). The views about nonmarital births, however, according to Cherlin, are tied to views about morality, and nonmarital births thus are viewed as less acceptable. Not surprisingly, nonmarital births are more accepted in low-income communities than in middle-income neighborhoods. It is expected by some that, in the future, views will change and the ambivalent acceptance of divorce will likely extend to women having children outside of marriage.

The Impact of Divorce on Adults

There are potentially multiple issues that divorced adults deal with as they move on after a failed marriage. The legal divorce is usually not the end of stress and unhappiness. Some of these issues include having major responsibility for children as the custodial parent, decreased contact with children for the noncustodial parent, difficulty dealing with reduced income, decreased social support, and potentially continued conflict with the ex-spouse over child support or custody issues (Amato, 2007). People differ in their ability to address these issues. For example, the ability to develop social support is dependent upon one's social skills and one's ability to construct new social networks. Individuals' ability to define their new status as a single person will also affect their ability to move on. Those who see their singlehood as an opportunity for personal growth, rather than a tragedy, will adjust more readily and successfully to life after divorce.

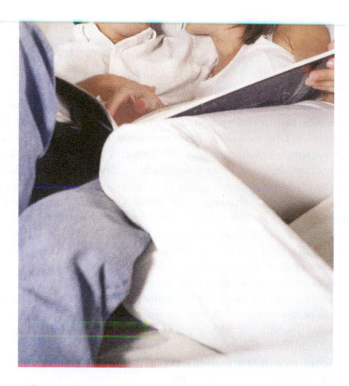

In the largest follow-up study of divorce to date, Mavis Hetherington and John Kelly (2002) followed over 1,400 people who experienced divorce for up to 30 years. In their book *For Better or Worse: Divorce Reconsidered*, they found that the majority of adults (70%) who divorced felt that they were doing at least as well or better than before the divorce.

They identified six different styles of adjusting to the divorce. The first three types (70%) were doing better, and they were called the enhanced, competent loners, and good enoughs. The *enhanced type* (20%) felt that the divorce helped them focus on their strengths and develop themselves more fully. The *competent loners* (10%) never remarried but led rather full and happy lives as single persons. The largest group was the *good enoughs* (40%), who felt that divorce was like a speed bump, but that they were survivors and it did not negatively impact their lives.

Less than one-third of the adults (30%) felt their lives were more negatively impacted by the divorce. The *seekers* (13%) felt that remarriage brought them the security and meaning that they wanted in their lives. The *libertines* (6%) coped by living life in the fast lane and not focusing on the past but enjoying the present. The *defeateds* (11%) were most negatively impacted and experienced poverty, depression, drug abuse, and bitterness.

This major study provides the best evidence to date that most adults who get divorced eventually adjust and manage well over time. This study is important because it used a large sample, followed people for many years, and was done well. It is in striking contrast to many other studies, which have been limited in scope and have focused on the more negative impact of divorce.

The Impact of Divorce on Children

The increase in divorce and the resulting impact on the well-being of children have been a major focus of research for many years. It is estimated that 40% of all children will experience divorce before reaching adulthood (Amato, 2007). Most studies show that children with divorced parents have higher rates of emotional and social problems than children from intact families.

Some of the most vocal professionals describing the negative impact of divorce on children include Judith Wallerstein and her colleagues (Wallerstein & Blakeslee, 2003, Wallerstein & Lewis, 2004). They conducted a longitudinal study of children of divorce using a small sample of families and concluded that divorce has a long-term impact on children. Even 5 years after a divorce, they found more than one-third of the children showed signs of moderate-to-severe depression. After 10 years, some of the adult children were underachieving and having emotional problems, and after 15 years, some adult children were having problems in their love relationships. This study had a small and biased sample of 60 families and no control group, although it did follow the same people over time, and provided a negative perspective on divorce.

While most of the studies have emphasized the negative impact of divorce on children, Hetherington and Kelly (2002) identified both the negative and the more positive aspects of divorce on children. In their study, *For Better or Worse: Divorce Reconsidered*, they investigated the impact of divorce on children with over 1,400 adults and 2,500 children. They found that between 75% and 80% of the children were doing rather well 6 years after the divorce. So resiliency was much more prominent than pathology in the children.

A recent longitudinal study looked at how parental separation affected children's behavioral and emotional problems (Stadelmann, Perren, Groeben, & von Klitzing, 2010). In this large study of almost 200 5 and 6-year-old children, researchers investigated parental separation, family conflict, and children's views of their parents' relationships as these variables related to behavioral problems. The researchers found that parental separation and family conflict predicted and increased the level of behavior problems. They also found that if parents got along well, the behavioral problems were diminished.

Constance Ahrons, a long-time researcher of divorce, concludes that the effect of divorce on children varies depending on a multitude of interactive factors (Ahrons, 2006). These factors take into account the child, the parents, the pre- and postdivorce family, and the environmental and social factors. She concludes that most children of divorced parents grow up to be healthy and well adjusted, while another smaller group does less well.

The personalities of children affect how they react and respond to divorce (Ahrons, 2006). For example, the child's temperament and ways of coping have an impact on his or her ability to deal with this major family change. Is the child easy going, or does he or she respond dramatically to family transitions? Has the child developed ways of coping with difficulties? A child's emotional health before the divorce also affects his or her ability to deal with divorce. In addition, to fend for themselves.

On the other hand, Norval Glenn found that some children whose parents were not in a high-conflict marriage before the divorce also experienced trauma (Bryant, 2006). Children whose parents did not get along sometimes felt relief that their parents would not be fighting anymore, and welcomed a divorce (Amato, 2007). As one person said, "I was glad when they got divorced because they were so unhappy together." However, children whose parents appeared to get along before the divorce were taken by surprise when their parents separated, because they had no idea their parents had a problem. One adult child whose parents divorced unexpectedly said, "If my parents couldn't make it in a marriage, no one can. I don't think I will ever get married."

Ahrons (2007) reported on a longitudinal interview study following 173 children of divorce over 20 years. Because longitudinal studies are rare, and the sample is relatively large, this study is very telling of what we know about the effects of divorce on children over time. This study focused on the long-term effects of divorce and the impact of a new partner in their parents' lives.

A focus of the Ahrons (2007) study was how well their divorced parents got along. Sixty percent of the adult children said their parents were cooperative, whereas when the divorce occurred only 40% were cooperative. Children whose parents did not get along describe the effort they had to make to maneuver relationships between both parents. They talked retrospectively about not being able to talk about one parent when they were in the presence of the other. They also talked about dreading the transition times when moving between households. As adults they had to deal with weddings, funerals, and other family celebrations, often wondering how their divorced parents would behave toward each other. The major factor related to their personal well-being was how well their divorced parents got along. If the parents did not get along, the children did not do well. This finding supports other short-term findings, but according to this study, it was also true 20 years later. Not surprisingly, the relationships they had with their extended family also depended on how well their parents got along. This is consistent with the knowledge that family can be an important support system in getting through difficult times in life.

It does need to be noted that this study was conducted with adults whose parents divorced in the 1970s and 1980s. Times have changed, when it comes to parent custody issues and views about divorce and remarriage. Children whose parents divorce today may have a slightly different experience.

A more recent study by Amato, Kane, and James (2011) compared three groups of parents following divorce. The three groups were cooperative parenting, parallel parenting, and single parenting to see how children did in terms of behavior problems following a divorce. Cooperative parenting meant that parents worked together after the divorce and was coined by these authors as the *good divorce*. Youth who had parents who worked together in a positive way had fewer behavior problems and had better relationships with their fathers than the other two groups. However, these youth were no better off than the other two groups in terms of self-esteem, substance abuse, or early sexual activity. In conclusion, these authors question whether there really is such a thing as a good divorce.

Because same-sex relationships are becoming more prevalent, studies are now appearing that focus on the breakup of same-sex couples. A recent study of lesbian couple breakups, most of whom did not have a legal marriage relationship, indicated that if the children had been adopted by the nonbiological parent there was a closer relationship with both mothers after the separation (Gartrell, Bos, Preyser, Deck, & Rodas, 2011).

We might conclude from all of these findings regarding the impact of divorce on children that breakup and divorce can affect kids in negative ways. However, if parents get along the outcomes for kids are more positive.

Binuclear Families Compared to Single-Parent Families. Terminology often can help in understanding how families are reorganized after divorce. Constance Ahrons (2004) sometimes prefers the term *binuclear family* to *single-parent family* because it acknowledges the positive outcome that results from divorce or separation of biological parents. Divorce or separation is a process that results in family reorganization rather than disintegration of the family system. This reorganization of the nuclear family frequently results in the establishment of two households, the mother's and the father's. If one ex-partner does not drop out of the family after the separation and the two households continue to interrelate, then a **binuclear family** has been established.

In some binuclear families, children have a primary and a secondary home: One parent has **sole custody**, and the children live with that parent in the primary home; the other parent in the secondary home has rights of visitation with the children. In a smaller proportion of families, the homes of both parents have equal importance—"one child, two homes." This arrangement has been termed **joint custody**. In an even smaller proportion of families, one parent has sole custody of one or more of the children, and the other parent has sole custody of the other child or children—an arrangement called **split custody** (McBride, 2003).

In binuclear families, relationships between the two households can vary greatly. Some ex-partners continue the preseparation wars into the postseparation years, whereas others get along wonderfully. A few binuclear families even share some holidays. The majority, however, rarely get together as a group. Ahrons (2003) identified four types of relationships in binuclear families: *perfect pals, cooperative colleagues, angry associates,* and *fiery foes.* Ahrons also uses the term *dissolved duo* to describe a relationship that is completely over.

Joint Custody. Joint custody is defined as either physical custody, where the child spends about equal time with both parents, or shared legal custody, where the child spends more time with one parent but both parents are involved in the child's life. In general, joint custody can be successful only if both parents are willing and able to work together in the best interests of the child or children.

Joint custody has been found to have more positive outcomes for children than sole custody. In a meta-analysis of 33 studies that examined 1,846 sole-custody and 814 joint-custody families, Robert Bauserman (2002) found that child adjustment was more positive with joint custody than with sole custody. Children in joint custody had fewer emotional problems, higher self-esteem, better school performance, and more positive family relationships than children under sole custody.

children and both parents feel it best that both parents continue to have contact with the children after the divorce? (2) Are both parents capable of maintaining an adequate home for the children? (3) Can the parents get along with each other well enough to manage a joint-custody arrangement after the divorce? If all members of the family can honestly answer yes to all three questions, then joint custody can potentially be successful.

Joint-custody parents report less stress than sole-custody parents. Joint-custody parents also have more time to pursue their own interests, because the ex-spouse assumes a share of the child care responsibilities. Joint-custody parents are more likely to come from a devitalized or burned-out marriage; they are likely to neither love nor hate each other but are able to deal rationally with each other.

Coping Successfully as a Single Parent. Single parents have developed a number of successful strategies for coping with their unique station in life and offer the following suggestions for other single parents:

- Don't rush into a new couple relationship, particularly in an attempt to transfer your dependence onto another person. Let go of the past and move on.
- Realistically face what has happened. Learn from it; don't repeat it.
- Don't succumb to feelings of failure and worthlessness. Make the best of the situation and don't blame yourself completely.
- Keep busy with constructive activities. Take up new (or old) activities you always wanted to find time to enjoy.
- Listen to others but make your own decisions.
- Take one day at a time, setting small goals at first.
- Consider going back to school.
- Be flexible, adaptable, and independent.

Single-Parent Families

The number of children who at some point live in single-parent families increased from 1960 through 2000, and then began to level off (see Figure 15.2). Figure 15.2 indicates that there are differences in different cultural groups, with a higher rate of single parenthood for Blacks than Whites. In 1960, 9% of all children lived with one parent, and in 2008 it was 26% (Wilcox, 2009), with the majority of these families being headed by mothers. The percentage of single-parent families headed by fathers has increased substantially in recent years, with the number currently at 18%. It needs to be noted, however, that in 20% of separations and divorces, parents have joint legal custody of children and children share equal time with both parents (Kelly, 2007).

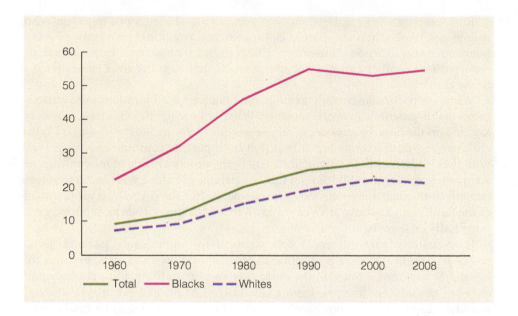

FIGURE 15.2

Percentage of children under age 18 living with a single parent, by year, United States

Because it is estimated that 40% of all children will live in single-parent families at some point in their lives (Amato, 2007), and 26% of children in 2008 were living in single-parent families (Wilcox, 2009), single parenthood is one of the most dramatic family trends in recent history. The increase in single-parent families has resulted from divorce, cohabitation, and births outside of marriage. Children born to cohabiting couples account for the largest increase in single-parent families. Multiple studies point to the varying ways single-parent families manage time with children and the varying factors that impact nonresidential parents' involvement in the lives of their children.

The literature is clear that unless there is abuse or neglect on the part of the noncustodial parent, most children want to have a relationship with both parents (Kelly, 2007). Because most of the noncustodial parents are fathers, studies have typically focused on the time children are allowed to spend with their fathers. Generally, the quality of the parent–child relationship, the amount of contact, the amount of active involvement, and the type of parenting provided are related to more positive outcomes for children. This involvement usually results in fewer behavioral problems, better communication skills, and better academic performance.

Based upon existing literature, Kelly (2007) describes three types of coparenting relationships following separation or divorce. First, there is *conflicted coparenting*, which makes up approximately one-quarter of parents. These couples experience frequent conflicts and poor communication and focus more on their own needs than their children's needs. Approximately half of parents are in *parallel coparenting relationships* and have low conflict with each other but have limited communication regarding parenting issues. They ultimately parent children when they are with them but have limited involvement when the children are with the other parent. Finally, approximately one-fourth of parents may be categorized as practicing *cooperative coparenting*, which involves planning together for their children's lives and supporting each other in their parenting roles. Children whose parents who are coparenting cooperatively seem to be most resilient.

Fathers

Because the majority of children still end up residing with their mothers, the fathers often have less time with their children and typically are the noncustodial parent (Kelly, 2007). This often creates a disparity between biological mothers and fathers in terms of the time spent with children. Because the amount of time fathers spend with children has important implications for their development, much research has focused on father–child relationships. From 1976 to 2002 the amount of time spent with 6- to 12-year-olds increased (Amato, Meyers, & Emery, 2009). In 1976 mothers reported that 18% of noncustodial fathers saw their children at least once a week, and in 2002 the percentage had increased to 31%. Some noncustodial fathers spend little time with their children because it is too painful to have a minimal visiting role in the lives of their children. Mothers are often referred to as *gatekeepers* of children, and control how much time fathers spend with their children. This may be due to beliefs, held by both mothers and fathers, that caring for children is the mother's responsibility and that fathers are less competent in this regard.

Fathers' involvement with their biological children is influenced by many factors (Kelly, 2007), one of which is the degree to which they are paying child support. If fathers are paying child support, they are more likely to be spending time with their children. Fathers who were once married to their children's mother are also more likely to be involved in their children's lives. Hostility over a separation or divorce is also directly related to involvement with their children—with less contact if there was hostility during the breakup. For couples who were not married, better relationships between parents and the parents' relationships with each other's extended family are positively related to increased involvement with their children (Ryan, Kalil, & Ziol-Guest, 2008).

Several other factors can affect the involvement of the noncustodial parent in the lives of the children (Kelly, 2007). Moving away, especially more than 75 miles, can affect time with children. This may be a substantial barrier for parents with limited economic resources or whose work does not allow for flexibility in spending time

Many people who remarry have children from a previous marriage, and the resulting combination can be a large stepfamily with complex dynamics. The children must establish relationships with their stepparent and their stepsiblings, and the adults must learn new roles as stepparents.

with children. If the parents are hostile toward each other or have coparenting conflict, it can lead to breakdown in communication and complicates the planning and execution of time with children. Finally, remarriage or having a new romantic relationship can also affect time together. Typically, when such problems or barriers interfere with spending time with children, time together decreases and closeness between the noncustodial parent and children diminishes.

Here are several research findings that help us understand the role of fathers in the lives of their noncustodial children:

Fathers rely on others for support. Noncustodial divorced fathers relied more on relatives and former spouses regarding parenting than did custodial parents. Custodial parents relied more on romantic partners for parenting support. This support, no matter where it came from, helped fathers buffer the daily stresses of role overload (DeGarmo, Patras, & Eap, 2008).

Shared physical placement supports the father–child relationship long term. A study of over 1,500 mothers and fathers found that fathers who have shared placement, meaning their children live with them part of the time, are likely to continue to maintain the initial shared physical placement 3 years later (Berger, Brown, Joung, Melli, & Wimer, 2008). It appears that the court-ordered shared physical placement supports fathers in continuing to have quality time with their children.

Close relationships with mother are related to close relationships with the noncustodial father. In one study of almost 500 adolescents, it was found that children were more likely to have a close relationship with their noncustodial father if they had a close relationship with their mother (Scott, Booth, King, & Johnson, 2007). These relationships were maintained long term.

Relationships with children have positive effects on the father's well-being. In a study of economically disadvantaged new fathers, it was found that increased commitment to fathering led to fathers having more religious participation, improved well-being, and increased work hours. In other words, fathers' contact with their children improved the fathers' lives—a relationship between parent and child is beneficial to both parent and child (Knoester, Petts, & Eggebeen, 2007).

the divorce rate in the United States to be somewhere between 40% and 50%, resulting in many single-parent families. However, in recent years the number of single-parent families has increased dramatically because of the number of children born to unmarried parents and children born in cohabiting relationships (Sugarman, 2003; Wilcox, 2009).

The largest increase in single-parent families is currently coming from cohabiting couples who have children, and who are legally defined as single-parent families. It is estimated that 60% of all adults cohabit at some time during their lifetime, and 40% of those who cohabit have children (Wilcox, 2010). It is also estimated that half of nonmarital births are to mothers in cohabiting relationships (Pew Research Center, 2007). Many of these couples, even though they are not married, see themselves as being in a stable couple relationship with children they parent together (Sugarman, 2003). Therefore, for many of the cohabiting couples, both parents may be very involved in the life of the child/children and in all aspects of family life and family responsibilities.

Currently, approximately 40% of all children are born to single mothers (Pew Research Center, 2007), with that percentage having increased dramatically in recent years. But keep in mind what we have just stated, half of the children born to single mothers are in cohabiting households. Therefore, we are left with 20% of children born to mothers who we might assume have limited or no support from a significant other.

We also are aware that some single-parent families live in extended family households, which means there may be multiple sources of support in terms of raising children and/or financial support. For example, there has been an increase in multi-generational family households in recent years. The percentage of the U.S. population living in households that include at least two adult generations has increased from 12% several years ago to 16%, according to recent figures (Pew Research Center, 2010). Although some of this increase may be because of adult children returning home or never leaving home, some is attributed to the increase in single-parent families who seek help and support from their parents.

Single-parent families from diverse cultures are likely to look different from those from White middle-class single-parent families. Do Latino, African American, and Asian American single-parent families have differing living arrangements than the members of the European American culture? We expect that to be true. For example, African Americans have the highest percentage of single-parent families (52%) of any major ethnic group in the United States (Fields, 2003). We also know, however, that the institution of the family is highly valued in African American culture. Family is also highly valued in other cultural groups as well. Family, for African Americans, means nuclear family, extended family, and friends who may be viewed as family members (Skogrand, Barrios-Bell, & Higginbotham, 2009). Therefore, single-parent families are often living with extended family members who support them in parenting and provide other resources. Moreover, in Black communities there is a strong religious orientation among many families

(Taylor, Lincoln, & Chatters, 2005). It has been found that many members of the Black community view their church as an important means of support, and churches actually function as families and supplement the efforts of the family network. Churches in the African American culture help and support single-parent families. Other ethnic groups in the United States have similar family and informal community support systems in place and are a strength and resource for members of single-parent families.

One more component of single-parent families is the non-residential fathers' involvement in the lives of the children. Approximately 35% of divorced parents have joint custody of children. We also know anywhere from 30% (Amato, Meyers, & Emery, 2009) to 60% (Kelly, 2007) of children have at least weekly contact with their fathers, and this percentage has increased in recent years. These percentages vary so much because fathers tend to over-report the time spent with children and mothers tend to under-report the time fathers spent with children (Amato et al., 2009). Historically, we have had a stereotypical view of the "deadbeat dad," but in the United States there is evidence this is changing. There have been policy changes that support father involvement with their children because we know more about the important role fathers play in their lives—because dads want to spend time with their kids.

We also have a significant number of gay and lesbian families that include a second, same-sex parent, who in many states in the United States is not recognized as a legal parent. However, a recent ruling by the United States Supreme Court recognizes same-sex marriages at the federal level. An estimated 25% of gay and lesbian couples have children living with them, and another 45% of these couples want to have children. In many cases, these children are legally living in single-parent families, even though there may be a very involved and active second parent living in the home (Gates, 2008).

There is much lamenting about the increase of single-parent families. We should be concerned about this change in family structure. However, single-parent families do not only result from divorce. They may involve a second parent who lives in the home, but where the couple is not married, as in the case of cohabiting couples. They are choosing to create a family without marriage—or as in the case of gay and lesbian couples, are not allowed to marry in many states. Non-residential parents, usually fathers, are often very involved in the life of children even if he or she does not live in the home. There may be other caring adults who are considered *family* who provide love, resources, and support in single-parent families. We may conclude, therefore, that it is not about family structure, but it is about family function. We need to look at how single-parent families function and who is part of what is considered *family*. We need to see what strengths and resources are available to family members.

Challenges of Being in Single-Parent Families

Challenges in single-parent families may be more evident for those who truly feel like they are *going it alone,* with little or no support from others. Even those who are not going it alone may be able to relate to the challenges identified in the literature. It is important to note that research is still mostly about how poorly single-parent families are doing, and how the outcomes for children in single-parent families are not very promising. The research talks about outcomes, not the multiple challenges families encounter and the strength it takes to meet those challenges. The challenges identified below have been identified in the literature:

Financially, many single-parent families struggle (Anderson, 2003). Most children in single-parent homes live primarily with their mothers (approximately 80%).

working multiple—sometimes dead-end jobs—the parent is likely to feel tired and depressed. Children may not get enough time or supervision from an adult, and basic needs such as health care, food, shelter, and clothing may not be optimal. This can also mean that single-parent families live in communities that are unsafe (and environment does count), less likely to go to the best schools, and are less likely to be involved in high-quality and supervised activities (Anderson, 2003). Financial issues also tend to have a domino effect. Here is an example: A single-mother is working two jobs, driving an old car that often breaks down, has health insurance with one of her jobs, but generally has no money left over after paying bills. The car breaks down, with no money to repair the car. Jobs are lost, health insurance is lost, and soon housing will be lost. There is no safety net when finances are really tight.

Lack of financial resources can affect all areas of well-being. Parents become depressed, exhausted, burned out. Self-esteem diminishes. A person who has low self-esteem and is depressed is not a good parent (Anderson, 2003) and, therefore, there is stress on all family members. Lack of financial security may be the single most important issue for single-parent families, because it has such far-reaching effects (Anderson, 2003).

Experiencing the stigma of being in a single-parent family (Amato, 2007; Anderson, 2003). Much is written about the problems of both adults and children in single-parent families. Adults and children often feel a sense of failure for not being successful in marriage, not providing a second parent for their child, for not living up to society's family standards. Even at a young age, children experience the stigma. Recently, a single mom talked about how she gave her little boy so many things he did not need to compensate for being in a single-parent family. The single mom added, "I could never do enough to compensate for him not having a dad in his life."

Single parents also sometimes talk about how hard it is to attend family events, because most people there are in two-parent families. Or how hard it is to go to any kind of event where nuclear families—two parents and children—are present, because they are faced with the fact they are alone and their children do not have two married parents. Even though the number of people marrying in the United States has decreased in recent years, due to delaying marriage and cohabitation, still the majority of people, over 90%, want to be married—they still see marriage as *the prize* (Waite, Luo, & Lewin, 2009) and 90% of adults will eventually marry (Pew Research Center, 2007). To not be in a two-parent family is a stigma felt by many single-parent families.

Having to juggle everything alone and making decisions alone. If there is a supportive other parent or a significant *other* in their lives, it may not be as difficult. However, many single parents talk about juggling many activities and obligations alone. They talk about always feeling they are in a survival mode, always feeling unsettled. There often is no time to nurture oneself, or even have time or energy to go on a date. This can result in feeling vulnerable. *What if I make a poor financial decision? What if I choose the wrong school for my child? What if I make the wrong decision regarding a child's well-being?* There is often the feeling of not having someone to bounce ideas off, and the feeling of not having anyone to help out when schedules get out of hand. This can affect emotional well-being and can contribute to feelings of being inadequate.

Benefits of Being in Single-Parent Families

There are several benefits of being in a single-parent family that are identified in the literature and they include the following:

There is closeness between the parent and child/children (Anderson, 2003). Members of single-parent families often have a strong family bond. Because they need to work together to make things happen, they understand and empathize with each other and they become close. The parent and child or children also need to do most things together, since children cannot be left with the other parent. They often rely on each other exclusively when they need comfort and experience joys. They have a bond because they are aware of struggles and challenges that no one else knows about.

The parent and child/children "get to do hard things." Being a child in a single-parent family should not necessarily mean you have to do adult things such as taking on added household responsibility, moving to a new neighborhood, or taking care of one's own needs. There are, however, times when children in single-parent families have to experience these *hard things* to a greater degree than children in two-parent families. These hard things may include mowing the lawn earlier than other children, having to learn to walk to school rather than getting a ride, or having to earn their own money to buy clothes. These things may seem like negative experiences; however, these children may experience the positive result of accelerated growth and development that can help them in life (Anderson, 2003). This may mean children develop social skills and learn to empathize with people at an earlier age. For example, one single mom said her child learned what it meant to be poor as a result of being in a single-parent family, and developed an increased capacity to empathize with people who had little money. As this child became an adult, he expressed his appreciation for this experience.

Parents, of course, also do hard things. They may *go without* because money does not stretch. They may not be able to spend as much time with adult friends because they need to focus on children's needs. They may need to sacrifice their own needs for the benefit of the family, because there just are not enough resources to go around. Both children and adults may learn coping skills that prepare them for all kinds of challenges.

Everyone, adults and children, may be forced into situations that are ultimately beneficial. Sometimes parents are pushed to use skills and abilities they did not know they had or are forced, in all kinds of ways, to move out of their comfort zone. A single-parent may decide to get an advanced degree to better provide for the family. As a result, this person meets new and interesting people, and the person experiences a whole new world—and children get the experience of seeing their parent do this. What a single-parent was at one point forced into

What Resources do Single-Parent Families Rely On?

Research in this area is very limited, almost nonexistent. Some resources, however, can be gleaned from the literature. It needs to be noted, however, that some resources may be useful to one single-parent family and this same resource may not be useful to another:

Family and friends. Family members, especially parents of the single parent, often help out with finances and emotional support. In some cases the single-parent resides with parents in the early years as a single-parent. Friends may also become like family and help each other with any needs that arise. Single parents often have a network of friends that all help each other with child care, finances, getting children to important events, moving, and any other issue or challenge that arises. What is assumed with this group of friends is that "I will help you, because you have been there for me when I needed help." Having a social network is critical for maintaining a successful single-parent family (Anderson, 2003).

Spiritual and/or religious resources. Strong families of all kinds rely on spiritual and religious resources for strength and guidance. Although this can be a religion, it can also be a common set of values that help the family work together toward a common goal. For example, a family may be dedicated to caring for the environment, and even though this is not religion it is a shared value. Family members work together toward a common goal. In terms of religion, however, a single parent may view a higher being as someone to go to, to ask for guidance, support, or comfort. As one single parent said, "Without God in my life, I would never make it." This parent feels less alone in making important decisions because she relies on answers to prayer to help her with these decisions.

A positive attitude. There is little in the literature about the importance of members of single-parent families having a positive attitude. Family stress theory, however, indicates that how one perceives a crisis is an important component determining the outcome for the family. How a single parent views the challenges they face and their family situation is an important determinant of well-being and hope for the entire family. Some single parents see themselves and their families as victims of some injustice on the part of the ex-partner, or someone else who got them into this *less than optimal* family situation. Lots of energy goes into those feelings, with less remaining for positive family interactions. It can lead to depression and low self-esteem. Many single parents indicate the importance of seeing things in a positive light, and sometimes it is for the sake of their children—so that they, too, feel positive. A positive attitude leads to positive communication, positive interaction, and hope for the future.

Members of single-parent families generally have reason to be positive. They are accomplishing amazing things. They are addressing challenges, they are doing well. For example, relying on an older study, 20% of children who experience divorce have problem behaviors versus 10% from nondivorce households (Hetherington, 1992). That means 80% of children who experienced divorce do not have problems and have been resilient to the changes in family structure. We know that approximately 25% of single mothers live in poverty compared with 15% of the general population (National Poverty Center, n.d.). Therefore, 75% of single mothers do not live in poverty. That is something to feel positive about. These families, given all the challenges, are generally doing well.

A sense of humor. Although single-parent families may experience more stress than two-parent families, having a sense of humor helps. A sense of humor goes with a positive attitude. If you view something in a positive light, you are more likely to laugh about it. We know that laughter helps us physically and chemically—it releases health-enhancing hormones into our system and reduces stress hormones. So it is healthy to laugh. It is often said, "If I didn't laugh, I would cry." That comment can be made by anyone, not just single parents. It seems that members of single-parent families who have a sense of humor as a response to some of the challenges they face do better.

We need more research to better understand the dynamics and strengths of single-parent families especially cohabiting families, non-residential parent-supported families, and other families that have other adults and support systems in place. We need research to learn more about how children and adults use the strengths they develop to meet future challenges—how these strengths benefit them in the long run.

Stepfamilies

A **stepfamily** is a family in which one or both partners in a relationship have a child or children from a previous relationship. Although some stepfamilies result when there is a divorce involving a child and one of the partners remarries, more recently the term includes children who came from or become part of a cohabiting relationship. For example, a child may have been born to a single mother. The mother then cohabits with a man and brings the child into that new relationship. This new relationship is a stepfamily relationship because one partner (she) had a child from a previous relationship. The increase in the number of single-parent and cohabiting families has contributed to this evolution of the definition of stepfamilies.

Approximately 9% of married couples have a stepchild in their family, and approximately 11.5% of cohabiting households that have a stepchild (Teachman & Tedrow, 2008). These data are cross-sectional and reflect the number of stepfamilies at any given point in time. It is estimated that 40% of all mothers and 30% of all children will at some point be in a stepfamily, if we look at individuals' lifetime experiences.

The joining together of two families in a second or subsequent relationship adds considerable complexity to a family system. A child of divorced parents who both remarry will have two stepparents; a range of possible combinations of biological siblings, stepsiblings, and half-siblings; up to eight grandparents; and numerous extended relatives (aunts, uncles, cousins, etc.).

Stepfamilies are also formed in gay and lesbian relationships. A common same-sex stepfamily results from a child who was born in a heterosexual relationship and is now part of a same-sex stepfamily.

Differences Between Nuclear Families and Stepfamilies

Many stepfamilies assume that they are like nuclear families, but there are differences between nuclear families and stepfamilies. Because there are usually two biological parents in a nuclear family, the children are clearer about their biological heritage. In a stepfamily, one parent is not a biological parent, which can increase children's feelings of attachment to their biological parent. In a nuclear family the parents' marriage or relationship is ongoing and may have lasted many years, but in a stepfamily, one partner may have changed. The new couple have to balance their investment in the new relationship with the handling of parenting and stepparenting issues.

Healthy single-parent families share the same strengths that contribute to the well-being of strong two-parent families. This father genuinely enjoys spending leisure time with his children.

Although fewer men than women have sole custody of the children after a divorce, research shows that single fathers do just as good a job of childrearing as single mothers do and that they experience the same stresses of loneliness and limited time and money.

Children from previous relationships put stepfamily couples at higher risk for divorce or separation (Whitton, Nicholson, & Markman, 2008). Unlike nuclear families, the relationship with stepchildren can create challenges that make it more difficult for couples to maintain a healthy relationship. Issues of expectations of how the stepfamily should function, consensus about child rearing, biological parent–child relationships, and stepparent–stepchildren relationships all create additional stress for couples in stepfamilies, compared to nuclear families (Whitton et al., 2008).

The bonds that children feel with their parents and vice versa are often stronger in nuclear families than in stepfamilies. There are often loyalty issues in stepfamilies, with children, particularly adolescents, feeling greater loyalty to their biological parents than to the stepparent. Many stepfamilies struggle with complex and sometimes conflictual dynamics. Issues regarding grandparents and stepgrandparents add to the complexity. There can also be struggles between stepsiblings when both spouses bring children to the new family. Financial issues can also be complex. When both parents in a stepfamily have children, the financial resources available for child support payments and for meeting the financial demands of all the children can be limited.

Though they may be fearful of entering into a new relationship most single parents want to find a new mate. Even more difficult than finding a new partner is finding one who cares about the children, and one whom the children like also. Single parents who marry again then face the challenge of developing a stepfamily system that works.

Children in Stepfamilies

It has been well documented that children in stepfamilies are more likely to experience emotional and behavioral problems than children in nuclear families. This is comparable to children in single-parent families (Nicholson, Sanders, Halford, Phillips, & Whitton, 2008). According to Ahrons (2007), for many children a remarriage is more stressful than the parents' divorce. From the perspective of a child living in a stepfamily, life can be extremely challenging (Nicholson et al., 2008). Children often need to share

TABLE 15.1	Factors Influencing the Adjustment of Children in Stepfamilies*

Fears of Being Replaced or Unloved

Being hurt by Mom wanting to spend time alone with stepdad

Feeling sad when stepdad appears more loving toward his own children

Feeling jealous of Mom spending time with stepchildren

Grief over Losing Original Family

Feeling sad about Mom and Dad not getting back together

Resentment at stepdad for causing the divorce

Loyalty Conflicts

Feeling compelled to stick up for Mom when Dad is criticizing her

Feeling upset that stepdad is trying to replace Dad

Being afraid that liking stepdad will make Dad angry

Being anxious about saying the wrong things when asked about the other household

Uncertainty over Family Relationships

Being afraid of being expected to love stepdad and his kids

Being unsure what stepdad can and can't do

Being confused when stepdad is sometimes nice and at other times is cross

Uncertainty About the Future

Hearing Mom and stepdad fight and being afraid the new family will break up

Feeling it is pointless getting to know the stepdad because he will leave, just like Dad did

Worrying about being responsible for family fights

Exposure to Conflict

Feeling upset by Mom and Dad saying bad things about each other

Feeling caught in the middle passing messages between parents

Changes in Roles and Status

Losing that special feeling of not being the youngest or oldest anymore

Resentment of the stepdad taking over

Feeling rejected when Mom confides in stepdad and not me

Feeling Invaded

Feeling resentful over having to share room or possessions with stepsiblings

Changes in Rules and Expectations

Resentment about changes in what is expected and what is okay

Being uncertain about whether I will get yelled at

Being confused when Mom overrides what stepdad says

* Examples written for biological mother/stepfather family.

Source: From J. Pryor (Ed.), The International Handbook of Stepfamilies: Policy and practice in legal, research, and clinical environments. Copyright © 2008 by John Wiley & Sons. Reproduced with permission of John Wiley & Sons, Inc.

Many children in stepfamilies become adopted by a nonbiological parent. In fact, 25% of all adoptions include children who are adopted by a stepparent (Stewart, 2010). Stewart learned from her study that children adopted by a stepparent at an early age had about the same number of emotional problems as children in two-parent biological families. However, children who were older when they were adopted were similar in terms of well-being as children who lived in stepfamilies but were not adopted—both having more behavioral problems than children in families with both biological parents. Therefore, when children are older there does not seem to be an advantage to going through the adoption process.

It has been suggested that children be included in stepfamily education so they can be part of learning about the many adjustments all family members are experiencing (Higginbotham, Skogrand, & Torres, 2010). According to Higginbotham et al. (2010), children participating in a research-based stepfamily education program were able to learn to better express their feelings, develop relationship skills, and feel support from peers and facilitators. They felt *normal* after realizing other children in stepfamilies had similar experiences. Parents also benefited in stepfamily education that included their children. They were more able to empathize with the issues children were experiencing, they became more engaged in family activities, and they were able to improved parent–child relationship skills. Because the challenge of meeting the needs of children in stepfamilies is so great, it is important for educational programming to include children, because a more unified family is likely to be a result.

Couples in Stepfamilies

Couple relationships are more difficult to maintain in stepfamilies than in nuclear families. The multiple challenges of children and ex-partners create stress for the couple's relationship. In a national sample of more than 50,000 couples in stepcouple relationships, *remarriage stumbling blocks* were identified (Deal & Olson, 2010). These anticipated problems of stepcouples are listed in rank order below:

- They expect difficulty dealing with complex stepfamily issues. (88%)
- They believe having children from previous relationships will put an additional strain on their marriage. (66%)
- Creating a stepfamily puts more strain on their relationship. (85%)
- Having different patterns of childrearing in their birth family can be problematic. (82%)
- They expect stepfamily adjustment to be difficult. (78%)
- They don't have a specific plan for money management. (73%)
- They have concerns over unpaid bills, debts, or settlements. (66%)
- They feel their partner is too stubborn. (65%)
- One or both of the partners goes out of their way to avoid conflict with the other. (63%)
- They have a fear of another marital failure. (63%)

The above problems identified by couples are real, and many couples in stepfamilies encounter challenges related to these issues.

Deal and Olson (2010) also identified the top five strengths that distinguish great relationships from unhappy relationships. They are provided in Figure 15.3. The personality of each partner is the factor most often identified as distinguishing happy from unhappy stepcouples. Personality refers to such things as stubbornness or being withdrawn, jealous, critical, or controlling. These characteristics

Happy Couples (*n* = 15,056)   Unhappy Couples (*n* = 15,433)

make relationships difficult and are likely to contribute to unhappiness. The other factors that make a difference for couples in stepfamilies include healthy communication, ability to resolve conflict and solve problems, spending leisure time together, and the ability to be flexible.

In a study of the reasons why couples attended stepfamily courses, it was found that most couples attend because they are seeking information about children, stepchildren, and parenting issues (Skogrand, Reck, Higginbotham, Adler-Baeder, & Dansie, 2010). As mentioned previously, the parent–child and stepparent–stepchild relationships are often the most troublesome, and these relationships will impact the couple relationships.

A study by Skogrand, Mendez , and Higginbotham (in press) explored the benefits of two lesbian couples in stepfamilies attending a stepfamily course with other members of the course being heterosexual couples. These two lesbian couples found the course very helpful in that stepparent/stepchildren relationships were the most problematic before attending the course. These couples benefited by learning how to address these challenges resulting in improved parent/child relationships and, thus, resulting in improved family relationships. These researchers concluded that the shared experience of being in a stepfamily created a bond with heterosexual couples that was more important than the nonshared experience of being lesbian couples in stepfamilies.

Stepfamilies in Diverse Populations

It is difficult to know the ethnic makeup of stepfamilies in this country. In some cultures, such as the African American and Latino populations, cohabitation is more common than in the European American population, which would result in more unidentified stepfamilies in these populations (Coltrane, Gutierrez, & Parke, 2008).

Although limited research exists about stepfamilies in various cultures, Coltrane et al. (2008) studied Mexican stepfamilies and identified specific issues that were unique to this population. One of the issues they identified was that children often had little or no contact with their noncustodial birth father, which is different from children in European American stepfamilies. According to Skogrand, Barrios-Bell, and Higginbotham (2009), this may be due to the strong influence of religion and familism in Latino culture. It is suggested by these authors that beliefs about the sanctity of marriage can negatively affect feelings about divorce and remarriage and, as a result, that Latino stepfamilies mimic the nuclear family structure. Stepfamilies may come together with little acknowledgment of past marriage or couple relationships. This would also mean that relationships with nonresidential parents may be discouraged. The Mexican stepfathers in the Coltrane study took on more of a father role than was typical of European American stepfathers. Other unique qualities of Mexican stepfamilies included recent immigration issues and dealing with language barriers.

Little is known about how stepfamilies function in other ethnic cultures. We might speculate, however, that values about family and religion will differ and, thus, impact stepfamily relationships. More research needs to be conducted to learn more about stepfamilies in diverse populations.

Boundary Ambiguity in Stepfamilies

Family boundary ambiguity refers to a lack of clarity regarding who is included and who is not included in the family, and this lack of clarity regarding family composition is associated with stress for family members (Stewart, 2007). Because of the multiple and complex family compositions that can result in stepfamilies, boundary ambiguity is likely to result.

Stewart (2007) found that boundary ambiguity is rare in remarriages or new couple relationships where couples only have shared children with no other children being brought into the marriage. However, boundary ambiguity is more prevalent where there are nonresidential stepchildren. It seems that people have a tendency to define family as those who live with you, and those who are out of sight are also out of mind. In addition, when the stepfamily is structurally more complex, there is likely to be more boundary ambiguity, such as when parents have multiple sets of children.

Stepfamilies in Later Life

Stepfamilies are increasing as a family structure in later life, which adds complexity to relationships with adult stepchildren, care of elderly stepparents, and inheritance issues. Couples are experiencing the opportunity for a second chance as they find love and remarriage in later years, but they are also faced with unique and complex challenges in the new multifamily relationships. There are no clear rules for these relationships because it is a relatively new phenomenon (Sherman, et al., 2006). Family members may not know who they are to each other. For example, if the remarriage occurs after all the children are adults, are they still stepbrothers and -sisters to their stepparent's children? They are faced with new responsibilities. Who cares for an aging stepmother? They are also faced with issues around finances and inheritance. Who inherits the family business? These relationships require increased patience, communication, and commitment to navigate this new territory.

Stepparents face many challenges in dealing with the offspring of their new spouse (Ahrons, 2003, 2004). Stepparents must remember that they are taking on someone else's child and many of the childrearing responsibilities formerly held by a biological parent. Stepparents often find themselves either overidealized by their stepchildren early in the relationship or the victim of displaced hostility.

Not all members of a stepfamily are biologically related. This is an obvious enough fact and one that should, in theory, be relatively simple to deal with. But our culture considers biological family ties special. "Blood is thicker than water," the old saying goes. Biological family bonds are difficult to break. Many children of divorce keep hoping that Mom and Dad will reunite, and the new marriage of one of the parents dashes those hopes. When a stepparent enters the family, children truly know that their mother and father will never get back together. This can cause despair and bitterness toward the stepparent. The stepparent can become the personification of evil in the child's mind: "If only *she* weren't around, Mom and Dad would get back together."

Even though the relationships between biological parent and child are well established, the couple in a stepfamily are newlyweds. It can be very difficult for the couple to balance marital needs and the children's needs. Family members' loyalties are divided in new and complex ways when a new family member comes on the scene. If a stepparent does not recognize the stepchildren's long-standing bonds with the biological parent and move carefully, the stepparent can end up in a very difficult love triangle.

A common example is a single mother who lives alone with her children for a number of years before marrying again. The mother may have developed strong ties and a comfortable pattern of parenting with her children. If she has an adolescent son or daughter, the mother's relationship with the child may be more like that of a big sister than that of a parent. The adolescent may become very jealous of the new spouse. "She always used to want to talk to me after school. Now she spends all her time with him!"

In the case of single-parent families headed by a male, girls may develop an almost "wifelike" relationship with their father during the single-parent period, according to Geoffrey Greif (2000). Daughters often serve as confidante and household manager for their father, and many enjoy their new status. When the father marries again, the daughter may see the stepmother as a competitor for Dad's time and affection and an intruder on her wifelike roles.

Stepparents must avoid the tendency to try too hard; bonding takes a good deal of time. Newlyweds generally go out of their way to please each other, but the same approach taken with the stepchildren can create problems for the new stepparent. The stepparent knows that his or her new spouse's children are a major hurdle in establishing a successful marriage and feels that if she or he can only get along with the children, the chances for success in this new marriage are vastly improved. But children do not easily forsake the love of their birth parent for a stepparent. Adolescents, in particular, are often not very open to including an "outsider" in their family.

The stepparent needs to avoid the trap of trying to replace the former parent. In reality, the stepparent is not so much a new parent in the family as a new adult in the family. The parent role has to develop slowly. The urge to build a solid new marriage can spur stepparents to play the "superstepmother" or "superstepfather" role, which is neither realistic nor beneficial.

Stepparents must also avoid favoritism in dealing simultaneously with their "real" children and their stepchildren. Children are not always pleasant to be around; they can at times be selfish, whiney, disobedient, and intrusive. Just as many parents have difficulty loving their own children when they are not acting lovable, so it is difficult for stepparents to love someone else's children at times. It is also important that stepparents not overcompensate for their tendency to favor their biological children by being more lenient with their stepchildren.

Stepparents also need to develop skills in dealing with complex financial realities in their new families. Although people who are marrying again are usually painfully aware of how challenging family money problems can be, few feel comfortable discussing money matters and financial planning before remarriage. Some even prefer to avoid talking about minor financial issues until they become more serious problems. Money problems are common in stepfamilies. For example, a father who remarries is sometimes in the difficult position of sending child support payments to his biological children, supporting his new family, and hoping that his new spouse's former husband will continue to provide financial support for the stepchildren.

Summary

- The number of divorces was at its highest peak around 1980, with rates declining slowly but steadily through 2005. In 2007 they increased slightly.
- The number of people cohabiting has increased in recent years, which may have implications for the declining divorce rate. If fewer people marry, fewer people will divorce. Couples who cohabit and then separate are not identified and may historically been reflected in divorce statistics.
- No-fault divorce laws eliminated (1) fault as grounds for divorce, (2) gender-based division of responsibilities, (3) the adversarial nature of divorce, and (4) linkage of the financial settlement to the determination of fault. Some argue, however, that no-fault's principle of equity between the sexes penalizes divorced women financially.
- Individuals differ greatly in their ability to address the issues of divorce. However, most go on to do as well as or better than before the divorce.
- Children, however, do not always do as well as adults in the aftermath of divorce. Although most are doing well 6 years after the divorce, the first few years were often difficult. A key factor in how well children do after a divorce is related to how well their parents get along.
- In one 20-year study, Ahrons found that, looking back, children felt caught between their parents when they did not get along postdivorce. They felt they could not talk to one parent about the other. Even into adulthood they felt they had to manage family events so their parents did not cause problems. Clearly, when parents got along after a divorce, children's well-being improved, even into adulthood.
- The duration and experience of the entire process of divorce vary with each individual. It appears, however, that when people can talk openly about divorce and accept it as an important part of their lives, they can move on as happy single individuals.
- At any given time, 26% of children are living in single-parent households. It is estimated, however, that 40% of all children will live in a single-parent household at some point in their lives.
- Generally, children want to have contact with both of their biological parents.
- Of the children whose biological parents do not live together, the majority end up living with their mothers. Fathers, however, are increasingly taking a more active role in the lives of their noncustodial children.

- Stepfamilies are created when one or both partners in a relationship have a child or children from a previous relationship.
- Stepfamilies are not only created when there is a divorce and remarriage. The number of stepfamilies has increased because many children are part of or become part of cohabiting relationships.
- Children brought into a stepfamily increase the risk for divorce or separation. Issues around parenting and parent–child relationships contribute to this stress.
- Children in stepfamilies experience multiple stresses and challenges. It is important for parents and stepparents to understand what children are experiencing.

Key Terms

no-fault divorce

tender years doctrine

divorce culture

binuclear family

sole custody

joint custody

split custody

stepfamily

Activities

1. Interview someone who has been divorced. Ask her or him to recount experiences encountered throughout the entire divorce process. Determine whether that person's experience was similar to or different from the literature in this chapter.

2. Interview a member of a single-parent family. Ask not only about the stresses the family faces but also about the strengths in the family. How is the family different from a two-parent family? How is it similar? Discuss your findings with other students.

Suggested Readings

Ahrons, C. (2007). Family ties after divorce: Long-term implications for children. *Family Process, 46,* 53–65.

Coontz, S. (2005). *Marriage, a history: From obedience to intimacy or how love conquered marriage.* New York: Viking.

Deal, R. L., & Olson, D. (2010). *The remarriage checkup.* Minneapolis: Bethany House.

England, P., & Edin, K. (Eds.). (2007). *Unmarried couples with children.* New York: Russell Sage Foundation.

Ford, M., Ford, A. , & Ford, S. (2006). *My parents are divorced too.* Washington, DC: American Psychological Association.

Joanning, H., & Keoughan, P. (2006, May/June). The divorce process and therapeutic interventions. *Family Therapy Magazine,* pp. 14–16.

Popenoe, D. (2008). *Cohabitation, marriage, and child wellbeing: A cross-national perspective.* Retrieved from the National Marriage Project Web site: http://www.virginia.edu/marriageproject/pdfs/NMP2008CohabitationReport.pdf.

Pryor, J. (2008). (Ed.). *The international handbook of stepfamilies: Policy and practice in legal, research, and clinical environments.* Hoboken, NJ: John Wiley & Sons.

Wallerstein, J. S., & Blakeslee, S. (2003). *What about the kids? Raising your children before, during, and after divorce.* New York: Hyperion.

Wilcox, B. (2009). *The state of our unions: Marriage in America 2009.* Retrieved from the National Marriage Project Web site: http://www.stateofourunions.org.

 Visit the text-specific Online Learning Center at **www.mhhe.com/olson8e** for practice tests, chapter summaries, and PowerPoint slides.

16. *S*trengthening Marriages and Families Worldwide

Global Perspectives on
Family, Community, and
Cultural Strengths

Premarital and Marriage
Programs

Marital and Family Therapy

Strengthening Your Marriage
and Family Relationships

The Future of Your Family

Summary

Activities

Suggested Readings

Olson-Sigg, & Larson, 2008).

Therefore, the need for strengthening couple and family relationships is a global concern that unites all of us on planet Earth, and the work we can do together needs to be done on multiple levels simultaneously: work strengthening our personal relationships as couples and families; work building communities that are more supportive of couple and family relationships; and work to grow our national and international networks to be more cognizant of the critical importance of positive human relationships that begin in families of one kind or another.

In this final chapter of *Marriages and Families: Intimacy, Diversity, and Strengths*, we will begin by taking a broad look at the strengths and challenges couples and families face, from the *micro level* to the *macro level*. New global-level research has discovered that family strengths, community strengths, and the broader cultural strengths from country to country around the world are remarkably similar. After this discussion from a world perspective, we will return once again to the micro level and look at premarital and marriage programs that serve individual couples. These programs aim to build a strong foundation for couples in the early years of their relationship, and to strengthen the connections of those couples who are not in the midst of a marital crisis but would like to prevent difficulties and enhance their love for each other in a group educational setting. This section on educational prevention programs will be followed by a section on therapeutic intervention: a discussion of marital and family therapy for those who have significant challenges. Research has shown that the vast majority of couples who have experienced marital therapy find the process useful in helping them to overcome difficulties they are facing and improving their communication and conflict resolution skills. We then present a summary of the best advice experts around the world have for strengthening marriage and family relationships. The chapter ends with some very personal stories about different people's views of the future of their couple and family relationships.

Global Perspectives on Family, Community, and Cultural Strengths

Research on couple and family strengths and challenges around the world confirms what investigators have long suspected: that family strengths from culture to culture are remarkably similar—much more similar than different. The research team working on this project included 43 investigators in 18 countries, including countries in each of the world's seven major geocultural areas: Africa (Botswana, Kenya, Somalia, South Africa); Asia (China, India, Korea); Europe (Greece, Romania, Russia); the Middle East (Israel, Oman); Latin America (Brazil, Mexico); North America (Canada, USA); and Oceania (Australia, New Zealand). This research also shows that community strengths and cultural strengths worldwide also look much the same from a global perspective (DeFrain & Asay, 2007).

Family Strengths

The reader is well aware by now of the International Family Strengths Model, which includes six major qualities or strengths. When people around the world describe the qualities that make their family strong, they commonly talk about:

1. Appreciation and affection
2. Positive communication
3. Commitment to the family
4. Enjoyable times together
5. A sense of spiritual well-being and shared values
6. The ability to manage stress and crisis effectively

Family members in each country tend to talk about strengths in unique and different ways; and strengths are manifested somewhat differently from culture to culture in the ways people in families behave toward each other. But broadly speaking, it is difficult to deny the basic premise that the strengths concepts family members talk about around the world share a great deal in common with each other no matter where they are on Earth. In terms of family strengths, human beings speak a common language.

Community Strengths

This research also found that when talking about the strengths of the community in which they live, people around the world also share a common language. A qualitative analysis of community strengths in the 18 countries in the world's seven major geocultural areas indicates that what makes a community work well in a particular culture is quite similar to what makes a community effective globally. Five basic community strengths emerged from the research:

1. A supportive environment that genuinely values families, and a general willingness and natural generosity infused in the culture to help when families are in need
2. An effective educational delivery system
3. Religious communities for families seeking this kind of support
4. Family service programs developed by government and nongovernmental organizations for families who cannot find the help they need from their own extended family, friends, and neighbors
5. A safe, secure, and healthful environment

Cultural Strengths

Finally, the global research team found that cultural strengths also were remarkably similar from country to country and culture to culture. The study discovered five worldwide cultural strengths:

1. A rich cultural history
2. Shared cultural meanings
3. A stable political process
4. A viable economy
5. An understanding of the global society

London: Routledge, Taylor & Francis Group. Copyright © 2007 The Haworth Press. Reproduced by permission of Taylor and Francis Group, LLC, a division of Informa plc.

Two Visual Models Integrating Family, Community, and Cultural Strengths

How do family strengths, community strengths, and cultural strengths fit together? How do these strengths interact with and influence each other? We believe that strong families help build strong communities and that strong communities contribute significantly to the health of nations. Figure 16.1 simplifies the very complex processes involved in the interactions among family strengths, community strengths, and cultural strengths. In this model the three areas of strengths move out and away from the single-family unit to the broader cultural contexts in a concentric fashion. The health of each level of society from the micro level of the family to the community that surrounds the family and on to the macro level of the national-level social culture is affected by what is happening in each other level. The three concentric circles not only interact with each other but have depth, indicating complex interactions on various levels. (See Figure 16.1.)

Figure 16.2 shows the relationships among family strengths, community strengths, and cultural strengths in another way, a Venn diagram with intersecting strengths. The intersection of the three areas of strengths represents the strong family (the black area). Although families can have many strengths even when they live in a community or a culture without significant strengths, the most fortunate families are those where significant family strengths, community strengths, and cultural strengths intersect. In this way of thinking about families, a family caught up by the terrible forces of war or economic depression can still be strong, in spite of the difficult environment in which they live. Conversely, in a healthy community and healthy national cultural environment there will be troubled families without many significant family strengths. (See Figure 16.2.)

FIGURE 16.2

The Relationship of Family, Community, and Cultural Strengths: A Venn Diagram

Source: *Strong Families Around the World: Strengths-Based Research and Perspectives* (p. 462) by J. DeFrain & S. M. Asay, 2007, London: Routledge, Taylor & Francis Group. Copyright © 2007 The Haworth Press. Reproduced by permission of Taylor and Francis Group, LLC, a division of Informa plc.

FIGURE 16.3

Family Strengths and
Universal Values Around
the World: A Proposed
Model

Source: Adapted with permission
from an illustration by Amie
DeFrain.

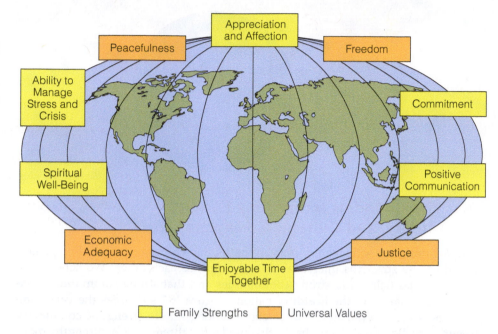

Another global perspective that fits well here is the work of Kenneth Boulding (1985), an economist and philosopher who believes that human betterment is the end toward which we individually and collectively should strive. Human betterment is an increase in the *ultimate good,* that which is good in itself. Four great virtues make up this ultimate good:

- *Economic adequacy.* "Riches," in contrast to poverty; nourishment, in contrast to starvation; adequate housing, clothing, health care, and other essentials of life
- *Justice,* in contrast to injustice; equality, rather than inequality, in access to work, education, and health
- *Freedom,* in contrast to coercion and confinement
- *Peacefulness,* in contrast to war and strife

The four great virtues from Boulding and the International Family Strengths Model of DeFrain and Stinnett are illustrated in Figure 16.3. And for another discussion of universal values, see The Perennial Philosophy in Box 16.1.

FOR BETTER OR FOR WORSE © Lynn Johnston. Reprinted with the permission of Universal Uclick. All rights reserved.

and philosophers have argued since at least the sixteenth century that there is a perennial philosophy—an eternal philosophy, if you will—that all great world religions share and that unites them in a common view of what is sacred in life.

In 1540, Augustinus Steuchis, the librarian of the Vatican in Rome, wrote of a *philosophia perennis*—a way of thinking about the world and our lives that is "universal and inclusive, internally coherent, fruitful of new insights and applications, and reasoned so conclusively that attacks cannot refute, and written or presented so convincingly that reasonable minds cannot resist it" (*The Dictionary of the History of Ideas*, 2003).

Gottfried Leibniz (1646–1716), a German philosopher and mathematician, expanded upon Steuchis's thinking about a perennial philosophy, one with qualities that would ensure its survival through time and change and become, by generalization, a permanently significant philosophy. Analysis of all religions and philosophies both ancient and modern would "draw the gold from the dross, the diamond from its mine, the light from the shadows; and this would be in effect a kind of perennial philosophy."

Aldous Huxley (1894–1963), an English writer, was the most prominent person in the 20th century to look for the gold, the diamond, the light. He studied world religions at length and in 1945 wrote of the enduring intellectual and personal insights that, he argued, are repeated in all variations of thought and conviction and that can serve

- the *psychology* that "finds in the soul something similar to, or even identical with, divine Reality," and
- the *ethic* or principle of moral living that places human beings' final purpose in life as seeking knowledge of "the immanent and transcendent Ground of all being." (Huxley, 1945, p. vii)

Huxley wrote that this belief system came from time immemorial, beginning so far back in the past that its origins could not be traced. He argued that this perennial philosophy is universal. Rudiments of it could be found in the traditional lore of all ancient and modern peoples in every region of the world. In its fully developed forms it could be found in the texts of every one of the great religions of the world. Each belief system might express these ideas using different terminology and examples reflecting different cultural contexts, but Huxley was convinced that the core concepts were similar.

What relevance does this so-called perennial philosophy, with roots going back literally thousands of years, have for us today? The theologians and philosophers arguing from this perspective believe that the core beliefs of all the world's religions are much more alike than different, and that if we recognize this common spiritual ground, we can use this knowledge to find ways of living peacefully with each other in our families, in our communities, and among nations. Our personal religious beliefs can bring us together.

We give strength to each other as individuals, family members, and citizens of our communities. Novelist James A. Michener, a self-described citizen of the world, dedicated a lifetime to understanding people around the world. Michener and his wife Mari Yoriko Sabusawa would live in an area for many months and write about what they saw and learned. Some of his internationally acclaimed novels and stories include: *Tales of the South Pacific, Caravans, The Source, Caribbean, Mexico, Centennial, Poland, Texas, Alaska,* and *Hawaii.* Late in his long life Michener concluded:

> We are all brothers [and sisters]. We all face the same problems and find the same satisfactions. We are united in one great band. I am one with all of them, in all lands, in all climates, in all conditions. Since we brothers [and sisters] occupy the entire earth, the world is our home. (Michener, 1991, p. 249)

Premarital and Marriage Programs

Today's families live in a global society that is complex, interconnected, and continuously evolving because of the rapid pace of change in the world economy, technology, and migration. Change worldwide affects couples and families everywhere. Therefore international efforts, aided by technology, are growing as researchers and family educators work together around the globe to develop programs to help strengthen couple and family relationships. One study of global family concerns and the role of family life education represented six continents and 50 countries. The researchers found that family education and related coursework were available in all the continents of the world, and there was worldwide public interest in the need for family life education programs (Darling & Turkii, 2009).

In the rest of this chapter we will shift our focus from the macro level, the global perspective on couples and families, back to the micro level. We will see how couples can find effective premarital and marriage education programs to enhance their relationships. Then we will look at marital and family therapy and how it can be helpful for those facing more difficult challenges. Finally, we will be summing up the best advice that can be found today for strengthening couple and family relationships, and think a bit about the future—what the future will bring for each of us in our own personal quest to create strong, loving, and caring couple and family relationships.

Programs and services for couples and families range from informal networks to couple and family therapy. Table 16.1 lists program types in order of their therapeutic impact, from least to most intensive. As couple and family issues become more serious and chronic, a higher intensity of treatment is recommended. For example, it would be more appropriate for a couple who has been having marital problems for several years and has seriously considered divorce to see a couple therapist rather than to attend a self-help group.

Couple education programs can be very useful resources for couples without serious problems. These programs can help couples meet and learn from other couples. They can also learn from skill-building programs that focus on communication and conflict-resolution skills. These are relationship skills that couples can use to improve their relationships and resolve the differences that inevitably arise in any close relationship.

Couple therapy and family therapy are recommended when relationship problems between partners or among family members are chronic and intense. When

TABLE 16.1	Programs for Couples and Families		
	Service	**Goal**	**Provider**
Education courses for students	Functional marriage and family courses	Awareness and knowledge	High school and college teachers
Couple education programs	Premarital and marital programs	Insight and skills in communication and conflict resolution	Clergy, counselors, and marital therapists
Couple and family therapy	Marital and family therapy	Insight and change in relationship dynamics	Marital and family therapists, psychologists

Failing to prepare is like preparing to fail.

This quote emphasizes the importance of being prepared for marriage, which is one of the most challenging tasks that you will experience in your life. Because the risk of divorce is still very high and because of the considerable value couples place on a happy marriage, more couples are seeking premarital counseling from the clergy performing their marriage ceremony or from a professional counselor.

There is increasing evidence that skill-based premarital and couples education programs can increase satisfaction and enhance the maintenance of healthy, committed relationships (Halford, Markman, & Scott, 2008; Knutson & Olson, 2003; Murray, 2006). Marriage education evaluation studies indicate that participants from a wide variety of ethnic/cultural groups, levels of household income, and family structure types can benefit from involvement in these types of programs. These benefits include an increased knowledge of relationships, including the ability to identify unhealthy relationship patterns. Participants also can develop more realistic beliefs about relationships/marriages and decrease their level of verbal aggression (Adler-Baeder, Kerpelman, Schramm, Higginbotham, & Paulk, 2007).

As discussed in Chapter 11, an effective premarital program has at least three essential components: (1) a premarital inventory with individual feedback for each couple, (2) a skill-building component that focuses on communication and problem solving, and (3) small-group discussions in which couples can air their mutual issues. The program should last 6 to 8 weeks and should be started a year before the marriage so that the partners have time to develop their relationship skills and deal with any important issues.

Concerned by continuing high divorce rates, the federal government and many states began working in the early 2000s to develop premarital counseling and marriage education programs. One survey of premarital counseling providers, primarily members of the clergy and mental health professionals, held favorable opinions of the government efforts to help strengthen marriages (Murray, 2006). Good candidates for marriage preparation programs include couples who value marriage, are kind and considerate to each other, and are both mature in their judgments and views of the world (Duncan, Holman, & Yang, 2007).

One of the most popular premarital programs in the United States is the *PREPARE Program*, which is offered by over 75,000 counselors and clergy. As mentioned in Chapter 11, more than 3 million couples have participated in this program since 1980. The program is also available in 13 other countries around the world. The six goals of the program are to (1) help the couple explore their relationship strengths and growth areas; (2) teach the couple the communication skills of assertiveness and active listening; (3) help the couple learn to resolve conflict effectively using a 10-step conflict resolution model; (4) help the couple discuss their families of origin; (5) develop a workable budget and financial plan; and (6) develop personal, couple, and family goals. The PREPARE Program focuses on 20 important

Educational programs for couples are increasingly popular, both as a means for helping couples learn new relationship skills and as a way to strengthen an already effective relationship. Either way, there is always room for improvement.

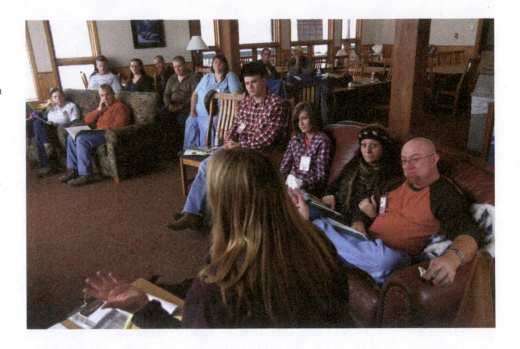

relationship areas, including communication, conflict resolution, financial management, and egalitarian roles. For more information on the PREPARE Program and the location of a professional in your community, and to take a sample *Couple Quiz*, visit the Web site at www.prepare-enrich.com.

Couple Education Programs

Interest in couple programs is on the rise. There are two types of couple programs. One type, referred to simply as a couple enrichment program, usually lasts 1 or 2 days and often takes place on a weekend. The focus is on motivating the couple to increase the amount of personal information they share with each other. These relatively brief programs are helpful to some couples who already have a good marriage and want to improve it. However, for couples with more serious relationship issues, such programs can create problems by raising expectations for a better relationship, but not providing the relationship skills to achieve it.

The second type of program, couple education, focuses on teaching communication and conflict resolution skills. These programs are more effective than the 1- or 2-day couple enrichment programs. They usually last about 6 weeks and meet each week for about 2 hours. Skill-building programs have demonstrated their effectiveness and value to couples.

The following five marriage education programs are high quality and have developed and been refined over the last 20 years:

- *Couple Communication Program*—Sherod Miller and Phyllis Miller (2012)
- *PAIRS Program*—Lori Gordon (Gordon & Durana, 1999)
- *PREP Program*—Howard Markman and Scott Stanley (2012)
- *PREPARE/ENRICH Program*—David Olson and Peter Larson (2012)

To learn more about these programs and other couple education programs, go to the Smart Marriages Web site at www.smartmarriages.com.

as possible. Couples and families who receive help with problems before they become too severe have a much better chance of overcoming the difficulties and building a stronger relationship than do those who wait. An analogy can be made to treating cancer and a problematic marriage: the sooner you seek treatment, the more effective the treatment and the better the outcome.

Common Problems in Couple Relationships

The national survey of 21,501 married couples identified 10 of the most common marital problems for married couples from newlyweds to retired couples (Olson & Olson, 2000). The top 10 issues or stumbling blocks were obtained across both happy and unhappy couples and they are summarized in Table 16.2.

In reviewing the common stumbling blocks for married couples, it is striking that a high percentage of both happy and unhappy couples (ranging from 78% to 93%) have these problems. The most problematic issue for couples is sharing leadership equally, with 93% agreeing that this is a problem. Over 80% of the couples agreed that their partner was too stubborn, that children reduced their marital satisfaction, that their partner was too negative or critical, that they wish they had more time to be together, that they wish their partner would share more feelings, and that they often ended up feeling responsible for problems. Three other very common issues were avoiding conflict with their partner, having difficulty completing tasks, and that differences never seemed to get resolved.

When clustering these 10 items into topic areas, the most common areas were regarding conflict resolution (3 items); couple flexibility (2 items); personality issues (2 items); and 1 item in communication, leisure activities, and parenting. These are

TABLE 16.2	Top 10 Stumbling Blocks for Couples

A nationwide survey of 21,501 married couples from newlyweds to retirees uncovered the 10 most common difficulties they face:

Issue/Problem	Percentage of Couples
1. We have problems sharing leadership equally.	93%
2. My partner is sometimes too stubborn.	87
3. Having children reduces our marital satisfaction.	84
4. My partner is too negative or critical.	83
5. I wish my partner had more time and energy for recreation with me.	82
6. I wish my partner were more willing to share feelings.	82
7. I always end up feeling responsible for the problem.	81
8. I go out of my way to avoid conflict with my partner.	79
9. We have difficulty completing tasks or projects.	79
10. Our differences never seem to get resolved.	78

issues that marital and family therapists often observe when working with couples having marital problems.

Problems Related to Closeness and Flexibility

Marital and family therapists working with couples and families with problems often use the Couple and Family Map. Because it focuses on the key dimensions of cohesion, flexibility, and communication, the Couple and Family Map provides a useful framework for diagnosing and treating several common problems in marital and family systems.

One frequent problem couples seeking counseling describe is the feeling that they are at opposite extremes on the same dimension of the model. On the cohesion dimension, for example, one partner may want more togetherness, whereas the other partner may want more autonomy. Similarly, on the flexibility dimension, one partner may desire more flexibility in the family, whereas the other partner may want more rules (i.e., rigidity). When couples disagree on the balance of separateness (autonomy) and togetherness in their relationship, they can negotiate by jointly planning their schedules. When couples disagree on flexibility issues (rules or roles), they might try reversing roles at home for a week.

Another common problem for couples occurs when both partners are at the same extreme on one or both model dimensions. Both may be disengaged from the relationship because they are so heavily involved in career or outside interests that they have little time or energy for the marriage. Or both may be enmeshed, so invested in the partner that they have little room to develop personal interests and skills. When couples are disengaged, it is important for them to assess their commitment to the relationship. When couples are too enmeshed, one solution is for each of them to develop more separate interests and spend more time apart.

This all may sound quite simple, but difficulties arise because people see their relationships differently and have conflicting expectations about them. For example, the wife and the husband often offer different couple and family descriptions and goals. Add a teenage child, and the child's description will tend to be different from

Family gatherings can be a great way for different generations to connect and build a stronger family network.

with the conflicting perspectives of all the family members. This approach produces a more valid—and also a more complex—picture of the family's dynamics.

Common Questions About Marital and Family Therapy

The American Association for Marriage and Family Therapy (AAMFT), which is the professional organization representing the interests of approximately 25,000 marriage and family therapists nationally, argues that research studies have repeatedly demonstrated the effectiveness of marriage and family therapy for treating a wide range of mental and emotional disorders and health problems. Marriage and family therapists treat not only marital distress and conflict, but also adolescent drug abuse, depression, alcoholism, obesity, and dementia in the elderly, because these issues all have a family component (AAMFT, 2012).

People have many questions about marriage and family therapy; therefore, we will pose several of these here and offer the best answers we found (DeFrain and the University of Nebraska Family Action Research and Writing Team, 2012).

What happens in marital counseling? The counselor sometimes plays the role of referee, helping partners calm down and really listen to each other. In other cases where the couple has closed down communication the approach is to help them open up and learn what is happening in their relationship. Basically, the purpose is to help couples learn to communicate effectively with each other and resolve conflicts effectively. A good counselor knows how to smooth the waters, help couples talk clearly and honestly with each other, and look for solutions to problems that they alone cannot seem to resolve.

Is something wrong with people who go to a professional counselor? One useful way of answering this question is to ask another question: Is there something wrong with a man who takes his car to a good mechanic when it is running poorly? Or another question: Is there something wrong with a woman who calls a doctor when she thinks she is having a heart attack? The fact of the matter is that none of us are experts in everything. We can't fix everything in our life, and this long list sometimes includes our marriage and family relationships. So, we do the wise thing and seek help from someone who is trained and highly experienced in dealing effectively with such difficulties.

What if one partner is willing to go to a therapist, but the other partner is not willing? Wives are often the ones who want the couple to seek counseling, and husbands sometimes are resistant (Eubanks Fleming & Córdova, 2012). The prognosis for healing a relationship is much better if both partners are intensely involved in the process. However, one partner may be totally resistant to seeking help, but in this case it is still useful for the other partner to spend some time with a professional to get some ideas of how to proceed in her or his situation.

What about marital therapy for situations in which violence is possible? In some volatile situations it is not wise to involve both partners in therapy. There may be genuine danger, usually for an abused wife. One therapist we know told the story of a couple who sought therapy with her. During the session it became very clear that the husband was abusive and that the wife needed help in telling her husband she was leaving him and wanted a divorce. Upon learning this, the husband stormed out of the counselor's office in a rage. Two days later he walked into a restaurant where his wife was having lunch and shot her.

She survived, but the marriage did not.

Marriage and family therapists have done a great deal of good for many couples. However, in the case of domestic violence the endangered spouse is encouraged to seek counsel from programs and professionals who specialize in dealing with family violence, because safety is a critical concern. The situation may be so dangerous for the woman that she and her children need to remain hidden in a secret family shelter provided by the community until the man is jailed by the police or calms down and is deemed nonviolent. And, as we saw earlier in this book, alcohol and other drug abuse problems often go hand-in-hand with domestic violence. When seeking help with these kinds of situations, it is important to approach programs and specialists who focus on substance abuse issues.

Not all marriages can be saved, even with professional help. And not all marriages should be saved.

What kinds of qualifications should the therapist have? Licensed marital and family therapists who are certified by the American Association of Marriage and Family Therapy (AAMFT) are specially trained to deal with relationship problems and work directly with couples and families. Some psychologists, psychiatrists, social workers, and other counselors have some additional training for work with couples and families, but these tend to be the minority in their professions. For more information about the AAMFT, visit their Web site at http://www.amft.org.

How can a person find a marital or relationship therapist? A good place to start the AAMFT Web site. There is a very handy *Therapist Locator* tool. Type in your zip code and check how far you would be willing to drive (5 miles, 10 miles, 25 miles, 50 miles, and so forth). The search can be done in several other ways, also: by city or state, or by the last name of the therapist. The *Therapist Locator* then lists professionals in your area and the qualifications of each therapist. If a computer is not available, in many cities and towns marital and family therapists are listed under "Marital and Family Counseling" in the yellow pages. A person could also consult a family service organization or the United Way for a list of names. And finally, a good way is to ask friends and loved ones. Someone you know and trust often will have experience with professional marriage and family therapists, and can give good advice.

Here are some useful, specific questions to ask the potential marital and family therapist:

- What is your professional training and degree?
- How much specialized training and experience have you had in marital and family therapy?
- Do you usually see couples and families together or as individuals?
- What procedure will you use to evaluate our relationship?
- How much will you charge for that assessment?
- How frequently will we have sessions, and how long will they last?
- What will each session cost?

one who both of them feel comfortable with and believe is competent to deal with their problems. If it doesn't go well with this first choice, we encourage the couple not to give up on therapy, but simply find another therapist.

Can I afford this? What is it going to cost? And how long will it take? The hourly cost of marriage and family therapy in the United States can vary widely, from perhaps $75 to $200 per hour, with an average cost of $100 per hour. The cost can sound steep to a couple living on a tight budget, but they need to remember that if you get the oil changed in your car it might be costing you $65 an hour or more. Fortunately, some therapists and family service agencies offer sliding fee scales and the cost of therapy can be quite reasonable for a couple on a limited budget. Also, health insurance policies cover marriage and family therapy with a small co-pay. A couple visiting with a counselor an hour a week for 3 months might expect to pay $1,200 at $100 per hour. Be sure you are very clear on the cost *before* therapy begins.

Is marriage and family therapy effective? The short answer to this question is, *Not always, but quite often.* A research team in the mid-1990s led by Bill Doherty at the University of Minnesota concluded that marital and family therapy is a rather cost-effective and efficient approach to dealing with a range of emotional and relationship problems in individuals, couples, and families (Doherty & Simmons, 1996). Similarly, a more recent study by Andrew Christensen (2010) at UCLA and other colleagues around the and others United States looked at traditional and nontraditional approaches to marriage and family therapy for troubled couples. The researchers found substantial positive effects as a result of the therapy. These positive effects proved true even for seriously and chronically distressed couples. However, the research team also concluded that going to a therapist is no guarantee that a marriage will be saved. Within 2 years of therapy, more than 25% of the couples in the study ended up separated or divorced.

We certainly do not want to sound repetitious, but it is important to stress that couples should be proactive in regard to marriage problems: When things aren't going right, don't be afraid to talk about the situation with your partner and work together toward a solution. Don't wait until it's too late. These problems just don't fix themselves. And finally, anything mentionable is manageable.

Family Therapy Case Study

The Davis family has five members: Mary and Don, the parents; 18-year-old Ann; 16-year-old Julie; and 9-year-old Peter. Mary drank to relieve feelings of inadequacy in a family dominated by high achievers: Don and the oldest daughter, Ann. The middle daughter, Julie, also felt inadequate but tried to console her mother and was responsible enough to be a surrogate mother to Peter, the youngest child. The family came in for therapy shortly after Mary began treatment for her dependence on alcohol. Ann subsequently left home, angry at Mary for all the problems she

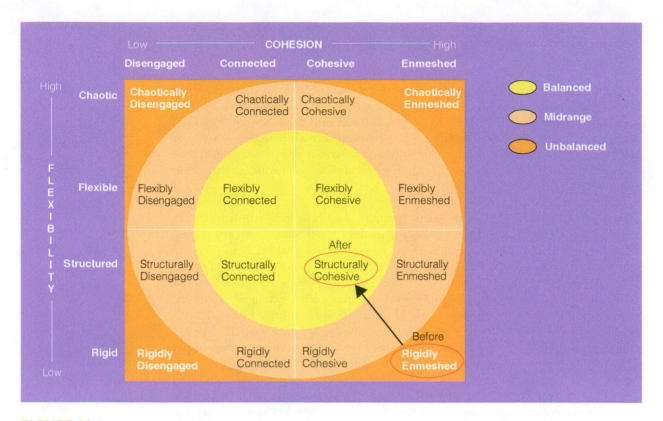

FIGURE 16.4

Couple and Family Map:
Before and After Therapy

had caused. Julie felt lost because her mother was being "taken care of" by other people and Julie's role as chief counselor had been usurped.

In terms of the Couple and Family Map, the Davis family would be classified as a *rigidly enmeshed* family, which is an unbalanced family type because they are at the extreme levels of both cohesion and flexibility. The goal for therapy in terms of their family system is to move them one level toward the balanced part of the model, which would move them to the *structurally cohesive* family type (see Figure 16.4).

Diagnosis. In terms of cohesion, the Davis family was *enmeshed*. They evidenced high emotional bonding as well as high mutual dependency. The mother and the two daughters competed intensely for approval from each other and from Dad. The family's external boundaries were closed. No one felt free to interact with people outside the family, partly because they were afraid Mary would be drunk and embarrass everyone. Friends and relatives were kept at a distance. The only time husband and wife made contact was when one of the children misbehaved. Then the two would team up as parents and support each other; otherwise, they did not interact much. The father–daughter coalitions, especially that between Don and Ann, were strong. In many ways, Don and Ann played the role of parents in the family, because Mary's drinking often made her incapable of parenting.

Individual activities were permitted but only within family-approved guidelines. Don and Ann spent a lot of time playing tennis together, but Julie's desire to spend the same amount of time away from the family *partying* with friends was not approved. Close friends, especially males, were not allowed. The family tried desperately to have fun at their cabin on the weekends. Everyone was required to go, and the implicit message was, "You *will* have fun!" The result was that nobody enjoyed the weekends at the cabin. Tending to Peter's needs kept Julie connected to the family after she became adrift when her mother entered the alcohol treatment program.

Much of the conflict in the family seemed to stem from its *rigidity*. The family system and each of its members could seldom think of new ways to solve problems. Also, no one in the family knew how to be appropriately assertive. Rather than making their point firmly but without malice or yelling, family members resorted to aggressive behaviors: screaming, throwing things, and occasionally striking each other.

Family roles were stereotypic and rigid. Mary saw herself as being in charge of the house, and she saw Don as the boss of the children, the rule enforcer. Mary made many threats but rarely carried them out. When things got out of hand, Don delivered punishment in a heavy-handed manner. When Mary felt upset about life, she tended to clean house or drink. She made life difficult for everyone by insisting that each be as compulsive about housekeeping standards as she was.

All in all, family leadership, rules, and roles were very rigid. As new situations developed in the family, the members did not have the flexibility to negotiate and create solutions that were reasonable. Ann and Julie could not discuss possible changes in a rational fashion with their parents. The Davises were locked in a dysfunctional family system that was *rigidly enmeshed*.

Treatment. The family therapist sought to focus on those issues in the family on which some positive movement was already under way. On the dimension of cohesion, the goal was to increase the level of individual autonomy in the family—in short, to give each member more space. A related goal was to strengthen the marriage.

In terms of flexibility, the family therapist taught family members how to negotiate and compromise with each other, rather than alternating between quiet passivity and conflict. Members were taught to see family rules as general guidelines to be discussed and interpreted as new situations arose in day-to-day living. This gave the children a chance to argue their points and even to change their parents' minds occasionally. When the family as a whole had improved on these dimensions, the focus shifted to the marriage.

Don and Mary continued in marital therapy as a couple. The therapist focused on ways the couple could learn to enjoy each other's company again. They were encouraged to go out on dates without the children and to do things they felt they hadn't had time to do together for many years. As the marriage improved, the number of disagreements with the children diminished. Why was this? As the marital coalition strengthened and Mary took back her rightful place on the parental team, it was less necessary for Julie and Ann to struggle for a position in coalition with Dad, and Julie no longer felt it necessary to try to fill the vacuum.

The family therapist got a good deal of help from Mary's alcohol counselors and from Alcoholics Anonymous. The chemical dependence specialists were adept at helping Mary maintain sobriety once she had attained it. Al-Anon, which focuses on the family of the alcoholic, gave Don and the children support and ideas in their struggle to live with an alcoholic. As Mary became more secure in her marriage with Don, she was able to be more supportive of Julie in her growth as an individual. The family became more adept at both separating from and connecting with each other.

As a result of couple therapy to strengthen the marriage and family therapy to improve the family functioning, after about 10 sessions the family was now functioning as a *structurally cohesive* family (see the Couple and Family Map, Figure 16.4). In terms of cohesion, they had moved from being *enmeshed* to being less connected as a *cohesive* family. Don and Mary became more emotionally connected to each other, and this helped to reduce the dysfunctional parent–adolescent coalition of Don and daughter Ann. In terms of flexibility, the family moved from being *rigid* to being *structured*. The parents started to work more as a cooperating team and gave their adolescents a little more freedom and autonomy. All family members were much happier with how the family had changed, and they were more clear about how they could continue to improve their family over time.

Families have a variety of ways that they interact with the outside world. Spending time with other families is a healthy way to teach children about the world outside of their own family.

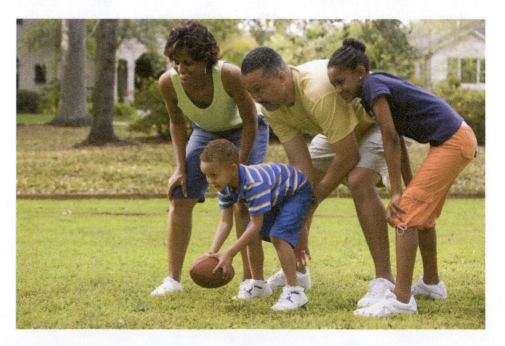

which their relationship was built. The 10 suggestions listed here can help couples keep relationships vital and healthy.

1. Give one or two compliments or more to your partner each day.
2. Find time to dialogue for 5 minutes each day about your relationship.
3. Have a weekly meeting for about 15 minutes with your partner and discuss one or two issues and one or two strengths of your relationship.
6. Share feelings with each other and listen, and listen.
7. Resolve issues as soon as possible.
8. If a problem persists for 2 to 3 months, use the 6 steps for resolving couple conflict (see Chapter 5 on conflict resolution).
9. If you are unable to resolve your conflict, seek professional counseling from a marital therapist.
10. At least once a year, try to attend a workshop to enrich your marriage.

Strengthening Your Marriage and Family Relationships

What is the best advice we can give about building stronger marriage and family relationships?

1. *Carefully choose a good partner, prepare for your marriage, and once you are married, continue to find ways to build a stronger marriage.* Read together, talk with other more experienced couples about marriage, attend educational programs for couples, and engage in premarital counseling with a skillful professional.
2. *Do things every day that continually build a stronger couple and marital relationship.* Praise your partner at least once or twice a day. This is just as important as going to school, going to work, eating, sleeping, and breathing.
3. *Work on building your family strengths, which ultimately impact the quality of your individual, couple, and parent-child relationships.* You don't marry an individual, you marry a whole family and the culture that surrounds that family. You can't afford to try to ignore or escape this fact, so find ways to get along well with your partner's family and your own family. Don't try to isolate yourselves as a couple from the rest of your families.

Building a Stronger Marriage

The couple relationship is the foundation of a strong family, so it is important that the couple develop a strong and healthy relationship. As we have seen earlier in this textbook, a strong marriage has a positive impact on the emotional and physical health of the individuals.

There are a variety of very specific things that couples can do to build a stronger relationship. Box 16.2 lists 10 suggestions that have been found to be important

BOX 16.3   Putting It Together

Building a Stronger Family

Families today are often mix-and-match affairs with any number—and type—of parents, grandparents, children, and siblings. In order for any family to work, no matter what its makeup, there has to be a conscious effort to instill positive feelings and a sense that every family member is equally important. Here are 10 suggestions for keeping families strong.

1. Give at least one compliment to each family member each day.
2. Do a daily dialogue for 5 to 10 minutes each day about what is happening with each family member.
3. Try to have your family meal together with everyone present.
4. Have a weekly family meeting for about 30 to 45 minutes with all family members attending. Each member should say one thing they like about the family and one issue they have with their family that everyone will work on during the session.
5. Give top priority to your marriage.
6. Be as assertive as your children are with you. (Not aggressive but assertive.)
7. Remember to listen, listen, and listen.
8. Spend 1 hour of quality time each week with each child (one on one).
9. If a problem persists, bring it to the family meeting and use the six-step model for resolving the conflict (see Chapter 5).
10. If a parenting problem lasts for 2 to 3 months, seek professional help from a family therapist.

across numerous studies. These suggestions include giving compliments, finding time to dialogue, having a weekly date, being assertive, listening with care, resolving issues before they become serious, and seeking help if you have problems that you are unable to resolve. Because marriages change over time, it is important to keep working on improving the relationship. One way is to look for opportunities to attend couple enrichment programs with other couples.

Building a Stronger Family

In numerous studies, we have found that strong families successfully manage life's difficulties in a variety of creative ways. These are some of their strategies:

- *Look for something positive in difficult situations.* No matter how difficult, most problems teach us something about ourselves and others that we can draw on in future situations.
- *Pull together.* Think of the problem not as one family member's difficulty, but as a challenge for the family as a whole.
- *Create open channels of communication.* Challenges cannot be met when communication shuts down.
- *Keep things in perspective.* "These things, too, shall pass."
- *Adopt new roles in a flexible manner.* Crises often demand that individuals learn new approaches to life and take on different responsibilities.
- *Focus to minimize fragmentation.* Look at the big picture. Focusing on the details rather than the essentials can make people edgy and anxious.
- *Create a life full of meaning and purpose.* We all face severe crises in life. These challenges are simply unavoidable. Our aim should be to live a useful life of service to our community. Giving of ourselves brings a richness and dignity to our lives, in spite of the troubles we endure.
- *Actively meet challenges head on.* Life's disasters do not go away when we try to hide our head in the sand.

The Future of Your Family

The future of couples and families around the world begins with each of us as we create the future in our own family.

Listen to people talk about the future of their families:

"That's a really hard question, Grandpa!" exclaimed Cole, age 6. But he quickly turned to his Mommie and Daddy and smiled: *"I want you guys to be alive with me forever because you always snuggle."*

* * * * *

"The future for my family?" 19-year-old Rachel replied. *"I'm not sure. My parents have been divorced for almost 15 years, and they're both remarried. My mom's happily remarried. My dad is not so happy. He always talks about my mom and what she's doing and what they'd be like if they were still together. My mom has done a really good job of showing us things are okay, even with stressful events. She has raised us very well, I believe. My father he had a girlfriend . . . he screwed up, and he's realizing it now. And I just don't know what to say to him. Yeah, Dad, you blew it. And I think he's going to get divorced again. For myself, I have the biggest hopes. I know everyone does."*

* * * * *

"As far as where we're going," 21-year-old Tanya noted, *"I think we'll be okay because my partner, Darren, has a strong family. But I don't want my dysfunctional family to overshadow our life because that's something I want to overcome. I want to overcome the statistics and have a strong marriage."*

* * * * *

"For the future," said 20-year-old Allan, *"I want to raise my family like my family did. We were a close family and had good communication. We had fun together and got much love from one another, because our family cared for each other."*

* * * * *

"I think we're a happier family than we were in the past because we laugh a lot," answered Marta, a 40-year-old divorced mother of three. *"The children think I have done really well as a single mom taking care of them and developing her career. That's pretty exciting. Young people need to hang in there with their parents and try to understand them, because they love you and they just want the very best for you."*

* * * * *

"Well, gosh, I haven't really thought much about the future," 62-year-old Richard said. *"But that's a great question, so here goes: I think I'll keep chugging along in a lot of ways pretty much as I have been for many, many years. I'll probably retire, as they say, in a couple years and that will give me much more time to enjoy with Lynn, and with our grown-up kids and grandkids. She's had some health problems the past few years and I learned never to take your loved ones for granted. So, we'll travel a bit more and I'll*

probably get involved in some volunteer activities I like that will help the community a bit. Mostly I'll enjoy being with Lynn. You know, we've been best friends, really, for just about forever."

* * * * *

"The future?" 92-year-old Helen pondered. "When you're my age it's pretty certain you have learned to live in the moment because anything can happen to older people any second. But, your question is a serious question, so I'll give you a serious answer: I'm not so concerned about my future. My life has been a long life, a good life. I miss Jim, just as lots of widows miss their husbands. I miss him terribly. But my life still has meaning because I am connected to my children and grandchildren and the few old friends that have lived as long as I have. I may go in a few years or I may go this afternoon. That's really not important. The important thing to me is that my family will survive after I'm gone. Their lives will go on and on. And I hope they will remember me and think kindly of me and remember how much I cared for them. That sums up a pretty good life."

It has been said that when our life comes to an end, all we really have left is our story. We won't be taking our money or possessions or resume with us when we make the transition from this world to whatever will come next for us. All we have at the end of a hopefully long and meaningful life will be the story of our journey. Will our story, as it comes to an end, be a happy one or a sad one? Will it include touching elements of warm and affectionate relationships, or will it be a story of loneliness and despair?

We hope you have seen as you were reading this book that happiness, in many ways, is a choice human beings make in life. And we also hope that it has become clear to you that loving couple and family relationships are created every day by people who have educated themselves to meet the challenges of intimate living. These fortunate souls have joined together with the special people in their world to write a family story full of life: meaningful work, significant opportunities to learn and grow, chances that were taken for adventure and reaching out, and much love given and received from people for whom they deeply care.

Summary

- As the world shrinks, the need for international cooperation expands. The family, in all its magnificent diversity, is the basic foundation for all known world cultures throughout history. Worldwide research on family strengths, community strengths, and cultural strengths, which began almost 40 years ago, is making it quite clear that what makes families work well is much more similar than different from culture to culture, giving human beings solid common ground upon which to build a better world together.

- Global-level research has discovered that family strengths, community strengths, and the broader cultural strengths are remarkably similar from country to country around the world.

- Family strengths worldwide include appreciation and affection; positive communication; commitment to the family; enjoyable times together; a sense of spiritual well-being and shared values; and the ability to manage stress and crisis effectively.

- Community strengths from a global perspective include a supportive environment that genuinely values families, and a general willingness and natural generosity infused in the culture to help when families are in need; an effective educational delivery system; religious communities for families seeking this kind of support; family service programs developed by government and nongovernmental organizations for families who cannot find the help they need from their own extended families, friends, and neighbors; and a safe, secure, and healthful environment.

the national-level social culture, is affected by what is happening in every other level.

- Although families can have many strengths even when they live in a community or a culture without significant strengths, the most fortunate families are those where significant family strengths, community strengths, and cultural strengths intersect. In this way of thinking about families, a family caught up by the terrible forces of war or economic depression can still be strong, in spite of the difficult environment in which they live. Conversely, in a healthy community and healthy national cultural environment there will be troubled families without many significant family strengths.
- Economist Kenneth Boulding believes that there are four great virtues that make up the *ultimate good* and we should individually and collectively strive to achieve these: *economic adequacy, justice, freedom,* and *peacefulness.*
- Within the world, focusing on our similarities as human beings can help unite us and understand one another. Within families, focusing on family strengths emphasizes these strengths and helps us build successful ways of relating to one another.
- There are many ways individuals, couples, and families seek support, advice, and education, ranging from *informal networks* to *professional therapy.* The intensity level of the program should correspond to the level of need.
- A good premarital program can reduce a couple's chances of divorce and improve their overall relationship. One important way we can strengthen marriages is to offer good premarital programs that give couples the skills to help them through their lives together.
- There are two types of couple programs: *couple enrichment programs* and *couple education programs.* Couple enrichment programs typically last 1 or 2 days and improve the couple relationship by increasing the sharing between the couple. Couple education programs are skill based, more comprehensive, and more effective in helping couples build stronger relationships.
- The top five stumbling blocks identified by couples in a national survey were the following: They have problems sharing leadership equally, they feel their partner is sometimes too stubborn, they are less satisfied with their marriage since having children, they feel their partner is too negative or critical, and they wish their partner had more time and energy for recreation.

research studies have repeatedly demonstrated the effectiveness of marriage and family therapy for treating a wide range of mental and emotional disorders and health problems. Marriage and family therapists treat not only marital distress and conflict, but also adolescent drug abuse, depression, alcoholism, obesity, and dementia in the elderly, because these issues all have a family component.

- Building strong marriages begins with your being proactive about your relationship skills and developing good relationships with others. Choosing a good partner and premarital education are the first steps you can take to develop a strong marriage. Then, as a couple, seek out couple education programs. When you have a family, remember to build on your strengths as individuals, as a couple, and as a family.
- Ways to build a strong family are to compliment each family member regularly; have a 5- to 10-minute daily dialogue about what is happening with each family member; try to have the family meal with everyone present; have a 30- to 45-minute weekly family meeting with all family members attending; give top priority to your marriage; be assertive like your children are with you; listen, listen, listen; spend 1 hour of quality time each week with each child one on one; if problems persist, use the 10-step model for resolving the conflict; seek professional help if a parenting problem lasts 2 or 3 months.

Activities

1. Draw a model outlining the strengths of your family, community, and culture. Pick either the concentric circles model or the Venn diagram model. Share your model with a small group of other people and discuss what you are seeing together.
2. Write down the strengths in your family of origin that you want to bring into your marriage.
3. Write down the problematic issues in your family of origin, and think about ways you can avoid bringing them into your marriage.
4. What are the pros and cons of premarital counseling?
5. Will cohabitation help you personally prepare for marriage?
6. Would you attend a couple program or go to marital therapy? Why? Why not?

Suggested Readings

American Association for Marriage and Family Therapy (AAMFT). (2012). Founded in 1942, AAMFT is the professional association for the field of marriage and family therapy, representing the professional interests of more than 24,000 marriage and family therapists in the United States, Canada, and abroad. AAMFT publishes the *Journal of Marital and Family Therapy* and *Family Therapy Magazine*. Web site: www.aamft.org.

American Family Strengths Inventory (AFSI). (2012). An at-home, free assessment of couple and family strengths. Take the inventory with your partner and other family members and plan how to enhance your strengths and improve areas of potential growth in your relationships. Web site: www.ianrpubs.unl.edu /epublic/live/g1881/build/g1881.pdf.

Atwood, J., & Genovese, F. (2006). *Therapy with single parents: A social constructivist approach.* New York: Haworth Press.

Bigner, J., & Gottlieb, A. (2007). (Eds.). *Interventions with families of gay, lesbian, bisexual, and transgender people: From the inside out.* Binghamton, NY: Haworth Press.

DeFrain, J., & the University of Nebraska–Lincoln Extension Family Action Research and Writing Team. (2007a). *Family treasures: Creating strong families.* New York: iUniverse, Inc. (Available online from the *University of Nebraska–Lincoln for Families* Web site at www .unlforfamilies.unl.edu.) Sixty-three couple and family activities keyed to each of the six major strengths.

DeFrain, J., & the University of Nebraska–Lincoln Extension Family Action Research and Writing Team. (2007b). *Family treasures: Creating strong families.* Resource Guide for Educators and Families (CD and DVD set). Lincoln: University of Nebraska Extension. (Available online from the *University of Nebraska–Lincoln for Families* Web site at www. unlforfamilies.unl.edu.) Explains the International Family Strengths Model and shows families using some of the 63 couple and family activities designed to strengthen relationships.

DeFrain, J., & the University of Nebraska–Lincoln Extension Family Action Research and Writing Team. (2012). *Getting connected, staying connected: Loving each other day by day.* Bloomington, IN: iUniverse. Very clear and specific activities to strengthen couple and family relationships.

Eubanks Fleming, C. J., & Córdova, J. V. (2012). Predicting relationship help seeking prior to a marriage checkup. *Family Relations, 61*(February), 90–100.

Ferrer, M. (2010). Stepping stones for stepfamilies. A six-lesson curriculum for enhancing stepfamily relationships developed by the University of Florida Extension. Web site: http://edis.ifas.ufl.edu /topic_program_stepping_stones_for_stepfamilies.

Gil, E. (2006). *Helping abused and traumatized children: Integrating directive and nondirective approaches.* New York: Guilford Press.

Gurman, A. (Ed.). (2008). *Clinical handbook of couple therapy* (4th ed.). New York: Guilford Press.

Halford, W. K., Moore, E., Wilson, K., Dyer, C., Farrugia, C., & Judge, K. (2008). *Couple-CARE: Couple commitment and relationship enhancement.* [Complete educator kit.] Queensland, Australia: Australian Academic Press.

Hecker, L. L., & Wetchler, J. L. (Eds.). (2003). *An introduction to marriage and family therapy.* London: Routledge, Taylor & Francis Group. Insight and analysis from 20 experts.

Hennon, C. B., & Wilson, S. M. (Eds.). (2008). *Families in a global context.* London: Routledge, Taylor & Francis Group. How are families the same or different around the world? An in-depth analysis of family life in 17 countries.

Huxley, A. (1944). *The perennial philosophy.* New York: Harper & Brothers.

Imber-Black, E. (Ed.). (2010) Couple and family therapy theory and practice: Innovations in 2010. *Family Process, 49* (3), 265–267. A special issue of the respected journal.

Kim, H. W., Markman, H. J., & Scott, S. (2008). Strengthening couples' relationships with education: Social policy and public health perspectives. *Journal of Family Psychology, 22*(4), 497–505. "There is some evidence that skill-based couples relationship education enhances couples' maintenance of healthy, committed relationships."

Minuchin, P., Colapinto, J., & Minuchin, S. (2007). *Working with families of the poor* (2nd ed.). New York: Guilford Press.

Moore, B. A. (2011). *Handbook of counseling military couples.* New York and London: Routledge, Taylor & Francis Group.

National Council on Family Relations. (2012). NCFR, founded in 1938, is the oldest multidisciplinary and nonpartisan professional organization focused solely on family research, practice, and education. NCFR publishes three scholarly journals: *Journal of Marriage and Family, Family Relations: Interdisciplinary Journal of Applied Family Studies,* and *Journal of Family Theory & Review.* Web site: www.ncfr.org.

Olson, D. H., Olson-Sigg, A., & Larson, P. J. (2008). *The couple checkup: Finding your relationship strengths.* Nashville, TN: Thomas Nelson.

Onedera, J. D. (2007). *The role of religion in marriage and family counseling.* London: Routledge, Taylor & Francis Group. Focuses on how each of the major world religions can influence family dynamics.

Paragament, K. I. (2007). *Spiritually integrated psychotherapy: Understanding and addressing the sacred.* New York: Guilford Press.

Rivett, M. (2009). *Family therapy: 100 key points and techniques.* London: Routledge, Taylor & Francis Group. Family therapy theory and practice; concise and jargon-free.

University of Nebraska–Lincoln Extension. (2012). Educational materials for strengthening couple and family relationships. Web site: www.ianrpubs.unl.edu/epublic /pages/index.jsp.

Visit the text-specific Online Learning Center at **www.mhhe.com/olson8e** for practice tests, chapter summaries, and PowerPoint slides.

Family Scales

Couple and Family Map

Couple and Family Map

The Couple and Family Map can be used to define the way in which a couple or a family interacts—that is, to describe the family system. The Couple and Family Scales are the tools an interviewer uses to place the couple or family in the Couple and Family Map. In this resource section we will outline the instructions for using these scales. The process consists of six steps:

1. Understanding the dimensions and concepts of the Couple and Family Map
2. Interviewing the couple or family
3. Completing the Coalition Rating Scale
4. Assigning a scale value for each concept
5. Assigning a global rating for each dimension
6. Plotting the global ratings on the Couple and Family Map

Step 1: Dimensions and Concepts

There are three primary dimensions in the Couple and Family Map: family cohesion, family flexibility, and family communication. Each dimension has several concepts that help define and describe it. Before doing an assessment of a couple or a family, the interviewer reviews all the concepts and their descriptions for each of the three dimensions.

Step 2: Interview Questions

To assess a couple or a family, the interviewer, usually through a semistructured interview, evaluates the couple's or family's interactions in terms of each of the concepts for each dimension. Those experienced in using the Family and Couple Scales find it helpful to encourage the couple or family to discuss with each other the interview questions in Table A.1. The questions focus on the two dimensions of cohesion and flexibility but not on communication. To assess communication, the interviewer simply observes how the couple or family communicates while they are discussing the interview questions. The interviewer should encourage the couple or the family to talk directly to each other—*not* to the interviewer—so that the interviewer can observe how they interact with each other.

Step 3: The Coalition Rating Scale

After the interview, the interviewer first completes the Coalition Rating Scale (shown in Table A.2), if it applies. It is necessary to use this scale if one or more family members function differently from the rest of the family. For example, it is possible to have a *rigidly enmeshed* family with a *chaotically disengaged* husband. If there is a disengaged member or a coalition (see definitions given in Table A.2), these family members are rated separately from the rest of the

---

TABLE A.1	Interview Questions for Assessing Family Cohesion and Flexibility

Questions for Assessing Family Cohesion

1. *Separateness/togetherness:* How much do family members go their own way versus spending time with the family?
2. *I–we balance:* Do family members have a good balance of time apart and together?
3. *Closeness:* Do people feel close to each other?
4. *Loyalty:* Is the family a top priority compared with work or friends?
5. *Activities:* Do people spend much time having fun together?
6. *Dependence/independence:* Do family members stay in close contact?

Other Useful Questions to Assess Family Cohesion

1. How does your family celebrate birthdays and holidays?
2. Describe your typical dinnertime meal in terms of who is present, who prepares the meal, who cleans up, and the type of family interaction that occurs.

3. What is a typical weekend like in your family?
4. Do you have special times when you get together as a family?

Questions for Assessing Family Flexibility

1. *Leadership:* Is leadership shared between parents?
2. *Discipline:* Is (was) discipline strict?
3. *Negotiation:* How do you negotiate differences in your family?
4. *Roles:* Does each spouse do only certain tasks?
5. *Rules:* Do rules change in your family?
6. *Change:* Is change upsetting to your family?

Other Useful Questions to Assess Family Adaptability

1. How open is your family to change?
2. Is your family good at problem solving?
3. Does your family seem disorganized?
4. Who is in charge—the parent(s) or the child(ren)?

This Coalition Rating Scale provides a way of noting coalitions' or disengaged individuals' patterns in family systems. After observing the family's interactions, any coalitions or disengaged individuals should be identified by checking the relevant categories below.

Definitions

Coalition. A coalition is two or more people with a high degree of emotional closeness to one another. During family interaction, the members of a coalition are very connected to one another and may at times exclude other family members.

____ Mother–son
____ Mother–daughter
____ Father–son
____ Father–daughter
____ Son–daughter
____ Same-sex siblings
____ Other

____ Disengaged mother
____ Disengaged father
____ Disengaged child(ren)
____ Other

(A husband–wife coalition is considered a positive dyad and is therefore not listed.)

family system. The interviewer completes the Coalition Rating Scale *first*, before completing the other scales.

Step 4: Assigning Scale Values

After interviewing the couple or family, the interviewer rates them on each of the concepts that make up the three dimensions, using the scales in Table A.3. Before selecting a value, the interviewer carefully reads the descriptions for each concept and then selects a value from 1 to 8 that most closely represents the couple or family as a unit.

Step 5: Assigning Global Ratings

After assigning a rating for each concept in each of the three dimensions and recording those ratings on Table A.4, the interviewer makes a global rating for each of the three dimensions (cohesion, flexibility,

and communication) and records the global ratings on Table A.4. The global rating for each dimension should be based on an overall evaluation rather than on a sum of the subscale (concept) ratings.

Step 6: Plotting a Family System Type on the Couple and Family Map

Finally, the interviewer plots the couple's or the family's global ratings on cohesion and flexibility on the Couple and Family Map (Figure A.1). This determines the marital or family system type. If, for example, the interviewer assigns a family a global rating of 5 on the cohesion dimension and 4 on the flexibility dimension, the model will identify the family as *structurally cohesive*, one of the four balanced family types on the Couple and Family Map. If the family contains a coalition or a disengaged member, the interviewer also plots the coalition or member on the map.

Levels of Family Cohesion

COHESION							
Disengaged (Unbalanced)		**Connected (Balanced)**		**Cohesive (Balanced)**		**Enmeshed (Unbalanced)**	
Score 1	2	3	4	5	6	7	8
Separateness/ togetherness High separateness		More separateness than togetherness		More togetherness than separateness		Very high togetherness	
I–we balance Primarily "I" Primarily "we"		More "I" than "we"				More "we" than "I"	
Closeness Little closeness		Low-to-moderate closeness		Moderate-to-high closeness		Very high closeness	
Loyalty Lack of loyalty		Some loyalty		Considerable loyalty		High loyalty	
Activities Mainly separate		More separate than shared		More shared than separate		Mainly shared	
Dependence/ independence High independence High dependence		More independence than dependence		More dependence than independence		High dependence	

Levels of Family Flexibility

FLEXIBILITY							
Rigid (Unbalanced)		**Structured (Balanced)**		**Flexible (Balanced)**		**Chaotic (Unbalanced)**	
Score 1	2	3	4	5	6	7	8
Leadership Authoritarian		Sometimes shared		Often shared		Lack of leadership	
Discipline Strict discipline		Somewhat democratic		Democratic		Erratic/inconsistent	
Negotiation Limited discussion		Organized discussion		Open discussion		Endless discussion	
Roles Roles very stable		Roles stable		Role sharing		Dramatic role shifts	
Rules Unchanging rules		Few rule changes		Some rule changes		Frequent rule changes	
Change Very little change		Moderate change		Some change		Considerable change	

Levels of Family Communication

COMMUNICATION					
Poor		**Good**		**Very Good**	
Score 1	2	3	4	5	6
Listening skills Poor listening skills		Appears to listen, but feedback is limited		Gives feedback, indicating good listening skills	
Speaking skills Often speaks for others		Speaks for oneself more than for others		Speaks mainly for oneself rather than for others	
Self-disclosure Low sharing of feelings		High sharing of feelings		Moderate sharing of feelings	
Clarity Inconsistent messages		Clear messages		Very clear messages	
Staying on topic Seldom stays on topic		Often stays on topic		Mainly stays on topic	
Respect and regard Low to moderate		Moderate to high		High	

I–we balance	☐	☐	☐	☐	☐	☐	☐	☐
Closeness	☐	☐	☐	☐	☐	☐	☐	☐
Loyalty	☐	☐	☐	☐	☐	☐	☐	☐
Activities	☐	☐	☐	☐	☐	☐	☐	☐
Dependence/independence	☐	☐	☐	☐	☐	☐	☐	☐
Global rating	☐	☐	☐	☐	☐	☐	☐	☐

FLEXIBILITY

	Rigid		Structured		Flexible		Chaotic	
Score	1	2	3	4	5	6	7	8
Leadership	☐	☐	☐	☐	☐	☐	☐	☐
Discipline	☐	☐	☐	☐	☐	☐	☐	☐
Negotiation	☐	☐	☐	☐	☐	☐	☐	☐
Roles	☐	☐	☐	☐	☐	☐	☐	☐
Rules	☐	☐	☐	☐	☐	☐	☐	☐
Change	☐	☐	☐	☐	☐	☐	☐	☐
Global rating	☐	☐	☐	☐	☐	☐	☐	☐

COMMUNICATION

	Poor		Good		Very Good	
Score	1	2	3	4	5	6
Listening skills	☐	☐	☐	☐	☐	☐
Speaking skills	☐	☐	☐	☐	☐	☐
Self-disclosure	☐	☐	☐	☐	☐	☐
Clarity	☐	☐	☐	☐	☐	☐
Staying on topic	☐	☐	☐	☐	☐	☐
Respect and regard	☐	☐	☐	☐	☐	☐
Global rating	☐	☐	☐	☐	☐	☐

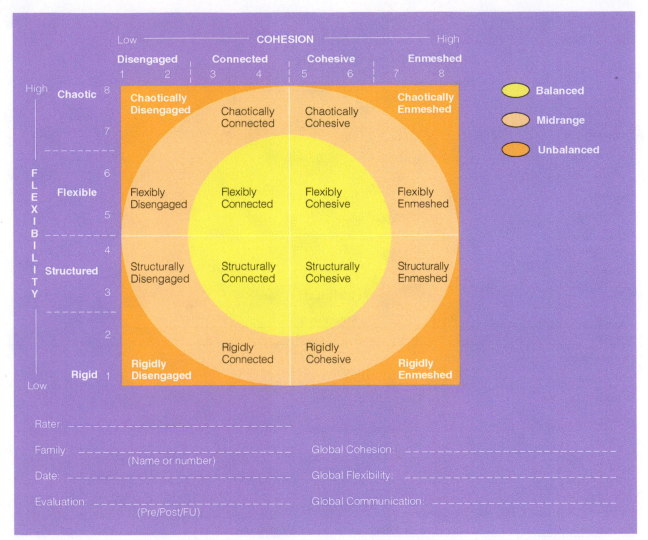

FIGURE A.1

Couple and Family Map

Source: The Harvard Guide to Women's Health by K.J. Carlson, S.A. Eisenstat, and T. Ziporyn, 1996, Cambridge, MA: Harvard University Press.

Research Methods

A Knowledge Explosion
Family Research Methods
Research Designs
A Final Word About Research

Family science, also called family studies, is growing rapidly, as a profession and as a social and behavioral science. In recent years, research on the family has improved in both quality and quantity. Family researchers use many of the same methods as other social scientists, but they tailor these methods to their own interests and purposes as they focus on couple and family issues. This section describes several research methods, including questionnaires, interviews, case studies, and observational approaches.

A Knowledge Explosion

Family science is a multidisciplinary field, which has an impact on many disciplines. These disciplines in turn contribute to the understanding of families (Table B.1). Over the past 35 years, this science has emerged as a genuine discipline unto itself. Its primary goal is to achieve a better understanding of families in order to enhance the quality of family life. Professionals whose main interests are research, theory, and the development of programs for families tend to call themselves *family scientists*. Those who develop educational programs for couples and families call themselves *family life educators*. Those who work clinically with troubled families are called *marital and family therapists*.

Family scientists have backgrounds in a wide variety of disciplines: human development, family science programs, human ecology, home economics, social work, nursing, educational psychology, psychology, sociology, psychiatry, and anthropology. Family scientists may be researchers, professors, teachers, family life educators, family therapists, ministers, nurses, social workers, or attorneys.

This multidisciplinary contribution to the field of family science has resulted in increased collaboration among researchers, with more articles being coauthored in recent years (Moody, 2004). Nearly half of all social science articles in family science are coauthored. This trend might be the result of funding requirements of projects in the field or the need for differing skills on any given article. Family science is also more likely to have coauthors than many of the other social science areas because it is already a multidisciplinary field of study.

Family Research Methods

The whole of science is nothing more than a refinement of everyday thinking.

—ALBERT EINSTEIN

It is primarily through research that new ideas and facts are discovered. The word *research* is derived from the Middle French word *recherché*, meaning "to investigate thoroughly." Science, in the final analysis, is an examination of events or information in an attempt to make new discoveries.

TABLE B.1	Disciplines Contributing to Family Science
Discipline	**Topics in Family Science**
Anthropology	Cross-cultural studies; kinship; diversity in families
Biology	Conception and reproduction; growth, development, and aging
Child development	Development of infant and child; interpersonal skills
Communication studies	Couple and family communication
Economics	Family finances; consumer behavior
Education	Family life education; marriage preparation
History	Historical perspectives on the family throughout time
Human sciences	Ecosystem perspectives on family, nutrition, housing, clothing
Law	Marriage and divorce laws; child custody laws
Literature	Marriages and families in fiction, present and past
Marital and family therapy	Treating couple and family relationships
Medicine and nursing	Families and health
Psychiatry	Treating mental health problems
Psychology	Family psychology; assessment of couples and families
Social work	Treating family problems; family policy
Sociology	Marriage and divorce statistics; sociological theories about families

Family researchers have a creative mix of tools and techniques for learning more about family realities, using both "insider" and "outsider" perspectives. An **insider perspective** is provided by family members when they describe how they see their relationships. An **outsider perspective** is provided by researchers or therapists observing and describing the activity from their point of view. Methods that tap the insider perspective are questionnaires, interviews, and case studies. Outsider perspectives are obtained through observational approaches. Family researchers often use only one method in a particular study, but there are advantages to a multimethod approach that uses both insider and outsider perspectives.

Family researchers study couple and family issues from both quantitative and qualitative perspectives. **Quantitative research** typically uses structured questionnaires and scales to assess people's description of their relationship (i.e., couple, marriage, family) attitudes and behaviors. Their responses are typically converted to numbers that can be summed and analyzed using statistical methods. Most family science researchers believe that in the past 15 years qualitative research has become more accepted as a legitimate and systematic mode of inquiry (Creswell, 2009, 2012). **Qualitative research** tends to be based on more or less open-ended interviews of people talking about how they see their relationships. Their verbal responses are analyzed looking for themes in their comments. Ultimately, quantitative studies produce numbers that can be analyzed, whereas qualitative studies are more often looking for themes in stories from persons about a given topic.

Because quantitative studies rely on questionnaires and scales rather than personal interviews, quantitative studies usually have a larger sample of participants than qualitative studies. In qualitative research, data collection is often more involved and time consuming, because the interviews or written testimony can be much longer and in depth. This usually requires a great deal more time to transcribe into written testimony from the participants. This is why it has been said that, "Quantitative research

called **mixed-methods research approaches,** rely on both qualitative and quantitative methods in the same study. For example, a research team focusing on marital quality might want to begin with 10 in-depth, face-to-face interviews, in which time is spent talking with couples about their marriages in a relatively unstructured and open-ended fashion. The researcher might ask a few broad, leading questions and then listen as the couple talk about how they view the particular issues, all of which is tape recorded or videotaped.

After completing a series of these in-depth interviews and transcribing the data—that is to say, the couples' thoughts about the issues—the researchers can then design the quantitative phase of the study. The open-ended interview questions can then be transformed into a more structured questionnaire with closed-end questions, that is, questions that have a series of fixed responses. The questionnaire can then be mailed to hundreds of couples in a wide geographic area. By using a qualitative approach, the researchers develop an in-depth understanding of the dynamics of marital quality based on a small sample of couples. Expanding the sample size and the breadth of the study to many more couples using the quantitative approach then increases the sample size and the ability to use statistical analysis with the data. The mixed-methods approach gives the investigator, in sum, "the best of both worlds."

Research methods need to be suitable for the population being studied. Written questions, for example, are inappropriate for people whose culture is predominantly oral.

Questionnaires

Perhaps the most common method of studying families is the questionnaire. The researcher carefully prepares a series of questions based on a review of previous research on the topic. *Fixed-response questions* require an individual to pick his or her response from a selection of possible responses; *open-ended questions* allow the individual to respond in her or his own words. A questionnaire might contain either or both types of questions.

Developing a questionnaire is a challenge. What questions one asks and the manner in which the questions are phrased can greatly influence the results of a study. Researchers are wise to do a trial run with a small sample of families to see whether the questions are clear and precise. Next, the process of **validating** a survey instrument—ensuring that the instrument measures what it is intended to measure—often takes researchers several months or even a number of years, depending on the complexity of the problem they are studying.

After the questionnaire is deemed satisfactory by the research team, it is distributed to a sufficiently large sample of family members. A number of factors determine the size of the sample, including how much money the research team has to spend on the project, how important the topic is to the researchers, and how difficult it is to find a group of families who are willing to participate in the study.

In the past, it was quite common for family researchers to limit their studies to what mothers thought was going on in their families. Fathers and children were often ignored. Researchers assumed that one individual could speak for the family as a whole. Furthermore, researchers favored this approach to studies of multiple family members because the latter were much more time consuming, expensive, and difficult to analyze. Today, most researchers recognize that fathers, mothers, and children often differ in their perceptions of family life and that a good study demands information and perceptions gathered from multiple family members.

Interviews

The interview—whether face to face or by telephone—is another family research method. Some investigators believe that interview data are more valid than data from questionnaires because the researcher can ask follow-up questions and get more information. On the other hand, some research has found that people are more honest on questionnaires. Furthermore, interviews tend to take more time, cost more money, and thus reach fewer people than is possible with questionnaires. Variation from one interviewer to another may also taint the results; questionnaires, of course, are standardized. Perhaps the best approach is to use both questionnaires and interviews. The results

can then be compared with each other to provide **cross-validation**.

Case Studies

Some of the most emotionally gripping research findings have come from family therapists and researchers using the case study method. A **case study** is a detailed description of a person or family whose interactions illustrate some specific idea, concept, or principle of family science. Using this method, researchers record in narrative form and analyze the complexities of family dynamics. Great care is taken to protect the privacy and anonymity of the family members, in part by concealing their names and disguising any identifying family characteristics.

The major problem with case studies is that the families described are probably not representative of all American families. For example, if a researcher were to analyze the case of a stepfamily in treatment at a counseling agency, the researcher might conclude that stepfamilies have numerous problems. This conclusion would be biased, however, because it was based on a family who had come for help. If the researcher were to question stepfamilies by randomly telephoning people in the community, the result would be a more **representative sample**—that is, a random selection—of stepfamilies and probably a more positive description of interactions in this type of family.

Observational Approaches

Social psychologists who study families and family therapists who treat families with problems tend to work by observing family interactions in natural settings, such as the home. Observational approaches, which tap the outsider perspective, have both strengths and limitations. One strength is that the researcher does not have to rely on family members' self-reports of their own behavior. One major limitation is that the presence of a stranger (the therapist or researcher) influences family members' behavior, making it less natural. Researchers also need to consider whether families who volunteer for such studies differ in some ways from families who do not. These are important issues in any research study, but they are more problematic in observational studies.

Sometimes a family is brought into a research laboratory for a study. Often the laboratory is set up like a living room or a dining room, and the family vational research, however, many creative observational family studies have contributed significantly to the field of family science.

Historical Studies

Studies of families from earlier generations are often useful and interesting to us today. As historians point out, we cannot know where we are going in the future unless we know where we have been. Historical research, which often relies on diaries and historical statistics about families, can help us understand families in the past.

Feminists argue that much of what has been presented as family history in the past has focused on the lives of men (*his*-story) and has neglected the lives of women (*her*-story). The history of the family, which in many cultures is traditionally the domain of women, has received little attention from historians (who have for the most part been men). But in recent decades, a resurgent feminist history movement has begun to look at the past from women's perspectives.

Multicultural Studies

Multicultural studies of families can contribute rich insights into family life and family interactions. The United States has innumerable family cultures: African American, Caucasian, Latino, Italian American, Chicago suburban, inner-city Boston, gay-male, lesbian, middle class, upper class, rural, urban, and so forth. Family life is different in each of these cultures. A family in the commuter culture of Los Angeles, for example, lives a life quite different from that of a family in rural Iowa. Diversity in families is discussed in greater detail in Chapter 2.

Conducting research with economically disadvantaged and diverse populations has been an area of focus in the social sciences in recent years (Knight, Roosa, & Umaña-Taylor, 2009; Trimble & Fisher, 2006). This increased interest is primarily because minority populations in this country are increasing.

ample, findings often are not reported within the context of cultural beliefs but instead are interpreted in terms of the dominant culture. Also, the people studied may not have received any reports of findings or received any benefit from the studies and feel "used" in the process. Therefore, there are new resources about how to ethically and appropriately conduct research with these populations. This usually means research needs to be conducted with an understanding about how a behavior might fit into the context of cultural values and beliefs, subjects must be compensated for their time, they must be adequately informed about the research process, and members of the community studied need to be part of or inform the research team (Trimble & Fisher, 2006).

Research Designs

Researchers are often interested in how particular families grow and change over time. Three types of research designs that take the passage of time into consideration are longitudinal studies, cross-sectional studies, and cross-sectional cohort studies.

Longitudinal Studies

In a longitudinal study, the researcher interviews or observes a family several times over a period of months or years. This approach obviously takes a considerable amount of time, effort, and money. For those reasons, only a small proportion of family research is longitudinal. The results of such projects, however, are often well worth the effort because they provide valuable information about long-term processes, such as the effect of the birth of a child on a marriage.

An example of a longitudinal study would be research on couples who came together to form a stepfamily and comparing marital satisfaction scores of those who attended family education and those who did not, over a 10-year period. Within a year of becoming a stepfamily, half of the couples attended a stepfamily course. There would be a control group that did not experience the intervention and a treatment group that did experience the intervention. Marital satisfaction was measured for all couples within 1 year of their becoming a stepfamily. All the couples were evaluated at 2-year intervals to measure their marital satisfaction scores, with the goal of determining whether those who attended the stepfamily course had higher marital satisfaction than those who did not, and whether those scores changed over a 10-year period.

Cross-Sectional Studies

In a cross-sectional study, a researcher selects couples or families at various stages of the family life cycle and compares the differences between the various stages. For example, a researcher could compare four stages of the life cycle by selecting some newlywed couples, some couples with young children, some couples with adolescents, and some older couples whose children had left home. The aim of this approach is to describe the similarities and differences between couples and families at these four stages.

The advantage of the cross-sectional design is efficiency: Data can be collected from all four groups at about the same time and then immediately compared. A disadvantage of this type of study is that it is not possible to know if identified similarities and differences are due only to the stage of the life cycle or to the characteristics of these specific families—a question that could only be answered by a longitudinal study that followed the same families over time. Furthermore, cross-sectional studies cannot reveal whether the historical context for each group (past experiences, crises, etc.) influenced the findings.

Cross-Sectional Cohort Studies

Because of the problems with both longitudinal and cross-sectional studies, researchers have designed a shortcut known as the cross-sectional cohort study. Using this approach, researchers do not follow a group of families for many years; instead, they study various families at different stages of the family life cycle for

shorter periods. They might, for example, study a group of families with a 10-year-old, another group with a 12-year-old, a third group with a 14-year-old, and a fourth group with a 16-year-old. If they follow these families for 5 years, they could analyze changes from age 10 to 15, 12 to 17, 14 to 19, and 16 to 21. The result would be an overview of an 11-year period (age 10 to age 21) achieved in only 5 years of research.

A Final Word About Research

No single study can provide definitive answers to important questions in family science. In fact, each study almost invariably raises new questions that are complex and difficult to answer. The advancement of scientific knowledge is a slow and painstaking process. People researching a particular topic in family science have to examine data from many related studies on the topic.

Sometimes studies produce findings that conflict with the results of other studies. These discrepancies may be due to variations in the type of questions asked, the method of research used, or the specific sample studied. For example, a sample of families drawn from the Midwest may look at gender-role issues in families somewhat differently from a sample of families drawn from Latino families living in California. Likewise, two-parent traditional American families may have a different way of looking at certain issues than do single-parent families.

Although studies on similar topics may have differing results, good studies tend to complement each other. When dozens of researchers from various parts of the United States or around the world look at a problem from many different theoretical approaches, using different research methods and different statistical analyses, a fairly comprehensive picture emerges. When the findings are similar in spite of all the differences in the sample, method, and analysis, the results are more conclusive and help build more valid findings and theories about couples and families.

Key Terms

family science
insider perspective

outsider perspective
quantitative research

qualitative research
mixed-methods research
validating
cross-validation

case study
representative sample

A

ability to manage stress and crisis effectively One of the six major qualities (commonly found in emotionally healthy families) identified by researchers working within the family strengths framework.

abortion Expulsion of a fetus from the uterus before it is sufficiently developed to survive on its own; commonly used to describe only artificially induced terminations of pregnancy.

accommodating style A style of conflict resolution characterized by nonassertive but cooperative behavior; accommodaters subjugate their own wants and needs to those of others.

acculturation The intermeshing of cultural traits and values with those of the dominant culture.

afterbirth The placenta and fetal membranes, which are expelled from the uterus during the third stage of labor.

ageism A form of prejudice or discrimination in which one judges an older person negatively solely on the basis of age.

aggressive communication A style of interpersonal communication that attempts to hurt or put down the receiver while protecting the aggressor's self-esteem.

agreeing to disagree A negotiating strategy in which two people are unable to agree on opposing courses of action and decide to take neither course of action.

Al-Anon A self-help group for families of alcoholics.

Alateen A support group for young people with alcoholic parents, based on the Alcoholics Anonymous model.

alcohol abuse A generic term that encompasses both alcoholism (addiction to alcohol characterized by compulsive drinking) and problem drinking (alcohol consumption that results in functional disability).

Alcoholics Anonymous (AA) A self-help group for alcoholics.

alcoholism Addiction to alcohol characterized by compulsive drinking.

alimony Court-ordered financial support to a spouse or former spouse following separation or divorce.

alzheimer's disease A progressive neurologic disease of the brain that leads to the irreversible loss of neurons and dementia. Clinical hallmarks of the disease include impairment in memory, judgment, decision making, orientation to physical surroundings, and language.

ambiguous loss When a family member is physically absent but psychologically present, the family experiences highly stressful feelings. People need to find ways to accept a loss before they can move on through the grieving process, but this is difficult when there is significant ambiguity in the situation. *See also* boundary ambiguity.

amniotic sac The membrane that encloses the fetus and holds the amniotic fluid, which insulates the fetus.

androgen Any of the hormones that develop and maintain male secondary sex characteristics.

anorgasmia A sexual dysfunction that prevents a woman from having an orgasm; failure to achieve orgasm (climax) during sexual intercourse.

appreciation and affection One of the six major qualities (commonly found in emotionally healthy families) identified by researchers working within the family strengths framework.

arranged marriage *See* parent-arranged marriage.

assertive communication A style of interpersonal communication that involves expressing one's self-interests and wishes without degrading or putting down the other person.

assertiveness A person's ability to express her or his feelings and desires.

assimilation Adopting the cultural traits and values of the dominant culture.

attachment theory This theory focuses on the ways that children develop attachment to their caregivers, usually their parents, during infancy. The most important tenet of attachment theory is that a young child needs to develop a relationship with at least one primary caregiver for social and emotional development to occur normally. This theory has recently been applied to adults in romantic relationships.

attentive listening A style of listening focused on fully understanding the speaker's point of view; characterized by encouragement rather than trying to direct or control the speaker.

authoritarian parenting A parenting style characterized by the demand for absolute obedience to rigid rules and the use of punitive, forceful disciplinary measures.

autonomic power pattern A power pattern in a marriage in which both partners have about equal authority but in different areas of life; both make decisions in their particular domains independent of each other.

avoidance A person's tendency to minimize issues and a reluctance to deal with issues directly.

avoidance style A style of conflict resolution characterized by nonassertive and passive behavior; avoiders often withdraw from the conflict or change the subject.

B

baby boomer A person who was born during the demographic post–World War II baby boom, between 1946 and 1964. The term is sometimes used in a cultural context and sometimes used in a demographic context.

balanced families Families who fit into the four central categories of the Couple and Family Map: families who are flexibly connected, flexibly cohesive, structurally connected, or structurally cohesive. *See also* midrange families; unbalanced families.

bankruptcy The state of being financially insolvent or unable to pay one's bills.

barrier methods of contraception Devices that prevent pregnancy by physically blocking the sperm from entering the uterus, including condoms, diaphragms, and cervical caps.

behaviorist A clinician who, based on learning theories, has developed practical, positive ways of dealing with children's behavior; rather than focusing on punishment, behaviorists encourage "accentuating the positive." *See also* reinforcement.

belief system One of the four major components of the sociocultural context in which families live, centering on religious/spiritual/ethical beliefs and other ideas about how to live successfully and happily in the world. *See also* extended-family system; family system; social system.

bidirectional effects Both the influence of the child on the parent and the influence of the parent on the child; child development specialists and family scientists concur that studying these effects is important to an understanding of parent–child dynamics.

bilateral descent A method of tracing the lineage of children equally through ancestors of both mother and father.

binuclear family A postdivorce family in which both parents participate in the raising of their children despite living in separate households; the children generally reside with one of the parents.

bisexual Sexual orientation toward members of both sexes.

blamer A person whose style of anger management is characterized by a short temper, emotionally intense responses to stress, and the belief that others are responsible for her or his feelings and problems.

blastocyst An early stage of the fertilized egg, containing about 100 cells; implants itself in the uterine lining (endometrium).

blended family A term used to describe a stepfamily. Some researchers object to the term because it creates unrealistic expectations that the new family will quickly and easily "blend" together harmoniously and because it assumes a homogeneous unit, one without a previous history or background. *See also* stepfamily.

boomerang kids Adult children who come back to their parents' home to live as a result of divorce, job loss, or an inability to make it in the "real world."

boundaries The lines that both separate systems from and connect systems to each other. The notion of a boundary implies a hierarchy of interconnected systems, each larger than the one before it.

boundary ambiguity Lack of clarity about whether a person is either in or out of the family system; related to family stress levels. The concept includes two variables: physical and psychological presence or absence. High ambiguity (conflicting variables) produces high levels of stress.

brainstorming A conflict resolution strategy that involves thinking of as many solutions to a problem as possible.

breastfeeding Feeding a baby from the mother's breast rather than from a bottle; usually better than bottle-feeding for the physical well-being of the baby.

budgeting The regular, systematic balancing of income and expenses.

C

cascading circumstances When one crisis has an impact on other issues in one's life. An example would be when a person loses a job, and the job loss results in losing one's apartment, and the loss of an apartment results in having one's children removed from the home.

case study A detailed description of a person or a family that illustrates a specific idea, concept, or principle of family science.

catharsis conflict The false belief that venting anger verbally prevents physical violence. Researchers who study family violence have found that verbal and physical violence are related.

centrifugal interaction Behavior that pushes system components away from one another, decreasing the system's connectedness.

centripetal interaction Behavior that pulls system components toward one another, resulting in the system's increasing connectedness.

cervical cap A thimble-shaped contraceptive device that fits snugly over the cervix; must be fitted by a physician and used with a spermicide.

cesarean section (C-section) Surgical delivery of the fetus by incising the mother's abdominal and uterine walls.

circular causality model An interpersonal communication model that describes an interaction pattern in which both parties view their behavior as a reaction to the other's behavior rather than as something for which they are each responsible. The first person sends out a message that causes a change in and a response from the second person. That response causes a new response in the first person, whose response initiates another response from the second person, and so on. This type of communication cycle can escalate into conflict.

closed system A family system that has the capacity to maintain the status quo and avoids change; also called a *morphostatic system*.

closure The resolution of an issue.

cluttered nest The period during which young adults return to their parental home until they are established professionally and financially and can move into an apartment or home of their own.

coculture A distinct cultural or social group living within a dominant culture but also having membership in another culture, such as gay men and lesbians.

cognitive development theory A model of child development that views growth as the mastery of specific ways of perceiving, thinking, and doing; growth occurs at discrete stages.

cohabitation The sharing of living quarters by unrelated and unmarried heterosexual or same-sex adults who have an emotional and sexual relationship.

Cohabiting The sharing of living quarters by unrelated and unmarried heterosexual or same-sex adults who have an emotional and sexual relationship.

cohesion *See* family cohesion.

collaborative style A style of conflict resolution characterized by a high degree of assertiveness about reaching one's own goals coupled with a concern for the other person.

collective worldview The group is viewed as more important than the individual.

commitment Attachment to another. One of the six major qualities (commonly found in emotionally healthy families) identified by researchers working within the family strengths framework; also, the cognitive component of Sternberg's three dimensions of love.

communication The way humans create and share meaning, both verbally and nonverbally; the foundation for developing and maintaining human relationships,

desire to "win" at all costs.

complex stepfamily A stepfamily that includes children from both parents. *See also* simple stepfamily.

compromise style A style of conflict resolution characterized by a willingness to give up something to resolve an issue.

conception The union of a sperm cell and the nucleus of an ovum (egg), which begins the development of the fetus; also called *fertilization*.

conceptual framework A set of interconnected ideas, concepts, and assumptions that helps organize thinking from a particular perspective. The field of family science includes a variety of major conceptual frameworks: family systems theory (or the family systems framework), the family strengths framework, the family development framework, the symbolic interaction framework, the social construction framework, and the feminist framework.

condom A rubber sheath placed over the penis before intercourse to prevent pregnancy and protect against sexually transmitted diseases.

conflicted couple A type of premarital and married couple characterized by few relationship strengths, low levels of relationship satisfaction, and a high risk of divorce.

conjugal family system A family consisting of a husband, a wife, and children; also called a *nuclear family*.

consanguineal family system A family system that emphasizes blood ties more than marital ties.

constructive intimacy games Games, or exercises, designed to increase intimacy in a relationship; people participate voluntarily, and they know the rules and goals of the game. *See also* destructive intimacy games.

consummate love A type of love relationship characterized by commitment, intimacy, and passion.

continuous partial attention To keep up with the relentless flow of information, ideas, and exchanges, we often find ourselves in a state of continuous partial attention. As we attend to our e-mail, cell phone, computer, television, laptop, iPod, and so forth, we also are often trying to hold a genuine conversation with a friend. This form of multitasking, when it comes to developing and maintaining intimate relationships, simply does not work.

contraception A deliberate action (use of a device, drug, or technique) taken to prevent conception (pregnancy).

contractions Tightenings of the muscles, especially those of the uterus, during labor.

coparenting A style of parenting in which both parents take on tasks and roles traditionally associated with only the mother or the father.

coping What we do when we identify something as potentially harmful or stressful.

Couple and Family Map A graphic representation of dynamic relationships within families, comprising three central dimensions: cohesion (togetherness), flexibility (ability to change), and communication (a facilitating dimension that helps families move between the extremes on the cohesion and flexibility dimensions). Identifies 16 types of family relationship.

couple-arranged marriage Freedom of choice in marriage. This approach is sometimes referred to as the *love match*, though love is not always the goal of marriage in Western industrialized societies. *See also* parent-arranged marriage.

crisis-loss stage of grief A period of chaotic shock; the first of Brubaker's three stages of the grieving process. *See also* new-life stage of grief; transition stage of grief.

cross-cultural family study A research study focused on how cultural context influences family issues, among them, values and behaviors, courtship and marriage patterns, communication, roles, work and the family, childrearing patterns, and sexuality.

cross-validation A comparison of the results from one research method with those of another research method to see if the findings are similar or identical.

cultural competence The ability to be effective in working with a variety of cultural groups. This ability involves awareness, knowledge, and skills.

cultural group A set of people who embrace core beliefs, behaviors, values, and norms and transmit them from generation to generation.

cultural identity A feeling of belonging that evolves from the shared beliefs, values, and attitudes of a group of people; the structure of the group's marital, sexual, and kinship relationships.

curvilinear relationship Researchers have found that the relationship between stress and effective outcomes for people is curvilinear—both too much and too little stress are problematic for individual and family functioning, but moderate levels of stress are usually positive.

D

dance of anger Lerner's metaphor to describe styles of managing anger and ways in which these styles interact.

dating A form of courtship involving a series of appointed meetings for social interaction and activities during which an exclusive relationship may evolve between two people. Also called *individual-choice courtship*.

definition of the situation The concept that a situation is based on a person's subjective interpretation; hence, people can have different views of the same situation.

delivery The second stage of labor, lasting from the time the cervix is completely dilated until the fetus is expelled or removed by cesarean section.

democratic parenting A parenting style that establishes the parents' legitimate power to set rules while also recognizing the child's feelings, individuality, and need to develop autonomy; uses positive reinforcement, seldom punishment, to enforce standards. Also called *authoritative parenting*.

Depo-Provera (DMPA) A progestin that is administered by injection.

destructive intimacy games Games that reduce intimacy because people are often unaware of the game, do not voluntarily participate, and are often manipulated to behave in certain ways. *See also* constructive intimacy games.

devitalized couple The unhappiest type of married couple; characterized by few couple strengths and the highest risk for divorce.

diaphragm A cup-shaped rubber contraceptive device that is inserted in the vagina before intercourse to cover the cervical opening and block sperm from entering the uterus; must be fitted by a physician and used with a spermicide.

dilation and curettage (D & C) An abortion technique used in the second trimester of pregnancy; performed in a hospital under general anesthetic. After the cervix is dilated (opened), the embryo is removed from the uterus with a sharp instrument (curette).

dilation and evacuation (D & E) An abortion technique used in the second trimester of pregnancy. Suction and forceps are used to remove the embryo or fetus.

DINS dilemma Inhibited or hypoactive sexual desire in couples with many demands on their time. DINS stands for *double income, no sex.*

directive listening A style of listening in which the listener attempts to control the direction of the conversation through the use of questions.

distancer An individual who (1) wants emotional space when stress is high, (2) is self-reliant rather than a help-seeker, and (3) values privacy.

distress Feelings of discomfort caused by high levels of stress.

divorce culture The notion that divorce has become so accepted in the United States that it is almost expected as the outcome of marriage.

double bind A situation in which the message relayed by the speaker calls into question the type of relationship the receiver has with the speaker.

double standard Different standards of appropriate sexual and social behavior for the two sexes; the belief that premarital sex is more acceptable for males than for females.

egalitarian roles Social equality between the sexes; equal sharing of practical responsibilities and decision making by men and women. Also called *equalitarian roles*.

emerging adulthood A new stage of development between childhood and adulthood that is the age from 18 to 25. This is a prolonged period of role exploration focusing on identity exploration.

emic perspective The analysis of a society from the inside. *See also* etic perspective.

empty love A type of love relationship involving commitment but no passion or intimacy.

empty-nest syndrome Feelings of malaise, emptiness, and lack of purpose that some parents experience when their last child leaves home. *See also* spacious nest.

endogamy The practice of choosing a mate from within one's own ethnic, religious, socioeconomic, or general age group.

enjoyable time together One of the six major qualities (commonly found in emotionally healthy families) identified by researchers working within the family strengths framework.

ENRICH A comprehensive marital inventory containing 125 questions in categories that are relevant to married couples and their satisfaction with their relationship. ENRICH is an acronym for **EN**riching **R**elationship **I**ssues, **C**ommunication, and **H**appiness.

episiotomy A surgical incision from the vagina toward the anus, performed to prevent tearing of the perineum during childbirth.

erectile dysfunction A sexual dysfunction in which a man has difficulty achieving or maintaining penile erection that is firm enough for intercourse.

estrogen Although often called the *female hormone*, any of a group of hormones, produced primarily by the ovaries, that are significant in controlling female physiological functions and directing the development of female secondary sex characteristics at puberty.

ethnic group A set of people who are embedded within a larger cultural group or society and who share beliefs, behaviors, values, and norms that are transmitted from generation to generation.

ethnic identity The geographic origin of a minority group within a country or culture; cultural identity transcends ethnic identity.

ethnocentrism The assumption that one's own culture is the standard by which to judge other cultures.

model of the modern family, the wife-mother's role is to be expressive—caring for the emotional well-being of the family, providing nurturing and comfort. *See also* instrumental role.

extended family A nuclear family and those related to its members by blood, such as aunts, uncles, cousins, and grandparents.

extended-family system One of the four major components of the sociocultural context in which families live; focuses on the degree of importance relatives outside the nuclear family have on the family's life. *See also* belief system; family system; social system.

F

family Two or more people who are committed to each other and who share intimacy, resources, decision-making responsibilities, and values; people who love and care for each other.

family cohesion The togetherness or closeness of a family; one of the three dimensions of the Couple and Family Map.

family communication Interaction; sharing of thoughts and feelings; the facilitating dimension of the Couple and Family Map.

family coping A family's ability to manage stressful events or situations as a unit with minimal or no detrimental effects on any individual members.

family coping resources Resources of a healthy family system on which the family can draw in times of stress, including cohesion, adaptability, and a willingness to adopt nontraditional family roles in the face of changing economic circumstances. *See also* personal coping resources.

family development framework A conceptual framework that focuses on how family members deal with roles and developmental tasks within the family unit as they move through the stages of the life cycle.

family flexibility A family's ability to change and adapt in the face of stress or crisis; one of the three dimensions of the Couple and Family Map.

family of origin The family in which a person is raised during childhood.

family power The ability of one family member to change the behavior of the other family members.

family science An interdisciplinary field whose primary focus is to better understand families in order to enhance the quality of family life. Professionals whose main focus of applied or action research is the family tend to call themselves *family scientists*; those who develop educational programs for families sometimes call themselves *family life educators* or *family educators*; those who work clinically with troubled families are called *marriage* (or *marital*) *and family therapists*.

family strengths framework A conceptual framework proposing that if researchers study only family problems, they will find only problems in families, but that if they are interested in family strengths, they must study strong families; identifies six qualities that strong families commonly demonstrate: commitment, appreciation and affection, positive communication, enjoyable time together, spiritual well-being, and the ability to manage stress and crisis effectively.

family system One of the four major components of the sociocultural context in which families live; focuses on the interconnectedness of family members. *See also* belief system; extended-family system; social system.

family systems theory (or family systems framework) A conceptual framework that views everything that happens to any family member as having an impact on everyone else in the family, because family members are interconnected and operate as a group, or family system.

family therapy An approach to helping families; based on the belief that the roots of an individual's problems may be traced to troubled family dynamics, and solutions can come by working with the whole family.

fatuous love A type of love relationship in which commitment is based on passion but in which there has not yet been time to develop true intimacy.

femininity A gender-linked constellation of personality traits and behavioral patterns traditionally associated with females in a society.

feminist framework A conceptual framework that emphasizes the value of women's perspectives on society and the family, that recognizes women's subordination, and that promotes change in that status.

fertility awareness A variety of contraceptive methods based on predicting a woman's fertile period and avoiding intercourse during that interval (or using an additional method of contraception during that time).

fertilization The union of a sperm cell and the nucleus of an ovum (egg); also known as *conception*.

fetal alcohol syndrome (FAS) Serious malformations (particularly of the facial features and the eyes) seen in children whose mothers drank excessively during their pregnancy.

flexibility *See* family flexibility.

G

gay and lesbian families Same-sex couples, such as two men or two women, develop an intimate, caring, loving relationship and include children in that relationship.

gender The learned characteristics and behaviors associated with biological sex in a particular culture. *See also* sex.

gender identity A person's internal sense of being female or male, which is expressed in personality and behavior.

gender role The traits and behaviors assigned to males and females in a culture.

gender-role stereotype A rigid, simplistic belief about the distinctive psychological characteristics and behavioral patterns attributable to a man or woman based exclusively on sex.

general systems theory A set of principles and concepts that can be applied to all types of systems, living and nonliving.

goals Specific, achievable objectives or purposes.

gunnysacking An alienating ("dirty") fighting tactic in which a person saves up unresolved grievances until he or she explodes, resulting in a major confrontation.

H

harmonious couple A type of premarital and married couple characterized by many couple strengths, relationship satisfaction, and a low risk of divorce.

heterosexual Sexual orientation toward members of the other sex.

historical trauma The loss, of things such as land, language, or culture, that results in loss of identity and social problems for individuals and families.

HIV *See* human immunodeficiency virus.

homogamy The tendency to marry someone of the same ethnic group, educational level, socioeconomic status, religion, and values.

homosexual Sexual orientation toward members of the same sex.

hooking up Having a sexual encounter with someone who is an acquaintance or someone who is a stranger. The sexual encounter may or may not include intercourse.

human ecosystem A model showing how various human subsystems interrelate among each other. To really understand a specific family system, one also needs to consider the various system levels it influences and that influence it.

human immunodeficiency virus (HIV) The virus that causes AIDS.

husband-dominant power pattern A power pattern in a marriage in which the man is the boss.

idiographic approach A theoretical approach that focuses on the study of individuals and individual differences. *See also* nomothetic approach.

incest taboo The nearly universal societal prohibition of intercourse between parents and children and between siblings.

incongruity humor Humor that points out things in life that don't fit together logically.

individualistic worldview The individual is viewed as more important than the group.

induced labor A method of abortion performed in the late second trimester, generally in a hospital, in which a saline solution or prostaglandins are injected into the amniotic sac to cause the woman's body to expel the fetus.

infatuation A type of love relationship characterized by passion and lacking both intimacy and commitment.

insider perspective How people inside the family describe their relationships. *See also* outsider perspective.

instrumental role According to the Parsons and Bales model of the modern family, the husband-father's role—being the breadwinner, the manager, and the leader of the family. *See also* expressive role.

interdependence of parts A characteristic of systems; the parts or elements of a system are interconnected in such a way that if one part is changed, other parts are automatically affected.

international family strengths framework A conceptual framework proposing that if researchers study only family problems, they will find only problems in families, but that if they are interested in family strengths, they must study strong families. The international family strengths framework identifies six qualities that strong families commonly demonstrate around the world: commitment, appreciation and affection, positive communication, enjoyable time together, spiritual well-being and shared values, and the ability to manage stress and crisis effectively.

intimacy Sharing intellectually, physically, and/or emotionally with another person; the emotional component of Sternberg's three dimensions of love.

intimate experience An experience in which one feels close to another or shares oneself in one area of life, such as intellectually, socially, emotionally, or sexually.

intimate relationship A partnership involving an emotional bond between two people, with proven mutual commitment and trust, that provides personal and relationship

jealousy The condition of being resentful and suspicious of a rival.

joint custody A legal child custody arrangement following a divorce in which children divide their time between the homes of both parents, with both homes having equal importance: "one child, two homes."

K

kinship The relatedness of certain individuals within a group. Cultures have norms and expectations that structure and govern kin behavior.

L

labor The stages of delivering a baby, consisting of contractions of the uterine muscles and dilation of the cervix, the birth itself, and the expulsion of the placenta.

learned helplessness theory A theory that a learned passivity develops from giving power over oneself to another; that passivity increases helplessness, reduces problem-solving abilities, and limits options.

learning theories Approaches to understanding human development that focus on how people learn to behave the way they do.

life course (as compared to life cycle or life stage) A term to describe the transitions that one makes through life. It is fluid to reflect the unpredictable changes such as divorce, remarriage, or early retirement that are not tied to traditional age stages.

liking A type of love relationship characterized by intimacy but lacking passion and commitment.

lineage Line of descent, influenced by cultural norms. Lineage determines membership in a kinship group, patterns of inheritance, and kinship obligations or responsibilities. *See also* matrilineal society; patrilineal society.

linear causality model An interpersonal communication model that assumes a direct, or linear, relationship between cause and effect.

living apart together A living arrangement for committed intimate couples who choose to maintain separate homes.

longevous marriage A long-term marriage that lasts 50 years or more.

looking-glass self The idea that you learn about yourself based on the feedback you receive from others.

low sexual desire The woman's desire to have sex is low or absent.

M

male menopause Physical changes in men related to age, similar to those that occur in women during menopause.

managing stress Pauline Boss's alternative to the phrase *coping with stress;* individual family members' use of their own resources to help their family deal with a stressor or work through a crisis.

marriage An emotional and legal commitment between two people to share emotional and physical intimacy, various tasks, and economic resources.

masculinity A gender-linked constellation of personality traits and behavioral patterns traditionally associated with males in a society.

masturbation Self-stimulation of the genitals; also called *autoeroticism.*

mating gradient The tendency of women to marry men who are better educated or more successful than they are.

matriarchal group A group in which the mother or eldest female is recognized as the head of the family, kinship group, or tribe. Descent is traced through this woman.

matrilineal society A society in which descent, or lineage, is traced through females.

matrilocal society A society that encourages newly married couples to live with or near the wife's kin, especially her mother's kinship group.

menopause The cessation of ovulation, menstruation, and fertility in women as a result of aging.

menses The menstrual flow in which the endometrial tissue is discharged.

menstruation The discharge from the uterus through the vagina of blood and the unfertilized ova; occurs about every 28 days in nonpregnant women between puberty and menopause.

metacommunication Communicating about communicating.

middle age Generally speaking, the years between the ages of 35 and 65; from the standpoint of the family development conceptual framework, the middle years of the family life cycle are the launching period for young-adult children and the period before the parents' retirement.

midlife crisis A period of questioning one's worth, values, and contributions in life, usually beginning in a person's 40s or early 50s.

midrange families Families who are extreme on one dimension of the Couple and Family Map but balanced on the other dimension. There are eight midrange family types. For example, a family might be structurally enmeshed: extreme on cohesion (enmeshed) but balanced on flexibility (structured). *See also* balanced families; unbalanced families.

midwife A nonphysician who attends and facilitates a birth.

minority group A social group that differs from the rest of the population in some ways and that often experiences discrimination and prejudice.

miscarriage The termination of a pregnancy from natural causes before the fetus is viable outside of the mother (during the first or second trimester of pregnancy).

mixed message A message in which there is a discrepancy between the verbal and the nonverbal components: The receiver hears one thing but simultaneously feels something else.

mixed-methods research This is a type of study in which family researchers use both qualitative and quantitative research techniques, thus benefiting from the strengths of both approaches to research.

monogamy A relationship in which a man or a woman has only one mate.

morning sickness Nausea experienced by many women during the first trimester of pregnancy, often but not exclusively in the morning.

morphogenic system A system that is open to growth and change; also called an *open system.*

morphostatic system A system that has the capacity to maintain the status quo, thus avoiding change; also called a *closed system.*

multicultural marriage Marriage between two people from two different cultural or ethnic groups.

multiple system levels General systems theory holds that systems are embedded within other systems, layer upon layer.

multiracial marriage Marriage between people from two different cultural or ethnic groups.

N

negative feedback Information or communication that is intended to minimize change in a system.

neolocal society In this type of group, norms encourage newly married couples to establish a separate, autonomous residence, autonomous of either partner's kinship group.

new-life stage of grief The period during which the bereaved establishes a new lifestyle and exhibits to society and himself or herself that he or she can live satisfactorily as a single person; the last of Brubaker's three stages of the grieving process. *See also* crisis-loss stage of grief; transition stage of grief.

no-fault divorce Divorce laws that do not place blame (fault) for the divorce on either spouse. One party's assertion that irreconcilable differences exist is sufficient grounds for dissolving the marriage.

nomothetic approach A theoretical approach that focuses on developing a theory that works for a great number of cases. Researchers using this approach believe it is possible to develop a general family theory. *See also* idiographic approach.

nuclear family A kinship group in which a husband, a wife, and their children live together in one household; also called a *conjugal family system*.

O

old age Arbitrarily defined as beginning at age 65, which coincides for most people with retirement.

open system A family system that is open to growth and change; also called a *morphogenic system*.

oral contraceptives Birth control pills taken by mouth that contain hormones that suspend ovulation and thus prevent conception.

organic sexual dysfunction Organic factors cause 10% to 20% of all cases of sexual dysfunction, and contribute to the dysfunction in another 15% of all cases, according to one source. For example, a man may have difficulty achieving or maintaining an erection as a result of numerous medical conditions, including diabetes and alcoholism.

organismic theory Developed by Jean Piaget and expanded by later theorists, a theory of child development emphasizing that children's minds develop through various stages and that children think very differently from adults; sees child-thought as primitive and mystical, with logical reasoning developing slowly into adulthood.

orgasmic disorder The woman cannot experience an orgasm.

orgasmic dysfunction Impairment of the ordinary physical responses of sexual excitement or orgasm as the result of physical or medical factors, such as illness, injury, or drugs.

outsider perspective How researchers or therapists perceive a family, in contrast with how family members perceive the family. *See also* insider perspective.

overfunctioner An individual who knows what is best not only for herself or himself but for everybody else as well; overfunctioners cannot let others solve their problems themselves.

oviduct In the female reproductive system, one of a pair of tubes through which ova (eggs) travel from an ovary to the uterus. Also called *fallopian tube*.

ovulation The regular monthly release in the female of one or more eggs from an ovary.

parental control The degree of flexibility exhibited by a parent in terms of enforcing rules and disciplining her or his child(ren).

parental support The amount of caring, closeness, and affection a parent exhibits or gives to her or his child(ren).

parent-arranged marriage A practice, common in non-industrialized societies, in which the parents of the bride and groom select the future spouse and arrange the marriage ceremony. Based on the principle that the elders in a community have the wisdom to select an appropriate spouse, this type of marriage generally extends existing family units rather than creating new units. *See also* couple-arranged marriage.

partner dominance The degree to which a person feels her or his partner tries to be controlling and dominant in their relationship.

passion Intense physiological arousal; the motivational component of Sternberg's three dimensions of love.

passive communication A style of interpersonal communication characterized by an unwillingness to say what one thinks, feels, or wants.

passive–aggressive behavior Feigning agreement or acting as if everything is okay but later becoming hostile or aggressive; an indirect way of expressing anger.

patriarchal group A group in which the father or eldest male is recognized as the head of the family, kinship group, or tribe. Descent is traced through this man.

patrilineal society A society in which descent, or lineage, is traced through males.

patrilocal society A society that encourages newly married couples to live with or near the husband's kin, especially his father's kinship group.

perennial philosophy Though religions around the world are remarkably diverse and fascinating to learn about, many theologians and philosophers have argued since at least the sixteenth century that there is a perennial philosophy—an eternal philosophy, if you will—that all great world religions share and that unites them in a common view of that which is sacred in life.

permissive parenting A style of parenting in which the parents (1) permit the child's preferences to take over their ideals and (2) rarely force the child to conform to their standards.

permissiveness The extent to which couples are physically intimate before marriage.

personal coping resources Qualities that help people deal with stressors across the life cycle, such as an individual's self-esteem and mastery (confidence in personal abilities). *See also* family coping resources.

personification The belief that everything one's partner does is a reflection on oneself; leads to attempts to control the partner's behavior.

persuasive listening A style of listening in which the "listener" is looking only for an opportunity to take over and control the direction of the conversation.

placenta A vascular organ that joins the fetus with the mother's uterus and through which the fetus receives nutrients and discharges wastes; expelled in the final stage of labor, following the birth of the baby.

plural marriage A marriage in which a man has more than one wife (polygyny) or a woman has more than one husband (polyandry).

polyandry A plural marriage in which a woman has more than one husband.

polygamy A marriage in which a man or a woman has more than one mate; a plural marriage.

polygyny A plural marriage in which a man has more than one wife.

positive communication One of the six major qualities (commonly found in emotionally healthy families) identified by researchers working from a family strengths perspective.

positive feedback Information or communication that is intended to create change in a system.

postmodernism A belief system that emphasizes multiple perspectives or "truths." Postmodernists are extremely skeptical in regard to questions of truth, meaning, and historical interpretation. No objective, universal truth can be seen, once and for all, and readily agreed upon. Instead, there is only a collection of subjective truths shaped by the particular subcultures in which we live. These multiple subjective truths are constantly competing for our attention and allegiance.

postpartum depression A feeling of depression after giving birth, characterized by irritability, crying, loss of appetite, and difficulty sleeping; thought to be a result of the many physiological changes that occur after delivery.

posttraumatic stress disorder (PTSD) A severe stress reaction characterized by the reexperiencing of past traumatic events.

power The ability of an individual in a social system to change the behavior of other members of the system through will, influence, or control.

prejudice Negative judgment or opinion having no or limited basis in fact; hostility to a person or a group based on physical characteristics.

premature ejaculation A sexual dysfunction in which a man is unable to control his ejaculation reflex voluntarily and reaches orgasm sooner than he or his partner wishes.

PREPARE A comprehensive premarital inventory that assesses a couple's relationship and determines how idealistic or realistic each person is in regard to marriage, how well the couple communicates, and how well the couple resolves conflicts and financial issues; acronym for **PRE**-marital **P**ersonal **A**nd **R**elationship **E**valuation.

problem drinking Alcohol consumption that results in functional disability.

progestin A hormone connected with pregnancy and contained in oral contraceptives.

pseudo–kin group A type of kinship group in which relationships resembling kinship ties develop among "unrelated" individuals.

psychodynamic theory Developed by Freud and his followers, a theory of human development that emphasizes the importance of providing a positive emotional environment during early childhood, when the foundation for later life is laid down.

psychosocial sexual dysfunction Impairment of the ordinary physical responses of sexual excitement or orgasm as a result of psychological, developmental, interpersonal, environmental, or cultural factors; these causes of sexual problems include untreated anxiety or depression and long-term stress.

pursuer An individual who wants a very high degree of togetherness and expression of feelings in a relationship.

Q

qualitative research Qualitative research in the field of family science tends to focus on family members' perceptions of their world and how they live in it. Data are recorded in the form of words and stories that the family members tell. These verbal or written perceptions are analyzed by researchers looking for common themes that explain the processes of life in families.

quantitative research Quantitative research in the field of family science reduces family members' attitudes and behaviors to numbers that can be analyzed using statistical methods. Rather than work with the words and stories collected in qualitative investigations, quantitative researchers work with data that are numerical.

quid pro quid A strategy for negotiating differences in which one person gets to do what he or she wants in exchange for doing something another person requests; "this for this."

quid pro quo A strategy for negotiating differences in which one person agrees to do something in exchange for the other person's agreement to do something else of equal value or importance; "this for that."

rejecting parenting A style of parenting in which parents pay little attention to their children's needs and set few or no expectations for their children's behavior.

remarriage A marriage in which one or both partners marry following divorce or the death of a spouse; in this book, remarriage refers to couples who have never been married to each other before.

representative sample A random selection of individuals who accurately reflect the characteristics of a particular group.

research study Careful, systematic, and patient investigation in a field of knowledge to establish facts or principles, test hypotheses, or better understand processes.

role The expected behavior of a person or group in a given social category, such as husband, wife, supervisor, or teacher.

role making The process of creating new roles or revising existing roles.

role taking The process whereby people learn how to play roles correctly by practicing and getting feedback from others.

romantic love A type of love relationship characterized by intimacy and passion but lacking commitment.

routinization A situation, often encountered in middle age, in which one's job lacks the challenge it once offered and becomes boring.

S

sandwich generation Parents, usually in their 50s and older, who are simultaneously responsible for child rearing and for caring for their own aging parents; individuals who are "caught in the middle" between two generations.

segregation Isolation of an ethnic group within the dominant culture.

self-confidence A measure of how a person feels about herself or himself and the ability to control things in her or his life.

self-disclosure Revealing to another person personal information or feelings that that individual could not otherwise learn.

sex Being biologically male or female; also, sexual activity or behavior. *See also* gender.

sex educator A trained teacher who provides information and principles about sex and sexuality, generally in a group setting.

aroused even when she wishes to have sex.

sexual dysfunction A state in which one's sexual behavior or lack of it is a source of distress; any malfunction of the human sexual response that inhibits the achievement of orgasm, either alone or with a partner.

sexual orientation A person's self-identification as a heterosexual, homosexual, bisexual, or transgender.

sexual pain disorder The woman experiences pain during sexual contact.

sexuality The set of beliefs, values, and behaviors by which one defines oneself as a sexual being.

sibling abuse Physical violence between siblings; probably the most common form of abuse of children.

SIDS *See* sudden infant death syndrome.

simple stepfamily A stepfamily that includes children from only one parent. *See also* complex stepfamily.

singlehood The state of being unmarried, divorced, or unattached to another person.

social construction framework A conceptual framework that proposes that human beings are profoundly immersed in the social world and that our understanding of this world and beliefs about this world are social products.

social environment All the factors, both positive and negative, in society that impact individuals and their relationships, such as mass media, the Internet, changing gender roles, and growing urban crowding.

social learning theory A psychological theory of development that focuses on learning through observation, imitation, and reinforcement.

social system One of the four major components of the sociocultural context in which families live; encompasses the influence of the community, laws, economic resources, educational opportunities, and other external factors on the family. *See also* belief system; extended-family system; family system.

sole custody A child custody arrangement following a divorce in which only one parent has legal and physical custody of the child or children; the other parent generally has visitation rights.

spacious nest A positive descriptive term for the time in a marriage when the children have left home. *See also* empty-nest syndrome.

sperm The male reproductive cells produced by the testes.

spermicide A contraceptive substance (gel, cream, foam, or vaginal insert) that is toxic to sperm; usually used with a barrier device; may protect against certain sexually transmitted diseases.

spiritual well-being One of the six major qualities (commonly found in emotionally healthy families) identified by researchers working within the family strengths framework.

split custody A legal child custody arrangement following a divorce in which each parent has sole custody of one or more of the children.

STD *See* sexually transmitted disease.

stepfamily The family created when one or both partners in a marriage have a child or children from a previous marriage. *See also* blended family.

stepparent An adult who is married to one's biological parent but who is not one's birth parent.

Stepping Ahead Program An eight-step program designed to build strengths in stepfamilies.

stereotype A standardized, oversimplified, often foolish and mean-spirited view of someone or something.

sterilization Any procedure, but usually a surgical one, by which an individual is made incapable of reproduction.

stress The nonspecific response of the body to any demand made upon it.

stress pileup The occurrence and after-effects of several stresses within a short period of time, which can strain an individual's or a family's coping abilities.

stressor An external event that causes an emotional and/or a physical response and that can precipitate a crisis.

strong family Two or more people who share significant relationship strengths, which are likely to include appreciation and affection for each other; commitment to the family; positive communication with each other; enjoyable time together; a sense of spiritual well-being; and the ability to manage stress and crisis effectively. Also can be defined as people who love and care for each other.

subsystem In the general systems theory, a small system that is part of a larger suprasystem.

sudden infant death syndrome (SIDS) The sudden, unexpected death of an infant, which cannot be explained by postmortem examination or tests.

suprasystem In the general systems theory, a large system that incorporates smaller subsystems.

symbolic interaction framework A conceptual framework that focuses on the internal perceptions of family members and examines how they learn roles and rules in society through interaction and shared meaning.

syncratic power pattern A power pattern in a marriage in which both partners share authority equally and make decisions jointly.

system A set of interconnected components that form a whole; what happens to one component affects all the other components.

T

tender years doctrine The legal presumption under traditional divorce laws that young children would do better with their mother than with their father after a divorce.

theory Systematically organized knowledge applicable in a wide variety of circumstances; especially, a system of assumptions, accepted principles, and rules of procedure devised to analyze, predict, or otherwise explain the nature or behavior of a specified set of phenomena.

traditional couple A type of premarital and married couple characterized by some external strengths (such as religion and friends) but fewer internal strengths (such as communication and conflict resolution skills).

transgender An individual who believes that he or she is a victim of a biologic accident that occurred before birth and has been living within a body incompatible with his or her real gender identity. A majority of transgender persons are biologic males who identify themselves as females, usually early in childhood.

transition stage of grief The period during which the bereaved's grief lessens and he or she begins to recognize that a new life is possible; the second of Brubaker's three stages of the grieving process. *See also* crisis-loss stage of grief; new-life stage of grief.

traumatic brain injury Damage to the brain, usually the result of a sudden, violent blow to the head that launches the brain on a collision course with the inside of the skull. This collision can bruise the brain, tear nerve fibers, and cause bleeding. The resulting symptoms can include severe headaches, problems with memory, confusion, an inability to follow directions, depression, and difficulty concentrating.

trimester One of three periods of about 3 months each into which pregnancy is divided.

tubal ligation A female sterilization procedure in which the oviducts (fallopian tubes) are cut or tied and sealed.

U

umbilical cord A flexible structure that connects the fetus to the placenta and through which nutrients pass to the fetus and waste products are discharged.

unbalanced families Families who fall at the extremes on both the flexibility and the cohesion dimensions of the Couple and Family Map: chaotically enmeshed, chaotically disengaged, rigidly enmeshed, or rigidly disengaged, families. *See also* balanced families; midrange families.

uncontested divorce Under traditional divorce law, a divorce in which one party would charge the other party with an infraction that was considered by the court as grounds for granting a divorce and the accused party would agree not to challenge the accuser in court. In many cases, parties were forced to collude and to perjure themselves in order to divorce.

V

vacuum aspiration An abortion method, used during the first trimester of pregnancy, in which the uterine contents are removed by suction.

vaginismus A sexual dysfunction in which a woman's vaginal muscles involuntarily constrict, preventing intercourse; a muscular contraction that causes the vagina to close. Vaginismus is usually an anxiety reaction before coitus or a pelvic examination.

validation The process of ensuring that a research instrument measures what it is intended to measure.

vasectomy A male sterilization procedure in which the vasa deferentia are severed and tied.

wholeness A characteristic of systems; general systems theorists believe that the whole is more than the sum of its parts.

wife-dominant power pattern A power pattern in a marriage in which the woman is the boss.

Z

zero-sum game A game in which one side's margin of victory equals the other side's margin of defeat, producing a final sum of zero; what one person wins, the other loses.

zygote The fertilized ovum (egg).

AARP. (2005). Sexuality at midlife and beyond. Web site: http://www.aarp.org.

AARP. (2013). Web site: http://www.aarp.org.

AARP. (n.d.). Sex and Intimacy. Retrieved from http://www.aarp.org/hom-family/sex-intimacy.

AARP. (n.d.). Sexuality at midlife and beyond. Web site: http://www.aarp.org.

AARP. (n.d.). Web site: http://www.aarp.org. AARP is a large, well-known, and politically powerful organization providing information and advocacy for people age 50 and older.

American Association of Sexuality Educators, Counselors and Therapists (AASECT). A not-for-profit, interdisciplinary professional organization promoting the understanding of human sexuality and healthy sexual behavior. "AASECT members include sexuality educators, sexuality counselors and sex therapists, physicians, nurses, social workers, psychologists, allied health professionals, clergy members, lawyers, sociologists, marriage and family counselors and therapists, family planning specialists and researchers, as well as students in relevant professional disciplines. Web site: http://www.aasect.org/.

ABC News. (2012). U.S. gun homicide rate higher than other developed countries. Web site: http:///abcnews.go.com/blogs/headlines/2012/12/us-gun-ownership-homicide-rate-higher-than-other-develo…

ABC News–Washington Post. (2001, January 11–15). Poll: Views about abortion. Cited in T. Raum. Associated Press (2001, January 23). Bush's early gamble: The new president will find it hard to finesse the thorny issue of abortion. Lincoln [NE] Journal Star, p. 5A.

Abma, J. C., et al. (2004). Teenagers in the United States: Sexual activity, contraceptive use, and childbearing, 2002. Vital and Health Statistics, 23(24). Web site: http://www.cdc.gov/nchs/data/series/sr_23/sr23_024.pdf.

Abma, J. C., Martinez, G. M., Mosher, W. D., & Dawson, B. S. (2004, December). Teenagers in the United States: Sexual activity, contraceptive use, and childbearing, Series 23, Number 24. Washington, DC: Centers for Disease Control and Prevention.

Abortion foes vow to fight: Maryland's governor OKs abortion-rights law. (1991, February 19). Lincoln [NE] Journal Star, p. 2.

About.com. (2012). 23.5 million Americans in recovery. Web site: http://www.alcoholism.about.com/b/2012/03/07/23-5-million-americans-in-recovery.htm.

Abrahms, S. (2012, June). Aarp.org/bulletin. Washington, D.C. American Association of Retired Persons.

Adams, M., & Coltrane, S. (2007). Framing divorce reform: Media, morality, and the politics of family. Family Process, 46, 17–34.

Addis, M. E. (2008). Gender and depression in men. Clinical Psychology: Science and Practice, 15(3), 153–168.

Addis, M. E., & Mahalik, J. R. (2003). Men, masculinity, and the context of help seeking. American Psychologist, 58(1), 5–14.

Adler-Baeder, F., Kerpelman, J. L., Schramm, D. G., Higginbotham, B., & Paulk, A. (2007). The impact of relationship education on adolescents of diverse backgrounds. Family Relations, 56 (July), 291–303.

Adler, N. E., David, H. P., Major, B. N., Roth, S. H., Russo, N. F., & Wyatt, G. E. (1992). Psychological factors in abortion: A review. American Psychologist, 47, 1194–1204.

Adler, N. E., Ozer, E. J., & Tschann, J. (2003, March). Abortion among adolescents. American Psychologist, 211–217.

Administration for Children and Families. (2003). Child maltreatment 2001. U.S. Department of Health and Human Services. Washington, DC: http://www.acf.hhs .gov/programs/cb/publications/cm01/index.htm.

Administration for Children and Families. (2004). Child maltreatment 2002. U.S. Department of Health and Human Services. Washington, DC: http://www.acf.hhs.gov.programs/cb/publications/cm02/chapterthree.htm.

Administration for Children and Families. (2007). The Healthy Marriage Initiative. Web site: http://www.acf.hhs.gov/healthymarriage/about/mission.html#ms.

Administration for Children and Families. (2010). The Healthy Marriage Initiative. Web site: http://www.acf.hhs.gov/healthymarriage.

Administration for Children and Families. (2012). The Healthy Marriage Initiative. Web site: http://www.acf.hhs.gov/healthymarriage/.

Administration on Aging. (2011). Aging statistics. Web site: http://www.aoa.gov/aoaroot/aging_statistics/index.aspx.

Advocates for Youth. "Established in 1980 as the Center for Population Options, Advocates for Youth champions efforts that help young people make informed and responsible decisions about their reproductive and sexual health. Advocates believes it can best serve the field by boldly advocating for a more positive and realistic approach to adolescent sexual health." The work focuses on 14- to 25-year-olds in the United States and internationally. Web site: http://www.advocatesforyouth.org.

Advocates for Youth. (2010a). Are parents and teens talking about sex? Web site: http://www.advocatesforyouth.org/index.php?option=com_content&task=view&id=136&Itemid=206.

Advocates for Youth. (2010b). Comprehensive sex education: Research and results. Web site: http://www.advocatesforyouth.org.

AFL-CIO and the Institute for Women's Policy Research. (1999). Equal pay for working families: National and state data. http://www.aflcio.org/issuepolitics/women/equalpay/EqualPayForWorkingFamilies.cfm.

Ahlburg, D. A., Jensen, E. R., & Perez, A. E. (1997). Determinants of extramarital sex in the Philippines. *Health Transition Review,* Suppl. to Vol. 7, pp. 467–479.

Ahrons, C. (2007). Family ties after divorce: Long-term implications for children. *Family Process, 46,* 53–65.

Ahrons, C. R. (2003). *The binuclear family study 1979–2000.* Harvard University, The Radcliffe Institute for Advanced Study, Murray Research Center.

Ahrons, C. R. (2004). *We're still family: What grown children have to say about their parents' divorce.* New York: HarperCollins.

Ahrons, C. R. (2006, May/June). Long-term effects of divorce on children. *Family Therapy Magazine,* pp. 24–27.

Aiken, L. R. (2004). *Dying, death, and bereavement* (4th ed.). Mahwah, NJ: Erlbaum. A brief but comprehensive survey of research, writings, and professional practices on death and dying.

Alan Guttmacher Institute. (1999). *Teenage pregnancy: Overall trends and state-by-state information* (Table 1). New York: Author.

Alan Guttmacher Institute. (2000). *Induced abortion.* New York: Author (http://www.agi-usa-org/pubs/fb_induced_abortion.html).

Alan Guttmacher Institute. (2002). Teen pregnancy: Trends and lessons learned. *The Guttmacher Report on Public Policy, 5*(1), 2.

Alan Guttmacher Institute. (2008). Facts on induced abortion in the United States. Web site: http://www.guttmacher.org/pubs/fb_induced_abortion.html.

Alan Guttmacher Institute. (2009a). Get "in the know": 20 questions about pregnancy, contraception and abortion. Web site: http://www.guttmacher.org/in-the-know/index.html.

Alan Guttmacher Institute. (2009b). Facts on contraceptive use. Web site: http://www.guttmacher.org/pubs/fb_contr_use.html.

Alan Guttmacher Institute. (2009c). Get "in the know": Questions about pregnancy, contraception and abortion. Web site: http://www.guttmacher.org/in-the-know/incidence.html.

Alan Guttmacher Institute. (2009d). Safety of abortion. Web site: http://www.guttmacher.org/in-the-know/safety.html.

Al-Anon/Alateen. (2010). Is your life affected by someone else's drinking? Web site: http://www.al-anon.alateen.org/english.html.

Al-Anon/Alateen. (2012a). About us. Web site: http://al-anon/alateen.org.

Al-Anon/Alateen. (2012b). Online Al-Anon outreach. Web site: http://www.ola-is.org/.

Al-Anon/Alateen. (2013). "For over 55 years, Al-Anon (which includes Alateen for younger members) has been offering strength and hope for friends and families of problem drinkers. It is estimated that each alcoholic affects the lives of at least four other people . . . alcoholism is truly a family disease. No matter what relationship you have with an alcoholic, whether they are still drinking or not, all who have been affected by someone else's drinking can find solutions that lead to serenity in the Al-Anon/Alateen fellowship." Web site: http://www.al-anon.alateen.-org/english.html.

Alberti, R., & Emmons, M. (2008). *Your perfect right: Assertiveness and equality in your life and relationships* (9th ed.). Atascadero, CA: Impact.

Alcoholics Anonymous. (2010). Information on A.A. Web site: http://www.aa.org/lang-/en/subpage.cfm?page=1.

Alcoholics Anonymous. (2012a). Estimates of A.A. groups and members as of January 1, 2012. Web site: http://www.aa.org/en_pdfs/smf-53_en.pdf.

Alcoholics Anonymous. (2012b). Welcome to AA. Web site: http://www.aa.org/ Education and support for alcoholics from other alcoholics.

Alcoholics Anonymous. (2012c). Welcome to AAOnline! Web site: http://www.aaonline.org/.

Alcoholics Anonymous Meetings in Los Angeles County, California. (2012). Web site: http://www.simeetings.com/LA/LAMtgs.html.

Alcoholics Anonymous. (2012a). Welcome to AA. Web site: http://www.aa.org/. Education and support for alcoholics from other alcoholics.Alcoholics Anonymous. (2012b). Welcome to AAOnline! Web site: http://www.aaonline.org/.

Alcoholics Anonymous. (2013). In their own words, AA is "a fellowship of men and women who share their experience, strength and hope with each other that they may solve their common problem and help others to recover from alcoholism. The only requirement for membership is a desire to stop drinking." AA charges no dues or fees for membership and is self-supporting through member contributions. It is not allied with any sect, denomination, politics, organization, or institution. AA does not wish to engage in any controversy, and neither endorses nor opposes any causes. "Our primary purpose is to stay sober and help other alcoholics to achieve sobriety." Web site: http://www.aa.org/lang/en/subpage.cfm/page=1.

Aldous, J. (1998). Public policy and grandparents: Contrasting perspectives. In M. E. Szinovacz (Ed.), *Handbook on grandparenthood* (pp. 230–246). Westport, CT: Greenwood.

Aldwin, C. M., & Levenson, M. R. (2001). Stress, coping, and health at midlife: A developmental perspective. In M. E. Lachman (Ed.), *Handbook of midlife development,* pp. 188–216. New York: John Wiley.

Aldwin, C. M., Park, C. L., Spiro, A. III, & Abeles, R. P. (2007). *Handbook of health psychology and aging.* New York: The Guilford Press. How biological, psychological, and social factors over the life course affect aging.

Allen, E. S., Rhoades, G., Stanley, S. M., Loew, B., & Markman, H. J. (2012). The effects of marriage education for army couples with a history of infidelity. *Journal of Family Psychology, 26,* 26–35.

Allen, K. (December, 2007). The missing right to same-sex divorce. *Family Focus, 2,* 17.

Allen, K. R., Blieszner, R., & Roberto, K. A. (2000). Families in the middle and later years: A review and critique of research in the 1990s. *Journal of Marriage and the Family, 62*(4), 911–926.

Allen, S. M., & Hawkins, A. J. (1999). Mothers' beliefs and behaviors that inhibit greater father involvement in family. *Journal of Marriage and the Family, 61,* 199–212.

Allen, W. D., & Olson, D. H. (2001). Five types of African-American marriages based on ENRICH. *Journal of Marital and Family Therapy, 27*(3), 301–314.

Allgeier, E. R., & Allgeier, A. R. (2000). *Sexual interactions: Basic understandings* (6th ed.). Boston: Houghton Mifflin.

Alzheimer's Foundation of America (n.d.). Web site: http://alzidn.org/index.htm.

Amato, P. (2007). Divorce and the well-being of adults and children. *Family Focus, 52*, F3–F4, F18.

Amato, P., Meyers, C. E., & Emery, R. E. (2009). Changes in nonresidential father-child contact from 1976 to 2002. *Family Relations, 58*, 41–53.

Amato, P. R. (2000). The consequences of divorce for adults and children. *Journal of Marriage and the Family, 62*(4), 1269–1287.

Amato, P. R., & Booth, A. (1997). *A generation at risk: Growing up in an era of family upheaval.* Cambridge, MA: Harvard University Press.

Amato, P. R., Kane, J. B., & James, S. (2011). Reconsidering the "Good Divorce." *Family Relations, 60*, 511–524.

American Academy of Pediatrics. (2005). Policy statement: Breastfeeding and the use of human milk. *Pediatrics, 115*(2), 496–506.

American Academy of Pediatrics. (2009). Breastfeeding initiatives. Web site: http://www.aap.org/publiced/BR_BFBenefits.htm.

American Academy of Pediatrics. (2013). Working mothers. Web site: http://www2aap.org/publiced/BK)_WorkingMothers.htm.

American Association for Marriage and Family Therapy. (n.d.). AAMFT is the key national organization for advancing the professional interests of marriage and family therapists, and it has excellent educational resources for professionals and laypersons on its Web site: http://www.aamft.org.

American Association for Marital and Family Therapy. (2010). Infidelity. Web site: http://www.aamft.org/.

American Association for Marital and Family Therapy. (2012a). Infidelity. Web site: http://www.aamft.org/imis15/content/Consumer_Updates/Infidelity.aspx.

American Association for Marital and Family Therapy (2012a). Infidelity. Web site: http://aamft.org/imis15/content/Consumer_Updates/Infidelity.aspx.

American Association for Marital and Family Therapy. (2012b). Online infidelity. Web site: http://www.aamft.org/imis15/Content/Consumer_Updates/Online_Infidelity.aspx.

American Association for Marriage and Family Therapy. (2012). Home page. Web site: http://aamft.org.

American Association for Marriage and Family Therapy (AAMFT). (2012). Founded in 1942, AAMFT is the professional association for the field of marriage and family therapy, representing the professional interests of more than 24,000 marriage and family therapists in the United States, Canada, and abroad. AAMFT publishes the *Journal of Marital and Family Therapy* and *Family Therapy Magazine*. Web site: www.aamft.org.

American Association for Marriage and Family Therapy (n.d.). Retrieved from http://www.aamft.org.

/epublic/live/g1881/build/g1881.pdf.

American Heritage Dictionary of the English Language (4th ed.). (2000). Boston: Houghton Mifflin.

American Heritage Dictionary of the English Language. (2012). Family. Web site: http://www.ahdictionary.com/word/search.html?q=family.

American Humane Association. (2012). Facts about animal abuse and domestic violence. Web site: http://www.americanhumane.org/interaction/support-the-bond/fact-sheets/animal-abuse-domestic-violen…

American Planning Association. (2011). *Child care and sustainable community development.* Retrieved from www.planning.org.

American Psychological Association. (2004). *Resolution on sexual orientation, parents and children.* Web site: www.apa.org/pi/lgbc.

American Psychological Association. (2008, August 13). Report of the APA Task Force on Mental Health and Abortion. Web site: http://www.apa.-org/releases/abortion-report.pdf.

American Psychological Association. (2010). Sexual orientation and homosexuality. Web site: http://www.apa.org/helpcenter/sexual-orientation.aspx.

amFAR AIDS Research. (2004). Global initiatives. Web site: http://www.amfar.org/cgi-bin/iowa/programs/globali/record.html?record=87.

Anderson, B. L. (2010). *Finances in strong African American marriages* (Unpublished master's thesis). Utah State University, Logan, Utah.

Anderson, C. (2003). The diversity, strengths, and challenges of single-parent households. In F. Walsh (Ed.), *Normal family process* (3rd ed., pp. 121–152). New York: Guilford Press.

Anderson, J. R., & Doherty, W. J. (2005). Democratic community initiatives: The case of overscheduled children. *Family Relations, 54*, 654–665.

Annenberg Center for the Digital Future, University of Southern California. (2009). Family time decreasing with Internet use. Web site: http://Annenberg.usc.edu/News%20and%Events/News/090615CDF.aspx.

Antonovics, K., & Town, R. (2004). Are all the good men married? Uncovering the sources of the marital wage premium. *American Economic Review, 68*(1), 137–154.

Apter, T. (2009). *What do you want from me?* New York: Norton.

Arditti, J., Burton, L., & Neeves-Botelho, S. (2010). Maternal distress and parenting in the context of cumulative disadvantage. *Family Process, 49*, 142–164.

Arias, E., Anderson, R. N., Kung, H., Murphy, S. L., & Kochanek, K. D. (2004). Deaths: Final data for 2001. *National Vital Statistics Reports, 50*(15). Hyattsville, MD: National Center for Health Statistics. Web site: http://www.cdc.gov/nchs/data/nvsr/nvsr52/nvsr52_03.pdf.

Arias, E., & Smith, B. L. (2003). Deaths: Preliminary data for 2001. *National Vital Statistics Reports, 52*(3), 21. Hyattsville, MD: National Center for Health Statistics. Web site: www.cdc.gov.

Arias, I., & Pape, K. T. (1999). Psychological abuse: Implications for adjustment and commitment to leave violent partners. *Violence and Victims, 14*(1), 55–67.

Arnett, J. J. (2000). Emerging adulthood: A theory of development from the late teens through the twenties. *American Psychologist, 55,* 469–480.

Arnett, J. J. (2004). *Emerging adulthood: The winding road from the late teen through the twenties.* New York: Oxford University Press.

Arnett, J. J. (2011). Emerging adulthood(s): The cultural psychology of a new life stage. In L. A. Jensen (Ed.), *Bridging cultural and developmental approaches to psychology: New syntheses in theory, research, and policy* (pp. 255–275). New York: Oxford University Press.

Arond, M., & Pauker, S. L. (1987). *The first year of marriage.* New York: Warner Books.

Asai, S. G. (2004). Culturally sensitive adaptation of PREPARE with Japanese premarital couples. *Journal of Marital and Family Therapy, 30*(4), 411–426.

Asai, S. G., & Olson, D. H. (2004). *National couple abuse study.* Roseville, MN: Life Innovations. Web site: http://lifeinnovations.com.

Asay, S. M., DeFrain, J., Metzger, M., & Moyer, B. (2013). *Family violence from a global perspective: A strengths-based approach.* Thousand Oaks, CA: Sage.

Asay, S. M., DeFrain, J., Metzger, M., & Moyer, R. (2013). *Family violence from a global perspective: Strengths-based research and case studies.* Thousand Oaks, CA: Sage.

Atwood, J., & Genovese, F. (2006). *Therapy with single parents: A social constructivist approach.* New York: Haworth Press.

Australian Government. (2008). *Families in Australia: 2008.* Canberra: Department of Prime Minister and Cabinet, p. 1.

Australian Institute of Family Studies. (2010). Effects of child abuse and neglect for children and adolescents. Web site: http://www.aifs.gov.au/nch/pubs/sheets/rs17/4s17.html.

Avenevoli, S., Sessa, F. M., & Steinberg, L. (1999). Family structure, parenting practices, and adolescent adjustment. In E. M. Hetherington (Ed.), *Coping with divorce, single parenting and remarriage* (pp. 65–90). Mahwah, NJ: Erlbaum.

Axtell, R. E. (2007). *Essential do's and taboos: The complete guide to international business and leisure travel.* Hoboken, NJ: Wiley.

Axtell, R. E. (2007). *Essential do's and taboos: The complete guide to international business and leisure travel.* Hoboken, NJ: Wiley. A fun and funny book.

Axtell, R. G. (1999). *Do's and taboos of humor around the world: Stories and tips from business and life.* New York: Wiley.

Azar, S. T., & Bober, S. L. (1999). Children of abusive parents. In W. K. Silverman & T. O. Ollendick (Eds.), *Developmental issues in the clinical treatment of children* (pp. 371–392). Needham Heights, MA: Allyn & Bacon.

Azar, S. T., & Gehl, K. S. (1999). Physical abuse and neglect. In R. T. Ammerman et al. (Eds.), *Handbook of prescriptive treatments for children and adolescents* (2nd ed., pp. 329–345). Needham Heights, MA: Allyn & Bacon.

Babycenter. (2011, July). *How much you'll spend on childcare.* Retrieved from http://www.babycenter.com/0_how-much-youll-spend-on-childcare_1199776.bc.

Baca Zinn, M., & Pok, A. Y. H. (2002). Tradition and transition in Mexican-origin families. In R. L. Taylor (Ed.), *Minority families in the United States: A multicultural perspective* (pp. 77–100). Upper Saddle Creek, NJ: Prentice Hall.

Bach, G., & Wyden, P. (1969). *The intimate enemy: How to fight fair in love and marriage.* New York: Morrow.

Bachman, H. J., & Chase-Lansdale, P. L. (2005). Custodial grandmothers' physical, mental, and economic well-being: Comparisons of primary caregivers from low-income neighborhoods. *Family Relations, 54,* 475–487.

Bailey, S. J. (2003). Challenges and strengths in nonresidential parenting following divorce. *Marriage and Family Review, 35*(1/2), 59–80.

Baldry, A. C. (2003). Animal abuse and exposure to interpersonal violence in Italian youth. *Journal of Interpersonal Violence, 18*(3), 258–281.

Baldwin, S. E., & Baranoski, M. V. (1990). Family interactions and sex education in the home. *Adolescence, 25,* 573–582.

Bámaca, M. Y., Umaña-Taylor, A. J., Shin, N., & Alfaro, E. C. (2005). Latino adolescents' perception of parenting behaviors and self-esteem: Examining the role of neighborhood risk. *Family Relations, 54,* 621–632.

Barry, E. (2007, February). Eagerness and some resignation as Civil Union Law takes effect. *The New York Times.* Web site: http://www.nytimes.com/2007/02/20/nyregion/20civil.html.

Barta, P. L. (2001). Blended families: How to make sense of your new stepfamily. *In Touch.* Missoula, MT: APS Healthcare.

Bartholomae, S., & Fox, J. J. (2008, June). The "unbanked"— Families on the financial fringe. *Family Focus, 38,* 3, 5.

Bass, B. L., Butler, A. B., Grzywacz, J. G., & Linney, K. D. (2009). Do job demands undermine parenting? A daily analysis of spillover and crossover effects. *Family Relations, 58,* 201–215.

Bateson, G., Jackson, D. D., Haley, J., & Weakland, J. (1956). Toward a theory of schizophrenia. *Behavioral Science, 1,* 251–264.

Bauer, J. W., & Wollen, B. J. (1990). *Financial management extension consultant program: Young singles and young couples.* St. Paul: Minnesota Extension Service.

Baumbusch, J. L. (2004). Unclaimed treasures: Older women's reflections on lifelong singlehood. *Journal of Women and Aging, 16*(1/2), 105–121. Lifelong single women strongly emphasize their independence and "ability to be alone" as significant benefits, while discussing drawbacks, including loneliness and the absence of a social support network, which became more important as they experienced increasing age and frailty.

Baumrind, D. (1991). The influence of parenting style on adolescent competence and substance abuse. *Journal of Early Adolescence, 11*(1), 56–95.

Baumrind, D. (1995). *Child maltreatment and optimal caregiving in social contexts.* New York: Garland.

Baumrind, D. (1996). The discipline controversy revisited. *Family Relations, 45,* 405–414.

Bauserman, R. (2002). Child adjustment in joint-custody versus sole-custody arrangements: A meta-analytic review. *Journal of Family Psychology, 16*(1), 23–35.

BBC News. (2004, November 16). STUC urges gender pay gap action. Web site: http://news.bbc.co.uk/go/pr/fr/-/2/us_news/scotland/4013675.stm.

BBC News. (2012). Abused by their own children. Web site: http://news.bbc.co.uk/2/hi/uk_news/magazine/8366113.stm.

html.

Bell, R. Q. (1977). *Child effects on adults*. Hillsdale, NJ: Erlbaum.

Bellous, J. E. (2010). *Children, spirituality, loss and recovery*. New York: Routledge.

Belsky, J., & Hsieh, K. H. (1998). Patterns of marital change during the early childhood years: Parent personality, coparenting and division-of-labor correlates. *Journal of Family Psychology, 12*(4), 511–528.

Belsky, J., & Kelly, J. (1994). *The transition to parenthood: How a first child changes a marriage: Why some couples grow closer and others apart*. New York: Delacorte.

Belsky, J. (2006). Early child care and early child development: Major findings of the NICHD study of early child care. *European Journal of Developmental Psychology, 3*, 95–110.

Bem, S. L. (1995). Dismantling gender polarization and compulsory heterosexuality: Should we turn the volume down or up? *Journal of Sex Research, 32*(4), 329–334.

Bent-Goodley, T. B. (2005). An African-centered approach to domestic violence. *Families in Society, 86*, 197–206.

Berger, L. M., Brown, P. R., Joung, E., Melli, M. S., & Wimer, L. (2008). The stability of child physical placements following divorce: Descriptive evidence from Wisconsin. *Journal of Marriage and the Family, 70*, 273–283.

Berger, R., & Hannah, M. T. (1999). *Preventive approaches in couples therapy*. Philadelphia: Brunner/Mazel.

Bergstrom, A., Clery, L. M., & Peacock, T. D. (2003). *The seventh generation: Native students speak about finding the Good Path*. Charleston, WV: Educational Resources Information Center (ERIC), Clearinghouse on Rural Education and Small Schools.

Berkow, R. (Ed.). (1997). *The Merck manual of medical information: Home edition*. White House Station, NJ: Merck Research Laboratories.

Berkowitz, D. (2009). Theorizing lesbian and gay parenting: Past, present, and future scholarship. *Journal of Family Theory & Review, 1*, 117–132.

Berkowitz, D., & Marsiglio, W. (2007). Gay men: Negotiating procreative, father, and family identities. *Journal of Marriage and the Family, 69*, 366–381.

Berman, J. (2010, September 15). What makes a family? Children, say many Americans. *ABC World News*. Web site: http://abcnews.go.com/WN/defines-family-children-americans-survey/story?id=11644693.

Bernard, J. (1970). Women, marriage, and the future. *Futurist, 4*, 41–43.

Bernard, J. (1972). *The future of marriage*. New York: World.

Berscheid, E. (1999). The greening of relationship science. *American Psychologist, 54*(4), 260–266.

Berscheid, E. (2006). Seasons of the heart. In M. Mikulincer & G. S. Goodman (Eds.), *Dynamics of romantic love: Attachment, caregiving, and sex* (pp. 404–422). New York: Guilford.

of education. In *Understanding the issues around forced marriage: "16 days of action to end violence against women."* Stirling, Scotland, November 26. Web site: http://eprints.soton.ac.uk/64141/.

Bhugra, D., Popelyuk, D., & McMullen, I. (2010). Paraphilias across cultures: Contexts and controversies. *Journal of Sex Research, 47*, 242–256.

Biblarz, T. J., & Stacey, J. (2010). How does the gender of parents matter? *Journal of Marriage and Family, 72*, 3–22.

Bierstedt, R. (1950). An analysis of social power. *American Sociological Review, 6*, 7–30.

Bigner, J., & Gottlieb, A. (2007). (Eds.). *Interventions with families of gay, lesbian, bisexual, and transgender people: From the inside out*. Binghamton, NY: Haworth Press.

Billingsley, A. (1986). *Black families in White America*. Englewood Cliffs, NJ: Prentice Hall.

Billingsley, A. (1992). *Climbing Jacob's ladder: The ending legacy of African-American families*. New York: Touchstone.

Binner, J. M., & Dnes, A. W. (2001). Marriage, divorce, and legal change: New evidence from England and Wales. *Economic Inquiry, 39*(2), 298–306.

Binson, D., Michaels, S., Stall, R., Coates, T. J., Gagnon, J. H., & Catania, J. A. (1995). Prevalence and social distribution of men who have sex with men: United States and its urban centers. *Journal of Sex Research, 32*(3), 245–254.

Biracial couples find more tolerance. (2001, July 6). Lincoln [NE] *Journal Star*, p. 5A.

Birditt, K. S., Rott, L. M., & Fingerman, K. L. (2009). "If you can't say something nice, don't say anything at all": Coping with interpersonal tensions in the parent-child relationship during adulthood. *Journal of Family Psychology, 23*(6), 769–778.

Bissell, M. (2000). Socio-economic outcomes of teen pregnancy and parenthood: A review of the literature. *Canadian Journal of Human Sexuality, 9*(3), 191–204.

Bjorklund, G. (1977). Historical perspectives on parent education in America. Paper presented at *Toward the Competent Parent: An Interdisciplinary Conference on Parenting*, Atlanta, February 21–22.

Blackman, L., Clayton, O., Glenn, N., Malone-Colon, L., & Roberts, A. (2005). *The consequences of marriage for African Americans: A comprehensive literature review*. New York: Institute for American Values.

Blankenhorn, D. (1999, December 6). Fatherhood on the rebound. *Christianity Today*, pp. 70–71.

Blankenhorn, D. (2004). About David Blankenhorn. American Values.org Web site: http://www.americanvalues.org/htmolabout_david_blankenhorn.html.

Blankenhorn, D. (2007). *The future of marriage*. New York: Encounter Books.

Bloch, E. (2007). The daddy difference. *Parenting, 21*(5), 81–84. The author argues that fathers let kids take risks while mothers are too protective because of their attachment to the child, which developed during pregnancy. And fathers trust themselves more than experts, while mothers are more sensitive to getting it right; they tend to compare notes with other parents more than dads do.

Blow, A. J., & Hartnett, K. (2005). Infidelity in committed relationships II: A substantive review. *Journal of Marital and Family Therapy, 31,* 217–233.

Bock, J. D. (2000). Doing the right thing? Single mothers by choice and the struggle for legitimacy. *Gender and Society, 14*(1), 62–86.

Bogle, K. A. (2008a). *Hooking up: Sex, dating and relationships on campus.* New York: New York University Press.

Bogle, K. A. (2008b). The sociology of "hooking up": An interview with Kathleen Bogle. *Inside Higher Education.* Web site: ttp://www.insidehighered.com/news/2008/01/29/hookups.

Bohannan, P. (1970). The six stations of divorce. In P. Bohannan (Ed.), *Divorce and after* (pp. 29–55). New York: Doubleday.

Boonstra, H. (2000). Promoting contraceptive use and choice: France's approach to teen pregnancy and abortion. *The Guttmacher Report on Public Policy, 3*(3).

Boonstra, H. D. (2007a). The case for a new approach to sex education mounts: Will policymakers heed the message? *Guttmacher Policy Review, 10*(2), p. 4. Web site: http://www.guttmacher.org/pubs/gpr/10/2/gpr100202.html.

Booth, A., Crouter, A. C., & Clements, M. (Eds). (2001). *Couples in conflict.* Mahwah, NJ: Erlbaum. A collection of insightful articles on conflict and conflict resolution in couples.

Booth, S. (2010, February). They're golden. *Real Simple,* pp. 127–135. "There's nothing so nice as a new marriage," the screenwriter Ben Hecht once wrote. But the six couples featured in this magazine story beg to differ. More than 50 years into their marriages, they share their unforgettable moments and secrets of staying together, happily.

Borcherdt, B. (1996). *Head over heart in love: 25 guides to rational passion.* Sarasota, FL: Professional Resource Press.

Borcherdt, B. (2000). *You can control your anger! 21 ways to do it.* Sarasota, FL: Professional Resource Press.

Borcherdt, B. (2000). *You can control your anger! 21 ways to do it.* Sarasota, FL: Professional Resource Press. A practical guide for people who would like to change.

Borders, L. D., Penny, J. M., & Portnoy, F. (2000). Adult adoptees and their friends: Current functioning and psychosocial well-being. *Family Relations, 49,* 407–418.

Bornstein, R. F. (2006). The complex relationship between dependency and domestic violence. *American Psychologist, 61,* 595–606.

Boss, P. (1988). *Family stress management.* Newbury Park, CA: Sage.

Boss, P. (1992). Primacy of perception in family stress theory and measurement. *Journal of Family Psychology, 6*(2), 113–119.

Boss, P. (1999). *Ambiguous loss: Learning to live with unresolved grief.* Cambridge, MA: Harvard University Press.

Boss, P. (2002). *Family stress management: A contextual approach.* Thousand Oaks, CA: Sage.

Boss, P. (2006). *Loss, trauma, and resilience: Therapeutic work with ambiguous loss.* Dunmore, PA: Norton.

Boss, P. (2007). Ambiguous loss theory: Challenges for scholars and practitioners. *Family Relations, 56,* 105–111.

Boss, P. (2011). *Loving someone who has dementia: How to find hope while coping with stress and grief.* San Francisco, CA: Jossey-Bass.

Boss, P., et al. (2009). *Sourcebook of family theories and methods: A contextual approach.* St. Paul, MN: Springer.

Boss, P., et al. (2009). *Sourcebook of family theories and methods: A contextual approach.* St. Paul, MN: Springer. An outstanding collection of family theories and family research methods.

Boston Women's Health Book Collective. (1998). *Our bodies, ourselves for the new century: A book by and for women.* New York: Touchstone/Simon & Schuster.

Boston Women's Health Book Collective. (2006). *Our bodies, ourselves: Menopause.* New York: Simon & Schuster.

Boston Women's Health Book Collective. (2006). *Our bodies, ourselves: Menopause.* New York: Touchstone/Simon & Schuster.

Boston Women's Health Book Collective. (2008). *Our bodies, ourselves: Pregnancy and birth.* New York: Touchstone/Simon & Schuster.

Boston Women's Health Book Collective. (2011). *Our bodies, ourselves.* New York: Simon & Schuster.

Boston Women's Health Collective. (2005). *Our bodies, ourselves: A new edition for a new era.* (35th anniversary edition). New York: Simon & Schuster.

Boulding, K. (1985). *Human betterment.* Beverly Hills, CA: Sage.

Bowen, G. L., Pittman, J. F., Pleck, J. H., Haas, L., & Voydanoff, P. (Eds.). (1995). *The work and family interface: Toward a contextual effects perspective.* Minneapolis: National Council on Family Relations.

Boyd-Franklin, N. (2003). *Black families in therapy: Understanding the African American experience* (2nd ed.). New York: Guilford Press.

Boyd-Franklin, N., Franklin, A. J., & Toussaint, P. A. (2000). *Boys into men: Raising our African American teenage sons.* New York: Dutton.

Boyd-Franklin, N., Franklin, A., & Toussaint, P. (2000). *Boys into men: Raising our African American teenage sons.* New York: Penguin Putnam. "A convincing argument to parents that educating an African-American teenage son and keeping him alive, healthy, and out of jail past the age of 25 years is no small task."

Bradford, K., Higginbotham, B., & Skogrand, L. (2013). Evaluation data from pre-marital classes. Unpublished raw data.

Bradford, K., Vaughn, L., & Barber, B. (2008). When there is conflict. *Journal of Family Issues, 29,* 780–805.

Braithwaite, D. (2008, December 11). Braithwaite delves into voluntary kin. *Scarlet.* Web site: http://scarlet.unl.edu/p=872.

Brandeis University Institute for Health Policy. (1993). Substance abuse: The nation's number one health problem. Cited by National Council on Alcoholism and Drug Dependence: http://www.ncadd.org.

Brandeis University Institute for Health Policy. (2001). Substance abuse: The nation's number one health problem. Cited by National Council on Alcoholism and Drug Dependence: http://www.ncadd.org.

"Breasts Shaped by Evolution for Babies, Not Men." (2010). Breastfeeding.com. Web site: http://www.breastfeeding.com/reading_room/breasts_shaped_babies.html.

Brick, P., & Taverner, B. (2001). *Positive images: Teaching abstinence, contraception, and sexual health* (3rd ed.). Morristown, NJ: Planned Parenthood of Greater Northern New Jersey.

quality of father–child and stepfather–stepchild relationships. *Dissertation Abstracts International-A, 63*(11), 4091.

Brown University Center for Alcohol and Addiction Studies. (2000). Position paper on drug policy. Physician Leadership on National Drug Policy. Cited by National Council on Alcoholism and Drug Dependence: http://www.ncadd.org.

Browning, R. (1970). Grow old along with me! In I. Jack (Ed.), *Browning: Poetical works.* Oxford, UK: Oxford University Press. (Original work published 1864.)

Brubaker, T. H. (1985). *Later life families.* Beverly Hills, CA: Sage.

Brubaker, T. H. (Ed.). (1990). *Family relationships in later life* (2nd ed.). Newbury Park, CA: Sage.

Brubaker, T. H. (1991). Families in later life: A burgeoning research area. In A. Booth (Ed.), *Contemporary families: Looking forward, looking back* (pp. 226–248). Minneapolis: National Council on Family Relations.

Bruce, M. L. (2002). Psychosocial risk factors for depressive disorders in late life. *Biological Psychiatry, 52*(3), 175–184.

Bryan, A. A. (1998). *Facilitating couple relationships during the transition to parenthood.* Unpublished doctoral dissertation, University of Wisconsin, Eau Claire, Department of Family Health Nursing.

Bryant, M. (2006). The divorce dilemma. Feature Story. Retrieved from University of Texas. Web site: http://www.utexas.edu/features/2006/divorce/index.html.

Bryant, J., & Bryant, J. A. (2001). *Television and the American family.* (2nd ed.). Mahwah, NJ: Erlbaum.

Buchanan, C. M., & Heiges, K. L. (2001). When conflict continues after the marriage ends: Effects of post-divorce conflict on children. In J. H. Grych & F. D. Fincham (Eds.), *Interparental conflict and child development: Theory, research, and applications* (pp. 337–362). New York: Cambridge University Press.

Buchanan, C. M., Maccoby, E. E., & Dornbusch, S. M. (1996). *Adolescents after divorce.* Cambridge, MA: Harvard University Press.

Buckingham, M., & Clifton, D. O. (2005). *Now, discover your strengths.* Lincoln, NE: Gallup Press.

Bumpass, L. (1999, March). (Interviewed by Nadya Labi.) A bad start: Living together may be the road to divorce. *Time,* p. 61.

Bumpass, L., & Lu, H. H. (1998). *Trends in cohabitation and implications for children's family contexts.* Unpublished manuscript, University of Wisconsin, Madison, Center for Demography.

Bumpass, L., & Lu, H. H. (2000a). Cohabitation: How the families of U.S. children are changing. *Focus, 21*(1), 5–8.

Bumpass, L., & Lu, H. H. (2000b). Trends in cohabitation and implications for children's family contexts in the United States. *Population Studies, 54,* 29–41.

Buono, A. J., & Weisenbach, S. (Eds.). (2004). *We met online! Stories of married Catholics who met their spouses on the Internet.* Philadelphia: Xlibris.

Buss, D. M., Shackelford, T. K., Kirkpatrick, L. A., & Larsen, R. J. (2001). A half century of mate preferences: The cultural evolution of values. *Journal of Marriage and the Family, 63,* 491–503.

Butler, M. H., Harper, J. M., & Seedall, R. B. (2009). Facilitated disclosure versus clinical accommodation of infidelity secrets: An early pivot point in couple therapy. *Journal of Marital and Family Therapy, 35,* 125–143.

Buzzetti, A. L., & Associates. (2010). Children abusing elderly parents: A growing concern in New Jersey. Web site: http://www.24-7pressrelease.com/press-release/children-abusing-elderly-parents-a-growing-concern-in-...

Byrne, D. (1983). Sex without contraception. In D. Byrne & W. A. Fisher (Eds.), *Adolescents, sex, and contraception.* Hillsdale, NJ: Erlbaum.

Byrne, D. (2009). Professional profile. Web site: http://www.byrne.socialpsychology.org/.

Cacciatore, J., DeFrain, J., Jones, K., & Jones, H. (2008). The couple and the death of a baby. *Journal of Family Social Work, 11*(4), 351–370.

Cacioppo, J. T., & Patrick, W. (2008). *Loneliness: Human nature and the need for social connection.* New York: W. W. Norton.

Caldwell, J., Du Bois, B., Erickson, J., Goins, R., Hillabrant, W., Kendall, E., et al. (2005). Culturally competent research with American Indians and Alaska Natives. *American Indian and Alaska Native Mental Health Research: The Journal of the National Center, 12,* 1–21.

Campbell, R. (2010). *Leadership: Getting it done.* Web site: http://www.missouri.edu/-campbellr/Leadership/default.htm.

Cano, A., Christian-Herman, J., O'Leary, K. D., & Avery-Leaf, S. (2002). Antecedents and consequences of negative marital stressors. *Journal of Marital and Family Therapy, 28,* 145–151.

Caplin, J., & McGirt, E. (2004, August 1). Ephrata, Washington pays for the war: A small town's National Guard soldiers trained hard for duty in Iraq. No one trained their families for the financial burden of their absence. *Money.* Web site: www.guardfamily.org/A00_admin/A0017_news%5Chtm%5CNYCU_07_12_2004.htm#Homefront_dealing_with_deployment.

Carey, B. (2007). Stress on troops adds to U.S. hurdles in Iraq. *The New York Times.* Web site: http://topics.nytimes.com/top/reference/timestopics/subjects/v/veterans/posttraumatic_stress_disorder/in...

Carr, D. (2006). Good grief: Bouncing back from a spouse's death in later life. *Contexts, 5*(4), 22–27.

Carroll, J. (2007, December 31). Most Americans "very satisfied" with their personal lives. Gallup Poll. Web site: http://www.gallup.com/poll/103483/most-americans-very-satisfied-their-personal-lives.aspx.

Carson, D. K., Dail, P. W., Greeley, S., & Kenote, T. (1990). Stresses and strengths of Native American reservation families in poverty. *Family Perspective, 24*(4), 383–400.

Cassidy, J., & Shaver, P. R. (Eds.) (2008). *Handbook of attachment: Theory, research, and clinical application* (2nd ed.). New York: Guilford Press.

Castro, R. (2001). "When a man is with a woman, it feels like electricity": Subjectivity, sexuality and contraception among men in central Mexico. *Culture, Health and Sexuality, 3*(2), 149–165.

Caughy, M. O., O'Campo, P. J., Nettles, S. M., & Lohrfink, K. F. (2006). Neighborhood matters: Racial socialization of African American children. *Child Development, 77,* 1220–1236.

Cavedo, C., & Guerney, B. G. (1999). Relationship enhancement, enrichment and problem prevention. In R. Berger & M. T. Hannah (Eds.), *Preventive approaches in couple therapy* (pp. 73–105). Philadelphia: Brunner/Mazel.

Center for Problem-Oriented Policing. (2013). Child abuse and neglect in the home, Problem-Specific Guide for Police #45. Web site: http://www.popcenter.org.

Center for Problem-Oriented Policing. (2012). Factors contributing to domestic violence. Web site: http://www.popcenter.org/problems/domestic_violence/2.

Center for Problem-Oriented Policing. (2013). The problem of domestic violence, Guide No. 45. Web site: http://www.popcenter.org.

Centers for Disease Control. (2010a). HIV/AIDS in the United States. Department of Health and Human Services. Web site: http://www.cdc.gov/hiv/resources/factsheets/u.s.htm.

Centers for Disease Control. (2012). Alcohol and public health. Web site: http://www.cdc.gov/alcohol/faqs.htm.

Centers for Disease Control. (2012a). Alcohol and public health. Web site: http://www.cdc.gov/alcohol/faqs.htm.

Centers for Disease Control. (2012b). Child maltreatment prevention. Web site: http://www.cdc.gov./ViolencePrevention/childmaltreatment/index.html.

Centers for Disease Control. (2012c). Dating Matters Initiative. Web site: http://www.cdc.gov/ViolencePrevention/DatingMatters/index.html Dating Matters is a new teen dating violence prevention initiative.

Centers for Disease Control and Prevention. (2004a). Actual causes of death in the United States, 2000. National Center for Chronic Disease Prevention and Health Promotion. Web site: http://www.cdc.gov/nccdphp/factsheets/death_causes2000.htm.

Centers for Disease Control and Prevention. (2004c, May 21). Youth risk behavior surveillance—United States, 2003. *Morbidity and Mortality Weekly Report, 53*(SS-2).

Centers for Disease Control and Prevention. (2007). Illegal drugs. *Morbidity and Mortality Weekly Report, 57*(05), 93–96.

Centers for Disease Control and Prevention. (2009). Births and natality. Web site: http://www.cdc.gov/nchs/fastats/births.htm.

Centers for Disease Control and Prevention. (2009). Estimated pregnancy rates for the United States, 1990–2005: An update. *National Vital Statistics Reports, 58*(4), p. 1. U.S. Department of Health and Human Services. Web site: http://www.cdc.gov/nchs/data/nvsr/nvsr58/nvsr58_04.pdf.

Centers for Disease Control and Prevention. (2009a). National marriage and divorce rate trends. Department of Health and Human Services. Web site: http://www.cdc.gov/nchs/nvss-/marriage_divorce_tables.htm.

Centers for Disease Control and Prevention. (2009b). Suicide. Web site: http://www.cdc.-gov/violenceprevention.

Centers for Disease Control and Prevention. (2010). *HIV/AIDS surveillance report, 2010, 22.* Web site: http://www.cdc.gov/hiv/topics/surveillance/resources/reports.

Centers for Disease Control and Prevention. (2010). *HIV/AIDS surveillance report, 2010, 17.* Atlanta: Author. Web site: http://www.cdc.gov/hiv/topics/surveillance/resources/reports.

Centers for Disease Control and Prevention. (2010a). HIV/AIDS in the United States. Department of Health and Human Services. Web site: http://www.cdc.gov/hiv/resources/factsheets/u.s.htm.

Centers for Disease Control and Prevention. (2010b). Sexual risk behaviors. Web site: http://www.cdc.gov/-HealthyYouth/sexualbehaviors/index.htm.

Centers for Disease Control and Prevention. (2011, November). National Intimate Partner and Sexual Violence Survey: 2010 Summary Report. Web site: http://www.cdc.gov/violenceprevention/nisvs.

Centers for Disease Control and Prevention. (2012). Child maltreatment prevention. Web site: http://www.cdc.gov/violenceprevention/childmaltreatment/.

Centers for Disease Control and Prevention. (2013a). National marriage and divorce rate trends. Web site: http://www.cdc.gov/nchs/nvss/marriage_divorce_tables.htm.

Centers for Disease Control and Prevention. (2013b). Alcohol use and health. Web site: http://www.cdc.gov/alcohol/fact-sheets/alcohol-use.htm.

Centers for Disease Control and Prevention. (2013c). Tobacco use. Web site: http://www.cdc.gov/chronicdisease/resources/publications/aag/osh.htm.

Chaney, C., & Skogrand, L. (2009, June). *Strong Black marriages.* Paper presented at the African American Healthy Marriage Initiative Research to Practice Conference, Chapel Hill, NC.

Chang, I. (2003). *The Chinese in America: A narrative history.* New York: Viking. The 150-year history of a people's search for a better life.

Chapman, M., & Perreira, K. (2005). The well-being of immigrant Latino youth: A framework to inform practice. *Families in Society, 86,* 104–111.

Chase-Lansdale, P. L., Cherlin, A. J., & Kiernan, K. E. (1995). The long-term effects of parental divorce on the mental health of young adults: A developmental perspective. *Child Development, 66,* 1614–1634.

Cherlin, A. J. (2009). *The marriage-go-round: The state of marriage and family in America today.* New York: Random House.

Cherlin, A. (2009). *The marriage-go-round: The state of marriage and family in America today.* Clashing values have caused more partnering and repartnering in the United States than elsewhere in the world, Cherlin argues. The reason, in part, is that Americans value both marriage and individualism.

Cherlin, A. J. (2009a). *The marriage-go-round: The state of marriage and family in America today.* New York: Random House.

Cherlin, A. J. (2009b). The origins of the ambivalent acceptance of divorce. *Journal of Marriage and Family, 71,* 226–229.

Cherlin, A. J. (2010). Demographic trends in the United States: A review of research in the 2000s. *Journal of Marriage and Family, 72,* 403–419.

child abuse and neglect. State Statutes. Web site: http://www.childwelfare.gov/systemwide/laws_policies/statutes/define.cfm.

Child Welfare Information Gateway. (2012). What is child abuse and neglect? Web site: http://www.childwelfare.gov/can/defining/.

Child Welfare Information Gateway. (2012a). Definitions of child abuse and neglect. Web site: http://www.childwelfare.gov/can/defining/.

Child Welfare Information Gateway. (2012b). Long-term consequences of child abuse and neglect. Web site: http://www.childwelfare.gov/pubs/factsheets/long_term_consequences.cfm.

China.Org.CN. (2001). Extramarital sex top threat to marriage; and Unfaithful husband sentenced to prison. Web site: http://www.china.org.cn.

Chiriboga, D., Zettle, L., Connidis, I., Koropeckyj-Cox, T., Bluck, S., Luecking, G., Rook, K., Dykstra, P., DePaulo, B., Morris, W., & Hertel, J. (2004). The never-marrieds in later life: Potentials, problems, and paradoxes. The Gerontologist, 44(1), 145. A cross-national perspective on conceptual models and research findings, including discussions of social supports available to never-married men and women, advantages and disadvantages of never being married, how society views individuals representing this role status, and the variety of types of never-marrieds.

Christensen, A., Atkins, D. C., Baucom, B., & Yi, J. (2010). Marital status and satisfaction five years following a randomized clinical trial comparing traditional versus integrative behavioral couple therapy. Journal of Consulting and Clinical Psychology, 78(2), 225–235.

Axtell, R. E. (2007). Essential do's and taboos: The complete guide to international business and leisure travel. Hoboken, NJ: Wiley. A fun and funny book.

Christie-Mizell, C. A., Pryor, E. M., & Grossman, E. R. B. (2008). Child depressive symptoms, spanking, and emotional support: Differences between African American and European American youth. Family Relations, 57(July), 335–350.

Christopher, F. S. (2001). To dance the dance: A symbolic interactional exploration of premarital sexuality. Mahwah, NJ: Erlbaum.

Chu, K. (2006, December 15). How to escape card debt. USA Today, p. 3B.

Cicirelli, V. G. (2001). Intergenerational decision making by mother and adult child: Effects of adult child gender and age of dyad. The Gerontologist, 41(1), 12.

Cicirelli, V. G. (2003). Caregiving decision making by older mother and adult child: Process and expected outcome. The Gerontologist, 43(1), 364.

success in fertility assistance, adoption, and surrogacy. Baltimore: Johns Hopkins University Press.

Claxton, A., & Perry-Jenkins, M. (2008). No fun anymore: Leisure and marital quality across the transition to parenthood. Journal of Marriage and the Family, 70, 28–43.

Claxton-Oldfield, S. (2000). Deconstructing the myth of the wicked stepparent. Marriage and Family Review, 30(1–2), 51–58.

Clay, R. A. (2009). The debate over low libidos: Psychologists differ on how to treat a lack of desire among some women. APA Online Monitor on Psychology, 40(4), 32. Web site: http://www.apa.org/monitor/2009/04/libidos.html.

Clift, E. (1992, July 13). Abortion angst: How the court's ruling will affect women, doctors and activists on both sides. Newsweek, pp. 16–19.

Cohn, D'V. (2011, December 14). Barely half of U.S. adults are married—A record low. Pew Research Center. Web site: http://www.pewsocialtrends.org/2011/12/14/barely-half-of-u-s-adults-are-married-a-record-low/.

Cole, C. L., & Broussard, J. (2006, May/June). The social context and history of divorce in the U.S. Family Therapy Magazine, pp. 6–9.

Coleman, M., & Ganong, L. H. (2004). Handbook of contemporary families: Considering the past, contemplating the future. Thousand Oaks, CA: Sage.

Coleman, M., Ganong, L., & Fine, M. (2000). Reinvestigating remarriage: Another decade of progress. Journal of Marriage and the Family, 62(4), 1288–1307.

Coles, R. L. (2003). Black single custodial fathers: Factors influencing the decision to parent. Families in Society: The Journal of Contemporary Human Services, 84(2), 247–258.

Coley, R. L., & Chase-Lansdale, P. L. (1998). Adolescent pregnancy and parenthood: Recent evidence and future directions. American Psychologist, 53(2), 152–166.

Coles, R. L., & Green, C. (2010). The myth of the missing Black father. New York: Columbia University Press.

Coltrane, S., Gutierrez, E., & Parke, R. (2008). Stepfathers in cultural context: Mexican American families in the United States. In J. Pryor (Ed.), The international handbook of stepfamilies: Policy and practice in legal, research, and clinical environments (pp. 100–121). Hoboken, NJ: John Wiley.

Compassionate Friends. (2010). Through a network of more than 625 chapters, with locations in all 50 states, as well as Washington, D.C., and Puerto Rico, for the past four decades Compassionate Friends has been supporting bereaved families after the death of a child. Web site: http://www.compassionatefriends.org/.

Connidis, I. A., & McMullin, J. A. (1999). Permanent childlessness: Perceived advantages and disadvantages among older persons. Canadian Journal on Aging, 18, 447–465.

Constantine, N. A., Jerman, P., & Huang, A. X. (2007). California parents' preferences and beliefs regarding school-based sex education policy. *Perspectives on Sexual and Reproductive Health, 39*(3), 167–175.

Consumer Reports. (2005). CR's guide to contraception. *Consumer Reports* (February), 34–38. Sections on condoms for extra protection; birth control, more and safer choices; a comparative guide to contraceptives; and abortion options.

Cook, R., & DeFrain, J. (2005). Using discourse analysis to explore family strengths: A preliminary study. *Marriage and Family Review, 38*(1), 3–12.

Coontz, S. (2005). *Marriage, a history: From obedience to intimacy or how love conquered marriage.* New York: Viking.

Coontz, S. (Ed.). (2008). *American families: A multicultural reader.* New York: Routledge.

Cooper, C. L., & Dewe, P. (2007). Stress: A brief history from the 1950s. In A. Monat, R. S. Lazarus, & R. Reevy (Eds.), *The Praeger handbook on stress and coping* (vol. 1, pp. 7–32). Westport, CT: Praeger.

Cooper, M. L. (2002). Alcohol use and risky sexual behavior among college students and youth: Evaluating the evidence. *Journal of Studies of Alcohol, 14*, 101–117.

Coop Gordon, K., Hughes, F. M., Tomcik, N. D., Dixon, L. J., & Litzinger, S. C. (2009). Widening spheres of impact: The role of forgiveness in marital and family functioning. *Journal of Family Psychology, 23*(1), 1–13.

Copen, C. E., Daniels, K., Vespa, J., Mosher, W. D. (2012, March). *First marriages in the United States: Data from the 2006–2010 National Survey of Family Growth.* National Health Statistics Reports, U.S. Department of Vital Statistics, U. S. Department of Health and Human Services. Web site: http://www.cdc.gov/nchs/data/nhsr/nhsr049.pdf.

Cowan, P. A., & Cowan, C. P. (2011, summer). After the baby: Keeping the couple relationship alive. *Family Focus, 56.2(49)*, 1, 2, 5.

Cowley, G. (1989, March 13). How the mind was designed: Evolutionary theory is yielding rich new insights into everything from cognition to sexual desire. *Newsweek*, pp. 56–58.

Cox, C. B. (2007). Grandparent-headed families: Needs and implications for social work interventions and advocacy. *Families in Society: The Journal of Contemporary Social Services, 88*, 561–566.

Creswell, J. W. (2007). *Qualitative inquiry & research design: Choosing among five approaches* (2nd ed.). Thousand Oaks, CA: Sage.

Creswell, J. W. (2009). *Qualitative inquiry and research design: Choosing among five approaches* (3rd ed.). Thousand Oaks, CA: Sage.

Creswell, J. W. (2012). *Educational research: Planning, conducting, and evaluating quantitative and qualitative research* (4th ed.). Boston: Pearson.

Crittenden, A. (2001). *The price of motherhood: Why the most important job in the world is still the least valued.* New York: Metropolitan Books. "An easy, informative, enjoyable read."

Crockenberg, S. C. (2003). Rescuing the baby from the bathwater: How gender and temperament (may) influence how child care affects child development. *Child Development, 74*(4), 1034–1038.

Cross, T. (1997). Understanding the relational worldview in Indian families. *Pathways, 12*, 10–12.

Csikszentmihalyi, M. (1999). If we are so rich, why aren't we happy? *American Psychologist, 54*(10), 821–827.

Cullington, D. (2008). *Breaking up blues.* New York: Routledge.

Cummins, H. J. (2001). *Advice for those experiencing ambiguous loss.* Minneapolis: Minneapolis Star and Tribune.

CYFERnet. (2010). Financial literacy. Children, Youth and Families Education and Research Network. Web site: http://www.cnpp.usda.gov/ExpendituresonChildrenbyFamilies.htm.

Cynkar, A. (2007). Early-career insights: Seven steps to stomp out debt. *Monitor on Psychology, 38.* Web site: http://www.apa.org/monitor/may07/sevensteps.html.

Daggett, L. M. (2002). Living with loss: Middle-aged men face spousal bereavement. *Qualitative Health Research, 12*(5), 625–639.

Dahl, T. (1980). *Model of stress.* Unpublished manuscript University of Minnesota, Minneapolis.

Dailard, C. (2001). Sex education: Politicians, parents, teachers and teens. *The Guttmacher Report, 4*(1).

Dalla, R., DeFrain, J., Johnson, J., & Abbott, D. A. (Eds.). (2009). *Strengths and challenges of new immigrant families: Implications for research, education, policy, and service.* Lanham, MD: Lexington Press.

Dalla, R., DeFrain, J., Johnson, J., & Abbott, D. A. (2009). *Strengths and challenges of new immigrant families: Implications for research, education, policy, and service.* Lanham, MD: Lexington Books/Rowman & Littlefield. Explores the lives of East Indian, Sudanese, Somali, African, Asian Indian, Korean, Irish, Egyptian, Israeli, Chinese, Mexican, and other immigrants. "A wonderful introduction for those wanting to study or work with immigrant families."

Daly, M., & Wilson, M. I. (1996). *Current Directions in Psychological Science, 5*, 77–81.

Danes, S. M. (1992). Parental perceptions of children's financial socialization. In R. Imas (Ed.), *Proceedings of the Association for Financial Counseling and Planning Education* (pp. 16–35). Charleston, SC: Association for Financial Counseling and Planning Education.

Danes, S. M., & Haberman, H. R. (2007). Teen financial knowledge, self-efficacy, and behavior: A gendered view. *Financial Counseling and Planning, 18*(1), 48–60.

Danziger, S., & Rouse, C. E. (Eds.). (2007). *The price of independence: The economics of early adulthood.* Philadelphia: Network on Transitions to Adulthood.

Darkwa, O. (2004). Social welfare services for the aged. Chicago: University of Illinois. Web site: http://www.uic.edu/classes/socw/socw550/AGING/sld001.htm.

Darling, C. A., & Turkki, K. (2009). Global family concerns and the role of family life education: An ecosystemic analysis. *Family Relations: Interdisciplinary Journal of Applied Family Studies, 58* (February), 4–27.

Darroch, J. E., Frost, J. J., & Singh, S. (2001). Teenage sexual and reproductive behavior in developed countries: Can more progress be made? *Occasional Report, No. 3.* New York: Alan Guttmacher Institute.

Davis, K. E. (2004). *Love's many faces apprehended.* Washington, DC: American Psychological Association.

Davis, K. E. (2007). Professional profile. Web site: http://keith.davissocialpsychology.org.

Deal, R. L., & Olson, D. H. (2010). *The remarriage checkup: Tools to help your marriage last a lifetime*. Minneapolis: Bethany House. Ways in which remarried couples can build on their strengths and overcome relationship problems.

Dee, T. S. (2001). The effects of minimum legal drinking ages on teen childbearing. *Journal of Human Resources 36*(4), 824–838.

Deen, M. R. (2005, June). Family values reconsidered. *Family Focus*, pp. 5–6.

Deets, H. B. (1996). Aging in America: A women's issue. Workshop on social protection, poverty, and older persons at risk, American Association of Retired Persons and UN/ECE. Web site: http://www.unece.org/spot/deets.htm.

DeFrain, J. (2006). *Family treasures: Creating strong families*. Lincoln, NE: University of Nebraska Press.

DeFrain, J., and the University of Nebraska–Lincoln Extension Family Action Research and Writing Team. (2006). *Family treasures: Creating strong families*. Bloomington, IN: iUniverse.

DeFrain, J., and the University of Nebraska–Lincoln for Families Writing Team. (2007). *Family treasures: Creating strong families*. University of Nebraska–Lincoln Extension. New York: iUniverse.

DeFrain, J., & the University of Nebraska–Lincoln Extension Family Action Research and Writing Team. (2007a). *Family treasures: Creating strong families*. New York: iUniverse, Inc. (Available online from the *University of Nebraska–Lincoln for Families* Web site at www.unlforfamilies.unl.edu.) Sixty-three couple and family activities keyed to each of the six major strengths.

DeFrain, J., & the University of Nebraska–Lincoln Extension Family Action Research and Writing Team. (2007b). *Family treasures: Creating strong families*. Resource Guide for Educators and Families (CD and DVD set). Lincoln: University of Nebraska Extension. (Available online from the *University of Nebraska–Lincoln for Families* Web site at www.unlforfamilies.unl.edu.) Explains the International Family Strengths Model and shows families using some of the 63 couple and family activities designed to strengthen relationships.

DeFrain, J., and the University of Nebraska–Lincoln Extension Family Action Research and Writing Team. (2012). *Getting connected, staying connected: Loving each other day by day* Bloomington, IN: iUniverse.

DeFrain, J., & The University of Nebraska Extension Family Action Research and Writing Team. (2012). *Getting connected, staying connected: Loving each other day by day*. Bloomington, IN: iUniverse. A practical guide for couples and families built around the research-based six key couple and family strengths.

DeFrain, J., & Asay, S. (Eds.). (2007). *Strong families around the world: The family strengths perspective*. New York: Haworth.

DeFrain, J., Ernst, L., & Nealer, J. (1997). The family counselor and loss. In J. R. Woods, Jr. (Ed.), *Loss in pregnancy or the neonatal period: Principles of care with clinical cases and analyses* (pp. 499–520). Pitman, NJ: Jannetti.

DeFrain, J., Fricke, J., & Elmen, J. (1987). *On our own: A single parent's survival guide*. Lexington, MA: Lexington Books/Heath.

DeFrain, J., Martens, L., Stork, J., & Stork, W. (1986). *Stillborn: The invisible death*. Lexington, MA: Lexington Books/Heath.

DeFrain, J., Millspaugh, E., & Xie, X. (1996). The psychosocial effects of miscarriage: Implications for health professionals. *Families, Systems, and Health: Journal of Collaborative Family Health Care, 14*(3), 331–347.

DeFrain, J., & the University of Nebraska Extension Family Action Team. (2012). *Getting connected, staying connected: Loving one another day by day*. Indianapolis, IN: iUniverse.

DeGarmo, D. S., Patras, J., & Eap, S. (2008). Social support for divorced fathers' parenting: Testing a stress-buffering model. *Family Relations, 57*, 35–48.

DeLuccie, M. (1995). Mothers as gatekeepers: A model of maternal mediators of father involvement. *Journal of Genetic Psychology, 156*(1), 115–131.

DeNavas-Walt, C., Proctor, B., & Lee, C. (2006). Income, poverty, and health insurance coverage in the United States: 2005. *Current population reports*. Washington, DC: Government Printing Office.

DePaulo, B. (2004, November 21). Singles shall overcome. Web site: http://www.unmarriedamerica.org/News-About-Us/singles_shall_overcome.htm.

DePaulo, B. M. (2006). *Singled out: How singles are stereotyped, stigmatized, and ignored and still live happily ever after*. New York: St. Martin's.

Dettwyler, K. (1995). A time to wean: The hominid blueprint for the natural age of weaning in modern human populations. In P. Stuart-Macadam & K. Dettwyler (Eds.), *Breastfeeding: Biocultural perspectives*. New York: Aldine DeGruyter.

de Vries, J. M., Swenson, L., & Walsh, R. P. (2007). Hot picture or self-description: Predicting mediated dating success with Parental Investment Theory. *Marriage and Family Review, 42*, 7–33.

Dew, J. (2007). Two sides of the same coin? The differing roles of assets and consumer debt in marriage. *Journal of Family and Economic Issues, 28*, 89–104.

Dew, J. (2008a). Debt change and marital satisfaction change in recently married couples. *Family Relations, 57*, 60–71.

Dew, J. (2008b). Themes and trends of *Journal of Family and Economic Issues:* A review of twenty years (1988–2007). *Journal of Family and Economic Issues, 29*, 496–540.

Dew, J. (2009). The gendered meanings of assets for divorce. *Journal of Family and Economic Issues, 30*, 20–31.

Dew, J. (2011). Financial issues and relationship outcomes among cohabiting individuals. *Family Relations, 60,* 178–190.

Diamond, M. (2007). *My father before me: How fathers and sons influence each other throughout their lives.* New York: W. W. Norton. Suggested reading from the American Association for Marital and Family Therapy.

DiCenso, A., Guyatt, G., Willan, A., & Griffith, L. (2002). Interventions to reduce unintended pregnancies among adolescents: Systematic review of randomized controlled trials. *British Medical Journal, 324*(7351), 1426–1430.

Dickler, J. (2012, May 15). Boomerang kids: 85% of college grads move home. *CNNMoney.* Web site: http://money.cnn.com/2010/10/14/pf/boomerang_kids_move_home/index.htm.

Dick-Read, G. (1984). *Childbirth without fear: The original approach to natural childbirth.* New York: Harper & Row. (Original work published 1932.)

Dienhart, A. (2001). Make room for daddy: The pragmatic potentials of the tag-team structure for sharing parenting. *Journal of Family Issues, 22*(8), 973–999.

Dindia, K. (2000). Self-disclosure, identity, and relationship development: A dialectic perspective. In K. Dindia & S. Duck (Eds.), *Communication and personal relationships* (pp. 147–162). New York: Wiley.

Dinger, M. K., & Parsons, N. (1999). Sexual activity among college students living in residence halls and fraternity or sorority housing. *Journal of Health Education, 30*(4), 242–246.

Dingfelder, S. (2006). Violence in the home takes many forms. *Monitor in Psychology, 37,* 18.

Dirie, W. (1998). *Desert flower.* New York: Morrow.

Divorce rate climbs among middle-aged Chinese. (2004, February 1). *The Epoch Times.* Web site: http//www.asianresearch.org/articles/1846.htm.

Divorce rate on the increase in Shanghai. (2004, December 16). *Shanghai Daily.* Web site: http://www.china.org.cn/english/Life/115127.htm.

Dobson, J. C. (1999). *Love must be tough: New hope for families in crisis.* Nashville: Word.

Doherty, W. (2013). Bill Doherty on citizen engagement. Web site: http://www.drbilldoherty.org/citizenengagement.php.

Doherty, W. J. (2000). *Take back your kids.* Notre Dame, IN: Sorin Books.

Doherty, W. J. (2001). *Take back your marriage: Sticking together in a world that pulls us apart.* New York: Guilford.

Doherty, W. J., & Allen, W. (1994). Family functioning and parental smoking as predictors of adolescent cigarette use: A six-year prospective study. *Journal of Family Psychology, 8*(3), 347–353.

Doherty, W. J., & Anderson, J. R. (2004). Community marriage initiatives. *Family Relations, 53,* 425–432.

Doherty, W. J., Erickson, M. F., & LaRossa, R. (2006). An intervention to increase father involvement and skills with infants during the transition to parenthood. *Journal of Family Psychology, 20*(3), 438–447.

Doherty, W. J., & Simmons, D. S. (1996). Clinical practice patterns of marriage and family therapists: A national survey of therapists and their clients. *Journal of Marital and Family Therapy, 22,* 9–25.

Dolbin-MacNab, M., & Keiley, M. K. (2009). Navigating interdependence: How adolescents raised solely by grandparents experience their family relationships. *Family Relations, 58,* 172–175.

Dolbin-MacNab, M. L. (2006). Just like raising your own? Grandmothers' perceptions of parenting a second time around. *Family Relations, 55,* 564–575.

Domestic Abuse Intervention Programs (n.d.). Equality wheel. Web site: http://www.theduluthmodel.org/wheelgallery.php.

Douglas, S. J., & Michaels, M. W. (2004). *The mommy myth: The idealization of motherhood and how it has undermined women.* New York: Free Press. Cultural forces are at work to "return women to the Stone Age."

Downs, B. (2003). *Fertility of American women: June 2002.* Current Population Reports, P20–548. Washington, DC: U.S. Census Bureau.

Drago, R. W. (2007). *Work, family, life.* Boston, MA: Dollars & Sense Publishers.

Dreby, J. (2010). *Divided by borders: Mexican migrants and their children.* Berkeley, CA: University of California Press.

Driver, J., Tabares, A., Shapiro, A., Nahm, E. Y., & Gottman, J. M. (2003). Interactional patterns in marital success or failure: Gottman Laboratory studies. In F. Walsh (Ed.), *Normal family processes* (3rd ed., pp. 493–513). New York: Guilford Press.

Dugas, C. (2012, October 24). Gender pay gap persists. *USA Today.* Web site: http://www.usatoday.com/story/money/personalfinance/2012/10/24/gender-pay-gap/1652511/.

Duly, A. (2003). Consumer spending for necessities. *Consumer Expenditure Survey Anthology,* pp. 35–38.

Duncan, S. F., Holman, T. B., & Yang, C. (2007). Factors associated with involvements in marriage preparation programs. *Family Relations: Interdisciplinary Journal of Applied Family Studies, 56* (July), 270–278.

Durham, W., & Braithwaite, D. O. (2009). Communication privacy management with the family planning trajectories of voluntarily child-free couples. *Journal of Family Communication, 9,* 43–65.

Duvall, E. M. (2001). Evelyn Duvall's life. *Marriage and Family Review, 32*(1/2), 7–23.

Duvander, A.-Z. E. (1999). The transition from cohabitation to marriage: A longitudinal study of the propensity to marry in Sweden in the early 1990s. *Journal of Family Issues, 20*(5), 698–717.

Dye, J. L. (2008). Fertility of American women: 2006. *Current Population Reports,* P20-558. U.S. Census Bureau. Web site: https://www.census.gov/prod/2008pubs/p20-558.pdf.

Dykstra, P. A. (2007a). Pathways to childlessness and late-life outcomes. *Journal of Family Issues, 28*(11), 1487–1517.

Dykstra, P. A. (2007b). Childlessness and parenthood in two centuries: Different roads—different maps? *Journal of Family Issues, 28*(11), 1518–1532.

Dykstra, P. A., & Hagestad, G. O. (2007). Roads less taken: Developing a nuanced view of older adults without children. *Journal of Family Issues, 28,* 1275–1310.

Economics and Statistics Administration. (2011). Exploring the digital nation—Computer and Internet use at home. Web site: http://www.esa.doc.gov/Reports/exploring-digital-nation-computer-and-internet-use-home.

Edmondson, B. (2010). All the lonely people. American Association of Retired Persons. Web site: http://www.aarp.org/personal-growth/transitions/info-09-2010/all_the_lonely_people.html.

Edmondson, B. (2010). All the lonely people. *AARP Magazine.* Researchers find a rise in loneliness in recent years. Web site: http://www.aarp.org/personal-growth/transitions/info-09-2010/all_the_lonely_people.html.

Ellison, C. G., & Bradshaw, M. (2009). Religious beliefs, socio-political ideology, and attitudes toward corporal punishment. *Journal of Family Issues, 30,* 320–340.

Emmers-Sommer, T. M., Rhea, D., Triplett, L., & O'Neil, B. (2003). Accounts of single fatherhood: A qualitative study. *Marriage and Family Review, 35*(1/2), 99–115.

Encyclopedia Britannica. (2004). Biography: Dirie, Waris. Web site: http://www.britannica.com/eb/article?eu=368479.

Encyclopedia Britannica. (2010). Biography: Dirie, Waris. Web site: http://www.britannica.com/EBchecked/topic/711244/Waris-Dirie.

England, P., & Edin, K. (Eds.). (2007). *Unmarried couples with children.* New York, NY: Russell Sage Foundation.

Ennis, S. R., Rios-Vargas, M., & Albert, N. G. (2011, May). *The Hispanic population: 2010.* (U. S. Census Bureau Report C2010BR-04). Retrieved from http://www.census.gov/prod/cen2010/briefs/c2010br-04.pdf.

Enright, E. (2004, July and August). A house divided. *American Association of Retired Persons Magazine,* pp. 60, 64–66, 68, 81.

Erickson, R. (2005). Why emotion work matters: Sex, gender, and the division of household labor. *Journal of Marriage and the Family, 67,* 337–351.

Erikson, E. H. (1950). *Childhood and society.* New York: Norton.

Esteinou, R. (2009). *Construyendo relaciones y fortalezas familiares: Un panorama internacional.* Mexico, D.F.: Centro de Investigaciones y Estudios Superiores en Anthropologia Social. This book, published in Spanish in Mexico City, is the first book in Latin America to focus on family strengths. The book is the result of the Mexican Family Strengths Conference held in Cuernavaca, and includes articles from Mexico, Australia, Botswana, China, Italy, Korea, and the United States.

Eubanks Fleming, C. J., & Córdova, J. V. (2012). Predicting relationship help seeking prior to a marriage checkup. *Family Relations, 61* (February), 90–100.

Eunice Kennedy Shriver National Institute of Child Health and Human Development, NIH, DHHS. (2006). *The NICHD study of early child care and youth development (SECCYD): Findings for children up to age 4½ years (05-4318).* Washington, DC: U.S. Government Printing Office. This government-funded $200 million study, which began in 1991, is by far the most ambitious study of the effects of nonmaternal child care, and about families who use child care as well as those who do not. A free 62-page report is available on the Web site at http://www.nichd.nih.gov/publications/.

Faces and Voices of Recovery. (2012). Organizing the recovery community. Web site: http://www.facesandvoicesofrecovery.org/about.

go to war—A systemic perspective on harm and healing. *Journal of Family Psychology, 19,* 233–236.

Family Action Centre, University of Newcastle, Australia. (2010). Useful information and resources on parenthood. Web site: www.newcastle.edu.au-/centre/fac.

Family Focus. (2005, June). American families: By the numbers. *Family Focus,* pp. 6, 14.

Family Service Association. (2012). How do you define your family? Web site: http://www.fsabc.org/mission/family/.

Family violence tops health issue. (1991, October 17). Lincoln [NE] *Journal Star,* p. 3.

Faris, E. (1940, summer). Seven pillars of family strength. *Living,* 69–76.

Fawcett, N. R., Gullone, E., & Johnson, J. (2002, March). The relationship between animal abuse and domestic violence: Implications for animal welfare agencies and domestic violence. *Australian Domestic and Family Violence Clearinghouse Newsletter, 10,* 4–7.

Fay, R., Turner, C., Klassen, A., & Gagnon, J. (1989). Prevalence and patterns of same-gender sexual contact among men. *Science, 246,* 338–348.

Federal Reserve Bank of New York. (2012). *Credit card debt.* Retrieved from http://www.newyorkfed.org/household-credit/index.html.

Fehr, B. (2004). A prototype model of intimacy interactions in same-sex friendships. In D. J. Mashek & A. Aron (Eds.), *Handbook of closeness and intimacy* (pp. 9–26). Mahwah, NJ: Erlbaum.

Fenell, D. L., & Weinhold, B. K. (1997). *Counseling families: An introduction to marriage and family therapy* (2nd ed.). Denver, CO: Love.

Ferguson, S. J. (2000). Challenging traditional marriage: Never married Chinese American and Japanese American women. *Gender and Society, 14*(1), 136–159. Why do some heterosexual Chinese American and Japanese American women never marry? The four most significant reasons are the effect of their parents' marriages, their status as eldest daughter, their pursuit of education, and the lack of eligible suitors. Parents' traditional marriages and duties as eldest daughter caused many to have negative views of marriage and childbearing. The number of suitors was limited for 46 of 62 respondents because their parents placed strict restrictions on them concerning the types of men they are allowed to marry.

Fergusson, D. M., Horwood, L. J., & Ridder, E. M. (2005). Rejoinder. *Journal of Marriage and the Family, 67,* 1131–1136.

Ferrer, M. (2010). Stepping stones for stepfamilies. A six-lesson curriculum for enhancing stepfamily relationships developed by the University of Florida Extension. Web site: http://edis.ifas.ufl.edu/topic_program_stepping_stones_for_stepfamilies.

Fields, J. (2003, June). *Children's living arrangements and characteristics: March 2002.* Current Population Reports, P. 20–547. Washington, DC: U.S. Census Bureau.

Fields, J., & Casper, L. M. (2001). *America's families and living arrangements: March 2000.* Current Population Reports, P20-537. Washington, DC: U.S. Census Bureau.

Fill, S. K. (2002). Single mothers by choice: An exploratory study. *Masters Abstracts International, 40*(06), 1420.

Fincham, F. D., Hall, J., & Beach, S. R. (2006). Forgiveness in marriage: Current status and future directions. *Family Relations, 55,* 415–427.

Fincham, F. D., Stanley, S. M., & Beach, S. R. (2007). Transformative processes in marriage: An analysis of emerging trends. *Journal of Marriage and the Family, 69,* 275–292.

Finer, L. (2007). Trends in premarital sex in the United States, 1954–2003. *Public Health Reports, 122,* 73–78.

Finer, L., et al. (2006). Disparities in rates of unintended pregnancy in the United States, 1994 and 2001. *Perspectives on Sexual and Reproductive Health, 38*(2), 90–96.

Finer, L. B., Frohwirth, L. F., Dauphinee, L. A., Singh, S., & Moore, A. M. (2006). Timing of steps and reasons for delay in obtaining abortions in the United States. *Contraception, 74,* 334–344.

Fisher, H. E., Aron, A., & Brown, L. (2006). Romantic love: A mammalian brain system for mate choice. *Philosophical Transactions of the Royal Society B, 361,* 2173–2186.

Fitzpatrick, L. (2004, March 29). Getting out. *Time Asia.* Web site: http://www.time.com/time/asia/magazine/printout/0,13675,501040405-605534,00.html.

Fletcher, W. L., & Hansson, R. O. (1991, March). Assessing the social components of retirement anxiety. *Psychology and Aging, 6,* 76–85.

Flynn, C. P. (2000a). Why family professionals can no longer ignore violence toward animals. *Family Relations, 49*(1), 87–95.

Flynn, C. P. (2000b). Woman's best friend: Pet abuse and the role of companion animals in the lives of battered women. *Violence Against Women, 6*(2), 162–177.

Folbre, N. (2008). *Valuing children: Rethinking the economics of the family.* Cambridge, MA: Harvard University Press.

Ford, M., Ford, A., & Ford, S. (2006). *My parents are divorced too.* Washington, DC: American Psychological Association.

Fowers, B., & Davidov, B. (2006). The virtue of multiculturalism: Person transformation, character, and openness to the other. *American Psychologist, 61,* 581–594.

Fowers, B. J., Montel, K. H., & Olson, D. H. (1996). Predicting marital success for premarital couple types based on PREPARE. *Journal of Marital and Family Therapy, 22*(1), 103–119.

Fowers, B. J., & Olson, D. H. (1986). Predicting marital success with PREPARE: A predictive validity study. *Journal of Marital and Family Therapy, 12*(4), 403–413.

Fowers, B. J., & Olson, D. H. (1992). Four types of premarital couples: An empirical typology based on PREPARE. *Journal of Family Psychology, 6*(1), 10–21.

Fox, G. L., & Murry, V. M. (2000). Gender and families: Feminist perspectives and family research. *Journal of Marriage and the Family, 62*(4), 1160–1172.

Francoeur, R. T. (1982). *Becoming a sexual person.* New York: Wiley.

Francoeur, R. T. (Ed.). (1997). *International encyclopedia of sexuality.* New York: Continuum.

Franklin, A. J. (2004). *From brotherhood to manhood: How Black men rescue their relationships and dreams from the invisibility syndrome.* New York: Wiley.

Franklin, A. J. (2006). A dialogue about gender, race, and invisibility in psychotherapy with African American men. In J. C. Muran (Ed.). *Dialogues on difference: Diversity studies of the therapeutic relationship* (pp. 117–131). Washington DC: American Psychological Association Books.

Fravel, D. L. (1995). *Boundary ambiguity perceptions of adoptive parents experiencing various levels of openness in adoption.* Unpublished doctoral dissertation, University of Minnesota, St. Paul.

Freedom to Marry. (2012a). The freedom to marry internationally. Web site: http://freedomtomarry.org/landscape/entry/c/international.

Freedom to Marry. (2012b). State by state. Web site: http://www.freedomtomarry.org/.

Freedom to Marry. (2013a). What's happening now with marriage. Web site: http://www.freedomtomarry.org.

Freedom to Marry. (2013b). Marriage at the Supreme Court in 2013. Web site: http://www.freetomarry.org/landscape/entry/c/supreme-court.

Frias, S. M., & Angel, R. J. (2005). The risk of partner violence among low-income Hispanic subgroups. *Journal of Marriage and the Family, 67,* 552–564.

Friedan, B. (1963). *The feminine mystique.* New York: Norton.

Friedan, B. (1997). *Beyond gender: The new politics of work and family.* Washington, DC: The Woodrow Wilson Center Press, book jacket.

Frieden, T. (2012). U.S. violent crime down for fifth straight year. *CNN Justice.* Web site: http://www.cnn.com/2012/10/29/justice/us-violent-crime/index.html.

Friedlin, J. (2002). Second and third wave feminists clash over the future. *Women's E-News.*

Fromm, E. (2000). *The art of loving.* New York: Continuum.

Frost, D. M. (2011). Stigma and intimacy in same-sex relationships: A narrative approach. *Journal of Family Psychology, 25,* 1–10.

Fry, R., Cohn, D'V., Livingston, G., & Taylor, P. (2011). The rising age gap in economic well-being: The old prosper relative to the young. *Pew Social & Demographic Trends.* Web site: http://www.pewsocialtrends.org/2011/11/07/the-rising-age-gap-in-economic-well-being/.

Fu, V. K. (2008). Interracial-interethnic unions and fertility in the United States. *Journal of Marriage and the Family, 70* (August), 783–795.

Fusaro, M. A. (2008). Hidden consumer loans: An analysis of implicit interest rates on bounced checks. *Journal of Family and Economic Issues, 29,* 251–263.

Gagnon, J. (2010). John Gagnon, personal profile. Web site: http://www.stonybrook.edu/sociology/?faculty/Gagnon/gagnon.

Gagnon, J. H. (2004). *An interpretation of desire: Essays in the study of sexuality.* Chicago: University of Chicago Press.

Gallup, Inc. (1989). *Love and marriage.* Princeton, NJ: The Gallup Organization.

Gallup, Inc. (2004, June 22). The cultural landscape: What's morally acceptable? Web site: http://www.gallup.com/content/login.aspx?ci=12061.

Gallup poll. (1996). *Gender and society: Status and stereotypes.* Princeton, NJ: The Gallup Organization.

Ganong, L. H., & Coleman, M. (1994). *Remarried family relationships*. Thousand Oaks, CA: Sage.

Ganong, L. H., & Coleman, M. (1999). *Changing families, changing responsibilities: Family obligations following divorce and remarriage*. Mahwah, NJ: Erlbaum.

Ganong, L. H., & Coleman, M. (2000). Remarried families. In C. Hendrick & S. S. Hendrick (Eds.), *Close relationships: A sourcebook* (pp. 155–168). Thousand Oaks, CA: Sage.

Garbarino, J. (2000). The soul of fatherhood. *Marriage and Family Review, 29*(2/3), 11–21.

Graves, J. L., Jr. (2004). *The race myth: Why we pretend race exists in America*. New York: Dutton. Dr. Graves, an evolutionary biologist at Fairleigh Dickinson University in New Jersey, argues,

We have paid dearly for the policies of racism, and are continuing to pay in a currency of despair, unfulfilled dreams, and blood. . . . Every time we pay, we slide closer toward hell on a road paved with our racial misconceptions. We will continue to pay until we reject the notion that there are biological races in the human species, and that race determines an individual's worth.

Garcia, A. M. (2003). *Narratives of Mexican American women*. Walnut Creek, CA: AltaMira Press. This is an insightful narrative of Chicana college students' struggle with their personal and family lives.

Garman, E. T., & Forgue, R. E. (1997). *Personal finance* (5th ed.). Boston: Houghton Mifflin.

Garman, E. T., & Forgue, R. E. (2002). *Personal finance* (7th ed.). Boston: Houghton Mifflin.

Gartrell, N., Bos, H., Peyser, H., Deck, A., & Rodas, C. (2011). Family characteristics, custody arrangements, and adolescent psychological well-being after lesbian mothers break up. *Family Relations, 60*, 572–585.

Gary, L. E., Beatty, L. A., & Berry, G. L. (1986). Strong Black families: Models of program development for Black families. In S. Van Zandt, H. Lingren, G. Rowe, P. Zeece, L. Kimmons, P. Lee, D. Shell, & N. Stinnett (Eds.), *Family strengths 7: Vital connections* (pp. 453–468). Lincoln: University of Nebraska Press.

Gates, G. (2008). Diversity among same-sex couples and their children. In S. Coontz, M. Parson, & G. Raley (Eds.), *American families* (pp. 394–399). New York: Routledge.

Gates, G. J. (2006). Same-sex couples and the gay, lesbian, bisexual population: New estimates from the American community survey. The Williams Institute. Web site: http://www.law.ucla.edu/williamsinstitute/publications/samesexcouplesandglbpopacs.pdf.

Gaunt, R. (2009). Maternal gatekeeping: Antecedents and consequences. *Journal of Family Issues, 29*(3), 373–395.

Gay and Lesbian Times. (2003, October 9). Sex clampdown proposed in Indonesia. Web site: http://www.gaylesbiantimes.com/?id=1167&issue=824.

sociations with child behaviors and ineducation by perceived normativeness. *Child Development, 81*, 487–502.

Gerson, K. (2010). *The unfinished revolution: How a new generation is reshaping family, work, and gender in American*. New York, New York: Oxford University Press.

Gibbs, N. (2001, July 30). Who's in charge here? *Time*, pp. 40–49.

Gibran, K. (1976). *The prophet*. New York: Knopf. (Original work published 1923.)

Gibson, P. A. (2002). Caregiving role affects family relationships of African-American grandmothers as new mothers again: A phenomenological perspective. *Journal of Marital and Family Therapy, 28*(3), 341–353.

Gibson, P. A. (2005). Intergenerational parenting from the perspective of African American grandmothers. *Family Relations, 54*, 280–297.

Gil, E. (2006). *Helping abused and traumatized children: Integrating directive and nondirective approaches*. New York: Guilford Press.

Gilbert, N. (2008). *A mother's work: How feminism, the market, and policy shape family life*. New Haven, CT: Yale University Press.

Giles, J. (2008). *The nature of sexual desire*. Landham, MD: University Press of America.

Glenn, N., & Marquardt, E. (2001). *Hooking up, hanging out, and hoping for Mr. Right*. New York: Institute for American Values.

Glick, J. (2010). Connecting complex processes: A decade of research on immigrant families. *Journal of Marriage and Family, 72*, 498–515.

Goldberg, A. E. (2007). Talking about family: Disclosure practices of adults raised by lesbian, gay, and bisexual parents. *Journal of Family Issues, 28*, 100–131.

Goldberg, A. E., Downing, J. B., & Sauck, C. (2008). Perceptions of children's parental preferences in Lesbian twom-other households. *Journal of Marriage and the Family, 70*(May), 419–434.

Goldenberg & Goldenberg Eunice Kennedy Shriver National Institute of Child Health and Human Development, NIH, DHHS. (2006). The NICHD study of early child care and youth development (SECCYD): Findings for children up to age 4½ years (05-4318). Washington, DC: U.S. Government Printing Office.

Goldenberg, H., & Goldenberg, I. (2011). *Family therapy: An overview* (8th ed.). Belmont, CA: Brooks/Cole.

Goldstein, S. (1940, winter). The family as a dynamic factor in American society. *Living*, 8–19.

Gomel, J. N., Tinsley, B. J., Parke, R. D., & Clark, K. M. (1998). The effects of economic hardship on family relationships among African American, Latino, and Euro-American families. *Journal of Family Issues, 19*(4), 436–476.

Goodman, C. C., & Silverstein, M. (2006). Grand-mothers raising grandchildren. *Journal of Family Issues, 27*, 1605–1626.

Goodman, E. (2001, February 26). Clear up contraceptive issue before it's 2-LATE. Lincoln [NE] *Journal Star*, p. 4B.

Goodwin, R. (2009). *Changing relations*. New York: Cambridge University Press.

Gordon, K., Baucom, D. H., & Snyder, D. K. (2005). Forgiveness in couples: Divorce, infidelity, and couples therapy. In E. L. Worthington (Ed.), *Handbook of forgiveness* (pp. 407–422). New York: Routledge.

Gordon, K. C., & Baucom, D. H. (2003). Forgiveness and marriage: Preliminary support for a synthesized model of recovery from a marital betrayal. *American Journal of Family Therapy, 31*, 179–199.

Gordon, L., & Durana, C. (1999). The PAIRS Program. In R. Berger & M. T. Hannah (Eds.), *Preventive approaches in couples therapy*. Philadelphia: Brunner/Mazel.

Gordon, P. A. (2003). The decision to remain single: Implications for women across cultures. *Journal of Mental Health Counseling, 25*(1), 33–45.

Gordon, S., & Gordon, J. (2000). *Raising a child responsibly in a sexually permissive world* (2nd ed.). Cincinnati, OH: Adams Media.

Gotta, G., Green, R., Rothblum, E., Solomon, S., Balsam, K., & Swartz, P. (2011). Heterosexual, lesbian, and gay male relationships: A comparison of couples in 1975 and 2000. *Family Process, 50*, 353–376.

Gottlieb, L. (2006). How do I love thee? *The Atlantic* (March), 58, 60, 62–68, 70.

Gottman, J. (2010). What we've learned: What makes same-sex relationships succeed or fail? The Gottman Institute. Web site: http://www.gottman.com/research/gaylesbian/self_help/.

Gottman, J. M. (2007). *And baby makes three: The six-step plan for preserving marital intimacy and rekindling romance after baby arrives*. New York: Crown.

Gottman, J. M. (2011). *The science of trust: Emotional attunement for couples*. New York: W. W. Norton.

Gottman, J. M. (2011). *The science of trust: Emotional attunement for couples*. New York: W. W. Norton. *Journal of Family Communication*. Philadelphia: Routledge. Web site: http://www.tandf.co.uk/journals/hjfc.

Gottman, J. M., & DeClaire, J. (2001). *The relationship cure: A five-step guide for building better connections with family, friends, and lovers*. New York: Crown.

Gottman, J. M., Gottman, J. S., & DeClaire, J. (2006). *Ten lessons to transform your marriage: America's love lab experts share their strategies for strengthening your relationship*. New York: Crown Publishers.

Gottman, J. M., & Notarius, C. I. (2000). Decade review: Observing marital interaction. *Journal of Marriage and the Family, 62*, 927–947.

Gottman, J. M., Schwartz Gottman, J., & DeClaire, J. (2006). *Ten lessons to transform your marriage: America's love lab experts share their strategies for strengthening your relationship*. New York: Crown.

Gottman, J. M., Schwartz Gottman, J., & DeClaire, J. (2006). *Ten lessons to transform your marriage: America's love lab experts share their strategies for strengthening your relationships*. New York: Crown. The latest book from the University of Washington research team.

Gottman, J. M., & Silver, N. (1994). *Why marriages succeed or fail*. New York: Simon & Schuster.

Gouin, J.-P., Kiecolt-Glaser, J. K., Malarkey, W. B., & Glaser, R. (2008). The influence of anger expression on wound healing. *Brain, Behavior, and Immunity, 22*, 699–708.

Graham, L. (1998, December 13). Where have all the small towns gone? *Parade*, pp. 6–9.

Gray, P. (1998, January 18). Paradise found. *Time*, p. 67.

Green, R. (2012). Gay and lesbian family life. In F. Walsh (Ed.), *Normal family process* (4th ed., pp. 172–195). New York: Guilford Press.

Greenspan, S. I. (2003). Child care research: A clinical perspective. *Child Development, 74*(4), 1064–1068.

Greer, M. (2005). A new kind of war. *Monitor on Psychology, 36*, 38.

Greif, G. L. (2000). How do I involve fathers? In D. DePanfilis (Ed.), *Handbook for child protection practice*. Thousand Oaks, CA: Sage.

Grieco, E. M. (2010, January). *Race and Hispanic origin of the foreign-born population in the United States: 2007*. (U. S. Census Bureau Report ASC-11). Retrieved from http://www.census.gov/prod/2010pubs/acs-11.pdf.

Grotevant, H. D. (2003). Counseling psychology meets the complex world of adoption. *The Counseling Psychologist, 31*(6), 753–762.

Grotevant, H. D. (2008, September). Open adoption: What is it and how is it working? *National Council on Family Relations Report, 53*(3), F1–F2, F17–F19.

Gudmunson, C. G., Beutler, I. F., Israelsen, C. L., McCoy, J. K., & Hill, E. J. (2007). Linking financial strain to marital instability: Examining the roles of emotional distress and marital interaction. *Journal of Family and Economic Issues, 28*, 357–376.

Gurman, A. (Ed.). (2008). *Clinical handbook of couple therapy* (4th ed.). New York: Guilford Press.

Gustafson, R. (2005). Is pornography addictive? Web site: http://www.parentstov.org.

Guttmacher Institute. Created four decades ago "to advance sexual and reproductive health in the United States and worldwide through an interrelated program of social science research, policy analysis and public education designed to generate new ideas, encourage enlightened public debate, promote sound policy and program development and, ultimately, inform individual decision making." Web site: http://www.guttmacher.org/.

Guttmacher Institute. (2006). U.S. teenage pregnancy statistics: National and state trends and trends by race and ethnicity. Web site: http://www.guttmacher.org/pubs/2006/09/11/USTPstats.pdf.

Guttmacher Institute. (2007a). Strong evidence favors comprehensive approach to sex ed. Web site: http://guttmacher.org/media/nr/2007/05/23/index.html.

Guttmacher Institute. (2007b). Changing direction: Support sex education that works. Web site: http://www.guttmacher.org/media/presskits/2007/05/10/sexed.html/.

Haddock, S. A., Zimmerman, T. S., Ziemba, S. J., & Lyness, K. P. (2006). Practices of dual earner couples successfully balancing work and family. *Journal of Family and Economic Issues, 27*, 207–234.

Hagestad, G. O., & Call, V. (2007). Pathways to childlessness: A life perspective. *Journal of Family Issues, 28*, 1338–1361.

Queensland, Australia: Australian Academic Press.

Halgunseth, L. C., Ispa, J. M., & Rudy, D. (2006). Parental control in Latino families: An integrated review of the literature. *Child Development, 77*, 1282–1297.

Hall, M., & Havens, B. (2004). Social isolation and social loneliness. Division of Aging and Seniors, Health Canada. Web site: http://www.hc-sc.gc.ca/seniors-aines/naca/writings_gerontology/writ18/writ18_3_e.htm.

Halpern, D. F., & Cheung, F. M. (2008). *Women at the top: Powerful leaders tell us how to combine work and family.* West Sussex, United Kingdom: Wiley-Blackwell.

Hammack, P., & Cohler, B. (2009). *The story of sexual identity: Narrative perspectives on the gay and lesbian life course.* New York: Oxford University Press.

Hamon, R. R., & Ingoldsby, B. B. (Eds.). (2003). *Mate selection across cultures.* Thousand Oaks, CA: Sage. The meaningful processes, traditions, and practices related to couple formation around the world, including chapters from North America, the Caribbean and South America, Africa, the Middle East, Europe, and Asia.

Hanna, S. L., Suggett, R., & Radtke, D. (2008). *Person to person: Positive relationships don't just happen* (5th ed.). Upper Saddle River, NJ: Pearson/Prentice Hall.

Hao, L. (2007). *Color lines, country lines: Race, immigration and wealth stratification in America.* New York: Russell Sage Foundation.

Hare, J., & Skinner, D. (2008). "Whose child is this?" Determining legal status for lesbian parents who used assisted reproductive technologies. *Family Relations, 57*, 365–375.

Harmon, A. (1998, August 30). Researchers say cyberspace sad, lonely: People who spend time online are more depressed. Lincoln [NE] *Journal Star*, p. 5A.

Harris, A. H., & Thoresen, C. E. (2005). Forgiveness, unforgiveness, health and disease. In E. L. Worthington (Ed.), *Handbook of forgiveness* (pp. 321–334). New York: Routledge.

Harris, G. (2004, May 1). FDA restricts pill's availability. *New York Times* report in the Minneapolis *Star Tribune*, p. A2.

Harris, J. (2003). *I kissed dating goodbye.* Sisters, OR: Multnomah.

Harris, J. R. (2009). *The nurture assumption* (2nd ed.). New York: Free Press/Simon & Schuster.

Hart, A. D., Weber, C. H., & Taylor, D. (1998). *Secrets of Eve: Understand the mystery of female sexuality.* Nashville: Word.

Harter, P. (2004, August 4). Divorce divides Morocco and W Sahara. *BBC News.* Web site: http://news.bbc.co.uk/go/pr/fr/-/1/hi/world/africa/3532612.stm.

Hartshorne, J. K., Salem-Hartshorne, N., & Hartshorne, T. (2009). Birth order effects in the formation of long-term relationships. *Journal of Individual Psychology, 65*, 156–176.

Harvey, J. H. (Ed.). (2004). *The handbook of sexuality in close relationships.* Mahwah, NJ: Erlbaum. Enhances the dialogue about the centrality of sexual issues in close relationships.

Hatcher, R. A., Trussell, J., Stewart, F., Stewart, G. K., Kowal, D., Guest, F., Cates, W., & Policar, M. S. (1998). *Contraceptive technology* (17th ed.). New York: Irvington.

Hawley, D. R., & Olson, D. H. (1995). Enriching newlyweds: An evaluation of three enrichment programs. *American Journal of Family Therapy, 23*, 129–147.

Hawthorne, B. (2000). Split custody as a viable post-divorce option. *Journal of Divorce and Remarriage, 33*(4), 1–19.

He, W., Sengupta, M., Velkoff, V. A., & DeBarros, K. A. (2005). 65+ in the United States: 2005. *Current population reports.* Washington, DC: Government Printing Office.

Hecker, L. L., & Wetchler, J. L. (Eds.). (2003). *An introduction to marriage and family therapy.* London: Routledge, Taylor & Francis Group. Insight and analysis from 20 experts.

Helburn, S. W., & Bergmann, B. R. (2002). *America's childcare problem: The way out.* New York: Palgrave. A holistic overview of all aspects of child care in America.

Hellmich, N. (1990, April 4). Marriage is no. 1 with men. *USA Today*, p. 1D.

Hennon, C. B., & Wilson, S. M. (Eds.). (2008). *Families in a global context.* London: Routledge, Taylor & Francis Group. How are families the same or different around the world? An in-depth analysis of family life in 17 countries.

Henry J. Kaiser Family Foundation/ABC Television. (1998, September). Sex in the 90s: 1998 National survey of Americans on sex and sexual health. Web site: http://www.kff.org.

Henshaw, S. K. (1999). *U.S. teenage pregnancy statistics with comparative statistics for women aged 20–24* (p. 5). New York: Alan Guttmacher Institute.

Herbenick, D., Reece, M., Schick, V., Sanders, S. A., Dodge, B., & Fortenberry, J. D. (2010). Sexual behavior in the United States: Results from a national probability sample of men and women ages 14–94. *Journal of Sexual Medicine, 7*, 255–265.

Herbert, W. (1999, February 22). Not tonight, dear: Americans say their sex lives leave a lot to be desired. *U.S. News and World Report*, pp. 57–59.

Herbst, P. G. (1952). The measurement of family relationships. *Human Relations, 5*, 3–35.

Herek, G. M. (2006). Legal recognition of same-sex relationships in the United States. *American Psychologist, 61* (6), 607–621.

Hernandez, D. J. (1997). Child development and the social demography of childhood. *Child Development, 68*(1), 149–169.

Heron, M. P., Hoyert, D. L., Xu, J., Scott, C., & Tejada-Vera, B. (2008). Deaths: Preliminary data for 2006. *National Vital Statistics Reports, 56*(18). Hyattsville, MD: National Center for Health Statistics.

Herz, R. S., & Inzlicht, M. (2002). Sex differences in response to physical and social factors involved in human mate selection: The importance of smell for women. *The Evolution of Human Behavior, 23*, 359–364.

Hetherington, E. M. (1992). Coping with marital transitions: A family systems perspective. *Monographs of the Society for Research in Child Development, 57.*

Hetherington, E. M., & Kelly, J. (2002). *For better or worse: Divorce reconsidered.* New York: W. W. Norton.

Higginbotham, B., Skogrand, L., & Torres, E. (2010). Stepfamily education: Perceived benefits for children. *Journal of Divorce & Remarriage, 51,* 36–49.

Higginson, J. G. (1998). Competitive parenting: The culture of teen mothers. *Journal of Marriage and the Family, 60,* 135–149.

Hill, M. S., Freedmen, S. R., & Enright, R. D. (2007). Towards a feminist empowerment model of forgiveness psychotherapy. *Psychotherapy: Theory, Research, Practice, Training, 44,* 14–29.

Hill, R. (1949). *Families under stress: Adjustment to the crises of war separation and reunion.* New York: Harper.

Hill, R. (1958). Generic features of families under stress. *Social Casework, 49,* 139–150.

Hill, R. (1971). *The strengths of Black families.* New York: Emerson Hall.

Hill, Z. E., Cleland, J., & Ali, M. M. (2004). Religious affiliation and extramarital sex among men in Brazil. *International Family Planning Perspectives, 30*(1), 20–26.

Hine, D. C. (2007). Family first, then the world. In H. McAdoo (Ed.) *Black families* (4th ed, pp. 238–247). Thousand Oaks, CA: Sage.

Hines, P. M., & Boyd-Franklin, N. (1996). African American families. In M. McGoldrick, J. Giordano, & J. K. Pearce (Eds.), *Ethnicity and family therapy* (pp. 66–84). New York: Guilford.

Hingson, R. W., & Howland, J. (2002). Comprehensive community interventions to promote health: Implications for college-age drinking problems. *Journal of Studies on Alcohol,* Suppl. No. 14, 226–240.

Hird, M. J., & Abshoff, K. (2000). Women without children: A contradiction in terms? *Journal of Comparative Family Studies, 31*(3), 347–366.

Hobfoll, S. E., & Spielberger, C. D. (1992). Family stress: Integrating theory and measurement. *Journal of Family Psychology, 6*(2), 99–112.

Hochshild, A. (2009, October 16). The state of families, class and culture. *New York Times.* Web site: http://www.nytimes.com/2009/10/18/books/review/Hochshild-t.html/_r=2.

Hochschild, A. (2010). Berkeley sociology faculty profile. Web site: http://sociology.berkeley.-edu/profiles/hochschild/.

Hochschild, A. R. (1997). *The time bind: When work becomes home and home becomes work.* New York: Metropolitan Books.

Hoffman, L., & Rainville, A. (2004, December 15). Children of the fallen. Scripps Howard News Service. Web site: www.shns.com/shns/warkids.

Hogan, M. J. (1993). Family futures: Possibilities, preferences and probabilities. *Marriage and Family Review, 18,* 255–262.

Holmes, T. H., & Ella, D. M. (Eds.). (1989). *Life change, life events, and illness: Selected papers.* New York: Praeger.

Holmes, T. H., & Rahe, R. H. (1967). The social readjustment rating scale. *Journal of Psychosomatic Research, 11,* 213–218.

Holstein, J. A., & Gubrium, J. F. (Eds.). (2008). *Handbook of constructionist research.* New York: Guilford Press.

Holtzman, M. (2005, June). The family definitions continuum. *Family Focus,* pp. 1, 3.

Holtzworth-Munroe, A. (2005). Male versus female intimate partner violence: Putting controversial findings into context. *Journal of Marriage and the Family, 67,* 1120–1125.

Holzner, C., Jameson, K., Maloney, T., Abebe, B., Lund, M., & Schaub, K. (2006). *The economic impact of the Mexico–Utah relationship.* University of Utah. Web site: http://www.ipia.utah.edu/utah_mexico_final_version.pdf.

Homer, M. M., Freeman, P. A., Zabriskie, R. B., & Eggett, D. L. (2007). Rituals and relationships: Examining the relationship between family of origin rituals and young adult attachment. *Marriage and Family Review, 42,* 5–27.

Hood Center for Children and Families, Dartmouth Medical College. (2012). Smoking. Web site: http://hoodcenter.dartmouth.edu/research-programs/smoking/parent-family_influences.html.

Horn, W. (2010). "Wade Horn." Wikipedia. Web site: http://en.wikipedia.org/wiki/-Wade_Horn.

Horn, W. F. (1995). *Father facts.* Lancaster, PA: The National Fatherhood Initiative.

Hornik, D. (2001). Can the church get in step with stepfamilies? *US Catholic, 66*(7), 30–31.

Hosek, J. (Ed.). (2011). How is deployment to Iraq and Afghanistan affecting U.S. service members and their families? An overview of early RAND research on the topic. RAND National Defense Research Institute. Web site: rand.org/content/dam/rand/occasional_papers/2011/RAND_OP316.pdf.

Hoskins, M. (2005, winter). Merger of minds: Buffet/Gates. *Nebraska Magazine,* 30–35. Web site: http://ncsu.edu/ffci/publications/2009/v14-n1-2009-spring/olsen-skogrand.php.

Houseknecht, S. K., & Lewis, S. K. (2005). Explaining teen childbearing and cohabitation: Community embeddedness and primary ties. *Family Relations, 54,* 607–620.

Houseknecht, S. K., & Sastry, J. (1996). Family decline and child well-being: A comparative analysis. *Journal of Marriage and the Family, 58,* 726–739.

Howard, J. (2002). In A. Gore and T. Gore, *The spirit of family.* New York: Henry Holt (back cover).

Howden, L. M., & Meyer, J. A. (2011, May). *Age and sex composition: 2010.* U.S. Census Bureau, U. S. Census Briefs. Web site: http://www.census.gov/prod/cen2010/briefs/c2010br-03.pdf.

Huebner, A. J., Mancini, J. A., Bowen, G. L., & Orthner, D. K. (2009). Shadowed by war: Building community capacity to support military families. *Family Relations, 58,* 216–228.

Huebner, A. J., Mancini, J. A., Wilcox, R. M., Grass, S. R., & Grass, G. A. (2007). Parental deployment and youth in military families: Exploring uncertainty and ambiguous loss. *Family Relations, 56,* 112–122.

Hull, E. (2011). Military service and marriage: A review of research. National Healthy Marriage Resource Center. Web site: http://www.healthymarriageinfo.org.

Human Rights Watch. (2004, November 29). Divorced from justice: Women's unequal access to divorce in Egypt. Web site: http://hrw.org/reports/2004/egypt1204/1.htm.

Humes, K. R., Jones, N. A., & Ramirez, R. R. (2011, March). *Overview of race and Hispanic origin: 2010* (U.S. Census Bureau Report C2010BR-02). Retrieved from http://www.census.gov/prod/cen2010/briefs/c2010br-02.pdf.

Hyde, J. S., & DeLamater, J. D. (2008). *Understanding human sexuality* (10th ed.). Boston: McGraw-Hill Higher Education. An excellent comprehensive textbook.

Hyde, J. S., & DeLamater, J. D. (2010). *Understanding human sexuality* (11th ed.). New York: McGraw-Hill.

Iasenza, S. (2010). What is queer about sex?: Expanding sexual frames in theory and practice. *Family Process, 49,* 291–308.

Ihinger-Tallman, M., & Pasley, K. (1987). *Remarriage.* Newbury Park, CA: Sage.

Ihinger-Tallman, M., & Pasley, K. (1997). Stepfamilies in 1984 and today: A scholarly perspective. *Marriage and Family Review, 27*(1–2), 19–40.

Ikkink, K. K., van Tilburg, T., & Knipscheer, K. C. P. M. (1999). Perceived instrumental support exchanges in relationships between elderly parents and their adult children: Normative and structural explanations. *Journal of Marriage and the Family, 61,* 831–844.

Imber-Black, E. (Ed.). (2010). Couple and family therapy theory and practice: Innovations in 2010. *Family Process, 49*(3), 265–267.

Infoplease (2012). *Hispanic Americans by the numbers, from the U.S. Census Bureau.* Retrieved from http://www.infoplease.com/spot/hhmcensus1.html.

Inman, A. G., Altman, A., Kaduvettoor-Davidson, A., Carr, A., & Walker, J. (2011). Cultural intersections: A qualitative inquiry into the experience of Asian Indian–White interracial couples. *Family Process, 50,* 248–266.

Insel, P. M., & Roth, W. T. (2010). *Connect Core Concepts in Health* (Brief 11th Ed.). New York: McGraw-Hill Higher Education.

Insel, P. M., & Roth, W. T. (2014). *Core concepts in health* (13th ed.). New York: McGraw-Hill.

Institute for Women's Leadership, Rutgers University. (2011). Women heads of state. Web site: http://www.iwl.rutgers.edu/documents/njwomencount/womenHeadsofstates.pdf.

Jackson, J. K. (1954). The adjustments of the family to the crisis of alcoholism. *Quarterly Journal of Studies on Alcohol, 15,* 562–586.

Jacobs, N. N. (2006). *Coping with infertility: Clinically proven ways of managing the emotional roller coaster.* Routledge Mental Health. Web site: http://www.routledgementalhealth.com. For couples trying to better understand and cope with issues involving infertility.

Janus, S. S., & Janus, C. L. (1993). *The Janus report on sexual behavior.* New York: Wiley.

Jayson, S. (2010). Free as a bird and loving it. In K. Gilbert (Ed.), *Annual edition: The family 10/11* (pp. 47–48). Boston: McGraw-Hill.

Jervis, L. L., Beals, J., Croy, C. D., Klein, S. A., Manson, S. M., & AI-SUPERPFP Team. (2006). Historical consciousness among two American Indian tribes. *American Behavioral Scientist, 50,* 526–549.

Focus, 40, F17–F19.

Johnson, M. P. (2008). A typology of domestic violence: Intimate terrorism, violent resistance, and situational couple violence. Boston: Northeastern University Press.

Johnson, M. P. (2012). Professional. Web site: http://www.personal.psu.edu/MPJ/Welcome.html.

Joint United Nations Programme on HIV/AIDS and World Health Organization. (2009, November). 09 AIDS epidemic update. Web site: unaids.org.

Jones, E. F., & Stahmann, R. F. (1994). Clergy beliefs, preparation, and practice in premarital counseling. *Journal of Pastoral Care, 48,* 181–186.

Jones, F., & Bright, J. (2007). Stress: Health and illness. In A. Monat, R. S. Lazarus, & R. Reevy (Eds.), *The Praeger handbook on stress and coping* (vol. 1, pp. 141–168). Westport, CT: Praeger.

Jones-Sanpei, H., Holmes, E. K., & Day, R. D. (2009). Family process environmental measures. In the NLSY97: Variation by race and socioeconomic conditions. *Marriage & Family Review, 45,* 160–180.

Jouriles, E. N., Norwood, W. D., McDonald, R., & Peters, B. (2001). Domestic violence and child adjustment. In J. H. Grych & F. D. Fincham (Eds.), *Interparental conflict and child development: Theory, research, and applications* (pp. 315–336). New York: Cambridge University Press.

Julien, D., Chartrand, E., Simard, M., Bouthillier, D., & Begin, J. (2003). Conflict, social support, and relationship quality: An observational study of heterosexual, gay male and lesbian couples' communication. *Journal of Family Psychology, 17*(3), 419–428.

Journal of Family Communication. Philadelphia: Routledge. *JFC* publishes original empirical and theoretical papers that advance the understanding of the communication processes within or about families. *JFC* is also committed to publishing manuscripts that address issues related to the intersection between families, communication, and social systems, such as mass media, education, health care, and law and policy. Web site: http://www.tandf.co.uk/journals/hjfc.

Kagan, J. (1964). *The nature of the child.* New York: Basic Books.

Kaminer, Y., & Bukstein, O. G. (2008). *Adolescent substance abuse.* New York: Routledge.

Kansas State University at Manhattan. (2010). Useful information on parenting and families on the KSU Extension Web site: www.oznet.ksu.edu/.

Kantrowitz, B. (2006). Sex and love: The new world. *Newsweek, 147*(8), 50–54, 58–60.

Kantrowitz, B., & Springen, K. (2007, June 18). Confronting Alzheimer's. *Newsweek,* 55–61.

Kapungu, C. T., Baptiste, D., Holmbeck, G., McBride, C., Robinson-Brown, M., Sturdivant, A., Crown, L., & Paikoff, R. (2010). Beyond the "birds and the bees": Gender differences in sex-related communication among urban African-American adolescents. *Family Process, 49,* 251–264.

Karger, H. (2005). *Shortchanged: Life and debt in the fringe economy.* San Francisco: Berrett-Koehler.

Karis, T. A., & Killian, K. D. (2008). *Intercultural couples.* London: Routledge, Taylor & Francis Group. Cross-cultural relationships were once shunned and assumed to be inherently problematic. But in recent years intercultural couples have grown in numbers and social acceptance.

Kartemquin Films. (2008). *The new Americans.* Web site: kartemquin.com. Follows 4 years in the lives of a diverse group of contemporary immigrants and refugees as they start new lives in America. An Indian couple is viewed through the dot-com boom and bust in Silicon Valley. A Mexican meatpacker struggles to reunite his family in rural Kansas. Two families of Nigerian refugees escape government persecution. Two Los Angeles Dodgers prospects follow their big dreams of escaping the barrios of the Dominican Republic. And a Palestinian woman marries into a new life in Chicago, only to discover that in the wake of September 11, she cannot leave behind the pain of the conflict in her homeland.

Kasolowsky, R. (2010). British couple arrested in Dubai for extramarital sex. Reuters. Web site: http://www.msnbc.msn.com/id/34823864.

Kaufman, A. (2011). *Personality, partner similarity and couple satisfaction: Do opposites attract or birds of a feather flock together.* Prepare Enrich. Web site: https://www.prepare-enrich.com/pe/pdf/research/2011/personality_and_couple_satisfaction_kaufmann_2011.pdf.

Kaufman, M. (2000, September 30). RU-486 user: It's easier, but not easy. *Washington Post* article published in the Lincoln [NE] *Journal Star,* p. 6A.

Keillor, G. (1994, October 17). It's good old monogamy that's really sexy. *Time,* p. 71.

Keillor, G. (2005). *Lake Wobegon days.* New York: Viking Penguin.

Keillor, G. (2009). *A Prairie Home Companion* with Garrison Keillor. Web site: http://prairiehome.publicradio.org/.

Kelly, G. F. (2008). *Sexuality today* (9th ed.). New York: McGraw-Hill Higher Education.

Kelly, J. B. (2007). Children's living arrangements: Following separation and divorce: Insights from empirical and clinical research. *Family Process, 46,* 35–52.

Kendig, H., Dykstra, P. A., Gaalen, P. A., & Melkas, T. (2007). Health of aging parents and childless individuals. *Journal of Family Issues, 28,* 1457–1486.

Kennedy, J. F. (1990). Inaugural address. In D. B. Baker (Ed.), *Political quotations.* Detroit: Gale Research. (Original work published 1961.)

Kensinger-Rose, K., & Elicker, J. (2008). Parental decision making about child care. *Journal of Family Issues, 29*(9), 1161–1184.

Kersting, K. (2005, March). Happiness in men usually drops after age 65, study finds. *American Psychological Association Monitor.* Web site: apa.org/monitor/march05/happiness.aspx.

Kiang, L., Gonzales-Backen, M., Yip, T., Witkow, M., & Fuligni, A. (2006). Ethnic identity and the daily psychological well-being of adolescents from Mexican and Chinese backgrounds. *Child Development, 77,* 1338–1350.

Kilmann, R., & Thomas, K. (1975). Interpersonal conflict: Handling behavior as reflections of Jungian personality dimensions. *Psychological Reports, 37,* 971–980.

Kim, H. W., Markman, H. J., & Scott, S. (2008). Strengthening couples' relationships with education: Social policy and public health perspectives. *Journal of Family Psychology, 22*(4), 497–505. "There is some evidence that skill-based couples relationship education enhances couples' maintenance of healthy, committed relationships."

Kindlon, D. (2001). *Too much of a good thing: Raising children of character in an indulgent age.* New York: Talk Miramax.

King, V., & Scott, M. E. (2005). A comparison of cohabiting relationships among older and younger adults. *Journal of Marriage and the Family, 67*(May), 271–285.

Kinsey Institute for Research in Sex, Gender, and Reproduction. The Kinsey Institute at Indiana University promotes interdisciplinary research and scholarship in the fields of human sexuality, gender, and reproduction. Web site: http://www.kinseyinstitute.org/.

Klein, D. M., & White, J. M. (1996). *Family theories.* Thousand Oaks, CA: Sage.

Klein, M., & Gordon, S. (1992). Sex education. In C. E. Walker & M. C. Roberts (Eds.), *Handbook of clinical child psychology* (2nd ed., pp. 933–949). New York: Wiley.

Kleinke, C. L. (2007). What does it mean to cope? In A. Monat, R. S. Lazarus, & R. Reevy (Eds.), *The Praeger handbook on stress and coping* (vol. 2, pp. 289–308). Westport, CT: Praeger.

Kline, G. H., Stanley, S. M., Markman, H. J., Olmos-Gallo, P. A., St. Peters, M., Whitton, S. W., & Prado, L. M. (2004). Timing is everything: Pre-engagement cohabitation and increased risk for poor marital outcomes. *Journal of Family Psychology, 18*(2), 311–318.

Knapp, M. L., & Vangelisti, A. L. (2009). *Interpersonal communication and human relationships* (6th ed.) Boston: Pearson/Allyn & Bacon.

Knight, G. P., Roosa, M. W., & Umaña-Taylor, A. J. (2009). *Studying ethnic minority and economically disadvantaged populations: Methodological challenges and best practices.* Washington, D.C: American Psychological Association.

Knoester, C., Petts, R. J., & Eggebeen, D. J. (2007). Commitments to fathering and the well-being and social participation of new, disadvantaged fathers. *Journal of Marriage and the Family, 69,* 991–1004.

Knudson-Martin, C. (2012). Changing gender norms in families and society. In F. Walsh (Ed.), *Normal family process* (4th ed., pp. 297–323). New York: Guilford Press.

Knutson, L., & Olson, D. H. (2003). Effectiveness of PREPARE Program with premarital couples in a community setting. *Marriage and Family, 6*(4), 529–546.

Kohlberg, L. (1966). Cognitive stages and preschool education. *Human Development, 9,* 5–17.

Kolak, A. M., & Volling, B. L. (2007). Parental expressiveness as a moderator of coparenting and marital relationship quality. *Family Relations, 56* (December), 467–478.

Koropeckyj-Cox, T., & Pendell, G. (2007). The gender gap in attitudes about childlessness in the United States. *Journal of Marriage and the Family, 69* (November), 899–915.

Koropeckyj-Cox, T., & Pendell, G. (2009). Attitudes about childlessness in the United States. *Journal of Family Issues, 28*(8), 1054–1082.

Kostelnik, M. (2005). *What is a high quality early childhood program?* Lincoln: University of Nebraska, College of Education and Human Sciences.

Kottak, C. P. (2004). *Anthropology: The exploration of human diversity* (10th ed.). Boston: McGraw-Hill.

Kraut, R., Patterson, M., Lundmark, V., Kiesler, S., Mukopadhyay, T., & Scherlis, W. (1998). Internet paradox: A social technology that reduces social involvement and psychological well-being? *American Psychologist, 53*(9), 1017–1031.

Kuba, C. A. (2006). *Navigating the journey of aging parents: What care receivers want.* New York: Taylor & Francis.

Kulthau, K., & Mason, K. O. (1996). Market child care versus care by relatives: Choices made by employed and non-employed mothers. *Journal of Family Issues, 17*(4), 561–578.

Kurdek, L. A. (1998). The nature and predictors of the trajectory of change in marital quality over the first 4 years of marriage for first-married husbands and wives. *Journal of Family Psychology, 12*(4), 594–610.

Kurdek, L. A. (2000). Attractions and constraints as determinants of relationship commitment: Longitudinal evidence from gay, lesbian, and heterosexual couples. *Personal Relationships, 7*(3), 245–262.

Kurdek, L. A. (2003). On being insecure about the assessment of attachment styles. *Journal of Social and Personal Relationships, 19*(6), 811–834.

Kurdek, L. A. (2004). Are gay and lesbian cohabiting couples really different from heterosexual married couples? *Journal of Marriage and the Family, 66*, 880–900.

Kurdek, L. A. (2005). Gender and marital satisfaction early in marriage: A growth curve approach. *Journal of Marriage and the Family, 67*, 68–84.

Kurdek, L. A. (2006). Differences between partners from heterosexual, gay, and lesbian cohabiting couples. *Journal of Marriage and the Family, 68*, 509–528.

Kurdek, L. A. (2008). Change in relationship quality for partners from lesbian, gay male, and heterosexual couples. *Journal of Family Psychology, 22*(5), 701–711.

Lacayo, R. (1997, April 14). The kids are all right: Day care—A new study says it's mostly harmless, sometimes helpful and less important than home. *Time*, p. 76.

Lachman, M. E. (2004). Development in midlife. *Annual Review of Psychology, 55*, 305–331.

LaMastro, V. (2001). Childless by choice? Attributions and attitudes concerning family size. *Social Behavior and Personality, 29*(3), 231–243.

Web site: http://times.hankooki.com/, cgi-bin/, hnppna cgi?pa=/1page/opinion/200408/kt2004080916572054130.htm&ur=times.hankooki.com&fo=print_kt.htm.

Larsen, A. S., & Olson, D. H. (1989). Predicting marital satisfaction using PREPARE: A replication study. *Journal of Marital and Family Therapy, 15*, 311–322.

Larson, P. J., & Olson, D. H. (2004). Spiritual beliefs and marriage: A national survey based on ENRICH. *The Family Psychologist, 20*(2), 4–8.

Larson, P. J., & Olson, D. H. (2012). Top five stressors for couples. Web site: http://www.prepare-enrich.com/research.

Larson, R. W., Branscomb, K. R., & Wiley, A. R. (2006). Forms and function of family mealtimes: Multidisciplinary perspectives. In R. W. Larson, A. R. Wiley, & K. R. Branscomb (Eds.), *Family mealtimes as a context of development and socialization* (pp. 1–15). San Francisco: Jossey-Bass.

Larson, R. W., Wilson, S., Brown, B. B., Furstenberg, F. F., Jr., & Verma, S. (2002). Changes in adolescents' interpersonal experiences: Are they being prepared for adult relationships in the twenty-first century? *Journal of Research on Adolescence, 12*(1), 31–68.

Lasswell, M., & Lasswell, T. (1991). *Marriage and the family* (3rd ed.). Belmont, CA: Wadsworth.

Laughlin, L. (2010). Who's minding the kids? Child care arrangements: Spring 2005/Summer 2006. Household Economic Studies, U.S. Census Bureau. Web site: http://www.census.gov/hhes/childcare/.

Laumann, E. O. (2010). Edward O. Laumann, Department of Sociology, University of Chicago. Web site: http://sociology.uchicago.edu/people/faculty/laumann.shtml.

Laumann, E. O., et al. (Eds.). (2004). *The sexual organization of the city.* Chicago: University of Chicago Press.

Laumann, E. O., Gagnon, J. H., Michael, R. T., & Michaels, S. (1994). *The social organization of sexuality: Sexual practices in the United States.* Chicago: University of Chicago Press.

Laumann, E. O., Gagnon, J. H., Michael, R. T., Michaels, S., & Kolata, G. (1995). *Sex in America: A definitive survey.* Boston: Little, Brown.

Laumann, E. O., & Michael, R. T. (2000). *Sex, love, and health in America: Private choices and public policies.* Chicago: University of Chicago Press.

Laumann, E. O., Paik, A., & Rosen, R. C. (1999). Sexual dysfunction in the United States: Prevalence and predictors. *Journal of the American Medical Association, 28*(6), 537–544.

Lawrence, E., Rothman, A. D., Cobb, R. J., Rothman, M. T., & Bradbury, T. N. (2008). Marital satisfaction across the transition in parenthood. *Journal of Family Psychology, 22*(1), 41–50.

Lazarony, L. (2002, August 15). Credit cards: Big debt on campus. Web site: http://www.bankrate.com/brm/news/cc/20020815a.asp.

Lazarus, R. S. (2007). Stress and emotion: A new synthesis. In A. Monat, R. S. Lazarus, & R. Reevy (Eds.), *The Praeger handbook on stress and coping* (vol. 1, pp. 33–52). Westport, CT: Praeger.

Leboyer, F. (1995). *Birth without violence: The book that revolutionized the way we bring our children into the world.* Rochester, VT: Healing Arts Press.

Lee, C. Y. S., & Doherty, W. J. (2007). Marital satisfaction and father involvement during the transition to parenthood. *Fathering, 5,* 75–98.

Lee, E., & Mock, M. (2005). Asian families: An overview. In M. McGoldrick, J. Giordano, N. Garcia-Preto (Eds.). *Ethnicity and family therapy* (3rd ed.). New York: Guilford Press.

Lee, G. R., Peek, C. W., & Coward, R. T. (1998). Race differences in filial responsibility expectations among older parents. *Journal of Marriage and the Family, 60,* 404–412.

Lee, V. (1996). Asian American families: An overview. In M. McGoldrick, J. Giordano, & J. K. Pearce (Eds.), *Ethnicity and family therapy* (pp. 227–248). New York: Guilford.

Lee, Y., & Waite, L. (2005). Husbands' and wives' time spent on housework: A comparison of measures. *Journal of Marriage and the Family, 67,* 328–336.

Leiblum, S. R. (2002). *Getting the sex you want: A woman's guide to becoming proud, passionate, and pleased in bed.* New York: Crown.

Leiblum, S. R. (Ed.). (2007). *Principles and practice of sex therapy.* New York: Guilford Press.

Leiblum, S., & Rosen, R. (2000). *Principles and practices of sex therapy.* New York: Guilford.

Leifer, M. (1980). *Psychological effects of motherhood: A study of first pregnancy.* New York: Praeger.

LeMasters, E. E. (1957). Parenthood as crisis. *Marriage and Family Living, 19,* 325–355.

Leon, K., & Jacobvitz, D. B. (2003). Relationships between adult attachment representations and family ritual quality: A prospective, longitudinal study. *Family Process, 42*(3), 419–432.

Lerner, H. G. (2005). *The dance of anger: A woman's guide to changing the patterns of intimate relationships.* New York: Perennial Currents.

Lerner, H. G. (2005). *The dance of anger: A woman's guide to changing the patterns of intimate relationships.* New York: Perennial Currents. A new edition of the classic.

Lerner, H. G. (2012). *Marriage rules: A manual for the married and the coupled up.* New York: Gotham Books.

Lerner, H. G. (2012). *Marriage rules: A manual for the married and the coupled up.* New York: Gotham Books. Good advice from the much-admired couple and family therapist.

Letiecq, B. L., Bailey, S. J., & Kurtz, M. A. (2008). Depression among rural Native American and European American grandparents rearing their grandchildren. *Journal of Family Issues, 29,* 334–356.

Levaro, E. B. (2011). Theorizing age and gender in the pursuit of love in later life. Doctoral dissertation. Corvallis, OR: Oregon State University. Web site: http://www.ir.library.oregonstate.edu/xmlui/bitstream/handle/1957/22664/L.

Levaro, L. B. (2009, summer). Living together or living apart together: New choices for old lovers. *Family Focus,* 9–10.

Levin, D. E., & Kilbourne, J. (2008). *So sexy so soon: The new sexualized childhood and what parents can do to protect their kids.* New York: Ballantine Books. Sex is everywhere in American commercial culture. How to help children live in such an environment.

Levine, J. A., & Pitt, E. W. (1995). *New expectations: Community strategies for responsible fatherhood.* New York: Families and Work Institute.

Levine, J. A., & Pleck, J. H. (2002). Masculinity and fatherhood. Sloan Work and Family Research Network, Boston College. Web site: http://wfnetwork.bc.edu/The_Network_News-/4-1/TNN4-1_Pleck.pdf.

Levine, J. R., & Markman, H. J. (Eds.). (2001). *Why do fools fall in love? Experiencing the magic, mystery, and meaning of successful relationships.* San Francisco: Jossey-Bass.

Levy, K., Kelly, K. M., & Jack, E. L. (2006). Sex differences in *Jealousy:* A matter of evolution or attachment theory? In M. Mikulincer & G. S. Goodman (Eds.), *Dynamics of romantic love: Attachment, caregiving, and sex* (pp. 128–145). New York: Guilford.

Limb, G. E., & Hodge, D. R. (2008). Developing spiritual competency with Native Americans: Promoting wellness through balance and harmony. *Journal of Contemporary Social Sciences, 89,* 615–622.

Lindau, S. T., Schumm, L. P., Laumann, E. O., Levinson, W., O'Muircheartaigh, C. A., & Waite, L. J. (2007). A study of sexuality and health among older adults in the United States. *New England Journal of Medicine, 357,* 762–774.

Lino, M. (2004). *Expenditures on children by families, 2003.* U.S. Department of Agriculture, Center for Nutrition Policy and Promotion. Miscellaneous Publication No. 1528-2003. Washington, DC. Web site: http://www.cnpp.usda.gov.

Lino, M., & Carlson, A. (2009). *Expenditures on children by families, 2008.* U.S. Department of Agriculture, Center for Nutrition Policy and Promotion. Miscellaneous Publication No. 1528-2008. Web site: http://www.cnpp.usda.gov/ExpendituresonChildrenbyFamilies.htm.

Lippa, R. A. (2001). *Gender, nature, and nurture.* Mahwah, NJ: Erlbaum.

Lisle, J. (2004, November 24). Single women become a force in home buying. Web site: http://www.realestatejournal.com/buysell/salestrends/20041124-lisle.html.

Livingston, G., & Parker, K. (2010, September 9). Since the start of the Great Recession, more children raised by grandparents. Pew Research Center. Web site: http://www.pewsocialtrends.org.

Loseke, D. R., Gelles, R. J., & Cavanaugh, M. M. (Eds.). (2005). *Current controversies on family violence.* Thousand Oaks, CA: Sage.

Lunneborg, P. (1999). *The chosen lives of childfree men.* Westport, CT: Bergin & Garvey/Greenwood.

Luthra, R., & Gidycz, C. A. (2006). Dating violence among college men and women: Evaluation of a theoretical model. *Journal of Interpersonal Violence, 21*(6), 717–731.

Lykken, D. (1999). *Happiness.* New York: Golden Books.

Maccoby, E. E., & Lewis, C. C. (2003). Less day care or different day care? *Child Development, 74*(4), 1069–1075.

MacDonald, W. L., & DeMaris, A. (1995). Remarriage, stepchildren, and marital conflict: Challenges to the incomplete institutionalization hypothesis. *Journal of Marriage and the Family, 57,* 387–398.

couples. *Family Process, 48,* 9–23.

Madden, M., & Lenhart, A. (2006). Online dating. Washington, DC: Pew Internet & American Life Project. Web site: http://www.pewinternet.org/.

Mahoney, A. (2010). Religion in families, 1999–2009: A relational spirituality framework. *Journal of Marriage and Family, 72* (August), 805–827. The role of religion "for better and worse," in marital and parent-child relationships.

Malinowski, B. (1929). *The sexual life of savages.* New York: Harcourt.

Manning, R. D. (2001). Credit cards on campus. Web site: http://www.newdream.org/newsletter/creditcards.php.

Manning, W., & Brown, S. (2006). Children's economic well-being in married and cohabiting parent families. *Journal of Marriage and the Family, 68,* 345–362.

Manning, W., & Smock, P. (2005). Measuring and modeling cohabitation: New perspectives from qualitative data. *Journal of Marriage and the Family, 67,* 989–1002.

Manning, W. D., Longmore, M. A., & Giordano, P. C. (2007). The changing institution of marriage: Adolescents' expectations to cohabit and to marry. *Journal of Marriage and the Family, 69* (August), 559–575.

Manning, W. D., Stewart, S. D., & Smock, P. J. (2003). The complexity of fathers' parenting responsibilities and involvement with nonresident children. *Journal of Family Issues, 24*(5), 645–667.

Mansfield, A. J., Kaufman, J. S., Marshall, S. W., Gaynes, B. N., Morrissey, J. P., & Engel, C. C. (2010). Deployment and the use of mental health services among U. S. Army wives. *New England Journal of Medicine, 362,* 101–109.

Manzi, C., Vignoles, V. L., Regalia, C., & Scabini, E. (2006). Cohesion and enmeshment revisited: Differentiation, identity, and well-being in two European cultures. *Journal of Marriage and the Family, 68,* 673–689.

March of Dimes. (2009). Stillbirth. Web site: http://www.marchofdimes.com-/professionals/14332_1198.asp.

Marelich, W. D., Gaines, S. O., & Banzet, M. R. (2003). Commitment, insecurity and arousability: Testing a transactional model of jealousy. *Representative Research in Social Psychology, 27,* 23–31.

Markman, H. (2010). *Fighting for your marriage: A deluxe revised edition of the classic bestseller for enhancing marriage and preventing divorce* (3rd ed.). San Francisco: Jossey-Bass.

Markman, H. J. (2010). *Fighting for your marriage: A deluxe revised edition of the classic bestseller for enhancing marriage and preventing divorce* (3rd ed.). San Francisco: Jossey-Bass.

Markman, H. J., Stanley, S. M., Jenkins, N. H., & Blumberg, S. L. (2004). *12 hours to a great marriage: A step-by-step guide for making love last.* San Francisco: Jossey-Bass. Most recent popular book from Markman, the marriage communication authority, and his colleagues.

tative study of happy, enduring African American marriages. *Family Relations, 57,* 172–185.

Marks, L. D., Swanson, M., Nesteruk, O., & Hopkins-Williams, K. (2006). Stressors in African American marriages and families: A qualitative study. *Stress, Trauma, and Crisis: An International Journal, 9,* 203–225.

Marmot, M. (2004). *Status syndrome: How your social standing directly affects your health and life expectancy.* New York: Times Books.

Marquardt, E., Blankenhorn, D., Lerman, R., Malone-Colon, L., & Wilcox, B. (2012). *The state of our unions 2012: The president's marriage agenda for the forgotten sixty percent.* University of Virginia, The National Marriage Project. Retrieved from http://www.stateofourunions.org/.

Marquardt, E., Blankenhhorn, D., Lerman, R., Malone-Colon, L., & Wilcox, B. (2012). *The state of our unions 2012: The president's marriage agenda for the forgotten sixty percent.* University of Virginia, The National Marriage Project. Web site: http://www.stateofourunions.org/.

Marquardt, E., Blankenhorn, D., Lerman, R. I., Malone-Colon, L., & Wilcox, W. B. (2012). The President's marriage agenda for the forgotten sixty percent. *The State of Our Unions.* Charlottesville, VA: National Marriage Project and Institute for American Values.

Marsh, J. C. (2003). Arguments for family strengths research. *Social Work, 48*(2), 147–149.

Martin, J. A., Hamilton, B. E., Sutton, P. D., Ventura, S. J., et al. (2009). Births: Final data for 2006. *National Vital Statistics Reports, 57*(7). Hyattsville, MD: National Center for Health Statistics.

Martinez-Brawley, E. E., & Zorita, P. (2011). Immigration and human services: The perils of professionalization. *The Journal of Contemporary Social Services, 92,* 133–137.

Mashek, D. J., & Aron, A. (Eds.). (2004). *Handbook of closeness and intimacy.* Mahwah, NJ: Erlbaum. Written by scholars in the field, this book provides the most comprehensive summary of a wealth of ideas about closeness and intimacy.

May, R. (1969). *Love and will.* New York: Norton.

Mayo Clinic. (n.d.) Excellent resources on extramarital sex, male and female sexual dysfunction. Web site: http://www.mayoclinic.com.

Mayo Clinic. (2009a). Coping with pregnancy loss. Web site: http://www.mayoclinic.com-/health/pregnancy-loss/PR00098.

Mayo Clinic. (2009b). Miscarriage. Web site: http://www.mayoclinic.com-/health/miscarriage/DS01105.

Mayo Clinic. (2010a). Female sexual dysfunction. Web site: http://www.mayoclinic.com/health/female-sexual-dysfunction/DS0070.

Mayo Clinic. (2010b). Female orgasm: Why can't I climax during sexual intercourse? Web site: http://www.mayoclinic.com/health/female-orgasm/AN0172/METHO.

Mayo Clinic. (2010c). Viagra for women: Why doesn't it exist? Web site: http://www.mayoclinic.com/health/viagra-for-women/AN01987?ME.

Mayo Clinic. (2012, May 31). Hormone therapy: Is it right for you? Web site: http://mayoclinic.com/health/hormone-therapy/WO00046.

Mayo Clinic (n.d.). Mayo Clinic Health Information. Retrieved from http://www.mayoclinic.com/health-information/.

McAdoo, H. P. (Ed.). (2007). *Black families* (4th ed.). Thousand Oaks, CA: Sage.

McBride, E. K. (2003). Splitting heirs: Reforming the custodial treatment of identical twins in divorce. *Family Law Quarterly, 37*(3), 515–526.

McCarthy, B. (2001). Male sexuality after fifty. *Journal of Family Psychotherapy, 12*(1), 29–37.

McCarthy, B. (2003). Marital sex as it ought to be. *Journal of Family Psychotherapy, 14*(2), 1–12.

McCarthy, B. W. (2003). *Rekindling desire: A step-by-step program to help low-sex and no-sex marriages.* London: Routledge Mental Health, Taylor & Francis Group.

McCarthy, B. W. (2007). *Men's sexual health: Fitness for satisfying sex.* London: Routledge Mental Health, Taylor & Francis Group.

McCarthy, B. W. (2009). *Discovering your couple sexual style: Sharing desire, pleasure, and satisfaction.* New York: Routledge.

McConaghy, N., Hadzi-Pavlovic, D., Stevens, C., & Manicavasagar, V. (2006). Fraternal birth birth order and ratio of heterosexual/homosexual feelings in women and men. *Journal of Homosexuality, 4*(51), 161–174.

McCullough, M. (2000, September 29). RU-486 wins FDA approval: Abortion pill available in a month. Knight Ridder Newspapers article published in the Lincoln [NE] *Journal Star,* p. 1A.

McGinley, E., & Sabbadini, A. (2006). *Play Misty for Me* (1971): The perversion of love. *International Journal of Psychoanalysis, 87*(2), 589–597.

McGirk, T. (2009, November 30). The hell of PTSD. *Time,* 41–43.

McGoldrick, M., Giordano, J., & Preto, N. G. (2008). *Ethnicity and family therapy.* New York: Guilford.

McGoldrick, M., & Hardy, K. V. (Eds.). (2008). *Re-visioning family therapy: Race, culture, and gender in clinical practice.* New York: Guilford Press.

McLeod, B. (1986, July). The oriental express. *Psychology Today,* pp. 48–52.

Mead, M. (1935). *Sex and temperament in three primitive societies.* New York: Morrow/Quill.

Mead, M. (1995). *Blackberry winter.* New York: Kodansha International.

Medved, C. E. (2009). *Journal of Family Communication.* Philadelphia: Routledge / Taylor & Francis Group. This professional journal publishes research on all aspects of communication within and about families, including communication in family systems, communication in family relationships, and families managing communication with social systems such as the mass media, education, health care, and law and policy.

Meier, J. A., McNaughton-Cassill, M., & Lynch, M. (2006). The management of household and childcare tasks and relationship satisfaction in parenting couples. *Marriage and Family Review, 40,* 61–88.

Meier, P. (1991, January 6). War of words: Women talk about how men and women talk. Minneapolis *Star Tribune,* p. 8.

Melby, J. N., Conger, R. D., Conger, K. J., & Lorenz, F. O. (1993). Effects of parental behavior on tobacco use by young male adolescents. *Journal of Marriage and the Family, 55,* 439–454.

Mendenhall, T. J., Grotevant, H. D., & McRoy, R. G. (1996). Adoptive couples: Communication and changes made in openness levels. *Family Relations, 45,* 223–229.

Merck & Co. (2009c). *Merck manuals online medical library, home edition for patients and caregivers.* Infertility. Web site: http://www.merck.com/mmhe/sec22/ch254/ch254a.html.

Merck & Co. (2009a). *Merck manuals online medical library, home edition for patients and caregivers.* Contraception. Web site: http://www.merck.com/mmhe/sec22/ch255/-ch255b.html?qt=calendar%20method&alt=sh.

Merck & Co. (2009b). *Merck manuals online medical library, home edition for patients and caregivers.* Abortion. Web site: http://www.merck.com/mmhe/sec22/ch255/ch255d.html.

Mertensmeyer, C., & Fine, M. (2000). ParentLink: A model of integration and support for parents. *Family Relations, 49,* 257–265.

Michener, J. A. (1991). *The world is my home.* New York: Random House.

Mickish, J., & Schoen, K. (2004). Colorado Alliance for Cruelty Prevention: Safe pets, safe families, safe communities. *The Colorado Lawyer, 33*(1), 37–40.

Miedzian, M. (2002). *Boys will be boys: Breaking the link between masculinity and violence.* New York: Lantern Books.

Mikulincer, M., & Shaver, P. R. (2007). *Attachment in adulthood.* New York: Guilford Press.

Mikulincer, M., & Shaver, P. R. (2007). *Attachment in adulthood.* New York: Guilford Press.

Miller, B. C. (2002). Family influences on adolescent sexual and contraceptive behavior. *Journal of Sex Research, 39*(1), 22–26.

Miller, B. C., Benson, B., & Galbraith, K. A. (2001). Family relationships and adolescent pregnancy risk: A research synthesis. *Developmental Review, 21*(1), 1–38.

Miller, B. C., Sage, R., & Winward, B. W. (2006). Teen childbearing and public policy. In L. Kowaleski-Jones & N. H. Wolfinger (Eds.), *Fragile families and the marriage agenda.* New York: Springer, 47–72.

Miller, R. B. (2000). Misconceptions about the U-shaped curve of marital satisfaction over the life course. *Family Science Review, 13*(1–2), 60–73.

Miller, S., & Miller, P. A. (1997). *Core communication: Skills and processes.* Littleton, CO: Interpersonal Communication Programs.

Miller, S., & P. (2010). Couple communication program. Web site: http://www.smartmarriages.com/directory/17.

Miller, S., & Miller, P. (2012). Couple communication program. Web site: http://www.smartmarriages.com/directory/17.

Mindel, C. H., Habenstein, R. W., & Wright, R., Jr. (Eds.). (1988). *Ethnic families in America: Patterns and variations* (3rd ed.). New York: Elsevier.

Minuchin, P., Colapinto, J., & Minuchin, S. (2007). *Working with families of the poor* (2nd ed.). New York: Guilford Press.

Mohatt, G., & Thomas, L. (2006). "I wonder, why would you do it that way?" In J. E. Trimble & C. B. Fisher (Eds.), *The handbook of ethical research with ethnocultural populations and communities.* Thousand Oaks, CA: Sage.

Monaghan, L., Goodman, J. E., & Robinson, J. M. (Eds.). (2012). *A cultural approach to interpersonal communication: Essential readings.* Malden, MA: Wiley-Blackwell.

Monat, A. Lazarus, R. S., & Reevy, G. (Eds.). (2007). *The Praeger handbook on stress and coping* (vol. 1). Westport, CT: Praeger.

Monserud, M. A. (2008). Intergenerational relationships and affectual solidarity between grandparents and young adults. *Journal of Marriage and the Family, 70,* 182–195.

Montagu, A. (1964). *Man's most dangerous myth: The fallacy of race.* Cleveland: World.

Montenegro, X. P. (2004). *The divorce experience: A study of divorce at midlife and beyond.* Washington, D.C.: American Association of Retired Persons. Web site: http://www.assets.arp.org.rgcenter/general/divorce.pdf.

Moody, J. (2004). The structure of social science collaboration network: Disciplinary cohesion from 1963 to 1999. *American Sociological Review, 69,* 213–238.

Moore, B. A. (2011). *Handbook of counseling military couples.* New York and London: Routledge/Taylor & Francis Group.

Moore, F. (2009). *The effects of female control of resources on sex-differentiated mate preferences.* Evolution and Human Behavior (May).

Moore, K. A. (1998). What a difference a dad makes. *Child trends report.* Washington, DC: Child Trends.

Moore, K. A. (2010). *Kristin A. Moore, senior scholar and program area director. Child Trends.* Web site: http://www.childtrends.org/_staffmemdisp_page.cfm?LID=05A6959E-2D9F-470F-804052FAE261DD83.

Morbidity and Mortality Weekly Report. (2006, June). Epidemiology of HIV/AIDS—United States, 1981–2005. *Morbidity and Mortality Weekly Report, 55,* 589–592.

Morgan, S. P., & Chen, R. (1992). Predicting childlessness for recent cohorts of American women. *International Journal of Forecasting, 8,* 477–493.

Morrill, P. (2006). *Couples in great marriages with a traditional structure and egalitarian relationship.* Unpublished master's thesis, Utah State University, Logan.

Morrill, P., Bradford, K., Higginbotham, B., & Skogrand, L. (2013). Evaluations of "How to Avoid Falling for a Jerk (ette)." Unpublished raw data.

Mroczek, D. K., & Spiro, A., III. (2003). Modeling intra-individual change in personality traits: Findings from the Normative Aging Study. *Journals of Gerontology: Series B: Psychological Sciences and Social Sciences, 58B*(3), 153–165.

Murray, C. L. (2006). Professional responses to government-endorsed premarital counseling. *Marriage & Family Review, 40*(1), 53–67.

Murry, V. M., Smith, E. P., & Hill, N. E. (2001). Race, ethnicity, and culture in studies of families in context. *Journal of Marriage and Family, 63,* 911–914.

Murstein, B. I. (1980). Mate selection in the 1970s. *Journal of Marriage and the Family, 42,* 52–54.

Mussen, P. H. (1969). Early sex-role development. In D. A. Goslin (Ed.), *Handbook of socialization theory and research.* Chicago: Rand McNally.

Mydans, S. (2004, November 20). There she is, "Miss Spinster of Thailand" and proud of it. *The New York Times.*

Myers, J. E., Madathil, J., & Tingle, L. R. (2005). Marriage satisfaction and wellness in India and the United States: A preliminary comparison of arranged marriages and marriages of choice. *Journal of Counseling & Development, 83,* 183–190.

Myerson, B. (1987). *Miss America, 1945: Bess Myerson's own story.* New York: Newmarket Press.

Nadeau, J. W. (1998). *Families making sense of death.* Thousand Oaks, CA: Sage. Well written and provides a rich qualitative analysis of how families make meaning after a significant death.

Najman, J. M., Dunne, M. P., Purdie, D. M., Boyle, F. M., & Coxeter, P. D. (2006). Sexual partner preferences: Evolutionary imperative, emotional attachment or hedonism? *Marriage & Family Review, 40,* 5–23.

Nakonezny, P. A., Shull, R. D., & Rodgers, J. L. (1995). The effect of no-fault divorce law on the divorce rate across the 50 states and its relation to income, education, and religiosity. *Journal of Marriage and the Family, 57*(2), 477–488.

Nance-Nash, S. (2012). Five survival tips for parents with "boomerang" kids. Forbes. Web site: http://www.forbes.com.

National Center for Health Statistics. (2009). National Vital Statistics Reports. *Births: Final data for 2006, 57*(7), January 7, and *Births: Preliminary data for 2007, 57*(12), March 18.

National Center for Injury Prevention and Control. (2005). Violence. Web site: http://www.cdc.gov/ncipc/default.htm.

National Center for Victims of Crime. (2012). Help for crime victims. Web site: http://www.victimsofcrime.org/.

National Center on Elder Abuse. (2012). Administration on Aging. Web site: http://www.ncea.aoa.gov/ncearoot/Main_Site/Index.aspx.

National Child Care Information and Technical Assistance Center. (2008, June). National Task force on Early Childhood Education for Hispanics in the United States. Web site: http://nccic.acf.hhs.gov/library/index.cfm/do=oll.viewitem&itemid=41292http://nccic.acf.hhs.gov/library/index.cfm?do=oll.viewitem&itemid=41292.

National Child Care Information Center. (2004a, September). Hispanics and child care: The changing landscape. U.S. Department of Health and Human Services, Washington, DC.

National Child Care Information Center. (2004b). National Leadership Forum on Child Care Issued of the Hispanic Community. Child Care Bulleting Issue 24. U.S. Department of Health and Human Services, Washington, DC.

National Coalition Against Domestic Violence. (2012). Domestic violence facts. Web site: http://www.ncadv.org/.

National Coalition for the Homeless. (2004, September). How many people experience homelessness? NCH Fact Sheet #2. Washington, DC. Web site: http://www.nationalhomeless.org/numbers.html.

National Coalition for the Homeless. (2009, July). Web site: http://www.nationalhomeless.org/-factsheets/.

National Coalition Against Domestic Violence. (2012a). Domestic violence facts. Web site: http://www.ncadv.org/.

National Coalition Against Domestic Violence. (2012b). Psychological abuse. Web site: http://www.ncadv.org/.

National Council on Alcoholism and Drug Dependence. (2004). Alcohol and drug dependence are America's number one health problem. Web site: http://www.ncadd.org/facts/numbroneproblem.html.

National Council on Alcoholism and Drug Dependence. (2012). Welcome to NCADD. Web site: http://ncadd.org.

National Council on Alcoholism and Drug Dependence. (2012a). 2.5 million alcohol-related deaths worldwide – annually. Web site: http://www.ncadd.org/index.php/in-the-news/155-25-million-alcohol-related-deaths-world-wide-annually.

National Council on Alcoholism and Drug Dependence. (2012b). Helping a family or friend. Web site: http://www.ncadd.org/index.php/for-friends-and-family/helping-someone.

National Council on Family Relations. (2010). Certified Family Life Educator certification. Web site: http://www.ncfr.org/cert/index.asp.

National Council on Family Relations. (2010). The premier U.S. organization focusing on family life education and the preparation and certification of professionals in the field. Web site: www.ncfr.org.

National Council on Family Relations. (2012). NCFR, founded in 1938, is the oldest multidisciplinary and nonpartisan professional organization focused solely on family research, practice, and education. NCFR publishes three scholarly journals: *Journal of Marriage and Family, Family Relations: Interdisciplinary Journal of Applied Family Studies,* and *Journal of Family Theory & Review.* Web site: www.ncfr.org.

National Crime Victimization Survey. (2002). *Crime and victims statistics.* Washington, DC: U.S. Department of Justice, Office of Justice Programs. Web site: http://www.ojp.usdoj.gov/bjs/cvict.htm.

National Dating Abuse Helpline. (2012). About the National Dating Abuse Helpline. (2012). Web site: http://www.loveisrespect.org/about-national-dating-abuse-helpline.

National Domestic Violence Hotline. (2012). Is this abuse? Web site: http://www.thehotline.org/.

National Healthy Marriage Resource Center. (2012). Web site: http://www.healthymarriageinfo.org.

National Healthy Marriage Resource Center. (2013). Remarriage trends in the United States. Web site: http://www.healthymarriageinfo.org.

National Healthy Marriage Resource Center (n.d.). Web site: http://www.healthymarriageinfo.org/curricula/index.cfm.

National Institute of Child Health Research Network. (2003). *Child Development,* 74(4), 976–1005.

National Institutes of Health. (2009a). Research on miscarriage and stillbirth. National Institute of Child Health and Human Development. Web site: http://www.nichd.nih.gov/womenshealth/-research/pregbirth/miscarriage_stillbirth.cfm.

National Institutes of Health (2009b). Medline Encyclopedia: Sudden Infant Death Syndrome. Web site: http://www.nlm.nih.gov/medlineplus/ency/article/001566.htm.

National Institute of Mental Health. (2013). Suicide in the U.S.: Statistics and prevention. Web site: http://www.nimh.nih.gov/health/publications/suicide-in-the-us-statistics-and-prevention/index.shtml.

National Institute on Alcohol Abuse and Alcoholism. (2012). Alcoholism and health. Web site: http://www.niaaa.nih.org.

National Institute on Alcohol Abuse and Alcoholism. (2012). A guide for marriage and family therapists. Web site: http://www.niaaa.nih.org.

National Institute on Drug Abuse. (2012). General questions about drug abuse. Web site: http://drugfactsweek.drugabuse.gov/chat/chatfaqs_topics/general_questions.php.

National Marriage Project. (2007, July). *The state of our unions 2007: The social health of marriage in America.* Web site: http://www.virginia.edu/marriageproject/pdfs/SOOU2007.pdf.

National Marriage Project. (2009, February). *The state of our unions 2008: The social health of marriage in America.* Web site: www.virginia.edu/marriageproject/pdfs/2008update.pdf.

National Marriage Project. (2012). *The state of our unions: Marriage in America 2012.* Web site: http://www.stateofourunions.org/.

National Marriage Project. (2012). *The state of our unions: Marriage in America 2012.* Web site: http://www.nationalmarriageproject.org.

National Opinion Research Center. (1996). *General social survey.* Chicago: University of Chicago.

National Poverty Center. (2010). Poverty in the United States: Frequently asked questions. Web site: http://www.npc.umich.edu/poverty/.

National Poverty Center (n.d.). National Web site: http://www.npc.umich.edu/poverty.

National Poverty Center (n.d.). *Poverty in the United States.* Retrieved from http://npc.umich.edu/poverty/.

National Right to Life Committee. Founded in 1973 in response to a U.S. Supreme Court decision released on January 22 of that year, legalizing abortion in all 50 states. "The ultimate goal of the National Right to Life Committee is to restore legal protection to innocent human life. The primary interest of the National Right to Life Committee and its members has been the abortion controversy; however, it is also concerned with related matters of medical ethics which relate to the right to life issues of euthanasia and infanticide." NRLC does not have positions on other issues, such as contraception, sex education, capital punishment, and national defense. Web site: http://www.nrlc.org/.

National Stepfamily Resource Center. (2013). Web site: http://www.stepfamilies.org.

from Papua New Guinea; and the Casimiro-Branco family from East Timor. The families share their personal stories, their family traditions, and how they have dealt successfully with the challenges of life they face in Australia today.

National Women's Hall of Fame. (2013). Betty Friedan. Web site: http://greatwomen.org/women-of-the-hall/search-the-hall/details/2/61-Friedan.

National Youth Violence Prevention Resource Center. (2009). Dating violence warning signs. Web site: http://www.safeyouth.org/scripts/faq/datingwarning.asp.

Nation's legal drugs may be its worst drugs. (1986, November 23). Lincoln [NE] Journal Star, pp. 1D, 3D.

Nelson, L. J., & Barry, C. M. (2005). Distinguishing features of emerging adulthood: The role of self-classification as an adult. Journal of Adolescent Research, 20, 242–262. New York: Touchstone.

Neugarten, B. (1968). The awareness of middle age. In B. Neugarten (Ed.), Middle age and aging. Chicago: University of Chicago Press.

Neumaier, J. (2001). Coronary heart disease patients and sex: Death in the extramarital bed. MMW—Fortschritte der Medizin, 143(20), 18–19.

Newport, F. (2013, January 3). Americans optimistic about life in 2013. Gallup Poll. Web site: http://www.gallup.com/poll/159698/americans-optimistic-life-2013.aspx.

New York Life. (2012). Adult children moving back home: Don't let "boomerang kids" derail your goals. Web site: http://www.newyorklife.com/.

New York State Administrative Regulations. (1995). 9 N.Y.C.R.R. 2104.6(d)(3).

Nicholson, J. M., Sanders, M. R., Halford, W. K., Phillips, M., & Whitton, S. W. (2008). The prevention and treatment of children's adjustment problems in stepfamilies. In J. Pryor (Ed.), The international handbook of stepfamilies: Policy and practice in legal, research, and clinical environments (pp. 485–521). Hoboken, NJ: John Wiley & Sons.

Nicholson, T. (2001). 50+ world—Bright scene with shadows. AARP Bulletin, p. 25.

Niebuhr, R. (1988). Serenity prayer. In G. Carruth & E. Ehrlich (Eds.), Harper book of American quotations. New York: Harper & Row. (Original work published 1951.)

Niehuis, S., Skogrand, L., & Houston, T. (2006). When marriages die: Premarital and early marriage precursors to divorce. Forum of Family and Consumer Issues, 11. Online journal: http://www.ces.ncsu.edu/depts/fcs/pub/forum.html.

Niemeyer, R. A. (2011). Grief and bereavement in contemporary society: Bridging research and practice. New York: Routledge.

Nord, C. W., & Zill, N. (1996). Non-custodial parents' participation in their children's lives: Evidence from the Survey of Income and Program Participation. Washington, DC: U.S. Department of Health and Human Services. Web site: ftp://aspe.os.dhhs.gov/cyp.

Notes, 11(2). Web site: http://www.practicenotes.org/vol11_no2.htm.

Norwood, E. (1998). Poor folks have dreams. In C. L. Nelson & K. A. Wilson (Eds.), Seeding the process of multicultural education (pp. 73–78). Plymouth, MN: Minnesota Inclusiveness Program.

Notter, M. L., MacTavish, K. A., & Shamah, D. (2008). Pathways toward resilience among women in rural trailer parks. Family Relations, 57, 613–624.

NPR. (2004). Sex education in America: An NPR/Kaiser/Kennedy School poll. Web site: http://www.npr.org/templates/story/story.php?storyID=1622610.

Ochs, E., & Shohet, M. (2006). The cultural structuring of mealtime socialization. In R. W. Larson, A. R. Wiley, & K. R. Branscomb (Eds.), Family mealtimes as a context of development and socialization (pp. 35–49). San Francisco: Jossey-Bass.

O'Farrell, T. J., & Fals-Stewart, W. (2001). Family-involved alcoholism treatment: An update. Recent Developments in Alcoholism, 15, 329–356.

O'Farrell, T. J., & Fals-Stewart, W. (2007). Alcohol abuse. Journal of Marital and Family Therapy, 29(1), 121–146.

Office of Population Research and Association of Reproductive Health Professionals. (2009). Web site: http://www.ec.princeton.edu/questions/dose.html.

Olds, S. B., London, M. L., & Ladewig, P. (2004). Maternal–newborn nursing and women's healthcare (7th ed.). Upper Saddle River, NJ: Pearson/Prentice Hall.

Olsen, C., & Skogrand, L. (2009). Cultural implications and guidelines for Extension and family life programming with Latino/Hispanic audiences. The Forum for Family and Consumer Issues, 14. Online journal: http://ncsu.edu/ffci/publications/2009/v14n1-2009-spring/olsen-skogrand.php.

Olson, A., & Olson, D. H. (2001). Ten traits of love. In J. R. Levine & H. J. Markman (Eds.), Why do fools fall in love? Experiencing the magic, mystery, and meaning of successful relationships. San Francisco: Jossey-Bass.

Olson, D., & Gorall, D. M. (2003). Circumplex model of marital and family patterns. In F. Walsh (Ed.), Normal family processes (3rd ed., pp. 514–548). New York: Guilford Press.

Olson, D., & Larson, P. (2012). PREPARE/ENRICH Program. Web site: http://www.smartmarriages.com/directory/122.

Olson, D., Olson-Sigg, A., & Larson, P. (2008). The couple checkup. Nashville, TN: Thomas Nelson.

Olson, D. H. (1996). Clinical assessment and treatment using the Circumplex Model. In F. W. Kaslow (Ed.), Handbook in relational diagnosis (pp. 59–80). New York: Wiley.

Olson, D. H. (1997). Family stress and coping: A multisystem perspective. In S. Dreman (Ed.), The family on the threshold of the 21st century: Trends and implications (pp. 259–280). Mahwah, NJ: Erlbaum.

Olson, D. H. (2011). FACES IV and the Circumplex Model: Validation study. *Journal of Marital & Family Therapy, 3,* 64–80.

Olson, D. H., Fournier, D. G., & Druckman, J. M. (2001). *PRE-PARE, PREPARE-MC and ENRICH inventories* (4th ed.). Minneapolis: PREPARE/ENRICH.

Olson, D. H., Fye, S., & Olson, A. (1999). *National survey of happy and unhappy married couples.* Minneapolis: Life Innovations.

Olson, D. H., & Gorall, D. M. (2003). Circumplex model of marital and family patterns. In F. Walsh (Ed.), *Normal family processes* (3rd ed.) (pp. 514–548). New York Guilford Press.

Olson, D. H., Larson, P. J., & Olson-Sigg, A. (2009). *PREPARE-ENRICH Program: Customized Version.* Minneapolis, MN.: Life Innovations, Inc. Web site: http:// www.prepare-enrich.com.

Olson, D. H., McCubbin, H. I., Barnes, H., Larsen, A., Muxen, M., & Wilson, M. (1989). *Families: What makes them work* (2nd ed.). Los Angeles: Sage.

Olson, D. H., & Olson, A. K. (2000). *Empowering couples: Building on your strengths.* Minneapolis: Life Innovations.

Olson, D. H., Olson-Sigg, A., & Larson, P. J. (2008). *The couple checkup: Finding your relationship strengths.* Nashville: Thomas Nelson.

Olson, D. H., Olson-Sigg, A., & Larson, P. J. (2008). *The couple checkup.* Nashville: Thomas Nelson. Based on a survey of 50,000 couples, the book is an effort to help couples find the strengths in their relationship and build on these strengths.

Olson, D. H., Olson-Sigg, A., & Larson, P. J. (2008). *The couple checkup: Finding your relationship strengths.* Nashville: Thomas Nelson. Based on a national survey of 50,000 marriages.

Olson, D. H., Olson-Sigg, A., & Larson, P. J. (2009). National survey of marriage: Based on over 50,000 couples who took ENRICH. Unpublished manuscript. Minneapolis, MN: Live Innovations.

Olson, D. H., & Stewart, K. L. (1991). Family systems and health behaviors. In H. E. Schroeder (Ed.), *New directions in health psychology assessment. Series in applied psychology: Social issues and questions* (pp. 27–64). Washington, DC: Hemisphere.

O'Malley, C. J., Blankemeyer, M., Walker, K. K., & Dellmann-Jenkins, M. (2007). Children's reported communication with their parents about war. *Journal of Family Issues, 28,* 1639–1662.

Onah, H. E., Iloabachie, G. C., Obi, S. N., Ezugwu, F. O., & Eze, J. N. (2002). Nigerian male sexual activity during pregnancy. *International Journal of Gynecology and Obstetrics, 76*(2), 219.

Onedera, J. D. (2007). *The role of religion in marriage and family counseling.* London: Routledge, Taylor & Francis Group. Focuses on how each of the major world religions can influence family dynamics.

Ooms, T. (1998). *Toward more perfect unions: Putting marriage on the public agenda.* Washington, DC: Family Impact Seminar.

Ooms, T., Bouchet, S., & Parke, M. (2004). *Beyond marriage licenses: Efforts in states to strengthen marriage and two-parent families.* Washington, DC: Center for Law and Social Policy.

Oord, T. J. (2008) (Ed.). *The altruism reader: Selections from writings on love, religion, and science.* West Conshohocken, PA: Templeton Foundation Press.

Ordoñez, J. (2007, May 14). Baby needs a new pair of shoes. *Money,* 50, 51, 54.

Orwell, G. (1951). *Animal farm.* New York: Penguin.

Osborn, F. (1939, Spring and Summer). The comprehensive program of eugenics and its social implications. *Living,* 33–38.

Oswald, R. F., & Kuvalanka, K. A. (2008). Same-sex couples: Legal complexities. *Journal of Family Issues, 29,* 1051–1066.

Owens, T. J., & Suitor, J. J. (Eds.). (2007). *Advances in life course research: Vol. 12. Interpersonal relations across the life course.* Amsterdam: Elsevier.

Padgett, D. (1997). The contribution of support networks to household labor in African American families. *Journal of Family Issues, 18*(3), 227–250.

Pan, P. A. (2000, December 26). Thoroughly modern women disconcert many in China. *The Washington Post,* p. A20.

Pan, Y. (2002). *On the freedom of mate selection.* Paper presented at the Building Family Strengths Conference, Shanghai Academy of Social Sciences, Shanghai, China.

Paragament, K. I. (2007). *Spiritually integrated psychotherapy: Understanding and addressing the sacred.* New York: Guilford Press.

Parents Without Partners. (2010). Home page. Web site: http:// www.parentswithoutpartners.org/.

Parkman, A. M. (1995). The deterioration of the family: A law and economics perspective. In G. B. Melton (Ed.), *The individual, the family, and social good: Personal fulfillment in times of change* (pp. 21–52). Lincoln: University of Nebraska Press.

Parkman, A. M. (2000). *Good intentions gone awry: No-fault divorce and the American family.* Lanham, MD: Rowman & Littlefield.

Parsons, T. (1955). The American family: Its relations to personality and the social structure. In T. Parsons & R. F. Bales (Eds.), *Family socialization and interaction process* (pp. 3–21). Glencoe, IL: Free Press.

Parsons, T. (1965). The normal American family. In S. M. Farber, P. Mustacchi, & R. H. L. Wilson (Eds.), *Man and civilization: The family's search for survival* (pp. 31–50). New York: McGraw-Hill.

Parsons, T., & Bales, R. F. (1955). *Family socialization and interaction process.* Glencoe, IL: Free Press.

Partnership at Drugfree.org. (2012). Support and resources for parents dealing with teen drug and alcohol abuse. Web site: http://www.drugfree.org.

Peele, S., with Brodsky, A. (1991). *Love and addiction.* New York: Taplinger.

Peluso, P. (Ed.) (2007). *Infidelity: A practitioner's guide to working with couples in crisis.* London: Routledge Mental Health, Taylor & Francis Group. When one partner in a relationship is unfaithful to the other, salvaging the relationship takes a lot of work by both parties.

Pence, E. L., & McDonnell, C. (2000). Developing policies and protocols in Duluth, Minnesota. In J. Hanmer & C. Itzin (Eds.), *Home truths about domestic violence: Feminist influences on policy and practice* (pp. 249–268). London: RoutledgeFalmer.

Pensanti, H. (2001). *Better sex for you: A natural approach to finding new levels of sexual satisfaction.* Lake Maru, FL: Siloam Press.

Peplau, L. A., & Fingerhut, A. W. (2007). The close relationships of lesbians and gay men. *Annual Review of Psychology, 58,* 405–424. Web site: http://www.ppcok.org/brochure.php?id=2.

American parent: Overcoming challenges and finding strength in a new immigrant Latino community. *Journal of Family Issues, 27,* 1383–1414.

Peters, M. F. (1981). Strengths of Black families. In N. Stinnett, J. DeFrain, K. King, P. Knaub, & G. Rowe (Eds.), *Family strengths 3: Roots of well-being* (pp. 73–91). Lincoln: University of Nebraska Press.

Peterson, G. W., Steinmetz, S., & Wilson, S. M. (2005). *Parent–youth relations: Cultural and cross-cultural perspectives.* New York: Haworth.

Peterson, K. S. (1992a, March 12). Adults should know status of parents. *USA Today,* p. 1D.

Peterson, K. S. (1992b, March 12). Parents hand down financial attitudes. *USA Today,* p. 4D.

Pew Forum on Religion and Public Life. (2008). A slight but steady majority favors keeping abortion legal: But most also favor restrictions. Pew Research Center. Web site: http://pewforum.org/Abortion/A-Slight-but-Steady-Majority-Favors-Keeping-Abortion-Legal.aspx.

Pew Research Center. (2006, February 13). Are we happy yet? Web site: http://pewsocialtrends.org/assets/pdf/AreWeHappyYet.pdf.

Pew Research Center (2007). *As marriage and parenthood drift apart, public is concerned about social impact.* Web site: http://pewresearch.org.

Pew Research Center (2010). *The return of multi-generational family household.* Web site: http://pewsocialtrends.org.

Pew Research Center for the People and the Press. (2005, August 3). Abortion and rights of terror suspects top court issues. Web site: http://people-press.org/reports/display.php3?ReportID=253.

Physician Leadership on National Drug Policy. (2000). Position paper on drug policy. Providence, RI: Brown University Center for Alcohol and Addiction Studies.

Pick Program (n.d.). *Love Thinks.* Web site: http://www.lovethinks.com/PICK/PICK_Program.

Pieve, L. (2001). An ethnographic study of the perceptions of Puerto Rican pregnant teenagers. *Dissertation Abstracts International-A, 62*(03), 1226.

Pines, A. M. (1998). *Romantic jealousy: Causes, symptoms, cures.* New York: Routledge.

Pitt-Catsouphes, M., Kossek, E. E., & Sweet, S. (2006). *The work and family handbook.* Mahwah, NJ: Erlbaum.

PlanetSave.com. (2001, August 13). Women sentenced to 100 lashes for extramarital sex in Nigeria. Web site: http://www.planetsave.com/ViewStory.asp?ID=1165.

Planned Parenthood. (2006). 5 ways to prevent abortion (and one way that won't work). Web site: http://www.jhu.edu/choice/files/5waystopreventabortion.pdf.

Planned Parenthood of Central Oklahoma. (2010). Ten ridiculous ideas that will make a father out of you. Web site: http://www.ppcok.org/brochure.php?id=2.

Planned Parenthood Federation of America. Planned Parenthood describes itself as "a trusted health care provider, an informed educator, a passionate advocate, and a global partner helping similar organizations around the world." The organization has delivered reproductive health care, sex education, and information for more than 90 years. Ninety locally governed affiliates nationwide operate 850 health centers. Web site: http://www.plannedparenthood.org/index.htm.

Poduska, B. (2001, August). The credit trap. *Marriage and Families,* pp. 22–28.

Pool, J. N., & Olson-Sigg, A. (2010). *PREPARE-ENRICH-INSPIRE for Teens: Preparing Youth, Enriching Relationships and Inspiring Futures.* Berkeley, CA: The Dibble Institute.

Poortman, A., & van der Lippe, T. (2009). Attitudes toward housework and child care and the gendered division of labor. *Journal of Marriage and Family, 71,* 526–541.

Popenoe, D. (2008). *Cohabitation, marriage, and child wellbeing: A cross-national perspective.* Retrieved from the National Marriage Project Web site: http://www.virginia.edu/marriageproject/pdfs/NMP2008 CohabitationReport.pdf.

Popenoe, D., & Whitehead, B. D. (1999a), *Should we live together? What young adults need to know about cohabitation before marriage.* New Brunswick, NJ: Rutgers University, National Marriage Project.

Popenoe, D., & Whitehead, B. D. (1999b). *The state of our unions.* 1996 New Brunswick, NJ: Rutgers University, National Marriage Project.

Popenoe, D., & Whitehead, B. D. (2000). *The state of our unions 2000.* New Brunswick, NJ: Rutgers University, National Marriage Project.

Popenoe, D., & Whitehead, B. D. (2004). *The state of our unions 2004.* New Brunswick, NJ: Rutgers University, National Marriage Project.

Popenoe, D., & Whitehead, R. D. (2010). *The state of our unions 2010.* Piscataway, NJ: National Marriage Project, Rutgers University.

Population Reports. (1999, April). Condom use. Baltimore: Johns Hopkins School of Public Health, Center for Communication Programs, Population Information Program.

Porche, M. V., & Purvin, D. M. (2008). "Never in our lifetime": Legal marriage for same-sex couples in long-term relationships. *Family Relations, 57,* 144–159.

Porter, J. (1999, January 10). It's time to start thinking about electing a female president. Lincoln [NE] *Journal Star,* p. 6D.

PREPARE-ENRICH (n.d.). PREPARE-ENRICH by Life Innovations. Retrieved Online: http://www.prepare-enrich.com.

Prevent Child Abuse America. (2012). Making the case: Why prevention matters. Web site: http://www.preventchildabuse.org/index.shtml.

Prevent Child Abuse. (2012). Making the case: Why prevention matters. Web site: http://www.preventchildabuse.org/index.shtml.

Proctor, B. D., & Dalaker, J. (2003). *Poverty in the United States: 2002*. Current Population Reports, Consumer Income. Washington, DC: U.S. Census Bureau.

Pryor, J. (2008). (Ed.). *The international handbook of stepfamilies: Policy and practice in legal, research, and clinical environments.* Hoboken, NJ: John Wiley & Sons.

Public Broadcasting Service. (2012). Senior living. *Independent Lens*. Web site: http://www.pbs.org/independentlens/almosthome/senior.html.

Puente, S., & Cohen, D. (2003). Jealousy and the meaning (or nonmeaning) of violence. *Personality and Social Psychology Bulletin, 29*(4), 449–460.

Purplefairy, L. (2012). The silent suffering of parent abuse: When children abuse parents. Web site: http://222.loupurplefairy.hubpages.com/hub/The-Silent-Suffering-of-Parent-Abuse-When-Children-Abuse-P...

Qian, Z. (2005). Breaking the last taboo: Interracial marriages in America. *Contexts, 4*, 33–37.

Qian, Z., Blair, S. L., & Ruf, S. D. (2001). Asian American interracial and interethnic marriages: Differences by education and nativity. *International Migration Review, 35*(2), 557–586.

Qian, Z., & Lichter, D. T. (2007). Social boundaries and marital assimilation: Interpreting trends in racial and ethnic intermarriage. *American Sociological Review, 72*, 68–94.

Qian, Z., & Lichter, D. T. (2011). Changing patterns of interracial marriage in a multiracial society. *Journal of Marriage and Family, 73*, 1065–1083.

Raetz, K. (2011). *Birth order and couple satisfaction.* Prepare Enrich. Web site: https://www.prepare-enrich.com/pe/pdf/research/2011/birth_order_and_couple_satisfaction_Raetz_2011.pdf.

Rainville, G. (2009, May). *AARP Bulletin survey on employment status of the 45+ population: Executive summary.* Web site: http://www.aarp.org/research/surveys/money/work/employment/articles/bulletin_jobs_0.html.

Raley, S. B., Mattingly, M. J., & Bianchi, S. (2006). How dual are dual-income couples? Documenting change from 1970–2001. *Journal of Marriage and the Family, 68*, 11–28.

Rank, M. R., & Hirschl, T. A. (1999). The economic risk of childhood in America: Estimating the probability of poverty across the formative years. *Journal of Marriage and the Family, 61*, 1058–1067.

Rank, M. R., & Williams, J. H. (2010). A life course approach to understanding poverty among older American adults. Families in Society: *The Journal of Contemporary Social Services, 91*(4), 337–441.

Rank, M. R., & Williams, J. H. (2010). A life course approach to understanding poverty among older American adults. Families in Society. *The Journal of Contemporary Social Services, 91*, 337–341. Nearly half of all elderly Americans will encounter at least 1 year of poverty or near poverty between the ages of 60 and 90.

Recker, N. K. (2001). The wicked stepmother myth. Family Life Month Packet. Columbus: Ohio State University Extension Web site: http://ohioline.osu.edu/flm01/FS04.html.

Red Horse, J. (1997). Traditional American Indian family systems. *Families, Systems & Health, 15*, 243–249.

Reinisch, J., & Beasley, R. (1994). *The Kinsey Institute new report on sex* (p. 45). New York: St. Martin's.

Remez, L. (1998). In Turkey, women's fertility is linked to education, employment and freedom to choose a husband. *International Family Planning Perspectives, 24*(2), 97–98.

Rennison, C. M. (2003, February). Intimate partner violence, 1993–2001. U.S. Department of Justice, Office of Justice Programs. Web site: http://www.ojp.usdoj.gov/bjs.

Rettig, K. D., Christensen, D. H., & Dahl, C. M. (1991). Impact of child support guidelines on the economic well-being of children. *Family Relations, 40*, 167–175.

Rettig, K. D., Leichtentritt, R. D., & Stanton, L. M. (1999). Understanding noncustodial fathers' family and life satisfaction from resource theory perspective. *Journal of Family Issues, 20*(4), 507–538.

Reynolds, M. (2002, April 3). Kandahar's lightly veiled homosexual habits. *Los Angeles Times.* Web site: http://www.globalgayz.com/g-afghanistan.html.

Rich, J. (2003). *The couple's guide to love and money.* Oakland, CA: New Harbinger.

Ridley, C. A., Peterman, D. J., & Avery, A. W. (1978, April). Cohabitation: Does it make for a better marriage? *Family Coordinator*, pp. 129–136.

Riemer, F. G., & Siegel, D. H. (2007). Ethical issues in open adoption: Implications for practice. *Families in Society: The Journal of Contemporary Social Services, 88*(1), 11–18.

Rilke, R. M. (1904). *Letters to a young poet.* Letter 7, March 14. New York: W. W. Norton.

Risman, B. J., & Johnson-Sumerford, D. (1998). Doing it fairly: A study of postgender marriages. *Journal of Marriage and the Family, 60*, 23–40.

Rivett, M. (2009). *Family therapy: 100 key points and techniques.* London: Routledge, Taylor & Francis Group. Family therapy theory and practice; concise and jargon-free.

Robbins, R., Scherman, A., Holman, H., & Wilson, J. (2005). Roles of American Indian grandparents in times of cultural crises. *Journal of Cultural Diversity, 12*, 62–68.

Roberts, L. (2005). Alcohol and the marital relationship. *Family Focus*, pp. 12–13.

Roberts, S. (2006, October 15). To be married means to be outnumbered in America. *The New York Times*, p. A22.

Roberts, S., Sabar, A., Goodman, B., & Balleza, M. (2007, January 16). 51% of women are now living without spouse. NYTimes.com. Web site: http://select.nytimes.com.

Robinson, P. W., Davidson, L. J., & Drebot, M. E. (2004). Parent abuse on the rise: A historical review. *American Association of Behavioral Social Science Online Journal.* Web site: http://www.aabss.org.

Robles, B. J. (2003). *Latino families: Net worth.* Baltimore: Annie Casey Foundation.

Rodgers, J. L., Nakonezny, P. A., & Shull, R. D. (1997). The effect of no-fault divorce legislation on divorce rates: A response to a reconsideration. *Journal of Marriage and the Family, 59*(4), 1026–1030.

Rogers, F. (2009). *Good reads.* Web site: http://www.goodreads.com/quotes/show/157666.

Rokach, A. (2005). Coping with loneliness during pregnancy and motherhood. *Psychology and Education, 42*(1), 1–12.

dren. *Journal of Family Issues, 27,* 912–932.

Rowe, C. L. (2003). Family-based interventions for substance abuse: A profile of two models. *The Family Psychologist, 19*(4), 4–9.

Rowe, D. (2007). *My dearest enemy, my dangerous friend: Making and breaking sibling bonds.* Routledge Mental Health. Web site: http://www.routledgementalhealth.com. A book for those who have struggled with the pain and pleasure of brotherhood and sisterhood.

Rowe, D. (2008). *What should I believe? Why our beliefs about the nature of death and the purpose of life dominate our lives.* London and New York: Routledge. If we use our beliefs as a defense against our feelings of worthlessness, we feel compelled to force our beliefs on other people by coercion or aggression. But if we can create a set of beliefs expressed in religious or philosophical metaphors that are meaningful to us, we can live in peace with ourselves and others.

Rudy, D., & Grusec, J. E. (2006). Authoritarian parenting in individualist and collectivist groups: Associations with maternal emotion and cognition and children's self-esteem. *Journal of Family Psychology, 20*(1), 68–78.

Russell, B. (1938). *Power: A new social analysis.* New York: Norton.

Russo, N. F., & Dabul, A. J. (1997). The relationship of abortion to well-being: Do race and religion make a difference? *Professional Psychology: Research and Practice, 28*(1), 23–31.

Ryan, R. M., Kalil, A., Ziol-Guest, K. M. (2008). Longitudinal patterns of nonresident fathers' involvement: The role of resources and relations. *Journal of Marriage and the Family, 70,* 962–977.

Saad, L. (2011). Most Americans believe crime in U.S. is worsening. Gallup Poll. Web site: http://www.gallup.com/poll/150464/americans-believe-crime-worsening.aspx.

Sager, C. J., Brown, H. S., Crohn, H., Engel, T., Rodstein, E., & Walker, L. (1983). *Treating the remarried family.* New York: Brunner/Mazel.

Saluter, A. (1996). *Marital status and living arrangements.* Washington, DC: United States Bureau of the Census.

Sammons, M. T. (2005). Psychology in the public sector: Addressing the psychological effects of combat in the U.S. Navy. *American Psychologist, 162,* 123–129.

Sandler, L. (2010, July 19). One and done. *Time, 176*(3), 34–41.

Sarkisian, N. (March, 2007). Race, class, and extended family involvement. *Family Focus,* 14–15.

Sarkisian, N., Gerena, M., & Gerstel, N. (2006). Extended family ties among Mexicans, Puerto Ricans, and Whites: Superintegration or disintegration? *Family Relations, 55,* 331–344.

Sassler, S. (2010). Partnering across the life course: Sex, relationships, and mate selection. *Journal of Marriage and Family, 72,* 557–574.

Saving 2 Invest (n.d.). *A look at the average American income, earnings and poverty by household, gender and race.* Web site: http://www.savingtoinvest.com/2010/10/income-earnings-and-poverty-by-household-gender-and-race.html.

Schachner, D. A. (2006). *Attachment and long-term singlehood.* Unpublished doctoral dissertation, University of California, Davis.

Scheinkman, M. (2005). Beyond the trauma of betrayal: Reconsidering affairs in couples therapy. *Family Process, 44,* 227–244.

Schmitt, D. P., & Buss, D. M. (2001). Human mate poaching: Tactics and temptations for infiltrating existing mateships. *Journal of Personality and Social Psychology, 80*(6), 894–917.

Schnell, R. (2000). The representation and treatment of adultery in medieval literature. *International Academy for Marital Spirituality Review, 6,* 17–33.

Schooler, J. E., & Atwood, T. C. (2008). *The whole life adoption book: Realistic advice for building a healthy adoptive family.* Colorado Springs, CO: NavPress.

Schoppe-Sullivan, S. (2010, Summer). Maternal gatekeeping: Listening for the "creeaak." *NCFR Report, 55.2,* F6–F8.

Schoppe-Sullivan, S. (2010, Winter). Maternal gatekeeping: Listening for the "creeaak." *Family Focus, Issue, 55.3*(47), 24, 26.

Schramm, D. G. (2006). Individual and social costs of divorce in Utah. *Journal of Family and Economic Issues, 27,* 133–151.

Schramm, D. G., Marshall, J. P., Harris, V. W., & Lee, T. R. (2005). After "I do": The newlywed transition. *Marriage and Family Review, 38,* 45–67.

Schultz, N. C., Schultz, C. L., & Olson, D. H. (1991). Couple strengths and stressors in complex and simple stepfamilies in Australia. *Journal of Marriage and the Family, 53,* 555–564.

Schwartz, J., Raine, G., & Robins, K. (1987, May 11). A "superminority" tops out. *Newsweek,* pp. 48–49.

Scott, M., Booth, A., King, V., & Johnson, D. (2007). Postdivorce father-adolescent closeness. *Journal of Marriage and the Family, 69,* 1194–1209.

Scott, M. J. (2007). *Moving on after trauma.* New York: Routledge.

Search Institute. (2006). *Introduction to assets.* Minneapolis: Author. Web site: http://www.search-institute.org/assets.

Search Institute. (2013). Discovering what kids need to succeed. Web site: http://www.search-institute.org/.

Sedlak, A. J., Mettenburg, J., Basena, M., Petta, I., McPherson, K., Greene, A., & Li, S. (2010). *Fourth national incidence study of child abuse and neglect (NIS-4): Report to Congress.* Washington, DC: U. S. Department of Health and Human Services, Administration for Children and Families. Web site: http://www.acf.hhs.gov/programs/opre/abuse_neglect/natl_incid/nis4_report_congress_full_pdf_jan2010.pdf.

Seiler, W. J., & Beall, M. L. (2011). *Communication: Making connections* (8th ed.). Boston: Pearson/Allyn and Bacon.

Seligman, M. E. (2002). *Authentic happiness.* New York: Free Press.

Selle, R. (1998, May). People in the news: Feminism's matriarch. *The World and I,* p. 51.

Selye, H. (1974). *The stress of life* (2nd ed.). New York: McGraw-Hill.

Sen, A. (2001, October 27–November 9). Many faces of gender inequality. *Frontline.* Web site: http://www.flonnet.com/fl18220040.htm.

Sex Information and Education Council of the U.S. (2001). Community action kit. Web site: http://www.siecus.org/advocacy/kits0005.html.

Sex Information and Education Council of the U.S. (2004). Adolescence and abstinence fact sheet. Web site: http://www.siecus.org/pubs/fact/fact0001.html.

Sexuality Information and Education Council of the United States (SIECUS). Founded by Dr. Mary S. Calderone in 1964, who was concerned about the lack of information about sexuality for both young people and adults. So, at the age of 60, "with determination to live in a world in which sexuality was viewed as a natural and healthy part of life," she founded SIECUS, which publishes books, journals, and resources for professionals, parents, and the public. Web site: http://www.siecus.org/.

Sharma, A. R., McGue, M. K., & Benson, P. L. (1998). The psychological adjustment of United States adopted adolescents and their nonadopted siblings. *Child Development, 69*(3), 791–802.

Sharp, E. A., & Ganong, L. (2011). "I'm a loser, I'm not married, let's just all look at me": Ever-single women's perceptions of their social environment. *Journal of Family Issues, 32,* 956–980.

Sheehy, G. (1998). *New passages: Mapping your life across time.* New York: Pocket Books.

Sheldon, A. (2009). *Big brother now: A story about me and our new baby* and *Big sister now: A story about me and our new baby.* Magination Press. Web site: http://www.magination-press.com.

Sherman, C. W. (2006, December). Remarriage and stepfamily in later life. *Family Focus,* pp. 8–9.

Sherman, C. W., & Bauer, J. W. (2008). Financial conflicts facing late-life remarried Alzheimer's disease caregivers. *Family Relations, 57,* 492–503.

Sherman, M. D., Sautter, F., Jackson, M. H., Lyons, J. A., & Han, X. (2006). Domestic violence in veterans with post-traumatic stress disorder who seek couples therapy. *Journal of Marital and Family Therapy, 32,* 479–490.

Shoemake, E. (2007). Human mate selection theory: An integrated evolutionary and social approach. *Journal of Scientific Psychology, Fall,* 35–41.

Shorris, E. (1992). *Latinos: A biography of the people.* New York: Norton.

Shostak, A. (1987). Singlehood. In M. Sussman & S. Steinmetz (Eds.), *Handbook of marriage and the family.* New York: Plenum.

Silva, M. (2002). The effectiveness of school-based sex education programs in the promotion of abstinent behavior: A meta-analysis. *Health Education Research, 17*(4), 471–481.

Silverman, J. (2001). Dating violence against adolescent girls. *Journal of the American Medical Association, 286*(5), 572–579.

Silverstein, L. B. (2010). Louise Bordeaux Silverstein, Yeshiva University. Web site: http://www.yu.edu/Ferkauf/people/Silverstein.asp.

Silverstein, L. B., & Auerbach, C. F. (2000). Continuing the dialogue about fathers and families. *American Psychologist, 55*(6), 683–684.

Silverstein, M., & Giarrusso, R. (2010). Aging and family life: A decade review. *Journal of Marriage and Family, 72* (October), 1039–1058. An excellent overview of recent trends in research.

Simons, J., & Carey, M. P. (2008). Prevalence of sexual dysfunction. Published at PubMed Central (PMC), and archive of the National Institutes of Health's National Library of Medicine. Retrieved from http://www.ncbi.nlh.gov/pmc/articles/PMC2426773/.

Singh, S., & Darroch, J. E. (2000). Adolescent pregnancy and childbearing: Levels and trends in developed countries. *Family Planning Perspectives, 32*(1), 14–23.

Singletary, M. (2003, August 27). Do college students need credit cards? Hardly. *The Washington Post.* Web site: http://www.washingtonpost.com/ac2/wp-dyn/A56633-2003Aug27.

Singletary, M. (2004, October 20). College students should steer clear of credit cards. *The Washington Post.* Web site: http://washingtonpost.com/wp-dyn/articles/A50054-2004(ct20.html).

Skogrand, L. (2004). A process for learning about and creating programming for culturally diverse audiences. *Forum of Family and Consumer Issues, 9.* Online journal: http://www.ces.ncsu.edu/depts/fcs/pub/forum.html.

Skogrand, L., Barrios-Bell, A., & Higginbotham, B. (2009). Stepfamily education for Latino families: Implications for practice. *Journal of Couple and Relationship Therapy: Innovations in Clinical and Educational Interventions, 8,* 113–128.

Skogrand, L., & Chaney, C. (2010). Strong marriages in African American culture. Unpublished raw data.

Skogrand, L., DeFrain, N., DeFrain, J., & Jones, J. (2007). *Surviving and transcending a traumatic childhood: The dark thread.* New York: Haworth.

Skogrand, L., DeFrain, N., DeFrain, J., & Jones, J. E. (2007). *Surviving and transcending a traumatic childhood: The dark thread.* New York: Routledge.

Skogrand, L., Hatch, D., & Singh, A. (2009). Strong marriages in Latino culture. In R. Dalla, J. DeFrain, J. Johnson, & D. Abbott (Eds.), *Strengths and challenges of new immigrant families: Implications for research, policy, education, and service.* (pp. 117–134). Lexington, MA: Lexington Press.

Skogrand, L., Henderson, K., & Higginbotham, B. (2006). Sandwich generation (fact sheet). Utah State University Cooperative Extension. Web site: http://extension.usu.edu/cooperative.

Skogrand, L., Johnson, A. C., Horrocks, A., & DeFrain, J. (2011). Financial management practices of couples with great marriages. *Journal of Family and Economic Issues, 32,* 27–35.

Skogrand, L., Mendez, E., & Higginbotham, B. (2012). *Stepfamily education: A case study of two lesbian couples.* Manuscript submitted for publication.

Skogrand, L., Mueller, L., Crook, R., Spotted Elk, D., Dayzie, I., LeBlanc, H., & Rosenband, R. (2007). *Strong marriages for Navajo couples: Couple activity book.* Available online at http://extension.usu.edu/files/publications/publication/pub__8139744.pdf.

Retrieve from http://www.ucdenver.edu/academics/colleges/PublicHealth/research/centers/CAIANH/journal/Documents/Volume%2015/15(2)_Skogrand_Strong_Navajo_Marriages_25–41.pdf.

Skogrand, L., Reck, K., Higginbotham, B., Adler-Baeder, F., & Dansie, L. (2010). Recruitment and retention for stepfamily education. *Journal of Couple & Relationship Therapy, 9*, 448–465.

Skogrand, L., Schramm, D. G., Marshall, J. P., & Lee, T. (2005). The effects of debt on newlyweds and implications for education. *Journal of Extension, 43*. Web site: http://www.joe.org/joe/2005june/rb7.shtml.

Skolnick, A. S., & Skolnick, J. H. (1977). *Family in transition.* Boston: Little, Brown.

Skutch, L. P. (2001). Childless-by-choice women and mothers-by-choice: A comparative study of attitudes and behaviors on quality of life and feminist perspectives. *Dissertation Abstracts International-B, 62*(2), 1145.

Slater, L. (2006, February). This thing called love. *National Geographic*, 32–49.

Smiler, A. P. (2008). "I wanted to get to know her better": Adolescent boys' dating motives, masculinity ideology, and sexual behavior. *Journal of Adolescence, 31*, 17–32.

Smith, J. (2003). The adopted child syndrome: A methodological perspective. *Families in Society: The Journal of Contemporary Human Services, 82*, 491–497.

Smith, J. A. (2009). *The daddy shift: How stay-at-home dads, breadwinning moms, and shared parenting are transforming the American family.* Boston: Beacon Press.

Smith, K. (2002). *Who's minding the kids? Child care arrangements: Spring 1997* (pp. 70–86). Washington, DC: U.S. Census Bureau.

Smith, S. R., & Hamon, R. R. (2012). *Exploring family theories* (3rd ed.). New York: Oxford University Press.

Smock, P. (2000). Cohabitation in the United States. *Annual Review of Sociology, 26*, 1–20.

Solheim, C. (2008, June). Family resource management through multicultural lenses. *Family Focus, FF38*, 1–2, 4.

Solot, D., & Miller, M. (2000). Ten ways to improve your chances for a good marriage after cohabitation. Alternatives to Marriage. Web site: http://www.unmarried.org/ten-ways-to-improve-your-chances-for-a-good-marrage.

Solot, D., & Miller, M. (2009). Sex discussed here! Sex education unlike any you've had before. Web site: http://www.sexualityeducation.com/.

Somer, E. (2007). Stress and diet. In A. Monat, R. S. Lazarus, & R. Reevy (Eds.), *The Praeger handbook on stress and coping* (vol. 2, pp. 509–528). Westport, CT: Praeger.

Somers, M. S. (1993). A comparison of voluntarily child-free adults and parents. *Journal of Marriage and the Family, 55*, 643–650.

159–183.

Stadelmann, S., Perren, S., Groeben, M., & von Klitzing, K. (2010). Parental separation and children's behavioral/emotional problems: The impact of parental representations and family conflict. *Family Process, 49*, 92–108.

Stanley, S. M., Whitton, S. W., Sadberry, S. L., Clements, M. L., & Markman, H. J. (2006). Sacrifice as a predictor of marital outcomes. *Family Process, 45*, 289–303.

Stauss, J. H. (1986). The study of American families: Implications for applied research. *Family Perspective, 20*(4), 337–350.

Stauss, J. H. (1993). Reframing and refocusing American Indian family strengths. *Family Perspective, 27*(4), 311–321.

Straus, M., Gelles, R., & Steinmetz, S. (2006). *Behind closed doors: Violence in the American family.* New Brunswick, NJ: Translation Publishers.

Sternberg, R. J. (2007a). Triangular theory of love. Web site: http://en.wikipedia.org/wiki/Triangular_theory_of_love.

Sternberg, R. J. (2007b). Robert J. Sternberg homepage. Web site: http://yale.edu/rjsternberg.

Sternberg, R. J. (2008). Triangulating love. In T. J. Oord (Ed.), *The altruism reader: Selections from writings on love, religion, and science* (pp. 331–347). West Conshohocken, PA: Templeton Foundation Press.

Sternberg, R. J., & Barnes, M. (Eds.). (1988). *The psychology of love.* New Haven, CT: Yale University Press.

Sternberg, R. J., & Weis, K. (Eds.). (2006). *The new psychology of love.* New Haven, CT: Yale University Press.

Sternberg, R., & Weis, K. (2008) (Eds). *The new psychology of love.* Yale University Press: New Haven, CT.

Stewart, K. L. (1989). Stress and adaptation: A multisystem model of individual, couple, family, and work systems. *Dissertation Abstracts International-A, 49*(08).

Stewart, S. (2010). The characteristics and well-being of adopted stepchildren. *Family Relations, 59*, 558–571.

Stewart, S. D. (2007). *Brave new stepfamilies.* Thousand Oaks, CA: Sage.

Stinnett, N., & DeFrain, J. (1985). *Secrets of strong families.* Boston: Little, Brown.

Stokes, B. (2007, July 24). Happiness is increasing in many countries—But why? Pew Research Center. Web site: http://pewglobal.org/commentary/display.php?AnalysisID=1020.

Stolzer, J. (2005). Breastfeeding in the 21st century: A theoretical perspective. *International Journal of Sociology and the Family, 31*(1), 39–55.

Stolzer, J. (2006). Breastfeeding: An interdisciplinary review of the literature. *International Review of Modern Sociology, 32*(1), 103–128.

Stone, A. A., Schwartz, J. E., Broderick, J. E., & Deaton, A. (2010). A snapshot of the age distribution of psychological well-being in the United States. *Proceedings of the National Academy of Sciences.* Web site: http://www.pnas.org/content/early/2010/05/04/1003744107.abstract.

Stone, P. (2007). *Opting out: Why women really quit careers and head home.* Berkeley: University of California Press. This book challenges the media stories about the "new traditionalism" that prompts high-achieving women to make the "choice" to quit work and return to full-time motherhood, "the most rewarding job in the world." Stone argues that women are often forced out of the workplace because it is still designed for "ideal workers" who are available to work 24–7 because they have no caregiving responsibilities.

Straus, J. (2006). *Unhooked generation: The truth about why we're still single.* New York: Hyperion.

Straus, M. (2007). Do we need a law to prohibit spanking? *National Council on Family Relations Family Focus* (June), F7, F19.

Straus, M. (2008, December). Ending spanking can make a major contribution to preventing physical abuse. *Family Focus, 40,* F14–F16.

Straus, M. A. (1990). The national family violence surveys. In M. Straus & R. J. Gelles (Eds.), *Physical violence in American families* (pp. 3–16). New Brunswick, NJ: Transaction.

Straus, M. A. (1994). *Beating the devil out of them: Corporal punishment in American families.* New York: Lexington Books.

Straus, M. A. (1998). Impulsive corporal punishment by mothers and antisocial behavior and impulsiveness of children. *Behavioral Sciences and the Law, 16*(3), 353–374.

Straus, M. A. (2001). *Beating the devil out of them: Corporal punishment in American families.* (with a new introduction by the author). New Brunswick, NJ.

Straus, M. A. (2002). Communicating the no-spanking message to parents. *Journal of Family Communication, 21*(5), 3–5.

Straus, M. A., & Gelles, R. J. (1986). Societal change and change in family violence from 1975 to 1985 as revealed by two national surveys. *Journal of Marriage and the Family, 48,* 465–479.

Straus, M. A., Gelles, R. J., & Steinmetz, S. K. (2006). *Behind closed doors: Violence in the American family.* New Brunswick, NJ. The classic research on family violence, with a new introduction by Murray Straus and Richard Gelles.

Straus, M. A., & Mathus, A. K. (1996). Social change and trends in approval of corporal punishment by parents from 1968 to 1994. In D. Frehsee, W. Horn, & K. Bussman (Eds.), *Violence against children* (pp. 91–105). New York: de Gruyter.

Straus, M. A., & Stewart, J. H. (1999). Corporal punishment by American parents: National data on prevalence, chronicity, severity, and duration, in relation to child and family characteristics. *Clinical Child and Family Psychology Review, 2*(2), 55–70.

Street, A. E., & Arias, I. (2001). Psychological abuse and post-traumatic stress disorder in battered women: Examining the roles of shame and guilt. *Violence and Victims, 16*(1), 65–78.

Strong, B., Yarber, W. L., Sayad, B. W., & DeVault, C. (2008). *Human sexuality: Diversity in contemporary America.* New York: McGraw-Hill Higher Education.

Struthers, C. B., & Bokemeier, J. L. (2000). Myths and realities of raising children and creating family life in a rural county. *Journal of Family Issues, 21*(1), 17–46.

Suárez-Oronzco, C., Suárez-Oronzco, M., Todorova, I. (2008). *Learning a new land: Immigrant students in American society.* Cambridge, MA: Belknap Press of Harvard University Press.

Substance Abuse and Mental Health Services Administration. (2004). The complicated relationship between substance abuse and violence. Center for Substance Abuse Prevention. Washington, DC: U.S. Department of Health and Human Services. Web site: http://www.samhsa.gov.

Substance Abuse and Mental Health Services Administration. (2012). Alcohol abuse. Web site: http://samhsa.gov.

Sue, D. W., & Sue, D. (2008). *Counseling the culturally diverse: Theory and practice* (5th ed.). Hokenboken, New Jersey: John Wiley & Sons.

Sugarman, S. D. (2003). Single-parent families. In M. A. Mason, A. Skolnick, & S. D. Sugarman (Eds.), *All our families: New policies for a new century* (pp. 14–39). New York: Oxford University Press.

Suter, E. A., Daas, K. L., & Bergen, K. M. (2008). Negotiating lesbian family identify via symbols and rituals. *Journal of Family Issues, 29,* 26–47.

Sutton, C. E. T., & Broken Nose, M. A. (1996). American Indian families: An overview. In M. McGoldrick & J. Giordano (Eds.), *Ethnicity and family therapy* (2nd ed., pp. 31–44). New York: Guilford.

Sutton, C. T., & Broken Nose, M. A. (2005). American Indian families: An overview. In M. McGoldrick, J. Giordano, N. Garcia-Preto (Eds.), *Ethnicity and family therapy* (3rd ed.). New York: Guilford Press.

Sweeney, J. (1982, June 21). Taking the long view of marriage: Why do some endure? *Los Angeles Times,* pp. 1, 21–23.

Switala, K. (2012). The feminist theory. Web site: http://www.cddc.vt.edu/feminism/enin.html. Research materials and information for students, activists, and scholars interested in women's conditions and struggles around the world.

Taffel, S. M., Placek, P. J., Moien, M., & Kosary, C. L. (1991). 1989 U.S. cesarean section rate steadies—VBAC rate rises to nearly one in five. *Birth, 18,* 73–77.

Tamis-Lemonda, C. S., & Cabrera, N. (2003). *Handbook of father involvement: Multidisciplinary perspectives.* Mahwah, NJ: Erlbaum. Experts from diverse scientific disciplines share their interests in the topic of father involvement in the lives of children.

Tannen, D., Kendall, S., & Gordon, C. (Eds.). (2007). *Family talk: Discourse and identity in four American families.* New York: Oxford University Press.

Tannen, D. (2001). *You just don't understand: Women and men in conversation.* New York: Quill.

Tannen, D. (2003). *Communication matters. Course one: He said / she said, women, men and language* [sound recording]. Prince Frederick, MD: Recorded Books. Deborah Tannen has focused our attention on the differences between male and female communication styles and how these differences affect our relationships with each other.

Tannen, D. (2005). *Conversational style: Analyzing talk among friends.* New York: Oxford University Press.

Tannen, D. (2007). *You're wearing that? Understanding mothers and daughters in conversation.* New York: Random House.

Tannen, D. (2009). *You were always mom's favorite: Sisters in conversation throughout their lives.* New York: Random House.

Tannen, D. (2012). The official web site of Deborah Tannen. Web site: http://www9.georgetown.edu/faculty/tannend/.

American and Japanese attitudes to extramarital sex, divorce—and Princess Diana. The Harris Poll: http://www.harrisinteractive.com/harris_poll1/index.asp?PID=193.

Taylor, J. L. (2009). Midlife impacts of adolescent parenthood. *Journal of Family Issues, 30,* 484–510.

Taylor, R. J., Jackson, J. S., and Chatters, L. M. (Eds.). (1997). *Family life in Black America.* Thousand Oaks, CA: Sage.

Taylor, R. J., Lincoln, K. D., & Chatters, L. M. (2005). Supportive relationships with church members among African Americans. *Family Relations, 54,* 501–511.

Teachman, J., & Tedrow, L. (2008). The demography of stepfamilies in the United States. In J. Pryor (Ed.), *The international handbook of stepfamilies: Policy and practice in legal, research, and clinical environments* (pp. 3–29). Hoboken, NJ: John Wiley & Sons.

The Dictionary of the History of Ideas. (2003). Electronic Text Center. Charlottesville: University of Virginia Library and the Gale Group. Web site: http://etext.virginia.edu/cgi-local/DHI/dhi.cgi?id=dv3-56.

The Economist, 2007. Where money seems to talk (2007, July 14). *The Economist, 384,* p. 63–64.

Theroux, P. (1996). *My other life: A novel.* Boston: Houghton Mifflin.

Thiele, D. M., & Whelan, T. A. (2006). The nature and dimension of the grandparent role. *Marriage and Family Review, 40,* 93–108.

Thomas, V., & Olson, D. H. (1993). Problem families and the Circumplex Model: Observational assessment using the clinical rating scale. *Journal of Marital and Family Therapy, 19*(2), 159–175.

Thompson, K. L., & Gullone, E. (2003). Promotion of empathy and prosocial behaviour in children through humane education. *Australian Psychologist, 38*(3), 175–182.

Thompson, M. (2008, February 25). Death at the Army's hands. *Time,* 40–42.

Thorne, D. (2010). Extreme financial strain: Emergent chores, gender inequality and emotional distress. *Journal of Family and Economic Issues, 31,* 185–197.

Thrift nation. (2009, April 27). *Time,* 20–23.

Tichenor, V. J. (1999). Status and income as gendered resources: The case for marital power. *Journal of Marriage and the Family, 61,* 638–650.

Tirman, J. (2012). The forgotten wages of war. *The New York Times.* Web site: http://www.nytimes.com/2012/01/04/opinion/the-forgotten-wages-of-war.html?_r=0.

Tong, R. (2009). *Feminist thought* (3rd ed.). Boulder, CO: Westview Press.

Treas, J., & Drobnic, S. (Eds). (2010). *Dividing the domestic: Men, women, and household work in cross-national perspective.* Stanford, CA: Stanford University Press.

Lonner, & J. Trimble (Eds.), *Counseling across cultures* (4th ed., pp. 93–112). Los Angeles: Sage.

Troll, L. E. (1997). Growing old in families. In I. Deitch & C. Ward Howell (Eds.), *Counseling the aging and their families* (pp. 3–16). Alexandria, VA: American Counseling Association.

Troll, L. E. (2001/2002). When the world narrows: Intimacy with the dead? *Generations, 25*(2), 55–58.

Troll, L. E. (2001). When the world narrows: Intimacy with the dead? *Generations, 25*(2), 55–58.

Tubbs, C. Y., Roy, K. M., & Burton, L. M. (2005). Family ties: Constructing family time in low-income families. *Family Process, 44,* 77–91.

Tudge, J. (2008). *The everyday lives of young children: Culture, class, and child rearing in sssdiverse societies.* New York: Cambridge University Press.

UK National Statistics. (2004, January 24). Marriage and divorce rates: EU comparison, 2002. Web site: http://www.statistics.gove.uk/STATBASE/ssdataset.asp?vlnk+17625&More=Y.

Ulker, A. (2008). Wealth holdings and portfolio allocation of the elderly: The role of marital history. *Journal of Family Economic Issues, 30,* 90–108. Death and divorce earlier in life can significantly affect the accumulation of wealth among the elderly.

Ulker, A. (2009). Wealth holdings and portfolio allocations of the elderly: The role of marital history. *Journal of Family and Economic Issues, 30,* 90–108.

United Nations AIDS. (2004). A global overview of the AIDS epidemic. Web site: http://www.unaids.org/EN/resources/epidemiology.asp.

United Nations International Labour Office. (2004a). *Breaking through the glass ceiling: Women in management—update 2004.* Geneva: Author.

United Nations International Labour Office. (2004b). *Global employment trends for women 2004.* Geneva: Author.

United States Courts (n.d.). *2011 BAPCPA report highlights.* Retrieved from http://www.uscourts.gov/Statistics/BankruptcyStatistics/bapcpa-report-highlights.aspx.

University of Michigan. (2003). Monitoring the future: National results on adolescent drug use: Overview of key findings, 2002. Cited by the U.S. Department of Justice, Office of Justice Programs, Bureau of Justice Statistics. Web site: http://www.ojp.us.doj.gov/bjs/dcf/du.htm.

University of Michigan Health System. (2012). Sibling abuse. Web site: http://www.med.umich.edu/yourchild/topics/sibabuse.htm.

University of Missouri at Columbia Extension. (2010). Information on parenthood and families. Web site: www.extension.missouri.edu-/main/family/.

University of Nebraska–Lincoln Extension. (2010). Parenting and family issues from a strengths-based perspective. Web site: www.ianrpubs.unl.edu/-epublic/pages/index.jsp.

University of Nebraska–Lincoln Extension. (2012). Educational materials for strengthening couple and family relationships. Web site: www.ianrpubs.unl.edu/epublic/pages/index.jsp.

Urban Institute. (2000, February 1). A new look at homelessness in America. Web site: http://www.urban.org.

U.S. Administration on Aging. (2009). A profile of older Americans: 2008. Web site: http://www.aoa.gov/AoARoot/Aging_Statistics/Profile/2008/3.aspx.

U.S. Advisory Board on Child Abuse and Neglect. (1990). *Child abuse and neglect: Critical first steps in response to a national emergency.* Washington, DC: U.S. Government Printing Office.

U.S. Census Bureau. (2000, June). Fertility in American women: Population characteristics. Web site: http://www.census.

U.S. Census Bureau. (2001a). Age: 2000. Census 2000 brief. Web site: http://www.census.gov.

U.S. Census Bureau. (2001b). Census 2000 shows America's diversity. Web site: http://www.census.gov/Press-Release/www.2001/cb01cn61.html.

U.S. Census Bureau. (2001c, March). Current population survey. Web site: http://www.census.gov.

U.S. Census Bureau. (2001d). Population by race and Hispanic/Latino status. Web site: http://census. gov/statab/www/part1a.html.

U.S. Census Bureau. (2001e). Population change and distribution. Web site: http://www.census.gov/population/cen2000/c2kbr01-2.pdf.

U.S. Census Bureau. (2001f). Population profile of the United States: 2000. Web site: http://www.census.gov.

U.S. Census Bureau. (2002a). Money income in United States—2001. Web site: http://www.census.gov.

U.S. Census Bureau. (2002b). Press release. Web site: http://www.census.gov/Press-Release/www/2002/cb02cn173.html.

U.S. Census Bureau. (2002c). *Statistical abstract of the United States* (122nd ed). Washington, DC: U.S. Government Printing Office.

U.S. Census Bureau. (2002d). Summary File 3 (SF 3). Poverty status in 1999 by sex by age. Web site: http://factfinder.census.gov.

U.S. Census Bureau. (2003a). American Indian and Alaska Native heritage month: November 2003. Web site: http://www.census.gov.

U.S. Census Bureau. (2003b). *Statistical abstract of the United States* (123rd ed.). Washington, DC: U.S. Government Printing Office.

U.S. Census Bureau. (2004a). Census Bureau projects tripling of Hispanic and Asian populations in 50 years; non-Hispanic Whites may drop to half of total population. Web site: http://www.census.gov/Press-Release/www/releases/archives/population/001720.html.

U.S. Census Bureau. (2004c). *Statistical abstract of the United States* (120th ed.). Washington, DC: U.S. Government Printing Office.

U.S. Census Bureau. (2004d, July 19). Unmarried and Single Americans Week. Web site: http://www.unmarriedamerica.org/usaweek/census-release.htm.

U.S. Census Bureau. (2005). Hispanic heritage month 2005: September 15–October 15. Web site: http://www.census.gov/Press-Release/www/releases/archives/.

U.S. Census Bureau. (2005a). Educational attainment in the United States: 2005. Web site: http://www.census.gov/population/www/socdemo/education/cps2005.html.

U.S. Census Bureau. (2005b). Family groups with children under 18 years old by race and Hispanic origin. *Statistical abstract of the United States*. Web site: http://www.census.gov/compendia/statab/tables/07s0062.xls.

U.S. Census Bureau. (2005c, May). Indicators of marriage and fertility in the United States from the American Community Survey: 2000–2003. Web site: http://www.census.gov/population/www/socdemo/fertility/mar-fert-slides.html.

U.S. Census Bureau. (2005d). Internet access and usage and online service usage: 1997–2005. *Statistical abstract of the United States*. Web site: http://www.census .gov/compendia/statab.

U.S. Census Bureau. (2005e). Marital status of the population by sex, race and Hispanic origin: 1990–2005. *Statistical abstract of the United States*. Web site: http://www.census.gov/compendia/statab.

U.S. Census Bureau. (2006). *Statistical abstract of the United States* (126th ed.). Washington, DC: U.S. Government Printing Office. Web site: http://www.census.gov.

U.S. Census Bureau. (2006a). Hispanic heritage month. *Facts for features.* Web site: http://www.census .gov/Press-Release.

U.S. Census Bureau. (2006b, February). Valentine's Day: February 14. Web site: http://census.gov/Press-Release/www/releases/archives/facts_for. . . .

U.S. Census Bureau. (2007). Marriage and divorce: 2004. Web site: http://www.census.gov-/Press-Release/www/releases/archives/.

U.S. Census Bureau. (2008). *Current population survey, 2008 annual social and economic supplement.* Current Population Reports, Series P20-537 and the U.S. Census Bureau. Retrieved from Web site: www.census.gov/population/socdemo/hh-fam/cps2008.

U.S. Census Bureau. (2008). *Statistical abstract of the United States* (128th ed.). Washington, DC: U.S. Government Printing Office. Web site: http://www.census.gov.

U.S. Census Bureau. (2008, February 28). Nearly half of preschoolers receive child care from relatives. Web site: http://www.census.gov/Press-Release/www/releases/archives/children/011574.html.

U.S. Census Bureau. (2008, May 1). U.S. Hispanic population surpasses 45 million: Now 15 percent of total. Web site: http://www.census.gov/Press-Release/www/releases/archives/.

U.S. Census Bureau. (2008, July 1). Median age of the population by race and Hispanic origin for the United States and states. Web site: http://data.iowadatacenter.org/datatables/UnitedStates/-usstmedianagebyrace 2008.pdf.

U.S. Census Bureau. (2009). *Statistical abstract of the United States* (129th ed.). Washington, DC: U.S. Government Printing Office. Web site: http://www.census.gov.

U.S. Census Bureau. (2009a). *Older Americans month: May 2009.* Web site: http://www.census.gov/Press-Release/www/releases/archives/-facts_for_features_special_editions/013384.html.

U.S. Census Bureau. (2009b). As baby boomers age, fewer families have children under 18 at home. Web site: http://www.census.gov/Press-Release/www/releases/archives/-families_households/013378.html.

census.gov/population/www/socdemo/hispanic/files/-Internet_Hispanic_in_US_2006.pdf.

U.S. Census Bureau (2010). *Asian/Pacific American heritage month: May 2010.* (Profile America: Facts for Features, CB10-FF.07). Retrieved from http://www.census.gov/newsroom/releases/archives/facts_for_features_special_editions/cb10-ff07.html.

U.S. Census Bureau. (2010). Census Bureau reports families with children increasingly face unemployment. Web site: http://www.census.gov/Press-Release/www/releases-/archives/families_households/014540.html.

U.S. Census Bureau. (2010). Family households with own children under age 18 by type of family and age of householder, Table 65. *Statistical Abstract of the United States: 2012.* Retrieved from http://www.census.gov/compendia/statab/cats/population/households_families_group_qu.

U.S. Census Bureau. (2010). *Statistical abstract of the United States* (130th ed.). Washington, DC: U.S. Government Printing Office. Web site: http://www.census.gov.

U.S. Census Bureau (2010a). American Community Survey 1-year estimates, Grandchildren under 18 years living with a grandparent householder by grandparent responsibility and presence of parent. Web site: http://www.census.gov/acs/www.

U.S. Census Bureau. (2010b). Older Americans Month: May 2010. Web site: http:P//www.census.gov/newsroom/releases/archives/facts_for_features_special_editions/cb10-ff06.html.

U.S. Census Bureau. (2011). Census Bureau reports 55 percent have married one time. Newsroom. Web site: http://www.census.gov/newsroom/releases/archives/marital_-status_liv...

U.S. Census Bureau. (2011). *State & county quickfacts.* Web site: http://quickfacts.census.gov/qfd/states/00000.html.

U.S. Census Bureau. (2011, Sept. 13). Frequently asked questions: What is the difference between households and families? Web site: http://www.census.gov/hhes/www.income/about/faqs.html.

U.S. Census Bureau. (2011a). Marital events of Americans: 2009. American Community Survey Reports. Web site: http://www.census.gov/prod/2011pubs/acs-13.pdf.

U.S. Census Bureau. (2012). *About poverty.* Retrieved from http://www.census.gov/hhes/www/poverty/about/overview/measure.html.

U.S. Census Bureau. (2012). *Average earnings of year-round, full-time workers by educational attainment: 2009* (Table 703). Statistical Abstract of the United States. Retrieved from http://www.census.gov/compendia/statab/2012/tables/12s0703.pdf.

U.S. Census Bureau. (2012). Educational attainment by race and Hispanic origin: 1970–2010, Table 229. *Statistical Abstract of the United States 2012.* Retrieved from http://www.census.gov/compendia/statab/2012/tables/12s0695.pdf.

U.S. Census Bureau. (2012). *Money income of families — Percent distribution by income level in constant (2009) dollars: 1980–2009* (Table 696). Statistical Abstract of the United States. Retrieved from http://www.census.gov/compendia/statab/2012/tables/12s0695.pdf.

U.S. Census Bureau. (2012). *Money income of families— Percent distribution by income level in constant (2009) dollars: 1980–2009* (Table 696). Statistical Abstract of the United States. Retrieved from http://www.census.gov/compendia/statab/2012/tables/12s0695.pdf.

U.S. Census Bureau. (2012). *Statistical abstract of the United States: 2012.* Table 133. Marriages and divorces: Number and rate by state: 1990 to 2009, p. 98. Web site: http://www.census.gov/compendia/statab/2012/tables/12s0133.pdf.

U.S. Census Bureau. (2012). Table 67. Family groups with children under 18 years old by race and Hispanic origin: 1990 to 2010. Web site: http://www.census.gov/compendia/statab/2012/tables/12s0067.pdf.

U.S. Census Bureau. (2012a). Population profile of the United States: The oldest old is the fastest growing segment of the elderly population. Web site: http://www.census.gov/population-profile/elderpop.html.

U.S. Census Bureau. (2012b). Table 104. Expectation of life at birth, 1970 to 2008, and projections, 2010 to 2020. *Statistical Abstract of the United States: 2012.* Web site: http://www.census.gov/compendia/statab/2012/tables/12s0104.pdf.

U.S. Census Bureau. (2012c). Older Americans Month: May 2010. *Profile America: Facts for Features.* Web site: http://www.census.gov/newsroom/releases/archives/facts_for_features_-special_editions_cb10-ff06.htm.

U.S. Census Bureau, Housing and Household Economic Statistics Division. (2008). Current population survey—Definitions and explanations. Web site: http://www.census.gov-/population/www/cps/cpsdef.html.

U.S. Census Bureau News. (2004, June 14). Hispanic and Asian American increasing faster than overall population.

Usdansky, M. L. (2009). A weak embrace: Popular and scholarly depictions of single-parent families. *Journal of Marriage and Family, 71,* 209–225.

U.S. Department of Agriculture, Economic Research Service. (2013). Food security in the U.S.: Key statistics and graphics. Web site: http://www.ers.usda.gov/topics/food-nutrition-assistance/food-security-in-the-us/key-statistics-graphics.aspx.

U.S. Department of Commerce, Economics and Statistics Administration & Executive Office of the President, Office of Management and Budget. (2011, March). *Women in America: Indicators of social and economic well-being.* Retrieved from http://www.whitehouse.gov/sites/default/files/rss_viewer/Women_in_America.pdf.

U.S. Department of Health and Human Services. (2010). Female genital cutting. Web site: http://www.womens-health.gov/faq/female-genital-cutting.cfm.

U.S. Department of Health and Human Services. (2011). Child maltreatment. Administration for Children and Families, Administration on Children, Youth and Families, Children's Bureau. Web site: http://www.acf.hhs.gov/programs/cb/resource/child-maltreatment-2011.

U.S. Department of Justice. (2005a). Victims of crime. Web site: http://www.usdoj.gov.

U.S. Department of Justice. (2005a, b). Bureau of Justice Statistics. Intimate homicide victims by gender. Web site: http://bjs.ojp.usdoj.gov/content/homicide/intimates.cfm.

U.S. Department of Justice. (2012). Domestic violence. Web site: http://www.ovw.usdoj.gov/domviolence.htm.

U.S. Department of Labor. (2010, February 5). The unemployment situation—January 2010. Web site: http://www.bls.gov/news.release/pdf/empsit.pdf.

U.S. General Accounting Office. (2003). *Women's earnings: Work patterns partially explain difference between men's and women's earnings.* Report to Congressional requesters. Washington, DC: Author.

U.S. National Center for Health Statistics. (2009). *Vital Statistics of the United States and National Vital Statistics Reports.* Web site: http://www.census.gov.compendia/-stab/tables/09s0077.pdf.

U.S. National Library of Medicine. (2010). Aging changes in the nervous system. *Medline Plus,* National Institutes of Health. Web site: http://nlm.nih.gov/medlineplus/ency/article/004023.htm.

Valente, J. (2009, May 9). Hooking up. *PBS: Religion and Ethics Newsweekly.* Interviews and discussion from the Public Broadcasting Service. Web site: http://www.pbs.org/wnet/religion-andethics/episodes/may-8-2009/hooking-up/2896/.

Van As, C. F. (2003). Facilitating the optimal academic achievement of the adolescent through parenting. *Dissertation Abstracts International-A, 63*(08), 2794.

Vandell, D. L., Burchinal, M., Vandergrift, N., Belsky, J., Steinberg, L., & NICHD Early Child Care Research Network. (2010). Do effects of early child care extend to age 15 years? Results from the NICHD study of early child care and youth development. *Child Development, 81,* 737–756.

Van Dorn, R. A., Bowen, G. L., & Blau, J. R. (2006). The impact of community diversity and consolidated inequality on dropping out of high school. *Family Relations, 55,* 105–118.

van Dulmen, M., Miller, B. C., Grotevant, H. D., Fan, X., & Christensen, M. (2000). Comparisons of adopted and non-adopted adolescents in a large, nationally representative sample. *Child Development, 71*(5), 1458–1473.

Van Epp, J. (2008). *How to avoid falling in love with a jerk.* New York: McGraw-Hill.

Van Volkom, M. (2006). Sibling relationships in middle and older adulthood: A review of the literature. *Marriage and Family Review, 40,* 151–170.

Vega, W. A., Patterson, T., Sallis, J., Nader, P., Atkins, C., & Abraham, I. (1986). Cohesion and adaptability in Mexican American and Anglo families. *Journal of Marriage and the Family, 48,* 857–867.

Veniegas, R. C., & Peplau, L. A. (1997). Power and the quality of same-sex friendships. *Psychology of Women Quarterly, 21*(3), 279–297.

Vincent, J. P., & Jouriles, E. N. (2000). *Domestic violence: Guidelines for research-informed practice.* London: Jessica Kingsley.

Visher, E. B. (1989). The Stepping Ahead Program. In M. Burt (Ed.), *Stepfamilies stepping ahead* (3rd ed., pp. 57–89). Lincoln, NE: Stepfamilies Press.

Visher, E. B., & Visher, J. S. (1992). *How to win as a stepfamily* (2nd ed.). New York: Brunner/Mazel.

Visher, E. B., Visher, J. S., & Pasley, K. (1997). Stepfamily therapy from the client's perspective. *Marriage and Family Review, 27*(1–2), 191–213.

von Bertalanffy, L. (1968). *General system theory: Foundation, development, applications.* New York: Braziller.

Vosburg, E. S. (2004). Toward triadic communication: A crisis in Japanese family relationships. In W. C. Nichols (Ed.), *Family therapy around the world* (pp. 105–117). Binghamton, NY: Haworth.

Voydanoff, P. (2005). Work demands and work-to-family and family-to-work conflict: Direct and indirect relationships. *Journal of Family Issues, 26,* 707–726.

Voydanoff, P. (2008). A conceptual model of the work-family interface. In K. Korabik, D. S. Lero, & D. L. Whitehead (Eds.), *Handbook of work-family integration,* chap. 2. St. Louis: Elsevier.

Waite, L. J. (1998). Why marriage matters. In T. Ooms (Ed.), *Strategies to strengthen marriage* (pp. 1–22). Washington, DC: Family Impact Seminar.

Waite, L. J. (2001, April). 5 marriage myths, 6 marriage benefits. *Marriage and Families,* pp. 19–25.

Waite, L. J. (2003, April). Uncommitted cohabitation versus marriage. *Terskel, 76,* 17–20.

Waite, L. J., & Gallagher, M. (2000). *The case for marriage: Why married people are happier, healthier, and better off financially.* New York: Doubleday.

Waite, L. J., & Lehrer, L. (2003). The benefits from marriage and religion in the United States: A comparative analysis. *Population and Developmental Review, 29*(2), 255–275.

Waite, L., Luo, Y., & Lewin, A. (2009). Marital happiness and marital stability: Consequences for psychological well-being. *Social Science Research, 38,* 201–212.

Waldegrave, C. (2009). Culture, gender, and socioeconomic context in therapeutic and social policy work. *Family Process, 48,* 85–101.

Waldrep, D. A., Cozza, S. J., & Chen, R. S. (2004, June). The impact of deployment on the military family. In *Iraq War Clinician Guide* (2nd ed., pp. 83–86). Washington, DC: Department of Veterans Affairs, National Center for PTSD.

Walker, A. J., & McGraw, L. A. (1999). Interdependence between mothers and daughters in middle and later life: Patterns of connection and autonomy. Poster presented at the 61st Annual Conference of the National Council on Family Relations, Irvine, CA, November 12–15.

Walker, L. E. (2000). *The battered woman syndrome* (2nd ed.). New York: Springer.

Walker, L. E. (2009). *The battered woman syndrome: With research associates.* New York: Springer.

Waller, M. R., & Peters, H. E. (2008). The risk of divorce as a barrier to marriage among parents of young children. *Social Science Research, 37,* 1188–1199.

Waller, W. (1951). *The family* [revised by R. Hill]. New York: Dryden.

Wallerstein, J. S., & Blakeslee, S. (2003). *What about the kids? Raising your children before, during, and after divorce.* New York: Hyperion.

Wang, R., Bianchi, S., & Raley, S. (2005). Teenagers' Internet use and family rules: A research note. *Journal of Marriage and the Family, 67*, 1249–1258.

Wang, W., & Morin, R. (2009, November 24). Home for the holidays . . . and every other day: Recession brings many young adults back to the nest. Pew Research Center Publications. Web site: http://pewresearch.org/pubs/1423/home-for-the-holidays-boomeranged-parents.

Washington Post. (2012). Faces of the fallen. Web site: http://apps.washingtonpost.com/national/fallen/.

Watamura, S. E., Sebanc, A. M., & Gunnar, M. R. (2002). Rising cortisol at childcare: Relations with nap, rest, and temperament. *Developmental Psychobiology, 40*(1), 33–42.

WebMD. (2009). Am I pregnant? Web site: http://www.webmd.com/baby/guide/pregnancy-am-i-pregnant.

Weinberg, D. (2008). The philosophical foundations of constructionist research. In J. A. Holstein & J. F. Gubrium (Eds.), *Handbook of constructionist research* (pp. 13–40). New York: Guilford Press.

Weinstock, H., et al. (2004). Sexually transmitted diseases among American youth: Incidence and prevalence estimates, 2000. *Perspectives on Sexual and Reproductive Health, 36*(1), 6–10.

Weitzman, L. J., & Dixon, R. B. (1992). The transformation of legal marriage through no-fault divorce. In A. S. Skolnick & J. H. Skolnick (Eds.), *Family in transition: Rethinking marriage, sexuality, child rearing, and family organization* (7th ed., pp. 217–289). New York: HarperCollins.

Wenger, G. C., Dykstra, P. A., Melkas, T., & Knipscheer, K. (2007). Social embeddedness and late-life parenthood: Community activities, close ties, and support networks. *Journal of Family Issues, 28*, 1419–1456.

Westman, J. C. (1998). Grandparenthood. Parenthood in America, General Library System, University of Wisconsin–Madison. Web site: http://parenthood.library.wisc.edu/Westman/Westman-Grandparenthood.html.

Where money seems to talk. (2009, July 14). *The Economist.* 63–64.

Whisman, M. A., Coop Gordman, K., & Chatav, Y. (2007). Predicting sexual infidelity in a population-based sample of married individuals. *Journal of Family Psychology, 21*(2), 320–324.

Whitaker, C. (1992). Symbolic experiential family therapy: Model and methodology. In J. K. Zeig (Ed.), *Evolution of psychotherapy: The second conference* (pp. 13–23). Philadelphia: Brunner/Mazel.

White, J. M., & Klein, D. M. (2002). *Family theories* (2nd ed.). Thousand Oaks, CA: Sage.

White, M., & Epston, D. (1990). *Narrative means to therapeutic ends.* New York: Norton.

White, M., & Morgan, A. (2006). *Narrative therapy with children and their families.* Adelaide, Australia: Dulwich Centre Publishers.

Whitman, C. T. (1995, May 31). Wheaton College commencement address. *Good Morning America.* New York: ABC Television.

Whitton, S., & Buzzella, B. A. (2011). Relationship education with same-sex couples. *Family Focus, 56.4*, F13–F115.

Whitton, S. W., Nicholson, J. M., & Markman, H. (2008). Research on interventions for stepfamily couples. In J. Pryor (Ed.), *The international handbook of stepfamilies: Policy and practice in legal, research, and clinical environments* (pp. 455–484). Hoboken, NJ: John Wiley & Sons.

Whorley, M., & Addis, M. E. (2006). Ten years of research on the psychology of men and masculinity in the United States: Methodological trends and critique. *Sex Roles, 55*, 649–658.

Wiener, N. (1956). *I am a mathematician.* New York: Doubleday.

Wilcox, B. (2009). *The state of our unions: Marriage in America 2009.* Retrieved from the National Marriage Project Web site: http://www.stateofourunions.org.

Wilcox, B. (2010). *The state of our unions: When marriage disappears.* Charlottesville, VA: The National Marriage Project, University of Virginia. Web site: http://nationalmarriageproject.org/wp-content/uploads/2012/06/Union_11_12_10.pdf.

Wilcox, B. (2010). *The state of our unions: When marriage disappears.* Retrieved from http://www.stateofourunions.org/2010/index.php.

Wilcox, B. (2010). *The state of our unions: When marriage disappears.* Retrieved from the National Marriage Project Web site: http://www.stateofourunions.org/2010/index.php.

Wilcox, B. (2011). *The state of our unions: When baby makes three.* Retrieved from http://www.stateofourunions.org/2011/SOOU2011.pdf.

Wilcox, W. B. (2009). The great recession's silver lining. In W. B. Wilcox (Ed.), *The state of our unions* (pp. 15–22). Charlottesville, VA: National Marriage Project. Web site: http://virginia.edu/marriageproject.

Wilcox, W. B., & Marquardt, E. (Eds.). (2011). The state of our unions 2011. National Marriage Project at the University of Virginia and the Center for Marriage and Families at the Institute for American Values. Web site: http://www.stateofourunions.org/.

Wildermuth, S. M., & Vogl-Bauer, S. (2007). We met on the Net: Exploring the perceptions of Online romantic relationships. *Southern Communication Journal, 72*, 211–227.

Williams, K. (2011). A socio-emotional relational framework for infidelity: The relational justice approach. *Family Process, 50*, 516–528.

Willoughby, B. J., & Dworkin, J. (2009). The relationship between emerging adults' expressed desire to marry and frequency of participation in risk-taking behaviors. *Youth & Society, 40*, 426–450.

Willows, J. (2008). *Moving on after childhood sexual abuse.* New York: Routledge.

Wilmot, W. W., & Hocker, J. L. (2011). *Interpersonal conflict* (8th ed.). New York: McGraw-Hill.

Wincze, J. P. (2009). *Enhancing sexuality: A problem-solving approach to treating dysfunction: Therapist guide* (2nd ed.). New York: Oxford University Press. An excellent overview of sex therapy today.

Wind, R. (2006, December). Premarital sex is nearly universal among Americans, and has been for decades. Media Center, Alan Guttmacher Institute. Web site: http://www.guttmacher.org/media/nr/2006/12/19/index.html.

Winslow, S. (2005). Work–family conflict, gender, and parenthood, 1977–1997. *Journal of Family Issues, 26*, 727–755.

Wolak, J., Mitchell, K., & Finkelhor, D. (2006). Online victimization of youth: Five years later. Web site: http://www.missingkids.com.

Wolfe, A. (1999, September). The mystique of Betty Friedan. *The Atlantic Online:* http://www.theatlantic.com/issues/99sep/9909friedan.htm.

Women in Leadership. (2010). Web site: http://www.guide2womenleaders.com/.

WomensLaw.org. Learning about abuse. Web site: http://www.womenslaw.org.

WomensLaw.org. (2012). Learning about abuse. Web site: http://www.womenslaw.org.

Wood, S., & Liossis, P. (2007). Potentially stressful life events and emotional closeness between grandparents and adult grandchildren. *Journal of Family Issues, 28*, 380–398.

Worthington, E. L. (Ed.). (2005). *Handbook of forgiveness.* New York: Routledge.

Wright, P. J. (2009). Father-child sexual communication in the United States: A review and synthesis. *Journal of Family Communication, 9*, 233–250.

Wrobel, G. M., Ayers-Lopez, S., Grotevant, H. D., & McRoy, R. G. (1996). Openness in adoption and the level of child participation. *Child Development, 67*(5), 2358–2374.

Wuerffel, J., DeFrain, J., & Stinnett, N. (1990, Fall). How strong families use humor. *Family Perspective*, pp. 129–142.

Wynne, L. (1958). Pseudo-mutuality in the family relations of schizophrenics. *Psychiatry, 21*, 205–222.

Xiao, J. J. (Ed.) (2008). *Handbook of consumer finance research.* New York: Springer.

Xu, A., Xie, X., Liu, W., Xia, Y., & Liu, D. (2007). Chinese family strengths and resiliency. In DeFrain, J., & Asay, S. M. (Eds.), *Strong families around the world: Strengths-based research and perspectives.* London: Routledge, Taylor & Francis Group.

Yalom, M. (1997). *A history of the breast.* New York: Alfred A. Knopf.

Yalom, M. (2001). *A history of the wife.* New York: HarperCollins.

Yarrow, P. (1972). River of Jordan. *PP&M Lifelines.* Mary Beth Music, ASCAP. Burbank, CA: Warner Bros. Records.

Zambrana, R. E. (Ed.). (1995). *Understanding Latino families.* Thousand Oaks, CA: Sage.

Zambrana, R. E., & Capello, D. (2003). Promoting Latino child and family welfare: Strategies for strengthening the child welfare system. *Children and Youth Services Review, 25*(10), 755–780.

Zaslow, M., & Eldred, C. (1998). Parenting behavior in a sample of young mothers in poverty. *APA Monitor.* Washington, DC: American Psychological Association.

Zhang, Y. (2010). A mixed-methods analysis of extramarital sex in contemporary China. *Marriage & Family Review, 46*, 170–190.

Zhang, Y., & Van Hook, J. (2009). Marital dissolution among interracial couples. *Journal of Marriage and the Family, 71*, 95–107.

Zhou, M., & Lee, J. (2008). Asian American youth: Culture, identity, and ethnicity. In S. Coontz (Ed.), *American families: A multicultural reader* (pp. 294–300). New York: Routledge, Taylor & Francis Group.

Zigler, E. F. (2004). Research interests. Yale University, Department of Psychology, New Haven, CT. Web site: http://www.yale.edu/psychology/FacInfo/Zigler.html.

Contents

Abbott, D. A., 32, 69
Abebe, B., 245
Abeles, R. P., 402
Abma, J. C., 173
Abrahms, S., 382
Abshoff, K., 341
Adams, M., 462, 465, 466
Aday, L. A., 386
Addis, M. E., 200
Adler-Baeder, F., 310, 485, 497
Ahrons, C., 468–470, 482, 487, 489
Aiken, L. R., 402
Albert, N. G., 43
Alberti, R., 158
Aldous, J., 384
Aldwin, C. M., 377, 402
Alfaro, E. C., 18
Ali, M. M., 186
Allen, E. S., 185
Allen, K., 39, 393
Allen, S. M., 199
Allen, W., 320, 454
Altura, J., 95
Amato, P., 12, 344, 466, 468, 469, 472, 473, 476, 477
Anderson, J. R., 310, 328
Anderson, N. B., 64
Angel, R. J., 429, 430, 433
Antonovics, K., 12
Apter, T., 328
Arditti, J., 353
Arias, E., 388
Arias, I., 431, 432
Arias, L., 431, 432
Aries, E., 114
Arnedt, C., 170
Arnett, J. J., 87, 104
Aron, A., 253, 275
Arrington, R., 92
Asai, S., 207, 209, 430
Asay, S. M., 2, 15, 18, 32, 33, 81, 406, 433, 434, 447, 457, 491, 493
Atwood, J., 512
Atwood, T. C., 339, 372
Auerbach, C. F., 364
Avenevoli, S., 346
Avery-Leaf, S., 150

Axtell, R. E., 116, 132
Bachman, H. J., 386
Bailey, S. J., 387, 435
Balleza, M., 268
Bámaca, M. Y., 18
Banzet, M. R., 252
Barber, B., 344, 437
Barrios-Bell, A., 56, 207, 311, 341, 475, 486
Bartholomae, S., 227
Bass, B. L., 219
Bateson, G., 120
Baucom, D. H., 150
Bauer, J. W., 395
Baumbusch, J. L., 274
Baumrind, D., 344, 346
Bauserman, R., 470, 471
Beach, S. R., 321, 324
Beach, S. R. H., 150
Beall, M. L., 132
Bean, R. A., 344
Becvar, D. S., 80
Becvar, R. J., 80
Beers, M. H., 287
Begin, J., 146
Bell, R., 347
Bellous, J. E., 371
Belsky, J., 322
Bem, S., 114
Benson, B., 177
Benson, P. L., 338
Bent-Goodley, T. B., 36
Bergen, K. M., 41
Berger, L. M., 474
Bergmann, B. R., 372
Bergstron, A., 68
Berkowitz, D., 38, 41
Berman, J., 6
Bernard, A., 197
Bernard, J., 7, 16, 88
Berscheid, E., 74
Berzon, B., 191
Bhopal, K., 277, 278
Bhugra, D., 167
Bianchi, S., 27, 202
Biblarz, T., 38, 39
Bigner, J., 512
Billingsley, A., 55
Birditt, K. S., 141

Bjorklund, G., 366
Blackman, L., 306
Blair, S. L., 58
Blakeslee, S., 468, 489
Blankenhorn, D., 270, 271, 302, 362
Blankenmeyer, M., 422
Blau, J. R., 18
Blieszner, R., 393
Bloch, E., 371
Blow, A. J., 160, 183, 192
Bluck, S., 274
Blumberg, S. L., 132, 158
Bock, J. D., 360
Bogle, K., 283, 284, 301
Bokemeier, J. L., 28
Booth, A., 158
Booth, S., 402
Borcherdt, B., 139, 140
Borders, L. D., 339
Bornstein, R., 429, 433
Bos, H., 470
Boss, P., 104, 402, 410–411, 424
Bouchet, S., 326
Boulding, K., 494
Bouthillier, D., 146
Bowen, G. L., 18, 417
Boyd-Franklin, N., 208, 219, 371
Boyle, F. M., 254
Bradford, K., 294, 437
Bradshaw, M., 353
Braithwaite, D. O., 342
Branscomb, K. R., 115
Bright, J., 408, 409
Broderick, C., 3
Broderick, J. E., 388
Broken Nose, M. A., 208
Brommel, B. J., 214
Broussard, J., 460
Brown, B. B., 352
Brown, E., 184
Brown, K. G., 344
Brown, L., 253
Brown, P. R., 474
Brown, S., 17
Browning, R., 390
Brubaker, T., 396, 397
Bryan, Audrey, 323
Bryant, J., 32

Bryant, J. A., 32
Bryant, M., 469
Buechner, F., 362
Buffett, W., 223
Bukstein, O. G., 457
Bumpass, L., 298
Buono, A. J., 274
Burgess, E., 7, 88
Burr, W. R., 425, 425
Burton, L., 20, 93, 353
Buss, D. M., 186, 206, 288
Butler, A. B., 219
Butler, M. H., 185
Buzzella, B. A., 37

Cabrera, N., 372
Cacioppo, J. T., 272, 274
Caldwell, J., 36, 45
Call, V., 378, 379
Campbell, R., 28
Cano, A., 150
Caplin, J., 421
Carey, B., 423
Carey, M. P., 187
Carlson, A., 337, 372
Carlson, K. J., A–6
Carr, D., 398
Cassidy, J., 266, 274, 294
Castro, R., 186
Catta-Preta, B., 132
Caughy, M. O., 18
Cavanaugh, M. M., 435
Chaney, C., 35, 55, 56
Chang, I., 68
Chapman, M., 36, 47
Chartrand, E., 146
Chatav, Y., 186
Chatters, L. M., 55, 476
Chen, R., 340, 420
Cher, 248
Cherlin, A., 32, 45, 93, 301, 382, 466, 480
Cheung, F. M., 219
Chiriboga, D., 274
Christensen, A., 132, 503
Christensen, M., 339
Christian-Herman, J., 150
Christie-Mizell, C. A., 351
Chse-Lansdale, P. L., 386
Chu, K., 239, 241
Cicirelli, V. G., 383
Cinotto, S., 115
Clark, R., 64, 371
Clark, V. R., 64
Claxton, A., 92
Clay, R. A., 188, 192
Clayton, O., 306
Cleland, J., 186
Clements, M., 158
Clery, L. M., 68
Cohen, D., 252, 275

Cohler, B., 69
Cohn, D'V., 308, 390, 402
Colapinto, J., 512
Cole, C. L., 460
Coles, R. L., 69
Coltrane, S., 462, 465, 466, 485, 486
Conger, K. J., 454
Conger, R. D., 454
Connidis, I., 274, 342
Constantine, N. A., 176
Cook, R., 81, 89
Cooley, Charles, 88
Coontz, S., 69, 267, 460, 489
Coop Gordon, K., 150, 158
Coop Gordman, K., 186
Cooper, C. L., 407, 408
Cooper, M. L., 179
Copen, C. E., 289, 297, 298
Córdova, J. V., 501
Cowan, C. P., 336
Cowan, P. A., 336
Cox, C. B., 386
Coxeter, P. D., 254
Cozza, S. J., 420
Crane, D. R., 344
Creswell, J. W., A–9
Crittenden, A., 372
Crook, R., 92
Crosby, J. F., 152
Cross, T., 59
Crouter, A. C., 158
Cullington, D., 457
Cynkar, A., 230

Daas, K. L., 41
Dailard, C., 176
Dalla, R., 32, 69
Daly, M., 444
Danes, S., 337, 338
Daniels, K., 289, 297, 298
Dansie, L., 485
Danziger, S., 245
Darkwa, O., 394
Darling, C. A., 496
Darroch, J. E., 174
Davidov, B., 47–49
Davidson, L. J., 448–449
Davis, K. E., 247
Davis, T., 55
Day, J. C., 13
Day, R. D., 223
De Staël, Madame, 248
de Vries, J. M., 255
Deal, R. L., 33, 484, 485, 489
Deaton, A., 388
Deck, A., 470
DeClaire, J., 121, 132, 158, 328
Dee, T. S., 180
DeFrain, A., 494
DeFrain, J., 147, 158

DeFrain, J., 2, 15, 18, 32, 33, 51, 53, 54, 62, 69, 81, 83, 115, 224, 348, 370, 406, 414, 433, 442, 443, 447, 457, 491, 493, 501, 509, 512
DeFrain, N., 74, 442, 443, 457
DeGarmo, D. S., 474
DeLamater, J. D., 165, 166, 180, 192, 380
Dellmann-Jenkins, M., 422
DeLuccie, M., 362
DeNavas-Walt, C., 45
DePaulo, B., 268, 274
Devahastin, S., 269
Dew, J., 221, 299
Dewe, P., 407, 408
Diamond, M., 372
Dickler, J., 382
Dienhart, A., 358
Dindia, K., 122
Dinger, M. K., 179
Dingfelder, S., 430
Dirie, W., 167
Dixon, L. J., 150, 158
Doherty, W., 30, 310, 323, 324, 328, 349, 364, 372, 454, 503
Dolbin-MacNab, M., 92, 386
Dole, B., 197
Dole, E., 197
Douglas, S. J., 372
Downing, J. B., 93, 363
Drago, R. W., 219
Drebot, M. E., 448–449
Dreby, J., 69
Driver, J., 314
Drobnic, S., 219
Dugas, C., 213
Duncan, S. F., 497
Dunn, L., 239
Dunne, M. P., 254
Durana, C., 498
Durham, W., 342
Duvall, E., 87
Dworkin, J., 87, 294
Dye, J. L., 360, 362
Dyer, C., 512
Dykstra, P., 274, 341, 378, 379

Eap, S., 474
Edin, K., 489
Edmondson, B., 393, 402
Eggebeen, D. J., 474
Eggett, D. L., 266
Einstein, A., 152
Eisenstat, S. A., A–6
Eldridge, K., 132
Elias, M., 391
Elicker, J., 354
Ella, D. M., 407
Ellison, C. G., 353
Emery, R. E., 473, 476
Emmons, M., 158
England, P., 489

Ezugwu, F. O., 186

Fadiman, G., 197
Faiola, A., 207, 269
Fals-Stewart, W., 423, 452
Fan, X., 339
Faris, E., 73
Farrugia, C., 512
Fawcett, N. R., 435
Fehr, B., 255
Ferguson, S. J., 274
Fergusson, D. M., 428
Ferrer, M., 512
Fields, J., 13, 475
Fill, S. K., 360
Fincham, F., 150
Fincham, F. D., 321, 324
Finer, L., 173, 174
Fingerman, K. L., 141
Finkelhor, D., 27
Fisher, C., 47, A–11
Fisher, H., 253
Fitzpatrick, L., 462, 463
Flynn, C. P., 352
Folbre, N., 245
Ford, A., 489
Ford, M., 489
Ford, S., 489
Fowers, B., 47–49, 321
Fox, G. L., 90
Fox, J. J., 227
Franklin, A., 208, 219, 371
Freedmen, S. R., 93
Freeman, P. A., 266
Frey, W. H., 267
Frias, S. M., 429, 430, 433
Friedan, B., 31, 90
Frieden, T., 22
Friedlin, J., 90
Fromm, E., 248
Frost, D. M., 40
Frost, J. J., 174
Fry, R., 390, 402
Fu, V. K., 293
Fuligni, A., 47
Furstenberg, F. F., Jr., 352
Fusaro, M. A., 227

Gaalen, P. A., 379
Gagnon, J. H., 185
Gaines, S. O., 252

Gaunt, R., 383
Gelles, R., 33, 433, 434, 435, 445, 449
Genovese, F., 512
Gerena, M., 36
Gershoff, E. T., 354
Gerson, K., 219
Gerstel, N., 36
Giarrusso, R., 403
Gibbs, N., 349
Gibran, K., 94, 264, 369
Gibson, P. A., 386, 387
Gidyez, C. A., 295
Gil, E., 512
Gilbert, N., 219
Giordano, J., 291–293
Giordano, P. C., 298
Glaser, R., 140
Glenn, N., 281, 283, 306, 469
Glick, J., 45, 46, 268
Goldberg, A. E., 37, 93, 363
Goldenberg, H., 74, 76, 77, 79, 80, 105
Goldenberg, I., 74, 76, 77, 79, 80, 105
Goldstein, S., 73
Gonzales-Backen, M., 47
Gonzalez, J., 59, 61
Gonzalez-Kruger, G., 81
Goodman, B., 268
Goodman, C. C., 386
Goodman, J. E., 132
Goodwin, R., 248, 249, 275, 324
Gorall, D., 315
Gordon, C., 133
Gordon, K. L., 150
Gordon, L., 498
Gordon, P. A., 268, 269
Gotta, G., 163, 164, 173
Gottlieb, A., 512
Gottlieb, L., 302
Gottman, J., 119, 121, 130, 132, 146, 158, 164, 314, 328, 372
Gouin, J.-P., 140
Graham, L., 28
Grass, G. A., 416
Grass, S. R., 416
Graves, J. L., Jr., 69
Gray, P., 41
Green, C., 69
Green, R., 163, 164, 173
Greer, M., 423
Greif, G., 487

Gustafson, K., 27
Gutierrez, D., 485

Haberman, H. R., 338
Haddock, S. A., 202
Hadzi-Pavlovic, D., 173
Hagestad, G. O., 378, 379
Haley, J., 97, 120
Halford, W. K., 482, 497, 512
Halgunseth, L. C., 57
Hall, J., 324
Hall, M., 393
Halpern, D. F., 202, 203, 219
Ham, J., 162
Hamilton, B. E., 360
Hammack, P., 69
Hamon, R. R., 105, 106, 302
Han, X., 423–424
Hao, L., 69
Hare, J., 41
Harper, J. M., 185
Harris, A. H., 324
Harris, J., 281, 350
Harris, S., 277
Harris, V. W., 318, 328
Hartnett, K., 160, 183, 192
Hartshone, T., 290
Hartshorne, J. K., 290
Harvey, J. H., 192
Hatch, D., 35, 47, 57, 69, 311
Havens, B., 393
Hawkins, A. J., 199
Hayes, J., 371
Hazan, C., 266
Hecker, L. L., 512
Helburn, S. W., 372
Hellmich, N., 182
Henderson, K., 374, 403
Hennon, C. B., 512
Herbenick, D., 160, 169, 170
Herbst, P. G., 215
Herlihy, J. L., 248
Heron, M. P., 217
Hertel, J., 274
Hertwig, O., 162
Herz, R. S., 288
Hetherington, E. M., 12, 467, 468, 480
Higginbotham, B., 38, 56, 207, 310, 311, 341, 374, 403, 475, 484, 485, 486, 497
Hill, N. E., 41
Hill, R., 55, 87, 412, 413

Hill, T. L., 387
Hill, Z. E., 186
Hills, M. S., 93
Hine, D. C., 55
Hingson, R. W., 180
Hird, M. J., 341
Hirschl, T. A., 12
Hobfoll, S. E., 424
Hochschild, A., 20
Hocker, J. L., 153, 154
Hodge, D. R., 59
Hoeffel, E. M., 45
Hoffman, L., 420
Hogan, M. J., 363
Holder-Taylor, C., 93
Holman, H., 385
Holman, T. B., 497
Holmes, E. K., 223
Holmes, T. H., 407, 408
Holstein, J. A., 105
Holtzman, M., 5
Holtzworth-Munroe, A., 428
Holzner, C., 227, 245
Homer, M. M., 266
Hopkins-Williams, K., 55
Horn, W., 362
Horrocks, A., 224
Horwood, L. J., 428
Hosek, J., 418
Hoskins, M., 223
Houseknecht, S. K., 18
Houston, T., 318
Howard, J., 6
Howden, L. M., 287, 289
Hsieh, K-H, 322
Huang, A. X., 176
Huebner, A. J., 416, 417, 422
Hughes, F. M., 150, 158
Hull, E., 421
Humes, K. R., 43
Hunt, S., 87, 88, 105
Husseini, R., 186
Huxley, A., 495
Hyde, J. S., 165, 166, 180, 192, 380

Iloabachie, G. C., 186
Imber-Black, E., 512
Ingoldsby, B. B., 106, 302
Insel, P. M., 188, 450
Inzlicht, M., 288
Ispa, J. M., 57

Jack, E. L., 252
Jackson, D. D., 120
Jackson, J. K., 450
Jackson, M. H., 423–424
Jacobs, N. N., 372
Jacobvitz, D. B., 85
James, S., 469
Jameson, K., 245
Jayson, S., 270

Jenkins, N. H., 132, 158
Jensen, L. A., 104
Jerman, P., 176
Jervis, L. L., 61
Joanning, H., 460, 489
Johnson, A. C., 224
Johnson, D., 474
Johnson, J., 32, 69, 435
Johnson, M., 428, 437, 457
Johnson, V., 182
Johnson-Sumerford, D., 358
Jones, F., 408, 409
Jones, J. E., 442, 443, 457
Jones, N. A., 43
Jones-Sanpei, H., 223
Joung, E., 474
Judge, K., 512
Julien, D., 146

Kagan, J., 210
Kalil, A., 473
Kaminer, Y., 457
Kane, J. B., 469
Kantrowitz, B., 288, 395
Kapungu, C. T., 177
Karger, H., 245
Karis, T. A., 302
Kasolowsky, R., 186
Kaufman, A., 290
Keiley, M. K., 92
Keillor, G., 201
Kelley, M., 423
Kelly, G. F., 190, 471–473, 476
Kelly, J., 12, 467, 468
Kelly, K. M., 252
Kendall, S., 133
Kendig, H., 379
Kensinger-Rose, K., 354
Keoughan, P., 460, 489
Kerpelman, J. L., 310, 497
Kersting, K., 388
Kiang, L., 47
Kiecolt-Glaser, J. K., 140
Killian, K. D., 302
Kilmann, R., 153, 153
Kim, H. W., 512
Kincaid, A. D., 113
Kindlon, D., 349
King, M. L., 55
King, V., 474
Kinsey, A., 169
Kirkpatrick, L. A., 206
Klein, D. M., 88
Klein, S. R., 425
Kleinke, C. L., 407
Kline, G. H., 298
Knight, G. P., A–11
Knipscheer, K., 379
Knoester, C., 474
Knudson-Martin, C., 196, 210
Knutson, L., 313, 328, 497

Kohlberg, L., 211
Kolak, A. M., 357
Kolodny, R., 182
Kornhaber, A., 402
Koropeckyj-Cox, T., 274, 340, 341, 378, 379
Kossek, E. E., 219
Kuba, C. A., 402
Kurdek, L., 37, 38, 163, 165, 318, 322
Kurtz, M. A., 387

Lachman, M. E., 377
LaMastro, V., 341
Landers, A., 181
Langer, G., 170
Lankov, A., 462
LaRossa, R., 364
Larsen, R. J., 206
Larson, P. J., 33, 85, 98, 99, 108, 109, 116, 127, 129–131, 132, 135, 136, 158, 160, 161, 196, 197, 216, 224, 258, 314, 320, 328, 330, 331, 332, 409, 410, 491, 498, 512
Larson, R. W., 115, 352
Lasswell, M., 396, 449
Lasswell, T., 449
Laughlin, L., 21
Laumann, E. O., 185
Lawrence, E., 336
Layden, M. A., 27
Lazarony, L., 240
Lazarus, R. S., 406, 407
Le Guin, U. K., 248
Lebow, J., 382
Lee, C., 45, 364
Lee, E., 209
Lee, J., 58
Lee, T., 226, 245, 328
Lee, T. R., 318
Lee, Y., 198
Lehrer, L., 15–17
Leiblum, S. R., 187
Leibniz, G., 495
LeMasters, E. E., 335–336
Lenhart, A., 254, 285
Leon, K., 85
Lerman, R., 270, 271, 302
Lerner, H. G., 143, 145, 158, 328
Letiecq, B. L., 387
Levaro, E. B., 398, 400
Levenson, M. R., 377
Levine, J., 250, 364
Levy, K., 252
Lewin, A., 15–17, 477
Lewis, C. S., 324
Lewis, S. K., 18
Lichter, D. T., 65, 294
Lim, V. R., 132
Limb, G. E., 59

Lohrfink, K. F., 18
Longmore, M. A., 298
Lorenz, F. O., 454
Loseke, D. R., 435
Lu, H. H., 298
Luecking, G., 274
Lund, M., 245
Luo, Y., 15–17, 477
Luthra, R., 295
Lynch, M., 198, 219
Lyness, K. P., 202
Lyons, J. A., 423–424

Mace, D., 7, 310
Mace, V., 7, 310
Maciel, J. A., 210
MacTavish, K. A., 223
Madathil, J., 278
Madden, M., 254, 285
Mahoney, A., 105
Malarkey, W. B., 140
Malone-Colon, L., 270, 271, 302, 306
Maloney, T., 245
Mancini, J. A., 416, 417
Manicavasagar, V., 173
Manning, R. D., 240
Manning, W., 17, 298
Mansfield, A. J., 417
Manzi, C., 344
Marelich, W. D., 252
Markman, H. J., 116, 117, 130, 132, 158, 185, 250, 325, 328, 482, 497, 498, 512
Marks, L., 55
Marmot, M., 389
Marquardt, E., 270, 271, 281, 283, 302, 307
Marsh, J. C., 81
Marshall, J. P., 226, 245, 318, 328
Marsiglio, W., 41
Martin, J. A., 360
Martinez, V., 420
Martinez-Brawley, E. E., 46
Mashek, D. J., 275
Masters, W., 182
Mathus, A. K., 351
Mattingly, M. J., 202
May, R., 139
McAdoo, H. P., 53, 55, 56, 69
McBride, E. K., 470
McCarthy, B., 182, 183, 192

McMullin, J. A., 342
McNaughton-Cassill, M., 198, 219
McRoy, R., 338
Mead, G., 88
Mead, M., 205, 362, 384
Medved, C. E., 132
Meier, J. A., 198, 199, 202, 219
Meier, P., 110
Melby, J. N., 454
Melkas, T., 379
Melli, M. S., 474
Mencken, H. L., 248
Mendez, E., 38, 485
Metzger, M., 15, 32, 433, 447, 457
Meyer, J. A., 287, 289
Meyers, C. E., 473, 476
Michael, R. T., 185
Michaels, M. W., 372
Michaels, S., 185
Michener, J. A., 495
Miedzian, M., 436
Mikulinger, M., 266, 275
Milanese, M., 282
Miller, A., 299
Miller, B., 177, 178, 339
Miller, J. E., 106
Miller, M., 300
Miller, P., 126, 498
Miller, R. B., 366
Miller, S., 126, 498
Minuchin, P., 512
Minuchin, S., 512
Mitchell, K., 27
Mock, M., 209
Mohatt, G., 47, 69
Monaghan, L., 132
Monat, A., 406
Monserud, M. A., 384
Montel, K. H., 321
Montenegro, X. P., 381, 382
Moody, J., A–8
Moore, B. A., 512
Moore, E., 512
Moore, K. A., 364
Morgan, A., 89
Morgan, S. P., 340
Mori, Yoshio, 269

Mueller, L., 92
Mueller, M. L., 92
Murphy, M., 371
Murray, C. E., 497
Murry, V. M., 41, 90
Mussen, P., 211
Mydans, S., 269
Myers, J. E., 278

Nadeau, J. W., 402
Nahm, E. Y., 314
Najman, J. M., 254, 255
Nance-Nash, S., 382
Neeves-Botelho, S., 353
Nelson, L. J., 87
Nesteruk, O., 55
Nettles, S. M., 18
Neugarten, B., 375
Neumaier, J., 186
Newton, R. H., 310
Nicholson, J. M., 482, 483
Niebuhr, R., 146
Niehuis, S., 318
Niemeyer, R. A., 402
Nord, C. W., 362
Norris, T., 45
Notarius, C. I., 119
Notter, M. L., 223

Obama, B., 292
Obi, S. N., 186
O'Campo, P. J., 18
Ochs, E., 115
O'Farrell, T. J., 452
O'Leary, K. D., 150
Olsen, C., 57, 311
Olson, D. H., 33, 51, 53, 85, 91, 96, 98, 99, 100, 108, 109, 116, 127, 129–131, 132, 135, 136, 158, 160, 161, 196, 197, 216, 224, 249, 250, 258, 313, 314, 315, 320, 321, 328, 330, 331, 332, 341, 344, 409, 410, 412, 416, 430, 484, 485, 489, 491, 497, 498, 499, 512
Olson-Sigg, A., 33, 98, 99, 108, 109, 116, 127, 129–131, 132, 135, 136, 158, 160, 161, 196, 197, 216, 224, 249, 250, 258, 314, 320, 321, 328, 330, 331, 332, 409, 491, 499, 512
O'Malley, C. J., 422
Onah, H. E., 186

Onedera, J. D., 512
Ooms, T., 304, 305, 326, 327
Oord, T. J., 248, 275
Ordoñez, J., 236
Orthner, D. K., 417
Orwell, G., 194
Osborn, F., 72
Owens, T. J., 105

Palacio, J., 79
Pan, P. A., 269
Pan, Y., 279
Pape, K. T., 431, 432
Paracelsus, 248
Paragament, K. I., 512
Park, C. L., 402
Parke, M., 326
Parke, R., 485
Parker, K., 386
Parshall, S., 42
Parsons, N., 179
Parsons, T., 90, 201
Patras, J., 474
Patrick, W., 272, 274
Paulk, A., 310, 497
Peacock, T. D., 68
Peluso, P., 192
Pence, E. L., 434, 435
Pendell, G., 340, 341
Penny, J. M., 339
Perez, L., 420
Perreira, K., 47
Perren, S., 468
Perry-Jenkins, M., 92
Peters, H. E., 294
Peterson, G. W., 117
Petts, R. J., 474
Peyser, H., 470
Phillips, W. K., 482
Piaget, J., 347
Pines, A. M., 252
Pitt, E., 364
Pitt-Catsouphes, M., 219
Pleck, J. H., 364
Poortman, A., 198
Popelyuk, D., 167
Popenoe, D., 8, 12, 268, 270, 297, 298,
    307, 461, 489
Porche, M. V., 37
Portnoy, F., 339
Powell, B., 6
Preto, N. G., 291–293
Proctor, B., 45
Pryor, E. M., 351
Pryor, J., 489
Pucheu Theall, K., 371
Puente, S., 252, 275
Purdie, D. M., 254
Purplefairy, L., 449
Purvin, D. M., 37

Qian, Z., 46, 58, 65, 69, 294

Raetz, K., 290
Rahe, R. H., 407, 408
Rainville, A., 420
Rainville, G., 377
Raley, S., 27, 202
Ramirez, R. R., 43
Rank, M. R., 12, 391, 403
Reck, K., 485
Red Horse, J., 59
Reevy, G., 406
Regalia, C., 344
Reynolds, M., 165
Rhoades, G., 185
Richard-Davis, G., 371
Ridder, E. M., 428
Riemer, F. G., 338
Rilke, R. M., 136
Rios-Vargas, M., 43
Risman, B. J., 358
Rivett, M., 512
Robbins, R., 385
Roberto, K. A., 393
Roberts, A., 306
Roberts, J. A., 240
Roberts, S., 8, 268
Robinson, J. M., 132
Robinson, P. W., 448–449
Rodas, C., 470
Rogers, F., 154
Rokach, A., 258
Rook, K., 274
Roosa, M. W., A–11
Rosato, D., 377
Ross, M. E., 386
Roth, W. T., 188, 450
Rott, L., 141
Rouse, C. E., 245
Rowe, C. L., 452
Rowe, D., 372, 403
Rowe, G., 396
Roy, K. M., 20
Rozema, H. J., 113
Rudy, D., 57, 345
Ruf, S. D., 58
Russell, B., 214
Russell, C., 99
Ryan, R. M., 473

Saad, L., 22
Sabar, A., 268
Sabbadini, A., 252
Sabusawa, M. Y., 495
Sadberry, S. L., 325, 328
Sage, R., 177
Saint Augustine, 252
Salem-Hartshorne, N., 290
Saluter, A., 387
Sammons, M. T., 423

Sand, G., 248
Sanders, M. R., 482
Sandler, L., 340
Santagata, R., 132
Sarkisian, N., 36, 55
Sassler, S., 286, 288,
    294, 299
Satir, V., 499
Sauck, C., 93, 363
Sautter, F., 423–424
Saval, M., 219
Scabini, E., 344
Schachner, D. A., 266
Schaub, K., 245
Scheinkman, M., 160
Scherman, A., 385
Schmitt, D. P., 186
Schnell, R., 186
Schoenherr, J., 370
Schooler, J. E., 339, 372
Schoppe-Sullivan, S., 199, 363
Schramm, D. G., 226, 228, 229, 245,
    307, 310, 318, 328, 497
Schwartz, J. E., 388
Schwartz, P., 288
Schwartz-Gottman, J.,
    132, 158
Scott, M., 457, 474
Scott, S., 497, 512
Sedlak, A. J., 438, 443
Seedall, R. B., 185
Seiler, W. J., 132
Sen, A., 213
Sessa, F. M., 346
Shackelford, T. K., 206
Shamah, D., 223
Shapiro, A., 314
Sharma, A. R., 338
Sharp, E. A., 271
Shaver, P. R., 266, 274,
    275, 294
Sheehy, G., 377–378
Sheldon, A., 372
Sherman, C. W., 395, 486
Sherman, M. D., 423–424
Shin, N., 18
Shoemake, E., 294
Shohet, M., 115
Siegel, D. H., 338
Signoret, S., 248
Silverman, J., 296
Silverstein, L. B., 364
Silverstein, M., 386, 403
Simard, M., 146
Simmons, D. S., 503
Simons, J., 187
Singh, A., 35, 47, 57, 69, 311
Singh, S., 174
Singletary, M., 240, 241
Skinner, D., 41

Smith, E. P., 41
Smith, J. A., 358, 372
Smith, N. R., 214
Smith, S. R., 105, 106
Smith, T., Jr., 420
Smock, P., 298
Solheim, C., 227, 228
Solot, D., 300
Somer, E., 409
Somers, M. S., 341
Sorokin, P., 7
Spencer, M., 47
Spielberger, C. D., 424
Spiro, A., III, 388, 402
Sprecher, S., 294
Sprenkle, D., 99
Springen, K., 395
Stacey, J., 38, 39
Stadelmann, S., 468
Stanley, S. M., 130, 132, 158, 185, 321, 325, 328, 498
Stauss, J. H., 60
Steinberg, L., 346
Steinmetz, S., 33, 117, 435
Sternberg, R. J., 249, 251, 275
Steuchio, A., 195
Stevens, C., 173
Stewart, S., 228, 484, 486
Stinnett, N., 53, 81, 83
Stokes, B., 221
Stone, A. A., 388
Stone, P., 219
Straus, J., 275
Straus, M., 33, 350–353, 435, 438–440
Street, A. E., 431, 432
Struthers, C. B., 28
Suárez-Oronzco, M., 69
Sue, D., 208, 209
Sue, D. W., 208, 209
Sugarman, S. D., 475, 477
Suitor, J. J., 105
Sullivan, H. S., 248
Sussman, D., 170
Suter, E. A., 41
Sutton, C. T., 208
Sutton, P. D., 360
Swanson, M., 55
Sweeney, J., 396
Sweet, S., 219

Teachman, J., 480
Tear, J., 110
Tedrow, L., 480
Theroux, Paul, 466
Thiele, D. M., 384, 385
Thomas, K., 153, 153
Thomas, L., 47, 69
Thomas, V., 100
Thomas, W., 88
Tomcik, N. D., 150, 158
Thompson, K. L., 435
Thoresen, C. E., 324
Thorne, D., 243, 244
Tingle, L. R., 278
Tirman, J., 420
Todorova, I., 69
Tong, R., 90, 106
Torres, E., 310, 484
Toussaint, P. A., 219, 371
Town, R., 12
Treas, J., 219
Trimble, J., 47, 59, 61, A–11
Troll, L. E., 384, 393, 398
Tubbs, C. Y., 20
Tudge, J., 69
Turkki, K., 496
Twain, M., 139

Ulker, A., 396, 403
Umaña-Taylor, A. J., 18, A–11

Valente, J., 302
Van As, C. F., 344
van der Lippe, T., 198
Van Dorn, R. A., 18
van Dulmen, M., 339
Van Epp, J., 293, 302
Van Hook, J., 465
van Leeuwenhoek, A., 162
Van Putten, Z., 210
Van Volkom, M., 400, 403
Vandell, D. L., 357
Vaughn, L., 437
Vega, W., 57
Ventura, S. J., 360
Verma, S., 352
Vespa, J., 289, 297, 298
Vignoles, V. L., 344
Vines, P. L., 45

Waldrep, A. J., 420
Walker, A. J., 383
Walker, K. K., 422
Walker, L. E., 435, 457
Waller, M. R., 294
Wallerstein, J. S., 468, 489
Wallin, P., 88
Walsh, F., 51, 52, 106
Walsh, R. P., 255
Wang, R., 27
Wang, W., 382
Watson, J. B., 7
Weakland, J., 120
Weinberg, D., 89
Weinstock, H., 174
Weis, K., 249, 275
Weisenbach, S., 274
Wenger, G. C., 379
West, R., 90
Wetchler, J. L., 512
Whelan, T. A., 384, 385
Whisman, M. A., 186
Whitaker, C., 75
White, J. M., 88
White, M., 89
Whitehead, B., 8, 12, 268, 290, 297, 298
Whitman, C. T., 330
Whitton, S., 37, 325, 328, 482
Whorley, M., 200
Wiener, N., 311
Wilcox, B., 223, 297, 298, 302, 330, 331, 372, 461, 471, 472, 475, 477, 489
Wilcox, R. M., 416
Wilcox, W. B., 307
Wildermuth, S. M., 285, 286
Wiley, A. R., 115
Williams, D. R., 64
Williams, J. H., 391, 403
Williams, K., 184
Williams, S., 6
Williams, V., 6
Willoughby, B. J., 87, 294
Willows, J., 457
Wilmot, W. W., 153, 154
Wilson, J., 385
Wilson, K., 512
Wilson, M. I., 444
Wilson, S., 352, 512

Wilson, S. M., 117
Wimer, L., 474
Wincze, J. P., 192
Wind, R., 181
Winn, D., 93
Winslow, S., 202
Winward, B. W., 177
Witkow, M., 47
Wolak, J., 27
Wood, S., 384
Worthington, E. L.,
    324, 328

Worthington, E. L., Jr., 150
Wright, P. J., 178
Wuerffel, J., 83
Wynne, L., 97

Xiao, J. J., 245
Xu, A., 279

Yalom, M., 166
Yang, C., 497
Yip, T., 47
Yolen, J., 370

Zabriskie, R. B., 266
Zettle, L., 274
Zhang, Y., 184, 465
Zhou, M., 58
Ziemba, S. J., 202
Zigler, E., 442, 443
Zill, N., 362
Zimmerman, C., 7
Zimmerman, T. S., 202
Ziol-Guest, K. M., 473
Ziporyn, T., A–6
Zorita, P., 46

Page numbers in *italics* denote figures and tables.

A Prairie Home Companion
        (radio show), 201
AA (Alcoholic Anonymous), 32, 123,
        452, 453
AAMFT. *See* American Association
        for Marital and Family Therapy
        (AAMFT)
AASECT (American Association of
        Sexuality Educators, Counselors,
        and Therapists), 189, 191
ABC News survey (American Sex
        Survey), 170–171
ABC-X Family Crisis Model, 412–413
Abrazo (hug), 116
Absent father, 362
Abstinence-only approach, 175
Abuse, 427
        See also Violence
Abusive behaviors, 427
Accelerated-consensus trajectory, 342
Accommodating style of conflict
        resolution, 154
Acculturation, 64
Acquired immunodeficiency syndrome
        (AIDS), 168–169
Adaptability, A–2
        See also Flexibility
Adolescents and young adulthood
        Alateen, 452, 453
        authoritarian parenting, 345
        child care, 357
        cigarette smoking, 454–455
        mate selection, 294–295
        out-of-wedlock births, 360
        pregnancy risk, 176, 177
        risky sexual behavior, *181*
        sex education, 175–179
        sexual behavior, 173–181
        teen parent educational programs, 368
        teen pregnancy, 174, 175, 334
        violence, 429
        See also Colleges/universities
Adoption, 338–339
Advantages of marriage, 15–18
Advocates for Youth, 179, 191
Afghanistan, 165

Africa
        breasts, 167
        buttocks, 167
        divorce, 463
        female circumcision, 167
        labia majora, 166
        love marriage, 279
African Americans
        Black-White marriage, 291, 465
        child abuse, 23, 438
        children, 341
        corporal punishment, 351
        divorce rate, 10
        domestic violence, 429
        egalitarian marriage, 56
        family network, 475–476
        family structures with minor
                children, *11*
        father-child communication about
                sex, 178
        financial security, 36
        gender roles, 208
        generally, 44–45
        grandparents raising
                grandchildren, 386
        historical trauma, 61
        kinship bonds, 55
        marital status, *8*
        marriage, 306
        median household income, *232*
        multiracial marriage, 65
        out-of-wedlock births, 360
        percentage of American
                population, 43
        poverty rate, 231
        refugees and immigrants, 44
        relationship education, 310
        religious orientation, 55
        same-sex relationships, 38
        school dropouts, 18
        sharing children, 379
        single-mother family, 13
        single-parent families, 471, *472*
        social environment, 18
        strengths, 55–56
        strong marriage, 35
        types of married couples, 320
        wage gap, 234
        women living with spouses, 267

AFSI (American Family Strengths
        Inventory), 512
Age at marriage, 8, 289, 304
Aggressive behavior, 128
Aggressive communication, 128
Agreeing to disagree, 130, 150, 156
Agriculturally oriented family, 67
AI/AN population. *See* American
        Indians and Alaska Natives
AIDS (acquired immunodeficiency
        syndrome), 168–169
Al-Anon, 32, 452, 453
Alaska (Michener), 495
Alaska Natives. *See* American Indians
        and Alaska Natives
Alateen, 452, 453
Alcohol use and abuse, 449–455
        alcohol-related deaths, 454
        college students, 179–180
        coping strategies for women, 452
        definitions, 449
        factoids, 24
        family violence, 433–434, 450
        family's reaction, 450–452
        gender, 450
        long-term health risks, 25
        married women, 305
        NCADD recommendations,
                453–454
        self-help groups, 452, 453
        treatment and prevention, 452–454
        warning signs, *450*
Alcoholics Anonymous (AA), 32, 123,
        452, 453
Alcoholism, 449
Alone time, 21
Alternatives to Marriage Project, 461
Alzheimer's disease, 395
Ambiguous loss, 410–411
Ambivalent acceptance of divorce, 466
American Association for Marital and
        Family Therapy (AAMFT)
        background/overview, 72, 191,
                501, 512
        certification of therapists, 502
        couple and family therapy, 366
        finding a therapist, 151
        infidelity, 185
        publications, 512

American Association of Sexuality Educators, Counselors, and Therapists (AASECT), 189, 191
American dream, 28, 223
American economy, 29
American Family Strengths Inventory (AFSI), 512
American Indians and Alaska Natives
    bilingual language skills, 59, 60
    children, 341
    communal living, 208
    community-wide ceremonies, 86
    "cultural recovery," 61
    cultural values, 208–209
    custodial grandparents, 386–387
    disciplining children, 60
    extended family, 60, 405
    gender roles, 208–209
    generally, 45
    grandparenthood, 385
    historical trauma, 61
    legacy of trauma, 36
    median age, 45
    multiracial marriage, 65
    Navajo couples, 92
    officially sanctioned marriage, 60–61
    percentage of American population, 43
    respect for elders, 59, 60
    sharing children, 379
    "soul wounds," 61
    sovereign political entities, 45
    spiritual beliefs, 59
    spiritual practices, 59–60
    strengths, 59–61
    tribal community, 60
    tribal support system, 59
American Sex Survey (ABC News), 170–171
American society. See United States
Anal intercourse, 169
Androgen, 379
Anger
    dance metaphor, 143–145
    double-edged sword, 140
    health, and, 140
    love, and, 142–143
    myths and facts, 140, 141
    repressed, 138
    See also Conflict and conflict resolution
Anger and conflict taboos, 138–139
Angry associates, 470
Animal abuse, 352, 434–435
Annie (film), 182
Annual household expenses, 235
Anxious attachment, 266
Appearance, 288–289
Appreciation and affection, 52, 54, 82–83
Arguing. See Resolving disagreements

Arapesh tribe, 205
Army Child and Youth Services, 422
Arranged marriage, 249–251, 277–279
Asian Americans
    family loyalty, 58
    family structures with minor children, 11
    father-child communication about sex, 178
    filial piety, 58
    gender roles, 209
    generally, 45
    marital status, 8
    median age, 45
    median household income, 232
    multiracial marriage, 65
    out-of-wedlock births, 360
    poverty rate, 231
    resettlement of Japanese Americans, 58
    single-mother family, 13
    strengths, 57–59
    women living with spouses, 267
Asian countries, 269
Asking questions, 83
Assertive communication, 127–128
Assertiveness, 127–128, 129–130, 131
Assets, 225
Assimilation, 64
Association for Couples in Marriage Enrichment, 310
Attachment, 253
Attachment figures, 266
Attachment theory, 265–267, 294
Attentive listening, 126
Attraction, 250
Attractiveness, 255, 288–289
Authoritarian parenting, 345, 346
Authoritative (democratic) style of parenting, 344, 346–347
Autonomic power pattern, 215, 215, 216
Avoidance, 129, 130
Avoidance style of conflict resolution, 154
Avoidant attachment, 266

Baby boomers, 376, 395, 398
Bad memories, 314
Bad to worse group, 322
Balance of power, 27–28
Balanced family, 99, 101
Bank account, 227
Bankruptcy, 243–244
Basic institutional inequality, 213
Beatles (musical group), 262
Behavioral exercises and sex, 190
Behaviorists, 348
Belief system, 53
Bereaved spouses, 397–398
Best-friend couples, 183
Bidirectional effects, 347
Big Brothers Big Sisters, 30, 31

Bilateral descent, 51
Bilateral-persuasion trajectory, 342–343
Binuclear family, 470
Biracial couples, 65–66, 290–293
Birth order, 290
Bisexual, 162
Black-White marriage, 291, 465
Blacks. See African Americans
Blamer, 144, 145
Blaming, 117, 411
Body exploration, 189
Bond of affection and closeness, 20
Boomerang kids, 382
Boundaries, 75
Boundary ambiguity, 410, 486
Brain and love, 253
Brainstorming, 155, 156
Breast, 166–167
Breast cancer, 408–409
Budget counselors, 244
Budgeting, 230, 237–238
Bulldozing the other into agreement, 157

Canada, aggressiveness, 200
Cancer, 408–409
Caravans (Michener), 495
Cardiovascular disease, 409
Careless or impulsive spending, 243
Caribbean (Michener), 495
Cascading circumstances, 353
Case for Marriage, The (Waite/Gallagher), 15
Case study, A–10
    See also Family therapy case study
Catharsis, 141
Catharsis conflict, 435
Caucasian Americans
    Black-White marriage, 291, 465
    child abuse, 23
    childlessness, 340
    family structures with minor children, 11
    father-child communication about sex, 178
    grandparents raising grandchildren, 386
    individualism and self-determination, 35
    marital status, 8
    median household income, 232
    net worth, 235
    nursing homes, 392
    out-of-wedlock births, 360
    poverty rate, 231
    single-mother family, 13
    strengths, 53–54
    wage gap, 234
    women living with spouses, 267
CCC (Civilian Conservation Corps), 73
CCCS (Consumer Credit Counseling Service), 244

stress, and, 418

Changing the social environment, 30
Chaotic relationships, 96, 97, 98
Chaotically cohesive relationships, 100
Chaotically connected relationships, 100
Checking account, 227
Chicano/a families. *See* Hispanic
    Americans
Child abuse and neglect, 437–445
    alternatives to spanking, 440
    behavioral consequences, 441
    child fatalities, 23
    cross-generational transmission, 442
    defined, 437
    families at risk, 443–444
    family characteristics, 438
    family structure, 438
    physical health consequences, 441
    psychological aggression, 438–439
    psychological consequences, 441
    race and ethnicity, 23
    societal consequences, 441
    spanking, 439–440
    surviving/transcending abuse,
        442–443
    treatment and prevention, 445
Child abuse hotline, 445
Child care, 354–357
    caregiver education level, 359
    child care centers, 354–355
    cost of, 236
    effect of, on teenagers, 357
    employer-sponsored care centers, 356
    equality, 199, 200
    follow-up study (teenagers), 357
    generally, 20–21
    high quality programs, 358
    Hispanics, 355
    in-home day care, 354
    minimum-wage jobs, 357
    most care is "fair," 357
    NICHD study, 356–357
    positive caregiving, 359
    questions to ask, 21
    relatives, 354
    statistics, 354, 355
Child care centers, 354–355
Child-centered approach to
    childrearing, 350
Child Effects on Adults (Bell), 347
Child fatalities, 23

statistics, 340
stereotypical characteristics of
    parents, 379
unilateral-persuasion trajectory, 342
Child support, 473
Child support payments, 362
Child-thought, 347
Child-to-parent abuse, 448–449
Childbirth education, 366
Childfree, 378
Childlessness. *See* Child-free alternative
Childrearing, 347–354
    behaviorists, 348
    bidirectional effects, 347
    corporal punishment, 350–354
    discipline, 349–354
    family systems perspective, 347
    learning theories, 348
    organismic theory, 347–348
    parent-dominant *vs.* child-centered
        approach, 350
    positive discipline, 350, 353
    psychodynamic theory, 347
    reinforcement, 348–349
    TLC approach, 350
Children
    abuse. *See* Child abuse and neglect
    accentuate the positive, 440
    cohabitation, 475
    cost of raising, 236, 337–338
    cultural diversity, 67
    death of a child, 365
    discipline, 349–354
    divorce, 362
    domestic violence, 428, 436
    gays and lesbians, 38–39, 41, 476
    happiness, 330–331
    Hispanics, 57
    homelessness, 29
    how many?, 13
    importance of, to successful
        marriage, 339, 340
    joint custody, 464, 470–471
    military families, 422
    self-concept, 84
    sons *vs.* daughters, 344
    stepfamily, 482–484, 487–488
    See also Childrearing
China
    aggression in children, 354
    aggressiveness, 200

Choosing a mate. *See* Mate selection
Cigarettes. *See* Tobacco use
Circular causality model, 117
Circumplex model of marital and
    family systems, 99
Civilian Conservation Corps (CCC), 73
Closed system, 77
Closeness, 94
Cluttered nest, 383
Coalition rating scale, A–2, A–3
Coed dorms, 283
Cognitive coping resources, 425, 425
Cognitive development theory,
    211–212
Cohabitation, 296–300
    breaking up, 299–300
    childlessness, 343
    children, 475
    cohabiting and then marriage,
        297–298, 307
    defined, 9, 296
    factors to consider, 300
    late adulthood and old age, 400
    length, 298
    marriage rate, and, 270
    multicultural couples, 65
    popularity, 297–298
    religious orientation, 298
    Scandinavian countries, 280
    socioeconomic class, 299
    stepchildren, 480
    stigma, 298
    supporters/detractors, 300
    temporary arrangement, 17
    trends, 8–9
    why people cohabit, 298
Cohesion, 91–96
    activities, 94
    closeness, 94
    commitment, 52
    defined, 91
    dependence-independence, 94
    family systems theory, 78–80
    I-we balance, 94
    loyalty, 94
    questions for assessing family
        cohesion, A–2
    separateness-togetherness, 91–96
    spending time together, 52
Cohesive relationships, 93, 94
Cohort study, A–12

Collaborative style of conflict
    resolution, 153–154
Colleges/universities
    coed dorms, 283
    credit cards, 239, 240
    cultural conflicts (female Chicana
        student), 79
    fraternities/sororities, 180, 283
    hooking up, 281–284
    let loose and party attitude, 283
    marriage aspirations, *281*, 283
    preparation for parenting classes, 368
    sexual behavior and alcohol, 179–180
    walk of shame, 284
Commitment
    cohesion, 52
    death of a child, 365
    family members, 14
    family strengths framework, 83
    love triangle, 251
    widowhood, 398
Common cold, 409
Communication, 52
    aggressive, 128
    assertive, 127–128, 129–130
    avoidance, 130
    blaming, 117
    clarity, *98*
    cohesion and flexibility, and, 99
    content (message), 118
    continuous partial attention, 121
    cooperative endeavor, 117
    cultural differences, 114–116
    defined, 108
    directness, 119
    double bind, 119–121
    family, 52
    family strengths framework, 83–84
    feedback. *See* Feedback
    gender communication quotient, 113
    gender differences, 109–114
    intimacy, 128, 256–257, 258–259
    intimate relationship, 111, 258–259
    listening, *98 See also*
        Listening
    metacommunication, 149
    mixed message, 119
    nationwide survey, 108
    noncommunication, 117
    nonverbal. *See* Nonverbal
        communication
    passive, 128
    positive, 52, 54, 83
    positive/negative comments,
        124–125, *125*
    positive/negative communication
        style, 129, *129*
    relationship component, 118
    report component, 118
    respect and regard, *98*
    self-disclosure. *See* Self-disclosure

    speaking skills, *98*
    staying on topic, *98*
    stonewalling, 130
    strengths/problems, *109*
Communication problems, *109*
Communication strengths, *109*
Community resources and stress,
    422–423, *425*, 426
Community strengths, 492
Community system, *76*
Companionate love, 251
Compassionate Friends, 371
Competent loners, 467
Competitive style of conflict
    resolution, 153
Complementary couples, 183
Compliments, 262
Composite gamily groups, 50
Comprehensive sex education, 175
Compromise style of conflict
    resolution, 154
Compulsive spending, 243
Conceptual framework, 71
    See also Models of couples and families
Conflict and conflict resolution, 134–158
    accommodating style, 154
    anger and conflict taboos, 138–139
    avoidance style, 154
    clarifying the issue, 155
    collaborative style, 153–154
    competitive style, 153
    compromise style, 154
    constructive/destructive
        approaches, *152*
    decision-making phase, 137
    finding out what each person
        wants, 155
    gay and lesbian couples, 146
    happy *vs.* unhappy couples, *135*, 146
    hierarchy of conflict, 136, *137*
    identifying various alternatives, 155
    intimacy, 260
    intimacy and conflict, 141–142
    marriage, 314
    nationwide survey, 135–136
    negotiating style, 155–157
    older people, 296
    problem-solving phase, 137
    resolving disagreements, 147–151
    reviewing and renegotiating, 157
    solidifying agreements, 157
    steps in process, 154–157
    top five conflict problems, *136*
    See also Anger
Conflict-avoiding style of conflict
    resolution, 314
Conflict-minimizing couples, 183
Conflicted coparenting, 472
Conflicted couples, *320*, 321, 323
Conjugal family system, 49
Connected relationships, 93, *94*

Conquest mentality, 283
Consanguineal family systems, 50
Constructive intimacy games, 262
Consumer Credit Counseling Service
    (CCCS), 244
Consumer culture, 20
Consumer Reports, 192
Consummate love, 251
Contemporary *vs.* traditional dating
    and marriage patterns, *204*
Contempt, 146, 314
Continuity in marriage and the
    family, 14
Continuous partial attention, 121
Conventional couples, *320*, 321
Conversational style
    gays and lesbians, 112
    men, 111, 112
    women, 111, 112
Cooperative colleagues, 470
Cooperative coparenting, 469–470, 472
Coparenting, 357–360, 469–470, 472
Coping abilities, 52
Corporal punishment, 350–354, 439–440
    African Americans, 351
    animal abuse, 352
    depression, 351, *352*
    harmful effect of, on society, 351
    harmful effect of, on the child, 352, 354
    international studies, 354
    no-spanking laws, 352–353
    parental stress, 353
    public opinion, 351, 353
    sons *vs.* daughters, 350–351, *351*
Corporate takeover, 20
Counseling, 395, 396, 501
    See also Marital and family therapy
Couple and family enrichment
    programs, 367, 498
Couple and Family Map, 98–103,
    A–1–A–6
    advantages, 101
    balanced *vs.* unbalanced families, 99
    change in relationships over time,
        102–103
    coalition rating scale, A–2, *A–3*
    Couple and Family Rating Form, *A–5*
    Couple and Family Scales, A–2, *A–4*
    couples at opposite extremes on
        same dimension, 500
    families of origin, 315
    family systems theory, 99
    family therapy case study, *504*
    graphic model, *100, A–6*
    healthy relationships, 99–101
    interview questions, A–2, *A–2*
    9/11 attacks, *415*
    parenting styles, *343*
    plotting the family system type, A–3
    steps in process, A–2–A–3
    working themes, 101

education programs
Couple flexibility, 259
See also Flexibility
Courtship, 280, 300
    See also Dating; Mate selection
Covenant marriage, 465
Credit card, 230, 239, 240–241
Credit card debt, 29
Credit card trap, 241
"Credit Cards on Campus," 240
Credit clinics, 244
Credit spending, 243
Credit uses and abuses, 239–244
Crisis-loss stage of grief, 397
Crisis nurseries, 367
Crisis spending, 243
Criticism, 146, 314
Cross-country comparisons.
    See International comparisons
Cross-cultural family studies, 63
Cross-sectional cohort study, A–12
Cross-sectional study, A–12
Cross-validation, A–10
Cultural competence
    acquiring knowledge, 49
    awareness, 48
    knowledge, 48–49
    skills, 49
Cultural diversity, 34–69
    acculturation, 64
    AI/ANs. *See* American Indians and
        Alaska Natives
    Asian Americans. *See* Asian
        Americans
    assimilation, 64
    attractiveness, 165–166
    blacks. *See* African Americans
    challenges for ethnic groups, 63–67
    communication, 114–116
    cross-cultural family studies, 63
    cultural competence, 48–49
    domestic violence, 429–430
    education, *44*
    ethnocentrism, 63
    etic/emic perspective, 63
    family power structures, 67
    female circumcision, 167
    gays and lesbians. *See* Gays and
        lesbians
    immigration, 45–46
    income, *44*

multicultural feminism, 91
multicultural study, A–11
parent-child relationships, 67
personal story (going from the
    majority to the minority), 62
population trends, 46, *46*
poverty, *44*
prejudice, 64
racism, 64
refugees, 46
research, 47
same-sex behavior, 167
segregation, 64
sexual attitudes, 167
sexual behavior, 166–167
sexuality, 165–168
stereotypes, 64
tolerance, 63
two-parent families, *44*
whites. *See* Caucasian Americans
why culture matters, 35–36
See also International comparisons
Cultural groups, 36, 41
Cultural norms and expectations, 18
Cultural strengths, 492
Culture, 41
Custodial grandparents, 385–387
Cyberdating, 285–286

Dance of anger, 144
Dance of Anger, The (Lerner), 143
Dating, 280–288
    communication, 124–125
    conflict resolution, 296
    do's and don'ts, 286
    e-dating (text messaging, etc.), 283
    historical overview, 280
    hooking up, 281–284
    Internet dating and matchmaking
        services, 254–255, 285–286
    limitations, *281*
    money talk, 229
    older people, 286–288
    online dating services, 254–255,
        285–286
    serial daters, 250
    sluts/players, 284
    stressors, 409
    traditional *vs.* contemporary view, *204*
    violence, 295–296, 297, 429
    See also Mate selection

tobacco use, and, 25, 454
Debit card, 241
Debt, 225, 226
    See also Financial issues
"Decision to Remain Single: Implications
    for Women Across Cultures, The"
    (Gordon), 269
Defeateds, 467
Defense of Marriage Act, 37
Defensiveness, 146, 314
Definition of the situation, 88
Democratic parenting, 344,
    346–347
Demographic revolution, 388
Demographics, 43
Denmark, 461
Dependence-independence, *94*
Deployment, 416, 418, 419, 421
Depression
    bereaved spouses, 397
    children (divorce), 468
    corporal punishment, 351, *352*
    grandparents raising
        grandchildren, 387
    loneliness, 272
    marital satisfaction, 322
    passion, 251
Desert Flower (Dirie), 167
Destructive intimacy games, 260, 261,
    262–264
Devitalized couples, *320*, 321, 323
DINS (double income, no sex)
    dilemma, 182
Directive listening, 126
Discipline, 349–354
    accentuate the positive, 440
    alternatives to spanking, 440
    corporal punishment, 350–354
    deprivation of privileges, 352
    explaining, 352
    historical overview, 353
    indulgence, 350
    international studies, 354
    positive, 350, 353
    timeout, 352, 440
Disciplines contributing to family
    science, *A–8*
Disengaged relationships, 93,
    94, 96
Dissolved duo, 470
Distancer, 143–144

Diversity
    ethnic groups. *See* Cultural diversity
    financial style, 226–228
    variety of family structures, 2
Divorce, 460–471
    age, 462
    ambivalent acceptance, 466
    assets, 225
    binuclear family, 470
    children, 362, 468–471
    cohabitation, and, 461
    coparenting, 358
    covenant marriage, and, 465
    custodial arrangements,
        470–471, 472
    danger signs, 146
    financial costs, 228–229
    financially challenging times, 461
    gays and lesbians, 470
    globalization, 461, 462–463
    historical trends, 460
    impact, 466–470
    industrialized, urban-oriented
        societies, 66
    interracial marriage, 465
    length of first marriage, 462
    middle and later years, 381–382
    military families, 420–421
    no-fault system, 463–464
    predicting, 314
    rate of, 460, *460*
    single parent, coping strategies, 471
    soul mate mentality, 461
    statistics/factoids, *12*
    styles of adjusting, 467
    trends, 9–10
    waiting period/parental
        counseling, 465
    women's independence, 460
Divorce culture, 466
"Doing your own thing," 96
Domestic violence, 427–437
    alcohol, 433–434
    animal abuse, 434–435
    catharsis conflict, 435
    children, 428, 436
    cultural differences, 429–430
    dating relationship, 429
    defined, 427
    economic impact, 429
    economic stress, 433
    effects of, 427–428
    equality wheel, 436, *436*
    financial dependency, 433
    incidence of, 428–429
    isolation, 433
    learned helplessness theory, 433
    male dominance, 434
    marital therapy, 502
    national survey, 430–431
    psychological abuse, 431–432

reporting the crime, 429, 430
    self-esteem, 433
    three-phase cyclical pattern, 435
    treatment and prevention,
        435–436, 502
    types, 428
    verbal aggression, 435
    violence in family of origin,
        432–433
    youth, 433
Dominant truth, 89
Dopamine, 253
Double bind, 119–121
Double income, no sex (DINS)
    dilemma, 182
Double standard, 280
Downsizing, 20, 202
Drifting apart, 323
Dysfunctional family, 82, 83
Dyspareunia, 188

Eclectic approach, 71
Ecofeminism, 91
Ecological approach to human
    systems, *76*
Ecology, 76
Economic abuse, 427
Economic adequacy, 494
Economic distress
    child abuse, 443
    detrimental to family relationship, 29
    spouse abuse, 433
    See also Financial issues
Economic issues. *See* Financial issues
Economic recession, 221, 223, 377
Education
    childbirth, 366
    cultural diversity, *44*
    income, 233, *233*
    marriage. *See* Marriage education
        programs
    parenthood. *See* Parent education
    premarital. *See* Premarital education
    relationship, 310
    sex, 175–179
    sexuality, 368
    Smart Marriages Web site, 498
Egalitarian groups, 51
Egalitarian haven, 28
Egalitarian marital relationship, 14
Egalitarian marriage, 56
Egalitarian roles, 203
Egalitarian roles and marital
        satisfaction, 215–216
Egalitarianism, 194
Egypt, 463
Elder abuse, 383, 388
Elderly. *See* Late adulthood and old age
Emerging adulthood, 87
Emic perspective, 63
Emotional abuse, 427

Emotional closeness, 96
Emotional coping strategies, *425*,
        425–426
Emotional intimacy, 266
Emotionally expressive
        couples, 183
Employee assistance programs, 366
Empty love, 251
Empty-nest syndrome, 335, 382
Endogamy, 290
Endorphins, 250
Enhanced type (divorce), 467
Enjoyable time together, 84–85
Enmeshed relationships, 93–96
ENRICH inventory, 85, 258, 315, 323
Equal Pay Act, 213
Equal pay for comparable work
        approach, 234
Equalitarian roles, 203
Equality wheel, 436, *436*
Equity theory, 294
Erectile dysfunction, 188
Essential Life Skills for Military
        Families, 422
Ethnic groups, 35, 41
        See also Cultural diversity
Ethnic identity, 47, 66
Ethnically mixed couples, 65–66,
        290–293
Ethnicity, 41
Ethnocentrism, 63
Etic perspective, 63
Eugenics, 72
European ancestry, 48
Exchange theory, 294
Exclusionists, 6
Exogamy, 290, 291
Expressive role, 90, 201
Extended family, 5, 50
Extended-family system, 53
Extramarital sex, 183–185, 186
Extreme stability and extreme change,
        97–98
Extreme togetherness and extreme
        separateness, 94–96
"Extreme Togetherness Poem"
        (Altura), 95
Eye contact, 116

Facebook, 283
FACES (Family Adaptability and
        Cohesion Evaluation Scales), 57
"Falling in love," 94
Families and Democracy
        Model, 30
Families of color
        social system, 53
        socioeconomic status, 53
        spiritual belief system, 53
        See also Cultural diversity
Familism, 56

extent, 39, 50
future of (personal stories), 509–510
nuclear, 49–50
personal stories, 509–510
suggestions for keeping family
strong, 508
therapy. *See* Marital and
family therapy
top 10 stumbling blocks, 499, *499*
value system, 14
Family Action Centre, University of
Newcastle, Australia, 367, 372
Family adaptability, *A–2*
See also Flexibility
Family Adaptability and Cohesion
Evaluation Scales (FACES), 57
Family boundary ambiguity, 486
Family cohesion, 52
See also Cohesion
Family communication, 52
See also Communication
Family coping strategies, 424–426
cognitive coping resources,
425, *425*
community resources, *425, 426*
emotional coping strategies, *425,*
425–426
individual development, *425*
overview, 427
relationship coping resources,
425, 426
spiritual beliefs, *425, 426*
theoretical perspectives, 424–425
Family development framework, 86–88,
92–93
Family education classes, 336–337
Family flexibility, 52
See also Flexibility
Family forms, 203
Family gatherings, 500
Family in Transition (Skolnick/
Skolnick), 7
Family income, 231–235
Family life. *See* Gender roles
Family life cycle, 87
Family life education programs,
72, 496
Family life educators, 365, 366, A–8
Family mealtime, 115
Family of origin, 315–317
Family of origin rituals, 266

mixed-methods research, A–9
multicultural study, A–11
observational approaches,
A–10–A–11
qualitative/quantitative research, A–9
questionnaire, A–9–A–10
research designs, A–11–A–12
See also Research
Family science, 71–74, A–8
family life education, 72
historical overview, 72–73
journals, 72
other disciplines, and, *73, A–8*
professional associations, 72
relationships, 74
See also Family research methods;
Research
Family scientists, A–8
Family service programs, 364
Family strengths, 492
Family strengths framework, 81–86
ability to manage stress and crisis
effectively, 86
appreciation and affection, 82–83
asking questions, 83
commitment, 83
communication, 83–84
enjoyable time together, 84–85
humor, 83–84
listening, 83
overview, *81*
research, 92
shared values, 85
spiritual well-being, 85
therapists/counselors, 81
worldview, 83
Family Strengths Inventory, 54
Family strengths perspective, 2
See also Strengths
Family stress theory, 479
Family structure
child abuse, 438
factoids, 12–13
impact of, on children, 346–347
overview, *11*
trends, 11–13
various types, 2
See also specific family structures
Family studies, A–8
Family support programs. *See* Parent
education

childrearing, 347
cohesion, 78–80
concentric circles, 76
flexibility, 77–78
gender roles, 212
general systems theory, 75
hierarchy of connected systems,
75–77
human ecosystem, 76
reorganization of family system
after a car accident, 78
research, 92
wholeness, 76
Family therapists
AAMFT, 501, 512
balance of separateness and
connectedness, 79
fair fighting, 152
family strengths framework, 81
family systems theory, 75
growing edge, 142
infidelity, 185
resistance to change, 77
resolving disagreements, 147
See also Therapy/therapists
Family therapy, 365, 366, 369
See also Marital and family therapy
Family therapy case study, 503–506
Family-to-work influence, 202–203
"Family tree" approach to descent, 51
Farm and ranch families, 367
FAS (fetal alcohol syndrome), 449
Fatherhood, 361–364
absent father, 362
coparenting, 357–360
divorce, 362
effect of good fathering, 364
nurturing and caring for children,
362–364
responsible fathers, 364
Fatuous love, 251
Federal Healthy Marriage Initiative,
310, 313, 325–326, 328
Federal Trade Commission
Web site, 241
Feedback
family systems theory, 80–81
negative, 80
positive, 80
Female circumcision, 167
Female genital mutilation (FGM), 167

Feminine Mystique, The (Friedan), 90
Feminine qualities, 195
Femininity, 194
Feminism
    definition of family, 90
    ecofeminism, 91
    full range of masculine and
        feminine qualities, 90
    gender-based distinctions, 90
    gender roles, 212–214
    historical study, A–11
    multicultural, 91
Feminist framework, 90–91, 93
Feminist movement, 90
Feminist theory and mate
    selection, 294
Fetal alcohol syndrome (FAS), 449
FGM (female genital mutilation), 167
Fiery foes, 470
Fight/fighting, 152
Fighting dirty, 148
Financial counseling, 244
Financial dependency, 433
Financial issues, 29, 220–225
    annual household expenses, 235
    assets, 225
    bankruptcy, 243–244
    budgeting, 230, 237–238
    child abuse, 423
    child care, 236, 237
    collective/individualistic
        worldview, 226
    credit cards, 230, 239, 240–241
    credit uses and abuses, 239–244
    dating, 229
    debt, 225, 226
    divorce, 228–229
    education, 233, *233*
    ethnic groups, 226, 227, 231, *232*,
        234, 235
    family income, 231–235
    financial counseling, 244
    gender, 233–234
    happy *vs.* unhappy couples, *224*
    home ownership, 240–243
    late adulthood and old age, 390–391
    living within your means, 224
    marital satisfaction, 224
    money and happiness, 221–223
    necessities, expenditures on, *235*
    net worth, 235
    pooling money, 238–239
    problem areas, 229
    raising children, 236, 337–338
    renting a home, 242
    smart money management, 237–239
    spouse abuse, 433
    stepfamilies, 488
    steps to financial freedom, 230
    working outside the home, 236
First wave of feminist movement, 90

Fixed-response questions, A–9
Flexibility, 52, 96–98
    change, *97*
    defined, *96*
    discipline, *97*
    family systems theory, 77–78
    intimacy, 259
    leadership, *97*
    negotiation, *97*
    questions for assessing family
        flexibility, *A–2*
    roles, *97*
    rules, *97*
    stability-change continuum, 96–98
Flexible relationships, *96, 97, 97*
Flexibly cohesive relationships, *100*
Flexibly connected relationships, *100*
Flexibly disengaged relationships, *100*
Flexibly enmeshed relationships, *100*
"Floating on air," 250
Flooding, 314
Food security, 29
For Better or Worse: Divorce Reconsidered
    (Hetherington/Kelly), 467, 468
"For Every Woman" (Smith), 214
Forgiveness, 150–151, 324–325
Forgiveness therapy model, 93
Four horsemen, 314
*Fourth National Incidence Study of Child
    Abuse and Neglect* (Sedlak et al), 438
France
    cheek-to-cheek greeting, 116
    homicide by firearm, 23
    nonverbal gestures, 114
Fraternities, 180, 283
Freedom, 494
Friendship
    acceptance, 247
    collectivist cultures, 249
    confiding, 248
    enjoyment, 247
    immigrants, 249
    individualistic cultures, 249
    love relationships, 247
    mutual assistance, 248
    opposite-sex relationships, 248, 255
    respect, 248
    self-disclosure, 123–124, 255
    spontaneity, 248
    superficiality, 248
    trust, 248
    understanding, 248
Friendship network, 272
Fun, 151
Future of Marriage, The (Bernard), 16
Future of the family (personal stories),
    509–510

Gatekeeping, 363
Gay and lesbian parenting,
    360–361, 476

Gays and lesbians, 36–41, 163–165
    breakup, 470
    challenges, 39–41
    children, 38–39, 41, 476
    conflict and supportiveness, 146
    conversational style, 112
    couple education, 37
    dissolution of relationships, 38
    heterosexual couples, compared,
        164–165
    how many?, 163, 173
    intimacy, 40–41
    monogamous relationships, 173
    parent education programs, 368
    parenting, 360–361
    past and current life
        circumstances, 164
    regular family activities, 41
    same-sex marriage, 4, 37
    sperm donor, 41
    stepfamily, 480
    stigma, 40–41, 173
    strengths, 163–164
    surrogate mother, 41
    terminology, 172
Gender
    alcohol use and abuse, 450
    defined, 90
    double standard, 280
    financial assets, 225
    hookup culture, 283–284
    infidelity, 184
    life expectancy, *217*
    listening style, *110*
    matriarchal/patriarchal groups, 51
    matrilocal/patrilocal societies, 51
    patrilineal/matrilineal societies, 50
    speaking style, *110*
    wage gap, 213, 233–234
    See also Gender roles; Men; Women
Gender-biased language, 195
Gender communication quotient, 113
Gender identity, 194
Gender inequality, 213
Gender inequity, 213
Gender-role stereotypes, 194, 195, 205
Gender roles, 194–214
    African Americans, 208
    American Indian culture, 208–209
    Asian Americans, 209
    child care, 199
    cognitive development theory,
        211–212
    defined, 194
    distribution of family work,
        198–199
    egalitarian roles, 203
    family systems theory, 212
    feminist framework, 212–214
    Gallup survey of male/female
        traits, 200

masculinity/femininity, 194–195
maternal gatekeeping, 199
nationwide survey, 196–197
Parsons theory, 201–202
in process of changing, 27–28
social learning theory, 210
top five role problems, *197*
traditional *vs.* contemporary view,
    202–203, *204*
General systems theory, 75
"Giving Compliments," 262
Giving to others, 30
Global economy, 29
"Global Employment Trends for
    Women 2004," 213
Global measure of well-being, 388
Global perspectives, 491–495
    community strengths, 492
    cultural strengths, 492
    family strengths, 492
    human betterment, 494
    integrating family, community, and
      cultural strengths, 493
    Michener (citizen of the world), 495
    perennial philosophy, 495
    See also International comparisons
Gonorrhea, 174
Good divorce, 469, 470
Good enoughs, 467
Good gets worse group, 322
Good listener, 127
Goofing off together, 151
Grandfamilies, 385–387
Grandparents/grandparenthood, 383–387
    adolescents, 92
    attitudes and expectations, 384
    cultural differences, 385, 386
    depression, 387
    educational resources, 367
    grandparent behavior, 384
    grandparent satisfaction, 384
    grandparents raising grandchildren,
      385–387
    stress, 386
    symbolic meaning of
      grandparenthood, 384
Gray divorce, 382
Great Britain
    aggressiveness, 200
    nonverbal gestures, 114

Happiness, 510
    aging, 388
    childlessness, 341
    communication, 258–259
    conflict, *135, 146,* 260
    finances, 224, *224*
    gender roles, *197, 216*
    international comparisons, 221
    middle age, 377
    money, 221–223
    parenthood, 330–331
    relationship characteristics, *258*
    sexual intimacy, *161*
    stepfamily, *485*
Happy memories, 84–85
Harmonious couples, 320, *320,* 323
Hawaii (Michener), 495
Healthy Marriage Initiative, 310, 313,
    325–326, 328
Hereditary defectives, 72
Heterosexual, 162
Heterosexual-homosexual
    continuum, 172
Hispanic Americans
    bank account, 227
    child abuse, 23
    child care, 355
    children, 57, 341
    collectivist society, 57, 226
    cultural conflicts (female Chicana
      college student), 79
    domestic violence, 429–430
    familism, 56
    family structures with minor
      children, *11*
    father-child communication about
      sex, 178
    gender roles, 207–208
    generally, 43
    grandparents raising
      grandchildren, 386
    hugging, 114
    marital status, *8*
    median household income, *232*
    multiracial marriage, 65
    net worth, 235
    out-of-wedlock births, 360
    percentage of American
      population, 43
    poverty rate, 231

women living with spouses, 267
Historical study, A–11
Historical trauma, 61
HIV (human immunodeficiency virus),
    168–169
Holmes and Rahe Stress Test, 407, *408*
Home loan, 242–243
Home ownership, 240–243
Homelessness, 29
Homosexuality, 162, 172
    See also Gays and lesbians
Honest communication, 256
Honesty, 260
*Hooking Up, Hanging Out, and Hoping
    for Mr. Rights: College Women on
    Dating and Mating Today* (Glenn/
    Marquardt), *281*
*Hooking Up: Sex, Dating and Relationships
    on Campus* (Bogle), *283*
Hormonal conditions and sex,
    187–188
Household expenses, 235
Household inequality, 213
Housework, 198
Hugging, 114, 116
Human betterment, 494
Human ecosystem, 76
Human immunodeficiency virus (HIV),
    168–169
Human mate poaching, 186
Human systems, 76
Humiliations and betrayal, 150
Humor, 83–84, 150
Husband-dominant power pattern, 215,
    215, 216
Hypothesis, 71

"I Don't Care; You Decide" game,
    262–264
I Kissed Dating Goodbye (Harris), *281*
I-we balance, *94*
Idiographic approach, 71
"If You Really Love Me, You'll Know
    What I Want" game, 265
*Illusion and Disillusion: The Self in Love
    and Marriage* (Crosby), 147
Immigrants/immigration
    documentation, 45
    friendship, 249
    gender roles, 210
    refugees, 46

Implied threats, 157
Impotence, 188
Impulsive spending, 243
In-home day care, 354
Incest taboos, 165
Inclusionists, 6
Income
    bank account, 227
    collective/individualistic
        worldview, 226
    cultural diversity, *44*
    domestic violence, 430
    education, 233, *233*
    ethnic group, *232*
    family income (2009), *231*
    gender, 233
    social problems, 223
    stress, 20
    See also Financial issues
India
    divorce, 462
    love marriage, 279
    reincarnation, 279
    semiarranged marriage, 279
Individual-choice courtship. *See* Dating
Individual sense of well-being, 20
Infatuation, 251
Infidelity, 183–185, 186
Influenza, 409
Insider perspective, A–9
Instability of couple and family
        relationships, 22
Instant messaging, 283
Instrumental role, 90, 201
Integrating family, community, and
        cultural strengths, 493
Interdependence of parts, 77
International comparisons
    discipline, 354
    divorce, 461, 462–463
    eye contact, 116
    family violence, 446–447
    female heads of state, 28
    gender inequity, 213
    gender roles, 205–206
    greeting, 116
    gun violence, 23
    happiness, 221
    infidelity, 184, 186
    interconnectedness of countries, 29
    national day care policies, 357
    nonverbal gestures, 114, 116
    same-sex marriage, 4
    singlehood, 269
    spanking, 353
    teenage sex, 174
    See also Global perspectives; *specific
        country names*
International family strengths
        framework, 81–86
    See also Family strengths framework

Internet
    dating services, 255, 285–286
    negative impacts, 27
    sexual exploitation, 27
    trends, 26
    villagelike atmosphere, 28
Internet dating and matchmaking
        services, 254–255, 285–286
Interpersonal communication, 107–133
    See also Communication
Interpersonal trust, 93
Interracial/interfaith marriages, 65–66,
        290–293
    acculturation, 292
    Black-White marriages, 291, 465
    cohabitation, 65
    cultural familiarity, 293
    divorce, 465
    extended-family agreement, 293
    race, 292
    religion, 292
    sex and sex roles, 293
    socioeconomic differences, 293
    values, 292
Interview, A–10
Intimacy
    attachment theory, 265–267
    communication, 128, 256–257, 258–259
    conflict, 141–142
    couple relationships, 258–260
    defined, 255
    diversity, 36
    divorce, 459
    equality/balance of power, 194
    family problems, and, 405
    gays and lesbians, 40–41
    love, and, 251
    marriage, 124, 255, 257–258, 304
    middle and later years, 374
    opposite-sex relationships, 255–256
    partner attachment, 253
    same-sex relationships, 255
    self-disclosure, 122–123, 255, 256
    sex. *See* Sexual intimacy
    sharing information, 2
    See also Love
Intimacy games, 260–265
    constructive games, 262
    destructive games, 262–264
    dimensions, *261*
    disguised objectives, 265
    implicit rules, 265
    limiting destructive games, 264–265
    naming the game, 264–265
    unveiling game strategies, 265
Intimate experience, 257
Intimate partner violence. *See* Domestic
        violence
Intimate relationship, 257, 260
Intimate terrorism, 428
Iraq war, 420

Iraq War Clinician Guide, 420
Israel, 279
"I" statements, 149
Italy
    aggression in children, 354
    hugging, 116
    marriage and divorce rates, 461
    nonverbal gestures, 114

Japan
    bowing, 116
    dating, 280
    divorce, 462–463
    extramarital sex, 186
    eye contact, 116
    gender roles, 207
    love-based marriage, 279–280
    nape of the neck, 167
    singlehood, 269
"Japanese Women Live, and Like It, on
        Their Own" (Faiola), 269
Jealousy, 95, 252–254
Jews, 42–43
Joint custody, 464, 470–471
Jordan, 186
Journal of Family Communication, 132
Journal of Family Issues, 72
Journal of Family Psychology, 72
Journal of Family Theory & Review, 72
Journal of Marital and Family Therapy, 72
Journal of Marriage and Family, 72
Journals, 72
"Journey of happy memories," 348–349
Junteenth Day celebrations, 49
Just-say-no programs, 175
Justice, 494

Kansas State University at Manhattan,
        368, 372
Kenya, 354
Kin relationships, 49–51
Kindness, 151
Kinsey Institute, 192
Kinship, 49
Kinship groups, 49–50
Kissing, 166
Knowledge-positions, 89
Korea
    divorce, 462
    singlehood, 269

Labeling, 194
Lack of time, 20–21
Late adulthood and old age, 388–401
    Alzheimer's, 395
    biological reality, 389
    cohabitation, 400
    couple relationships, 398–400
    dating, 286–288
    death of a spouse, 397–398, 399
    divorce, 396

middle-old, 389
myths and reality, 390–393
nursing homes, 392
old-old, 389
proms and dances, 297
psychological phenomenon, 389
retirement, 393–396
senility, 392, 395
sex, 297, 391
sexuality, 171–172
sibling relationships, 400–401
social phenomenon, 389
stepfamily, 486
young-old, 389
younger family members, and, 393
Latino/a families. *See* Hispanic
    Americans
Laughing, 151
Law of enlightened self-interest, 309
Learned helplessness theory, 433
Learners, 353
Learning theories, 348
Leisure-work balance, 20
Lesbians. *See* Gays and lesbians
Let loose and party attitude, 283
Libertines, 467
Life course, 88
Life course theory, 294
Life cycle, 87
Life events, 407–409
Life expectancy, 217, 388–389
Life satisfaction, 388
Life stages, 87
Liking, 251
Lineage, 50
Linear causality model, 117
Lines of descent, 50, 51
Listening, 125–127
    attentive, 126–127
    conflict resolution, 147, 155
    directive, 126
    females, *110*
    males, *110*
    persuasive, 126
    poor/good, *98*
    strong families, 83
Living, 72
Living apart together, 400
Living together. *See* Cohabitation
Living within your means, 224

Looking-glass self, 88
Love
    anger, and, 142–143
    arranged marriage, 249
    brain, and, 253
    changing nature of, 250
    characteristics, 250
    chemicals, release of, 250
    companionate, 251
    consummate, 251
    empty, 251
    famous quotations, *248*
    fatuous, 251
    hate, and, 139
    language, 250
    paradoxical nature of, 250
    real *vs.* superficial, 250
    romantic, 251, 266
    scientific findings, 250, 253
    See also Intimacy
Love and War (Korea), 462
Love-based marriage, 250
Love match, 279
Love relationships, 251
Love triangle, 249–251
    commitment, 251
    intimacy, 251
    passion, 251
Loving Someone Who Has Dementia
    (Boss), 410
Loyalty, 94

Malaysia, 279
Male dominance, 434
Male menopause, 379–380
Managing stress, 424
    See also Family coping strategies
Marital and family therapists, A–8
Marital and family therapy, 496–497,
    499–506
    case study, 503–506
    closeness/flexibility, 500–501
    common problems, 499, *499*
    common questions and answers,
        501–503
    cost, 503
    effectiveness, 503
    how to find a therapist, 502–503
    overview, *496*
    stigma, 369, 501

emotionally expressive couples, 183
Marriage, 303–328
    advantages, 15–18
    African Americans, 306
    age, 8, 289, 304
    arranged, 249–251, 277–279
    benefits of, 305
    characteristics, 3
    children. *See* Parenthood
    cohabitation, compared, 17
    conflict resolution, 314
    coparenting, 359–360
    couple-arranged, 279
    covenant, 465
    daily routines. *See* Gender roles
    defined, 3
    drifting apart, 323
    educational programs. *See* Marriage
        education programs
    egalitarian marital relationship, 14
    family of origin, 315–317
    forgiveness, 150–151, 324–325
    gender-role differences, 113
    happiness, 322–323
    healthy/successful, 308–309,
        339, *340*
    income/wealth, 17
    infidelity, 183–185, 186
    intimacy, 124, 257–258, 304
    late adulthood and old age, 400
    long-term, 396–397
    marital satisfaction, 322–323
    middle and later years, 380–381
    newlywed years, 317–318
    number one priority, as, 323–324
    older people, 298
    popularity, 307
    predicting a successful marriage,
        314–315
    premarital education.
        See Premarital education
    premarital fantasies and marital
        realities, 319
    pre-marriage cohabitation, 9,
        297–298, 307
    PREPARE, 313, 497–498
    sacrifice, 325
    semiarranged, 279
    sex, 16, 181–183, 305
    Smart Marriages Web site, 498

Marriage —*Cont.*
  state laws to strengthen marriage, 326–327
  statistics/factoids, *12*, 304, *308*
  suggestions for keeping marriage vital and healthy, 507–508
  top 10 stumbling blocks, 499, *499*
  traditional *vs.* contemporary view, *204*
  trends, 8
  two-marriage concept, 16–17
  types of married couples, 320–321
  unhealthy/destructive, 306–307
  wedding, 317
  See also Remarriage
Marriage and Family Review, 72
Marriage education evaluation studies, 497
Marriage education inventories, 304
Marriage education programs, 310–313
  benefits, 185, 496, 497
  Healthy Marriage Initiative, 310
  infidelity, and, 185
  marital satisfaction/marriage adjustment, 320
  overview, *496*
  premarital education. *See* Premarital education
  PREPARE Program, 310, 497–498
  recommended programs, 313, 498
Marriage movement, 310
Marriage Preparation and Preservation Act (Florida), 326–327
Marriage resource web sites, 313
Martin Luther King, Jr., Memorial, 55
Masculine qualities, 194, 195
Masculinity, 194
Masturbation, 167, 391
Masturbation exercises, 189–190
Mate selection, 288–295
  adolescent years, 294–295
  age, 289
  birth order, 290
  career women, 290
  China, 279
  endogamy/exogamy, 290–291
  finding a good mate, 293–294
  intercultural marriages, 290–293
  personality, 290
  physical attractiveness, 288–289
  questions to ask, 296
  sex ratio, 289
  six-hour pre-marital course, 293–294
  theory, 294
  See also Dating
Material possessions, 20
Maternal gatekeeping, 199
Mating gradient, 289
Matriarchal group, 51
Matrilineal society, 50
Matrilocal society, 51
Mayo Clinic, 192

"Me generation," 96
Mealtime, 115
Men
  career/financial success, 16
  childlessness, 379
  conversational style, 111, 112
  coparenting, 357–360
  distancers, 144
  fatherhood, 361–364
  health problems, 218
  home as egalitarian haven, 28
  instrumental role, 201
  jealousy, 252
  male menopause, 379–380
  preferential characteristics of mate, 255
  reactions to beautiful women, 116
  sexual behaviors, 169–170
  sexual dysfunction, 188–189
  stereotypical characteristics, 194
  traits (Gallup Poll), *200*
  See also Gender; Women
Menopause, 187, 377–379
Metacommunication, 149
Mexican Americans. *See* Hispanic Americans
Mexican Family Strengths Conference, 33
Mexico (Michener), 495
Middle age, 375–383
  baby boomers, 376
  boomerang kids, 382
  childlessness, 378–379
  cluttered nest, 383
  defined, 375
  divorce, 381–382
  emotional intimacy, 374
  empty-nest syndrome, 382
  generativity *vs.* stagnation, 375
  happiness, 377
  male menopause, 379–380
  marriage, and, 380–381
  menopause, 377–379
  middlescence, 375
  midlife crisis, 376–377
  sandwich generation, 383
  sexual intimacy, 374
  sexuality, 377–380
  solo parenthood, 360
  spacious nest, 382
  working world, and, 377
Middle-aged marriage, 380–381
Middle-old, 389
Middlescence, 375
Midlife crisis, 376–377
Midrange family, 99, *101*
Military families, 416–424
  children, 422
  community support, 422–423
  deployment, 418, 419, 421
  divorce, 420–421

  emotional cycle, 421
  family support programs, 367
  National Guard, 421
  PTSD, 423–424
  retirement, 419
  traumatic brain injury, 420
Minority populations. *See* Cultural diversity
MISS Foundation, 372
Mixed message, 119
Mixed-methods research, A–9
Mixed race marriage, 65–66, 290–293
Models of couples and families, 74–91
  family development framework, 86–88
  family strengths framework, 81–86
  family systems theory, 74–81
  feminist framework, 90–91
  overview, 74
  social construction framework, 89
  symbolic interaction framework, 88
Moderates, 6
Money management, 237–239
Money matters. *See* Financial issues
Monogamy, 50
More modern societies, 67
Morocco, 463
Morphogenic system, 77
Morphostatic system, 77
Mortality inequality, 213
Mortgage, 242–243
Mother's Book, The (Mrs. Child), 353
Motor vehicle accident, *414*
Mrs. Doubtfire (film), 466
Multicultural feminism, 91
Multicultural intellectual movements, 89
Multicultural study, A–11
Multiple subjective truths, 89
Multiple system levels, 75
Multiracial marriage, 65–66, 290–293
Multitasking, 121
Mundugumor tribe, 205
Mutual-negotiation trajectory, 342
Mutual support, 266

Nagging, 111–112
Nagging-and-avoidance, 147
Nakode, 279
Narrative therapy, 89
Natality inequality, 213
National 4-H, 422
National Center for Health Statistics, 372
National Council on Family Relations (NCFR), 72, 366, 368, 372, 512
National day care policy, 357
National Guard, 421
National Healthy Marriage Resource Center, 313, 328

Necessities, expenditures on, *235*
Negative comments, 124, 125, *125*
Negative communication cycle, 129, *129*
Negative emotions, 138–139
Negative feedback, 80
Negative health behaviors, 409
Negotiating style, 155–157
Neighborhood system, *76*
Neolocal society, 51
Net worth, 235, *391*
Netherlands, 4
Never married women raising children alone, 271, 360, 362
New-life stage of grief, 397
Newlywed years, 317–318
Newsletters, 367
NICHD child care study, 356–357, 372
Nigeria, 186
9/11 attacks. *See* September 11 terrorist attacks
No-fault divorce, 463–464
No-spanking laws, 352–353
Nomothetic approach, 71
Non-love, 251
Noncommunication, 117
Nonindulgent parents, 350
Nonmarital childbearing, 271, 360, 362
Nonparenthood, 339–343
Nonsexual dating violence, 296
Nonverbal communication
    eye contact, 116
    greeting, 116
    hugging, 114, 116
    international comparisons, 114, 116
    male reaction to beautiful women, 116
    mixed message, 119
    relationship component, 119
    spoken communication, 118
    what is it, 119
    written communication, 118–119
Nuclear family, 49–50
Nursing homes, 392

Observational approaches, A–10 to A–11
Obsessive-compulsive disorder, 253
Officially sanctioned marriage, 60–61
Old age, 389
    See also Late adulthood and old age

Operation: Military Kids, 422
Oral sex, 169
Organismic theory, 347–348
Orgasmic disorder
    men, 188
    women, 187
Outsider perspective, A–9
Overcrowding, 28
Overdraft charges, 227
Overfunctioner, 144
Owl Moon (Yolen/Schoenherr), 370
Owl moon walk, 370
Ownership inequality, 213
Oxytocin, 253

Pacific Islanders. *See* Asian Americans
Painful intercourse, 188
PAIRS Program, 313, 498
Parallel coparenting relationships, 472
Parent-arranged marriage, 277–279
Parent-dominated approach to childrearing, 350
Parent education, 365–369
    abusive and neglectful parents, 366
    adoptive parents, 366
    alcohol and other drugs, 366
    bereaved parents, 366
    blue-collar parents, 366
    business community programs, 366
    childbirth education, 366
    children with developmental disabilities, 368
    couple and family enrichment programs, 367
    crisis nurseries, 367
    family therapy, compared, 366
    farm and ranch families, 367
    foster parents, 367
    grandparents, 367
    Internet resources, 367–368
    lower-income parents, 366
    mass media, 367
    military families, 367
    minority-group parents, 367
    newsletters, 367
    parenthood decision making, 368
    preparation for parenting classes, 368
    respite care facilities, 367
    sexual minority children, 368

adoption, 338–339
bidirectional effects, 347
child care, 354–357
child-free alternative, 339–343
childrearing. *See* Childrearing
coparenting, 357–360
death of a child, 365
discipline, 349–354
educational programs and resources, 365–369
empty-nest syndrome, 335
family education classes, 336–337
family structure, 346–347
fatherhood, 361–364
financial issues, 236, 337–338
gays and lesbians, 360–361
goal for most couples, 14
happiness, 330–331
happy *vs.* unhappy couples, *332*
"journey of happy memories," 348–349
joy and enduring satisfaction, 369–370
leisure patterns, 92–93
marital happiness, 330–331
myths and realities, 333–335
one-child family, 334
parental control, 343, 344
parental support, 343
passing problems on to next generation, 333
"second shift," 362
sons *vs.* daughters, 344
styles of parenting, 343–347
teenage parents, 334
TLC approach, 350
top five parenting issues, *332*
transition to, 335–337
"Parenthood as Crisis" (LeMasters), 335
Parenting styles, 343–347
    authoritarian style, 345, 346
    Couple and Family Map, *343*
    democratic style, 344, 346–347
    overview, *344*
    permissive style, 345, 346
    rejecting style, 345
    uninvolved style, 345
Parents Without Partners, 368
Parsons theory, 201–202

Partner dominance, 129
Partnered masturbation, 169
Passion, 251
Passive behavior, 128
Passive communication, 128
Paternal responsibility, 364
Patriarchal group, 51
Patrilineal society, 50, 51
Patrilocal society, 51
Peacefulness, 494
Pearl Harbor, 58
Pedophiles, 27
Perennial philosophy, 495
Perfect pals, 470
Permissive parenting, 345, 346
Permissiveness, 280
Persona theory, 250
Personal happiness, 73
    See also Happiness
Personal stories (future of the family),
    509–510
Personality compatibility,
    259, 290
Personification, 95
Persuasive listening, 126
Philippines, 354
Philosophia perennis, 495
Physical, mental and social
    inadequacy, 72
Physical abuse, 427
Physical attractiveness, 288–289
Physiological stress, 406
Planned Parenthood Federation of
    America, 176, 192
Pleasurable time together, 84–85
Plural marriage, 50
Poland (Michener), 495
Polyandry, 50
Polygamy, 50
Polygyny, 50
Pooling money, 238–239
Population distribution, 43
Population trends, 46, 46
Pornography, 27
Positive caregiving, 359
Positive comments, 124, 125, 125
Positive communication, 52, 54, 83
Positive communication cycle, 129, 129
Positive complementary cycle, 262
Positive discipline, 350, 353
Positive feedback, 80
Positive reinforcement, 348
Postdeployment, 421
Postmodernism, 89
Posttraumatic stress disorder (PTSD),
    423–424
Poverty
    cultural diversity, 44
    financial survival, 231
    stresses, 223
    See also Financial issues

Pow-wows, 49
Power, 214–217
    defined, 214
    dynamic process, 214
    egalitarian roles and marital
        satisfaction, 215–216
    interactive process, 214
    men vs. women, 28
    minimizing power issues, 217–218
    system property, 214
    type of power patterns, 215–216
Predeployment, 421
Pregnancy risk, 176, 177
Prejudice, 64
Premarital education, 311–313
    benefits, 497
    components, 497
    effectiveness of program, 312
    PREPARE Program, 497–498
    recommended programs, 313
    state involvement, 327
Premarital fantasies and marital
    realities, 319
Premarital sex, 173, 174
Premature ejaculation, 188, 189
PREP Program, 130, 310, 313, 498
PREPARE, 313, 315, 497–498
PREPARE Couple Questionnaire, 313
PREPARE/ENRICH Program, 313, 498
Prescription drug abuse, 454
Pressure tactics, 157
Prevention and Relationship
    Enhancement Program (PREP),
    130, 310, 313, 498
Problem drinking, 449
    See also Alcohol use and abuse
Professional associations, 72
Professional inequality, 213
Property crimes, 22
Pseudo-kin group, 50
Psychodynamic theory, 347
Psychological abuse, 427, 431–432
Psychological aggression, 438–439
Psychological stress, 406
PTSD (posttraumatic stress disorder),
    423–424
Pursuer, 143

Qualitative research, A–9
Quantitative research, A–9
Questionnaire, A–9–A–10
Quid pro quid, 156
Quid pro quo, 156

Race, 41, 42
    See also Cultural diversity
Racism, 64
Rape, 23
    See also Domestic violence
Rapid ejaculation, 188
Real love, 250

Recession, 221, 223, 377
Recognizing others' strengths, 64
Redeployment, 421
Reframing, 425
Refugees, 46
Reinforcement, 348–349
Rejecting parenting, 345
Relationship characteristics, 258–260
Relationship coping resources,
    425, 426
Relationship Enhancement, 310, 313
Relationship power balances, 28
Relationship science, 74
Relationship services, 285
Relationship strengths, 14, 15
    See also Strengths
Relationships, 74
Relationships map. See Couple and
    Family Map
Religion
    cohabitation, 298
    interfaith marriage, 290–293
    perennial philosophy, 495
    spanking, 353
    stress, and, 425, 426
Religious beliefs, 85
Religious or spiritual group, 85
Remarriage
    age, 10
    factoids, 10–11
    trends, 10–11
    See also Stepfamily
Remarriage stumbling blocks, 484
Renting a home, 242
Representative sample, A–10
Repressed anger, 138
Research, A–12
    family development framework,
        92–93
    family strengths framework, 92
    family systems theory, 92
    feminist framework, 93
    minority populations, 47
    mixed-methods approach, A–9
    qualitative, A–9
    quantitative, A–9
    social construction framework, 93
    symbolic interaction framework, 93
    See also Family research methods
Research designs
    cross-sectional cohort study, A–12
    cross-sectional study, A–12
    longitudinal study, A–11 to A–12
Research study, 71, 92–93
Resolving disagreements, 147–151
Respite care facilities, 367
Responsible fathers, 364
Restructuring of economy and
    society, 31
Retirement, 393–396
Reviewing and renegotiating, 157

Same-sex marriage, 4, 37
Same-sex parenting, 360–361
Same-sex relationships.
	See Gays and lesbians
Sandwich generation, 374, 383
Sarcasm, 84
Saving and investment plan, 29
Savings, 230
Savings account, 230
Say what you really mean, 147
Scandinavian countries, 280
Scotland, 213
Search Institute, 30
SECCYD (Study of early child care and
	youth development), 356–357, 372
Second marriage. See Remarriage
"Second shift," 362
Second wave of feminist movement, 90
Secondhand smoke exposure, 25
Secret, 119
Secure romantic attachment, 266
Secured card, 241
Seekers, 467
Segregation, 64
Self-assessment, rate the strengths in
	your family, 54
Self-concept, 84
Self-confidence, 129
Self-disclosure
	defined, 122
	friendship, 123–124
	gender, 122
	intimacy, 122–123, 255, 256
	intimate relationship, 124
	poor/good, 98
	relationship type, 125
	strangers, 123
Self-esteem, 252, 308, 433
Self-stimulation, 189–190
Semiarranged marriage, 279
Senility, 392, 395
Seniors. See Late adulthood and old age
Sensate focus, 190
Separateness-togetherness continuum,
	91–96
September 11 terrorist attacks
	coping mechanisms, 425–426
	Couple and Family Map, 415
	family systems changes, 414–416
	overview, 414

marriage, 16
national obsession, as, 27
older people, 297
	See also Sexual intimacy
Sex and Temperament in Three Primitive
	Societies (Mead), 205
Sex and the City (TV), 268
Sex drive, 253
Sex education, 175–179
	abstinence-only approach, 175
	effectiveness, 179
	just-say-no programs, 175
	parent-child communication, 176–179
	pregnancy risk, 176, 177
Sex educators, 189
Sex ratio, 289
Sex-selective abortion, 213
Sex therapists, 189
Sex therapy, 189–190
"Sex Without Strings, Relationships
	Without Rings" (Popenoe/
	Whitehead), 297
Sexual abuse, 427
Sexual arousal disorder, 187
Sexual dysfunction, 187–189
Sexual exploitation, 27
Sexual identity, 161
Sexual infidelity, 183–185
Sexual intimacy, 159–192
	ABC News Survey, 170–171
	adolescents/young adulthood,
		173–181
	cultural differences, 165–168
	extramarital sex, 183–185, 186
	gays and lesbians, 163–165, 172–173
	happy vs. unhappy couples, 161
	healthy marital relationships, 160
	heterosexual-homosexual
		continuum, 172
	historical overview, 162–163
	HIV/AIDS differences, 168–169
	later life, in, 171–172
	nationwide survey, 160–161,
		169–170
	premarital sex, 173, 174
	self-help techniques, 189–190
	sex education, 175–179
	sex therapy, 189–190
	sex within marriage, 181–183
	sexual dysfunction, 187–189

(SIECUS), 192
Sexually-charged language, 195
Sexually transmitted infections
	(STIs), 174
Shaming, 354
Shanghai, 463
Shared meaning, 88
Sibling abuse, 445–448
Sibling relationships (middle and older
	adulthood), 400–401
SIECUS (Sexuality Information and
	Education Council of the United
	States), 192
Silent treatment, 148
Singing together, 84–85
Single-parent births, 360
Single-parent families, 335,
	471–480
	African Americans, 471, 472
	benefits of, 478–479
	challenges, 476–478
	child abuse, 444
	child support, 473
	coping strategies, 471
	financial resources, 476–477
	increase in numbers, 12–13
	male, families headed by, 487
	noncustodial fathers, 473–475
	non-residential fathers, 476
	parent education, 368
	positive attitude, 479–480
	race and ethnicity, 13
	sense of humor, 480
	single mothers, 360, 475
	social network, 479
	spiritual/religious resources, 479
	stigma, 477
	strengths, 475–476
	suggestions for keeping family
		strong, 508, 509
Single-parent mothers, 360, 475
Singlehood, 267–273, 461
	cohabitation, 270
	ethnic groups, 267
	factoids/statistics, 267, 268, 270
	historical perspective, 269–270
	loneliness, 272–273
	stigma, 271
"Singles Shall Overcome" (DePaulo), 268
Situational couple violence, 428
Smart Marriages Web site, 498

Social construction framework, 89, 93
Social environment
    changing, 30
    defined, 18
    effect of, 18–19
    elements, *19*
    positive response to, 30–31
Social exchange theory, 250
Social isolation, 433, 444
Social learning theory, 210
Social system, 53
Sociobiological theory, 294
Sociocultural characteristics, 52–53
    belief system, 53
    extended-family system, 53
    social system, 53
Sociocultural stress, 406
Sole custody, 470
Solidifying agreements, 156
Solo parenthood, 271, 360, 362
Somali immigrants, 227
Sons *vs.* daughters, 344
Sorority, 180
Soul mate mentality, 461
"Soul wounds," 61
Source, The (Michener), 495
Spacious nest, 382
Spain, 461
Spanking, 350–354, 439–440
Speaking skills, 98, *98*
Speaking style, *109*
Special opportunity inequality, 213
Spending time together, 52, 84–85
Spinster, 270
    See also Singlehood
Spiritual beliefs, 85
Spiritual well-being, 52, 53, 85
Split custody, 470
Spouse abuse. *See* Domestic violence
Squeeze technique, 190
Stability-change continuum, 96–98
Stalking, 22, 23
Statins, 391
Stay-at-home moms, 13
Staying on topic, *98*
Stays good group, 322
Stepfamily, 480–488
    boundary ambiguity, 486
    child abuse, 444
    children, 482–484, 487–488
    defined, 480
    diverse populations, 485–486
    educational courses, 310–311, 368, 485
    favoritism, 488
    financial issues, 488
    gays and lesbians, 480
    happy *vs.* unhappy couples, *485*
    Hispanics, 486
    later life, in, 486
    nuclear family, compared, 481–482
    parent education, 368

remarriage stumbling blocks, 484
    suggestions for keeping family
        strong, 508, 509
Stepfamily education, 310–311
Stereotypes, 64
Stigma
    cohabitation, 298
    gays and lesbians, 40–41, 173
    marital and family therapy, 369, 501
    single-parent families, 477
    singlehood, 271
STIs (sexually transmitted infections), 174
Stonewalling, 130, 146, 314
Stop-and-go technique, 190
Straightforwardness, 260
Strain-based demands, 202
Strengths, 2
    African Americans, 55–56
    American Indians and Alaska
        Natives, 59–61
    Asian Americans, 57–59
    Caucasian Americans, 53–54
    communication, *109*
    community, 492
    conceptual framework. *See* Family
        strengths framework
    cultural, 492
    factoids, 15
    family, 492
    generally, 2
    Hispanic Americans, 56–57
    single-parent families, 475–476
    Venn diagram, *493*
Stress
    ABC-X model, 412–413
    cancer, and, 408–409
    cardiovascular disease, and, 409
    change, and, 416
    common cold, and, 409
    coping, 407. *See also* Family coping
        strategies
    dating couples, 409, *410*
    defined, 19, 406
    emotion, and, 407
    engaged couples, 409–411
    generally, 406
    grandparents raising
        grandchildren, 386
    Holmes and Rahe Stress Test, 407, *408*
    influenza, and, 409
    levels of, 406
    life events, and, 407–409
    married couples, *410*, 411
    negative health behaviors, and, 409
    poverty, 223
    repressed anger, 138
    sandwich generation, 383
    spanking, 353
    technological changes, 20
    work-family balance, 20
Strong family, 2, 5

Strong marriage, 14, 35
Structurally cohesive relationships, *100*
Structurally connected relationships, *100*
Structurally disengaged relationships, *100*
Structurally enmeshed relationships, *100*
Structured relationships, *96, 97, 97*
Study of early child care and youth
    development (SECCYD),
    356–357, 372
Styles of parenting. *See* Parenting styles
Subsystem, 75
Successful marriages, 308–309, 339, *340*
Suicide, 23, 296
Superficial love, 250
Superior heredity capacity, 72
Supermoms, 28
Supportive couples, 183
Suprasystem, 75
Sweden
    cohabitation, 280, 461
    marriage rate, 280
    no-spanking law, 352–353
Symbolic interaction framework, 88, 93
Syncratic power pattern, 215, *215*, 216
System, 75
    See also Family systems theory

Tabula rasa, 333
Taiwan, 463
Take Back Your Kids (Doherty), 349
Take Back Your Marriage (Doherty),
    323, 324
Tales of the South Pacific (Michener), 495
Tchambuli tribe, 205
Teaser rate, 241
Technological changes, 20
Teen pregnancy, 174, 175, 334
Teenagers. *See* Adolescents and young
    adulthood
Tender years doctrine, 464
Texas (Michener), 495
Text messaging, 283
Thailand
    aggression in children, 354
    "Miss Spinster," 269
The Coordinator, 72
The new Americans (film), 33
"The Ties That Bind" game, 264
Theory, 71
    See also Models of couples
        and families
Therapist Locator, 502
Therapy/therapists
    AAMFT, 501, 512
    family strengths framework, 81
    family therapists. *See* Family therapists
    marital and family therapy.
        See Marital and family therapy
    narrative therapy, 89
    sex therapy, 189–190
    terminology, A–8

economic burden, 25
nonsmokers, 25
tobacco-related deaths, 25, 454
Togetherness-separateness continuum, 91–96
Tolerance of traditions of other ethnic groups, 63
Too Much of a Good Thing: Raising Children of Character in an Indulgent Age (Kindlon), 349
Traditional couples, 321, 323
Traditional family, 3
Transgender, 162
Transition stage of grief, 397
Transition to parenthood, 335–337
Traumatic brain injury, 420
Trends, 6–11
  cohabitation, 8–9
  divorce, 9–10
  family structure, 11–13
  Internet, 26, 27
  marriage, 8
  pessimists/optimists, 7
  remarriage, 10–11
Trust, 93, 248
Truth statement, 89
12 Hours to a Great Marriage (Markman/ Stanley), 130
Two-marriage concept, 16–17
Two-parent families, cultural diversity, 44

Ultimate good, 494
Ultimatum, 147–148
Unbalanced family, 99, 101
"Under love's spell," 247
Underfunctioner, 144
Unemployment, 29
Unhappy couples. *See* Happiness
Unilateral-persuasion trajectory, 342
Uninvolved parenting, 345
United States
  adopted children, 338
  age of marriage, 289
  aggressiveness, 200
  Americans who are 65 years and older, 376
  child fatalities, 23

happiness, 211
individuality, 65
life expectancy, 217
marital status, 8
marriage rate, 298
minority populations, 43
net worth, 391
nursing home residents, 392
open communication about sex, 160
population distribution, 43
premarital sex, 173, 174
rural societies, 28
same-sex marriage, 4
sex ratio, 289
sexual activity, 173
singlehood, 267, 270
strengths/weaknesses of American culture, 64
traditional family, 3
two-adult-generation households, 475
wage gap, 213
widowhood, 398
  See also International comparisons
Universal values, 494
University. *See* Colleges/universities
University of Missouri at Columbia Extension, 368, 372
University of Nebraska-Lincoln Extension, 368, 372, 512
Unmarried couples. *See* Cohabitation
Unmarried women raising children alone, 271, 360, 362
Up in the Air (film), 271
Urban migration, 28

Validating, A–10
Validating couples, 183
Validating style of conflict resolution, 314
Value system, 53
Verbal aggression, 435
Villagelike atmosphere, 28
Violence
  alcohol, and, 450
  child abuse. *See* Child abuse and neglect
  child-to-parent abuse, 448–449
  dating, 295–296, 297, 429

Volatile style of conflict resolution, 314
Voluntary childlessness, 340
  See also Child-free alternative
Voluntary family, 6
Voluntary kin, 6

Wage gap, 213, 233–234
Walk of shame, 284
War. *See* Military families
Wedding, 317, 409
Weight Watchers, 123
Welcome Baby programs, 369
Well-functioning family, 4–5
Wellness programs, 366
Western ideal of rugged individualism, 18
White-Asian couples, 465
White families. *See* Caucasian Americans
Wholeness, 76
"Who's In Charge Here?" (Gibbs), 349
Why There Are No Good Men Left (Whitehead), 290
Widowhood, 397–398
Wife battering. *See* Domestic violence
Wife-dominant power pattern, 215, 215, 216
Women
  assets, 225
  career women and mate selection, 290
  childlessness, 379
  circumcision, 167
  cohabitation, 270
  conversational style, 111, 112
  dating violence, 296, 297
  expressive role, 201
  gatekeeping, 363, 473
  gender inequality, 213
  gender revolution, 28
  intimate partner violence, 23
  jealousy, 252
  mating gradient, 289
  menopause, 377–379
  nagging, 111–112
  never married, but raising children alone, 271, 360, 362
  positions of power, 28

Women—*Cont.*
  preferential characteristics of mate, 254–255
  pursuers/underfunctioners, 145
  rape, 23
  "second shift," 362
  sexual behaviors, 170
  sexual dysfunction, 187–188
  singlehood, 268
  stalking, 23
  stay-at-home moms, 13
  stereotypical characteristics, 194–195
  stress-related health problems, 217
  supermoms, 28
  traits (Gallup Poll), *200*
  walk of shame, 284
  working mothers, 202, 236
  working outside the home, 90
  See also Gender; Men
Win-lose, 149
Win-win, 149
Work-family balance, 20
Work-family interface, 202–203
Working mothers, 202, 236

Working outside the home, 236
Work-to-family influence, 202
Worldview, 83–84

You Just Don't Understand: Women and Men in Conversation (Tannen), 110
Young adulthood. *See* Adolescents and young adulthood
Young-old, 389
"You" statements, 149
You've Got Mail (film), 26